edited by

EDWARD E. SAMPSON

University of California, Berkeley

A BOOK OF READINGS

PRENTICE-HALL, INC.

Englewood Cliffs, N.J.

Approaches, Contexts,
and Problems
of Social Psychology

Approaches, Contexts, and Problems of Social Psychology

PRENTICE-HALL PSYCHOLOGY SERIES
RICHARD S. LAZARUS, EDITOR

APPROACHES, CONTEXTS, AND PROBLEMS OF SOCIAL PSYCHOLOGY
A Book of Readings
Edited by Edward E. Sampson

Second printing .... February, 1965

© 1964 by

PRENTICE-HALL, INC., *Englewood Cliffs, N.J.*

Library of Congress Catalog Card No.: 64-17196

Printed in the United States of America C-04368

PRENTICE-HALL INTERNATIONAL, INC., *London*
PRENTICE-HALL OF AUSTRALIA, PTY., LTD., *Sydney*
PRENTICE-HALL OF CANADA, LTD., *Toronto*
PRENTICE-HALL OF JAPAN, INC., *Tokyo*
PRENTICE-HALL OF INDIA (Private) LTD., *New Delhi*

Preface

Any collection of readings in any field is subject to the particular and perhaps, at times, peculiar biases of its editor. In a field like social psychology, having historical and extant roots in psychology, sociology, and anthropology, such a collection is especially subject to these psychological, sociological, or even anthropological biases.

Although those whom I hold responsible for giving me my own biases might vigorously wish to dissociate themselves from such a role as they glance through this collection of readings, I must point my accusing finger toward a select group of people at the University of Michigan for prejudicing my view of the field. Michigan social psychology contained heavy doses of both sociology and psychology (with psychology being of the cognitive variety), and a general atmosphere of cross-field-fertilization that has forever blinded me to a social psychology which does not pay its due to sociology and psychology.

I find that I am also forever blinded to any atheoretical, purely empirical approach to anything. It may be simply that I never quite know what to do with all those data matrices; it may be that I never did really understand what "purely empirical" meant; it may be that I lack that *third ear* required for hearing when you sit back and "let the data speak." Whatever the reasons, when faced with a selective choice between another data-collection study or a more fanciful theoretical article, more often than not I let theoretical fancy sway my decision. This is not to imply, however, that the theoretical selections in this book, taken together, form a systematic, integrated whole. But rather, they sample what I see to be some current conceptual frameworks in the field. Nor should this theoretical bent be taken to imply that empirical studies have not found their way into this collection, as over half of the selections are researches.

Although I point accusingly at Michigan as the source of my academic biases, I must take full responsibility for this particular selection of readings and this manner of organizing and introducing them. For his help in reviewing and commenting upon the original outline for the book, however, I am grateful to Professor John W. Thibaut. Some of his suggestions have been incorporated into the final product. I would also like to express my appreciation to Miss Sari Wade for her assistance in the many detailed chores connected with preparing such a collection. And finally, I would like to offer thanks to those anonymous, prospective, but as yet unfullfilled authors of another book of readings, the outline of which I once reviewed and so vigorously damned in a five page point-by-point critique, that the stage was suddenly set for me to attempt to answer the challenging cries of, "Well, could you do any better?"

E.E.S.

Contents

Approaches, Contexts,

and Problems

of Social Psychology

An Introduction to the Field of Social Psychology

As is the case with most efforts to trace the historical roots of present-day disciplines, with social psychology there is no simple event to which one may point and with confidence state, "This is how and where it all began." However, it is possible to point to 1908 as the year which marks the advent of a significant event in the historical development of social psychology. In that year two men, Edward Ross a sociologist and William McDougall a psychologist, independently published books entitled *An Introduction to Social Psychology*. Capturing in their separate works the long histories of their two parent fields, each set forth his conception of this "new field." For Ross, influenced by a tradition of concern with suggestion, crowd behavior, and other forms of human interaction, the field of social psychology focused upon the development of human thought and upon the uniformities of human behavior which arose from interpersonal associations and interactions. For McDougall, influenced by the Darwinian conceptions of instinct and the nonrationality of man and by a psychological tradition of concern with the conditions which motivated individual behavior, social psychology studied the manner by which nonrational, instinctually motivated individuals became changed in society.

Both Ross and McDougall had defined a field which dealt with relationships between the individual and society. Ross turned to the social processes of interaction, suggestion, and imitation to account for the observed uniformities in human behavior. McDougall, on the other hand, saw social life and the uniformities of human behavior as springing not from the social processes of suggestion and interaction, but rather from the dynamic instincts with which man was born.

Ross and McDougall were important in the history of social psychology not so much for what they had to say in 1908 as for the fact that their books served to crystallize two traditions which are with us today: from the directions laid down by McDougall and the reactions it evoked we have a *psychological social psychology,* while from the directions laid down by Ross we have what now exists as a *sociological social psychology*. No clearer evidence of the present day survival of this initial diversity in focus can be found than in the presence of social psychology courses in both psychology and sociology departments of most universities.

The historical diversity reflected in present-day social psychology may leave many persons puzzled over the precise nature of the field. One might legitimately ask, "What is social psychology all about?" "Does it differ from what I've learned in psychology?" "Doesn't it refer to the same things I've just read in sociology?"

There is neither an obvious nor a simple answer to these legitimate queries. Speaking ideally, the domain of social psychology builds upon the accumulated knowledges of both psychology and sociology plus other related social sciences (e.g., anthropology, political science, etc.), and seeks to form an integration or synthesis of these fields which are in themselves broad and diverse. This would mean that a social psychologist ideally is concerned with both the impact of a psychologically meaningful individual upon a structurally meaningful environment as well as with the impact of that structurally meaningful environment upon the psychologically meaningful individual. Thus, unlike a very extreme psychological view which sees a complexly structured organism facing an empty or minimally structured environment, or a very extreme sociological view which sees an empty or minimally structured organism facing a complexly structured environment, the social psychologist ideally seeks to formulate concepts and units which permit equal complexity of structure and process for the individual and the society and which deal with the additional complexities developing from the interactions of the two. As such, not only must it draw heavily upon strictly psychological theory to understand the nature of the individual (thus its similarity to much of psychology); not only must it draw heavily upon strictly sociological theory to understand the nature of society (thus its similarity to much of sociology); but also, and perhaps most importantly, it must draw upon the emergent units arising from the point of juncture, contact, or interaction between *person-in-society* or *society-in-person*.

In order to present more clearly the scope of the field of social psychology, it is useful to differentiate between concepts or units of analysis which take different levels of phenomena as their referent. Figure 1 presents

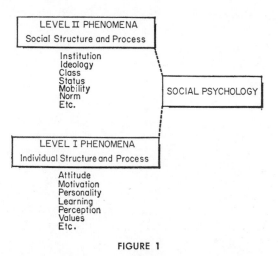

FIGURE 1

an example of two such levels and a sampling of concepts on each level.

Level I concepts take as their major point of reference structures and processes which characterize the functioning of the individual. Level II concepts, on the other hand, take as their major reference point structures and processes which characterize the functioning of the culture, society, or social system. Strictly speaking, the domain of social psychology lies in the region formed out of the interaction between Levels I and II. That is, it properly focuses upon concepts involving the interactive relationships between phenomena at Level I and those at Level II. Because the field at present does not have concepts which, strictly speaking, lie in this interactive region, the social psychologist must continually refer to and make use of Level I and Level II concepts. Although there are many such concepts, typically the social psychologist only utilizes those Level I concepts which have implications for or ties with Level II concepts or Level II concepts which have implications for or ties with Level I. Thus, for example, Level I concepts which postulate individual personality dispositions, motivations, attitudes, beliefs, or values, are of interest to the social psychologist as these are seen to have both their origins and development within the context of Level II phenomena, or to refer directly to individual relations to other individuals. In a similar manner, Level II concepts which postulate societal events such as institutions, ideologies, normative patterns, and role structures, are of interest to the social psychologist as these are seen to refer to the contexts in which individual social behavior takes place.

As just presented, the field of social psychology necessarily overlaps with many of the other social sciences. It overlaps with a strictly individualistic psychology as it focuses its attention upon the nature of the individual who enters the social domain. It overlaps with a strictly structural sociology and a cultural anthropology as it focuses its attention upon the nature of the social contexts in which behavior occurs. And finally, it presumably has as one of its goals development of its own particular concepts and units as it seeks to explore and to understand the new phenomena created out of this meeting of what T. M. Newcomb has referred to as *protoplasm and society*. (T. M. Newcomb. *Social Psychology*. New York: Holt, Rinehart & Winston, Inc., 1950, p. 483.)

In the collection of readings which follow, an attempt is made to convey this scope and focus of the field by presenting material involving concepts which characterize the individual (e.g., his cognitive structures, his motivations, his self concept, his attitudes); which characterize the contexts in which social behavior occurs (e.g., contexts provided by the small group, the organization, the community, and the society); and finally, which characterize the manner by which the individual interacts with and relates to others and develops within a social context (e.g., interpersonal perception, interaction, influence, and socialization).

Given the rather complex subject matter which stems from the breadth and scope of the field of social psychology, it is of interest to examine the manner by which investigations of a social psychological nature can be carried out.

Let us assume that the aim of a scientific discipline is to seek to understand or explain the phenomena with which it deals; and that explanation itself involves the development of a theoretical framework to which specific, new phenomena may be referred and thus be understood. This, therefore, requires the development *both* of theories to specify the

manner by which the phenomena of social psychology are to be conceptualized, in terms of a set of concepts and relationships, and of research methods to test empirically the hypotheses derived from these theoretical frameworks. The readings in this collection reflect both approaches to scientific understanding and explanation, in that some attempt to develop purely theoretical schemes for conceptualizing the individual, the societal contexts, or the relation between these, whereas others attempt to conduct empirical investigations of individual, societal, or relational events.

The precise methods for conducting the empirical investigations of social psychology borrow heavily from the laboratory techniques developed by the experimental psychologist, the survey and other field techniques developed by the sociologist, and the intense observational and interview techniques developed by the cultural anthropologist. Although there are some who would maintain strongly that strict laboratory experimentation, in which there is a maximum of control and a minimum of confounding errors, is the only proper method for the scientific testing of hypotheses or the gathering of empirical data, it seems rather apparent that all *systematic* techniques of data collection, including the highly complex processes involved in observation, have an important place in the *repertoire* of the social psychological investigator. It is thus with an openness to all methods that we have included, side-by-side, readings of a strictly experimental, strictly field observational, and strictly survey and correlational nature.

As has already been stated, the collection of readings which follows is a reflection of the complexity and scope of the present state of social psychology, including psychological, sociological, and anthropological theories, concepts, and methods. To provide an organization to a field with such scope, the readings are grouped into three major sections.

In the first section, "Approaches," we cover the major existing approaches to studying the phenomena of interest to social psychology. In this section, readings which deal mainly with individualistic concepts (such as cognition, motivation, and attitude), developmental concepts (such as socialization, cognitive development, and the development of the self concept), and interactional or relational conceptions (such as interpersonal perception and influence) are represented.

In the second section, "Contexts," we cover the major contexts in which social behavior may be seen to occur. Material dealing with the small group, the large scale organization, the community, and the society are represented. The contexts presented in this second section provide the framework within which the action of the actors outlined in the first section occurs. The performance we as social psychologists witness is a function of the actor, characterized by the section one approaches and the stage-audience situation upon or within which his action takes place, characterized by the section two contexts.

In the third and final section, we take a brief but important look at certain significant social problems and issues which confront each of us living within a complexly organized system. Given what information we now have about the actor and his stage, we are ready to examine the manner by which such social psychological information aids our understanding of these problem areas of pressing importance.

If there is a theme which runs throughout the entire book and which provides the thread by which one may better grasp the field of social psychology, it is embodied within the previously mentioned actor analogy. The social psychologist is witness to a performance which he seeks to understand and explain. He is aware that what he witnesses can only be understood in terms of the actor performing, the stage on which the performance takes place, and the audience which is witness to that performance. Given a different actor, a different stage, or a different audience, and the play witnessed is itself different.

SECTION ONE

Social Psychological Approaches

to the Study of Behavior

In this major section, we examine five approaches employed by social psychologists in studying the phenomena of their field. The number five should not be assumed to have any magic connotations, for in actuality, it represents a somewhat arbitrary manner of dividing up and organizing the significant areas of social psychological inquiry into: Linguistic and cognitive processes; interpersonal perception, interaction, and influence; motivation and emotion; socialization, role taking, and the self concept; and the concept of attitude.

These five approaches, although presented separately, are better seen as interdependent groupings which reflect present foci in the field. Each basically reflects the social psychologists' interest in the characteristics of the individual entering the interactive arena.

A. Via Linguistic and Cognitive Processes

I. Cognitive Processes

An early Platonic trichotomy describes all mental processes in terms of three major aspects: (1) Cognitive, involving knowing, thinking, perceiving; (2) Affective, involving feelings and emotions; and (3) Conative, involving acting, doing, striving. In this section we examine this first aspect.

Cognitive theories in psychology, similar in many respects to the subjective orientation approach in sociology, deal with the manner by which the individual cognizes, maps, organizes, or defines the world in which he behaves. Cognition, therefore, refers to the basic processes whereby an individual structures and knows his environment.

In somewhat oversimplified terms, one can differentiate between two basic approaches to the study of man. In one, the individual organism is seen as a passive recipient of stimuli presented to him from without and to which he reacts much as a billiard ball does when hit with a cue in the hands of a skillful player. In the other, the individual organism is seen as an active participator in and constructor of a world of stimuli which he selectively processes and to which he selectively responds. According to this latter view, the manner by which the individual actively processes the stimulus input, or in other words his processes of cognition, play an extremely significant role in his behavior. These cognitive processes, therefore, become basic to the full understanding of a social psychological being who is engaged in actively coming to grips with a physical and a social environment.

The study of these cognitive processes importantly enters a social psychology which takes this active view of the individual. For how the individual cognizes or defines his world is one of the major determinants of his manner of responding in that world. Two individuals entering a situation, one defining it as threatening, the other as friendly, would be expected to act differently in that situation. To understand fully how they react requires, therefore, an understanding of the manner by which each processes the information in that situation to arrive at different categorization schema: For one it is categorized as threatening; for the other, as friendly.

Not only may the *manner* by which two people categorize, cognize, or define a situation differ, but as importantly, the *number* of categories each has available for processing the data from the situation may differ. Thus, for example, one person may have only two categories for classifying people, "good vs. bad," while another person may have a multitude of such categories along a "good-bad" dimension. Undoubtedly the manner by which these two persons define situations and interact with others in those situations will be importantly influenced by this factor.

In addition to the number and kind of cognitive categories an individual has for defining a situation, the actual processes of cognitive interaction by which such categories function are important to examine. Do category systems for processing the environment function to maintain simplicity, to maintain a degree of balance or internal consistency, to maintain a degree of fit with additional information, to maintain a congruence with one's self concept?

Each of the readings included in this section has as its major interest some aspect of this cognitive process. The Festinger reading on cognitive dissonance presents his formulation of a principle by which cognitive processes are assumed to operate. In his reading, he discusses the nature of cognitive dissonance and the manner by which such dissonance may be reduced by the individual. In addition, he discusses the implications of this principle for the overt behavior of the individual, citing experimental evidence supporting his position.

The Harvey, Hunt, and Schroder reading presents a framework for discussing the manner by which the individual develops a cognitive or conceptual framework for organizing his environment.

II. Linguistic Processes

Language behavior, by which we refer to the spoken rather than the written representation, is a universal aspect of culture in which each of us has a continuous and vital participation. By listening to and recording the speech utterances of a speech community, and from these detailed records abstracting the patterns of speaking, linguists have been able to learn a great deal about language behavior. While structural linguists have demonstrated the existence of certain basic sound, meaning, and order or grammatical units into which all known languages may be analyzed, historical linguists have focused their attention on language clusters or families and on the historical changes which languages undergo.

Whereas these preceding interests developed mainly within branches of anthropology, a concern with language development within the individual has occupied the attention of many in psychology. Coupling an interest in the sheer facts of language learning and development which marked early psychological concern, with an interest in language as a shared cognitive system for processing the environment, we have what presently exists in social psychology as the field of psycholinguistics. The development of what has come to be called the Sapir-Whorf hypothesis, or the hypothesis of linguistic relativity, reflects this social psychological interest in language as a process which structures the environment, yielding somewhat different "environmental realities" for speakers of different languages: Hence a linguistic relativity principle, with reality being made relative to the linguistic system of the speakers.

The article by Fishman attempts to offer a more comprehensive and systematic way of examining this linguistic relativity principle and its implications. Unlike the Fishman reading which focuses mainly upon the relativity principle, the article by Church more broadly examines the nature of language as a cognitive mode of the organism including in his discussion a treatment of the relation between linguistic development and the development of the individual's concept of himself, or his identity.

To the social psychologist, interested in understanding and explaining the manner by which the individual relates to an environment in which he actively participates and which he actively structures, the study of the culturally shared modes of such organization provided by the linguistic system provides an extremely important area of inquiry.

Although we include only these four readings in this section dealing with linguistic and cognitive processes, it will be helpful to the reader to take note of readings in other sections which also have the flavor of this cognitive approach: (1) The readings in section B on interpersonal perception and interaction generally involve an aspect of the individual's cognitive structure, including situational definitions involving the individual's perception of and consequent reactions to other persons. (2) The approach of White's motivation article, dealing with the concepts of competence, exploration, and mastery of the environment suggest the importance to motivation of these cognitive processes of "knowing" the environment and one's relation to it. (3) The Schachter and Singer article on emotional states contains a section which discusses the role of cognitive factors on structuring the situation and providing one component of the individual's emotional experience. (4) The cognitive approaches to attitude formation and change, especially the principle of congruity proposed by Osgood and Tannenbaum and the theory and research of Rosenberg, are further instances of the generality of the study of cognitive processes in present day social psychology.

Cognitive Dissonance / Leon Festinger

It is the subject of a new theory based on experiments showing that the grass is usually not greener on the other side of the fence and that grapes are sourest when they are in easy reach.

There is an experiment in psychology that you can perform easily in your own home if you have a child three or four years old. Buy two toys that you are fairly sure will be equally attractive to the child. Show them both to him and say: "Here are two nice toys. This one is for you to keep. The other I must give back to the store." You then hand the child the toy that is his to keep and ask: "Which of the two toys do you like better?" Studies have shown that in such a situation most children will tell you they prefer the toy they are to keep.

This response of children seems to conflict with the old saying that the grass is always greener on the other side of the fence. Do adults respond in the same way under similar circumstances or does the adage indeed become true as we grow older? The question is of considerable interest because the adult world is filled with choices and alternative courses of action that are often about equally attractive. When they make a choice of a college or a car or a spouse or a home or a political candidate, do most people remain satisfied with their choice or do they tend to wish they had made a different one? Naturally any choice may turn out to be a bad one on the basis of some objective measurement, but the question is: Does some psychological process come into play immediately after the making of a choice that colors one's attitude, either favorably or unfavorably, toward the decision?

To illuminate this question there is another experiment one can do at home, this time using an adult as a subject rather than a child. Buy two presents for your wife, again choosing things you are reasonably sure she will find about equally attractive. Find some plausible excuse for having both of them in your possession, show them to your wife and ask her to tell you how attractive each one is to her. After you have obtained a good measurement of attractiveness, tell her that she can have one of them, whichever she chooses. The other you will return to the store. After she has made her choice, ask her once more to evaluate the attractiveness of each of them. If you compare the evaluations of attractiveness before and after the choice, you will probably find that the chosen present has increased in attractiveness and the rejected one decreased.

Such behavior can be explained by a new theory concerning "cognitive dissonance." This theory centers around the idea that if a person knows various things that are not psychologically consistent with one another, he will, in a variety of ways, try to make them more consistent. Two items of information that psychologically do not fit together are said to be in a dissonant relation to each other. The items of information may be about behavior, feelings, opinions, things in the environment and so on. The word "cognitive" simply emphasizes that the theory deals with relations among items of information.

Such items can of course be changed. A person can change his opinion; he can change his behavior, thereby changing the information he has about it; he can even distort his perception and his information about the world around him. Changes in items of information that produce or restore consistency are referred to as dissonance-reducing changes.

Cognitive dissonance is a motivating state of affairs. Just as hunger impels a person to eat, so does dissonance impel a person to change his opinions or his behavior. The world, however, is much more effectively arranged for hunger reduction than it is for dissonance reduction. It is almost always possible to find something to eat. It is not always easy to reduce dissonance. Sometimes it may be very difficult or even impossible to change behavior or opinions that are involved in dissonant relations. Consequently there are circumstances in which appreciable dissonance may persist for long periods.

To understand cognitive dissonance as a motivating state, it is necessary to have a clearer conception of the conditions that produce it. The simplest definition of dissonance can, perhaps, be given in terms of a person's expectations. In the course of our lives we have all accumulated a large number of expectations about what things go together and what things do not. When such an expectation is not fulfilled, dissonance occurs.

For example, a person standing unprotected in the rain would expect to get wet. If he found himself in the rain and he was not getting wet, there would exist dissonance between these two pieces of information. This unlikely example is one where the expectations of different people would all be uniform. There are obviously many instances where different people would not share the same expectations. Someone who is very self-confident might expect to succeed at whatever he tried, whereas someone who had a low opinion of himself might normally expect to fail. Under these circumstances what would produce dissonance for one person might produce consonance for another. In experimental investigations, of course, an effort is made to provide situations in which expectations are rather uniform.

Perhaps the best way to explain the theory of cognitive dissonance is to show its application to specific situations. The rest of this article, therefore, will be devoted to a discussion of three examples of cognitive dissonance. I shall discuss the effects of making a decision, of lying and of temptation. These three examples by no means cover all the situations in which dissonance can be created. Indeed, it seldom happens that everything a person knows about an action he has taken is perfectly consistent with his having taken it. The three examples, however, may serve to illustrate the range of situations in which dissonance can be expected to occur. They will also serve to show the kinds of dissonance-reduction effects that are obtained under a special circumstance: when dissonance involves the person's behavior and the action in question is difficult to change.

Let us consider first the consequences of making a decision. Imagine the situation of a person who has carefully weighed two reasonably attractive alternatives and then chosen one of them—a decision that, for our purposes, can be regarded as irrevocable. All the information this person has concerning the attractive features of the rejected alternative (and the possible unattractive features of the chosen alternative) are now inconsistent, or dissonant, with the knowledge that he has made the given choice. It is true that the person also knows many things that are consistent or consonant with the choice

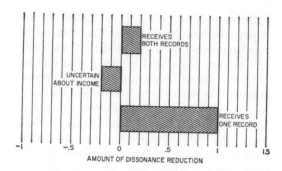

AMOUNT OF DISSONANCE REDUCTION

Dissonance reduction is a psychological phenomenon found to occur after a person has made a choice between two approximately equal alternatives. The effect of the phenomenon is to enhance the attractiveness of the chosen object or chosen course of action. The chart summarizes the results of an experiment in which high school girls rated the attractiveness of 12 "hit" records before and after choosing one of them as a gift. Substantial dissonance reduction occurred under only one of three experimental conditions described in the text. Under two other conditions no systematic reduction was observed.

he has made, which is to say all the attractive features of the chosen alternative and unattractive features of the rejected one. Nevertheless, some dissonance exists and after the decision the individual will try to reduce the dissonance.

There are two major ways in which the individual can reduce dissonance in this situation. He can persuade himself that the attractive features of the rejected alternative are not really so attractive as he had originally thought, and that the unattractive features of the chosen alternative are not really unattractive. He can also provide additional justification for his choice by exaggerating the attractive features of the chosen alternative and the unattractive features of the rejected alternative. In other words, according to the theory the process of dissonance reduction should lead, after the decision, to an increase in the desirability of the chosen alternative and a decrease in the desirability of the rejected alternative.

This phenomenon has been demonstrated in a variety of experiments. A brief description of one of these will suffice to illustrate the precise nature of the effect. In an experiment performed by Jon Jecker of Stanford University, high school girls were asked to rate the attractiveness of each of 12 "hit" records. For each girl two records that she

had rated as being only moderately attractive were selected and she was asked which of the two she would like as a gift. After having made her choice, the girl again rated the attractiveness of all the records. The dissonance created by the decision could be reduced by increasing the attractiveness of the chosen record and decreasing the attractiveness of the rejected record. Consequently a measurement of dissonance reduction could be obtained by summing both of these kinds of changes in ratings made before and after the decision.

Different experimental variations were employed in this experiment in order to examine the dynamics of the process of dissonance reduction. Let us look at three of these experimental variations. In all three conditions the girls, when they were making their choice, were given to understand there was a slight possibility that they might actually be given both records. In one condition they were asked to rerate the records after they had made their choice but before they knew definitely whether they would receive both records or only the one they chose. The results for this condition should indicate whether dissonance reduction begins with having made the choice or whether it is suspended until the uncertainty is resolved. In a second condition the girls were actually given both records after their choice and were then asked to rerate all the records. Since they had received both records and therefore no dissonance existed following the decision, there should be no evidence of dissonance reduction in this condition. In a third condition the girls were given only the record they chose and were then asked to do the rerating. This, of course, resembles the normal outcome of a decision and the usual dissonance reduction should occur.

The chart on this page shows the results for these three conditions. When the girls are uncertain as to the outcome, or when they receive both records, there is no dissonance reduction—that is, no systematic change in attractiveness of the chosen and rejected records. The results in both conditions are very close to zero—one slightly positive, the other slightly negative. When they receive only the record they chose, however, there is a large systematic change in rating to reduce dissonance. Since dissonance reduction is only observed in this last experimental condition, it is evident that dissonance reduction does not occur during the process of making a decision but only after the decision is made and the outcome is clear.

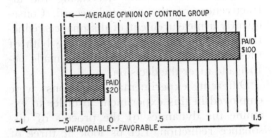

Consequences of lying are found to vary, depending on whether the justification for the lie is large or small. In this experiment students were persuaded to tell others that a boring experience was really fun. Those in one group were paid only $1 for their cooperation; in a second group, $20. The low-paid students, having least justification for lying, experienced most dissonance and reduced it by coming to regard the experience favorably.

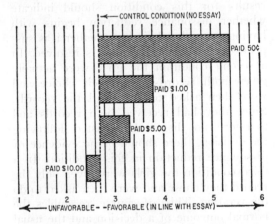

Graded change of opinion was produced by paying subjects various sums for writing essays advocating opinions contrary to their beliefs. When examined later, students paid the least had changed their opinion the most to agree with what they had written. Only the highest paid group held to their original opinion more strongly than did a control group.

Let us turn now to the consequences of lying. There are many circumstances in which, for one reason or another, an individual publicly states something that is at variance with his private belief. Here again one can expect dissonance to arise. There is an inconsistency between knowing that one really believes one thing and knowing that one has publicly stated something quite different. Again, to be sure, the individual knows things that are consonant with his overt, public behavior. All the reasons that induced him to make the public statement are consonant with his having made it and provide him with some justification for his behavior. Nevertheless, some dissonance exists and, according to the theory, there will be attempts to reduce it. The degree to which the dissonance is bothersome for the individual will depend on two things. The more deviant his public statement is from his private belief, the greater will be the dissonance. The greater the amount of justification the person has for having made the public statement, the less bothersome the dissonance will be.

How can the dissonance be reduced? One method is obvious. The individual can remove the dissonance by retracting his public statement. But let us consider only those instances in which the public statement, once made, cannot be changed or withdrawn; in other words, in which the behavior is irrevocable. Under such circumstances the major avenue for reduction of the dissonance is change of private opinion. That is, if the private opinion were changed so that it agreed with what was publicly stated, obviously the dissonance would be gone. The theory thus leads us to expect that after having made an irrevocable public statement at variance with his private belief, a person will tend to change his private belief to bring it into line with his public statement. Furthermore, the degree to which he changes his private belief will depend on the amount of justification or the amount of pressure for making the public statement initially. The less the original justification or pressure, the greater the dissonance and the more the person's private belief can be expected to change.

An experiment recently conducted at Stanford University by James M. Carlsmith and me illustrates the nature of this effect. In the experiment, college students were induced to make a statement at variance with their own belief. It was done by using students who had volunteered to participate in an experiment to measure "motor performance." The purported experiment lasted an hour and was a boring and fatiguing session. At the end of the hour the experimenter thanked the subject for his participation, indicating that the experiment was over. The real purpose of the hour-long session, however, was to provide each subject with an identical experience about which he would have an unfavorable opinion.

At the end of the fatiguing hour the experimenter enlisted the subject's aid in preparing the next person for the experiment. The subject was led to believe that, for experimental purposes, the next person was supposed to be given the impression that the hour's session was going to be very interesting and lots of fun. The subject was persuaded to help in this deception by telling the next subject, who was waiting in an adjoining room, that he himself had just finished the hour and that it had indeed been very interesting and lots of fun. The first subject was then interviewed by someone else to determine his actual private opinion of the experiment.

Two experimental conditions were run that differed only in the amount of pressure, or justification given the subject for stating a public opinion at variance with his private belief. All subjects, of course, had the justification of helping to conduct a scientific experiment. In addition to this, half of the subjects were paid $1 for their help—a relatively small amount of money; the other subjects were paid $20—a rather large sum for the work involved. From the theory we would expect that the subjects who were paid only $1, having less justification for their action, would have more dissonance and would change their private beliefs more in order to reduce the dissonance. In other words, we would expect the greatest change in private opinion among the subjects given the least tangible incentive for changing.

The illustration on page 12 shows the results of the experiment. The broken line in the chart shows the results for a control group of subjects. These subjects participated in the hour-long session and then were asked to give their private opinion of it. Their generally unfavorable views are to be expected when no dissonance is induced between private belief and public statement. It is clear from the chart that introducing such dissonance produced a change of opinion so that the subjects who were asked to take part in a deception finally came to think better of the session than did the control subjects. It is also clear that only in the condition where they were paid a dollar is this opinion change appreciable. When they were paid a lot of money, the justification for misrepresenting private belief is high and there is correspondingly less change of opinion to reduce dissonance.

Another way to summarize the result is to say that those who are highly rewarded for doing something that involves dissoance change their opinion less in the direction of agreeing with what they did than those who are given very little reward. This result may seem surprising, since we are used to thinking that reward is effective in creating change. It must be remembered, however, that the critical factor here is that the reward is being used to induce a behavior that is dissonant with private opinion.

To show that this result is valid and not just a function of the particular situation or the particular sums of money used for reward, Arthur R. Cohen of New York University conducted a similar experiment in a different context. Cohen paid subjects to write essays advocating an opinion contrary to what they really believed. Subjects were paid either $10, $5, $1 or 50 cents to do this. To measure the extent to which dissonance was reduced by their changing their opinion, each subject was then given a questionnaire, which he left unsigned, to determine his private opinion on the issue. The extent to which the subjects reduced dissonance by changing their opinion to agree with what they wrote in the essay is shown in the lower illustration on page 12. Once again it is clear that the smaller the original justification for engaging in the dissonance-producing action, the greater the subsequent change in private opinion to bring it into line with the action.

The final set of experiments I shall discuss deals with the consequences of resisting temptation. What happens when a person wants something and discovers that he cannot have it? Does he now want it even more or does he persuade himself that it is really not worth having? Sometimes our common general understanding of human behavior can provide at least crude answers to such questions. In this case, however, our common understanding is ambiguous, because it supplies two contradictory answers. Everyone knows the meaning of the term "sour grapes"; it is the attitude taken by a person who persuades himself that he really does not want what he cannot have. But we are also familiar with the opposite reaction. The child who is not allowed to eat candy and hence loves candy passionately; the woman who adores expensive clothes even though she cannot afford to own them; the man who has a hopeless obsession for a woman who spurns his attentions. Everyone "understands" the behavior of the person who longs for what he cannot have.

Obviously one cannot say one of these reactions is wrong and the other is right; they both occur. One might at least, however, try to answer the question: Under what circumstances does one reaction take place and not the other? If we examine the question from the point of view of the theory of dissonance, a partial answer begins to emerge.

Imagine the psychological situation that exists for an individual who is tempted to engage in a certain action but for one reason or another refrains. An analysis of the situation here reveals its similarity to the other dissonance-producing situations. An individual's knowledge concerning the attractive aspects of the activity toward which he was tempted is dissonant with the knowledge that he has refrained from engaging in the activity. Once more, of course the individual has some knowledge that is consonant with his behavior in the situation. All the pressures, reasons and justifications for refraining are consonant with his actual behavior. Nevertheless, the dissonance does exist, and there will be psychological activity oriented toward reducing this dissonance.

As we have already seen in connection with other illustrations, one major way to reduce dissonance is to change one's opinions and evaluations in order to bring them closer

in line with one's actual behavior. Therefore when there is dissonance produced by resisting temptation, it can be reduced by derogating or devaluing the activity toward which one was tempted. This derivation from the theory clearly implies the sour-grapes attitude, but both theory and experiment tell us that such dissonance-reducing effects will occur only when there was insufficient original justification for the behavior. Where the original justification for refraining from the action was great, little dissonance would have occurred and there would have been correspondingly little change of opinion in order to reduce dissonance. Therefore one might expect that if a person had resisted temptation in a situation of strong prohibition or strong threatened punishment, little dissonance would have been created and one would not observe the sour-grapes effect. One would expect this effect only if the person resisted temptation under conditions of weak deterrent.

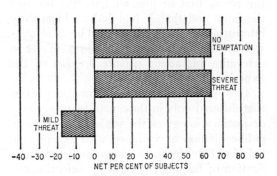

NO TEMPTATION

SEVERE THREAT

MILD THREAT

-40 -30 -20 -10   0   10 20 30 40 50 60 70 80 90
NET PER CENT OF SUBJECTS

Consequences of temptation were explored by prohibiting children from playing with a desirable toy. Later the children were asked to re-evaluate the attractiveness of the forbidden toy. In one case the prohibition was enforced by removing the toy from the child's presence. In the second case the prohibition took the form of a threat of severe punishment; in the third case, a threat of mild punishment. The chart shows the net per cent of children who thought the forbidden toy more attractive after the experiment than before. ("Net per cent" means the per cent who found the toy more attractive minus the per cent who found it less so.) Evidently only those threatened mildly experienced much dissonance, and they reduced it by downgrading toy's desirability. Others thought the toy more desirable.

This line of reasoning leaves open the question of when the reverse effect occurs— that is, the situation in which desire for the "unattainable" object is increased. Experimentally it is possible to look at both effects. This was done by Elliot Aronson and Carlsmith, at Stanford University, in an experiment that sheds considerable light on the problem. The experiment was performed with children who were about four years old. Each child was individually brought into a large playroom in which there were five toys on a table. After the child had had an opportunity to play briefly with each toy, he was asked to rank the five in order of attractiveness. The toy that the child liked second best was then left on the table and the other four toys were spread around on the floor. The experimenter told the child that he had to leave for a few minutes to do an errand but would be back soon. The experimenter then left the room for 10 minutes. Various techniques were employed to "prohibit" the child from playing with the particular toy that he liked second best while the experimenter was out of the room.

For different children this prohibition was instituted in three different ways. In one condition there was no temptation at all; the experimenter told the child he could play with any of the toys in the room and then took the second-best toy with him when he left. In the other two conditions temptation was present: the second-best toy was left on the table in the experimenter's absence. The children were told they could play with any of the toys in the room except the one on the table. The children in one group were threatened with mild punishment if they violated the prohibition, whereas those in the other group were threatened with more severe punishment. (The actual nature of the punishment was left unspecified.)

During his absence from the room the experimenter observed each child through a one-way mirror. None of the children in the temptation conditions played with the prohibited toy. After 10 minutes were up the experimenter returned to the playroom and each child was again allowed to play briefly with each of the five toys. The attractiveness of each toy for the child was again measured. By comparing the before and after measurements of the attractiveness of the toy the child originally liked second best, one can assess the effects of the prohibition. The results are shown in the chart on page 14.

When there was no temptation—that is, when the prohibited toy was not physically present—there was of course no dissonance, and the preponderant result is an increase in the attractiveness of the prohibited toy. When the temptation is present but the prohibition is enforced by means of a severe threat of punishment, there is likewise little dissonance created by refraining, and again the preponderant result is an increase in the attractiveness of the prohibited toy. In other words, it seems clear that a prohibition that is enforced in such a way as not to introduce dissonance results in a greater desire for the prohibited activity.

The results are quite different, however, when the prohibition is enforced by only a mild threat of punishment. Here we see the result to be expected from the theory of dissonance. Because the justification for refraining from playing with the toy is relatively weak, there is appreciable dissonance between the child's knowledge that the toy is attractive and his actual behavior. The tendency to reduce this dissonance is strong enough to more than overcome the effect apparent in the other two conditions. Here, as a result of dissonance reduction, we see an appreciable sour-grapes phenomenon.

The theory of cognitive dissonance obviously has many implications for everyday life. In addition to throwing light on one's own behavior, it would seem to carry useful lessons for everyone concerned with understanding human behavior in a world where everything is not black and white.

Stages of Conceptual Development /

O. J. Harvey (*University of Colorado*)
David E. Hunt (*Syracuse University*)
Harold M. Schroder (*Princeton University*)

How do concepts develop? We view concepts as jointly determined by the internal state of the organism and conditions of the relevant environment. Out of this interdependent totality of dispositional and situational determinants our emphasis shall be on those internal states represented by the stage of development of the individual at the particular time and on those external factors embodied in the training conditions to which the individual is exposed. The present chapter deals specifically with the stages of development.

FIRST STAGE: UNILATERAL DEPENDENCE

Conceptual systems in the first stage are characterized by external control, by the acceptance of externally derived concepts or schemata not built up through experience with the actual stimuli, and by the absolutistic nature of such concepts. In a new or relatively unstructured situation, a person's functioning is maximally anchored in external control and is therefore characterized by seeking external criteria for evaluating his behavior. The term unilateral is intended to convey the fact that functioning in this stage is adjusted to match absolutistic, ready-made conceptual criteria. Unilateral dependence implies a lack of differentiation between a rule and its purpose; between authority and one's own experience; between one's thoughts about authority and oneself. First stage functioning is assumed to have the following characteristics: things are endowed with power as in magical thought; answers to questions are accepted more in the sense of absolutes (Werner, 1957); thinking is more concrete ("this is the way it is because it is"); behavior associated with this stage is characterized by a greater immediacy, by greater sensitivity to limits, to what is right and wrong, to what is tolerated and not tolerated, and by greater submissiveness to external control.

According to Bennis and Shepard (1956) the first stage in the development of a group involves a preoccupation with authority and submission, or in their words, ". . . the characteristic expectations of group members are that the trainer will establish rules of the game and distribute rewards. He is presumed to know what the goals are or ought to be" (p. 420). At this stage these authors view the group's behavior as a plea for the leader to tell them what to do. In problem solving the beginning stage of conceptual functioning is characterized by rigidity and all-or-none shifting. In the initial stage of psychotherapy, patients begin by seeking a direct solution (Rogers, 1951), or as Rotter (1954) observed, they hope that ". . . the therapist will . . . either in some magical way provide him with a better personality or in some way or other remove the frustrations from his external circumstances" (p. 355).

In the study of the moral development of the child, Piaget (1932) refers to this stage as moral realism. According to Piaget, this stage possesses three features:

. . . In the first place, duty, as viewed by moral realism, is essentially heteronomous. Any act that shows obedience to a rule or even to an adult, regardless of what he may command, is good; any act that does not conform to rules is bad. A rule is therefore not in any way something elaborated, or even judged or interpreted by the mind; it is given as such, readymade and external to the mind. It is also conceived of as revealed by the adult and imposed by him. The good, therefore, is rigidly defined by obedience.

In the second place, moral realism demands that the letter rather than the spirit

Reprinted with permission from the senior author, O. J. Harvey, *Conceptual Systems and Personality Organization,* Copyright © 1961 by John Wiley & Sons, Inc., pp. 85, 94–109.

of the law shall be observed. This feature derives from the first. . . .

In the third place, moral realism induces an objective conception of responsibility. We can even use this as a criterion of realism, for such an attitude toward responsibility is easier to detect than the two that precede it. For since he takes rules literally and thinks of good only in terms of obedience, the child will at first evaluate acts not in accordance with the motive that has prompted them, but in terms of their exact conformity with established rules (pp. 106–107).

According to the normative observations made by the staff at the Gesell Institute of Child Development (Ilg and Ames, 1955), characteristics of conceptual functioning similar to those in the first stage are first observed at about the age of two. The normative two-year-old ". . . can occasionally put another person's wishes above his own. . . . though he cannot as yet share with other children. . . ." (p. 25). As the authors point out, however, early child development is characterized by rapid and violent swings from one extreme of functioning to another. The stages are close together so that the normative two-and-a-half-year-old child is stubborn and domineering.

It appears from the observational data that a child encountering a relatively new environmental demand is likely to begin an entirely new developmental cycle. Thus behavior typical of this first stage of functioning was reported to be characteristic of children of two, five, ten, and sixteen years of age. (See Table 2.) The relationship of first stage functioning to new environmental demands may be seen when we note that these ages approximate the normative years when children (1) begin to talk, (2) begin school, group play, (3) begin to look to peers as

TABLE 2

Cycle	Age	Stages of Conceptual Development			
		First Stage External Control	Second Stage Negativism	Third Stage Mutuality	Fourth Stage Interdependence
I Infancy	1½ 2 2½ 3 3½–4½				
II Childhood	5 6 7–8 9				
III† Late Childhood	10 11 12–14 15–16				

This table is based on an interpretation of the normative observations taken at the Gesell Institute (Ilg and Ames, 1955).

† This part of the graph is hypothetical to show the expected progression to more abstract functioning in the third cycle.

opposed to the family as a model, and (4) begin to take on the adult role, respectively. For example, the normative five-year-old is described as "... a good age.... His mother is the center of his world.... He likes to do things with her and for her, likes to obey her commands. He likes to be instructed and get permission" (p. 33). And the normative ten-year-old, after passing through all ranges of behavior, as "... his parents' word is so utterly law ... He not only obeys easily and naturally, but he seems to expect to obey and gains status in his own eyes by his obedience" (Ilg and Ames, p. 40). Naturally first stage behavior at five is different from first stage behavior at ten, particularly if progression through more abstract levels has occurred between these ages. Less difference between first stage functioning at different ages would be expected if arrestation occurred at an early age. Developmental norms representing a return to an earlier stage of organization after progression to varying levels of abstractness would be required for diagnosis or a statistical description of development.

Since first stage functioning may be quite desirable from the source's standpoint (for example, the parents' wishes) he may attempt to prevent the subject's progression beyond this stage. Procedures that prevent progression beyond the first stage may be implicitly justified by conceiving of first stage functioning as highly desirable and valued. For example, in education, absolutistic functioning is often confused with development; in dogma it can be viewed as faith; in totalitarian states as being a good citizen; and in personal development as being "good," obedient, or trustworthy. Although this early level of functioning represents some degree of all these "positive" characteristics and may be advantageous in certain situations, the nature of relatedness in the first stage is nonetheless concrete, unilateral, and absolutistic.

TRANSITION TO THE SECOND STAGE (FIRST TRANSITION)

In order for development to progress beyond this unilateral level of functioning, new differentiations must evolve and become integrated with old differentiations. From pole A of first stage concepts, the opposite pole of the conceptual system, which represents the simplest and next most abstract differentiation, is resistance to external control (pole B). Training that induces sufficient openness to such oppositional tendencies, and simultaneously sufficient openness to and trust in external control, maximizes the potential for integrating these opposing motivational tendencies and for developmental progression to the second stage. In common language, parents whose behavior both promotes trust and gives permission and encouragement to develop assertiveness, opposition, and age-appropriate independence provide the necessary basis for developmental progress to what we refer to as the second stage.

Through the integration of differentiations based on unilateral absolutistic control and opposition to external control, the subject is able (1) to free himself from the constraints of symbiotic dependence, (2) to differentiate between external and internal control, and (3) to manipulate the criterion applied to his own behavior through the potential of generating different systems of ordering outside the framework of external control. Under conditions of progression, first stage tendencies are less absolutistic and second stage tendencies are less negativistic, compared to functioning that is arrested at these stages.

The emergence of second stage concepts involves the differentiation of the subject from the source, thus opening the possibility of dependency at a different level of abstraction. The difference between dependency in the form of evaluating others as supportive and dependency in the form of viewing others in terms of absolutistic control is similar to the difference between imitation and symbiotic relatedness. Dependency in the form of mutuality cannot be experienced until the self and the source have been differentiated.

SECOND STAGE: NEGATIVE INDEPENDENCE

Negative independence represents functioning that is negatively related to external constraints. Since such functioning represents a lessening of the importance of external control and the initial budding of internal control, we use the term, negative independence; the term does not imply any necessary hostility or aggression. Hostile reactions represent the extreme manifestations of closed second stage relatedness, which denotes the arrestation of development at this stage. For progression to occur beyond the first stage, the subject must test the limits of absolute solutions and rules in order to avoid complete reliance on externally given conceptual systems; otherwise he will remain dependent upon external control. A person working in a problem-solving situation, for example, would never attempt an alternative solution unless he resisted or questioned the initial solution. Such questioning cannot occur if the person feels that the original solution is absolute and under the control of the source.

Second stage concepts represent a differentiation from external forces, but such concepts are not highly articulated. However, they are the foundations on which informational and interdependent standards can develop and represent the initial form of internal control. Put in the language of the present conception of development, the person must successfully progress through second stage concepts in order to move on to the third and fourth stages.

This stage has been referred to as "freedom from" authoritarian control and contrasted with positive freedom, independence, or "freedom to" (Fromm, 1941). Coffey (1954) refers to an early stage of "resistance" in group psychotherapy, and Bennis and Shepard (1956) report that group development proceeds from a preoccupation with submission to a preoccupation with rebellion. Functioning at this stage is characterized by such clichés as "I'll do it myself"; by the emergence of "self will."

A comprehensive study of the emergence of a period of resistance in infants and young children has been carried out by Levy (1955). He gives many examples, such as "the battle of the spoon" and "clash of wills" and includes certain forms of "shyness" in this class. According to Levy:

Whatever the measure of non-compliance, —the intelligence test, the physical examination, observations of spontaneous behavior, experiments, the clinical case record or ordinary inquiry—all studies confirm the existence of a period in the early childhood of most children in which negativism is more frequent than in the period preceding or following. . . . There was a clear rise in frequency as the age of 18 months was reached, and a decided fall in frequency when the age of two years was past. The findings were also consistent with the mother's accounts of the child's behavior at home (p. 210). [And later in considering the common features of oppositional behavior he states] A number of them appear to have a common function of resistance to external influence. This influence would determine when an act is to begin, . . . and when it is to end. . . . (p. 213).

Observations at the Gesell Institute (Ilg and Ames, 1955) indicate a period of negativism directly following the "obedient" stages outlined under the first stage (see Table 2). The first onset of second stage functioning was observed at about eighteen months and again at two and one-half, six, and presumably again, at about eleven. At two and one-half behavior was described as:

He wants exactly what he wants when he wants it. . . . Everything has to be done just so. Everything has to be right in the place he considers its proper place. . . . With no ability to choose between alternatives . . . the child at this age shuttles back and forth endlessly between any two extremes, seeming to be trying to include both in his decision. "I will—I won't." . . . He wants to go on and on with whatever he is doing (pp. 25–26).

This behavior, characterized by conflict between compliance and opposition and rituals and stubbornness, is an excellent example of the transition between first and second stage functioning, which is described in detail in the chapters to follow.

At two and one-half the conflicting first and second stage tendencies do not appear to be well integrated, as shown by the continued vacillation between "will-ing" and "won't-ing" as well as by ritualistic behavior. In the next cycle of development from five to ten (second swing of the pendulum in

Table 2) children demonstrate the characteristics of a more successful transition to second stage conceptual functioning. At six years of age, typical behavior is much closer to our description of negative independence, internal control, and the avoidance of dependency. Normative functioning is described as:

> . . . *he* wants to be the center of his world, even though he hasn't yet developed a secure sense of himself [negative independence]. . . . Whatever is wrong, Mother gets the blame [externalization of blame]. . . . he tends to be extremely negative in his response to others. That he has been asked to do something is in his eyes sufficient reason for refusing to do it [internal control and avoidance of dependency] (Ilg and Ames, 1955, pp. 34–35).

The progression to second stage functioning is perhaps the most critical point in child development, education, and group development. As Levy states, "Without this resistant character the organism's response would be determined entirely by external stimuli. . . . The capacity to resist external influence thus enables the organism to use and develop inner controls" (p. 213). Levy also quotes a study by Hetzer (1929) who compared two groups of seven-year-old children divided on the presence or absence of a "stubborn period" in development. Children who had not gone through the "stubborn period" were significantly more dependent on the teacher's help than others.

The value, therefore, of second stage functioning lies primarily in its providing the essential basis for the development of mutuality, dependence, and later interdependence. In order to appreciate this value, the observer must view this stage in developmental perspective. The immediate quality of second stage functioning may strike the observer as disagreeable. In contrast to first stage functioning which may be viewed as desirable by certain sources, the oppositional quality of second stage functioning may be strongly resisted by power-oriented, absolutistic sources or by sources who are insecure regarding their own status and competence. The immature quality of second stage functioning may also prove threatening since it is likely to be less predictable or dependable. Despite these immediate, potentially disagreeable qualities, second stage functioning is an essential stage in development. The overthrow of feudalism, authoritarian control, or the divine right of kings is analogous to the transition to second stage functioning. As Fromm (1941) has so eloquently described, however, such revolutions do not magically lead to true independence or interdependence. In nations, as in individuals, development is assumed to proceed through stages, but national development is slower because the controlling authority of nations is generally very effective in prohibiting oppositional behavior. Indeed, first stage functioning, on the part of the masses, is usually enforced and held up as a model of citizenship. In this sense many revolutions, regardless of the change in creed, do not represent what we mean by progression; they are power battles within the first stage in which the outcome merely changes the external authority.

TRANSITION TO THE THIRD STAGE (SECOND TRANSITION)

The extreme pole of second stage concepts would allow for such differentiations as evaluating others as interfering with negative independence on the one hand and as models or supportive agents on the other. Progression to third stage represents approach tendencies toward, openness to, and the successful integration of differentiations based on these opposite poles of the second stage. Only those training conditions that simultaneously generate differentiations based on opposition to external control and dependency on others lead to the emergence of third stage concepts; such concepts are open to differentiations based on both mutuality and autonomy and allow further progression of the second stage conceptual system to dependency ties. The integration of the two opposing motivational tendencies in level II transition represents the emergence of a new conceptual system in which the form of relatedness to objects involves conditional dependence and mutuality. As development progresses through these stages the form of relatedness becomes progressively less stimulus bound, more relativistic, and less unilateral. Although the third stage represents a swing toward dependency, this form of dependency is markedly different from that described in the first stage.

THIRD STAGE: CONDITIONAL DEPENDENCE AND MUTUALITY

This stage may be characterized by conditional or "as if" functioning, in that it involves learning about one's relationship to the environment in a more objective way. The progression is from externally derived structure (first stage) through resistance to external control (second stage) and, if this can be achieved, to a more empirical approach in the third stage. The history of science appears to follow a similar developmental course, beginning first with primitive forms of dogma, then going through a stage of questioning, and then adopting empiricism. In experimental work on problem solving the questioning or oppositional second stage may be momentary because of the peripheral relationship of the subject to the problem. However, in science, in the development of groups, and in child development, the second stage may be the most critical.

In social behavior the transition is from a stage of opposition to other people's attitudes or intentions (an exaggerated bifurcation of self and external forces) to a stage in which other people's intentions and wishes are taken into account. As third stage concepts emerge, a more objective view of the social environment becomes possible. The person in the third stage views other people less subjectively (that is, less in terms of his own motives and less in terms of absolute standards) and more in terms of other's standards and past experience. His understanding of other points of view, rather than resisting or submitting to them, makes mutual relationships possible. Third stage functioning also involves holding alternative views of the self, of events, and of others simultaneously with a minimum of concern for ambiguity.

Piaget's study of the development of moral concepts in children is illustrative:

There is no doubt that by adopting a certain technique with their children, parents can succeed in making them attach more importance to intentions than to rules conceived as a system of ritual interdictions. . . . It is when the child is accustomed to act from the point of view of those around him, when he tries to please rather than to obey, that he will judge in terms of intentions. So that taking intentions into account presupposes cooperation and mutual respect. . . . In order to remove all traces of moral realism, one must place oneself on the child's own level, and give him a feeling of equality by laying stress on one's own obligations and one's own deficiencies . . . thus creating an atmosphere of mutual help and understanding. In this way the child will find himself in the presence, not of a system of commands requiring ritualistic and external obedience, but of a system of social relations such that everyone does his best to obey the same obligations, and does so out of mutual respect. The passage from obedience to cooperation thus marks a progression analogous to that of which we saw the effects in the evolution of the game of marbles: only in the final stage does the morality of intention triumph over the morality of objective responsibility (Piaget, 1932, pp. 133–134).

In this passage Piaget is emphasizing a form of relatedness between the subject and the rule rather than changes in behavior toward a rule. The two forms of relatedness he describes are very similar to the present first and third stages. In describing moral realism, Piaget points out that justice is defined in terms of adult authority or an external criterion that is absolute and does not change with situational changes. This stage is equivalent to our first stage functioning and, according to Piaget, is typical of children below seven or eight years of age;[1] on the other hand, the functioning described by Piaget above, which is similar to the third stage, is more typical of children between the ages of eight and eleven. Studies indicate that reciprocity, defined as "eye for an eye" and representing aspects of the first and

[1] It should be noted that the age at which children pass through these stages will vary across different content areas. Here Piaget is speaking of the development of the abstractness of moral concepts. Earlier we were speaking of the abstractness of a child's level of functioning in relationship to his parents.

second stages in our sense, decreases with age (Durkin, 1959a, 1959b) whereas empathic behavior or mutuality increases (Piaget, 1932). Also, younger children are more absolutistic, whereas older children (eighth graders) show overt concern for possible mitigating factors in the interpersonal situation being judged (Durkin, 1959b).

Group functoning in the third stage is characterized by cooperation instead of submission and by competition rather than dominance and opposition. Although third stage functioning is essential for the occurrence of cooperation, many individuals use the words cooperation and competition for functioning that is clearly at the unilateral or oppositional level and, as Bennis and Shepard (1956) observe, it is just such individuals who tend to retard group development. These authors observe that at this third stage:

> The power problem is resolved by being defined in terms of member responsibilities, . . . [and,] at least within the life of the group, later activity is rarely perceived in terms of submission and rebellion (Bennis and Shepard, 1956, p. 424), [and further that] any slight increase in tension is instantly dissipated by joking and laughter. The fighting of Phase I [the second stage] is still fresh in the memory of the group, and the group's efforts are devoted to patching up differences, healing wounds, and maintaining a harmonious atmosphere (Bennis and Shepard, 1956, p. 429).

One of the most significant aspects of the transition from the second to the third stage is the change in the conception of causality. Although the foundation for this change is established by earlier stages, at the third stage the individual's behavior becomes the independent rather than the dependent variable. In attempting to integrate counterpersonal and mutual evaluations the person functioning at this stage is more likely to think in terms of the locus of causality residing primarily in his own behavior.

> The rule of constraint, which is bound up with unilateral respect, is regarded as sacred and produces in the child's mind feelings that are analogous to those which characterize the compulsory conformity of primitive communities [first stage]. But this rule of constraint remains external to the child's spirit and does not lead to as effective an obedience as the adult would wish. Rules due to mutual agreement and cooperation, on the contrary, take root inside the child's mind and result in an effective observance in the measure in which they are incorporated in an autonomous will [third stage] (Piaget, 1932, p. 365).

In social behavior the third stage represents an empirical phase, similar to the data-gathering phase in science. The person reacts in alternative ways toward others in order to experience their reactions. By observing the reactions of others to his own reactions and finding out more about their standards, he is better able to control the consequences of his own behavior and learn about his own characteristics and limitations. It is as if he were using the environment, or other people's standards, as a mirror to develop a more abstract criterion of his own behavior. Cooley (1912) refers to this procedure as the "looking-glass self." During this stage mutuality, obtaining satisfaction from pleasing others, and empathy replace unilateral functioning and concern with dominance and power. A new basis for relating to people is established.

Taking on the roles of other persons can be viewed in terms of the subject's setting up hypotheses and carrying out experiments on the effects of his own social behavior. An excellent account of this process, referred to as "conversation of gestures," has been given by G. H. Mead (1934) and more recently by Sarbin (1954). The net effect is the emergence of a more objective understanding of the relationships between the subject and his environment. Make-believe play in childhood and the intensive role-taking behavior of adolescents are characteristic of third stage functioning. On this basis, we would expect that the absence of make-believe play and role taking would be associated with arrestation of progressive development at some more concrete level. The significance of third stage functioning for social development is impressively demonstrated by Kelly (1955) who utilizes the technique of role-therapy to induce modifications in conceptual organization.

In child development functioning more typical of the transition from the second to the third stage and of the third stage is modal at ages three, seven and eight, and again perhaps at fourteen and fifteen. Observations indicate that each phase or cycle of third stage functioning is preceded by a stage of opposition, "out of bounds behavior" or negative independence (Ilg and Ames, 1955). For the infant at age three typical functioning is described as:

> Quiet. . . . seems to love to conform. . . . uses the word "Yes" quite as easily as he formerly used the word "No" . . . likes to give as well as take . . . "We" is another word he uses frequently. It expresses his cooperative, easy-going attitude towards life in general. . . . He no longer seems to need the protection of rituals [that is, he has progressed beyond level II transitional functioning]. . . . The child is no longer rigid, inflexible, domineering. . . . He likes to make friends and will often willingly give up a toy or privilege in order to stay in the good graces of some other person. . . . (p. 27).

No doubt the advent of language has much to do with this initial progression to third stage functioning in infancy, and we would expect an association between speech problems and increasing difficulties in developmental transition to the third stage.

As we found in second stage functioning in the first infant cycle (age two to four and one-half), the first cycle of third stage functioning does not represent a complete transition. When this stage is reached in early childhood it is less differentiated from the first stage and does not represent the level of empathy and "subjective responsibility" described above. In the second cycle in Table 2, the occurrence of third stage functioning at around seven or eight years of age, the effect of the conflicting differentiations (based on the counter personal and dependent poles of the concepts) and representing transition to the third stage, is more clearly apparent.

At age seven the modal behaviors observed (Ilg and Ames, 1955) are typically transitional (between second and third stages) as illustrated by the following descriptions:

> Seven . . . has calmed down [from earlier oppositional tendencies]. . . . But he is more likely to complain [seek support]. . . . More apt to retreat from the scene muttering than to stay and demand his own [more covert oppositional tendencies]. Opposition has been tempered by conflicting dependency evaluations]. . . . He often demands too much of himself [over-striving represents self-assertion and insures that he will be cared for]. . . . tends to feel that people are against him, that they don't like him [*emergence of sensitization to rejection by others due to his oppositional tendencies*] (Ilg and Ames, 1955, p. 36).

As we indicate in later chapters, these characteristics, along with the tendency to dramatize everything, are typical of the transition from the second to the third stage and characterize the functioning of individuals when progressive development is arrested at this transitional level.

Following the difficult transition period at seven, modal behavior at eight is described as less conflicting and, in some respects, more characteristic of third stage functioning:

> . . . he is constantly busy and active . . . enjoying new experiences . . . trying out new friends [the empirical attitude]. . . . with his newly increased powers of evaluation, he may recognize his all-too-frequent failures. Then, tears and self-disparagement! [the emergence of internal causation and self-blame]. . . . He needs protection both from trying to do too much and from too excessive self-criticism when he meets with failure [behavior leading to support and protection from others and the emergence of depressive feelings]. . . . Now he is interested, not just in how people treat him, but in his *relationships* with others. He is ready for, and wants, a good two-way relationship [mutuality]. Furthermore, it is not just what people do which concerns him, but also what they think [sensitization to relationships and learning about the effect of his own reactions on others] (Ilg and Ames, 1955, pp. 37–38).

TRANSITION TO THE FOURTH STAGE (THIRD TRANSITION)

Since the evaluations and judgments at the third stage are based largely on the effect that one's reactions have on others, we have used such terms as conditional dependence, empiricism, and "the looking-glass self." Just as empiricism is tied to data, so the third stage evaluations are dependent upon the standards of others. The subject is dependent upon external conditions or upon observations of the effect of his own behavior.

The extreme pole of this conceptual system would represent evaluations based on autonomous standards. Transition to the fourth stage requires openness to differentiations based on autonomy and represents the integration of differentiations based on mutuality and autonomy.

In order for a person to experience autonomy as positive and not conflicting with mutuality, he must view both poles of the third stage as positive. If the training conditions have produced such structure, then the way is open for the integration of mutuality and autonomy, which leads to the emergence of a fourth stage conceptual system involving interdependence of informational standards. Interdependent evaluations represent what we assume to be the most abstract level of conceptual development.

FOURTH STAGE: INTERDEPENDENCE

In the fourth stage mutuality and autonomy are integrated so that neither interferes with the other and yet both are important. We refer to this integration as positive interdependence. The nature of subject-object linkages at this level is abstract, interdependent, and informational. The abstractness and lack of subjectivity are exemplified by the characteristics of group functioning that Bennis and Shepard (1956), following Sullivan (1953), call "consensual validation," which was observed to follow the more compulsively cooperative phase.

> Its chief characteristic is the willingness and ability of group members to validate their self-concepts with other members. The fear of rejection fades when tested against reality. The tensions that developed as a result of these fears diminish in the light of actual discussion of member roles. . . . what ensues is a serious attempt by each group member to verbalize his private conceptual

scheme for understanding human behavior—his own and that of others. Bringing these assumptions into explicit communication is the main work of subphase 6. This activity demands a high level of work and of communicative skill. Some of the values that appear to underlie the group's work during this subphase are as follows: 1. Members can accept one another's differences without associating "good" and "bad" with the differences. 2. Conflict exists but is over substantive issues rather than emotional issues. 3. Consensus is reached as a result of rational discussion rather than through a compulsive attempt at unanimity. 4. Members are aware of their own involvement, and of other aspects of group process, without being overwhelmed or alarmed. 5. Through the evaluation process, members take on greater personal meaning to each other. This facilitates communication and creates a deeper understanding of how the other person thinks, feels, behaves; it creates a series of personal expectations, as distinguished from the previous, more stereotyped, role expectations (Bennis and Shepard, 1956, p. 433).

In the field of personality Fromm (1941) and Erikson (1950) describe higher levels of development as involving the interdependence of mutuality (love) and autonomous informational standards against which instrumental activity (work) is judged. Such interdependence frees relationships from constrictions due to power, resistance to control, or fears of rejection, thus permitting a more abstract and objective form of understanding and participation with others. On the basis of the development of autonomous informational standards the individual can experience rewards, as a result of instrumental activity or work, in terms of his own past experience rather than being dependent on some external source. Erikson (1950) portrays the significance of this level of development as follows:

> I know no better word for it than ego integrity. Lacking a clear definition, I shall point to a few constituents of this state of mind. . . . It is a postnarcissistic love of the human ego—not of the self—as an experience which conveys some world order and spiritual sense, no matter how dearly paid for. It is the acceptance of one's one and

only life cycle as something that had to be and that, by necessity, permitted of no substitutions: it thus means a new, and different love of one's parents. . . . Although aware of the relativity of all the various life styles which have given meaning to human striving, the possessor of integrity is ready to defend the dignity of his own life style against all physical and economic threats. For he knows that an individual life is the accidental coincidence of but one life cycle with but one segment of history; and that for him all human integrity stands or falls with the one style of integrity of which he partakes (Erikson, 1950, pp. 231–232).

In child development the earliest observations of behavior typical of the transition to fourth stage functioning are reported around nine years old, that is, in the second cycle of development shown in Table 2. In the first cycle of development in infancy the modal child appears to show tendencies toward the development of third stage concepts but this development is an insufficient base for progression to any form of interdependence. Instead, the child's growing confidence in his abilities leads to a negative form of independence between the ages of three and one-half and four and one-half. But with the new social conditions and problems that arise around five the pendulum swings back to a greater reliance on external control. During this cycle (cycle II) conceptual development approaches or reaches the fourth stage for some children as illustrated by the following descriptions of modal behavior for nine-year-old children:

> He lives more within himself, is surer in his contacts with the outside world, is more self-contained and self-sufficient . . . often insists on being extremely independent [conflict over autonomy] . . . though [he] may be interested in adults . . . he is much less interested than he was earlier in the relationship itself [less sensitivity to maintaining relationships and rejections]. . . . He wants and needs to have his maturity, his independence and his separateness [autonomy] respected. . . . if treated as the mature creature he considers himself to be, the 9-year-old usually gets along pretty well and does display a remarkable amount of self-reliance and capability. . . . However, there is a disquieting side . . . He does tend

> to worry . . . and . . . can be extremely anxious. . . . (Ilg and Ames, 1955, pp. 38–39).

It will be noted that these descriptive statements are quite different from functioning at the earlier three stages. The functioning of typical nine-year-olds represents a transition to the fourth stage rather than progression to full interdependence. Progression to interdependent functioning of the fourth stage is more likely in the adolescent cycle of development. The increasing reliance upon internal causation in the fourth stage is characterized by a strengthened capacity to face problems and to tolerate anxiety. The initial transition to the fourth stage may produce anxiety and worry, as observed above, but once the conceptual system becomes stabilized, such reactions are much less likely. Therefore, the subject not only develops autonomous skills and informational standards for problem solution but also a high degree of tolerance of anxiety and resistance to stress. The implication is that future adaptation to threat involves progressive development, as opposed to the warding off or defensive tendencies that lead to increasingly closed conceptual functioning.

The most general characteristic of such abstract functioning is resistance to stress. As more abstract forms of subject-object linkages develop there is greater self-awareness. It is this greater self-awareness or attribution of internal causation that is critical for stress tolerance as will become increasingly clear in later chapters. More abstract functioning is based on a conceptual system that has been open to a variety of conflicting forms of subject-object relatedness that have been progressively integrated during development. Consequently there is a greater reservoir of resources to overcome and withstand stress of various forms—failure, control, rejection, or isolation. An individual approaching a problem in a concrete way, with a single fixed solution, will continue to use the same solution in spite of situational changes. However, when he eventually fails, he will develop avoidance and other defensive orientations including the blind acceptance of some other externally anchored solution because of his undifferentiated conceptual structure and his lack of self-awareness. Concrete functioning may be characterized by more decisiveness, but it breaks down more rapidly under stress. Abstract functioning is less categorical, but it has a greater potential to mobilize under the impact of stress.

In problem solving as in science we would associate this level of development with that of theory, if the term "theory" is used in the sense of a systematic body of abstract informational standards that develop over time. Like any other area, however, scientific theory or problem solution can be taught to produce arrestation at any stage, for example, so that the subject would accept theoretical tenets concretistically in terms of the first stage, as fixed and beyond his control.

Fourth stage functioning is characterized by abstract standards developed through the exploration of alternative solutions against a variety of criteria. These standards are systematically related to the informational consequences of exploration and as such are "tools," not masters, since they are subject to change under changing conditions. Abstract functioning is characterized both by the availability of alternate conceptual schemata as a basis for relating and by the ability to hold a strong view or attitude that does not distort incoming information.

REFERENCES

1. Bennis, W. G., & Shepard, H. A. A theory of group development. *Human Relations,* 1956, 9, 415–437.
2. Coffey, H. S. Group psychotherapy. In L. A. Pennington & I. A. Berg (Eds.), *An introduction to clinical psychology.* New York: Ronald Press, 1954, pp. 586–607.
3. Cooley, C. H. *Human nature and the social order.* New York: Scribner, 1912.
4. Durkin, Dolores. Children's concept of justice: A comparison with the Piaget data. *Child Develpm.,* 1959, 30, 58–67 (a).
5. Durkin, Dolores. Children's acceptance of reciprocity as a justice principle. *Child Develpm.,* 1959, 30, 289–296 (b).
6. Erikson, E. H. *Childhood and society.* New York: W. W. Norton, 1950, pp. 213–220.
7. Fromm, E. *Escape from freedom.* New York: Rinehart, 1941.
8. Hertzer, H. Entwicklungsbedinkte Erziehungsschwirigkeiten. *Ztschr. Pädagog. Psychol.,* 1929, 30, 77–85.
9. Ilg, Frances L., & Ames, Louise B. *Child Behavior.* New York: Harper, 1955.
10. Kelly, G. *The psychology of personal constructs.* New York: Norton, 1955.
11. Levy, D. M. Oppositional syndromes and oppositional behavior. In P. H. Hoch & J. Zubin (Eds.) *Psychopathology of childhood.* New York: Grune and Stratton, 1955, pp. 204–226.
12. Mead, G. H. *Self, mind and society.* Chicago: University of Chicago Press, 1934.
13. Piaget, J. *The moral judgment of the child.* New York: Harcourt Brace, 1932.
14. Rogers, C. R. *Client-centered therapy.* New York: Houghton-Mifflin, 1951.
15. Rotter, J. B. *Social learning and clinical psychology.* New York: Prentice-Hall, 1954.
16. Sarbin, T. R. Role theory. In G. Lindzey (Ed.), *Handbook of social psychology,* Vol. I. Cambridge, Mass.: Addison-Wesley, 1954, pp. 253–258.
17. Sullivan, H. S. *The interpersonal theory of psychiatry.* New York: Norton, 1953.
18. Werner, H. *Comparative psychology of mental development.* (Rev. Ed.) New York: International Universities Press, 1957.

A Systematization of the Whorfian Hypothesis /

Joshua A. Fishman (*Yeshiva University*)

Interest in the Whorfian hypothesis—that the characteristics of a language have determining influences on cognitive processes—is increasing, not only among linguists and social anthropologists, but also among general semanticists, psychologists, social psychologists, and sociologists. Here is an interesting attempt by a social psychologist to systematize some of the work in this problem area, by proposing a double dichotomy which gives rise to a discussion of the hypothesis at four levels.

INTRODUCTION

During the late 20's and throughout the 30's two American linguists—Edward Sapir and Benjamin Lee Whorf—strikingly formulated anew the view that the characteristics of language have determining influences on cognitive processes. Since the languages of mankind differ widely with respect to their structural, lexical, and other characteristics, it followed that monolingual individuals speaking widely different languages should, therefore, differ with respect to their symbolically mediated behaviors. This formulation immediately rekindled interest in this topic area among linguists and social anthropologists and, with the passage of time, their interest has been increasingly transmitted to general semanticists, psychologists, social psychologists, and sociologists. Currently, interest in the Whorfian hypothesis (at times also referred to as the Sapir-Whorf hypothesis, the Korzybski-Sapir-Whorf hypothesis, the linguistic Weltanschauung hypothesis, and the linguistic relatively hypothesis) is high—although there is no little difference of opinion as to its proper interpretation, its limits, its verifiability, and its validity. This essay represents an attempt by a social psychologist to systematize some of the work in this problem area.

SOME LANGUAGE-THOUGHT RELATIONSHIPS NOT SUBSUMABLE UNDER THE WHORFIAN HYPOTHESIS

Since psychologists have been crucially interested in the impact of verbal habits on other kinds of behavior from the very beginning of the emergence of psychology as a scientific discipline [viz., Ebbinghaus's work with nonsense syllables (1897) and Galton's with word association (1879)], it is probably desirable to begin our deliberations with a clear indication as to why most of these studies are *not* concerned with the phenomena of interest to students of the Whorfian hypothesis. The classical psychological interest in this area is in terms of language as a human capacity. Psychologists have not been noticeably concerned with the unique "Englishness" of English and how it affects cognition—in the individual and in the culture—differently than the "Navahoness" of Navaho. For the large number of American psychologists who have in recent years reported on the impact of verbal habits on perception (e.g., Solomon and Howes, 1951; Miller, Bruner and Postman, 1951; Postman and Conger, 1954; Postman and Rosenzweig, 1957), the fact that the language involved was English was of no particular concern. The same is true of those who have earlier and also recently studied the relationship between language and learning (e.g., Lyon, 1914; Gates, 1917; Tsao, 1948), language and memory (e.g., Reed, 1924; Miller and Selfridge, 1950), and language and thinking (e.g., Eidens, 1929; Sells, 1936; Wilkins, 1928). Similarly, the studies of Piaget (1924), Vigotsky (1939), Luria (1959), and other European psychologists in this tradition have not been interested in the unique or characteristic verbal habits of *French* speaking or *Russian* speaking individuals and how such habits uniquely

Reprinted from *Behavioral Science*, 1960, 5, pages 323–339 by permission of author, Joshua A. Fishman, Yeshiva University Graduate School of Education and publisher, The Mental Health Research Institute.

or characteristically affect *French* thinking or *Russian* thinking. Even those studies that have worked with various "levels of approximation" (in an information theory sense) to the actual word sequences or letter sequences of some language (usually American English) have not been reacting to anything different in this respect than they would have been interested in were they working with some entirely different written or spoken language.

Furthermore, the "other variable" in all of these studies (whether this other variable be perception, learning, memory, reasoning, etc.) is of interest to the psychologist only as it is manifested through verbal habits. Thus, Woodworth and Sells (1935) are not concerned with the impact of verbal or symbolic habits on non-verbal reasoning. Rather, they are interested in *reasoning with verbal or symbolic materials* to determine how such reasoning is affected by our long ingrained verbal or symbolic habits. Similarly, Postman and his students and colleagues (references cited above) have been concerned not with the impact of *verbal* habits on the perception (visual or auditory) or *non-verbal* stimuli, but, rather, with the extent to which and the ways in which verbal habits control the perception of verbal stimuli. In other words, most classical psychological research in this area is not really concerned with the relationship between verbal habits on the one hand and certain non-verbal or non-linguistic behaviors on the other.

Although the Whorfian hypothesis has been discussed via data at various levels of linguistic and non-linguistic behavior, it differs from most psychological research dealing with the impact of verbal habits on behavior either in *one* or in *both* of the respects indicated above:

a. Research pertaining to the Whorfian hypothesis is concerned with those verbal habits that derive not from the mere fact of having acquired language but, rather, with those verbal habits that derive from some characteristic or unique aspect of one or more *given* languages. Thus, the Whorfian hypothesis is not so much concerned with verbal determinism in general as it is with relative linguistic determinism based upon contrasts between the characteristics of specific languages.

b. Much, though by no means all, research on the Whorfian hypothesis is concerned with relating these data pertaining to the unique characteristic nature of one or more given languages to some non-linguistic behaviors of the individual speakers of these languages.

THE WHORFIAN HYPOTHESIS: A BRIEF HISTORICAL INTRODUCTION

As is the case with many of the most fertile ideas of interest to social scientists today, it is possible to trace back some of the ingredients which go to make up the Whorfian hypothesis at least to the mid-nineteenth century, if not further. That multifaceted genius, Wilhelm von Humboldt, ventured to say in 1848 that "man lives with the world about him principally, indeed . . . exclusively, as language presents it." (Cited by Trager, 1959.) Although we may not now agree that von Humboldt demonstrated this proposition, we must admit that he and his followers amassed a wealth of linguistic evidence from language groups all over the globe in the process of their dedication to this proposition. In fact, it is from their early efforts that ethnolinguistics arose as a recognizably separate area of scholarly activity. It was also in reaction to this activity that a particular brand of logical and scientific criticism developed which long steered the major body of American linguistics away from ethnolinguistic concerns. This criticism was derived from the superficiality of the data and the prematureness of the conclusions via which ethnolinguistics arrived at the conclusion that the "soul of a people" and the "mind of a people" was not only reflected by its language but, indeed, shaped by it.

Humboldtian ethnolinguistics itself has long and intricate roots in the folklores of many peoples. The association between a people's individuality and its language is certainly an ancient one in the history of Western and Near Eastern civilizations. The ancient Greeks applied the term "barbarians" (those who say ba-ba, i.e., speak an incomprehensible tongue) to those to whom the gods had denied the gift of Greek, and the ancient Hebrews believed that their language was a uniquely holy vehicle that was created even before the world was brought into being and awarded to them as a particular gift of God. Certainly, linguistic awareness, linguistic pride, a belief in linguistic specialness and in the inherent untranslatability of one's own vernacular or some other superposed language have been frequent components of the ethnocentrism and the world-views of many peoples, past and present. The Whorfian hypothesis represents a groping toward the scientific restatement and the objective evaluation of language-and-behavior phenomena that are related to this ill-defined, pre-scientific, and value-laden area that has hitherto been shaped primarily by strong beliefs and emotions. The Whorfian hypothesis essentially represents an attempt to study linguistic relativity by the means of modern social science methods.

Among the earliest post-Humboldtian attempts to point out the linguistic relativity of symbolically mediated behavior were those made by the father of American anthropology, Franz Boas. An accomplished comparative linguist (i.e., a disciplined student of the structures of various languages), even by present-day standards, Boas claimed that a "purely linguistic inquiry" provided the data for "a thorough investigation of the psychology of the peoples of the world" (1911). The linguistic data obtained for this purpose Boas considered as superior even to that derivable from psychology directly, due to the fact that informants are more nearly unconscious of the categories in their thinking which language as such reveals.

With the writings of Edward Sapir, we approach the more direct and immediate antecedents of the Whorfian hypothesis. Sapir was a student of Boas and, like his teacher, firmly convinced that language could be regarded as the raw material of which a people's outlook on the world is fashioned. In 1929 Sapir wrote:

> ". . . The 'real world' is to a large extent unconsciously built up on the language habits of the group. The worlds in which different societies live are *distinct* worlds, not merely the same world with different labels attached. We [as individuals] see and

hear and otherwise experience very largely as we do because the language habits of our community predispose certain choices of interpretation."

Here we find clearly expressed a theme to which Whorf and others have returned time and again, namely that language is not "merely" a vehicle of communication by which man talks about some objective reality "out there" that exists previous to and independently of his language, but, rather, that language itself represents an objective reality by means of which man structures and organizes the "out there" in certain characteristic ways. Thus, when languages differ maximally, the organizing schemata which their speakers impose on the non-linguistic world should also differ maximally. In his own words, Sapir claims that language "does not as a matter of actual behavior stand apart from or run parallel to direct experience—but completely penetrates with it" (1933).

Although Sapir was certainly interested in linguistic relativity and convinced of its validity, his primary scientific and speculative contributions were made in connection with other topic areas. Benjamin Lee Whorf, on the other hand, devoted himself to the advancement of the hypothesis that now carries his name almost from the very beginning of his systematic work in linguistics up until the time of his premature death. In a series of articles—most of which have at long last been gathered together in one publication (Carroll, 1956)—based primarily on analyses of American Indian languages (but also, at times, based on other non-European languages), Whorf constantly reiterated his conviction that a generally unrecognized "principle of relativity" was operative. In accord with this principle, "observers are not led by the same picture of the universe, unless their linguistic backgrounds are similar or can in some way be calibrated" (1940).

Whorf's writings have become a common ground on which the interests of many linguists, anthropologists, social psychologists, and sociologists come together. Its attraction lies both in its dimly recognized reference to the classical problems of cultural differences, cultural relativity, and cultural universality as well as in its provocativeness for modern, interdisciplinary, objective research. When

Whorf says that "there is a precarious dependence of all we know upon linguistic tools which themselves are largely unknown or unnoticed," he hits all of us where it hurts most—at the foundations of our certainty in our scientific findings and in our everyday decisions. When he attacks the view that grammars are "merely norms of conventional and social correctness" and claims that they are, instead, the cement out of which we fashion experience, we feel that he must either be pointing at an unnoticed and potentially dangerous popular fallacy or tilting at nonexistent windmills. When he says that "we cut up nature—organize it into concepts—and ascribe significances as we do . . . largely because of the . . . absolutely obligatory . . . patterns of our [own] language," he stirs in us both our ethnocentric group-pride as well as our universalistic anti-ethnocentrism. In short, Whorf (like Freud) impugns our objectivity and rationality. It is not surprising then that recent years have seen many logical as well as not a few experimental efforts to evaluate and re-evaluate both the conceptual and the empirical grounds upon which the Whorfian hypothesis rests.

LEVEL 1. LINGUISTIC CODIFIABILITY AND CULTURAL REFLECTIONS (THE FIRST LANGUAGE-LANGUAGE LEVEL)

The weakest level of the Whorfian hypothesis (in the sense of being least pretentious or least novel) is that which provides evidence that languages differ "in the same ways" as the general cultures or surrounding environments of their speakers differ. Evidence along these lines has long been provided by ethnologists and folklorists, and its fragmentary and belated presentation by Whorfians can hardly be considered as either a serious contribution to the social sciences generally or as a substantiation of higher levels of the Whorfian hypothesis specifically.

From the point of view of the language data presented at this first level of argumentation, it is not the grammatical structure as such that is under consideration but, rather, the lexical store or the so-called "semantic structure." Actually, that which is dealt with

at this level might be referred to in present-day terms as contrasts in *codifiability*. Language X has a single term for phenomenon x, whereas language Y either has no term at all (and therefore refers to the phenomenon under consideration—if at all—only via a relative circumlocution) or it has three terms, y_1, y_2, and y_3, all within the same area of reference. As a result, it is much *easier* to refer to certain phenomena or to certain nuances of meaning in certain languages than in others. Thus, codifiability is also related to the question of translatability and to "what gets lost" in translation from one language to another.

The examples that have been given at this level of analysis are legion and no attempt needs to be made to exhaustively catalog them here. At times they are not accompanied by any explicit claims as to how the noted codifiability differences are related to implicit or explicit cultural differences. The fact that there is no handy English equivalent for the German *Gemütlichkeit* is rarely explained as an indication that Germans *are* more *gemütlich*. The fact that there may not be an exact semantic ("connotative") equivalence between *horse, cheval,* and *pferd* is not seriously attributed to different cultural roles for horses or for man-horse relationships in the three cultures from which these words are derived.

Nevertheless, there have been attempts to relate codifiability differences of the above type to behavioral differences. Usually, the behavior under scrutiny in this connection is *language behavior,* and the evidence advanced as to the parallelism between *selective codifiability as an aspect of a given language* and *the language behavior of the speakers of that language* is, at this level of analysis, of an anecdotal or fragmentary variety. Thus, the fact that the German language does have the term *Gemütlichkeit* does make it *easier* for Germans to be aware of and to express this phenomenon. Americans can also struggle toward a circumlocutious formulation of this concept but the very fact that it is a struggle may mean that the concept is less clearly formulated and less aptly as well as less frequently expressed. Gastil's concept of *polysemy* (1959) is also relevant at this level. In some languages, certain words have additional shades or ranges of meaning than their cognates or best equivalents in other languages. Thus, in French, one term is used for both "conscience" and for "consciousness." On the one hand, this means that French speakers do not have as *easily* available to them a distinction that we have. On the other hand, it means that they have more easily available to them a partial identity of these two terms that it is very difficult for us to fully appreciate. Lindeman (1938) has demonstrated from textual analysis how this linguistic identity has led to a greater conceptual fusion between these two usages on the part of French philosophers than is true for English or German thinkers. Gastil gives several other examples of polysemy (1959), particularly as between English and Persian, which convincingly demonstrate that code efficiency is differentially selective in different languages with the result that what is easily expressible in one language is not necessarily easily or accurately expressible in another.[1]

Assuming that the above holds true, the question still remains as to whether these observations are really pertinent to the Whorfian hypothesis. Seemingly so, for Whorf himself frequently presents data of this variety. Admittedly Whorf's examples are largely drawn from American Indian languages (and contrasted with American English), and the implication is therefore strong that we are not only dealing with groups whose languages differ markedly but whose lives and outlooks also differ greatly. Nevertheless, at *this* level of analysis, Whorf (and others even more frequently than he) does not take pains to relate linguistic factors to non-linguistic ones, but merely presents an enchanting catalog of codifiability differences. English has separate words for "pilot," "fly (n.)," and "airplane," but Hopi

has only one. Eskimo has many words for different kinds of "snow" but English has only two. On the other hand, Aztec has only one basic word for our separate words "cold," "ice," and "snow." We have one word for "water," whereas Hopi has two, depending on whether the water is stationary or in motion. English has such words as "speed" and "rapid," whereas Hopi has no real equivalents for them and normally renders them by "very" or "intense" plus a verb of motion. English has separate terms for "blue" and "green" but only one term for all intensities of "black" short of "gray." Navaho, on the contrary, does not have separate highly codeable terms for "blue" and "green" but does have two terms for different kinds of "black." English has the generic term "horse" but Arabic has only scores of different terms for different breeds or conditions of horses. The kinship terminology in some languages is certainly vastly different (and in certain respects both more refined and more gross) than it is in English. In all of these cases, it is not difficult to relate the codifiability differences to gross cultural differences. Obviously, Eskimos are more interested in snow, and Arabs in horses, than are most English speakers. Obvious, also, is the fact that these codifiability differences help speakers of certain languages to be more easily aware of certain aspects of their environment and to communicate more easily about them. This, essentially, was the lesson we learned from Bartlett's early work on remembering (1932). In this sense, then, their languages structure their verbal behavior in a non-trivial way and ostensibly also structure their pre-verbal conceptualizations as well.

Other Phenomena

Before proceeding to a summary and evaluation of this particular level of the Whorfian hypothesis, it might be well briefly to point out other phenomena that are subsumable under it. The "phatic communion" concept which Malinowski introduced so long ago (1923), and which so many have quoted but which few have elaborated, may in large part be seen as a codifiability phenomenon at the language-language level. It is probable that all traditioned groups, particu-

---

[1] I have previously pointed to codifiability as a precursor of language behavior in such diverse areas as social stereotyping (Fishman, 1956) and witness performance (Fishman, 1957). In general, to the degree that we are here dealing with codifiability in the absence of any consistent cultural context, our concern with the impact of language habits on language performance is only a shade different than that of the studies that we have previously characterized as not being subsumable under the Whorfian hypothesis.

larly those sharing many intimate and heightened experiences, develop differential codifiability in their languages. As a result, it is quite likely that they then find it easier, more meaningful, and more accurate to communicate their unique or characteristic experiences in their own language than in any other. The elliptic, highly abbreviated, seemingly mysterious, and non-verbal aspects of "phatic communion" (to outsiders) may be no more than a result of the differences between what are readily encodeable messages (verbal and non-verbal) for any group in its own language, and what are readily encodeable (and therefore decodeable) messages for some other group of observers who are "outsiders." In a sense, we are dealing once more with the relative translatability of the supposedly untranslatable. Since differential codifiability is so very often a correlate of distinctive cultural patterns, it seems quite understandable why most speakers of a language come to feel that no other language can as adequately cope with the very nuances of meaning and the very experiential patterns which are most significant to them in terms of their cultural distinctiveness. From this awareness it is but a short jump to language loyalty and language glorification. Thus, "word magic" may not be nearly as primitive, childish, or illogical as Freud suggests. There is magic indeed in a language whose differential codifiability makes it peculiarly suitable for the expression of an individual's most central personal and cultural experiences. In contrast to such a language, all others must seem pale indeed.

In conclusion, it must be said that the evidence for the Whorfian hypothesis at this first level is concerned neither with a truly *structural* analysis of language nor with a full-blooded analysis of the *non-linguistic concomitants* or resultants of language structure. In dealing with language-language relationships, the data are presented in a seemingly anecdotal and selective manner which fails to convince those who require more disciplined and organized approaches both to data and to demonstration. Nothing as grandiose as a "world-view" is produced by data at this level, although quite frequently we must admit that the reporter gives much evidence of having fully immersed himself

in the language and culture under study. Whorf himself is truly amazing in this last respect. Nevertheless, this first level is certainly a comedown from the more advanced levels of argumentation that he pursued. Perhaps this can be explained by his sheer fascination—often quite emotional in tone— with the American Indian languages which he had mastered. Undoubtedly the great structural differences between these languages and those that he almost disdainfully called "Standard Average European" (1941) provided much of the intellectual stimulation for his linguistic relativity hypothesis. On the other hand, he seems so fond of "playing" with these languages, fondling and dissecting their units of expression, that he may have been unable to withstand the temptation to do so even when he was not contributing thereby to the ultimate argument that he sought to advance. If we are to be satisfied only with the first level just discussed, then we can conclude no more than has Gastil in his discussion of polysemy, namely that

> "Languages differ as to the presence or absence of the field distinctions which they make. A language may be seen as a limited group of words and forms available for the use of a man thinking or expressing himself in the medium of that language. If he does not have the means to do a certain job of thinking or expressing, that job will not be accomplished as well as if he had such means." (1959)

Whorf would probably not have settled for as limited a claim as the foregoing.

LEVEL 2. LINGUISTIC CODIFIABILITY AND BEHAVIORAL CONCOMITANTS

At the second level of analysis of the Whorfian hypothesis, we leave behind the limitations of *inference* from codifiability in language to ease of formulation or expression via language. That is to say, we leave behind the *language-language behavior* level for the level in which *language-nonlanguage behavior* becomes of paramount interest to us. That this is a necessary direction for our inquiry to take has been recognized by Carroll and Casagrande who write in a recent preview of a forthcoming book:

"In order to find evidence to support the linguistic relativity hypothesis it is not sufficient merely to point to differences between languages and to assume that users of these languages have correspondingly different mental experiences. If we are not to be guilty of circular inference, it is necessary to show some correspondence between the presence or absence of a certain linguistic phenomenon and the presence or absence of a certain kind of non-linguistic response." (1958)

Note that the above quotation merely refers to *"a certain linguistic phenomenon"* rather than restricting the *type* of linguistic phenomenon that requires attention. The hallmark of the second level is that the "predictor" variables seem once more to be of the lexical or semantic codifiability type (and in this respect similar to Level 1, discussed above), whereas the "criterion variables" are of the non-linguistic behavior type (and in this respect different from, and an advance over, those encountered at Level 1). Thus far, there have been only a very few studies which strike me as operating at this level of analysis. The earliest one by far is that of Lehmann (1889) who demonstrated that identifying a different number with each of nine different shades of gray was of substantial help in behaviorally discriminating between these shades of gray. In essence, then, the numbers functioned as verbal labels. The availability (codifiability) of such labels for some *S*s resulted in much better discrimination-identification of the shades of gray than that which obtained in other *S*s who had to perform the same discrimination-identification task without being provided with such labels.

Some exceptionally interesting and sophisticated work with the codifiability concept in the color area has more recently been reported by Brown and Lenneberg (1954) and by Lenneberg alone (1953, 1957). These investigators have shown that culturally encoded colors (i.e., colors that can be named with a single word) require a shorter response latency when they need to be named than do colors that are not culturally encoded (i.e., that require a phrase—often an individually formulated phrase—in order to be described). At this point, their evidence

pertains to Level 1 that we have previously discussed. In addition, these investigators have gone on to show that the more highly codified colors are more readily recognized or remembered when they must be selected from among many colors after a period of delay subsequent to their original presentation. This finding was replicated among speakers of English and speakers of Zuni, although somewhat different segments of the color spectrum were highly codeable for the two groups of *S*s. The investigators summarize their findings to this point as follows:

"It is suggested that there may be general laws relating codability to cognitive processes. All cultures could conform to these laws although they differ among themselves in the values the variables assume in particular regions of experience." (Brown and Lenneberg, 1954)

Going on from this original statement, Lenneberg (1957) has further refined its experimental underpinnings by showing that the *learning* of color-nonsense syllable associations was predictably easier or harder as the learning task involved color categories that varied in degree from the ones that were most commonly recognized by his English-speaking *S*s. He therefore concluded that "there is good evidence that the shape of word frequency distributions over stimulus continua regulates the ease with which a person learns to use a word correctly." This conclusion should be as applicable to original language learning as it is to second and to artificial language learning, for it basically pertains not to language usage per se but to concept formation as such.

The color continuum seems to be a particularly fortunate area in which to study codifiability-cognition phenomena precisely because it is a real continuum. As such, no "objective" breaks occur in it and it is a matter of cultural or sub-cultural consensus as to just which breaks are recognized, just where on the spectrum they are located, and how much of a range they include. The demonstration that these various codifiability considerations influence recognition, recall, and learning has been most fortunately executed. Lenneberg and Brown are also alert to the fact that at this level it is perfectly acceptable to work with intralinguistic designs rather than to necessarily utilize the interlinguistic designs in terms of which the Whorfian hypothesis is most frequently approached. What is easily codifiable, and the specific range and content of easily codeable categories, does depend on the particular language under consideration. It also depends on the particular experiences of subgroups of speakers. As a result, contrasts in rate, ease or accuracy of various cognitive functions should be (and are) demonstrable both intralinguistically and interlinguistically as a function of codeability norms. Intralinguistic codifiability-cognition differentials in various natural population groupings should be of particular interest to students of social stratification.

Brown and Lenneberg have conducted their work with a conscious awareness of the Whorfian hypothesis and how it must be further specified or delimited. On the other hand, there have been other investigators who have also worked in the language-behavior domain at this level without any particular awareness of the Whorfian hypothesis as such. If the organizational framework here being advanced has been insightfully developed, it should nevertheless be possible to subsume their findings within it. In fact, it may turn out that within the context of the Whorfian hypothesis these other studies will obtain a new coherence and provocativeness. As a start in this direction (and an exhaustive search of the literature would be necessary in order to seriously go beyond such a start), I would classify the oft-cited work of Carmichael, Hogan, and Walter (1932) on memory for visual stimuli to which different verbal labels have been attached, as well as the problem-solving work of Maier (1930), and the transactional studies summarized by Kilpatrick (1955) on perceptual learning and problem-solving with and without verbal set as belonging at this level of analysis. These three last-mentioned studies also utilize intralinguistic designs.

The only study at this level that is directly inspired by the Whorfian hypothesis while utilizing an *interlinguistic* design is the one which Carroll and Casagrande refer to as "Experiment I" (1958). In this study, fluent Hopi speakers were compared with two different groups of English speakers with respect to sorting or picture classifying behavior. Utilizing the kind of lexic data that we have discussed in connection with Level 1, Carroll hypothesized that in each set of three stimulus plates Hopi speakers would more usually classify a certain subset of two as belonging together (because in Hopi the seemingly dissimilar activities depicted were nevertheless commonly "covered" by a single verb) whereas English speakers would more frequently classify another subset of two as belonging together (because in English a single verb was commonly used in referring to them). Although Carroll's data are quite far from revealing a uniform association between "Hopi categorizing responses" and Hopi speakers, or between "English categorizing responses" and English speakers, they nevertheless do reveal quite a substantial tendency in that direction. In addition, his graduate student Ss, whom we might have expected to be more "verbally minded," give the predicted "English categorizing responses" much more frequently than do his rural white Ss.

All in all, this is certainly an experimentally exciting level of analysis and one which will undoubtedly develop further in the years ahead. It will certainly be subject to improved experimental techniques since those now working in it are themselves aware of improvements that they hope to introduce into their future work in this area. This would seem to be the level of the Whorfian hypothesis most likely to attract social psychologists and sociologists with empirical interests in language phenomena.

LEVEL 3. LINGUISTIC STRUCTURE AND ITS CULTURAL CONCOMITANTS

When we turn our attention from the second to the third and fourth levels of the Whorfian hypothesis, we progress from lexical differences and so-called "semantic structure" to the more "formal" and systematized grammatical differences to which linguists have most usually pointed when considering the structure of a language or structural differences between languages. There is some evidence that although Whorf and others may, at times, have reverted to lower levels of presentation and documentation they, nevertheless, did associate linguistic relativity in its most pervasive sense with structural (i.e., grammatical) rather than merely with lexical aspects of language. This is suggested by such formulations as Sapir's that meanings are "not so much discovered in experience as imposed upon it, because of the tyrannical hold that linguistic *form* has upon our orientation to the world" (1919, my italics). Somewhat more forcefully stated is Whorf's claim that "the world is presented in a kaleidoscopic flux of impressions which has to be organized . . . largely by the linguistic *systems* in our minds" (1940, my italics). More forceful still—and there are a large number of possible quotations of this kind—is Whorf's statement that

> ". . . the background linguistic system (in other words, the grammar) of each language is not merely a reproducing instrument for voicing ideas, but rather is itself the shaper of ideas, the program and guide for the individual's mental activity, for his analysis of impressions, for his synthesis of his mental stock in trade. Formulation of ideas is not an independent process, strictly rational in the old sense, but it is part of a particular grammar and differs, from slightly to greatly, between grammars." (1940)

Finally, we may offer in evidence the paraphrasings of the Whorfian hypothesis by two eminent American linguists who have been both interested in and sympathetic to this hypothesis. The first of these says simply that "It is in the attempt properly to interpret the *grammatical categories* of Hopi that Whorf best illustrates his principle of linguistic relativity" (Hoijer, 1954, my italics). The other, as part of a more extended and systematic argument, says

> "Language as a whole has structure and all of its parts and subdivisions also have structure . . . [if] the rest of cultural behavior has been conditioned by language, then there must be a relationship between the *structure* of language and the *structure* of behavior." (Trager, 1959)

The emphasis on language *structure* as the critical feature in his linguistic relativity

hypothesis is actually a later and more mature level of Whorf's own thinking in this area. Sapir, on the other hand, as a professionally trained and professionally oriented linguist, was quite probably interested in language structure from the very outset. Whorf's intellectual and technical development in this topic area shows a transition from diffuse and unsystematic lexical analyses to more focused and interrelated grammatical analyses, the turning point coming most noticeably after his studies with Sapir. Be this as it may, both levels of argumentation do appear in Whorf's writings and even his later writings reveal many instances of regression to the first level discussed above. Thus, it is not strange that in the deliberations of many other students of this problem, whether in the roles of protagonists or detractors, the distinction between the lexical and the grammatical levels of analysis has not been fully exploited.

At the third level of analysis, we once more find ourselves in a realm of rich though ambiguous anthropological and ethnological data. As was the case with Level 1, above, the direct association or chain of reasoning between grammatical structure on the one hand and "something else" (be it *Weltanschauung* or even some less embracing segment of culture or values) on the other is not explicitly stated. Often, the "something else" is not stated at all and yet there is the general implication that grammatical oddities of the type presented cannot help but be paralleled by unique ways of looking at or thinking about or reacting to the surrounding environment. Thus, one encounters such evidence as that Chinese has no singular and plural or that it has no relative clauses (which we English speakers *do* have), whereas other languages have more levels of grammatical number (including singular, dual, tri-al, and plural forms—which we English speakers do *not* have). In this vein, the cataloging of grammatical differences can continue at great length (languages that do recognize gender of nouns and those that do not, languages that have tenses and those that do not, etc.) ; for both anthropologists, linguists, and a variety of nonspecialists have contributed to the fund of knowledge of phenomena of this type, always with the implication that it is clearly illogical to seriously suggest that linguistic phenomena such as these would have no relationship to life, to thought, and to values.

On the other hand, there are also several investigators that *have* attempted to indicate what the "something else" might be. In contrasting Hopi with English, Whorf (1940) has pointed to such odd grammatical features in Hopi as the absence of tenses, the classification of events by duration categories such that "events of necessarily brief duration (lightning, wave, flame, meteor, puff of smoke, pulsation) cannot be anything but verbs," the presence of grammatical forms for indicating the type of validity the speaker intends to attribute to his utterance (statement of current fact, statement of fact from memory, statement of expectation, and statement of generalization or law), etc. To Whorf all of these grammatical features seemed congruent with an outlook on life that was "timeless" and a historical in the sense that past, present, and future are seen as a continuity of duration, experience being cumulative and unchanging for countless generations. As a result of the "timelessness" of Hopi life, it is of greater importance for Hopi speakers to distinguish between the duration of events and their certainty than to indicate when they occurred (1941). A similarly ingenious and sensitive analysis is followed by Hoijer (1951, 1954) in connection with the Navaho verb system in which there is no clean separation between actors, their actions, and the objects of these actions. As Hoijer sees it, the Navaho verb links the actor to actions which are defined as pertaining to classes-of-beings. Thus it would appear that people merely "participate in" or "get involved in" somehow pre-existing classes of actions rather than serve as the initiators of actions. Hoijer interprets these grammatical characteristics as being consistent with the "passivity" and "fatefulness" of Navaho life and mythology in which individuals adjust to a universe that is given. Finally, in Nootka, Whorf finds a connection between the absence of noun-verb distinctions and "a monistic view of nature" (1940).

An example of work of this kind with modern European languages is provided by Glenn (1959). He points to the fact that the adjective most commonly precedes the noun in English whereas it most commonly follows it in French. The former pattern Glenn considers to be descriptive in a narrow or particularistic sense, more in keeping with inductive thought. The latter pattern he considers to be classificatory in a manner that moves from broader to narrower categories, as is the case with deductive thought. Glenn then proceeds to find "inductiveness" in English behaviors of various kinds (an inductive legal system in which many minute precedents culminate in the inductive formation of the common law, local governmental jurisdictions, and greater attention to pragmatic detail rather than to all-embracing theoretical unities, etc.) and "deductiveness" in diverse areas of French behavior (a broad legal code first and then individual decisions deduced from it, centralized governmental authority, the primacy of broad theoretical and philosophical interests, etc.). Whorf, too, has dealt with the world view of Standard Average European speakers, concluding from grammatical analyses that it emphasizes the concrete or material and the quantifiable (1941).

The efforts by Whorf, Hoijer, Glenn and similar scholars (see, e.g., Boas, 1938; Lee, 1944) merit considerable respect. They must be separated in our evaluation from pseudo-serious efforts to attribute or relate the musicalness of Italians to the light, melodious nature of the Italian language, or the stodginess of Germans to the heavy, lugubrious quality of the German language, or the warm, folksiness of Eastern European Jews to the intimate emotional quality of Yiddish, etc.[2] Superficially, the two approaches may seem similar, but the latter approach does not even have a serious structural analysis of language to recommend it. Nevertheless, the appeal of the Whorfian hypothesis for some lies precisely in the fact that it attempts to apply modern scientific methods and disci-

[2] Whorf himself makes a disclaimer along these lines when he states "I should be the last to pretend that there is anything so definite as 'a correlation' between culture and language, and especially between enthnological rubrics such as 'agricultural, hunting,' etc. and linguistic ones like 'inflected,' 'synthetic,' or 'isolating.' " (1941)

plined thought to such "old chestnuts" as the presumed "naturalness" that Hebrew (or Greek, or Latin, or Old Church Slavonic) be the language of the Bible, given its "classic ring" and its "otherworldly purity." However, with all of our admiration for those who have had the temerity as well as the ingenuity to attempt a rigorous analysis at this level, we must also recognize the limitations which are built into this approach. As many critics have pointed out (see, e.g., Lenneberg, 1953; Gastil, 1959), the third level of analysis has not normally sought or supplied independent confirmation of the existence of the "something else" which their grammatical data is taken to indicate. As a result, the very same grammatical designata that are said to have brought about (or merely to reflect) a given *Weltanschauung* are also most frequently the only data advanced to prove that such a *Weltanschauung* does indeed exist. Thus, once more, we are back at a language-language level of analysis (language structure $\rightleftarrows$ language-behavior-as-indication-of-world-view). Perhaps social scientists working together with linguists (or individuals trained in both fields) will ultimately be able to overcome this limitation as other evidence concerning national character and cultural mainsprings is amassed and systematized. As soon as there is sufficient "other" data (based on analysis of folklore materials, personality data, value-orientation measurements, etc.) and sufficient agreement as to how such data should be interpreted, there might well be a kind of Human Relations Area Files from which systematic variations in grammatical structure and systematic variations in value structure or lifestyle might be determined. This may not be too different from what Trager (1959) has had in mind in calling for greater attention to the recognition of structure in non-verbal areas of culture in order to push forward with research on the Whorfian hypothesis.

Pending the availability of such data, we might well consider that it is not the language-language nature of argumentation at this level that is, per se, its greatest drawback but rather its suspceptibility to selective presentation and to biased interpretation. Verbal behavior may long continue as our major avenue of insight into values and

motives. What we must be ever more dissatisfied with, however, are the self-selected lists of grammatical examples and the self-selected enumerations of cultures, cultural values or themes, and the evidence pertaining to the existence of such themes. In attempting to avoid these particular pitfalls, students of the Whorfian hypothesis have increasingly come to express a preference for a study design which investigates the relationship between grammatic structure on the one hand and *individual* non-linguistic behavior on the other. Although this is both a logical and a very promising solution to many of the above-mentioned problems, there is nevertheless no need to conclude at this point in our knowledge that it is the only one possible.

LEVEL 4. LINGUISTIC STRUCTURE AND ITS BEHAVIORAL CONCOMITANTS

The conceptual and methodological superiority of the fourth level of the Whorfian hypothesis is one thing. The accessibility of this level for study may well be quite another thing. It does seem that this level is in some ways the most demanding of all, for it requires detailed technical training at both the predictor and the criterion ends of the relationship to be investigated. This may be the reason why there currently appears to be only one study which might possibly be said to be an example of work at this level,[3] although in the future we might expect it to elicit greatly increased interest among sociolinguists and social psychologists with technical linguistic training. This is the study by Carroll and Casagrande which they refer to as Experiment II (1958). The grammatic features of interest to Carroll and Casagrande in this study are the particular verb forms required in Navaho verbs for handling materials in accord with the shape or other physical attribute (flexibility, flatness, etc.) of the object being handled. Note that Carroll and Casagrande are concerned here with distinctions in verb *forms* rather than dis-

---

[3] Related to this level of demonstration, but dealing with artistic structure rather than linguistic structure, are the findings summarized by Hallowell (1951) on the impact of culturally defined artistic styles on individual perceptions of reality.

tinctions between mere lexical absence or presence of verbs as such. Presumably it is this fact which permits us to consider Experiment II as a Level 4 study rather than as a Level 2 study. The non-linguistic data utilized by Carroll and Casagrande are the object-classifying behaviors of their Ss when presented first with a pair of objects which differ from each other in *two* respects (e.g., color and shape) and then with a third object similar to each member of the original pair in one of the two relevant characteristics. The Ss were asked to indicate "which member of the (original) pair went best with the (third) object shown him." If the S's reaction was governed by the requirements of Navaho verbal form, he would have to select a certain one of the original set of objects.

Carroll and Casagrande's hypotheses are quite explicitly stated: "(a) . . . that this feature of the Navaho language would affect the relative potency or order of emergence of such concepts as color, size, shape or form, and number in the Navaho-speaking child (specifically, that shape or form would develop earlier and increase more regularly with age, since this is the aspect provided for in the verb forms themselves), and (b) that he (i.e., the Navaho child) would be more inclined to perceive formal similarities (i.e., shape or form similarities) between objects than would English-speaking Navaho children of the same age." Carroll and Casagrande also assure us that the verb stems in question

> "compromise what Whorf has called a *covert class* and in the absence of native grammarians the pertinent grammatical rules operate well below the level of conscious awareness. Although most Navaho-speaking children, even at age 3 or 4, used these forms unerringly, they were unable to tell *why* they used a particular form with any particular object. Even when a child could not name an object—or may not have seen one like it before—in most cases he used the right verb form according to the nature of the object."

This last concern points up the importance of using unsophisticated Ss in this area of research in the same way as this is an important requirement in many attitudinal, motivational, or other dynamic fields of inquiry.

Carroll and Casagrande's original Ss were two very different groups of Navaho children—one being described as "Navaho dominant" (i.e., Ss who were either monolingual speakers of Navaho or else were bilinguals in whom Navaho speaking was dominant over speaking English) and the other as "English dominant." Finally, a further control group was obtained consisting of white middle class children in the Boston area. All subjects were of roughly comparable ages. In many respects Carroll and Casagrande's findings are extremely favorable for the Whorfian hypothesis. The Navaho-dominant Navaho Ss make the choices predicted by Navaho verb-stem requirements significantly more frequently than do the English-dominant Navaho Ss. In addition, there is quite a consistent increase in the "Navaho required responses" with age, although the Navaho-dominant Ss make such responses more frequently at every age from 3 through 10. Thus, when only these two groups of Ss are considered, the evidence is quite favorable to the Whorfian hypothesis—even though there is far from a one-to-one relationship between language dominance and object-classifying behavior. However, when the data from the Bostonian Ss are considered, some provocative difficulties appear. The white middle class children from the Boston area are even more Navaho in their object-classifying behavior than the Navaho-dominant Ss.[4] This superficially embarrassing finding is nevertheless of great provocative value both to Carroll and Casagrande and to all of those with concerns in this area, for it forces a consideration not only of the absence or presence of linguistic relativity in cognitive processes but of the degree ("strength") of this relativity as well as of its relative strength in comparison to other factors that may affect the direction of cogni-

[4] Note: "I have just within the past couple of months gotten additional data from an age and sex matched group of Harlem school children. Though by no means affording a perfect control group, I think it is a closer match to my English dominant Navahos than educationally advanced middle class youngsters from Boston. . . . On inspection the results show the Harlem group to be very close to the English dominant Navahos and, of course, the same age trend shows up." (Casagrande, 1960)

tive processes in various human groups. Perhaps, then, this may be the appropriate place to pause to consider this very matter.

THE DEGREE OF LINGUISTIC RELATIVITY

The fascination of the Whorfian hypothesis is in some ways compounded of both delights and horrors. We have already speculated concerning the delights. Let us now mention the horrors. The first is the *horror of helplessness,* since all of us in most walks of life and most of us in all walks of life are helplessly trapped by the language we speak. We cannot escape from it—and, even if we could flee, where would we turn but to some other language with its own blinders and its own vice-like embrace on what we think, what we perceive, and what we say. The second horror is the *horror of hopelessness*— for what hope can there be for mankind?; what hope that one group will ever understand the other?; what hope that one nation will ever fully communicate with the other? This is not the place for a full-dressed philosophical attack on these issues. Let us merely consider them from the point of view of the kinds of evidence supplied by some of the very studies we have mentioned.

The most "reassuring" facts that derive from Levels 1 and 2, the lexical and semantic codifiability levels of the Whorfian hypothesis, are that the noted non-translatability and the selective codifiability really pertain not so much to all-or-none differences between languages as to differences in relative ease or felicity of equivalent designation. Whenever we argue that there is no English word (or expression) for ——, which means so-and-so (or approximately so-and-so, or a combination of Y and Z) in English, we are partially undercutting our own argument. In the very formulation of our argument that there is "no English word (or expression) for ——" we have gone on to give an English approximation to it. This approximation may not be a very successful one but if that becomes our concern we can go through the contortions (both intellectual and gesticulational) that are required for an inching up on or a zeroing in on the non-English word or expression that we have in mind. The amount of effort involved may, at times, be

quite considerable and even the final approximation may leave us dissatisfied. However, after all is said and done, this is not so different, in terms of both process and outcome, as the communication problems that we face with one another even within our *own* speech community. We can do no better than to quote Hockett's conclusions at this point, in support of what has just been said.

"Languages differ not so much as to what *can* be said in them, but rather as to what it is *relatively easy* to say in them. The history of Western logic and science constitutes not so much the story of scholars hemmed in and misled by the nature of their specific languages, as the story of a long and fairly successful struggle *against* inherited linguistic limitations. Where everyday language would not serve, special sub-systems (mathematics, e.g.) were devised. However, even Aristotle's development of syllogistic notation carries within itself aspects of Greek language structure.

"The impact of inherited linguistic pattern on activities is, in general, *least* important in the most practical contexts and most important in such "purely verbal" goings-on as story-telling, religion, and philosophizing. As a result, some types of literature are extremely difficult to translate accurately, let alone appealingly." (1954)

Turning now to Levels 3 and 4, where we become concerned with the imbedded structural features of a language, it seems to be important that we realize that Whorf never proposed that *all* aspects of grammatical structure must *inevitably* have direct cognitive effects. Thus, to begin with, we are faced with the task of locating those few grammatical features which might have definable but unconscious functional correlates in our unguarded behavior. This is what Hoijer has in mind when he points to

"Mark Twain's amusing translation of a German folktale into English, where he regularly translates the gender of German nouns by the English forms *he, she,* and *it*. [This] illustrates in caricature the pitfalls of labeling the purely grammatical categories of one language in terms of the active structural-semantic pattern in another." (1954)

Lenneberg too has pointed to this very same principle (1953) when cautioning us that differences in metaphorical development in various languages may not only have no differential conscious correlates, but no differential unconscious ones as well.

If we look to Levels 2 and 4, these being the levels in which the behavioral concomitants of linguistic features are experimentally derived, we once more must reach the conclusion that linguistic relativity, where it does exist, is not necessarily an awesomely powerful factor in cognitive functioning. The relationships that have been encountered, though clear-cut enough, seem to be neither very great nor irreversible in magnitude. The very fact that increased infant and early childhood experience with toys and objects requiring primarily a form reaction can result in a *Navaho-like classifying preference* among monolingual English-speaking children also means that other kinds of environmental experiences might very well produce an *English-like classifying preference* among monolingual Navaho-speaking children. No one has yet directly studied the success with which behaviors predicted on the basis of linguistic relativity can be counteracted by either (a) simply making *S*s aware of how their language biases affect their thinking or (b) actively training *S*s to counteract these biases. It may be, after all, that this is an area in which *S*s can, with relatively little effort, learn how to "fake good." Furthermore, one might suspect that the impact of language *per se* on cognition and expression ought somehow to be greater and more fundamental than the impact of one or another language feature. Thus the impact of language *determinism* upon cognition ought to be more pervasive

and more difficult to counteract than that of language *relativity*.

None of the foregoing should be interpreted as implying that linguistic relativity, wherever it exists, is an unimportant factor in human experience or one that deserves no particular attention except from those who are professionally committed to unravelling the unimportant in painful detail. Quite the contrary; just because it is such a seemingly innocuous factor it is very likely to go unnoticed and, therefore, requires our particular attention in order that we may appropriately provide for it.

SUMMARY AND CONCLUSIONS

The four levels of the Whorfian hypothesis that have been presented here are essentially subsumable under a double dichotomy. As Figure 1 reveals, we have essentially been dealing with two factors—one pertaining to characteristics of a given language or languages and the other pertaining to behavior of the speakers of the language or languages under consideration. The first factor has been dichotomized so as to distinguish between lexical or semantic structure on the one hand (both of these being considered as codeability features) and grammatical structure on the other. The second factor has been dichotomized so as to distinguish between verbal behavior per se (frequently interpreted in terms of cultural themes or *Weltanschauungen*) and individual behavioral data which is other than verbal in nature.

In a rough way, we might say that Levels 1 and 3 are concerned with *large group phenomena* whereas Levels 2 and 4 are con-

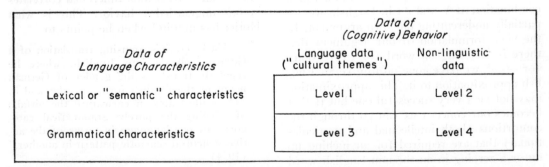

Data of Language Characteristics	Data of (Cognitive) Behavior	
	Language data ("cultural themes")	Non-linguistic data
Lexical or "semantic" characteristics	Level 1	Level 2
Grammatical characteristics	Level 3	Level 4

Fig. 1. Schematic Systematization of the Whorfian Hypothesis

cerned with *individual behavior*. Whorf was aware of and interested in both kinds of data, for he held that "our linguistically determined thought world not only collaborates with our *cultural idols and ideals* but engages even our unconscious *personal reactions* in its patterns and gives them certain typical character(istic)s" (1941, my italics).

In general, Whorf is not deeply concerned with "which was first, the language patterns or the cultural norms?" He is content to conclude that "in the main they have grown up together, constantly influencing each other" (1941).[5] Nevertheless, he does state that if these two streams are to be separated from each other for the purposes of analysis he considers language to be by far the more impervious, systematic, and rigid of the two. Thus, after a long association between culture and language, innovations in the former will have but minor impact on the latter, "whereas to inventors and innovators it (i.e., language) legislates with the decree immediate" (1941). Although Whorf is leary of the term correlation it seems most likely that he considered language structure not only as interactingly reflective of "cultural thought" but as directly formative of "individual thought." With proper cautions, the four levels of the Whorfian hypothesis that have been differentiated in this review may be seen as quite consistent with this conclusion.

Some of the characteristics, difficulties, and potentials of further empirical and theoretical study at each of the four differentiated levels have been considered. All levels can make use of both interlinguistic or intralinguistic designs, although Levels 1 and 3 most commonly employ the former— if only for purposes of contrast.

Although evidence favoring the Whorfian hypothesis exists at each level, it seems likely that linguistic relativity, though affecting some of our cognitive behavior, is nevertheless only a moderately powerful factor and a counteractable one at that. Cer-

tainly much experimental evidence has accumulated that points to a large domain of contra-Whorfian universality in connection with the relationships between *certain* structures of particular languages and *certain* cognitive behaviors of their speakers (see Osgood, 1960, e.g.). The time might, therefore, now be ripe for putting aside attempts at grossly "proving" or "disproving" the Whorfian hypothesis and, instead, focusing on attempts to delimit more sharply the types of language structures and the types of nonlinguistic behaviors that do or do not show the Whorfian effect as well as the degree and the modifiability of this involvement when it does obtain.

Because of Whorf's central role in making us aware of this phenomenon so that we may now better come to grips with it, both intellectually and practically, none can deny that he richly deserves to be characterized by his own standard for what constitutes a real scientist.

> "All real scientists have their eyes primarily on background phenomena in our daily lives; and yet their studies have a way of bringing out a close relation between these unsuspected realms . . . and . . . foreground activities." (1940)

REFERENCES

Bartlett, F. C. *Remembering*. London: Cambridge, 1932.

Boas, F. *Handbook of American Indian languages, Part 1*. Washington, D.C.: Government Printing Office, 1911.

Boas, F. (Ed.) Language. In *General anthropology*. Boston: Heath, 1938.

Brown, R. W. & Lenneberg, E. H. A study in language and cognition. *J. abnorm. soc. Psychol.*, 1954, 49, 454–462.

Carmichael, L., Hogan, H. P., & Walter, A. A. An experimental study of the effect of language on the reproduction of visually perceived form. *J. exp. Psychol.*, 1932, 15, 73–86.

Carroll, J. B. (Ed.) *Language, thought and reality; selected writings of Benjamin Lee Whorf*. New York: Wiley, 1956.

Carroll, J. B. and Casagrande, J. B. The function of language classifications in behavior. In Maccoby, Newcomb, & Hartley (Eds.),

---

[5] Sapir also takes this view in his article on language and environment (1912), in which he concludes that grammatical features once did correspond to environmental circumstances but have subsequently developed at a pace and in directions unrelated to environmental changes.

Readings in social psychology. New York: Holt, 1958.

Casagrande, J. B. Personal communication. March 18, 1960.

Ebbinghaus, H. Über eine neue Methode im Prüfunt geistiger Rühigkeiten und ihre Awendung bei Schulkindern. *Z. Psychol.,* 1897, 13, 401–457.

Eidens, H. Experimentelle Untersuchungen über den Denkuerlauf bei unmittelbarren Folgerungen. *Arch, ges. Psychol.,* 1929, 71, 1–66.

Fishman, J. A. An examination of the process and function of social stereotyping. *J. soc. Psychol.,* 1956, 43, 27–64.

Fishman, J. A. Some current research needs in the psychology of testimony. *J. soc. Issues,* 1957, 13, 60–67.

Galton, F. Psychometric experiments. *Brain,* 1879, 2, 149–162.

Gastil, R. D. Relative linguistic determinism. *Anthropological Linguistics,* 1959, 1, No. 9, 24–38.

Gates, A. I. Recitation as a factor in memorizing. *Arch. Psychol.,* 1917, 6, No. 40.

Glenn, E. S. Paper presented at the American Psychological Association meeting, Cincinnati, 1959.

Hallowell, A. Cultural factors in the structuralization of perception. In Rohrer & Sherif (Eds.), *Social psychology at the crossroads.* New York: Harper, 1951.

Hockett, C. F. Chinese versus English: an exploration of the Whorfian theses. In H. Hoijer (Ed.), *Language in culture.* Amer. Anthropological Assn., Memoir 79, 106–123, 1954.

Hoijer, H. Cultural implications of some Navaho linguistic categories. *Language,* 1951, 27, 11–120.

Hoijer, H. The Sapir-Whorf hypothesis. In H. Hoijer (Ed.), *Language in culture.* Amer. Anthropological Assn., Memoir 79, 92–104, 1954.

Kilpatrick, F. P. Perception theory and general semantics. *Etc.,* 1955, 12, 257–264.

Lee, D. D. Linguistic reflection of Wintu thought. *Int. J. Amer. Linguistics,* 1944, 10, 181–187.

Lehmann, A. Über Wiedererkennen. *Philos. Stud.* (Wundt), 1889, 5, 96–156.

Lenneberg, E. H. Cognition in ethnolinguistics. *Language,* 1953, 29, 463–471.

Lenneberg, E. H. A probabilistic approach to language learning. *Behav. Sci.,* 1957, 2, 1–12.

Lindeman, R. *Der Begriff der Conscience im Französichen Denken.* Jena-Leipzig, 1938.

Luria, A. R. The directive function of speech in development and dissolution. Part I: Development of the directive function in speech in early childhood. *Word,* 1959, 15, 341–352.

Lyon, D. O. The relation of length of material to time taken for learning and the optimum distribution of time. *J. educ. Psychol.,* 1914, 5, 1–9, 85–91, 155–163.

Maier, N. R. F. Reasoning in humans. I. On direction. *J. comp. Psychol.,* 1930, 10, 115–143.

Malinowski, B. The problem of meaning in primitive languages. In Ogden & Richards, *The meaning of meaning.* New York: Harcourt-Brace, 1923.

Miller, G. A., Bruner, J. S. & Postman, L. Familiarity of letter sequences and tachistoscopic identification. In G. A. Miller, *Language and communication.* New York: McGraw-Hill, 1951.

Miller, G. A. and Selfridge, J. A. Verbal context and the recall of meaningful material. *Amer. J. Psychol.,* 1950, 63, 176–185.

Osgood, C. E. The cross-cultural generality of visual-verbal synesthetic tendencies. *Behav. Sci.,* 1960, 5, 146–169.

Piaget, J. *Le language et la pensée chez l'enfant.* Neuchâtel and Paris: Belachaux et Niestle, 1924.

Postman, L. & Conger, B. Verbal habits and the visual recognition of words. *Science,* 1954, 119, 671–673.

Postman, L. & Rosenzweig, M. P. Perceptual recognition of words. *J. Speech and Hearing Disorders,* 1957, 22, 245–253.

Reed, H. B. Repetition and association in learning. *Ped. Sem.,* 1924, 31, 147–155.

Sapir, E. Language and environment. *Amer. Anthrop.,* 1912, n.s., 14, 226–242.

Sapir, E. The status of linguistics as a science. *Language,* 1929, 5, 207–214.

Sapir, E. Language. *Encycl. Soc. Scs.,* 1933, 9, 155–169.

Sells, S. B. The atmosphere effect. *Arch. Psychol.,* 1936, 29, No. 200.

Solomon, R. L. & Howes, D. H. Word frequency, personal values, and visual duration thresholds. *Psychol. Rev.,* 1951, 58, 256–270.

Trager, G. L. The systematization of the

Whorf hypothesis. *Anthrop. Ling.,* 1959, 1, No. 1, 31–35.

Tsao, J. C. Studies in spaced and massed learning: II. Meaningfulness of material and distribution of practice. *Quart. J. exp. Psychol.,* 1948, 1, 79–84.

Vigotsky, L. S. Thought and speech. *Psychiatry,* 1939, 2, 29–54.

Whorf, B. L. Science and linguistics. *Technology Review,* 1940, 44, 229–231, 247, 248.

Whorf, B. L. The relation of habitual thought and behavior to language. In L. Spier (Ed.), *Language, culture and personality.* Menasha, Wisc.: 1941, Pp. 75–93.

Wilkins, M. C. The effect of changed material on the ability to do formal syllogistic reasoning. *Arch. Psychol.,* 1928, 16, No. 102.

Woodworth, R. S. & Sells, S. B. An atmosphere effect in formal syllogistic reasoning. *J. exp. Psychol.,* 1935, 18, 451–460.

The Verbal Organism / Joseph Church (*Vassar College*)

We have in effect posed two polar modes of experience, the preverbal and the verbal. It is clear that when the child first begins to speak, it is merely as a way of extending forms of behavior in which he is already engaged; that is, language is assimilated and subordinated to the child's preverbal orientation. But the ontogenesis of language is interesting because of the opposite tendency, the way language opens up new orientations and new possibilities for learning and for action, dominating and transforming preverbal experience. We must emphasize that language is not just one function among many. One does not speak in the same sense that he walks, or eats, or makes love. Language is an all-pervasive characteristic of the individual, such that he becomes a verbal organism, whose walking, eating, love-making, and the rest are altered in keeping with his symbolic experience.

Language transforms experience first by creating new channels through which the human environment can act on the child. The sounds that formerly brought him only excitement or amusement or fear or irritation now bring him information and instructions as well. Through language one can manipulate the child's behavior, one can shape his objective and subjective reality, and one can, in time, induct him into a

purely symbolic realm of past and future, of remote places, of ideal relationships, of hypothetical events, of imaginative literature, of values, of imaginary entities ranging from werewolves to psi-mesons, and of alternative systems of symbolization such as mathematics.

At the same time, the learning of language transforms the individual in such a way that he is enabled to do new things for himself, or to do old things in new ways. Language permits us to deal with things at a distance, to act on them without physically handling them. This action at a distance takes two forms. First, we can act on other people, or on objects through people. This kind of action is not new, although language expresses our wants far more precisely than affective vocalizations or gestures. But action on people is not confined to getting what we want out of them. We can edify or amuse people as well as persuade them, we can apprise them of facts, or flatter them, or delude them with language. Second, we can manipulate symbols in ways impossible with the things they stand for, and so arrive at novel and even creative versions of reality, as in a scientific theory, a work of art, or a joke. Word realism and word magic, although an essential part of the symbolic attitude, can also impede effective verbal action, since it often seems that, in acting on things verbally, we are acting on the things themselves.

The real value of symbolic action, of course, is that we can verbally rearrange

From *Language and the Discovery of Reality,* by Joseph Church. © Copyright 1961 by Joseph Church. Reprinted by permission of Random House, Inc.

situations which in themselves would resist rearrangement, as when we discuss social or political or educational reforms; we can isolate features which in fact cannot be isolated, as when, in criticizing a work of art, we can talk separately about the artist's technical competence and his particular "vision"; we can juxtapose objects and events far separated in time and space, as when we try to relate infantile experience to adult personality, or look for regularities in historical events; we can, if we will, turn the universe symbolically inside out, as, in effect, such innovators as Copernicus and Einstein have done.

THE THEMATIZATION OF EXPERIENCE

Egocentrism, as we have said, reflects the ambiguous localization of experience, and an important feature of development is the progressive internalization of one's own functioning and feeling, together with the systematization of the outer world. This process is largely a matter of language, and a major change in the child's symbolic functioning occurs when he becomes able to communicate with himself.

It has been noted that certain of the toddler's first denominations and predicative utterances—"Baby crying"—seem to be not so much assertions as requests for confirmation. In effect, the toddler is talking for his own benefit, but he needs another person to mediate and verify his observations and phrasings. Within a few months, however, he is able to talk to himself without an intermediary, and there begins a period of frequent soliloquy, the child giving a running commentary on his own doings. In addition, the child begins to engage in verbal self-direction, telling himself what to do and how to do it—he even, somewhat later, scolds himself for his own misdeeds. Adults also direct themselves verbally, especially when learning a new skill. But although the toddler presumably hears what he is saying, he does not yet answer himself back. The first sign of solitary dialogue comes at about age two and a half or three, in dramatic play, when the child carries on "conversations," speaking now for this character and now for that one. (Here we see another ex-

ample of how the child acquires a whole class of behavior, not by deliberate instruction or by external reinforcement, but by empathically observing and absorbing the styles of those around him.)

By age three, the child deals very well symbolically with his familiar pragmatic world. By about age four, he begins once more to find his language inadequate to his experience. He is now learning—through accounts by adults and older children, through his travels, through television, through stories—about a great many things which may not fit established schemata of his existence, his familiar world-picture. He learns about bad men and ghosts and rockets and magic and football and religion and war and surgery and wild animals (some gentle and some fierce). His body boundaries are becoming more stable and by that very fact more vulnerable—perhaps this is the reason for the marked increase in fears, phobias, nightmares, and so forth, around age four, noted by a number of observers. It is apparent that many of the dynamisms of the child's world are being given explicit shape, and these incarnations are often frightening. The conflict between feelings of omnipotence and impotence, and between conservatism—wanting to live in a narrow, safe, familiar groove—and progressivism—wanting to grow, explore, experiment, and be independent (this conflict is called "growth ambivalence")—which dates at least from the toddler's first strivings for "autonomy," likewise becomes more pronounced. The child is becoming increasingly aware of the complexity and inconsistency of adult behavior, and he finds that the world keeps taking away his privileges and making new demands on him as he matures. By the same token, he becomes more aware of past and future, of growth and change, and of temporal relationships in general. Life keeps him off balance, and he is driven to wonder and to ask questions.

It is worth emphasizing that the solution to the child's perplexities lies in *thematizing* them—reducing them to manageable symbolic forms—which is, after all, the goal of the philosopher, the artist, and the scientific theorist. As he thematizes his experience, he reforges the schematic framework within which his existence is oriented. Again, like the nominalistic toddler, the four-year-old cannot undertake the job of thematization singlehanded, but needs an adult participant in his dialectic with reality: "Are gorillas fierce?" "What would happen if you fell into the deep water and you couldn't swim?" "When I grow up to be a big man [this from a little girl], will I have a penis like my daddy's?" It can be seen that the child's concerns are still largely (although not exclusively) personal, but that, if only for selfish reasons of orientation, he is trying to decipher and order the world, to classify things and make generalizations. He is still at the stage of phenomenalism and realism and does not yet seek out the systematic links between events. Nevertheless, he is beginning to suspect, to doubt, to sense that things are not always just as they seem.

Just as the toddler acquires confidence in his capacity for denomination and predication and learns to dispense with an adult sounding board, so the older preschool child learns to try answering his own questions. Not that he gives up asking his parents— but his questions come increasingly after an attempt at a formulation of his own, in the form of hypotheses. Also, whereas the toddler's monologues tend to be a verbal parallel of his concrete actions, the preschool child's thoughts are more often detached from the immediate situation and given to things in general—mostly in the form of reveries and fantasies, let it be noted, but also sometimes in an approximation of analytic thought.

It is not until considerably later, usually in adolescence, that the child's interior monologue becomes an interior dialogue. The adolescent's interior dialogues usually postulate a receptive audience which listens admiringly and feeds him cues while he displays his wit and wisdom and deploys a splendid future. In the same way, an adult who has fared badly in a debate may later, in solitude, reenact the discussion, this time, however, marshaling his arguments with perfect logic and acid clarity, backing them up with brilliantly conceived illustrations and analogies, quoting fluently from the pertinent authorities, and in general dumfounding his opponent. Despite the childish, egotistical nature

of much interior dialogue, it is the prototype of dialectical and synthetic thinking. It is the device by which we apprehend our own thoughts, criticize them, revise them, organize them, and make them our own. Until our thoughts have been formulated symbolically they are only elusive feelings and impulses to action; once we have said them, no matter how imperfectly, we have objectified and externalized them and can work with them. Obviously, it is not easy to view one's own ideas objectively, since they continue to resonate with feelings and connotations and associations that may be very vivid to their creator but completely hidden from everyone else. Authors are driven to various stratagems to counteract this effect— they can ask someone else to read and criticize a manuscript, or they can set it aside for a while and let it "cool off," after which they can return to it with rather more detachment.

It is impossible to say when the stream of symbolic consciousness takes firm hold, but in many adults—especially those who are described as "verbal"—we find an almost uninterrupted flow of internal verbalization by which the individual orders, integrates, and embroiders his experience as it is happening, in the manner of a critic who writes his review simultaneously with watching a play or reading a book, or of the psychologist who, in the course of an ordinary conversation, finds himself analyzing and classifying the other person's attitudes, motives, defenses, role identifications, style of thought, and so forth. Many people can deal with routine situations while their thoughts are, as the saying goes, miles away—thus, of course, the absent-minded professor.

THE VERBAL SELF

It is clear that thematization deals not only with the environment but also with the child himself. The child's verbal self is at least partially distinct from the schematic self, discussed earlier, that arises out of action and feeling and observation—we have already mentioned how the child can know explicitly that he has two eyes, whereas functionally he experiences himself as a Cyclops. The verbalization of self begins when the child learns the names of body parts—here again, if asked to show his ear, he is at great pains to show first one ear and then the other; but it will be a year before this concrete knowledge of having two ears can be voiced, even though the child will long since have been able to say that he has two cookies. It is interesting, too, that not much before age three can the child correctly answer such questions as "What do you see with?" and "What do you hear with?" The toddler's verbal identity receives a focus when he learns his name—indeed, the proper name seems to retain through life a pregnant importance: note how school-age children write their names on every available surface, how adolescents lovingly practice elegant signatures, how resentful the adult feels if his name is misspelled or mispronounced or forgotten, how when we meet someone who shares our name we feel a thrill either of kinship or of resentment at the usurpation. It is a dogma of salesmanship that one call the client by name as often as possible; what the salesman may not realize is that overdoing this may strike the customer as a desecration, a taking of his name in vain. It is reported that many primitive peoples give their children a real name, known only to the family, and, as a shield against nominal sorcery, a public pseudonym. Many adolescents adopt pseudonyms and nicknames which they feel represent their new true selves more accurately than the names chosen by their parents.

STAGES IN THE FORMATION OF A THEMATIC IDENTITY

Self-verbalization is closely linked to what is called the "search for identity." In primitive, closed societies the individual's identity is defined from birth by the social role he occupies. In Western societies, by contrast, each member must find his own place in the scheme of things, his own goals and meanings and values, his own functions and roles—in sum, his own unique identity. Even when, in our society, a family offers a child a more or less complete identity—as exemplified in the novels of John P. Marquand, notably *The Late George Apley*—

he is likely to repudiate it and go questing, at least temporarily, after his own.

Toddlerhood and Autonomy

Early schemata of the self are founded on practical competences, on control, on the bringing of implicit body experience into awareness, on the pain and pleasure that arise out of action on the environment and the environment's action on the child. For we must bear in mind the inexorable reciprocity of experience: it is always experience of a world vis-à-vis me, and of me vis-à-vis the world.

As the body schema becomes more stable, there arises the experience not only of self in the momentary situation but of self in relation to the world at large. This awareness is expressed in general orientations or attitudes of passivity, mastery, vulnerability, persistence, playfulness, helplessness, deviousness, flexibility, resignation, resistance, and so forth. However, according to Erikson—and the evidence supports him—the child who has in infancy acquired a trustful attitude toward the world will, as a toddler, characteristically develop an attitude of autonomy. Autonomy is sometimes equated with one of its most striking manifestations, negativism—an occasional obstinate resistance to adult commands, requests, questions, and suggestions. Negativism has its antecedents in early infancy: the hungry two-month-old, for instance, may turn his head away and cry angrily when the parent tries to give him a pacifier in lieu of a bottle. Slightly later, the child may vigorously refuse unfamiliar foods or foods that he finds distasteful. Still later, when he has become mobile, he scampers away and hides, or is suddenly very preoccupied with a plaything, when his parents summon him. Such behavior is sometimes whimsical and sometimes in earnest, but even playful negativism shows the child's growing sense of autonomy. Negativism reaches full flower when the child learns, early in his linguistic career, to say No, which he does to every remark which is even faintly interrogatory or imperative in tone. It is interesting that most children use *no* some months in advance of *yes*. The child's verbal No may be quite independent of his actual wants, intentions, and actions, but he seems called upon to assert at least a token autonomy on every possible occasion. The child refuses not only direction and coercion but also help and support—he wants to do it himself. On the other hand, he likes to make his parents do for him things, such as feeding him, of which he is perfectly capable. He wants to control not only himself but others as well.

Autonomy rests upon a schematic, unverbalized self-knowledge. As we have said, the toddler's early active vocabulary refers only to things external to himself. His first self-references are a matter of defining ownership or giving accounts of things he has done or seen—such accounts, let it be remembered, are usually comprehensible only to adults who know the child well or have been present on the particular occasion. It is some time before the toddler makes any attempt to define himself objectively or to give explicit voice to his inner states. He does not say "Hungry," but "Eat" or "Lunch"; if he feels good, he smiles; if he feels bad, he cries or fusses—but in neither case does he say what he feels. If he is eating a favorite foodstuff, he devours it avidly; if a disliked one, he spits it out—but he at first has no way of verbalizing "pleasant" or "unpleasant." He echoes what his parents say about him—"Good boy," "Big boy"—but the words have only affective meaning. Even though he can say quite early whether he is a boy or a girl, the difference is for him strictly a matter of minor externals, such as coiffure. Even a five-year-old, seeing a picture of a nude girl, may insist that it is a boy because "he" has his hair cut like a boy's.

Role-playing begins while self-verbalization is still in a nascent state. The child may strut about, shoulders back and chest outthrust, proclaiming himself to be Superman or Mighty Mouse; or he may drop to all fours and alternate barks with cries of "Dog, dog." It would appear that even the schematic self can be sufficiently stable and conscious to serve as a plaything; we would guess, however, that it is still highly dependent on immediate environmental feedback and would dissolve rapidly if external conditions changed markedly. Again we must remember that the organism cannot function psychologically without its environ-mental context, as in conditions of sensory deprivation, and that even adults change character markedly from one situation to the next. It is a commonplace that a man may be a tiger in the office and a mouse at home (or vice versa), the life of the party among strangers and a sphinx with his own family.

The Preschool Years

During the preschool years, the child begins to acquire and to apply to himself explicit notions of temperamental differences, tastes and preferences, life goals and life styles, physical attributes, and so forth. Also, he becomes able to talk about his own feeling states—he now not only has feelings about objects but feels his own feelings and knows what they feel like. Of course, like everybody else, the preschool child attends to himself only in times of inactivity, of recollection, and of preparation for action, or when he is at odds with his environment; once he is in action, his self-awareness ceases to be focal and becomes part of the background against which he perceives the figural object with which he is dealing. Unlike adults, the preschool child feels no need to idealize himself verbally, although fear of censure may force him into silence. Even though, at this age, the child is far from able to describe himself in terms of personality traits, there does seem to be a concrete knowledge of himself as a total person, implicit in such chronic attitudes as smugness, anxiety, guilt, self-assurance, strength, and so forth.

The School Years

In children of all ages, the stability of the self-image derives both from pragmatic feedback and from the regard of other people. As long as people view the child with approval, he does not question himself; if others disapprove him, he is made uncomfortable, defensive, and anxious. Or, if he is too long ignored, he may feel the threat of disintegration. The toddler and the preschool child orient themselves to parental affection. So, of course, do school-age children; but, in addition, they measure themselves against the standards of the school and, perhaps more important, of the children's society of which they become a part.

The school child's self-descriptions are largely in terms of his acceptability to his contemporaries, as gauged by his physical characteristics, his competences, his mastery of the tribal ways, and his commitment to the tribal morality (which may differ radically from that of adults). This means that he is becoming skilled in the duplicity that is so important a part of adult functioning, the ability to adapt oneself to the changing demands of different situations and to mask one's true feelings when these conflict with the standards of one's surroundings. We might mention that the school-age child's duplicity may be a peril to empirical research, since he has no qualms about giving misleading answers and telling his age-mates about procedures which he has sworn to keep secret. We might also say that this very gift of duplicity may, in adolescence, be a source of guilt and self-reproach—even while the adolescent is charging the adult world with hypocrisy and insincerity, he senses the seeds growing in himself.

The school-age child has not yet learned to ask, "Who am I?" but can give quite an elaborate answer to "What am I?" He is becoming explicitly aware of some of the peculiarities of his body, as shown by his delight in such stunts as crossing his eyes, testing his patellar reflex, holding his arm pressed against a wall and then, as he steps away, watching the arm rise unbidden, and turning the flow of urine on and off by an act of will. Yet he has only the most rudimentary notion of himself as a person apart from his body, as a consciousness, and as an agent rather than a reagent. If he has been taught that he has a soul, he does not conceive of it as his own vital essence, his psychism, but as some vaporous stuff, vaguely human in shape, that effuses from the body at death. If he imagines the torments of hell, it is not because he sees his sentience trapped in his soul and carried to damnation, but because he imagines his own corporeal self among the flames. Although the school child vehemently disowns his infantile past and talks grandiosely of the future, adult life and its concerns are still wholly remote and essentially meaningless for him.

During the school years, nevertheless, the child becomes increasingly the master of language. Not only does he learn to deal with written language and with quantitative and schematic symbolizations, but he begins to apprehend and exploit the possibilities of language as an abstract sphere: he enjoys puns and *double-entendres,* he is intrigued to discover that foreigners use different words to designate the things he knows, he revels in codes and ciphers, he grasps figures of speech, and, above all, he becomes more proficient at translating his own thoughts and feelings into words.

Adolescence and Adulthood

It is in adolescence that the youngster begins to define himself as a psychological entity different from—and even in conflict with—his body, and explicitly to question his own identity: Do I really exist? Why do I behave the way I do and can I really control my behavior? Why am I so different from everyone else? What do I believe in? Will independence to decide for myself be a blessing or a curse? Whom can I count on? What do people really think of me? What does it all mean?

Needless to say, the adolescent does not spend all his time brooding about such matters. His practical knowledge carries him along very nicely most of the time. But these questions do lurk in the background, ready to assail him in moments of solitude, in moments of confidential intimacy with friends, and whenever reminders occur in the form of failures, temptations, vocational and educational choices, draft calls, and so on. The adolescent is usually able to define at least some of his own salient personality traits, especially those that he worries about—shyness, moodiness, impulsiveness, stinginess, attitudes out of keeping with his sex role, and the like.

While the adolescent's self-esteem continues to be dependent on public opinion, he is beginning, too, to define more abstract, ideal standards to which he compares himself. The adolescent's self-judgments include some which are factually quite accurate, some which are much too harsh, and some which give him rather more credit than he deserves.

Like the adult, the adolescent seeks self-understanding only up to a point. There are some things he would rather not know about, because they conflict with either the standards of the group or his own professed ideals. In addition, to acknowledge some impulses is tantamount to approving them, and approving them to acting on them. In short, a portion of the adolescent's (and adult's) self-knowledge is cast in the form of the "defense mechanisms" mentioned earlier—denial, reaction formation, rationalization, projection, displacement, and so forth. The defense mechanisms work in either of two ways. One can refuse to give a name to a wish, impulse, attitude, or idea, thus denying its existence; or else one can give it a verbal formulation which masks its true nature and so neutralize it. We can see an early defense mechanism in the legalistic quibble of the school-age child: "You said not to hit him. I only gave him a little shove." However, the use of defense mechanisms in the construction of a stable verbal self-image, including the secondary elaborations by which one integrates partial self-insights, does not seem to occur before the adolescent years.

Lest we seem to have detached the young person and his development too much from environmental conditions, it should be made clear that the normal person cannot sustain a self-image by verbiage alone but must bolster it by some actual accomplishment. Our notions about ourselves are always full of doubts and contradictions and ambiguities. What most of us try to do, more or less consciously, is to find the sort of setting that will evoke and support and reflect back to us a coherent and pleasing self-image. But the behavior we engage in to fortify our self-image is futile unless the environment gives back the proper echoes. Unlike the normal person, the schizophrenic defends his precarious intactness by avoiding any real test of his self-image or else by trying to destroy the surroundings that mirror his behavior in such an intolerable way. The individual in an environment alien or hostile to his style of life may find his behavior and his self-image shifting as he takes on the coloration of his surroundings. In trying to resist the process of adaptation, the individual may be driven to extremes, until he becomes a caricature of what he is trying to stand for—like the legendary British colonial who, to avoid going native, dressed for dinner even in the middle of the jungle and allotted himself a single copy of the *Times* at breakfast each morning.

B. Via Processes of Interpersonal Perception, Interaction, and Influence

If we as social psychologists are concerned with the manner by which individuals structure and organize their environment and then react and interact within it, it is of the utmost importance to examine one particularly important feature of that environment, other people.

The process of perception in general and the process of person perception in particular has occupied an important place in the field of social psychology. Initially, social psychologists concentrated on the issue of perceptual accuracy—e.g., how accurately does one person perceive an emotion or reaction in another. Only more recently has the focus shifted to the actual process involved rather than the outcome of accuracy-inaccuracy. If we maintain that the manner by which an individual defines a situation, especially the person-objects in that situation, is basic to understanding how he will behave in it, it seems to be of importance to examine the manner by which such definitions come about and function rather than simply to determine if they are correct or not. This is especially the case when the object defined is another person, a difficult object indeed about which to determine objectively perceptual accuracy.

The Jones and Thibaut reading included in this section presents a conceptual framework for understanding the process involved in this most important act of interpersonal perception. They reject the over-simplified idea that each of us is involved in a continuous processing of all information provided by another, suggesting rather that certain components of an interaction between two or more people—especially the particular goals of that interaction—make certain kinds of information-processing more salient. Their approach most excellently reflects the social psychological concern with the determinants of the process of interpersonal perception.

The provocative essay by Goffman, provides what he refers to as a dramaturgic analysis to defining situations. He focuses his attention for the most part upon the presentation provided by the stimulus object, e.g., the person being perceived.

Given our social psychological approach to this area, it is of obvious importance to be concerned with the perceiver, the perceived, and the interactive situation in which these are involved.

The nature of the individual's definition of the situation, especially his conceptualization of the other actors present, is assumed to be an important determinant of the outcomes of his interaction in that situation.

As a concept, interaction denotes the formation of a relationship between two or more persons, A and B, such that A's behavior serves both as a stimulus for B and a response to B's behavior which in turn may serve as both a stimulus and as a response for A. Interaction, therefore, involves a reciprocal relationship in which each person may produce effects for the other person.

By combining interaction and interpersonal influence in the same section, we intend to suggest that influence and conformity may be meaningfully interpreted within a context of these effects of A on B and of B on A. As A's behavior effects B's behavior, A is serving as a stimulus which influences B. This may involve an intentional act on the part of A to influence or effect B—e.g., A says to B, "Would you please open the door?"—or it may be a less intentional act of influence—e.g., A unwittingly frowns and B changes the topic of their conversation.

Two readings most general in their treatment of this topic of interaction and influence are those by Gouldner and by Jahoda. In his theoretical article, Gouldner examines a normative component of many forms of interpersonal interaction, discussing some of its implications for the stable functioning of dyadic relationships as well as the larger context provided by the social system. Further implications of "the norm of reciprocity" for deviance and conformity are also examined. In contrast to the sociological approach to relationships in general taken by Gouldner is the more strictly social psychological approach to the specific areas of conformity and deviation discussed by Jahoda.

The remaining selection by Izard examines one form of interactive relationship, friendship, as this is related to similarity of personality.

Interaction Goals as Bases of Inference in Interpersonal Perception[1] / Edward E. Jones (*Duke University*) John W. Thibaut (*University of North Carolina*)

It is quite possible to surface after brief immersion in the literature on "social perception" with the impression that people, when they are with other people, are preoccupied with the cognitive task of assessing each other's fundamental nature. This is essential, so the argument is likely to run, because appropriate and adjustive reactions depend on accurate perceptions of the characteristics of the other persons in our social environment. Steiner (19) has seriously

Reprinted from PERSON PERCEPTION AND INTERPERSONAL BEHAVIOR, edited by Renato Tagiuri and Luigi Petrullo, by permission of the authors and publisher, Stanford University Press. © Copyright 1958 by the Board of Trustees of the Leland Stanford Junior University.

[1] The writing of the present paper was in many ways facilitated by the Ford Foundation and the Office of Naval Research. Some of the research reported here was supported in part by ONR Contract No. Nonr–855(04).

questioned the validity of this latter assumption, which would seem to depend to an important degree on the stimulus attributes chosen as criteria of accuracy. The question thus arises: accurate in what respect? with regard to which set of characteristics?

The development of research and theory dealing with interpersonal perception has thus far been constrained by an overemphasis on perceiving the personality characteristics and behavior tendencies of a particular other. Proceeding on the assumption that the particular responses made by another provide the primary clues for drawing inferences about his nature, many research designs in the perception area seem to foster the implication that we view others as though through a reduction screen, to eliminate the disturbing effects of context. In order to be more faithful to the typical situation of social interaction, however, we should recognize that in many interaction situations, considerable information is conveyed by cues about the situation and the roles of the participants. Even if we restrict social perception to the perception of persons per se, we will have to deal with inferences about their behavior in relation to the interaction context.

It also seems unwise to assume that our social effectiveness in an interaction situation grows as a monotonic function of the amount of information available about the other actors. This assumption fails to consider the fact that not all information is equally useful and that a redundancy of cues, when we are only concerned with a few, can operate as distracting noise. A study by Leventhal (14) provides support for this qualification, and Cronbach (4) discusses various statistical reasons why an increase in information may sometimes lead to an actual decline in accuracy.

Our present approach rests on the observation that social interactions are rarely communicative free-for-alls which require large amounts of information to be intelligently maintained. For the most part, we interact with others within fairly well-defined situations and in terms of rather constraining roles. Our main requirement, therefore, is for information *relevant* to adequate role performance, and, fortunately for cognitive economy, we need not be indiscriminately attentive to all the cues provided by the other actor(s).

Two assumptions underlying the subsequent development of this argument may now be stated as a conclusion of the foregoing remarks:

1. Interpersonal perception can most fruitfully be treated as both instrumental to social interaction and conditioned by it. Thus the strategic focus in social perception will vary as a function of the type of social interaction it supports. If we can successfully identify the goals for which an actor is striving in the interaction situation, we can begin to say something about the cues to which he will attend, and the meaning he is most likely to assign them.

2. The perceiver in any social situation will act in such a way as to reduce the need for information to sustain the interaction process. This blanket statement, which de-

serves at least a *ceteris paribus,* implies a general tendency to adopt simplifying strategies in our interactions with others, strategies which are in the service of cognitive and emotional economy. Much stabilization and simplification of the interaction process results from role-playing strategies of various kinds, but other strategies may actually be the expressions of enduring personality characteristics. The unresponsive, passive person has in this sense a lowered need for information when he is interacting with someone else.

In keeping with the focus of the present symposium, our main concern in this paper will be with the inferences one person draws about another person in a social situation, but we shall examine the inference process with consistent reference to the interaction context in which the perceiver finds himself vis-à-vis the person being judged. In particular, we shall discuss some of the conditions and circumstances which affect our assessment of others by giving rise to the premises from which cognitive inferences proceed. We shall attempt to explore, that is, some of the reasons why different inferences are drawn when the same behavior appears in varying social interaction contexts.

SOME RELEVANT PROPERTIES OF THE INFERENCE PROCESS

In some ways it is unfortunate that we have become accustomed to talking about social or interpersonal *perception.* The processes in which most of us are interested seem to be primarily those of inference, induction, and deduction, rather than isomorphic reflections of social reality, as the word perception somehow suggests. Recognition that we are mainly interested in the nature of cognitive inferences about interpersonal events points us toward an investigation of the learning processes which lie behind categorization, the attachment of significance to cues, and the cognitive redintegration of wholes through exposure to their parts.

One of the most crucial determinants of the inference process is certainly that of association on the basis of past experience. Thus, the more frequent the occurrence of behavior X and behavior Y in the same stimulus persons, the more likely we are to predict Y when X occurs, or vice versa. Similarly, the more frequently we have associated certain overt behavioral cues with certain internal states or traits, the more will we treat these cues as symptomatic of a trait, a state of mind, or a syndrome. A great deal can be learned about individual differences in association links and patterns through the use of such devices as Osgood's *Semantic Differential* (15) and Kelly's *Role Repertory Test* (13). Both of these devices have actually been applied to the study of problems in interpersonal perception (cf. 16, 2, 14). The particular semantic framework in terms of which an individual structures his inferences about interpersonal events is obviously a crucial and suitable focus for detailed empirical study.

In studying the inference process in social perception, however, we should not only be concerned with the most probable if-then sequences of behavior as they are structured by the perceiver. It is also important to examine the conditions which affect the selection of information at the origin of the inference process. Here questions of attention, selective perception, deliberate decisions of relevance, etc., enter the picture. The perceiver does not passively assign equal priority to incoming cues, but actively seeks out information which is relevant to his purposes in the situation of interaction. The perceiver is tuned or set to process certain kinds of information but not others.

Once cue selection has occurred, furthermore, the inference process is not entirely dependent on a stable matrix of associations which are in some mechanical way tripped off by the selected information. Again, depending on the interaction context, the same information may be treated in different ways at different times by the same observer. This is particularly true when we deal with inferences resulting in evaluative conclusions. The same behavior may be viewed with opprobrium in one context and with approval in another. We may dislike a person when he thwarts us but feel quite neutral and objective when he thwarts another.

Thus the context of interaction conditions both the *selection* and the *transformation* of information. In subsequent discussions we shall use the term *inferential set* (10) to cover these two functions as they are conditioned by the interaction goals of the perceiver. We assume that each participant in an interaction must come to an initial decision (no matter how tentative or erroneous) regarding the nature of the social situation in which he is involved. Out of this decision will evolve a set to attend to, and to utilize in certain ways, the information provided by the other person. This carries us abruptly to the next problem, that of specifying the conditions which arouse various inferential sets and exploring the dimensions along with these conditions appear to vary. This will involve us in an attempt to classify social interaction, but our primary attention will be directed to consequent perceptual variations.

CLASSES OF SOCIAL INTERACTION AND THEIR PERCEPTUAL IMPLICATIONS

Any attempt to classify social interactions will naturally reflect the biases, goals, and theoretical priorities of the classifier. In addition, one can focus on the contents of interaction, the roles of the participants, the formal tempo of the interchange, the fundamental personal needs being served, the contributions of interactive behavior to social equilibrium, and so on. Concerned as we are with the perceptual concomitants of interaction, we have found it useful to work within a two-way classification scheme. On the one hand, there are important variations in the "fullness" or mutuality of interaction—the extent to which the behavior of each actor is contingent on the behavior of each other actor. On the other hand, one can distinguish different interactions in terms of the dominant interpersonal goals of the participants involved. This dual classification scheme is thus both formal and substantive, but we shall attempt to show later that form and substance are empirically interdependent.

Interactions Classified in Terms of the Reciprocality of Behavior

It is customary to speak of social interaction whenever two or more persons are behaving in orientation to each other. The basic defining criterion is simply that the presence of one person affects the behavior of another person. Such a definition covers a broad array of social phenomena, however, and it is necessary to make certain further distinctions based on the degree to which the moment-to-moment behavior of one actor is contingent on the moment-to-moment behavior of the other actor. Although we shall talk hereafter in terms of dyadic situations only, the same considerations should apply in situations of three or more actors. If we reflect on the determinants of behavior in a social situation, we can typically allocate some variance to the general response hierarchy which the actor imports into the situation, to various nonsocial features of the environment, to the social structure of the situation as perceived by the actor, and to the particular behavior of the other actor which becomes a stimulus for the perceiver. The question now becomes, how important a determinant *is* the behavior of the other actor and the personal characteristics he reveals through his behavior? In some social situations, what the other actor says or does plays a minor role in determining what the perceiver says or does. In other situations it may be vitally important. In order to deal with this dimension of variation, we propose three formal types of interaction ranging from the extreme of independent to the extreme of mutually interdependent social behavior: *noncontingent interactions, asymmetrically contingent interactions, and reciprocally contingent interactions.*

A *noncontingent interaction* is actually something of a contradiction in terms, since it implies that people are interacting in such a way that the behavior of one actor is not a determinant of the behavior of the other actor. However, there is a class of social situations where interaction is simulated in this fashion but where the behavior of each actor is actually quite rigorously determined by detailed role prescriptions. The *appearance* of interaction is accomplished through a simple synchronization of responses, so that both actors do not talk at the same time or in inappropriate orders. In such a situation, we can say that the behavior of each actor is determined by a clearly defined S.O.P. (from the military nomenclature, "standing operating procedure") and thus the content of the other's behavior is irrelevant to the unfolding of his own responses. Many ceremonial interactions, or interactions appearing within highly formalized social organizations, would approximate this extreme. Noncontingent interactions may also arise whenever the participants are characterized by extreme behavioral perseveration or intense personal preoccupation. Thus, noncontingent interactions may be observed between detached schizophrenic patients or mental defectives where the form of social interaction is apparent, but the content of one actor's speech is not contingent on the content of the other's.

When the interaction situation is basically simulated or noncontingent, regardless of its origin, the requirements for social perception in a functional sense are practically nonexistent. Very little sensitivity to the other is required, over and above the minimal amount of monitoring which is essential for temporal synchronization. In this sense, the noncontingent interaction situation is comfortably stable for both participants, and, most important, continuous monitoring of behavioral content is unnecessary. If the perceiver is aware of the S.O.P. which governs himself and the S.O.P. which governs the other, no immediate, instrumental purpose is served by coming to any conclusions about the personality characteristics of the other.

Asymmetrically contingent interactions are considerably more common than noncontingency interactions and also take a greater variety of forms. "Asymmetrical contingency" suggests a type of interaction in which the behavior of one actor is fully contingent on the behavior of another, but the other's behavior is independently determined (as if one person was "shadowing" another). If this were the case, then the situation would be "noncontingent" from one actor's point of view and "fully contingent" as far as the other actor was concerned. This denotation is somewhat misleading, however, and it implies a type of interaction which would be extremely unstable.

It is more meaningful, we believe, to approach asymmetrical contingency interactions by making an initial distinction between standard and variable responders. A standard responder is one whose response potentialities are largely determined by an S.O.P. The S.O.P. does not completely define his behavior, as in the noncontingency situation (except for synchronization cues), but it vastly reduces his range of improvisation. A variable responder, on the other hand, is one whose behavior is unfettered by a constraining S.O.P. and is consequently open to interpersonal influence. With this distinction in mind, then, we can define a situation as asymmetrically contingent when it involves interaction between a standard and a variable responder.

One example of asymmetrical contingency is the typical interaction between an interviewer and a respondent. The interviewer is a standard responder—his behavior is governed by an S.O.P. which may be highly detailed (a schedule of specific questions) or more broadly delimiting (a topic check list). The interviewer's behavior may, at various points, be partly dependent on the respondent's behavior, but he does operate with a set of behavior categories definitely restricted and to some extent sequentially specified by the purpose of his interview. The interviewee, of course, is a variable responder, attuned both to the questions asked and the perceived intent behind them.

Experiments which involve the use of role-playing confederates provide another example, since the naïve subject (variable responder) is confronted with a "stooge" whose behavior is largely determined by an S.O.P. established by the experimenter.

The perceptual consequences of such asymmetrically contingent interactions naturally depend on whether we focus on the cognitive task of the variable responder or the standard responder. Turning first to the latter, the standard responder is of course confronted with a stimulus person whose responses cannot be predicted in terms of any knowledge of a governing S.O.P. If the standard responder's S.O.P. completely specifies his own response sequence, however, there is no need for inference-building information. His behavior is by definition unaffected by the behavior of the variable responder. If the S.O.P. merely restricts the standard responder to a limited set of be-

havior categories, without specifying the sequence of behaviors, then we have a situation in which a complex stimulus pattern must be "coded" into response-relevant information. In this latter case, the behavior of the variable responder will be perceived in a highly selective fashion. Thus in spite of the complexity of the stimulus, the cognitive burden of the standard responder will be light even if the sequence in which he should make his responses is not specified.

The perceptual implications of being a variable responder depend on the degree to which the responder is aware of the nature of the situation. If he is aware that the standard responder's behavior is covered by an S.O.P., he will presumably concentrate initially on those cues which will help him determine the nature of the S.O.P. The continuity and intensity of the variable responder's monitoring will depend on feedback about the complexity of the S.O.P. If the variable responder is unaware of the existence of an S.O.P., he will be in the same position, subjectively, as any actor in a situation of full, mutual contingency.

At least in our democratic, "other-directed" culture, asymmetrical contingency relationships are likely to be quite unstable. Thus some interactions start out being asymmetrically contingent and end up being noncontingent. If we think of the course of an argument between a liberal and a party-line communist, it might well be that the liberal tries to counter the communist's arguments in a flexible and "contingent" way, but the communist responds largely in terms of his own ideological S.O.P. In time, it seems plausible to assume, the liberal will reduce his contingency on the specific content of the communist's argument, and a decline in continuous monitoring will result. In the military, and many other hierarchical organizations, an attempt is characteristically made to push asymmetrical contingency situations in the direction of noncontingent ones by emphasizing the S.O.P.s which govern interactions between status levels.

Other interactions start out asymmetrically contingent and end up being doubly contingent, as in the case where the interviewer is drawn into controversy with the interviewee.

Reciprocally contingent interactions.— Here we refer to those "full" interactions in which the behavior of one actor is contingent on the behavior of the other and vice versa. Parsons and Shils (17) apparently wish to restrict the term interaction to such "double contingency" situations, but we prefer to treat reciprocal contingency as an extreme point on a broad continuum. Nevertheless, reciprocal contingency is neither a rare nor unimportant phenomenon. In such clearly social situations the full range of human emotions is most likely to be engaged, and the intricate complexities of shared and nonshared perspectives become critically relevant.

As contrasted with noncontingent interactions, the search requirements in reciprocal contingency situations are naturally more demanding as far as interpersonal perception itself is concerned. Because each response of Actor A is partially dependent on the preceding response of Actor B, A will naturally have to monitor continuously the behavior of B. Since the situation is by nature fluid, the perceiver has to be constantly alert to incoming cues from the other in order to respond in an effective manner. There are also two, somewhat contradictory additional implications for interpersonal perception or inference:

1. Actor A and Actor B are by definition in a situation where each actor is a partial, but only a partial, cause of the other's behavior. If we assume that A and B perceive each other as modifiable from moment to moment, cues of social reinforcement and acceptance by the other actor will take on greater significance because they will be perceived as spontaneous, at least in part. In line with this, inferences about the other's intentions, motives, and "true nature" will take on added significance, i.e., will become an increasingly important determinant of interaction behavior. Parsons and Shils (17) seem to be making the same point when they propose that double contingency interactions imply "the normative orientation of action, since alter's reaction of punishment or reward is super-added to alter's 'intrinsic' or direct behavioral reaction to ego's original selection" (p. 16). Their argument, however, involves a somewhat different derivation.

2. On the other hand, in reciprocal contingency situations the need for information is immediate, and it must be quickly processed since neither actor has much time to think about the preceding act before having to act himself. As a consequence of this "urgency" consideration, we suggest that much of the perceiver's attentive energy will be directed to his own future responses and not to the stable characteristics of the other. Thus the main moment-to-moment problem is not "What is he like?" but "What am I going to do next?"

These two considerations suggest that the perceiver is typically placed in a certain amount of cognitive conflict when in reciprocal contingency situations. As long as he is in the situation and responding directly to the other person, concentration on his own responses will likely be the dominant factor. Certainly some information about the motives and character of the other actor will "filter through" and in part determine his own reactions, but much of this information will not be processed and evaluated at the time. In retrospect, however, when there is no longer the urgency which comes with response planning and execution, information about the stable characteristics of the other will command greater attention and certain conclusions will likely be drawn about the other actor for future reference. How often do we engage in a pleasant and smooth interchange with some other person only to realize later, upon reflection, that we have been crassly manipulated? It is probably good selling technique to force such a rapid interchange upon the prospect that he cannot devote his full attention to a calm consideration of the merits of the product (or the salesman).

To summarize our position briefly, we feel that certain classificatory distinctions may be made in terms of the degree to which the behaviors of parties to an interaction are mutually contingent. Furthermore, these distinctions appear to have considerable relevance for the continuity and urgency of perceptual search, as well as for the kinds of cues most available as a basis for inference. It is difficult, however, to make any precise predictive statements about the inference process, knowing only the degree of mutual contingency. For this reason, we would like to introduce another, more substantive, basis for classification which will move us closer to empirically verifiable statements.

Interactions Classified in Terms of Mediated Purpose

Certainly the goals or purposes that one person wants and expects to achieve by interaction with another are highly complex in the concrete instance, and difficult to disentangle. It nevertheless seems convenient to classify interactions in terms of three different *kinds* of goals toward which the interaction is directed: the facilitation of personal goal attainment, the deterministic analysis of personality, and the application of social sanctions.

Assuming that these are important classes of interaction goals, there are characteristic cognitive problems associated with each class of goals. If the goal is facilitation of goal attainment, the associated problem may be summarized by the question, "What is he doing to me or for me that makes me want to approach or avoid him?" The attempt to solve this problem promotes the arousal of what we shall call a *value-maintenance* inferential set, whose selective and transformative properties will be fully discussed below. Given the second goal of analyzing the determinants of personality, from the perceiver's point of view arises the functionally related question, "How did he get the way he is?" or, "What features in his past experiences cause him to behave as he now does?" The inferential activities to which this kind of concern gives rise may be referred to under the heading *causal-genetic set.* Finally, when the perceiver decides that his goal in the interaction involves the application of social sanctions, presumably he becomes concerned with the appropriateness of the stimulus person's behavior in terms of the generalized norms which he considers to be applicable to the present behavior setting. Such a concern conditions the inference process in ways which we shall subsume under the label *situation-matching set.*

These distinctions have a variety of implications, many of which will be discussed below, but an important set of implications may be organized around considerations of perceived cause and perceived effect. Fritz Heider (8) has drawn attention to the nature and determinants of personalized "phenomenal causality"—i.e., the location of cause or responsibility in the behaving person—but he has done so, in our opinion, at the expense of underestimating the frequency of situations in which phenomenal causality does not take this form. We know that in some circumstances, particularly those favoring a detached objectivity, causality may be perceived as "distributed" among a variety of determinants including the actor as well as other features of the total situation. The *value-maintenance set,* for example, clearly involves the attribution of substantial cause to the other actor, who is thereby seen as in some personal sense responsible for abetting or thwarting the perceiver. The perceiver in a *causal-genetic set* conceives an act as emanating from a personality which has complex origins in a variety of social, physical, and biological determinants. In the *situation-matching set,* the causal locus of behavior is more or less irrelevant to the inference process, or at least the extent to which causation is phenomenally personalized will depend on other conditions.

In a similar fashion, certain distinctions may be drawn which involve the way in which the actual or most probable *effects* of an act are perceived. Defining the consequences of an act involves the invocation of certain standards or norms of evaluation. The *causal-genetic set,* as we have described it, is alone in its relative avoidance of such evaluation. While the other two sets both involve comparison with a standard, the standard is that of a generalized norm in the *situation-matching set* and one of personal or idiosyncratic criteria in the *value-maintenance set.*

It is now our purpose to show how each of these various sets arises out of particular kinds of interaction situations and how some fairly precise empirical predictions can be derived from a consideration of the interaction context. We now turn, therefore, to a second way of classifying interaction.

Facilitation of personal goal attainment.— The search for personal gratification is obviously a ubiquitous feature of social interaction. In general, it is fair to assume that the party to any interaction has a persistent interest in the gratification of his personal needs. H. A. Murray (17) has made a beginning attempt to classify interactions in terms of the various personal needs which are likely to be facilitated or obstructed in behavioral interplay. It may be more fruitful, however, and certainly it is easier, to approach the problem of classification by considering a small number of intermediate interaction goals each of which may serve a variety of different personality needs. We shall refer in the following four categories, therefore, to the actor's primary purpose in the interaction rather than the specific personal needs which are likely to be fulfilled therein. Each of these four interaction types, all falling under the general rubric of "facilitation of goal attainment," represents an instance of interaction situations in which the *value-maintenance set* is likely to be aroused and maintained.

1. One important goal, which may on occasion dominate the concerns of the actor, is *gaining cognitive clarity about the shared environment.* The main feature of interactions having this as a goal will be the attempt of one actor to elicit information from the other actor about relevant aspects of the environment, and about those characteristics of the other which would qualify him to serve as a reliable information mediator. The actor's primary orientation to the environment is informational, and he is set to use the behavior of others as an extension or surrogate of his own perceptual, reality-testing apparatus. Festinger's (7) "A Theory of Social Comparison Processes" deals at length with this pervasive feature of interaction, but his emphasis is on social influence and self-evaluation rather than on the consequences of the social comparison motive for social perception. The findings of a long line of researchers, stemming from Sherif's (18) and Asch's (1) work, provide ample evidence that most of us are to some extent influenced by the judgments of others with regard to social reality. A similarly impressive list of findings—many of

which are presented in Hovland, Janis, and Kelly (9)—makes it clear that not all sources of social influence are equally effective in causing conformity or attitude change. This suggests the importance of a decision, on the part of the actor, regarding the relevance and reliability of the information provided him.

The implications for social perception, inference, and evaluation are fairly straightforward: the stronger the need for cognitive clarity about the shared environment, the more will another be positively evaluated if he is informative and provides reliable evidence about the environment. Thus the perceiver will be particularly sensitive to cues which aid in assessing such personal characteristics as reliability, candor, objectivity, perceptiveness, relevant expertise, etc.

2. A second important goal which may provide a focus for a given interaction is *securing motivational and value support.* Here the main concern of the actor is *not* with immediately external reality, but rather with the consensual validity of his own values, attitudes, and aspirations. His behavior, therefore, will be directed toward eliciting support and agreement for his views on issues which are important to him. To the extent that the values of others are perceived to be congruent with his own, the actor will feel relaxed, comfortable, and righteous in the interaction. The interaction itself will tend to be leisurely and prolonged, and the actor will give every indication of wanting to maintain his relationship with the other. To the extent that the other's values are perceived to be incongruent, however, the difference in shared perspectives will result in mutual withdrawal and avoidance. No attempt will be made to sustain the interaction. An attempt by Actor *A* to elicit information about the values and attitudes of *B* may be common to several interaction types, but in the present case there is a particular interest in coming to an approach-avoidance decision—"Is he on my side (does he believe the way I do) or not? Is he for me or against me?"

One perceptual implication of this interaction subclass is obvious: the stronger our need to verify and validate our own beliefs and values, the more will others be positively evaluated if they are seen as similar in values to the perceiver. The individual who is secure in his own value orientation, in other words, can afford to be positively attracted to persons with values differing from his own. In general, we do tend to attribute positive characteristics to those perceived to have values congruent with our own. A study by Fensterheim and Tresselt (6), as well as an unpublished study by Jones, Bruner, and Tagiuri, indicates that this is clearly the case. The further assumption we are making is that the congruence of actors' values will be a much more crucial issue in some interaction settings than in others, and the extent to which the issue is relevant will have important consequences for the inference process.

It should be noted that we are not contending that dissimilarity of values always leads to negative cathexis, or even that similarity of values necessarily leads to positive cathexis. As we shall see below, there are other considerations which affect the relevance for evaluation of value congruence between actors. It is also true that the extent to which congruence is desired by both actors will vary with the particular values involved. Thus a person whose dominant orientation is toward power and exploitation is less likely to be attracted to a person having congruent values than the highly aesthetic person will be attracted to a fellow aesthete. Even the power-oriented actor, however, may gain feelings of support and virtue from the knowledge that others are power-oriented too—particularly if some kind of tacit agreement may be reached between actors not to manipulate each other.

3. A third "intermediate" interaction goal is *directly maximizing beneficent social response*. In situations where this goal is dominant, the actor will behave in such a way as to elicit positive affective evaluation from other actors. While it is obvious that Actor A will usually be more effective in this activity if he is aware of Actor B's values and criteria for personal evaluation, the basic nature of this goal is the elicitation of cues of liking, acceptance, support, respect, etc. This goal will be pursued regardless of the consequences for obtaining other information or maintaining one's own values and beliefs.

The interaction goal of maximizing beneficent response may be instrumental to a variety of more basic concerns of the actor. The fact that Actor A perceives that B likes him is comforting to A for perhaps two fundamental reasons. On the one hand, when someone else likes you, this more or less automatically increases your potential power or control over his responses to you—i.e., if you know that a person likes you, you also tend to assume that he will "do things for you." On the other hand, to be liked by others is a comforting index of one's own worth and virtue. If A's primary reason for wanting others to like him is that his sense of virtue is thereby enhanced, the *manner* in which he has elicited the "like" response from B will take on importance. Thus, if A deviously presents a false front to increase the likelihood that B will like him, he will not know whether B would have liked him otherwise, and therefore B's response will lose its value as an index of A's worth. The cue-eliciting behavior of A will presumably be much less relevant if A is primarily concerned with the augmentation of his personal power.

A number of perceptual implications stem from these considerations. The stronger a person's need for dependence on others, for control over others, or for establishing his own worth, the more will another person be positively evaluated if he gives signs of liking the perceiver, "choosing" him, or otherwise supporting and accepting him (cf. 22). The distinction between liking as a sign of potential nurturance and liking as an index of worth does not suggest any differential implications for perceptual search activities, but the inference process will vary as a function of the perceiver's prior cue-eliciting behavior (the extent to which the perceiver has been deviously ingratiating, etc.). Whatever the source or motive for securing positive affect from others, however, the perceiver will be most sensitive to such traits as friendliness, acceptance, tolerance, and supportiveness.

A recent study by Thibaut and Strickland (24) indicates quite clearly the value of distinguishing between situations in which the interaction goal is that of gaining cognitive clarity about the shared environment, and situations in which beneficent social response is the dominant issue. In this study, subjects whose need for acceptance by others was aroused by pre-experimental procedures showed less resistance to group pressure, in a rigged conformity situation, than subjects who were primarily concerned with their accuracy as individuals. Similar results have been reported by Deutsch and Gerard (5), and by Jones, Wells, and Torrey (12).

4. A final interaction goal which we believe needs to be distinguished is *accomplishing some outcome external to the interaction itself*. In a sense, the first of the intermediate interaction goals we have discussed, gaining cognitive clarity about the environment, should fall under the present rubric, but here we are concerned with performance activities which actually effect some change in the environment. The great majority of experiments on group problem solving involve the type of interaction to which we are here referring. There are two variants of this class of interaction, however, that bear separate discussion since their perceptual implications differ.

The first possibility is that Actor *A* is working toward some individually attainable goal which *B* can either prevent or allow *A* to obtain. Thus Actor *A* may be seeking permission to do something which falls within the "gatekeeping" prerogatives of *B*. In such a case, *A*'s interaction strategy might well involve learning the sources of resistance or compliance in *B*, so that activities to produce acquiescence will have more effective direction. The stronger the need to attain the goal in question, the more will the stimulus person (the gatekeeper) be positively evaluated if he gives signs of tractability, permissiveness, and compliance. As Thibaut and Riecken (23) have shown, this positive evaluation will be especially enhanced if the compliance is perceived to be voluntary or spontaneous rather than forced by the situation or by some power of the perceiver.

A second possibility, however, is that Actor *A* needs supporting activity from *B* in order to obtain a "group goal." In such a case, there will again be some emphasis on tractability, but *A* will also be vitally interested in *B*'s competence and dependability. In order to make precise predictions here

about the traits in which *A* will be most interested, a variety of additional considerations would also have to be taken into account: the individual's general desire to lead or to follow, his self-confidence in directing others, etc. In general, however, we might expect *A* to be most sensitive to *B*'s cooperativeness, dependability, and his willingness to work.

A study by Jones and deCharms (11) provides a demonstration of the arousal of a value-maintenance set in this type of interaction situation. In this study, subjects worked toward the solution of a series of problems in groups. In half of the groups, all subjects worked toward individual rewards based on their individual performances. In the remaining groups, however, all members had to succeed or no one would obtain a reward. In all cases one member failed by prearrangement, following which the subjects rated each other on a number of personality traits. One finding was that the failing subject was seen as significantly less dependable when his failure affected the group (in spite of the fact that his behavior was, of course, identical in both kinds of groups). When the tasks were presented as tests of motivation, this difference was markedly greater than when the tasks were presented as tests of intelligence. The reason for this last finding was apparently that motivation is perceived to be internally caused, i.e., under the control of the actor himself. Competence, on the other hand, represents a more stable, externally imposed cluster of attributes for which the actor cannot be held personally responsible. The assumption that the *value-maintenance set* involves the attribution of cause to the other actor (see above) is thus supported. When *B* behaves in a manner which prevents *A*'s goal attainment, the degree to which the *value-maintenance set* is aroused will depend on the degree to which causation is attributed to the frustrator.

Each of the above interaction subclasses involves the facilitation of personal goal attainment in some instrumental or intermediate way. The range of interactions covered is fairly broad, and we feel that there are few serious omissions as far as most day-to-day interaction situations are concerned. What this implies, in effect, is that most of our interactions, and the social inference activities deriving from them, are apt to proceed largely from value-maintenance sets of varying content. We do not feel, however, that the facilitation of goal attainment is the only activity providing grounds for the substantive classification of interaction types. The remaining two classes add important, and often overlooked, ingredients to the conceptual picture.

Deterministic analysis of personality.— The second broad purpose which may be mediated by social interaction involves a concern with behavior causation. These are the interactions which characteristically give rise to the causal-genetic inferential set, since the main goal of the perceiver is to establish the pertinent historical and situational determinants of a person's behavior, or, more accurately, the personality characteristics giving rise to that behavior.

While the psychotherapist and the psychoanalytically oriented diagnostician are professionally prone to adopt the causal-genetic set, a concern with behavior and personality determinants is certainly not restricted to these specialized roles. There are many situations in which we are faced with the necessity of making a prediction about another's behavior in order to program our own activities. In some cases, we may predict future behavior on the basis of simple and straightforward generalizations from past behavior. More often, however, prediction is mediated by some kind of personality conception, which provides a matrix from which probability statements may be drawn.

The desire for prediction may stem from a variety of sources other than the need to plan and regulate social interaction with someone else. The interest in understanding the determinants of others' behavior may be simply an expression of aesthetic fulfillment or scientific curiosity. Or, it may stem from a desire for power through social control.

Whatever the particular source of the motive to analyze another's personality determinants, there are several perceptual implications of this type of interaction which merit discussion. All of the situations which we have described as having the goal of "facilitating personal goal attainment" quite

clearly involved inferences leading up to an evaluative decision with regard to the stimulus person. Here we turn to a class of situations, however, which do *not* involve the evaluation of a person in terms of the consequences of his behavior for the perceiver. Since the stimulus person will not be seen as the ultimate causal agent of his own behavior, the often seductive practice of inferring intent from consequence will tend to be inhibited.

It is obvious that not all consequences of a person's behavior are direct reflections of his intentions. Because of his primary interest in personal history and personality factors, the causal-genetic observer has a clear stake in discriminating intended from unintended behavioral consequences. Accidental behavior, or behavior which is completely dictated by the situation, provides little information of relevance to causal-genetic goals.

The observer in the value-maintenance set is less concerned with the "true" nature of the stimulus person than he is with the latter's personal meaning or significance for him. Therefore, his overt response to the stimulus person will be dictated by the kind of consequences the stimulus person's behavior has for him. The stronger the consequence, whether positive (e.g., obvious flattery) or negative (e.g., an accidental slur on the perceiver's nationality), the less relevant the underlying intent in conditioning evaluative conclusions.

The situation-matching observer presents the most complicated picture of all, with regard to this issue. In most everyday situations where one is in a position to apply social sanctions to the behavior of others, the intent which underlies "good" or "bad" behavior is a relevant determinant of the application of sanctions (i.e., praise or punishment). The perceiver's cognitive impression of the stimulus person will be quite congruent with the responses made to the stimulus person. There are some situations, however, where the perceiver must fill a clearly prescribed role which constrains him quite automatically to apply positive sanctions to "good acts" and negative sanctions to "bad acts." This might characterize the shop foreman, the ship captain, or the jury member.

Such a role often, as one feature of its constraining characteristics, specifically declares the irrelevance of intent for the application of sanctions. So the sanctions presumably will be applied. The sloppy worker will lose his job, the nervous sailor will get shore duty, and the drunk driver who killed a pedestrian will get life imprisonment. But what effect will the behavioral constraints of such a role have on perception and judgment of the stimulus person? This is clearly an empirical question, but our guess is that the observer's *impressions* will be contingent on the intentions of the stimulus person more than on the consequences of his behavior, the reverse being true for his overt sanctioning *responses*. The jury member, for example, may have strong feelings of compassion and personal warmth for the criminal he helps send to the chair. Nevertheless, we would expect some tendency for one's impression to press toward congruence with one's behavior in this case. Intention will only be relevant to a degree which does not conflict too strongly with the prescribed response. Thus, for example, the degree of compassion would be tempered by the seriousness of the crime regardless of the perceived intent behind the criminal behavior.

While the causal-genetic perceiver will thus utilize cues regarding intent as a basis for his inferences, knowledge about intent will be purely instrumental to his analytic purpose. But if intentions are not causes of behavior as far as the determinist is concerned, what are the determinants and how is information about them elicited? It is clear that, even if all the determinants of a particular person's behavior were known, the causal sequence would have to be truncated at some point so as to avoid infinite causal regress. Theories of personality can be characterized, essentially, in terms of the particular schedule of priorities assigned to causal determinants. The layman's phenomenal conceptions of personality or behavior causation are not dissimilar to more systematic theories in this regard. Just as theories of personality differ in structuring and delimiting the causal sequence, so there are differences between individuals in their preference for certain causal determinants rather than others.

Partly because of the great variety of ways in which causation may be attributed in the assessment of personality, it is not possible to make precise predictive statements about the traits to which the causal-genetic perceiver will be most sensitized. It is important to note that, in one sense, the purely causal-genetic perceiver, A, has no intrinsic concern with the stimulus person, B. As we have said before, B is merely the physical locus of converging causal forces. B will not be perceived as deliberately and voluntarily causing his own behavior as is typically the case in the value-maintenance set. Because of this the natural tendency to treat another person as an active, behaving unit may be somewhat inhibited. There will be perceived unity, of course, but it will not be so clearly structured in phenomenal experience nor so completely taken for granted. The unity will tend to be imposed on the stimulus person by the perceiver; the missing links in the inference chain will be supplied by the perceiver's own "theory" of personality. As a consequence, it might be tentatively hypothesized that the causal-genetic observer's inferential conclusions are apt to be more systematic, consistent, and logical than those of the observer in a value-maintenance set. To the value-maintenance observer, contradictory inferences are less apt to be ruthlessly eliminated.

A final consequence of the distinction between emergent and imposed unity is that, given an observer in a value-maintenance set, we can make better predictions of the perceiver's inferences by studying the stimulus person than by studying the perceiver. That is, we can assume that perceivers in general will respond to affronts, flattery, or innuendo with similar kinds of reactions. Given a causal-genetic observer, however, the inference process can be more fully predicted from a knowledge of the perceiver and his mode of approaching the explanation problem.

The application of social sanctions.—The third broad purpose which may be mediated by social interaction is that of applying social sanctions to others. In many social situations, an actor may behave as an agent of social control in dispensing social rewards and punishments or in "passing judgment" on the appropriateness of another's behavior. The actor's main goal is to establish whether or not the other person is behaving appropriately, whether the person's behavior "matches" the norms which apply in the situation. For this reason, we have spoken of the *situation-matching set* as the cognitive resultant of such interactions. In order to speak of this set having been aroused or adopted, it is not necessary that the perceiver be in a position of authority over the stimulus person or that the perceiver actually be in a position to apply sanctions. The important criterial feature is that Actor A evaluates Actor B (whether or not it is to his face) positively or negatively in terms of relevant situational norms.

An example will perhaps best clarify some of the differences between situations giving rise to the three different types of inferential set. Let us assume that the stimulus person (B) is a suspect in a criminal case. X, who is a spectator in the trial courtroom, looks at B and says to himself, "I wouldn't want to meet him in a dark alley" or "He looks like a nice, clean-cut chap; the kind of person I'd like to get to know." Y, on the other hand, is a court-appointed psychiatrist who is preoccupied with assessing B's sanity and his responsibility for the crime allegedly committed. Y might say to himself, "The utter lack of motive for this crime makes me suspect the man's sanity" or "The instability of this man's home environment is clearly a crucial factor behind his impulsiveness and irrationality." Z, finally, is a member of the jury. As he looks at B he is primarily concerned with B's legal innocence or guilt—deciding *what* B did for one thing, and deciding whether this action violates the law for another. Needless to say, in terms of the foregoing descriptions, we would say that the value-maintenance set is dominant with X, the causal-genetic set with Y, and the situation-matching set with Z. One of the reasons why the courtroom appears to be such a favorite setting for the plot denouement of many plays may be precisely because of the dramatic potential of the dilemma between inferential sets.

While the jurist provides one of the purest examples of roles primarily concerned with social control, there are many other, less specialized roles which also typically involve the application of sanctions. The position of parent, for example, involves an extremely complex set of functions, but among these the role of disciplinarian and socializer is clearly very important. Much of the time, the parent's interactions with his child are colored by normative evaluation: is the child obedient and responsible, has he developed the self-control appropriate to his age, etc. Other interaction situations such as those involving fitness evaluations, promotion decisions, school or program failures, etc., are also clearly situation-matching in nature. By the very nature of the role relationship, normative evaluation and the application of sanctions will play a critical part in the interactions between superiors and subordinates. If the superior does not, or cannot, apply negative and positive sanctions to the subordinate, it is indeed difficult to see how the hierarchy could maintain itself.

Turning to the perceptual implications of such interactions, we have already discussed some of the conditions affecting the judged importance of intent versus consequence when the two are dissimilar. In general, the situation-matching observer should place less emphasis on whether or not a particular action was intended than should observers in either value-maintenance or causal-genetic sets.

In order to make predictive statements about the inference process of a perceiver in the role of a dispenser of sanctions, it is obviously necessary to know something about how he perceives the norms. Since the perceiver is primarily concerned with the consequences of the other's behavior, perceptions of the person himself involve relatively uncomplicated cognitive requirements. However, this may be more than outweighed by cognitive complexities from another source: the task of evaluating the situation and apprehending the most relevant norms. In any concrete instance, this may be difficult because even though the situation is objectively clear, it may be one to which conflicting norms apply. The dilemma between "universalistic" and "particularistic" standards (20, 21) is an especially clear example of this. Or the situation may be essentially normless—the perceiver is hard put to trade on any normative precedents or to make generalizations from more clearly structured normative situations. The "brain-washing" phenomenon would seem to be a good example of this, in that the average person does not know whether to refer to turncoats as "traitors" and "cowards" or to conclude that every person has his breaking point. While the government has moved rapidly to shore up the norms for prisoners of war, there was confusion on this score throughout most of the Korean war.

Much of the foregoing may be restated by acknowledging that no norm is categorically imperative. Not only is it unlikely that any situation involves only one norm, or only congruent norms; as implied above, the applicability of a norm is always to some extent dependent on the intentions of the transgressor, the degree to which he was cognizant of the norm in question, and the degree to which extenuating circumstances are involved. Since norms are basically generalizations constructed with reference to recurrent social situations, they are thereby not likely to be totally applicable in any concrete case. It is precisely because norms are not tailor-made that arbitration, personal judgment, and social consensus are typically involved in judicial decisions.

Relationship Between Formal and Substantive Classes of Interaction

Having to this point outlined a dual system for classifying social interactions, it is now pertinent to inquire into the extent to which classification in terms of the formal criteria of contingency is independent of classification in terms of the substantive criteria of mediated goals. As we have presented the classification schemes, they appear to be *logically* independent. That is, it is one thing to classify interaction in terms of the extent to which the behavior of each actor is dependent on that of the other. It is quite another thing to inquire into the content of the actors' expectancies and to assay their goals and purposes in the interaction.

Characteristically, however, there would seem to be an empirical relation between the two modes of classification such that the more specialized roles leading to the causal-genetic and situation-matching sets will be more easily maintained in noncontingent and asymmetrically contingent interactions. Double contingency interactions, on the other hand, are more apt to arouse and perpetuate value-maintenance sets of various types. We have already noted, for example, that inferences about the intentions and motives of others take on added significance in double contingency situations. The evaluation of another person in terms of his motivation is, we have also seen, a critical feature of value-maintenance sets. On the other hand, in situations where the goal of the perceiver is to establish the determinants of another's behavior *or* to act as an agent of society in the application of sanctions, the mutuality of interpersonal involvement which is assumed to accompany double contingency interactions would seem to add further complication to the cognitive task and make the maintenance of a causal or situation-matching set that much more difficult.

While these relationships are to some extent self-evident, it will probably be helpful to illustrate them in terms of concrete instances. Take, for example, the case of an interviewer concerned with the deterministic analysis of the interviewee's personality. Typically this role would be carried out in the context of asymmetrically contingent interaction. That is, the behavior of the interviewer is determined largely by an S.O.P. which guides him in asking a certain pattern of questions. Even if the "next" question is a function of the last answer, the degree of double contingency is apt to be limited. The stronger the interviewer's S.O.P. the easier it will be to maintain the causal-genetic set. If the interviewer has a weak S.O.P., or if the interviewee forces the interviewer into double contingency by eliciting reactions not covered by the S.O.P. (when the interviewee says, for example, "You seem to know all the answers; why don't you tell me"), value-maintenance criteria are likely to enter the picture.

A second set of roles—those of the parent, the teacher, the administrator, the foreman, etc.—more definitely suggest the dominance of situation-matching in contexts involving role behavior. Persons in each of these roles spend some portion of their time in the application of normative sanctions. Once again, to the extent that the norms are clearly specified by an S.O.P. and do not have to be generated from moment to moment, the situation-matching set can be more easily maintained. An exclusive emphasis on the application of sanctions will tend to break down, however, whenever the child, the student, or the worker succeeds in turning the interaction into a double contingency one. This will tend to happen whenever the target person questions the legitimacy or the rationale of the norms (as when little Johnny says, "Why?" to his mother's request that he clean his room), or when the target person tries to curry favor with the applier of sanctions (the employee buys the foreman a drink). The implication of this increase in the "fullness" of interaction is that value-maintenance criteria will color the application of sanctions. Thus, Johnny may be considered impertinent, and even greater pressure put on him, and the drink-buying employee may be given a high productivity rating by the foreman.

The most natural social context for the arousal of a value-maintenance set is that in which interaction between peers, colleagues, neighbors, "fellow members," etc., is involved. We have already commented on the ubiquitousness of value-maintenance criteria—they obtrude persistently in causal-genetic and situation-matching settings. However, an interesting final consideration concerns what happens to the typical process of interaction over time. It will now be recalled that, in the introduction, we offered the assumption that "the perceiver in any social situation will act in such a way as to reduce the need for information to sustain the interaction process." A derivative of this assumption is the proposition that efforts will be made, during the typical interaction, to reduce the mutuality of contingency. That is, we would expect some kind of drift from double contingency to asymmetrical or non-contingency in the interests of cognitive economy. More specifically, given the desire or need to predict and control aspects of the social environment, the typical person has some investment in maximizing the stability of that environment. The actor in a double contingency situation is by definition faced with the complex cognitive problem of abstracting diverse behavioral determinants. Phenomenally, the behavior of Actor B is "caused" by Actor A, by various features of the situation and by B's own personal expectancies and intentions in the interaction. As we move away from double contingency, however, into interactions involving stronger and more clearly specified behavioral S.O.P.s, the task of prediction entails more and more exclusively the ability to specify the controlling S.O.P.s. Basically the argument resolves into the proposition that interaction is more predictable between actors who share common conceptions about each other's social role. Beginning with a fresh, fluxional interaction context, then, attempts will be made by each actor to crystallize the S.O.P.s governing each other's behavior and to achieve some consensus about them.

On the other hand, there is counterpressure from another source promoting a value-maintenance set. We have described the value-maintenance set as ubiquitous for the probable and apparent reason that this is the most natural, primitive egocentric orientation. (It may well be fruitful to consider the developmental implications of the different sets herein described. There is, for example, a definite parallel between a value-maintenance orientation and Piaget's stage of egocentrism. Furthermore, it seems true that much of socialization involves the gradual substitution of causal-genetic and situation-matching criteria for more primitive value-maintenance standards.)

While the value-maintenance set is likely to be aroused in a variety of "ego"-involving contexts, orientations in which situation-matching or causal-genetic considerations are dominant seem to require the support of specialized training (legal, psychological, etc.) and/or the force of group pressure for their maintenance. Even with these supports, however, no one would claim that the therapist never expresses anger toward his patient or that the parent never overlooks transgressions which do not prevent the attainment of his own goals.

We have, then, a condition for the development of an equilibrium as far as the temporal trend of interaction, and the accompanying perceptions, are concerned. The expected drift away from mutual contingency is inhibited by the actor's tendency to reinforce those acts of others which have beneficent consequences for him. The expected "regression" to value maintenance is inhibited by the socially important tendency to behave in terms of normative, role-determined requirements.

The implications of this equilibrium between conflicting "drifts" are not at all clear. A logical possibility is that many interactions would "stabilize" at some point between double contingency and noncontingency but that value-maintenance overtones would be quite prominent. This might take the form, for example, of being irritated with a friend solely because he departs from your expectations of him and not because his behavior is intrinsically irritating. Or it might take the form of A belittling B's arguments by engaging in a pseudo-psychoanalysis of B's motives or the determinants of his behavior. The underlying desire in this latter case is not to further mutual understanding, but to express value-maintenance conclusions in the guise of a causal-genetic formulation. Whether or not these examples are plausible and representative, it does seem clear that various checking and balancing forces do operate to inhibit or prevent the exclusive, long-term adoption of any inferential set in social interaction.

THE CONDITIONS AND CONSEQUENCES OF SET AROUSAL

Working from the premise that it is the actual process of social interaction which shapes the form and emphases of social perception, it has been necessary to categorize and delimit, to abstract from a complex and ever-changing set of behaviors. In doing so, we have inevitably over-emphasized the unitary quality of interaction types and their related inferential sets. A given pattern of interaction is likely to serve several functions for each actor, and we can never expect to find a "pure set" in operation—at least for any psychologically meaningful unit of time. While it is therefore wrong to talk literally about the adoption of a certain inferential set, it is still meaningful to speak of the relatively predominating effects of one set over

others in so far as these effects can be reliably indexed.

It was our intention, in the foregoing discussion, to develop a number of themes from which empirically verifiable statements of relationship might be drawn. It is quite clear, however, that the problem of establishing operational indexes for many of the variables introduced will not be easily solved. Indeed, we have deliberately freed ourselves from the responsibility of making detailed empirical statements in favor of a broader conceptual outline. We do believe, however, that many of the relationships implied in the foregoing discussion are testable and some of the evidence for this belief has already been presented. While we have barely scratched the surface in exploring the empirical consequences of the above formulation, there appear at present to be three broad and feasible lines of research.

Our first concern has been with demonstrating that different inferential sets can be aroused experimentally, having at least some of the consequences outlined above. The most straightforward methodology for accomplishing this involves placing different perceivers in different social roles vis-à-vis the person being judged or observed. By holding constant the behavior of the stimulus person, any differences in evaluation or inference may be attributed to the sets themselves. One method of establishing different perceiver roles is, of course, by variations in instruction. In a second experiment by Jones and deCharms, just recently completed, Naval Air Cadets were exposed to a tape-recorded interview between a psychologist and an ex-prisoner of war who had signed several communistic propaganda statements. Subjects in one group were told to imagine that they were members of a judicial board of inquiry empowered to study the case and to decide what the formal charges should be (an attempt to arouse the situation-matching set). Subjects in a second group were told to imagine that they were members of a medical-psychological board of review empowered to determine *why* the prisoner did what he did (causal-genetic set). Other subjects were told to think of him in terms of whether or not they would like the prisoner as a friend (value-maintenance set). A final group of S's were told nothing (control). The adoption of one or another set was further strengthened by requesting the subjects to express a preference among several questions to obtain further information. If the subject under situation-matching instructions chooses a question on the norms and legal precedents involved, we not only have evidence that the instructions were effective (which was true in the experiment described); we also assume that the very act of expressing a preference has given the set further momentum. While the use of instructions for set-arousal seems superficial and somewhat naïve, with proper pretesting and postquestioning it seems to be a moderately effective way of arousing the subject's interest in certain features of the stimulus person rather than in others. There are undoubtedly many other ways of arousing inferential sets, ways which will suggest themselves in the context of a particular experimental problem.

It is obvious that procedures to encourage role simulation will not have the potent perceptual consequences of actual role playing. It is clearly possible to arrange cognitively realistic social situations (with the aid of confederates or other deception devices) in which a certain set is most likely to be promoted. There are two kinds of problems in maintaining experimental control, however. First of all, if any kind of genuine interaction is allowed between naïve subject and confederate, it would be impossible to hold the confederate's (and stimulus person's) behavior constant across replicated subjects. Second, the methodological separation of set and interaction content seems to make conceptual sense as well. If we want to study the effects of set, we confound things by arousing set through variations in the interaction itself. Resulting differences in perception probably will be more a function of shifts in interaction content than of shifts in inferential set—but, in any event, one would never know. For these reasons, we have tended to make the convenient assumption that the *goals* of interaction are present prior to the actual interaction itself. Therefore, in our research we have either held constant or systematically varied the actual content of interaction, while treating set arousal as the independent variable.

As for the dependent or outcome variables, our interest naturally is in measures which reflect the workings and results of the inference process. But the specific outcome variable of interest will depend in an intimate way on the specific design of the experiment: the particular sets that are being compared, the information which has been conveyed in the process of interaction, the relevant personality characteristics of the perceiver, and so on. It is possible to generalize two main types of hypotheses which will determine the outcome variable of interest: sensitivity hypotheses and evaluation hypotheses. It will be noted that these hypotheses are respectively concerned with the selective and transformative function of sets.

Sensitivity hypotheses include specific propositions that people in one set will "pay more attention to" and will be more affected by certain kinds of information presented than people in another set. When set-relevant information is varied, therefore, rating changes will be greater than when the varied information is more relevant to some other set. In the first Jones and deCharms experiment, for example, the confederate is seen as declining more in competence when his low performance prevents the reward attainment of the naïve subjects than when it does not. The interpretation here is that subjects who are interdependent in the solution of problems will be much more "concerned with" each other's problem-solving competence than will subjects who do not share an inevitably common fate.

Evaluation hypotheses propose that the degree to which a person is liked or disliked will be a joint function of the actual information presented by or about him and the set which the perceiver has adopted. There is, of course, a close relationship between sensitivity hypotheses and evaluation hypotheses. Modifying the evaluative potential of set-relevant information will produce a greater shift in evaluative rating than will changes in nonrelevant information.

The attempted arousal of various inferential sets by experimental manipulation is not the only appropriate research tactic. We are quite prepared to assume that some people, or people in different cultures, will find it more difficult to adopt a certain set than others will. This suggests that culture and personality variables are important determinants of set adoption. Not only is this of theoretical importance in its own right, but it provides a means for learning more about the validity of set-arousal procedures. If, for example, highly prejudiced people are hypothetically incapable of adopting a causal-genetic set, we should find them unaffected by arousal procedures designed to promote that set. If subjects at the nonprejudiced extreme of an attitude scale are markedly affected by the procedures, on the other hand, we have a coherent picture in which the predicted effects of one independent variable support the predicted effects of the other independent variable and vice versa. In such a circumstance, one's confidence in the validity of the arousal procedures *and* the attitude scale would be enhanced.

Prejudice and authoritarianism are not the only "personality" variables of obvious relevance. In the prisoner-of-war study, a version of the Stouffer-Toby Universalism-Particularism Scale was administered to all subjects to test the hypothesis that universalists would find it easier to adopt the situation-matching set, particularists the value-maintenance set. The results on this point have yet to be analyzed. The dimension of simplicity-complexity of "interpersonal constructs," which has been studied by Bieri (2) and Leventhal (14), also suggests itself as a relevant focus for analyzing individual differences in the case of set adoption. The cognitively complex person should prove himself more capable of shifting sets as the occasion demands, and he should adopt the causal-genetic set with less strain than the cognitively simple subject. The experimental choice of the personality or attitude dimension most likely to bring order to the data of individual differences will naturally depend on the particularly experimental design and the content of the social stimulus material. In the first Jones-deCharms experiment, for example, subjects who were low in need for achievement were more negative in their evaluation of a failing confederate than those subjects who were high in need for achievement. While this particular result was un-

anticipated, it could be plausibly explained after the fact. The point is that a variety of personality variables may, at one time or another, seem relevant to the experimenter who wishes to investigate individual differences in interpersonal perception.

While our research to this point has been experimental in nature, a second hopeful avenue of investigation should involve parallel field research. There are a number of hypotheses which can be investigated by studying the perceptual consequences of role adoption in the natural environment. In approaching these "field" problems, of course, it should be useful to employ some of the indexes devised to handle the experimental data in the research discussed above.

One problem of striking interest and importance is the perceptual consequences of the psychotherapeutic role. We need to know a great deal more about the details of the therapeutic interaction process. In terms of our scheme for classifying interaction, the therapeutic relationship is an exceedingly complex one. In a sense, the interaction is doubly contingent and yet the therapist generally operates in terms of a more or less well-defined S.O.P. We are perhaps justified in describing the therapeutic relationship as *simulated* double contingency. While it is generally the therapeutic ideal to keep the interaction simulated, in the sense that the therapist tries to limit his personal involvement, there are several reasons why it is difficult to keep the interaction "asymmetrical."

First of all, in the process of simulating double contingency, the therapist calls for reactions in the patient which are appropriate to double-contingency interactions. It is difficult for the therapist not to be affected by these reactions.

Second, the natural drift away from double contingency is partially inhibited in therapy because of the motive of the therapist to bring about some kind of change in the patient. In order to bring about such change, the therapist has to interact with the patient in a personally relevant and significant way.

Finally, there is a fundamental value of the therapist at stake in such interactions, namely, the importance of being able to bring about a cure or decided improvement in mental condition. The therapist's reputation and self-esteem are anchored to this capacity to change and improve the well-being of another. In the service of this value, the normal drift toward value maintenance is quite likely to produce feelings and reactions which are inconsistent with a purely causal-genetic orientation as well as with keeping the double contingency only simulated. Thus the therapist is apt to feel positive toward a tractable patient and negative toward a resistive one.

Keeping these considerations in mind, it would be most interesting to examine the therapist's perception of his patients *in relation to* the actual content of interaction. The general hypothesis would be that the inferences drawn about the patient by the therapist would depend on the extent to which the patient has threatened, challenged, or vilified the therapist's values (used broadly) *and* the extent to which the therapist has been drawn into double contingency throughout the process of therapy.

Another set of problems involves the whole area of role conflict. Using the psychotherapist again as an example, it would be interesting to explore the extent to which the causal-genetic orientation of the therapist's office carries over into interactions with non-patients, and the extent to which this orientation actually becomes maladaptive. Whether or not fatherhood is an exhausting burden depends, perhaps, on the ease with which the father can shift from the role of disciplinarian (situation matching) to playmate (value maintenance). Situation-matching and value-maintenance conflicts are also clearly involved in many "gatekeeping" roles such as journal editor, critic, personnel selector, etc. Causal-genetic and situation-matching conflicts are presumably prevalent in the observer and student of court cases, and a study of legal precedents themselves, from this point of view, might be most rewarding.

A final area of research would involve a more detailed investigation of the inference process—plotting the actual chain from input through inference to judgment by correlational means. Here the task would be to establish which traits "go with" which other traits in the minds of social perceivers under

different conditions of set adoption. Here we would consider the interplay between "search requirements" and "probability considerations," as Bruner (3) has classified them.

Engaging in research in any of these directions will undoubtedly produce data which call for a restatement of the foregoing conceptual scheme. We would indeed be unhappy if the scheme could encompass *any* result without needing to be changed. Nevertheless, we do feel that the analysis presented here points up some issues in interpersonal perception which have heretofore been neglected.

SUMMARY

In this paper we have presented a theory of interpersonal perception which is closely geared to the different kinds of social interaction which affect and are affected by one's perception of another. Acknowledging the paramount importance of stimulus content and purely associative inferential linkages in the process of perceiving another, we have concentrated on the role of *inferential sets* as a determinant both of the information selected and the inferential use to which it is put. As a function of the type of interaction in which an individual finds himself, he becomes set to process incoming information about the other person in different ways.

In order to move toward verifiable statements concerning the specific functions that inferential sets might play, we have introduced a two-way classification scheme for handling different kinds of social interaction. One mode of classification is in terms of the rather formal criterion, the degree of contingency between the actors' behavior. Generally speaking, the more contingent A's behavior on B's behavior, the greater the need for inferences concerning B's motives and personality.

A second mode of classification is in terms of a more substantive criterion, the personal goal which is mediated by the interaction. Here we proposed three different *kinds* of goals, each giving rise to a different inferential set: (*a*) the facilitation of personal goal attainment, giving rise to the *value-maintenance* set; (*b*) the deterministic analysis of personality, giving rise to the *causal-genetic* set; and (*c*) the application of social sanctions, giving rise to the *situation-matching* set. While formal and substantive classifications are logically independent, it would seem difficult to maintain either a causal-genetic or a situational-matching set under circumstances where there is a high degree of mutual or double contingency.

An attempt was made to describe various hypothetical ways in which the adoption of inferential sets conditions the process of understanding another person. While most of the supporting examples presented were anecdotal, the consequences of the present theoretical position for both laboratory and field research were discussed.

REFERENCES

1. Asch, S. E. Studies of independence and conformity: I. A minority of one against a unanimous majority. *Psychol. Monogr.,* 1956, 70, No. 9 (Whole No. 416).
2. Bieri, J. Cognitive complexity-simplicity and predictive behavior. *J. abnorm. soc. Psychol.,* 1955, 51, 263–268.
3. Bruner, J. S. On perceptual readiness. *Psychol. Rev.,* 1957, 64, 123–152.
4. Cronbach, L. J. Processes affecting scores on "understanding of others" and "assumed similarity." *Psychol. Bull.,* 1955, 52, 177–193.
5. Deutsch, M., and Gerard, H. B. A study of normative and informational social influences upon individual judgment. *J. abnorm. soc. Psychol.,* 1955, 51, 629–636.
6. Fensterheim, H., and Tresselt, M. E. The influence of value systems on the perception of people. *J. abnorm. soc. Psychol.,* 1953, 48, 93–98.
7. Festinger, L. A theory of social comparison processes. *Hum. Relat.,* 1954, 7, 117–140.
8. Heider, F. Social perception and phenomenal causality. *Psychol. Rev.,* 1944, 51, 358–374.
9. Hovland, C. I., Janis, I. L., and Kelly, H. H. *Communication and persuasion.* New Haven: Yale Univ. Press, 1953.
10. Jones, E. E. Inferential sets in social perception. *Amer. Psychol.,* 1955, 10, 393 (abstr.).
11. Jones, E. E., and deCharms, R. Changes in social perception as a function of the personal relevance of behavior. *Sociometry,* 1957, 20, 75–85.
12. Jones, E. E., Wells, H. H., and Torrey, R. Some effects of feedback from the experimenter on conformity behavior. *J. abnorm. soc. Psychol.,* in press.
13. Kelly, G. A. *The psychology of personal constructs.* 2 vols. New York: Norton, 1955.
14. Leventhal, H. Effects of setting factors and judges' interpersonal constructs on predictive behavior. Unpublished doctoral dissertation, Univ. North Carolina, 1956.
15. Osgood, C. E. The nature and measurement of meaning. *Psychol. Bull.,* 1952, 49, 192–237.
16. Osgood, C. E., and Luria, Zella. A blind analysis of a case of multiple personality using the semantic differential. *J. abnorm. soc. Psychol.,* 1954, 49, 579–591.
17. Parsons, T., and Shils, E. *Toward a general theory of action.* Cambridge: Harvard Univ. Press, 1954.
18. Sherif, M. A study of some social factors in perception. *Arch. Psychol.,* 1935, No. 187.
19. Steiner, I. Interpersonal behavior as influenced by accuracy of social perception. *Psychol. Rev.,* 1955, 62, 268–275.
20. Stouffer, S. A. An analysis of conflicting social norms. *Amer. sociol. Rev.,* 1949, 14, 707–717.
21. Stouffer, S. A., and Toby, J. Role conflict and personality. *Amer. J. Sociol.,* 1951, 41, 395–406.
22. Tagiuri, R. Relational analysis: An extension of sociometric method with emphasis upon social perception. *Sociometry,* 1952, 15, 91–104.
23. Thibaut, J. W., and Riecken, H. W. Some determinants and consequences of the perception of social causality. *J. Pers.,* 1955, 24, 113–133.
24. Thibaut, J. W., and Strickland, L. H. Psychological set and social conformity. *J. Pers.,* 1956, 25, 115–129.

The Presentation of Self in Everyday Life /

Erving Goffman (*University of California, Berkeley*)

When an individual enters the presence of others, they commonly seek to acquire information about him or to bring into play information about him already possessed. They will be interested in his general socio-economic status, his conception of self, his attitude toward them, his competence, his trustworthiness, etc. Although some of this information seems to be sought almost as an end in itself, there are usually quite practical reasons for acquiring it. Information about the individual helps to define the situation, enabling others to know in advance what he will expect of them and what they may expect of him. Informed in these ways, the others will know how best to act in order to call forth a desired response from him.

For those present, many sources of information become accessible and many carriers (or "sign-vehicles") become available for conveying this information. If unacquainted with the individual, observers can glean clues from his conduct and appearance which allow them to apply their previous experience with individuals roughly similar to the one before them or, more important, to apply untested stereotypes to him. They can also assume from past experience that only individuals of a particular kind are likely to be found in a given social setting. They can rely on what the individual says about himself or on documentary evidence he provides as to who and what he is. If they know, or know of, the individual by virtue of experience prior to the interaction, they can rely on assumptions as to the persistence and generality of psychological traits as a means of predicting his present and future behavior.

However, during the period in which the individual is in the immediate presence of the others, few events may occur which directly provide the others with the conclusive information they will need if they are to direct wisely their own activity. Many crucial facts lie beyond the time and place of interaction or lie concealed within it. For example, the "true" or "real" attitudes, beliefs, and emotions of the individual can be ascertained only indirectly, through his avowals or through what appears to be involuntary expressive behavior. Similarly, if the individual offers the others a product or service, they will often find that during the interaction there will be no time and place immediately available for eating the pudding that the proof can be found in. They will be forced to accept some events as conventional or natural signs of something not directly available to the senses. In Ichheiser's terms,[1] the individual will have to act so that he intentionally or unintentionally *expresses* himself, and the others will in turn have to be *impressed* in some way by him.

The expressiveness of the individual (and therefore his capacity to give impressions) appears to involve two radically different kinds of sign activity: the expression that he *gives,* and the expression that he *gives off*. The first involves verbal symbols or their substitutes which he uses admittedly and solely to convey the information that he and the others are known to attach to these symbols. This is communication in the traditional and narrow sense. The second involves a wide range of action that others can treat as symptomatic of the actor, the expectation being that the action was performed for reasons other than the information conveyed in this way. As we shall have to see, this distinction has an only initial validity. The individual does of course intentionally convey misinformation by means of both of these types of communication, the first involving deceit, the second feigning.

Taking communication in both its narrow and broad sense, one finds that when the individual is in the immediate presence of

[1] Gustav Ichheiser, "Misunderstandings in Human Relations," Supplement to *The American Journal of Sociology,* LV (September, 1949), pp. 6–7.

others, his activity will have a promissory character. The others are likely to find that they must accept the individual on faith, offering him a just return while he is present before them in exchange for something whose true value will not be established until after he has left their presence. (Of course, the others also live by inference in their dealings with the physical world, but it is only in the world of social interaction that the objects about which they make inferences will purposely facilitate and hinder this inferential process.) The security that they justifiably feel in making inferences about the individual will vary, of course, depending on such factors as the amount of information they already possess about him, but no amount of such past evidence can entirely obviate the necessity of acting on the basis of inferences. As William I. Thomas suggested:

> It is also highly important for us to realize that we do not as a matter of fact lead our lives, make our decisions, and reach our goals in everyday life either statistically or scientifically. We live by inference. I am, let us say, your guest. You do not know, you cannot determine scientifically, that I will not steal your money or your spoons. But inferentially I will not, and inferentially you have me as a guest.[2]

Let us now turn from the others to the point of view of the individual who presents himself before them. He may wish them to think highly of him, or to think that he thinks highly of them, or to perceive how in fact he feels toward them, or to obtain no clear-cut impression; he may wish to ensure sufficient harmony so that the interaction can be sustained, or to defraud, get rid of, confuse, mislead, antagonize, or insult them. Regardless of the particular objective which the individual has in mind and of his motive for having this objective, it will be in his interests to control the conduct of the others, especially their responsive treatment of him.[3]

This control is achieved largely by influencing the definition of the situation which the others come to formulate, and he can influence this definition by expressing himself in such a way as to give them the kind of impression that will lead them to act voluntarily in accordance with his own plan. Thus, when an individual appears in the presence of others, there will usually be some reason for him to mobilize his activity so that it will convey an impression to others which it is in his interests to convey. Since a girl's dormitory mates will glean evidence of her popularity from the calls she receives on the phone, we can suspect that some girls will arrange for calls to be made, and Willard Waller's finding can be anticipated:

> It has been reported by many observers that a girl who is called to the telephone in the dormitories will often allow herself to be called several times, in order to give all the other girls ample opportunity to hear her paged.[4]

Of the two kinds of communication—expressions given and expressions given off—this report will be primarily concerned with the latter, with the more theatrical and contextual kind, the non-verbal, presumably unintentional kind, whether this communication be purposely engineered or not. As an example of what we must try to examine, I would like to cite at length a novelistic incident in which Preedy, a vacationing Englishman, makes his first appearance on the beach of his summer hotel in Spain:

> But in any case he took care to avoid catching anyone's eye. First of all, he had to make it clear to those potential companions of his holiday that they were of no concern to him whatsoever. He stared through them, round them, over them—eyes lost in space. The beach might have been empty. If by chance a ball was thrown his way, he looked surprised; then let a smile of amusement lighten his face (Kindly Preedy), looked

---

[2] Quoted in E. H. Volkart, editor, *Social Behavior and Personality*, Contributions of W. I. Thomas to Theory and Social Research (New York: Social Science Research Council, 1951), p. 5.

[3] Here I owe much to an unpublished paper by Tom Burns of the University of Edinburgh. He presents the argument that in all interaction a basic

underlying theme is the desire of each participant to guide and control the responses made by the others present. A similar argument has been advanced by Jay Haley in a recent unpublished paper, but in regard to a special kind of control, that having to do with defining the nature of the relationship of those involved in the interaction.

[4] Willard Waller, "The Rating and Dating Complex," *American Sociological Review*, II, p. 730.

round dazed to see that there *were* people on the beach, tossed it back with a smile to himself and not a smile *at* the people, and then resumed carelessly his nonchalant survey of space.

But it was time to institute a little parade, the parade of the Ideal Preedy. By devious handlings he gave any who wanted to look a chance to see the title of his book—a Spanish translation of Homer, classic thus, but not daring, cosmopolitan too—and then gathered together his beach-wrap and bag into a neat sand-resistant pile (Methodical and Sensible Preedy), rose slowly to stretch at ease his huge frame (Big-Cat Preedy), and tossed aside his sandals (Carefree Preedy, after all).

The marriage of Preedy and the sea! There were alternative rituals. The first involved the stroll that turns into a run and a dive straight into the water, thereafter smoothing into a strong splashless crawl towards the horizon. But of course not really to the horizon. Quite suddenly he would turn on to his back and thrash great white splashes with his legs, somehow thus showing that he could have swum further had he wanted to, and then would stand up a quarter out of water for all to see who it was.

The alternative course was simpler, it avoided the cold-water shock and it avoided the risk of appearing too high-spirited. The point was to appear to be so used to the sea, the Mediterranean, and this particular beach, that one might as well be in the sea as out of it. It involved a slow stroll down and into the edge of the water—not even noticing his toes were wet, land and water all the same to *him!*—with his eyes up at the sky gravely surveying portents, invisible to others, of the weather (Local Fisherman Preedy).[5]

The novelist means us to see that Preedy is improperly concerned with the extensive impressions he feels his sheer bodily action is giving off to those around him. We can malign Preedy further by assuming that he has acted merely in order to give a particular impression, that this is a false impression, and that the others present receive either no impression at all, or, worse still, the impression that Preedy is affectedly trying to cause them to receive this particular impression.

But the important point for us here is that the kind of impression Preedy thinks he is making is in fact the kind of impression that others correctly and incorrectly glean from someone in their midst.

I have said that when an individual appears before others his actions will influence the definition of the situation which they come to have. Sometimes the individual will act in a thoroughly calculating manner, expressing himself in a given way solely in order to give the kind of impression to others that is likely to evoke from them a specific response he is concerned to obtain. Sometimes the individual will be calculating in his activity but be relatively unaware that this is the case. Sometimes he will intentionally and consciously express himself in a particular way, but chiefly because the tradition of his group or social status require this kind of expression and not because of any particular response (other than vague acceptance or approval) that is likely to be evoked from those impressed by the expression. Sometimes the traditions of an individual's role will lead him to give a well-designed impression of a particular kind and yet he may be neither consciously nor unconsciously disposed to create such an impression. The others, in their turn, may be suitably impressed by the individual's efforts to convey something, or may misunderstand the situation and come to conclusions that are warranted neither by the individual's intent nor by the facts. In any case, in so far as the others act *as if* the individual had conveyed a particular impression, we may take a functional or pragmatic view and say that the individual has "effectively" projected a given definition of the situation and "effectively" fostered the understanding that a given state of affairs obtains.

There is one aspect of the others' response that bears special comment here. Knowing that the individual is likely to present himself in a light that is favorable to him, the others may divide what they witness into two parts; a part that is relatively easy for the individual to manipulate at will, being chiefly his verbal assertions, and a part in regard to which he seems to have little concern or control, being chiefly derived from the expressions he gives off. The others may then use what are considered to be the ungovernable aspects of his expressive behavior as a check upon the validity of what is conveyed by the governable aspects. In this a fundamental asymmetry is demonstrated in the communication process, the individual presumably being aware of only one stream of his communication, the witnesses of this stream and one other. For example, in Shetland Isle one crofter's wife, in serving native dishes to a visitor from the mainland of Britain, would listen with a polite smile to his polite claims of liking what he was eating; at the same time she would take note of the rapidity with which the visitor lifted his fork or spoon to his mouth, the eagerness with which he passed food into his mouth, and the gusto expressed in chewing the food, using these signs as a check on the stated feelings of the eater. The same woman, in order to discover what one acquaintance (A) "actually" thought of another acquaintance (B), would wait until B was in the presence of A but engaged in conversation with still another person (C). She would then covertly examine the facial expressions of A as he regarded B in conversation with C. Not being in conversation with B, and not being directly observed by him, A would sometimes relax usual constraints and tactful deceptions, and freely express what he was "actually" feeling about B. This Shetlander, in short, would observe the unobserved observer.

Now given the fact that others are likely to check up on the more controllable aspects of behavior by means of the less controllable, one can expect that sometimes the individual will try to exploit this very possibility, guiding the impression he makes through behavior felt to be reliably informing.[6] For example, in gaining admission to a tight social circle, the participant observer may not only wear an accepting look while listening to an informant, but may also be careful to wear the same look when observing the informant talking to others; observers of the

observer will then not as easily discover where he actually stands. A specific illustration may be cited from Shetland Isle. When a neighbor dropped in to have a cup of tea, he would ordinarily wear at least a hint of an expectant warm smile as he passed through the door into the cottage. Since lack of physical obstructions outside the cottage and lack of light within it usually made it possible to observe the visitor unobserved as he approached the house, islanders sometimes took pleasure in watching the visitor drop whatever expression he was manifesting and replace it with a sociable one just before reaching the door. However, some visitors, in appreciating that this examination was occurring, would blindly adopt a social face a long distance from the house, thus ensuring the projection of a constant image.

This kind of control upon the part of the individual reinstates the symmetry of the communication process, and sets the stage for a kind of information game—a potentially infinite cycle of concealment, discovery, false revelation, and rediscovery. It should be added that since the others are likely to be relatively unsuspicious of the presumably unguided aspect of the individual's conduct, he can gain much by controlling it. The others of course may sense that the individual is manipulating the presumably spontaneous aspects of his behavior, and seek in this very act of manipulation some shading of conduct that the individual has not managed to control. This again provides a check upon the individual's behavior, this time his presumably uncalculated behavior, thus reestablishing the asymmetry of the communication process. Here I would like only to add the suggestion that the arts of piercing an individual's effort at calculated unintentionality seem better developed than our capacity to manipulate our own behavior, so that regardless of how many steps have occurred in the information game, the witness is likely to have the advantage over the actor, and the initial asymmetry of the communication process is likely to be retained.

When we allow that the individual projects a definition of the situation when he appears before others, we must also see that the others, however passive their role may seem to be, will themselves effectively project

---

[6] The widely read and rather sound writings of Stephen Potter are concerned in part with signs that can be engineered to give a shrewd observer the apparently incidental cues he needs to discover concealed virtues the gamesman does not in fact possess.

a definition of the situation by virtue of their response to the individual and by virtue of any lines of action they initiate to him. Ordinarily the definitions of the situation projected by the several different participants are sufficiently attuned to one another so that open contradiction will not occur. I do not mean that there will be the kind of consensus that arises when each individual present candidly expresses what he really feels and honestly agrees with the expressed feelings of the others present. This kind of harmony is an optimistic ideal and in any case not necessary for the smooth working of society. Rather, each participant is expected to suppress his immediate heartfelt feelings, conveying a view of the situation which he feels the others will be able to find at least temporarily acceptable. The maintenance of this surface of agreement, this veneer of consensus, is facilitated by each participant concealing his own wants behind statements which assert values to which everyone present feels obliged to give lip service. Further, there is usually a kind of division of definitional labor. Each participant is allowed to establish the tentative official ruling regarding matters which are vital to him but not immediately important to others, e.g., the rationalizations and justifications by which he accounts for his past activity. In exchange for this courtesy he remains silent or noncommittal on matters important to others but not immediately important to him. We have then a kind of interactional *modus vivendi*. Together the participants contribute to a single over-all definition of the situation which involves not so much a real agreement as to what exists but rather a real agreement as to whose claims concerning what issues will be temporarily honored. Real agreement will also exist concerning the desirability of avoiding an open conflict of definitions of the situation.[7] I will refer to this level of

agreement as a "working consensus." It is to be understood that the working consensus established in one interaction setting will be quite different in content from the working consensus established in a different type of setting. Thus, between two friends at lunch, a reciprocal show of affection, respect, and concern for the other is maintained. In service occupations, on the other hand, the specialist often maintains an image of disinterested involvement in the problem of the client, while the client responds with a show of respect for the competence and integrity of the specialist. Regardless of such differences in content, however, the general form of these working arrangements is the same.

In noting the tendency for a participant to accept the definitional claims made by the others present, we can appreciate the crucial importance of the information that the individual *initially* possesses or acquires concerning his fellow participants, for it is on the basis of this initial information that the individual starts to define the situation and starts to build up lines of responsive action. The individual's initial projection commits him to what he is proposing to be and requires him to drop all pretenses of being other things. As the interaction among the participants progresses, additions and modifications in this initial informational state will of course occur, but it is essential that these later developments be related without contradiction to, and even built up from, the initial positions taken by the several participants. It would seem that an individual can more easily make a choice as to what line of treatment to demand from and extend to the others present at the beginning of an encounter than he can alter the line of treatment that is being pursued once the interaction is underway.

In everyday life, of course, there is a clear understanding that first impressions are important. Thus, the work adjustment of those in service occupations will often hinge upon a capacity to seize and hold the initiative in the service relation, a capacity that will require subtle aggressiveness on the part of

---

[7] An interaction can be purposely set up as a time and place for voicing differences in opinion, but in such cases participants must be careful to agree not to disagree on the proper tone of voice, vocabulary, and degree of seriousness in which all arguments are to be phrased, and upon the mutual respect which disagreeing participants must carefully continue to express toward one another. This debaters' or academic definition of the situation may also be invoked suddenly and judiciously as a way of translating a serious conflict of views into one that can be handled within a framework acceptable to all present.

the server when he is of lower socio-economic status than his client. W. F. Whyte suggests the waitress as an example:

The first point that stands out is that the waitress who bears up under pressure does not simply respond to her customers. She acts with some skill to control their behavior. The first question to ask when we look at the customer relationship is, "Does the waitress get the jump on the customer, or does the customer get the jump on the waitress?" The skilled waitress realizes the crucial nature of this question. . . .

The skilled waitress tackles the customer with confidence and without hesitation. For example, she may find that a new customer has seated himself before she could clear off the dirty dishes and change the cloth. He is now leaning on the table studying the menu. She greets him, says, "May I change the cover, please?" and, without waiting for an answer, takes his menu away from him so that he moves back from the table, and she goes about her work. The relationship is handled politely but firmly, and there is never any question as to who is in charge.[8]

When the interaction that is initiated by "first impressions" is itself merely the initial interaction in an extended series of interactions involving the same participants, we speak of "getting off on the right foot" and feel that it is crucial that we do so. Thus, one learns that some teachers take the following view:

You can't ever let them get the upper hand on you or you're through. So I start out tough. The first day I get a new class in, I let them know who's boss . . . You've got to start off tough, then you can ease up as you go along. If you start out easy-going, when you try to get tough, they'll just look at you and laugh.[9]

Similarly, attendants in mental institutions may feel that if the new patient is sharply put in his place the first day on the ward and made to see who is boss, much future difficulty will be prevented.[10]

Given the fact that the individual effectively projects a definition of the situation when he enters the presence of others, we can assume that events may occur within the interaction which contradict, discredit, or otherwise throw doubt upon this projection. When these disruptive events occur, the interaction itself may come to a confused and embarrassed halt. Some of the assumptions upon which the responses of the participants had been predicated become untenable, and the participants find themselves lodged in an interaction for which the situation has been wrongly defined and is now no longer defined. At such moments the individual whose presentation has been discredited may feel ashamed while the others present may feel hostile, and all the participants may come to feel ill at ease, nonplussed, out of countenance, embarrassed, experiencing the kind of anomy that is generated when the minute social system of face-to-face interaction breaks down.

In stressing the fact that the initial definition of the situation projected by an individual tends to provide a plan for the co-operative activity that follows—in stressing this action point of view—we must not overlook the crucial fact that any projected definition of the situation also has a distinctive moral character. It is this moral character of projections that will chiefly concern us in this report. Society is organized on the principle that any individual who possesses certain social characteristics has a moral right to expect that others will value and treat him in an appropriate way. Connected with this principle is a second, namely that an individual who implicitly or explicitly signifies that he has certain social characteristics ought in fact to be what he claims he is. In consequence, when an individual projects a definition of the situation and thereby makes an implicit or explicit claim to be a person of a particular kind, he automatically exerts a moral demand upon the others, obliging them to value and treat him in the

---

[8] W. F. Whyte, "When Workers and Customers Meet," Chap. VII, *Industry and Society*, ed. W. F. Whyte (New York: McGraw-Hill, 1946), pp. 132–33.

[9] Teacher interview quoted by Howard S. Becker, "Social Class Variations in the Teacher-Pupil Relationship," *Journal of Educational Sociology*, XXV, p. 459.

[10] Harold Taxel, "Authority Structure in a Mental Hospital Ward" (unpublished Master's thesis, Department of Sociology, University of Chicago, 1953).

manner that persons of his kind have a right to expect. He also implicitly forgoes all claims to be things he does not appear to be[11] and hence forgoes the treatment that would be appropriate for such individuals. The others find, then, that the individual has informed them as to what is and as to what they *ought* to see as the "is."

One cannot judge the importance of definitional disruptions by the frequency with which they occur, for apparently they would occur more frequently were not constant precautions taken. We find that preventive practices are constantly employed to avoid these embarrassments and that corrective practices are constantly employed to compensate for discrediting occurrences that have not been successfully avoided. When the individual employs these strategies and tactics to protect his own projections, we may refer to them as "defensive practices"; when a participant employs them to save the definition of the situation projected by another, we speak of "protective practices" or "tact." Together, defensive and protective practices comprise the techniques employed to safeguard the impression fostered by an individual during his presence before others. It should be added that while we may be ready to see that no fostered impression would survive if defensive practices were not employed, we are less ready perhaps to see that few impressions could survive if those who received the impression did not exert tact in their reception of it.

In addition to the fact that precautions are taken to prevent disruption of projected definitions, we may also note that an intense interest in these disruptions comes to play a significant role in the social life of the group. Practical jokes and social games are played in which embarrassments which are to be taken unseriously are purposely engineered.[12] Fantasies are created in which devastating exposures occur. Anecdotes from the past— real, embroidered, or fictitious—are told and retold, detailing disruptions which occurred, almost occurred, or occurred and were admirably resolved. There seems to be no grouping which does not have a ready supply of these games, reveries, and cautionary tales, to be used as a source of humor, a catharsis for anxieties, and a sanction for inducing individuals to be modest in their claims and reasonable in their projected expectations. The individual may tell himself through dreams of getting into impossible positions. Families tell of the time a guest got his dates mixed and arrived when neither the house nor anyone in it was ready for him. Journalists tell of times when an all-too-meaningful misprint occurred, and the paper's assumption of objectivity or decorum was humorously discredited. Public servants tell of times a client ridiculously misunderstood form instructions, giving answers which implied an unanticipated and bizarre definition of the situation.[13] Seamen, whose home away from home is rigorously he-man, tell stories of coming back home and inadvertently asking mother to "pass the fucking butter."[14] Diplomats tell of the time a nearsighted queen asked a republican ambassador about the health of his king.[15]

To summarize, then, I assume that when an individual appears before others he will have many motives for trying to control the impression they receive of the situation. This report is concerned with some of the common techniques that persons employ to sustain such impressions and with some of the common contingencies associated with the employment of these techniques. The specific content of any activity presented by the individual participant, or the role it plays in the interdependent activities of an on-going social system, will not be at issue; I shall be concerned only with the participant's dramaturgical problems of presenting the activity before others. The issues dealt with by stagecraft and stage management are sometimes

[11] This role of the witness in limiting what it is the individual can be has been stressed by Existentialists, who see it as a basic threat to individual freedom. See Jean-Paul Sartre, *Being and Nothingness,* trans. by Hazel E. Barnes (New York: Philosophical Library, 1956), p. 365 ff.

[12] Goffman, *op. cit.,* pp. 319–27.

[13] Peter Blau, "Dynamics of Bureaucracy" (Ph.D. dissertation, Department of Sociology, Columbia University, forthcoming, University of Chicago Press), pp. 127–29.

[14] Walter M. Beattie, Jr., "The Merchant Seaman" (unpublished M.A. Report, Department of Sociology, University of Chicago, 1950), p. 35.

[15] Sir Frederick Ponsonby, *Recollections of Three Reigns* (New York: Dutton, 1952), p. 46.

trivial but they are quite general; they seem to occur everywhere in social life, providing a clear-cut dimension for formal sociological analysis.

It will be convenient to end this introduction with some definitions that are implied in what has gone before and required for what is to follow. For the purpose of this report, interaction (that is, face-to-face interaction) may be roughly defined as the reciprocal influence of individuals upon one another's actions when in one another's immediate physical presence. *An* interaction may be defined as all the interaction which occurs throughout any one occasion when a given set of individuals are in one another's continuous presence; the term "an encounter" would do as well. A "performance" may be defined as all the activity of a given participant on a given occasion which serves to influence in any way any of the other participants. Taking a particular participant and his performance as a basic point of reference, we may refer to those who contribute the other performances as the audience, observers, or co-participants. The pre-established pattern of action which is unfolded during a performance and which may be presented or played through on other occasions may be called a "part" or "routine."[16] These situational terms can easily be related to conventional structural ones. When an individual or performer plays the same part to the same audience on different occasions, a social relationship is likely to arise. Defining social role as the enactment of rights and duties attached to a given status, we can say that a social role will involve one or more parts and that each of these different parts may be presented by the performer on a series of occasions to the same kinds of audience or to an audience of the same persons.

[16] For comments on the importance of distinguishing between a routine of interaction and any particular instance when this routine is played through, see John von Neumann and Oskar Morgenstern, *The Theory of Games and Economic Behaviour* (2nd ed.; Princeton: Princeton University Press, 1947), p. 49.

The Norm of Reciprocity: A Preliminary Statement* /
Alvin W. Gouldner (*Washington University at St. Louis*)

The manner in which the concept of reciprocity is implicated in functional theory is explored, enabling a reanalysis of the concepts of "survival" and "exploitation." The need to distinguish between the concepts of complementarity and reciprocity is stressed. Distinctions are also drawn between (1) reciprocity as a pattern of mutually contingent exchange of gratifications, (2) the existential or folk belief in reciprocity, and (3) the generalized moral norm of reciprocity. Reciprocity as a moral norm is analyzed; it is hypothesized that it is one of the universal "principal components" of moral codes. As Westermarck states, "To requite a benefit, or to be grateful to him who bestows it, is probably everywhere, at least under certain circumstances, regarded as a duty. This is a subject which in the present connection calls for special consideration." Ways in which the norm of reciprocity is implicated in the maintenance of stable social systems are examined.

"There is no duty more indispensable than that of returning a kindness," says Cicero,

Reprinted from The *American Sociological Review*, 1960, 25, pages 161–178, by permission of author and publisher, The American Sociological Association.

* Sections of this paper were read at the annual meeting of the American Sociological Association, September, 1959. The author is indebted to Robert

adding that "all men distrust one forgetful of a benefit."—Men have been insisting on the importance of reciprocity for a long time. While many sociologists concur in this judg-

K. Merton, Howard S. Becker, John W. Bennett, Louis Schneider, and Gregory Stone for reading an earlier draft but knows of no adequate "reciprocity" for their many valuable suggestions.

ment, there are nonetheless few concepts in sociology which remain more obscure and ambiguous. Howard Becker, for example, has found this concept so important that he has titled one of his books *Man in Reciprocity* and has even spoken of man as *Homo reciprocus,* all without venturing to present a straightforward definition of reciprocity. Instead Becker states, "I don't propose to furnish any definition of reciprocity; if you produce some, they will be your own achievements."[1]

Becker is not alone in failing to stipulate formally the meaning of reciprocity, while at the same time affirming its prime importance. Indeed, he is in very good company, agreeing with L. T. Hobhouse, who held that "reciprocity . . . is the vital principle of society,"[2] and is a key intervening variable through which shared social rules are enabled to yield social stability. Yet Hobhouse presents no systematic definition of reciprocity. While hardly any clearer than Hobhouse, Richard Thurnwald is equally certain of the central importance of the "principle of reciprocity": this principle is almost a primordial imperative which "pervades every relation of primitive life"[3] and is the basis on which the entire social and ethical life of primitive civilizations presumably rests.[4] Georg Simmel's comments go a step further, emphasizing the importance of reciprocity not only for primitive but for all societies. Simmel remarks that social equilibrium and cohesion could not exist without "the reciprocity of service and return service," and that "all contacts among men rest on the schema of giving and returning the equivalence."[5]

Were we confronted with only an obscure concept, which we had no reason to assume to be important, we might justifiably consign it to the Valhalla of intellectual history, there to consort eternally with the countless incunabula of sociological ingenuity. However convenient, such a disposition would be rash, for we can readily note the importance attributed to the concept of reciprocity by such scholars as George Homans, Claude Lévi-Strauss, and Raymond Firth,[6] as well as by such earlier writers as Durkheim, Marx, Mauss, Malinowski, and von Wiese, to name only a few masters.

Accordingly, the aims of this paper are: (1) to indicate the manner in which the concept of reciprocity is tacitly involved in but formally neglected by modern functional theory; (2) to clarify the concept and display some of its diverse intellectual contents, thus facilitating its theoretical employment and research utility; and (3) to suggest concretely ways in which the clarified concept provides new leverage for analysis of the central problems of sociological theory, namely, accounting for stability and instability in social systems.

RECIPROCITY AND FUNCTIONAL THEORY

My concern with reciprocity developed initially from a critical reexamination of current functional theory, especially the work of Robert Merton and Talcott Parsons. The fullest ramifications of what follows can best be seen in this theoretical context. Merton's familiar paradigm of functionalism stresses that analysis must begin with the identification of some problematic pattern of human behavior, some institution, role, or shared pattern of belief. Merton stipulates clearly the basic functionalist assumption, the way in which the problematic pattern is to be understood: he holds that the "central orientation of functionalism" is "expressed in the

[1] Howard Becker, *Man in Reciprocity,* New York: Prager, 1956, p. 1.

[2] L. T. Hobhouse, *Morals in Evolution: A Study in Comparative Ethics,* London: Chapman & Hall, 1951, First edition, 1906, p. 12.

[3] Richard Thurnwald, *Economics in Primitive Communities,* London: Oxford University Press, 1932, p. 106.

[4] *Ibid.,* p. 137. See also, Richard Thurnwald, "Banaro Society: Social Organization and Kinship System of a Tribe in the Interior of New Guinea," *Memoirs of the American Anthropological Association,* 8, 1916; among other matters of relevance to the analysis of reciprocity, Thurnwald's discussion here (p. 275) opens the issue of the "exchange of women," which Lévi-Strauss later developed.

[5] Georg Simmel, *The Sociology of Georg Sim-*

mel, translated and edited by Kurt H. Wolff, Glencoe, Ill.: Free Press, 1950, p. 387.

[6] See, respectively, George Homans, "Social Behavior as Exchange," *American Journal of Sociology,"* 63 (May, 1958), pp. 597–606; C. Lévi-Strauss, *Les Structures élémentaires de la parenté,* Paris: Presses Universitaires, 1949; and Raymond Firth, *Primitive Polynesian Economy,* New York: Humanities Press, 1950.

practice of interpreting data by establishing their consequences for larger structures in which they are implicated."[7] The functionalist's emphasis upon studying the *existent* consequences, the ongoing functions or dysfunctions, of a social pattern may be better appreciated if it is remembered that this concern developed in a polemic against the earlier anthropological notion of a "survival." The survival, of course, was regarded as a custom held to be unexplainable in terms of its existent consequences or utility and which, therefore, had to be understood with reference to its consequences for social arrangements no longer present.

Merton's posture toward the notion of a social survival is both pragmatic and sceptical. He asserts that the question of survivals is largely an empirical one; if the evidence demonstrates that a given social pattern is presently functionless, then it simply has to be admitted provisionally to be a survival. Contrariwise, if no such evidence can be adduced, "then the quarrel dwindles of its own accord."[8] It is in this sense that his position is pragmatic. It is also a sceptical position in that he holds that "even when such survivals are identified in contemporary literate societies, they seem to add little to our understanding of human behavior or the dynamics of social change. . . ."[9] We are told, finally, that "the sociologist of literate societies may neglect survivals with no apparent loss."[10]

This resolution of the problem of survivals does not seem entirely satisfactory, for although vital empirical issues are involved there are also important questions that can only be clarified theoretically. Merton's discussion implies that certain patterns of human behavior are already known to be, or may in the future be shown to be, social survivals. How, then, can *these* be explained in terms of functional theory? Can functional theory ignore them on the grounds that they are not socially consequential? Consequential or not, such social survivals would in themselves entail patterns of behavior or

belief which are no less in need of explanation than any other. More than that, their very existence, which Merton conceives possible, would seem to contradict the "central orientation" of functional theory.

Functionalism, to repeat, explains the persistence of social patterns in terms of their ongoing consequences for existent social systems. If social survivals, which by definition have no such consequences, are conceded to exist or to be possible, then it would seem that functionalism is by its own admission incapable of explaining them. To suggest that survivals do not help us to understand other patterns of social behavior is beside the mark. The decisive issue is whether existent versions of functional theory can explain social survivals, not whether specific social survivals can explain other social patterns.

It would seem that functionalists have but one of two choices: either they must dogmatically deny the existence or possibility of functionless patterns (survivals), and assert that all social behavior is explainable parsimoniously on the basis of the same fundamental functionalist assumption, that is, in terms of its consequences for surrounding social structures; or, more reasonably, they must concede that some social patterns are or may be survivals, admitting that existent functional theory fails to account for such instances. In the latter case, functionalists must develop further their basic assumptions on the generalized level required. I believe that one of the strategic ways in which such basic assumptions can be developed is by recognizing the manner in which the concept of *reciprocity* is tacitly involved in them, and by explicating the concept's implications for functional theory.

The tacit implication of the concept of reciprocity in functional theory can be illustrated in Merton's analysis of the latent functions of the political machine in the United States. Merton inquires how political machines continue to operate, despite the fact that they frequently run counter to both the mores and the law. The *general* form of his explanation is to identify the consequences of the machine for surrounding structures and to demonstrate that the machine performs "positive functions which

[7] R. K. Merton, *Social Theory and Social Structure*, Glencoe, Ill.: Free Press, 1957, pp. 46–47.
[8] *Ibid.*, p. 33.
[9] *Ibid.*, p. 34.
[10] *Ibid.*

are at the same time not adequately fulfilled by other existing patterns and structures."[11] It seems evident, however, that simply to establish its consequences for other social structures provides no answer to the question of the persistence of the political machine.[12] The explanation miscarries because no explicit analysis is made of the feedback through which the social structures or groups, whose needs are satisfied by the political machine, in turn "reciprocate" and repay the machine for the services received from it. In this case, the patterns of reciprocity, implied in the notion of the "corruption" of the machine, are well known and fully documented.

To state the issue generally: the demonstration that A is functional for B can help to account for A's persistence only if the functional theorist tacitly assumes some principle of reciprocity. It is in this sense that some concept of reciprocity apparently has been smuggled into the basic but unstated postulates of functional analysis. The demonstration that A is functional for B helps to account for A's own persistence and stability only on two related assumptions: (1) that B *reciprocates* A's services, and (2) that B's service to A is *contingent* upon A's performance of positive functions for B. The second assumption, indeed, is one implication of the definition of reciprocity as a transaction. Unless B's services to A are contingent upon the services provided by A, it is pointless to examine the latter if one wishes to account for the persistence of A.

It may be assumed, as a first approximation, that a social unit or group is more likely to contribute to another which provides it with benefits than to one which does not; nonetheless, there are certain general conditions under which one pattern may provide

benefits for the other despite a *lack* of reciprocity. An important case of this situation is where power arrangements constrain the continuance of services. If B is considerably more powerful than A, B may force A to benefit it with little or no reciprocity. This social arrangement, to be sure, is less stable than one in which B's reciprocity *motivates* A to continue performing services for B, but it is hardly for this reason sociologically unimportant.

The problem can also be approached in terms of the functional autonomy[13] of two units relative to each other. For example, B may have many alternative sources for supplying the services that it normally receives from A. A, however, may be dependent upon B's services and have no, or comparatively few, alternatives. Consequently, the continued provision of benefits by one pattern,[14] A, for another, B, depends not only upon (1) the benefits which A in turn receives from B, but also on (2) the power which B possesses relative to A, and (3) the alternative sources of services accessible to each, beyond those provided by the other. In short, an explanation of the stability of a pattern, or of the relationship between A and B, requires investigation of mutually contingent benefits rendered and of the manner in which this mutual contingency is sustained. The latter, in turn, requires utilization of two different theoretical traditions and general orientations, one stressing the significance of power differences and the other emphasizing the degree of mutual dependence of the patterns or parties involved.

Functional theory, then, requires some assumption concerning reciprocity. It must, however, avoid the "Pollyanna Fallacy" which optimistically assumes that structures securing "satisfactions" from others will invariably be "grateful" and will always reciprocate. Therefore it cannot be merely hypostatized that reciprocity will operate in every case; its occurrence must, instead, be

11 *Ibid.*, p. 73. Among the functions of the political machine to which Merton refers are: the organization and centralization of power so that it can be mobilized to satisfy the needs of different groups, provision of personalized forms of assistance for lower-class groups, giving political privileges and aid to business groups, and granting protection for illicit rackets.

12 An initial statement of this point is to be found in A. W. Gouldner, "Reciprocity and Autonomy in Functional Theory," in L. Gross, editor, *Symposium on Sociological Theory*, New York: Harper & Row Publishers, 1959, pp. 241–270.

13 For fuller discussion of this concept, see Gouldner, *ibid.*

14 Use of terms such as "pattern" or "unit" is intended to indicate that the present discussion deliberately collapses distinctions between institutional, interpersonal, group, or role reciprocities, treating them here under a single rubric for reasons of space.

documented empirically. Although reciprocal relations stabilize patterns, it need not follow that a lack of reciprocity is socially impossible or invariably disruptive of the patterns involved. Relations with little or no reciprocity may, for example, occur when power disparities allow one party to coerce the other. There may also be special mechanisms which compensate for or control the tensions which arise in the event of a breakdown in reciprocity. Among such compensatory mechanisms there may be culturally shared prescriptions of one-sided or unconditional generosity, such as the Christian notion of "turning the other cheek" or "walking the second mile," the feudal notion of *"noblesse oblige,"* or the Roman notion of "clemency." There may also be cultural prohibitions banning the examination of certain interchanges from the standpoint of their concrete reciprocity, as expressed by the cliché, "It's not the gift but the sentiment that counts." The major point here is that if empirical analysis fails to detect the existence of functional reciprocity, or finds that it has been disrupted, it becomes necessary to search out and analyze the compensatory arrangements that may provide means of controlling the resultant tensions, thereby enabling the problematic pattern to remain stable.

A RECONCEPTUALIZATION OF "SURVIVALS"

Thus far reciprocity has been discussed as a mutually contingent exchange of benefits between two or more units, as if it were an "all or none" matter. Once the problem is posed in this way, however, it is apparent that reciprocity is not merely present or absent but is, instead, quantitatively variable— or may be treated as such. The benefits exchanged, at one extreme, may be identical or equal. At the other logical extreme, one party may give nothing in return for the benefits it has received. Both of these extremes are probably rare in social relations and the intermediary case, in which one party gives something more or less than that received, is probably more common than either of the limiting cases.

Having cast the problem of reciprocity in these quantitative terms, there emerges an important implication for the question of

social survivals. The quantitative view of reciprocity. These functionalists made the cogent of the *earlier* notion of a survival. It may now be seen that there a survival was tacitly treated as one of the limiting cases of reciprocity, that is, one in which a pattern provides *nothing* in exchange for the benefits given it.

The polemical opposition of the earlier functionalists to this view of a survival rests implicitly on an unqualified principle of reciprocity. These functionalists made the cogent assumption that a social pattern which persists must be securing satisfaction of its own needs from certain other patterns. What was further and more dubiously assumed, however, was that if this pattern continues to be "serviced" this could only be because it reciprocally provided *some* gratifications to its benefactors. In the course of the polemic, the question of the degree of such gratification—the relation between its output and input—became obscured. To the early functionalists, the empirical problem became one of unearthing the hidden contributions made by a seeming survival and, thereby, showing that it is not in fact functionless. In effect, this enjoined the functionalist to exert his ingenuity to search out the hidden reciprocities for it was assumed that there must be some reciprocities somewhere. This led, in certain cases, as Audrey Richards states, to "some far-fetched explanations. . . ."[15]

If, however, it had been better understood that compensatory mechanisms might have been substituted for reciprocity, or that power disparities might have maintained the "survival" despite its lack of reciprocity, then many fruitful problems may well have emerged. Above all, the early functionalists neglected the fact that a survival is only the limiting case of a larger class of social phenomena, namely, relations between parties or patterns in which functional reciprocity is *not equal*. While the survival, defined as the extreme case of a *complete* lack of reciprocity, may be rare, the larger class of *unequal* exchanges, of which survivals are a part, is frequent. The tacit conception of survivals as entailing no reciprocity led the

15 Raymond Firth, editor, *Man and Culture: An Evaluation of the Work of Bronislaw Malinowski,* New York: The Humanities Press, 1957, p. 19.

early functionalists to neglect the *larger class of unequal exchanges*. It is this problem which the functionalist polemic against survivals has obscured to the present day.

THE "EXPLOITATION" PROBLEM

It was, however, not only the functionalist polemic against the concept of survivals that obscured the significance and inhibited the study of unequal exchanges. A similar result is also produced by the suspicion with which many modern sociologists understandably regard the concept of "exploitation." This concept of course is central to the traditional socialist critique of modern capitalism. In the now nearly-forgotten language of political economy, "exploitation" refers to a relationship in which unearned income results from certain kinds of unequal exchange.

Starting perhaps with Sismondi's notion of "spoliation," and possibly even earlier with the physiocrat's critique of exchange as intrinsically unproductive, the concept of exploitation can be traced from the work of the Saint-Simonians to that of Marx and Proudhon.[16] It is also present in Veblen's notion of the Vested Interest which he characterizes as "the right to something for nothing" or, in other words, as *institutionalized* exploitation. Even after the emergence of sociology as a separate discipline the concept of exploitation appears in the works of E. A. Ross,[17] von Wiese and Howard Becker.[18] As it passed into sociology, how-

ever, the concept was generalized beyond its original economic application. Ross and Becker-von Wiese, for example, speak of various types of exploitation: economic, to be sure, but also religious, "egotic," and sexual. However, just as the concept of exploitation was being generalized and made available for social analysis, it almost disappeared from sociological usage.

"*Almost* disappeared" because there remains one area in which unabashed, full-scale use of the concept is made by sociologists. This is in the study of sexual relations. As Kanin and Howard remark, "It has been the *practice* to speak of exploitation when males were found to have entered sexual liaisons with women of comparative lower status."[19] Kingsley Davis also uses the notion of exploitation implicitly in his discussion of the incest taboo, remarking that ". . . father-daughter incest would put the daughter in a position of subordination. While she was still immature the father could use his power to take advantage of her."[20] What Davis is saying is that one function of the incest taboo is to prevent sexual exploitation. He goes on to add that "legitimate sexual relations ordinarily involve a certain amount of reciprocity. Sex is exchanged for something equally valuable."[21] This is an interesting commentary, first, because Davis is quite clear about treating exploitation in the context of a discussion of reciprocity; and second, because he explicitly uses a notion of reciprocity in a strategic way even though it is not systematically explored elsewhere in his volume, once again illustrating the tendency to use the concept and to assume its analytic importance without giving it careful conceptualization.[22]

[16] The views of these and other analysts of exploitation are ably summarized in C. Gide and C. Rist, *A History of Economic Doctrines*, translated by R. Richards, Boston: Heath, revised edition, 1918.

[17] See, e.g., E. A. Ross, *New-Age Sociology*, New York: Appleton-Century, 1940, esp. Chapter 9.

[18] Note von Wiese and Becker's comment: "The Marxians trace the social process of exploitation to the 'capitalistic' economic order; their thesis is that capitalism creates exploitation. We, on the other hand, do not deny the existence of capitalistic exploitation, but it is for us only one of the forms which are found among the phenomena of exploitation. The destruction of capitalism will not signalize the end of exploitation, but will merely prevent the appearance of some of its forms and will open up new opportunities for others." L. von Wiese and Howard Becker, *Systematic Sociology*, New York: Wiley, 1932, p. 700. It would seem that 20th century history amply confirms this view.

[19] E. Kanin and D. H. Howard, "Postmarital Consequences of Premarital Sex Adjustments," *American Sociological Review*, 23 (October, 1958), p. 558. (My italics.)

[20] Kingsley Davis, *Human Society*, New York: Macmillan, 1949, p. 403.

[21] *Ibid.*, p. 404.

[22] Note Davis's tendency to assume that legitimate sexual relations entail an exchange of *equal* values even though his previous sentence indicates that there may be no more than "a *certain amount* of reciprocity" involved. The latter is a way of talking about *unequal* exchanges and thus implies that these occur in institutionalized and not only in illicit relations. This is an important problem that cannot be developed here.

The continued use of the concept of exploitation in sociological analyses of sexual relations stems largely from the brilliant work of Willard Waller on the dynamics of courtship. Waller's ambivalent comments about the concept suggest why it has fallen into sociological disrepute. "The word exploitation is by no means a desirable one," explains Waller, "but we have not been able to find another which will do as well. The dictionary definition of exploitation as an 'unfair or unjust utilization of another' contains a value judgment, and this value judgment is really a part of the ordinary sociological meaning of the term."[23] In short, the concept of exploitation may have become disreputable because its value implications conflict with modern sociology's effort to place itself on a value-free basis, as well as because it is a concept commonly and correctly associated with the critique of modern society emphasized by the political left. But the concept *need* not be used in such an ideological manner; it can be employed simply to refer to certain transactions involving an exchange of things of unequal value. It is important to guarantee that the ordinary value implications of a term do not intrude upon its scientific use. It is also important, however, to prevent our distaste for the ideological implications of exploitation from inducing a compulsive and equally ideological neglect of its cognitive substance.

The unsavory implications of the concept of exploitation have *not* excluded it from studies of sexual relations, although almost all other specializations in sociology eschew it. Why this is so remains a tempting problem for the sociology of knowledge, but cannot be explored here. In the present context, the important implications are the following: If the possible sexual exploitation of daughters by fathers gives rise, as Davis suggests, to mechanisms that serve to prevent this, then it would seem that *other* types of exploitation may also be controlled by *other* kinds of mechanisms. These may be no less important and universal than the incest taboo. If the exploitation of women by men

(or men by women) is worthy of sociological attention, then also worth studying is the exploitation of students by teachers, of workers by management or union leaders, of patients by doctors,[24] and so on. If the notion of exploitation, in a value-free sense, is useful for the analysis of sexual relations then it can be of similar aid in analyzing many other kinds of social relations.

Doubtless "exploitation" is by now so heavily charged with misleading ideological resonance that the term itself can scarcely be salvaged for purely scientific purposes and will, quite properly, be resisted by most American sociologists. This is unimportant. Perhaps a less emotionally freighted—if infelicitous—term such as "reciprocity imbalance" will suffice to direct attention once again to the crucial question of unequal exchanges.

In any event, the present analysis of reciprocity opens up long-neglected questions, yielding a new perspective on the relation between functional theory and the concepts of "survival" and "exploitation." In the latter case, moveover, intimations emerge of some of the ways in which two diverse theoretical traditions contain surprising convergences.

These two traditions are, first, that which is commonly if questionably[25] held to begin with Comte, was developed by Durkheim, and reaches its fullest current expression in the work of Parsons. The second tradition, while often ideologically distorted nevertheless retains significant sociological substance, derives from Marx and Engels, was developed by Kautsky, and ended in Bukharin. The latent convergence between these two schools involves the implicit stress that each gives to reciprocity, albeit to polar ends of its continuum.

[24] The point is not to stress, as Parsons does, the unique exploitability of the patient or the peculiar power of the physician, but to see this relationship as but one dramatic case of a larger class of phenomena of basic theoretic significance which should be explicitly dealt with in systematic theory rather than given only *ad hoc* treatment in specific empirical contexts. See Talcott Parsons, *The Social System*, Glencoe, Ill.: Free Press, 1951, p. 445.

[25] The thesis that this is more mythological than real is developed in my introduction to Emile Durkheim, *Socialism and Saint-Simon*, translated by C. Sattler and edited by A. W. Gouldner, Yellow Springs: Antioch Press, 1958, esp. p. ix.

[23] Willard Waller, *The Family: A Dynamic Interpretation*, revised by Reuben Hill, New York: Dryden, 1951, p. 163.

The "Comteian" tradition, of course, approached reciprocity through its emphasis on the division of labor, viewed as a major source of social cohesion. Characteristically focusing on the problem of social instability and change, rather than stability and cohesion, the "Marxian" tradition emphasized the opposite end of reciprocity, namely, exploitation. This, I suspect, is one of the major but overlooked convergences in the history of sociological theory.

This latent convergence becomes most evident in Durkheim's lectures on "Professional Ethics and Civic Morals."[26] Durkheim contends that the existence of social classes, characterized by significant inequalities, in principle makes it impossible for "just" contracts to be negotiated. This system of stratification, Durkheim argues, constrains to an unequal exchange of goods and services, thereby offending the moral expectations of people in industrial societies. The exploitation rendered possible by notable disparities of power among the contracting parties encourages a sense of injustice which has socially unstabilizing consequences. Thus both Durkheim and Marx use a concept of "exploitation" for analyzing social instabilities. Durkheim, however, adds an important element that was systematically neglected by Marx, namely, that unequal exchanges of goods and services are socially disruptive because they violate certain pervasive *values*. But the specific nature of this value element is never fully confronted and explored by Durkheim; we must here take as problematic what Durkheim took as given.

COMPLEMENTARITY AND RECIPROCITY

First, however, the question of the meaning of the concept of reciprocity should be reexamined. Consideration of some of the ways in which the reciprocity problem is treated by Parsons helps to distinguish reciprocity from other cognate concepts. "It is inherent in the nature of social interaction," writes Parsons, "that the gratification of ego's need-dispositions is contingent on al-

ter's reaction and vice versa."[27] Presumably, therefore, if the gratification of either party's needs is not contingent upon the other's reactions, the stability of their relation is undermined. This, in turn, implies that if a social system is to be stable there must always be some "mutuality of gratification."[28] Social system stability, then, presumably depends in part on the mutually contingent exchange of gratifications, that is, on reciprocity as exchange.

This, however, remains an insight the implications of which are never systematically explored. For example, the implications of differences in the *degree* of mutuality or in the symmetry of reciprocity are neglected. Again, while the concept of "exploitation" assumes *central* importance in Parsons' commentary on the patient-doctor relation, it is never precisely defined, examined, and located in his *general* theory.

One reason for Parsons' neglect of reciprocity is that he, like some other sociologists, does not distinguish it from the concept of complementarity. Parsons uses the two concepts as if they are synonymous[29] and, for the most part, centers his analysis on complementarity to the systematic neglect of reciprocity rigorously construed. The term complementarity, however, is itself an

26 Emile Durkheim, *Professional Ethics and Civic Morals,* translated by C. Brookfield, Glencoe, Ill.: Free Press, 1958; see esp. pp. 209–214.

27 Parsons, *op. cit.,* p. 21.
28 Talcott Parsons and Edward A. Shils, editors, *Toward a General Theory of Action,* Cambridge: Harvard University Press, 1951, p. 107.
29 Parsons' tendency to equate complementarity and reciprocity may be illustrated by his comment that "Role expectations organize . . . the reciprocities, expectations, and responses to these expectations in the specific interaction systems of ego and one or more alters. This reciprocal aspect must be borne in mind since the expectations of an ego *always* imply the expectations of one or more alters. It is in this *reciprocity* or *complementarity* that sanctions enter. . . ." *Ibid.,* pp. 190–191 (my italics) ; see also p. 105. The burden of Parsons' analysis attends to the conditions and consequences of complementarity, by which he means that a role player requires of himself what his role partner requires of him. It is precisely for this reason that Parsons emphasizes that values must be held in common by the actors, if their expectations are to be compatible. The equation of reciprocity with complementarity is not peculiar to Parsons. It is evident in the work of other sociologists who sometimes speak of the rights and obligations in a pair of roles as "reciprocal" and other times as "complementary." And, like Parsons, others state that rights and duties, or role expectations, are *always* complementary.

ambiguous one and is not, in all of its meanings, synonymous with reciprocity. Complementarity has at least four distinct meanings:[30]

Complementarity[1] may mean that a right (x) of Ego against Alter implies a duty (—x) of Alter to Ego. Given the often vague use of the term "right," it is quite possible that this proposition, in one aspect, is only an expansion of some definition of the concept "right." To that degree, of course, this is simply an analytic proposition. The interesting sociological questions, however, arise only when issues of empirical substance rather than logical implication are raised. For example, where a group shares a belief that some status occupant has a certain right, say the right of a wife to receive support from her husband, does the group in fact also share a belief that the husband has an obligation to support the wife? Furthermore, even though rights may logically or empirically imply duties, it need not follow that the reverse is true. In other words, it does not follow that rights and duties are always transitive. This can be seen in a second meaning of complementarity.

Complementarity[2] may mean that what is a duty (—x) of Alter to Ego implies a right (x) of Ego against Alter. On the *empirical* level, while this is often true, of course, it is also sometimes false. For example, what may be regarded as a duty of charity or forbearance, say a duty to "turn the other cheek," need not be *socially* defined as the *right* of the recipient. While a man may be regarded as having an unconditional obligation to tell the truth to everyone, even to a confirmed liar, people in his group might not claim that the liar has a *right* to have the truth told him.

The other two meanings of complementarity differ substantially. Complementarity[3] may mean that a right (x) of Alter against Ego implies a duty (—y) of Alter to Ego. Similarly, complementarity[4] may mean that a duty (—x) of Ego to Alter implies a right (y) of Ego against Alter.

In these four implications of complementarity—sometimes called reciprocal rights and obligations—there are two distinctive types of cases. Properly speaking, *complementarity* refers only to the first two meanings sketched above, where what is a right of Ego implies an obligation of Alter, or where a duty of Alter to Ego implies a right of Ego against Alter. Only the other two meanings, however, involve true instances of *reciprocity,* for only in these does what one party receives from the other require some return, so that giving and receiving are mutually contingent.

In short, complementarity connotes that one's rights are another's obligations, and *vice versa*. Reciprocity, however, connotes that *each* party has rights *and* duties. This is more than an analytic distinction: it is an *empirical* generalization concerning role systems the importance of which as a datum is so elemental that it is commonly neglected and rarely made problematic. The English philosopher MacBeath suggests that this empirical generalization may be accounted for by the principle of reciprocity.[31] This would seem possible in several senses, one of which is that, were there only rights on the one side and duties on the other, there need be no exchange whatsoever. Stated differently, it would seem that there can be stable patterns of reciprocity *qua* exchange only insofar as *each* party has both rights and duties. In effect, then, reciprocity has its significance for *role systems* in that it tends to structure *each* role so as to include both rights and duties. It is now clear, at any rate, that reciprocity is by no means identical with complementarity and that the two are confused only at theoretic peril.

MALINOWSKI ON RECIPROCITY

Renewing the effort to clarify the diverse meanings of reciprocity, we turn to Malinowski's seminal contribution. This is most fully elaborated in his *Crime and Custom,*[32] which opens with the following question: Why is it that rules of conduct in a primitive society are obeyed, even though they are

[30] The analysis here closely follows W. D. Ross, *The Right and the Good,* Oxford: Clarendon Press, 1950.

[31] Alexander MacBeath, *Experiments in Living,* London: Macmillan, 1952; see esp. pp. 127 ff.

[32] Bronislaw Malinowski, *Crime and Custom in Savage Society,* London: Paul, Trench, Trubner, 1932.

hard and irksome? Even under normal conditions, the savage's compliance with his moral code is at best partial, conditional, and evasive. These, says Malinowski, are the elementary facts of ethnography, and consequently we cannot assume that the savage's conformity is due only to his awe and reverence for traditional custom, or that he slavishly and spontaneously complies with its dictates.

Above all, Malinowski rejects the assumption that it is the sacred authority of the moral code, or the "collective conscience," which accounts for the conformity given it. It is to this anti-Durkheimian point that he directs the brunt of his polemic. Conformity, says Malinowski, is not sanctioned "by a mere psychological force, but by a definite social machinery. . . ."[33] Thus Malinowski expressly rejects a psychological account of conformity and seeks instead a distinctively sociological explanation.[34] This he finds in the "principle of reciprocity."

One of Malinowski's central theses holds that people *owe obligations to each other* and that, therefore, conformity with norms is something they give *to each other*. He notes for example, that almost every religious or ceremonial act is regarded as an obligation between groups and living individuals, and not only to the immortal gods. For Malinowski, therefore, one meaning of reciprocity refers to the interlocking status duties which people owe one another. Thus he speaks of reciprocity as taking place "within a standing partnership, or as associated with definite social ties or coupled with mutuality in noneconomic matters."[35]

Reciprocity also entails a "mutual dependence and [is] realized in the equivalent arrangement of reciprocal services. . . ."[36] Here reciprocity is conceived as the complement to and fulfillment of the division of labor. It is the pattern of exchange through which the mutual dependence of people, brought about by the division of labor, is realized. Reciprocity, therefore, is a mutually gratifying pattern of exchanging goods and services.

As noted above, Malinowski speaks of reciprocity as involving an exchange of *equivalent* services; he further stresses this by insisting that "most if not all economic acts are found to belong to some chain of reciprocal gifts and counter-gifts, which in the long run balance, benefiting both sides equally."[37] For Malinowski, then, the exchange of goods and services is not only mutually gratifying but is equally so, "in the long run."

Speaking of the reciprocal exchange of vegetables and fish between inland communities and fishing villages, Malinowski remarks that there is a "system of mutual obligations which forces the fisherman to repay whenever he has received a gift from his inland partner, and vice versa. Neither partner can refuse, neither may stint, neither should delay."[38] This is seen to be related to the group's existential beliefs about reciprocity. That is, men are not regarded as blindly involving themselves in reciprocal transactions; they are viewed as having some presentiment of the consequences of reciprocity and of its breakdown. In this vein, Malinowski writes: "Though no native, however intelligent, can formulate this state of affairs in a general abstract manner, or present it as a sociological theory, yet everyone is well aware of its existence and in each concrete case he can foresee the consequences."[39] More specifically, it seems to be implied that people believe that (a) in the long run the mutual exchange of goods and

[33] *Ibid.,* p. 55.

[34] This, by the way, is why I cannot concur in Parsons' judgment that Malinowski never disentangled a social system level of analysis from an encyclopedic concept of culture. See Talcott Parsons, "Malinowski and the Theory of Social Systems," in *Man and Culture . . . , op. cit.,* pp. 53–70. Malinowski's *Crime and Custom* transcends a clinical case analysis of specific primitive societies and presents a generalized and basic contribution to the theory of social systems when it addresses itself to the problem of *reciprocity.* Parsons, however, does not mention the significance of reciprocity in Malinowski's work and is able to support his claim that it ignores social system analysis only by this noteworthy omission. Parsons' neglect of the principle of reciprocity in Malinowski's work, it would seem, is consistent with his own neglect of the distinction between reciprocity and complementarity.

[35] Malinowski, *op. cit.,* p. 39.

[36] *Ibid.,* p. 55.

[37] *Ibid.,* p. 39.

[38] *Ibid.,* p. 22.

[39] *Ibid.,* p. 40. This is not to say, however, that Malinowski regards reciprocity *qua* transaction as *always* intended by all the actors or as something of which they are always aware. In brief—and I agree—there are both latent and manifest reciprocities.

services *will* balance out; or (b) if people do not aid those who helped them certain penalties will be imposed upon them; or (c) those whom they have helped *can* be expected to help them; or (d) some or all of these.

It is clear that two basically different elements were caught up in Malinowski's "principle of reciprocity." One of these is a set of sentiments or existential folk beliefs about reciprocity. The other is a mutually contingent exchange of benefits or gratifications. (The latter conception converges, though it is not completely identical, with the ecological concept of symbiosis). There is, however, a third analytically distinct element which, if implicit in Malinowski, remained murky. This is a *value* element, the same value that Durkheim, as mentioned earlier, invoked but did not clarify. Like Durkheim, Malinowski never fully disentangles it from the other elements.

In the exchanges between the fishing and the inland villages, cited above, we may suggest that each side lives up to its obligations, not simply because of constraints imposed by the division of labor with its attendant mutual dependency, but also because the partners share the higher level *moral norm:* "You *should* give benefits to those who give you benefits." Note that this norm does not simply make it unconditionally imperative, say, for the fisherman to give the inland gardeners fish. I refer here not to the *specific* obligation to give fish but rather to a *general* obligation to repay benefits.

In sum, beyond reciprocity as a pattern of exchange and beyond folk beliefs about reciprocity as a fact of life, there is another element: a generalized moral norm of reciprocity which defines certain actions and *obligations* as repayments for benefits received.

Malinowski frequently seems to confuse this general norm with the existence of complementary and concrete status rights and duties. It is theoretically necessary, however, to distinguish specific status duties from the general norm. Specific and complementary duties are owed by role partners to one another by virtue of the socially standardized roles they play. These may require an almost unconditional compliance in the sense that they are incumbent on all those in a given status simply by virtue of its occupancy. In contrast, the generalized norm of reciprocity evokes obligations toward others on the basis of their past behavior. In the first case, Ego's obligations to Alter depend upon Ego's status vis-à-vis Alter; in the second case, Ego's obligation toward Alter depend upon what Alter has done for Ego. There are certain duties that people owe one another, not as human beings, or as fellow members of a group, or even as occupants of social statuses within the group but, rather, because of their prior actions. We owe others certain things because of what they have previously done for us, because of the history of previous interaction we have had with them. It is this kind of obligation which is entailed by the generalized norm of reciprocity.

THE NORM OF RECIPROCITY

Contrary to some cultural relativists, it can be hypothesized that a norm of reciprocity is universal. As Westermarck stated, "To requite a benefit, or to be grateful to him who bestows it, is probably everywhere, at least under certain circumstances, regarded as a duty."[40] A norm of reciprocity is, I suspect, no less universal and important an element of culture than the incest taboo, although, similarly, its concrete formulations may vary with time and place.

Specifically, I suggest that a norm of reciprocity, in its universal form, makes two interrelated, minimal demands: (1) people should help those who have helped them, and (2) people should not injure those who have helped them. Generically, the norm of reciprocity may be conceived of as a dimension to be found in all value systems and, in particular, as one among a *number* of "Principal Components" universally present in moral codes. (The task of the sociologist, in this regard, parallels that of the physicist who seeks to identify the basic particles of matter, the conditions under which they vary, and their relations to one another.)

[40] Edward Westermarck, *The Origin and Development of the Moral Ideas,* London: Macmillan, 1908, Vol. 2, p. 154.

To suggest that a norm of reciprocity is universal is not, of course, to assert that it is unconditional. Unconditionality would, indeed, be at variance with the basic character of the reciprocity norm which imposes obligations only contingently, that is, in response to the benefits conferred by others. Moreover, such obligations of repayment are contingent upon the imputed *value* of the benefit received. The value of the benefit and hence the debt is in proportion to and varies with— among other things—the intensity of the recipient's need at the time the benefit was bestowed ("a friend in need . . ."), the resources of the donor ("he gave although he could ill afford it"), the motives imputed to the donor ("without thought of gain"), and the nature of the constraints which are perceived to exist or to be absent ("he gave of his own free will . . ."). Thus the obligations imposed by the norm of reciprocity may vary with the *status* of the participants within a society.

Similarly, this norm functions differently in some degree in different *cultures*. In the Philippines, for example, the *compadre* system cuts across and pervades the political, economic, and other institutional spheres. *Compadres* are bound by a norm of reciprocity. If one man pays his *compadre's* doctor's bill in time of need, for example, the latter may be obligated to help the former's son to get a government job. Here the tendency to govern all relations by the norm of reciprocity, thereby undermining bureaucratic impersonality, is relatively legitimate, hence overt and powerful. In the United States, however, such tendencies are weaker, in part because friendship relations are less institutionalized. Nonetheless, even in bureaucracies in this country such tendencies are endemic, albeit less legitimate and overt. Except in friendship, kinship, and neighborly relations, a norm of reciprocity is not imposed on Americans by the "dominant cultural profile," although it is commonly found in the latent or "substitute" culture structure in all institutional sectors, even the most rationalized, in the United States.

In otherwise contrasting discussions of the norm of reciprocity one emphasis is notable. Some scholars, especially Homans, Thur-

wald, Simmel, and Malinowski, assert or imply that the reciprocity norm stipulates that the amount of the return to be made is "roughly equivalent" to what had been received. The problem of equivalence is a difficult but important one. Whether in fact there is a reciprocity norm specifically requiring that returns for benefits received be *equivalent* is an empirical question. So, too, is the problem of whether such a norm is part of or distinct from a more general norm which simply requires that one return some (unspecified) benefits to benefactors. Logically prior to such empirical problems, however, is the question of what the meaning of equivalence would be in the former norm of equivalent reciprocity.

Equivalence may have at least two forms, the sociological and psychodynamic significance of which are apt to be quite distinct. In the first case, heteromorphic reciprocity, equivalence may mean that the things exchanged may be concretely different but should be equal in *value,* as defined by the actors in the situation. In the second case, homeomorphic reciprocity, equivalence may mean that exchanges should be concretely alike, or identical in form, either with respect to the things exchanged or to the circumstances under which they are exchanged. In the former, equivalence calls for "tit for tat"; in the latter, equivalence calls for "tat for tat." Historically, the most important expression of homeomorphic reciprocity is found in the *negative* norms of reciprocity, that is, in sentiments of retaliation where the emphasis is placed not on the return of benefits but on the return of injuries, and is best exemplified by the *lex talionis*.[41]

Finally, it should be stressed that equivalence in the above cases refers to a definition of the exchangeables made by actors in the situation. This differs of course, from holding that the things exchanged by people, in the long run, will be *objectively* equal in value, as measured by economists or other

[41] It is further indicative of our terminological difficulties in this area that this is often what Piaget spoke of as "reciprocity." For example, ". . . reciprocity stands so high in the eyes of the child that he will apply it even where to us it seems to border on crude vengeance." J. Piaget, *The Moral Judgment of the Child*, New York: Harcourt, Brace, 1932, p. 216.

social scientists. Here, again, the adequacy of these conceptual distinctions will be determined ultimately by empirical test. For example, can we find reciprocity norms which, in fact, require that returns be equivalent in value and are these empirically distinguishable from norms requiring that returns be concretely alike? Are these unidimensional or multi-dimensional? Similarly, only research can resolve the question whether a norm of retaliation exists in any given group, is the polar side of the norm of reciprocity, or is a distinctive norm which may vary independently of the reciprocity norm. These conceptual distinctions only suggest a set of research possibilities and have value primarily as guides to investigation.[42]

RECIPROCITY AND SOCIAL SYSTEMS

As mentioned above, sociologists have sometimes confused the notion of complementarity with that of reciprocity and have recently tended to focus on the former. Presumably, the reason for this is because of the importance of complementarity in maintaining the stability of social systems. Clearly, if what one party deems his right is accepted by the other as his obligation, their relation will be more stable than if the latter fails to so define it. But if the group

stabilizing consequences of complementarity are the basis of its theoretical significance, then the same consideration underwrites with equal potency the significance of reciprocity. For reciprocity has no less a role in maintaining the stability of social systems.

Note that there are at least two ways, not merely one, in which complementarity as such can break down. In the one case, Alter can refuse to acknowledge Ego's rights as his own duties. In the other case, however, Ego may not regard as rights that which Alter acknowledges as duties. The former is commonly viewed as the empirically more frequent and as the theoretically more significant case. That this often seems to be taken as a matter of course suggests the presence of certain tacit assumptions about basic human dispositions. It seems to assume, as Aristotle put it, that people are more ready to receive than to give benefits. In short, it premises a common tendency toward what used to be called "egoism," a salient (but not exclusive) concern with the satisfaction of one's own needs.

This or some cognate assumption appears to be eminently reasonable and empirically justified. There can be no adequate systematic sociological theory which boggles at the issue; indeed, it is one of the many virtues of Parsons' work that it confronts the egoism problem. His solution seems to be sidetracked, however, because his overwhelming focus on the problem of complementarity leads to the neglect of reciprocity. If assumptions about egoistic dispositions are valid, however, a complementarity of rights and obligations should be exposed to a persistent strain, in which each party is somewhat more actively concerned to defend or extend his own rights than those of others. There is nothing in complementarity as such which would seem able to control egoism.

One way out may be obtained by premising that socialization internalizes complementary rights and obligations in persons, before they fully assume responsible participation in a social system. Even if socialization were to work perfectly and so internalize such rights and obligations, there still remains the question as to what mechanism can sustain and reinforce these during full participation in the social system. The con-

---

[42] A further point that fuller discussion should develop concerns the terms "roughly" equivalent. Use of the term "roughly," in one part, indicates that a certain range of concrete behavior will be viewed by the actors as compliance with this reciprocity norm and that more than one specific return will be acceptable and defined as equivalent. The norm of reciprocity *qua* equivalence is thus like most other norms which also tolerate a range of variability. The demand for *exact* equality would place an impossible burden even on actors highly motivated to comply with the reciprocity norm and would yield endemic tensions. Conversely, a notion of "rough" equivalence held by the actors allows for easier compliance with the norm and can be regarded as one of the mechanisms sustaining it. Recognition that the requirement is for "rough" equivalence, however, should not be allowed to obscure the fact that there may be a specific reciprocity norm which does in fact call for equivalence. This would be a distinguishing feature of the hypothesized norm and should no more be concealed by reference to a "rough" equivalent than should be the distinctive content of any other norm be obscured by the fact that a variable range of behaviors will be acceptable to those holding it.

cept of complementarity takes mutually compatible expectations as given; it does not and cannot explain how they are maintained once established. For this we need to turn to the reciprocities processes because these, unlike pure complementarity, actually mobilize egoistic motivations and channel them into the maintenance of the social system. Benthamite utilitarianism has long understood that egoism can motivate one party to satisfy the expectations of the other, since by doing so he induces the latter to reciprocate and to satisfy his own. As Max Gluckman might put it with his penchant for Hegelian paradox, there is an altruism in egoism, made possible through reciprocity.

Furthermore, the existential belief in reciprocity says something like this, "People will usually help those who help them." Similarly, the *norm* of reciprocity holds that people should help those who help them and, therefore, those whom you have helped have an obligation to help you. The conclusion is clear: if you want to be helped by others you must help them; hence it is not only proper but also expedient to conform with the specific status rights of others and with the general norm. Both the existential belief in and the norm of reciprocity enlist egoistic motivations in the service of social system stability.[43]

A full analysis of the ways in which the whole reciprocities complex is involved in the maintenance of social systems would require consideration of the linkages between each of its various elements, and their relation to other general properties of social systems. There is no space for such consideration here. Instead, I examine only one part of the complex, namely, the generalized *norm* of reciprocity, and suggest some of the ways in which it contributes to social system stability.

[43] I suppose that one can take two different attitudes toward this transmutation of the base metal of egoism. One can deplore the situation and say with Eliot:
  "The last temptation is the greatest treason;
  To do the right thing for the wrong reason."
Or one can adopt the older and perhaps sociologically wiser view that here, once more, "private vices make public benefits," and provide an indispensable basis for the *spontaneous self-regulation* of social systems.

If, following Parsons, we suppose that social systems are stable to the extent that Ego and Alter conform with one another's expectations, we are confronted with the problem of why men *reciprocate* gratifications. Parsons holds that once a stable relation of mutual gratification has been established the system is self-perpetuating; presumably, no special mechanisms are necessary to maintain it. Insofar as this is not simply postulated in analogy with the principle of inertia in physics, apparently reciprocity is accounted for by Parsons, and also by Homans, as a result of the development of a beneficent cycle of mutual reinforcement. That is, Ego's conformity with Alter's expectations reinforces Alter's conformity with Ego's expectations, and so on.

This explanation of reciprocity *qua* transaction is particularly strange in Parsons' case since he often stresses, but here neglects, the significance of shared values as a source of stability in social systems. So far as the question here is not simply the general one of why men conform with the expectations of others but, rather, the more specific problem of why they *reciprocate* benefits, part of the answer would seem to be that they have commonly internalized some general *moral norm*. In short, the suggestion is that the motivation for reciprocity stems not only from the sheer gratification which Alter receives from Ego but also from Alter's internalization of a specific norm of reciprocity which morally obliges him to give benefits to those from whom he has received them. In this respect, the *norm* of reciprocity is a concrete and special mechanism involved in the maintenance of any stable social system.

Why should such a norm be necessary? Why it is that expedient considerations do not suffice to mobilize motivations to comply with other's expectations, thereby inducing them to provide reciprocal compliances? One major line of analysis here would certainly indicate the disruptive potentialities of power differences. Given significant power differences, egoistic motivations may seek to get benefits without returning them. (It is notable that Parsons fails to define the power situation in his basic model of Ego-Alter equilibrium.) The situation is then ripe for the breakdown of reciprocity and for the development of system-disrupting exploitation. The norm of reciprocity, however, engenders motives for returning benefits even when power differences might invite exploitation. The norm thus safeguards powerful people against the temptations of their own status; it motivates and regulates reciprocity as an exchange pattern, serving to inhibit the emergence of exploitative relations which would undermine the social system and the very power arrangements which had made exploitation possible.[44]

As we have seen, Parsons stresses that the stability of social systems largely derives from the *conformity* of role partners to each other's expectations, particularly when they do their duty to one another. This formulation induces a focus on conformity and deviance, and the degrees and types of each. Presumably, the more that people pay their social debts the more stable the social system. But much more than conformity and deviance are involved here.

The idea of the reciprocities complex leads us to the historical or genetic dimension of social interaction. For example, Malinowski, in his discussion of the Kula Ring, carefully notes that the gifts given are not immediately returned and repayment may take as long as a year. What is the significance of this intervening time period? It is a period governed by the norm of reciprocity in a double sense. First, the actor is accumulating, mobilizing, liquidating, or earmarking resources so that he can make a suitable re-

payment. Second, it is a period governed by the rule that you should not do harm to those who have done you a benefit. This is a time, then, when men are morally constrained to manifest their gratitude toward, or at least to maintain peace with, their benefactors.

Insofar as men live under such a rule of reciprocity, when one party benefits another, an obligation is generated. The recipient is now *indebted* to the donor, and he remains so until he repays. Once interaction is seen as taking place over time, we may note that the norm of reciprocity so structures social relations that, between the time of Ego's provision of a gratification and the time of Alter's repayment, falls the shadow of indebtedness. An adequate analysis of the dynamics of social interaction is thus required to go beyond the question of deviance from or conformity with the parties' obligations to one another. A second basic dimention needs to be examined systematically, namely, the time period when there is an obligation still to be performed, when commitments which have been made are yet to be fulfilled.

These outstanding obligations, no less than those already given compliance, contribute substantially to the stability of social systems. It is obviously inexpedient for creditors to break off relationships with those who have outstanding obligations to them. It may also be inexpedient for *debtors* to do so because their creditors may not again allow them to run up a bill of social indebtedness. In addition, it is *morally* improper, under the norm of reciprocity, to break off relations or to launch hostilities against those to whom you are still indebted.

If this conclusion is correct, then we should not only look for mechanisms which constrain or motivate men to do their duty and to pay off their debts. We should also expect to find mechanisms which induce people to *remain* socially indebted to each other and which *inhibit* their complete repayment. This suggests another function performed by the requirement of only *rough* equivalence of repayment that may be involved in one of the norms of reciprocity. For it induces a certain amount of ambiguity as to whether indebtedness has been repaid and, over time, generates uncertainty about who is in whose

---

[44] This line of analysis is further strengthened if we consider the possibility that Ego's continued conformity with Alter's expectations may eventually lead Alter to take Ego's conformity for "granted" and thus lead Alter to reciprocate less for later acts of conformity by Ego. In short, the value of Ego's conformity may undergo an inflationary spiral in which his later conforming actions are worth less than earlier ones, in terms of the reciprocities they yield. As reciprocities tend to decline, the social system may experience mounting strain, either collapsing in apathy or being disrupted by conflict. In this connection, the general norm of reciprocity may serve as a brake, slowing the rate at which reciprocities decline or preventing them from declining beyond a certain (unknown) level, and thus contributing to the stability of the system. This is more fully developed in A. W. Gouldner, "Organizational Analysis," in R. K. Merton *et al.*, editors, *Sociology Today*, New York: Basic Books, 1959, esp. pp. 423 ff.

debt.[45] This all hinges, however, on a shared conception of the moral propriety of repayment, engendered by the norm of reciprocity.

Still another way in which the general norm of reciprocity is implicated in the maintenance of social system stability is related to an important attribute of the norm, namely, its comparative indeterminancy. Unlike specific status duties and like other general norms, this norm does not require highly specific and uniform performances from people whose behavior it regulates. For example, unlike the status duties of American wives, it does not call upon them to cook and to take care of the children. Instead, the concrete demands it makes change substantially from situation to situation and vary with the benefits which one party receives from another.

This indeterminancy enables the norm of reciprocity to perform some of its most important system-stabilizing functions. Being indeterminate, the norm can be applied to countless *ad hoc* transactions, thus providing a flexible moral sanction for transactions which might not otherwise be regulated by specific status obligations. The norm, in this respect, is a kind of plastic filler, capable of being poured into the shifting crevices of

social structures, and serving as a kind of all-purpose moral cement.

Not only does the norm of reciprocity play a stabilizing role in human relations in the *absence* of a well developed system of specific status duties, but it contributes to social stability even when these are *present* and well established. Status duties shape behavior because the status occupant believes them binding in their own right; they possess a kind of *prima facie* legitimacy for properly socialized group members. The general norm of reciprocity, however, is a second-order defense of stability; it provides a further source of motivation and an additional moral sanction for conforming with specific status obligations. For example, the employer may pay his workers not merely because he has contracted to do so; he may also feel that the workman has earned his wages. The housewife may take pains with her husband's meals not merely because cooking may be incumbent on her as a wife; she may also have a particularly considerate husband. In each case, the specific status duties are complied with not only because they are inherent in the status and are believed to be right in themselves, but also because each is further defined as a *"repayment."* In sum, the norm of reciprocity requires that if others have been fulfilling their status duties to you, you in turn have an additional or second-order obligation (repayment) to fulfill your status duties to them. In this manner, the sentiment of gratitude joins forces with the sentiment of rectitude and adds a safety-margin in the motivation to conformity.

The matter can be put differently from the standpoint of potential deviance or non-conformity. All status obligations are vulnerable to challenge and, at times, may have to be justified. If, for any reason, people refuse to do their duty, those demanding compliance may be required to justify their claims. Obviously, there are many standardized ways in which this might be done. Invoking the general norm of reciprocity is one way of justifying the more concrete demands of status obligations. Forced to the wall, the man demanding his "rights," may say, in effect, "Very well, if you won't do this

---

[45] An interesting case of a mechanism serving to create and maintain outstanding obligations is part of the Vartan Bhanji, a form of ritual gift exchange in Pakistan and other parts of India. Eglar's study of this pattern makes it clear that a fundamental rule of Vartan Bhanji is reciprocity, that a gift should be returned for a gift, and a favor for a favor. It is also notable that the system painstakingly prevents the total elimination of outstanding obligations. Thus, on the occasion of a marriage, departing guests are given gifts of sweets. In weighing them out, the hostess may say, "These five are yours," meaning "these are a repayment for what you formerly gave me," and she then adds an extra measure, saying, "These are mine." On the next occasion, she will receive these back along with an additional measure which she later returns, and so on. See Z. E. Eglar, *Vartan Bhanji: Institutionalized Reciprocity in a Changing Punjab Village,* Ph.D. thesis, Columbia University, 1958.

Other mechanisms for maintaining outstanding obligations may be found in cultural prescriptions which require men not to be overly eager to repay their social obligations. It still seems to be understood that there is a certain impropriety in this, even if we do not go as far as Seneca in holding that "a person who wants to repay a gift too quickly with a gift in return is an unwilling debtor and an ungrateful person."

simply because it is your duty, then remember all that I have done for you in the past and do it to repay your debt to me." The norm of reciprocity thus provides a second-order defense of the stability of social systems in that it can be used to overcome incipient deviance and to mobilize auxiliary motivations for conformity with existent status demands.[46]

STARTING MECHANISMS

Two distinct points have been made about the social functions of the norm of reciprocity. One is that this norm serves a group *stabilizing* function and thus is quite familiar in functional theory. The second point, however, is the view that the norm is not only in some sense a defense or stabilizing mechanism but is also what may be called a "starting mechanism." That is, it helps to initiate social interaction and is functional in the early phases of certain groups before they have developed a differentiated and customary set of status duties.

In speaking of the norm of reciprocity as a "starting mechanism," indeed in conceiving of starting mechanisms, we find ourselves outside the usual perspective of functional theory. Functional theory commonly focuses on already-established, on-going systems, and on the mechanisms by means of which an established social system is enabled to maintain itself. Although functional theory is concerned with the problems of how individual actors are prepared by socialization to play a role in social systems, its general theoretical models rarely, if ever, include systematic treatment of the beginnings of a social system as such and, consequently, do not formally raise the question of the na-

ture of the mechanisms needed to start such a system.[47]

Every social system of course has a history, which means that it has had its beginnings even if these are shrouded in antiquity. Granted that the question of origins can readily bog down in a metaphysical morass, the fact is that many concrete social systems do have determinate beginnings. Marriages are not made in heaven, and whether they end in divorce or continue in bliss, they have some identifiable origins. Similarly, corporations, political parties, and all manner of groups have their beginnings. (Recent studies of friendship and other interpersonal relations in housing projects have begun to explore this problem.)

People are continually brought together in new juxtapositions and combinations, bringing with them the possibilities of new social systems. How are these possibilities realized? Is such realization entirely a random matter? These are the kinds of questions that were familiar to the earlier students of "collective behavior," who, in focusing on crowds, riots, and rumors, were often primarily concerned with investigating the development of groups in *statu nascendi*.[48] Although this perspective may at first seem somewhat alien to the functionalist, once it is put to him, he may suspect that certain kinds of mechanisms, conducive to the crystallization of social systems out of

---

[46] A cogent illustration of this is provided by William F. Whyte: "When life in the group runs smoothly, the obligations binding members are not explicitly recognized. . . . It is only when the relationship breaks down that the underlying obligations are brought to light. While Alec and Frank were friends I never heard either one of them discuss the services he was performing for the other, but when they had a falling out . . . each man complained to Doc that the other was not acting as he should in view of the services which had been done for him." *Street Corner Society,* Chicago: University of Chicago Press, 1945, p. 256.

[47] Modern functionalism emerged in a world in which Newtonian mechanics was the overshadowing scientific achievement and a basic model for the development of social science. The Newtonian standpoint was not, of course, a cosmology concerned with the question of planetary origins but took the existent relations among planets as given. Today, however, two developments of global significance encourage and perhaps require a shift in social perspectives. In one, rocket engineering, the question is raised as to how new, man-made, planets may be "shot" into stable orbits. Second, international politics require us to help "underdeveloped" countries to *begin* a beneficent cycle of capital accumulation which will be self-sustaining. In both instances, practical "engineering" problems forcefully direct attention to the question of "starting mechanisms" and would seem likely to heighten dissatisfaction with general sociological models that largely confine themselves to already established systems.

[48] I am indebted to Howard S. Becker for this and many other insights into what seemed to be the guiding impulses of the "Chicago School" of collective behavior.

ephemeral contacts, will in some measure be institutionalized or otherwise patterned in any society. At this point he would be considering "starting mechanisms." In this way, I suggest, the norm of reciprocity provides one among many starting mechanisms.

From the standpoint of a purely economic or utilitarian model,[49] there are certain difficulties in accounting for the manner in which social interaction begins. Let us suppose two people or groups, Ego and Alter, each possesses valuables sought by the other. Suppose further that each feels that the only motive the other has to conduct an exchange is the anticipated gratification it will bring. Each may then feel that it would be advantageous to lay hold of the other's valuables without relinquishing his own. Furthermore, suppose that each party suspects the other of precisely such an intention, perhaps because of the operation of projective or empathic mechanisms. At least since Hobbes, it has been recognized that under such circumstances, each is likely to regard the impending exchange as dangerous and to view the other with some suspicion.[50] Each may then hesitate to part with his valuables before the other has first turned his over. Like participants in a disarmament conference, each may say to other, "You first!" Thus the exchange may be delayed or altogether flounder and the relationship may be prevented from developing.

The norm of reciprocity may serve as a starting mechanism in such circumstances by preventing or enabling the parties to break out of this impasse. When internalized in both parties, the norm *obliges* the one who has first received a benefit to repay it at some time; it thus provides some realistic grounds for confidence, in the one who first parts with his valuables, that he will be repaid. Consequently, there may be less hesitancy in being the first and a greater facility with which the exchange and the social relation can get underway.

CONCLUSION

I have limited this discussion of the norm of reciprocity to its functions and its contribution to the stability of social systems, omitting examination of its dysfunctions and of the manner in which it induces tensions and changes in social systems. That the norm commonly imposes obligations of reciprocity only "when the individual is able" to reciprocate does not guarantee agreement concerning the individual's "ability." Furthermore, there may be occasions when questions as to whether the individual's return is appropriate or sufficient (apart from whether it is equivalent) that arise by virtue of the absence of common yardsticks in terms of which giving and returning may be compared. Moreover, the norm may lead individuals to establish relations only or primarily with those who can reciprocate, thus inducing neglect of the needs of those unable to do so. Clearly, the norm of reciprocity cannot apply with full force in relations with children, old people, or with those who are mentally or physically handicapped, and it is theoretically inferable that other, fundamentally different kinds of normative orientations will develop in moral codes. I hope to explore these and related problems in subsequent discussions.

[49] Some indications of the utilitarian approach to this problem may be derived from the stimulating paper by T. C. Schelling, "An Essay on Bargaining," *American Economic Review,* 46 (June, 1956), pp. 281–306.
[50] Cf. M. Deutsch, "A Study of Conditions Affecting Cooperation," New York: Research Center for Human Relations, 1955, p. 25, dittoed.

Conformity and Independence: A Psychological Analysis / Marie Jahoda

The rapidly growing psychological literature on conditions producing conformity raises a major new question: How is non-conformity possible? Curiosity about this question sets the stage for this paper.[1]

To be curious about the conditions under which independence occurs presupposes a belief in its existence. I admit to this belief, even though it receives small support from the literature. Not only is there widespread consensus among many diagnosticians of the climate of our times that this is an age of conformity; the relevant psychological literature is almost unanimous in its emphasis on conditions accounting for conformity. Actually, there is, of course, ample evidence for the existence of independence not only in common-sense observations but also in every single experiment which rejects the null-hypothesis of independence on statistically impressive levels of confidence. There is a tacit implication in many of these experiments that those insubordinate subjects who are outside the hypothesis-confirming majority are a nuisance. The fewer there are of them, the less said about them, the better. Unless, of course, one can think of an additional experimentally manipulable variable which will bring the recalcitrants into line. Concern with statistical significance has, to be sure, helped to increase immeasurably the level of rigour in psychological thought; but it also has at least one undesirable consequence: it threatens to interfere with the general task of psychology which is to understand human behaviour, and not merely the behaviour of majorities, however large or significant.

In any case, I submit that it makes psychological sense to speak of nonconformity, and hence to inquire into the conditions which make it possible.

Reprinted from *Human Relations,* 1959, 12, pages 99–120, by permission of author and publisher, Tavistock Publications, Ltd.

[1] Thanks are due to my colleagues Isidor Chein, Stuart W. Cook, and George S. Klein whose constructive suggestions and cogent criticisms helped me in the writing of this paper.

I shall have to take a lengthy detour before I come to terms with this question, and it may at times appear that I am running away from it rather than moving toward it. Let me, therefore, first briefly outline the route I propose to follow:

I will first examine the proposition that conformity versus non-conformity is a meaningless dichotomy which has been created by social value biases, and which defies the principle of determinism in human behaviour.

Next, I will examine some aspects of the contemporary psychological literature on conformity and identify the major types of variables which have been demonstrated to produce conformity.

This examination will lead to the identification of several distinct social-psychological processes which are frequently lumped together under the label of conformity or independence.

Finally, I shall try to formulate some tentative answers to the major question: How is non-conformity possible?

I. IS THE DISTINCTION BETWEEN CONFORMITY AND NON-CONFORMITY VALID?

There is an easy general answer to this question: it all depends on what is meant by conformity. No doubt. But as one looks into the meaning given to the term in various contexts, matters become more difficult. In the current debate on political conformity, confusion is great because the term conformity is contaminated by value judgements on the issue with regard to which conformity is diagnosed. On that level, 'good' and 'bad' or 'right' and 'wrong' are often used synonymously with 'independent' and 'conforming'.

On a barely more sophisticated level, those who agree with the majority are called conformists, those who agree with the minority independents. For example, we learn from Stouffer's study (55), that the majority of the adult population think that a communist should not be permitted to be a sales clerk. Personally, I am convinced that most of the people adhering to this opinion actually are conformists, at least in this respect. But to prove the point by reference to the size of the majority is committing 'high treason: to be right for the wrong reason'.

On a higher level of insight, conformity is regarded as the reduction of diversity through social influence processes. But it is on this more sophisticated level where value and majority views are discarded as criteria that serious doubts arise about the wisdom of the distinction between independence and conformity. In the political and cultural debate Trilling has used gentle but none the less devastating mockery to show that when value judgments and deviations from majority opinions are rejected as criteria of non-conformity, nothing much but conformity remains. In his essay on *Freud and the Crisis of our Culture* (56) he says:

'The American educated middle class is firm in its admiration of non-conformity and dissent. The right to be non-conformist, the right to dissent, is part of our conception of community. Everybody says so: in the weekly, monthly, quarterly magazines, and in the *New York Times*, at the cocktail party, at the conference of psychiatrists, at the conference of teachers. How good that is, and how right! And yet, when we examine the content of our idea of non-conformity, we must be dismayed at the smallness of the concrete actuality this very large idea contains. The rhetoric is as sincere as it is capacious, yet we must sometimes wonder whether what is being praised and defended is anything more than the right to have had some sympathetic connection with Communism ten or twenty years ago. Men of principle have opposed reactionary tendencies in our society and some have taken risks in their opposition, but for most of us our settled antagonism to that instance of reactionary tendency we call McCarthyism is simply the badge of our class. Our imagination of dissent from our culture can scarcely go beyond this. We cannot really imagine non-conformity at all, not in art, not in moral or social theory, certainly not in the personal life—it is probably true that there never was a culture which required so entire an eradication of personal differentiation, so bland a uniformity of manner. Admiring non-conformity and loving community, we have decided that we are all non-conformists together.

Trilling exempts from the general charge of conformity 'men of principle'. There is no doubt that Trilling approves of them; or that they are in a small minority; or that they are not just conforming to non-conformity. There is a mere suggestion in the passage that some crucial other factor is involved in their behaviour. If we can identify this crucial factor in a man of principle, we may be nearer to a useful distinction between independence and conformity. Perhaps an example will help. I have chosen one from Senator Kennedy's book *Profiles in Courage* (40).

It is the case of Senator Edmund G. Ross of Kansas. In 1868 in the frenzied aftermath of the Civil War, impeachment proceedings were brought against President Andrew Johnson. A two-thirds majority of the Senate was necessary to confirm the impeachment vote of the House of Representatives. The Republicans—Ross was a Republican—had brought the charges. They needed 36 votes; they were sure of 35. Ross's vote was to be decisive. Every conceivable pressure was brought to bear on him. His residence was watched; his social associations were suspiciously scrutinized; his political career was at stake; a fearful avalanche of telegrams came from his constituents and from people in other parts of the country; his party and the press cajoled, bribed, and threatened. Senator Ross later on described the moment of voting: 'I almost literally looked down into my open grave. Friendships, position, fortune, everything that makes life desirable to an ambitious man were about to be swept away by the breath of my mouth, perhaps forever. It is not strange that my answer was carried waveringly over the air and failed to reach the limits of the audience, or that repetition was called for by distant Senators on the opposite side of the Chamber.' But the answer was 'not guilty'. Several others who had been undecided when impeachment proceedings first started had also been exposed to severe pressure. Their vote was 'guilty'. Senator Edmund Ross manifested what most people would regard as independent behaviour. What is the psychological variable which distinguishes him from others who started off with the same hesitation and were subjected to the same pressures, but yielded in the end?

To say that other forces were stronger than the external pressure is certainly not a satisfactory answer. What other forces? Two types of explanatory concept come to mind: the impact of an absent reference group and some enduring personality characteristic. Let us consider the adequacy of each.

The unsatisfactory nature of the reference group concept lies in the fact that, unless we are very careful, it leads to a sort of reductionist thinking which can do away with the distinction between Ross and his colleagues. At least, this can be concluded from Cooley's discussion, some 50 years ago, of conformity and non-conformity (12). The non-conformist, he says, is the one who seems to be out of step with the procession because he is keeping time to another music. Cooley calls this behaviour 'remote conformity', and concludes that 'there is, therefore, no definite line between conformity and non-conformity; there is simply a more or less characteristic and unusual way of selecting and combining accessible influences'. In other words, we are back at assuming fundamentally similar events in conformist and independent behaviour. This is not to imply that this reduction of independence to conformity is illogical or impossible; on the contrary, it is tantamount to asserting that all human behaviour is determined. Nor do I deny the valuable sensitizing function that the more current term 'reference group behaviour' has for social-psychological work. All I want to emphasize is that if one is interested in specifying the *difference* between Ross and his colleagues, one does not want to commit oneself too readily to a viewpoint which may lead to the conclusion that they are basically alike.

What about personality characteristics as a decisive variable to account for the difference? Terms like ego-strength, superego, sense of security, or more superficially stubbornness and the like suggest themselves. To be sure, it would be of great help to have a Rorschach, an MMPI, or a TAT of Ross, or of somebody committing an equally independent action, just as it would be useful to know his reference groups. But I am doubtful whether such personality measures would give us a fully satisfactory answer. On the most concrete level my doubt stems from what Kennedy says about Ross's personality which he presents, of course, not in psychological terms. Ross's own description of his faltering voice at the dramatic moment does not suggest a personality free from anxiety or happy in defying the world. In other less dramatic situations he occasionally demonstrated independence, occasionally conformity.

In more general terms, the problem then is, which among the numerous possible approaches to personality yields the best tool for predicting conforming behaviour? The very fact that one and the same person conforms on some occasions but not on others, even though the results of psychodiagnostic testing must be assumed to be identical on both occasions, raises doubt as to the help such tests can provide for the task. Again, I should limit my heresy: this is not to say that psychodiagnostic measures are invalid. All I wish to say is that as far as I understand their rationale they are after more or less enduring attributes of a person. These attributes are modifiable by external factors, and do not necessarily win the day, as Tolstoy already sensed when he wrote in *Resurrection*:

> 'One of the most widespread superstitions is that every man has his own special qualities; that a man is kind, cruel, wise, stupid, energetic, apathetic, etc. Men are not like that. We may say of a man that he is more often kind than cruel, more often wise than stupid, more often energetic than apathetic, or the reverse . . . Every man carries in himself the germs of every human quality, and sometimes one manifests itself; sometimes another, and the man often becomes unlike himself, while still remaining the same man.'

Tolstoy implies that situational factors can prove so powerful that they break through habitual response patterns. To be sure, Tolstoy did not deny the power of enduring attributes of the personality either. He explicitly recognizes it in the phrase 'remaining the same man'. But remaining the same man in what respect? Surely not only as a physical organism; and equally surely not in overt behaviour. Tolstoy suggests it is not traits. Is it the psychodynamics underlying behaviour and traits? Is the basic organization of motives, as Chein (10) suggests, or are cognitive controls, as George Klein (41) suggests, the best indicator of what remained the same in Senator Ross while he was first a respected member of the Republican party and then a rebel? Clinical psychology will have to teach us in what the identifiable sameness consists which a person carries from one situation to the other.

But the possible types of answer to the question as to what remains the same in a man as he moves from one situation to the other do not yet promise help in predicting conforming behaviour. For none of the alternatives mentioned above promises to discriminate between the situations in which persons like Senator Ross choose to conform or not to conform.

R. Bendix (5) draws attention to this power of a person to make choices. People can respond to an external factor, he states, either because or in spite of their personality predisposition. On both counts one and the same enduring personality attribute may— under unspecified conditions—be related either to acceptance or to resistance of external influences. A person with a strong ego, for example, may conform to a majority view of his colleagues but not to the political climate of his times. If his job is at stake he may act in accordance with his convictions, or against them.

Thus far the explanatory concepts which I have examined as possible major determinants of independent or conforming behaviour have not proved adequate. But, perhaps, the difficulty lies less with these concepts than with the fact that the phenomenon which they are supposed to explain has not been sufficiently clarified. Let us consider Senator Ross again for a lead as to the characteristics of the special type of behaviour in which he engaged.

From Kennedy's description (only briefly summarized here) it becomes clear that *the most significant matter in his action was that he cared very much about the issue at stake.*

To be sure, he had a reference group, he was a 'remote conformist', or, if you will, he conformed to his own conscience. To be sure, he had a strong ego. But these enduring personality attributes came into play against overwhelming pressures only because he really cared about the impeachment issue. This condition—the close link between a person and an object in the external world (object, because the issue existed independent of Senator Ross's existence)—permitted him to act as he did. For this process, the term ego-involvement suggests itself. Some of its connotations, however, make it not entirely appropriate: the emphasis on ego implies a contrast to, or an exclusion of, other aspects of the personality. As one reconstructs in imagination Senator Ross's experience it becomes quite clear that the entire personality organization of the man was related to the issue. Not only his mind or his ego; but intense emotional forces and conflicts were involved. For this affective and rational link between a person and an object, psycho-analysis uses the term cathexis.

Recently, the term cathexis has been introduced into systematic social-science thinking. In the introductory statement to the book *Toward a General Theory of Action,* all the contributors to the volume agree to call the 'tendency to react positively or negatively to objects the cathectic mode of orientation. Cathexis, the attachment to objects which are gratifying and rejection of those which are noxious, lies at the root of the selective nature of action.' And somewhat later: 'The term cathexis is broader . . . than affect. It is affect plus object.'

In the psycho-analytic literature the term is used in various ways, and the underlying concept not clearly defined. This is why I shall only note in passing the similarity to cathexis of what I regard as a crucial and critical attribute of independent behaviour. Here, I shall rather use the term *emotional and intellectual investment in the issue.*

One advantage of regarding such central investment in an issue as a necessary attribute of what is widely but vaguely meant by independent behaviour, lies in the fact that it immediately helps us to clarify the universal diagnosis of conformity in our public life. There, the question should perhaps be reformulated to the effect of asking: have people lost the ability to develop such investments in issues or is the general diagnosis based on the fact that the types of issue which provoke investment have changed? Both questions could be empirically answered without leading to a confusion about implicit value judgements or to the untenable over-simplification that independent behaviour is identical with agreeing with a minority, conforming behaviour with agreeing with a majority.

To regard emotional and intellectual investment in an issue as an attribute of independence, and its absence as an attribute of conformity, implies a shift from a unidimensional description of the phenomenon to a more complex notion, which I will elaborate later on. Before doing so, it is appropriate to turn to the experimental literature on conformity.

To the extent that the experimental literature is largely limited to manipulating conditions of influence with regard to matters in which the individual has no investment, it now becomes understandable why we know in psychology so much more about conformity than about independence. What actually do we know about conformity?

II. A SURVEY OF RESEARCH ON SOME ASPECTS OF CONFORMITY

The operational criterion of conformity which underlies most empirical research on the topic is the private and/or public agreement of an individual with an opinion which he had not held before it was presented to him. The existence of this phenomenon is, of course, the basis of all human society and undoubtedly accounts for the direction of the overwhelming majority of all human behaviour. Sherif's early experiment on the autokinetic effect (53) and Blake's experiments (7), which ingeniously use real-life settings in a controlled manner, have demonstrated that when people are exposed to social influences they tend to yield to them. Whether you want to call this conformity or trust in others is a terminological question which I want to avoid at this point. The ubiquity of conforming behaviour has also

been demonstrated from a different point of view by Barker and Wright (4) in their ecological studies of the behaviour of children in the Middle West. Barker and Wright state that 95 per cent of the behaviour of children during an ordinary day is determined by behaviour settings in which they find themselves. They define a behaviour setting as a locale for role performance which has the quality of eliciting largely similar responses from persons who find themselves in that locale; the corner drugstore, for example, is a behaviour setting. It is reasonable to expect that a similar proportion of adult behaviour is also so regulated.

These demonstrations that conformity is indeed the rule make, at least by implication, another point of interest: persons who do not thus conform show some deficiency or deviation from the normal. The point has been made explicitly in a number of recent experimental studies with psychoneurotics and schizophrenics. Such persons do not show the general trend toward conforming behaviour that others demonstrate. Hovland, Janis, and Kelley (28), for example, say that 'persons with acute psychoneurotic symptoms are predisposed to be resistant to persuasive communications'. Levine and colleagues (42) repeated the autokinetic experiments with neurotics, whom they found to be less influenced by group judgements than non-neurotics. Sarbin and Hardyck (51) found perceptual conformance negatively correlated with schizophrenia. Anybody who has ever visited a mental hospital will find his observations there in complete accord with these experimental findings. Non-conformity in this sense is sometimes indeed the first indication of incipient mental disease.

The point to be kept in mind here is that it may be reasonable to distinguish first between ability and inability to conform. Those who are able to conform may then be further studied as to whether they also have the ability not to conform—for example, whether their conforming behaviour expresses a compulsive need to go along with the opinions of others or whether the ability can be used discriminatingly in a variety of circumstances. The experimental literature is mainly concerned with specifying these circumstances.

It is convenient to discuss the available empirical research under the following headings: *inducing agent; situational context; reference group behaviour and group membership; personality predispositions; variations in issues; types of response.*

Inducing Agents

By inducing agent I mean both the source of the opinion to which experimental subjects finally agree and the nature and manner of presentation of this opinion. The most systematic series of studies here are the Yale studies. Among other things we learn from them that sources of high credibility have a greater immediate effect in producing conformity of opinion than sources of low credibility; the difference tends to disappear, however, with time.

As to the nature of the communication, the Yale group distinguishes between arguments on the one hand, and rewards or punishment on the other. Their published experiments, as far as I know, have not tried to combine these two types of variable in one experiment. Rather, variations have been tested within each type. With regard to the arguments, they have established that if the conclusions of an argument are explicitly presented, the communication will result in greater conformity if the issue is very complex and if the audience is on an intellectually relatively low level.

With regard to the reward-punishment variables their experiments on different degrees of fear-arousing appeals are relevant. They suggest that a moderate amount of fear-appeal is probably more successful in producing conformity than a high amount.

Other studies on the inducing agent have frequently utilized group opinions as the agent. Goldberg (21), for example, experimented with the size of the group which presents the opinion to which subjects conform. He found that 'the degree of conformity to groups of four is not different from the degree of conformity to groups of two'. Asch (1) likewise found that the conformity effect was not increased by enlarging the number of group members. Both authors also varied the number of exposures to group opinion

divergent from individual opinion and found, by and large, that conformity occurs within the first few exposures. Additional exposures do not increase the conformity effect significantly.

Kelman (37) used an authority figure with seventh-grade students in an effort to get them to conform. Two conditions were compared: high and low pressure to conform. In the high-pressure group it was made clear to the children that they were to write an essay agreeing with the authority figure. In the low-pressure group it was explained that although the best agreeing essays would be rewarded, non-agreement was quite permissible. He found that the high-pressure group showed more immediate conformity in their essays, but less attitude change as separately ascertained. Here, we come across for the first time the important distinction between private and public conformity which has been made in many other experiments. The finding that low pressure from the inducing agent has more enduring conformity effects than high pressure agrees with the Yale fear-appeal studies, as well as with a number of other investigations. Jerome Frank (18), for example, also came to the conclusion that low pressure and a step-by-step approach were more effective than high pressure in having people accept the demand of the experimenter.

In the light of such consensus it is particularly interesting that some studies show greater conformity effects in response to high pressure. Festinger, for example (16), reports high pressure as being most effective. There are, of course, many non-experimental observations and studies which support Festinger. Galileo would certainly not have yielded to anything but the stake. Some federal employees in their excessive self-imposed restrictions (22) would not have yielded to anything but the threat of loss of their jobs and the danger of not finding new ones. The whole notion of a 'breaking-point' for all stress experiences also is in line with the statement that the higher the pressure, the higher the degree of conformity. I believe that these apparently contradictory results could be reconciled if we distinguished behaviour on an issue according to the degree of cathexis of that issue, and in terms of several other qualifications which will be introduced later.

Another variable that has been used when groups are the inducing agent is the attractiveness of the group to the member or the liking he has for it. Bovard (8), for example, finds that leader-centred groups are less effective in inducing conformity than group-centred groups. Since liking for the group was greater in the latter, he suggests that this is a major factor in producing conformity to group norms. Back (2) confirms this point explicitly: the more cohesive a group, the greater its influence on opinions of members. In the same vein, the Yale studies conclude that 'persons who are most highly motivated to maintain their membership [in groups] tend to be most susceptible to influence by other members within the group'.

There are many other studies demonstrating the power of the group to induce conformity. Deutsch and Gerard (14) criticize some of this work in pointing out that in several of these experiments the presence of others is regarded as tantamount to the existence of a group. They distinguish conceptually between inducing agents which exercise a normative social influence, i.e. an influence to conform with the positive expectations of another, and those which exercise an informational social influence, i.e. the acceptance of information from another as evidence. Their experimental work does not actually compare the relative impact of these two types of influence. On the basis of their theorizing, however, they hypothesize and find that social influences produce more conformity in individuals forming a group than in an aggregation of unrelated persons; that the effect will be less under conditions of anonymity or when no pressure from others is perceived; that social influence to conform to one's own judgement will reduce the impact of influence to conform to that of others; and that a personal commitment to conform to one's own judgment is strengthened when supported by another person.

Situational Context

Most experimental studies are, as we all know and deplore, conducted among college students. But some have made efforts to use groups of other kinds: high-school students, youth groups, airmen, navy draftees, officers, industrial managers, etc. The effort of many investigators goes in the direction of working in 'realistic' situational contexts. But there is relatively little comparative work on conformity behaviour of the same individual in different situations. Situational contexts vary mostly in the degree of artificiality of the situation used for experimental purposes. Comparisons here are difficult because of the difference in methodology and criteria used.

It might be pointed out here that survey-type research has used the most realistic settings. Stouffer's study on *Conformity, Communism and Civil Liberties* (55) shows, for example, a higher degree of conformity with regard to current political pressures in the population at large than in the leadership of voluntary organizations. Jahoda and Cook (31), in their exploratory study of the impact of the loyalty and security measures on federal employees, also suggest a high degree of conformity to current pressures; in addition they raise the hypothesis that situations in which there is emotional and factual support from colleagues and superiors, and where the group atmosphere is frank and trusting, lead to *less* conformity with the general climate of opinion than do reverse conditions. Altogether, however, we know less about variations in situational contexts than about variations in the inducing agent.

Reference Group Behaviour and Group Membership

A number of investigators have drawn attention to the importance of an individual's reference groups as a factor related to the tendency to conform. The Yale group (28), for example, mentions the salience of group norms as a matter of importance in producing conformity. The findings among Catholic high-school students, for whom Catholicism was made salient by giving them pre-experimentally Catholic material to read, suggest 'that the use of contents which arouse awareness of a reference group can have a marked effect on the audience's tendency to accept or reject the recommended opinion'. However, the authors add: 'The absence of a similar effect for the college students raises some question as to whether the phenomenon is a general one or occurs only for persons who are strongly attached to a group but have relatively little understanding of its norms.' In his analysis of juvenile delinquency among lower-class gangs, Albert K. Cohen (11) uses—at least by implication—also the power of a reference group as an explanatory factor for conformity. Delinquency becomes a possible solution to the juvenile's life problems only to the extent that his gang, i.e. his reference group, shares his values and norms. The same point has been made fifteen hundred years ago by St. Augustine (50) when he explains a pear-stealing episode he was involved in as a lad in terms of his membership in a group.

In general, these findings raise the question as to the conditions under which different reference groups become factors in determining opinions. As far as I know, this central question of reference group theory has not yet been tackled in research. As a rule, the concept is used as if the individual had only one group with whom he shared norms, namely the one deliberately built into the research design.

Kelley and Woodruff (35) indicate that opinions that were perceived as being expressed by a reference group, even when these opinions contradicted the expected norms of the group, had a profound influence on an individual's stand. The investigators are careful to point out that conforming to such opinions is only one way of dealing with the situation; another is to reinterpret the unexpected opinion of the reference group.

In a sense, the status of an individual in a group can also be regarded under this heading. Kelley and Shapiro (34) have experimented with this variable in a group situation where conformity was detrimental to the goals of the group. They found that the persons most secure in their group membership, that is those who were liked best by the others, were more likely to deviate from the norm than members who were less acceptable to the others.

Personality Predispositions

There are a number of studies dealing with personality predispositions to conformity. Janis (32) states that persons with low self-esteem tend to be more readily influenced than others. On the other hand, he finds, in line with what was previously described as inability to conform, that persons with acute symptoms of neurotic anxiety tend to conform less. Hoffman (26) finds that conformity has an anxiety-reducing function for compulsive conformists, i.e. those whose conformity is based on non-rational needs to agree with one's peer group. He distinguishes from this compulsive conformity conformity based on such realistic factors as external pressure, greater task-relevant information or skills on the part of other group members, etc. Interestingly he finds no difference in the frequency of conformity behaviour, whether compulsive or realistic conformity is involved. Hoffman's findings on the anxiety-reducing function of conformity are in line with Riesman's idea that anxiety is the self-inflicted punishment for non-conformity in other-directed persons (49).

Crutchfield's (13) findings on personality correlates of conformity show authoritarian attitudes and behaviour to be positively correlated with conformity, a conclusion which agrees with those in *The Authoritarian Personality*. The independent person he finds to have more intellectual effectiveness, ego-strength, leadership ability, and maturity in social relations, together with a conspicuous absence of inferiority feelings, of rigid and excessive self-control, and of authoritarian attitudes. More elaborate is Barron's list of personality differences between conformists and non-conformists (3) : 'Independents and Yielders were found to be equally stable in personality, but *do* differ in their values and self-descriptions. Independents see themselves primarily as original, emotional, and artistic; Yielders characterize themselves as obliging, optimistic, efficient, determined, patient, and kind. Yielders tend to be practical-minded, somewhat physicalistic in their thinking, and group-oriented; Independents placed higher values on creativity, close inter-personal relations, and the individual as opposed to the group.' Goldberg (20) suggests a hypothesis on cognitive functioning to account for variations in conformity. He assumes that the individual performs some sort of probability calculation as to the likelihood that one's own or the other person's judgement is correct, and acts in the light of the outcome.

On the perceptual level, Harriet Linton finds certain styles of perception related to a tendency to conform (44). She says: 'The tendency for behaviour to be modified by an external stimulus regardless of whether the external stimulus is personal or impersonal in nature, is a function of enduring attributes of the person; consequently, subjects whose performance in perceptual tasks is highly affected by the perceptual field will be those whose behaviour in other situations is most likely to be modified so as to conform to an external standard.'

It is beyond question that all these results are meaningful on some level of human functioning. But in the light of the preceding analysis of the distinction between independence and conformity, it is still an open question how they bear on our central problem here, i.e. on the relation of independence and conformity to the significance of the issue for a person. It is interesting to note that hardly any of the studies reported so far concern themselves with the nature of the issue on which independence or conformity is observed apart from mentioning it in the description of procedures, let alone with the relation of the individual to that issue, emotionally and intellectually invested or otherwise. It is hence with particular curiosity that one turns to what is known from current research about the effects of variation in the issue.

Variations in the Issue

Crutchfield (13), in his elaboration of the Asch experiments, varied systematically the nature of the problem on which conformity or independence was observed. He used perceptual judgements, logical solutions, vocabulary, attitudes, opinions, preferences for ornamental designs, etc. In the course of his experiments he told the group immediately after each judgement what the 'right' answer was. Actually, the experimenter reinforced as 'right' the pretended group consensus on the wrong answer. The effect of this additional pressure was striking in increasing the group's conformity behaviour. But there is an exception to this regularity. As Crutch-

field states: 'The enhanced power of the group does *not* carry over to increase the influence on expression of opinions and attitudes. The subjects exposed to this "correction" method (the experimenter's false announcement of the "right" answer) do not exhibit greater conformity to group pressure on opinion and attitudes than that found in other subjects.' In other words, the information about the 'right' answer was effective only on those items where 'right' answers were possible. Crutchfield's speculation on this result is interesting, even though I question whether his emphasis on the rational element alone gives the full picture. He says:

'This crucial finding throws some light on the nature of the psychological processes involved in the conformity situation. For it seems to imply that conformity behaviour under such group pressure, rather than being solely an indiscriminate and irrational tendency to defer to the authority of the group, has in it important rational elements. There is something of a reasonable differentiation made by the individual. He may be led to accept the superiority of the judgement of the group on matters where there is an objective frame of reference against which the group can be checked. But he does not, thereby, automatically accept the group's superiority on matters of a less objective sort. To some degree, therefore, it can be argued that the individual is functioning with respect to his group in a manner which strikes a sensible balance by sometimes making relevant use of the group's judgements as a resource in his own judgements, without at the same time becoming indiscriminately dependent upon the group's judgements in all matters.'

'The sensible balance' which the individual sometimes strikes between his own judgement and the judgement of the group raises a crucial question: When is 'sometimes'? Surely 'sometimes' cannot mean when attitudes and opinions are involved. Most other studies have, after all, established conformity with regard to attitudes and opinions. Unless we can find an approach to an answer to this question, this important qualification makes us doubt whether we actually know as much about conformity as the literature suggests.

It should be noted that Luchins (45) in a

relatively early study already pointed to related ideas. He used children 11 to 13 years of age as subjects in the interpretation of ambiguous drawings. A confederate's answer preceded the subject's response. The children tended to see what the confederate said when the drawing left enough scope for ambiguity. But when the drawing presented a clearly structured object, subjects tended to remain independent of the confederate's pronouncement.

The Asch experiments themselves (1) implicitly make a contribution to the question 'When is sometimes?' This series of experiments is outstanding in several ways, but particularly in relation to one point which, perhaps, Asch himself has not sufficiently emphasized. In addition to the conventional statistical treatment of the variations in his basic design, there is hidden in his data a perfect correlation of $+1$, a result of 100 per cent, which it will be admitted, is a rarity in psychological research. The implicit result I refer to is the creation of intense conflict in all his experimental subjects. The evidence for this result comes from the interviews Asch conducted with all his subjects after the experiment.

But how is this related to the question of the issue on which conformity and independence were observed? As you know, the issue in the Asch experiments was a perceptual judgement on length of lines. Disagreement by the group on these judgements produced intense conflicts in the individuals because reliance on one's perceptual judgement is the deeply anchored basis of all our relations to the world around us. Woodworth, as quoted by Hilgard (24), has made the point: 'To see, to hear—to see clearly, to hear distinctly—to make out what it is one is seeing or hearing—moment by moment, such concrete, immediate motives dominate the life of relation with the environment.' And Hilgard conjectures 'that perceptual goals are intimately related to the other goals of the learner. The basic reason for achieving a stable world is that such a world is the most convenient one in which to satisfy our needs.' Much in line with these statements is Festinger's (16) statement on a basic human motive, to know one's environment and to know oneself. He speaks of 'a motiva-

tion in the human organism to hold *correct* opinions, beliefs and ideas about the world in which he lives and to know *precisely* what his abilities enable him to do in this world'.

In any case, these statements demonstrate that there is reason to believe that the Asch situation attacked an immensely cathected issue for the individual. Hence the universality of deep conflict in his subjects and the curious fact that, notwithstanding the strength of the pressure, only about one-third of all subjects yielded, though the percentage of yielders is as a rule much greater in other experiments on other issues. Nevertheless, there are, even under these conditions, differences in responses.

Occasionally, the judgement as to the relevance or importance of an issue is made in terms of the investigator's judgement rather than in psychological terms from the point of view of the acting person. This leads to confusions of the following kind. In discussing the psychology of voting, Lipset and colleagues (45) say: 'We do know, in a general way, that decisions which are not ego-involved are more easily influenced from the outside, a fact which explains the great success of commercial advertising as compared with the failure of many campaigns to improve race relations or attitudes toward international issues.' The implication is clear that the general population is assumed to be ego-involved with international issues and not with the goods offered in advertising campaigns. Of course, the opposite is the case. Housewives care very much about coffee and very little about our relations with China. I shall try to clear up this confusion later on.

Types of Response

Many investigators have, of course, been aware of the variety of behaviours which are commonly called conformity, and have accordingly tried to distinguish between them. The most frequent distinction is that between private and public conformity. On a basis of statements by Lewin (43) and research by French (19), Festinger (15) has conceptualized this distinction. He summarizes the major points of a theory of compliant behaviour thus: '1. Public compliance without private acceptance will occur if the person in question is restrained from leaving the situation and if there is a threat of punishment for noncompliance. 2. Public compliance with private acceptance will occur if there is a desire on the part of the person to remain in the existing relationship with those attempting to influence him.' These generalizations are true for some people in some circumstances. Not for all, of course. It is easy enough to imagine a situation where public compliance without private acceptance occurs where one wishes to remain in the existing relation with those attempting to influence one. For example, a person may wish to remain on good terms with a friend. Just because of this wish he complies publicly with a statement by his friend, even though he privately regards it as unsound.

This is, of course, not to say that the distinction between private and public acceptance is unimportant. On the contrary: it is of crucial significance. But its importance derives more from viewing it in conjunction with cathexis to the issue than in conjunction with group membership. Note, for example, the remarkable challenge to social psychologists offered by such historical episodes as that of the Marrano Jews in Spain who, for almost five centuries, maintained secret adherence to Judaism while publicly adhering to the Roman Catholic faith—a situation which, to say the least, gives us some perspective about the magnitude of the effects we are able to create experimentally.

Another distinction made by Hoffman (26) between compulsive and realistic conformity has already been mentioned. Brodbeck and colleagues (9) also speak of two kinds of conformity: conformity to the individual's standards and conformity to others. This distinction within the concept of conformity leads to a reductionism unsuitable for our purposes here, as suggested earlier in connection with Cooley's 'remote conformity'.

More recently another type of distinction has been introduced, which is based on the realization that one and the same outcome of a social influence can be the result of a variety of processes. Kelley (33), for example, has developed a scheme to deal with the fact of resistance to efforts of persua-

sion. Using as an example Kendall and Wolf's (39) ingenious analysis of resistance to the message in the Mr Biggot's cartoon series, he has suggested that resistance can come about through distortion or misunderstanding of content, through cognitive restructuring (in line with Asch's position in his discussion of the suggestion literature), or through changing interpretations of the inducing agent or his social prestige.

When the phenomenon to be explained is not resistance but conformity several authors have also distinguished separate processes. Asch speaks of conformity to a rule, either because a person is convinced that the rule is right, or because it is the thing that everybody does, or because it is dangerous not to observe that rule. Kelman (36) has elaborated on three processes which he calls internalization, identification, and compliance. In an earlier paper I (30) have distinguished four processes, three of which correspond to Asch's and Kelman's distinctions: consentience, roughly corresponding to Asch's conviction and Kelman's internalization; conformance, corresponding to Asch's 'what-everybody-does' and Kelman's identification; compliance, corresponding to Asch's 'it-is-dangerous-not-to-conform' and Kelman's identical term. The fourth, convergence, is a sort of strategy an individual uses in going along for the sake of other related consequences.

All three authors have made it clear that the distinctions between these processes are necessary for understanding the different meaning of conformity behaviour. Kelman and Jahoda have stated that the consequences of conformity vary for each process, as do the conditions under which they can be changed.

III. CONFORMITY AND INDEPENDENCE: A COMPLEX CRITERION

In the light of the foregoing remarks it must be obvious that I have some doubts whether the customary operational criterion by which independence is distinguished from conformity—agreement or disagreement with a presented opinion not previously held by the individual—is the best possible criterion in efforts to extend our knowledge in the area. This criterion is at the root of the confusion in the public debate on the subject. It has led only to partial understanding, and, I believe, cannot stand up under logical or psychological scrutiny. I have tried to show that the inadequacy of the agreement

ence has been brought to bear on these people, some adhere to their old position, some have changed. What has happened?

A combination of these three dimensions— dichotomized for purposes of simplicity —yields eight distinguishable processes, as follows:

Types of Conformity and Independence

Initial investment in issue			Yes				No	
Adoption of advocated position		No		Yes		No		Yes
Private opinion differs from public opinion	No	Yes	No	Yes	No	Yes	No	Yes
Designation of process	a	b	c	d	e	f	g	h

criterion stems from the fact that one and the same position taken by different individuals can have completely different meaning, that is, different antecedents, different contexts, and different consequences. If this is correct, the classification of persons according to this unidimensional criterion or the study of factors related to it must lead into a blind alley. Position-taking on an issue in which the individual has intellectual and emotional investment is psychologically so different a process from position-taking on an issue which is not so invested, that they must be assumed to manifest different regularities. If this is granted, then the first task, obviously, is to specify the dimensions which have to enter into a criterion distinguishing these different processes.

Though I have particularly emphasized the investment in an issue, a relatively neglected aspect in research, the review of the literature makes it clear that at least two further dimensions need to be taken note of: the actual position arrived at by an individual under the impact of social influences, and a qualification of this position corresponding to the distinction between private and public opinion on the issue.

Let us keep a concrete example in mind, say the position of people on the issue of capital punishment. Let us assume that, before some external influence is brought to bear, the people we are interested in all take the position implied in the law of the land that capital punishment is proper punishment for certain crimes. After some influ-

It remains to be seen whether these eight logical possibilities are also psychological possibilities. Processes a–d occur in persons who have an emotional and intellectual investment in the issue of capital punishment. It had a place in their life space with some salience even before the campaign started. Process a designates a person who, though reached by the campaign, does not change his mind, and is at ease with himself about the final position he takes. This is *independent dissent.*

Process b implies a person who adheres to his original position but feels less comfortable with it than he used to. Publicly he gives the impression of independence; but privately the influence process has undermined his stand. He experiences conflict. The nonyielders in the Asch experiment who continued to say what they saw but developed doubts about their eyesight are an example to the point. This position may be called *undermined independence.*

Process c describes a person who changed his mind as a result of the pressures in the campaign. He emerges from the internal turmoil in which the realization that others disagree with him may have thrown him into a changed position with which he is again completely at ease. To make this plausible in the light of his investment in the issue we must assume that he has restructured the manner in which he sees the issue. For example, he may have thought about capital punishment in relation to the nature of the crime. Challenged by public pressure, he may have re-examined the arguments against capital punishment in relation to the punisher and the morality of society. Given investment in the issue, nothing but such a restructuring of the issue could result in a conflict-free change of mind. I suspect that Senator Cain[2] has undergone exactly this process in his recent change of opinion on the effects of the internal security procedures. This position may be termed *independent consent*.

Process *d* implies taking a stand against one's own conviction; there is no cathexis to the new position. Private opinion remains what it was. Galileo is the prime example for this sort of *compliance*. To undergo this process presupposes extremely strong pressures on a person, ordinarily severe threats.

The next four positions are taken by persons for whom the issue of capital punishment was either very much on the periphery of their life space or never in it. Process *e* is one where such a person does not change his position, and does not feel any conflict about it. This position appears unreasonable. One would expect this type of behaviour in those who lack the essential ability to respond to external pressure, or in those who reject a stand just because it is demanded by others. Such people show *compulsive resistance*.

Process *f*—no investment in the issue, no change, and conflict—is psychologically not immediately plausible within the present scheme. The process becomes conceivable if one enters into the complex relationship which other issues bear to the one under discussion.

An ordinary American liberal may serve as an example. He has never given the matter much thought when he is reached by the Rosenberg campaign. He feels that an example should be set in view of what he regards as the overwhelming threat of communism. He may also think that the campaign has been organized by communists. Both these factors touch on issues in which he has considerable intellectual and emotional investment, but which are different from the

issue of capital punishment. His apparent independence of efforts to get him to oppose capital punishment results from considerations related to other issues. A shift in frame of reference has occurred. His is *expedient resistance*.

Process *g* may well be the most frequent one when there is no involvement with the issue, and the position is changed without creating conflict. It is a very reasonable type of behaviour which goes with a certain amount of trust in other people. This is *conformity* in the narrow sense of the word. These people may be involved with other persons rather than have investments in the issue under consideration. No strong influence is necessary to move them to another position.

Finally, process *h* is again not immediately plausible. With little, if any, investment the position is changed, but conflict results. A person sympathetic to communism may serve as an example in his attitude to the Rosenberg campaign. He gives in to pressures to change his opinion because of incidental special issues in the Rosenberg case. Here again a shift in the frame of reference occurs. He can see no particular reason to take a stand against capital punishment which he knows is used in communist countries. But he can see great advantage in using the counter-arguments in this particular case, for obvious reasons. Emotional and intellectual investment in his system of political beliefs makes it expedient to go along with social pressures. His agreement is *expedient conformity*.

The empirical identification of these eight patterns will not be easy. But I cannot see a simpler scheme within which it makes sense to talk about political independence and conformity. It remains to be demonstrated through experimental work that our understanding of social influence processes will be advanced by the adoption of this multidimensional criterion.

Let me briefly demonstrate the usefulness of thinking in these terms to clear the confusion about why commercial advertising is successful though the same methods fail in efforts to influence opinions on international relations. What happens, I believe, is that advertising campaigns concerned with heav-

---

[2] Senator Cain had originally supported the security measures, but in the course of investigating one or two cases among his own constituents he became convinced of their detrimental effect and changed his position on the issue.

ily invested matters such as cosmetics, result in type *c* responses, independent consent. Women want to be beautiful. When confronted with a pressure to use X to soften their skin they deliberately decide to comply. Advertising campaigns concerned with matters in which people have little investment, such as international relations, result in type *g* responses, conformity. That is, people do not deliberately relate themselves to the issue. Everything goes that is suggested. The confusion arises from the value judgement of the observer who understandably prefers independent consent to conformity. An additional point, often made implicitly in the literature, accounts for the difference in the two responses: it is apparently easier to reach persons in a public campaign on an issue in which they have emotional and intellectual investment than on one which is of no significance to them. Advertising campaigns on cosmetics are followed with intelligent interest; campaigns on international problems are not.

We now turn finally to the central question with which this paper started.

IV. HOW IS INDEPENDENCE POSSIBLE?

The scheme I have outlined defines eight distinguishable acts. It is in the nature of these definitions that one and the same person can perform any one of these acts, depending on the subject-matter with regard to which social influence processes are exercised and on the conditions under which this occurs. At this stage, then, it does not make sense to speak of independent persons; only of independent actions of a person. Even the term independent action may be a misleading oversimplification in view of the distinction made between independent dissent, independent consent, and undermined independence.

To take actions rather than persons as the unit of study does certainly not imply an underrating of the personality factor in response to social influence processes. On the contrary. The concept of investment, or cathexis, is a personality concept, referring, as it does, to the habitual relationship to an idea or issue of a total personality, not just of his ego or conscious knowledge.

Research on social influence processes re-

sulting in one or the other of the eight types of action depends, then, on the possibility of identifying the three components of the multidimensional criterion we have established. Two of these components—position-taking and correspondence between private and public opinion—have often been used in research and do not present special difficulties. The identification of degrees of investment, however, is a major problem. It is necessary to develop methods which permit one to locate an issue in a person's life space.

The term 'life space' has become a shibboleth in social psychology. We all use it freely, but we know very little about it. It is mainly referred to as a boundary condition without much concern for its content and structure. Lewin has spoken of the growing differentiation of the life space from infancy both in terms of content and in terms of its time dimension. If we are to discover whether a given political or social issue is cathected for an individual we ought to investigate his life space before he is exposed to any influence, be that influence nothing more than the direct question by an interviewer with regard to the issue, a question which, of course, introduces the issue into the life space. With some such notion in mind, a number of studies concerned with independence and conformity in political and social matters have appropriately started the interview with general and open-ended questions. Thus the Stouffer study began with questions designed to find out what kind of things people worry about, and what problems they discussed with their friends. Stouffer found that communism, conformity, and civil liberties were mentioned spontaneously by only 1 per cent of the population. Similarly in a study of attitudes towards blacklisting in the entertainment industry (29), questions about satisfactions and frustrations preceded questions about the topic proper. Here 6 per cent of the people interviewed mentioned blacklisting spontaneously.

These techniques go undoubtedly in the right direction. But in both cases, I now feel uncertain whether the existence or the absence of investment can be safely inferred from this rather crude effort. First of all, existence of an issue in the life space does not necessarily imply emotional and intellectual investment; and second, not everything that is so invested will come out into the open in response to such questions. When it comes down to it, we do not know what people really care about; nor have we sharpened our methodological tools to find this out. Somewhere in the social science literature—but I cannot recall where—I remember a statement to the effect that the majority of people know only two activities which elicit total investment because they are immediately gratifying; ends in themselves, not means to an end: sex among adults and play among children. Whether or not this pessimistic view of the world is justified, I do not know. However, I have less doubt that ideas are a relatively rare occurrence as objects of investment, and, hence, that the conformity in political and social matters of our times is largely a result of lack of such investment.

The difficulty in empirically identifying whether an issue is cathected by an individual lies largely in the fact that reasonably normal human beings do not invest all their emotional and intellectual energies in one object. Material things, human relations, other ideas, life itself can be cathected. The relationship of such diverse investments to each other needs to be explored empirically and broadly before more standardized measures of the degree of investment in an issue can be designed. At present, I can only speculate on the nature of measurable variables which may prove helpful in identifying investment in an issue. Two such variables come to mind: 1. the degree of compartmentalization or interconnectedness of factors in the life space, in other words, its spatial organization; and 2. the time-span of the life space with regard to the issue, in other words, its temporal organization. I am about to explore the usefulness of a free-association method, starting from the issue, with regard to both organizational principles. Here, I only want to add a remark about the time dimension of the life space. We know as an empirical generalization from research that the narrow present situation tends to dominate the life space for persons relatively free from neurosis. To be able to meet a current situation on its own terms, and not with the obsolete and infantile cathexes acquired in

early life, is actually the goal of psychotherapy and one relatively clear distinction between neurosis and absence of neurosis. Yet Heinz Hartmann (23) speaks of another tendency in human behaviour:

'In stressing the importance of factors like anticipation, postponement of gratification, and the like, in the development of action, we at the same time give action its place in a general trend of human development, the trend toward a growing independence from the immediate impact of present stimuli, the independence from the "hic et nunc". This trend can also be described as one toward "internalization" . . . a process of inner regulations replaces the reactions and actions due to fear of the social environment.'

It is possible to think of this longer time-span of which Hartmann speaks as characteristic for behaviour with regard to cathected issues. For only to the extent that the scope of the life space extends beyond the physically given present situation can past experiences, absent reference groups, anticipations of consequences of one's actions, shifts in frame of reference, and other such factors support the position on a cathected issue. When the life space is dominated by the past to the exclusion of present and future, we have the inability to conform which early in this paper was deliberately excluded from consideration. When the present dominates to the exclusion of past and future, independent dissent will be unlikely, conformity the rule. When the time dimension of the life space is balanced between past, present, and future, independent action is most likely.

Tentatively, then, I suggest that the interconnectedness of an issue with other matters in the life space, and the large time-span of the life space with regard to an issue should be regarded as criteria for investment.

What does all this mean for research? As I see it, the first task is the development of methods for the identification of investment in an issue. If and when such methods are developed, the experiments on conformity in the literature must be repeated, replacing the unidimensional criterion with the more complex definition I have attempted. Doing so will, I am confident, increase our knowledge of social influence processes, and sharpen the diagnosis of what is now all too easily called an 'age of conformity'.

REFERENCES

1. Asch, Solomon. *Social Psychology.* Prentice-Hall, 1952.
2. Back, K. W. The exertion of influence through social communication. *J. abnorm. soc. Psychol.,* Vol. 46, 1951.
3. Barron, Frank K. Some personality correlates of independence of judgment. *J. Personality,* Vol. 21, 1953.
4. Barker, Roger G., and Wright, Herbert F. *Midwest and its Children; The Psychological Ecology of an American Town.* Evanston, Ill.: Row, Peterson, 1955.
5. Bendix, R. Compliant behavior and individual personality. *Amer. J. Sociol.,* Vol. 58, 1952.
6. Berenda, Ruth. *The Influence of the Group on the Judgments of Children; An Experimental Investigation.* King's Crown Press, Columbia University, New York, 1950.
7. Blake, R. R., and Mouton, J. S. Present and future implications of social psychology for law and lawyers. *J. Public Law.* Emory University, 1954.
8. Bovard, Everett W., Jr. Group structure and perception. *J. abnorm. soc. Psychol.,* Vol. 46, 1951.
9. Brodbeck, A. J., Nogee, P., DiMascio, A. Two kinds of conformity: a study of the Riesman typology applied to standards of parental discipline. *J. Psychol.,* Vol. 41, 1956.
10. Chein, I. Personality and typology. *J. soc. Psychol.,* Vol. 18, 1943.
11. Cohen, Albert K. *Delinquent Boys: The Culture of the Gang.* Glencoe: Free Press, 1955.
12. Cooley, Charles H. *Social Organization.* Scribner's, 1909.
13. Crutchfield, Richard. Conformity and character. *Amer. Psycholog.,* Vol. 10, 1955.
14. Deutsch, M., and Gerard, H. B. A study of normative and informational social influences upon individual judgment. *J. abnorm. soc. Psychol.,* Vol. 51, 1955.
15. Festinger, Leon. An analysis of compliant behavior. In M. Sherif and M. O. Wilson (Eds.), *Group Relations at the Crossroads.* New York: Harper, 1953.
16. Festinger, Leon. Motivation leading to social behavior. In M. R. Jones (Ed.), *Nebraska Symposium on Motivation.* University of Nebraska Press, 1954.
17. Festinger, L., Back, K., Schachter, S., Kelley, H. H., and Thibaut, J. Theory and experiment in social communication. Research Center for Group Dynamics, Institute for Social Research, University of Michigan, 1950.
18. Frank, Jerome D. Experimental studies of personal pressure and resistance. *J. gen. Psychol.,* 1944.
19. French, J. R. P., Jr. Organized and unorganized groups under fear and frustration. *Studies in Topological and Vector Psychology,* III. Iowa City: University of Iowa, 1944.
20. Goldberg, Solomon C. *Some Cognitive Aspects of Social Influence; A Hypothesis.* Manuscript, undated.
21. Goldberg, Solomon C. Three situational determinants of conformity to social norms. *J. abnorm. soc. Psychol.,* Vol. 49, 1954.
22. Grodzins, Morton. *The Loyal and the Disloyal: Social Boundaries of Patriotism and Treason.* University of Chicago Press, 1956.
23. Hartmann, Heinz. On rational and irrational action. In *Psychoanalysis and the Social Sciences,* Vol. 1, 1947.
23a. Hartmann, Heinz. Notes on a theory of sublimation. In *The Psychoanalytic Study of the Child,* Vol. X, 1955.
24. Hilgard, E. R. The role of learning in perception. In Blake, R. R., and Ramsey, G. V. (Eds.), *Perception, an Approach to Personality.* New York: Ronald Press, 1951.
25. Hoch, P., and Zubin, J. (Eds.), *Psychiatry and the Law.*
26. Hoffman, Martin L. *Compulsive Conformity as a Mechanism of Defense and a Form of Resistance to Group Influence.* Manuscript.
27. Hoffman, Martin L. Some psychodynamic factors in compulsive conformity. *J. abnorm. soc. Psychol.,* Vol. 48, 1953.
28. Hovland, C. I., Janis, I. L., Kelley, H. H. *Communication and Persuasion.* Yale University Press, 1953.
29. Jahoda, M. In *Report on Blacklisting—* Vol. II. Meridian Books, July 1956.

30. Jahoda, M. Psychological issues in civil liberties. *Amer. Psychologist,* May 1956.

31. Jahoda, M., and Cook, S. W. Security measures and freedom of thought. *Yale Law Journal,* March 1952.

32. Janis, I. Personality correlates of susceptibility to persuasion. *J. Personality,* Vol. 22, 1954.

33. Kelley, H. H. *Resistance to Change and the Effects of Persuasive Communications.* Manuscript, 1954.

34. Kelley, H. H., and Shapiro, M. M. An experiment on conformity to group norms where conformity is detrimental to group achievement.

35. Kelley, H. H., and Woodruff, C. L. Members' reactions to apparent group approval of a counternorm communication. *J. abnorm. soc. Psychol.,* Vol. 52, 1956.

36. Kelman, Herbert C. *A Discussion of Three Processes of Opinion Change.* Manuscript, 1954.

37. Kelman, Herbert C. Attitude change as a function of response restriction. *Hum. Relat.,* Vol. 6, 1953.

38. Kelman, Herbert C. *Individual Liberties in an Atmosphere of Conformity.* Manuscript, 1955.

39. Kendall, P. L., and Wolf, K. M. The analysis of deviant cases in communications research. In P. F. Lazarsfeld and F. N. Stanton (Eds.), *Communications Research, 1948–9.* New York: Harper, 1949.

40. Kennedy, John F. *Profiles in Courage.* New York: Harper, 1955.

41. Klein, George S. Need and regulation. In M. R. Jones (Ed.), *Nebraska Symposium on Motivation.* University of Nebraska Press, 1954.

42. Levine, J., Laffal, J., Berkowitz, M., Lindemann, J., and Drevdah, J. Conforming behavior of psychiatric and medical patients. *J. abnorm. soc. Psychol.,* Vol. 49, 1954.

43. Lewin, K. Behavior and development as a function of the total situation. In D. Cartwright (Ed.), *Field Theory in Social Science.* New York: Harper, 1951; London: Tavistock Publications, 1952.

44. Linton, Harriet B. Correlates in perception, attitudes and judgment. *J. abnorm. soc. Psychol.,* Vol. 51, 1955.

45. Lipset, S. M., Lazarsfeld, P. F., Bonton, A. B., and Linze, J. The psychology of voting: an analysis of political behavior. In Lindzey, G. (Ed.), *Handbook of Social Psychology.* Addison Wesley, 1954.

46. Luchins, A. S. Social influence on perception of complex drawings. *J. soc. Psychol.,* Vol. 21, 1945.

47. McBride, D. *An Experimental Study of Overt Compliance without Private Acceptance.* Ph.D. thesis, 1955.

48. Parsons, T., and Shils, E. A. (Eds.), *Toward a General Theory of Action.* Cambridge, Mass.: Harvard University Press, 1951.

49. Riesman, D. *The Lonely Crowd.* Yale University Press, 1950.

50. St. Augustine. *Confessions.* New York: Sheed & Ward, 1943.

51. Sarbin, T. R., and Hardyck, C. D. Conformance in role perception as a personality variable. *J. Consult. Psychol.,* Vol. 19, 1955.

52. Schachter, S. Deviation, rejection and communication. *J. abnorm. soc. Psychol.,* Vol. 46, 1951.

53. Sherif, M. *The Psychology of Social Norms.* New York: Harper, 1936.

54. *Social Science and Freedom; a Report to the People.* Social Science Research Center of the Graduate School, Univ. of Minnesota, 1955.

55. Stouffer, S. A. *Communism, Conformity and Civil Liberties.* Doubleday, 1955.

56. Trilling, Lionel. *Freud and the Crisis of our Culture.* Boston: The Beacon Press, 1955.

57. Wallace, M. Future time perspective in schizophrenia. *J. abnorm. soc. Psychol.,* Vol. 52, 1956.

58. Wylie, Ruth. *Pressure toward Uniformity as a Variable in Making Evaluations of Self.* Manuscript, 1956.

ACKNOWLEDGMENTS

The passage from *Freud and the Crisis of our Culture* by Lionel Trilling is reprinted by kind permission of The Beacon Press.

The passage from "Conformity and Character" by Richard S. Crutchfield is reprinted by kind permission of the author.

Personality Similarity and Friendship[1] /

Carroll E. Izard[2] (*Vanderbilt University*)

Why do Person A and Person B find each other attractive and each other's company a satisfying experience? Two antithetical answers have been formulated to this question in recent years. Winch (1958) argued that the principle of complementarity explains attraction between marriage partners: successful marriages are made up of people whose needs and characteristics complement each other. Newcomb (1956), working with college males who were brought together as strangers and shared common quarters for several months, pointed to perceived similarity as the most significant factor in interpersonal attraction: Person A is attracted to Person B if A perceives B as like A. Newcomb's similarity thesis was given some support by Kelly (1955), who, like Winch, used married couples as *S*s. Several other studies have found real or assumed similarity to be a significant factor in interpersonal relations (Fiedler, 1958; Rosenfeld & Jackson, 1959); however, Morton (1959)[3] reviewed the literature concerned specifically with personality similarity and friendship and found contradictory conclusions.

Reprinted from *Journal of Abnormal and Social Psychology,* 1960, 61, pages 47–51, by permission of author and publisher, The American Psychological Association.

[1] This paper was presented at the 1959 meeting of the APA.
Three additional articles by Professor Izard dealing with this same subject matter are: "Personality Profile Similarity as a Function of Group Membership." *Journal of Abnormal and Social Psychology.* Expected date of publication, 1964. "Personality Similarity, Positive Affect, and Interpersonal Attraction." *Journal of Abnormal and Social Psychology,* 1960, 61, 484–485. "Personality Similarity and Friendship: A Follow-up Study." *Journal of Abnormal and Social Psychology,* 1963, 66, 598–600.
[2] The author is indebted to C. I. Bliss, Yale University and Connecticut Agricultural Experiment Station, for invaluable assistance in developing the analysis of variance procedure for comparing profiles; and to Dudley Peeler, Edna Johnson, David Catron, and Billie Farmer for assistance in obtaining and analyzing the data for this study.
[3] Gulliksen was principal investigator under Office of Naval Research (Contract Nonr. 1858 (15)), and National Science Foundation Grant G-642, Princeton: Princeton University and Educational Testing Service, 1959.

The principal thesis underlying the present study is a variant of Newcomb's similarity principle but differs in its emphasis on similarity of affective personality factors and on actual rather than perceived similarity. The affective component in interpersonal attraction has come to seem more important with the recent work of Tagiuri (1958) and Schutz (1958) on the significance of affective rapport—"mutuality," "congruency," "compatibility"—in interpersonal relations and group productivity.

These developments support the basic postulate of the present work, that interpersonal positive affect—the expression of favorable feeling, self-involving interest, acceptance, or esteem in relation to another person—is a significant determinant of individual and interpersonal behavior. A further underlying assumption is that personality similarity facilitates the expression of interpersonal positive affect.

The aim of this study was to throw some light on the general problem of interpersonal attraction by studying personality (affective) variables in relation to friendship. The specific hypotheses were (*a*) mutual friends have similar personality profiles, and (*b*) mutual friends have significant positive correlations on some of the separate personality characteristics that make up the profile.

METHOD

Over 200 students from a high school and a private college, both of which draw largely from the white middle and upper classes, were asked to list their closest personal friends in rank order. They were then given Edwards' (1954) Personal Preference Schedule (PPS), a forced choice personality inventory that measures 15 manifest needs originally defined by Murray (1938). Various PPS scales have been found significantly related to other personality tests (Silverman, 1957) and to relevant criteria derived from actual behavioral situations (Bernardin & Jessor, 1957; Gisvold, 1958; Izard, in press).

TABLE 1

ANALYSIS OF VARIANCE OF PPS SCORES OF FRIEND AND RANDOM PAIRS

Source	df	Sum of Squares	MS	F	P
Between Variables	14	$\Sigma V^2_t/N - T^2/N_o = A$	805.338	47.803	.001
Variables × Groups	14	$(\Sigma v^2_{t1} + \Sigma v^2_{t2})/N_g - C - A$	16.847	<1.000	
Variables × Pairs (Friends)	406	$\Sigma y^2_{t1}/N_p - \Sigma v^2_{t1}/N_g$	23.143	1.529	.01
Variables × Pairs (Random)	406	$\Sigma y^2_{t2}/N_p - \Sigma v^2_{t2}/N_g$	22.811	1.226	.05
Variables × Ss (Friends)	420	$\Sigma y^2_1 - \Sigma y^2_{t1}/N_p$	15.138	1.229	.05
Variables × Ss (Random)	420	$\Sigma y^2_1 - \Sigma y^2_{t2}/N_p$	18.599		
C (Correction)	1	T^2/N_o			

The sociometric data made possible the selection of 30 pairs who chose each other as best friends. In addition, a control group of 60 Ss from an entering college class were selected and paired at random, with the restriction that there be the same number of male and female pairs as in the 30 pairs of friends.

An analysis of variance technique, described in detail in connection with presenting the results, was used to test the hypothesis that mutual friends have similar personality profiles. This method made it possible to test for profile similarity between pairs of friends and between random pairs, and to compare the group of friend pairs to the group of random pairs with respect to similarity. The technique gives considerably more information and tests of significance based on more degrees of freedom than would the more conventional series of profile correlations or D measures. An r or D is useful as an index of similarity for a single pair, but neither is as powerful as the analysis of variance technique for studying a series of pairs and for comparing one such series with another with respect to profile similarity.

The hypothesis that mutual friends have significant correlations on some of the individual personality variables was tested by computing intraclass correlation (r_i) for each of the 15 personality characteristics. Corresponding correlations were computed for the Ss paired randomly. The significance of an r_i was determined by Fisher's (1948) method: transform r_i to z, compute corrected z or $z_c = z + \dfrac{1}{2n' - 1}$, and then compare z_c with $s_{z_c} = \dfrac{1}{n' - \frac{3}{2}}$. The acceptable level of significance was set at .025, since

testing the hypothesis required the computation of 30 r_i's.

RESULTS

The hypothesis that mutual friends have similar personality profiles was supported by the analysis of variance for comparing profiles. For this analysis, profiles were entered in adjacent rows of the data sheet. Since entries in a given row were not independent and summed to a constant, the terms usually based on row totals drop out. To compute the terms in the analysis, let y_1 and y_2 represent the scores of friends and random Ss respectively on a given personality variable, y_{t1} and y_{t2} the respective totals for a friend and random pair on a variable, v_{t1} and v_{t2} the variable total for the friend group and random group respectively, V_t the total for both groups on a variable, T the grand total for all observations, N_p the number in a unit (pair), N_g the number in a group, N the number of Ss, and N_o the total number of observations. The analysis of variance together with the computational formulas for the sums of squares is presented in Table 1.

The Between Variables term simply represents the variance associated with the average profile for the 120 Ss. This term is of no consequence in the present study. It simply indicates that on the average the Ss responded significantly differently to the 15 PPS scales. It was expected to be quite large in comparison with its error—the Variables × Groups term.

The Variables × Groups term is similar to a simple Between Groups term in a single variable analysis of variance. The principal difference is that here each group is measured on 15 separate variables. Hence, the variance due to variables can be isolated (Between Variables term) and the groups compared in terms of their differential interaction to the 15 variables (Variables × Groups term). The same logic applies to the other interaction terms in the analysis. The Variables × Groups term was tested against the pooled variance of the two Variables × Pairs terms. The resulting F was less than 1.000. This indicated that the average profile for the friend group did not differ significantly from that of the random group.

The test for profile similarity of friends

$$F = \frac{\text{Variables} \times \text{Pairs (Friends)}}{\text{Variables} \times Ss \text{ (Friends)}}$$

can be interpreted as a between variance—with variance ratio. The variance within pairs of friends (Variables + Ss) was significantly smaller ($P < .01$) than the variance between friends (Variable × Pairs). However, the corresponding F for the random Ss was also significant, though less so ($P < .05$). It was considered that this significant F for similarity of random pairs was possibly due to chance fluctuations in random sampling. However, two additional samples of random pairs from the same population had significant profile correlations. While further research is needed to determine the meaning of this finding, it makes it necessary to test whether friend pairs are significantly more alike than Ss paired at random.

In order to compare the relative similarity of friend and random pairs, it was necessary to check whether the two groups were homogeneous with respect to overall variability. This test

$$F = \frac{\begin{array}{c}\text{Variables} \times \text{Pairs (Random)} \\ + \text{ Variables} \times Ss \text{ (Random)}\end{array}}{\begin{array}{c}\text{Variables} \times \text{Pairs (Friends)} \\ + \text{ Variables} \times Ss \text{ (Friends)}\end{array}}$$

($P > .025$), indicated that the profiles of the 60 Ss in the friend group did not differ on the average from those of the 60 Ss in the random group. The comparison of the within variances of the two groups of pairs

$$F = \frac{\text{Variables} \times Ss \text{ (Random)}}{\text{Variables} \times Ss \text{ (Friends)}}$$

($P < .05$), showed that mutual friends considering a pair as a unit, were significantly more similar than Ss paired at random.

Table 2 presents the intraclass correlations testing the hypothesis that mutual friends have significant positive correlations on some of the personality characteristics that make up the profile. As shown in the table, no r_i was significant for the Ss randomly paired. For mutual friends, r_i was significant at the .025 level for Exhibition, at approximately the .01 level for Deference, and beyond the .01 level for Endurance.

The results from both the analysis of variance and intraclass correlation are evidence for similarity and contrary to what would be expected from complementarity; namely, that the scores of friend pairs on a particular variable should correlate negatively. However, they do not completely rule out the possibility of another less well defined type of complementarity, in which a given personality characteristic (e.g., Dominance) complements another (e.g., Abasement). To test for the presence of such complementarity across characteristics, it is necessary to identify characteristics that are psychologically complementary. There is little theoretical or empirical basis for making these

TABLE 2

INTRACLASS CORRELATIONS FOR FRIENDS AND FOR RANDOM Ss

PPS	Intraclass Correlations	
Variable	Friends	Random Ss
Achievement	.200	.031
Deference	.435*	.347
Order	.279	−.157
Exhibition	.386*	.179
Autonomy	−.001	.060
Affiliation	.022	.138
Intraception	.113	−.183
Succorance	−.082	−.077
Dominance	.112	.201
Abasement	.168	.296
Nurturance	.100	.223
Change	.253	.212
Endurance	.473*	−.248
Heterosexuality	.116	.193
Aggression	.167	−.049

* $P < .025$.

pairings. The most appropriate empirical basis available for these pairings is the magnitude of the negative intercorrelations of the 15 variables in the standardization group. These negative correlations might be interpreted as evidence of within person complementarity. Primarily on this basis, the seven most relevant of the 105 possible combinations were tested. The intraclass correlation is again appropriate, since there is no logical basis for assigning Ss to x and y columns for an ordinary product moment correlation (Fisher, 1948). The estimate of correlation for a given pair of characteristics would be obtained by pooling the two r_is for that combination, and the acceptable level of P would be somewhat less than .01. The 14 r_is were essentially zero, the largest having a sign in the opposite direction to that predicted by the complementarity principle.

There is a possibility that the social desirability of characteristics may be a factor in the friendship pairings, although the fact that Edwards employed the forced choice technique to eliminate social desirability at the item level makes this unlikely. To check on the possibility, the 98 students in a general psychology course were asked to rank the 15 characteristics in terms of social desirability. The final ranks based on the Ss' individual rankings were normalized by means of Fisher's rankit transformation (Fisher & Yates, 1953). Since the rankits for the 49 men correlated .984 with the corresponding values for the 49 women, final rankits for social desirability were based on all 98 Ss. The rankits for social desirability were correlated with rankits derived from the rank order of the characteristics in terms of the magnitude of the r_is for the friend group. This correlation was only .002, indicating that on the average there is no relationship between the social desirability of a given personality characteristic and the degree to which friends are similar on that characteristic. Further, it is interesting to note that the profile based on this index of social desirability did not correlate significantly with the obtained average profile for a large sample of college males or with the average profile for a large sample of college females.

DISCUSSION

There is some support for the importance of perceived similarity, assumed similarity, and actual similarity in interpersonal attraction and friendship. Newcomb (1956) found that perceived similarity was a key factor in interpersonal attraction, and Fiedler (1958) reported that assumed similarity was significantly related to leader attitudes and team effectiveness. Rosenfeld and Jackson (1959) showed that similarity on three scales from the Guilford-Zimmerman Temperament Survey (Sociability-Unsociability, Ascendance-Submissiveness, Security-Insecurity) was significantly related to friendship ratings of female office employees. The present study showed that mutual friends, people who are attracted to one another over an extended period of time, have personality profiles as measured by the 15 scale PPS that are significantly more similar than those of Ss paired at random and that they have significant positive correlations on some of the separate personality characteristics.

The question arises as to why personality similarity is a factor in friendship or interpersonal attraction and as to how this factor operates in interpersonal dynamics. The role of personality similarity may be understood by viewing it in relation to the underlying hypotheses of the present study. It was postulated that interpersonal positive affect is an important determinant of interpersonal behavior and that personality similarity facilitates the expression of positive affect. It seems reasonable that the expression of positive affect—favorable feeling, self-involving interest, acceptance, esteem—enhances interpersonal attraction. But how does personality similarity facilitate positive affect? If Person A and Person B have similar personality profiles, they have vested affect or affect needs in common. More dynamically, they have similar ways of expressing and receiving affect, and this actual similarity of affective characteristics might reasonably be expected to facilitate mutually satisfying interactions and experiences. For one thing, the same individuals, groups and interpersonal situations that evoke positive affect in one member of an affectively similar pair would tend to evoke positive affect in the other. Actual personality similarity should also increase the accuracy of interpersonal perception and communication, particularly the perception and communication of attitudes, values and other affective aspects of experience. This is almost tantamount to saying that Ss can perceive and communicate that which is similar to their own experience more readily than the dissimilar, the familiar more readily than the unfamiliar. This formulation is in keeping with Newcomb's (1956) conception that accurate interpersonal communication and perception of similarity are interdependent rewarding conditions. Insofar as a person sees his self-involving, affect laden desires and actions confirmed by the desires and actions of another, his perceptions of self and others receives confirmation. This line of thinking is also consonant with the concept of congruency—"the tendency, correctly based on experience, to perceive a person's feelings for us as congruent with our feelings for him"—the factor which Tagiuri (1958, p. 321) has considered the most significant determinant of social preference. In fine, personality similarity, or similar affect needs and similar ways of expressing and receiving affect, should facilitate interpersonal positive affect and make for effective communication, compatibility and cohesiveness in the two person group.

SUMMARY

The present study was designed to test the hypotheses that mutual friends (a) have similar personality profiles, and (b) significant positive correlations on some of the separate personality characteristics that make up the profile. Mutual "best" friends were determined by a sociometric procedure, and personality characteristics were measured by the 15 scale PPS.

An analysis of variance technique for comparing personality profiles showed that pairs of friends were significantly more similar than pairs established by random assignment. Hypothesis b was supported by significant intraclass correlations among friends on Exhibition, Deference, and Endurance and no significant correlations

among the random Ss. These results tend to rule out the possibility of within characteristics complementarity, and an additional analysis yielded evidence against across characteristics complementarity. Further analysis showed that the social desirability of the personality characteristics was not significantly related to the degree to which friends are alike on the characteristics or to the degree to which the characteristics are actually present in the population sampled.

Accepting friendship as a criterion of attraction between people and the PPS as a measure of affective characteristics, the present findings may be restated as follows: personality similarity or similarity of affect needs and of ways of expressing and receiving affect is a significant factor in interpersonal attraction. These findings were discussed in relation to Newcomb's similarity principle and Tagiuri's concept of congruency. Personality similarity was interpreted as essentially a facilitator of interpersonal positive affect, the latter being postulated as a key determinant of attraction as well as other aspects of interpersonal behavior.

REFERENCES

Bernardin, A. C., & Jessor, R. A construct validation of the Edwards Personal Preference Schedule with respect to dependency. *J. consult. Psychol.*, 1957, 21, 63–67.

Edwards, A. L. *Manual, Edwards Personal Preference Schedule.* New York: Psychological Corp., 1954.

Fiedler, F. E. *Leader attitudes and group effectiveness.* Urbana: Univer. Illinois Press, 1958.

Fisher, R. A. *Statistical methods for research workers.* London: Oliver, Boyd, 1948.

Fisher, R. A., & Yates, F. *Statistical tables for biological, agricultural and medical research.* New York: Hafner, 1953.

Gisvold, D. A validity study of the Autonomy and Deference subscales of the EPPS. *J. consult. Psychol.*, 1958, 22, 445–447.

Izard, C. E. Personality characteristics associated with resistance to change. *J. consult. Psychol.*, in press.

Kelly, E. L. Consistency of the adult personality. *Amer. Psychologist*, 1955, 10, 659–681.

Morton, A. S. Similarity as a determinant of friendship: A multidimensional study. *USN tech. Rep.,* 1959, Nonr 1858 (15), Princeton.

Murray, H. A. *Explorations in personality.* A clinical and experimental study of fifty men of college age. New York: Oxford, 1938.

Newcomb, T. M. The prediction of interpersonal attraction. *Amer. Psychologist,* 1956, 11, 575–586.

Rosenfeld, H., & Jackson, J. Effect of similarity of personalities on interpersonal attraction. *Amer. Psychologist,* 1959, 14, 366–367 (Abstract).

Schutz, W. C. *FIRO: A three dimensional theory of interpersonal behavior.* New York: Rinehart, 1958.

Silverman, R. E. The Edwards Personal Preference Schedule and social desirability. *J. consult. Psychol.,* 1957, 21, 402–404.

Tagiuri, R. Social preference and its perception. In R. Tagiuri & L. Petrullo (Eds.), *Person perception and interpersonal behavior.* Stanford, Calif.: Stanford Univer. Press, 1958.

Winch, R. F. *Mate-selection: A study of complementary needs.* New York: Harper, 1958.

C. Via Motivation and Emotion

The two areas of motivation and emotion are classics in the history of human thought, having their foundations in philosophical speculation, later to enter a more empirically oriented psychology. The topic of motivation, basically focusing on the "why" or causes of behavior overlaps with almost every area of psychology, including social psychology. Emotion, focusing upon the affective side of the Platonic trichotomy, has a similar broad range of application. They are commonly linked in that similar physiological and psychological processes are seen to underlie each.

Early conceptions of motivation turned towards a doctrine of instincts to answer the question, "why." As psychology moved towards an experimental behaviorism, rejecting the instinct doctrine, conceptions of motivation turned to certain primary or basic survival drives such as hunger, thirst, and sex for answers to this same question. A period of theory and research postulating the existence of need tensions which resulted in activity directed towards their reduction lent support to this tension-reduction motivational model. Even the more psychoanalytic approaches to motivation were founded upon a somewhat similar tension-reduction, survival model. More recently, with a series of experiments on both

animals and humans and with a changing orientation within the formerly strict psychoanalytic theory of motivation, we may note a change in the psychological treatment of motivation. The article by White most aptly expresses this changing conception of both animal and human motivation, suggesting what appears to be a more social psychological treatment. In this newer model, man the active explorer and seeker of mastery over his environment is not motivated solely by efforts to reduce tension, but rather, he seeks to come to grips with and learn about the world, a social world, in which he lives.

Not only has this newer conception of motivation turned more towards the cognitive functions of perceiving, learning, and knowing, thus fitting in with the preceding topics central to social psychology, but in addition, it has suggested the extreme importance of social rather than simple biological conditions of motivation.

The reading by Feather deals with what may rightly be called a social psychological condition of motivation, the need for achievement: A need which in this instance finds its gratification only within a social context; a need which is particularly significant in a society highly oriented towards an achievement-success theme. The Feather reading examines the effects of this achievement motivation on persistence in an experimental situation.

Unlike the preceding article which deals with the effects of a single motive in an experimental setting within a single culture, the Whiting article examines cross-culturally the broader implications of the conditions of motivation used as a means of social control. By examining the child-rearing conditions which produce and maintain the motivational mechanisms of control with which he deals, Whiting presents a theme which we next encounter in section D on socialization. But the broader message imparted in his article suggests that the topic of motivation is of necessary concern to the social psychologist not only because there are social origins to individual states of motivation, but also, and most importantly, because the motivational systems socialized within a culture provide a basic control mechanism for maintaining and integrating the social system and its organization.

The final reading included in this section presents a most interesting study which attempts to determine the factors producing the particular emotional state we report feeling. Is our feeling of joy or anger, for example, simply a function of a state of physiological arousal or must certain cognitive and social cues be present in addition? Of particular interest to the social psychologist is the authors' conclusion which suggests that cognitive factors may be a major determinant of the emotional labels we apply to common states of physiological arousal.

Motivation Reconsidered: The Concept of Competence / Robert W. White (*Harvard University*)

When parallel trends can be observed in realms as far apart as animal behavior and psychoanalytic ego psychology, there is reason to suppose that we are witnessing a significant evolution of ideas. In these two realms, as in psychology as a whole, there is evidence of deepening discontent with theories of motivation based upon drives. Despite great differences in the language and concepts used to express this discontent, the theme is everywhere the same: Something important is left out when we make drives the operating forces in animal and human behavior.

The chief theories against which the discontent is directed are those of Hull and of Freud. In their respective realms, drive-reduction theory and psychoanalytic instinct theory, which are basically very much alike, have acquired a considerable air of orthodoxy. Both views have an appealing simplic-

ity, and both have been argued long enough so that their main outlines are generally known. In decided contrast is the position of those who are not satisfied with drives and instincts. They are numerous, and they have developed many pointed criticisms, but what they have to say has not thus far lent itself to a clear and inclusive conceptualization. Apparently there is an enduring difficulty in making these contributions fall into shape.

In this paper I shall attempt a conceptualization which gathers up some of the important things left out by drive theory. To give the concept a name I have chosen the word *competence*, which is intended in a broad biological sense rather than in its narrow everyday meaning. As used here, competence will refer to an organism's capacity to interact effectively with its environment. In organisms capable of but little learning, this capacity might be considered an innate attribute, but in the mammals and especially man, with their highly plastic nervous systems, fitness to interact with the environment is slowly attained through prolonged feats of learning. In view of the directed-

Reprinted from *Psychological Review*, 1959, 66, pages 297–333, by permission of author and publisher, The American Psychological Association. This is an edited version of the original article. (E.E.S.)

ness and persistence of the behavior that leads to these feats of learning, I consider it necessary to treat competence as having a motivational aspect, and my central argument will be that the motivation needed to attain competence cannot be wholly derived from sources of energy currently conceptualized as drives or instincts. We need a different kind of motivational idea to account fully for the fact that man and the higher mammals develop a competence in dealing with the environment which they certainly do not have at birth and certainly do not arrive at simply through maturation. Such an idea, I believe, is essential for any biologically sound view of human nature.

As a first step, I shall briefly examine the relevant trends of thought in several areas of psychology. From this it will become clear that the ideas advanced in this paper have already been stated, in one way or another, by workers in animal behavior, child development, cognitive psychology, psychoanalytic ego psychology, and the psychology of personality. If there is novelty in this essay, it lies in putting together pieces which are not in themselves new. They already lie before us on the table, and perhaps by looking once more we can see how to fit them into a larger conceptual picture.

THE TREND IN ANIMAL PSYCHOLOGY

One of the most obvious features of animal behavior is the tendency to explore the environment. Cats are reputedly killed by curiosity, dogs characteristically make a thorough search of their surroundings, and monkeys and chimpanzees have always impressed observers as being ceaseless investigators. Even Pavlov, whose theory of behavior was one of Spartan simplicity, could not do without an investigatory or orientating reflex. Early workers with the obstruction method, such as Dashiell (1925) and Nissen (1930), reported that rats would cross an electrified grid simply for the privilege of exploring new territory. Some theorists reasoned that activity of this kind was always in the service of hunger, thirst, sex, or some other organic need, but this view was at least shaken by the latent learning experiments, which showed that animals

learned about their surroundings even when their major needs had been purposely sated. Shortly before 1950 there was a wave of renewed interest not only in exploratory behavior but also in the possibility that activity and manipulation might have to be assigned the status of independent motives.

Exploratory Behavior

In 1953 Butler reported an experiment in which monkeys learned a discrimination problem when the only reward was the opening of a window which permitted them to look out upon the normal comings and goings of the entrance room to the laboratory. The discriminations thus formed proved to be resistant to extinction. In a later study, Butler and Harlow (1957) showed that monkeys could build up a series of four different discriminations solely for the sake of inspecting the entrance room. Butler concluded that "monkeys—and presumably all primates—have a strong motive toward visual exploration of their environment and that learning may be established on the basis of this motive just as it may be established on the basis of any motive that regularly and reliably elicits responses." Montgomery, in 1954, reported a study with rats in which the animals, their major organic needs satiated, learned to avoid the short arm of a Y maze and to take the path which led them into additional maze territory suitable for exploration. Similar findings have been described by Myers and Miller (1954), whose rats learned to press a bar for the sake of poking their heads into a new compartment and sniffing around. Zimbardo and Miller (1958) enlarged upon this study by varying the amount of novelty in the two compartments. In their report "the hypothesis advanced is that opportunity to explore a 'novel' environment or to effect a stimulus change in the environment is the reinforcing agent."

These experiments make a strong case for an independent exploratory motive. The nature of this motive can be more fully discerned in situations in which the animals are allowed a varied repertory of behavior. In 1950 Berlyne published a searching paper on curiosity, a theme which he further developed in subsequent years (1955, 1957,

1958). The rats in his experiments were confronted with an unfamiliar space and later with various novel objects placed in it. Approaching, sniffing, and examining were readily elicited by each novelty, were fairly rapidly extinguished, but were restored nearly to original strength when a fresh novelty was added. Exploration on the part of chimpanzees has been studied by Welker (1956), who put various pairs of objects before the animals and observed the course of their interest. The objects were often first approached in a gingerly manner, with signs of uneasiness, then examined and handled quite fully, then discarded. Introducing a new pair of objects promptly reproduced the whole sequence, just as it did with the rats in Berlyne's experiments. Welker used pairs of objects to find out whether or not the chimpanzees would have common preferences. Bigness and brightness evoked more interest, and greater time was spent upon objects which could be moved, changed, or made to emit sounds and light.

Activity and Manipulation

Exploration is not the only motive proposed by critics of drive orthodoxy, and novelty is not the only characteristic of the environment which appears to incite motivated behavior. Some workers have suggested a need for activity, which can be strengthened by depriving animals of their normal opportunities for movement. Kagan and Berkun (1954) used running in an activity wheel as the reward for learning and found it "an adequate reinforcement for the instrumental response of bar pressing." Hill (1956) showed that rats will run in an activity wheel to an extent that is correlated with their previous degree of confinement. It is certain that the activity wheel offers no novelty to the animals in these experiments. Nevertheless, they seem to want to run, and they continue to run for such long times that no part of the behavior can readily be singled out as a consummatory response

Changing Conceptions of Drive

In a brief historical statement, Morgan (1957) has pointed out that the conception of drive as a noxious stimulus began to lose its popularity among research workers

shortly after 1940. "On the whole," he says, "the stimulus concept of drive owed more to wishful thinking than to experimental fact." When technical advances in biochemistry and brain physiology made it possible to bring in an array of new facts, there was a rapid shift toward the view that "drives arise largely through the internal environment acting on the central nervous system." One of the most influential discoveries was that animals have as many as a dozen specific hungers for particular kinds of food, instead of the single hunger demanded by Cannon's model of the hunger drive. If an animal's diet becomes deficient in some important element such as salt, sugar, or the vitamin-B complex, foods containing the missing element will be eagerly sought while other foods are passed by, a selectivity that obviously cannot be laid to contractions of the stomach. Similarly, a negative food preference can be produced by loading either the stomach or the blood stream with some single element of the normal diet. The early work of Beach (1942) on sexual behavior brought out similar complications in what had for a time been taken as a relatively simple drive. Hormone levels appeared to be considerably more important than peripheral stimulation in the arousal and maintenance of the sex drive. Further work led Beach (1951) to conclude that sexual behavior is "governed by a complex combination of processes." He points out that the patterns of control differ tremendously from one species to another and that within a single species the mechanisms may be quite different for males and females. Like hunger, the sex drive turns out to be no simple thing.

New methods of destroying and of stimulating brain centers in animals have had an equally disastrous effect on the orthodox drive model. The nervous system, and especially the hypothalamus, appears to be deeply implicated in the motivational process. Experimental findings on hypothalamic lesions in animals encourage Stellar (1954) to believe that there are different centers "responsible for the control of different kinds of basic motivation," and that in each case "there is one main excitatory center and one inhibitory center which operates to depress the activity of the excitatory center." As research findings accumulate, this picture may seem to be too cleanly drawn. Concerning sexual behavior, for example, Rosvold (1959) concludes a recent review by rejecting the idea of a single center in the cerebrum; rather, the sex drive "probably has a wide neural representation with a complex interaction between old and new brain structures and between neural and humoral agents." Nevertheless, Miller's (1958) careful work seems to leave little doubt that motivated behavior in every way similar to normal hunger and normal pain-fear can be elicited by electrical stimulation of quite restricted areas of the hypothalamus. It is clear that we cannot regress to a model of drives that represents the energy as coming from outside the nervous system. Whatever the effects of peripheral stimulation may be, drives also involve neural centers and neural patterns as well as internal biochemical conditions.

What sort of model becomes necessary to entertain these newly discovered facts? In 1938 Lashley expressed the view that motivation should not be equated with disturbance of organic equilibrium but rather with "a partial excitation of a very specific sensorimotor mechanism irradiating to affect other systems of reaction." Beach (1942) postulated that there must be in the nervous system "a condition analogous to Sherrington's central excitatory state." Morgan, in 1943, undertook to capture the facts in a systematic theory which seems to have been well sustained by subsequent research (Morgan, 1957). He distinguished two types of process which he called *humoral motive factors* and *central motive states*. The humoral factors consist of chemical or hormonal constituents of the blood and lymph, and they are conceived to influence behavior chiefly by a direct sensitizing action on neural centers. The central motive states have several properties: They are partly self-maintaining through neural circuits, they tend to increase the organism's general activity, they evoke specific forms of behavior not strongly controlled by the environment, and they prime or prepare consummatory responses which will occur when adequate stimulation is found. This is a far cry from the orthodox model, but we must nowadays

admit that the orthodox model is a far cry from the facts.

In view of this radical evolution of the concept of drive, it is not surprising to find the drive reduction hypothesis in serious difficulties. The earlier identification of reinforcement with drive reduction has been directly attacked in a series of experiments designed to show that learning takes place when drive reduction is ruled out.

In 1950 Sheffield and Roby showed that instrumental learning would take place in hungry rats when the reward consisted not of a nutritive substance but of sweet-tasting saccharine in the drinking water. This finding appeared to be "at variance with the molar principle of reinforcement used by Hull, which identifies primary reinforcement with 'need reduction.'" The authors naturally do not question the vital importance of need reduction, but they point out that need-reducing events may accomplish reinforcement through a mechanism more direct and speedy than the reduction of the need itself. They think that "stimulation and performance of a consummatory response appears to be more important to instrumental learning—in a primary, not acquired, way—than the drive satisfaction which the response normally achieves." Their findings are in line with an earlier experiment with chickens by Wolfe and Kaplon (1941), who used different sizes of food pellets so that the number of pecks and the amount of food received could be thrown out of their usual close connection. The chickens, we might say, would rather peck than eat; learning was more strongly reinforced when four pecks were necessary than when one peck was enough to take the same amount of food.

The substitution of the consummatory response for need reduction as the immediate reinforcing mechanism is a step in advance, but it soon turns out that another step is required. Can it be shown that an aroused need which does not reach consummation has a reinforcing effect? To test this possibility Sheffield, Wulff, and Backer (1951) provided male rats with the reward of copulating with a female, but not enough times to produce ejaculation. This reward was favorable to instrumental learning even though there was no need reduction and no performance of the final consummatory act. The results were supported by Kagan (1955), whose animals showed substantial learning under the same conditions, though learning was still faster when ejaculation was permitted. Sheffield, Roby, and Campbell (1954) have proposed a *drive-induction* theory according to which the property of reinforcement is assigned to the excitement of an aroused drive. We have already seen that some such assumption is essential if exploration is to be assigned the status of a drive. Here it can be added that the whole theory of pregenital sexuality involves motivation without consummatory acts and without any but the most gradual need reduction. And as a final blow to the orthodox hypothesis comes the finding by Olds and Milner (1954) that positive reinforcement can be brought about by direct electrical stimulation of certain areas of the brain. Once again we learn that neural centers are deeply implicated in the plot of motivation. The simple mechanics of need reduction cannot possibly serve as the basis for a theory of learning.

Twenty years of research have thus pretty much destroyed the orthodox drive model. It is no longer appropriate to consider that drives originate solely in tissue deficits external to the nervous system, that consummatory acts are a universal feature and goal of motivated behavior, or that the alleviation of tissue deficits is the necessary condition for instrumental learning. Instead we have a complex picture in which humoral factors and neural centers occupy a prominent position; in which, moreover, the concept of neurogenic motives without consummatory ends appears to be entirely legitimate.

THE TREND IN PSYCHOANALYTIC EGO PSYCHOLOGY

Rather an abrupt change of climate may be experienced as we turn from the animal laboratory to the psychoanalytic treatment room, but the trends of thought in the two realms turn out to be remarkably alike. Here the orthodox view of motivation is to be found in Freud's theory of the instincts—they might be known to us as drives if an early translator had been more literal with the German *Trieb*.

Freud's Theories of Instinct and Ego

In his final work, Freud (1949) described instincts as "somatic demands upon mental life" and as "the ultimate cause of all activity." He wrote further:

It is possible to distinguish an indeterminate number of instincts and in common practice this is in fact done. For us, however, the important question arises whether we may not be able to derive all of these instincts from a few fundamental ones. . . . After long doubts and vacillations we have decided to assume the existence of only two basic instincts, *Eros* and the *destructive instinct* (Freud, 1949, p. 20).

The history of Freud's long doubts and vacillations has been lucidly related by Bibring (1941). Up to 1914 Freud used a two-fold classification of sexual instincts and ego instincts. The ego instincts made their appearance in his case histories in a somewhat moral character, being held responsible for the disastrous repression of sexual needs, but in systematic usage they were conceived as serving the goal of self-preservation, and hunger was generally taken as an appropriate model. In 1914, when he evolved the concept of narcissism and saw that it threatened to blur the line between sexual and ego tendencies, Freud (1925b) still expressed himself as unwilling to abandon an idea which followed the popular distinction of love and hunger and which reflected man's dual existence "as reproducer and as one who serves his own ends." Various facts, particularly those of sadism and masochism, served to overcome his reluctance, so that he finally united self-preservation and preservation of the species under the heading of Eros or life instincts, establishing destructiveness or the death instinct as the great antagonist in a profound biological sense (Freud, 1948). This highly speculative step proved to be too much for some of his otherwise loyal followers, and the earlier orthodoxy did not become entirely extinct.

Freud's tendency to revise his thinking makes it difficult to pin down an orthodox doctrine, but most workers will probably agree that his main emphasis was upon somatically based drives, a mental apparatus which received its power from the drives, and, of course, the multitude of ways in which the apparatus controlled, disguised, and transformed these energies. His treatment of the ego was far from complete, and it was not long before voices were raised against the conception that so vital and versatile a part of the personality could be developed solely by libidinal and aggressive energies.

An Instinct to Master

In 1942 Hendrick proposed that this difficulty be met by assuming the existence of an additional major instinct. "The development of ability to master a segment of the environment," he wrote, and the need to exercise such functions, can be conceptualized as an "instinct to master," further characterized as "an inborn drive to do and to learn how to do." The aim of this instinct is "pleasure in exercising a function successfully, regardless of its sensual value." The simpler manifestations are learning to suck, to manipulate, to walk, to speak, to comprehend and to reason; these functions and others eventually become integrated as the ego.

The instinct to master has an aim—to exercise and develop the ego functions—and it follows hedonic principles by yielding "primary pleasure" when efficient action "enables the individual to control and alter his environment." It is to this extent analogous to the instincts assumed by Freud. But just as an exploratory drive seemed radically to alter the whole conception of drive, so the instinct to master implied a drastic change in the psychoanalytic idea of instinct. Mastery, the critics agreed, could not be an instinct, whatever else it might be.

It is of interest that Fenichel (1945), who definitely rejected Hendrick's proposal, gives us another close parallel to the animal work by attributing mastering behavior to anxiety-reduction. He argued that mastery is "a general aim of every organism but not of a specific instinct." He agreed that there is "a pleasure of enjoying one's abilities," but he related this pleasure to cessa-

tion of the anxiety connected with not being able to do things. "Functional pleasure," he wrote, "is pleasure in the fact that the exercise of a function is now possible without anxiety," and he contended that when anxiety is no longer present, when there is full confidence that a given situation can be met, then action is no longer accompanied by functional pleasure. We must certainly agree with Fenichel that anxiety *can* play the part he assigns it, but the proposal that all pleasure in ego functions comes from this source raises the same difficulties we have already considered in connection with exploratory behavior. That we exercise our capacities and explore our surroundings only to reduce our fear of the environment is not, as I have already argued, an assumption that enjoys high probability on biological grounds.

Hartmann on the Ego

A less radical change in the orthodox model is proposed by Hartmann, who, in a series of papers since 1939, often in conjunction with Kris and Loewenstein, has been refining and expanding Freud's views on the ego and the instincts. While the ego is conceived as a "substructure" of the personality, this term is somewhat metaphorical because in practice the ego has to be defined by its functions. The list of functions, which includes grasping, crawling, walking, perceiving, remembering, language, thinking, and intention, covers much the same ground that was indicated by Hendrick, but Hartmann does not attribute their growth to an instinct. On the other hand, Hartmann (1950) early came to the conclusion that development could not be explained, as Freud had seemed to conceive it, simply as a consequence of conflict between instinctual needs and frustrating realities. The instincts alone would never guarantee survival; they require mediation by the innate ego apparatus if they are to meet "the average expectable environmental conditions." He therefore proposed that we conceive of an autonomous factor in ego development, an independent maturation of functions taking place in a "conflict-free ego sphere." Functions such as locomotion ripen through maturation and through learning even when they are not caught up in struggles to obtain erotic and aggressive gratification or to avoid anxiety. As Anna Freud (1952) has pointed out, walking becomes independent of instinctual upheavals a few weeks after its beginning; thereafter, it serves the child impartially in situations of conflict and those that are free from conflict.

Hartmann's emphasis on adaptation permits him to perceive much more that is autonomous about the ego than was ever seriously included in Freud's systematic thought. He allows, for instance, that aims and interests which develop in the beginning as defenses against instincts may later become part of conflict-free spheres of activity—become interests in their own right—and thus achieve "secondary autonomy." a concept very close to Allport's (1937) functional autonomy of motives (Hartmann, 1950). He deals with the possibility that adaptive skills developing in the conflict-free sphere may have a decisive influence on the handling of conflicts. These skills have a history of their own, shaped jointly by the child's abilities and by the responses evoked from parents. As Monroe (1955) has expressed it, they have "a very important role in the development of the conscious and semiconscious psychological self." They may thus have a direct influence upon the outcome when a child becomes involved in conflict. Rapaport (1958) sees Hartmann's ideas on the autonomy of the ego as vital to the proper understanding not only of healthy development but also of psychopathology itself.

Glancing back over these trends in psychoanalytic ego psychology, we cannot fail to be impressed by striking similarities to the trend in animal work. Using Reik's familiar metaphor, we might say that those who listen with their two ears and those who listen with the third ear have apparently been hearing much the same sounds. In both realms there is discontent with drive orthodoxy. In both there is persistent pointing to kinds of behavior neglected or explained away by drive orthodoxy: exploration, activity, manipulation, and mastery. Similar theories have been proposed to account for the energies in such behavior: (a) they are derived or transformed in some

way from the primary drives or instincts (secondary reinforcement, neutralization of drive energies); (b) they are powered by the need to reduce anxiety; (c) they can be accounted for only by postulating a new primary drive (exploratory drive, instinct to master). When these explanations are considered to have failed, the one remaining course is to work out a different idea of motivation.

I believe that the difficulties in this undertaking can be greatly reduced by the concept of competence, to which we shall shortly turn.

Needs for Excitement and Novelty

Human experience provides plentiful evidence of the importance of reducing excessive levels of tension. Men under wartime stress, men under pressure of pain and extreme deprivation, men with excessive work loads or too much exposure to confusing social interactions, all act as if their nervous systems craved that utterly unstimulated condition which Freud once sketched as the epitome of neural bliss. But if these same men be granted their Nirvana they soon become miserable and begin to look around for a little excitement. Human experience testifies that boredom is a bad state of affairs about which something must be done. Hebb (1949) has been particularly insistent in reminding us that many of our activities, such as reading detective stories, skin diving, or driving cars at high speeds, give clear evidence of a need to raise the level of stimulation and excitement. Men and animals alike seem at times bent on increasing the impact of the environment and even on creating mild degrees of frustration and fear. Hebb and Thompson (1954) reflect upon this as follows:

Such phenomena are, of course, well known in man: in the liking for dangerous sports or roller coasters, where fear is deliberately courted, and in the addiction to bridge or golf or solitaire, vices whose very existence depends upon the level of difficulty of the problems presented and an optimal level of frustration. Once more, when we find such attitudes toward fear and frustration in animals, we have a better basis for supposing that we are dealing with something fundamental if a man prefers skis to the less dangerous snowshoes, or when we observe an unashamed love of work (problem solving and frustration included) in the scientist, or in the business man who cannot retire. Such behavior in man is usually accounted for as a search for prestige, but the animal data make this untenable. It seems much more likely that solving problems and running mild risks are inherently rewarding, or, in more general terms, that the animal will always act so as to produce an optimal level of excitation (Hebb & Thompson, 1954, p. 551).

The child at play, like the young chimpanzee and the exploring rat, needs frequent novelty in the stimulus field in order to keep up his interest—in order to maintain pleasant discrepancies from whatever adaptation level he has reached. Hebb's (1949) theory of the neurological correlates of learning also deals with novelty, though in a somewhat different way. He equates sustained interest with a state of neural affairs in which "phase sequences" are relatively complex and are growing in the sense of establishing new internal relations. Such a state follows most readily from a stimulus field characterized by difference-in-sameness, that is, containing much that is familiar along with certain features that are novel. If the field is entirely familiar, phase sequences run off quickly, are short-circuited, and thus fail to produce sustained interest. Hebb's theory, which has the engaging quality of being able to explain why we enjoy reading a detective story once but not right over again, expresses in a neurological hypothesis the familiar fact that well-learned, habituated processes do not in themselves greatly interest us. Interest seems to require elements of unfamiliarity: of something still to be found out and of learning still to be done.

It seems to me that these contributions, though differing as to details, speak with unanimity on their central theme and would force us, if nothing else did, to reconsider seriously the whole problem of motivation. Boredom, the unpleasantness of monotony, the attraction of novelty, the tendency to vary behavior rather than repeating it rigidly, and the seeking of stimulation and mild excitement stand as inescapable facts of human experience and clearly have their parallels in animal behavior. We may seek rest and minimal stimulation at the end of the day, but that is not what we are looking for the next morning. Even when its primary needs are satisfied and its homeostatic chores are done, and organism is alive, active, and up to something.

Dealing with the Environment

If we consider things only from the viewpoint of affect, excitement, and novelty, we are apt to overlook another important aspect of behavior, its effect upon the environment. Moving in this direction, Diamond (1939) invites us to consider the motivational properties of the sensorineural system, the apparatus whereby higher animals "maintain their relations to the environment." He conceives of this system as demanding stimulation and as acting in such a manner as to "force the environment to stimulate it." Even if one thinks only of the infant's exploring eyes and hands, it is clear that the main direction of behavior is by no means always that of reducing the impact of stimulation. When the eyes follow a moving object, or when the hand grasps an object which it has touched, the result is to preserve the stimulus and to increase its effect. In more elaborate explorations the consequence of a series of actions may be to vary the manner in which a stimulus acts upon the sense organs. It is apparent that the exploring, manipulating child produces by his actions precisely what Hebb's theory demands as a basis for continuing interest: he produces differences-in-sameness in the stimulus field.

High pressure of need or anxiety is the enemy of exploratory play and is a condition, as every scientist should know, under which we are unlikely to achieve an objective grasp of the environment. Low need pressure is requisite if we are to perceive objects as they are, in their constant character, apart from hopes and fears we may at other times attach to them.

Hence an autonomous capacity to be interested in the environment has great value for the survival of a species.

Being interested in the environment implies having some kind of satisfactory interaction with it. Several workers call attention to the possibility that satisfaction might lie in having an effect upon the environment, in dealing with it, and changing it in various ways. Groos (1901), in his classical analysis of play, attached great importance to the child's "joy in being a cause," as shown in making a clatter, "hustling things about," and playing in puddles where large and dramatic effects can be produced. "We demand a knowledge of effects," he wrote, "and to be ourselves the producers of effects." Piaget (1952) remarks upon the child's special interest in objects that are affected by his own movements. This aspect of behavior occupies a central place in the work of Skinner (1953), who describes it as "operant" and who thus "emphasizes the fact that the behavior *operates* upon the environment to generate consequences." These consequences are fed back through the sense organs and may serve to reinforce behavior even when no organic needs are involved. A rat will show an increased tendency to press a bar when this act produces a click or a buzz. A baby will continue to investigate when his efforts produce rattling or tinkling sounds or sparkling reflections from a shiny object. The young chimpanzees in Welker's experiment spent the longest time over objects which could be lighted or made to emit sounds. Skinner finds it "difficult, if not impossible, to trace these reinforcing effects to a history of conditioning." "We may plausibly argue," he continues, "that a capacity to be reinforced by any feedback from the environment would be biologically advantageous, since it would prepare the organism to manipulate the environment successfully before a given state of deprivation developed."

Woodworth's Behavior-Primacy Theory

The most far-reaching attempt to give these aspects of behavior a systematic place in the theory of motivation is contained in Woodworth's recent book, *Dynamics of Behavior* (1958). Woodworth takes his start from the idea that a great deal of human behavior appears to be directed toward producing effects upon the environment without immediate service to any aroused organic need. "Its incentives and rewards are in the field of behavior and not in the field of homeostasis." This is illustrated by exploratory behavior, which is directed outward toward the environment.

> Its long-range value as the means of making the child acquainted with the world he has to deal with later, and so equipping him through play for the serious business of life, can scarcely lie within the little child's horizon. His goals are more limited and direct: to see this or that object more closely, to find what is behind an obstacle, to hear the noise an object makes when it strikes the floor, to be told the name of a thing or person (Woodworth, 1958, p. 78).

COMPETENCE AND THE PLAY OF CONTENTED CHILDREN

A backward glance at our survey shows considerable agreement about the kinds of behavior that are left out or handled poorly by theories of motivation based wholly on organic drives. Repeatedly we find reference to the familiar series of learned skills which starts with sucking, grasping, and visual exploration and continues with crawling and walking, acts of focal attention and perception, memory, language and thinking, anticipation, the exploring of novel places and objects, effecting stimulus changes in the environment, manipulating and exploiting the surroundings, and achieving higher levels of motor and mental coordination. These aspects of behavior have long been the province of child psychology, which has attempted to measure the slow course of their development and has shown how heavily their growth depends upon learning. Collectively they are sometimes referred to as adaptive mechanisms or as ego processes, but on the whole we are not accustomed to cast a single name over the diverse feats whereby we learn to deal with the environment.

I now propose that we gather the various kinds of behavior just mentioned, all of which have to do with effective interaction with the environment, under the general heading of competence. According to Webster, competence means fitness or ability, and the suggested synonyms include capability, capacity, efficiency, proficiency, and skill. It is therefore a suitable word to describe such things as grasping and exploring, crawling and walking, attention and perception, language and thinking, manipulating and changing the surroundings, all of which promote an effective—a competent—interaction with the environment. It is true, of course, that maturation plays a part in all these developments, but this part is heavily overshadowed by learning in all the more complex accomplishments like speech or skilled manipulation. I shall argue that it is necessary to make competence a motivational concept; there is a *competence motivation* as well as competence in its more familiar sense of achieved capacity. The behavior that leads to the building up of effective grasping, handling, and letting go of objects, to take one example, is not random behavior produced by a general overflow of energy. It is directed, selective, and persistent, and it is continued not because it serves primary drives, which indeed it cannot serve until it is almost perfected, but because it satisfies an intrinsic need to deal with the environment.

No doubt it will at first seem arbitrary to propose a single motivational conception in connection with so many and such diverse kinds of behavior. What do we gain by attributing motivational unity to such a large array of activities? We could, of course, say that each developmental sequence, such as learning to grasp or to walk, has its own built-in bit of motivation—its "aliment," as Piaget (1952) has expressed it. We could go further and say that each item of behavior has its intrinsic motive—but this makes the concept of motivation redundant. On the other hand, we might follow the lead of the animal psychologists and postulate a limited number of broader motives under such names as curiosity, manipulation, and mastery. I believe that the idea of a competence motivation is more adequate than any of these alternatives and that it points to very vital common properties which have been lost from view amidst the strongly analytical tendencies that go with detailed research.

In order to make this claim more plausible, I shall now introduce some specimens of playful exploration in early childhood.

I hope that these images will serve to fix and dramatize the concept of competence in the same way that other images—the hungry animal solving problems, the child putting his finger in the candle flame, the infant at the breast, the child on the toilet, and the youthful Oedipus caught in a hopeless love triangle—have become memorable focal points for other concepts. For this purpose I turn to Piaget's (1952) studies of the growth of intelligence from its earliest manifestations in his own three children. The examples come from the first year of life, before language and verbal concepts begin to be important. They therefore represent a practical kind of intelligence which may be quite similar to what is developed by the higher animals.

As early as the fourth month, the play of the gifted Piaget children began to be "centered on a result produced in the external environment," and their behavior could be described as rediscovering the movement which by chance exercised an advantageous action upon things" (1952, p. 151). Laurent, lying in his bassinet, learns to shake a suspended rattle by pulling a string that hangs from it. He discovers this result fortuitously before vision and prehension are fully coordinated. Let us now observe him a little later when he has reached the age of three months and ten days.

> I place the string, which is attached to the rattle, in his right hand, merely unrolling it a little so that he may grasp it better. For a moment nothing happens. But at the first shake due to chance movement of his hand, the reaction is immediate: Laurent starts when looking at the rattle and then violently strikes his right hand alone, as if he felt the resistance and the effect. The operation lasts fully a quarter of an hour, during which Laurent emits peals of laughter (Piaget, 1952, p. 162).

Three days later the following behavior is observed.

> Laurent, by chance, strikes the chain while sucking his fingers. He grasps it and slowly displaces it while looking at the rattles. He then begins to swing it very gently, which produces a slight movement of the hanging rattles and an as yet faint sound inside them. Laurent then definitely

increases by degrees his own movements. He shakes the chain more and more vigorously and laughs uproariously at the result obtained. (Piaget, 1952, p. 185).

Very soon it can be observed that procedures are used "to make interesting spectacles last." For instance, Laurent is shown a rubber monkey which he has not seen before. After a moment of surprise, and perhaps even fright, he calms down and makes movements of pulling the string, a procedure which has no effect in this case, but which previously has caused interesting things to happen. It is to be noticed that "interesting spectacles" consist of such things as new toys, a tin box upon which a drumming noise can be made, an unfolded newspaper, or sounds made by the observer such as snapping the fingers. Commonplace as they are to the adult mind, these spectacles enter the infant's experience as novel and apparently challenging events.

Moving ahead to the second half of the first year, we can observe behavior in which the child explores the properties of objects and tries out his repertory of actions upon them. This soon leads to active experimentation in which the child attempts to provoke new results. Again we look in upon Laurent, who has now reached the age of nine months. On different occasions he is shown a variety of new objects—for instance a notebook, a beaded purse, and a wooden parrot. His carefully observing father detects four stages of response: (a) visual exploration, passing the object from hand to hand, folding the purse, etc.; (b) tactile exploration, passing the hand all over the object, scratching, etc.; (c) slow moving of the object in space; (d) use of the repertory of action: shaking the object, striking it, swinging it, rubbing it against the side of the bassinet, sucking it, etc., "each in turn with a sort of prudence as though studying the effect produced" (1952, p. 255).

Here the child can be described as applying familiar tactics to new situations, but in a short while he will advance to clear patterns of active experimentation. At 10 months and 10 days Laurent, who is unfamiliar with bread as a nutritive substance, is given a piece for examination. He manipulates it, drops it many times, breaks off fragments and lets them fall. He has often done this kind of thing before, but previously his attention has seemed to be centered on the act of letting go. Now "he watches with great interest the body in motion; in particular, he looks at it for a long time when it has fallen, and picks it up when he can." On the following day he resumes his research.

> He grasps in succession a celluloid swan, a box, and several other small objects, in each case stretching out his arm and letting them fall. Sometimes he stretches out his arm vertically, sometimes he holds it obliquely in front of or behind his eyes. When the object falls in a new position (for example on his pillow) he lets it fall two or three times more on the same place, as though to study the spatial relation; then he modifies the situation. At a certain moment the swan falls near his mouth; now he does not suck it (even though this object habitually serves this purpose), but drops it three times more while merely making the gesture of opening his mouth. (Piaget, 1952, p. 269).

These specimens will furnish us with sufficient images of the infant's use of his spare time. Laurent, of course, was provided by his studious father with a decidedly enriched environment, but no observant parent will question the fact that babies often act this way during those periods of their waking life when hunger, erotic needs, distresses, and anxiety seem to be exerting no particular pressure. If we consider this behavior under the historic headings of psychology we shall see that few processes are missing. The child gives evidence of sensing, perceiving, attending, learning, recognizing, probably recalling, and perhaps thinking in a rudimentary way. Strong emotion is lacking, but the infant's smiles, gurgles, and occasional peals of laughter strongly suggest the presence of pleasant affect. Actions appear in an organized form, particularly in the specimens of active exploration and experimentation. Apparently the child is using with a certain coherence nearly the whole repertory of psychological processes except those that accompany stress. It would be arbitrary indeed to say that one was more important than another. These specimens have a meaningful unity when seen as transactions between the child and his environment, the child having some influence upon the environment and the environment some influence upon the child. Laurent appears to be concerned about what he can do with the chain and rattles, what he can accomplish by his own effort to reproduce and to vary the entertaining sounds. If his father observed correctly, we must add that Laurent seems to have varied his actions systematically, as if testing the effect of different degrees of effort upon the bit of environment represented by the chain and rattles. Kittens make a similar study of parameters when delicately using their paws to push pencils and other objects ever nearer to the edge of one's desk. In all such examples it is clear that the child or animal is by no means at the mercy of transient stimulus fields. He selects for continuous treatment those aspects of his environment which he finds it possible to affect in some way. His behavior is selective, directed, persistent—in short, motivated.

Motivated toward what goal? In these terms, too, the behavior exhibits a little of everything. Laurent can be seen as appeasing a stimulus hunger, providing his sensorium with an agreeable level of stimulation by eliciting from the environment a series of interesting sounds, feels, and sights. On the other hand we might emphasize a need for activity and see him as trying to reach a pleasurable level of neuromuscular exercise. We can also see another possible goal in the behavior: the child is achieving knowledge, attaining a more differentiated cognitive map of his environment and thus satisfying an exploratory tendency or motive of curiosity. But it is equally possible to discern a theme of mastery, power, or control, perhaps even a bit of primitive self-assertion, in the child's concentration upon those aspects of the environment which respond in some way to his own activity. It looks as if we had found too many goals, and perhaps our first impulse is to search for some key to tell us which one is really important. But this, I think, is a mistake that would be fatal to understanding.

We cannot assign priority to any of these goals without pausing arbitrarily in the cycle of transaction between child and environment and saying, "This is the real point." I propose instead that the real point is the transactions as a whole. If the behavior gives satisfaction, this satisfaction is not associated with a particular moment in the cycle. It does not lie solely in sensory stimulation, in a bettering of the cognitive map, in coordinated action, in motor exercise, in a feeling of effort and of effects produced, or in the appreciation of change brought about in the sensory field. These are all simply aspects of a process which at this stage has to be conceived as a whole. The child appears to be occupied with the agreeable task of developing an effective familiarity with his environment. This involves discovering the effects he can have on the environment and the effects the environment will have on him. To the extent that these results are preserved by learning, they build up an increased competence in dealing with the environment. The child's play can thus be viewed as serious business, though to him it is merely something that is interesting and fun to do.

Bearing in mind these examples, as well as the dealings with environment pointed out by other workers, we must now attempt to describe more fully the possible nature of the motivational aspect of competence. It needs its own name, and in view of the foregoing analysis I propose that this name be *effectance*.

EFFECTANCE

The new freedom produced by two decades of research on animal drives is of great help in this undertaking. We are no longer obliged to look for a source of energy external to the nervous system, for a consummatory climax, or for a fixed connection between reinforcement and tension-reduction. Effectance motivation cannot, of course, be conceived as having a source in tissues external to the nervous system. It is in no sense a deficit motive. We must assume it to be neurogenic, its "energies" being simply those of the living cells that make up the nervous system. External stimuli play an important part, but in terms of "energy" this part is secondary, as one can see most clearly when environmental stimulation is actively sought. Putting it picturesquely, we might say that the effectance urge represents what the neuromuscular system wants to do when it is otherwise unoccupied or is gently stimulated by the environment. Obviously there are no consummatory acts; satisfaction would appear to lie in the arousal and maintaining of activity rather than in its slow decline toward bored passivity. The motive need not be conceived as intense and powerful in the sense that hunger, pain, or fear can be powerful when aroused to high pitch. There are plenty of instances in which children refuse to leave their absorbed play in order to eat or to visit the toilet. Strongly aroused drives, pain, and anxiety, however, can be conceived as overriding the effectance urge and capturing the energies of the neuromuscular system. But effectance motivation is persistent in the sense that it regularly occupies the spare waking time between episodes of homeostatic crisis.

In speculating upon this subject we must bear in mind the continuous nature of behavior. This is easier said than done; habitually we break things down in order to understand them, and such units as the reflex arc, the stimulus-response sequence, and the single transaction with the environment seem like inevitable steps toward clarity. Yet when we apply such an analysis to playful exploration we lose the most essential aspect of the behavior. It is constantly circling from stimulus to perception to action to effect to stimulus to perception, and so on around; or, more properly, these processes are all in continuous action and continuous change. Dealing with the environment means carrying on a continuing transaction which gradually changes one's relation to the environment. Because there is no consummatory climax, satisfaction has to be seen as lying in a considerable series of transactions, in a trend of behavior rather than a goal that is achieved. It is difficult to make the word "satisfaction" have this connotation, and we shall do well to replace it by "feeling of efficacy" when attempting to indicate the subjective and affective side of effectance.

It is useful to recall the findings about novelty: the singular effectiveness of novelty in engaging interest and for a time support-

ing persistent behavior. We also need to consider the selective continuance of transactions in which the animal or child has a more or less pronounced effect upon the environment—in which something happens as a consequence of his activity. Interest is not aroused and sustained when the stimulus field is so familiar that it gives rise at most to reflex acts or automatized habits. It is not sustained when actions produce no effects or changes in the stimulus field. Our conception must therefore be that effectance motivation is aroused by stimulus conditions which offer, as Hebb (1949) puts it, difference-in-sameness. This leads to variability and novelty of response, and interest is best sustained when the resulting action affects the stimulus so as to produce further difference-in-sameness. Interest wanes when action begins to have less effect; effectance motivation subsides when a situation has been explored to the point that it no longer presents new possibilities.

We have to conceive further that the arousal of playful and exploratory interest means the appearance of organization involving both the cognitive and active aspects of behavior. Change in the stimulus field is not an end in itself, so to speak; it happens when one is passively moved about, and it may happen as a consequence of random movements without becoming focalized and instigating exploration. Similarly, action which has effects is not an end in itself, for if one unintentionally kicks away a branch while walking, or knocks something off a table, these effects by no means necessarily become involved in playful investigation. Schachtel's (1954) emphasis on focal attention becomes helpful at this point. The playful and exploratory behavior shown by Laurent is not random or casual. It involves focal *attention* to some object—the fixing of some aspect of the stimulus field so that it stays relatively constant—and it also involves the focalizing of *action* upon this object. As Diamond (1939) has expressed it, response under these conditions is "relevant to the stimulus," and it is change in the *focalized* stimulus that so strongly affects the level of interest. Dealing with the environment means directing focal attention to some part of it and organizing actions to have some effect on this part.

In our present state of relative ignorance about the workings of the nervous system it is impossible to form a satisfactory idea of the neural basis of effectance motivation, but it should at least be clear that the concept does not refer to any and every kind of neural action. It refers to a particular kind of activity, as inferred from particular kinds of behavior. We can say that it does not include reflexes and other kinds of automatic response. It does not include well-learned, automatized patterns, even those that are complex and highly organized. It does not include behavior in the service of effectively aroused drives. It does not even include activity that is highly random and discontinuous, though such behavior may be its most direct forerunner. The urge toward competence is inferred specifically from behavior that shows a lasting focalization and that has the characteristics of exploration and experimentation, a kind of variation within the focus. When this particular sort of activity is aroused in the nervous system, effectance motivation is being aroused, for it is characteristic of this particular sort of activity that it is selective, directed, and persistent, and that instrumental acts will be learned for the sole reward of engaging in it.

Some objection may be felt to my introducing the word *competence* in connection with behavior that is so often playful. Certainly the playing child is doing things for fun, not because of a desire to improve his competence in dealing with the stern hard world. In order to forestall misunderstanding, it should be pointed out that the usage here is parallel to what we do when we connect sex with its biological goal of reproduction. The sex drive aims for pleasure and gratification, and reproduction is a consequence that is presumably unforeseen by animals and by man at primitive levels of understanding. Effectance motivation similarly aims for the feeling of efficacy, not for the vitally important learnings that come as its consequence. If we consider the part played by competence motivation in adult human life we can observe the same parallel. Sex may now be completely and purposefully divorced from reproduction but nevertheless pursued for the pleasure it can yield. Similarly, effectance motivation may lead to continuing exploratory interests or active adventures when in fact there is no longer any gain in actual competence or any need for it in terms of survival. In both cases the motive is capable of yielding surplus satisfaction well beyond what is necessary to get the biological work done.

In infants and young children it seems to me sensible to conceive of effectance motivation as undifferentiated. Later in life it becomes profitable to distinguish various motives such as cognizance, construction, mastery, and achievement. It is my view that all such motives have a root in effectance motivation. They are differentiated from it through life experiences which emphasize one or another aspect of the cycle of transaction with environment. Of course, the motives of later childhood and of adult life are no longer simple and can almost never be referred to a single root. They can acquire loadings of anxiety, defense, and compensation, they can become fused with unconscious fantasies of a sexual, aggressive, or omnipotent character, and they can gain force because of their service in producing realistic results in the way of income and career. It is not my intention to cast effectance in the star part in adult motivation. The acquisition of motives is a complicated affair in which simple and sovereign theories grow daily more obsolete. Yet it may be that the satisfaction of effectance contributes significantly to those feelings of interest which often sustain us so well in day-to-day actions, particularly when the things we are doing have continuing elements of novelty.

THE BIOLOGICAL SIGNIFICANCE OF COMPETENCE

The conviction was expressed at the beginning of this paper that some such concept as competence, interpreted motivationally, was essential for any biologically sound view of human nature. This necessity emerges when we consider the nature of living systems, particularly when we take a longitudinal view. What an organism does at a given moment does not always give the right clue as to what it does over a period of time. Discussing this problem, Angyal (1941) has proposed that we should look for the general pattern followed by the total organismic process over the course of time. Obviously this makes it necessary to take account of growth. Angyal defines life as "a process of self-expansion"; the living system "expands at the expense of its surroundings," assimilating parts of the environment and transforming them into functioning parts of itself. Organisms differ from other things in nature in that they are "self-governing entities" which are to some extent "autonomous." Internal processes govern them as well as external "heteronomous" forces. In the course of life there is a relative increase in the preponderance of internal over external forces. The living system expands, assimilates more of the environment, transforms its surroundings so as to bring them under greater control. "We may say," Angyal writes, "that the general dynamic trend of the organism is toward an increase of autonomy. . . . The human being has a characteristic tendency toward self-determination, that is, a tendency to resist external influences and to subordinate the heteronomous forces of the physical and social environment to its own sphere of influence." The trend toward increased autonomy is characteristic so long as growth of any kind is going on, though in the end the living system is bound to succumb to the pressure of heteronomous forces.

Of all living creatures, it is man who takes the longest strides toward autonomy. This is not because of any unusual tendency toward bodily expansion at the expense of the environment. It is rather that man, with his mobile hands and abundantly developed brain, attains an extremely high level of competence in his transactions with his surroundings. The building of houses, roads and bridges, the making of tools and instruments, the domestication of plants and animals, all qualify as planful changes made in the environment so that it comes more or less under control and serves our purposes rather than intruding upon them. We meet the fluctuations of outdoor temperature, for example, not only with our bodily homeostatic mechanisms, which alone would be painfully unequal to the task, but also with

clothing, buildings, controlled fires, and such complicated devices as self-regulating central heating and air conditioning. Man as a species has developed a tremendous power of bringing the environment into his service, and each individual member of the species must attain what is really quite an impressive level of competence if he is to take part in the life around him.

We are so accustomed to these human accomplishments that it is hard to realize how long an apprenticeship they require. At the outset the human infant is a slow learner in comparison with other animal forms. Hebb (1949) speaks of "the astonishing inefficiency of man's first learning, as far as immediate results are concerned," an inefficiency which he attributes to the large size of the association areas in the brain and the long time needed to bring them under sensory control. The human lack of precocity in learning shows itself even in comparison with one of the next of kin: as Hebb points out, "the human baby takes six months, the chimpanzee four months, before making a clear distinction between friend and enemy." Later in life the slow start will pay dividends. Once the fundamental perceptual elements, simple associations, and conceptual sequences have been established, later learning can proceed with ever increasing swiftness and complexity. In Hebb's words, "learning at maturity concerns patterns and events whose parts at least are familiar and which already have a number of other associations."

This general principle of cumulative learning, starting from slowly acquired rudiments and proceeding thence with increasing efficiency, can be illustrated by such processes as manipulation and locomotion, which may culminate in the acrobat devising new stunts or the dancer working out a new ballet. It is especially vivid in the case of language, where the early mastery of words and pronunciation seems such a far cry from spontaneous adult speech. A strong argument has been made by Hebb (1949) that the learning of visual forms proceeds over a similar course from slowly learned elements to rapidly combined patterns. Circles and squares, for example, cannot be discriminated at a glance without a slow apprenticeship involving eye movements, successive fixations, and recognition of angles. Hebb proposes that the recognition of visual patterns without eye movement "is possible only as the result of an intensive and prolonged visual training that goes on from the moment of birth, during every moment that the eyes are open, with an increase in skill evident over a period of 12 to 16 years at least."

On the motor side there is likewise a lot to be cumulatively learned. The playing, investigating child slowly finds out the relationships between what he does and what he experiences. He finds out, for instance, how hard he must push what in order to produce what effect. Here the S-R formula is particularly misleading. It would come nearer the truth to say that the child is busy learning R-S connections—the effects that are likely to follow upon his own behavior. But even in this reversed form the notion of bonds or connections would still misrepresent the situation, for it is only a rare specimen of behavior that can properly be conceived as determined by fixed neural channels and a fixed motor response. As Hebb has pointed out, discussing the phenomenon of "motor equivalence" named by Lashley (1942), a rat which has been trained to press a lever will press it with the left forepaw, the right forepaw, by climbing upon it, or by biting it; a monkey will open the lid of a food box with either hand, with a foot, or even with a stick; and we might add that a good baseball player can catch a fly ball while running in almost any direction and while in almost any posture, including leaping in the air and plunging forward to the ground. All of these feats are possible because of a history of learning in which the main lesson has been the effects of actions upon the stimulus fields that represent the environment. What has been learned is not a fixed connection but a flexible relationship between stimulus fields and the effects that can be produced in them by various kinds of action.

One additional example, drawn this time from Piaget (1952), is particularly worth mentioning because of its importance in theories of development. Piaget points out that a great deal of mental development depends upon the idea that the world is made up of objects having substance and permanence. Without such an "object concept" it would be impossible to build up the ideas of space and causality and to arrive at the fundamental distinction between self and external world. Observation shows that the object concept, "far from being innate or ready-made in experience, is constructed little by little." Up to 7 and 8 months the Piaget children searched for vanished objects only in the sense of trying to continue the actions, such as sucking or grasping, in which the objects had played a part. When an object was really out of sight or touch, even if only because it was covered by a cloth, the infants undertook no further exploration. Only gradually, after some study of the displacement of objects by moving, swinging, and dropping them, does the child begin to make an active search for a vanished object, and only still more gradually does he learn, at 12 months or more, to make allowance for the object's sequential displacements and thus to seek it where it has gone rather than where it was last in sight. Thus it is only through cumulative learning that the child arrives at the idea of permanent substantial objects.

The infant's play is indeed serious business. If he did not while away his time pulling strings, shaking rattles, examining wooden parrots, dropping pieces of bread and celluloid swans, when would he learn to discriminate visual patterns, to catch and throw, and to build up his concept of the object? When would he acquire the many other foundation stones necessary for cumulative learning? The more closely we analyze the behavior of the human infant, the more clearly do we realize that infancy is not simply a time when the nervous system matures and the muscles grow stronger. It is a time of active and continuous learning, during which the basis is laid for all those processes, cognitive and motor, whereby the child becomes able to establish effective transactions with his environment and move toward a greater degree of autonomy. Helpless as he may seem until he begins to toddle, he has by that time already made substantial gains in the achievement of competence.

Under primitive conditions survival must

depend quite heavily upon achieved competence. We should expect to find things so arranged as to favor and maximize this achievement. Particularly in the case of man, where so little is provided innately and so much has to be learned through experience, we should expect to find highly advantageous arrangements for securing a steady cumulative learning about the properties of the environment and the extent of possible transactions. Under these circumstances we might expect to find a very powerful drive operating to insure progress toward competence, just as the vital goals of nutrition and reproduction are secured by powerful drives, and it might therefore seem paradoxical that the interests of competence should be so much entrusted to times of play and leisurely exploration. There is good reason to suppose, however, that a strong drive would be precisely the wrong arrangement to secure a flexible, knowledgeable power of transaction with the environment. Strong drives cause us to learn certain lessons well, but they do not create maximum familiarity with our surroundings.

This point was demonstrated half a century ago in some experiments by Yerkes and Dodson (1908). They showed that maximum motivation did not lead to the most rapid solving of problems, especially if the problems were complex. For each problem there was an optimum level of motivation, neither the highest nor the lowest, and the optimum was lower for more complex tasks. The same problem has been discussed more recently by Tolman (1948) in his paper on cognitive maps. A cognitive map can be narrow or broad, depending upon the range of cues picked up in the course of learning. Tolman suggests that one of the conditions which tend to narrow the range of cues is a high level of motivation. In everyday terms, a man hurrying to an important business conference is likely to perceive only the cues that help him to get there faster, whereas a man taking a stroll after lunch is likely to pick up a substantial amount of casual information about his environment. The latent learning experiments with animals, and experiments such as those of Johnson (1953) in which drive level has been systematically

varied in a situation permitting incidental learning, give strong support to this general idea. In a recent contribution, Bruner, Matter, and Papanek (1955) make a strong case for the concept of breadth of learning and provide additional evidence that it is favored by moderate and hampered by strong motivation. The latter "has the effect of speeding up learning at the cost of narrowing it." Attention is concentrated upon the task at hand and little that is extraneous to this task is learned for future use.

These facts enable us to see the biological appropriateness of an arrangement which uses periods of less intense motivation for the development of competence. This is not to say that the narrower but efficient learnings that go with the reduction of strong drives make no contribution to general effectiveness. They are certainly an important element in capacity to deal with the environment, but a much greater effectiveness results from having this capacity fed also from learnings that take place in quieter times. It is then that the infant can attend to matters of lesser urgency, exploring the properties of things he does not fear and does not need to eat, learning to gauge the force of his string-pulling when the only penalty for failure is silence on the part of the attached rattles, and generally accumulating for himself a broad knowledge and a broad skill in dealing with his surroundings.

The concept of competence can be most easily discussed by choosing, as we have done, examples of interaction with the inanimate environment. It applies equally well, however, to transactions with animals and with other human beings, where the child has the same problem of finding out what effects he can have upon the environment and what effects it can have upon him. The earliest interactions with members of the family may involve needs so strong that they obscure the part played by effectance motivation, but perhaps the example of the well fed baby diligently exploring the several features of his mother's face will serve as a reminder that here, too, there are less urgent moments when learning for its own sake can be given free rein.

In this closing section I have brought together several ideas which bear on the evolutionary significance of competence and of its motivation. I have sought in this way to deepen the biological roots of the concept and thus help it to attain the stature in the theory of behavior which has not been reached by similar concepts in the past. To me it seems that the most important proving ground for this concept is the effect it may have on our understanding of the development of personality. Does it assist our grasp of early object relations, the reality principle, and the first steps in the development of the ego? Can it be of service in distinguishing the kinds of defense available at different ages and in providing clues to the replacement of primitive defenses by successful adaptive maneuvers? Can it help fill the yawning gap known as the latency period, a time when the mastery of school subjects and other accomplishments claim so large a share of time and energy? Does it bear upon the self and the vicissitudes of self-esteem, and can it enlighten the origins of psychological disorder? Can it make adult motives and interests more intelligible and enable us to rescue the concept of sublimation from the difficulties which even its best friends have recognized? I believe it can be shown that existing explanations of development are not satisfactory and that the addition of the concept of competence cuts certain knots in personality theory. But this is not the subject of the present communication, where the concept is offered much more on the strength of its logical and biological probability.

SUMMARY

The main theme of this paper is introduced by showing that there is widespread discontent with theories of motivation built upon primary drives. Signs of this discontent are found in realms as far apart as animal psychology and psychoanalytic ego psychology. In the former, the commonly recognized primary drives have proved to be inadequate in explaining exploratory behavior, manipulation, and general activity. In the latter, the theory of basic instincts has shown serious shortcomings when it is stretched to account for the development of the effective ego. Workers with animals have attempted to meet their problem by invoking secondary reinforcement and anxiety reduction, or by adding exploration and manipulation to the roster of primary drives. In parallel fashion, psychoanalytic workers have relied upon the concept of neutralization of instinctual energies, have seen anxiety reduction as the central motive in ego development, or have hypothesized new instincts such as mastery. It is argued here that these several explanations are not satisfactory and that a better conceptualization is possible, indeed that it has already been all but made.

In trying to form this conceptualization, it is first pointed out that many of the earlier tenets of primary drive theory have been discredited by recent experimental work. There is no longer any compelling reason to identify either pleasure or reinforcement with drive reduction, or to think of motivation as requiring a source of energy external to the nervous system. This opens the way for considering in their own right those aspects of animal and human behavior in which stimulation and contact with the environment seem to be sought and welcomed, in which raised tension and even mild excitement seem to be cherished, and in which novelty and variety seem to be enjoyed for their own sake. Several reports are cited which bear upon interest in the environment and the rewarding effects of environmental feedback. The latest contribution is that of Woodworth (1958), who makes dealing with the environment the most fundamental element in motivation.

The survey indicates a certain unanimity as to the kinds of behavior that cannot be successfully conceptualized in terms of primary drives. This behavior includes visual exploration, grasping, crawling and walking, attention and perception, language and thinking, exploring novel objects and places, manipulating the surroundings, and producing effective changes in the environment. The thesis is then proposed that all of these behaviors have a common biological significance: they all form part of the process whereby the animal or child learns to interact effectively with his environment. The word *competence* is chosen as suitable to indicate this common property. Further, it is maintained that competence cannot be fully acquired simply through behavior instigated by drives. It receives substantial contributions from activities which, though playful and exploratory in character, at the same time show direction, selectivity, and persistence in interacting with the environment. Such activities in the ultimate service of competence must therefore be conceived to be motivated in their own right. It is proposed to designate this motivation by the term effectance, and to characterize the experience produced as a *feeling of efficacy*.

In spite of its sober biological purpose, effectance motivation shows itself most unambiguously in the playful and investigatory behavior of young animals and children. Specimens of such behavior, drawn from Piaget (1952), are analyzed in order to demonstrate their constantly transactional nature. Typically they involve continuous chains of events which include stimulation, cognition, action, effect on the environment, new stimulation, *etc*. They are carried on with considerable persistence and with selective emphasis on parts of the environment which provide changing and interesting feedback in connection with effort expended. Their significance is destroyed if we try to break into the circle arbitrarily and declare that one part of it, such as cognition alone or active effort alone, is the real point, the goal, or the special seat of satisfaction. Effectance motivation must be conceived to involve satisfaction—a feeling of efficacy— in transactions in which behavior has an exploratory, varying, experimental character and produces changes in the stimulus field. Having this character, the behavior leads the organism to find out how the environment can be changed and what consequences flow from these changes.

In higher animals and especially in man, where so little is innately provided and so much has to be learned about dealing with the environment, effectance motivation independent of primary drives can be seen as an arrangement having high adaptive value. Considering the slow rate of learning in infancy and the vast amount that has to be learned before there can be an effective level of interaction with surroundings, young animals and children would simply not learn enough unless they worked pretty steadily at the task between episodes of homeostatic crisis. The association of interest with this "work," making it play and fun, is thus somewhat comparable to the association of sexual pleasure with the biological goal of reproduction. Effectance motivation need not be conceived as strong in the sense that sex, hunger, and fear are strong when violently aroused. It is moderate but persistent, and in this, too, we can discern a feature that is favorable for adaptation. Strong motivation reinforces learning in a narrow sphere, whereas moderate motivation is more conducive to an exploratory and experimental attitude which leads to competent interactions in general, without reference to an immediate pressing need. Man's huge cortical association areas might have been a suicidal piece of specialization if they had come without a steady, persistent inclination toward interacting with the environment.

REFERENCES

Allport, G. W. *Personality: A psychological interpretation.* New York: Holt, 1937.

Allport, G. W. Effect: A secondary principle of learning. *Psychol. Rev.,* 1946, 53, 335–347.

Angyal, A. *Foundations for a science of personality.* New York: Commonwealth Fund, 1941.

Ansbacher, H. L., & Ansbacher, R. R. (Eds.) *The individual psychology of Alfred Adler.* New York: Basic Books, 1956.

Beach, F. A. Analysis of factors involved in the arousal, maintenance and manifestation of sexual excitement in male animals. *Psychosom. Med.,* 1942, 4, 173–198.

Beach, F. A. Instinctive behavior: Reproductive activities. In S. S. Stevens (Ed.), *Handbook of experimental psychology.* New York: Wiley, 1951. Pp. 387–434.

Berlyne, D. E. Novelty and curiosity as determinants of exploratory behavior. *Brit. J. Psychol.,* 1950, 41, 68–80.

Berlyne, D. E. The arousal and satiation of perceptual curiosity in the rat. *J. comp. physiol. Psychol.,* 1955, 48, 238–246.

Berlyne, D. E. Attention to change, conditioned inhibition ($S^I R$) and stimulus satiation. *Brit. J. Psychol.,* 1957, 48, 138–140.

Berlyne, D. E. The present status of research on exploratory and related behavior. *J. indiv. Psychol.,* 1958, 14, 121–126.

Bibring, E. The development and problems of the theories of the instincts. *Int. J. Psychoanal.,* 1941, 22, 102–131.

Bruner, J. S., Matter, J., & Papanek, M. L. Breadth of learning as a function of drive level and mechanization. *Psychol. Rev.,* 1955, 62, 1–10.

Bühler, C. The reality principle. *Amer. J. Psychotherap.,* 1954, 8, 626–647.

Bühler, K. *Die geistige Entwicklung des Kindes.* (4th ed.) Jena: Gustav Fischer, 1924.

Butler, R. A. Discrimination learning by rhesus monkeys to visual-exploration motivation. *J. comp. physiol. Psychol.,* 1953, 46, 95–98.

Butler, R. A. Exploratory and related behavior: A new trend in animal research. *J. indiv. Psychol.,* 1958, 14, 111–120.

Butler, R. A. & Harlow, H. F. Discrimination learning and learning sets to visual exploration incentives. *J. gen. Psychol.,* 1957, 57, 257–264.

Cofer, C. N. Motivation. *Ann. Rev. Psychol.,* 1959, 10, 173–202.

Colby, K. M. *Energy and structure in psychoanalysis.* New York: Ronald, 1955.

Dashiell, J. F. A quantitative demonstration of animal drive. *J. comp. Psychol.,* 1925, 5, 205–208.

Diamond, S. A neglected aspect of motivation. *Sociometry,* 1939, 2, 77–85.

Dollard, J., & Miller, N. E. *Personality and psychotherapy.* New York: McGraw-Hill, 1950.

Erikson, E. H. *Childhood and society.* New York: Norton, 1952.

Erikson, E. H. Growth and crises of the healthy personality. In C. Kluckhohn, H. A. Murray, & D. Schneider (Eds.), *Personality in nature, society, and culture.* (2nd ed.) New York: Knopf, 1953. Pp. 185–225.

Fenichel, O. *The psychoanalytic theory of neurosis.* New York: Norton, 1945.

French, T. M. *The integration of behavior.* Vol. I. *Basic postulates.* Chicago: Univer. Chicago Press, 1952.

Freud, A. The mutual influences in the development of ego and id: Introduction to the discussion. *Psychoanal. Stud. Child,* 1952, 7, 42–50.

Freud, S. *Wit and its relation to the unconscious.* New York: Moffat, Yard, 1916.

Freud, S. Formulations regarding the two principles in mental functioning. *Collected papers.* Vol. 4. London: Hogarth Press and Institute of Psycho-analysis, 1925. Pp. 13–21. (a)

Freud, S. On narcissism: An introduction. *Collected papers.* Vol. 4. London: Hogarth Press and Institute of Psycho-analysis, 1925. Pp. 30–59. (b)

Freud, S. Instincts and their vicissitudes. *Collected papers.* Vol. 4. London: Hogarth Press and Institute of Psycho-analysis, 1925. Pp. 60–83. (c)

Freud, S. *The ego and the id.* (Trans. by J. Riviere) London: Hogarth Press, 1927.

Freud, S. *Beyond the pleasure principle.* London: Hogarth Press, 1948.

Freud, S. *An outline of psycho-analysis.* (Trans. by J. Strachey) New York: Norton, 1949.

Goldstein, K. *The organism.* New York: American Book, 1939.

Goldstein, K. *Human nature in the light of psychopathology.* Cambridge, Mass.: Harvard Univer. Press, 1940.

Gross, K. *The play of man.* (Trans. by E. L. Baldwin) New York: D. Appleton, 1901.

Harlow, H. F. Mice, monkeys, men, and motives. *Psychol. Rev.,* 1953, 60, 23–32.

Harlow, H. F., Harlow, M. K., & Meyer, D. R. Learning motivated by a manipulation drive. *J. exp. Psychol.,* 1950, 40, 228–234.

Hartmann, H. Comments on the psychoanalytic theory of the ego. *Psychoanal. Stud. Child,* 1950, 5, 74–95.

Hartmann, H. Notes on the theory of sublimation. *Psychoanal. Stud. Child,* 1955, 10, 9–29.

Hartmann, H. Notes on the reality principle. *Psychoanal. Stud. Child,* 1956, 11, 31–53.

Hartmann, H. *Ego psychology and the problem of adaptation.* (Trans. by D. Rapaport) New York: International Univer. Press, 1958.

Hartmann, H., Kris, E., & Loewenstein, R. Notes on the theory of aggression. *Psychoanal. Stud. Child,* 1949, 3 & 4, 9–36.

Hebb, D. O. *The organization of behavior.* New York: Wiley, 1949.

Hebb, D. O. Drives and the c.n.s. (conceptual nervous system). *Psychol. Rev.,* 1955, 62, 243–254.

Hebb, D. O. The motivating effects of exteroceptive stimulation. *Amer. Psychologist,* 1958, 13, 109–113.

Hebb, D. O., & Thompson, W. R. The social significance of animal studies. In G. Lindzey (Ed.), *Handbook of social psychology.* Vol. I. Cambridge, Mass.: Addison-Wesley, 1954. Pp. 532–561.

Hendrick, I. Instinct and the ego during infancy. *Psychoanal. Quart.,* 1942, 11, 33–58.

Hendrick, I. Work and the pleasure principle. *Psychoanal. Quart.,* 1943, 12, 311–329. (a)

Hendrick, I. The discussion of the 'instinct to master.' *Psychoanal. Quart.,* 1943, 12, 561–565. (b)

Hill, W. F. Activity as an autonomous drive. *J. comp. physiol. Psychol.,* 1956, 49, 15–19.

Johnson, E. E. The role of motivational strength in latent learning. *J. comp. physiol. Psychol.,* 1953, 45, 526–530.

Kagan, J. Differential reward value of incomplete and complete sexual behavior. *J. comp. physiol. Psychol.,* 1955, 48, 59–64.

Kagan, J., & Berkun, M. The reward value of running activity. *J. comp. physiol. Psychol.,* 1954, 47, 108.

Kardiner, A., & Spiegel, H. War stress and neurotic illness. New York: Hoeber, 1947.

Lashley, K. S. Experimental analysis of instinctive behavior. *Psychol. Rev.,* 1938, 45, 445–471.

Lashley, K. S. The problem of cerebral organization in vision. In H. Klüver, *Visual mechanisms.* Lancaster, Pa.: Jaques Cattell, 1942. Pp. 301–322.

Leuba, C. Toward some integration of learning theories: The concept of optimal stimulation. *Psychol. Rep.,* 1955, 1, 27–33.

Lilly, J. C. Mental effects of reduction of ordinary levels of physical stimuli on intact, healthy persons. *Psychiat. res. Rep.,* 1956, No. 5.

Maslow, A. H. *Motivation and personality.* New York: Harper, 1954.

Maslow, A. H. Deficiency motivation and growth motivation. In M. R. Jones (Ed.), *Nebraska symposium on motivation 1955.* Lincoln, Neb.: Univer. Nebraska Press, 1955. Pp. 1–30.

McClelland, D. C., Atkinson, J. W., Clark, R. A. & Lowell, E. I. *The achievement motive.* New York: Appleton-Century, 1953.

McDougall, W. *Introduction to social psychology.* (16th ed.) Boston: John Luce, 1923.

McReynolds, P. A restricted conceptualization of human anxiety and motivation. *Psychcl. Rep.,* 1956, 2, 293–312. Monogr. Suppl. 6.

Miller, N. E. Learnable drives and rewards. In S. S. Stevens (Ed.), *Handbook of experimental psychology.* New York: Wiley, 1951. Pp. 435–472.

Miller, N. E. Central stimulation and other new approaches to motivation and reward. *Amer. Psychologist,* 1958, 13, 100–108.

Mittelmann, B. Motility in infants, children, and adults. *Psychoanal. Stud. Child,* 1954, 9, 142–177.

Montgomery, K. C. The role of the exploratory drive in learning. *J. comp. physiol. Psychol.,* 1954, 47, 60–64.

Montgomery, K. C., & Monkman, J. A. The relation between fear and exploratory behavior. *J. comp. physiol. Psychol.,* 1955, 48, 132–136.

Morgan, C. T. *Physiological psychology.* New York: McGraw-Hill, 1943.

Morgan, C. T. Physiological mechanisms of motivation. In M. R. Jones (Ed.), *Nebraska symposium on motivation 1957.* Lincoln, Neb.: Univer. Nebraska Press, 1957. Pp. 1–35.

Mowrer, O. H. *Learning theory and personality dynamics.* New York: Ronald, 1950.

Munroe, R. *Schools of psychoanalytical thought.* New York: Dryden, 1955.

Murphy, G. *Personality: A biosocial approach to origins and structure.* New York: Harper, 1947.

Murray, H. A. *Explorations in personality.* New York & London: Oxford Univer. Press, 1938.

Murray, H. A. & Kluckhohn, C. Outline of a conception of personality. In C. Kluckhohn, H. A. Murray, & D. M. Schneider (Eds.), *Personality in nature, society, and culture.* (2nd ed.) New York: Knopf, 1953.

Myers, A. K., & Miller, N. E. Failure to find a learned drive based on hunger; evidence for learning motivated by "exploration." *J. comp. physiol. Psychol.,* 1954, 47, 428–436.

Nissen, H. W. A study of exploratory behavior in the white rat by means of the obstruction method. *J. genet. Psychol.,* 1930, 37, 361–376.

Olds, J., & Milner, P. Positive reinforcement produced by electrical stimulation of septal area and other regions of rat brain. *J. comp. physiol. Psychol.,* 1954, 47, 419–427.

Piaget, J. *The origins of intelligence in children.* (Trans. by M. Cook) New York: International Univer. Press, 1952.

Rapaport, D. *Organization and pathology of thought.* New York: Columbia Univer. Press, 1951.

Rapaport, D. On the psychoanalytic theory of thinking. In R. P. Knight & C. R. Friedman (Eds.), *Psychoanalytic psychiatry and psychology.* New York: International Univer. Press, 1954. Pp. 259–273.

Rapaport, D. The theory of ego autonomy: A generalization. *Bull. Menninger Clin.,* 1958, 22, 13–35.

Rosvold, H. E. Physiological psychology. *Ann. Rev. Psychol.,* 1959, 10, 415–454.

Schachtel, E. G. The development of focal attention and the emergence of reality. *Psychiatry,* 1954, 17, 309–324.

Sheffield, F. D., & Roby, T. B. Reward value of a non-nutritive sweet taste. *J. comp. physiol. Psychol.,* 1950, 43, 471–481.

Sheffield, F. D., Roby, T. B., & Campbell, B. A. Drive reduction vs. consummatory behavior as determinants of reinforcement. *J. comp. physiol. Psychol.,* 1954, 47, 349–354.

Sheffield, F. D., Wulff, J. J., & Backer, R. Reward value of copulation without sex drive reduction. *J. comp. physiol. Psychol.,* 1951, 44, 3–8.

Skinner, B. F. *Science and human behavior.* New York: Macmillan, 1953.

Steller, E. The physiology of motivation. *Psychol. Rev.,* 1954, 61, 5–22.

Tolman, E. C. Cognitive maps in rats and men. *Psychol. Rev.,* 1948, 55, 189–208.

Welker, W. L. Some determinants of play and exploration in chimpanzees. *J. comp. physiol. Psychol.,* 1956, 49, 84–89.

Whiting, J. W. M. & Mowrer, O. H. Habit progression and regression—a laboratory study of some factors relevant to human socialization. *J. comp. Psychol.,* 1943, 36, 229–253.

Wolfe, J. B., & Kaplon, M. D. Effect of amount of reward and consummative activity on learning in chickens. *J. comp. Psychol.,* 1941, 31, 353–361.

Woodworth, R. S. *Dynamics of behavior.* New York: Holt, 1958.

Yerkes, R. M. & Dodson, J. D. The relation of strength of stimulus to rapidity of habit-formation. *J. comp. Neurol. Psychol.,* 1908, 18, 459–482.

Young, P. T. Food-seeking drive, affective process, and learning. *Psychol. Rev.,* 1949, 56, 98–121.

Young, P. T. The role of hedonic processes in motivation. In M. R. Jones (Ed.), *Nebraska symposium on motivation 1955.* Lincoln, Neb.: Univer. Nebraska Press, 1955. Pp. 193–238.

Zimbardo, P. G., & Miller, N. E. Facilitation of exploration by hunger in rats. *J. comp. physiol. Psychol.,* 1958, 51, 43–46.

The Relationship of Persistence at a task to Expectation of Success and Achievement Related Motives[1] / N. T. Feather[2] (*University of Michigan*)

The present study investigates the relationship of persistence at a task both to its apparent difficulty and to the relative

strength within an individual of the motives to achieve success and to avoid failure (Feather, 1960). The situation to be considered is one in which a subject comes to an objectively insoluble puzzle either believing it to be easy or very difficult. He works at this achievement task under test conditions and suffers repeated and consistent failure in his attempts to get the solu-

Reprinted from *Journal of Abnormal and Social Psychology,* 1961, 63, pages 552–561, by permission of author and publisher, The American Psychological Association.

[1] This paper is based upon a doctoral dissertation submitted to the department of psychology at the University of Michigan.

The research was part of a project on Personality Dynamics financed by a grant from the Ford Foundation.

The author wishes to thank John W. Atkinson,

dissertation chairman, for his advice and criticism; and J. David Birch, Dorwin Cartwright, Clyde C. Coombs, and John B. Lansing for their suggestions.

[2] Now at the University of New England, Armidale, New South Wales, Australia.

tion. Persistence is measured in terms of the total time or total trials which the subject works at the task before he turns to an alternative achievement activity. The former measure is sometimes referred to in the literature as temporal persistence; the latter is analogous to resistance to extinction.

The hypotheses of the present investigation are developed from the theory of achievement motivation (Atkinson, 1957, 1960) together with certain additional assumptions. This theory relates characteristics of motivated behavior to the interaction of relatively stable personality dispositions (motives) and more transient situational influences (expectations and incentive values). As such, this approach belongs to a class of "expectancy value" theories which all involve somewhat similar concepts (Feather, 1959a). Within this context, the present research attempts to clarify the relationship of persistence at a task to expectations and motives by providing answers to the following two questions:

1. How is persistence at a task affected by the initial subjective probability of success among subjects in whom the motive to achieve success is stronger than the motive to avoid failure ($M_s > M_{af}$)? Do such subjects tend to persist longer at the task when it initially appears easy to them than when it initially appears very difficult?

2. Conversely, how is persistence at a task affected by the initial subjective probability of success among subjects in whom the motive to avoid failure is stronger than the motive to achieve success ($M_{af} > M_s$)?

The present investigation goes beyond the earlier studies of French and Thomas (1958) and Atkinson and Litwin (1960) in its attempt to vary both motive and expectation simultaneously. Furthermore, it provides assumptions about the dynamics of changing motivation as expectations of success and failure change, and an explicit analysis of why the subject stops performing the task.

THEORETICAL ASSUMPTIONS

Consider a subject who is performing the initial achievement task. It is assumed that

he will continue to persist at this task as long as total motivation to perform it is stronger than total motivation to perform the alternative available to him.

Total motivation to perform the initial achievement task is attributable to the following component motivations[3]: (a) achievement related motivation to perform the task, and (b) extrinsic motivation to perform the task. Similarly, since the alternative is also an achievement task, total motivation to perform it is attributable to analogous component motivations.

Achievement related motivation to perform a task refers to the *resultant* of motivation to achieve success at the task and motivation to avoid failure at the task. According to the theory of achievement motivation (Atkinson, 1957, 1960) these two motivations summate algebraically to give *positive* achievement related motivation (approach) for subjects in whom the motive to achieve success is stronger than the motive to avoid failure (i.e., when $M_s > M_{af}$), and *negative* achievement related motivation (avoidance) for subjects in whom $M_{af} > M_s$. Further, achievement related motivation whether positive or negative is at its maximum when subjective probability of success at the task is intermediate (i.e., when $P_s = .50$) and decreases monotonically as P_s becomes either smaller or larger than .50. If achievement related motivation were the only motivation elicited in the situation it is apparent that a subject with stronger motive to avoid failure should not even undertake performance of an achievement task. Instead he should avoid the task and choose activities which do not arouse anxiety about failure. In contrast, a subject with stronger motive to achieve success should show some positive interest in performing an achievement task.

The concept of extrinsic motivation to perform a task is introduced to account for the fact that the subject is in a social situation in which he has the role of a subject in

[3] It should be noted that a distinction is made between motivation, which refers to a particular act or response, and motive. Differences in strength of motive (a latent disposition of personality) are assumed to be only one factor influencing the strength of motivation, the other influences being level of expectation and incentive value.

an experiment and knows he is expected to make some attempt at the task. In any test situation there are certain extrinsic constraints that influence the subject to perform the task irrespective of the nature of his achievement related motivation. Studies by French (1955), and by Atkinson and Raphelson (1956) have shown, for example, that other motives like n Affiliation are sometimes systematically related to task performance in a situation where no achievement orientation is given but cooperation is requested. The usual social constraints (i.e., desire for approval, fear of disapproval) provide an important source of motivation for subjects in whom $M_{af} > M_s$. If these subjects are to perform the task at all, some positive motivation must exist to oppose their tendency to avoid an achievement task. For subjects in whom $M_s > M_{af}$, the extrinsic motivation to perform an assigned task enhances their normally positive motivation to perform achievement related tasks. In both cases, task performance may be considered overdetermined, that is, the result of two or more different kinds of motivation to perform or not to perform the task (cf. Atkinson & Reitman, 1956).

In the light of this analysis of the components of total motivation, the basic condition for performance of the initial task rather than the alternative task is as follows:

INITIAL TASK
Achievement related   Extrinsic
                +
motivation   motivation

ALTERNATIVE TASK
$>$ Achievement related   Extrinsic
                +
motivation   motivation

It is assumed that the subject will turn to the alternative achievement task when:

INITIAL TASK
Achievement related   Extrinsic
                +
motivation   motivation

ALTERNATIVE TASK
$<$ Achievement related   Extrinsic
                +
motivation   motivation

How then does total motivation to perform the initial achievement task become weaker than total motivation to perform the alternative, so that the subject gives up persisting at the initial task and turns to the alternative? To permit derivation of hypotheses the following three assumptions are made:

1. Both extrinsic motivation to perform the initial task and extrinsic motivation to perform the alternative task are assumed to be constant across experimental conditions.

2. Extrinsic motivation to perform the initial task is assumed to be stronger than extrinsic motivation to perform the alternative task. This is a strong assumption that at least acknowledges the fact that the subject is asked by the experimenter to begin the initial task first.

3. The subjective probability of success for the alternative achievement task is assumed to be constant across experimental conditions. Hence, achievement related motivation to perform the alternative task is a positive constant for subjects in whom the motive to achieve success is stronger (i.e., when $M_s > M_{af}$), and has the same value (but negative) for subjects in whom $M_{af} > M_s$.

It follows that any decrease in total motivation to perform the initial task must be related to change in achievement related motivation to perform the initial task. Since, in the theory of achievement motivation, the motives to achieve success (M_s) and to avoid failure (M_{af}) are considered relatively *stable* dispositions of the personality, change in achievement related motivation to perform the initial task must be mediated by variation in the subject's expectation of success at the task as he works at it unsuccessfully. Repeated unsuccessful attempts at the initial task are assumed to produce successive decreases in subjective probability of success at the task (P_s). Decrease in P_s is thus the basic dynamic principle assumed to mediate decrease in total motivation to perform the initial task.

The following two specific assumptions are made about this decrease in expectation of success:

1. When the task is presented as a test of skill, reduction in P_s to a particular value is

assumed to require more unsuccessful attempts at the task when P_s is initially high than when P_s is initially low.[4]

2. The rate at which decrease in P_s occurs is assumed not to be systematically related to the strength of either the motive to achieve success (M_s) or the motive to avoid failure (M_{af}).

HYPOTHESES

The following four hypotheses are tested in the present investigation:

Hypothesis 1 states that when the motive to achieve success is stronger than the motive to avoid failure ($M_s > M_{af}$), persistence at the initial achievement task should be greater when initial subjective probability of success is high (i.e., some $P_s > .50$) than when initial P_s is low (i.e., some $P_s < .50$).

Hypothesis 2 states that when $M_{af} > M_s$, persistence at the initial achievement task should be greater when initial P_s is low (i.e., some $P_s < .50$) than when initial P_s is high (i.e., some $P_s > .50$).

Hypothesis 3 states that when initial P_s is high (i.e., some $P_s > .50$), subjects in whom $M_s > M_{af}$ should persist longer at the initial achievement task than subjects in whom $M_{af} > M_s$.

Hypothesis 4 states that when initial P_s is low (i.e., some $P_s < .50$), subjects in whom $M_{af} > M_s$ should persist longer at the initial achievement task than subjects in whom $M_s > M_{af}$.

The detailed derivation is presented for Hypotheses 1 and 2 only. The derivation of Hypotheses 3 and 4 follows the same line of argument.

Derivation of Hypothesis 1

Consider a subject in whom the motive to achieve success is stronger than the motive to avoid failure (i.e., $M_s > M_{af}$), and to whom the initial achievement task is presented as easy (i.e., some $P_s > .50$). For this subject, achievement related motivation to perform the task is *positive* (approach) and becomes increasingly positive as his sub-

[4] This assumption is consistent with the distinction between tasks involving skill and tasks involving a degree of external control (e.g., chance) presented by James and Rotter (1958).

jective probability of success (P_s) at the task falls to .50 with successive failures. Hence, total motivation to perform the initial task should increase as the task appears more difficult to the subject up to the point at which his $P_s = .50$. At this point positive achievement related motivation and, hence, total motivation to perform the task would be maximum. Thereafter, as P_s gets lower and the task appears more and more difficult to the subject, positive achievement related motivation decreases until at some low level of P_s total motivation to perform the initial task becomes weaker than total motivation to perform the alternative. The subject should then quit the initial task and turn to the alternative.

In contrast, if the initial task were presented to this subject as very difficult (i.e., some $P_s < .50$), there would be an immediate decrease in the positive achievement related motivation to perform the task as his P_s drops with repeated failure. Hence, total motivation to perform the initial task would decrease immediately. In this condition it should take less unsuccessful attempts at the task to reduce P_s to the low level at which total motivation to perform the initial task becomes less than total motivation to perform the alternative. Hence, we would expect a subject in whom $M_s > M_{af}$ to persist longer at the initial achievement task when his P_s is initially high than when his P_s is initially low.

Derivation of Hypothesis 2

Consider a subject in whom the motive to avoid failure is stronger than the motive to achieve success (i.e., $M_{af} > M_s$), and to whom the initial achievement task is presented as easy (i.e., some $P_s > .50$). For this subject, achievement related motivation to perform the task is *negative* (avoidance) and becomes increasingly negative as his P_s at the task drops to .50 with repeated failure. Hence, total motivation to perform the initial task should decrease as the task appears more difficult to the subject up to the point at which his $P_s = .50$, where negative achievement related motivation would be maximum. At this point total motivation to perform the initial task should therefore be minimum. It follows that, if the subject is to quit the task at all, he should do so as his P_s at the task falls to .50 since it is during this stage of task performance that total motivation to perform the task is decreasing.

In contrast, if the initial task were presented to this subject as very difficult (i.e., some $P_s < .50$), there would be an immediate decrease in negative achievement related motivation as his P_s drops with repeated failure. Hence, total motivation to perform the initial task would increase immediately, and the subject should continue to perform the task indefinitely. We would therefore expect a subject in whom $M_{af} > M_s$ to persist longer at the initial achievement task when his P_s is initially low than when his P_s is initially high.

In the preceding analysis, differences in persistence have been related to differences in the way in which total motivation to perform the initial achievement task changes with decrease in P_s as a subject experiences repeated failure at the task. The different types of change in total motivation are summarized in Table 1 in relation to differences in motive and differences in initial P_s.

Adequate tests of the hypotheses of the study clearly require development of procedures which communicate to the subjects that they are expected to perform the initial achievement task first, but that they may

TABLE 1

Changes in Total Motivation to Perform the Initial Achievement Task as P_s Decreases in Relation to Differences in Motive ($M_s > M_{af}$ and $M_{af} > M_s$) and Differences in Initial Subjective Probability of Success ($P_s > .50$ and $P_s < .50$)

Initial P_s	Motive relationship	Change in total motivation as P_s decreases
> .50	$M_s > M_{af}$	Increase followed by decrease
< .50	$M_s > M_{af}$	Immediate decrease
> .50	$M_{af} > M_s$	Decrease followed by increase
< .50	$M_{af} > M_s$	Immediate increase

feel free to move on to the alternative achievement task whenever they choose to do so. If extrinsic motivation to perform the initial task were very strong in relation to

extrinsic motivation to perform the alternative task, none of the differences in persistence predicted here would be expected to occur.

METHOD

Subjects

Thematic apperceptive stories under neutral conditions and Mandler-Sarason Test Anxiety Questionnaire provided measures of strength of n Achievement (M_s) and Test Anxiety (M_{af}) for 89 male college students from an introductory psychology course at the University of Michigan in 1959.[5] The TAT was administered according to the standard procedure (McClelland, Atkinson, Clark, & Lowell, 1953). Six pictures were presented in the following order (using numbers assigned by Atkinson, 1958): 2, 48, 1, 7, 100, 24. Interscorer reliability for scoring n Achievement was .93.[6]

In subjects classified High n Achievement-Low Test Anxiety (in terms of median splits) it was assumed $M_s > M_{af}$; in subjects classified Low n Achievement-High Test Anxiety it was assumed $M_{af} > M_s$.

Task

A task consisting of four items and labeled the Pereceptual Reasoning test was presented to 34 of these preselected subjects in individual test sessions of one hour duration. Subjects were randomly assigned so that approximately half of each of the High n Achievement-Low Test Anxiety and Low n Achievement-High Test Anxiety groups came to the first item of the Perceptual Reasoning test with a high initial subjective probability of success (P_s); the other half came to the first item with a low initial P_s. The procedure adopted in assigning subjects guaranteed that the experimenter would be unaware when testing a subject for persistence of his n Achievement and Test Anxiety scores. The initial P_s for each item of the test was experimentally induced by using fictitious group norms and the subject could leave each item as he wished and turn to the next one in the series.

Each item of the Perceptual Reasoning

[5] The author wishes to thank Charles P. Smith for administering the TAT and Test Anxiety Questionnaire.
[6] The author wishes to thank William Larkin for his assistance in scoring the TAT protocols.

test involved a line diagram approximately 1.5 inches square printed on a white card 6″ × 4″. Copies of a particular item were stacked in a pile 2″ high and the four piles of cards were placed in line on the desk immediately in front of the subject. The piles were designated 1–4 from left to right and the subject could not see the content of any item until he began to work at it, i.e., the precise content of the alternatives to which he could turn if he wished to quit an item was unknown to him.

For each item the subject's task was to trace over all the lines of the diagram with a red pencil according to two rules: he was not permitted to lift his pencil from the figure; he was not permitted to trace over any line twice. It is a simple matter to construct figures for which the problem is *insoluble* but which are sufficiently complex so that the subject is unable to see this. The subject was allowed to take as many trials at an item as he wished. If he wanted another trial at the item, he simply took another copy of the same item from the top of its pile and worked at it. The following instructions to the subject summarize the restrictions placed on task performance:

Naturally there are certain restrictions involved in this test. You can only work at an item for 40 seconds at a time, and I shall be timing you on that. But you can have as many of these 40 second trials as you want. If you fail on a trial, that is if you don't succeed in tracing over all the lines in the figure, you will then have the choice of continuing or going on to the next item. If you want to go on to the next item you should let me know at once. Once you've stopped working at an item you can't go back to it again. If you want to continue with the item you should turn the *failed* copy face downwards. You can then take another copy of the same item from the pile and you will again have 40 seconds to work at that.

Obviously, for an insoluble item, each trial the subject took resulted in failure. Using this procedure, one can obtain two measures of persistence for an insoluble item: total time spent in working at the item; and number of trials taken at the item before turning to the next one in the series. The former measure is akin to the typical temporal measure used in studies of persistence; the latter is analogous to resistance to extinction.

It will be noted that the alternative activity to which the subject could turn was another *achievement* task similar in content to the one at which he had been working.

Of the four items involved in the Perceptual Reasoning test the first and third were *insoluble,* the second and fourth items were soluble.

Experimental Induction of Subjective Probability of Success

The following instructions were given:

Now the four items vary in difficulty. Some are harder than others, and you're not expected to be able to solve all of them, but do the best you can. Before I present each item I'm going to let you know the percentage of college students who are able to pass that item. . . . Well, let's look at the norms for the first item. These go by age. How old are you? The tables show that at your age level——per cent, that is approximately——per cent of college students are able to get the solution.

Table 2 presents the fictitious norms for each of the four items of the Perceptual Reasoning test that were reported to Groups A, B, C, and D. These norms were assumed to be sufficiently different to determine differences in initial P_s for each of the four items. It should be noted that initial P_s on items following the first may be influenced not only by the norms reported to the subject but also by the subject's actual experience with the preceding items.

The following final instructions were given before Item 1 was presented to the subject:

Try to get the solution if you can. It's quite OK for you to take as many 40 second trials as you want at the item. But remember that the four items do vary in difficulty, some are harder than others and you may not be able to solve all of them. So if you should feel that you're not getting anywhere with the item you should let me know at once so that we can move on to the next one. Here is Item 1. You should find it fairly easy/ difficult.

For each insoluble item the subject was timed from when he started the item until when he nominated to try the next item in the set. When he quit an insoluble item, the copies of the item he had attempted were stacked to one side out of sight and their number was later recorded.

Effectiveness of Reported Norms

Norm procedure: After reporting the fictitious group norm but before presenting the item, the experimenter gave the following instruction: ". . . I'm also going to ask you to let me know what you think your own chances are of solving the problem. You can do this very simply by marking a number along this scale. I'll get you to do this before I present each item and I'll also get you to check here how confident you are about that estimate." To obtain the probability estimates a 20-point rating scale was used, numbered from 0 to 100 in steps of five. The

TABLE 2

FICTITIOUS PERCENTAGES[a] OF SUCCESS REPORTED TO SUBJECTS IN THE EXPERIMENTAL INDUCTION OF INITIAL DIFFICULTY FOR EACH OF FOUR TEST ITEMS

Group	Motivation		Reported percentages of success for each of four items			
	n Achievement	Test Anxiety	1	2	3	4
A	High	Low	70	50	5	50
B	High	Low	5	50	70	50
C	Low	High	70	50	5	50
D	Low	High	5	50	70	50

[a] Actual percentages reported deviated slightly from tabulated values in that they were given to one decimal place to add to authenticity (e.g., 69.4%).

subject made his rating of confidence in his probability estimate on a five-category Likert-type scale ranging from "Not certain at all" to "No doubt about it at all."

Time Limits for Insoluble Items 1 and 3

Data concerning persistence at Item 1 were from the very outset considered more crucial for the test of the hypotheses since results for other items would be complicated by differential sequence effects. For this reason each subject was allowed to persist at Item 1 for 20 minutes (if he so desired) so as to increase the possibility of obtaining a wide variance in persistence scores. If the subject was still persisting at Item 1 after 20 minutes it was suggested that he move on

to Item 2. This interruption procedure for Item 1 necessarily introduced a time differential for Item 3, some subjects having more time to work at this item than others, depending on how long they had worked at Item 1. Subjects still working at Item 3 were interrupted at approximately 15 minutes before the hour to allow sufficient time for administration of a postperformance questionnaire.

Postperformance Questionnaire

Finally, the experimenter administered a questionnaire to each subject specifically designed to provide information about the assumptions involved in the hypotheses. The majority of questions were presented in Likert-type form and were related to Item 1. When the subject had completed the questionnaire he was thanked for his participation in the experiment, commended on his performance at a fairly difficult task, and requested to keep details of the experiment in confidence. A report of the experiment was sent to each subject at a later date.

RESULTS

The basic data relevant to the hypotheses of the present investigation are the persistence scores of the four groups in terms of time and trials for the first insoluble item (Item 1). The results of analysis of persistence scores for the second insoluble item (Item 3) are presented in less detail since the necessity for unanticipated interruption of a sizable number of extremely persistent subjects on the first and third items, and the possibility of uncontrolled sequence effects, make interpretation of results for the third item equivocal.

Analysis of Persistence at Item 1

Since time and trials scores are perfectly correlated for Item 1, only the analysis of persistence trials is presented. By persistence trials is meant the number of trials the subject took at Item 1 before he quit to move on to the second item or before he was interrupted. The median of these persistence trials at Item 1 for all subjects is 20 with a range from 2 to 41+.[7] Persistence trials for

[7] The + indicates that the subject has to be interrupted. Due to the interruption procedure some scores are open-ended. Hence, results are classified on the basis of median splits and relationships in the resulting frequency tables analyzed using χ^2 as the basic statistic.

subjects of each of Groups A, B, C, and D are classified as high and low in terms of whether they are above or below this median, and the resulting frequencies are presented in Table 3. Below Table 3 are presented the results of a partitioned χ^2 analysis (Sutcliffe, 1957) applied to these data.

Table 3 shows that only the χ^2 representing the interactive effect of motivation and expectation on persistence is significant ($p < .01$). While the proportion of subjects classified high in persistence *increases* as the reported norm varies from 5% to 70% (i.e., from difficult to easy) for subjects high in n Achievement and low in Test Anxiety, this proportion *decreases* for subjects low in n Achievement and high in Test Anxiety with the same variation in the reported norm. This implies a basic difference in the way persistence is related to the initial difficulty of the item among subjects in whom $M_s > M_{af}$ versus subjects in whom $M_{af} > M_s$.

Relationships in Table 3 are clearly consistent with Hypotheses 1, 2, 3, and 4. Subjects in whom it is assumed that $M_s > M_{af}$

(the High-Low subjects) show greater persistence at the task when the reported norm defines it as easy (70% norm) than when the norm defines it as difficult (5% norm). This result supports Hypothesis 1 in implying that subjects in whom $M_s > M_{af}$ tend to persist longer at the item when initial expectation of sucess is high rather than low. In contrast, subjects in whom it is assumed that $M_{af} > M_s$ (the Low-High subjects) show greater persistence at the task when the reported norm defines it as difficult (5% norm) than when the norm defines it as easy (70% norm). This result supports Hypothesis 2 in implying that subjects in whom $M_{af} > M_s$ tend to persist longer at the item when initial expectation of success is low rather than high. Furthermore, among subjects for whom the reported norm defines the item as easy, the proportion of subjects showing high persistence is greater for those classified as high in n Achievement and low in Test Anxiety. This result is consistent with Hypothesis 3 in implying that, when the initial expectation of success is high, subjects in whom $M_s > M_{af}$ tend to persist longer at the item than subjects in whom

TABLE 3

NUMBER OF SUBJECTS WHO WERE HIGH AND LOW IN PERSISTENCE ON ITEM 1 IN RELATION TO STATED DIFFICULTY OF THE TASK AND NATURE OF MOTIVATION

Group	Motivation		Stated difficulty of task	Persistence trials	
	n Achievement	Test Anxiety		High (above median)	Low (below median)
A	High	Low	70% (easy)	6	2
B	High	Low	5% (difficult)	2	7
C	Low	High	70% (easy)	3	6
D	Low	High	5% (difficult)	6	2
A and B	High	Low	70%, 5%	8	9
C and D	Low	High	70%, 5%	9	8
A and C	Both conditions		70% (easy)	9	8
B and D	Both conditions		5% (difficult)	8	9

Partition of χ^2

Source	Value	df	p
Motivation × Persistence	.12	1	> .05
Expectation × Persistence	.12	1	> .05
Motivation × Expectation × Persistence	7.65	1	< .01
Total	7.89	3	< .05

$M_{af} > M_s$. Finally, among subjects for whom the reported norm defines the item as difficult, the proportion of subjects showing high persistence is greater for those classified as low in n Achievement and high in Test Anxiety. The result is consistent with Hypothesis 4 in implying that, when the initial expectation of success is low, subjects in whom $M_{af} > M_s$ tend to persist longer at the item than subjects in whom $M_s > M_{af}$.

Analysis of Persistence at Item 3

Persistence data for Item 3 compared across Groups A, B, C, and D show no significant trends. However, when comparisons of persistence scores for Items 1 and 3 are made within the same group, subjects of Group B (High-Low subjects) persist longer at Item 3 which for them is defined by the reported norm as easy than at Item 1 which is defined by the norm as difficult. This change is consistent with Hypothesis 1. Subjects of Group C (Low-High subjects) persist longer at Item 3 which for them is defined by the reported norm as difficult than at Item 1 which is defined by the norm as easy. This change is consistent with Hypothesis 2. However, when ambiguous comparisons of persistence scores are excluded (due to the interruption procedure), there is a tendency for all subjects to persist longer at Item 3 than at Item 1. This suggests that an influence common to all subjects might have operated to increase persistence at Item 3.

When such an influence is assumed and ambiguous differences in persistence scores (due to the interruption procedure) are excluded, the data support the qualified prediction that Groups A and D should at least tend to increase relatively less in persistence from Item 1 to Item 3 than do Groups B and C. However, this result is equivocal since, as a result of limitations of time, subjects of Group A and D who persist relatively longer at Item 1 may not have had the same opportunity to increase in persistence at Item 3 as did subjects of Groups B and C.

Analysis of Supplementary Data

Analysis of data concerned with effectiveness of experimental procedures supports the assumption that the different reported norms determined widely different initial subjective probabilities of success. The probability estimates given by subjects in all four groups tend to follow the reported norms very closely. Data obtained from the postperformance questionnaire are generally consistent with assumptions involved in hypotheses. For example, subjects in all four groups report decreases in estimates of probability of success as they work at Item 1 with repeated failure. This decrease is consistent with the basic dynamic assumption that expectation of success should diminish with repeated failure at the task. In addition, there is no evidence that the rate of decrease in probability estimates with failure at Item 1 differs between the two motivation conditions (High-Low subjects versus Low-High subjects). This implies that rate of decrease in P_s is independent of the relative strength of M_s and M_{af} within the individual.

DISCUSSION

Where the present investigation permits unequivocal test of the four hypotheses (i.e., for Item 1), results are consistent with predictions. Furthermore, postperformance questionnaire data generally support the basic assumptions involved in these predictions.

The investigation stands in marked contrast to the typical trait studies of persistence and extinction studies with human subjects since hypotheses are based on a consideration of personality and situational factors in interaction. Trait studies of persistence typically concentrate on the relatively stable aspects of persons by looking for consistencies in behavior and they tend to neglect the role of the situation. In contrast, extinction studies usually attempt to relate persistence of behavior to characteristics of the acquisition stage and they tend to ignore the influence on resistance to extinction of relatively stable personality characteristics. The contribution of the present study is to investigate persistence as a phenomenon determined by the interaction of both personality and situational influences.

The present investigation also differs from the usual extinction investigation by using a task that could be seen by the subject as involving personal skill (cf. James & Rotter, 1958) and that provided a relatively inexhaustible range of alternative responses following failure. In contrast, extinction studies with humans have often used tasks in which the subject may see success and failure as largely beyond his control (e.g., the Humphrey's apparatus) and where the response is restricted to a particular action (e.g., pulling down a lever). Furthermore, in the present investigation initial expectation of success was varied by using fictitious norms. In contrast, in extinction studies the expectation may be considered as based mainly on frequency and pattern of reinforcement and nonreinforcement in the acquisition series.

The theoretical analysis may be extended to a consideration of persistence under conditions that differ from those of the present investigation in important respects. The general paradigm of the persistence situation is that in which the subject has some expectation of attaining a goal, is unrestricted in the number of attempts he can have at attaining it, and has an alternative activity to turn to as he wishes. Within this general framework the following differences may be noted which in turn imply specific types of persistence situation worthy of investigation:

1. Performance of the alternative to which the subject may turn may involve motives that are the same or different from those involved in the performance of the activity at which he is presently engaged. The persistence situation studied in the present investigation is one in which initial task and alternative activity belong to the same class of activity. Total motivation to perform the initial task and total motivation to perform the alternative task are both attributable to the *same* motivational components. In contrast, we can consider a type of persistence situation in which the initial task and the alternative task do not belong to the same class of activity, i.e., where the alternative is *motivationally different* in the sense that total motivation to perform the alternative is influenced by motives which are not involved in performance of the initial activity. Investigations of persistence by French and Thomas (1958) and by Atkinson and Litwin (1960) appear to fall in this latter class since in both of these studies the alternative activity to which the subject can turn does not necessarily involve achievement related motivation.

2. The situation does or does not involve types of motivational tendency in which incentive values and expectations are assumed to be dependent. In the achievement context dependencies are assumed between the positive incentive value of success and the subjective probability of success, and between the negative incentive value of failure and the subjective probability of failure (cf. Feather, 1959a, 1959b). But, in the more general case (e.g., efforts to get food when hungry), there would be no dependency between incentive value and expectation, and, hence, no increase to a maximum motivation followed by a decrease as expectation of goal attainment (P_g) changes from $P_g > .50$ to $P_g < .50$ (as occurs for achievement related motivation). Instead we would expect motivation to perform the activity to decrease continuously with decrease in the strength of expectation of goal attainment, providing strength of motive and incentive remained constant.

3. Persistence situations may differ according to whether or not the incentive is objectively present. One can consider a persistence situation in which the incentive is actually in view, e.g., young children attempting to overcome an obstacle in order to get a candy. In the present investigation and in the human extinction type of study, the incentive is not objectively present. In the Perceptual Reasoning test, the subject has to solve the puzzle; he cannot see the solution. In the extinction situation the reinforcement does not appear in the extinction series. Hence, it is possible for the subject to develop the expectation that there is in fact no incentive, e.g., that the puzzle is insoluble or that the experimenter has "fixed" the apparatus so that no more reinforcements will occur. In other words, the subject may conceive of these situations as beyond his control, as not involving skill. Consequently, special care is required to ensure that the subject retains the belief that only his efforts will influence the outcome.

These three differentiating characteristics, in combination, yield the eight specific types of persistence situation summarized in Table 4. The persistence situation investi-

TABLE 4

Types of Persistence Situation According to Whether or not the Alternative Is Motivationally the Same or Different from the Present Activity, Dependencies between Incentive Values and Expectations Exist or do Not Exist, and the Incentive is Objectively Present or Absent

Persistence situation	Alternative (motivationally same or different)	Dependency between expectation and incentive value (present or absent)	Incentive (objectively present or absent)
1	same	present	present
2	different	present	present
3	same	absent	present
4	different	absent	present
5	same	present	absent
6	different	present	absent
7	same	absent	absent
8	different	absent	absent

gated in the present study corresponds to 5, i.e., performance of the alternative involves the same kind of motivation as the activity at which the subject is presently engaged, dependencies are assumed between incentive values and expectations, and the incentive is not objectively present. In contrast, the persistence situation studied by French and Thomas (1958) and by Atkinson and Litwin (1960) corresponds to 6 since performance of the alternative in these studies probably involves different motivation from that involved in the activity at which the subject is engaged. It should be possible to construct experimental situations corresponding to the other six cases and to analyze persistence behavior in each of these in terms of the interaction of motives, expectations, and incentives. Such an approach would require (a) specification of the nature of the motives, expectations, and incentives involved in the situation; (b) measures of

the strength of these motives, expectations, and incentives; (c) assumptions concerning how these basic variables combine to determine the various component motivations; (d) specification of the manner in which expectation changes with experience at the activity; and (e) assumptions concerning the resolution of the set of component motivations into a resultant motivation.

The present study has shown that this strategy does work for the type of persistence situation investigated here. Detailed specification of the components of total motivation to perform a task in relation to total motivation to perform the available alternative, in conjunction with a dynamic principle of expectation change, has permitted differential predictions about persistence. This type of analysis, which takes account of both personality dispositions and situational influences in interaction according to an "expectancy value" model, may also be required to explain persistence in the other types of situation.

SUMMARY

This investigation examines the relationship of persistence at a task both to its apparent difficulty and to the relative strength within an individual of the motives to achieve success and to avoid failure. A subject performs a task presented to him as part of an important test, undergoes repeated failure at it (because it is in fact insoluble), but may turn to an alternative achievement task whenever he desires. Strength of motive to achieve success is assessed by the TAT n Achievement procedure; strength of motive to avoid failure is assessed by Mandler-Sarason Test Anxiety Questionnaire. Apparent difficulty of the task (i.e., initial expectation of success) is varied by use of fictitious group norms. Persistence is measured by total trials or total time the subject works at the task before turning to the alternative.

Hypotheses are derived from Atkinson's theory of achievement motivation with additional assumptions. The following hypotheses are tested:

Hypothesis 1 states that when motive to achieve success (M_s) is stronger in the subject than motive to avoid failure (M_{af}) he should be more persistent at a task when his initial subjective probability of success (P_s) is high (easy task, $P_s > .50$) than when his initial P_s is low (difficult task, $P_s < .50$).

Hypothesis 2 states that when $M_{af} > M_s$, the subject should be more persistent when his initial P_s is low than when his initial P_s is high.

Hypothesis 3 states that when initial P_s is high, a subject in whom $M_s > M_{af}$ should be more persistent than one in whom $M_{af} > M_s$.

Hypothesis 4 states that when initial P_s is low, a subject in whom $M_{af} > M_s$ should be more persistent than one in whom $M_s > M_{af}$.

Results are generally consistent with hypotheses and with assumptions involved in the predictions.

As a guide to future research a theoretical scheme is presented in which different classes of persistence situations are identified. The present investigation indicates the importance of specifying the components of total motivation to perform a task in relation to the components of total motivation to perform the alternative when attempting to predict degree of persistence. The theoretical analysis suggests the possibility of conceptualizing each component motivation in "expectancy value" terms, and the importance of change in expectation as a dynamic principle mediating change in motivation. The factual evidence clearly provides a demonstration that persistence can be conceptualized as an interaction of personality dispositions and situational influences.

REFERENCES

Atkinson, J. W. Motivational determinants of risk-taking behavior. *Psychol. Rev.,* 1957, 64, 359–372.

Atkinson, J. W. (Ed.) *Motives in fantasy, action, and society.* Princeton: Van Nostrand, 1958.

Atkinson, J. W. Personality dynamics. *Annu. Rev. Psychol.,* 1960, 11, 255–290.

Atkinson, J. W., & Litwin, G. H. Achievement motive and test anxiety as motives to approach success and to avoid failure. *J. abnorm. soc. Psychol.,* 1960, 60, 52–63.

Atkinson, J. W., & Raphelson, A. C. Individual differences in motivation and behavior in particular situations. *J. Pers.,* 1956, 24, 349–363.

Atkinson, J. W., & Reitman, W. R. Performance as a function of motive strength and expectancy of goal attainment. *J. abnorm. soc. Psychol.,* 1956, 53, 361–366.

Feather, N. T. Subjective probability and decision under uncertainty. *Psychol. Rev.,* 1959, 66, 150–164. (a)

Feather, N. T. Success probability and choice behavior. *J. exp. Psychol.,* 1959, 58, 257–266. (b)

Feather, N. T. Persistence in relation to achievement motivation, anxiety about failure, and task difficulty. Unpublished doctoral dissertation, University of Michigan, 1960.

French, Elizabeth G. Some characteristics of achievement motivation. *J. exp. Psychol.,* 1955, 50, 232–236.

French, Elizabeth G., & Thomas, F. H. The relation of achievement motivation to problem solving effectiveness. *J. abnorm. soc. Psychol.,* 1958, 56, 46–48.

James, W. H., & Rotter, J. B. Partial and 100% reinforcement under chance and skill conditions. *J. exp. Psychol.,* 1958, 55, 397–403.

McClelland, D. C., Atkinson, J. W., Clark, R. A., & Lowell, E. L. *The achievement motive.* New York: Appleton-Century-Crofts, 1953.

Sutcliffe, J. P. A general method of analysis of frequency data for multiple classification design. *Psychol. Bull.,* 1957, 54, 134–137.

Sorcery, Sin, and the Superego: A Cross-Cultural Study of Some Mechanisms of Social Control /

John W. M. Whiting (*Laboratory of Human Development, Harvard University*)

If one is to consider the problem of motivation in cross-cultural perspective, there are a number of different approaches one might take. The first would be to investigate primary drives and to explore the habits and behavior systems that have developed as a means for satisfying these drives. This would lead to, for example, a study of the economic institutions that have been built up in various societies for the satisfaction of the hunger drive; a study of marriage customs as they relate to the satisfaction of the sex drive; shelter and clothing as a response to extremes of temperature. Another important aspect of motivation, as it is manifested at the cross-cultural level, is a consideration of those motives opposed to the immediate satisfaction of primary drives— motives which have been referred to as fear, anxiety, guilt, shame, and the sense of sin— that is, those motives which underlie social control. It is a consideration of some aspects of this latter type of motivation which will be the theme of this paper.

It is apparent from a study of cultures the world over that positive reinforcement alone cannot maintain a complex social system. Tabus and negative sanctions oppose the desire for immediate gratification of the members of any society and seem to be, therefore, a requirement for social living. It seems also that simple punishment for wrong-doing does not create enduring enough inhibitions for the maintenance of social order. Perhaps if the punishment were severe enough, the fear of wrong-doing might be, as was apparently the case with Solomon's dogs, partially irreversible (19). It is not unlikely that certain types of behavior in some societies are very resistant to extinction for this reason. However, the prevalence of cultural institutions for social

control suggests that this is not the case for all behavior systems in any society. Perhaps such traumatic treatment would have other consequences, such as that of making the members of the society incapable of performing the tasks required to maintain themselves.

Another method might be used by a society to prevent the extinction of inhibition—that of continuous negative reinforcement. If it could be arranged that every time a member of a society deviated from the cultural rules he was immediately punished, this should be a very effective method of social control. This, however, would require that each member have a policeman shadowing him every moment of the day and night—and who would control the policeman?

There are, of course, policemen or the equivalent in every society. In fact, it is characteristic of the members of a society to police the actions of others. "If I can't do wrong, why should I permit my neighbor to?" Our cross-cultural evidence suggests, however, that policing by either officials or neighbors is not enough to maintain the system, and this paper will be concerned with a consideration of three other devices which have been invented by mankind to solve the problem of social control. They are sorcery, sin, and the superego. How these cultural mechanisms operate to control the deviations in the individual and the child-rearing conditions required to produce and maintain them is, then, the thesis of this paper.

1. SORCERY

As Beatrice Whiting has shown (22), the belief in sorcery and witchcraft operates in many societies to prevent crime. She points out in her discussion of the Paiute that they have no chief, no council of elders or other judiciary law-enforcing body, and that crime is, in the first instance, controlled only by the

Reprinted from *Nebraska Symposium on Motivation*, 1959, pages 174–195, by permission of author and publisher, University of Nebraska Press.

fear of retaliation from the victim or his relatives. There is, however, in Paiute the belief that anyone in the society may have magical powers which can be employed to kill or injure another person. This belief greatly enhances the fear of retaliation. One might defend oneself from the natural powers of retaliation from a victim, but not from his supernatural powers. Thus, the belief in sorcery tends to exaggerate the fear of retaliation and to deter crime. Finally, the only capital crime in Paiute, that is the only crime which will result in public execution by the whole group, is the accusation and conviction of sorcery. A person so convicted is stoned to death or driven from the band, in which case he will often die of starvation. Since one is convicted of sorcery on the basis of being exceptionally "mean," that is, being a thief or a murderer, this too is a deterrent to crime. Thus, the belief in sorcery acts in Paiute to deter crime where no formal means except retaliation is present for this purpose.

Sorcery and witchcraft are widespread in societies the world over, and the function of these beliefs has been described in detail by Kluckhohn (11) for the Navaho, Evans-Pritchard (6) for the Azande, and Smith and Roberts (18) for the Zuni. A cross-cultural test of the hypothesis that sorcery operates as a means of social control was made by Whiting (22). The relationship between the importance of sorcery and the absence of a formal judiciary system yielded a tetrachroic r of .85.

On the psychological side, one of the features which is most striking in a society that has a strong belief in witchcraft is the suspicion and distrust of others that it engenders. If one were to describe clinically the personality of a strong believer in witchcraft, he would be judged as paranoid. Not only does he grant magical and exaggerated powers to others to do harm, but he also feels that he too may have access to such powers, and thus exaggerates his own ability to do harm. Both of these traits are, clinically speaking, characteristic of the paranoid, and our search for a psychological hypothesis to account for the origins of the belief in sorcery leads us to a consideration of those child-training mechanisms which might produce paranoia.

This general hypothesis was previously explored by Whiting and Child (23) in a chapter on the origins of the fear of others, and in this chapter we concluded that cross-cultural evidence most strongly supported the hypothesis that sorcery was a manifestation, in part at least, of the projection of aggression. The strongest relationship between "fear of human being," our label for the belief that sorcerers can cause sickness, and any child-training variable was that with the severity of the socialization of aggression. The value of the Pearson r for this relation was +.43 which was significant at the 1% point.

The hypothesis that sorcery could be interpreted as a defense against sexual anxiety, suggested by Freud's derivation of paranoia, was also supported. The relation between sorcery and the severity of socialization in the area of sex yielded a Pearson r of +.37, significant at the 5% point. This relationship was not only less strong and significant than the relationship of sorcery to the punishment of aggression, but also less stable, since another child-training measure, that of initial sex anxiety, was not related to sorcery.

Since the punishment for aggression accounts for less than 20% of the variance, and since the punishment for sex is ambiguous, it was decided for the purposes of this paper to re-explore the problem to see if other factors could be discovered which singly, or in interaction, could better predict the belief in sorcery. Three recent cross-cultural studies (3, 24, 21) have been concerned, in part, with a consideration of cultural manifestations of conflict in the sexual area. Two of these studies have demonstrated the importance of the so-called post-partum sex tabu in this regard.

Societies the world over may be divided into three groups with regard to the time at which a woman resumes sexual intercourse with her husband following parturition. First, there are those societies, like our own, where intercourse is resumed as soon as the woman's wounds are healed, or as soon as her regular menstrual cycle is regained. In these cases the duration of the period of sexual abstinence is from a few weeks to a few months. This pattern is generally found in societies with a monogamous system of marriage. Polygynous societies generally have a much longer period of abstinence. These societies may be divided into two groups: first, those generally residing in the tropics who have a belief that sexual intercourse will sour or poison the mother's milk, whose tabu on sexual intercourse thus lasts as long as the mother nurses the child, generally from two to three years. The other group of polygynous societies which have a long post-partum sex tabu are the nomads. The rationalization for the tabu in this case is quite different. In nomadic societies, women are generally the burden carriers, freeing men to hunt and defend themselves against hostile bands and wild animals. In such wandering groups, a woman cannot afford to carry two children, and thus they have a conscious policy of not having a second child until the first can take care of himself on a long march. The duration of the post-partum sex tabu in these societies is often four years or more. As was shown in Whiting, Kluckhohn, and Anthony (24), a long post-partum sex tabu is strongly associated with exclusive mother-child sleeping arrangements. In other words, the nursing infant in these societies ordinarily sleeps in the mother's bed, while the husband sleeps elsewhere—often in another building with his co-wife, a hut of his own, or in the men's club house. The assumption that a mother sleeping alone with her infant at a time when she is deprived of sexual intercourse with her husband may unconsciously seduce the child, was made both by Whiting, Kluckhohn, and Anthony (24), and by Stephens (21), and the predicted consequences of such an assumption—male initiation rites and elaborate menstrual tabus—were confirmed by both studies.

The above analysis suggests a source for sexual anxiety and conflict other than that used in Whiting and Child (23), and thus provides another test for the psychoanalytic hypothesis that paranoia, and hence sorcery, is a defense against sexual anxiety. In other words, those societies with a long post-partum sex tabu, if this hypothesis is correct, should be those who have the strongest belief in sorcery.

To test this hypothesis, the scores obtained on the duration of the post-partum sex tabu in the Whiting, Kluckhohn, and Anthony study (24) were correlated with the scores on sorcery (fear of others) obtained in the Whiting and Child (23) study. The results of this test are presented in Table 1.

Our hypothesis is thus rather strongly confirmed. The association obtained in this table is much stronger than any yielded by a nonparametric test in the Whiting and Child study. In fact, a chi-square test of the relationship between sorcery and either severity of socialization for sex or aggression did not yield significant results when broken into a four-by-four table, even though they were significant when tested by correlational techniques.

It might be interesting, however, to present the interaction of the duration of the post-partum sex tabu with the two factors found to be associated with a strong belief in sorcery in Whiting and Child, that is, the severity of punishment for aggression and for sex during childhood. It might be expected on theoretical grounds that seduction in infancy followed by the severe punishment for sexual behavior in childhood might increase the probability of paranoid projection. The interactions between post-partum sex tabu and severity of sex and aggression training are presented in Table II.

It will be seen from Table II that the punishment for aggression in childhood, when combined with the post-partum sex tabu, does not yield any stronger prediction of the importance of sorcery than does the post-partum sex tabu alone. The severity of sex training, however, does somewhat strengthen the relationship. The Bena, Thonga, and Masai, all of whom (see Table I) had a long post-partum sex tabu, but a weak belief in sorcery, were relatively mild in sex training, whereas only the Lesu and Trobrianders of the group with the long post-partum sex tabu and sorcery were mild in sex training. Although the relationship of severity of sex training to sorcery in societies with a long post-partum sex tabu is not significant with the reduced number

TABLE 1

POST-PARTUM SEX TABU		*SORCERY* (*Whiting and Child* [23])			
		Low (0 — 8)		*High (9 and 10)*	
(Whiting, Kluckhohn, and Anthony [24])				12 Arapesh	10
				18 Azande	10
				36 Chagga	9
				21 Chiricahua	9
				24 Kurtachi	9
				18 Kwakiutl	10
	Long			24 Kwoma	10
		22 Bena	7	30 Lesu	9
		24 Dahomeans	6	18 Tiv	9
		18 Masai	6	18 Trobrianders	10
		48 Teton	0	42 Venda	9
		21 Thonga	7	30 Wogeo	10
		9 Alorese	5	0 Baiga	10
		3 Ashanti	5	0 Maori	9
		1 Balinese	4	1 Sanpoil	9
		2 Chamorro	6	9 Yagua	11
		1 Chewa	8		
		1 Hopi	8		
	Short	0 Lakher	7		
		1 Lamba	4		
		1 Lepcha	7		
		2 Navaho	7		
		2 Ontong Java	6		
		0 Papago	4		
		1 Siriono	2		
		6 Tanala	7		
		1 Yukaghir	4		

This table shows the relationship between the duration of the post-partum sex tabu and the strength of the belief that sorcerers can cause illness. The numbers at the left of the name of each society represent the duration in months of the post-partum sex tabu. The numbers at the right indicate the average judgment of two raters on the importance of sorcery. $P = .004$ (Fischer exact test).

TABLE II

POST-PARTUM SEX TABU Whiting, Kluckhohn and Anthony (24)	SEVERITY OF AGGRESSION TRAINING Whiting and Child (23)	FEAR OF SORCERY Whiting and Child		SEVERITY OF SEX TRAINING Whiting and Child (23)	FEAR OF SORCERY Whiting and Child	
		Low	*High*		*Low*	*High*
Long	high	2	7	high	2	10
	low	3	6	low	3	2
Short	high	8	3	high	8	2
	low	6	1	low	7	2

This table shows the joint effect of the duration of the post-partum sex tabu and the severity of socialization of aggression and sex on the belief that sorcerers can cause sickness. The effect of the severity of sex training in societies with long sex tabus is the only condition where a child-rearing variable approaches significance in predicting sorcery.

of cases, the association is reasonably strong in the predicted direction. In no other instance does either child-rearing variable approach significance when the duration of the post-partum sex tabu is controlled.

The interaction of the punishment for sex with the duration of the post-partum sex tabu suggests that the paranoid theory of the development of a fear of sorcery is more tenable than the hypothesis of simple projection of aggression, which was our conclusion in Whiting and Child. Thus, there seems to be reasonable evidence that one of the mechanisms of social control found strongly developed in many of the simpler societies is a defense against sexual anxiety produced by a combination of seduction in infancy followed by the punishment for sex during childhood.

2. THE FEAR OF GHOSTS

A somewhat different mechanism of social control found in many societies consists of the belief that gods, ghosts, and spirits are concerned with the moral behavior of the living and will punish them for wrong-doing. Beliefs in supernatural sanctions of this kind are so familiar to us in the western world that we need not illustrate them. The sin of transgression against the rules of the gods and the belief that retribution will follow either here or in the afterlife is widespread throughout the world and clearly operates to maintain conformity to social rules in many societies.

No cross-cultural rating is available which directly estimates the degree to which a belief in gods and spirits operates as a mechanism of social control. An indirect estimate of this factor is, however, available from the Whiting and Child study. It is a scale designed to measure the degree to which gods, ghosts, and spirits can cause illness. It may be assumed that societies which believe that supernaturals are relatively harmless cannot use this belief as a sanction against wrong-doing. The converse, of course, cannot be assumed. Powerful and harmful gods may not be concerned with the moral behavior of the living. Even if this measure were accepted as being to a degree

at least an index of social control by the gods, the relation of the Whiting and Child measure to child-rearing variables was disappointing. Except for the fear of animal spirits, which was found to be significantly associated with the punishment for aggression in the Whiting and Child study (23), no child-rearing factor was discovered which related to the belief that either ghosts or spirits could cause illness.

This failure to find a relationship may be due to the low reliability of the judgments of our raters on the belief that spirits or ghosts can cause illness or to the fact that we chose inappropriate child-rearing variables to predict them. It is probable that both of these factors contributed to our failure. In the first place, our method of coding fear or ghosts and spirits was complex, involving not only various subcategories of spiritual beings, but also a judgment of the degree to which each category could cause illness, and the agreement between judges in making both of these decisions at once was not high. We attempted to obtain a more reliable score by combining various of the subcategories of supernatural beings, and although this increased the reliability somewhat, it was still far less satisfactory in this regard than many of the other judgments used in the study.

In this paper, another estimate of the fear of ghosts will be used. This is a rating made by Friendly (8) in a cross-cultural study of mourning customs. Although she does not report the reliability of her judgments on this particular scale, it has the distinct advantage over the Whiting and Child scores of being specifically related to fear of ghosts of the dead at the funeral. Thus the cultural context for the belief was much more rigorously specified and therefore should be more comparable from one society to another. The Friendly measure of ghost fear, like the Whiting and Child measure, does not, of course, specifically relate to the fear of the supernatural as a consequence of wrong-doing. As was suggested above, it must be presumed that societies which have a strong fear of ghosts at the funeral are more likely to believe that the supernatural are concerned with their moral behavior than are societies in which this fear is lacking. This assumption, however, will not be tested in this paper.*

As was the case in our analysis of the fear of sorcerers stated above, the hypothesis that the fear of ghosts is a simple matter of projection of aggression is rejected. It is assumed, however, that anxiety about the direct expression of aggression may lead to its projection and displacement onto other objects than the frustrater. This has been shown cross-culturally in a study of folk tales by Wright (26). He pointed out that societies with severe aggression training were more likely to portray strangers to the hero as objects of aggression than as friends of the hero.

The displacement or projection of aggression hypothesis, however, only tells us that with severe anxiety about aggression the object will be dissimilar from the frustrater; it does not tell us precisely who or what the object of such aggression shall be. The problem, then, is to predict the child-training circumstances which should lead to a preoccupation with ghosts of the dead.

By the time an individual in any society reaches late adulthood, the chances are that he will have been to the funeral of each of his parents, but much less likely that he will have been to the funeral of a spouse or sibling or, except for those who have died in infancy, a child. This set of probabilities suggests that mourning ceremonies are designed for children responding to the death of a parent, and the modal ghost to be feared is a parental ghost. It should be pointed out that the high infant mortality found in many societies may change this probability ratio, but it may also be said that funerals of children dying in infancy are very often quite different from the funerals of adults and aged.

The above analysis enables us to be more precise in our search for antecedents to the fear of ghosts of the dead. We can restate our problem as follows: What are the child-rearing conditions that should lead to a pre-occupation with parental ghosts?

It was suggested in a recent theoretical paper (25) that if a parent in caring for a child and satisfying his needs was frequently absent when he was in a high state of need—that is, hungry, cold, or suffering from some other discomfort—he would be very likely to engage in fantasies which would represent his mother or other caretaker satisfying his needs. Assuming that the mother eventually comes and feeds him or covers him up, this act should reinforce his magical thinking and increase the probability that he will produce fantasy images of his mother when she is absent and he is in need. It is our hypothesis that this type of magical thinking underlies a preoccupation with ghosts and spirits of the dead at the cultural level of abstraction.

Specifically, then, our hypothesis may be stated as follows: Those societies which are relatively neglectful of infants should be more afraid of ghosts at funerals than those societies in which children are treated indulgently during their infancy. To test this hypothesis we chose a scale prepared by Bacon, Barry, and Child (4), which they named "Overall Indulgence During Infancy," to measure the manner in which an infant was cared for. The rating instructions for this scale are as follows:**

The initial period will be defined as approximately the first year (and as long thereafter as the treatment of the infant remains approximately constant, but if there is any change it is the first year that is dealt with). This means that if there is a change in treatment at the end of the *neonatal* period, the treatment characteristic of the rest of infancy is what will be dealt with here, not the treatment of the neonate.

Separate ratings should be made of as many as possible of the following variables:

1. Display of affection toward the infant: to what extent is he held, fondled, caressed, played with?
2. Protection from environmental discomforts: e.g., excessive heat or cold, bright light, insects. To what extent are such

---

* A recent cross-cultural study by Spiro and D'Andrade (20) attacked the problem of supernatural social control. There are not, however, enough overlapping cases to determine whether or not fear of ghosts at funerals is related to contingent reward and punishment by the gods.

** The authors were kind enough to give us the original ratings on this scale.

discomforts either not experienced, usually prevented, or quickly eliminated?

3. Degree of drive reduction: considering particularly hunger, thirst, and unidentified discomforts, how fully are the infant's needs reduced?

4. Immediacy of drive reduction: how quickly are these needs reduced?

5. Consistency of drive reduction: how consistently are drives reduced? Here it is necessary to take into account not only drives which parents can always reduce (e.g., in most cases hunger) but also drives which parents may be unable to reduce (e.g., chronic discomfort from illness).

6. Constancy of presence of nurturant agent: if the mother is not always present, the rating of constancy will then be affected by whether the infant is then alone, left with a moderately nurturant substitute, a highly nurturant substitute, etc.

7. Absence of pain inflicted by the nurturant agent: e.g., cold baths, depilation, rough handling, or physical punishment.

A rating is then to be made of *overall indulgence* during infancy, based on the separate variables listed above, weighted as seems proper, and on any other pertinent information including general statements about infantile indulgence. The duration of the initial period should be given some slight weight here.

A test of the relationship between this scale and Friendly's judgment of the fear of ghosts is presented in Table III.

It will be seen from Table III that although the relationship is not strong, our prediction is confirmed at least at an acceptable level of confidence.

The hypothesis as phrased above, however, only specified that a member of a society with relatively low indulgence during infancy would be *preoccupied* with ghostly images of his parents, not that he would fear them. In other words, the independent variable that we have selected should be a necessary but not sufficient cause for the fear of ghosts at a funeral. A second factor should be added, that of the projection of aggression. The child neglected in infancy may well have magical fantasies about his parents but not necessarily attribute malevolence to these fantasy figures. We wish to assume

that such malevolence is a consequence of severe punishment for aggression and the consequent need to displace it. Specifically, then, societies where parents, relatively speaking, neglect their children during infancy and punish them severely for aggression during childhood, should be the societies that fear the ghosts of the dead at funerals. To test this hypothesis, the Whiting and Child scores on the punishment for aggression, the Bacon, Barry, and Child scores on indulgence during infancy, and the Friendly scores on the fear of ghosts were used. The number of societies for which all three of these scores were available was reduced from the 46 in the previous table to 32. The interaction between these two variables is presented in Table IV.

This table confirms both parts of our prediction. Considering the 18 cases where initial indulgence is low, that is, the top half of the table, there is a significant relation between punishment for aggression and the fear of ghosts (P = .039). No prediction was made concerning the effect of aggression with high initial indulgence, that is, the bottom half of the table, and no significant relationship was found. Finally, if one contrasts the cases where both factors are present (the top line) with the cases where both factors are absent (the bottom line) we find a very strong relationship indeed— 15 out of 17 cases being in the predicted cells (P = .002). Thus it appears that again the interaction between two child-training variables has more powerful predictive value than was generally found with the single-factor approach used in Whiting and Child, and we can conclude that there is strong support for the hypothesis that societies where children are neglected in infancy and later punished for aggression have mourning customs designed to protect the living from dangerous ancestral ghosts.

Two recent cross-cultural studies by Lambert, Triandis, and Wolf (12) and by Spiro and D'Andrade (20) have also been concerned with the relationship between the nature of the gods and child-rearing practices. In the former study it was found that gods were mainly aggressive rather than benevolent in societies low on Subscale #7 of the Bacon, Barry, and Child scores (see

TABLE III

DEGREE OF OVER-ALL INDULGENCE Bacon, Barry, and Child (4)		FEAR OF GHOSTS AT FUNERAL CEREMONIES Friendly (8)			
	Low		*High*		
Low			5 Ainu	3	
			4 Alorese	3	
			10 Ashanti	3	
			6 Aymara	3	
	10 Azande	1	7 Chaga	3	
	9 Balinese	2	7 Dahomeans	3	
	10 Flathead	2	10 Kwakiutl	3	
	9 Ganda	2	10 Navaho	3	
	10 Lamba	2	10 Paiute	3	
	9 Mbundo	2	9 Tanala	3	
	9 Pukapuka	2	9 Venda	3	
	10 Siriono	2	10 Western Apache	3	
	13 Andamanese	2	11 Cheyenne	3	
	12 Arapaho	2	12 Chiricahua	3	
	11 Araucanians	2	11 Jivaro	3	
	11 Arunta	2	12 Lepcha	3	
	13 Bena	2	12 Tupinamba	3	
	11 Chenchu	2			
	11 Chuckchee	2			
	11 Crow	2			
	12 Cuna	2			
High	13 Hopi	2			
	11 Kaska	2			
	12 Kurtachi	2			
	11 Kwoma	2			
	11 Lesu	2			
	11 Maori	1			
	12 Omaha	1			
	14 Papago	2			
	12 Trobrianders	1			
	12 Yagua	1			
	12 Zuni	2			

This table shows the relationship between the degree of indulgence during infancy and the degree to which ghosts of the dead are feared at funerals. The number before the name of each society indicates its score on over-all indulgence, that following the fear of ghosts scale. $P < .01$ (Fischer exact test).

TABLE IV

OVER-ALL INDULGENCE DURING INFANCY (Bacon, Barry, and Child)	SEVERITY OF SOCIALIZATION OF AGGRESSION (Whiting and Child)	FEAR OF GHOSTS AT FUNERALS (Friendly)	
		Low	*High*
Low	Severe	2	9
	Mild	5	2
High	Severe	4	3
	Mild	6	0

This table shows the interaction between indulgence during infancy and the punishment of aggression during childhood as predictors of the fear of ghosts at funerals. Where initial indulgence is low, the severity of punishment for aggression in childhood is significantly and positively related to the fear of ghosts at funerals. $P = .039$ (Fischer exact test).

above). In other words, societies in which socializing agents gave infants cold baths, handled them roughly, and punished them physically believed in aggressive rather than benevolent gods. The Friendly fear of ghosts at the funeral scale used in this study was not significantly related to Subscale #7, nor was the aggressiveness of the gods significantly related to the over-all indulgence scale.

Spiro and D'Andrade found that societies with high initial indulgence (Whiting and Child scale) had gods who could be influenced by ritual ($r = .82$) or compulsion ($r = .72$) to benefit the living. Low initial indulgence did not predict punitive gods, however.

Thus, although the details differ, these two studies generally support the finding of the present paper that indulgence in infancy is related to beliefs about gods and spirits.

The relationship between ghost fear and the punishment of aggression in childhood was not replicated either by Lambert et al., or by Spiro and D'Andrade. High pressure for self-reliance and independence as well as general rigidity in child rearing predicted aggressive gods in the former study, while severe weaning and severe toilet training predicted punitive gods in the latter study.

Moreover, although all three studies indicate that the nature of the gods reflect in some way the relationship between parent and child, the details of this relationship depend upon the method of determining the nature of the gods.

3. THE SUPEREGO

The third mechanism of social control to be considered, the superego or conscience, has been a subject of considerable interest in recent years, particularly as it relates to the process of identification. Most research in this field rests on the assumption that internalized moral values are a consequence of identification with the parents, and that guilt, remorse, or the readiness to accept blame is a measurable consequence of the degree of parental identification.

A number of specific hypotheses have been put forward as to the child-rearing factors which should produce strong parental identification and subsequent guilt, and empirical research has supported some of these hypotheses.

Freud, in his original formulation of identification, suggested that it was a conversion of cathexis. This has been interpreted by some theorists to mean that identification should be related to parental warmth or nurturance. Empirical tests of this hypothesis have been generally negative. Sears, Maccoby, and Levin (17), using the mother's estimate of the strength of a child's conscience, found a positive relationship between these two variables which, although significant at the 5% level, yielded a correlation of but .10, thus accounting for only 1% of the variance; Whiting and Child, using an index of guilt to be discussed below, found no relation at all between these variables; and Heinicke (10), using doll play to measure guilt, found a significant negative relation between these variables.

Another interpretation of the Freudian theory has produced more empirical support. This interpretation relates to the technique of discipline. The hypothesis that the relative importance of love-oriented or psychological techniques of discipline should be a precondition for guilt has been confirmed by Sears, Maccoby, and Levin (17), when it is employed by relatively warm mothers; by Whiting and Child (23); by Allinsmith and Greening (2); and by Faigin and Hollenberg (7).

The age of socialization has been considered as a variable in a number of studies. Allinsmith (1) found that early weaning and early toilet training were related to high guilt. Whiting and Child (23) found that early weaning, early sex training, and early independence training were the best predictors of their cross-cultural measure of guilt.

Finally, a number of studies have considered the status relationship between parents. Faigin and Hollenberg (7) in a comparative study of three societies in New Mexico found evidence that guilt is positively related to the prestige of the father. Heinicke (10) found guilt to be positively related to the mother's evaluation of the father. Although Goethals (9) in a similar study did not confirm this relationship, his findings were in the predicted direction; however, they did not reach an acceptable level of confidence.

It is the last of these hypotheses that will be considered here. In a recent theoretical paper on identification and the control of resources (25), this has been labelled the *status envy* hypothesis. Suggested by Freud's formulation of the Oedipal conflict, the hypothesis is simply that a person will identify with, and hence accept the moral values of, any person who is a successful rival with respect to resources which he covets but cannot control. Specifically, here it is assumed that where a child and a father frequently compete for love, affection, recognition, food, care, and even sexual gratification from the mother, and where the father is often successful—that is, he is nurtured by the mother at a time when the child is in need—then the child should envy the father and hence identify with him.

Variations in family structure and household composition luckily provide an opportunity to test this hypothesis. Murdock (14) in a recent study of 565 societies has rated these two variables. He made a number of distinctions as to family structure, but the distinction between monogamy and polygyny is the one of particular relevance here. By his definition, any society in which 20% or more of the families consist of a man and two or more wives has been considered polygynous, less than 20% as having either limited polygyny or monogamy. There are, in his sample, 232 polygynous societies, 184 societies with limited polygyny, and 134 societies with strict monogamy. For the test of this hypothesis we have combined limited polygyny with monogamy, thus yielding a total of 318 monogamous societies.

The monogamous family is familiar to us. It epitomizes the eternal triangle. In this type of family, the three statuses—father, mother, and children—are bound in intimate relation with one another. It is in such a family that father and children are most likely to compete for the love and affection of the mother.

Polygynous families are organized in a different pattern. Here the father has two or more wives to care for him, and rivalry with his children should therefore be cut in half at least. In such a family, when the child is tired, hungry, and demanding attention from his mother at the same time that the father is in need of attention, the mother can say to him: "I'm busy. Get it from your other wife." A contrast between monogamous and polygynous societies should provide a test, then, of the status envy hypothesis.

Household structure also provides a definition of the conditions which should maximize status envy between father and child. Murdock has again made a number of distinctions as to the relatives who live together under one roof. Again we are not concerned with all the fine distinctions that he has made, but have grouped them, with reference to their bearing on our hypothesis, in the following four categories: nuclear, extended, polygynous, and mother-child. In his sample, these types occur with the following frequencies:

172 extended households
141 nuclear households
123 mother-child households
 89 polygynous households

Some of the extended families, however, are also polygynous, and we have reclassified them on this basis. Thus, the proportion of extended families stated above is an overestimate, and that of polygynous families an underestimate.

Again, we are familiar with the nuclear family household. Here the mother, father, and children eat, sleep, and entertain under one roof. Grandparents and siblings of the parents live elsewhere. Monogamous extended families consist of two or more nuclear families living together under one roof. A typical extended family consists of an aged couple with their married sons or daughters together with their spouses and children. The polygynous household consists of a man living with his wives and their children. Finally, the mother-child household occurs in societies with polygyny where each wife has a separate house and establishment and lives in it with her children. In these societies, the father either has a hut of his own, sleeps in the men's club house, or rotates among the houses of his various wives. It is of particular importance here that the husband generally does not sleep in the house of any wife who has a nursing infant, and also that in these societies the nursing period lasts from two to three years.

Considering these household arrangements in the light of the status envy hypothesis, it seems clear that maximal status rivalry between father and child should occur in nuclear households; somewhat less in monogamous extended families where the presence of grandparents and married siblings provides a condition of diffused nurturance and a less intense and intimate relationship among the members of the nuclear family. With polygynous households the fact of polygyny, as has been shown above, decreases the intensity of the rivalry even more, but not so much as in the mother-child household where the father is seldom present to compete with his children for the love and affection of the mother. We would predict, then, that if our hypothesis is correct, the greatest identification and guilt should be found in societies with nuclear households, next with monogamous extended households, next with polygynous households, and least of all with mother-child households.

To test this hypothesis the measure of guilt used in Whiting and Child has been chosen as a dependent variable. The general definition of this measure was stated as follows:

> As a cultural index of the degree to which guilt feelings characterize the members of a society, we have used a measure of the extent to which a person who gets sick blames himself for having gotten sick. Self-recrimination, as a response to illness, seemed to us a probably useful index of the degree to which guilt feelings are strong and widely generalized (p. 227).

The details of making this judgment are presented in Whiting and Child (p. 221, ff.) and will not be reviewed here. It should be stated, however, that the intent of this index was to obtain an estimate of the degree to which a member of any society was ready to accept personal responsibility for wrongdoing. It should be pointed out that this is by no means a direct measure of such a tendency, and although we are not satisfied with this method of measuring the strength of the superego, it is the only one presently available.

A test of the status envy hypothesis as measured by family organization and household membership is presented in Table V.

TABLE V

PATIENT RESPONSIBILITY Whiting and Child (23)	FAMILY AND HOUSEHOLD STRUCTURE Murdock (14)			
	Family: *Household:*	*Polygynous* *Mother-Child*	*Polygynous* *Polygynous*	*Monogamous* *Extended*	*Monogamous* *Nuclear*
High			11 Arapesh 11 Chiricahua 14 Kwoma	15 Hopi 10 Lepcha 21 Maori 10 Papago	16 Alorese 13 Chamorro 14 Lakher 14 Manus 17 Navaho 18 Pukapuka
		12 Dahomeans			
Low		9 Azande 8 Bena 3 Chagga 6 Kurtachi 5 Lesu 4 Thonga	5 Commanche 8 Kwakiutl 6 Tanala 9 Teton 8 Wogeo	3 Chenchu 9 Samoans	5 Trobrianders
% High		14%	38%	67%	86%

This table shows the relationship between family and household structure with patient responsibility, the index of guilt used by Whiting and Child. The number before each society is its value for this score. The order of the percentages is as predicted, and the differences between monogamous and polygynous family structure are significant, $P = .009$ (Fischer exact test).

TABLE VI

FAMILY STRUCTURE (Murdock)	AGE OF WEANING (Whiting and Child)	PATIENT RESPONSIBILITY (Whiting and Child)	
		Low	*High*
Monogamous	Early	1	6
	Late	4	2
Polygynous	Early	5	1
	Late	6	3

This table shows the interaction between family structure and age of weaning in producing patient responsibility. It will be seen that the age of weaning is related to patient responsibility only in monogamous societies. Although a nonparametric test does not yield significant results, a Pearson r between these variables yields a coefficient of $-.71$, which is significant at the 5% point.

It will be seen from this table that our hypothesis is rather strikingly confirmed. Only one monogamous nuclear household society had low guilt, and only one polygynous mother-child society had high guilt. The proportions of societies having high guilt are in the predicted order. Both the contrast between polygynous and monogamous societies and that between nuclear and mother-child households are highly significant statistically, P values being .009 and .015 respectively.

These social structure variables, however, do not control all the variance, and it would be interesting to discover how the other variables presumed to be related to identification and guilt interact with the conditions of status envy. To test this hypothesis, the societies were divided by family structure into those which were polygynous and monogamous. Tests were then run between patient responsibility and the following variables: degree of initial nurturance, the relative importance of love-oriented techniques, and the age of weaning. The first two of these factors did not yield a significant relationship, although there was a strong tendency for patient responsibility to be related to low initial indulgence in monogamous societies, but not in polygynous societies. This relationship should be explored on a larger sample. The interaction between family structure and age of weaning, however, did yield significant results even on our small sample, and is presented in Table VI.

As is shown in this table, monogamous societies with early weaning are more likely to have high patient responsibility than monogamous societies with late weaning. Although a nonparametric test of this relationship does not yield a significant result, a Pearson product moment correlation gives an r value of $-.71$, which is significant at the 5% level of confidence. This value for r can be compared with $-.42$, the value reported in Whiting and Child for the same relationship when monogamous and polygynous societies were grouped. This is not surprising, since it will be seen from the above table that the age of weaning has no effect on patient responsibility in polygynous societies. In fact, the relationship is in the reverse direction.

Thus, if patient responsibility be taken as an index of identification and guilt, cross-cultural exidence supports the hypothesis that the maximization of rivalry between father and child and early socialization combine to produce the strong internalization of moral values and readiness to accept blame.

4. SUMMARY AND DISCUSSION

Before reviewing and summarizing the above findings, let us consider an interesting question which arises here: How are these three types of social control related to one another? Are they alternatives—that is to say, if a society has one mechanism, does it lack either or both the others? If this is not the case, do certain combinations of the three occur more frequently than others? The answer to these questions is that they are all essentially independent of one another. Although there is some tendency for societies with strong fear of ghosts also to have a high patient responsibility score, the correlation between these two methods of social control does not approach significance. Similarly, both of these factors are by direction slightly negatively related to the fear of sorcery, but again, the relationship does not approach significance.

For the last two decades, it has been a fashion to classify societies into guilt or shame cultures—Mead (13), Benedict (5), and Singer (15). More recently, Riesman (16) has suggested the other-oriented and inner-oriented as labels for making similar distinctions. The analysis in this paper suggests that the problem may be somewhat more complex. The paper in this symposium by Levin and Baldwin on shame and pride suggests that this too is a complex set of motivations. And we have shown, I think, that guilt and the acceptance of blame are equally complex. Secondly, if one wishes to distinguish between internalized values and the fear of external danger, it seems clear that the source of external danger may be quite different and produced by quite different techniques of socialization. Although ghosts and sorcerers may both be defined as external sources of danger, they are clearly not the same. Finally, it seems evident that any given society may have all of these anxiety-producing mechanisms at least to some degree, and some societies may have two or more of them as dominant mechanisms of social control.

Essentially, then, there seem to be three independent motivational systems which occur in societies over the world: (1) the exaggerated and paranoid fear of retaliation from other humans; (2) the sense of sin deriving from the projected dread of punishment by gods or ghosts; and (3) the sense of guilt and readiness to accept blame deriving from a sense of personal responsibility for one's actions. The first of these, paranoid fear, seems to be in part produced by early seduction followed by severe punishment for sex; the second, ghost fear, by early neglect followed by severe punishment for aggression; and the last, guilt, by early socialization and a monogamous family structure and nuclear household, which accentuates rivalry between father and child for the nurturance of the mother.

REFERENCES

1. Allinsmith, W. Conscience and conflict: The moral force in personality, *Child Developm.*, 1957, 28, 469–476.
2. Allinsmith, W., & Greening, T. C. Guilt over anger as predicted from parental discipline: A study of super-ego development. *Amer. Psychologist*, 1955, 10, 320 (Abstract).
3. Ayres, Barbara C. Personality determinants of food and sex tabus during pregnancy. Unpublished doctoral dissertation, Radcliffe Coll., 1954.
4. Bacon, Margaret, Barry, H. III, & Child, I. L. Rater's instructions for analysis of socialization practices with respect to dependence and independence. Unpublished typescript, Yale Univer., 1952.
5. Benedict, Ruth. *The chrysanthemum and the sword.* Boston: Houghton Mifflin, 1946.
6. Evans-Pritchard, E. E. *Witchcraft, oracles, and magic among the Azande.* London: Oxford Univer. Press, 1937.
7. Faigin, Helen, & Hollenberg, Eleanor. Child rearing and the internalization of moral values. Unpublished typescript, Harvard Univer., 1953.
8. Friendly, Joan P. A cross-cultural study of ascetic mourning behavior. Unpublished honors thesis, Dept. of Social Relations, Radcliffe Coll., 1956.
9. Goethals, G. W. A study of the relationship between family esteem patterns and identification, the internalization of values, and aggression of a group of four-year-old children. Unpublished doctoral dissertation. Grad. School of Educ., Harvard Univer., 1953.
10. Heinicke, C. M. Some antecedents and correlates of guilt-fear in young boys. Unpublished doctoral dissertation, Dept. of Social Relations, Harvard Univer., 1953.
11. Kluckhohn, C. Navaho witchcraft. *Papers of the Peabody Museum of American archaeology and ethnology, Harvard Univer.,* 1944, 22, No. 2.
12. Lambert, W. W., Triandis, L. M., & Wolf, Margery. Some correlates of beliefs in the malevolence and benevolence of super-

natural beings: A cross-societal study. *J. abnorm. and soc. Psychol.*, 1959, 58, 162-169.

13. Mead, Margaret. *Cooperation and competition among primitive peoples.* New York: McGraw-Hill, 1937.

14. Murdock, G. P. World ethnographic sample. *Amer. Anthrop.*, 1957, 59, 664–687.

15. Piers, G., & Singer, M. B. *Shame and guilt.* Springfield, Ill.: Thomas, 1953.

16. Riesman, D. *The lonely crowd.* New Haven: Yale Univer. Press, 1950.

17. Sears, R. R., Maccoby, Eleanor E., & Levin, H. *Patterns of child rearing.* Evanston, Ill.: Row, Peterson, 1957.

18. Smith, W., & Roberts, J. M. Zuni law: A field of values. *Papers of the Peabody Museum of archaeology and ethnology, Harvard Univer.* 1943, 43, No. 1.

19. Solomon, R. L., & Wynne, L. C. Traumatic avoidance learning: The principles of anxiety conservation and partial irreversibility. *Psychol. Rev.*, 1954, 61, 353-385.

20. Spiro, M. E., & D'Andrade, R. G. A cross-cultural study of some supernatural beliefs. *Amer. Anthrop.*, 1958, 60, 456–466.

21. Stephens, W. M. Cross-cultural evidence on the Oedipus complex. Unpublished doctoral dissertation, Harvard Univer., Grad. School of Educ., 1959.

22. Whiting, Beatrice B. Paiute sorcery. New York: *Viking Fund Publ. Anthrop.*, No. 15, 1950.

23. Whiting, J. W. M., & Child, I. L. *Child training and personality: A cross-cultural study.* New Haven: Yale Univer. Press, 1953.

24. Whiting, J. W. M., Kluckhohn, R. P. R. H., & Anthony, A. A. The function of male initiation ceremonies at puberty. In Maccoby, Newcomb, and Hartley (Eds.), *Readings in social psychology.* New York: Holt, 1958.

25. Whiting, J. W. M. Resource mediation and learning by identification. Unpublished theoretical paper, Lab. of Human Develop., Harvard Univer., 1959.

26. Wright, G. O. Projection and displacement: A cross-cultural study of the expression of aggression in myths. Unpublished doctoral dissertation, Grad. School of Educ., Harvard Univer., 1952.

Cognitive, Social, and Physiological Determinants of Emotional State[1] / Stanley Schachter (*Columbia University*)
and
Jerome E. Singer (*Penn. State University*)

The problem of which cues, internal or external, permit a person to label and identify his own emotional state has been with us since the days that James (1890) first tendered his doctrine that "the bodily changes follow directly the perception of the exciting fact, and that our feeling of the

same changes as they occur *is* the emotion" (p. 449). Since we are aware of a variety of feeling and emotion states, it should follow from James' proposition that the various emotions will be accompanied by a variety of differentiable bodily states. Following James' pronouncement, a formidable number of studies were undertaken in search of the physiological differentiators of the emotions. The results, in these early days, were almost uniformly negative. All of the emotional states experimentally manipulated

Reprinted from *Psychological Review*, 1962, 69, pages 379–399, by permission of the senior author and publisher, The American Psychological Association.

[1] This experiment is part of a program of research on cognitive and physiological determinants of emotional state which is being conducted at the Department of Social Psychology at Columbia University under PHS Research Grant M-2584 from the National Institute of Mental Health, United States Public Health Service. This experiment was

conducted at the Laboratory for Research in Social Relations at the University of Minnesota.

The authors wish to thank Jean Carlin and Ruth Hase, the physicians in the study, and Bibb Latané and Leonard Weller who were the paid participants.

were characterized by a general pattern of excitation of the sympathetic nervous system but there appeared to be no clear-cut physiological discriminators of the various emotions. This pattern of results was so consistent from experiment to experiment that Cannon (1929) offered, as one of the crucial criticisms of the James-Lange theory, the fact that "the same visceral changes occur in very different emotional states and in non-emotional states" (p. 351).

More recent work, however, has given some indication that there may be differentiators. Ax (1953) and Schachter (1957) studied fear and anger. On a large number of indices both of these states were characterized by a similarly high level of autonomic activation but on several indices they did differ in the degree of activation. Wolf and Wolff (1947) studied a subject with a gastric fistula and were able to distinguish two patterns in the physiological responses of the stomach wall. It should be noted, though, that for many months they studied their subject during and following a great variety of moods and emotions and were able to distinguish only two patterns.

Whether or not there are physiological distinctions among the various emotional states must be considered an open question. Recent work might be taken to indicate that such differences are at best rather subtle and that the variety of emotion, mood, and feeling states are by no means matched by an equal variety of visceral patterns.

This rather ambiguous situation has led Ruckmick (1936), Hunt, Cole, and Reis (1958), Schachter (1959) and others to suggest that cognitive factors may be major determinants of emotional states. Granted a general pattern of sympathetic excitation as characteristic of emotional states, granted that there may be some differences in pattern from state to state, it is suggested that one labels, interprets, and identifies this stirred-up state in terms of the characteristics of the precipitating situation and one's apperceptive mass. This suggests, then, that an emotional state may be considered a function of a state of physiological arousal[2]

and of a cognition appropriate to this state of arousal. The cognition, in a sense, exerts a steering function. Cognitions arising from the immediate situation as interpreted by past experience provide the framework within which one understands and labels his feelings. It is the cognition which determines whether the state of physiological arousal will be labeled as "anger," "joy," "fear," or whatever.

In order to examine the implications of this formulation let us consider the fashion in which these two elements, a state of physiological arousal and cognitive factors, would interact in a variety of situations. In most emotion inducing situations, of course, the two factors are completely interrelated. Imagine a man walking alone down a dark alley, a figure with a gun suddenly appears. The perception-cognition "figure with a gun" in some fashion initiates a state of physiological arousal; this state of arousal is interpreted in terms of knowledge about dark alleys and guns and the state of arousal is labeled "fear." Similarly a student who unexpectedly learns that he has made Phi Beta Kappa may experience a state of arousal which he will label "joy."

Let us now consider circumstances in which these two elements, the physiological and the cognitive, are, to some extent, independent. First, is the state of physiological arousal alone sufficient to induce an emotion? Best evidence indicates that it is not. Marañon[3] (1924), in a fascinating study (which was replicated by Cantril & Hunt, 1932, and Landis & Hunt, 1932), injected 210 of his patients with the sympathomimetic agent adrenalin and then simply asked them to introspect. Seventy-one percent of his subjects simply reported their physical symptoms with no emotional overtones; 29% of the subjects responded in an apparently emotional fashion. Of these the great majority described their feelings in a

---

[2] Though our experiments are concerned exclusively with the physiological changes produced by the injection of adrenalin, which appear to be primarily the result of sympathetic excitation, the term physiological arousal is used in preference to the more specific "excitation of the sympathetic nervous system" because there are indications, to be discussed later, that this formulation is applicable to a variety of bodily states.

[3] Translated copies of Marañon's (1924) paper may be obtained by writing to the senior author.

fashion that Marañon labeled "cold" or "as if" emotions, that is, they made statements such as "I feel *as if* I were afraid" or *"as if* I were awaiting a great happiness."* This is a sort of emotional "déjà vu" experience; these subjects are neither happy nor afraid, they feel "as if" they were. Finally a very few cases apparently reported a genuine emotional experience. However, in order to produce this reaction in most of these few cases, Marañon (1924) points out:

> One must suggest a memory with strong affective force but not so strong as to produce an emotion in the normal state. For example, in several cases we spoke to our patients before the injection of their sick children or dead parents and they responded calmly to this topic. The same topic presented later, during the adrenal commotion, was sufficient to trigger emotion. This adrenal commotion places the subject in a situation of 'affective imminence' (pp. 307-308).

Apparently, then, to produce a genuinely emotional reaction to adrenalin, Marañon was forced to provide such subjects with an appropriate cognition.

Though Marañon (1924) is not explicit on his procedure, it is clear that his subjects knew that they were receiving an injection and in all likelihood knew that they were receiving adrenalin and probably had some order of familiarity with its effects. In short, though they underwent the pattern of sympathetic discharge common to strong emotional states, at the same time they had a completely appropriate cognition or explanation as to why they felt this way. This, we would suggest, is the reason so few of Marañon's subjects reported any emotional experience.

Consider now a person in a state of physiological arousal for which no immediately explanatory or appropriate cognitions are available. Such a state could result were one covertly to inject a subject with adrenalin or, unknown to him, feed the subject a sympathomimetic drug such as ephedrine. Under such conditions a subject would be aware of palpitations, tremor, face flushing, and most of the battery of symptoms associated with a discharge of the sympathetic nervous system. In contrast to Marañon's (1924) subjects he would, at the same time,

be utterly unaware of why he felt this way. What would be the consequence of such a state?

Schachter (1959) has suggested that precisely such a state would lead to the arousal of "evaluative needs" (Festinger, 1954), that is, pressures would act on an individual in such a state to understand and label his bodily feelings. His bodily state grossly resembles the condition in which it has been at times of emotional excitement. How would he label his present feelings? It is suggested, of course, that he will label his feelings in terms of his knowledge of the immediate situation.[4] Should he at the time be with a beautiful woman he might decide that he was wildly in love or sexually excited. Should he be at a gay party, he might, by comparing himself to others, decide that he was extremely happy and euphoric. Should he be arguing with his wife, he might explode in fury and hatred. Or, should the situation be completely inappropriate he could decide that he was excited about something that had recently happened to him or, simply, that he was sick. In any case, it is our basic assumption that emotional states are a function of the interaction of such cognitive factors with a state of physiological arousal.

This line of thought, then, leads to the following propositions:

1. Given a state of physiological arousal for which an individual has no immediate explanation, he will "label" this state and describe his feelings in terms of the cognitions available to him. To the extent that cognitive factors are potent determiners of emotional states, it could be anticipated that precisely the same state of physiological arousal could be labeled "joy" or "fury" or "jealousy" or any of a great diversity of emotional labels depending on the cognitive aspects of the situation.

2. Given a state of physiological arousal for which an individual has a completely ap-

---

[4] This suggestion is not new for several psychologists have suggested that situational factors should be considered the chief differentiators of the emotions. Hunt, Cole, and Reis (1958) probably make this point most explicitly in their study distinguishing among fear, anger, and sorrow in terms of situational characteristics.

propriate explanation (e.g., "I feel this way because I have just received an injection of adrenalin") no evaluative needs will arise and the individual is unlikely to label his feelings in terms of the alternative cognitions available.

Finally, consider a condition in which emotion inducing cognitions are present but there is no state of physiological arousal. For example, an individual might be completely aware that he is in great danger but for some reason (drug or surgical) remain in a state of physiological quiescence. Does he experience the emotion "fear"? Our formulation of emotion as a joint function of a state of physiological arousal and an appropriate cognition, would, of course, suggest that he does not, which leads to our final proposition.

3. Given the same cognitive circumstances, the individual will react emotionally or describe his feelings as emotions only to the extent that he experiences a state of physiological arousal.[5]

PROCEDURE

The experimental test of these propositions requires (a) the experimental manipulation of a state of physiological arousal, (b) the manipulation of the extent to which the subject has an appropriate or proper explanation of his bodily state, and (c) the creation of situations from which explanatory cognitions may be derived.

In order to satisfy the first two experimental requirements, the experiment was cast in the framework of a study of the effects of vitamin supplements on vision. As soon as a subject arrived, he was taken to a private room and told by the experimenter:

In this experiment we would like to make various tests of your vision. We are particularly interested in how certain vitamin compounds and vitamin supplements affect the visual skills. In particular, we want to find out how the vitamin compound called 'Suproxin' affects your vision.

[5] In his critique of the James-Lange theory of emotion, Cannon (1929) also makes the point that sympathectomized animals and patients do seem to manifest emotional behavior. This criticism is, of course, as applicable to the above proposition as it was to the James-Lange formulation. We shall discuss the issues involved in later papers.

What we would like to do, then, if we can get your permission, is to give you a small injection of Suproxin. The injection itself is mild and harmless; however, since some people do object to being injected we don't want to talk you into anything. Would you mind receiving a Suproxin injection?

If the subject agrees to the injection (and all but 1 of 185 subjects did) the experimenter continues with instructions we shall describe shortly, then leaves the room. In a few minutes a physician enters the room, briefly repeats the experimenter's instructions, takes the subject's pulse and then injects him with Suproxin.

Depending upon condition, the subject receives one of two forms of Suproxin—epinephrine or a placebo.

Epinephrine or adrenalin is a sympathomimetic drug whose effects, with minor exceptions, are almost a perfect mimicry of a discharge of the sympathetic nervous system. Shortly after injection systolic blood pressure increases markedly, heart rate increases somewhat, cutaneous blood flow decreases, while muscle and cerebral blood flow increase, blood sugar and lactic acid concentration increase, and respiration rate increases slightly. As far as the subject is concerned the major subjective symptoms are palpitation, tremor, and sometimes a feeling of flushing and accelerated breathing. With a subcutaneous injection (in the dosage administered to our subjects), such effects usually begin within 3–5 minutes of injection and last anywhere from 10 minutes to an hour. For most subjects these effects are dissipated within 15–20 minutes after injection.

Subjects receiving epinephrine received a subcutaneous injection of ½ cubic centimeter of a 1 : 1000 solution of Winthrop Laboratory's Suprarenin, a saline solution of epinephrine bitartrate.

Subjects in the placebo condition received a subcutaneous injection of ½ cubic centimeter of saline solution. This is, of course, completely neutral material with no side effects at all.

Manipulating an Appropriate Explanation

By "appropriate" we refer to the extent to which the subject has an authoritative, unequivocal explanation of his bodily condition. Thus, a subject who had been informed by the physician that as a direct consequence of the injection he would feel palpitations, tremor, etc. would be considered to have a completely appropriate explanation. A subject who had been informed only that the injection would have no side effects would have no appropriate explanation of his state. This dimension of appropriateness was manipulated in three experimental conditions which shall be called: Epinephrine Informed (Epi Inf), Epinephrine Ignorant (Epi Ign), and Epinephrine Misinformed (Epi Mis).

Immediately after the subject had agreed to the injection and before the physician entered the room, the experimenter's spiel in each of these conditions went as follows:

Epinephrine Informed. I should also tell you that some of our subjects have experienced side effects from the Suproxin. These side effects are transitory, that is, they will only last for about 15 or 20 minutes. What will probably happen is that your hand will start to shake, your heart will start to pound, and your face may get warm and flushed. Again these are side effects lasting about 15 or 20 minutes.

While the physician was giving the injection, she told the subject that the injection was mild and harmless and repeated this description of the symptoms that the subject could expect as a consequence of the shot. In this condition, then, subjects have a completely appropriate explanation of their bodily state. They know precisely what they will feel and why.

Epinephrine Ignorant. In this condition, when the subject agreed to the injection, the experimenter said nothing more relevant to side effects and simply left the room. While the physician was giving the injection, she told the subject that the injection was mild and harmless and would have no side effects. In this condition, then, the subject has no experimentally provided explanation for his bodily state.

Epinephrine Misinformed. I should also tell you that some of our subjects have experienced side effects from the Suproxin. These side effects are transitory, that is, they will only last for about 15 or 20 minutes. What will probably happen is that your feet will feel numb, you will have an itching sensation over parts of your body, and you may get a slight headache. Again these are side effects lasting 15 or 20 minutes.

And again, the physician repeated these symptoms while injecting the subject.

None of these symptoms, of course, are consequences of an injection of epinephrine and, in effect, these instructions provide the subject with a completely inappropriate explanation of his bodily feelings. This condition was introduced as a control condition of sorts. It seemed possible that the description of side effects in the Epi Inf condition might turn the subject introspective, self-examining, possibly slightly troubled. Differences on the dependent variable between the Epi Inf and Epi Ign conditions might, then, be due to such factors rather than to differences in appropriateness. The false symptoms in the Epi Mis condition should similarly turn the subject introspective, etc., but the instructions in this condition do not provide an appropriate explanation of the subject's state.

Subjects in all of the above conditions were injected with epinephrine. Finally, there was a placebo condition in which subjects, who were rejected with saline solution, were given precisely the same treatment as subjects in the Epi Ign condition.

Producing an Emotion Inducing Cognition

Our initial hypothesis has suggested that given a state of physiological arousal for which the individual has no adequate explanation, cognitive factors can lead the individual to describe his feelings with any of a diversity of emotional labels. In order to test this hypothesis, it was decided to manipulate emotional states which can be considered quite different—euphoria and anger.

There are, of course, many ways to induce such states. In our own program of research, we have concentrated on social determinants of emotional states and have been able to demonstrate in other studies that people do evaluate their own feelings by comparing themselves with others around them (Schachter 1959; Wrightsman 1960). In this experiment we have attempted again to manipulate emotional state by social means. In one set of conditions, the subject is placed together with a stooge who has been trained to act euphorically. In a second set of conditions the subject is with a stooge trained to act in an angry fashion.

Euphoria

Immediately after the subject had been injected, the physician left the room and the experimenter returned with a stooge whom he introduced as another subject, then said:

Both of you have had the Suproxin shot and you'll both be taking the same tests of vision. What I ask you to do now is just wait for 20 minutes. The reason for this is simply that we have to allow 20 minutes for the Suproxin to get from the injection site into the bloodstream. At the end of 20 minutes when we are certain that most of the Suproxin has been absorbed into the bloodstream, we'll begin the tests of vision.[6]

The room in which this was said had been deliberately put into a state of mild disarray. As he was leaving, the experimenter apologetically added:

The only other thing I should do is to apologize for the condition of the room. I just didn't have time to clean it up. So, if you need any scratch paper or rubber bands or pencils, help yourself. I'll be back in 20 minutes to begin the vision tests.

As soon as the experimenter had left, the stooge introduced himself again, made a series of standard icebreaker comments and then launched his routine. For observation purposes, the stooge's act was broken into a series of standard units, demarcated by a change in activity or a standard comment. In sequence, the units of the stooge's routine were the following:

1. Stooge reaches for a piece of paper and starts doodling saying, "They said we could use this for scratch, didn't they?" He doodles a fish for some 30 seconds, then says:

2. "This scrap paper isn't even much good for doodling" and crumples paper and attempts to throw it into wastebasket in far corner of the room. He misses but this leads him into a "basketball game." He crumples up other sheets of paper, shoots a few baskets, says "Two points" occasionally. He gets up and does a jump shot saying, "The old jump shot is really on today."

3. If the subject has not joined in, the stooge throws a paper basketball to the subject saying, "Here, you try it."

4. Stooge continues his game saying, "The trouble with paper basketballs is that you don't really have any control."

5. Stooge continues basketball, then gives it up saying, "This is one of my good days. I feel like a kid again. I think I'll make a plane." He makes a paper airplane saying, "I guess I'll make one of the longer ones."

6. Stooge flies plane. Gets up and retrieves plane. Flies again, etc.

7. Stooge throws plane at subject.

8. Stooge, flying plane, says, "Even when I was a kid, I was never much good at this."

9. Stooge tears off part of plane saying, "Maybe this plane can't fly but at least it's good for something." He wads up paper and making a slingshot of a rubber band begins to shoot the paper.

10. Shooting, the stooge says, "They [paper ammunition] really go better if you make them long. They don't work right if you wad them up."

11. While shooting, stooge notices a sloppy pile of manila folders on a table. He builds a tower of these folders, then goes to the opposite end of the room to shoot at the tower.

12. He misses several times, then hits and cheers as the tower falls. He goes over to pick up the folders.

13. While picking up, he notices, behind a portable blackboard, a pair of hula hoops which have been covered with black tape with a few wires sticking out of the tape. He reaches for these, taking one for himself and putting the other aside but within reaching distance of the subject. The stooge tries the hula hoop, saying, "This isn't as easy as it looks."

14. Stooge twirls hoop wildly on arm, saying, "Hey, look at this—this is great."

15. Stooge replaces the hula hoop and sits down with his feet on the table. Shortly thereafter the experimenter returns to the room.

This routine was completely standard, though its pace, of course, varied depending upon the subject's reaction, the extent to which he entered into this bedlam and the extent to which he initiated activities of his own. The only variations from this standard routine were those forced by the subject. Should the subject originate some nonsense of his own and request the stooge to join in, he would do so. And, he would, of course, respond to any comments initiated by the subject.

[6] It was, of course, imperative that the sequence with the stooge begin before the subject felt his first symptoms for otherwise the subject would be virtually forced to interpret his feelings in terms of events preceding the stooge's entrance. Pretests had indicated that, for most subjects, epinephrine-caused symptoms began within 3–5 minutes after injection. A deliberate attempt was made then to bring in the stooge within 1 minute after the subject's injection.

Subjects in each of the three "appropriateness" conditions and in the placebo condition were submitted to this setup. The stooge, of course, never knew in which condition any particular subject fell.

Anger

Immediately after the injection, the experimenter brought a stooge into the subject's room, introduced the two and after explaining the necessity for a 20 minute delay for "the Suproxin to get from the injection site into the bloodstream" he continued, "We would like you to use these 20 minutes to answer these questionnaires." Then handing out the questionnaires, he concludes with, "I'll be back in 20 minutes to pick up the questionnaires and begin the tests of vision."

Before looking at the questionnaire, the stooge says to the subject,

I really wanted to come for an experiment today, but I think it's unfair for them to give you shots. At least, they should have told us about the shots when they called us; you hate to refuse, once you're here already.

The questionnaires, five pages long, start off innocently requesting face sheet information and then grow increasingly personal and insulting. The stooge, sitting directly opposite the subject, paces his own answers so that at all times subject and stooge are working on the same question. At regular points in the questionnaire, the stooge makes a series of standardized comments about the questions. His comments start off innocently enough, grow increasingly querulous, and finally he ends up in a rage. In sequence, he makes the following comments.

1. Before answering any items, he leafs quickly through the questionnaire saying, "Boy, this is a long one."

2. Question 7 on the questionnaire requests, "List the foods that you would eat in a typical day." The stooge comments, "Oh for Pete's sake, what did I have for breakfast this morning?"

3. Question 9 asks, "Do you ever hear bells? _____. How often? _____."
The stooge remarks, "Look at Question 9. How ridiculous can you get? I hear bells every time I change classes."

4. Question 13 requests, "List the childhood diseases you have had and the age at which you had them" to which the stooge remarks, "I get annoyed at this childhood disease question. I can't remember what childhood diseases I had, and especially at what age. Can you?"

5. Question 17 asks, "What is your father's average annual income?" and the stooge says, "This really irritates me. It's none of their business what my father makes. I'm leaving that blank."

6. Question 25 presents a long series of items such as "Does not bathe or wash regularly," "Seems to need psychiatric care," etc. and requests the respondent to write down for which member of his immediate family each item seems most applicable. The question specifically prohibits the answer "None" and each item must be answered. The stooge says, "I'll be damned if I'll fill out Number 25. 'Does not bathe or wash regularly'—that's a real insult." He then angrily crosses out the entire item.

7. Question 28 reads:
"How many times each week do you have sexual intercourse?" 0–1 _____ 2–3 _____ 4–6 _____ 7 and over _____. The stooge bites out, "The hell with it! I don't have to tell them all this."

8. The stooge sits sullenly for a few moments then he rips up his questionnaire, crumples the pieces and hurls them to the floor, saying, "I'm not wasting any more time. I'm getting my books and leaving" and he stamps out of the room.

9. The questionnaire continues for eight more questions ending with: "With how many men (other than your father) has your mother had extramarital relationships?"
4 and under _____: 5–9 _____: 10 and over _____.

Subjects in the Epi Ign, Epi Inf and Placebo conditions were run through this "anger" inducing sequence. The stooge, again, did not know to which condition the subject had been assigned.

In summary, this is a seven conditions experiment which, for two different emotional states, allows us (a) to evaluate the effects of "appropriateness" on emotional inducibility and (b) to begin to evaluate the effects of sympathetic activation on emotional inducibility. In schematic form the conditions are the following:

EUPHORIA	ANGER
Epi Inf	Epi Inf
Epi Ign	Epi Ign
Epi Mis	Placebo
Placebo	

The Epi Mis condition was not run in the Anger sequence. This was originally conceived as a control condition and it was felt that its inclusion in the Euphoria conditions alone would suffice as a means of evaluating the possible artifactual effect of the Epi Inf instructions.

Measurement

Two types of measures of emotional state were obtained. Standardized observation through a one-way mirror was the technique used to assess the subject's behavior. To what extent did he act euphoric or angry? Such behavior can be considered in a way as a "semiprivate" index of mood for as far as the subject was concerned, his emotional behavior could be known only to the other person in the room—presumably another student. The second type of measure was self-report in which, on a variety of scales, the subject indicated his mood of the moment. Such measures can be considered "public" indices of mood for they would, of course, be available to the experimenter and his associates.

Observation

Euphoria. For each of the first 14 units of the stooge's standardized routine an observer kept a running chronicle of what the subject did and said. For each unit the observer coded the subject's behavior in one or more of the following categories:

Category 1: Joins in activity. If the subject entered into the stooge's activities, e.g., if he made or flew airplanes, threw paper basketballs, hula hooped, etc., his behavior was coded in this category.

Category 2: Initiates new activity. A subject was so coded if he gave indications of creative euphoria, that is, if, on his own, he initiated behavior outside of the stooge's routine. Instances of such behavior would be the subject who threw open the window and, laughing, hurled paper basketballs at passersby; or, the subject who jumped on a table and spun one hula hoop on his leg and the other on his neck.

Categories 3 and 4: Ignores or watches stooge. Subjects who paid flatly no attention to the stooge or who, with or without comment, simply watched the stooge without joining in his activity were coded in these categories.

For any particular unit of behavior, the subject's behavior was coded in one or more of these categories. To test reliability of coding two observers independently coded

two experimental sessions. The observers agreed completely on the coding of 88% of the units.

Anger. For each of the units of stooge behavior, an observer recorded the subject's responses and coded them according to the following category scheme:

Category 1: Agrees. In response to the stooge the subject makes a comment indicating that he agrees with the stooge's standardized comment or that he, too, is irked by a particular item on the questionnaire. For example, a subject who responded to the stooge's comment on the "father's income" question by saying, "I don't like that kind of personal question either" would be so coded (scored $+2$).

Category 2: Disagrees. In response to the stooge's comment, the subject makes a comment which indicates that he disagrees with the stooge's meaning or mood; e.g., in response to the stooge's comment on the "father's income" question, such a subject might say, "Take it easy, they probably have a good reason for wanting the information" (scored -2).

Category 3: Neutral. A noncommittal or irrelevant response to the stooge's remark (scored 0).

Category 4: Initiates agreement or disagreement. With no instigation by the stooge, a subject, so coded, would have volunteered a remark indicating that he felt the same way or, alternatively, quite differently than the stooge. Examples would be "Boy I hate this kind of thing" or "I'm enjoying this" (scored $+2$ or -2).

Category 5: Watches. The subject makes no verbal response to the stooge's comment but simply looks directly at him (scored 0).

Category 6: Ignores. The subject makes no verbal response to the stooge's comment nor does he look at him; the subject, paying no attention at all to the stooge, simply works at his own questionnaire (scored -1).

A subject was scored in one or more of these categories for each unit of stooge behavior. To test reliability, two observers independently coded three experimental sessions. In order to get a behavioral index of anger, observation protocol was scored according to the values presented in parentheses after each of the above definitions of categories. In a unit-by-unit comparison, the two observers agreed completely on the scoring of 71% of the units jointly observed. The scores of the two observers differed by a value of 1 or less for 88% of the units coded and in not a single case did the two observers differ in the direction of their scoring of a unit.

Self Report of Mood and Physical Condition

When the subject's session with the stooge was completed, the experimenter returned to the room, took pulses and said:

Before we proceed with the vision tests, there is one other kind of information which we must have. We have found, as you can probably imagine, that there are many things beside Suproxin that affect how well you see in our tests. How hungry you are, how tired you are, and even the mood you're in at the time—whether you feel happy or irritated at the time of testing will affect how well you see. To understand the data we collect on you, then, we must be able to figure out which effects are due to causes such as these and which are caused by Suproxin.

The only way we can get such information about your physical and emotional state is to have you tell us. I'll hand out these questionnaires and ask you to answer them as accurately as possible. Obviously, our data on the vision tests will only be as accurate as your description of your mental and physical state.

In keeping with this spiel, the questionnaire that the experimenter passed out contained a number of mock questions about hunger, fatigue, etc., as well as questions of more immediate relevance to the experiment. To measure mood or emotional state the following two were the crucial questions:

1. How irritated, angry or annoyed would you say you feel at present?

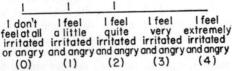

2. How good or happy would you say you feel at present?

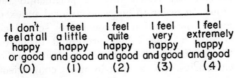

To measure the physical effects of epinephrine and determine whether or not the injection had been successful in producing the necessary bodily state, the following questions were asked:

1. Have you experienced any palpitation (consciousness of your own heart beat)?

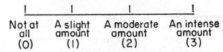

2. Did you feel any tremor (involuntary shaking of the hands, arms or legs)?

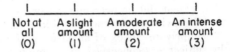

To measure possible effects of the instructions in the Epi Mis condition, the following questions were asked:

1. Did you feel any numbness in your feet?

2. Did you feel any itching sensation?

3. Did you experience any feeling of headache?

To all three of these questions was attached a four-point scale running from "Not at all" to "An intense amount."

In addition to these scales, the subjects were asked to answer two open-end questions on other physical or emotional sensations they may have experienced during the experimental session. A final measure of bodily state was pulse rate which was taken by the physician or the experimenter at two times—immediately before the injection and immediately after the session with the stooge.

When the subjects had completed these questionnaires, the experimenter announced that the experiment was over, explained the deception and its necessity in detail, answered any questions, and swore the subjects to secrecy. Finally, the subjects answered a brief questionnaire about their experiences, if any, with adrenalin and their previous knowledge or suspicion of the experimental setup. There was no indication that any of the subjects had known about the experiment beforehand but 11 subjects were so extremely suspicious of some crucial feature of the experiment that their data were automatically discarded.

Subjects

The subjects were all male, college students taking classes in introductory psychology at the University of Minnesota. Some 90% of the students in these classes volunteer for a subject pool for which they receive two extra points on their final exam for every hour that they serve as experimental subjects. For this study the records of all potential subjects were cleared with the Student Health Service in order to insure that no harmful effects would result from the injections.

Evaluation of the Experimental Design

The ideal test of our propositions would require circumstances which our experiment is far from realizing. First, the proposition that: "A state of physiological arousal for which an individual has no immediate explanation will lead him to label this state in terms of the cognitions available to him" obviously requires conditions under which the subject does not and cannot have a proper explanation of his bodily state. Though we toyed with such fantasies as ventilating the experimental room with vaporized adrenalin, reality forced us to rely on the disguised injection of Suproxin—a technique which was far from ideal for no matter what the experimenter told them, some subjects would inevitably attribute their feelings to the injection. To the extent that subjects did so, differences between the several appropriateness conditions should be attenuated.

Second, the proposition that: "Given the same cognitive circumstances the individual will react emotionally only to the extent that he experiences a state of physiological arousal" requires for its ideal test the manipulation of states of physiological arousal and of physiological quiescence. Though there is no question that epinephrine effectively produces a state of arousal, there is also no question that a placebo does not prevent physiological arousal. To the extent that the experimental situation effectively produces sympathetic stimulation in placebo subjects, the proposition is difficult to test, for such a factor would attenuate differences between epinephrine and placebo subjects.

Both of these factors, then, can be expected to interfere with the test of our several propositions. In presenting the results of this study, we shall first present condition by condition results and then evaluate the effect of these two factors on experimental differences.

RESULTS

Effects of the Injections on Bodily State

Let us examine first the success of the injections at producing the bodily state required to examine the propositions at test. Does the injection of epinephrine produce symptoms of sympathetic discharge as compared with the placebo injection? Relevant data are presented in Table 1 where it can be immediately seen that on all items subjects who were in epinephrine conditions show considerably more evidence of sympathetic activation than do subjects in placebo conditions. In all epinephrine conditions pulse rate increases significantly when compared with the decrease characteristic of the placebo conditions. On the scales it is clear that epinephrine subjects experience considerably more palpitation and tremor than do placebo subjects. In all possible comparisons on these symptoms, the mean scores of subjects in any of the epinephrine conditions are greater than the corresponding scores in the placebo conditions at better than the .001 level of significance. Examination of the absolute values of these scores makes it quite clear that subjects in epinephrine conditions were, indeed, in a state of physiological arousal, while most subjects in placebo conditions were in a relative state of physiological quiescence.

The epinephrine injection, of course, did not work with equal effectiveness for all subjects; indeed for a few subjects it did not work at all. Such subjects reported almost no palpitation or tremor, showed no increase in pulse and described no other relevant physical symptoms. Since for such subjects the necessary experimental conditions were not established, they were automatically excluded from the data and all further tabular presentations will not include such subjects. Table 1, however, does include the data of these subjects. There were four such subjects in euphoria conditions and one of them in anger conditions.

In order to evaluate further data on Epi Mis subjects it is necessary to note the results of the "numbness," "itching," and "headache" scales also presented in Table 1.

TABLE 1

THE EFFECTS OF THE INJECTIONS ON BODILY STATE

Condition	N	Pulse		Self-rating of				
		Pre	Post	Palpitation	Tremor	Numbness	Itching	Headache
Euphoria								
Epi Inf	27	85.7	88.6	1.20	1.43	0	0.16	0.32
Epi Ign	26	84.6	85.6	1.83	1.76	0.15	0	0.55
Epi Mis	26	82.9	86.0	1.27	2.00	0.06	0.08	0.23
Placebo	26	80.4	77.1	0.29	0.21	0.09	0	0.27
Anger								
Epi Inf	23	85.9	92.4	1.26	1.41	0.17	0	0.11
Epi Ign	23	85.0	96.8	1.44	1.78	0	0.06	0.21
Placebo	23	84.5	79.6	0.59	0.24	0.14	0.06	0.06

Clearly the subjects in the Epi Mis condition do not differ on these scales from subjects in any of the other experimental conditions.

Effects of the Manipulations on Emotional State

Euphoria: Self-report. The effects of the several manipulations on emotional state in the euphoria conditions are presented in Table 2. The scores recorded in this table

TABLE 2

SELF-REPORT OF EMOTIONAL STATE IN
THE EUPHORIA CONDITIONS

Condi-tion	N	Self-Report scales	Comparison	p[a]
Epi Inf	25	0.98	Epi Inf vs. Epi Mis	<.01
Epi Ign	25	1.78	Epi Inf vs. Epi Ign	.02
Epi Mis	25	1.90	Placebo vs. Epi Mis,	ns
Placebo	26	1.61	Ign, or Inf	

[a] All *p* values reported throughout paper are two-tailed.

are derived, for each subject, by subtracting the value of the point he checks on the irritation scale from the value of the point he checks on the happiness scale. Thus, if a subject were to check the point "I feel a little irritated and angry" on the irritation scale and the point "I feel very happy and good" on the happiness scale, his score would be +2. The higher the positive value, the happier and better the subject reports himself as feeling. Though we employ an index for

expositional simplicity, it should be noted that the two components of the index each yield results completely consistent with those obtained by use of this index.

Let us examine first the effects of the appropriateness instructions. Comparison of the scores for the Epi Mis and Epi Inf conditions makes it immediately clear that the experimental differences are not due to artifacts resulting from the informed instructions. In both conditions the subject was warned to expect a variety of symptoms as a consequence of the injection. In the Epi Mis condition, where the symptoms were inappropriate to the subject's bodily state the self-report score is almost twice that in the Epi Inf condition where the symptoms were completely appropriate to the subject's bodily state. It is reasonable, then, to attribute differences between informed subjects and those in other conditions to differences in manipulated appropriateness rather than to artifacts such as introspectiveness or self-examination.

It is clear that, consistent with expectations, subjects were more susceptible to the stooge's mood and consequently more euphoric when they had no explanation of their own bodily states than when they did. The means of both the Epi Ign and Epi Mis conditions are considerably greater than the mean of the Epi Inf condition.

It is of interest to note that Epi Mis subjects are somewhat more euphoric than are Epi Ign subjects. This pattern repeats itself in other data shortly to be presented. We would attribute this difference to differences in the appropriateness dimension. Though, as in the Epi Ign condition, a subject is not provided with an explanation of his bodily state, it is, of course, possible that he will provide one for himself which is not derived from his interaction with the stooge. More reasonably he could decide for himself that he feels this way because of the injection. To the extent that he does so he should be less susceptible to the stooge. It seems probable that he would be less likely to hit on such an explanation in the Epi Mis condition than in the Epi Ign condition for in the Epi Mis condition both the experimenter and the doctor have told him that the effects of the injection would be quite different from what he actually feels. The effect of such instructions is probably to make it more difficult for the subject himself to hit on the alternative explanation described above. There is some evidence to support this analysis. In open-end questions in which subjects described their own mood and state, 28% of the subjects in the Epi Ign condition made some connection between the injection and their bodily state compared with the 16% of subjects in the Epi Mis condition who did so. It could be considered, then, that these three conditions fall along a dimension of appropriateness, with the Epi Inf condition at one extreme and the Epi Mis condition at the other.

Comparing the placebo to the epinephrine conditions, we note a pattern which will repeat itself throughout the data. Placebo subjects are less euphoric than either Epi Mis or Epi Ign subjects but somewhat more euphoric than Epi Inf subjects. These differences are not, however, statistically significant. We shall consider the epinephrine-placebo comparisons in detail in a later section of this paper following the presentation of additional relevant data. For the moment, it is clear that, by self-report manipulating appropriateness has had a very strong effect on euphoria.

Behavior. Let us next examine the extent to which the subject's behavior was affected by the experimental manipulations. To the extent that his mood has been affected, one should expect that the subject will join in the stooge's whirl of manic activity and initi-

ate similar activities of his own. The relevant data are presented in Table 3. The column

TABLE 3

Behavioral Indications of Emotional State in the Euphoria Conditions

Condition	N	Activity index	Mean Number of acts initiated
Epi Inf	25	12.72	.20
Epi Ign	25	18.28	.56
Epi Mis	25	22.56	.84
Placebo	26	16.00	.54

	p value	
Comparison	Activity index	Initiates[a]
Epi Inf vs. Epi Mis	.05	.03
Epi Inf vs. Epi Ign	*ns*	.08
Placebo vs. Epi Mis, Ign, or Inf	*ns*	*ns*

[a] Tested by X^2 comparison of the proportion of subjects in each condition initiating new acts.

labeled "Activity index" presents summary figures on the extent to which the subject joined in the stooge's activity. This is a weighted index which reflects both the nature of the activities in which the subject engaged and the amount of time he was active. The index was devised by assigning the following weights to the subject's activities: 5—hula hooping; 4—shooting with slingshot; 3—paper airplanes; 2—paper basketballs; 1—doodling; 0—does nothing. Pretest scaling on 15 college students ordered these activities with respect to the degree of euphoria they represented. Arbitrary weights were assigned so that the wilder the activity, the heavier the weight. These weights are multiplied by an estimate of the amount of time the subject spent in each activity and the summed products make up the activity index for each subject. This index may be considered a measure of behavioral euphoria. It should be noted that the same between-condition relationships hold for the two components of this index as for the index itself.

The column labeled "Mean number of acts initiated" presents the data on the extent to which the subject deviates from the stooge's routine and initiates euphoric activities of his own.

On both behavioral indices, we find precisely the same pattern of relationships as those obtained with self-reports. Epi Mis subjects behave somewhat more euphorically than do Epi Ign subjects who in turn behave more euphorically than do Epi Inf subjects. On all measures, then, there is consistent evidence that a subject will take over the stooge's euphoric mood to the extent that he has no other explanation of his bodily state.

Again it should be noted that on these behavioral indices, Epi Ign and Epi Mis subjects are somewhat more euphoric than placebo subjects but not significantly so.

Anger: Self-report. Before presenting data for the anger conditions, one point must be made about the anger manipulation. In the situation devised, anger, if manifested, is most likely to be directed at the experimenter and his annoyingly personal questionnaire. As we subsequently discovered, this was rather unfortunate, for the subjects, who had volunteered for the experiment for extra points on their final exam, simply refused to endanger these points by publicly blowing up, admitting their irritation to the experimenter's face or spoiling the questionnaire. Though as the reader will see, the subjects were quite willing to manifest anger when they were alone with the stooge, they hesitated to do so on material (self-ratings of mood and questionnaire) that the experimenter might see and only after the purposes of the experiment had been revealed were many of these subjects willing to admit to the experimenter that they had been irked or irritated.

This experimentally unfortunate situation pretty much forces us to rely on the behavioral indices derived from observation of the subject's presumably private interaction with the stooge. We do, however, present data on the self-report scales in Table 4. These figures are derived in the same way as the figures presented in Table 2 for the euphoria conditions, that is, the value checked on the irritation scale is subtracted from the value checked on the happiness scale. Though, for the reasons stated above, the absolute magnitude of these figures (all positive) is relatively meaningless, we can, of course, compare condition means within the set of anger conditions. With the happiness-irritation index employed, we should, of course, anticipate precisely the reverse results from those obtained in the euphoria

TABLE 4

SELF-REPORT OF EMOTIONAL STATE IN THE ANGER CONDITIONS

Condition	N	Self-Report scales	Comparison	p
Epi Inf	22	1.91	Epi Inf vs. Epi Ign	.08
Epi Ign	23	1.39	Placebo vs. Epi Ign or Inf	ns
Placebo	23	1.63		

conditions; that is, the Epi Inf subjects in the anger conditions should again be less susceptible to the stooge's mood and should, therefore, describe themselves as in a somewhat happier frame of mind than subjects in the Epi Ign condition. This is the case; the Epi Inf subjects average 1.91 on the self-report scales while the Epi Ign subjects average 1.39.

Evaluating the effects of the injections, we note again that, as anticipated, Epi Ign subjects are somewhat less happy than Placebo subjects but, once more, this is not a significant difference.

Behavior. The subject's responses to the stooge, during the period when both were filling out their questionnaires, were systematically coded to provide a behavioral index of anger. The coding scheme and the numerical values attached to each of the categories have been described in the methodology section. To arrive at an "Anger index" the numerical value assigned to a subject's responses to the stooge is summed together for the several units of stooge behavior. In the coding scheme used, a positive value to this index indicates that the subject agrees with the stooge's comment and is growing angry. A negative value indicates that the subject either disagrees with the stooge or ignores him.

The relevant data are presented in Table 5. For this analysis, the stooge's routine has been divided into two phases—the first two units of his behavior (the "long" questionnaire and "What did I have for breakfast?") are considered essentially neutral revealing nothing of the stooge's mood; all of the following units are considered "angry" units for they begin with an irritated remark about the "bells" question and end with the stooge's fury as he rips up his questionnaire and stomps out of the room. For the neutral units, agreement or disagreement with the stooge's remarks is, of course, meaningless as an index of mood and we should anticipate no difference between conditions. As can be seen in Table 5, this is the case.

TABLE 5

BEHAVIORAL INDICATIONS OF EMOTIONAL STATE IN THE ANGER CONDITIONS

Condition	N	Neutral units	Anger units
Epi Inf	22	+0.07	−0.18
Epi Ign	23	+0.30	+2.28
Placebo	22[a]	−0.09	+0.79

Comparison for anger units	p
Epi Inf vs. Epi Ign	<.01
Epi Ign vs. Placebo	<.05
Placebo vs. Epi Inf	ns

[a] For one subject in this condition the sound system went dead and the observer could not, of course, code his reactions.

For the angry units, we must, of course, anticipate that subjects in the Epi Ign condition will be angrier than subjects in the Epi Inf condition. This is indeed the case. The Anger index for the Epi Ign condition is positive and large, indicating that these subjects have become angry, while in the Epi Inf condition the Anger index is slightly negative in value indicating that these subjects have failed to catch the stooge's mood at all. It seems clear that providing the subject with an appropriate explanation of his bodily state greatly reduces his tendency to interpret his state in terms of the cognitions provided by the stooge's angry behavior.

Finally, on this behavioral index, it can be seen that subjects in the Epi Ign condition are significantly angrier than subjects in the Placebo condition. Behaviorally, at least, the injection of epinephrine appears to have led subjects to an angrier state than comparable subjects who received placebo shots.

Conformation of Data to Theoretical Expectations

Now that the basic data of this study have been presented, let us examine closely the extent to which they conform to theoretical expectations. If our hypotheses are correct and if this experimental design provided a perfect test for these hypotheses, it should be anticipated that in the euphoria conditions the degree of experimentally produced euphoria should vary in the following fashion:

$$\text{Epi Mis} \geqq \text{Epi Ign} > \text{Epi Inf} = \text{Placebo}$$

And in the anger conditions, anger should conform to the following pattern:

$$\text{Epi Ign} > \text{Epi Inf} = \text{Placebo}$$

In both sets of conditions, it is the case that emotional level in the Epi Mis and Epi Ign conditions is considerably greater than that achieved in the corresponding Epi Inf conditions. The results for the Placebo condition, however, are ambiguous for consistently the Placebo subjects fall between the Epi Ign and the Epi Inf subjects. This is a particularly troubling pattern for it makes it impossible to evaluate unequivocally the effects of the state of physiological arousal and indeed raises serious questions about our entire theoretical structure. Though the emotional level is consistently greater in the Epi Mis and Epi Ign conditions than in the Placebo condition, this difference is significant at acceptable probability levels only in the anger conditions.

In order to explore the problem further, let us examine the experimental factors identified earlier, which might have acted to restrain the emotional level in the Epi Ign and Epi Mis conditions. As was pointed out earlier, the ideal test of our first two hypotheses requires an experimental setup in which the subject has flatly no way of evaluating his state of phsysiological arousal other than by means of the experimentally provided cognitions. Had it been possible to physiologically produce a state of sympathetic activation by means other than injection, one could have approached this experimental ideal more closely than in the present setup. As it stands, however, there is always a reasonable alternative cognition available to the aroused subject—he feels the way he does because of the injection. To the extent that the subject seizes on such an explanation of his bodily state, we should expect that he will be uninfluenced by the stooge. Evidence presented in Table 6 for the anger condition and in Table 7 for the euphoria conditions indicates that this is, indeed, the case.

As mentioned earlier, some of the Epi Ign and Epi Mis subjects in their answers to the open-end questions clearly attributed their physical state to the injection, e.g., "the shot gave me the shivers." In Tables 6 and 7 such subjects are labeled "Self-informed." In Table 6 it can be seen that the self-informed subjects are considerably less angry than are the remaining subjects; indeed, they are not angry at all. With these self-informed subjects eliminated the difference between the Epi Ign and the Placebo conditions is significant at the .01 level of significance.

Precisely the same pattern is evident in Table 7 for the euphoria conditions. In both the Epi Mis and the Epi Ign conditions, the self-informed subjects have considerably lower activity indices than do the remaining subjects. Eliminating self-informed subjects, comparison of both of these conditions with the Placebo condition yields a difference significant at the .03 level of significance. It should be noted, too, that the self-informed subjects have much the same score on the activity index as do the experimental Epi Inf subjects (Table 3).

It would appear, then, that the experimental procedure of injecting the subjects, by providing an alternative cognition, has, to some extent, obscured the effects of epinephrine. When account is taken of this artifact, the evidence is good that the state of physiological arousal is a necessary component of an emotional experience for when self-informed subjects are removed, epinephrine subjects give consistent indications of greater emotionality than do placebo subjects.

Let us examine next the fact that consistently the emotional level, both reported and behavioral, in Placebo conditions is greater

TABLE 6

THE EFFECTS OF ATTRIBUTING BODILY STATE TO THE INJECTION ON ANGER IN THE ANGER EPI IGN CONDITION

	N	Anger index
Self-informed subjects	3	−1.67
Others	20	+2.88
Self-informed versus Others		$p = .05$

TABLE 7

THE EFFECTS OF ATTRIBUTING BODILY STATE TO THE INJECTION ON EUPHORIA IN THE EUPHORIA EPI IGN AND EPI MIS CONDITIONS

Epi Ign		
	N	Activity index
Self-informed subjects	8	11.63
Others	17	21.14
Self-informed versus Others		$p = .05$

Epi Mis		
	N	Activity index
Self-informed subjects	5	12.40
Others	20	25.10
Self-informed versus Others		$p = .10$

than that in the Epi Inf conditions. Theoretically, of course, it should be expected that the two conditions will be equally low, for by assuming that emotional state is a joint function of a state of physiological arousal and of the appropriateness of a cognition we are, in effect, assuming a multiplicative function, so that if either component is at zero, emotional level is at zero. As noted earlier this expectation should hold if we can be sure that there is no sympathetic activation in the Placebo conditions. This assumption, of course, is completely unrealistic for the injection of placebo does not prevent sympathetic activation. The experimental situations were fairly dramatic and certainly some of the placebo subjects gave indications of physiological arousal. If our general line of reasoning is correct, it should be anticipated that the emotional level of subjects who give indications of sympathetic activity will be greater than that of subjects who do not. The relevant evidence is presented in Tables 8 and 9.

TABLE 8

SYMPATHETIC ACTIVATION AND EUPHORIA IN THE EUPHORIA PLACEBO CONDITION

Subject whose:	N	Activity index
Pulse decreased	14	10.67
Pulse increased or remained same	12	23.17
Pulse decreasers versus pulse increasers or same		$p = .02$

As an index of sympathetic activation we shall use the most direct and unequivocal measure available—change in pulse rate. It can be seen in Table 1 that the predominant pattern in the Placebo condition is a decrease in pulse rate. We shall assume, therefore, that those subjects whose pulse increases or remains the same give indications of sympathetic activity while those subjects whose pulse decreases do not. In Table 8, for the euphoria condition, it is immediately clear that subjects who give indications of sympathetic activity are considerably more euphoric than are subjects who show no sympathetic activity. This relationship is, of course, confounded by the fact that euphoric subjects are considerably more active than noneuphoric subjects—a factor which independent of mood could elevate pulse rate. However, no such factor operates in the anger condition where angry subjects are neither more active nor talkative than calm subjects. It can be seen in Table 9 that Placebo subjects who show signs of sympathetic activation give indications of considerably more anger than do subjects who show no such signs. Conforming to expectations,

TABLE 9

SYMPATHETIC ACTIVATION AND ANGER IN ANGER PLACEBO CONDITION

Subjects whose:	N[a]	Anger index
Pulse decreased	13	+0.15
Pulse increased or remained same	8	+1.69
Pulse decreasers versus pulse increasers or same		$p = .01$

[a] N reduced by two cases owing to failure of sound system in one case and experimenter's failure to take pulse in another.

sympathetic activation accompanies an increase in emotional level.

It should be noted, too, that the emotional levels of subjects showing no signs of sympathetic activity are quite comparable to the emotional level of subjects in the parallel Epi Inf conditions (see Tables 3 and 5). The similarity of these sets of scores and their uniformly low level of indicated emotionality would certainly make it appear that both factors are essential to an emotional state. When either the level of sympathetic arousal is low or a completely appropriate cognition is available, the level of emotionality is low.

DISCUSSION

Let us summarize the major findings of this experiment and examine the extent to which they support the propositions offered in the introduction of this paper. It has been suggested, first, that given a state of physiological arousal for which an individual has no explanation, he will label this state in terms of the cognitions available to him. This implies, of course, that by manipulating the cognitions of an individual in such a state we can manipulate his feelings in diverse directions. Experimental results support this proposition for following the injection of epinephrine, those subjects who had no explanation for the bodily state thus produced, gave behavioral and self-report indications that they had been readily manipulable into the disparate feeling states of euphoria and anger.

From this first proposition, it must follow that given a state of physiological arousal for which the individual has a completely satisfactory explanation, he will not label this state in terms of the alternative cognitions available. Experimental evidence strongly supports this expectation. In those conditions in which subjects were injected with epinephrine and told precisely what they would feel and why, they proved relatively immune to any effects of the manipulated cognitions. In the anger condition, such subjects did not report or show anger; in the euphoria condition, such subjects reported themselves as far less happy than subjects with an identical bodily state but no adequate knowledge of why they felt the way they did.

Finally, it has been suggested that given constant cognitive circumstances, an individual will react emotionally only to the extent that he experiences a state of physiological arousal. Without taking account of experimental artifacts, the evidence in support of this proposition is consistent but tentative. When the effects of "self-informing" tendencies in epinephrine subjects and of "self-arousing" tendencies in placebo subjects are partialed out, the evidence strongly supports the proposition.

The pattern of data, then, falls neatly in line with theoretical expectations. However, the fact that we were forced, to some extent, to rely on internal analyses in order to partial out the effects of experimental artifacts inevitably makes our conclusions somewhat tentative. In order to further test these propositions on the interaction of cognitive and physiological determinants of emotional state, a series of additional experiments, published elsewhere, was designed to rule out or overcome the operation of these artifacts. In the first of these, Schachter and Wheeler (1962) extended the range of manipulated sympathetic activation by employing three experimental groups—epinephrine, placebo, and a group injected with the sympatholytic agent, chlorpromazine. Laughter at a slapstick movie was the dependent variable and the evidence is good that amusement is a direct function of manipulated sympathetic activation.

In order to make the epinephrine-placebo comparison under conditions which would rule out the operation of any self-informing tendency, two experiments were conducted on rats. In one of these Singer (1961) demonstrated that under fear inducing conditions, manipulated by the simultaneous presentation of a loud bell, a buzzer, and a bright flashing light, rats injected with epinephrine were considerably more frightened than rats injected with a placebo. Epinephrine-injected rats defecated, urinated, and trembled more than did placebo-injected rats. In nonfear control conditions, there were no differences between epinephrine and placebo groups, neither group giving any indication of fear. In another study, Latané and Schachter (1962) demonstrated that rats injected with epinephrine were notably more capable of avoidance learning than were rats injected with a placebo. Using a modified Miller-Mowrer shuttlebox, these investigators found that during an experimental period involving 200 massed trials, 15 rats injected with epinephrine avoided shock an average of 101.2 trials while 15 placebo-injected rats averaged only 37.3 avoidances.

Taken together, this body of studies does give strong support to the propositions which generated these experimental tests. Given a state of sympathetic activation, for which no immediately appropriate explanation is available, human subjects can be readily manipulated into states of euphoria, anger, and amusement. Varying the intensity of sympathetic activation serves to vary the intensity of a variety of emotional states in both rats and human subjects.

Let us examine the implications of these findings and of this line of thought for problems in the general area of the physiology of the emotions. We have noted in the introduction that the numerous studies on physiological differentiators of emotional states have, viewed en masse, yielded quite inconclusive results. Most, though not all, of these studies have indicated no differences among the various emotional states. Since as human beings, rather than as scientists, we have no difficulty identifying, labeling, and distinguishing among our feelings, the results of these studies have long seemed rather puzzling and paradoxical. Perhaps because of this, there has been a persistent tendency to discount such results as due to ignorance or methodological inadequacy and to pay far more attention to the very few studies which demonstrate *some* sort of physiological differences among emotional states than to the very many studies which indicate no differences at all. It is conceivable, however, that these results should be taken at face value and that emotional states may, indeed, be generally characterized by a high level of sympathetic activation with few if any physiological distinguishers among the many emotional states. If this is correct, the findings of the present study may help to resolve the problem. Obviously this study does *not* rule out the possibility of physiological differences among the emotional states. It is the case, however, that given precisely the same state of epinephrine-induced sympathetic activation, we have, by means of cognitive manipulations, been able to produce in our subjects the very disparate states of euphoria and anger. It may indeed be the case that cognitive factors are major determiners of the emotional labels we apply to a common state of sympathetic arousal.

Let us ask next whether our results are specific to the state of sympathetic activation or if they are generalizable to other states of physiological arousal. It is clear that from our experiments proper, it is impossible to answer the question for our studies have been concerned largely with the effects of an epinephrine created state of sympathetic arousal. We would suggest, however, that our conclusions are generalizable to almost any pronounced internal state for which no appropriate explanation is available. This suggestion receives some support from the experiences of Nowlis and Nowlis (1956) in their program of research on the effects of drugs on mood. In their work the Nowlises typically administer a drug to groups of four subjects who are physically in one another's presence and free to interact. The Nowlises describe some of their results with these groups as follows:

> At first we used the same drug for all 4 men. In those sessions seconal, when compared with placebo, increased the checking of such words as expansive, forceful, courageous, daring, elated, and impulsive. In our first statistical analysis we were confronted with the stubborn fact that when the same drug is given to all 4 men in a group, the N that has to be entered into the analysis is 1, not 4. This increases the cost of an already expensive experiment by a considerable factor, but it cannot be denied that the effects of these drugs may be and often are quite contagious. Our first attempted solution was to run tests on groups in which each man had a different drug during the same session, such as 1 on seconal, 1 on benzedrine, 1 on dramamine, and 1 on placebo. What does seconal do? Cooped up with, say, the egotistical benzedrine partner, the withdrawn, indifferent dramamine partner, and the slightly bored lactose man, the seconal subject reports that he is distractible, dizzy, drifting, glum, defiant, languid, sluggish, discouraged, dull, gloomy, lazy, and slow! This is not the report of mood that we got when all 4 men were on seconal. It thus appears that the moods of the partners do definitely influence the effect of seconal (p. 350).

It is not completely clear from this description whether this "contagion" of mood is more marked in drug than in placebo groups, but should this be the case, these results would certainly support the suggestion that our findings are generalizable to internal states other than that produced by an injection of epinephrine.

Finally, let us consider the implications of our formulation and data for alternative conceptualizations of emotion. Perhaps the most popular current conception of emotion is in terms of "activation theory" in the sense employed by Lindsley (1951) and Woodworth and Schlosberg (1958). As we understand this theory, it suggests that emotional states should be considered as at one end of a continuum of activation which is defined in terms of degree of autonomic arousal and of electro-encephalographic measures of activation. The results of the experiment described in this paper do, of course, suggest that such a formulation is not completely adequate. It is possible to have very high degrees of activation without a subject either appearing to be or describing himself as "emotional." Cognitive factors appear to be indispensable elements in any formulation of emotion.

SUMMARY

It is suggested that emotional states may be considered a function of a state of physiological arousal and of a cognition appropriate to this state of arousal. From this follows these propositions:

1. Given a state of physiological arousal for which an individual has no immediate explanation, he will label this state and describe his feelings in terms of the cognitions available to him. To the extent that cognitive factors are potent determiners of emotional states, it should be anticipated that precisely the same state of physiological arousal could be labeled "joy" or "fury" or "jealousy" or any of a great diversity of emotional labels depending on the cognitive aspects of the situation.

2. Given a state of physiological arousal for which an individual has a completely appropriate explanation, no evaluative needs will arise and the individual is unlikely to label his feelings in terms of the alternative cognitions available.

3. Given the same cognitive circumstances, the individual will react emotionally or describe his feelings as emotions only to the extent that he experiences a state of physiological arousal.

An experiment is described which, together with the results of other studies, supports these propositions.

REFERENCES

Ax, A. F. Physiological differentiation of emotional states. *Psychosom. Med.,* 1953, 15, 433–442.

Cannon, W. B. *Bodily changes in pain, hunger, fear and rage.* (2nd ed.) New York: Appleton, 1929.

Cantril, H., & Hunt, W. A. Emotional effects produced by the injection of adrenalin. *Amer. J. Psychol.,* 1932, 44, 300–307.

Festinger, L. A theory of social comparison processes. *Hum. Relat.,* 1954, 7, 114–140.

Hunt, J. McV., Cole, M. W., & Reis, E. E. Situational cues distinguishing anger, fear, and sorrow. *Amer. J. Psychol.,* 1958, 71, 136–151.

James, W. *The principles of psychology.* New York: Holt, 1890.

Landis, C., & Hunt, W. A. Adrenalin and emotion. *Psychol. Rev.,* 1932, 39, 467–485.

Latané, B., & Schachter, S. Adrenalin and avoidance learning. *J. comp. physiol. Psychol.,* 1962, 65, 369–372.

Lindsley, D. B. Emotion. In S. S. Stevens (Ed.), *Handbook of experimental psychology.* New York: Wiley, 1951. Pp. 473–516.

Marañon, G. Contribution à l'étude de l'action émotive de l'adrénaline. *Rev. Francaise Endocrinol.,* 1924, 2, 301–325.

Nowlis, V., & Nowlis, H. H. The description and analysis of mood. *Ann. N. Y. Acad. Sci.,* 1956, 65, 345–355.

Ruckmick, C. A. *The psychology of feeling and emotion.* New York: McGraw-Hill, 1936.

Schachter, J. Pain, fear, and anger in hypertensives and normotensives: A psycho-physiologic study. *Psychosom. Med.,* 1957, 19, 17–29.

Schachter, S. *The psychology of affiliation.* Stanford, Calif.: Stanford Univer. Press, 1959.

Schachter, S., & Wheeler, L. Epinephrine, chlorpromazine, and amusement. *J. abnorm. soc. Psychol.,* 1962, 65, 121–128.

Singer, J. E. The effects of epinephrine, chlorpromazine and dibenzyline upon the fright responses of rats under stress and non-stress conditions. Unpublished doctoral dissertation, University of Minnesota, 1961.

Wolf, S., & Wolff, H. G. *Human gastric function.* New York: Oxford Univer. Press, 1947.

Woodworth, R. S., & Schlosberg, H. *Experimental psychology.* New York: Holt, 1958.

Wrightsman, L. S. Effects of waiting with others on changes in level of felt anxiety. *J. abnorm. soc. Psychol.,* 1960, 61, 216–222.

D. Via Socialization, Role Taking, and the Self Concept

The developmental core of social psychology is embodied within this section which deals with concepts emerging from the interaction of protoplasm and society. The topic of socialization focuses upon the manner by which that dehumanized organic blob of potentials which is the infant participates in those child-rearing events which lead him to become a humanized societal being. Child-rearing practices, whereby one generation imparts its culture upon the next, involve training the individual to learn those habits and expectations for his behavior which are related to the roles he will play as he develops within the society. Out of these training procedures and his role-taking behavior, the individual develops a self concept, an identity which provides a point of differentiation of self from non-self or environment and a point of reference which becomes central to his ongoing interactions within this environment.

Because processes of socialization provide a most critical juncture between the individual and his society, having continuing consequences for the individual's behavior and for the transmission and maintenance of the social system itself, it has been a topic of great concern to psychologists, anthropologists, and sociologists. The usual study of socialization attempts to do one or both of two things: (1) It focuses its attention on the effects of differential socialization techniques upon a specific form of child or later adult personality and behavior. (2) It focuses its attention on the effects of certain social structural variables upon the particular socialization practices employed. In the first approach, the researcher examines such factors as the *age* at which a given practice is employed (e.g. the age of weaning, the age of toilet training, the age of independence training, etc.), the *nature* of the technique employed (e.g. reward as a means of training, physical vs. psychological punishment as a means of training, etc.), the *agent* of socialization (e.g. the mother, the father, sibs, extended family, other institutionalized agents, etc.), and the *continuity* of the socialization procedure (e.g. early training procedures which are continuously reinforced as appropriate vs. early training procedures which must later be unlearned). He then attempts to relate these general variables or factors to the development of certain specific characteristics of personality or behaviors in the child or in the adult. He thus seeks to understand the social psychological process of individual and cultural development.

Studies of basic personality structure, national character and modal personality (cf. the Inkeles *et al.* reading in Section II, part D) provide an example of the application of this first type of focus to the personality of an entire culture rather than of a single individual within that culture.

Studies employing the second focus are concerned with the relationships between existing social structural variables (e.g., social class, ethnic status, etc.) and particular socialization practices. In this approach, the researcher seeks to discover, for example, the existence of different socialization practices as a function of the differential social class of the socializing agent (e.g., Are Middle or Lower Class parents more permissive in toilet training? Do Lower Class parents employ more physical than psycho-logical punishment as compared with Middle Class parents?).

It should be rather apparent that the two approaches mentioned above are complementary and interdependent. For example, one may begin by examining the relationship between social structure and general socialization practices which lead to the development of a particular set of personality characteristics and behaviors in adults. These in turn may feed back to reinforce or stabilize the existing social structure and its particular practices, and so on around again.

The readings included in this section by Sewell and Aronfreed deal with some combination of type one and type two approaches to the study of socialization. The readings by Turner and Shibutani, on the other hand, focus more upon the relationship between socialization practices, conceptualized in terms of symbolic interaction and role-taking behavior, and the development of personal and group identifications.

Social Class and Childhood Personality[1] /
William H. Sewell (*University of Wisconsin*)

INTRODUCTION

During the past twenty-five years there has been a great deal of interest in the relationship between social class and personality—particularly in the bearing of social class on the personality of the child and the relationship between social class and adult mental illness. Because of space and time limitations, this paper will concentrate on social class influences on childhood personality and will not be concerned with the literature on youth and adults. The product of this interest in social class influences on childhood

personality has been numerous books, monographs, research articles and essays—often with contradictory emphases and conclusions depending on the convictions, theoretical orientations, and research styles of the authors.[2]

The theoretical basis for expecting a substantial relationship between social class and personality rests on three major assumptions upon which there seems to be widespread agreement among social scientists. The first is that in all societies some system of social stratification exists whereby the members of the society are differentiated

Reprinted from *Sociometry*, 1961, 24, pages 340–356, by permission of author and publisher, The American Sociological Association.

[1] This paper was presented at the Berkeley Conference on Personality in Childhood, arranged by the late Professor Harold E. Jones, on May 5, 1960. It was prepared while the writer was a Fellow at the Center for Advanced Study in the Behavioral Sciences.

[2] An extensive bibliography, consisting of 195 items, has been deposited with the American Documentation Institute Auxiliary Publications Project, Photo Duplication Service, Library of Congress, Washington 25, D.C. Order Document no. 6906 remitting $1.75 for 35 mm microfilm or $2.50 for photo copies. Advance payment is required. Make checks or money orders payable to: Chief, Photo Duplication Service, Library of Congress.

into subgroups or classes which bear to one another a relationship of social inequality. It is further generally acknowledged that persons in the society can be more or less located in the stratification system in terms of the characteristic social roles they play. Consequently it is possible to infer, crudely at least, the social class position of most individuals in terms of readily ascertainable criteria. The particular criteria will be dependent on the culture of the society in question.[3] There are rather wide differences among writers as to the origins of stratification, the functions of stratification, the criteria of social classes, the meaning of the term class,[4] the number of classes, the rigidity of any particular stratification system, and almost any other aspect of theory, substance, or measurement which could possibly be raised, but almost everyone seems agreed that some system of stratification based on social inequality is an inevitable product of organized group life. The empirical basis of this proposition is strong in that no society has yet been studied in which a stratification system, fulfilling at least the minimum requirements stated above, has not been found.

The second assumption is that the position of the child's family in the stratification system determines in considerable measure not only the social learning influences to which he will be subjected during the early period of his life, and in later life for that matter, but greatly affects also the access that he will have to certain opportunities that are socially defined as desirable. Certainly, there seems to be ample evidence

that this is true even in societies in which the stratification structure is not particularly rigid or the differences between the social classes extreme. While many social scientists would deny that American society has fixed classes each with its own distinctive subculture, none would claim that the learning environment of the child whose family is highly placed in the stratification structure does not differ materially from that of the child whose social class position is low. Also it is readily apparent that the styles of life, the material comforts, the value systems and the instruction, both intentional and unintentional, which the child receives about the roles available to him in society differ depending on the social class position of his family. And finally even his treatment in the neighborhood, community and larger society will depend for some time, at least, on his social status origins.

The third assumption on which there is general agreement is that the early experiences of the individual will be of considerable importance in determining his later social behavior. To be sure, there is rather massive disagreement about the particular psychodynamics of the relationship between early experience and later behavior, the specific or patterned experiences which produce other patterns or traits of later personality, or even the critical periods in terms of days, months and years in which the individual is most susceptible to influence. However, these details and differences of theory and commitment have not led to any widespread rejection of the basic notion of the primary importance of early experiences in shaping later personality. The experimental evidence on animal behavior and the somewhat more inferential knowledge about human learning furnish the empirical foundation for this assumption.

On the basis of these assumptions, the reasonable expectation would be that some distinct personality traits, configurations, or types might be found which would differentiate the children of the several social classes, or at least that the incidence of certain personality characteristics would be different for the children of the various social classes. The results of research efforts to elucidate these relationships have been disappointing

[3] A number of books, summarizing contemporary theory and research in social stratification, have appeared in recent years. See, for example, references 2, 3, 15, 19, 22, and 26.

[4] The writer is not convinced that social class is the best term for describing the socio-economic levels treated in most of the literature covered in this paper. Actually, the term social class implies much more than has been established concerning the existence of classes with distinctive boundaries and subcultures. What is meant operationally by social class in most studies is simply a convenient category of socioeconomic status. While the writer would prefer to use the more accurate term socioeconomic status or simply social status, he bows to the trend in the literature and will use the term social class in this paper except in referring to those studies where the authors have themselves used socioeconomic status or social status.

for a number of methodological and theoretical reasons. It would be impossible and is unnecessary to review each of the numerous writings which have direct bearing on the problem, but it does seem worthwhile to examine some of the most important of them to see if it is possible to reach any valid conclusions on the extent and nature of the relationship between social class and childhood personality, to point out some of the weaknesses of the research in the field, and to make some suggestions for future research. This is the purpose of the present paper.

AN EXAMINATION OF SELECTED STUDIES

A convenient point of departure might be to look at examples of studies which illustrate various approaches to the problem. As a minimum these would seem to include (a) work based primarily on typological and informal observational procedures, (b) those in which detailed observations on class-related child-training procedures have been made and personality characteristics inferred, observed or systematically assessed, and, finally (c) studies in which some measure of social class position has been related directly to some independent assessments of personality.

Perhaps the best-known example of the first type of study mentioned is Arnold Green's "The Middle-Class Male Child and Neurosis" (11) which was originally published in 1946 and has been republished in numerous collections of readings. Green, stimulated by the neo-Freudian writers Horney and Fromm, and on the basis of his recollections of his childhood and young adulthood in a Massachusetts industrial community of about 3,000 persons, delineated a set of social psychological conditions that he had observed in middle-class families which he believed predisposed middle-class male children to neurosis. He observed that the middle-class parent is caught up in a life-long struggle for improvement of personal position in the class structure. The father's work takes him away from the home and involves the manipulation of others around him to further his personal career. He is ambivalent toward his son because the child

takes time, money and energy that could be used for the father's social advancement and also interferes with his role as a partner and companion to his wife. The mother, too, is ambivalent toward her child. He interferes with her career aspirations and her individual pleasures. Also, he causes worries and demands great care and attention. Despite the socially structured ambivalence of both parents toward their son, they train him to love them for the care and sacrifices they have made for him and force him to feel lost without their love. Thus, the middle-class boy suffers "personality absorption" to such an extent that he cannot turn to others for genuine emotional satisfaction. Moreover, he is faced with the constant threat of withdrawal of parental love. Little wonder, then, that he feels small, insignificant, unworthy, inferior, helpless and anxious! He can never escape his parents' norms at home, in school or in his play groups—always he must try to live up to their high expectations of him, or he will lose their love. Thus, he lives "alone and afraid in a world he never made." The lower-class (Polish-American) child suffers no such fate. Although parental authority is often harsh and brutal, it is also casual and external to the "core of the self." The children avoid their parents, in fact have contempt for them and band together in common defense against their cruelty. Consequently the parents do not have the opportunity or the techniques to absorb the personalities of their children. Thus, the lower-class boys do not suffer from the guilt, anxiety and extreme sense of insecurity from which the middle-class boy suffers as a result of his extreme dependency on his parents.

This is possibly an all too brief portrayal of Green's argument, but it summarizes his main points. Although the paper purports to be based on careful observation, no indication is given about the number of observations made of the socialization practices of either lower- or middle-class families, nor is there any indication of the frequency of neurosis or neurotic behavior among either lower- or middle-class boys—much less any direct evidence on the incidence of neurotic behavior among those middle-class boys (or lower-class boys) who have, as against those who have not, been socialized in the "middle-class way." Consequently the article might well be dismissed as a provocative and speculative essay except for the fact that it has served as one of the principal supports for the currently widely-held stereotype of the neurotic middle-class child and has fostered the idea that the lower-class child in our culture is relatively less subject to neurotic tendencies and symptoms. It also illustrates something of the current state of the field in that a paper which is based essentially on speculation and retrospection should be widely accepted as portraying an accurate account of the influence of social class on childhood personality.

The second type of study is perhaps most conveniently illustrated by the research done by members of the Committee on Human Development at the University of Chicago and originally reported in 1948 in two articles, one by Allison Davis and Robert J. Havighurst (8),[5] "Social Class and Color Differences in Child Rearing," and another by Martha C. Ericson (10), "Child Rearing and Social Status." These studies were the first to report systematic empirical findings indicating that child-rearing practices of middle-class parents differ significantly from those of lower-class families. The findings of the Davis-Havighurst study were based on interviews with 98 middle-class (48 white and 50 Negro) and 102 lower-class (52 white and 50 Negro) mothers and dealt with a wide variety of child-training questions and the mothers' expectations concerning their children. Perhaps the most important finding of the study was the restrictiveness of the middle-class mothers in the critical early training of the child. They were shown to be less likely to breast-feed, more likely to follow a strict nursing schedule, to restrict the child's sucking period, to wean earlier and more sharply, to begin bowel and bladder training earlier and to complete toilet training sooner than were lower-class mothers. In addition, they generally followed stricter regimes in other areas of behavior and expected their children to take responsibility for themselves earlier. From these results the inference was drawn that

middle-class children encounter more frustration of their impulses and that this is likely to have serious consequences for their personalities. Their findings regarding the differences in nursing and toilet training between the middle and lower classes were widely heralded and served to strengthen the conviction, especially of psychoanalytically oriented workers in the field—particularly those at the forefront of the culture and personality movement—that the socialization of the middle-class child in America was producing neurotic middle-class children and adults.[6] Davis and Havighurst themselves did not make this assertion. Their own conclusions were rather equivocal concerning the supposed consequences of these differences in training for the middle-class child. Actually, the inference they drew regarding personality effects was that the training influences to which middle-class children are subjected are likely to produce an orderly, conscientious, responsible, tame, but frustrated child. The only direct evidence they presented about the personalities of the children studied was that thumb-sucking, which may be seen as an evidence of oral deprivation, and masturbation, which may indicate general frustration, are both much more frequently reported for middle-class than for lower-class children.

The findings of the Chicago group and the inferences made from their findings as to the personality consequences of class-related child-training practices were widely accepted and held sway without competition for some time. However, they were finally challenged by the results of two carefully designed empirical studies with quite different research objectives. The first of these was the attempt by the present writer to determine the consequences of a variety of infant-training practices on independently assessed childhood personality characteristics and the second was the careful study of patterns of child rearing made by a group of behavioral scientists at Harvard under the leadership of Robert R. Sears.

The study of infant training and personality, published in 1952, was based on

---

[5] See also reference 9.

[6] For a summary and critique of personality and culture literature see references 14 and 18.

interviews conducted in 1947 with the mothers of 165 rural Wisconsin children concerning the practices they followed in rearing their children and subsequently relating the data thus obtained to the personality characteristics of the same children as these were determined from scores on both paper-and-pencil and projective tests of personality and ratings of the children's behavior by their mothers and teachers.[7] The specific infant-training practices studied were those most stressed in the psychoanalytic literature, including: feeding, weaning, nursing schedule, bowel training, bladder training and punishment for toilet accidents. These experiences were not found to be significantly related to childhood personality characteristics as assessed in the study. Moreover, two carefully constructed factor-weighted indexes measuring permissiveness in toilet training and feeding produced even less positive results.[8] In all only 18 out of 460 relationships tested in the study were significant at the .05 level and, of these, seven were opposite from the predicted direction.[9] These results, along with evidence from studies not so directly focused on the problem, tended to undermine the confidence of many who had made the inferential leap from class-determined early training practices to class-linked childhood personality characteristics and types.

Equally upsetting evidence came in 1954 with the publication of a preliminary report from the Harvard study (21) by Eleanor E. Maccoby and P. K. Gibbs on "Methods of Child Rearing in Two Social Classes," and later when the more complete report of the study (30) was published by Robert Sears, Eleanor Maccoby and Harry Levin in their well-known book, *Patterns of Child Rearing*. Their results, based upon careful interviews with 379 New England middle-class and lower-class mothers (labeled "upper-middle" and "upper-lower" by Maccoby and Gibbs), clearly indicated no dif-

ferences in infant-feeding practices between the two social classes, more severity in toilet training in the lower-class families, less permissiveness in sex training in the lower-class families, more restriction of aggression toward parents and peers (and more punitiveness where such aggression took place) in lower-class families, greater imposition of restrictions and demands on the child in the lower-class family, more physical punishment, deprivation of privileges and ridicule by lower-class parents, but no differences between the two groups on isolation and withdrawal of love. Needless to say, these results were in important respects directly contradictory to the findings of the Chicago group and provided little factual basis for continued acceptance of the stereotyped version of the middle-class mother as a rigid, restrictive, demanding and punitive figure whose behavior can but result in frustrated, anxious, conforming and overly dependent children (30, Ch. 12). Neither was there any evidence whatever to support Green's contention about personality absorption of the child in the middle-class family or its supposed consequent—the neurotic middle-class child.

As might well be expected, the findings of the Harvard group provoked considerable debate and Havighurst and Davis did a comparison of the data of the two studies after adjusting to make the age groups more comparable, but they still found substantial and large differences between the results of the Chicago and Harvard studies (12). A number of other studies (16, 17, 20, 40) have appeared in recent years that generally confirm the findings of the Harvard group. Finally, Urie Bronfenbrenner (4), on the basis of an examination of a whole battery of studies, both published and unpublished, found a basis for explaining some of the differences, particularly in infant feeding and toilet training, in terms of a trend toward greater permissiveness in these areas on the part of lower-class mothers up to World War II but with a reversal since then, middle-class mothers subsequently becoming more permissive in infant training. The data gathered over the 25-year period on the training of the young child seem to him to show that middle-class mothers have been

---

[7] For another paper dealing with the effects of feeding techniques on oral symptoms, see reference 36. Other papers reporting on theoretical, methodological and substantive aspects of this study include references 31, 33 and 37.

[8] For the indexes, see (37), page 144.

[9] A replication of the study in Ceylon (38) resulted in the same conclusions.

consistently more permissive towards the child's expressed needs and wishes, less likely to use physical punishment and more acceptant and equalitarian than have lower-class mothers. Finally, he sees indications that the gap between the social classes may be narrowing. While one might disagree with some of his interpretations and question some of the data on which his trends are based, it is clear from his review that in the present situation the evidence clearly supports the findings of the Harvard group and furnishes little basis for the belief that the training practices of middle-class parents are more likely than those of lower-class parents to produce neurotic personalities in their children.

One other important study which carries the analysis of class-related child rearing a step forward has recently been reported (1958) by Daniel R. Miller and Guy E. Swanson, in *The Changing American Parent* (23, 24). In their study of child rearing in Detroit, Michigan, they add to the stratification position represented by social class a second variable dealing with integrative position in the social structure which they have called "entrepreneurial-bureaucratic integration." Families with entrepreneurial orientations are those in which the husband works in organizations that are relatively small in size, with a simple division of labor, have relatively small capitalization, and provide for mobility and income through individual risk-taking and competition. Families with bureaucratic orientations are those in which the father works in a large and complex organization employing many specialists, paying fixed wages or salaries for particular jobs, and, in place of reward for individual risk-taking, provides security in continuity of employment and income for those who conform with organizational demands. Miller and Swanson feel there is reason to believe that this aspect of status interpenetrates the family and influences child-rearing practices. Consequently, in their analysis they classify their families not only by social class but also by entrepreneurial-bureaucratic position. The addition of this new dimension of status produced results which were not nearly as clear-cut and definite as they had expected.

In keeping with their predictions, entrepreneurial middle-class mothers were not less permissive than entrepreneurial lower-class mothers and there were no differences between bureaucratic lower-class and middle-class families in this regard. Their predictions that entrepreneurial middle-class mothers would be more likely to train their children in an active and manipulative view of the world was not supported. Moreover, enterpreneurial and bureaucratic lower-class mothers did not differ to any appreciable extent in the way they trained their children. If only the class differences are considered, their results are quite similar to those of the Harvard group. It seems quite probable that the relative failure of the new dimension to add much to the predictive power of social class was to some extent due to the inadequacy of their scheme for determining entrepreneurial-bureaucratic orientation.[10] Consequently, in future studies, better categorization and assessment of this dimension may produce greater associations.[11] In any event the idea of introducing other dimensions of status than social class position seems to be a good one and should be tested in other studies.

A third type of research bearing directly on the relationship between social class and personality involves the correlation between measures of socioeconomic status (henceforth referred to as SES) and children's scores on personality tests and is perhaps well illustrated by a study by the present writer and A. O. Haller, "Social Status and the Personality Adjustment of the Child"

[10] Apparently the use of this variable was something of an afterthought and consequently its operational definition for purposes of the research had to be based on data available from the interview rather than what might have been more pertinent information. See (23), pp. 67–70.

[11] Possibly it would be a better test of the hypothesis to simply compare the personality characteristics, for a large number of cases, of children brought up in families more clearly representing the entrepreneurial and bureaucratic ends of the continuum, i.e., children of owner-operators of independent retail establishments vs. children of government clerks. It might even be more rewarding to drop the bureaucratic-entrepreneurial orientation entirely and to examine the influence of specific occupations on socialization norms and practices, on the assumption that occupations differ in the extent to which they interpenetrate family life and influence the behavior of members.

(34; see also 1, 5, 6). A comprehensive review of the studies in which SES had been measured objectively and correlated with independent assessments of the personality of the child indicated that middle-class children consistently made a better showing than lower-class children. For the most part the correlations were low or the differences were small and often there was no indication that the association was statistically significant, that sampling was adequate, that the tests of status and personality were dependable, or that variables known to be related to status or personality or both were controlled (34, pp. 114–115).

Consequently it was decided to make a rigorous test of the hypothesized relation between SES and personality using a design in which both variables were measured objectively and independently for a large sample (1,462) of grade-school children in a culturally homogeneous community with a fairly wide range of SES. Correlation analysis techniques were used to determine the relationship between SES, as measured by father's occupation and a rating of the prestige of the family in the community, and personality adjustment as indicated by a factor-weighted score on the California Test of Personality. The zero-order correlation coefficients between the two status measures and the personality scores were determined. Then the multiple correlation coefficient of the two status measures and personality score was computed, and, finally, the relationship was determined with sibling position, intelligence, and age controlled. The results indicated a low but significant association between status and measured personality (.16 for father's occupation and child's personality score, .23 for prestige position and child's personality score, .25 for the multiple correlation of the two status measures and child's personality score). The combined effect of the two status measures was not significantly reduced when the controls were introduced. The direction of the correlations indicated that the lower the SES of the child's family the less favorable his personality test score.

Certainly these results indicate that only a relatively small amount of the variance in measured personality found in this group of children can be accounted for by their SES. However, the test of the hypothesis was stringent and the correlations might well be higher in communities with more distinct stratification systems, and if more refined measures of status and personality were used. In any event the correlations, particularly since they are not markedly different from those reported by others who have followed similar methods, should not be dismissed. They at least help to explain some of the variance in measured personality—an area in which little measured variance has been explained by other measured variables. However, the results do not provide much encouragement for the view that social class is a major determinant of childhood personality and they offer still another instance of evidence against the claim that middle-class children suffer greater personality maladjustment than lower-class children.

In an attempt to explore further the relationship between SES and personality, the writers (35) next did a factor analysis of the 30 personality test items which had been found to be most highly correlated with SES. The results of this analysis indicated that four factors explained approximately 90 per cent of the common variance among the items. These factors were tentatively identified as (a) *concern over status,* (b) *concern over achievement,* (c) *rejection of family,* and (d) *nervous symptoms.* Each factor was negatively correlated with SES, their respective correlations being −.31, −.18, −.12 and −.26, indicating that the lower the status of the child the greater the tendency to score high (unfavorably) on each of the factors. The intercorrelation between the factors ranges from +.25 to +.59. Thus, there seems to be a tendency for children who are concerned about their social status to worry about their achievements, to reject their families and to display nervous symptoms. The evidence from this study points to the fact that these characteristics are more common among lower- than higher-status children. Again the correlations between SES and the personality characteristics indicated by the factors, although statistically significant, are low and offer only limited support for the notion that the position of the child in the stratification system has bearing on his personality pattern. They are, however, suggestive of a line of attack on the problem which may be somewhat more rewarding than some of the approaches employed thus far.

CONCLUSIONS REGARDING SOCIAL CLASS AND CHILDHOOD PERSONALITY

On the basis of this brief review of studies of the bearing of social class on the personality of the child, the following conclusions seem justified:

First, there is a growing body of evidence from empirical studies of several types indicating a relatively low correlation between the position of the child in the stratification system (social class) and some aspects of personality, including measured personality adjustment. The relationship has not been shown to be nearly as close as might have been expected, but there is mounting evidence that at least some of the variance in childhood personality can be explained by the social status position of the child. Possibly when better measures are used the relationship will prove to be higher. The present crude techniques of measuring both variables doubtless result in underestimation of the correlation.

Second, the direction of the relationships found offer absolutely no support for the notion that middle-class children more commonly exhibit neurotic personality traits than do children of lower-class origins. Indeed all of the empirical evidence points to the opposite conclusion.

Third, the studies of child rearing in relation to social class, made since the publication of the Chicago studies, have found fewer class-related differences in infant training than might have been expected and those differences that have been found tend to indicate greater permissiveness in feeding and toilet training on the part of middle-class mothers rather than lower-class mothers. The findings in relation to early childhood training indicate less impulse control, less punitiveness, less reliance on strict regime, less restrictiveness in sex behavior and less restriction on aggression—in other words, generally greater permissiveness on the part of middle-class mothers.

Fourth, empirical studies of the consequences of child training have given a great deal of attention to such aspects of infant discipline as manner of nursing, weaning, scheduling, bowel and bladder training, but have found very little or no relationship between these experiences and childhood personality traits and adjustment patterns. Much less attention has been given to the consequences of other aspects of child training, but some low correlations have been found between such factors as patterns of punishment, permissiveness for aggression and mother's affectional warmth for the child and such aspects of personality as feeding problems, dependency and aggression. Although these correlations explain only a small portion of the variance in childhood personality, they cannot be entirely dismissed and, to the extent that the child-training practices are class-linked, they must be credited with having some bearing on the relationship between social class and personality. Certainly, however, the empirical evidence does not permit any lavish claims regarding the influence of the child-training variables studied on the personality of the child.

Fifth, a final inescapable conclusion from reading these and other writings on social class and childhood personality is that, with a few notable exceptions, the level of research and theoretical sophistication in this area has been appallingly low. Some of the most influential work has had little or no acceptable empirical basis. The evidence upon which widely accepted claims have been founded is sometimes from samples that are so small or so clearly biased that no reliable conclusions could possibly be reached. In fact there is not a single study that can claim to be representative of the whole society or any region of the country and only a small handful are clearly representative of any definable social system. The statistical techniques in some of the studies are clearly inappropriate for the data. The theoretical guide-lines for most of the studies are seldom specified and often are not even discernible. The chain of inference from theory to data, to conclusions, to wider generalizations is sometimes unclear and instances can be cited in which links in the chain are entirely missing. Great lack of conceptual clarity, particularly concerning the two principal variables, social class and personality, is generally apparent. Thus, statistical categories of socioeconomic status measured by crude techniques are treated as social classes in the broader meaning of that term, and inferences are drawn about sub-cultures, learning environments, value systems and other social class characteristics without the necessary empirical evidence of their existence. Likewise the term personality is used in a variety of ways but with little attention to definition and specification. Often inferences are made about deeper levels of personality from more or less surface variables. Because of these weaknesses in theory and method, more definitive conclusions about the relationship between social class and childhood personality must await better designed studies.

SUGGESTED DIRECTION FOR FUTURE RESEARCH

In the light of the present situation in the field and because of the basic importance of the problem, both from the theoretical and practical points of view, a few suggestions regarding future research may be helpful.

First, although the available evidence concerning the relationship between child training and personality does not provide much of a basis for explaining personality variation and despite the fact that the present evidence concerning the relationship between social class and child training does not seem to indicate a very close correspondence, further studies of social class and child rearing are desirable and necessary. With our present knowledge of sampling procedures, data-gathering methods, and analysis techniques, a carefully designed large-scale study using a sample of sufficient size to permit racial and ethnic breakdowns and other needed controls and concentrating on various aspects of child rearing ranging over the whole period of childhood is the indicated next step. In such a study additional attention should be given to assessment of the behavioral correlates of

child-training practices and to appropriate delineation of larger personality configurations. Additional studies of small local communities with relatively narrow stratification systems or studies in larger communities with samples that are inadequate to represent the full range of the stratification system are not likely to add much to the knowledge already available from existing studies and could well be dispensed with.

Second, despite the fact that many studies have been made of the relationship between the SES and the measured personality of school children, there is still need for a definitive study in a large community with a heterogeneous population. Since it would be an overwhelming task to map the actual class structure of such a community, several objective SES indicators might be employed singly and in combination, using modern multivariate statistical analysis techniques to determine their relationship to measured personality as indicated by personality test results. With large samples, a number of variables could be controlled and some definitive conclusion might be reached regarding the relationship between SES and childhood personality. Further analysis, following the general model used by Sewell and Haller in their most recent study of test items having high correlations with SES, could be done to determine the factors which account for variance in responses to personality tests.

Third, there is need for an intensive study of the relationship between social class and personality in some community or society in which a functionally existing class system with well established sub-cultures is present, if indeed such can be found. It is clear from the literature that classes in this sense have been assumed to be operative but in no case have they been properly delineated, validated and sampled in any study of social class and personality. Such a task would be a major undertaking and probably could be carried out only in a modest-sized community, but, if an appropriate community were found, this would provide a more critical test of the theoretical relationship between social class and personality than any yet attempted. Unless and until such a study is done, no one is really justified in implying that social class is more than a convenient statistical category in discussing its relation to personality.

Fourth, it now seems clear that scientific concern with the relation between social class and personality has perhaps been too much focused on global aspects of personality and possibly too much on early socialization. Therefore, it is suggested that the more promising direction for future research will come from a shift in emphasis, toward greater concern with those particular aspects of personality which are most likely to be directly influenced by the position of the child's family in the social stratification system, such as attitudes, values and aspirations, rather than with deeper personality characteristics. It also is suggested that instead of focusing so much attention on the very young child, more research should be done on older children and adolescents—on the assumption that whatever differences one's social class position makes to the above-mentioned aspects of personality are likely to be the product of later and more gradual socialization experiences rather than the more proximate effect of specific aspects of early experiences (39). Evidence already available from a number of studies seems to clearly indicate that adolescents' belief systems and values differ rather clearly in relation to their social status positions: adolescents of lower-class backgrounds appear to have lower need-achievement, lower achievement values (27, 28), are much less likely to place high value on a college education, less frequently aspire to high level achievement in educational pursuits and occupational activities (13, 36) and are less willing to defer their gratifications than are middle- and upper-class adolescents (7, 29). Recent studies by the writer and others have shown that there is a marked positive correlation between the socioeconomic status and the educational and occupational aspirations of high school seniors and that relationship remains even when sex and intelligence are controlled (36, pp. 70–72). As yet unpublished, results from a more recent study which the writer is currently conducting on a statewide sample of Wisconsin high school seniors indicate that other variables such as parental pressure, rural-urban background, community and peer group in-

fluences may also be introduced without negating the influencing of SES on these aspirations. It may well be that it is precisely in the area of attitudes, values, and aspirations that social class influences are most pronounced. If so, it would be profitable to study children of different social-class backgrounds to determine when and how these characteristics of personality develop and how responsive they may be to other influences.

Fifth, it is suggested that it might be more revealing and more promising in terms of the knowledge that may be gained about social influences on personality to focus some attention on intraclass differences instead of being concerned exclusively with interclass variations. The data of most empirical studies of social class in relation to personality and related variables indicate the existence of considerable intraclass variation. Thus in the writer's studies of social status and personality, there were many children in each social status level who made favorable scores on the personality measures and some at each level who made unfavorable scores. Even in the study of differences in educational and occupational aspirations, where sizeable differences were found between SES groups, there were important differences within each status group (36). Obviously, it is not intelligence or sex which accounts for the within-class differences found in this study, because these variables have been controlled, but it may well be that family attitudes and values, peer-group influences, and community forces will be found to explain a sizeable portion of the variance. Another interesting series of questions suggested by these results is: What are the personality effects of having values and aspirations that are deviant from those of one's social class? Does it mean that the lower-class child has to reject the values of his family and neighborhood in order to be socially mobile? If so, what are the dimensions and what is the nature of the stress experienced by the upwardly mobile lower-class child and what personality consequences flow from such striving? If he is successful in his mobility aspirations, will the lower-class child find it possible to internalize the values of his new status position or will he be constantly plagued by the conflict between his old values and the new? These are just a few of the kinds of questions that could be studied in relation to intraclass differences in personality.

Sixth, it is suggested that, as basic a variable as social class is for social behavior, there are other important aspects and dimensions of social structure that cut across the social stratification system which should not be neglected in the study of the personality development of the child.[12] Among the more important of these are the mobility and the occupational orientations of the family. In addition, there are other traditional social structure variables such as age, sex, family size, sibling position, race, ethnic background and religion which probably play a signficant role but have been taken into account insufficiently in studies of social structure and childhood personality. Moreover, much theoretical and analytical work is needed on the possible influence of various combinations of social structure variables and their joint as well as independent influence on the personalities of children.

REFERENCES

1. Angelino, H., J. Dollins, and E. V. Mech. Trends in the "fears and worries" of school children as related to socioeconomic status and age. *Journal of Genetic Psychology,* 1956, 89, 263–277.
2. Barber, B. *Social Stratification.* New York: Harcourt, Brace, 1957.
3. Bendix, R., and S. M. Lipset (eds.). *Class, Status and Power: A Reader in Social Stratification.* Glencoe, Ill.: Free Press, 1953.
4. Bronfenbrenner, U. Socialization and social class through time and space, in E. E. Maccoby, T. M. Newcomb, and E. L. Hartley (eds.), *Readings in Social Psychology,* New York: Holt, 1958, 400–425.
5. Burchinal, L. G. Social status, measured intelligence, achievement, and personality adjustment of rural Iowa girls. *Sociometry,* 1959, 22, 75–80.
6. Burchinal, L. G., B. Gardner, and G. R. Hawkes. Children's personality adjustment and the socio-economic status of their families. *Journal of Genetic Psychology,* 1958, 92, 149–159.
7. Davis, A., and J. Dollard. *Children of Bondage: The Personality Development of Negro Children in the Urban South.* Washington, D.C.: American Council on Education, 1940.
8. Davis, A., and R. J. Havighurst. Social class and color differences in child-rearing. *American Sociological Review,* 1946, 11, 698–710.
9. Davis, A., and R. J. Havighurst. *Father of the Man: How Your Child Gets His Personality.* Boston: Houghton Mifflin, 1947.
10. Ericson, Martha C. Child rearing and social status. *American Journal of Sociology,* 1946, 52, 190–192.
11. Green, A. W. The middle-class male child and neurosis. *American Sociological Review,* 1946, 11, 31–41.
12. Havighurst, R. J., and A. Davis. A comparison of the Chicago and Harvard studies of social class differences in child rearing. *American Sociological Review,* 1955, 20, 438–442.
13. Hyman, H. H. The value systems of different classes: a social psychological contribution to the analysis of social classes, in Bendix and Lipset (see 3 above), 426–442.
14. Inkeles, A., and D. J. Levinson. National character: the study of modal personality and sociocultural systems, in G. Lindzey (ed.), *Handbook of Social Psychology,* Cambridge, Mass.: Addison Wesley, 1954, Ch. 26.
15. Kahl, J. A. *The American Class Structure,* New York: Rinehart, 1953.
16. Kohn, M. L. Social class and the exercise of parental authority. *American Sociological Review,* 1954, 24, 352–366.
17. Kohn, M. L. Social class and parental values. *American Journal of Sociology,* 1959, 64, 337–351.
18. Lindesmith, A. R., and A. L. Strauss. A critique of culture-personality writings. *American Sociological Review,* 1950, 15, 587–600.
19. Lipset, S. M., and R. Bendix. *Social Mobility in Industrial Society.* Berkeley: University of California Press, 1959.
20. Littman, R. A., R. A. Moore, and J. Pierce-Jones. Social class differences in child rearing: a third community for comparison

---

[12] Some provocative suggestions along these lines are given in (25).

with Chicago and Newton, Massachusetts. *American Sociological Review,* 1957, 22, 694–704.

21. Maccoby, E. E., P. K. Gibbs, *et al.,* Methods of child rearing in two social classes, in W. E. Martin and C. B. Stendler (eds.). *Readings in Child Development.* New York: Harcourt, Brace, 1954, 380–396.

22. Mayer, K. B. *Class and Society,* New York: Doubleday, 1951.

23. Miller, D. R., and G. E. Swanson. *The Changing American Parent.* New York: Wiley, 1958

24. Miller, D. R., and G. E. Swanson. *Inner Conflict and Defense.* New York: Holt, 1960.

25. Morris, R. T., and R. J. Murphy. The situs dimension in occupational structure. *American Sociological Review,* 1959, 24, 231–239.

26. Reissman, L. *Class in American Society.* Glencoe, Ill.: Free Press, 1959.

27. Rosen, B. C. The achievement syndrome: a psychocultural dimension of social stratification. *American Sociological Review,* 1956, 21, 203–211.

28. Rosen, B. C. Race, ethnicity and the achievement syndrome. *American Sociological Review,* 1959, 24, 47–60.

29. Schneider, L., and S. Lysgaard. The deferred gratification pattern: a preliminary study. *American Sociological Review,* 1953, 18, 142–149.

30. Sears, R. R., E. E. Maccoby, and H. Levin. *Patterns of Child Rearing.* Evanston. Ill.: Row, Peterson, 1957.

31. Sewell, W. H. Field techniques in social psychological study in a rural community. *American Sociological Review,* 1949, 14, 718–726.

32. Sewell, W. H. Infant training and the personality of the child. *American Journal of Sociology,* 1952, 58, 150–159.

33. Sewell, W. H. Some observation on theory testing. *Rural Sociology,* 1956, 21, 1–12.

34. Sewell, W. H., and A. O. Haller. Social status and the personality adjustment of the child. *Sociometry,* 1956, 19, 114–125.

35. Sewell, W. H., and A. O. Haller. Factors in the relationship between social status and the personality adjustment of the child. *American Sociological Review,* 1959, 24, 511–520.

36. Sewell, W. H. and P. H. Mussen. The effects of feeding, weaning and scheduling procedures on childhood adjustment and the formation of oral symptoms. *Child Development,* 1952, 23, 185–191.

37. Sewell, W. H., P. H. Mussen, and C. W. Harris. Relationships among child-training practices. *American Sociological Review,* 1955, 20, 137–148.

38. Straus, M. A. Anal and oral frustration in relation to sinhalese personality. *Sociometry,* 1957, 20, 21–31.

39. Strodtbeck, F. L. Family interaction values and achievement, in D. C. McClelland *et al., Talent and Society.* New York: Van Nostrand, 1958, Ch. II.

40. White, M. S. Social class, child-rearing practices and child behavior. *American Sociological Review,* 1957, 22, 704–712.

The Nature, Variety, and Social Patterning of Internalized Responses to Transgression /
Justin Aronfreed[1] (*University of Pennsylvania*)

Contemporary conceptions of the development of internalized control over social

A revised version of an article originally published in *Journal of Abnormal and Social Psychology,* 1961, 63, pages 223–240, by permission of author and publisher, The American Psychological Association.

[1] The author is indebted to Helene Aaronson, Nina Chaiken, Joseph Denny, and Kirby Smith for their assistance in the collection of data.

behavior have characteristically emphasized the role of moral judgment. Piaget's (1948) original observations of developmental changes in moral cognition have been followed by numerous assessments of children's perceptions of evaluative social standards and of the rationale for their application and enforcement (Boehm, 1962; Johnson, 1962; Kohlberg, 1963; MacRae, 1954). Of course, the knowledge of standards of conduct, as it is conveyed through the child's verbal report, is a step removed from actual social behavior. But psychological treatments of internalization which have been more directly concerned with its behavioral manifestations have also tended to assume that internalized control of conduct rests upon standards with respect to which actions, thoughts, and feelings may be evaluated as "good" and "bad" or "right" and "wrong." The more behaviorally oriented empirical studies are inclined to employ concepts such as conscience or "superego" to designate the evaluative substrate of conduct. These concepts are often used in such a way as to embrace dimensions of value somewhat broader than those which might properly be called moral, but they also reflect the assumption that evaluative cognition is fundamental to internalization.

The central position that is commonly accorded to guilt, in theoretical accounts of internalized reactions to transgression, reveals the importance that is given to the cognitive foundations of conduct. Guilt refers to an affective state whose cognitive properties take the form of self-evaluation. And many psychologists have taken the view that self-criticism is a prerequisite of reactions to transgression which are internalized in the sense that they occur even in the absence of any explicit or threatened external punishment. Freud (1936), for example, clearly distinguished the self-mediated consequences of transgression from those dependent upon external sanctions. He portrayed the child's conscience as an autonomous internalized representation of prohibitions and punishments formerly present in its parents' behavior. The same kind of distinction has been made by Sears, Maccoby, and Levin (1957, Ch. 10), who used mothers' reports of their children's reactions to transgression as evidence of whether the children were responding to self-instruction based on their own standards or were merely anticipating the external consequences of their misdeeds. In a cross-cultural study of a number of different societies, Whiting and Child (1953, Ch. 11) similarly described two distinct mechanisms of social control, one of "moral anx-iety" or guilt and the second of "objective anxiety" or fear of external punishment.

Other investigators have concurred in equating internalized reactions to transgression with the presence of self-criticism. Henry and Short (1954), in their study of societal influences upon the direction of aggression, speculated that self-punitive and self-critical tendencies were proportionate to the extent of internalization of parental sanctions. Heinecke (1953) took the intensity of the expression of guilt, in a group of four- and five-year-olds, as a measure of "strength of superego formation." Allinsmith (1960) has attempted to relate a variety of the internalized reactions to transgression of older children to an extensive network of evaluative standards. All of these approaches share the view that a response to transgression is internalized when it follows from the child's judgment of its own behavior and no longer requires the support of external punishment or surveillance.

Responses to transgression comprise only one of the types of conduct to be understood in any general account of internalization. They provide, however, a revealing perspective on various kinds of behavior to which the term moral is usually collectively applied. For many of the forms which these responses assume, even when they appear independent of any objective risk or threat of punishment, reflect an absence of self-evaluation and an external orientation inconsistent with what one might expect if they were entirely internally mediated. Common observation of children, for example, indicates quite clearly that they often perceive or anticipate punishment or criticism in the responses of other people or in impersonal fortuitous events, even though their actions were not really directly known to others. Children also often appear uncomfortable until they have confessed their transgressions or have done something that brings about discovery or punishment. Even their self-critical or self-corrective behavior may be dependent on external cues and resources for its initiation and performance. Another more indirect suggestion of children's reliance on their social environment, in responding to their own transgressions, is apparent in their tendency to localize the responsibility for their misbehavior in external sources or to blame others for the same offenses which they have committed.

These externally oriented reactions to transgression cannot be regarded as transitory phenomena of childhood. The findings of various studies (Adorno, Frenkel-Brunswik, Levinson, & Sanford, 1950; Allinsmith, 1960; Aronfreed, 1960) indicate that individuals frequently continue beyond childhood to perceive the source of criticism or punishment for their actions in the behavior of other people, to interpret impersonal events as punishment, and to blame others rather than themselves for wrongdoing. Whiting (1959) points out, in a recent report on cross-cultural variations on social control, that while no society can rely completely on direct external supervision of behavior, not all societies inculcate guilt as the effective mechanism of internalized control. He suggests that externally oriented forms of internal control, such as the fear of ghosts or sorcerers, are more typical of some cultural groups. Within our own western society, although it is thought of as a society that values the more internally oriented kinds of control, there is also considerable variation in the extent to which conduct that is essentially internalized is nevertheless initiated and carried out in a way that is highly conditioned by its external social context.

The many internalized reactions to transgression which show an external orientation call into serious question the assumption that self-evaluation is a prerequisite of such reactions. The sensitive observer is aware that even the verbalization of self-critical statements sometimes appears, if one looks further into its underpinnings, to follow not from an articulate standard of judgment, but rather from the tendency to make the critical response automatically, as though it were a necessary consequence of having committed a transgression. Such a tendency can be especially transparent in the behavior of young children, who may literally reproduce their parents' critical or punitive responses before they have any substantial cognitive resources for evaluating their own actions. We know, too, that a person may feel shame, disgust, or generalized anxiety, without a clear awareness of precisely what is wrong about his behavior. And it frequently seems that people do not need to engage in a great deal of judgment or conscious reflection in order to experience unpleasant feelings, and even to carry out self-corrective behavior, in response to some of their actions. The minimal role that explicit standards play in some reactions to transgression is undoubtedly attributable to the limited verbal and cognitive auspices under which much of socialization takes place.

As an initial approach to exploring and circumscribing a wide range of internalized responses to transgression, naturalistic observation seems to have certain advantages over experimental methods. In order to examine the role of self-evaluation in such responses and, more generally, the extent of their internal or external orientation, what is required are systematic distinctions among the various forms and patterns which they assume. The survey of children's responses to transgressions that is to be described here provides an analysis of the variety and distribution of these responses in a sample of children chosen to represent both sexes and the two major socioeconomic classes. The findings of the survey will be used to illustrate a general theoretical conception of the relationship between internal vs. external orientation in conduct and the individual's positions in society. The patterns of social reinforcement which establish this relationship, as they are reflected in the disciplinary practices of mothers, will also be examined.

Social Position and Social Experience

The basic proposition to be set forth here concerning the relationship between social position and the orientation of conduct can be very simply stated: whenever there is a significant differential of status or power among groups of people within a social structure, there will also be a corresponding difference in the relative internal vs. external orientation that characterizes their control and modification of their own behavior. The status differential must be, of course, a sustained feature of the social structure and not merely a transient phenomenon. Social class is the most sharply defined dimension of status along which such a difference of orientation is apparent. The people who hold the higher positions in a socioeconomic hierarchy have greater power and responsibility to evaluate and determine their own behavior as well as to act upon their external environment. The requirements of their work tend to encourage independence from immediate external supervision. Their opportunities for realizing their aspirations through modifying their circumstances would make their use of internal resources meaningful and rewarding. In contrast, the occupational roles held by individuals of lower status tend not to encourage initiative or self-reliance. Their opportunities for affecting their environment are more restricted. Their work is bounded by its concrete material nature, and its performance is more highly specified, within fairly narrow limits, by sources outside of their own control. They should, therefore, be more prone to perceive external dangers, gratifications, and restraints as determinants of their behavior. There is considerable evidence that differences of social orientation, in the direction described, do distinguish between the middle and the working classes in our society, and characterize their values and practices in socializing their children (Davis & Havighurst, 1946; Henry & Short, 1954; Kohn, 1959; McClelland, Rindlisbacher, & de Charms, 1955; Miller & Swanson, 1958). These differences would certainly be expected to have implications for the child's internal or external orientation in conduct.

If the relative status of different social positions does generate differences in the orientation of social conduct, then the significance of masculine and feminine sex roles should be, in some respects, parallel to the significance of social class membership. Despite the increasing equality afforded the two sexes in western society, it still remains true that greater status and self-direction of action attach to the masculine role and that children are sensitive to the differential activities and privileges of the two sexes (Brown, 1958; Lynn, 1959; Parsons, 1953; Rabban, 1950). Men are expected to have more control over their own actions as well as over their external environment. Women are expected to be responsive to direction from without rather than to show self-reliance. They must be more sensitive, and ready to accommodate themselves, to external influences (Barry, Bacon, & Child, 1957; Parsons, 1942). A woman's daily activities in her primary roles of wife and mother are very much conditioned by her husband's social status, and they usually do not permit her as much freedom of movement and decision making power as accrue to his more crucial occupational role.

The orientation of the child's conduct can be determined by its prospective positions in society only to the extent that values and expectations surrounding those positions are translated into patterns of social reinforcement which affect the child's response dispositions. And the search for the antecedents of internalized control in the child's socialization experience has generally focussed on parental disciplinary practices. The prevailing view of social class differences in child rearing, that was held for some years after the well-known study by Davis and Havighurst (1946), was that the working class was more permissive and less frustrating than the middle class. Recent surveys (Bronfenbrenner, 1958; Maccoby, Gibbs, et al., 1954) have tended to challenge that view and to suggest that inconsistencies between different studies of the socialization practices of the two classes may be attributable to uncontrolled sampling factors or to processes of social change over time. It is therefore rather striking that in all of the surveys cited, as well as in others (Littman, Moore, & Pierce-Jones, 1957; Miller, Swanson, et al., 1960), one persistent difference between the two classes continues to be found in their disciplinary techniques. Lower-class parents are more likely to use direct and explicit punishments in their discipline, particularly physical punishment. Middle-class parents are more prone to use techniques variously described as "love oriented" or "psychological" and consisting primarily of withdrawal of love, isolation, ignoring the child, reasoning, and explanation. On the basis of the little evidence available, it does not appear, in contrast, that there are consistent differences between boys and girls in the methods of punishment which they experience, although the survey by Sears et al. (1957, Ch. 10) suggested that the specific technique of withdrawal of love might be used somewhat more frequently with girls.

Many studies (Allinsmith, 1960; Heinecke, 1953; Sears et al. 1957, Ch. 10; Whiting & Child, 1953, Ch. 11) have indicated a limited degree of association between parental discipline and the child's internalized reactions to transgression. The implications of these studies for the distinctions made here among specific forms of response are somewhat difficult to assess, since typically a general index of conscience or internalization was used. In each case, however, the use of love oriented or psychological methods was positively related to reactions to transgression which the investigators regarded as evidence of "high internalization." The aim of distinguishing specific responses with respect to their internal or external orientation suggested that disciplinary techniques might be divided, for the purposes of the present study, into the two broad categories of *induction* and *sensitization*.

The induction category subsumes methods that should tend to induce in the child reactions to his own transgressions which could readily become independent of their original external stimulus sources. A mother who indicates her disapproval by rejecting or ignoring her child, or by showing that she is hurt or disappointed, is stimulating unpleasant feelings that are not closely tied to her physical proximity or its imminence. The arousal and termination of these feelings are less well defined by externally explicit punitive events conveyed through her immediate presence than would be the case if she were to punish the child with a direct attack. Likewise, if she reasons with the child or explains why his behavior is unacceptable, she is using a verbal and cognitive medium of exchange that can provide the child with his own resources for evaluating and modifying his behavior. Finally, if she asks the child why he behaved as he did, insists that he correct the consequences of his acts, or refrains from punishment when he takes the initiative in correcting himself, she is encouraging him to examine his actions and accept responsibility for them.

The term sensitization is applied to the more direct techniques of physical punishment and verbal assaults such as yelling, screaming, or "bawling out." Such techniques should give greater weight to the mother's punitive presence and be unlikely to induce reactions to transgression that could easily become separated from their original external elicitation. They should instead merely sensitize the child to the anticipation of painful external events and to the importance of external demands and expectations in defining appropriate responses.

In view of the significance attributed to socioeconomic status and the emphasis on self-evaluative resources as one aspect of internal orientation, the role that intelligence might play in the anticipated relationships was explored by examining the relationship between intelligence and each of the specific forms of response to transgression.

METHOD

There are certain obvious difficulties in trying to elicit and systematically observe a variety of different internalized reactions to transgression. It is unlikely, for example, that children would commit many of the necessary transgressions in situations where observation would be feasible. Moreover, some kinds of response to transgression would not be easily discernible in the child's behavior without resorting to techniques of verbal report and accepting the inherent limitations of these techniques. To meet these problems, a projective story completion device was constructed, consisting of five incomplete stories. The advantages of such a technique have been demonstrated in previous studies (Allinsmith, 1960; Aronfreed, 1960). The story completions written by the children can be analyzed for various responses to transgression occurring in the perception and behavior of the central figures, and these can be taken to represent the subject's own strongest response tendencies. This projective method tends to minimize the child's awareness that his own reactions are the center of interest. It also permits a fairly precise structuring of the variety of stimulus conditions under which children ordinarily show internalized responses to their own actions.

The transgressions which occurred in the stories were acts of aggression. Because such a considerable part of socialization in our society is devoted to the control of aggression, it was expected that the range of elicited responses would be fairly broad and generally representative of internalized reactions to transgression. Each story beginning was roughly 100 words in length and related, in simple language, an incident in which a child (the central figure) had become very angry with little or no justification by ordinary social standards. The child then committed an act of aggression of a kind generally socially prohibited but not uncommon among children. The aggression was directed against parents, a friendly neighbor, or a close companion, and the stories varied in the overtness and directness of the aggressive response. In one case, for example, a child is about to join friends at a playground and is angered at the slight delay occasioned by the mother's request to examine a rosebush and to pick any blooms which may have appeared. Rather than take the time to return with the roses, the child takes them and throws them into a trash can at the playground. In another story, a child chalks a "nasty" word on a neighbor's step because the neighbor's absence prevents the child from having a piece of play equipment that is usually generously provided.

All of the stories attempted to convey that the child's action was not directly observed by others, so that externally oriented responses occurring in the story completions would reflect the child's own perspective and not be invited by the context of the story. Likewise, provocation of the aggression in each of the stories was absent or negligible, so that there would be no realistic support for holding others responsible for the actions of the central figure.

Two sets of stories were used, so that the sex of the central figures could correspond to the sex of the child completing the stories. The two sets were otherwise almost identical, with the exception of minor variations introduced to insure that the stories would be sex appropriate. For example, in two stories where the transgression was provoked by the child's being reasonably refused some-

thing, or inadvertently deprived of it, the specific nature of the object was made to accord with the interests of the two sexes.

Subjects

The subjects of the study were 122 white children drawn from the sixth grade classes of two public schools in a large urban school system.[2] The sample was composed of comparable numbers of children from the middle and working classes, and was equally divided between the two sexes. There were 34 middle-class and 27 working-class boys. Among the girls, 28 were middle class and 33 were working class. Socio-economic status was determined on the basis of the fathers' occupations as reported in questionnaire interviews with the children's mothers. The working class group consisted of those children whose fathers earned their living through manual labor, factory work, or service and maintenance occupations. The fathers of the middle-class children were salesmen, office workers, owners and managers, and a few men engaged in professions.

Procedure

Story completion technique. The stories were given in written form to small groups of five or six children, sitting widely separated from one another in a large room. Each child individually read each of the five story beginnings and wrote a completion to it, finishing a given story before going on to the next. The task was put into a context of creativity by asking the children to write "the most interesting kinds of stories for sixth graders," and anonymity was preserved by having each child place the completed stories, without any name attached, in a large pile of already completed sets. Since each child completed five stories, 610 stories in all were obtained from the children.

Questionnaire interview. The mothers of the 122 children in the sample represented those who, among 124 originally solicited, were willing to participate in a questionnaire

[2] The author is grateful to a number of administrators and teachers in the Philadelphia public school system, whose cooperation made this study possible.

interview, the purpose of which was described to them as "finding out about the different things which mothers do to help their children grow up." Sampling biases attributed to the criterion of voluntary participation were thus virtually eliminated. When the mother's agreement to participate was received, she was visited at her home by one of four interviewers, two of whom were male and two female. Though the majority of the interviews were conducted by the male interviewers, there was no difference between the subsamples of mothers seen by the two sets of interviewers in their social class or sex of child characteristics.

After about 5 minutes of relatively informal questions aimed at attaining rapport with the mother and establishing the nature of her husband's occupation, the interview turned to a series of 12 distinct questions designed to elicit the mother's report of specific disciplinary techniques used with the child who was the subject of the study. Each question described a particular form of aggressive behavior and the circumstances under which it occurred, and then asked the mother how she usually responded when her child behaved in that way. The interviewers were provided with standardized probes for additional techniques or more detailed information. The situations described to the mother included not only obvious misbehavior such as throwing food or being verbally offensive toward her, but also more subtle incidents involving friends or property, where the child's responsibility was somewhat ambiguous. Two of the questions were phrased to explore conditions under which the mother might withhold punishment or make it contingent upon the child's subsequent actions, but even these commonly brought forth further disciplinary methods. Some of the questions dealt with the mother's current methods, while others asked about her methods in response to the kind of behavior more characteristic of the earlier years of childhood.

Intelligence measure. Scores on the sixth grade form of a test of verbal intelligence were available for almost all of the children in the sample. This test is a standardized instrument used throughout the entire school system from which the children were drawn.

It has a test-retest reliability of .91, a correlation of .78 with the Otis Quick-Scoring Inventory, and a correlation of .72 with the child's average standing across all sixth grade achievement tests.

Classification of Responses to Transgression

The broad outlines of the classification to be described were determined by the theoretical orientation of the survey, although some of the details of categorization were empirically adapted to accommodate the distinct form of typical responses in the story completions. Each story was individually scored for the presence of a number of independently defined forms of response. For some types of response, further distinctions were made among the story conditions defining their pattern of occurrence, in order to examine more closely the extent of their internal or external orientation. A single story almost invariably showed more than one form of response, and was therefore entered in more than one subcategory within the system of classification. A given subcategory was used only once, however, in the scoring of a particular story. The primary subcategories, and the major categories of classification under which they were organized, were as follows:

Self-criticism. This category was used whenever the reactions of the central figures showed evidence of self-criticism, self-blame, the explicit recognition of wrongdoing, or any form of self-appraisal of the kind associated with the experience of guilt. A slightly more liberal interpretation was made of this category than of others, so as to be certain that there would be no underestimation of the presence of self-evaluation. Disturbances of thought or action, for example, were included when they appeared to be associated with reflection upon transgression. Being "sorry" was not in itself taken as an indication of self-criticism, since it might actually be a response to external pressures or anticipated unpleasant external consequences. But remorse was included when it was felt specifically for the act of transgression and seemed to imply self-evaluation.

Correction of deviance. A wide range of

responses was classified here, all of them indicating an attempt to return to the appropriate social boundaries of behavior. These took the form of admission to others of responsibility for the transgression (*confession*), expression of remorse for actions or intentions (*apology*), removal or amelioration of injurious consequences (*reparation*), either concretely or through affection or helpfulness toward those perceived as harmed by the transgression, and resolutions or commitments to act more acceptably in the future (*modification of future behavior*).

Degree of activity in self-correction. This index was a crude continuum constructed to use the total pattern of responses in each story completion. Its purpose was to evaluate the extent to which responses to transgression were self-defined and initiated in the child's own behavior in a way that indicated active acceptance of responsibility, or, conversely, the extent to which they revealed a passive reliance on external events. A story was classified as *high* on the index if the sequence of responses included one of the more active forms of self-correction, such as reparation or modification of future behavior, without any dependence on external events. Stories were scored as *intermediate* if the sequence of responses was self-initiated but did not include an active form of self-correction (for example, if only confession or apology occurred), or if the sequence was externally initiated but subsequently included an active self-correction not imposed or required by external conditions. Stories were classified as *low* if they contained only externally defined consequences of transgression, or if such consequences were followed only by corrective actions that were relatively passive and essentially required by the external situation (for example, if confession or apology occurred only after the transgression had been discovered and punishment threatened).

For all of the other categories in the classification system, social class and sex comparisons could be made on the basis of the subjects' total scores, which were obtained simply by counting the number of instances of a given category occurring over the five stories. This index, however, was an attempt to express the degree to which a certain property of reactions to transgression was present rather than its mere presence or absence. It was therefore necessary to devise a means of combining the evaluations of individual stories so as to arrive at a composite evaluation of a subject's entire set of stories. Accordingly, values of zero, one, and two were arbitrarily assigned to stories scored, respectively, in the low, intermediate, and high categories. These values were then summated across the five stories to represent each subject's total degree of activity in self-correction.

External resolution. This category was used to describe responses characterized by the central figure's perception of the consequences of transgression as being primarily defined by external events. Three basic forms were distinguished. In the first type, *discovery and punishment,* other people discovered the transgression and responded with punishment or criticism. In some cases, discovery was invited or punishment provoked by the central figure's actions subsequent to the transgression. The second type consisted of experiences of *unpleasant fortuitous consequences* following the transgression, through indirect effects of impersonal circumstances. The central figure might, for example, suffer a painful accident, or be left with an unpleasant task, or have something of value lost or destroyed. The third type of external resolution was a *focus on external responsibility,* in which the actions of others were held responsible for the transgression or were used to justify it.

Externally oriented initiation and performance. A set of somewhat more refined distinctions was developed to describe various ways in which even the central figure's self-critical or self-corrective responses could show some degree of reliance on the external social environment. Thus, certain reactions received an *external initiation* in that they occurred only upon the influence or demands of other people. Likewise, public expressions of remorse and promises of conformity were considered a *display* (often with the result of being forgiven). And acts of reparation were characterized as dependent on a *use of external resources* when the assistance of other people (and occasionally even of God) was sought in carrying them out.

Classification of Maternal Discipline

The disciplinary practices reported by the mothers were divided into the two broad categories of induction and sensitization techniques on the basis of the conceptions already described. Three types of techniques were classified as induction: withdrawal of love in the form of rejecting or ignoring the child, indicating disappointment, refusing to speak to the child, or telling the child that he ought to feel bad; techniques influencing the child to assume or examine his own responsibility, such as asking him to report or account for his behavior, insisting upon his making reparation, or encouraging him in various ways to define transgressions for himself or to initiate his own moral responses; explanation of relevant standards (including "reasoning" and "talking things over"), describing the consequences of his actions to the child, suggesting appropriate alternative actions, or simply telling the child what aspects of his behavior were unacceptable. All forms of physical punishment and uncontrolled verbal assaults such as yelling, shouting, screaming, or "bawling out," were classified as sensitization techniques.

Other techniques used by the mothers which could not be clearly coordinated to the behavioral impact ascribed to induction and sensitization methods were excluded from the classification. Among the most frequent of these were various forms of restriction and deprivation, the effects of which were considered to be highly dependent on their behavioral context and style of administration. Discipline described with such terms as "scolding," "lecturing," or "criticism," without further elaboration, was also viewed as ambiguous within the induction-sensitization framework, since it was not obvious that it provided self-evaluative resources for the child. Nor could it, on the other hand, be assumed to represent a direct attack with the function of merely eliminating the offending behavior.

For each mother, two separate counts were made across the 12 disciplinary situations used in the questionnaire—one for the number of situations in which she reported induction techniques and the second for the number in which she reported sensitization techniques. In some instances, of course, the mother's response to a single situation contributed to both counts. Each situation was permitted to enter only once into each count, however, even though mothers often mentioned more than one specific kind of induction or sensitization technique in a given situation. The entire sample of mothers was then divided into two groups on the basis of which of the two counts was higher. Three mothers whose induction and sensitization counts were identical were placed in the group showing a predominance of sensitization techniques in order to have the two groups as nearly equal in size as possible.

Reliability of Classification

The entire classification of responses to transgression was independently applied by two judges,[3] one of whom was the writer, to the 100 stories written by a subsample of 20 children. The children were selected so as to equally represent both sexes and the two social classes, but were randomly chosen within this restriction. Each specific subcategory of responses scored by either of the judges was treated as an instance of classification, and was entered as a disagreement if not scored by both. In the case of the index of degree of activity in self-correction, failure of the two judges to score the same degree of activity was counted as a disagreement. Percentages of agreement were computed over the total number of instances of classification in each of the five major categories of the system. These percentages of agreement, summarized in Table 1, indicate that the classification system can be objectively and consistently used. The rather high reliability of classification probably reflects the fact that the system was specified in great detail and left little room for inference or interpretation. Comparable reliability has been obtained with a similar system in a previous study (Aronfreed, 1960).

[3] The author is indebted to Stephanie Manning for her work in establishing the reliability of classification.

TABLE 1

Percentage of Agreement between Two Independent Judges for Each Major Category of Classification of Responses to Transgression

Category of response to transgression	Percentage of agreement[a]
Self-criticism	94
Correction of deviance	96
Degree of activity in self-correction	90
External resolution	97
Externally oriented initiation and performance	98

[a] Based on a sample of 100 stories completed by 20 subjects.

The same two judges independently classified the disciplinary techniques reported by a randomly selected subsample of 20 mothers. Although the techniques were eventually to be grouped into the two broad types of induction and sensitization, reliability was based on the identification of specific forms of discipline, and a disagreement was entered whenever a particular form was scored by one judge but not by the other. The judges agreed on 97% of the total number of instances of classification induction techniques and on 98% of the instances of sensitization techniques.

RESULTS AND DISCUSSION

Table 2 shows, for each of the subcategories in the classification of responses to transgression and for the major types into which they were grouped, the frequencies and percentages of occurrence among both subjects and stories. In order to assess the role of self-evaluation in correction of deviance and in external resolution, instances of each specific form of these two types of response were separately tabulated with respect to the presence or absence of self-criticism in the stories in which they occurred. In computing percentages, a common basis for comparing different forms and patterns of response was provided by taking all frequencies as proportions either of the total number of subjects or the total number of stories.

The entries given for the broad response types in Table 2 represent frequencies and percentages of occurrence of these types in *any* specific form. A given subject, and even a single story, frequently showed multiple instance of responses classified within the same major type. Consequently, the entries presented for any major type are always smaller, and often considerably so, than the sum that would be obtained by adding the totals recorded for each of its specific forms. The single exception to this pattern occurs, in the case of the stories only, for the index of degree of activity in self-correction, since there a rating of degree is given to every story and is applied to the whole story as a unit. Similarly, for those forms of response which are separately tabulated according to whether or not they are accompanied by self-criticism, the entries for subjects showing any instance of a response are smaller than the combined entries for the presence and absence of self-criticism, since a particular subject may show some instances of the response that are accompanied by self-criticism and others that are not. The entries for stories showing any instance of a response do, however, represent the combined entries for the presence and absence of self-criticism, since in a single story self-criticism can only be either present or absent.

The most immediately obvious feature of the distribution in Table 2 is the great number and variety of internalized reactions to transgression which are shown by the children. Even if we restrict our attention to self-criticism, correction of deviance, and external resolution, and temporarily exclude the more refined patterning of responses, we can see that each story-trangression must be followed by multiple, sequential reactions. It is apparent that a single form of response was generally not sufficient, from the children's point of view, to define the consequences of transgression.

Self-criticism

Over one-fourth of the children show no evidence at all of self-criticism. The 90 subjects who do show evidence of self-criticism, while they are clearly in the majority, do not use it as a recurrently characteristic response, as can be seen from the fact it oc-

TABLE 2

FREQUENCY AND PERCENTAGE OF SUBJECTS AND STORIES SHOWING EACH
CATEGORY OF CLASSIFICATION OF RESPONSES TO TRANSGRESSION

Category of response to transgression	Subjects		Stories	
	N	%[a]	N	%[a]
Self-criticism	90	73.8	171	28.0
Correction of deviance (any form)				
Self-criticism present	84	68.8	160	26.2
Self-criticism absent	113	92.6	325	53.3
Any instance	117	95.9	485	79.5
Confession				
Self-criticism present	58	47.5	91	14.9
Self-criticism absent	94	77.1	182	29.8
Any instance	108	88.5	273	44.7
Apology				
Self-criticism present	18	14.7	18	2.9
Self-criticism absent	46	37.7	55	9.0
Any instance	54	44.3	73	11.9
Reparation				
Self-criticism present	56	46.2	79	12.9
Self-criticism absent	99	81.1	165	27.1
Any instance	110	90.2	244	40.0
Modification of future behavior				
Self-criticism present	38	31.1	53	8.7
Self-criticism absent	56	46.2	89	14.6
Any instance	71	58.2	142	23.3
Degree of activity in self-correction				
Low	105	86.1	212	34.8
Intermediate	116	95.1	248	40.7
High	89	72.9	150	24.5
External resolution (any form)				
Self-criticism present	79	64.8	125	20.5
Self-criticism absent	96	78.7	168	27.5
Any instance	118	96.7	293	48.0
Discovery and punishment				
Self-criticism present	58	47.5	70	11.5
Self-criticism absent	84	68.8	122	20.0
Any instance	107	87.7	192	31.5
Unpleasant fortuitous consequences				
Self-criticism present	34	27.9	36	5.9
Self-criticism absent	33	27.1	38	16.2
Any instance	60	49.2	74	12.1
Focus on external responsibility				
Self-criticism present	43	35.2	52	8.5
Self-criticism absent	47	38.5	52	8.5
Any instance	75	61.5	104	17.0
Externally oriented initiation and performance (any form)	93	76.2	150	24.6
External initiation	55	45.1	75	12.3
Display	51	41.8	75	12.3
Use of external resources	43	35.2	46	7.5

[a] Percentages based on Ns of 122 subjects and 610 stories.

curs in only 28% of the stories. The restricted role of self-criticism is also reflected in the limited extent to which it accompanies corrections of deviance and external resolution. For each of the specific forms of correction of deviance, and in the entries for instances of any form, the percentage of subjects for whom there is an accompanying self-criticism is uniformly considerably smaller than the percentage of subjects for whom there is not. Among the stories, also, self-criticism is typically absent roughly twice as frequently as it is present when corrections of deviance occur, and the disproportion is even greater in the case of apology. It would certainly not seem that any of the different kinds of correction of deviance presuppose the presence of self-evaluation. Corrections of deviance should not, therefore, be necessarily taken as indicating the operation of cognitive resources of moral judgment. They should instead be viewed as ambiguous in their implications for the orientation of conduct. Apparently, they can be used rather mechanically, either because they have become instrumental in reducing what are simple unpleasant feelings or perhaps because they have been successful in avoiding anticipated external punishment.

The tendency for self-criticism to be absent more often than present is less consistent as a context for the various forms of external resolution. In the case of each form, however, it is absent at least as often as, if not more often than, it is present. The substantial extent to which each of the different forms of external resolution is accompanied by self-criticism is a finding of special interest. There have been some attempts (Allinsmith, 1960; Aronfreed, 1960; Flugel, 1947) to conceptualize externally oriented reactions to transgression in such a way as to make self-evaluation a necessary condition of their occurrence. The concept of "defense against guilt," for example, specifies that the more "externalized" reactions to transgression defend the individual against the painful experience of the self-criticism which is presumed to accompany any degree of internalization, but which may somehow not find conscious expression. But the patterning of the different types of response

does not, under close examination, support the view that the reactions subsumed under external resolution are merely secondary elaborations whose function is to avoid self-criticism. It would appear, rather, that self-criticism and the various forms of external resolution are parallel and complementary consequences of transgression, and that neither type of response precludes or rests upon the presence of the other. There is no reason to assume that all internalized responses to transgression are to be interpreted as transformations of the experience of guilt.

Corrections of Deviance

Corrections of deviance are clearly indispensable to almost all of the children and are more characteristic of their behavior than any other type of response. They occur in almost 80% of the stories. Confession and reparation are decidedly the most common forms. Either of these kinds of reaction would, in itself, come close to accounting for the number of subjects who show correction of deviance in any form. It is also interesting to note that over 40% of the children give no indication at all of the modification of future behavior following a transgression.

The various levels of degree of activity in self correction are each manifested by very large proportions of the total group of children and are fairly well distributed throughout the stories. There is discernible, nevertheless, some tendency for responses showing a self-defined and active acceptance of responsibility to be less typical of the sample as a whole. Such responses occur in only about one-fourth of the stories and do not appear at all for over 25% of the subjects. The entire pattern of findings on this index points to the heavy situational determination of corrections of deviance and to their very uncertain value as indicators of autonomously sustained conduct.

Externally Oriented Responses

External resolution, like correction of deviance, is a component of the responses to transgression of virtually every child. Its various forms, while not as pervasive as corrections of deviance, are present in almost half of the stories. Discovery of the transgression and punishment by others are more common than unpleasant fortuitous consequences or a focus on external responsibility, but all of the forms are substantially present. What cannot be conveyed in the formal presentation of responses is the frequency with which external resolution is brought about through the most devious and artificial means, particularly in view of the fact that the story beginnings make it explicit that only the central figure knows of the transgression. Just as in actual life situations, however, there generally remains in the stories some minimal possibility of external consequences. This possibility is commonly seized upon and exploited in those instances where external resolution occurs. Apparently, this kind of reaction is sometimes an indispensable part of the child's equipment for responding to a transgression.

The importance of external events in defining the consequences of transgression is further attested by the extent to which even actions carried out by the central figure, such as corrections of deviance, show an external orientation. The initiation of responses through the influence or demands of other people, the public display of some of these responses, and the use of external resources in carrying out reparation each occur in the stories of a sizable percentage of subjects. Over three-fourths of the subjects show evidence of some form of reliance on an external social context in the initiation and performance of their responses to transgression.

The Nature of Internalized Responses to Transgression

The findings of the survey indicate that self-evaluation of the kind implied in the concept of guilt is not a prerequisite of internalized responses to transgression and that such responses frequently take a variety of forms in which external events are used to define the consequences of transgression. These findings do not contravene the fact that cognitive resources of moral judgment often do play an important role in reactions to transgression and have special implica-

tions for social behavior. But the use of such resources, however salient they may seem in the responses of some individuals, would appear to constitute only a special case of the more general psychological processes which are needed to describe internalization. The intimate dependence on external events that characterizes so many internalized reactions to transgression is, in some sense, just what one might expect. It would be much more paradoxical if such reactions were to assume properties which were entirely divorced from the external socializing situations in which they were originally learned.

If self-criticism is not to be given a fundamental status among internalized responses to transgression, but is to be viewed instead as only one form of these responses, then we are left with the problem of how to conceptualize their common foundations. To resolve the problem in a way that takes account of their variety and patterning, we may define an act as a transgression to the extent that it has been followed, in the individual's experience, by any form of social punishment. The punishment results in the attachment of anxiety to the act itself. When the anxiety is elicited in the absence of direct social surveillance, it may be considered the primary and invariant component of the internalized consequences of punishment.[4] The anxiety is endowed with motivating properties, and it is reducible through a number of different kinds of responses. The instrumental anxiety-reducing value of these responses is contingent on their production of cues which were originally associated with the attenuation of anxiety during the sociali-

[4] This affect should not in itself be referred to as guilt, since it is not necessarily accompanied by the cognitive phenomena usually associated with that term. To refer to the affect as anxiety seems more warranted, though such a general characterization possibly obscures a variety of qualities of experience dependent on the specific nature of the punishment from which they derive.

The term punishment is not used here in any restricted sense, but rather to convey the entire range of aversive stimuli which may induce painful feelings in a person. In this broad sense, the application of aversive control may take place through the most subtle and indirect kinds of interaction between people (as when, for example, a mother unintentionally withdraws from a close physical contact with her child because of something that it is doing).

zation process. The anxiety-reduction that becomes independently attached to some responses is derived from their having initially received direct external reinforcement through the prevention or arrest of punishment (or through the elimination of social cues which portended punishment). This path toward intrinsic reinforcement undoubtedly makes a substantial contribution to the internalization of corrections of deviance such as confession or reparation.

In the case of other responses, however, children actually learn to reproduce components of the punishments to which they have been previously exposed, because these components have become cues which signify the attenuation of the anxiety that occurs in the interval between transgression and punishment. Self-criticism is one example of such an instrumental response. Its acquisition is determined, in part, by the extent to which the patterns of socialization which the child has experienced around transgressions have been characterized by explicit verbalization of standards and their application to its behavior. When a child's punishment incorporates verbal criticism, the criticism itself will acquire some value as a signal for the termination of the anxiety that accompanies its anticipation. The child can then, on subsequent occasions when it commits a transgression, reduce its anxiety by reproducing the criticism in its own responses.[5] The capacity of punishment to assume anxiety-reducing cue properties also accounts for the various forms of response in which children rely on punitive external events to define the consequences of their transgressions. Attention to the role of anxiety and anxiety-reduction in the internalization of responses to transgression shows us, then, that externally oriented responses share important functional attributes with responses which clearly exhibit self-evaluation.

The Social Patterning of Responses to Transgression

Table 3 shows the frequencies with which children in each of the four subgroups defined by social class and sex role received high scores on the various subcategories in the classification of responses to transgression.[6] High and low scores were determined, independently for each subcategory, by splitting the range of scores for the subcategory into the two segments that would most nearly equally divide the entire sample of 122 subjects. Chi square values for each of the possible social class and sex comparisons are presented in Table 4.

Inspection of Tables 3 and 4 reveals a series of significant differences which are, almost without exception, those anticipated. The most consistent differences are found among those responses to transgression which are the most unequivocal indicators of internal or external orientation. Thus, middle-class children, regardless of their sex, show more evidence of self-criticism than do working-class children and are considerably less likely to resolve transgressions through the perception of unpleasant fortuitous consequences or a focus on external responsibility. Similarly, the boys, irrespective of their socioeconomic status, do not emphasize external responsibility as frequently as do the girls and appear much less dependent on an external initiation of their own moral actions. The tendency of girls to publicly display their reactions more often than boys is also fairly uniform, though it does not attain statistical significance in the working class group.

The appearance of consistent social class differences across both sexes, and of sex differences not confined to a particular social class, suggests that each of these two dimensions of social position has a general and independent bearing on the child's responses

---

[5] Sears et al. (1957, Ch. 10), and Whiting and Child (1953, Ch. 11) provide an interesting contrast to this interpretation of the role of self-criticism. They suggest that the child reproduces the critical application of its parents' standards to its own behavior, not because the criticism is associated with the termination of negative affect, but rather because there is a generalized positive affect attached to parental presence and actions.

[6] Social class and sex comparisons are not shown for the cumulative frequencies in the broader response types (major category headings). Significant variations in these frequencies could easily be generated by the response distributions in certain specific subcategories. Thus, they could not be interpreted as providing any information beyond that already conveyed in the subcategories, and would actually tend to inflate the apparent number of significant differences.

TABLE 3

FREQUENCY BY SOCIAL CLASS AND SEX OF CHILDREN SCORING HIGH IN EACH
CATEGORY OF CLASSIFICATION OF RESPONSES TO TRANSGRESSION

Category of response to transgression		Middle Class		Working class	
		Boys	Girls	Boys	Girls
	N =	34	28	27	33
Self-criticism		16	18	6	13
Confession		15	19	10	11
Apology		12	16	9	18
Reparation		18	20	14	16
Modification of future behavior		19	18	15	22
Degree of activity in self-correction		19	16	13	17
Discovery and punishment		13	9	9	20
Unpleasant fortuitous consequences		13	7	18	24
Focus on external responsibility		12	17	18	29
External initiation		9	15	9	23
Display		13	18	7	15
Use of external resources		10	14	10	11

Note.—A subject's score on any category is the number of instances of that
category occurring across the five story completions, where each category may
be counted only once in a given story. The single exception is in the case of
degree of activity in self-correction, where a subject's score is the summation
of values assigned to the total pattern of moral responses in each of the five
stories (see Method section).

TABLE 4

CHI SQUARE VALUES FOR SOCIAL CLASS AND SEX COMPARISONS OF CHILDREN SCORING HIGH
IN EACH CATEGORY OF CLASSIFICATION OF RESPONSES TO TRANSGRESSION

Category of response to transgression	Middle class vs. Working Class			Boys vs. Girls		
	Boys	Girls	Total	Middle class	Working class	Total
Self-criticism	3.02*	2.83*	5.75**	1.21	1.31	2.14
Confession	0.09	5.91**	4.08*	2.60	0.00	0.53
Apology	0.01	0.00	0.03	2.14	1.91	4.77*
Reparation	0.03	2.42	1.15	0.14	0.00	0.33
Modification of future behavior	0.06	0.01	0.00	0.17	0.38	0.86
Degree of activity in self-correction	0.12	0.03	0.28	0.02	0.00	0.00
Discovery and punishment	0.02	3.85*	1.57	0.05	3.40*	1.21
Unpleasant fortuitous consequences	3.80*	11.96**	15.90**	0.70	0.05	0.03
Focus on external responsibility	4.74*	4.65*	12.93**	3.03*	2.79*	7.85**
External initiation	0.09	1.06	2.07	3.68*	6.50**	11.92**
Display	0.55	0.14	1.70	3.19*	1.67	4.80*
Use of external resources	0.13	1.12	0.06	1.94	0.00	0.56

Note.—Chi square values for 2×2 contingency tables (employing correction for continuity) based on
frequencies in Table 3.
* $p < .05$, one-tailed test.
** $p < .01$, one-tailed test.

to transgression. At the same time, the marked parallelism of the orientations associated with the two kinds of status distinction supports the view that their similar effects are mediated through common elements of social reinforcement defining the extent of opportunity to evaluate and determine one's own actions or, conversely, the extent of one's dependence on the external environment. The common effects are especially striking when both are exhibited in the same form of response, as happens in the tendency to focus on external responsibility.

It can be seen that the parallel variations of internal vs. external orientation associated with social class and sex role are not identical in the specific response forms which they assume. Social class differences appear to center primarily on the distinction between consequences of transgression defined by the child's own resources and consequences defined by external events. Sex differences, in contrast, seem to reflect more of the variability in the extent to which the child's self-corrective actions are dependent on the support of the external environment. It is hardly surprising that the particular forms of response which vary with the two indices of status are not the same. Despite the similarity of their effects on the general orientation of conduct, social class and sex role have very different behavioral correlates which would certainly influence the specific way in which the child's orientation is expressed. It should also be noted that many of the social class and sex differences are not extreme even when they are statistically significant. The moderate degrees of difference may simply indicate that the social experiences which affect the orientation of the child's reactions to transgression are only moderately distinct with respect to variations in either socioeconomic status or sex role.

The least evidence of significant effects of social position occurs among the various forms of correction of deviance. The absence of the marked associations with status found among other responses accords with the view that corrections of deviance are, in themselves, ambiguous with respect to internal or external orientation. Although they represent the individual's own actions in defining the consequences of transgres-

sion, they are frequently highly influenced by external events. In fact, a central distinction between the responses of boys and girls, as has already been pointed out, lies in the extent to which they are externally initiated and displayed to others.

The social class differences include, in addition to those consistent across both sexes, some which are restricted only to girls. Middle-class girls show more evidence of confession and working-class girls more frequently perceive discovery and punishment by others as defining the consequences of their actions. The entire pattern of differences between the two classes provides an instructive contrast with the findings of two other surveys of children's reactions to transgressions that failed to reveal significant social class variations. One of these (Allinsmith, 1960) used a story completion device, similar to the one employed in the present study, with junior high school children. Many specific reactions, including self-criticism, corrections of deviance, and those characterized here as external resolution, were combined to derive a single broad evaluation of "intensity of guilt." In the second survey (Sears et al., 1957, Ch. 10), a general rating of the extent of development of conscience in kindergarten children was based on their mothers' reports of various overt behavioral manifestations of reactions to transgressions. It would seem that the use of a concept like internal vs. external orientation to treat different kinds of responses to transgression as distinct forms of behavior introduces a meaningful social patterning into their variety. Such a patterning is not apparent when all internalized responses to transgression are presumed to be equivalent reflections of some underlying unitary phenomenon such as guilt or conscience.

That girls are more externally oriented than boys in their reactions to transgression is a finding of considerable interest, since it is a contradictory and commonly held belief that girls, in our society, show greater conscientiousness and moral sensitivity. Perhaps it should be emphasized that the sex differences reported here represent variations not in the qualitative presence or breadth of internalization, but rather in the extent to which social support is sought for specific forms of response, all of which are internalized in that they occur in the absence of direct surveillance or application of punitive sanctions. The fact that the external orientation of girls is localized in their use of external resources to support their own actions may be helpful in resolving an apparent discrepancy with the findings of one other study in which sex differences have been described.

Sears et al. (1957, Ch. 10) reported that, among the roughly 20% of their 5–6 year old children showing evidence of "highly developed conscience," there was a slightly but significantly higher percentage of girls. It seems quite possible, however, that their use of the mother's observations to assess the child's reactions to transgression tended to put a premium on the kinds of response that would be easily discernible to the mother and perhaps even oriented toward her approval. Expressions of guilt were, in fact, defined in their study so as to include not only overt self-criticism and attempts at restitution, but also other behavioral manifestations which seem more externally oriented (for example, asking for forgiveness, looking "sheepish," seeking punishment, or acting in such a way as to invite inquiry or discovery). One of their most heavily used indices of conscience was confession. Responses such as confession and apology may be regarded as somewhat externally oriented corrections of deviance since, even though they represent the individual's own actions, they do require the presence of an external figure (and they often result in resolution of the transgression through restoration of the mother's affection). The response distributions found in the present study indicate, for example, that the more frequent use of confession among middle-class children than among working-class children is restricted to girls. Indeed, the tendency of the girls in the middle class to employ confession more often than the boys also comes close to attaining statistical significance. In the combined responses for both social classes, girls likewise show significantly more evidence of apology than do boys. If the internalized responses of boys are somewhat less manifest to mothers than those of

girls, the apparent difference might conceivably indicate the boys' greater independence of the mother as an external reinforcer rather than a lesser degree of internalization.

From the point of view of parents and other socializing agents, the visibility of internalized responses to transgression may be considerably enhanced by the child's use of overt self-criticism and appropriate verbalization of standards. These particular forms of response might in turn be conditioned by differences in the quality and rate of development of verbal facility. The fact that girls may show in their behavior an observable conscientiousness that easily flows into verbal expression is certainly one kind of evidence of internalization. The findings of the present study suggest, however, that internalization is not monolithic. The conscientiousness of girls need not obviate the possibility that their internalized responses are also dependent on their external situation in a way that conforms to the more general characteristics of their feminine role. Terman and his co-workers (1925) found, for example, in their studies of gifted and control children, that boys did not score as well as girls on five of seven character tests based essentially on verbalized knowledge of moral standards. But the girls were somewhat poorer on actual performance tests of honesty (when it appeared that their actions would not be known to others). Similarly, Hartshorne and May (1928) observed that boys were more resistant to temptation than girls on performance tests of "good" and "bad" behavior and were more consistent in their actions from one test to another. They concluded that differences in moral reputation favorable to girls were discrepant with differences in performance. Perhaps Terman and Tyler (1954) are correct in asserting, in their summary of sex differences, that the moral opinions expressed by girls result in their being inaccurately credited with a more internalized orientation in their behavior.

Finally, it should be pointed out that the nature of the relationships between social positions and reactions to transgression does not easily lend itself to the view, suggested by Piaget's (1948) interpretation of moral development, that different types of moral orientation sequentially emerge with advancing age or experience. It would seem more appropriate that internal and external orientation in social conduct be understood as relatively stable end-results of different patterns of social reinforcement. Such an understanding would be consistent with the findings of many other studies (Boehm, 1962; Havighurst & Neugarten, 1955; Kohlberg, 1963; Lerner, 1937; MacRae, 1954) in which, as in Piaget's investigation, attention has been devoted primarily to moral judgment. These studies, when taken together as a group, indicate that the child's evaluative social cognition is, like its conduct, closely associated with social status and other indicators of cultural expectation, and that it is not merely the natural consequence of increasing exposure to the general features of human society.

INTELLIGENCE

In order to answer the question of whether intelligence could be a factor in accounting for either the social class or sex differences, the total sample was divided into two equal groups on the basis of the verbal intelligence test on which IQ scores for all but three of the children were available. One group consisted of children whose scores were less than 110. In the other group were children whose scores were 110 or greater. These two groups were compared with respect to their frequencies of high and low scores on each category in the classification of responses to transgression. The comparisons indicated no relationship whatsoever between verbal IQ and any of the categories of response.

MATERNAL DISCIPLINE

Table 5 shows, for children in each of the four groups defined by social class and sex, the frequencies with which the disciplinary techniques predominantly used by their mothers fall into the induction or sensitization categories. The comparisons in Table 6 indicate that with children of both sexes, middle class mothers use more induction techniques and lower-class mothers use more sensitization techniques. There are no sig-

TABLE 5

FREQUENCY OF PREDOMINANT USE OF INDUCTION OR SENSITIZATION TECHNIQUES BY MOTHERS OF CHILDREN IN EACH SOCIAL CLASS AND SEX GROUP

Predominant maternal discipline	Middle class		Working class	
	Boys	Girls	Boys	Girls
Induction	21	20	9	14
Sensitization	13	7	18	18

Note.—Total $N = 120$. Adequate interview data on discipline not available for two girls.

TABLE 6

CHI SQUARE VALUES FOR SOCIAL CLASS AND SEX OF CHILD COMPARISONS OF PREDOMINANT MATERNAL DISCIPLINE
(Induction vs. Sensitization)

Comparison	Chi square value
Middle class vs. Working class	
Boys	3.80*
Girls	4.34*
Both sexes	8.50**
Boys vs. Girls	
Middle class	0.55
Working class	0.30
Both classes	0.55

Note.—Chi square values for 2×2 contingency tables (employing correction for continuity) based on frequencies in Table 5.
* $p < .05$, one-tailed test.
** $p < .01$, one-tailed test.

nificant differences in the types of discipline used with the two sexes. The social class differences are in agreement with the findings of other studies in which techniques respectively subsumed here under induction and sensitization were related in the same direction to the mother's socioeconomic status.

The frequencies of high and low scores on three indices of response to transgression among children whose mothers use predominantly induction or sensitization techniques, are presented in Table 7. Only categories of response are shown for which the associations with maternal discipline are statistically significant when taken over the entire sample. There is only one instance in which a significant variation limited to a single subgroup is eliminated from presentation by

TABLE 7

COMPARISON OF SCORES ON CATEGORIES OF MORAL RESPONSES OF CHILDREN WHOSE MOTHERS USE
PREDOMINANTLY EACH OF THE TWO TYPES OF MATERNAL DISCIPLINE
(Induction vs. Sensitization)
(I = Induction; S = Sensitization)

Category of moral responses	Middle class			Working class			Boys			Girls			Total sample		
	I	S	p^a	I	S	p^a	I	S	p^a	I	S	p^a	I	S	p^a
Reparation			*			ns			ns			*			**
High	30	8		14	16		19	13		25	11		44	24	
Low	11	12		9	20		11	18		9	14		20	32	
Degree of activity in self-correction			*			**			**			*			**
High	27	7		17	13		21	11		23	9		44	20	
Low	14	13		6	23		9	20		11	16		20	36	
Unpleasant fortuitous consequences			*			*			*			**			**
High	10	10		12	29		11	20		11	19		22	39	
Low	31	10		11	7		19	11		23	6		42	17	

Note.—Only those categories of moral responses are shown for which the association with maternal discipline was statistically significant when taken over the total sample (see Results and Discussion.

[a] p values for chi square tests (employing correction for continuity).
* $p < .05$, one-tailed test.
** $p < .01$, one-tailed test.

this criterion—girls whose mothers use predominantly sensitization techniques are more likely to focus on external responsibility than are girls whose mothers use induction techniques. The association of the children's responses with maternal discipline, while less striking and extensive than their association with social position, is generally consistent and in the expected direction. The response of reparation and a high degree of self-initiated acceptance of responsibility are more characteristic of children whose mothers use induction techniques. Children whose mothers use sensitization techniques are more likely to perceive external consequences of transgression in the form of unpleasant fortuitous events.

The patterning of internal vs. external orientation with respect to maternal discipline is generally consistent across the various social class and sex subgroups, thus indicating that it cannot be regarded as merely coincidental to the relationships between social position and reactions to transgression. Actually, neither the use of reparation nor the degree of activity in correction of deviance is directly related to the social class or sex of the child, despite the significant association between social class and discipline. These findings, when considered together with the fact that many of the types of response related to social position do not vary with maternal discipline, may indicate that the cataloguing of specific methods of punishment captures only some of the more visible aspects of the total pattern of social reinforcement bearing upon the child's moral orientation. The crucial elements of the pattern may conceivably lie, for example, in the nature of certain response cues in the behavior of either the child or the socializing agent, or in the place of these cues in the sequence of onset and termination of anxiety. An understanding of how these elements of social reinforcement affect the child's responses to transgression may require discriminations that are beyond the parent's capacity as a retrospective observer and demand the more exact control that is possible with experimental methods.

SUMMARY

Contemporary conceptions of the development of internalized control over social conduct characteristically take the view that internalization requires the child to exercise self-evaluation in terms of explicit standards of moral judgment, without the support of external punishment or surveillance. Common observation and the findings of a number of studies suggest, however, that responses to transgression, even when they are internalized, often reveal an absence of self-evaluation and a marked orientation toward the resolution of the transgression through external events. The survey of children's internalized reactions to transgression described in this paper examined the nature and variety of these reactions, particularly with respect to their internal vs. external orientation, and their relationship to both the child's positions in society and the disciplinary practices of its mother.

In the context of a theoretical framework built around hypothesized variations in patterns of social reinforcement, it was proposed that individuals occupying positions of differential status or power within a social structure would show corresponding differences of orientation in the control and modification of their own conduct. The implications of this proposition were developed for socioeconomic status and sex role. Higher status positions, as located in the middle class and the masculine sex role, were viewed as providing greater reinforcement of responses characterized by control over one's own actions as well as over the external environment. Lower status positions, as located in the working class and the feminine sex role, were considered more likely to foster responses characterized by the perception of one's actions, and their reinforcements, as externally determined. Parental disciplinary techniques were singled out as one of the means by which values and expectations surrounding the child's prospective social positions might be translated into the child's internal or external orientation in its responses to its own transgressions. A distinction was made between two major types of discipline. *Induction* techniques subsumed methods that would tend to induce reactions to transgression that could readily become independent of their original external stimulus sources. *Sensitization* techniques were those that would merely sensitize the child to the painful external consequences of transgression.

In order to circumscribe a wide variety of responses to transgression, a highly structured projective story completion device was constructed and administered to 122 sixth grade children drawn in comparable numbers from the two major socioeconomic classes and both sexes. In each story, the central figure committed, with minimal or no justification, a socially prohibited act of aggression. The responses to transgression occurring in the story completions, which could be classified with high reliability, were assumed to reflect the subjects' own strongest response tendencies. The methods of discipline applied to the children, as reported in questionnaire interviews with their mothers, were also reliably classified, and the mothers were divided into two groups according to whether they used predominantly induction techniques or sensitization techniques.

Self-evaluation was found to play only a restricted role in internalized responses to transgression; many forms of response did not seem to require the use of cognitive resources for self-criticism. The most common kind of response, correction of deviance, occurred very often without any evidence of self-criticism. Various forms of external resolution, in which the consequences of transgression were perceived in discovery and punishment by other people, or in unpleasant fortuitous events, or in which others were held responsible for the transgression or for similar actions, were also pervasive among the response to transgression. The frequent coincidence of such externally oriented responses with self-criticism indicated that they were not merely "defenses against guilt" whose function was to avoid self-evaluation. The importance of external cues and resources in determining responses to transgression was again confirmed by the many instances in which the responses were initiated upon the influence or demands of others, publicly displayed, or carried out with the assistance of external agents.

The limited occurrence of self-evaluation among internalized responses to transgression, and the extensive evidence of their frequent external orientation, suggested a theoretical perspective in which self-criticism was not viewed as a prerequisite of their occurrence. Instead, all of the various forms of reaction to transgression were considered to be complementary and functionally equivalent responses, instrumental to the reduction of the anxiety that becomes attached to transgressions as a consequence of social punishment.

The two dimensions of status represented in social class and sex role distinctions had the expected parallel significance for the child's internal or external orientation. The middle-class children and the boys showed more evidence of independence of external events in responding to transgression, while the working class children and the girls revealed a greater degree of external orientation. Social class differences were generally consistent across both sexes and sex differences were consistent at both social class levels. None of the differences was attributable to the variable of intelligence.

Obvious differences in the behavioral correlates of social class and sex role, despite similarities along the status dimension, were emphasized by the fact that the parallel variations in responses to transgression were not identical in the specific forms which they assumed. The marked social patterning of the responses clearly confirmed that their different forms should be treated as distinct phenomena and not as equivalent reflections of an underlying unitary phenomenon such as "conscience." The relationships between the responses and social positions also indicated that different orientations of conduct do not emerge sequentially with advancing age or social experience, as has been argued in some interpretations of moral development, but are rather the stable end-results of different patterns of social reinforcement.

The relationships between internalized responses to transgression and maternal discipline, while significant and in the expected direction, were somewhat less extensive than their relationships to social position. It appeared that disciplinary techniques in themselves provided only a partial view of the patterns of social reinforcement through which differences in the orientation of conduct are generated, and it was suggested that experimental methods would be necessary in order to examine these patterns more closely.

REFERENCES

Adorno, T. W., Frenkel-Brunswik, Else, Levinson, D. J., & Sanford, R. N. *The authoritarian personality*. New York: Harper, 1950.

Allinsmith, W. The learning of moral standards. In D. R. Miller, G. E. Swanson, et al. *Inner conflict and defense*. New York: Holt, 1960. Pp. 176–177.

Aronfreed, J. Moral behavior and sex identity. In D. R. Miller, G. E. Swanson, et al. *Inner conflict and defense*. New York: Holt, 1960. Pp. 177–193.

Barry, H., III, Bacon, Margaret K., & Child, I. L. A cross-cultural survey of some sex differences in socialization. *J. abnorm. soc. Psychol.*, 1957, 55, 327–333.

Boehm, Leonore. The development of conscience: A comparison of American children of different mental and socioeconomic levels. *Child Developm.*, 1962, 33, 575–590.

Bronfenbrenner, U. Socialization and social class through time and space. In Eleanor E. Maccoby, T. M. Newcomb, & E. L. Hartley (Eds.), *Readings in social psychology*. (3rd ed.) New York: Holt, 1958. Pp. 400–425.

Brown, D. G. Sex-role development in a changing culture. *Psychol. Bull.*, 1958, 55, 232–242.

Davis, A., & Havighurst, R. J. Social class and color differences in child-rearing. *Amer. sociol. Rev.*, 1946, 11, 698–710.

Flugel, J. C. *Man, morals, and society*. New York: International Univer. Press, 1947.

Freud, S. *The problem of anxiety*. New York: Norton, 1936.

Hartshorne, H., & May, M. A. *Studies in the nature of character*. Vol. I. *Studies in deceit*, New York: Macmillan, 1928.

Havighurst, R. J., & Neugarten, Bernice. *American Indian and white children*. Chicago: Univer. of Chicago Press, 1955.

Heinecke, C. M. Some antecedents and correlates of guilt and fear in young boys. Unpublished doctoral disseration, Harvard University, 1953.

Henry, A. F., & Short, J. F., Jr. *Suicide and homicide: Some economic, sociological, and psychological aspects of aggression.* Glencoe, Ill.: Free Press, 1954.

Johnson, Ronald C. A study of children's moral judgments. *Child Developm.,* 1962, 33, 327–354.

Kohlberg, L. Moral development and identification. In H. W. Stevenson (Ed.), *Yearb. nat. Soc. Stud. Educ.*: Vol. I. *Child psychology.* Chicago: Univer. of Chicago Press, 1963.

Kohn, M. L. Social class and the exercise of parental authority. *Amer. sociol. Rev.,* 1959, 24, 352–366.

Lerner, E. The problem of perspective in moral reasoning. *Amer. J. Sociol.,* 1937, 43, 248–269.

Littman, R. A., Moore, R. A., & Pierce-Jones, J. Social class differences in child-rearing: A third community for comparison with Chicago and Newton, Massachusetts. *Amer. sociol. Rev.,* 1957, 22, 694–704.

Lynn, D. B. A note on sex differences in the development of masculine and feminine identification. *Psychol. Rev.,* 1959, 66, 126–135.

McClelland, D. C., Rindlisbacher, A., & de Charms, R. Religious and other sources of parental attitudes toward independence training. In D. C. McClelland (Ed.), *Studies in motivation.* New York: Appleton-Century-Crofts, 1955. Pp. 389–397.

Maccoby, Eleanor E., Gibbs, Patricia K., et al. Methods of child-rearing in two social classes. In W. E. Martin & Celia B. Stendler (Eds.), *Readings in child development.* New York: Harcourt, Brace, 1954. Pp. 380–396.

MacRae, D., Jr. A test of Piaget's theories of moral development. *J. abnorm. soc. Psychol.,* 1954, 49, 14–18.

Miller, D. R., & Swanson, G. E. *The changing American parent.* New York: Wiley, 1958.

Miller, D. R., & Swanson, G .E., et al. *Inner conflict and defense.* New York: Holt, 1960.

Parsons, T. Age and sex in the social structure of the United States. *Amer. sociol. Rev.,* 1942, 7, 604–616.

Parsons, T. A revised analytical approach to the theory of social stratification. In R. Bendix & S. M. Lipset (Eds.), *A reader in social stratification.* Glencoe, Ill.: Free Press, 1953. Pp. 92–128.

Piaget, J. *The moral judgment of the child.* Glencoe, Ill.: Free Press, 1948.

Rabban, M. Sex-role identification in young children in two diverse social groups. *Genet. psychol. Monogr.,* 1950, 42, 81–158.

Sears, R. R., Maccoby, Eleanor E., & Levin, H. *Patterns of child rearing.* Evanston, Ill.: Row, Peterson, 1957.

Terman, L. M., & Tyler, Leona E. Psychological sex differences. In L. Carmichael (Ed.), *Manual of child psychology.* (2nd ed.) New York: Wiley, 1954. Pp. 1064–1114.

Terman, L. M., et al. *Genetic studies of genius.* Vol. I. *Mental and physical traits of a thousand gifted children.* Stanford, Calif.: Stanford Univer. Press, 1925.

Whiting, J. W. M. *Sorcery, sin and the super-ego.* In M. R. Jones (Ed.), *Nebraska symposium on motivation: 1959.* Lincoln, Nebr.: Univer. Nebraska Press, 1959. Pp. 174–195.

Whiting, J. W. M., & Child, I. L. *Child training and personality: A cross-cultural study.* New Haven: Yale Univer. Press, 1953.

Role-Taking, Role Standpoint, and Reference-Group Behavior[1] / Ralph H. Turner

In order to clarify the meaning and usefulness of the concept of "role-taking," some major types of role-taking behavior are differentiated and their relations to the concepts of "empathy" and "reference group" are explored. Role-taking may or may not include adoption of the standpoint of the other as one's own and may or may not be reflexive, these distinctions being related to its functions in the acquisition or implementation of values and to the element of self-consciousness in behavior. Coincidence of certain reference-group meanings with types of role-taking and possibilities for enhancing the usefulness of the reference-group concept are discussed.

For decades sociologists have made reference to "taking the role of the other" ("role-taking" for short) as a basic explanatory concept in relating the acts of the individual to the social contexts of his actions. In general, the term has been employed as a broadly "sensitizing concept"[2] rather than with precise denotations suitable to empirical research. Some years after these terms had become commonplace in sociological literature a new school of social relations appropriated the term "role-taking" to describe the particular procedures involved in the psychodrama and sociodrama.[3] On top of this earlier vagueness have been superimposed recent discussions of "role-taking capacity" and "empathic ability."[4] Finally, a new concept of "reference group," which has achieved meteoric prominence, quite obviously overlaps in some respects the earlier role-taking.

In this paper we shall consider the value of the concept "role-taking" in its more traditional senses by an examination of some of the special variations in meaning which can be assigned to it. We shall suggest some conceptual distinctions which, by differentiating types of role-taking activity, can render use of the concept more specific and more precise. Based on this discussion, we can then suggest boundaries to forestall tendencies which broaden the concept beyond all usefulness. Finally, we shall note the light which our analysis of role-taking may shed upon the idea of reference group and attempt to designate the specific scope of each concept.

THE MEANING OF ROLE-TAKING

Role-taking in its most general form is a process of looking at or anticipating another's behavior by viewing it in the context of a role imputed to that other. It is thus always more than simply a reaction to another's behavior in terms of an arbitrarily understood symbol or gesture.

By *role* we mean a collection of patterns of behavior which are thought to constitute a meaningful unit and deemed appropriate to a person occupying a particular status in society (e.g., doctor or father), occupying an informally defined position in interpersonal relations (e.g., leader or compromiser), or identified with a particular value in society (e.g., honest man or patriot).[5] We

Reprinted from *The American Journal of Sociology,* 61, 1956, pages 316–328, by Ralph H. Turner by permission of The University of Chicago Press. Copyright 1956 by University of Chicago. Printed in U.S.A.

---

[1] The author is indebted to Helen P. Beem for a critical reading of the manuscript.

[2] Cf. Herbert Blumer, "What Is Wrong with Social Theory?" *American Sociological Review,* XIX (February, 1954), 3–9.

[3] Cf. J. L. Moreno, *Psychodrama* (New York: Beacon House, 1946).

[4] Cf. Leonard S. Cottrell, Jr., and Rosalind F. Dymond, "The Empathic Responses: A Neglected Field for Research," *Psychiatry,* XII (1949), 355–59; Rosalind F. Dymond, "A Scale for the Measurement of Empathic Ability," *Journal of Consulting Psychology,* XIII (1949), 127–33; Harrison G. Gough, "A Sociological Theory of Psychopathy," *American Journal of Sociology,* LIII (March, 1948), 359–66.

[5] Role is conceived more inclusively here than in Linton's famous definition (Ralph Linton, *The Study of Man* [New York: Appleton-Century Co., 1936], pp. 113 ff.). The term "appropriate" in the

shall stress the point that a role consists of behaviors which are regarded as making up a meaningful unit. The linkage of behaviors within roles is the source of our expectations that certain kinds of action will be found together. When people speak of trying to "make sense" of someone's behavior or to understand its meaning, they are typically attempting to find the role of which the observed actions are a part.

Role will be consistently distinguished from status or position or value type as referring to the whole of the behavior which is felt to belong intrinsically to those subdivisions. Role refers to behavior rather than position, so that one may *enact* a role but cannot *occupy* a role. However, role is a normative concept. It refers to expected or appropriate behavior and is distinguished from the manner in which the role is actually enacted in a specific situation, which is *role behavior* or *role performance*.[6] While a norm is a directive to action, a role is a *set of norms,* with the additional normative element that the individual is expected to be consistent. The role is made up of all those norms which are thought to apply to a person occupying a given position. Thus, we return to our initial emphasis that the crucial feature of the concept of role is its reference to the assumption that certain different norms are meaningfully related or "go together."

With only unimportant qualifications, we shall accept the delimited meaning of role-taking proposed by Walter Coutu,[7] which

distinguishes the imaginative construction of the other's role (role-taking) from the overt enactment of what one conceives to be one's own appropriate role in a given situation (role-playing) and from the overt enactment of a role as a form of pretense ("playing-at" a role). Role-taking may proceed from identifying a position to inferring its role and in this manner anticipating the behavior of an individual. Or it may proceed from observing a segment of behavior to identifying the feelings or motives behind the behavior or to anticipating subsequent behavior. In either case certain actions are interpreted or anticipated upon the basis of the entire role of which they are assumed to be a part.

In the present discussion the manner in which an individual conceives the role of another will not be examined as an isolated form of behavior. The self-other relationship will be viewed as an aspect of a total social act.[8] The actor takes the role of another in carrying out some behavior of his own; role-taking is an adjunct to the determination or application of one's own role in a given situation. Accordingly, for present purposes we shall disregard the usage of role-taking as the enactment of roles in the sociodramatic setting when the usage detaches the roles from their specific implications for the way in which the actor will define his own role.[9] Furthermore, our purpose in understanding how the role-taking process shapes the actor's own behavior will determine the basis on which we shall distinguish types of role-taking activity. The critical differentiae for types of role-taking will revolve about the manner in which the

---

definition is purposely left without a further referent, since the particular content of the role (i.e., that which is regarded as appropriate) will vary depending upon the vantage point of the person or persons formulating the role conception. Cf. also Theodore R. Sarbin, "Role Theory," in *Handbook of Social Psychology,* ed. Gardner Lindzey (Cambridge, Mass., Addison-Wesley Publishing Co., 1954), I, 223–58.

[6] Cf. Theodore M. Newcomb, *Social Psychology* (New York: Dryden Press, 1950), p. 330.

[7] "Role-playing vs. Role-taking: An Appeal for Clarification," *American Sociological Review,* XVI (April, 1951), 180–87. Coutu's reference to role-taking as "imagining what the other person 'thinks he is supposed to do'" (p. 181) corresponds to our usage if the word "supposed" is used in a broad sense. However, the distinction between attitude and role that Coutu mentions (p. 181) is well taken but need not be applied in the manner he suggests. If an attitude is a tendency to act toward

a particular category of objects, a role is made up of attitudes. When one seeks to identify a particular attitude of some other person, he does so by placing himself in that other person's position, imaginatively reviewing that other's role until the attitude in question is indicated. Thus, taking the attitude of the other is part of a role-taking process, and Mead's usage does not do violence to contemporary use of the concept of role.

[8] "Social act" is used in the sense indicated by Ellsworth Faris and George Herbert Mead. For a brief statement of this conception see Ellsworth Faris, *The Nature of Human Nature* (New York: McGraw-Hill Book Co., 1937), pp. 144 ff.

[9] E.g., Theodore R. Sarbin, "The Concept of Role-taking," *Sociometry,* VI (August, 1943), 273–85.

self-other relationship affords a directive to the individual in the formulation of what his own behavior shall be.

ALTERNATIVE CLASSIFICATIONS OF ROLE-TAKING

It will help to convey the boundaries of the concept of role-taking as we are using it and clarify the major task of this paper if we first mention two alternative schemes for classifying role-taking behavior which we do not plan to emphasize, although we recognize their great importance. First, role-taking is frequently used to refer to an ability or capacity, and attention is accordingly centered about the accuracy with which the role of the other is inferred. Studies dealing with role-taking capacity or *empathic ability*[10] attempt to measure the degree to which the other-role as imaginatively constructed corresponds to the actual role as that other experiences it, and the individual is said to be taking the role of the other only when he accurately infers the other's feelings or anticipates his behavior.

From our standpoint, however, the process of role-taking is not inherently different when the inference is accurate from when it is inaccurate. Furthermore, once the actor formulates a conception of the role of the other, the manner in which that conception serves to shape his own behavior is unaffected by the accuracy or inaccuracy of the conception. Accordingly, we shall speak of the actor as taking the role of the other irrespective of whether his imputation is accurate or not.

Another important basis for classifying role-taking behavior which will not be elaborated here has to do with the criteria which are used to infer the role of the other. (a) As we have already noted, role-taking may be a matter of first observing some behavior of the other and then inferring the total role of which that behavior is assumed to be a part. In this sense one responds to the behavior of the other as a *gesture*, as an "incomplete act" which one completes in imagination by supplying the role of which it is

an indication.[11] (b) Or role-taking may take place without any visible behavior on the part of the other, the role being inferred from a knowledge of the situation, from the supposed status or value. Role-taking of these two types undoubtedly calls upon somewhat different skills, so that the individual who has high facility in identifying the meanings of gestures may not be equally adept at supplying the role from a mere knowledge of the situation.

The criteria used to infer the role of the other may also be either projection or knowledge of the other. (a) In the case of projection, one constructs the other-role as he would if he himself were in the situation or had made the particular gesture. When role-taking proceeds in this manner, the particular identity of the other is immaterial to the role content, since the role conceptions of the actor are simply imputed to the other. (b) In contrast to projection one may interpret the other's gesture on the basis of prior experience with that individual or other individuals assumed to be like him. Or one infers the other's role from prior experience with that other's behavior in similar situations or from prior experience with the behavior of people like him in comparable situations.

Again, these distinctions are of considerable importance. But from our present standpoint the manner in which the role of the other is inferred must be distinguished from the manner in which the inferred other-role shapes the enactment of the self-role. In focusing upon the latter in this paper, we shall disregard the former. And we shall use the concept of role-taking to include these varied bases for inferring the other-role—whether from gesture or from situation and whether by projection or by knowledge of the other.

Distinctions which we shall discuss in greater detail have to do with the ways in which the imputed other-role is related to the choice or enactment of the self-role. We assume that two persons may identify and imaginatively construct the role of a relevant other in the same manner and yet

[10] Cottrell and Dymond, *op. cit.;* Dymond, *op. cit.;* Gough, *op. cit.*

[11] George Herbert Mead, *Mind, Self, and Society* (Chicago: University of Chicago Press, 1934), pp. 42 ff.

themselves act in quite different ways. We shall emphasize two major axes for distinguishing types of other-determining-self relationships. The first of these is the *standpoint* which is adopted in the process of taking the role of the other.

STANDPOINT IN ROLE-TAKING

Taking the role of another may or may not include adopting the standpoint of the other as one's own. The role of the other may remain an object to the actor, so that he understands and interprets it without allowing its point of view to become his own, or the actor may allow the inferred attitudes of the other to become his own and to direct his behavior. Another way of stating the distinction is to note that an individual who is taking the role of another may identify with the role of that other, or else he may retain a clear separation of identity between the self-attitudes and the attitudes of the other. When role-taking includes adoption of the standpoint of the other, the role-taking process is an automatic determiner of behavior. One simply acts from the standpoint of the role. When the standpoint of the other is not adopted, some other factor must intervene to determine the kind of influence which the role imputed to the other will have on the actor.

An occasional confusion between taking the role of another and adopting the standpoint of another is partly responsible for the view that facility in role-taking necessarily results in altruistic or sympathetic behavior or eliminates divergence of purpose between opposing factions. Certain types of exploitation, for example, require elaborate role-taking behavior on the part of the exploiter. The "confidence man" frequently succeeds because of his ability to identify accurately the feelings and attitudes of the person with whom he is dealing while completely avoiding any involvement or identification with these feelings.

The standpoint is not, of course, something apart from the role. It is the core of the role. The difference to which we are referring concerns the ability to engage in an imaginative construction of the role of another while maintaining the separation of personal identities.

The early role-taking activity of the child does not make such a separation. To the degree to which he thinks or feels himself into a situation of another, he adopts as his own the attitudes appropriate to that situation. The more complex behavior in which the actor is able to see the other's role while maintaining a separation of identities appears to develop through two processes. First, the individual becomes concerned simultaneously with *multiple others*. As he takes the roles of two others simultaneously, he cannot simultaneously adopt the standpoints of each. Thus, in simultaneously taking the roles of his mother and his playmate, he cannot orient himself from each standpoint at the same time. Hence he may take the role of a playmate, but, in reacting to the imputed role, he may adopt the standpoint of his mother. The existence of conflicting standpoints in the varied roles which the individual has learned to take forces upon him a separation between taking the role and adopting its standpoint.

On the other hand, the presence of *stable purposes or needs* gradually leads the individual to engage in role-taking in an adaptive context. Such rudimentary understandings of the roles of others as the child may achieve are quite early put to use in the attempted pursuit of his own objectives. Role-taking makes possible both the manipulation of others and adjustment to them, becoming a means to a pre-existing end of some sort. The attitude and skill of role-taking which were learned in a relationship of identification become divorced from that relationship as it is discovered to be useful in promoting the individual's own purposes.

These two ways in which role-taking is divested of identification remain as two somewhat different kinds of standpoint which can be adopted toward the imputed role of the other. (1) In the former instance the standpoint adopted is that of a third party. The third-party standpoint indicates what behavior is expected of the actor, depending upon the inferences made concerning the role of the other. The point of view of the mother, for example, may be that her child should be friends with a neighbor only if that neighbor conceives his role as being a decent and respectable child. The role of the other, when divorced from adoption of its standpoint, becomes a datum in carrying out the standpoint of the third party.

The third-party standpoint may be recognized as that of a specific person or group, or it may be depersonalized into a norm. Such a norm provides the individual with a directive to action which is contingent upon his placing some construction on the role of the relevant other. In a study of college students' reactions toward a friend who had committed a hypothetical breach of the mores, for example, the majority volunteered some estimate of the role context in which the friend had committed the disapproved act. Some respondents found it appropriate not to report their friend's theft to the authorities when it could be assumed that the general role of the friend was still that of an honest, law-abiding person whose inconsistent behavior reflected unusual stress. For these respondents the norms defining their own responsibility were more dependent upon the role of the other than on any specific behavior in which he had engaged.[12] Whether the third-party standpoint is personalized or not, the actor engages in role-taking in order to determine how he *ought* to act toward the other.

(2) When role-taking is in the adaptive context, however, the standpoint consists of a purpose or objective rather than a specific directive. The actor must examine the probable interaction between the self-role and the other-role in terms of the promotion of a purpose. He lacks a specific or detailed directive supplied by the standpoint of a third party and consequently must shape his own role behavior according to what he judges to be the probable *effect of interaction* between his own role and the inferred role of the other.

This latter kind of role-taking behavior may be clarified with George Herbert Mead's classic distinction between "play" and the "game," as illustrated in baseball.[13] The skillful player in a game such as base-

ball cannot act solely according to a set of rules. The first baseman can learn in general when he is to field the ball, when to run to first base, etc. But, in order to play intelligently and to be prepared for less clearly defined incidents in the game, he must adjust his role performance to the roles of all the other players. The adjustment is in terms of the effect of interaction among roles toward the end of minimizing the score of the opposing team. Whether the first baseman fields the ball, runs to first, throws to home, etc., will depend upon what he thinks each of the other players will do and how his action will combine most effectively with theirs to keep the score down.

Mead has pointed out that in the "game" the actor must have in mind the roles of all the other players. However, there is more which is distinctive about this kind of role-taking than merely the simultaneous attention to multiple other-roles. The manner in which the actor relates his own role to the others is in terms of their *interactive effect* rather than simply in terms of accepting their direction. It is not so much what the pitcher wants him to do that determines the first baseman's action as what the first baseman judges will be the consequences if each acts in a particular way.[14]

This type of role-taking can be even more clearly illustrated in the case of exploitation or of salesmanship directed toward a reluctant buyer, in which cases the actor's purpose is not shared by the relevant other. In these instances the actor holds constantly in mind his imaginative construction of the role of the other and adjusts his own behavior so as to elicit and take advantage of behavior in the other which will enhance his own objectives. He sensitizes himself to the attitudes of the other while divesting himself of any identification with these attitudes. And these attitudes enter into determination of his own behavior through the

12 "Moral Judgment: A Study in Roles," *American Sociological Review*, XVII (January, 1954), 72–74.
13 *Op. cit.*, pp. 149 ff.

14 The anticipation of approval or disapproval from others may operate simultaneously with the mechanism being described here. However, the determination of a specific course of action to be followed at a particular instant in the game requires a more precise indication. This indication is afforded by viewing the consequences of particular combinations of roles involving self and others against the criterion of winning the game.

criterion of effect in interaction with potential self-behavior.

Recapitulating this section, we have observed that an individual who in some sense puts himself in the position of another and imaginatively constructs that other's role may do so from one of three general standpoints. First, he may adopt the other's standpoint as his own, in which case he is identifying with the other-role and allowing it to become an automatic guide to his own behavior. Second, the role of the other may remain an object viewed from the standpoint of some personalized third party or depersonalized norm, in which case the role of the relevant other becomes a datum necessary in implementing the third-party directive. Third, the role of the relevant other may be viewed from the standpoint of its effect in interaction with potential self-behavior, as contributing toward some individual or shared purpose. The standpoint of the actor in role-taking may change in the course of a single act, or he may be plagued by alternative standpoints. But the manner in which the imagined other-role affects the actor's behavior will be different with each standpoint.

REFLEXIVENESS IN ROLE-TAKING

Borrowing a term from George Herbert Mead, we shall suggest that a second major distinction be made between reflexive and nonreflexive role-taking.[15] Mead uses the term "reflexive" in referring to the "characteristic of the self as an object to itself." When the role of the other is employed as a mirror, reflecting the expectations or evaluations of the self as seen in the other-role,[16] we may speak of *reflexive role-taking*.

While role-taking is a process of placing specific behaviors of the other in the context of his total role, the attention of the actor is never equally focused upon all the attitudes implied by that role. Rather, one's orientation determines that only certain attitudes of the other-role will be especially relevant to the determination of his own behavior. Role-taking in abstraction is importantly different from role-taking in a situation which calls for a determination of how the actor's role should be played, for the demands of the actor's role determine the selection of aspects of the other-role for emphasis. In one context one particular set of attitudes may be relevant to the determination of the actor's behavior; in another context the same set of attitudes may be irrelevant.

One of the most important distinctions which can be made among the kinds of other-attitudes is between those which are expectations or evaluations or images directed toward the self and those which are not. When the attention of the role-taker is focused upon the way in which he appears to the other, the role-taking is reflexive.

Reflexiveness is connected with what we popularly call "self-consciousness." When role-taking is reflexive, the individual is led not merely to consider the effects of his action or their compatibility with some standard or code but to picture himself specifically as an object of evaluation by someone else. An additional perspective is added to his conception of his own behavior.

The criteria of reflexiveness and standpoint placed in combination serve to delineate more sharply the different ways in which the self-other relationship can determine behavior. We shall examine role-taking from each of the three standpoints in order in its nonflexive and reflexive forms.

1. When the standpoint of the other-role is adopted, the other may serve as a model or standard which is accepted without self-consciousness either in the absence of alternative models or because of prestige or dependence in the relationship. Role-taking which is nonreflexive and identifying is probably the simplest and earliest form. The child's "playing-at" various roles shifts fairly imperceptibly into such role-taking in real-life situations. When confronted with situations like those in which he has seen a parent or older sibling enact a role, the child adopts as his own the attitudes of the role as he understands them. For example, a child of three or four who has been taught in a

---

[15] *Op. cit.,* pp. 136 ff.
[16] The identity between reflexive role-taking and Cooley's "looking glass self" should be evident (Charles Horton Cooley, *Human Nature and the Social Order* [New York: Charles Scribner's Sons, 1922], p. 184).

firm but kindly manner not to touch various objects will suddenly adopt as his own the entire role and standpoint of the parent when he finds himself in company with a younger and less responsible child. The behavior of the younger child calls up in the older the role which adults have taken toward him. Accordingly, he naïvely acts toward the younger child as he has learned to understand the role of the parent toward himself.

The same pattern of role-taking continues to be a major source of the values and attitudes of the individual. Whenever there is close attachment of one person to another, there is a tendency for the standpoint of the other to be adopted. Probably the attachment need not be positive in character. An attachment loaded with negative affect giving rise to intense rivalry leads each person to take the role of his rival and unwittingly adopt that rival's standpoint in many respects. Whenever prestige is accorded to someone, there is a tendency to take the role of the prestigeful person without disentangling that other's standpoint.

2. In contrast to this nonreflexive relationship a desire to conform to the other's expectations or to appear favorably in the other's eyes may shape the self-behavior into conformity with the other.

When role-taking involves identification and is reflexive, the self becomes specifically an object evaluated from the standpoint of the other. The attitudes of the other which are adopted as one's own are the attitudes toward one's self rather than toward external objects and values in the environment. At this stage a self-image is beginning to be formed, though it is not yet independent of the particular other whose role is being taken. From reflexive identifying role-taking the individual begins to develop an estimate of his own adequacy and worth. His own self-esteem is the adoption of the estimate of himself which he infers from the standpoint of the role of the other. The bonds of intimacy and prestige or the absence of alternative standpoints determine that the evaluations of relevant others will become the self-evaluations of the individual.

3. The distinction in self-consciousness is also important when the standpoint of a third party or norm is being adopted. Nonreflexive role-taking of this sort directs attention to attitudes in the role of the other whose recognition makes it possible to act according to a pre-existing directive. This pre-existing directive (incorporated in the third-party standpoint) may be of two sorts. It may, as already illustrated, make the appropriate self-behavior conditional upon the role of the other. Or it may direct the actor to employ the roles of certain others as standards or models to compare with his own behavior. The third-party standpoint enables the actor to react discriminatingly toward the aspirations and attitudes of others in determining which shall be used as standards for his own aspirations and attitudes.

4. When role-taking from a third-party standpoint is reflexive, the standpoint enables the actor to react selectively to his audiences. His concern is not merely how he compares with the other but how he appears to the other. But his appearance to the other does not direct his own behavior in an automatic manner as in the case of identification. Instead, he can accept the evaluations of certain others as legitimate and reject the evaluations and expectations of different others as lacking legitimacy.[17]

As the third-party standpoint becomes stabilized and generalized so as to become a fairly consistent standpoint in the individual, it operates in reflexive role-taking as a fully evolved self-conception or self-image. Such a self-conception permits the actor to react selectively on two bases. First, it may tell the subject whose approval is worth seeking and whose is not. The parent tries to teach his child, for example, to seek the respect of his teachers and the children from "good" homes, while disregarding the opinions that children "without breeding" have of him. Second, it may designate the type of image one wishes to see reflected in the other's conception of one's self. The individual may wish to appear to all as an honest man, as an independent person, or as a good fellow. The self-conception directs the in-

[17] "Legitimacy" in role-taking is discussed in Ralph H. Turner, "Self and Other in Moral Judgment," *American Sociological Review*, XIX (June, 1954), 254-55, 258.

dividual to behave in a manner which will evoke such an image of himself in the role of his audience. The two bases of selection may also operate together. Thus, the self-image (or third-party standpoint) may tell the actor that he should appear strong and distant to others in subordinate relations with himself, easy to get along with to others who are his peers and intimates, liked by others who are loyal citizens, and hated by others who are not loyal citizens.

5, 6. When role-taking occurs from the standpoint of interactive effect, it becomes reflexive when the reflected self-image is manipulated by the actor as a means of achieving his ends. The salesman who tries to create the impression that he would rather lose the sale than sell a person what he does not want, the propagandist attempting to appear "folksy," and the counselor responding nonevaluatively to his client are all trying to manipulate the image of themselves held by the other so as to foster their purposes. On the other hand, in baseball the role-taking is more concerned with the attitudes of the others toward the game than toward each other and is therefore nonreflexive. The difference between reflexive and nonreflexive role-taking of this sort appears in two levels of playing a game such as poker. Each player will attempt to judge what other players are likely to do. But the superior player will also attempt by such techniques as bluffing, conspicuous misplay, randomized strategies, or the "poker face" to establish a false image of himself which will modify the play of others in anticipated directions.

SIGNIFICANCE OF THE TYPES

The types we have suggested are important because each finds the actor in a somewhat different relationship to the relevant other whose role he is attempting to infer. The types also differ in the complexity of the process and in the kind of discretion they permit the actor in shaping his own behavior. Though they are analytically distinguishable, however, the types are not characteristically found in complete empirical separation. They are importantly interrelated in the behavior of any individual in

two ways: (a) hierarchically and (b) as alternative orientations to the other.

a) The fundamental source of social values appears to be the *standpoint of the other*. Accordingly, we may speak of role-taking which involves identification as being *derivative* with respect to the values of the individual. The person derives his values through adopting others' standpoints. In contrast, the other types of role-taking are implementive or validative with respect to values. They serve as means through which the values already acquired may be validated by reference to some standard or implemented in practice. Hence, these types are dependent upon role-taking with identification in two ways. They are dependent upon some prior role-taking as the source of values they express. And they are dependent upon prior learning of the skills of role-taking before the role-taking can be detached from adoption of the role standpoint.

Validation has to do with determining the personal relevance of values which one already accepts. One may adopt a value without making it a demand upon one's self. Or one may adopt a value with varying levels of aspiration regarding its achievement. Such validation—setting degrees of personal relevance and levels of aspiration—takes place in part through the simple laws of effect in learning theory and in part through role-taking. To the extent that it occurs through role-taking, it does so either via the reflexive attention to what others expect of the individual or through the comparison of the self with designated standards.

Part of the particular significance of reflexive role-taking lies in its validative function. When one adopts the other's standpoint in reflexive role-taking, he does more than simply adopt certain values; he adopts a definition of what is expected of him regarding that value. The child, for example, who identifies with the parent and adopts his attitudes toward others often does not see the personal relevance of these attitudes except in limited situations. The child is typically "hypocritical" and is distressed when the parent directs attention to his own behavior. At other times the child attempts to make every value a directive to his own behavior and must learn that what he admires in others is not necessarily required of himself.

The values derived in identification role-taking also point to certain groups or persons who serve as standards of comparison in performing the validation function. The individual takes the role of those to whom his attention is thus directed in order to judge what their attitudes are toward the values they profess, what their aspirations are, what effort they put forth, so that he may use these estimates comparatively in setting his own levels.

The *implementive function* of role-taking is carried out, as we have already described, either as demanded by a norm which makes the actor's behavior conditional upon the role of the relevant other or through the consideration of probable effects of the interaction of roles in promoting a given objective. Such implementation is dependent upon both the derivative and the validative functions. The individual must have both adopted values and formed some conception of their personal relevance before he proceeds to carry them out.

b) The hierarchical relationship among types of role-taking is important from the point of view of socialization or the genetic backgrounds of current attitudes. But, from the point of view of the act in process, the important relationship among types of role-taking lies in the fact that they are *alternative relationships* which the individual can establish to the role of the other which will make the effect of that other's attitudes quite different. In order to predict the behavior of a person, it is not sufficient to know that he will take the role of another or to know how accurately he will take that role. A small cue may change his relationship toward the perceived other-role. The high-pressure salesman who is exploiting the attitudes in the other-role to the full may suddenly begin to identify with the attitudes of that other and be rendered incapable of continuing his sales talk. Or an individual identifying with the role of another who is in misfortune may suddenly remember a social norm which leads him to detach himself and treat the other-role as an object.

The alternative relationships to the other-role may exist as recognized conflicts to the individual. The most frequently noted conflict between standpoints is between adopting the standpoint of the other and subjecting the role of the other to the scrutiny indicated by some norm. For example, a subject who inferred a set of attitudes in a friend which would account for his having committed a theft concluded that his obligation was to report the friend to the authorities. By adding that "he will probably hate me for it," he gave explicit recognition to the conflict.[18] Important also is the conflict between derivative and validative orientations, when the values adopted as part of a standpoint are not adequately supported in the indicated validating relationships. Conflicts also frequently exist between role-taking from the standpoint of interactive effect and the other types.

From the distinction among types of role-taking emerges a major theoretical problem for the study of role behavior. The problem is to isolate the variables which determine what kind of role-taking relationship the individual will assume with respect to any specific relevant other. We have already suggested that strong affect directed toward the other makes the more complex forms less likely to take place and that according prestige to the other has a similar effect. Another determinant is the degree to which the roles of different statuses receive normative sanction from the standpoint of a generalized other. For example, the tendency for a parent to identify with the role of his child when the latter has been hurt is reinforced by the fact that this is in keeping with the generalized standpoint in the society. Thus there is a more generalized imperative operating on the parent than the spontaneous identification arising out of affective involvement. There are also differences in the situational focus of attention which affect role-taking relationships.

[18] To conceptualize such a situation as merely a conflict between norms or roles would be an oversimplification. The third-party standpoint is experienced as a fully sanctioned norm conveying obligation. It is opposed by the discomfort of having to think of one's self in a bad light to the degree to which one identifies with the other-role. The latter does not carry a sense of obligation such as the former.

BOUNDARIES TO ROLE-TAKING

The coexistence of different relationships in role-taking leads us to the further question of whether the concept has been so broadened in application as to lose its analytic utility. If we say, as some writers have, that, whenever an individual experiences an attitude toward some object, he is taking the role of some relevant other toward that object, then every action has been made into role-taking. On the other hand, if we limit role-taking to instances in which the subject recognizes and can conceptualize what he is doing, we make a dividing line which is indefensible in light of modern psychological understanding. The criterion of consciousness, then, is too narrow and the criterion of attitude source is too broad.

The key to a useful delimitation of the term becomes clear when we distinguish between a genetic or socialization framework in which we look into past experiences for the explanation of present behavior and an action framework in which we examine the dynamic interrelations among the elements contemporarily operating to determine action. The concept of role-taking belongs in the latter framework, designating a kind of relationship which may be contemporarily assumed toward a relevant other in the context of an act in process. Within the action framework we may say that a person is engaged in role-taking whenever the individual's conception or performance of his own role is altered by modifying his construction of the other-role.[19]

Even though we may suppose that all attitudes originate in some role-taking, the self-role can become autonomous; that is, it can become independent of the role-taking relationship which originally gave rise to it. Under the latter circumstance the self-role becomes stabilized so that the role-taking process is omitted or role-taking ceases to modify the self-role. One form of this autonomy is indicated when a person is said to have interiorized a social norm, meaning that an earlier process of role-taking has become truncated. The self-role may then persist unchanged even if the perceived attitudes of the relevant other change or if the affective relationship between self and other change.

A NOTE ON EMPATHY

Of the many senses in which *empathy* has been used, five can be particularly related to our current discussion. (1) By most traditional usage empathy refers to nonreflexive identifying role-taking, in which the individual unwittingly puts himself in the position of another and adopts his standpoint. (2) Sometimes empathy is presented as an ability that is desirable in personnel relations, in which case it designates the ability to understand the role of another while retaining one's personal detachment. According to this usage, empathy includes all role-taking except that in which the standpoint of the other is adopted as one's own. (3) Empathy is sometimes used to designate the process of seeing one's self as others see one, the ability to react to one's own behavior as others are reacting to it. This usage makes empathy identical with reflexive role-taking, regardless of standpoint. (4) Empathic capacity is sometimes used synonymously with role-taking capacity, to include all the forms of the process we have described. (5) When empathy is distinguished from projection, it refers to one criterion for inferring the other-role. In this usage all our types would be included so long as the role-taking is not based upon projection.

To make a choice among these usages by fiat would be an empty gesture. However, there are at least three implications of our present discussion for the current work dealing with empathy. First, the *tendency* to empathize, in whatever sense this is meant, is at least as important a variable as the *ability* to empathize. Under what circumstances will a person employ such empathic abilities as he has rather than merely enact a rigidly predetermined role or react to the other's gestures with standardized responses? Second, given the tendency and

[19] Merton and Kitt point out that "individuals *unwittingly* respond to different frames of reference introduced by the experimenter" (Robert K. Merton and Alice Kitt, "Contributions to the Theory of Reference Group Behavior," in *Continuities in Social Research*, ed. Robert K. Merton and Paul F. Lazarsfeld [Glencoe, Ill.: Free Press, 1950], p. 69).

ability to empathize (using the term in its broader senses), what relationship to the inferred other-role will determine its effect on the individual's behavior? The tendency and ability in role-taking must be seen in combination with the tendency to assume certain kinds of relations with relevant others. Third, the standpoint in role-taking operates to focus attention selectively on the role being taken. Consequently, certain aspects of the other-role are seen more clearly or are more salient than others, depending upon the standpoint governing the emphatic process. Since empathy or role-taking is not normally performed in a vacuum, the accuracy of empathic behavior will vary according to the focus of attention supplied by the governing standpoint. Consideration of empathic ability might profit from taking this observation into account. A quite tentative suggestion from one study of empathic ability that empathy is more accurate with respect to reflexive than nonreflexive aspects of the other-role may tell something about the focus of attention in the role-taking process within a clinical counseling situation.[20]

REFERENCE-GROUP BEHAVIOR

Two commentaries have recently pointed out different usages of the term "reference group."[21] Both have noted that a reference group may mean a group with which one compares himself in making a self-judgment. This usage prevails in the original work of Hyman and the more recent discussion by Merton and Kitt.[22] Both commentaries have also noted an alternative usage of reference group to mean the source of an individual's values (Kelley) or per-

spectives (Shibutani). Sherif, Newcomb, and Hartley have employed the concept chiefly in this sense.[23] A third usage suggested by Shibutani refers to a group whose acceptance one seeks. In the literature, however, the desire to be accepted is depicted as the mechanism which leads to the adoption of the values and perspectives of the reference group.[24] These are not, therefore, separate usages of the term but merely definitions, on the one hand, in terms of the effect of the reference group and, on the other hand, in terms of the mechanism of the reference group.

When a reference group is the source of values and perspectives, the identity of meaning with role-taking is apparent. One takes the role of a member of the group, which is synonymous with having "a psychologically functioning membership"[25] in the group, and one adopts the group's standpoint as one's own. Thus, except for emphasizing that the source of values need not be a group of which the individual is objectively a member, this use of reference group corresponds to one traditional usage of role-taking.

Reference group as a point of comparison corresponds partially to certain meanings of role-taking. The self-other relationship is essentially that which we have described as role-taking from a third-party standpoint. Merton and Kitt note the operation of a third-party standpoint in "the institutional definitions of the social structure which may focus the attention of members of a group or occupants of a so-

[20] Thomas G. Macfarlane, "Empathic Understanding in an Interpersonal Interview Situation" (unpublished Ph.D. dissertation, Department of Psychology, University of California, Los Angeles, 1952), pp. 115–16.

[21] Harold H. Kelley, "Two Functions of Reference Groups," in Readings in Social Psychology, ed. Guy E. Swanson, Theodore M. Newcomb, and Eugene L. Hartley (New York: Henry Holt & Co., 1952), pp. 410–14; Tamotsu Shibutani, "Reference Groups as Perspectives," American Journal of Sociology, LX (May, 1955), 562–69.

[22] Herbert Hyman, "The Psychology of Status," Archives of Psychology, No. 269, June, 1942; Merton and Kitt, op. cit.

[23] Muzafer Sherif, An Outline of Social Psychology (New York: Harper & Bros., 1948), pp. 105–6, 123, et passim; Sherif, "The Concept of Reference Groups in Human Relations," in Group Relations at the Crossroads, ed. Muzafer Sherif and M. O. Wilson (New York: Harper & Bros., 1953), pp. 203–31; Newcomb, op. cit., pp. 220–32; Eugene Hartley, "Psychological Problems of Multiple Group Membership," in Social Psychology at the Crossroads, ed. John H. Rohrer and Muzafer Sherif (New York: Harper & Bros., 1951), pp. 371–86.

[24] "A fraternity or sorority to which you hope some day to belong is a reference group for you if your attitudes are in any way influenced by what you take to be its norms" (Newcomb, op. cit., p. 226).

[25] Newcomb, "Social Psychological Theory," in Social Psychology at the Crossroads, ed. Rohrer and Sherif, p. 48.

cial status upon certain *common* reference groups."[26] However, the actor may or may not take the role of a member of the reference group. So long as the actor is using the reference group only as a point of comparison in estimating his own social standing or in deciding whether to be satisfied or dissatisfied with his lot, external attributes of the other alone are involved. The role of the relevant other is not being taken. But when levels of aspiration, degrees of determination, and the like are being compared, the individual must necessarily take the role of the other in order to make a comparison.

In the preceding sense reference group as a point of comparison is a broader concept than role-taking from a third-party standpoint. However, in our discussion of role-taking we recognized that the standpoint of the third party might direct attention to the relevant other in more ways than simple comparison. Comparable relations of individual to group appear not to have been included in reference-group usages.

Dispute over the proper meaning of "reference group" seems to center about the acceptable generality of the concept. The limited usage which Sherif and Shibutani prefer, referring to the source of the individual's major perspectives and values, might well be named the *identification group.* The identification group is the source of values, since the individual takes the role of a member while adopting the member's standpoint as his own.

At the opposite extreme the individual's behavior is affected somewhat by groups whose members constitute merely conditions to his action. The groups are neutrally toned to the actor; he must merely take them into account in order to accomplish his purposes. The manner in which he takes them into account may or may not require role-taking, and they may or may not constitute his membership group. Such a group might well be designated by some such neutral term as *interaction group.*

In between are those groups which acquire value to the individual because the standpoint of his identification groups designates them as points of reference. Con-

forming to the standpoint of his identification group (or of an autonomous self-image which has become stabilized independently of the identification group from which it was derived), the individual compares himself with certain groups or notes the impression he is making on them or in some other way takes account of them. Again, whether this relationship does or does not involve role-taking will depend upon the directive supplied by the identification group or self-conception. These groups might be called *valuation groups,* since their effect upon the individual's behavior is determined by the valuation which his more basic orientations lead him to place upon them.

Finally, if reference-group theory is to encompass the ways in which individual-group relationships shape the roles and role behaviors of the individual, we should note a dichotomy cross-cutting the preceding distinctions. Certain reference groups within each of the preceding types might usefully be regarded as *audience groups* to the individual. These are the groups by whom the actor sees his role performance observed and evaluated, and he attends to the evaluations and expectations which members of the group hold toward him. The actor takes the role of his audience reflexively. An individual's relations with his identification groups may place the latter on some occasions as his audience and on other occasions not. The reaction to the audience may be that of uncritical acceptance of their evaluations and expectations toward him, or the responses of his audience may be interpreted in an interactive context or as directed by his identification group or self-conception.

In general, then, it appears that the concepts of reference group and role-taking are closely related. In the broadest sense reference-group behavior is somewhat more inclusive than role-taking, since one may take account of a reference group without taking the role of a member. The terms "reference group" and "relevant other" refer to essentially the same phenomena. The reference group is a *generalized other* which is viewed as possessing member roles and attributes independently of the specific individuals who compose it. The same general differentiations seem applicable on the bases of standpoint and reflexiveness (audience).

Likewise, the same theoretical problems apply, and a similar principle regarding the boundaries of the concepts seems applicable.

The Structure of Personal Identity /
Tamotsu Shibutani (*University of California, Santa Barbara*)

Among the *Exemplary Novels* of Miguel de Cervantes is a fascinating tale of a man, temporarily deranged, who believed that he was made of glass. Whenever people approached him, he screamed and implored them to keep their distance lest they shatter him. He always walked in the middle of the street, glancing apprehensively at the rooftops for loose tiles that might fall upon him. On one occasion, when a wasp stung him on the neck, he did not dare strike it nor shake it off for fear of breaking himself. He refused to eat anything as hard as meat or fish and insisted upon sleeping only in beds of straw. Since glass is not only thinner than the skin but also transparent, he claimed that the peculiar construction of his body enabled his soul to see things more clearly, and he offered to assist those facing perplexing problems. Before long he became famous for his astonishingly astute observations. People followed him everywhere, seeking his advice. Whenever mischievous boys threw stones at him, he cried so loudly and desperately that adults came running to his assistance, and finally a wealthy patron hired a bodyguard to follow him about and to protect him against hoodlums.

Not many people outside of mental hospitals believe that they are made of glass, but there are persons who regard themselves as being somewhat fragile. Those who believe that they are unusually susceptible to colds, heat rashes, blisters, or freckles go out of their way to avoid exposure. Those who believe that their angelic children might become contaminated by contact with the filthy urchins who live in poorer neighborhoods take special care to see that their youngsters play exclusively with others of their own kind. All this suggests that much of what men do voluntarily depends upon what they conceive of themselves to be; Cervantes was merely pointing to an exaggerated instance of a common process.

It has already been noted that acts are inhibited or facilitated on the basis of self-images. Self-images vary from situation to situation, but each man also has a stable sense of personal identity. What he is willing or unwilling to do depends upon the kind of human being he thinks he is. Most persons, if lost and hungry in a strange city, would balk at searching garbage cans for food; they would rather remain hungry than do something that they regard as being beneath their dignity. A man who considers himself "no good," however, will certainly not resist temptations with the same determination as someone who is convinced that he is a decent person. An adequate theory of motivation, then, requires getting at the manner in which a man identifies himself.[1]

PERSONAL IDENTITY AND SOCIAL STATUS

Self-images are specific and differ from one context to another; one visualizes himself as playing a game, talking to his friends, reciting in a classroom, or whatever else he may be doing. In spite of the variety of things that one does he experiences all of these deeds as being performed by the same person. Even though self-images are constantly changing and never twice exactly the same, one has no difficulty in recognizing himself. Each can identify himself as a par-

Reprinted from *Society and Personality* by Tamotsu Shibutani, 1961, pages 213–221, by permission of Prentice-Hall, Inc., Englewood Cliffs, N.J.

[1] Cf. Nelson N. Foote, "Identification as the Basis for a Theory of Motivation," *American Sociological Review,* XVI (1951), 14–21.

ticular human being, characterized by a distinctive set of attributes; he regards himself as an individual of a unique sort. Each person, then, has a relatively stable *self-conception*. He knows that there are other people somewhat like him, especially if he thinks of himself as being "just average," but he also assumes that there is no one else who is exactly like him—who looks and acts the same, and has the same background. In our society it is taken for granted that there never has been anyone else like him in the past, and never will be in the future.

Very few people ever have occasion to ask themselves who they are. Each takes his personal identity so much for granted that he does not realize the extent to which his life is structured by the working conception he forms of himself. The things that a man does voluntarily, and in some cases even involuntarily, depend upon the assumptions he makes about the kind of person he is and about the way in which he fits into the scheme of things in his world. This becomes apparent under unusual circumstances—in an odd dream, in amnesia, or in temporary dissociation under hypnosis—when once familiar behavior patterns appear strange, incongruent, and out of place. A man is able to act with reasonable consistency in a wide variety of situations because of the relative stability of his self-conception.

Thus, flexible coordination rests upon the capacity of men to form self-images, and considerable regularity is introduced into the life of each person by virtue of a stable self-conception. Some psychologists have been reluctant to study these phenomena, frequently on the ground that they are too elusive to be examined objectively. To be sure, the study of what a person experiences as himself is difficult, but it is paradoxical that these scholars in their capacity as investigators should ignore such phenomena, when in their daily lives they are never so foolish. If a psychologist were confronted by a powerful drunk who insisted that he could "lick anybody in the house," he probably would not challenge the contention by claiming that self-images cannot be measured with precision. Should he go home and find his wife in the arms of a strange man

who insisted he was her husband, it is unlikely that he would shrug his shoulders and say that personal identity has never been demonstrated to be important. Many of the difficulties in the study of these phenomena begin when a search is made for some physical object located somewhere in the body, when the concepts of self-image and self-conception both refer to complex forms of *behavior*. Each person can imagine what he has done, what he is doing, what he is able to do, or what he proposes to do and can respond to his own imagination. These concepts refer, then, not to some part of the human body but to uniformities in behavior.

Even casual observation reveals that all human beings, with the possible exception of infants and some patients in psychotic wards, have some kind of working orientation toward themselves. The personal world of every individual is centered around himself. In making judgments and decisions, in speaking of space and time, he uses himself as the central point of reference. This is true not only of egotistical persons, but of everyone, even the most considerate and unselfish. Each is able to recognize his own aspirations, disappointments, and fears, and can differentiate between these and similar experiences on the part of other people. Strictly speaking, a person can only experience his own sensations, but there is a bipolarization of this experience into what is acknowledged as one's own and what is imputed to the outside world. In spite of the complexity of the processes involved, most adults have little difficulty in making this distinction, although from time to time one may become a bit confused.

Each person regards himself as a separate entity, and this belief is reinforced by the fact that the human body can readily be set off as an organic unit. Actually, the boundaries of the organism are not as clearly demarcated as we believe. Is the air in our lungs or the food in our digestive tract a part of us or merely passing through? Physiologists contend that virtually every cell in a human body is replaced within ten years or less. The relationship between any living organism and its environment is one of continual interaction. But the fact that men regard themselves as independent entities greatly facilitates organized social life. Concerted action is possible because each participant is able to control himself. Self-control involves the formation of a perceptual object of oneself and imputing to this object certain responsibilities. This entire procedure is greatly facilitated when men conceive of themselves as separate, independent entities. The fact that bodies are separate units, even if the boundaries are blurred, makes the isolation and pinpointing of responsibilities possible.

A man's sense of identity also arises from the continuity of his experiences in time. There are memories of the past that cannot be escaped, and there are reasonable aspirations for the future. Secret inner thoughts enjoy continuity along with those which are shared. The consistency of all such experiences enables each person to integrate them into a unit, a whole which is also treated as a distinct entity by other people. This sense of continuity is broken only under very unusual circumstances; in most cases it is cut off only with death.

The feeling of being a distinct object also arises from one's sense of personal autonomy. Each person believes that he is able to exercise some measure of control over his own destiny. He is capable of making decisions and of selecting among alternative lines of action. It is this widespread belief that provides the basis for the philosophical doctrine of "free will" and for the concept of moral responsibility. Since men are assumed to be capable of making choices, they are held accountable for their deeds. It should be noted, however, that they usually refuse to accept responsibility for conduct which occurred while they were "not themselves"—such as what they did under the influence of alcohol or drugs, in a condition of severe strain or shock, in a hypnotic trance, or in the power of some "evil spirit." The argument is that it would be unfair for anyone to be blamed for acts over which he did not have full control. This suggests that the limits of a man's conception of himself are often set by the area over which he feels he can exercise control.[2]

Self-conceptions are reinforced by recurrent social relationships. By virtue of who he is, one is related to each person he knows and to various categories of people in understood ways. A woman expects her husband to treat her with special consideration and occasionally to make intimate disclosures to her, but she would be disturbed if he granted similar privileges to other women. Imagine how shaken anyone would be if he were to enter his home only to find his parents staring blankly at him as if he were a complete stranger. In a series of experiments on inducing dissociation of personality through hypnosis, Harriman found it necessary to tell his subjects that the hypnotist was a "man who lives down the street" to account for his presence in the room. Whenever a subject successfully transformed his identity, he was no longer able to define his relationship to the experimenter and became puzzled.[3] It is through being recognized as a particular human being that each individual gains status within a community.

In all communities there is some kind of differentiation of the participants into ranks. Although the concept of *social status* has been utilized in a variety of ways, it may be used here to refer to a person's standing in a community, identifiable in terms of the rights, duties, privileges, and immunities that he enjoys by virtue of his position.[4] Status is a social process; one can have status only in relation to others who recognize his place and approach him in an understood way. Status, no matter how lowly, is important, for without it one becomes an outsider without claims upon anyone. For example, custodians are often held in low esteem in American communities, but when they are in the buildings in their charge they can expel intruders and can get the police to enforce their prerogatives. Having status, then, enables a person to anticipate the manner in which he will be treated.

Even in democratic communities, human beings are ordered into positions of relative superiority and inferiority. There are many criteria for evaluation, such as occupation of

[2] Cf. Thomas D. Eliot, "The Use of Psychoanalytic Classification in Analysis of Social Behavior: Identification," *Journal of Abnormal and Social Psychology*, XXII (1927), 67–81.

[3] Harriman, *op. cit.*, p. 640.
[4] Cf. Max Weber, *Essays in Sociology*, Hans H. Gerth and C. Wright Mills, trans. (New York: Oxford University Press, 1946), pp. 186–94.

the head of the household, size of income, lineage and ethnic identity, or level of intellectual attainment. In the United States, people are placed largely in terms of vocation and income; other criteria prevail elsewhere. Since such positions are placed in a rough hierarchy, each can be identified in terms of the prestige and influence the incumbents enjoy as well as the deference with which they are addressed. It should be noted that a person is often approached in a given manner by virtue of the position he occupies, quite apart from his personal qualities; many Army officers are addressed with respect even by enlisted men who look upon them in contempt. One's standing in a community, then, is largely a matter of accepted social usuage.

Some systems of social differentiation are stable, but in the modern world many are undergoing change. In relatively stable communities, status is not only clearly defined but can be acquired only through inheritance or through well-established sequences of training and achievement. One cannot become a warrior simply by picking up a spear. Furthermore, characteristic patterns of conduct that are expected of incumbents are also clearly defined. Warriors are expected to display courage, and those who desire such status must learn to inhibit their impulses to flee in the face of danger. A singer aspiring to become a prima donna must undergo incredibly strenuous training; should she succeed, she is expected to be temperamental and to comport herself in regal fashion. Doctors undergo a prescribed program of training, pass standardized examinations, and fall into already delineated specialties; once established, they must observe a code of professional ethics and are expected to behave in a dignified manner. Somewhat more flexible career lines can be found for those who desire to become writers, professional athletes, senators, or racketeers. In a changing society there is less consensus over the rights and duties of those in various positions, and the avenues of advancement are not so clearly marked.[5]

The concept of social status, which refers to a person's standing in a community, is not to be confused with the concept of conventional role, which refers to a participant's contribution to an organized enterprise.[6] Status, once it is established, remains relatively constant; it can be enhanced, but slowly, and lowered only through degrading performances. But each man in the course of a single day plays many different roles. To be sure, there are a limited set of interrelated roles played only by those who occupy a given position. For example, a man who is practicing medicine in an American city plays fairly well-defined roles in a number of standardized transactions—examining patients, giving instructions to nurses, consulting with colleagues, checking reports with laboratory technicians, urging hospital administrators to purchase new equipment, or referring patients to other doctors. Outside of these established contexts the expectations become less clear; indeed, the further he moves from situations involving medical care, the less clear his obligations become. But a doctor, by virtue of the high estimate placed upon his services to a community, enjoys considerable prestige; even when he is at an informal gathering he is expected to maintain the general demeanor considered proper for professional men. The role a person is called upon to play and the manner in which he is expected to perform may rest in part upon his status, but these concepts refer to different aspects of human behavior.

Personal identification is the basis of organized social life, for it is only when a person can be identified and placed in his niche that his responsibilities can be fixed. Whenever strangers meet, the first thing that they do is to ascertain one another's identity and status. This is essential, for there is no other way of knowing what to anticipate. Personal identity, then, constitutes one's only tie with the rest of society; each person has status in a community only in so far as he can identify himself as a specific human being who belongs in a particular place.

[5] Cf. Everett C. Hughes, *Men and Their Work* (Glencoe: Free Press, 1958), pp. 102–15. Typical difficulties faced by people in such situations will be discussed in Chapter XVII.

[6] Cf. Albert Pierce, "On the Concepts of Role and Status," *Sociologus*, VI (1956), 29–34; and Robert K. Merton, *Social Theory and Social Structure* (Glencoe: Free Press, 1957), pp. 368–84.

Furthermore, by virtue of his identity each person is also related in understood ways to various physical objects. This is what is meant by property. There is no necessary physical or biological connection between a man and the various things he owns. He can destroy or give away his belongings only because conventional norms permit owners relative freedom of action concerning their chattel. But a man can exercise his property rights only when he can identify himself as a specific human being. If men were not able to identify themselves and one another with consistency, our entire social and economic system would be in jeopardy.

The crucial importance of personal identity is demonstrated by an unusual form of dissociation popularly called amnesia. There are apparently many forms of amnesia, but the cases that attract attention are those in which a person finds himself walking about in a daze and approaches a police officer to report that he has forgotten who he is. There is a loss of memory, but in most instances the victims have not forgotten everything. They are usually able to perform a number of complex tasks, such as feeding and dressing themselves and speaking with conventional linguistic symbols to psychiatrists. Furthermore, those who approach police officers presumably remember that it is the duty of men in such uniforms to aid those in distress. There is a selective forgetting in which the victim is unable to recall only those items that would disclose his identity—his name, his place of residence, his place of employment, and his friends.[7] A person suffering from amnesia is a stranger. Since he has no ties with anyone, he has no claims on anyone other than those of any human being. He has no home to which to return, no firm in which he can count on steady employment, no one with whom he can relax; his life does not fit into any organized routine, for without personal identity there is no community in which he has definite status.

Because each man can conceive of himself in a consistent manner he can locate himself within the patterned activities of the groups in which he participates. As others respond to him in the manner that he regards as appropriate, this reinforces his sense of identity and enables him to continue to meet his obligations as he sees them. Concerted action then takes on a routine character, even when made up of voluntary contributions.

[7] Cf. Milton Abeles and Paul Schilder, "Psychogenic Loss of Personal Identity: Amnesia," *Archives of Neurology and Psychiatry,* XXXIV (1935), 587–604; and L. F. Beck, "Hypnotic Identification of an Amnesia Victim," *British Journal of Medical Psychology,* XVI (1937), 36–42. An account of some of the problems confronting a man who does not know who he is can be found in Sheperd I. Franz, *Persons One and Three* (New York: McGraw-Hill Book Co., 1933).

E. Via the Concept of Attitude

What the concept of habit was to early psychology, the concept of attitude was to social psychology: It provided one of the basic units of the field. Originating historically in a concern with psychological sets, motor sets, or readinesses to action, the concept of attitude slowly shifted its meaning until presently there is general agreement that "attitude" is a concept having at least cognitive and affective (evaluative) components. That is, an attitude involves the individual's positive or negative evaluation of some object of reference. Whether the concept of attitude so defined additionally has the motivational or dispositional properties it had historically, leading its holder to act in a particular manner, is still open to some dispute.

The entire area of attitude measurement, attitude formation, and attitude change has occupied a fantastic degree of time and effort on the part of social psychologists. The entire survey research movement and much of the applied end of the field have been concerned with assessing, forming, or changing attitudes. Public opinion, propaganda, and education all involve to varying degrees the concept of attitude. It would not be too far from the truth to state that to date some of the major contributions of social psychology

have involved research and theory in this area of attitudes and opinions.

There is an increasing trend today towards treating attitudes within the framework of general cognitive theory, postulating that the mechanisms of attitude formation and change are the same as the more general processes of cognitive development and reorganization. Thus it is that many of the readings included in this section are framed within this cognitive orientation. The Osgood and Tannenbaum principle of congruity provides an excellent example of a general cognitive theory and method of measurement applied to the study of attitudes. Building upon a principle which in many respects is similar to Festinger's theory of cognitive dissonance, the Rosenberg selection presents a theory of attitude dynamics which deals with the motivating properties stemming from an inconsistency created between the cognitive and the affective component of an attitude.

Framing his theory of attitude formation and change within the context of social influence, the Kelman selection presents three basic processes involved in adopting and expressing particular opinions. These are three intervening mechanisms which when taken into consideration permit a fuller understanding of the nature of the attitude or opinion change achieved, its endurance through time, and the degree of predictability of the individual's subsequent behavior given information about his attitude or opinion. As Kelman further differentiates these three mechanisms, he discusses the psychological processes that result in a basic attitudinal change at the level of the individual's personality as distinct from a more public level of change. The Katz, Sarnoff, and McClintock selection pursues this level further as they relate the process of attitude change to changes in the individual's personality dynamics. That attitude formation and change may not be a unitary process subject to a single principle of operation is an underlying theme expressed in these readings.

Given the years of social psychological study of attitudes, both in stringently controlled laboratories and in less well controlled field settings, there exists vast amounts of comparative data presumably dealing with the same attitudinal variables in these two settings. The lack of comparability of the experimental and field findings however, provides a significant problem for the social psychologist interested in understanding the basic processes involved in attitude formation and change. The Hovland article discusses these conflicting findings and offers reasonable explanations for such differences. Above all, it suggests the methodological necessity of utilizing laboratory and field studies in a complementary manner in order to arrive at conclusions which may be expanded into more general laws or principles.

The Principle of Congruity in the Prediction of Attitude Change /
Charles E. Osgood and Percy H. Tannenbaum
(*Institute of Communications Research, University of Illinois*)

The theoretical model presented in this paper, while not pretending to take account of all variables relating to attitude change, does attempt to cover those variables believed to be most significant with respect to the direction of change to be expected in any given situation. These variables are (*a*) existing attitude toward the source of a message, (*b*) existing attitude toward the concept evaluated by the source, and (*c*) the nature of the evaluating assertion which relates source and concept in the message. Predictions generated by the theory about the directions and relative amounts of attitude change apply to both sources and the concepts they evaluate.

UNDERLYING NOTIONS

Our work on attitude theory and measurement is an outgrowth of continuing research on experimental semantics, particularly the development of objective methods for measuring meaning (4, 5). From this viewpoint, the *meaning* of a concept is its location in a space defined by some number of factors or dimensions, and *attitude* toward a concept is its projection onto one of these dimensions defined as "evaluative." In the factor analytic work we have done so far, the first and most heavily loaded factor is always one clearly identifiable as evaluative by the labels of the scales it represents, e.g., good-bad, fair-unfair, valuable-worthless, pleasant-unpleasant, and the like. This conception of attitude as a dimension or factor in total meaning has a number of implications, including those explored in the present paper. It implies, for example, that people having the same attitude toward a concept, such as NEGRO, may be sharply differentiated in terms of other dimensions of the semantic space (e.g., some perceiving NEGRO as powerful and active, others as weak and passive).[1]

Reprinted from *Psychological Review*, 1955, 62, pages 42–55, by permission of the senior author and the publisher, The American Psychological Association.

[1] A study in progress exhibits precisely this phenomenon with respect to the concept NEGRO. Similar findings are evident with respect to THE CHURCH and CAPITAL PUNISHMENT.

Attitudes toward the various objects of judgment associated in messages must be measured in the same units if comparative statements about attitude change are to be made. There have been attempts to devise *generalized attitude scales* in the history of this field (cf. 6, 7), but if one is to judge by the criterion of acceptance and use, they have not been outstandingly successful. In applying the *semantic differential* (a label that has come to be applied to our measuring instrument), various objects of judgment, sources and concepts, are rated against a standard set of descriptive scales. To the extent that location on the evaluative dimension of the semantic differential is a reliable and valid index of attitude (as determined by correlation with other criteria), it is then necessarily a generalized attitude scale. We have some evidence for validity[2] and more is being obtained; reliability of the differential, particularly the evaluative dimension, is reasonably high, running in the .80's and .90's in available data.

Another underlying notion about human thinking we have been exploring is that *judgmental frames of reference tend toward maximal simplicity*. Since extreme, "all-or-nothing" judgments are simpler than finely discriminated judgments of degree, this implies a continuing pressure toward polarization along the evaluative dimension (i.e., movement of concepts toward either entirely good or entirely bad allocations). We have evidence that extreme judgments have shorter latencies than more discriminative judgments (5), and that extreme judgments are charatceristic of less intelligent, less mature, less well educated, or more emotionally oriented individuals (8). Furthermore, since assumption of identity is a simpler process than maintenance of distinction, this also implies a continuing pressure toward elimination of differences among concepts which are localized in the same direction of the evaluative framework. We have evidence that in the judging of emotionally polarized concepts all scales of judgment tend to rotate toward

the evaluative, e.g., their correlations with good-bad tend to increase and therefore the relative loading on the evaluative factor tends to increase (5).

The most "simple-minded" evaluative frame of reference is therefore one in which a tight cluster of highly polarized and undifferentiated good concepts is diametrically opposed in meaning to an equally tight and polarized cluster of undifferentiated bad concepts. The same underlying pressure toward simplicity operates on any new or neutral concept to shift it one way or the other. For example, there is the tendency in American thinking, about which Pandit Nehru complains, requiring that India be either "for us or agin' us." This is, of course, the condition referred to by the general semanticists (e.g., Johnson, 2) as a "two-valued orientation," and it is unfortunately characteristic of lay thinking in any period of conflict and emotional stress. The more sophisticated thinker, according to this view, should show less tendency to polarize, more differentiation among concepts, and thus greater relative use of factors other than the evaluative.

THE PRINCIPLE OF CONGRUITY

The principle of congruity in human thinking can be stated quite succinctly: *changes in evaluation are always in the direction of increased congruity with the existing frame of reference*. To make any use of this principle in specific situations, however, it is necessary to elaborate along the following lines: When does the issue of congruity arise? What directions of attitude change are congruent? How much stress is generated by incongruity and how is it distributed among the objects of judgment?

The issue of congruity. Each individual has potential attitudes toward a near infinity of objects. It is possible to have varying attitudes toward diverse concepts without any felt incongruity or any pressure toward attitude change, as long as no association among these objects of judgment is made. As anthropologists well know, members of a culture may entertain logically incompatible attitudes toward objects in their culture (e.g., ancestor worship and fear of the dead) with-

[2] For example, the correlations between scores on the evaluative scales of the semantic differential and scores on the Thurstone scales on attitude toward THE CHURCH, NEGRO and CAPITAL PUNISHMENT are .74, .82, and .81, respectively.

out any stress, as long as the incompatibles are not brought into association. The issue of congruity arises whenever a message is received which relates two or more objects of judgment via an assertion.

The simplest assertion is merely a *descriptive statement:* "Chinese cooking is good," "Jefferson was right," "This neurotic modern art." To the extent that the evaluative location of a particular qualifier differs from that of the thing qualified, there is generated some pressure toward congruity. Similar pressure is generated by ordinary *statements of classification:* "Senator McCarthy is a Catholic," "Tom is an ex-con," "Cigarettes contain nicotine." To the extent that the evaluative locations of instance and class are different, some pressure toward congruity exists. A more complex situation is that in which *a source makes an assertion about a concept:* "University President Bans Research on Krebiozen"; "Communists like strong labor unions." This is the most commonly studied situation, and one for which we have some empirical data against which to test our hypotheses. Assertions may be explicit linguistic statements of evaluation or implicit behavioral, situational statements. A newsphoto of Mrs. Roosevelt smiling and shaking hands with a little colored boy is just as effective in setting up pressures toward congruity as a verbal statement on her part.

Directions of congruence and incongruence. To predict the direction of attitude change fom this general principle it is necessary to take into account simultaneously the existing attitudes toward each of the objects of judgment prior to reception of the message and the nature of the assertion which is embodied in the message. Attitudes can be specified as favorable $(+)$, neutral (0), and unfavorable $(-)$. Assertions can be specified as positive or associative $(+)$ or negative or disassociative $(-)$. They may also, of course, include evaluative loading (e.g., when X denounces Y, we have both a disassociative assertion and negative evaluation of Y). When attitudes toward both objects of judgment are polar, the nature of the assertion determines congruence or incongruence. For EISENHOWER $(+)$ to come out in favor of FREEDOM OF THE PRESS $(+)$ is, of course, congruent with the existing frame of reference of most

people in this country, but for THE DAILY WORKER $(-)$ to speak in favor of FREEDOM OF THE PRESS $(+)$ is attitudinally incongruent. In this simplest of states in which human thinking operates, sources we like should always sponsor ideas we like and denounce ideas we are against, and vice versa.

When the existing attitude toward one of the objects of judgment is neutral and the other polar, we must speak of what directions *would be* congruent. If, for example, a favorable source like EISENHOWER were to make a favorable assertion about the MINISTER FROM SIAM (a neutral notion to most of us), it would be congruent *if* the latter were also favorable—hence pressure is generated toward attitude change in this direction. If PRAVDA $(-)$ sponsors GRADUAL DISARMAMENT (0), the pressure is such as to make the relatively neutral notion of disarmament less favorable; similarly, if a PROFESSOR (0) as a source favors PREMARITAL SEXUAL RELATIONS $(-)$ as making for better marriages, it is the PROFESSOR that becomes less favorable (this is not unlike the "guilt by association" technique). Conversely, for our neutral PROFESSOR (0) to speak out against MORAL DEPRAVITY $(-)$ must have the effect of raising his esteem (this is the familiar "I am against sin" technique).

When both objects of judgment are neutral, there is no question of congruity between them, and movement is determined solely by the nature of the assertion, i.e., this becomes a case of simple qualification or classification. If MR. JONES denounces MR. SMITH, neither of whom is known, there is presumably some negative pressure on MR. SMITH by virtue of the sheer devaluation of "being denounced." Since the evaluation applies to the concept and not the source, the effect should be chiefly upon the concept. We shall find evidence for such an "assertion effect" in the available data.

We may now make a general statement governing the direction of congruence which will hold for any object of judgment, source or concept, and any type of assertion.

1. *Whenever one object of judgment is associated with another by an assertion, its congruent position along the evaluative dimension is always equal in degree of polari-*

zation (d) *to the other object of judgment and in either the same (positive assertion) or opposite (negative assertion) evaluative direction.*

This is to say that we have attitude scores toward two objects of judgment, OJ_1 and OJ_2, and to each of these scores we assign a value, d, which represents the degree of polarization of that attitude. Thus we have d_{OJ_1} and d_{OJ_2}. Since the measuring instrument which has been used in our quantitative work so far (the semantic differential) treats the evaluative dimension as a 7-step scale with "4" defined as the neutral point, we have three degrees of polarization in each direction, i.e., $+3, +2, +1, 0, -1, -2, -3$. Given OJ_1 and OJ_2 associated with one another through either a positive $(OJ_1A^+OJ_2)$ or negative $(OJ_1A^-OJ_2)$ assertion, we define the congruent position (C) of either object of judgment as follows:

If $OJ_1A^+OJ_2$, then

$$dc_{OJ_1} = d_{OJ_2}, \qquad [1]$$

$$dc_{OJ_2} = d_{OJ_1}, \qquad [2]$$

If $OJ_1A^-OJ_2$, then

$$dc_{OJ_1} = -d_{OJ_2}, \qquad [3]$$

$$dc_{OJ_2} = -d_{OJ_1}, \qquad [4]$$

Figure 1 provides some graphic illustrations. In example 1, we have a positive assertion (indicated by the + on the bar connecting source and concept) associating two equally favorable objects of judgment; in this situation maximum congruity already exists. In all the other illustrations given, the existing positions are not those of maximum congruence, and those positions which would be maximally congruent for each object of judgment are shown by dashed circles. In situation 3, for example, a congruent source would be at −2 and a congruent concept would be at +3, given the favorable assertion between two items of opposite sign.

Magnitude and distribution of pressure toward congruity. Knowing the existing locations of maximum congruence under the given conditions (by applying Principle 1), it becomes possible to state the amount and direction of application of total available pressure toward congruity.

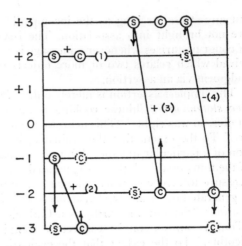

Fig. 1. Graphic examples of four situations in which a source (s) makes an assertion (+ or −) about a concept (c.). Positions of maximum congruity are indicated by dashed circles; predicted changes in attitude are indicated by arrows. See discussion in text.

2. *The total available pressure toward congruity* (P) *for a given object of judgment associated with another by an assertion is equal to the difference, in attitude scale units, between its existing location and its location of maximum congruence along the evaluative dimension; the sign of this pressure is positive* (+) *when the location of congruence is more favorable than the existing location and negative* (−) *when the location of congruence is less favorable than the existing location.*

That is,

$$P_{OJ_1} = dc_{OJ_1} - d_{OJ_1} \qquad [5]$$

$$P_{OJ_2} = dc_{OJ_2} - d_{OJ_2}. \qquad [6]$$

Therefore, substituting from equations 1 through 4,

if $OJ_1A^+OJ_2$,

$$P_{OJ_1} = d_{OJ_2} - d_{OJ_1}, \qquad [7]$$

$$P_{OJ_2} = d_{OJ_1} - d_{OJ_2}. \qquad [8]$$

If $OJ_1A^-OJ_2$,

$$P_{OJ_1} = -d_{OJ_2} - d_{OJ_1}, \qquad [9]$$

$$P_{OJ_2} = -d_{OJ_1} - d_{OJ_2}. \qquad [10]$$

The resulting signs of equations 7 through 10 then represent the direction of P.

For example 2 in Fig. 1, the total pressure

toward congruity available for the source is −2 units and for the concept is +2 units. As can be seen by inspection of these examples, the total pressures toward congruity for both objects associated by an assertion are always equal in magnitude, although they may be the same or different in sign (i.e., $|P_{oJ_1} = |P_{oJ_2}|$). The upper figures in each cell of Table 2 give the total pressures and directions of application for all possible relations among sources and concepts and both types of assertions. These computations are based upon the assumption of a 7-step scale with three degrees of polarization possible in each evaluative direction; they may be treated as general index numbers.

The third principle with which we shall operate incorporates the empirical generalization that intense attitudes are more resistant to change than weakly held ones (cf., 1, 3, 9), but does so in a way which generates more detailed predictions.

3. *In terms of producing attitude change, the total pressure toward congruity is distributed between the objects of judgment associated by an assertion in inverse proportion to their separate degrees of polarization.*

In other words, relatively less polarized objects of judgment, when associated with relatively more polarized objects of judgment, absorb proportionately greater amounts of the pressure toward congruity, and consequently change more.

Applying Principle 3 above, it is possible to predict relative attitude change according to the following formulas:

$$AC_{oJ_1} = \frac{|d_{oJ_2}|}{|d_{oJ_1}| + |d_{oJ_2}|} \quad P_{oJ_1}, \quad [11]$$

$$AC_{oJ_2} = \frac{|d_{oJ_1}|}{|d_{oJ_1}| + |d_{oJ_2}|} \quad P_{oJ_2}, \quad [12]$$

where AC refers to attitude change; where d_{oJ_1} and d_{oJ_2} are taken at their absolute values regardless of sign, and where P_{oJ_1} and P_{oJ_2} are determined from equations 7 through 10. Thus, the sign of the right-hand side of the equation is always that of the particular P_{oJ} under consideration, and thus represents the direction of change. In example 1 in Fig. 1, there is no pressure and hence no change. In the other examples solid arrows indicate the direction and magnitude of predicted change. In example 2, the source must absorb twice as much pressure as the more polarized concept, and in a negative rather than a positive direction (e.g., BULGARIA −1 sponsors HATE CAMPAIGN −3). The unexpected prediction here, that the even more unfavorable concept, HATE CAMPAIGN, actually becomes a little less unfavorable under these conditions, derives directly from the theoretical model and will be discussed later.

If we associate OJ_1 with the source of an assertion, and OJ_2 with the concept, the numbers in Table 1 represent the results of applying formula 12 to the prediction of attitude change toward the concept for all combinations of original attitude toward source and concept when the assertion is positive.

Note that for all *incongruous relations* the predicted change is constant for a given

TABLE 1

PREDICTED ATTITUDE CHANGE FOR CONCEPT AS A FUNCTION OF ORIGINAL LOCATIONS OF BOTH SOURCE AND CONCEPT—POSITIVE ASSERTION
(Uncorrected for incredulity)

Original Attitude Toward Source	Original Attitude Toward Concept						
	+3	+2	+1	0	−1	−2	−3
+3	0.0	+0.6	+1.5	+3.0	+3.0	+3.0	+3.0
+2	−0.4	0.0	+0.7	+2.0	+2.0	+2.0	+2.0
+1	−0.5	−0.3	0.0	+1.0	+1.0	+1.0	+1.0
0	0.0	0.0	0.0	0.0	0.0	0.0	0.0
−1	−1.0	−1.0	−1.0	−1.0	0.0	+0.3	+0.5
−2	−2.0	−2.0	−2.0	−2.0	−0.7	0.0	+0.4
−3	−3.0	−3.0	−3.0	−3.0	−1.5	−0.6	0.0

original attitude toward source (upper right and lower left corners of matrix)—a highly favorable source favoring a negative concept produces just as much attitude change when that concept is -3 as when it is -1. This prediction assumes complete credulity of the message on the part of the receiver, a condition that exists only rarely, in all probability, for incongruous messages. Certainly, when presented with the incongruous message, EISENHOWER sponsors COMMUNISM, in an experimental situation, very few subjects are going to give it full credence. If we are going to make predictions, it is apparent that the variable of credulity must be taken into account.

4. *The amount of incredulity produced when one object of judgment is associated with another by an assertion is a positively accelerated function of the amount of incongruity which exists and operates to decrease attitude change, completely eliminating change when maximal.*

Since incongruity exists only when similarly evaluated concepts are associated by negative assertions or when oppositely evaluated concepts are associated by positive assertions, the correction for incredulity is limited to the upper right and lower left corners of the matrix in Table 1. Within these situations, the *amount* of this correction is assumed to increase with the degree of incongruity, e.g., with the total pressure toward congruity available. It is assumed that no incongruity, and hence no incredulity, can exist where one of the objects of judgment is neutral, e.g., EISENHOWER may come out either for or against a neutral concept like ST. LAWRENCE WATERWAY without the issue of incredulity arising. It is realized, of course, that other factors than those discussed here may affect incredulity.

Figure 2 provides graphic illustration of the corrections made for incredulity. The original curves, level for the neutral point and beyond, derive from the upper right corner of Table 1 and represent three degrees of favorable original attitude toward the source (OJ_1). The dashed lines represent postulated incredulity, positively accelerated functions of total pressure toward congruity. The shape of this function is, of course, based on pure hunch and will probably have to be modified;

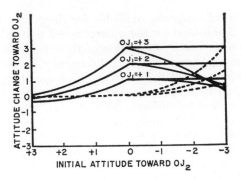

Fig. 2. Predicted change in attitude toward OJ_2 and correction for incredulity (postulated incredulity indicated by dashed lines).

it simply seems reasonable that a person's tendency to reject a message will be relatively much less for slightly incongruous relations (e.g., EISENHOWER $+3$ praises BULGARIANS -1) than for grossly incongruous ones (e.g., EISENHOWER $+3$ praises COMMUNISM -3). The light solid curves represent the result of subtracting incredulity functions from predicted attitude changes. The corrected values are given in Table 2. The same corrections, with appropriate regard to sign, apply to the lower left corner of Table 1 and are made in Table 2. For incongruous situations, then, the formulas for predicting attitude change become:

$$AC_s = \frac{|d_c|}{|d_s| + |d_c|} \; P_s \mp i, \quad [13]$$

$$AC_c = \frac{|d_s|}{|d_s| + |d_c|} \; P_c \mp i, \quad [14]$$

where the sign of the second factor $(i =$ correction for incredulity) is always opposite to that of the first factor, i.e., of P, and thus serves to diminish the effect. The notations s and c refer, of course, to source and concept, respectively.

It is to be emphasized that formulas 13 and 14 apply only to situations of incredulity, or, to put it another way, $i = 0$ for all credulous situations. The precise nature of the i function remains to be empirically determined. The curve we have assumed for i approximates the function $i = a(d_s^2 + b) \, (d_c^2 + d_c)$, where the constants a and b are 1/40 and 1 respectively. It is clear, however, that $i = f (d_s, d_c)$, and hence the attitude change is still

TABLE 2

TOTAL PRESSURE TOWARD CONGRUITY (UPPER NUMBERS) AND PREDICTED CHANGES IN ATTITUDE (LOWER NUMBERS) AS CORRECTED FOR INCREDULITY* (Positive assertion)**

Initial Location of OJ_2	Initial Location of OJ_1							
	+3	+2	+1	0	−1	−2	−3	M
+3	0	+1	+2	+3	+4	+5	+6	
	0.0	+0.6	+1.5	+3.0	+2.6	+1.5	0.0	+1.3
+2	−1	0	+1	+2	+3	+4	+5	
	−0.4	0.0	+0.7	+2.0	+1.8	+1.3	+0.5	+0.8
+1	−2	−1	0	+1	+2	+3	+4	
	−0.5	−0.3	0.0	+1.0	+0.9	+0.7	+0.4	+0.3
0	−3	−2	−1	0	+1	+2	+3	
	0.0	0.0	0.0	0.0	0.0	0.0	0.0	0.0
−1	−4	−3	−2	−1	0	+1	+2	
	−0.4	−0.7	−0.9	−1.0	0.0	+0.3	+0.5	−0.3
−2	−5	−4	−3	−2	−1	0	+1	
	−0.5	−1.3	−1.8	−2.0	−0.7	0.0	+0.4	−0.8
−3	−6	−5	−4	−3	−2	−1	0	
	0.0	−1.5	−2.6	−3.0	−1.5	−0.6	0.0	−1.3
/M/	0.3	0.6	1.1	1.7	1.1	0.6	0.3	

* The OJ whose change is being predicted, either source or concept, is always OJ_1 and the other is OJ_2.

** When dealing with negative assertions, reverse the sign of OJ_2 and look in that row.

a function of the two degrees of polarization and of direction of the assertion.

Incredulity, to the extent it is present, will not only operate to "damp" changes in attitude but should also appear in expressions of disbelief and rationalization. This makes it possible to ascertain the incredulity function independent of attitude change. A proposed experiment along these lines might be as follows: If subjects are persented with a number of messages and told that some are valid and others faked, we would expect the frequency of "fake" judgments to be some increasing function of the measured amount of incongruity (e.g., in terms of locations of original attitudes toward the associated objects of judgment). It is the shape of this function in which we would be particularly interested. If the same subjects were then assured that certain of the "fake" messages were actually valid, we would expect to record rationalizations and other attempts to interpret the message without modifying the evaluative frame of reference; e.g., told that RUSSIA is actually sponsoring a PEACE CONFERENCE, the subject is likely to rationalize this event as some subterfuge on the part of the Soviets in the Cold War. Use of the same messages on another group of subjects in a standard pre- and postmessage attitude change design should serve to test the prediction that attitude change for incongruous assertions is damped in proportion to the degree of incredulity produced.

This independence of credulity as a variable also means that it should be possible to approximate the attitude change values in Table 1 (uncorrected) under special conditions where credulity is made more probable. For example, if EISENHOWER were actually to invite important COMMUNIST PARTY OFFICERS to a friendly dinner at the White House, the effects on devaluating EISENHOWER and vice versa should be extreme. The greater effectiveness of "event" as compared to "word" propaganda follows directly.

The lower numbers in each cell in Table 2 represent the predicted magnitudes and directions of attitude change for all combinations of original attitude—for SOURCES or CONCEPTS and for either positive assertions or negative assertions (see instructions in table footnotes)—as computed by applying formulas 11 and 12, or 13 and 14 in the case of incongruous assertions. Let us take illustration 2 in Fig. 1 as an example: the original attitudes in this case are -1 (source) and -3 (concept), so we will be concerned with the cell defined by these values. Looking first for SOURCE CHANGE (e.g., SOURCE as OJ_1), we find a total pressure toward congruity of -2 (upper figure in cell) and a predicted attitude change of -1.5; looking then for CONCEPT CHANGE (e.g., CONCEPT as OJ_1), we find a total pressure of $+2$ and a predicted attitude change of $+0.5$. If this were the message BULGARIA praises COMMUNISM, we might expect a considerable increase in unfavorableness toward BULGARIA and a slight decrease in unfavorableness toward COMMUNISM. The reader may check the other illustrations against Table 2 if he wishes.

Predictions about attitude change are assumed to hold for *any* situation in which one object of judgment is associated with another by an assertion. In the special source-concept situation, we must take one additional factor into account—the fact that the *assertion itself,* whether positive or negative, typically applies to the concept rather than to the source. When X praises Y, the favorable effect of "praise" applies chiefly to Y; when X denounces Y, similarly, the unfavorable effect of "denounce" applies chiefly to Y. In other words, we must add to the equation predicting attitude change for concepts a constant $(\pm A)$ whose sign is always the same as that of the assertion. In the data we have available, the existence of such an assertion constant applying to the concept but not the source is clearly evident.

A TEST OF THE CONGRUITY PRINCIPLE[3]

On the basis of a pretest of 36 potential objects of judgment, three source-concept pairs were selected which met the criteria of (a) approximately equal numbers of subjects holding favorable, neutral, and unfavorable original attitudes toward them, and (b) lack of correlation between attitude toward the source and the concept making up each pair. The three source-concept pairs finally selected were: LABOR LEADERS with LEGALIZED GAMBLING, CHICAGO TRIBUNE with ABSTRACT ART, and SENATOR ROBERT TAFT with ACCELERATED COLLEGE PROGRAMS. Another group of 405 college students was given a *beforetest,* in which the 6 experimental concepts along with 4 "filler" concepts were judged against a form of the semantic differential including 6 scales highly loaded on the evaluative factor. The sum of ratings on these six 7-step scales constituted the attitude score for each concept, these scores ranging from 6 (most unfavorable) to 42 (most favorable). Five weeks later the same subjects were given highly realistic newspaper stories including positive or negative assertions involving the experimental source-concept pairs. Immediately afterward the subjects were given the *after-test,* again judging the same concepts against the semantic differential.

Original attitudes toward each source and concept were determined from the before-test scores, subjects being distributed into nine cells, s_+c_+, s_+c_0, s_+c_-, s_0c_+, etc. Attitude change amounts, for both source and concept, were obtained by substracting the before-test score from the after-test score for each subject, a positive value thereby indicating increased favorableness.

Table 3 compares predicted attitude change scores (upper number in each cell) with obtained attitude change scores (lower number in each cell) for both sources and concepts and for both positive and negative assertions. The predicted values represent the algebraic mean of the attitude change scores in appropriate cells of Table 2 (e.g., the value for s_+ c_+ with a positive assertion equals the average for the nine cells in the upper left corner); the obtained values

[3] This experiment is described in detail in a separate report by one of the authors (9).

TABLE 3

Predicted (Upper Values in Cells) and
Obtained (Lower Values in Cells)
Changes in Attitude

Original Attitude Toward Source	Positive Assertions			Negative Assertions		
	Original Attitude Toward Concept			Original Attitude Toward Concept		
	+	0	−	+	0	−
	Source Changes					
+	+ 0.2	0.0	− 1.1	−1.1	0.0	+0.2
	+ 25	+ 16	− 42	− 45	+ 1	+ 34
0	+ 2.0	0.0	− 2.0	−2.0	0.0	+2.0
	+150	+ 25	− 94	− 68	+ 17	+ 96
−	+ 1.1	+ 0.0	− 0.2	−0.2	− 0.0	+1.1
	+ 49	+ 13	− 7	− 33	− 3	+ 34
	Concept Changes					
+	+ 0.2	+ 2.0	+ 1.1	−1.1	− 2.0	−0.2
	+ 51	+245	+107	− 88	−180	− 39
0	0.0	0.0	0.0	0.0	0.0	0.0
	+ 39	+ 80	+ 48	− 72	− 79	− 34
−	− 1.1	− 2.0	− 0.2	+0.2	+ 2.0	+1.1
	− 24	− 52	− 10	+ 19	+ 22	+ 16

represent the total attitude change scores, summed algebraically, for 45 subjects (15 subjects on each of 3 stories) on 6 evaluative scales. The reason for the gross difference in absolute magnitudes of predicted and obtained scores is therefore that the former are expressed in scale units and the latter in group totals. The general correspondence between predicted and obtained directions of attitude change is apparent from inspection of Table 3. In every case predicted positive changes (+) and predicted negative changes (−) show corresponding signs in the obtained data, and predicted lack of change (0) generally yields obtained changes of small magnitude.

The predictions obviously hold better for source changes than for concept changes, and it will be recalled that it was also predicted that *an assertion constant* (±A) would apply to the concept but not the source. This would mean that for comparable situations (e.g., s_+c_0 vs. s_0c_+, s_0c_- vs. s_-c_0, etc.) concept changes should be more

in the favorable direction than source changes for positive assertions and more in the negative direction for negative assertions. Table 4 provides a test of this prediction. As can be seen, when comparable con-

TABLE 4

Effects of Assertion Itself (A)

Source	Concept	Difference (A)
	Positive Assertions (Predicted that A is +)	
s_+c_+ + 25	s_+c_+ + 51	+ 26
s_0c_+ +150	s_+c_0 +245	+ 95
s_-c_+ + 49	s_+c_- +107	+ 58
s_+c_0 + 16	s_0c_+ + 39	+ 23
s_0c_0 + 25	s_0c_0 + 80	+ 55
s_-c_0 + 13	s_0c_- + 48	+ 35
s_+c_- − 42	s_-c_+ − 24	+ 18
s_0c_- − 94	s_-c_0 − 52	+ 42
s_-c_- − 7	s_-c_- − 10	− 3
	Negative Assertions (Predicted that A is −)	
s_+c_+ − 45	s_+c_+ − 88	− 43
s_0c_+ − 68	s_+c_0 −180	−112
s_-c_+ − 33	s_+c_- − 39	− 6
s_+c_0 + 1	s_0c_+ − 72	− 73
s_0c_0 + 17	s_0c_0 − 79	− 96
s_-c_0 − 3	s_0c_- − 34	− 31
s_+c_- + 34	s_-c_+ + 19	− 15
s_0c_- + 96	s_-c_0 + 22	− 74
s_-c_- + 34	s_-c_- + 16	− 18

ditions for source and concept changes are arranged, the differences in magnitudes of attitude change are regularly positive for positive assertions (concept changes more toward favorable direction) and regularly negative for negative assertions (concept changes more toward unfavorable direction). With 17 of the 18 values in the predicted direction, this is obviously significant.

A rough estimate of the size of this constant can be obtained from the average difference between source and concept changes for comparable situations: it turns out to be $A = ±46$ in total change score or $A = .17$ in units of the 7-step attitude scale employed. In other words, under the general conditions of this experiment, the assertion constant applied to concept changes equals about 1/6 of a scale unit.

That the magnitudes of attitude changes as well as their directions tend to follow predictions is also evident by inspection of Table 3. This can be seen more clearly in the correlation plot between predicted changes and obtained changes given as Fig. 3. The predicted values are here treated as categorical and the obtained as continuous,

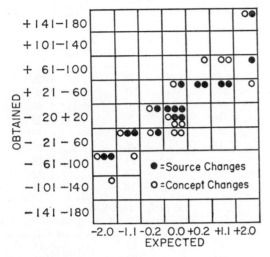

Fig. 3. Correlation plot between predicted and obtained attitude changes after corrections for incredulity and for constant effect of assertion.

and the latter have been corrected for the assertion constant by adding 46 to concept changes with negative assertions and subtracting 46 from concept changes with positive assertions. The correlation between predicted and obtained changes in attitude is high ($r = .91$).

A number of corollaries derive from the congruity principle, some of which can be tested against Tannenbaum's data and others of which cannot. They are as follows:

1. *Shifts in evaluation always tend toward equalization of the degrees of polarization of the objects of judgment associated by an assertion.* If two unequally polarized concepts are associated, the less polarized one becomes more so and the more polarized less so; if a neutral concept is associated with a polarized one, it always becomes more polarized. In Tannenbaum's data this means that the polarized object of judgment (neutral) should always change more than the more polarized object of judgment (plus or

minus); this holds for all relevant conditions except one (s_0c_+, negative assertion), and even here when correction for the assertion constant is made. The comparisons shown in Table 5, where concept changes have been corrected for the assertion constant, clearly substantiate this prediction in every case the neutral member shows a large shift and the polar member a small shift.

TABLE 5

COMPARISON OF ATTITUDE CHANGES FOR NEUTRAL AND POLAR OBJECTS OF JUDGMENT

Situation	Change for Neutral	Change for Polar
Positive Assertions		
s_0c_+	+150 (s)	− 7 (c)
s_+c_0	+199 (c)	+16 (s)
s_-c_0	− 98 (c)	+13 (s)
s_0c_-	− 94 (s)	+ 2 (c)
Negative Assertions		
s_0c_+	− 68 (s)	−26 (c)
s_+c_0	−134 (c)	+ 1 (s)
s_-c_0	+ 48 (c)	− 3 (s)
s_0c_-	+ 96 (s)	+12 (c)

2. *When the total pressure toward congruity is constant, it is easier to make an object of judgment more polarized than less so.* That this prediction follows from the theory can be seen in Table 2 by comparing magnitudes of attitude change within the same row or column (for a given location of source or concept) when the total pressure is the same in amount but opposite in sign—amount of attitude change is always larger in the same direction as the sign of the row or column. This cannot be checked in Tannenbaum's data because he does not differentiate between degrees of original attitude in the same direction. It would be expected, however, from our general notion that evaluative frames of reference tend toward maximum simplicity.

3. *Attitude change toward an object of judgment is an inverse function of intensity of original attitude toward that object.* That weakly held attitudes are more susceptible to change is a widely held notion, but it is only valid, according to the present theory, for the

average of all degrees of attitude toward the other object with which a given one is associated *regardless of sign* (the absolute means, $|M|$, given at the bottom of Table 2) or for maximally polarized attitudes toward the other object (+3 and —3 rows in Table 2). The "law" definitely does not hold for other degrees of attitude toward the second object of judgment, as can be seen by inspection of this table. The data in Table 6 compare predicted values (absolute means

TABLE 6

ATTITUDE CHANGE TOWARD AN OBJECT OF
JUDGMENT AS A FUNCTION OF ORIGINAL
ATTITUDE TOWARD THAT OBJECT
ITSELF

	Original Attitude Toward Object of Judgment		
	+	0	—
Predicted	0.6	1.7	0.6
Obtained (Source)	0.2	0.5	0.2
Obtained (Concept)	0.3	0.7	0.2

at bottom of Table 2) with those obtained by Tannenbaum, both being expressed in attitude scale units in this case. The close correspondence in trend is apparent, and the obtained trend is statistically significant. The difference in absolute magnitude presumably represents the limited effect of a single message upon attitude change. The theoretical model as developed so far takes account of neither learning via successive messages nor of intensity of assertions.

4. *Attitude change for a given object of judgment in the direction of the assertion is an approximately linear function of the favorableness of the original attitude toward the other object of judgment with which it is associated.* The more favorable the attitude toward a source, the greater the effect of a positive assertion on raising attitude toward the concept and the greater the effect of a negative assertion upon lowering attitude toward the concept. Strongly unfavorable sources have just the opposite effects. The same statements hold for changes in attitude toward sources when original attitudes toward concepts are varied. Table 7 compares

TABLE 7

ATTITUDE CHANGE TOWARD ONE OBJECT OF
JUDGMENT AS A FUNCTION OF ORIGINAL
ATTITUDE TOWARD THE OTHER OBJECT
OF JUDGMENT

Assertions	Original Attitude Toward Other Object		
	+	0	—
Positive			
Predicted	+0.8	0.0	—0.8
Obtained (Source)	+0.3	0.0	—0.2
Obtained (Concept)	+0.3	0.0	—0.3
Negative			
Predicted	—0.8	0.0	+0.8
Obtained (Source)	—0.2	0.0	+0.2
Obtained (Concept)	—0.2	—0.1	+0.2

predicted and obtained values. Again, the generally lower levels of obtained changes as compared with predicted changes are presumably due to the limited effects of a single message. Changes in attitude have been corrected for the assertion constant, here as in Table 6. The obtained functions are in the direction predicted, and their trend is statistically significant.

5. *Whenever a congruent assertion associates two differently polarized objects of judgment, and neither of them is neutral, the more polarized object of judgment becomes less so.* This deduction includes the rather paradoxical situations noted earlier in this paper in which, for example, a highly favorable source comes out in favor of somewhat less favorable concept and becomes slightly less favorable itself in doing so, according to theory. The locations in Table 2 where this prediction arises are italicized. Here we are forced to predict, for example: when EISENHOWER +3 praises GOLFING +1, he loses a little prestige while giving a big boost to the concept; when EISENHOWER +3 denounces COMIC BOOKS —1, he may make the latter considerably more unfavorable, but he loses a little ground himself in the exchange. It is as if a highly favorable source should only favor equally good things or be against extremely bad things and a highly unsavory concept should be only sponsored by equally

unsavory sources or condemned by highly noble sources.

If such an effect could be demonstrated, it would be convincing evidence for the whole theory. Tannenbaum's study provides only a partial test for this phenomenon in that the experimental situation probably lacked the necessary sensitivity to get at the very minimal changes predicted. However, of 38 cases that met the necessary conditions, 21 (55.3 per cent) showed relatively small changes in the predicted direction, 15 (39.5 per cent) showed no change, and only 2 (5.3 per cent) changed in the opposite direction.

SUMMARY

This paper describes a general theory of attitude change which takes into account original attitude toward the source of a message, original attitude toward the concept evaluated by the source, and the nature of the evaluative assertion. Predicted changes in attitude toward both source and concept are based upon the combined operation of a principle of congruity, a principle of susceptibility as a function of polarization, and a principle of resistance due to incredulity for incongruous messages. Comparison of predictions with data obtained in a recent experiment provides a test of the theory. No attempt has been made to integrate this particular theoretical model with more general psychological theory, and we feel no urge at this time to attempt such detailed translations. We are, of course, aware that there are many variables other than those considered here which contribute to attitude change.

REFERENCES

1. Birch, H. G. The effect of socially disapproved labeling upon well-structured attitudes. *J. abnorm. soc. Psychol.,* 1945, 40, 301–310.
2. Johnson, W. The communication process and general semantic principles. In W. Schramm (Ed.), *Mass communications.* Urbana: Univer. of Illinois Press, 1949. Pp. 261–274.
3. Klapper, J. T. The effects of mass media. Mimeographed manuscript, Bureau of Applied Social Research. Columbia Univer., 1949.
4. Osgood, C. E. The nature and measurement of meaning. *Psychol. Bull.,* 1952, 49, 197–237.
5. Osgood, C. E. Report on development and application of the semantic differential. Unpublished manuscript, Institute of Communications Research, Univer. of Illinois, 1953. Privately distributed.
6. Remmers, H. H. (Ed.) Generalized attitude scales: studies in socio-psychological measurements. *Bull. Purdue Univer. Stud. higher Educ.,* 1934, 36, No. 4.
7. Remmers, H. H., & Silance, E. B. Generalized attitude scales. *J. soc. Psychol.,* 1934, 5, 298–312.
8. Stagner, R., & Osgood, C. E. An experimental analysis of a nationalistic frame of reference. *J. soc. Psychol.,* 1941, 14, 389–401.
9. Tannenbaum, P. H. Attitudes toward source and concept as factors in attitude change through communications. Unpublished doctor's dissertation, Univer. of Illinois, 1953.

A Structural Theory of Attitude Dynamics / Milton J. Rosenberg

If people seek congruence between their beliefs and feelings toward objects, then attitudes can be changed by modifying either the beliefs or feelings associated with them. The incongruity thereby aroused may, in the former case, result in the feeling changing to become consistent with the altered beliefs; in the latter case the beliefs may change to become consistent with the altered feeling. The first type of change has already been demonstrated in research studies. Experimental verification of the second type would lend support to the theoretical proposition that the disruption of structural consistency is a basic condition for the occurrence of attitude change. To test for the second type, changes in feeling toward objects were induced during hypnosis and in the posthypnotic sessions changes in belief were measured.

Common insight suggests that when stable feelings and beliefs refer to the same object they tend toward congruence with one another. This paper reports a structural theory of attitude dynamics that has been developed through elaboration and extension of this insight. The theory is "structural" because it is not so much concerned with variables influencing the acquisition or reorganization of attitudes as with the problem of what attitudes *are* and the related problem of what happens "inside" them as they undergo change.

In support of the theory, a few experimental studies are briefly reviewed and one recent experiment is presented in greater detail. The last section of this report examines the theory for its bearing upon some problems in attitude measurement and persuasion.

THEORY AND DATA

Most, though by no means all, definitions of the attitude concept have been restricted to the notion of emotional "einstellung": when some object or class of objects dependably elicits an affective evaluative set that can be characterized as either "pro" or "con," "positive" or "negative," the individual is said to hold an attitude.

The theory outlined here flows from the contention that typically such stable affective sets are integrated with other psychological processes and that a more useful approach to attitude is one in which these processes are somehow represented. (Among the writers who have discussed this point are Chein,[1] Katz and Stotland,[2] Krech and Crutchfield,[3] Peak,[4] and Tolman.[5]) One convenient way to do this is to conceive of an attitude as consisting of a *cognitive* as well as an affective component. Of the many possible kinds of cognitions about attitude objects one variety is here singled out as requiring representation in the minimum definition of the attitude concept: these are beliefs about the relations between the attitude object and the other "objects" of affective significance to the individual. Thus a physician's negative attitude toward Federal medical insurance involves not only the fact of his affectively colored opposition but also the fact that he believes that Federal medical insurance, if instituted, would lead to "socialism" and "debasement of medical standards," which for him are negatively evaluated conditions, and that it would tend also to defeat, or reduce the likelihood of, such positively valued conditions as "professional freedom" and "maintenance of my income."

It will be argued in a later section of this paper that the elicitation and measurement of such attitudinal cognitions would help to reduce some of the major problems encountered in survey and experimental studies of social attitudes. But the full relevance and import of this argument will be apparent only if it is first demonstrated that a concern with both the affective and cognitive components of attitudes leads to a useful clarification of their structural properties and to

A revised version of an article originally published in *Public Opinion Quarterly*, 1960, 24, pages 319–340, by permission of author and publisher, Princeton University.

[1] I. Chein, "Behavior Theory and the Behavior of Attitudes," *Psychological Review*, Vol. 55, 1948, pp. 175–188.
[2] D. Katz and E. Stotland, "A Preliminary Statement to a Theory of Attitude Structure and Change," in S. Koch, editor, *Psychology: A Study of a Science*, Vol. III, New York, McGraw-Hill, 1959.
[3] D. Krech and R. S. Crutchfield, *Theory and Problems of Social Psychology*, New York, McGraw-Hill, 1948.
[4] H. Peak, "Attitude and Motivation," in M. Jones, editor, *Nebraska Symposium on Motivation, 1955*, Lincoln, Neb., University of Nebraska Press, 1955.
[5] E. C. Tolman, "A Psychological Model," in T. Parsons and E. A. Shils, editors, *Toward a General Theory of Action*, Cambridge, Mass., Harvard University Press, 1951.

a useful formulation of the attitude-change process.

Attitude structure. As employed by behavioral scientists the word "structure" usually denotes some constellation of component events or processes so related to one another that the irreversible alteration of the quality or magnitude of a particular component will set in motion comparable changes in the other components. If the structure of an attitude is simply conceptualized in terms of two major components, the affective and the cognitive, confirmation of this conceptualization can be obtained by demonstrating that these components co-vary in close relation to each other. Evidence of such co-variation may be sought either with regard to stable attitudes or with regard to attitudes undergoing change.

The first-mentioned case is exemplified by a group of studies which show that within a population of persons varying in their attitudinal affects toward some social object there exist correlate and consistent variations in *beliefs* about that object.[6] A similar study was conducted by the author in which the attitudinal affects of a large number of subjects were measured with regard to two separate social issues.[7] One month later these same subjects took a "test of cognitive structure" requiring them to rate a group of "values" both for the degree of positive or negative reward each represented and also for the extent to which each value was believed to be fostered or defeated through the influence of each of the two attitude objects, respectively. From these judgments it was possible to compute an over-all "index of cognitive structure." By testing the relationship between this index and the independent measure of attitudinal affect it was shown that stable positive affect toward an attitude object is associated with beliefs relating that object to the attainment of posi-

tive values and the blocking of negative values, while stable negative affect toward an attitude object is associated with beliefs relating it to the attainment of negative values and the blocking of positive values. It was also confirmed that moderate attitudinal affects, as compared to extreme ones, are associated with beliefs that relate the attitude object to less important values, or if to important values then with less confidence as to the existence of clear-cut instrumental relationships between the attitude object and the values in question. Data from this study also indicated that variation in attitudinal affect is separately correlated with at least two aspects of the person's set of attitudinal cognitions. The first of these is the over-all believed potency of the attitude object for achieving or blocking the realization of his values; the second is the over-all felt importance of those values.

In general terms what emerged from this study was the conclusion that stable patterns of feeling toward social objects are accompanied by, or organized in close relationship with, stable beliefs consistent with those affects. The major key to such consistency appears to be that the individual tends to relate positive attitude objects to goal attainment and negative attitude objects to frustration of his goal orientations.

Attitude change. The conception of attitude as an affective-cognitive structure has utility not only because it fits correlational findings such as those reported above but also because it suggests a way of theorizing about attitude change. The author's approach to the formulation of a structural theory of attitude change is founded on the following basic propositions:

1. When the affective and cognitive components of an attitude are mutually consistent, the attitude is in a stable state.

2. When these components are mutually inconsistent, to a degree that exceeds the individual's "tolerance limit" for such inconsistency, the attitude is in an unstable state.

3. In such an unstable state the attitude will undergo reorganizing activity until one of three possible outcomes is achieved. These outcomes are: (a) rejection of the communications, or other forces, that engendered the original inconsistency between af-

6 D. Cartwright, "Some Principles of Mass Persuasion," *Human Relations,* Vol. 2, 1949, pp. 253–268. M. B. Smith, "Personal Values as Determinants of a Political Attitude," *Journal of Psychology,* Vol. 23, 1949, pp. 477–486. A. D. Woodruff and F. J. DiVesta, "The Relationship between Values, Concepts and Attitudes," *Education and Psychological Measurement,* Vol. 8, 1948, pp. 645–660.

7 M. J. Rosenberg, "Cognitive Structure and Attitudinal Affect," *Journal of Abnormal and Social Psychology,* Vol. 53, 1956, pp. 367–372.

fect and cognition and thus rendered the attitude unstable, i.e. restoration of the original stable and consistent attitude; (b) "fragmentation" of the attitude through the isolation from each other of the mutually inconsistent affective and cognitive components; (c) accommodation to the original inconsistency-producing change so that a new attitude, consistent with that change, is now stabilized, i.e. attitude change.

In broad terms it is possible to specify some of the conditions under which each of these three outcomes is most likely to occur. Thus on the assumption that an individual's attitudes (defined as his consistent and persisting affective-cognitive structures) usually enable effective regulation of his adaptive behavior and are thus of value to him, it would be predicted that he will attempt to preserve them intact. From this it follows that *if possible* an individual will ultimately reject influences which have caused a temporary alteration in either the affective or cognitive component of one of his attitudes.

Frequently, however, the potency of the force leading to the alteration of one of the major components of an attitude is so great, or so persistent, as to make it *impossible* of rejection. When this is the case, fragmentation of the attitude is likely to result if, by virtue of the needs or "objective realities" that maintain it, the component persisting from the original attitude structure is unalterable. However, when this component is capable of alteration, it would be expected to give way, and general reorganization leading to the erection of a new attitude (i.e. attitude change) will result.

Restricting our concern to the case in which attitude change *does* occur, it may be asked: What are the specific lawful relationships between its occurrence and such variables as the content and organization of the change-inducing communication, the individual's level of tolerance for affective-cognitive inconsistency, and the relation of the attitude to other attitudes held by the same individual? No answer to such questions will be attempted here except to indicate that a large part of the available experimental literature on attitude change may be interpreted as indicating some of the parameters and parameter values that are

associated with the attitude-change outcome in situations where inconsistency between attitude components has been produced.[8]

The validity of a theoretical perspective, however, is not established by the claim that data collected for other purposes can be fitted to it; rather it is necessary to show that hypotheses derived from it are directly supported by available experimental evidence. For the purposes of this report, then, it seems desirable to elaborate not upon details and extensions of the propositions given above but rather upon the main attitude-change hypothesis resident in that set of propositions. In its simplest form this hypothesis is that *the production of inconsistency between the affective and cognitive portions of an attitude will culminate in a general attitude reorganization (through which the affective-cognitive inconsistency is reduced or eliminated) when (1) the inconsistency exceeds the individual's present tolerance limit and (2) the force producing it cannot be ignored or avoided.* In the remainder of this paper these two qualifying conditions are assumed, though not necessarily restated, whenever this hypothesis or data bearing upon it are discussed.

Two different predictions can be derived from this hypothesis. The first is simply that if a person somehow undergoes an "irreversible" change in his beliefs about an attitude object his affect toward that object will show corresponding change. The second prediction is the converse: if a person somehow undergoes an "irreversible" change in his *affect* toward an object his beliefs about that object will show corresponding change.

At present there is much clearer and stronger evidence available for the former prediction than for the latter one. Some of this evidence is based upon the impression of applied workers in the persuasion professions that if an audience member's beliefs about the value-serving and value-blocking powers of an "object" (such as a consumer product, a social policy, or a political candidate) can be reorganized, his feelings toward that object, and ultimately his behavior

[8] For a useful review of this literature see C. I. Hovland, "Effects of the Mass Media of Communication," in G. Lindzey, editor, *Handbook of Social Psychology*, Vol. II, Cambridge, Mass., Addison-Wesley, 1954.

toward it, will undergo corresponding change. In addition to this kind of evidence there are scores of experimental studies in which communications designed to change cognitions about attitude objects are directed at subjects. A result found in the majority of these studies is that such communications, if potent enough, do produce further change effects in evaluative (affective) responses. Most of these studies, however, do not provide for a precise check of whether, and to what extent, the communications designed to alter cognitions actually do so. Recently, however, a number of methods for the measurement of the cognitive aspects of attitude structures have become available. The test of cognitive structure developed by the author for use in the aforementioned correlational study is one of these. It has since been employed in attitude change studies by Carlson[9] and Peak.[10] While neither of these experiments was intended as a test of the present theoretical formulation, both were concerned with the prediction that change in beliefs about an attitude object will generate change in feelings toward that object.

In Carlson's study subjects were tested on two separate occasions for their affective and cognitive responses toward the social object "Negroes being allowed to move into white neighborhoods." Intervening between the two testing sessions was a manipulation designed to produce changes in the "perceived instrumentality" aspect of a number of the subject's beliefs about the attitude object. Thus the typical anti-desegregation subject who at first believed that housing desegregation would *lower* the worth of property (a negative instrumental relation between the attitude object and the value "worth of property") was exposed to a special manipulation intended to transform his belief to one in which desegregation would be seen as *raising* the worth of property.

Comparison of the premanipulation and postmanipulation cognitive structure tests showed that the typical subject *did* alter his beliefs about the separate relationships of the

attitude object to each of a number of separate values. Furthermore, it was found that, along with the production of such changes in the cognitive component of the person's attitude, consistent change, of roughly corresponding magnitude, was also obtained in his *affective* response toward the attitude object. Thus these data lend support to the first of the two predictions stated above; they confirm the hypothesis that the production of inconsistency in an attitude structure through modification of its cognitive component does eventuate in correlated consistency-restoring modification of its affective component.

In the study by Peak an attempt was made to produce a temporary alteration in the strength or pertinence of a general value ("making good grades") seen by her subjects to be instrumentally served by such attitude objects as the use of discussion techniques in college courses. It was shown that when attitudinal cognition changes, in the sense that the goal seen as served by the attitude object increases in its importance to the person, the affective response toward that object undergoes corresponding change.

While it does not deal with the sort of large-scale affective-cognitive inconsistency that Carlson is concerned with, this study too seems to demonstrate that change in the cognitive portion of an attitude tends to generate consistent change in its affective portion. A further value is that it shows that affect modification will be fostered not only by changes in the "instrumentality" aspect of cognitions about attitude objects but also by changes in the felt importance of the goals believed to be attained through the attitude object's instrumental powers.

However, to demonstrate, as our basic hypothesis asserts, that affective-cognitive inconsistency (rather than mere cognitive reorganization) is an underlying condition for attitude change, the reverse prediction must also be confirmed: it must be shown that the production of an irreversible change in an attitude's *affective* component will generate corresponding change in its cognitive component.

This prediction, unlike its opposite, does not receive unequivocal confirmation in the available experimental literature. Neverthe-

[9] E. R. Carlson, "Attitude Change and Attitude Structure," *Journal of Abnormal and Social Psychology,* Vol. 52, 1956, pp. 256–261.

[10] H. Peak, "The Effects of Aroused Motivation on Attitudes," Technical Report to the Office of Naval Research, 1959, mimeographed document.

less, some of the attitude change techniques that have been reported, particularly those involving direct approval or disapproval from peer groups or prestigeful figures, might be interpreted as producing direct modification of affective responses. A similar impression is created when nonexperimental examples of "emotional" persuasion techniques are examined. But in either the experimental or nonexperimental case it is likely that such influence procedures also tend to directly modify some attitudinal cognitions.

A specific aim in two recent studies by the author was to develop and investigate the effects of a "pure" experimental manipulation of attitudinal affect, one which did not directly act upon the cognitive content of the attitude being modified. The intention was to test experimentally the second of the two predictions drawn from the main hypothesis given above. The manipulation used in these studies involved posthypnotic suggestion of affect change. The second of these studies will be described in detail both for its bearing upon the main hypothesis and also to provide some idea of the style of experimentation by which the theory is being more fully developed.

An experiment involving direct and sustained alteration of attitudinal affect. In the first study involving hypnotic manipulation of attitudinal affect eleven experimental and eleven control subjects were tested on two separate occasions for their affective and cognitive responses toward various attitude objects. Between the two testing sessions the experimental subjects (all of whom were capable of achieving deep hypnosis) were placed in hypnosis and then given the suggestion that upon awakening their affective reactions toward two separate attitude objects would be changed (from positive to negative, or vice versa) and that they would have no memory of the suggestion having been made until the presentation of an amnesia-removing signal. It was assumed that such posthypnotic suggestion would foster strong and "irreversible" affect change for as long as posthypnotic amnesia was maintained. In a control group which received no affect manipulation the affective and cognitive responses toward attitude ob-

jects remained stable from the first to the second test administrations. In the experimental group significant change occurred not only in the subjects' affects toward the attitude objects but also in their *beliefs* about the relationships between each of those objects and various "values" deemed important by the subjects. Additional control data ruled out the possibility that these changes could have been due to any general tendency toward response instability rather than to the effects of the affect manipulation.

By using a second control procedure in which subjects "role-played" the occurrence of affect change, and by interviewing conducted both before and after removal of the experimental subjects' posthypnotic amnesias, it was found that the affect and belief changes achieved by the experimental subjects were experienced by them as legitimate and veridical; the subjects really felt and *believed* differently about the attitude objects on which they had received the posthypnotic suggestions of affect change. Aspects of this study have been reported in a number of publications,[11] and it will not be further described or discussed here except to note that its replication and extension were the main purposes of the study described below.

In this second study[12] the hynotic manipulation of attitudinal affect was kept in force for a full week rather than for a period of one or two hours, as was the case in the earlier study. Eight new experimental subjects were used in this experiment and were tested for both their affective and cognitive responses to three different attitude objects on six different occasions. The first of these occasions came three days before the delivery of a posthypnotic suggestion of affect

[11] M. J. Rosenberg, "Affect and Cognition in Attitude Structure and Attitude Change," paper read before meeting of Eastern Psychological Association, April, 1957. M. J. Rosenberg and C. W. Gardner, "Some Dynamic Aspects of Posthypnotic Compliance," *Journal of Abnormal and Social Psychology*, Vol. 57, 1958, pp. 351–366. M. J. Rosenberg, "Cognitive Reorganization in Response to the Hypnotic Reversal of Attitudinal Affect," *Journal of Personality*, Vol. 28, 1960, pp. 39–63.

[12] This experiment was carried out under Contract 609(27) with the Group Psychology Branch of the Office of Naval Research. Thanks are due to Charles W. Gardner, Carl I. Hovland, and Irving L. Janis, for their useful advice and to Sheldon Feldman, who conducted the testing with all subjects.

change with regard to one of the three attitude objects. In all cases the subject's original affect toward this object ("the abandonment of the United States policy of giving economic aid to foreign nations") was originally negative and was hypnotically manipulated in the positive direction in a way that involved no reference to any of his beliefs about the attitude object's relationships with any of his values. Specifically each subject was told in hynosis:

> After you awake, and continuing until our next meeting, you will feel very strongly opposed to the United States policy of giving economic aid to foreign nations. The mere idea of the United States giving economic aid to foreign nations will make you feel very displeased and disgusted. Until your next meeting with me you will continue to feel very strong and thorough opposition to the United States policy of economic aid to foreign nations. You will have no memory whatsoever of this suggestion's having been made . . . until the amnesia is removed by my giving you the signal at our next session.

Following the delivery of the posthypnotic suggestion the subject was awakened from hypnosis and the measures of affect and cognition were readministered. Two days later, and two days after that, these tests were again administered. Exactly one week after the hypnotic session the subject's amnesia for that session was removed and the experiment fully explained to him. Up to this point in the sequence all subjects had been led to believe that the hypnotic session and the testing sessions (the former conducted by the author and the latter by an associate) had no connection with each other, that they represented different and unrelated experiments.

However, toward the end of the first week, two subjects did gradually develop vague and uncertain suspicions that some sort of hypnotic manipulation might have been used. But both insisted that they had no memory of any such event, that they were merely "reasoning" from the fact that they had undergone sudden and intense changes in their feelings and beliefs on the foreign aid issue.

Three days after amnesia removal, and seven days after that, the measures of affect and cognition were again administered to all subjects. Before presenting the data that bear on the prediction that the production of strong affect change generates corresponding change in associated cognitions it will be necessary to describe the separate measures of affect and cognition by which these data were obtained. These measures were similar to those used in the author's two earlier studies described above.

The measure of affect consisted of three scales covering a 16-point range from "extremely in favor" to "extremely opposed." One of these scales dealt with the issue on which the subjects received the hypnotic affect manipulation. The other two scales dealt with issues that were not subjected to any manipulation and thus served as control areas against which changes on the manipulated issue could be compared.

The measure of the cognitive component involved thirty-two so-called "value cards." Sample value items are "all human beings having equal rights," "people being well educated," "making one's own decisions," "attaining economic security." In taking this test the subject first judges each of the thirty-two values in terms of its importance to him, using a scale with a range of 21 points. The scale runs from -10 (which stands for "gives me maximum dissatisfaction") through 0 (which stands for "gives me neither dissatisfaction nor satisfaction") to $+10$ (which stands for "gives me maximum satisfaction"). He then judges each of these same values in terms of whether, and to what extent, he thinks it will be attained or blocked as a consequence of the attitude object. On this task he uses an 11-point scale running from -5 (which stands for "extreme blocking") through 0 (which stands for "neither blocked nor attained") to $+5$ (which stands for "extreme attainment"). Thus at the end of the testing procedure there are available for each value term the subject's judgment of its importance as a positive or negative state and his judgment of how that value's realization will be affected by the attitude object. These two judgments are algebraically multiplied for each value term respectively. In turn the thirty-two products are algebraically summed. The resulting quantity is taken as an index of the over-all import of the cognitive structure associated with the attitude object. In effect this index expresses, in a single number, the extent to which the subject sees the attitude object as serving the attainment or blocking of his values. This index was separately obtained for each of the three attitude objects (the one subjected to affect manipulation and the two not subjected to such manipulation) from the data collected during each of the six separate testing sessions.

To test the prediction that the production of a large and irreversible affect change will generate comparable changes in beliefs about the attitude object, affect-change scores and cognition-change scores were computed for the three separate attitude objects. These scores referred to the differences between the index obtained from the subject's premanipulation test performance and each of the five postmanipulation test performances respectively. By application of the Randomization Test for Matched Pairs[13] it was possible to determine whether the subject's affect-change and cognition-change scores for the manipulated attitude object were significantly greater than the means of their change scores for the two nonmanipulated attitude objects.

As shown in the table below, until the amnesia removal the subjects showed significant change not only in their affective responses toward "abandoning the United States policy of economic aid to foreign nations" but also in their beliefs about how such abandonment will affect the realization of their values. When the test records are examined it is found that these statistically significant differences are based upon large-scale shifts in both affect and cognition. Thus a typical subject changes his affective evaluation from extreme opposition to abandonment of foreign aid to extreme approval. At the same time he changes many of his related beliefs. For example, whereas before the affect manipulation he believes that abandoning foreign aid would defeat such positive goals (for him) as "the avoidance of economic depression" and would serve

[13] See S. Siegel, *Non-parametric Statistics for the Behavioral Sciences,* New York, McGraw-Hill, 1956.

PROBABILITIES OF THE DIFFERENCES BETWEEN THE CHANGE SCORES FOR THE MANIPULATED AND NONMANIPULATED ATTITUDES*

Testing Sessions from Which Change Scores Are Computed†	Affect Change	Cognitive Change
Session 1–Session 2	.008	.024
Session 1–Session 3	.008	.024
Session 1–Session 4	.008	.008
Session 1–Session 5	N.S.	.056
Session 1–Session 6	N.S.	.064

* All probabilities are two-tailed and are obtained through application of the Randomization Test for Matched Pairs. All significant differences are in the direction: manipulated attitude > mean of nonmanipulated attitudes.

† The first testing session occurred three days before hypnotic manipulation of affect toward "foreign aid"; the second testing session came immediately after the manipulation; and the third and fourth sessions came three and five days, respectively, after the manipulation. The fifth and sixth sessions came ten days and seventeen days after the manipulation (i.e. three days and ten days after "amnesia removal"). The same tests were used in each of the six sessions—the affective scales dealing with the foreign aid issue and with the two unmanipulated issues, and the cognitive structure measures for each of those issues.

N.S. = not significant.

such negative goals as "the open expression of disagreement between people" he now sees the abandonment of foreign aid as *fostering* the former goal and *defeating* the latter.

Nor is this the only kind of change observed in the subject's cognitions about the attitude object. He also alters his evaluation of some of the value terms, sometimes even to the extent of changing positive values to negative ones or negative values to positive ones. In the latter case beliefs about the relationship between the attitude object and such transformed values are usually left unaltered, thus reversing their import.

It should not be concluded however that *all* the beliefs expressed by the typical subject are consistent with the altered attitudinal affect. Usually some of his original beliefs persist within the new structure and are inconsistent with its over-all import, though typically the intensity with which these beliefs are held is reduced after the affect manipulation. But in the light of the theoretical propositions advanced above it is not assumed that total and perfect consistency need obtain in a stable attitude structure; all that is assumed is that in such a stable structure affective-cognitive inconsistency, if present at all, is at a level below the individual's tolerance limit. At any rate, examination of the postmanipulation attitude structures of the subjects reveals, in most cases, an impressive degree of cognitive reorganization in the direction consistent with the altered affect.

As in the first study involving affect manipulation, interview procedures revealed that the subjects' changes in affect and cognition were *experienced* by them rather than merely "role-played." Indeed, the findings reported in the last two rows of the table provide a special kind of evidence to this effect in connection with the subjects' cognitive changes. These findings refer to data obtained after the posthypnotic amnesia was removed and the nature of the experiment was fully explained to each subject. While the removal of amnesia for the affect manipulation is followed by a return to the initial affective response, enough of the cognitive changes persist to make for a significant difference between the cognition-change scores on the manipulated issue and the mean of the cognition-change scores on the two nonmanipulated issues.

Since after amnesia removal the subjects' affective responses reverted to their original scale positions it might be contended that the significant persistence of some of the cognitive changes calls into question our conception of attitude as an internally consistent affective-cognitive structure. Examination of the subjects' test performances reveals, however, that while a number of altered beliefs do persist, a still larger number are changed back to their original form. Thus, after amnesia removal, in seven out of the eight cases the over-all index of cognitive structure has a negative sign and is thus consistent with the restored negative affect.

Many other aspects of this study, including data drawn from a group of unhypnotized control subjects, have not been covered in this account but have been detailed in another report.[14] But the data that have been reported or reviewed in this paper seem to provide strong confirmation for the general hypothesis that the production of affective-cognitive inconsistency within a previously stable attitude makes for attitude change. The confirmation of this hypothesis argues for the validity of the more general set of theoretical propositions from which it was derived.

Some additional theoretical considerations. While it has been demonstrated that, under certain specified conditions, affective-cognitive inconsistency does lead to attitude change, it has not been demonstrated that attitude change is *always* due to the production of such inconsistency. Indeed, such a conclusion would be possible only by studying the underlying structural modifications involved in all phenotypically classified forms of attitude change. Nevertheless, it is the author's contention that commitment to an inconsistency-reduction analysis of the attitude-change process will prove heuristically useful in developing experimental programs looking toward the construction of an adequately detailed theory of attitude dynamics.

A number of additional matters of theory require clarification. One of these is the possible objection that the type of attitude-change sequence demonstrated in the affect-manipulation experiments is an uncommon, and thus unimportant, case. In this connection a point made earlier needs to be repeated: hypnotic suggestion was employed as an experimental analogue of a broad class of nonhypnotic experiences which seem to produce affect modification in everyday settings. It can be argued that whenever the expression of an old affective response is followed by negative reinforcement, or whenever the imitative or trial-and-error "rehearsal" of a new affective response is followed by positive reinforcement, affect change similar to that observed in the present experiment is fostered. Such reinforcement need not come only from external agencies. As the individual's inner needs and conflicts are altered through the vicissitudes of experience or of "growth," the expression of old affects may come to heighten frustration and tension while the expression of new affects may operate to reduce needs and resolve conflicts. Thus attitudinal affects may undergo transformation under control by

14 M. J. Rosenberg, "An analysis of affective-cognitive consistency," in M. J. Rosenberg, C. I. Hovland, *et al.*, *Attitude organization and change*, New Haven, Yale Univer. Press, 1960.

reinforcements issuing from "within" the person (from changes in his hierarchy of motives and conflicts) rather than from other persons. By this point, much of the present analysis may be tied to the kind of "psychodynamic" approach to attitude that is exemplified in the contributions of Frenkel-Brunswik and her colleagues,[15] Katz, Sarnoff, and McClintock,[16] and Smith, Bruner, and White.[17]

Another possible objection is that the reduction in this paper of all forms of attitude change to two underlying structural sequences has the status of an "ideal" typology. It must be acknowledged that in many instances attitude change does not begin with the manipulation of either the cognitive or the affective component but, rather, both may undergo manipulation at the same time. It should be clear, however, that from the present point of view the production of change in either major component will increase the likelihood of change in the other component. Furthermore, close analysis of attitude-change techniques and communications will probably indicate that they usually are specifically directed more toward one than toward the other of the two major components.

A third objection might be that this theoretical approach has said little or nothing about a number of variables usually assumed to be important in attitude-dynamic processes. Among these are such variables as the person's "cognitive style" and his orientation toward the sources of communication directed at him. Similarly, little attention has been given here to the ways in which such communications differ from one another. A general response to this objection is that the pertinence of such variables lies in the fact that they, together with many others, control and determine whether, and to what extent, a specific attitude in a specific individual can be rendered inconsistent to a degree that is discomforting and motivating to him. Some of these variables would be in-

volved also in determining whether intolerable affective-cognitive inconsistency, once aroused, would be reduced through true attitude change or through either "fragmentation" of the attitude structure or ultimate rejection of the forces which aroused the initial inconsistency.

A further qualification should be noted. The present conceptualization of attitude as a stable and consistent structure of affective and cognitive components may seem to be contradicted by two particular lines of evidence. The first is that subjects tested for their affects and beliefs toward an "attitude object" sometimes reveal apparent patterns of moderate or even extreme inconsistency. On this basis Scott, in a useful discussion, has recently questioned the generality of formulations such as the present one.[18] However, the kinds of data on which this objection is based are usually collected without regard for the obvious fact that just because a subject chooses a non-neutral point on an attitudinal affect scale it cannot be assumed that he actually *holds* that attitude. Frequently his scale choice or, for that matter, his response to an evaluation-eliciting interview question does not reflect a real attitudinal affect but rather is due to loose and unreliable reference to an associated object toward which he may have some affect. Just as often such pseudo-affective responses may be forced by the wording of the questions or by the subject's anticipations of the experimenter's or interviewer's own affective preferences. In the light of these considerations it can be argued that the presence of gross and extreme inconsistency between a subject's affective and cognitive responses to a given "attitude object" (except when he has just been exposed to potent inducements to change) is presumptive evidence that he does not really *have* an attitude toward that object. In such a case it would be expected that retesting at a later date would yield evidence of significant instability on measures of both "affect" and "cognition." The bearing of this argument on some problems of attitude research is developed in the last section of this paper.

A more impressive line of counterevidence

[15] T. W. Adorno, E. Frenkel-Brunswik, D. J. Levinson, and R. N. Sanford, *The Authoritarian Personality,* New York, Harper, 1950.

[16] D. Katz, I. Sarnoff, and C. McClintock, "Ego Defense and Attitude Change," *Human Relations,* Vol. 9, 1956, pp. 27–46.

[17] M. B. Smith, J. S. Bruner, and R. W. White, *Opinions and Personality,* New York, Wiley, 1956.

[18] W. A. Scott, "Cognitive Consistency, Response Reinforcement and Attitude Change," *Sociometry,* Vol. 22, 1959, pp. 219–229.

is that many persons are aware of holding a few strong and stable affects for which they cannot offer any impressive cognitive support. Depth psychological data of both the clinical and experimental varieties suggest, however, that "cognitionless" affects, such as phobias or certain kinds of intense feelings toward other persons, are embedded in structures composed of "unconscious" beliefs (or better, "percepts"). The inability to verbalize such percepts may be based on the fact that they were acquired preverbally or that they were derived and developed through symbol-substitution processes for which no consensual vocabulary is available; or such beliefs may involve various kinds of "magical-irrational" relationships that individuals are trained to disavow as they acquire the "ego habits" of realistic adjustment. Confirming this extended conjecture is the clear fact that, whether through the routines of psychoanalytic free association, hypnotic exploration, or dream investigation, ostensibly cognitionless affects are regularly found to be rich in associated cognitive material.

IMPLICATIONS FOR THE MEASUREMENT AND ALTERATION OF SOCIAL ATTITUDES

The major test of the utility of a theory is whether it fits available experimental data and suggests new and verifiable hypotheses. In the previous section of this report the present theory was examined in the light of this criterion. Another possible test of a theory's utility is whether it helps to clarify "practical" problems in its area of reference. In this last section an attempt is made to apply the present view of attitude structure and dynamics to some of the everyday problems encountered by those who are engaged in attempting to survey, or to alter, the social attitudes of other persons. Though couched largely in terms of the problems that confront the "pollster" and "propagandist," this discussion should also have considerable bearing upon comparable problems in designing and executing "basic research" on attitudes.

Increasing the validity of attitude measurement. Probably the most common approach to measuring attitudes in large populations is to elicit from the respondent some judgment on an affective-evaluative scale presented to him either in interview or printed form. It has already been pointed out that if, in such a situation, an individual characterizes himself as occupying a non-neutral position, there is no guarantee that this is truly the case; nor is there any guarantee, assuming the individual *does* have some present feeling toward the attitude object, that this feeling is, or will be, stable over time and in altered circumstances. Thus many persons engaged in studying the public's preferences on social issues or toward consumer products or political candidates have some difficulty in knowing how much, or in what ways, they ought to believe the "data" they have collected. For such researchers the most important aspect of attitudes is their stability; they are interested in locating and describing the *persisting* affective preferences and aversions of respondents.

One way to guard against the unsuspected presence of unstable "pseudo-attitudes" is to measure each respondent (or a good sample) on at least two, or preferably more, occasions. The present theoretical approach suggests an alternative, and possibly more economical, procedure. It is simply that when respondents are tested or interviewed they be required to reveal their *beliefs* as well as their affects. From the point of view of the theory and data presented above it would be expected that the greater the degree of consistency between these beliefs and the affect expressed toward their object, the greater the likelihood that the affective set is real and will remain stable.

Clearly, just such cognitive measurement is involved in the kind of "survey in depth" that involves extended interviewing. But a possibly less costly and (for the purpose of determining the presence of a truly stable affective orientation) more effective technique would be the use of a test device similar to the cognitive structure measure employed by the author in the studies reported in this paper.

There is opportunity for considerable inventiveness in both the design of such devices and in their application to problems of attitude measurement. To give only one example, Nowlis and Axelrod have recently adapted the author's procedure for the measurement of cognitive structure to the problem of characterizing a *group* of persons in terms of the mean content and mean stability of their attitudes toward specific consumer products.[19] In this procedure, affect is measured in one randomly selected portion of the group's population and cognitive structure in another subgroup. The general finding is one of high correlation between these measures of affect and cognition, and on this basis the *group* may be characterized as one in which the attitudes studied are stably held by the typical members.

Whatever the specific form of such test procedures, and however administered, it seems likely that they could help reduce the ambiguities inherent in much current work on social attitudes. By enabling more accurate estimation of the validity of expressed affective orientations they could help reduce the kinds of error that have sometimes hounded polling studies. As one illustration of this point, it seems likely that among the many factors involved in the failure of the election polls of 1948 was the fact that the evaluative orientations expressed by many respondents were only loosely supported, if at all, by consistent and detailed beliefs. If this had been clear at the time it would have been possible to predict that the vigorous and assertive campaign waged by the Democratic candidate was likely to have significant influence upon the *developing* attitudes of some portions of the electorate.

Up to this point the question of validity in attitude measurement has been restricted to the problem of how "pseudo-attitudes" may be discriminated from real (stable) attitudes. A related problem is that, where a stable affective orientation exists, its direct measurement may yield an invalid estimate of its extremity. Again the assessment of the cognitive content of the attitude may be useful. When some device such as that used in the author's studies, and in those by Peak, Carl-

son, Nowlis, and Scott, is employed, the extremity of an attitude may be estimated on more than one basis. Thus two persons may characterize themselves as equally extreme in their affective evaluations of a given object; but at the same time computation of an over-all index based on their associated cognitions may yield widely divergent index values. In such a case it would seem quite appropriate to conclude that the person with the larger (more extreme) score on the cognitive index holds a more extreme *attitude*.

Increasing the action-predicting power of attitude measurement. The study of public attitudes (the term "public opinion" is avoided to eliminate confusion with the study of beliefs about affectively insignificant objects) is frequently motivated by the desire to predict what people will *do,* how they will overtly behave toward the objects of their attitudes. Thus the political pollster wants to know for whom the respondent will actually vote; the market researcher wants to know whether the respondent will actually buy the commodity; the media research specialist wants to know whether the respondent actually reads all or most of the publication for which he has expressed a liking.

The point has often been made that attitudes are not the sole determinants of actual overt behavior toward their objects.[20] Situational factors and restraints may interfere with or redirect the action orientations implicit in attitudes. Similarly, a person may fail to act on, or "act out," an attitude because such action is countermanded by a competing dispositional state (i.e. a motive or scruple or, for that matter, some other attitude) whose implications militate against carrying out the attitude-based action.

Before we can begin to make precise predictions about when, and to what extent, persons will *act* upon their attitudes we will have to reach a solution to the vast problem (it is really one of the *main* problems of psychology) of ranking, patterning, and relating to one another the many variables that conceivably control and determine overt action.

[19] V. Nowlis, "Some Studies of the Influence of Films on Mood and Attitude," Technical Report to the Office of Naval Research, 1960, mimeographed document. See also J. Axelrod, "The Relationship of Mood and Mood Shift in Attitude," Technical Report to the Office of Naval Research, 1959, mimeographed document.

[20] For a recent discussion of this problem, see Katz and Stotland, *op. cit.*

In the face of this limitation in present knowledge, what is usually done is to follow a theoretical rule of thumb to the effect that the "stronger" the attitude, the more likely it will be that the subject will take consistent action toward the attitude object. Perhaps a more precise way of stating this relationship is that the more extreme (and thus, following Suchman,[21] the more intense) the attitude, the stronger must the action-opposing forces be for the action to fail to occur in the particular attitude-eliciting situation in which those forces are operative. If such a working rule seems applicable to any situation in which attitudes are studied so as to predict overt behavior, it follows clearly that improvement in the validity of estimates of attitude intensity will increase the likelihood of successful prediction. On this basis some of the considerations raised above take on an additional relevance. If the measurement of the cognitive as well as the affective components of attitudes provides more valid estimates of attitude extremity and intensity, it is clear that the use of such measurement will enable more effective prediction of the attitude holder's response in a situation which allows for overt action toward the attitude object. As an example, let us consider a group of farmers, all of whom, or a sample of whom, have been previously tested for both their affective and cognitive responses toward a particular political candidate. If they live far from their polling place and the forecast is for heavy rain on election day, it should be possible to predict who is more likely to vote, and who not to vote, on the basis of the extent to which any individual or subgroup is characterized by a rich and detailed set of affect-supporting cognitions.

Beyond this obvious illustration it may be worth noting that the relation between the cognitive component of an attitude and the likelihood of consistent action may be influenced not only by the over-all import of the set of attitudinal cognitions (as represented, for example, in the index of cognitive structure used in the experiments reported above) but by the *content* of those cognitions as well. Thus, in the example already posed, if our investigations of attitudinal cognition reveal that some individuals stress the belief that the candidate, if elected, will strive to reduce the danger of drought, they may be less likely to drive through heavy rain to vote for him than a group of individuals who stress the belief that the candidate will restore agricultural payments to full parity.

Increasing the effectiveness of attitude-change procedures. The main concern in the first section of this paper was to outline, and offer evidence in support of, a structural theory of attitude change. The production of inconsistency between the affective and cognitive portions of a previously consistent and stable attitude structure was posited as the basic condition for such change. But it was pointed out that such inconsistency must exceed the person's tolerance limit and be maintained by forces that cannot be avoided or ultimately rejected. With these considerations in the background it is possible to outline a number of more specific points about the production of attitude change. These points are applicable only to attempts to influence persons or groups whose attitudes have been previously measured in their cognitive as well as their affective aspects.

Two aspects of persuasion campaigns are, first, the problem of *locating* the person or persons to whom change communications are to be addressed and, second, the design of these communications. An occasional strategy in persuasion campaigns is to concentrate attention not on all members of the reference population but rather on persons within that population who are centrally located in terms of their power to influence others. A strategy that may be employed separately, or in combination with this one, is to direct the main persuasion effort toward those within the reference population who seem to be potentially most persuasible on the matters at issue. Disregarding the question of the personality correlates of general persuasibility,[22] we may pursue the implications of the proposition

21 E. A. Suchman, "The Intensity Component in Attitude and Opinion Research," in S. A. Stouffer, *et al., Measurement and Prediction,* Princeton, N.J., Princeton University Press, 1950.

22 On this problem see C. I. Hovland and I. L. Janis, editors, *Personality and Persuasibility,* New Haven, Conn., Yale University Press, 1959.

that the less uniform the cognitive content of an attitude the greater is the likelihood of producing an alteration in it.

Now in situations where it is possible to determine the cognitive aspect of attitudes (whether through formal test procedures or through content analysis techniques, or, for that matter, through direct interviewing) it will be found that, even among a group of persons all of whom might be characterized as "moderates," there exist a number of different types of attitude structure. For example, two bureaucrats in a new African republic may be roughly equal in holding moderately anti-American attitudes. For one the moderately negative affect may be organized with a number of separate beliefs in *each* of which the United States is seen as *partially* violating such positive goals as "the end of colonialism," "independence for Algeria," and "the rapid development of African economic potential." Another may see the United States as *strongly* opposed to Algerian independence but generally (and paradoxically) in favor of ending colonialism; and he may be confused as to whether the United States intends to aid African economic development. Which of these two would be the more likely person to whom to address communications designed to transform his over-all attitude toward the United States to a favorable one? On the principle that the production of "intolerable" affective-cognitive inconsistency is a necessary condition for attitude change, it would seem clear that the person whose attitude structure already features some "tolerable" inconsistency is the most likely target for persuasion. If any of his other beliefs can be reversed, the additional amount of inconsistency produced may be sufficient to render the consequent degree of inconsistency "intolerable" and thus may generate an accommodating change of affect in the consistency-restoring direction.

Turning to the question of the development of communications intended to produce attitude change, let us examine first some further aspects of the strategy involving direct alteration of attitudinal cognitions. An extension of the considerations presented above with regard to "tolerably" inconsistent attitude structures is that the cognitions making for this state of affairs may be utilized as "entering wedges." As an example let us consider a hypothetical person who consistently dislikes and resists appeals for contributions to medical research organizations. Assume that his tested beliefs with regard to such appeals have the following content: much of the money that is collected is kept by the professional fund raisers themselves; this way of financing medical research is chaotic; the money frequently goes to incompetent researchers, etc. But if at the same time he believes that the anti-polio vaccine was developed under support from such funds, and if the fact that he holds this belief is known, the implications for further communication are clear. Evidence can be pulled together and transmitted to the effect that many other important medical discoveries have been achieved under similar conditions of financial support. As the intensity and certainty of this generalized version of his originally inconsistent belief is increased, the level of inconsistency within the structure is increased so that arguments bearing on other matters of belief may now become more compelling.

A related point is that even when all of an individual's elicited beliefs are consistent with his expressed attitudinal affect, these beliefs will vary in the certainty with which they are held and in the significance of the values or goals to which they refer. Thus the use of some form of cognitive testing may reveal that a person who opposes medical fund-raising campaigns is less certain that professional fund raisers "take a large cut" than he is that the fund-raising situation is a chaotic one. Or it might be discovered that he is more offended by "chaos" than by "professional fund raisers." Advance knowledge on such matters would suggest just which of the person's beliefs are most likely to be modifiable when persuasive counterarguments are directed at him.

Further implications along these lines will not be elaborated here. The general proposition behind these points is the simple one that the more that is known about the contents and strengths of various portions of the total cognitive component of an attitude, the more effectively can persuasive communications be developed.

When attitudes are highly normative for a given group of persons it is likely that there will be considerable similarity not only in their over-all affective responses to the attitude object but also in their beliefs (both consistent and inconsistent) about it. To the extent that such a situation is uncovered by effective measurement of attitudinal cognitions, it can be used as a guide to the development of large-scale persuasion programs.

Usually, such programs are based upon attempts to alter old beliefs or set up new ones, but, as was noted above, these are sometimes combined with more direct attempts at affect modification. Campaigns that involve communicating the judgments of prestigeful figures or of reference groups are of this type. The achievement of any significant degree of alteration in the cognitive supports of an attitudinal affect is likely to render that affect more responsive to the influence of such direct inductions. On this basis all the aforementioned points on the design of cognitive appeals may have equal relevance to the situation in which such appeals are combined with attempts at more direct modification of attitudinal affect.

Decreasing the guilt feelings of propagandist. The conceptualization of attitude structure that has been employed in this paper seems to the writer to be useful in clarifying some of the ethical issues involved in the persuasion transaction. It is clear that among those who are professionally engaged in trying to alter the attitudes of others there are quite a few who experience moral agitation as they pursue their work. From what such persons say about their dilemmas (in articles, novels, and cocktail-party "mea culpas") their disturbance is rooted in seeing themselves as sometimes involved in communicating untruths or in propagating false values.

In this article the word "propaganda" has been used in its nonperjorative sense; it has referred to organized and systematic attempts to persuade. But clearly there are kinds of propagandistic activity which involve dishonesty and kinds which do not; there are kinds which assert values that

appear "false" to the propagandist and kinds which do not. An ethical person, capable of thinking clearly, can usually distinguish between these possibilities. But in the midst of the tension, disorder, and improvisation that characterize some areas of the persuasion professions the distinction may sometimes blur and evade the grasp of self-knowledge.

One expedient may be for the propagandist to study *his own* attitudinal cognitions; to rank them, if possible, for the certainty with which they are held; to order his awareness of his own values and of the hierarchies into which they are organized. The consequence of self-analysis conducted in some such terms may be that he will be better able to organize and design his propagandistic communications so that they will be consistent with his real images of the relationships between "objects" and "values" and with his own sense of what social goals are truly valuable.

Of course it has been argued that the exigencies of the propagandist's situation and the urgencies of his task make total ingenuousness impossible. To the extent that this is true, and in some part it certainly is, it denotes one of the main problems of modern existence: the pressure upon individuals to act out roles that estrange them from their own ideals. But the role of propagandist need not require cynicism and deceit. When the propagandist is aware of the exact scope of the inconsistency, if any, between what he propagandizes and what he believes, he is usually in a position to reduce or eliminate that inconsistency. And if he cannot, he is at least then in a position to clarify the moral meaning of continuing his commitment to his work.

An ethical use of propaganda requires, too, a respect for the cognitive processes and achievements of those to whom persuasive communications are directed. It has already been observed that propagandists' attempts to change attitudinal affects by direct manipulation are usually subordinated to accompanying cognitive appeals. But this is not always the case. Procedures intended to produce affect alteration by methods that evade any significant recourse to the evidence and data bearing upon attitudinal beliefs may violate, or at least bypass, that which is most admirable in man: his potential for informed thought. The proper sphere of such methods is in the *experimental study* of attitude dynamics, and only when, as in the case of the present studies involving hypnosis, considerable effort is applied after the data have been collected to clarifying for the subjects the nature of the phenomena that they have experienced.

Perhaps the ultimate utility of such experiments, apart from their contribution to theory development, is that they will equip us to defend ourselves better against some of the demeaning techniques by which persuasion is achieved through suppression of the claims of reason.

Processes of Opinion Change* / Herbert C. Kelman

Attitude and opinion data provide a basis for inferring the meaning of opinions held by individuals and groups and also for predictions about their future behavior. Such inferences and predictions, if they are to be made effectively, require a theoretical foundation which explains the processes by which people adopt and express particular opinions. Here is a theory of three processes by which persons respond to social influence.

Herbert C. Kelman is Lecturer on Social Psychology at Harvard University. Currently, he is spending the year at the Institute for Social Research in Oslo and devoting part of his time to a further study of the effects of a year's sojourn in the United States on the self-images of Scandinavian students. His theoretical and experimental work during the past eight years on the problems reported in this article will be published in a forthcoming book, an early draft of which was awarded the Socio-Psychological Prize of the American Association for the Advancement of Science in 1956.

A persistent concern in the analysis of public opinion data is the "meaning" that one can ascribe to the observed distributions and trends—and to the positions taken by particular individuals and segments of the population. Clearly, to understand what opinion data mean we have to know considerably more than the direction of an individual's responses or the distribution of responses in the population. We need information that will allow us to make some inferences about the characteristics of the observed opinions—their intensity, their salience, the level of commitment that they imply. We need information about the motivational bases of these opinions—about the functions that they fulfill for the individual and the motivational systems in which they are embedded.[1] We need information about the cognitive links of the opinions—the amount and the nature of information that supports them, the specific expectations and evaluations that surround them.

The need for more detailed information becomes even more apparent when we attempt to use opinion data for the prediction of subsequent behavior. What is the likelihood that the opinions observed in a particular survey will be translated into some form of concrete action? What is the nature of the actions that people who hold a particular opinion are likely to take, and how are they likely to react to various events? How likely

Reprinted from *Public Opinion Quarterly*, 1961, 25, pages 57–78, by permission of author and publisher, Princeton University.

* This paper is based on a research program on social influence and behavior change, supported by grant M–2516 from the National Institute of Mental Health.

[1] For discussions of the different motivational bases of opinion see I. Sarnoff and D. Katz, "The Motivational Bases of Attitude Change," *Journal of Abnormal and Social Psychology*, Vol. 49, 1954, pp. 115–124; and M. B. Smith, J. S. Bruner, and R. W. White, *Opinions and Personality*, New York, Wiley, 1956.

are these opinions to persist over time and to generalize to related issues? What are the conditions under which one might expect these opinions to be abandoned and changed? Such predictions can be made only to the extent to which we are informed about the crucial dimensions of the opinions in question, about the motivations that underlie them, and about the cognitive contexts in which they are held.

INFERRING THE MEANING OF OPINIONS

In a certain sense, the need for more detailed information about opinions can (and must) be met by improvements and refinements in the methodology of opinion assessment. A great deal of progress in this direction has already been made in recent years. Thus, many widely accepted features of interviewing technique are specifically designed to elicit information on which valid inferences about the meaning of opinions can be based: the creation of a relaxed, nonjudgmental atmosphere; the emphasis on open-ended questions; the progressive funneling from general to specific questions; the use of probes, of indirect questions, and of interlocking questions; and so on. These procedures facilitate inferences (1) by maximizing the likelihood that the respondent will give rich and full information and thus reveal the motivational and cognitive structure underlying the expressed opinions, and (2) by minimizing the likelihood that the respondent will consciously or unconsciously distort his "private" opinions when expressing them to the interviewer.

Similarly, when attitudes are assessed by means of questionnaires, it is possible to approximate these methodological goals. In part, this is accomplished by the instructions, which can motivate the subject to respond fully and honestly and assure him of confidentialness or anonymity. In part it is accomplished by the use of indirect and projective questions, and by the inclusion of a series of interrelated items in the questionnaire. And, in part, it is possible to make inferences about the meaning of opinions by the use of various scaling devices in the analysis of the data.

There is no question about the importance of these methodological advances, but in and of themselves they do not solve the problem of inference. They increase the investigator's ability to obtain rich and relatively undistorted information on which he can then base valid inferences. But, no matter how refined the techniques, they do not provide direct information about the meaning of the opinions and do not permit automatic predictions to subsequent behavior: the investigator still has to make inferences from the data.

To make such inferences, the student of public opinion needs a theoretical framework which accounts for the adoption and expression of particular opinions on the part of individuals and groups. Such a framework can serve as a guide in the collection of data: it can provide a systematic basis for deciding what information is relevant and what questions should be asked in order to permit the drawing of inferences. Similarly, it can serve as a guide for interpreting the data and deriving implications from them.

The need for such a framework is particularly apparent when one attempts to make predictions about subsequent behavior on the basis of opinion data. For example, in a relaxed interview situation a particular respondent may express himself favorably toward socialized medicine. What are the chances that he will take the same position in a variety of other situations? To answer this, we would need a theoretical scheme for the analysis of interaction situations, in terms of which we could make some inferences about the structure and meaning of this particular interview situation as compared to various other situations in which the issue of socialized medicine might arise. How would we expect this same respondent to react to a concerted campaign by the Medical Association which links Federal insurance programs with creeping socialism? To answer this, we would need a theory of opinion formation and change, in terms of which we could make some inferences about the characteristics of opinions formed under different conditions.

Progress in the analysis of public opinion, then, requires theoretical development along with methodological improvements. For this development, it should be possible to draw on some of the current theoretical thinking and associated research in social psychology. There are two foci of social-psychological theorizing and research that would appear to be particularly germane to the analysis of public opinion. One is the study of processes of social interaction as such. Such diverse approaches to the analysis of social interaction as those of Getzels,[2] Goffman,[3] and Jones and Thibaut,[4] for example, can be useful for conceptualizing the determinants of *opinion expression*. Thus, by using one or another of these schemes, the investigator can make some formulations about the expectations that the respondent brought to the interview situation and the goals that he was trying to achieve in this interaction. On the basis of such a formulation, he can make inferences about the meaning of the opinions expressed in this situation and about their implications for subsequent behavior—for example, about the likelihood that similar opinions will be expressed in a variety of other situations.

The second relevant focus of social-psychological theorizing and research is the study of processes of social influence and the induction of behavior change. Theoretical analyses in this area can be useful for conceptualizing the determinants of *opinion formation* and *opinion change*. They can help the investigator in making formulations about the sources of the opinions expressed by the respondent—the social conditions under which they were adopted, the motivations that underlie them, and the social and personal systems in which they are embedded. On the basis of such a formulation, again, he can make inferences about

the meaning and implications of the opinions ascertained.

The model that I shall present here emerged out of the second research focus—the study of social influence and behavior change. It is, essentially, an attempt to conceptualize the processes of opinion formation and opinion change. It starts with the assumption that opinions adopted under different conditions of social influence, and based on different motivations, will differ in terms of their qualitative characteristics and their subsequent histories. Thus, if we know something about the determinants and motivational bases of particular opinions, we should be able to make predictions about the conditions under which they are likely to be expressed, the conditions under which they are likely to change, and other behavioral consequences to which they are likely to lead. Ideally, such a model can be useful in the analysis of public opinion by suggesting relevant variables in terms of which opinion data can be examined and predictions can be formulated.

THE STUDY OF SOCIAL INFLUENCE

Social influence has been a central area of concern for experimental social psychology almost since its beginnings. Three general research traditions in this area can be distinguished: (1) the study of social influences on judgments, stemming from the earlier work on prestige suggestion;[5] (2) the study of social influences arising from small-group interaction;[6] and (3) the study of social influences arising from persuasive communications.[7] In recent years, there has been a considerable convergence between these three traditions, going hand in hand with an increased interest in developing general principles of social influence and socially induced behavior change.

One result of these developments has been that many investigators found it nec-

[2] J. W. Getzels, "The Question-Answer Process: A Conceptualization and Some Derived Hypotheses for Empirical Examination," *Public Opinion Quarterly*, Vol. 18, 1954, pp. 80–91.

[3] See, for example, E. Goffman, "On Face-work: An Analysis of Ritual Elements in Social Interaction," *Psychiatry*, Vol. 18, 1955, pp. 213–231; and "Alienation from Interaction," *Human Relations*, Vol. 10, 1957, pp. 47–60.

[4] E. E. Jones and J. W. Thibaut, "Interaction Goals as Bases of Inference in Interpersonal Perception," in R. Tagiuri and L. Petrullo, editors, *Person Perception and Interpersonal Behavior*, Stanford, Calif., Stanford University Press, 1958, pp. 151–178.

[5] See, for example, S. E. Asch, *Social Psychology*, New York, Prentice-Hall, 1952.

[6] See, for example, D. Cartwright and A. Zander, editors, *Group Dynamics*, Evanston, Ill., Row, Peterson, 1953.

[7] See, for example, C. I. Hovland, I. L. Janis, and H. H. Kelley, *Communication and Persuasion*, New Haven, Yale University Press, 1953.

essary to make qualitative distinctions between different types of influence. In some cases, these distinctions arose primarily out of the observation that social influence may have qualitatively different effects, that it may produce different kinds of change. For example, under some conditions it may result in mere public conformity—in superficial changes on a verbal or overt level without accompanying changes in belief; in other situations it may result in private acceptance—in a change that is more general, more durable, more intergrated with the person's own values.[8] Other investigators found it necessary to make distinctions because they observed that influence may occur for different reasons, that it may arise out of different motivations and orientations. For example, under some conditions influence may be primarily informational—the subject may conform to the influencing person or group because he views him as a source of valid information; in other situations influence may be primarily normative—the subject may conform in order to meet the positive expectations of the influencing person or group.[9]

My own work can be viewed in the general context that I have outlined here. I started out with the distinction between public conformity and private acceptance, and tried to establish some of the distinct determinants of each. I became dissatisfied with this dichotomy as I began to look at important examples of social influence that

could not be encompassed by it. I was especially impressed with the accounts of ideological conversion of the "true believer" variety, and with the recent accounts of "brainwashing," particularly the Chinese Communist methods of "thought reform."[10] It is apparent that these experiences do not simply involve public conformity, but that indeed they produce a change in underlying beliefs. But it is equally apparent that they do not produce what we would usually consider private acceptance—changes that are in some sense integrated with the person's own value system and that have become independent of the external source. Rather, they seem to produce new beliefs that are isolated from the rest of the person's values and that are highly dependent on external support.

These considerations eventually led me to distinguish three processes of social influence, each characterized by a distinct set of antecedent and a distinct set of consequent conditions. I have called these processes *compliance, identification,* and *internalization.*[11]

THREE PROCESSES OF SOCIAL INFLUENCE

Compliance can be said to occur when an individual accepts influence from another person or from a group because he hopes to achieve a favorable reaction from the other. He may be interested in attaining certain specific rewards or in avoiding certain specific punishments that the influencing agent controls. For example, an individual may make a special effort to express only "correct" opinions in order to gain admission into a particular group or social set, or in order to avoid being fired from his government job. Or, the individual may be concerned with gaining approval or avoiding disapproval from the influencing agent in a more general way. For example, some individuals may compulsively try to say the

[8] See, for example, L. Festinger, "An Analysis of Compliant Behavior," in M. Sherif and M. O. Wilson, editors, *Group Relations at the Crossroads,* New York, Harper, 1953, pp. 232–256; H. C. Kelman, "Attitude Change as a Function of Response Restriction," *Human Relations,* Vol. 6, 1953, pp. 185–214; J. R. P. French, Jr., and B. Raven, "The Bases of Social Power," in D. Cartwright, editor, *Studies in Social Power,* Ann Arbor, Mich., Institute for Social Research, 1959, pp. 150–167; and Marie Jahoda, "Conformity and Independence," *Human Relations,* Vol. 12, 1959, pp. 99–120.

[9] See, for example, M. Deutsch and H. B. Gerard, "A Study of Normative and Informational Social Influence upon Individual Judgment," *Journal of Abnormal and Social Psychology,* Vol. 51, 1955, pp. 629–636; J. W. Thibaut and L. Strickland, "Psychological Set and Social Conformity," *Journal of Personality,* Vol. 25, 1956, pp. 115–129; and J. M. Jackson and H. D. Saltzstein, "The Effect of Person-Group Relationships on Conformity Processes," *Journal of Abnormal and Social Psychology,* Vol. 57, 1958, pp. 17–24

[10] For instance, R. J. Lifton, " 'Thought Reform' of Western Civilians in Chinese Communist Prisons," *Psychiatry,* Vol. 19, 1956, pp. 173–195.

[11] A detailed description of these processes and the experimental work based on them will be contained in a forthcoming book, S*ocial Influence and Personal Belief: A Theoretical and Experimental Approach to the Study of Behavior Change,* to be published by John Wiley & Sons.

expected thing in all situations and please everyone with whom they come in contact, out of a disproportionate need for favorable responses from others of a direct and immediate kind. In any event, when the individual complies, he does what the agent wants him to do—or what he thinks the agent wants him to do—because he sees this as a way of achieving a desired response from him. He does not adopt the induced behavior—for example, a particular opinion response—because he believes in its content, but because it is instrumental in the production of a satisfying social effect. What the individual learns, essentially, is to say or do the expected thing in special situations, regardless of what his private beliefs may be. Opinions adopted through compliance should be expressed only when the person's behavior is observable by the influencing agent.

Identification can be said to occur when an individual adopts behavior derived from another person or a group because this behavior is associated with a satisfying self-defining relationship to this person or group. By a self-defining relationship I mean a role relationship that forms a part of the person's self-image. Accepting influence through identification, then, is a way of establishing or maintaining the desired relationship to the other, and the self-definition that is anchored in this relationship.

The relationship that an individual tries to establish or maintain through identification may take different forms. It may take the form of classical identification, that is, of a relationship in which the individual takes over all or part of the role of the influencing agent. To the extent to which such a relationship exists, the individual defines his own role in terms of the role of the other. He attempts to be like or actually to *be* the other person. By saying what the other says, doing what he does, believing what he believes, the individual maintains this relationship and the satisfying self-definition that it provides him. An influencing agent who is likely to be an attractive object for such a relationship is one who occupies a role desired by the individual—who possesses those characteristics that the individual himself lacks—such as control in

a situation in which the individual is helpless, direction in a situation in which he is disoriented, or belongingness in a situation in which he is isolated.

The behavior of the brainwashed prisoner in Communist China provides one example of this type of identification. By adopting the attitudes and beliefs of the prison authorities—including *their* evaluation of *him* —he attempts to regain his identity, which has been subjected to severe threats. But this kind of identification does not occur only in such severe crisis situations. It can also be observed, for example, in the context of socialization of children, where the taking over of parental attitudes and actions is a normal, and probably essential, part of personality development. The more or less conscious efforts involved when an individual learns to play a desired occupational role and imitates an appropriate role model would also exemplify this process. Here, of course, the individual is much more selective in the attitudes and actions he takes over from the other person. What is at stake is not his basic sense of identity or the stability of his self-concept, but rather his more limited "professional identity."

The self-defining relationship that an individual tries to establish or maintain through identification may also take the form of a reciprocal role relationship— that is, of a relationship in which the roles of the two parties are defined with reference to one another. An individual may be involved in a reciprocal relationship with another specific individual, as in a friendship relationship between two people. Or he may enact a social role which is defined with reference to another (reciprocal) role, as in the relationship between patient and doctor. A reciprocal-role relationship can be maintained only if the participants have mutually shared expectations of one another's behavior. Thus, if an individual finds a particular relationship satisfying, he will tend to behave in such a way as to meet the expectations of the other. In other words, he will tend to behave in line with the requirements of this particular relationship. This should be true regardless of whether the other is watching or not: quite apart from the reactions of the other, it is important to the individual's own self-concept to meet the expectations of his friendship role, for example, or those of his occupational role.

Thus, the acceptance of influence through identification should take place when the person sees the induced behavior as relevant to and required by a reciprocal-role relationship in which he is a participant. Acceptance of influence based on a reciprocal-role relationship is similar to that involved in classical identification in that it is a way of establishing or maintaining a satisfying self-defining relationship to another. The nature of the relationship differs, of course. In one case it is a relationship of identity; in the other, one of reciprocity. In the case of reciprocal-role relationships, the individual is not identifying with the other in the sense of taking over *his* identity, but in the sense of empathically reacting in terms of the other person's expectations, feelings, or needs.

Identification may also serve to maintain an individual's relationship to a group in which his self-definition is anchored. Such a relationship may have elements of classical identification as well as of reciprocal roles: to maintain his self-definition as a group member an individual, typically, has to model his behavior along particular lines and has to meet the expectations of his fellow members. An example of identification with a group would be the member of the Communist Party who derives strength and a sense of identity from his self-definition as part of the vanguard of the proletarian revolution and as an agent of historical destiny. A similar process, but at a low degree of intensity, is probably involved in many of the conventions that people acquire as part of their socialization into a particular group.

Identification is similar to compliance in that the individual does not adopt the induced behavior because its content per se is intrinsically satisfying. Identification differs from compliance, however, in that the individual actually believes in the opinions and actions that he adopts. The behavior is accepted both publicly and privately, and its manifestation does not depend on observability by the influencing agent. It does depend, however, on the role that an individual takes at any given moment in time. Only

when the appropriate role is activated—only when the individual is acting within the relationship upon which the identification is based—will the induced opinions be expressed. The individual is not primarily concerned with pleasing the other, with giving him what he wants (as in compliance), but he is concerned with meeting the other's expectations for his own role performance. Thus, opinions adopted through identification do remain tied to the external source and dependent on social support. They are not integrated with the individual's value system, but rather tend to be isolated from the rest of his values—to remain encapsulated.

Finally, *internalization* can be said to occur when an individual accepts influence because the induced behavior is congruent with his value system. It is the content of the induced behavior that is intrinsically rewarding here. The individual adopts it because he finds it useful for the solution of a problem, or because it is congenial to his own orientation, or because it is demanded by his own values—in short, because he perceives it as inherently conducive to the maximization of his values. The characteristics of the influencing agent do play an important role in internalization, but the crucial dimension here—as we shall see below—is the agent's credibility, that is, his relation to the content.

The most obvious examples of internalization are those that involve the evaluation and acceptance of induced behavior on rational grounds. A person may adopt the recommendations of an expert, for example, because he finds them relevant to his own problems and congruent with his own values. Typically, when internalization is involved, he will not accept these recommendations *in toto* but modify them to some degree so that they will fit his own unique situation. Or a visitor to a foreign country may be challenged by the different patterns of behavior to which he is exposed, and he may decide to adopt them (again, selectively and in modified form) because he finds them more in keeping with his own values than the patterns in his home country. I am not implying, of course, that internalization is always involved in the situations mentioned.

One would speak of internalization only if acceptance of influence took the particular form that I described.

Internalization, however, does not necessarily involve the adoption of induced behavior on rational grounds. I would not want to equate internalization with rationality, even though the description of the process has decidedly rationalist overtones. For example, I would characterize as internalization the adoption of beliefs because of their congruence with a value system that is basically *irrational*. Thus, an authoritarian individual may adopt certain racist attitudes because they fit into his paranoid, irrational view of the world. Presumably, what is involved here is internalization, since it is the content of the induced behavior and its relation to the person's value system that is satisfying. Similarly, it should be noted that congruence with a person's value system does not necessarily imply logical consistency. Behavior would be congruent if, in some way or other, it fit into the person's value system, if it seemed to belong there and be demanded by it.

It follows from this conception that behavior adopted through internalization is in some way—rational or otherwise—integrated with the individual's existing values. It becomes part of a personal system, as distinguished from a system of social-role expectations. Such behavior gradually becomes independent of the external source. Its manifestation depends neither on observability by the influencing agent nor on the activation of the relevant role, but on the extent to which the underlying values have been made relevant by the issues under consideration. This does not mean that the individual will invariably express internalized opinions, regardless of the social situation. In any specific situation, he has to choose among competing values in the face of a variety of situational requirements. It does mean, however, that these opinions will at least enter into competition with other alternatives whenever they are relevant in content.

It should be stressed that the three processes are not mutually exclusive. While they have been defined in terms of pure cases, they do not generally occur in pure form in real-life situations. The examples that have been given are, at best, situations in which a particular process predominates and determines the central features of the interaction.

ANTECEDENTS AND CONSEQUENTS OF THE THREE PROCESSES

For each of the three processes, a distinct set of antecedents and a distinct set of consequents have been proposed. These are summarized in the table below. First, with respect to the antecedents of the three processes, it should be noted that no systematic quantitative differences between them are hypothesized. The probability of each process is presented as a function of the same three determinants: the importance of the induction for the individual's goal achievement, the power of the influencing agent, and the prepotency of the induced response. For each process, the magnitude of these determinants may vary over the entire range: each may be based on an induction with varying degrees of importance, on an influencing agent with varying degrees of power, and so on. The processes differ only in terms of the *qualitative* form that these determinants take. They differ, as can be seen in the table, in terms of the *basis* for the importance of the induction, the *source* of the influencing agent's power, and the *manner* of achieving prepotency of the induced response.

1. The processes can be distinguished in terms of the basis for the importance of the induction, that is, in terms of the nature of the motivational system that is activated in the influence situation. What is it about the influence situation that makes it important, that makes it relevant to the individual's goals? What are the primary concerns that the individual brings to the situation or that are aroused by it? The differences between the three processes in this respect are implicit in the descriptions of the processes given above: (a) To the extent that the individual is concerned—for whatever reason —with the *social effect* of his behavior, influence will tend to take the form of compliance. (b) To the extent that he is concerned with the *social anchorage* of his behavior, influence will tend to take the form of identification. (c) To the extent that he

SUMMARY OF THE DISTINCTIONS BETWEEN
THE THREE PROCESSES

	Compliance	Identification	Internalization
Antecedents:			
1. Basis for the *importance of the induction*	Concern with social effect of behavior	Concern with social anchorage of behavior	Concern with value congruence of behavior
2. Source of *power of the influencing agent*	Means control	Attractiveness	Credibility
3. Manner of achieving *prepotency of the induced response*	Limitation of choice behavior	Delineation of role requirements	Reorganization of means-ends framework
Consequents:			
1. Conditions of performance of induced response	Surveillance by influencing agent	Salience of relationship to agent	Relevance of values to issue
2. Conditions of change and extinction of induced response	Changed perception of conditions for social rewards	Changed perception of conditions for satisfying self-defining relationships	Changed perception of conditions for value maximization
3. Type of behavior system in which induced response is embedded	External demands of a specific setting	Expectations defining a specific role	Person's value system

is concerned with the *value congruence* of his behavior (rational or otherwise), influence will tend to take the form of internalization.

2. A difference between the three processes in terms of the source of the influencing agent's power is hypothesized. (a) To the extent that the agent's power is based on his *means control,* influence will tend to take the form of compliance. An agent possesses means control if he is in a position to supply or withhold means needed by the individual for the achievement of his goals. The perception of means control may depend on the agent's *actual* control over specific rewards and punishments, or on his *potential* control, which would be related to his position in the social structure (his status, authority, or general prestige). (b) To the extent that the agent's power is based on his *attractiveness,* influence will tend to take the form of identification. An agent is attractive if he occupies a role which the individual himself desires[12] or if he oc-

cupies a role reciprocal to one the individual wants to establish or maintain. The term "attractiveness," as used here, does not refer to the possession of qualities that make a person likable, but rather to the possession of qualities on the part of the agent that make a continued relationship to him particularly desirable. In other words, an agent is attractive when the individual is able to derive satisfaction from a self-definition with reference to him. (c) To the extent that the agent's power is based on his *credibility,* influence will tend to take the form of internalization. An agent possesses credibility if his statements are considered truthful and valid, and hence worthy of serious consideration. Hovland, Janis, and Kelley[13] distinguish two bases for credibility: expertness and trustworthiness. In other words, an agent may be perceived as possessing credibility because he is likely to *know* the truth, or because he is likely to *tell* the truth. Trustworthiness, in turn, may

12 This is similar to John Whiting's conception of "Status Envy" as a basis for identification. See J. W. M. Whiting, "Sorcery, Sin, and the

Superego," in M. R. Jones, editor, *Nebraska Symposium on Motivation,* Lincoln, University of Nebraska Press, 1959, pp. 174–195. [Cf. pp. 153–166].
13 *Op. cit.,* p. 21.

be related to over-all respect, likemindedness, and lack of vested interest.

3. It is proposed that the three processes differ in terms of the way in which prepotency is achieved. (a) To the extent that the induced response becomes prepotent—that is, becomes a "distinguished path" relative to alternative response possibilities—because the individual's choice behavior is limited, influence will tend to take the form of compliance. This may happen if the individual is pressured into the induced response, or if alternative responses are blocked. The induced response thus becomes prepotent because it is, essentially, the only response permitted: the individual sees himself as having no choice and as being restricted to this particular alternative. (b) To the extent that the induced response becomes prepotent because the requirements of a particular role are delineated, influence will tend to take the form of identification. This may happen if the situation is defined in terms of a particular role relationship and the demands of that role are more or less clearly specified; for instance, if this role is made especially salient and the expectations deriving from it dominate the field. Or it may happen if alternative roles are made ineffective because the situation is ambiguous and consensual validation is lacking. The induced response thus becomes prepotent because it is one of the few alternatives available to the individual: his choice behavior may be unrestricted, but his opportunity for selecting alternative responses is limited by the fact that he is operating exclusively from the point of view of a particular role system. (c) Finally, to the extent that the induced response becomes prepotent because there has been a reorganization in the individual's conception of means-ends relationships, influence will tend to take the form of internalization. This may happen if the implications of the induced response for certain important values—implications of which the individual had been unaware heretofore—are brought out, or if the advantages of the induced response as a path to the individual's goals, compared to the various alternatives that are available, are made apparent. The induced response thus becomes prepotent because it has taken on a new meaning: as the

relationships between various means and ends become restructured, it emerges as the preferred course of action in terms of the person's own values.

Depending, then, on the nature of these three antecedents, the influence process will take the form of compliance, identification, or internalization. Each of these corresponds to a characteristic pattern of internal responses—thoughts and feelings—in which the individual engages as he accepts influence. The resulting changes will, in turn, be different for the three processes, as indicated in the second half of the table. Here, again, it is assumed that there are no systematic quantitative differences between the processes, but rather qualitative variations in the subsequent histories of behavior adopted through each process.

1. It is proposed that the processes differ in terms of the subsequent conditions under which the induced response will be performed or expressed. (a) When an individual adopts an induced response through compliance, he tends to perform it only under conditions of *surveillance* by the influencing agent. These conditions are met if the agent is physically present, or if he is likely to find out about the individual's actions. (b) When an individual adopts an induced response through identification, he tends to perform it only under conditions of *salience* of his relationship to the agent. That is, the occurrence of the behavior will depend on the extent to which the person's relationship to the agent has been engaged in the situation. Somehow this relationship has to be brought into focus and the individual has to be acting within the particular role that is involved in the identification. This does not necessarily mean, however, that he is consciously aware of the relationship; the role can be activated without such awareness. (c) When an individual adopts an induced response through internalization, he tends to perform it under conditions of *relevance of the values* that were initially involved in the influence situation. The behavior will tend to occur whenever these values are activated by the issues under consideration in a given situation, quite regardless of surveillance or salience of the influencing agent. This does not mean, of course, that the be-

havior will occur every time it becomes relevant. It may be out-competed by other responses in certain situations. The probability of occurrence with a given degree of issue relevance will depend on the strength of the internalized behavior.

2. It is hypothesized that responses adopted through the three processes will differ in terms of the conditions under which they will subsequently be abandoned or changed. (a) A response adopted through compliance will be abandoned if it is no longer perceived as the best path toward the attainment of social rewards. (b) A response adopted through identification will be abandoned if it is no longer perceived as the best path toward the maintenance or establishment of satisfying self-defining relationships. (c) A response adopted through internalization will be abandoned if it is no longer perceived as the best path toward the maximization of the individual's values.

3. Finally, it is hypothesized that responses adopted through the three processes will differ from each other along certain qualitative dimensions. These can best be summarized, perhaps, by referring to the type of behavior system in which the induced response is embedded. (a) Behavior adopted through compliance is part of a system of external demands that characterize a specific setting. In other words, it is part of the rules of conduct that an individual learns in order to get along in a particular situation or series of situations. The behavior tends to be related to the person's values only in an instrumental rather than an intrinsic way. As long as opinions, for example, remain at that level, the individual will tend to regard them as not really representative of his true beliefs. (b) Behavior adopted through identification is part of a system of expectations defining a particular role—whether this is the role of the other which he is taking over, or a role reciprocal to the other's. This behavior will be regarded by the person as representing himself, and may in fact form an important aspect of himself. It will tend to be isolated, however, from the rest of the person's values—to have little interplay with them. In extreme cases, the system in which the induced response is embedded may be encapsulated and function

almost like a foreign body within the person. The induced responses here will be relatively inflexible and stereotyped. (c) Behavior adopted through internalization is part of an internal system. It is fitted into the person's basic framework of values and is congruent with it. This does not imply complete consistency: the degree of consistency can vary for different individuals and different areas of behavior. It does mean, however, that there is some interplay between the new beliefs and the rest of the person's values. The new behavior can serve to modify existing beliefs and can in turn be modified by them. As a result of this interaction, behavior adopted through internalization will tend to be relatively idiosyncratic, flexible, complex, and differentiated.

RESEARCH BASED ON THE MODEL

The model itself and its possible implications may be seen more clearly if I present a brief summary of the research in which it was used. This research has moved in three general directions: experimental tests of the relationships proposed by the model, application of the model to the study of personality factors in social influence, and application of the model to the analysis of a natural influence situation.

Experimental tests of the proposed distinctions between the three processes. The relationships proposed by the model can be tested by experiments in which the antecedents postulated for a given process are related to the consequents postulated for that process. The first experiment on this problem[14] varied one of the antecedents—the source of the influencing agent's power—and observed the effects of this variation on one of the consequents—the conditions of performance of the induced response. Subjects (Negro college freshmen) were exposed to a tape-recorded interview dealing with an aspect of the Supreme Court decision on school segregation. Four versions of this communication were developed and played to different groups of subjects. The four communications contained the same

14 H. C. Kelman, "Compliance, Identification and Internalization: Three Processes of Attitude Change," *Journal of Conflict Resolution*, Vol. 2, 1958, pp. 51–60.

message, but they differed in the way in which the communicator was introduced and presented himself at the beginning of the interview. These differences were designed to vary the source and degree of the communicator's power: in one communication the speaker was presented as possessing high means control, in the second as possessing high attractiveness, in the third as possessing high credibility, and in the fourth (for purposes of comparison) as being low in all three of these sources of power.

The subjects filled out attitude questionnaires designed to measure the extent of their agreement with the communication. To vary the conditions of performance, we asked each subject to complete three separate questionnaires, one under conditions of salience and surveillance, one under conditions of salience of the communicator—but without surveillance, and a third under conditions of nonsurveillance and nonsalience. It was predicted that attitudes induced by the communicator high in means control would tend to be expressed only under conditions of surveillance by the communicator (the mediating process here being compliance), attitudes induced by the communicator high in attractiveness would tend to be expressed only when the subject's relationship to the communicator was salient (the mediating process here being identification), and attitudes induced by the communicator high in credibility would tend to be expressed when they were relevant in content, regardless of surveillance or salience (the mediating process here being internalization). These predictions were confirmed to a most encouraging degree.

One implication of this study for the analysis of public opinion is that we can make certain predictions about the future course of a given opinion if we know something about the interpersonal circumstances under which it was formed. An interview might reveal the predominant dimensions in terms of which the respondent perceives those individuals and groups to whom he traces the opinion in question. For example, does he see them primarily as potential sources of approval and disapproval? Or as potential reference points for his self-definition? Or as potential sources of information

relevant to his own concern with reality testing and value maximization? From the answers to these questions we should be able to predict the future conditions under which this opinion is likely to come into play.

The study also suggests possible "diagnostic" devices that would make it possible to infer the process by which a particular opinion was adopted and hence the level at which it is held. If, for example, an opinion is expressed only in the presence of certain crucial individuals, one can assume that it is probably based on compliance and one can make certain further inferences on that basis. In other words, by observing the "conditions of performance of the induced response" (one of the consequents in our model), we can deduce the process on which this response is based.

It would, of course, be considerably easier and safer to make such inferences if several diagnostic criteria were available. It would be useful, therefore, to derive—from the list of consequents postulated by the model —further indicators in terms of which compliance-based, identification-based, and internalized opinions can be distinguished from one another, and to test the validity of these indicators. This is particularly true for identification and internalization. Since both of these processes, presumably, produce changes in "private belief," it is difficult to pin down the distinction between opinions based on them. There is a need, therefore, to develop a number of indicators that can capture the qualitative differences in the nature of opinions produced by these two processes, subtle though these differences may be. A second experiment addressed itself to this problem.[15]

The experimental situation, again, involved the use of tape-recorded communications. Three versions of the communication were used, each presented to a different group of college students. In each of the communications a novel program of science education was described and the rationale behind it was outlined. The basic message was identical in all cases, but the communications

15 H. C. Kelman, "Effects of Role-orientation and Value-orientation on the Nature of Attitude Change," paper read at the meetings of the Eastern Psychological Association, New York City, 1960.

differed in terms of certain additional information that was included in order to produce different orientations. In one communication (*role-orientation* condition) the additional information was designed to spell out the implications of the induced opinions for the subject's relationship to certain important reference groups. Positive reference groups were associated with acceptance of the message, and—in a rather dramatic way —negative reference groups were associated with opposition to it. The intention here was to create two of the postulated antecedents for *identification:* a concern with the social anchorage of one's opinions, and a delineation of the requirements for maintaining the desired relationship to one's reference groups (see the table). In the second communication (*value-orientation* condition) the additional information was designed to spell out the implications of the induced opinions for an important value— personal responsibility for the consequences of one's actions. The communication argued that acceptance of the message would tend to maximize this value. The intention here was to create two of the postulated antecedents of *internalization:* a concern with the value congruence of one's opinions, and a reorganization of one's conception of means-ends relationships. The third communication was introduced for purposes of comparison and contained only the basic message.

On the basis of the theoretical model it was predicted that the nature of the attitude changes produced by the two experimental communications would differ. Role orientation would presumably produce the consequences hypothesized for identification, while value orientation would produce the consequences hypothesized for internalization. A number of measurement situations were devised to test these predictions: (1) In each group, half the subjects completed attitude questionnaires immediately after the communication, under conditions of salience, and half completed them a few weeks later, under conditions of nonsalience. As predicted, there was a significant difference between these two conditions of measurement for the role-orientation group but not for the value-orientation group. (2) The

generalization of the induced attitudes to other issues involving the same values, and to other situations involving similar action alternatives, was measured. The prediction that the value-orientation group would show more generalization than the role-orientation group on the value dimension tended to be confirmed. The prediction that the reverse would be true for generalization along the action dimension was not upheld. (3) Flexibility of the induced attitudes was assessed by asking subjects to describe their doubts and qualifications. As predicted, the value-orientation group scored significantly higher on this index. (4) Complexity of the induced attitudes was assessed some weeks after the communication by asking subjects to list the things they would want to take into account in developing a new science education program. The total number of items listed was greater for the role-orientation group, but the number of items showing an awareness of relevant issues (as rated by a naïve judge) was clearly greater in the value-orientation group. (5) Half the subjects in each group were exposed to a countercommunication presenting a new consensus, the other half to a countercommunication presenting new arguments. It was predicted that the role-orientation group would be relatively more affected by the first type of countercommunication, and the value-orientation group by the second. The predicted pattern emerged, though it fell short of statistical significance.

The results of this study are not entirely unambiguous. They are sufficiently strong, however, to suggest that it should be possible to develop a number of criteria by which identification-based and internalized attitudes can be distinguished from one another. On the basis of such distinctions, one can then make certain inferences about the meaning of these attitudes and further predictions about their future course.

The relation between personality factors and social influence. This research starts with the assumption that the specific personality variables that are related to the acceptance of influence will depend on the particular process of influence involved. There is a further assumption that relationships depend on the type of influence situation to which the person is exposed. In other words, the concern is with exploring the specific personality variables that predispose individuals to engage in each of the three processes, given certain situational forces.

In the first study of this problem[16] we were interested in the relationship between one type of personality variable—cognitive needs and styles—and the process of internalization. We wanted to study this relationship in a situation in which people are exposed to new information that challenges their existing beliefs and assumptions. This is a situation in which at least some people are likely to re-examine their beliefs and—if they find them to be incongruent with their values in the light of the new information—they are likely to change them. A change under these particular motivational conditions would presumably take the form of internalization.

It was proposed that people who are high in what might be called the *need for cognitive clarity* would react more strongly to a situation of this type. They would be made uncomfortable by the incongruity produced by such a situation and the challenge it presented to their cognitive structures. The *nature* of their reaction, however, may differ. Some people may react to the challenge by changing their beliefs, while others may react by resisting change. Which of these directions an individual would be likely to follow would depend on his characteristic *cognitive style*. A person who typically reacts to ambiguity by seeking clarification and trying to gain understanding (a "clarifier") would be likely to open himself to the challenging information and perhaps to reorganize his beliefs as a consequence. A person who typically reacts to ambiguity defensively, by simplifying his environment and keeping out disturbing elements (a "simplifier"), would be likely to avoid the challenging information.

Measures of cognitive need and cognitive style were obtained on a group of college students who were then exposed to a per-

suasive communication that presented some challenging information about American education. Change in attitudes with respect to the message of the communication was measured on two occasions for each subject: immediately after the communication, under conditions of salience, and six weeks later under conditions of nonsalience.

We predicted that, among people high in need for cognitive clarity, those whose characteristic style is clarification would be the most likely to manifest attitude change in the induced direction, while those whose characteristic style is simplification would be the most likely to manifest resistance to change and possibly even negative change. This difference should be especially marked under conditions of nonsalience, which are the conditions necessary for a reasonable test of internalization. Among the people who are low in need for cognitive clarity, it was predicted that cognitive style would be unlikely to produce consistent differences since they are less motivated to deal with the ambiguity that the challenging information has created.

The results clearly supported these predictions. High-need clarifiers showed more change than high-need simplifiers (who, in fact, changed in the negative direction). This difference was small under conditions of salience, but became significant under conditions of nonsalience—suggesting that the difference between clarifiers and simplifiers is due to a difference in their tendency to internalize. Among low-need subjects, no consistent differences between the two style groups emerged.

This study suggests that one can gain a greater understanding of the structure of an individual's opinions on a particular issue by exploring relevant personality dimensions. In the present case we have seen that, for some of the subjects (those concerned with cognitive clarity), the opinions that emerge represent at least in part their particular solution to the dilemma created by incongruous information. In studies that are now under way we are exploring other personality dimensions that are theoretically related to tendencies to comply and identify. If our hypotheses are confirmed in these studies, they will point to other ways in

[16] H. C. Kelman and J. Cohler, "Reactions to Persuasive Communication as a Function of Cognitive Needs and Styles," paper read at the meetings of the Eastern Psychological Association, Atlantic City, 1959.

which emerging opinions may fit into an individual's personality system. Opinions may, for example, represent partial solutions to the dilemmas created by unfavorable evaluations from others or by finding oneself deviating from the group. Since these relationships between opinions and personality variables are tied to the three processes of influence in the present model, certain predictions about the future course of the opinions for different individuals can be readily derived.

The application of the model to the analysis of a natural influence situation. We are currently engaged in an extensive study of Scandinavian students who have spent a year of study or work in the United States.[17] We are interested in the effects of their stay here on their self-images in three areas: nationality, profession, and interpersonal relations. Our emphasis is on learning about the processes by which changes in the self-image come about or, conversely, the processes by which the person's existing image maintains itself in the face of new experiences. Our subjects were questioned at the beginning of their stay in the United States and at the end of their stay, and once again a year after their return home.

This study was not designed as a direct test of certain specific hypotheses about the three processes of influence. In this kind of rich field situation it seemed more sensible to allow the data to point the way and to be open to different kinds of conceptualizations demanded by the nature of the material. The model of influence did, however, enter into the formulation of the problem and the development of the schedules and is now entering into the analysis of the data.

In a preliminary analysis of some of our intensive case material, for example, we found it useful to differentiate four patterns of reaction to the American experience which may affect various aspects of the self-image: (1) An individual may change his self-image by a reorganization of its internal structure; here we would speak of a

[17] Lotte Bailyn and H. C. Kelman, "The Effects of a Year's Experience in America on the Self-image of Scandinavians: Report of Research in Progress," paper read at the meetings of the American Psychological Association, Cincinnati, 1959.

change by means of the process of *internalization*. (2) His self-image may be changed by a reshaping of the social relationships in which this image is anchored; here we would speak of a change by means of *identification*. (3) The individual may focus on the internal structure of the self-image but maintain it essentially in its original form; here we would speak of the process of *confirmation*. Finally, (4) he may maintain his self-image through a focus on its original social anchorage; here maintenance by the process of *resistance* would be involved. We have related these four patterns to a number of variables in a very tentative way, but the analysis will have to progress considerably farther before we can assess the usefulness of this scheme. It is my hope that this kind of analysis will give us a better understanding of the attitudes and images that a visitor takes away from his visit to a foreign country and will allow us to make some predictions about the subsequent history of these attitudes and images. Some of these predictions we will be able to check out on the basis of our post-return data.

CONCLUSION

There is enough evidence to suggest that the distinction between compliance, identification, and internalization is valid, even though it has certainly not been established in all its details. The specification of distinct antecedents and consequents for each of the processes has generated a number of hypotheses which have met the experimental test. It seems reasonable to conclude, therefore, that this model may be useful in the analysis of various influence situations and the resulting opinion changes. It should be particularly germane whenever one is concerned with the quality and durability of changes and with the motivational conditions that produced them.

I have also attempted to show the implications of this model for the analysis of public opinion. By tying together certain antecedents of influence with certain of its consequents, it enables us to infer the motivations underlying a particular opinion from a knowledge of its manifestations, and to predict the future course of an opinion from a knowledge of the conditions under which it was formed. Needless to say, the usefulness of the model in this respect is limited, not only because it is still in an early stage of development but also because of the inherent complexity of the inferences involved. Yet it does suggest an approach to the problem of meaning in the analysis of public opinion data.

Ego-Defense and Attitude Change[1] / Daniel Katz, Irving Sarnoff, and Charles McClintock

In a previous paper the theoretical framework for a program of research on the motivational bases of attitude change was set forth (10). It was postulated that no single theory of motivation could adequately account for all of the ways in which attitudes are formed, maintained, and altered. Since it was held that identical attitudes often stem from a variety of differing motivational sources, an attempt was made to relate existing theories to the range of phenomena for which they were originally devised and for which they appear to offer the greatest insight. Specifically, it was felt that any attitude could be regarded as serving one or more of three major motivational determinants: 1. reality-testing and the search for meaning: the need to acquire consistent knowledge about the external world, 2. reward and punishment, including the need to gain social acceptance and to avoid social disapproval, and 3. ego-defense: the need to defend against inner conflict. In a recent paper, H. Kelman has called attention to three processes in attitude change that resemble this analysis of motivational patterns (8). Kelman distinguishes between (a) internalization or incorporating the ideational content of the attitude, (b) compliance induced by extraneous reward and punishment, and (c) identification through taking the role of others.

Because of the complexity of human functioning, it is probable that all three sets of motivational determinants contribute to the development of every attitude. Nevertheless, they tend to contribute in a differential manner. It follows, therefore, that the most effective techniques of attitude change would be those aimed at the particular motivational sources that support the attitude under investigation.

The attitudinal focus of our research, our major dependent variable, is anti-Negro bias. In keeping with our theoretical position, we postulated that negative attitudes toward Negroes could stem from any of the three motivational contexts previously listed (10). Hence the bias might: 1. reflect exposure to a limited and inaccurate range of information about Negroes, 2. reflect conformity to prevailing social pressures, or 3. represent the use of Negroes as social media for such ego-defensive purposes as the projection of unconscious and unacceptable impulses.

The work of Frenkel-Brunswik, Sanford, Levinson, and Adorno gives priority to the basis of prejudice in personality mechanisms (1). We should grant this priority for anti-Negro attitudes that greatly distort the actuality of the attitudinal object under conditions minimizing the operation of the other two motivational patterns. Where there is ample opportunity for reality-testing and interaction, as in a Northern college population, we should assume that misinformation about Negroes based upon old stereotypes is not the primary factor in most of the subjects. We should assume that where the social rewards and punishments for the maintenance of prejudice have been relaxed, as in a Northern college population, this type of motivational pattern would again not be the primary factor. But where these conditions do not hold we should expect that prejudice could

Reprinted from *Human Relations*, 1956, 9, pages 27–46, by permission of the senior author and publisher, Tavistock Publications, Ltd.

[1] This study was supported in part at the time of data collection by the Human Resources Research Institute of the Air University.

be maintained at a high level without being based upon ego-defensiveness.

It is difficult to test theories about the genetic acquisition of attitudes without longitudinal studies of personalities over time. A profitable attack upon this motivational problem can be made, however, by using the traditional experimental procedure of introducing different manipulations and testing their effects. Thus, our basic assumption was that to the extent attitudes have different motivational roots, they will be influenced in corresponding fashion by different experimental manipulations. Accordingly, two different influence procedures were devised.[2] The one attempt was *informational* and was directed at the cognitive reorganization postulated by the Gestalt approach. It presented information about Negroes in a neutral or perhaps slightly favorable framework of cultural relativity. W. H. Crockett has shown the importance of cognitive structure in changing attitudes. In his experiment, greater attitude change occurred when people were given a rationale for the announced group norm than when the group norm was presented without a rationale (6). The other attempt was *interpretive* and was designed to give insight into the mechanisms and motivations of an ego-defensive nature that could be the basis of prejudice. G. W. Allport used this type of approach in his *ABC's of Scapegoating* (2).

Since we assumed that anti-Negro bias in our experimental population would be related more to ego-defensiveness than to other motivational factors, we also assumed that the influence procedure of the interpretive sort would produce more favorable attitudes toward Negroes than the informational procedure.

In addition to this overall expectation concerning the relative effectiveness of these influence procedures, our theory holds that such procedures will have a differential effect

upon individuals of differing degrees of ego-defensiveness. Thus, in comparison with less defensive individuals, highly ego-defensive persons should resist change on the basis of the interpretive approach because it is too threatening to them. Janis and Feshbach have shown that high fear arousal is not a favorable condition for changing attitudes (7). Jahoda and Cooper have found that highly prejudiced people will react defensively and block and distort the materials directed at caricaturing their beliefs (5). Moreover, these highly defensive persons should be relatively unmoved by the informational approach since it by-passes the essential emotional core of their anti-Negro attitudes. On the other hand, as compared with the highly defensive individuals, low ego-defensive persons should be more open and receptive to new information about Negroes, and, lacking as strong an emotional need to persist in their distorted perceptions of Negroes, they should develop more positive attitudes toward Negroes once the facts are presented to them. Hence, in addition to the greater effectiveness of the interpretive approach compared with the informational materials, the predictions are: 1. that the people who are in the middle ranges in ego-defensiveness will show the most positive change to the interpretive approach, with the low group next, and with the high group showing the least change, and 2. that the low ego-defensive group will show the most positive change to the informative approach, with the middle group next, and the high group last.

PROCEDURE

Subjects for this study were 243 female college students at Michigan State Normal College. They were all volunteers solicited as members of sorority and dormitory groups. These groups were then assigned to one of two experimental treatments or to a control situation. The subjects were asked to participate in a series of three sessions, which took place at the Normal College during the Spring of 1953. The first two sessions were separated by an interval of one week. The third session was held six weeks after the sec-

---

[2] In this experiment no attempt was made to manipulate the second motivational pattern through reward or punishment. In a combination of the rational and reward approaches, Milton Rosenberg has shown that individuals' attitudes can be predicted from their hierarchy of values and the perceived instrumentality of certain activities for achieving these values (9). In a follow-up of this study, Earl Carlson demonstrated that attitudes can be changed by changing the perception of their instrumental function for moving the individual toward his preferred goals (4).

ond. All data were gathered in a group setting.

For the first session, each subject was given a booklet that contained measures of personality and attitudes toward Negroes, including the F-scale, a specially designed TAT card, a twenty-item check list of statements pertaining to the subject's emotional functioning, a Bogardus social distance scale, and a Negro stereotype scale. All booklets were identical and subjects were free to leave as soon as they had finished filling out the materials.

At the outset of the second session, subjects assigned to the two experimental situations were presented with different sets of written influence materials aimed at inducing more favorable attitudes toward Negroes. One experimental treatment consisted of an interpretation of the relationship between mechanisms of ego-defense and anti-Negro attitudes. The other experimental treatment presented information about Negroes in a setting of cultural relativity. The control group was not exposed to any influence procedure.

Immediately after reading the influence materials, subjects in both experimental groups were requested to fill out another set of the same attitude questionnaires as they had answered a week before. Similarly, but without prior presentation of influence materials, the control group also filled out the same questionnaires.

To begin the third session, all subjects (both experimental and control) were again required to fill out a set of the original attitude scales. Following this, all groups were subdivided for the purpose of trying out other techniques of attitude change, which are not to be described here since they are outside the scope of this initial report.

Personality Measures

Ego-defensiveness. Since there is no generally accepted measure of ego-defensiveness as it relates to prejudice, a TAT card in the tradition of Murray was designed.[3] It was hoped that a pictorial representation of the attitudinal object would evoke the motivational matrix associated with the subject's attitudes toward the object.

Instructions accompanying the card were as follows: "Please take the picture out and place it beside this folder. Then make up a story about it. Be sure to cover these three main questions: 1. What is going on in the present situation? 2. What has happened in the past? 3. What is going to happen in the future? Tell what the people are doing, thinking, and feeling. Try to tell us as complete a story as possible in about five minutes. You may use the rest of this sheet and that directly opposite. (When you have completed this, go on to the next section.)"

The stories based on the TAT card were coded on projection, denial, and extrapunitiveness; and a combined score on ego-defensiveness was computed. Specifically, the code for projection included the two categories: 1. attribution of hostile feelings to the Negro girl, and 2. attribution of hostile feelings to non-principals (seated figures) with respect to the Negro girl. Extrapunitiveness was defined as perceiving one or more characters in the picture as playing a punitive role. Failure to identify the Negro girl as a Negro and omission of essential story elements required by the instructions were code categories for denial. Two coders independently coded for these specific categories, and the inter-coder reliability was computed on the basis of the number of agreements vs. the number of disagreements in terms of assigning persons to High, Middle, and Low Ego-Defensive groups. For an N of 60 TAT protocols randomly selected from the total test population, there were 51 agreements (85 per cent) and 9 disagreements (15 per cent). None of the 9 disagreements were more than one unit away in terms of our three-point scale. That is to say, no individual was scored as low ego-defensive by one coder and high ego-defensive by another.

---

[3] The card presents an unstructured social situation with two female figures sitting in chairs at a table in the foreground and two female figures standing in the background. The ethnic identity of the seated figures is ambiguous. Standing in the background and turned slightly toward each other, with their faces seen by the viewer, are a Negro girl and a white girl. There are no definite expressions on their faces although their features are drawn in detail. All four figures are dressed in the fashion of college girls and the two standing figures appear to be of college age. Two empty chairs are shown at the table near the seated girls.

Conformity. The measure of a need to conform was based on two items, which were part of a twenty-item check list. This list consisted of statements pertaining to the subject's emotional functioning. Subjects were presented with the list and the following instructions: "The following are a number of things which often trouble people. Please check (√) all those items which apply to yourself at the present time." The two conformity items were: "——It makes me uncomfortable to be different"; "——People can pretty easily change me even though my mind is already made up on the subject." A need to conform was considered present if a subject checked one or both of the above items.

Attitude Measures

Negro Stereotypes. This Likert-type scale consisted of 15 anti-Negro statements in a twenty-one-item questionnaire. Six pro-Negro statements are interspersed in the questionnaire in order to prevent subjects from developing a rigid response set. Subjects were requested to express the extent of their agreement or disagreement with each statement. The statements follow:

1. The refreshing aspect of Negro music is its rhythm and spontaneity.
2. One good way for Negroes to overcome existing social barriers in America is to change the things about their behavior which other Americans find objectionable.
3. Because of their aggressiveness and enjoyment of physical contact, Negro youths run into more trouble with the law than White youths.
4. Negroes might be able to solve many of their social problems if they could overcome their own laziness and irresponsibility.
5. Cleanliness and courtesy are characteristics which are noticeably lacking in the behavior patterns of most Negroes.
6. In every field where they have been given an opportunity to advance, Negroes have shown that they are good sports and gentlemen.
7. Despite the oppressions which they have endured, Negroes tend to be more happy and carefree than other groups.
8. Superstition and ignorance are characteristics which alienate the Negroes from other groups.
9. Most Negroes let situations of complete equality go to their heads. They find it impossible to control their excessively strong sexual and aggressive desires.
10. Although education and training can do much to polish the rough edges off the Negro group, a certain amount of inherited primitiveness is bound to remain.
11. Because of the many obstacles which they have had to overcome in achieving success, outstanding Negro artists and athletes are often more capable than their White colleagues.
12. The problem of racial prejudice in America has been greatly overplayed by a few Negro malcontents.
13. The aggressiveness of most Negroes has certainly not helped to better the position of their group in America.
14. Perhaps the position of Negroes in America would become more secure if they stopped striving to gain entry into circles where they are not really wanted.
15. Negroes would be better citizens if they displayed as much self-control in the use of alcohol and narcotics as other Americans.
16. In spite of severe environmental handicaps, Negroes have proven that they can do as well as any other group.
17. Limited native intelligence among Negroes still remains an important factor in preventing them from making noteworthy contributions to our cultural heritage.
18. Because of their careless and slovenly habits, Negroes invariably decrease property values in any neighborhood.
19. Negro politicians and labor leaders would be doing their race a great service if they developed a bit more humility and reticence.
20. Negroes often make excellent maids and cooks, but they tend to be too unreliable for positions of greater responsibility.
21. When one considers its relatively small size, one is amazed by the proportion of outstanding musicians and athletes which has emerged from the Negro group.

Negro Bogardus. The preceding Negro Stereotype Scale tends to approach anti-Negro attitudes from the standpoint of the subject's perception of the attitudinal object. In order to get an attitude measure with more affinity to the action level, we utilized a modern version of the Bogardus social distance scale. This scale specifies the levels of social intimacy to which a Negro would be admitted by the subject.

Influence Procedures

I. Interpretation. This material consisted of eleven double-spaced typewritten pages entitled "Emotions and Attitudes." In the first part of this presentation, we described in general terms the dynamics of scapegoating, projection, and compensation with respect to the development of anti-minority attitudes. We then presented a case history of a college girl to illustrate how these mechanisms of defense were basic to her ethnic prejudices. In doing this, we attempted to maximize identification of the subjects with the hypothetical case.

II. Information. This untitled presentation, nine double-spaced typewritten pages in length, attempted to evoke a frame of reference, cultural relativity, in which the attitudinal object and information concerning it could be perceived in a new way. Hence, this material was also roughly divided into two parts. The first part, the evocation of the frame of reference, was a presentation of the concept of cultural relativity. This concept is illustrated by a number of references to various societies that have drastically different ways of looking at and reacting to identical human phenomena such as personal disputes and mother-child relationships. The second part is aimed at a reevaluation of the attitudinal object from the viewpoint of the new frame of reference. Thus the concept of cultural relativity is applied to the negative attitudes and unfavorable circumstances that have confronted Negroes in America. The article then goes on to explain the apparent differences between whites and Negroes in social terms and to point out that whenever Negroes have had genuine equality of opportunity, they have performed as well as whites. A number of outstanding Negroes in various professional fields were listed to illustrate the social contributions already made by Negroes. The attempt here is to produce cognitive restructuring that will take account of the new information and to

make the conditions for such restructuring favorable by first evoking a new and acceptable frame of reference for the evaluation of the cognitive object.

Control Variables

It is generally desirable to control attitude-change studies by breaking cases according to original attitude position. Change toward the positive end of the scale may have different qualitative meanings for people occupying different positions along the scale. It may be easier to move people who are already favorably disposed to the ideas in the influence attempt than those who have opposed views. On the other hand, there is much less room to move for those already near the favorable end of the scale. In this study we did not have enough cases to control by original attitude position. But we did relate the amount of change to the original position of the subjects and found no significant differences between the number of people changing and the original attitude position that they held (*Table 1*).

TABLE 1

Change on Negro Stereotypes, Sessions 1–3, by Original Attitude Position for Interpretation and Informational Approaches ($N = 197$)

Direction of Change	Interpretation			Information		
	Original Attitude Position					
	Low	Med.	High	Low	Med.	High
$+$	10	20	25	12	15	22
$-$, 0	4	8	10	13	13	18
N.A.	5	5	4	6	4	3

Approach	Original Attitude	χ^2	P
Interpretation	High vs. Low	<1.00	N.S.
	Middle vs. High	<1.00	N.S.
	Middle vs. Low	<1.00	N.S.
Information	High vs. Low	<1.00	N.S.
	Middle vs. High	<1.00	N.S.
	Middle vs. Low	<1.00	N.S.

While it was assumed that ego-defensiveness was the main motivational pattern for the majority of the subjects as the basis for prejudiced attitudes, a very high correlation between original attitude position and degree of ego-defensiveness would raise the question of the identity of the processes being measured. Therefore, ego-defensiveness was broken against original attitude position (*Table 2*). The results show that

TABLE 2

RELATIONSHIP BETWEEN TAT MEASURE OF DEFENSIVENESS AND ORIGINAL ATTITUDES ON NEGRO STEREOTYPE SCALE ($N = 241$)

Stereotype Scale	Defensiveness		
	Low	Middle	High
Low	22	21	13
Middle	28	25	27
High	41	38	26

$$\chi^2 = 2.47 \qquad P = \text{N.S.}$$

people who are higher in ego-defensiveness tend to be higher in prejudice but there is no statistically significant relationship between these factors.[4]

RESULTS AND INTERPRETATION

1. The approach utilizing interpretive materials proved to be a more powerful influence attempt in producing positive attitudes than the approach utilizing informational materials. *Table 3* shows that significantly more people changed in the direction of favorable beliefs about Negroes over a

[4] Methodological note:

a. Scores on the Negro Stereotype Scale were computed on the basis of the subject's responses to the fifteen negative stereotype items. The positive stereotypes were not used for this analysis.

b. For both the Negro Bogardus and Negro Stereotype Scales, + indicates change favorable to the attitude object, Negro, − indicates change unfavorable, and 0 indicates no change toward the attitude objects, Negro.

c. Because of the relative infrequency of 0 change on the Negro Stereotype Scale from Sessions 1 to 3, the 0 and − categories are combined in the tables, except for *Table 3*.

d. Statistical analysis was based on the use of chi square corrected for continuity.

e. In the computation of chi square, the 0 and − change categories were combined. Results should thus be interpreted in terms of positive change versus non-positive change.

f. All probabilities reported have been computed on the basis of one-tail tests. That is, they have all taken into consideration the directional predictions made.

TABLE 3

CHANGE ON NEGRO STEREOTYPES, SESSIONS 1–3
($N = 243$)

Direction of Change	Approach		
	Interpretation	Information	Control
+	55	49	21
0	4	11	5
−	18	33	14
N.A.	14	13	6
Total	91	106	46

Interpretation/Information $\chi^2 = 5.60$ $P = .01$
Interpretation/Control $\chi^2 = 3.38$ $P = .03$
Information/Control $\chi^2 = <1.00$ $P = \text{N.S.}$

six-week period (Sessions 1 to 3) after exposure to the interpretive approach than after exposure to the informational treatment. Though there was some positive change in the group receiving the informational material, it was not significantly greater than in the control group.

The second measure of the dependent variable, a slightly modified Bogardus scale, proved much more stable over the six-week period. Again, however, there was a significant difference between the people subjected to the interpretive approach compared with those subjected to the informational approach, and again it was in the expected direction (*Table 4*). Since the control group also shifted over time, the difference be-

TABLE 4

CHANGE ON NEGRO BOGARDUS, SESSIONS 1–3
($N = 243$)

Direction of Change	Approach		
	Interpretation	Information	Control
+	37	30	16
0	28	42	16
−	12	21	8
N.A.	14	13	6
Total	91	106	46

Interpretation/Information $\chi^2 = 3.76$ $P = .03$
Interpretation/Control $\chi^2 = <1.00$ $P = \text{N.S.}$
Information/Control $\chi^2 = <1.00$ $P = \text{N.S.}$
(χ^2 computed on the basis of combining 0 and − change.)

tween the interpretive approach and the control group is not, however, significant. The ratio of favorable to unfavorable change is three to one for the interpretive approach and two to one for the control situation, but the number of cases is too small to make this a statistically significant result. The greater stability of the scores on the Bogardus scale as against the measure of stereotypes (some twenty people did not change in either direction on their stereotype scores, whereas 86 did not shift on the Bogardus) is probably due to two factors. The Bogardus scale may have more reliability as a measure, and in addition it may be more difficult to move people on items relating to a change in behavior than on items of belief having little specific behavioral reference.

The greater effectiveness of interpretation as compared with information can of course be a function of using a greater amount of the one influence than of the other. In other words, we may have done a better job in mobilizing a strong set of interpretation materials than of informational materials. There is, however, suggestive evidence on this point in that the *immediate* effects of the two influence procedures were not significantly different, but over time there was more continuous gain and less backsliding among the people subjected to the interpretive approach than among those subjected to the informational approach. The immediate results (*Tables 5 and 6*) show that there were no significant differences between the two approaches immediately after their presentation. Both interpretation and information produced positive changes in over half of the group on beliefs about Negro characteristics. Six weeks later, however, the gains produced by interpretation were significantly greater than those produced by the information approach. The findings from the Bogardus scale are less clear-cut but they do tend to support the same trend. The immediate effects of the two approaches are not at an acceptable level of statistical significance, but the effects several weeks later do meet the conventional criterion of less than the .05 level. It would appear, therefore, that the superior power of the interpretation approach lies in its ability to effect more cognitive reorganization over time.

The detailed breakdown of the movements of people from the second to the third session (*Table 7*) shows that more of the people who changed positively after the presentation of the interpretive materials continue to change positively during the following weeks than is true of the people receiving the information materials. Similarly there is a tendency for more backsliding to occur among the subjects receiving the information than among those getting the interpretive materials, though this is not a significant difference.

TABLE 5

CHANGE ON NEGRO STEREOTYPES, SESSIONS 1–2
($N = 243$)

Direction of Change	Approach		
	Interpretation	Information	Control
+	60	60	20
0	13	17	8
−	18	28	17
N.A.	0	1	1
Total	91	106	46

Interpretation/Information $\chi^2 = <1.00$ $P = $ N.S.
Interpretation/Control $\chi^2 = \phantom{<}4.60$ $P = .01$
Information/Control $\chi^2 = \phantom{<}1.56$ $P = .11$
(χ^2 computed by combining 0 and − change and running against + change.)

TABLE 6

CHANGE ON NEGRO BOGARDUS, SESSIONS 1–2
($N = 243$)

Direction of Change	Approach		
	Interpretation	Information	Control
+	34	31	12
0	36	57	22
−	21	18	12
N.A.	0	0	0
Total	91	106	46

Interpretation/Information $\chi^2 = \phantom{<}1.10$ $P = .15$
Interpretation/Control $\chi^2 = \phantom{<}1.28$ $P = .13$
Information/Control $\chi^2 = <1.00$ $P = $ N.S.
(χ^2 computed by combining 0 and − change and running against + change.)

TABLE 7

CONSISTENCY OF DIRECTION OF ATTITUDE CHANGE
BASED ON CHANGE FROM SESSIONS 1–2 AND
CHANGE FROM SESSIONS 2–3 ($N = 243$)

| Direction of Change: Sessions 2–3 | Positive Change: Sessions 1–2 | | |
| | Approach | | |
	Interpre-tation	Informa-tion	Control
+	30	23	7
0, −	25	33	16
Sub-total	55	56	23

| Direction of Change: Sessions 2–3 | Negative or No Change: Sessions 1–2 | | |
| | Approach | | |
	Interpre-tation	Informa-tion	Control
+	14	21	9
0, −	9	16	9
Sub-total	23	37	18
N.A.	13	13	5
Total-total	91	106	46

(Positive Change: Sessions 1–2)/(+, (−, 0) change Sessions 2–3)

Interpretation/Information	$\chi^2 = 1.52$	$P = .11$
Interpretation/Control	$\chi^2 = 2.88$	$P = .05$
Information/Control	$\chi^2 = <1.00$	$P = $ N.S.

(Negative Change: Sessions 1–2)/(+, (−, 0) change Sessions 2–3)

Interpretation/Information	$\chi^2 = <1.00$	$P = $ N.S.
Interpretation Control	$\chi^2 = <1.00$	$P = $ N.S.
Information/Control	$\chi^2 = <1.00$	$P = $ N.S.

TABLE 8

CHANGE ON NEGRO STEREOTYPES, SESSIONS 1–3, BY
EGO-DEFENSIVENESS FOR INTERPRETATIONAL AND
INFORMATIONAL APPROACHES ($N = 197$)

| Direction of Change | Interpretation | | | Information | | |
| | Ego-Defensiveness | | | | | |
	Low	Med.	High	Low	Med.	High
+	24	20	11	16	17	11
−, 0	5	7	10	16	17	15
N.S.	6	4	4	6	4	5

Approach	Defensiveness	χ^2	P
Interpretation	High vs. Low	4.00	.02
	Middle vs. High	1.57	.10
	Middle vs. Low	<1.00	N.S.
	Middle and Low vs. High	3.92	.02
Information	No significant relations between High, Middle, Low	—	—
Interpretation vs. Informa-tion	Low vs. Low	5.83	.01
	Middle vs. Middle	2.67	.05
	High vs. High	<1.00	N.S.

interpretive materials. The comparable ego-defensive groups under the influence of informational materials gave a fifty-fifty split, 33 shifting positively and 33 shifting negatively or showing no change. Similarly, for the low and middle defensive groups, on the Bogardus scale the information approach moved only 18 subjects positively, with 48 showing zero or minus change; whereas the interpretation approach shifted 30 people positively, with 26 showing zero or negative change.

The difference in changed stereotype scores between the high ego-defensive people and the combined middle and low group is significant for the interpretation approach but the corresponding difference for the information approach is slight and insignificant. The same findings hold when the Bogardus scale is used as the dependent variable. In general, then, the prediction of change as a function of the relationship between influence process and personality mechanism seems confirmed. The more de-

2. The greater effectiveness of the interpretive approach seems to be differentially related to the ego-defensiveness of the individual subjects (*Tables 8* and *9*). If the subjects high in ego-defensiveness are excluded from consideration, then the superiority of the interpretive approach over the informational presentation becomes even clearer. Forty-four of the middle and low defensive groups changed positively on their stereotype score over the six-week period, and only twelve showed no change or shifted negatively under the influence of

TABLE 9

CHANGE ON NEGRO BOGARDUS, SESSIONS 1–3, BY
EGO-DEFENSIVENESS FOR INTERPRETATIONAL
AND INFORMATIONAL APPROACHES ($N = 197$)

Direction of Change	Interpretation Ego-Defensiveness			Information		
	Low	Med.	High	Low	Med.	High
+	16	14	7	8	10	11
0	10	10	8	14	18	10
−	3	3	6	10	6	5
N.S.	4	4	6	5	4	6

Approach	Defensiveness	χ^2	P
Interpretation	High vs. Low	1.54	.11
	Middle vs. High	<1.00	N.S.
	Middle vs. Low	<1.00	N.S.
	Middle and Low vs. High	2.14	.07
Information	High vs. Low	1.24	*
	Middle vs. High	<1.00	N.S.
	Middle vs. Low	<1.00	N.S.
	Middle and Low vs. High	1.32	*
Interpretation vs. Information	Low vs. Low	4.55	.02
	Middle vs. Middle	2.27	.05
	High vs. High	<1.00	N.S.

* Indicates that findings are in the reverse direction from that predicted.
(χ^2 computed by combining 0 and − change and running them against + change.)

tailed predictions, however, are in need of revision in a number of respects, as the following specific findings suggest.

Within the group receiving the interpretation approach, the subjects scoring high in ego-defensiveness were less amenable to change both on the measure of beliefs about Negroes and on the Bogardus scale than were the subjects scoring in the middle and low ranges on ego-defensiveness. The original prediction was that the high ego-defensive people would be more resistant because of the difficulty of breaching their defenses with anything less than prolonged individual therapy. This hypothesis was thus confirmed. It was predicted, however, that the middle group in defensiveness would show the most change under the interpretation approach, since it was expected

that the low group would not be characteristically using the defense mechanisms under exposure or would at least have more insight into these mechanisms. This prediction was not confirmed, and the low and middle groups responded equally well to the interpretation materials and were remarkably alike in their reactions. The failure to obtain the predicted difference between the low and middle groups may be due to the lack of sensitivity of the measure, or it may be that in most populations there are very few people so low in defensiveness that they cannot profit from exposure to interpretive materials.

Within the group receiving the informational approach there were no differences between the people of varying degrees of defensiveness on the measure of beliefs about Negroes. There was, however, a tendency for the combined middle and low groups in defensiveness to show less change than the high group on the Bogardus scale. It should be remembered that the informational materials were presented in an indirect manner through the activation of a new frame of reference about the problem, namely, the approach of cultural relativity and historical perspective. Thus there would be a minimal challenge to the effect-laden defenses of the highly defensive subjects. Nevertheless, it was assumed that the people lowest in ego-defensiveness would be the most amenable to change. The theory was that these people did not hold racial attitudes in the service of defense mechanisms and hence could be readily changed if given new facts and new information. Again this prediction was not confirmed and perhaps for the reason already suggested, namely, that we did not have in our population of girls in a normal college enough subjects of the type postulated. It is also possible that the group scoring low in defensiveness may have been relatively more sophisticated and more familar with the "new" information presented. This is speculation, in that there was no control on the "newness" of the materials for any of the subjects. Such controls are desirable, in that experimental influences for some subjects may already be forces to which they are already habituated and for others may represent new forces.

3. There is evidence to indicate that the unpredicted tendency of the high ego-defensive group to change under the influence of information materials was due to the conformity pressures generated in the experimental situation. The prestige of the experimenters from the state university, the resort to "scientific" facts in the presentation, and the general trend in the direction of more liberal attitudes toward Negroes in the academic world may have produced a perception that the *correct* opinions were at the favorable end of the scale. Not only did a majority of the students, subjected to experimental influences, shift in the expected direction but more of the control group shifted in a positive than a negative direction (though not significantly so). In other words, the experiment probably made the issue more salient on the campus, and the resulting interactions made it clear that the majority were clearly positive in their attitudes toward Negro students.

A partial test of this hypothesis, that the high ego-defenders were affected by conformity pressures, was possible through a measure of conformity tendencies obtained from two items in the personality inventory. When this personality measure of conformity is applied to the high ego-defensive group (*Table 10*) we find that the positive changers on the stereotype scale had significantly more high conformers among them than had the zero or negative changers. Among the low and middle groups in ego-defensiveness, however, there is no significant relationship between conformity and positive change, though there is a tendency in this direction. Thus the effect of the information approach on the high ego-defenders can be interpreted as due to the conformity aspects of the experimental setting. In general, moreover, the changes produced by the information approach were not significantly greater than the real changes occurring in the control group. It seems plausible, therefore, to account for the effect of the information approach as a function of conformity to the experimenter and to the changes in group norms, rather than as a function of a rational restructuring to take account of the new cognitive materials presented. The *differential effects* of the interpretive approach upon the high and low ego-defenders cannot be explained away on the basis of conformity, however, for here the difference is not due to differential conformity effects in the two groups. If conformity pressures were to account for the greater positive change among the low and middle defensive groups, then the conformers in these groups should be contributing more to the change than are the conformers in the high ego-defensive group. But the figures in *Table 11* indicate that the reverse tendency is manifest. The conform-

TABLE 10

Change on Negro Stereotypes, Sessions 1–3, by Ego-Defensiveness for Conformity and Non-Conformity within the Informational Approach
($N = 106$)

	Defensiveness					
	Low		Middle		High	
	+	−,0	+	−,0	+	−,0
Non-conformity	9	10	7	11	3	8
Conformity	7	6	10	6	12	3

N.A. = 14

Conformity/Non-conformity

Low Ego Group	$\chi^2 = <1.00$	$P = $ N.S.
Middle Ego Group	$\chi^2 = 1.06$	$P = .15$
High Ego Group	$\chi^2 = 5.23$	$P = .01$

TABLE 11

Change on Negro Stereotypes, Sessions 1–3, by Ego-Defensiveness for Conformity and Non-Conformity within the Interpretational Approach
($N = 91$)

	Defensiveness					
	Low		Middle		High	
	+	−,0	+	−,0	+	−,0
Non-conformity	11	5	12	5	5	9
Conformity	13	0	8	2	6	1

N.A. = 14

Conformity/Non-conformity

Low Ego Group	$\chi^2 = <1.00$	$P = $ N.S.
Middle Ego Group	$\chi^2 = <1.00$	$P = $ N.S.
High Ego Group	$\chi^2 = 2.96$	$P = .04$

ity effect in fact works against finding the differential relationship postulated.

The greater susceptibility of high ego-defenders to conformity pressures is an integral part of the theory of the authoritarian personality as developed by Frenkel-Brunswik, Sanford, Adorno, and Levinson (1). These authors include in their syndrome of authoritarian character structure both defensive reactions of repression, projection, and displacement, and conventionalism and conformity. Suggestive evidence about the susceptibility of high F-scores to conformity pressures comes from an experimental investigation by M. Wagman, in which he used authoritarian suggestion of two types. The one authoritarian suggestion was designed to move a group of subjects in the direction of more liberal attitudes; the second was designed to move another group of subjects in a less liberal direction (11). Low F-scorers could not be influenced in the direction of greater liberality by authoritarian suggestion, but high F-scorers could be influenced in either direction. F. Barlow, in a separate analysis of some of the data from the study here reported, found that high scorers in ego-defensiveness were more likely than low scorers to see themselves as very close to the group norm all through the change process (3).

SUMMARY

In this exploratory study, we tested several hypotheses derived from the theory that social attitudes are supported by one or more of three principal motivational determinants: reality-testing, reward and punishment, and ego-defense. Since identical attitudes have different motivational roots, we assumed that they would be influenced in corresponding fashion by different experimental manipulations. To test this assumption, we devised interpretive and informational techniques that would attack the ego-defensive and reality-testing components of anti-Negro attitudes in a differential manner. We presented these techniques to white college girls in an effort to produce more favorable attitudes toward Negroes. We tested the relative overall effectiveness of the two change procedures as well as their effects upon subjects of various degrees of ego-defensiveness.

In general the findings confirmed the theory that affect-laden attitudes are more effectively influenced through attempting to give insight into the self than through giving insight into the objective nature of the problem. Moreover, the people highest in ego-defensiveness are the most difficult to change through the self-insight procedure. But the prediction that the people lowest in ego-defensiveness would be most easily influenced by informational materials (insight into the objective problem) was not confirmed. The high ego-defenders were as susceptible to change under the informational approach as were the low ego-defenders. The interpretation of this result was that the high ego-defenders were affected by the conformity pressures in the experimental situation rather than by the informational materials themselves.

REFERENCES

1. Adorno, T. W., Frenkel-Brunswik, E., Levinson, D. J., and Sanford, R. N. *The Authoritarian Personality.* New York: Harper, 1950.
2. Allport, G. W. *ABC's of scapegoating.* Chicago: Central Y.M.C.A. College.
3. Barlow, M. F. Security and group approval as value systems related to attitude change. Ph.D. Dissertation, University of Michigan, 1954.
4. Carlson, E. R. A study of attitude change and attitude structure. Ph.D. Dissertation, University of Michigan, 1953.
5. Cooper, E., and Jahoda, M. The evasion of propaganda: How prejudiced people respond to anti-prejudice propaganda. *J. Psychol.,* 1947, Vol. 23, pp. 15–25.
6. Crockett, W. H. The effect of attitude change on cognitive differentiation, under conditions of norm-presentation with and without counter-argument. Ph.D. Dissertation, University of Michigan, 1952.
7. Janis, I. L., and Feshbach, S. Effects of fear-arousing communications. *J. abnorm. soc. Psychol.,* 1953, Vol. 48, No. 3, pp. 78–92.

8. Kelman, H. A discussion of three processes of opinion change through social influences. Paper read at the 1954 meetings of the American Association for Public Opinion.

9. Rosenberg, M. J. The experimental investigation of a value theory of attitude structure. Ph.D. Dissertation, University of Michigan, 1953.

10. Sarnoff, I., and Katz, D. The motivational bases of attitude change. *J. abnorm. soc. Psychol.*, 1954, Vol. 49, No. 1, pp. 115–24.

11. Wagman, M. An investigation of the effectiveness of authoritarian suggestion and non-authoritarian information as methods of changing the prejudiced attitudes of relatively authoritarian and non-authoritarian personalities. Ph.D. Dissertation, University of Michigan, 1953.

Reconciling Conflicting Results Derived from Experimental and Survey Studies of Attitude Change / Carl I. Hovland

(*Yale University*)

Two quite different types of research design are characteristically used to study the modification of attitudes through communication. In the first type, the *experiment,* individuals are given a controlled exposure to a communication and the effects evaluated in terms of the amount of change in attitude or opinion produced. A base line is provided by means of a control group not exposed to the communication. The study of Gosnell (1927) on the influence of leaflets designed to get voters to the polls is a classic example of the controlled experiment.

In the alternative research design, the *sample survey,* information is secured through interviews or questionnaires both concerning the respondent's exposure to various communications and his attitudes and opinions on various issues. Generalizations are then derived from the correlations obtained between reports of exposure and measurements of attitude. In a variant of this method, measurements of attitude and of exposure to communication are obtained during repeated interviews with the same individual over a period of weeks or months. This is the "panel method" extensively utilized in studying the impact of various mass media on political attitudes and on voting behavior (cf., e.g., Kendall & Lazarsfeld, 1950).

Generalizations derived from experimental and from correlational studies of communication effects are usually both reported in chapters on the effects of mass media and in other summaries of research on attitude, typically without much stress on the type of study from which the conclusion was derived. Close scrutiny of the results obtained from the two methods, however, suggests a marked difference in the picture of communication effects obtained from each. The object of my paper is to consider the conclusions derived from these two types of design, to suggest some of the factors responsible for the frequent divergence in results, and then to formulate principles aimed at reconciling some of the apparent conflicts.

DIVERGENCE

The picture of mass communication effects which emerges from correlational studies is one in which few individuals are seen as being affected by communications. One of the most thorough correlational studies of the effects of mass media on attitudes is that of Lazarsfeld, Berelson, and Gaudet published in *The People's Choice* (1944). In this report there is an extensive chapter devoted to the effects of various media, particularly radio, newspapers, and magazines. The authors conclude that few changes in attitudes were produced. They estimate that the political positions of only about 5% of their respond-

Reprinted from *American Psychologist*, 1959, 14, pages 8–17, by permission of the publisher, The American Psychological Association.

ents were changed by the election campaign, and they are inclined to attribute even this small amount of change more to personal influence than to the mass media. A similar evaluation of mass media is made in the recent chapter in the *Handbook of Social Psychology* by Lipset and his collaborators (1954).

Research using experimental procedures, on the other hand, indicates the possibility of considerable modifiability of attitudes through exposure to communication. In both Klapper's survey (1949) and in my chapter in the *Handbook of Social Psychology* (Hovland, 1954) a number of experimental studies are discussed in which the opinions of a third to a half or more of the audience are changed.

The discrepancy between the results derived from these two methodologies raises some fascinating problems for analysis. This divergence in outcome appears to me to be largely attributable to two kinds of factors: one, the difference in research design itself; and, two, the historical and traditional differences in general approach to evaluation characteristic of researchers using the experimental as contrasted with the correlational or survey method. I would like to discuss, first, the influence these factors have on the estimation of overall effects of communications and, then, turn to other divergences in outcome characteristically found by the use of the experimental and survey methodology.

Undoubtedly the most critical and interesting variation in the research *design* involved in the two procedures is that resulting from differences in definition of exposure. In an experiment the audience on whom the effects are being evaluated is one which is fully exposed to the communication. On the other hand, in naturalistic situations with which surveys are typically concerned, the outstanding phenomenon is the limitation of the audience to those who *expose themselves* to the communication. Some of the individuals in a captive audience experiment would, of course, expose themselves in the course of natural events to a communication of the type studied; but many others would not. The group which does expose itself is usually a highly biased one, since most in-

dividuals "expose themselves most of the time to the kind of material with which they agree to begin with" (Lipset *et al.,* 1954, p. 1158). Thus one reason for the difference in results between experiments and correlational studies is that experiments describe the effects of exposure on the whole range of individuals studied, some of whom are initially in favor of the position being advocated and some who are opposed, whereas surveys primarily describe the effects produced on those already in favor of the point of view advocated in the communication. The amount of change is thus, of course, much smaller in surveys. Lipset and his collaborators make this same evaluation, stating that:

> As long as we test a program in the laboratory we always find that it has great effect on the attitudes and interests of the experimental subjects. But when we put the program on as a regular broadcast, we then note that the people who are most influenced in the laboratory tests are those who, in a realistic situation, do not listen to the program. The controlled experiment always greatly overrates effects, as compared with those that really occur, because of the self-selection of audiences (Lipset *et al.,* 1954, p. 1158).

Differences in the second category are not inherent in the design of the two alternatives, but are characteristic of the way researchers using the two methods typically proceed.

The first difference within this class is in the size of the communication unit typically studied. In the majority of survey studies the unit evaluated is an entire program of communication. For example, in studies of political behavior an attempt is made to assess the effects of all newspaper reading and television viewing on attitudes toward the major parties. In the typical experiment, on the other hand, the interest is usually in some particular variation in the content of the communications, and experimental evaluations much more frequently involve single communications. On this point results are thus not directly comparable.

Another characteristic difference between the two methods is in the time interval used in evaluation. In the typical experiment the time at which the effect is observed is usually rather soon after exposure to the communication. In the survey study, on the other hand, the time perspective is such that much more remote effects are usually evaluated. When effects decline with the passage of time, the net outcome will, of course, be that of accentuating the effect obtained in experimental studies as compared with those obtained in survey researches. Again it must be stressed that the difference is not inherent in the designs as such. Several experiments, including our own on the effects of motion pictures (Hovland, Lumsdaine, & Sheffield, 1949) and later studies on the "sleeper effect" (Hovland & Weiss, 1951; Kelman & Hovland, 1953), have studied retention over considerable periods of time.

Some of the difference in outcome may be attributable to the types of communicators characteristically used and to the motive-incentive conditions operative in the two situations. In experimental studies communications are frequently presented in a classroom situation. This may involve quite different types of factors from those operative in the more naturalistic communication situation with which the survey researchers are concerned. In the classroom there may be some implicit sponsorship of the communication by the teacher and the school administration. In the survey studies the communicators may often be remote individuals either unfamiliar to the recipients, or outgroupers clearly known to espouse a point of view opposed to that held by many members of the audience. Thus there may be real differences in communicator credibility in laboratory and survey researches. The net effect of the differences will typically be in the direction of increasing the likelihood of change in the experimental as compared with the survey study.

There is sometimes an additional situational difference. Communications of the type studied by survey researchers usually involve reaching the individual in his natural habitat, with consequent supplementary effects produced by discussion with friends and family. In the laboratory studies a classroom situation with low postcommunication interaction is more typically involved. Several studies, including one by Harold Kelley reported in our volume on *Communication and Persuasion* (Hovland, Janis, & Kelley, 1953), indicate that, when a communication is presented in a situation which makes group membership salient, the individual is typically more resistant to counternorm influence than when the communication is presented under conditions of low salience of group membership (cf. also, Katz & Lazarsfeld, 1955, pp. 48–133).

A difference which is almost wholly adventitious is in the types of populations utilized. In the survey design there is, typically, considerable emphasis on a random sample of the entire population. In the typical experiment, on the other hand, there is a consistent overrepresentation of high school students and college sophomores, primarily on the basis of their greater accessibility. But as Tolman has said: "college sophomores may not be people." Whether differences in the type of audience studied contribute to the differences in effect obtained with the two methods is not known.

Finally, there is an extremely important difference in the studies of the experimental and correlational variety with respect to the type of issue discussed in the communications. In the typical experiment we are interested in studying a set of factors or conditions which are expected on the basis of theory to influence the extent of effect of the communication. We usually deliberately try to find types of issues involving attitudes which are susceptible to modification through communication. Otherwise, we run the risk of no measurable effects, particularly with small-scale experiments. In the survey procedures, on the other hand, socially significant attitudes which are deeply rooted in prior experience and involve much personal commitment are typically involved. This is especially true in voting studies which have provided us with so many of our present results on social influence. I shall have considerably more to say about this problem a little later.

The differences so far discussed have primarily concerned the extent of overall effectiveness indicated by the two methods: why survey results typically show little modification of attitudes by communication while experiments indicate marked changes. Let me now turn to some of the other differences in generalizations derived from the two alternative designs. Let me take as the second main area of disparate results the research on the effect of varying distances between the position taken by the communicator and that held by the recipient of the communication. Here it is a matter of comparing changes for persons who at the outset closely agree with the communicator with those for others who are mildly or strongly in disagreement with him. In the naturalistic situation studied in surveys the typical procedure is to determine changes in opinion following reported exposure to communication for individuals differing from the communicator by varying amounts. This gives rise to two possible artifacts. When the communication is at one end of a continuum, there is little room for improvement for those who differ from the communication by small amounts, but a great deal of room for movement among those with large discrepancies. This gives rise to a spurious degree of positive relationship between the degree of discrepancy and the amount of change. Regression effects will also operate in the direction of increasing the correlation. What is needed is a situation in which the distance factor can be manipulated independently of the subject's initial position. An attempt to set up these conditions experimentally was made in a study by Pritzker and the writer (1957). The method involved preparing individual communications presented in booklet form so that the position of the communicator could be set at any desired distance from the subject's initial position. Communicators highly acceptable to the subjects were used. A number of different topics were employed, including the likelihood of a cure for cancer within five years, the desirability of compulsory voting, and the adequacy of five hours of sleep per night.

The amount of change for each degree of advocated change is shown in Fig. 1. It will be seen that there is a fairly clear progression, such that the greater the amount of change advocated the greater the average amount of opinion change produced. Simi-

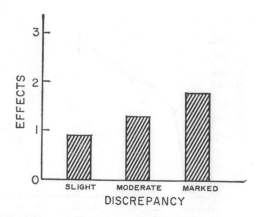

Fig. 1. Mean opinion change score with three degrees of discrepancy (deviation between subject's position and position advocated in communication). [From Hovland & Pritzker, 1957]

lar results have been reported by Goldberg (1954) and by French (1956).

But these results are not in line with our hunches as to what would happen in a naturalistic situation with important social issues. We felt that here other types of response than change in attitude would occur. So Muzafer Sherif, O. J. Harvey, and the writer (1957) set up a situation to simulate as closely as possible the conditions typically involved when individuals are exposed to major social issue communications at differing distances from their own position. The issue used was the desirability of prohibition. The study was done in two states (Oklahoma and Texas) where there is prohibition or local option, so that the wet-dry issue is hotly debated. We concentrated on three aspects of the problem: How favorably will the communicator be received when his position is at varying distances from that of the recipient? How will what the communicator says be perceived and interpreted by individuals at varying distances from his position? What will be the amount of opinion change produced when small and large deviations in position of communication and recipient are involved?

Three communications, one strongly wet, one strongly dry, and one moderately wet, were employed. The results bearing on the first problem, of *reception*, are presented in Fig. 2. The positions of the subjects are indicated on the abscissa in letters from A (extreme dry) to H (strongly wet). The

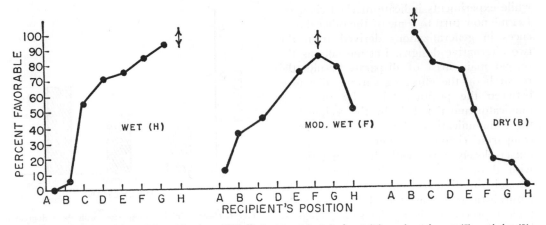

Fig. 2. Percentage of favorable evaluations ("fair," "unbiased," etc.) of wet (H), moderately wet (F), and dry (B) communications for subjects holding various positions on prohibition. Recipients position range from A (very dry) to H (very wet). Position of communications indicated by arrow. [From Hovland, Harvey, & Sherif, 1957]

positions of the communication are also indicated in the same letters, B indicating a strongly dry communication, H a strongly wet, and F a moderately wet. Along the ordinate there is plotted the percentage of subjects with each position on the issue who described the communication as "fair" and "unbiased." It will be seen that the degree of distance between the recipient and the communicator greatly influences the evaluation of the fairness of the communication. When a communication is directed at the pro-dry position, nearly all of the dry subjects consider it fair and impartial, but only a few per cent of the wet subjects consider the identical communication fair. The reverse is true at the other end of the scale. When an intermediate position is adopted, the percentages fall off sharply on each side. Thus under the present conditions with a relatively ambiguous communicator one of the ways of dealing with strongly discrepant positions is to *discredit* the communicator, considering him unfair and biased.

A second way in which an individual can deal with discrepancy is by distortion of what is said by the communicator. Thus is a phenomenon extensively studied by Cooper and Jahoda (1947). In the present study, subjects were asked to state what position they thought was taken by the communicator on the prohibition question. Their evaluation of his position could then be analyzed in relation to their own position. These results are shown in Fig. 3 for the moderately

wet communication. It will be observed that there is a tendency for individuals whose position is close to that of the communicator to report on the communicator's position quite accurately, for individuals a little bit removed to report his position to be substantially more like their own (which we call an "assimilation effect"), and for those with more discrepant positions to report the communicator's position as more extreme than it really was. This we refer to as a "contrast effect."

Now to our primary results on opinion change. It was found that individuals whose position was only slightly discrepant from the communicator's were influenced to a greater extent than those whose positions deviated to a larger extent. When a wet position was espoused, 28% of the middle-of-the-road subjects were changed in the direction of the communicator, as compared with only 4% of the drys. With the dry communication 14% of the middle-of-the-roaders were changed, while only 4% of the wets were changed. Thus, more of the subjects with small discrepancies were changed than were those with large discrepancies.

These results appear to indicate that, under conditions when there is some ambiguity about the credibility of the communicator and when the subject is deeply involved with the issue, the greater the attempt at change the higher the resistance. On the other hand, with highly respected com-

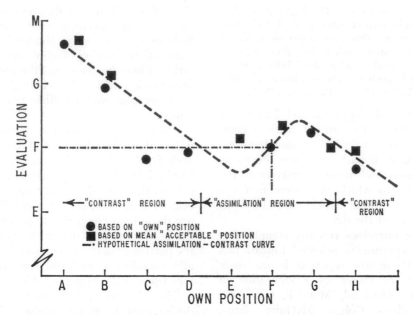

Fig. 3. Average placement of position of moderately wet communication (F) by subjects holding various positions on the issue, plotted against hypothetical assimilation-contrast curve. [From Hovland, Harvey, & Sherif, 1957]

municators, as in the previous study with Pritzker using issues of lower involvement, the greater the discrepancy the greater the effect. A study related to ours has just been completed by Zimbardo (1959) which indicates that, when an influence attempt is made by a strongly positive communicator (i.e., a close personal friend), the greater the discrepancy the greater the opinion change, even when the experimenter made a point of stressing the great importance of the subject's opinion.

The implication of these results for our primary problem of conflicting results is clear. The types of issues with which most experiments deal are relatively uninvolving and are often of the variety where expert opinion is highly relevant, as for example, on topics of health, science, and the like. Here we should expect that opinion would be considerably affected by communications and furthermore that advocacy of positions quite discrepant from the individual's own position would have a marked effect. On the other hand, the types of issues most often utilized in survey studies are ones which are very basic and involve deep commitment. As a consequence small changes in opinion due to communication would be expected. Here communication may have

little effect on those who disagree at the outset and function merely to strengthen the position already held, in line with survey findings.

A third area of research in which somewhat discrepant results are obtained by the experimental and survey methods is in the role of order of presentation. From naturalistic studies the generalization has been widely adopted that primacy is an extremely important factor in persuasion. Numerous writers have reported that what we experience first has a critical role in what we believe. This is particularly stressed in studies of propaganda effects in various countries when the nation getting across its message first is alleged to have a great advantage and in commercial advertising where "getting a beat on the field" is stressed. The importance of primacy in political propaganda is indicated in the following quotation from Doob:

The propagandist scores an initial advantage whenever his propaganda reaches people before that of his rivals. Readers or listeners are then biased to comprehend, forever after, the event as it has been initially portrayed to them. If they are told in a headline or a flash that the battle has been won, the criminal has been caught, or the bill is certain to pass the legislature, they will usually expect subsequent information to substantiate this first impression. When later facts prove otherwise, they may be loath to abandon what they believe to be true until perhaps the evidence becomes overwhelming (Doob, 1948, pp. 421–422).

A recent study by Katz and Lazarsfeld (1955) utilizing the survey method compares the extent to which respondents attribute major impact on their decisions about fashions and movie attendance to the presentations to which they were first exposed. Strong primacy effects are shown in their analyses of the data.

We have ourselves recently completed a series of experiments oriented toward this problem. These are reported in our new monograph on *Order of Presentation in Persuasion* (Hovland, Mandell, Campbell, Brock, Luchins, Cohen, McGuire, Janis, Feierabend, & Anderson, 1957). We find that primacy is often *not* a very significant factor when the relative effectiveness of the first side of an issue is compared experimentally with that of the second. The research suggests that differences in design may account for much of the discrepancy. A key variable is whether there is exposure to both sides or whether only one side is actually received. In naturalistic studies the advantage of the first side is often not only that it is first but that it is often then the only side of the issue to which the individual is exposed. Having once been influenced, many individuals make up their mind and are no longer interested in other communications on the issue. In most experiments on order of presentation, on the other hand, the audience is systematically exposed to both sides. Thus under survey conditions, self-exposure tends to increase the impact of primacy.

Two other factors to which I have already alluded appear significant in determining the amount of primacy effect. One is the nature of the communicator, the other the setting in which the communication is received. In our volume Luchins presents results indicating that, when the same communicator presents contradictory material, the point of view read first has more influence. One the other hand, Mandell and I

show that, when two different communicators present opposing views successively, little primacy effect is obtained. The communications setting factor operates similarly. When the issue and the conditions of presentation make clear that the points of view are controversial, little primacy is obtained.

Thus in many of the situations with which there had been great concern as to undesirable effects of primacy, such as in legal trials, election campaigns, and political debate, the role of primacy appears to have been exaggerated, since the conditions there are those least conducive to primacy effects: the issue is clearly defined as controversial, the partisanship of the communicator is usually established, and different communicators present the opposing sides.

Time does not permit me to discuss other divergences in results obtained in survey and experimental studies, such as those concerned with the effects of repetition of presentation, the relationship between level of intelligence and susceptibility to attitude change, or the relative impact of mass media and personal influence. Again, however, I am sure that detailed analysis will reveal differential factors at work which can account for the apparent disparity in the generalizations derived.

INTEGRATION

On the basis of the foregoing survey of results I reach the conclusion that no contradiction has been established between the data provided by experimental and correlational studies. Instead it appears that the seeming divergence can be satisfactorily accounted for on the basis of a different definition of the communication situation (including the phenomenon of self-selection) and differences in the type of communicator, audience, and kind of issue utilized.

But there remains the task of better integrating the findings associated with the two methodologies. This is a problem closely akin to that considered by the members of the recent Social Science Research Council summer seminar on *Narrowing the Gap Between Field Studies and Laboratory Studies in Social Psychology* (Riecken,

1954). Many of their recommendations are pertinent to our present problem.

What seems to me quite apparent is that a genuine understanding of the effects of communications on attitudes requires both the survey and the experimental methodologies. At the same time there appear to be certain inherent limitations of each method which must be understood by the researcher if he is not to be blinded by his preoccupation with one or the other type of design. Integration of the two methodologies will require on the part of the experimentalist an awareness of the narrowness of the laboratory in interpreting the larger and more comprehensive effects of communication. It will require on the part of the survey researcher a greater awareness of the limitations of the correlational method as a basis for establishing causal relationships.

The framework within which survey research operates is most adequately and explicitly dealt with by Berelson, Lazarsfeld, and McPhee in their book on *Voting* (1954). The model which they use, taken over by them from the economist Tinbergen, is reproduced in the top half of Fig. 4. For comparison, the model used by experimentalists is presented in the lower half of the figure. It will be seen that the model used by the survey researcher, particularly when he employs the "panel" method, stresses the large number of simultaneous and interacting influences affecting attitudes and opinions. Even more significant is its provision for a variety of "feedback" phenomena in which consequences wrought by previous influences affect processes normally considered as occurring earlier in the sequence. The various types of interaction are indicated by the placement of arrows showing direction of effect. In contrast the experimentalist frequently tends to view the communication process as one in which some single manipulative variable is the primary determinant of the subsequent attitude change. He is, of course, aware in a general way of the importance of context, and he frequently studies interaction effects as well as main effects: but he still is less attentive than he might be to the complexity of the influence situation and the numerous possibilities for feedback loops. Undoubtedly the real life communication situation is better described in terms of the survey type of model. We are all familiar, for example, with the interactions in which attitudes predispose one to acquire certain types of information, that this often leads to changes in attitude which may result in further acquisition of knowledge, which in turn produces more attitude change, and so on. Certainly the narrow question sometimes posed by experiments as to the effect of knowledge on attitudes greatly underestimates these interactive effects.

But while the conceptualization of the survey researcher is often very valuable, his correlational research design leaves much to be desired. Advocates of correlational analysis often cite the example of a science built on observation exclusively without experiment: astronomy. But here a very limited number of space-time concepts are involved and the number of competing theoretical formulations is relatively small so that it is possible to limit alternative theories rather drastically through correlational evidence. But in the area of communication effects and social psychology generally the variables are so numerous and so intertwined that the correlational methodology **is**

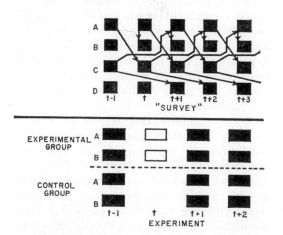

Fig. 4. Top Half: "Process analysis" schema used in panel research. (Successive time intervals are indicated along abscissa. Letters indicate the variables under observation. Arrows represent relations between the variables.) [From Berelson, Lazarsfeld, & McPhee, 1954]

Bottom Half: Design of experimental research. (Letters on vertical axis again indicate variables being measured. Unshaded box indicates experimentally manipulated treatment and blank absence of such treatment. Time periods indicated as in top half of chart.)

primarily useful to suggest hypotheses and not to establish casual relationships (Hovland *et al.*, 1949, pp. 329–340; Maccoby, 1956). Even with the much simpler relationships involved in biological systems there are grave difficulties of which we are all aware these days when we realize how difficult it is to establish through correlation whether eating of fats is or is not a cause of heart disease or whether or not smoking is a cause of lung cancer. In communications research the complexity of the problem makes it inherently difficult to derive causal relationships from correlational analysis where experimental control of exposure is not possible. And I do not agree with my friends the Lazarsfelds (Kendall & Lazarsfeld, 1950) concerning the effectiveness of the panel method in circumventing this problem since parallel difficulties are raised when the relationships occur over a time span.

These difficulties constitute a challenge to the experimentalist in this area of research to utilize the broad framework for studying communication effects suggested by the survey researcher, but to employ well controlled experimental design to work on those aspects of the field which are amenable to experimental manipulation and control. It is, of course, apparent that there are important communication problems which cannot be attacked directly by experimental methods. It is not, for example, feasible to modify voting behavior by manipulation of the issues discussed by the opposed parties during a particular campaign. It is not feasible to assess the effects of communications over a very long span of time. For example, one cannot visualize experimental procedures for answering the question of what has been the impact of the reading of *Das Kapital* or *Uncle Tom's Cabin*. These are questions which can be illuminated by historical and sociological study but cannot be evaluated in any rigorous experimental fashion.

But the scope of problems which do lend themselves to experimental attack is very broad. Even complex interactions can be fruitfully attacked by experiment. The possibilities are clearly shown in studies like that of Sherif and Sherif (1953) on factors influencing cooperative and competitive behavior in a camp for adolescent boys. They were able to bring under manipulative control many of the types of interpersonal relationships ordinarily considered impossible to modify experimentally, and to develop motivations of an intensity characteristic of real-life situations. It should be possible to do similar studies in the communication area with a number of the variables heretofore only investigated in uncontrolled naturalistic settings by survey procedures.

In any case it appears eminently practical to minimize many of the differences which were discussed above as being not inherent in design but more or less adventitiously linked with one or the other method. Thus there is no reason why more complex and deeply-involving social issues cannot be employed in experiments rather than the more superficial ones more commonly used. The resistance to change of socially important issues may be a handicap in studying certain types of attitude change; but, on the other hand, it is important to understand the lack of modifiability of opinion with highly-involving issues. Greater representation of the diverse types of communicators found in naturalistic situations can also be achieved. In addition, it should be possible to do experiments with a wider range of populations to reduce the possibility that many of our present generalizations from experiments are unduly affected by their heavy weighting of college student characteristics, including high literacy, alertness, and rationality.

A more difficult task is that of experimentally evaluating communications under conditions of self-selection of exposure. But this is not at all impossible in theory. It should be possible to assess what demographic and personality factors predispose one to expose oneself to particular communications and then to utilize experimental and control groups having these characteristics. Under some circumstances the evaluation could be made on only those who select themselves, with both experimental and control groups coming from the self-selected audience.

Undoubtedly many of the types of experiments which could be set up involving or simulating naturalistic conditions will be too ambitious and costly to be feasible even if possible in principle. This suggests the continued use of small-scale experiments which seek to isolate some of the key variables operative in complex situations. From synthesis of component factors, prediction of complex outcomes may be practicable. It is to this analytic procedure for narrowing the gap between laboratory and field research that we have devoted major attention in our research program. I will merely indicate briefly here some of the ties between our past work and the present problem.

We have attempted to assess the influence of the communicator by varying his expertness and attractiveness, as in the studies by Kelman, Weiss, and the writer (Hovland & Weiss, 1951; Kelman & Hovland, 1953). Further data on this topic were presented earlier in this paper.

We have also been concerned with evaluating social interaction effects. Some of the experiments on group affiliation as a factor affecting resistance to counternorm communication and the role of salience of group membership by Hal Kelley and others are reported in *Communication and Persuasion* (Hovland et al., 1953).

Starting with the studies carried out during the war on orientation films by Art Lumsdaine, Fred Sheffield, and the writer (1949), we have had a strong interest in the duration of communication effects. Investigation of effects at various time intervals has helped to bridge the gap between assessment of immediate changes with those of longer duration like those involved in survey studies. More recent extensions of this work have indicated the close relationship between the credibility of the communicator and the extent of post-communication increments, or "sleeper effects" (Hovland & Weiss, 1951; Kelman & Hovland, 1953).

The nature of individual differences in susceptibility to persuasion via communication has been the subject of a number of our recent studies. The generality of persuasibility has been investigated by Janis and collaborators and the development of persuasibility in children has been studied by Abelson and Lesser. A volume concerned with these audience factors to which Janis, Abelson, Lesser, Field, Rife, King, Cohen, Linton, Graham, and the writer have contributed will appear under the title *Personality and Persuasibility* (1959).

Lastly, there remains the question on how the nature of the issues used in the communication affects the extent of change in attitude. We have only made a small beginning on these problems. In the research reported in *Experiments on Mass Communication,* we showed that the magnitude of effects was directly related to the type of attitude involved: film communications had a significant effect on opinions related to straightforward interpretations of policies and events, but had little or no effect on more deeply intrenched attitudes and motivations. Further work on the nature of issues is represented in the study by Sherif, Harvey, and the writer (1957) which was discussed above. There we found a marked contrast between susceptibility to influence and the amount of ego-involvement in the issue. But the whole concept of ego-involvement is a fuzzy one, and here is an excellent area for further work seeking to determine the theoretical factors involved in different types of issues.

With this brief survey of possible ways to bridge the gap between experiment and survey I must close. I should like to stress in summary the mutual importance of the two approaches to the problem of communication effectiveness. Neither is a royal road to wisdom, but each represents an important emphasis. The challenge of future work is one of fruitfully combining their virtues so that we may develop a social psychology of communication with the conceptual breadth provided by correlational study of process and with the rigorous but more delimited methodology of the experiment.

REFERENCES

Berelson, B. R., Lazarsfeld, P. F., & McPhee, W. N. *Voting: A study of opinion formation in a presidential campaign.* Chicago: Univer. Chicago Press, 1954.

Cooper, Eunice, & Jahoda, Marie. The evasion of propaganda: How prejudiced people respond to antiprejudice propaganda. *J. Psychol.*, 1947, 23, 15–25.

Doob, L. W. *Public opinion and propaganda.* New York: Holt, 1948.

French, J. R. P., Jr. A formal theory of social power. *Psychol. Rev.*, 1956, 63, 181–194.

Goldberg, S. C. Three situational determinants of conformity to social norms. *J. abnorm. soc. Psychol.*, 1954, 49, 325–329.

Goswell, H. F. *Getting out the vote: An experiment in the stimulation of voting.* Chicago: Univer. Chicago Press, 1927.

Hovland, C. I. Effects of the mass media of communication. In G. Lindzey (Ed.), *Handbook of social psychology.* Vol. II. *Special fields and applications.* Cambridge, Mass.: Addison-Wesley, 1954. Pp. 1062–1103.

Hovland, C. I., Harvey, O. J., & Sherif, M. Assimilation and contrast effects in reactions to communication and attitude change. *J. abnorm. soc. Psychol.*, 1957, 55, 244–252.

Hovland, C. I., Janis, I. L., & Kelley, H. H. *Communication and persuasion.* New Haven: Yale Univer. Press, 1953.

Hovland, C. I., Lumsdaine, A. A., & Sheffield, F. D. *Experiments on mass communication.* Princeton: Princeton Univer. Press, 1949.

Hovland, C. I., Mandell, W., Campbell, Enid H., Brock, T., Luchins, A. S., Cohen, A. R., McGuire, W. J., Janis, I. L., Feierabend, Rosalind L., & Anderson, N. H. *The order of presentation in persuasion.* New Haven: Yale Univer. Press, 1957.

Hovland, C. I., & Pritzker, H. A. Extent of opinion change as a function of amount of change advocated. *J. abnorm. soc. Psychol.*, 1957, 54, 257–261.

Hovland, C. I., & Weiss, W. The influence of source credibility on communication effectiveness. *Publ. opin. Quart.*, 1951, 15, 635–650.

Janis, I. L., Hovland, C. I., Field, P. B., Linton, Harriett, Graham, Elaine, Cohen, A. R., Rife, D., Abelson, R. P., Lesser, G. S., &

King, B. T. *Personality and persuasibility.* New Haven: Yale Univer. Press, 1959.

Katz, E., & Lazarsfeld, P. F. *Personal influence.* Free Press of Glencoe, Inc., 1955.

Kelman, H. C., & Hovland, C. I. "Reinstatement" of the communicator in delayed measurement of opinion change. *J. abnorm. soc. Psychol.*, 1953, 48, 327–335.

Kendall, Patricia L., & Lazarsfeld, P. F. Problems of survey analysis. In R. K. Merton & P. F. Lazarsfeld (Eds.), *Continuities in social research: Studies in the scope and method of "The American Soldier."* Free Press of Glencoe, Inc., 1950. Pp. 133–196.

Klapper, J. T. *The effects of mass media.* New York: Columbia Univer. Bureau of Applied Social Research, 1949. (Mimeo.)

Lazarsfeld, P. F., Berelson, B., & Gaudet, Hazel. *The people's choice.* New York: Duell, Sloan, & Pearce, 1944.

Lipset, S. M., Lazarsfeld, P. F., Barton, A. H., & Linz, J. The psychology of voting: An analysis of political behavior. In G. Lindzey (Ed.), *Handbook of social psychology.* Vol. II. *Special fields and applications.* Cambridge, Mass.: Addison-Wesley, 1954. Pp. 1124–1175.

Maccoby, Eleanor E. Pitfalls in the analysis of panel data: A research note on some technical aspects of voting. *Amer. J. Sociol.*, 1956, 59, 359–362.

Riecken, H. W. (Chairman) Narrowing the gap between field studies and laboratory experiments in social psychology: A statement by the summer seminar. *Items Soc. Sci. Res. Council*, 1954, 8, 37–42.

Sherif, M., & Sherif, Carolyn W. *Groups in harmony and tension: An integration of studies on intergroup relations.* New York: Harper, 1953.

Zimbardo, P. G. Involvement and communication discrepancy as determinants of opinion change. Unpublished doctoral dissertation, Yale University, 1959.

SECTION TWO

Contexts of Interpersonal Behavior

The behavior of the actor examined in Section I obviously does not occur in a vacuum. As has already been stated in the introduction and implied in the nature of the research and theory presented in the first section of the readings, our actor behaves with reference to others in a total situational context. Our understanding of his performance comes only from an understanding of these contexts in which he is located. Thus the aim of this section is to deal with four convenient levels of social context: The small group, the large scale organization, the community, and the culture and society.

A. The Small Group

Perhaps one of the most ubiquitous of all social contexts is that provided by the small group. We are born into a small family group, are socialized within the context of such a group, as adults have a relatively small circle of friends and associates, and generally spend much of our lives in associations involving small numbers of persons. The two-person group or dyad, the three-person group or triad, and groups ranging in size up to about 8–15 have all generally been included under the rubric, small group. Typically, such groups are characterized by a general informality of relationships, rules, and norms, a flexible structure and division of labor, and a greater freedom and accessability of communication between members than the larger groups and organizations which are discussed in part B.

To provide some historical perspective to the present day studies of small groups, it is possible to outline four traditional emphases: (1) The early sociological concern with the small primary group as forming the basic unit of socialization. In C. H. Cooley's approach, such primary groups are characterized by face-to-face interaction, intimacy, and a sense of identification or "we-ness." This approach focuses upon the group as a source of cultural transmission and as one means of social cohesion and

control. (2) The early psychological concern with the small group as a location in which to study the interaction between two or more persons. In this tradition we have the beginnings of an experimental group dynamics. This latter movement was given additional impetus by Kurt Lewin and his followers who changed the focus to the emergent structures and processes of the small group itself rather than merely to the group as a collection of individuals which provided a setting for studying interpersonal behavior. (3) The more applied approach in which the group as a work or production unit is examined with an eye to improving group morale and productivity. (4) The therapeutic approach in which the small group is seen with respect to its abilities to effect changes in individual personality. Out of this latter tradition, we have the additional interests in individual sensitivity training, in which unstructured groups meet for a period of time in order to develop an increased sensitivity to group process.

Although these traditional approaches are not all represented in the readings we have selected, the experimental emphasis is dealt with in the first five studies, while the more therapeutic approach is exemplified by the provocative article by Bion.

Stemming from the early discussions of Simmel in which he utilized the facts of differential group size to reach interesting conclusions about differences between a condition of isolation, a dyadic relationship, a triadic relationship, and relationships involving four or more interacting individuals, we have the experiment of Kelley and Arrowood. Rather than focusing upon group size itself, however, they examine the effects of differential power distribution upon coalition formation in triads.

Moving away from the issues involved in triadic interactions, Schachter's research tackles the problem of group pressures towards uniformity of opinion, and the conditions which effect the magnitude and direction of these pressures.

The study by Hollander provides a further focus upon the issues of conformity and deviation within a small group and is especially relevant for its use of the concept of "idiosyncrasy credit."

That groups have structure—i.e. patterned modes of relationship among members—is an obvious fact. The effect of such structures upon the communication within the group is the main focus of the article by Cohen.

Though they employ a procedure involving only a dyadic relationship, the excellent series of studies reported by Deutsch and Krauss are intended to have general applicability to groups of larger size, including a specific reference to the international scene. By examining the bargaining relationship in a two-person game situation under varying conditions of threat and communication, the authors utilize the relative research ease of the small group context in order to discover underlying relationships applicable to contexts at all levels of interpersonal behavior.

The final selection by Bion presents the therapists' view of the first meeting with his therapy group. The view as expressed by Bion, the therapist, contains within it the rudiments of his theoretical framework for understanding this type of small group interaction.

Coalitions in the Triad: Critique and Experiment / Harold H. Kelley and A. John Arrowood

(*Laboratory for Research in Social Relations, University of Minnesota*[1])

Vinacke and Arkoff (4) have presented an experiment which tests some of Caplow's hypotheses (2) about how the relative power of three persons affects the formation of pair coalitions. The situation studied is one in which each person is trying to obtain for himself as much of some valuable but scarce commodity as he can. The three individuals differ in ways relevant to their ability to gain a share of the rewards (referred to as "power"). This work has been especially interesting because of the paradoxical result that with certain distributions of power among the three individuals, in

Reprinted from *Sociometry*, 1960, 23, pages 231-244, by permission of the senior author and publisher, The American Sociological Association.

[1] This research was supported by grant G–5553 to the senior author from the National Science Foundation.

Caplow's words, "the triadic situation often favors the weaker over the strong." Under certain conditions the stronger of the three is at a disadvantage and actually receives the smallest share of the available rewards.

The purpose of the present research is to state with greater precision than heretofore the conditions under which this phenomenon prevails and to test experimentally some of the limits of these conditions. In order to do so, it is necessary to clarify certain ambiguities in the concept of power as used in the Vinacke and Arkoff experiment. This clarification is accomplished through use of the analysis of power provided by Thibaut and Kelley (3).

The problem can best be illustrated by a brief description of the Vinacke and Arkoff procedure. Three subjects play a game in which each moves his counter along the spaces of a game board. The first one to reach the goal receives a prize of 100 points. On successive trials, the experimenter rolls a single die and each player advances a number of spaces determined by the product of two numbers: (a) the number of pips turned up on the die and (b) a "weight," ranging from 1 to 4, which was randomly assigned him at the beginning of the game. For example, in one game player A may have weight 4, player B, weight 2, and player C, weight 1. Since all players start at the same point on the board and move each time the die is cast, the person assigned the largest weight automatically wins. A further rule, however, enables any pair of players to form a coalition by combining their weights at any time during the game. When they do so, they are given a single counter placed at a position equal to the sum of the distances the two have attained at that time. On subsequent rolls, they advance according to the sum of their two weights. The formation of a coalition is acknowledged by the experimenter only when the two players have agreed upon how they will divide the 100 point prize, should they receive it; and, once formed, a coalition is indissoluble for the remainder of that game. Thus, the individual or coalition that can mobilize the largest weight automatically wins that game and there is really no need for going through the motions of rolling the die.

The weight each player receives is said to constitute his *power,* but consider this point more closely. In what sense does a player with a weight of 4 have more power than a player with a weight of 2? In the game where the three weights are 4, 2 and 1, the player with the 4 weight has power in the sense that he is able, regardless of the actions of the other two players, to induce his "environment" (the game) to give him the prize. However, in the game with weights 4, 3 and 2, the player with 4 weight can exercise this control over the environment only if the other two players fail to form a coalition. Since any pair can mobilize more weight than the remaining person, each pair has the same amount of power over the third person as does any other pair. The variability in 4's outcomes is as much under

the control of the joint actions of the other two players as is the variability in either 2 or 3's outcomes. Hence, as Vinacke and Arkoff point out, the initial weights in the 4–3–2 game are irrelevant with respect to the power a person has in the three-way bargaining situation.

In view of this logical analysis of the objective interdependency relations among the three players, Vinacke and Arkoff's results from the 4–3–2 and similar games are unexpected: The three players treat the weight 4 as if it does yield greater power. As his price for entering a coalition, player 4 apparently asks for a lion's share of the prize, because he typically receives more than 50 of the 100 points when he is in a coalition. Furthermore, players 2 and 3 tend to form the majority of the coalitions, presumably because each one can make a better deal with the other than he can with 4. From the point of view of rational analysis, then, the subjects act inappropriately, attributing to 4 a power that he does not in fact possess. The irony of the situation is that this erroneous belief about 4's advantage, which he usually shares, works to his disadvantage in the long run because of his exclusion from coalitions.

The first of the experiments reported below has the purpose of showing that Vinacke and Arkoff's data are, in a sense, spurious. They reflect a misunderstanding of the experimental situation that is not intrinsic to it, but results from the complexity of their total procedure. Confronted with the complexity, subjects erroneously equate initial weights with real power. (Our reasons for believing this erroneous assumption to be a reasonable one, considering the circumstances, are given in the Discussion.) The experimental hypothesis is that with a simpler procedure, subjects will acquire an adequate understanding of the true power relations and act more in accord with a rational analysis of the situation than the Vinacke and Arkoff data would suggest.

The second experiment has the purpose of testing Caplow's hypothesis under conditions where the power differences among the three persons are real rather than illusory. We expect the resulting bias in coalition formation (predominantly between the weaker members) to persist even though subjects are permitted thoroughly to familiarize themselves with the situation. (The limiting conditions under which the Caplow effect can be expected to appear are also described.)

EXPERIMENT I

In the Vinacke and Arkoff procedure, the relationship between weights and power is quite complicated. Each trio of subjects is required to play a series of games in which six different sets of weights are used. In the games played with a given set of values, a player need not have the same weight twice. With some sets of weights (such as 4–2–1) initial weight is relevant to power, and with others (such as 4–3–2) it is not.

In the present experiment, in order to simplify the subjects' task, only one set of weights was used (4–3–2) and each triad was given a lengthy series of trials, each player keeping the same weight throughout. It was expected that, with repeated experience in the single situation, the subjects' analyses of it would come to correspond with the analysis presented above, and their coalition formation and bargaining behavior would be increasingly consistent with an understanding that all players in the game have the same power.

Procedure

Ninety male students, volunteers from an introductory (sophomore) psychology class, served as subjects in thirty experimental triads. There is no reason to believe that the subjects were notably different from Vinacke and Arkoff's. Data were gathered first from 20 triads and, later, from ten additional triads. The first series were given a variable number of trials (10 to 70 trials, 26 on the average), and in the second series all groups completed 20 trials.

With the exceptions noted above, the experimental procedure followed that of Vinacke and Arkoff as closely as was possible from the available statements of their procedure. A major difference is that, whereas they gave very brief introductory instructions and relied on informal answers to questions to clarify the procedure, we gave rather full formal instructions and tried to minimize the necessity for subjects to ask questions. The subjects were given an individualistic orientation, it being emphasized that each was to accumulate as many points for himself as possible, attempting to maximize his outcomes without regard to those of any other players.

Results

In Table 1 are presented the frequencies of occurrence of the various coalitions. Data

TABLE 1

FREQUENCY OF OCCURRENCE OF VARIOUS COALITIONS IN THE THREE EXPERIMENTS

| | Vinacke and Arkoff's Three Trials | | Experiment I | | | | | Experiment II | | | |
| | | | First 3 Trials | | Last 3 Trials | | | First 3 Trials | | Last 3 Trials | |
Coalitions	N	%	N	%	N	%	(Coalitions)	N	%	N	%
2–3	59	66	41	46	37	41	(0–2)	24	53	29	64
2–4	20	22	24	27	26	29	(0–4)	12	27	13	29
3–4	9	10	21	23	27	30	(2–4)	9	20	3	7
No coalition	2	2	4	4	0	..		0	..	0	..
Totals	90	100	90	100	90	100		45	100	45	100

$$\frac{X^2 n = 88}{2\mathrm{df}} = 47.07$$
$$p<.001$$

$$\frac{X^2 n = 90}{2\mathrm{df}} = 2.47$$
$$.20<p<.30$$

$$\frac{X^2 n = 45}{2\mathrm{df}} = 22.93$$
$$p<.001$$

$$\frac{X^2 n = 86}{2\mathrm{df}} = 8.12$$
$$.01<p<.02$$

$$\frac{X^2 n = 45}{2\mathrm{df}} = 8.40$$
$$.01<p<.02$$

from our first and last three trials are presented for comparison with those from Vinacke and Arkoff's three trials in the 4–3–2 condition. They calculated a Chi-square for the 88 instances of coalition formation (excluding the two instances of "no coalition") to determine the likelihood of the departure of the observed distribution from a theoretical distribution in which the three possible coalitions occur equally often. This procedure is not strictly justified, inasmuch as each group of subjects provides three instances of coalition formation, hence the various entries are not independent. However, we present similar Chi-squares in order to provide some basis for comparing the two sets of results.

It appears that the present procedure yields a distribution of coalitions which, although biassed in a manner similar to Vinacke and Arkoff's, is closer to the chance distribution than is theirs. The divergence from the earlier experiment appears even on the first three trials. A comparison of our first three with theirs yields a Chi-square of 8.48, p = .02. (The distribution of first coalitions formed in each triad resembles their distribution most closely, the percentages, in order, being 63, 20 and 17.) These results suggest that, either because of the concentrated experience with the single situation, or perhaps because of greater clarity in the experimental instructions, a number of subjects became aware of the objective power relationships rather early in the game.

From the first to the last trials there is not a significant change in the incidence of the three coalitions, hence we cannot be sure that further experience increased their understanding of the situation. However, this result must be interpreted in the light of the rather limited degree to which the occurrence of the early coalitions departed from chance. To the extent that subjects achieved an understanding of their relationships very early, further improvement in this respect was limited. Upon examination of the data on a trial-by-trial basis, it is clear that the learning is very rapid, so that after the first three or four trials there is little more than chance exclusion of 4 from coalitions.

In Vinacke and Arkoff's experiment, associated with the tendency for 2 and 3 to be reluctant about forming coalitions with 4, was the tendency for him to receive more than half of the 100 point prize when he did manage to enter a coalition. This effect appears in the early trials of the present experiment and declines, though not significantly so, during its course. During the first three trials, player 4 was a member of a coalition in 26 triads and in 17 of these he managed to come out with more than 50 per cent of the rewards. During the last three trials of the experiment, this was true in only 10 of 29 possible instances. Of the 25 groups in which person 4 was in coalitions during both the first and last three trials, his share of the coalition reward declined in 13 instances, increased in six instances and did not change in the remaining six. Omitting the last six, the difference between the number of decreases and increases yields a p-value of .168 by the Sign test.

There are, then, two behavioral manifestations of the players' perception that 4 has the most power: (a) He is excluded from coalitions and, (b) when he is included in coalitions, he receives more than half the points. When early and later trials are compared, the extent to which 4's frequency of being included increases and the extent to which his percentage winnings per trial decrease provide two indicators of downgrading in the perception of his power. A comparison of the first and last three trials of the experiment reveals that in 18 triads the 4 man was downgraded on both of these indicators or downgraded on one with no change on the other; in six triads, he was upgraded on both indicators or upgraded on one with no change on the other; and in six triads, he did not change on either indicator or was upgraded on one and downgraded on the other. When the last six are omitted from the analysis, the Sign test indicates there was significantly more downgrading than upgrading (p = .026).

On the questionnaire at the end of the experiment all subjects were asked the following open-ended question: "Many subjects believe that 4 is more to be feared, has greater potential, etc. Did you at any time think that this was the case?" All but 14 of the 90 subjects admitted that they at some time had held this belief. This estimate of the extent of the belief, if it errs at all, is probably an underestimate because of the general realization at the end of the experiment of the incorrectness of this view. Most of those admitting to this belief reported having it "at first" or on the first one or two trials. Subjects with the three different weights were equally susceptible to this belief.

The next question asked when the subject realized that no position has any more power than any other and that nobody is justified in asking for more than half the 100 points. Forty-three of the 90 claimed to have realized this before or during the first three trials. Another 33 did not localize their insight so sharply in time. Only 13 admitted they had never realized this. On the basis of their answers to other questions about power relations, preferred position, position likely to win, and ease of bargaining with various positions, another nine subjects were added to the latter category of those who had failed to attain a correct understanding of the situation by the end of the experiment.

In brief, the self-report data suggest that, while some 85 per cent of our subjects believed at some time during the experiment (largely, in the early stages) that the 4 weight carries greatest power, only 25 per cent held this belief at the end of the experiment. As far as we could judge from their answers to questions asked after the experiment, the other 75 per cent had achieved a correct understanding of the power relations and apparently most of them did so during the actual trials of the experiment.

One may ask to what extent this change in belief about power relations reflects the subjects' direct experience with the game, as opposed to their being taught by the small number of their colleagues who had analyzed the situation correctly from the start. To answer this question, a comparison was made between those groups in which, from the sound recordings of the discussion, there appeared to have been some possibility of "teaching," and the remaining groups. There were no differences between the two sets of data either in the amount of learning that took place or in the coalitions formed. Hence, explicit teaching seems not to account for the observed effects.

A final open-ended question asked: "Why

do you think that many subjects would believe that 4 is more to be feared, has greater potential, etc.? What is there in the situation that leads to this belief?" The most frequent response, given by 34 of the 90 subjects, dealt with the fact that 4 would win invariably if no coalitions were formed. Another 13 merely stated, without further amplification, that 4 was the largest number. Nine subjects mentioned the multiplicative aspects of the game, pointing out that multiples of 4 are larger than multiples of 2 or 3. Apparently, the 56 responses in these three categories either discount or overlook the possibility of coalition formation. A fourth category of response deals with 4's "psychological" or "cultural" power. Seventeen of the 90 suggested that it was natural to react to 4's higher weight in the light of their previous experience in games that higher numbers are generally better ones and in everyday life that quantity often has the upper hand. This answer is silent concerning the possibility of coalitions but highlights the stereotype that "more" is "better."

It is difficult to evaluate the validity of these post-experiment explanations for the earlier misinterpretation. Because the misperception of 4's power is largely corrected by the end of the experiment, subjects may be somewhat reluctant or even unable to discuss the real basis for their mistaken views. Hence the reasons given by the 22 players who seem never to have realized the true nature of the power situation may be especially valuable indications of the source of the error. Seven of the 22 seemed to believe that coalitions including 4 were somehow more sure of obtaining the prize than were other coalitions or that 4 was the only player capable of bargaining and that the other players had either to accept his terms or receive nothing. We believe it noteworthy that it is only among these 22 players that we find the assertion (made by another seven of them) that a high-weight player is justified in demanding a majority share of the coalition reward because he *contributes more* to the coalition. One might guess that this interpretation figures more prominently in the early reaction to the situation than the overall figures would indicate. The comments about 4's larger number and the multiplicative aspects of the game may well be oblique references to earlier beliefs (which now appear to the subjects as totally unjustified) that the higher weight player makes a greater contribution to coalition success.

EXPERIMENT II

Under the Vinacke and Arkoff procedure, the alternative to being in a coalition on any given trial has the same value (zero) for each player regardless of his weight. Hence, 4's outcomes are as much subject to control through the joint actions of the other two players as are either 2 or 3's outcomes. It is in this sense that 4 has no more power than they. In the present experiment, real power differences are created by giving the three subjects differential ability to obtain rewards from the game, an ability that can not be attenuated by the actions of the other two persons. This is done by giving each person a specific alternative level of outcomes which he receives if he fails to gain membership in a coalition or if, once in a coalition, he and his partner fail to reach agreement on a division of the spoils. (The bargaining involved in the division of the prize *follows* rather than precedes the choice of coalition partners.) The person with a higher alternative value has high power in the sense that (a) he is less dependent upon getting into a coalition, and (b), during the bargaining following coalition formation, he can hold out for a larger share because he has less to lose if no agreement is reached. The long run effects of the latter, demanding a preponderant share of the reward, are of rather little concern to him because of the first fact. At the same time, factor (b) makes him less desirable than a weaker person as a coalition partner. Hence, we would expect that the poorer a player's alternative, the greater the likelihood of his being included in a pair coalition. Of course, this will be true only when the size of prize given a coalition does *not* increase in proportion to the power of its members. (In the present case, as in the Vinacke and Arkoff procedure, the prize is the same for all coalitions.) It is under these circumstances that Caplow's statement is relevant—that "the weakest member of the triad has a definite

advantage, being sure to be included in whatever coalition is formed."

Procedure

Forty-five male students, volunteers from an introductory (sophomore) psychology class, served as subjects in 15 experimental triads. The task was presented as a simple business game in which each player was a corporation chairman, controlling a certain share of the market each month. Each player's object was to accumulate as many points for himself as possible, not to compete but to attempt to maximize his own outcomes without regard to how this might affect the outcomes of the other players. Each subject was randomly assigned a weight—either 4, 2, or 0 —which represented the number of points he could earn on each trial if he chose to play the game independently. Any pair of subjects, however, had the option of forming a coalition which was then given one minute to decide in what manner to divide a ten-point prize between them. Coalitions were formed by a series of written choices. At the beginning of each trial, each subject privately indicated the number of the other player with whom he would most like to form a coalition. Reciprocated choices became coalition partners, thereby having the opportunity to attempt to decide how they wanted to divide the ten points between them. The third man, the player *not* in the coalition, was paid off immediately with the number of points equal to his weight or alternative and did not enter into the bargaining for that trial. (If there happened to be no reciprocated choices on a given trial, the subjects were requested to consider the problem again and indicate their choices once more. This procedure was continued until a reciprocated choice appeared. This was necessary on only 43 of the 300 trials. Most of the instances of non-reciprocation were found early in the game.) If the two members of the coalition reached some mutually satisfactory division of the ten points during the minute allotted for bargaining, they then received that number of points as their scores for that trial. If, however, they did not agree before the time limit, they forfeited the ten points and each received the number of points equal to their weights or alternatives. A time limit was placed on the bargaining so that the weaker player could not gain power by stalling and controlling time. Each subject retained the same weight throughout the game, and each triad completed 20 trials.

Although the weights employed in the present study differ from those used in the Vinacke-Arkoff experiment, they are comparable in at least two ways: first, if no coalitions are formed, or if no agreement is reached in the coalitions which are formed, the high-weight man will always win; and, second, the coalition is always assured a chance at a larger number of points than is any independent player. For certain analyses, then, we shall consider the present 0–2, 0–4, and 2–4 coalitions as equivalent, respectively, to the 2–3, 2–4, and 3–4 coalitions in the previous experiment.

Results

Table 1 presents the frequencies of occurrence of the various coalitions. Data from the first and last three trials of Experiment II

may be compared with those from Vinacke and Arkoff and Experiment I. The relative incidence of the various coalitions for the first three trials of Experiment II does not differ significantly from that of Experiment I. The difference between the two distributions for the last three trials of each experiment is significant at the .01 level with a Chi-square of 10.72. The difference between the two distributions for Experiment II is not significant (Chi-square = 3.48, p < .20).

It appears, then, that the present procedure yields a distribution of coalitions which, although departing initially from the Vinacke-Arkoff distribution, does not do so as markedly as does the distribution from Experiment I and comes to approximate the Vinacke-Arkoff distribution far more closely as the trials progress.

The data also suggest that this is not merely an illusory effect which disappears with repeated experience in the situation. Table 2 presents the mean frequencies per triad of the various coalitions, and the signifi-

TABLE 2

MEAN FREQUENCY OF OCCURRENCE OF VARIOUS COALITIONS OVERALL AND BY HALVES OF EXPERIMENT II WITH COMPARISONS*

Mean Frequency per Triad	Overall	First Half of Trials	Second Half of Trials
0–2	12.33	5.67	6.67
0–4	5.20	2.80	2.40
2–4	2.47	1.53	.93
	20 trials	10 trials	10 trials

Mean Difference per Triad			
0–2 > 0–4	7.13	2.87	4.27
	t = 10.62	t = 8.28	t = 9.19
	p < .02	p < .02	p < .02
0–2 > 2–4	9.87	4.13	5.73
	t = 14.68	t = 11.94	t = 12.35
	p < .02	p < .02	p < .02
0–4 > 2–4	2.73	1.27	1.47
	t = 4.07	t = 3.66	t = 3.16
	.02 < p < .10	p = NS	p = NS

*The t values in this table were calculated using the Tukey method for multiple comparisons.

cance levels for these differences. The 0–2 coalition occurs significantly more frequently than do either of the other possible pairs, both over the whole series of 20 trials and in both the first and second halves of the experiment; but only over the entire series of trials does the difference between the relative incidence of the 0–4 and 0–2 coalitions approach significance. Moreover, the average frequency of 0–2 coalitions tends to increase from the first to the second half of the experiment, while that of the 2–4 coalitions tends to decrease during the same period (in both instances $.05 < p < .10$, using the ordinary t-test for differences).

Another way of looking at the evidence is in terms of partnership choice data. Each of the positions predominantly chose the lower alternative man as a partner—i.e., 0 chose 2 66 per cent of the time, 2 chose 0 77 per cent of the time, and 4 chose 0 60 per cent of the time. Sign tests show that the results differ significantly from those expected by chance (equally frequent choice of the other two players) at beyond the .05 level in all three cases.

The previous experiments revealed an initial tendency for the 4 man to ask for and receive the majority of points from those coalitions which he did manage to enter. Over the entire series of 20 trials in the present experiment, there was a similar tendency for both 4 and 2 to receive more points than 0 in the 4–0 and 2–0 coalitions respectively (significant at better than the .02 level by the Tukey method for multiple comparisons). The slight tendency for 4 to receive more points than 2 from 2–4 coalitions proved non-significant. The over-all results are duplicated in the first half of the trials for each triad, but largely disappear during the second half—the only significant result remaining in the 4–0 coalition. As expected, on the average 4 received significantly more points per coalition from 0 than he did from 2, as did 2 from 0 over 4. The 0 man was slightly better rewarded by 2 than by 4, and especially during the second half of the game ($.05 < p < .10$). A comparison of first and second half scores reveals that 0's scores per coalition increase significantly ($p < .01$) while 4's scores per coalition decrease slightly ($.05 < p < .10$).

In a questionnaire administered at the end of the experiment the subjects were asked to indicate the following: which weight they would choose as a permanent partner; in general, which weight they believed each of the players should form coalitions with; which weight had the most power; which are the easiest and hardest weights with which to bargain; which weight would win in the long run; and which member, if either, of any coalition is justified in asking for a majority of the points. Their answers reflect the coalition formation and bargaining behavior discussed above. Only five of the 45 subjects, for example, failed to pick the available lower alternative player as a permanent coalition partner. The question: "Which of the three players has the most power?" was asked twice—once early in the questionnaire and once again at the end. At the first asking, four subjects responded that 0 had the most power, three picked 2, 36 chose 4, and two said that there were no power differences. At the later asking, 13 of the subjects who had previously singled out 4 as having power changed their answers to 2. The open-ended explanations accompanying these changes indicate a growing awareness of 2's ability to entice 0 into a coalition although still noting that, *if selected,* 4's higher weight becomes important. In general, however, subjects continue to view power as residing in a higher alternative.

DISCUSSION AND SUMMARY

It appears that Vinacke and Arkoff's procedure does initially give player 4 an illusory kind of power. In Experiment I, most of the subjects are initially subject to this misperception but apparently achieve a more correct understanding in a few trials. These results are in accord with our general contention that the phenomenon reported by Vinacke and Arkoff is limited to instances where the complexity of the learning task is so great in relation to the amount of contact and experience subjects have with it that they are not able properly to analyze it. In consequence, we witness actions that are "irrational" with respect to the analysis the experimenter makes at his leisure. However, these actions are not necessarily irrational when viewed in the light of the understanding subjects are able to achieve under the pressures of time and task complexity. Incomplete understanding is not to be confused with irrationality.

There are at least two possible interpretations of the initial erroneous attribution of power to player 4. The first is that the initial attribution of power to 4 reflects a general pessimism about the dependability of cooperative action. Logically, player 4 is more powerful *unless* the others join forces against him. Until one knows that joint action will be instituted dependably, attributing superior power to him is not wholly unwarranted. This interpretation is suggested by the most commonly given explanation for the attribution: 4 has more power because he would win if no coalitions were formed. The declining tendency to attribute power to 4 may reflect a growing confidence that in this situation, at least, cooperative action against him is to be taken for granted.

Another possible interpretation is that our subjects have learned to use a person's potentialities in a field of independent actors as an indication of his ability to contribute to cooperative efforts. This is explicitly suggested by the comments that he makes a larger contribution to any coalition he enters and is consistent with other more general explanations provided by the subjects. In view of their likely experiences with these matters, this conclusion is a highly reasonable one. It is probably true that in everyday situations a person's effectiveness, when everyone is acting for himself, is rather closely related to how much he can add to any joint effort. Thus, the common misperception in the Vinacke and Arkoff situation may reflect a positive correlation in the social environment of the typical subject. The reader may note the similarity of this interpretation to Brunswik's explanation (1) of, for example, the size-weight illusion as reflecting a correlation between size and weight over the universe of objects the person has experienced in his physical environment. In Brunswik's terms, we are suggesting that a person's effectiveness as an individual has "ecological validity" as a cue from which to predict his ability to contribute to joint efforts, and thus enjoys considerable "impression value" or "response-eliciting power." This is the case in

the Vinacke and Arkoff situation. In Experiment I, subjects initially utilize this cue extensively, but later learn that it is inappropriate in this situation and, hence, its subsequent degree of utilization declines.

The procedure of Experiment II, in contrast to that of Vinacke and Arkoff, appears to create large and lasting power differences among the members of the triad. Given differentially good alternatives to being in a coalition or, more important, to acquiescing to a coalition partner's demands, the predicted pattern of coalition formation emerges, and the weakest member of the triad is in the most favored position when it comes to joining pair coalitions. The score and self-report data, however, suggest certain minor trends worth brief consideration. We have noted a tendency for 0's average score per coalition to increase and 4's to decrease. This finding may be taken as an indication that during the course of the trials some 0's are beginning to capitalize on their status as preferred coalition partners by asking for a larger share of the prize and some 4's are recognizing that they must be more generous in dividing the prize if they are to be allowed to enter further coalitions. We have also noted some changes in subjects' perceptions of the most powerful player and in the reasons accompanying their answers. Mention of 2's greater ability to entice 0 into coalitions suggests that some subjects are becoming aware of the truth of Caplow's hypothesis. These findings raise the interesting side problem of how a high-power individual in a situation with limited communication possibilities would go about establishing trust. Once excluded from coalitions, the high-weight man would probably tend to remain excluded, since unless he could enter a coalition there would be no way for him to demonstrate to the others that he would not use his power against them.

It must be noted that in general 4 tends to accumulate the most points during the game —93 on the average as compared with 86 for 2 and 66 for 0. However, this is probably an artifact of the relative sizes of the alternatives and the prize to be divided. By making the coalition reward larger in relation to the largest weight, one could create a situation in which the highest alternative player would, by reason of his exclusion from coalitions, end up with the smallest accumulated score. However, as the coalition prize becomes larger, the differential power implications of any given set of weights becomes less important.

One might also manipulate the weights and coalition prize in such a manner that the highest alternative player would emerge as the most preferred partner. This is an important point because it indicates the boundary conditions for the phenomena observed in Experiment II. For example, different sizes of rewards might be given to different coalitions. If the various rewards were proportional to the weights of the persons comprising the various coalitions, one would expect no difference in the relative incidence of three possible types of coalition or even a bias in favor of coalitions including the high-power person. The latter effect would be expected, for example, if the 2–4 coalition received a prize of 12 points, the 0–4 coalition, 8 points, and the 0–2 coalition, 4 points. This would reproduce the situation where the more effective a person is as an independent actor, the more effective is the joint effort to which he contributes. It is not unreasonable to believe that, in many natural situations,

joint effectiveness is a direct function (and perhaps even a multiplicative one) of individual effectiveness. In these cases, if the above analysis is correct, coalitions would appear largely among persons of high power. On the other hand, the Caplow effect will appear when coalition effectiveness bears no relation (or a negative one) to the effectiveness of the component members.

REFERENCES

1. Brunswik, E., *Systematic and Representative Designs of Psychological Experiments,* Berkeley: University of California Press, 1949.
2. Caplow, T., A theory of coalitions in the triad," *American Sociological Review,* 1956, 21, 489–493.
3. Thibaut, J. W., and H. H. Kelley, *The Social Psychology of Groups,* New York: Wiley and Sons, Inc., 1959, Chapters 7 and 11.
4. Vinacke, W. E., and A. Arkoff, An experimental study of coalitions in the triad, *American Sociological Review,* 1957, 22, 406–414.

Deviation, Rejection, and Communication[1] /
Stanley Schachter (*University of Minnesota*)

The phenomenon of "group standards," uniformities of behavior and attitudes resulting from interaction among members of a group, is a widely documented finding in the social sciences. The gang studies of Shaw

Reprinted from *Journal of Abnormal and Social Psychology,* 1951, 46, pages 190–207, by permission of author and publisher, The American Psychological Association.

[1] This report is based on a dissertation presented in partial fulfillment of the requirements for the degree of Doctor of Philosophy at the University of Michigan. The writer is deeply indebted to Dr. Leon Festinger for generous advice and criticism. This study was conducted at the Research Center for Group Dynamics, as part of a program of research in social communication sponsored by the Office of Naval Research, Contract N6onr–23212, NR 151–698.

(9, 10), Thrasher (14), Whyte (16), and Zorbaugh (18) point up the existence of group codes and group standards. Community studies such as the Yankee City Series (15) or the Middletown books (5, 6) are in large part concerned with social conformities resulting from group membership and interaction.

In psychological circles interest in group standards was probably first stimulated by the experiments of Sherif (11, 12), which demonstrated the convergence of judgments as a function of group interaction. Sherif's approach has been chiefly that of restricting experimental work to small, carefully designed laboratory studies of perceptual phenomena. The principles derived have then been extended to more complex social phenomena. Others have studied these more complex social phenomena directly: several factory studies have demonstrated the existence of group standards about production level among industrial workers (2, 17); Newcomb (8) has found in a college community similarities of political attitudes which can plausibly be interpreted as group standards; Merei (7) has demonstrated that group standards arise in children's play groups and serve to increase the "strength" of the group.

The means by which the group imposes and maintains conformity have been an area of speculation. It has been suggested that non-conformity results in rejection from the group. Thrasher (16, p. 291) says: "Opinion in the gang manifests its pressure in the variety of methods through which group control is exerted, such as applause, preferment and hero-worshipping as well as ridicule, scorn, and ostracism . . . the member who has broken the code may be subjected to a beating or in extreme cases may be marked for death." Sherif and Cantril (13, p. 321) state: "Just as good members of any organized group uphold the values or norms of the group, . . . so the good members of gangs become conscious of their own norms and react violently against deviants and nonconformists."

The present study is concerned with the consequences of deviation from a group standard. Its immediate background is a study by Festinger, Schachter, and Back (4) of the relationships between group structure and group standards. Findings pertinent to the present study will be briefly reviewed.

1. Within each social group in a housing community there was homogeneity of attitude toward a community-wide problem. Among these groups, however, there was marked heterogeneity of attitude.

2. There was a high positive correlation between cohesiveness of the social group (measured by per cent of in-group sociometric choices) and strength of the group standard (measured by per cent of conformers to the standard).

3. Within a social group, deviates from the group standard received far fewer sociometric choices than did conformers.

The theory developed to explain these findings is as follows: Within any social group, pressures operate toward uniformity of attitude. The origins of such pressures are at least twofold: social reality and group locomotion.

Social reality. On any issue for which there is no empirical referent, the reality of one's own opinion is established by the fact that other people hold similar opinions. Forces exist to establish uniformity and thus to create "reality" for the opinion.

Group locomotion. Uniformity may be necessary or desirable for the group to locomote toward its goal. Locomotion will be facilitated if all members agree on a particular path to the goal.

The strength of the pressures toward uniformity that a group can exercise on its members will vary with the *cohesiveness* of the group and the *relevance* of the issue to the group. "Cohesiveness" is defined as the total field of forces acting on members to remain in the group. Stemming from cohesiveness is the property called the "internal power of the group," which is defined as the magnitude of change the group can induce on its members. The degree of internal power will be equal to the magnitude of the force on the member to remain in the group. If we assume that all groups are attempting to induce the same amount, we can derive that there will be fewer deviates from a group standard in highly cohesive groups than in less cohesive groups.

"Relevance" refers to the ordering, in terms of importance to the group, of the activities over which the internal power of the group extends. The conceptual dimension along which we can order particular activities as relevant or irrelevant to a particular group still remains unclear. There appear to be three possible bases for such ordering: the importance of the activity for group locomotion, the value which the group places upon the activity, and some hierarchy of needs common to group members in their roles as group members. Whatever the basis for ordering, we may anticipate that a group will exercise greater influence over relevant than over irrelevant activities.

It is assumed that there is a parallel between the process of induction and actual communication; that is, communication is the mechanism by which power is exerted. Therefore, one method by which deviation from a group standard may be maintained is cutting off the deviate from communication with the group. Lack of communication may result from little initial contact between the individual and the group or rejection from the group. In the latter case, if the magnitude of the change that the group attempts to induce is greater than the force on the individual to stay in the group, the deviate will want to leave the group, and/or the group will tend to push the deviate out of the group.

The present study is specifically concerned with the rejection of a deviate by the group. It is probable that not all groups reject to the same degree and that rejection is a consequence of deviation on only certain kinds of issues. To delineate more carefully some of the conditions affecting rejection, this experiment examines the effect of degrees of cohesiveness of the group and relevance of the issue on the degree of rejection of a deviate. The effects of these variables on communication and induction within the groups are also studied.

THE EXPERIMENT

The experiment was conducted as the first meeting of a club. Four types of clubs were set up, each representing a different degree and combination of cohesiveness and relevance. In each club paid participants deviated from and conformed to an experimentally created group standard. Discussion in each club was systematically observed. At the end of each meeting members were nominated for committees, and sociometric questionnaires were filled out. These served as measures of rejection.

The four types of clubs set up were case-study, editorial, movie, and radio clubs. There was a total of 32 clubs, eight of each type. Each club had from five to seven members and three paid participants who were perceived as fellow club members. All of the subjects (Ss) in the clubs were male college students.

In a typical meeting, after preliminary introductions, each club member read a short version of the "Johnny Rocco" case (3), the life history of a juvenile delinquent, which ended as Johnny was awaiting sentence for a minor crime. The case was presented as that of a real person. The leader of the club, in all instances the experimenter (E), asked the members to discuss and decide the question, "What should be done with this kid?" The discussion was guided by a seven-point scale made up of alternative suggestions ordered along a love-punishment dimension. Point 1 presented the "all-love" viewpoint, point 7 the "all-punishment" viewpoint. Between these extremes were graded variations of the two points of view.[2] This scale was used to point up the differences of opinion within the group. It was introduced to the club members as a convenient device for learning everyone's position and for channelizing discussion.

After reading the case, each club member announced the position on the scale that he had chosen. Then the three paid participants in each club announced their positions. One paid participant, the "deviate," chose a position of extreme deviation and maintained it throughout the discussion; the second, the "mode," chose and maintained the modal position of group opinion; and the third, the "slider," chose the position of extreme deviation but allowed himself to be gradually influenced, so that at the end of the discussion he was at the modal position.

The case was written sympathetically to ensure that the deviate paid participant would be a deviate. In all clubs almost all members chose positions on the scale emphasizing love and kindness (positions 2–4), and the deviate chose the position of extreme discipline (position 7).

The discussion, limited to 45 minutes, was largely a matter of thrashing out differences of opinion among club members. After 20 minutes the leader took a census to ensure that everyone was fully aware of everyone else's position. He took no part in the discussion except to answer the few questions directed to him. At the end of the discussion a final census was taken. Then the leader turned the discussion to the future of the club. At this time the committee nomination blanks and sociometric questionnaires were filled out.

After each meeting the Ss were told that

[2] For example, point 3 read: "He should be sent into an environment where providing Johnny with warmth and affection will be emphasized slightly more than punishing him, but discipline and punishment will be frequent if his behavior warrants it." For purposes of brevity the revised case study and the complete love-punishment scale are omitted from this paper. Interested readers may obtain copies by writing to the author.

this had been an experiment and not a club, and the purposes of the experiment and the various devices used were fully explained. The Ss were asked not to disclose the true nature of these "clubs." There was no indication that anyone gave away the experiment.

How the Variables, Cohesiveness and Relevance, Were Produced

"Cohesiveness" has been defined as the total field of forces acting on members to remain in the group. The greater the valence of the group for its members, the greater the cohesiveness. Valence of the group derives from at least two sources, the attractiveness of the activities the group mediates and the attractiveness of the members of the group. In this experiment two degrees of cohesiveness were produced by manipulating the attractiveness of the activities mediated by the groups.

Subjects were recruited for club membership from economics classes at the University of Michigan. The case-study and editorial clubs were described to half of these classes. The case-study clubs were purportedly being set up at the request of a group of lawyers, judges, and social workers to advise on the treatment and disposition of delinquents, sex offenders, etc. The editorial clubs were supposedly being organized at the request of a new national magazine to advise on feature articles, format, policy, etc. Interested students filled out a blank indicating which club they were interested in joining, and checked two rating scales noting the extent of their interest in each club. These were four-point scales—"not interested at all," "only mildly interested," "moderately interested," and "extremely interested."

The movie and radio clubs were described to the other half of these classes. The movie clubs were purportedly being set up for a local theatre. The club members were to see films and decide which ones the theatre could successfully program. Radio clubs were supposedly being formed to serve a similar market research function for a local radio station. Students indicated their interest in these two clubs in the manner described above.

The case-study and movie clubs were high cohesive groups, made up of students who had checked between "moderately" and "extremely interested" on the scales for these clubs. The editorial and radio clubs were low cohesive groups, made up of students who indicated high interest in joining the case-study or movie clubs and little or no interest in joining the editorial or radio clubs.[3] Students becoming members of clubs they were interested in joining made up the high cohesive groups. Those becoming members of clubs they were not interested in joining made up the low cohesive groups. In short, cohesiveness is defined here in terms of the valence of the activity.[4]

"Relevance" has been defined as an ordering of group activities along a dimension of "importance" to the group. Two degrees of relevance were produced experimentally. In one case, Ss were concerned with an activity corresponding to the purpose of the club. In the other case, Ss were concerned with an activity which had nothing to do with the purpose of the club.

Case-study and editorial clubs discussed a case study and a feature article, respectively. Movie and radio clubs discussed issues foreign to the purpose of the clubs; each began with an appropriate subject but was diverted to a side issue. The movie clubs saw a 15-minute film, and the radio clubs listened to a 15-minute recording. Then the leader introduced the observer as someone who had written up the Johnny Rocco case and wanted the help of the group to discuss what should be done with him. The group was assured that this had nothing to do with the club and would never happen again. With some enthusiasm from the paid participants, the group always agreed to discuss the case.

To make constant the time of interaction among Ss, radio and movie clubs were chosen as a setting for the irrelevant issue. The Ss were unable to interact while looking at a movie or listening to a recording. Therefore, their discussion time was the same as that of Ss discussing relevant issues.

To compare data obtained in the four types of clubs, it was necessary that the content be constant. This was done by using the "Johnny Rocco" case and the love-punishment scale in all the clubs. In case-study clubs, "Johnny Rocco" was the case for the

[3] A subject did not know which of the two clubs he had come to until the meeting was under way.
[4] This may seem a rather restricted definition of cohesiveness. Back (1), however, has demonstrated that cohesiveness, no matter what its source, can be considered a unitary concept. Whether cohesiveness is based on friendship, the valence of the activity mediated by the group, or group prestige, the consequences of increasing cohesiveness are identical.

day. In editorial clubs, "Johnny Rocco" was part of a feature article on juvenile delinquency. In movie and radio clubs, "Johnny Rocco" was the irrelevant issue. In all clubs the scale was the basis for discussing, "What should be done with the kid?"

In summary, there were four kinds of clubs, each reproducing a different combination of the experimental variables, as follows:

1. High cohesiveness–relevant issue (*Hi Co Rel*): Case-Study Club
2. Low cohesiveness–relevant issue (*Lo Co Rel*): Editorial Club
3. High cohesiveness–irrelevant issue (*Hi Co Irrel*): Movie Club
4. Low cohesiveness–irrelevant issue (*Lo Co Irrel*): Radio Club

In the procedure used there are two possible sources of selective error. (1) Possibly students interested in the case-study and editorial clubs were selectively different from those attracted to the movie and radio clubs. However, more than 80 percent of the students addressed asked to join one of the clubs. More than 90 per cent of these expressed preferences for case-study or movie clubs. (2) Students assigned to case-study and movie clubs rated editorial and radio clubs slightly more favorably than students assigned to editorial and radio clubs. Possibly students in case-study and movie clubs were more attracted to the idea of a club, any kind of club. This factor, however, probably had little effect on experimental results. In the degree of rejection of the deviate, no difference was found in high cohesive groups between students who rated the nonpreferred activity high and those who rated it low.

The Validity of the Manipulation of Cohesiveness

The manipulation of cohesiveness began with the canvassing for *S*s and their assignment to clubs on the basis of preliminary interest ratings. This method of assignment is summarized in Table 1, where figures were obtained by assigning numerical values to the four points of the rating scale. "Not interested at all" has the value 1; "extremely interested" has the value 4; and the two intermediate points, the values 2 and 3. The figures are the mean ratings of each club made by all *S*s assigned to a particular experimental condition. There is a marked difference between *S*s in high and low cohesive groups in their ratings of the clubs to which

TABLE 1

MEAN RATINGS ON SIGN-UP SHEETS

Group	Case-Study	Editorial
Hi Co Rel	3.27	2.20
Lo Co Rel	3.33	1.71
	Movie	Radio
Hi Co Irrel	3.53	2.24
Lo Co Irrel	3.34	1.59

they were assigned. In the low cohesive conditions, all but two *S*s rated the clubs in which they were placed between "not interested at all" and "only mildly interested." In the high cohesive conditions, all but two *S*s rated the clubs in which they were placed between "extremely interested" and "moderately interested."

How successful was this method in manipulating cohesiveness? At the end of each meeting, each *S* filled out a cohesiveness questionnaire designed to determine his intentions toward the club. There were three questions: (1) Do you want to remain a member of this group? (2) How often do you think this group should meet? (3) If enough members decide not to stay so that it seems this group might discontinue, would you like the chance to persuade others to stay?

Table 2 summarizes the data from this questionnaire and shows marked differences between high and low cohesive groups. In high cohesive groups 101 of the 102 *S*s wanted to continue their memberships; in low cohesive groups only 62 of 96 *S*s wanted to do so. There are differences, too, between *S*s in the two conditions who wanted to remain in their clubs. Such *S*s in low cohesive groups wanted to meet less often and were less willing to persuade others to stay in the club than were *S*s in high cohesive groups. The manipulation was clearly successful in producing groups with different degrees of cohesiveness.

The Paid Participants

The three paid participants in each group were perceived as fellow club members. Like the *S*s, they were male undergraduates. In each meeting, in each condition, they played three roles, deviate, mode, and slider. The deviate adopted the position of extreme discipline and maintained it throughout the discussion. The mode championed that position

TABLE 2

BREAKDOWN OF ANSWERS TO THE COHESIVENESS QUESTIONNAIRE

| Group | N | QUESTION 1 Want to remain member? | | QUESTION 2 Frequency of meetings? | | QUESTION 3 Want to induce others to stay in club? | |
		Yes	No	Once or twice a week	Once every 2, 3, or 4 weeks	Yes	No
Hi Co Rel	53	98%	2%	61%	39%	73%	19%
Lo Co Rel	50	68	32	54	46	51	34
Hi Co Irrel	49	100	0	73	27	61	35
Lo Co Irrel	46	61	39	36	64	21	71

which the modal number of members supported. If during the meeting the modal position shifted, he shifted. The slider began as an extreme deviate (position 7) and during the meeting moved step by step to the modal position.

The mode and slider roles were controls. The deviate and the mode provided evidence of the effect of deviation as contrasted to conformity. Comparison of the slider and the deviate tested whether rejection was a result of having at one time, but no longer, championed a deviate position, or of simply maintaining deviancy against all attempted influence.

The three roles were systematically rotated among four paid participants so that each played each role twice in each experimental condition. To assure constancy from meeting to meeting, rules of behavior guiding the paid participants in any role were carefully defined. (1) Each paid participant had to speak once every five minutes. If during any five-minute interval no one addressed a remark to him, he initiated a communication. (2) Where possible, all communications made by the paid participants, whether initiated or in response to someone, were rephrasings of the position he was maintaining at the time. (3) When it was impossible simply to rephrase the position, the paid participants at the deviate position were permitted two standard arguments: (a) Despite the fact that Johnny was shown love and affection, he went back to stealing. (b) It could not be said that discipline would not work, since it had not consistently been applied to Johnny.

Measures of Rejection

After the discussion the leader introduced the subject of the club's future and proposed

a plan by which a functioning group could be organized. To expedite such organization, each member filled out three mimeographed sheets: a committee nomination blank, a sociometric test, and the cohesiveness questionnaire described earlier.

Committee nominations. Three committees were set up, differing with respect to interest of the work, importance of the assigned functions, and delegated responsibility for club activities. They were called the Executive, Steering, and Correspondence Committees. In each club, the job of each committee was defined in much the same way, but with slightly different content. The Executive Committee was to decide what the group should discuss, to act as liaison agent between the club and its sponsoring agency, and to determine club policy. The Steering Committee was to prepare and present discussion materials and determine discussion procedure. The Correspondence Committee was to perform secretarial functions.[5]

The Ss were instructed to nominate persons whom they considered most capable of handling the work of each committee. They were not to nominate themselves or the same person for more than one committee. The number of members on each committee was manipulated so that no matter what number were present in any particular group, everyone had to nominate everyone else present for some committee. When ten people were present, each member nominated three peo-

[5] To check on whether or not jobs on these committees actually did vary in attractiveness, in several of the groups the members were asked to write their own names next to those committees in which they were most interested. Most requested the Executive Committee, a few the Steering, and none the Correspondence Committee.

ple for each committee; when nine people were present, only two people were nominated for the Correspondence Committee; and, when eight people were present, two people were nominated for the Steering Committee and two for the Correspondence Committee. The importance or unimportance of the committees to which the paid participants were nominated serves as an index of acceptance or rejection.

The sociometric test. Subjects were informed that it might become necessary to reduce the number of club members or to break up the group and portion out its members to one of the other clubs, and that therefore it would be helpful to know which people would like to remain together. They were asked to rank everyone present in order of preference for remaining in the same group with themselves. In contrast to committee nomination instructions, the emphasis here was on congeniality. These data provide a sociometric index of rejection.

The Observation Schedule

An observer, introduced as a friend interested in what the club was doing and who could be imposed upon to take notes, recorded the following aspects of the group process: (1) who spoke to whom; (2) the length, in time, of the communication; (3) whether the speaker attacked or supported the position of the person to whom he spoke; (4) whether a communication, even if not addressed to a person at a specific position, implied approval or disapproval of this position; and (5) whether the speaker talked about experiences from his own or his friends' personal histories.

Rationale

The setup described, while constituting a reasonably well controlled experimental situation, represented for the *S*s a real-life situation. What was for *E* a method of manipulating a variable was for *S* a club he was interested in joining. The measuring instruments were conventional methods of electing officers; and so on. In short, the experiment was fitted within a social framework completely consistent with the idea and operation of a club with no sacrifice of experimental control. The rationale for this procedure was the assumption that it would be possible to reproduce the variables and phenomena under study with greater intensity in a purportedly "real-life situation" than in a laboratory setup that was identi-

fied as such. It is possible to produce complex social phenomena in laboratory experiments. Which procedure is more "effective" in the study of particular social phenomena can only be determined by additional investigation.

THE THEORETICAL RELATIONSHIPS AMONG COHESIVENESS, RELEVANCE, AND REJECTION

The theory presented in the introduction can now be expanded to make specific derivations as to the degree of rejection anticipated in each experimental condition. The theory states that there are pressures toward uniformity of behavior and attitude among members of most social groups. If differences of opinion exist within a group, forces will arise on the members to restore uniformity. A number of corrective tendencies will develop; for example, pressures develop to change the opinions of members of the group holding opinions different from one's own; pressures arise to change one's own opinion to coincide more closely with those of other group members; a tendency develops to decrease one's dependence on deviant members as appropriate reference points in establishing the reality of one's own opinion. In any group where differences of opinion exist probably all of these tendencies exist and are, we shall say, simultaneously a function of the total pressures toward uniformity. In the present experimental situation where almost all *S*s were of similar opinions and there was only one deviate, it seems reasonable to suggest that the predominant tendencies acting on group members were the pressures to change the opinion of the deviate, and the tendency to decrease dependence on the deviate as a point of reference for establishing social reality.

A. *Pressures to change* (*Pch*) refer to the magnitude of pressures acting on group members to change a deviant opinion to conform more closely with their own. We make these assumptions about the relationship of *Pch* with the variables cohesiveness, relevance, and state of opinion:

1. *With increasing difference of opinion the magnitude of* Pch *should increase.*

If uniformity exists, *Pch* should have zero magnitude. As group opinion departs more and more from uniformity, *Pch* should correspondingly increase.

2. *With increasing cohesiveness, the magnitude of* Pch *should increase. At any point along a scale of difference of opinion,* Pch *should be greater for high than for low cohesive groups.*

Pressures to uniformity arise in part from a need for social reality within an appropriate reference group. A cohesive group, in which membership is valued, can be considered a more important reference group than a low cohesive group in which membership is not particularly cherished. Therefore, we can anticipate that pressures to uniformity will be greater in high than in low cohesive groups.

3. *With increasing relevance of issue, the magnitude of* Pch *should increase.*

Any set of activities can be ordered along some dimension of "importance" (relevance) for a particular reference group. It is plausible to assume that for activities which are of importance to the group, greater pressures to change will exist than for activitives which are unimportant.

B. *Dependence* (*Dep*) refers to the extent to which members of a group rely on one another as reference points in establishing social reality. We make these assumptions about the relationships of dependence with the variables cohesiveness, relevance, and state of opinion:

1. *With increasing difference of opinion the magnitude of* Dep *will decrease.*

If opinions are identical, dependence will be high. When persons have different opinions, it is unlikely that they will depend on one another to establish the reality of their opinions.

2. *With increasing cohesiveness, the magnitude of* Dep *will increase.*

Members of a high cohesive group (a valued and important reference group) will be more dependent on one another than will members of a low cohesive group.

3. *With relatively small differences of opinion the magnitude of* Dep *will increase with increasing relevance of issue. As difference of opinion increases,* Dep *for relevant issues decreases more rapidly than* Dep *for irrelevant issues, and a point of zero* Dep *will be reached with less difference of opinion for relevant than for irrelevant issues.*

The more "important" an issue to a particular group, the greater the extent to which group members depend on another for social reality. On relevant issues, it will be more important that the reference group which establishes social reality have similar opinions than on less relevant issues. Therefore, dependence should decrease more rapidly with increasing perceived difference and reach the point of zero dependence earlier for highly relevant issues than for irrelevant issues.

These relationships are presented graphically in Figure 1. The rising *Pch* curves and falling *Dep* curves with increasing difference

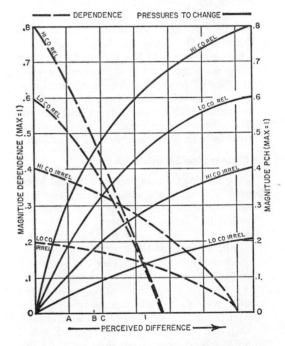

Fig. 1. Theoretical curves of the relationships between dependence, pressures to change, and cohesiveness, relevance, and perceived difference of opinion.

of opinion express assumptions A1 and B1 above. The greater magnitude of high cohesive than of low cohesive curves (relevance held constant), and of relevant than of irrelevant *Pch* curves (cohesiveness held constant), expresses assumptions A2, A3, and B2. At low levels of perceived difference with cohesiveness held constant, the magnitude of relevant *Dep* curves is greater than that of irrelevant *Dep* curves. Curves for relevant conditions drop at a faster rate and reach the point of zero dependence with far less perceived difference than do curves for irrelevant conditions. This is an expression of assumption B3.

For each condition, the maxima of the Pch and Dep curves are of the same magnitude. We assume that the maxima of both factors are similarly a function of total pressures to uniformity. The scale of magnitude along the ordinate of this graph has maximum $= 1$. The values assigned are, of course, arbitrary and purely illustrative.

From these curves we can make predictions concerning the interrelationships among cohesiveness, relevance, and degree of rejection.

We shall coordinate rejection to the amount of pressures to change that do not find public expression. The amount of pressures that do find public expression we call communication. Dependence defines the proportion of pressures to change that can be expressed. Multiplying these two factors, therefore, gives the amount of pressures that will actually be exerted.[6]

$$Comm = Pch \times Dep$$

Rejection, then, which is defined as the amount of pressures not exerted, is computed by multiplying Pch by the quantity $(1 - Dep)$.

$$Rej = Pch \times (1 - Dep)$$

The number 1 represents maximum dependence, the point at which all Pch will be communicated. The greater the pressures and the smaller the dependence, the greater the rejection. In effect, this formula suggests that rejection requires relatively little dependence on a person and, at the same time, relatively high pressures to change him. If pressures to change are high but dependence is high, rejection will be relatively slight. If dependence is low but there are no pressures to change, rejection will not occur.

Applying this formula to the postulated curves in Figure 1, we find these relationships. At point A in this figure:

$$Pch \times (1 - Dep) = Rej$$

Hi Co Rel	$.300 \times (1 - .650)$	$= .105$
Lo Co Rel	$.185 \times (1 - .513)$	$= .090$
Hi Co Irrel	$.110 \times (1 - .375)$	$= .069$
Lo Co Irrel	$.050 \times (1 - .185)$	$= .041$

At point B where the perceived difference is somewhat greater:

[6] This theory of communication will be developed and expanded in the following section.

$$Pch \times (1 - Dep) = Rej$$

Hi Co Rel	$.437 \times (1 - .487)$	$= .224$
Lo Co Rel	$.295 \times (1 - .409)$	$= .174$
Hi Co Irrel	$.175 \times (1 - .341)$	$= .115$
Lo Co Irrel	$.075 \times (1 - .175)$	$= .062$

These trends become clear: (1) As perceived difference increases, the degree of rejection in each of these conditions will increase. (2) At any point beyond zero, along the axis of perceived difference:

Rej in $Hi\ Co\ Rel > Rej$ in $Lo\ Co\ Rel$
Rej in $Hi\ Co\ Irrel > Rej$ in $Lo\ Co\ Irrel$
Rej in $Hi\ Co\ Rel > Rej$ in $Hi\ Co\ Irrel$
Rej in $Lo\ Co\ Rel > Rej$ in $Lo\ Co\ Irrel$[7]

Thus, the set of assumptions determining the shapes of these curves leads to these experimental predictions: (a) Persons in the mode and slider roles (who at the end of a meeting are close to zero perceived difference) will be rejected less (if at all) than will persons in the deviate role. (b) From experimental condition to condition the degree of rejection of persons in the deviate role will vary in the order noted in trend 2 above. With cohesiveness constant, rejection will be greater in relevant than in irrelevant groups. With relevance constant, rejection will be greater in high than in low cohesive groups.

RESULTS

The post-meeting nominations for committees and the sociometric rankings of all club members provide two indices of rejection, i.e., nominations to the less important committees and relatively low sociometric rankings.

Sociometric Rankings

At the end of each meeting the members of each club ranked everyone in the order of his desirability as a fellow club member. The instructions emphasized congeniality and compatibility as the basis for ranking. The lower the ranking, the greater the rejection.

[7] It is impossible to make an exact prediction about relative rejection between the $Lo\ Co\ Rel$ and $Hi\ Co\ Irrel$ conditions. Though the curves imply Rej in $Lo\ Co\ Rel > Rej$ in $Hi\ Co\ Irrel,$ this was done purely for illustrative simplicity. We have, of course, no way of determining the relative contributions of cohesiveness and relevance in a comparison of $Lo\ Co\ Rel$ and $Hi\ Co\ Irrel$ conditions.

Table 3 presents mean sociometric rankings of each paid participant in each condition. Each figure in the table is the mean of the mean sociometric rankings in each group. The N for each figure is 8, the number of groups in each condition. Since the groups varied in size from eight to ten members, all rankings were corrected to equivalent scores by adopting the nine possible rankings in a group of ten people as a basic scale and correcting rankings in smaller groups to equivalent scores. The mean rank in every group is 5.

These relationships emerge from Table 3: (1 In any condition, mean rankings of either mode or slider are considerably below mean

TABLE 3

MEAN SOCIOMETRIC RANKINGS OF THE PAID PARTICIPANTS

Group	Deviate	Mode	Slider
Hi Co Rel	6.44	4.65	5.02
Lo Co Rel	5.83	4.70	4.56
Hi Co Irrel	6.51	4.68	4.44
Lo Co Irrel	5.67	3.83	5.03

rankings of the deviate. All mode-deviate differences are significantly by a t-test at the 7 per cent level of confidence or better. Clearly, a penalty of relative rejection is imposed on a deviate. (2) There are no significant differences in rankings of either the mode or slider when comparisons are made between conditions.[8] The variables of cohesiveness and relevance have no effects on group evaluation of individuals who are at, or who adopt, the group norms. (3) The deviate is rejected more strongly in high than in low cohesive groups. Between rankings in high and low cohesive groups, the t is significant at the 12 per cent level for the difference between Hi Co Rel and Lo Co $Rel,$ and at the 1 per cent level for the difference between Hi Co $Irrel$ and Lo Co $Irrel.$[9] As predicted, greater cohesiveness produces greater rejection.

[8] The largest difference, that between the Hi Co $Irrel$ and Lo Co $Irrel$ conditions for the mode, is significant by t-test at only the 28 per cent level.

[9] In all tests of significance mentioned in this section, the group rather than the individual was considered the unit.

There is, however, no immediate evidence that the variable, relevance, affects the degree of rejection. The mean sociometric rankings of the deviate in the relevant and irrelevant condition, with cohesiveness constant, are about the same. This may be attributed in part to the fact that the measurement is a relative one, indicating only an individual's relative preference for one person over another, with no indication of the absolute intensity of like or dislike. There is, however, some indication of the relative intensities of the ratings in each condition. Occasionally a subject refused to fill in the sociometric sheet, or simply put in numbers in sequence, explaining that he was unable to discriminate among the people present. Random ranking implies that there was no genuine basis on which to express preference. If, therefore, any one experimental condition has a significantly greater number of random rankings than do the others, it may be inferred that, in general, all rankings in this condition were made with less basis for expressing preference and imply less intensity of like or dislike than in a condition where random responses are rare. More than twice as many random rankings were made in irrelevant conditions as in relevant. Of all subjects, 16 per cent ranked randomly in the irrelevant conditions and 6.8 per cent in the relevant conditions. This difference is significant by chi-square with 1 $d.f.$ at the 2 per cent level. There were no significant differences between Hi Co Rel and Lo Co Rel or between Hi Co $Irrel$ and Lo Co $Irrel.$ Though mean rankings are about the same for relevant and irrelevant conditions, random rankings of the deviate seem to imply less strong feelings of rejection in the irrelevant groups.

These sociometric data are in the directions predicted. (1) Paid participants in the mode and slider roles were not rejected; as deviates they were definitely rejected. (2) There is greater rejection of the deviate in high than in low cohesive groups. (3) Though sociometric rankings of the deviate are about the same for relevant and irrelevant conditions, random sociometric rankings indicate that the intensity of rejection in irrelevant conditions was less than in relevant conditions.

Assignment to Committees

With instructions emphasizing competence for the job, the members of each club nominated people for membership on the Executive, Steering, and Correspondence Committees. Rejection is coordinated to assignment to the least desirable committee. The Executive was the most attractive committee and the Correspondence the least attractive.

Tables 4, 5, and 6 present the data on the assignment of paid participants in the mode, slider, and deviate roles to the three committees. All figures in each table represent the percentage, above or below chance expectancy, of all Ss in each condition who assigned the various roles to the different committees. In Table 4, the mode was nominated for the Executive Committee by 4.56 per cent less than we would expect if nominations in the *Hi Co Rel* condition had been made on

TABLE 4

PERCENTAGE OF SUBJECTS ABOVE CHANCE ASSIGNING "MODE" TO COMMITTEES

Group	Executive	Steering	Correspondence
Hi Co Rel	−4.56	+6.76	−2.22
Lo Co Rel	−9.83	+20.15	−10.44
Hi Co Irrel	−0.08	+6.85	−6.93
Lo Co Irrel	+3.70	+3.70	−8.07

TABLE 5

PERCENTAGE OF SUBJECTS ABOVE CHANCE ASSIGNING "SLIDER" TO COMMITTEES

Group	Executive	Steering	Correspondence
Hi Co Rel	+1.76	−5.93	+4.16
Lo Co Rel	+7.32	−7.86	+0.50
Hi Co Irrel	−4.97	+4.38	+0.39
Lo Co Irrel	+2.69	−3.52	+0.16

TABLE 6

PERCENTAGE OF SUBJECTS ABOVE CHANCE ASSIGNING "DEVIATE" TO COMMITTEES

Group	Executive	Steering	Correspondence
Hi Co Rel	−14.00	−8.34	+22.31
Lo Co Rel	−17.58	−7.81	+25.26
Hi Co Irrel	−16.41	+4.83	+11.44
Lo Co Irrel	+10.16	−9.40	−1.30

some randomly determined basis. Varying group sizes, affecting the probability of any one person being assigned to a particular committee, necessitated computation of chance expectancies.

The standard errors of all chance percentages are close to 6.20.[10] Any score greater than 10.23 is significant at the 10 per cent level; greater than 12.09 is significant at the 5 per cent level; and greater than 15.93 is significant at the 1 per cent level. If the 5 per cent level is accepted, Table 5 reveals no significant fluctuations from chance in assigning the slider to any one particular committee. Similarly, for the mode, in Table 4, we find only one score that departs significantly from chance, assignment of the mode to the Steering Committee in the *Lo Co Rel* condition. With the large number of scores obtained, this may be interpreted as a chance fluctuation. There is no indication of systematic rejection for the mode or slider roles.

Table 6 for the deviate presents a completely different picture. In all conditions, except *Lo Co Irrel,* the deviate is over-nominated for the Correspondence Committee and under-nominated for the Executive Committee. Deviation results in assignment to a relatively peripheral position in the role structure of the group. Not only is the deviate considered relatively undesirable as a fellow club member, but also least capable of handling the important jobs in the club.

The degree of rejection, however, is affected by the experimental variables. Rejection is greater in both relevant conditions than in the irrelevant conditions. A *t*-test with 30 *d.f.* yields significance at the 2 per cent level of confidence for this difference. Differences between the degree of rejection in high cohesive groups and low cohesive groups, however, are less clear-cut. Although there is a difference between high and low cohesive irrelevant conditions significant by *t*-test at

[10] This score was computed using $\sqrt{\frac{p\,q}{n}}$, the customary formula for computing the standard error of a percentage. Since the number of cases varied slightly from condition to condition, and P varied slightly with the number of people in each group, the standard error 6.20 is a convenient approximation. The obtained standard errors for each committee in each condition are all quite close to this figure.

the 10 per cent level, there is no difference between the two relevant conditions. This is clearly inconsistent with theoretical expectations. Possibly the committee assignment measure should also be considered a relative measure that gives no indication of intensity of feeling. It is plausible that, though there is no difference between high and low cohesive relevant groups in the percentage of people assigning the deviate to the Correspondence Committee, the intensity of rejection is greater in high than in low cohesive groups. In contrast to the sociometric ranking, however, no S had difficulty in making these judgments, and there is no evidence of random assignment to committees. This may possibly be attributed to the different natures of the measures. A judgment of fitness for a particular job is a fairly everyday matter. Decisions about which people should be in or out of a group appear to be a more unusual sort of judgment to make.

Except for this single inconsistency, the data support the predictions. Neither the mode nor the slider was rejected. In all conditions except *Lo Co Irrel,* where we anticipated very little rejection, the deviate was over-nominated for the Correspondence Committee. Rejection of the deviate was greater in the relevant than in the irrelevant conditions, and greater in the *Hi Co Irrel* than in the *Lo Co Irrel* condition.

THE PROCESS OF COMMUNICATION

The previous section has treated the relationships between experimental manipulations and post-meeting measurements. This section relates the processes of induction and communication, as they occurred during the meetings, to the experimental variables, cohesiveness and relevance, and to the post-meeting measurements.

We shall consider communication, the process of one person talking to another, as the mechanism of induction, i.e., the means by which influence is exerted. There are, of course, other reasons why people communicate, but within the confines of this experiment and theory, we shall largely limit ourselves to communication as influence.

From the theoretical elaboration of "pressures to uniformity," specific derivations may be made about certain aspects of the patterns of communication that occurred in these meetings. Let us first relate the constructs, *Pch* and *Dep,* to the occurrence of communication.

1. Pressures to change others mean pressures to influence others, which we will consider identical with pressures to communicate. Our earlier assumptions may, therefore, be extended to communication pressures. The pressures to communicate to a deviate will rise with increasing perceived difference, increasing cohesiveness, and increasing relevance.

2. Dependence refers to the extent to which a person relies on another person or group of persons to establish social reality. It defines the proportion of pressure to change that can actually find public expression. Actual communication, then, is a function of both *Dep* and *Pch,* with dependence modifying the proportion of pressures to change that will be expressed publicly. Actual communication is formulated as $Comm = Pch \times Dep$.

In Figure 2, the heavily dotted lines, constructed by making the proper multiplications at each point, represent the magnitude or frequency of actual communication that should

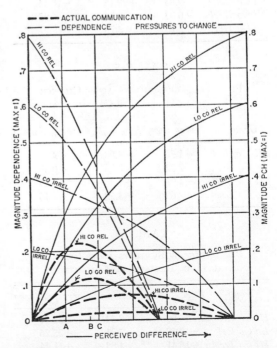

Fig. 2. Derived curves of actual communication in the four experimental conditions.

be directed at positions with different degrees of perceived difference in the four experimental conditions.[11] This figure is the same as Figure 1, with the curves for predicted communication added.

Let us examine more closely the meaning of "perceived difference." It refers to the phenomenological difference between two people rather than to the absolute difference between two points on the love-punishment scale. Two people may be at position 4 on the scale and perceive the difference between themselves and someone at position 7 as of very different orders of magnitude. We shall postulate that in this experiment perceived differences increased with discussion. In all club meetings the question, "How much do we really differ?" was frequently discussed, and attempts were made to reduce the distance between points on the scale. The deviates, however, were specifically instructed to resist attempts to minimize differences between themselves and people at other positions. The assumption that perceived difference increases with discussion seems reasonable, therefore, in this situation.

Accepting this assumption, we may say that the dotted curve of communication in Figure 2 represents the actual pattern of communication during the course of the meeting. From these considerations a number of testable derivations may be made about the frequency and pattern of communication to each paid participant in each condition.

Communication Patterns to the Deviate

A prediction previously developed was that rejection will increase with increasing perceived difference. Therefore, people who strongly reject the deviate perceive a greater difference between themselves and the deviate than do people who do not reject. In Figure 2, point C represents the position of a

rejector at the end of a meeting, point B the position of a mild rejector, and point A the position of a non-rejector. If perpendiculars are projected from these points, they intercept the communication curves at different relative positions.

If we accept the assumption that perceived difference increases with discussion time, and postulate that points C, B, and A in Figure 2 represent, respectively, the end-of-the-meeting perceptions of people who reject the deviate strongly, reject mildly, and do not reject, then we must say that the curves of actual communication up to points C, B, and A represent the patterns of communication from these three kinds of people to the deviate during the course of the meeting. In Figure 3 these predicted curves of communication, projected from Figure 2, are drawn for these three kinds of people for each experimental condition. These curves are specific predic-

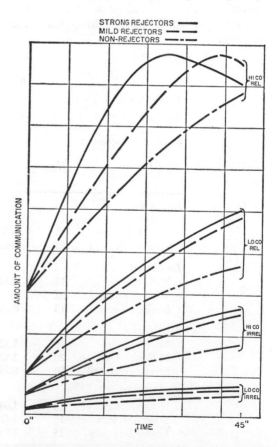

Fig. 3. Theoretical curves of communications from strong rejectors, mild rejectors, and non-rejectors to the deviate in the four experimental conditions.

[11] The coordination of rejection to the amount of pressures that are not publicly expressed can be demonstrated graphically in Figure 2. At any point along the axis of perceived difference, rejection is equal to the difference between the height of the appropriate derived curve of actual communication and the height of the corresponding curve for Pch. This relationship is simply stated algebraically:
$$Rej = Pch \times (1 - Dep)$$
$$= Pch - Pch \times Dep$$
$$Comm = Pch \times Dep$$
$$\therefore Rej = Pch - Comm$$

tions about the pattern and magnitude of communication to the deviate.

In Figure 3 the ordinate represents the amount of communication during the meeting, and the abscissa, the flow of time from zero to 45 minutes. A point on these curves represents the amount of communication that will be addressed to the deviate at a particular time in the course of the meeting by either the people who reject him strongly, reject mildly, or do not reject. All curves start slightly above the zero point, for it seems likely that even at the beginning of a meeting there is some perception of difference.

In the *Hi Co Rel* condition, the communication curve of non-rejectors increases continuously throughout the meeting. The curve of strong rejectors reaches a peak during the meeting and then declines continuously; and the mild rejectors' curve reaches a peak somewhat later and then declines. In all other conditions, all communication curves to the deviate rise continuously throughout the meeting.

The data testing these derivations are presented in Table 7. The meeting is here divided into ten-minute intervals and communications to the deviate during each interval tallied. The three categories of rejectors are determined by sociometric rankings of the deviate. Non-rejectors ranked the deviate from 1.0–3.72; mild rejectors from 4.0–7.92; and strong rejectors between 8 and 9. The figures in the table represent the total number of communications in each time interval made by all people in each rejector category, divided by the number of people in this category.

Let us examine first the data for the *Hi Co Rel* groups in Table 7. The strong rejectors reach their peak of communication to the deviate in the 15–25 minute interval and then decline steadily. The difference between the peak interval and the final time interval is significant at better than the 1 per cent level.[12]

[12] All of the levels of significance reported with this set of data were obtained by tabulating for each S in each category whether or not the num-

TABLE 7

Mean Number of Communications Addressed to "Deviate" during the Course of the Meeting by Subjects with Different Post-Meeting Reactions to Him

Group	N	Time Interval in Minutes			
		5–15*	15–25	25–35	35–45
Hi Co Rel					
Non-rejectors	13	1.15	0.92	2.15	1.54
Mild rejectors	15	0.40	1.27	1.87	0.86
Strong rejectors	25	0.68	1.60	1.52	0.76
Lo Co Rel					
Non-rejectors	13	0.38	0.54	0.84	0.46
Mild rejectors	22	0.58	0.50	1.23	1.73
Strong rejectors	15	0.26	0.47	1.27	2.99
Hi Co Irrel					
Non-rejectors	9	1.32	1.44	0.99	2.44
Mild rejectors	20	1.15	1.35	1.55	1.20
Strong rejectors	20	0.75	1.15	1.60	3.42
Lo Co Irrel					
Non-rejectors	16	1.69	1.69	2.34	2.12
Mild rejectors	15	1.47	0.94	2.20	3.74
Strong rejectors	15	1.20	0.74	2.47	2.87

* Because the first few minutes of many meetings were concerned with technical problems and deciding just what was to be done, data from the 0–5 time interval are not reported.

Mild rejectors reach their peak somewhat later, in the 25–35 minute interval, and then decline. The difference between this peak and the final time interval is significant at the 3 per cent level. Non-rejectors seem to reach a peak and then decline, but this difference is due entirely to one case and is significant at exactly the 50 per cent level of confidence. The data, then, essentially parallel theoretical expectations.

In the other experimental conditions the theory anticipates a steady rise in the number of communications addressed to the deviate by either mild, strong, or non-rejectors. The remaining data in Table 7 indicate that this is essentially correct. In six of these nine breakdowns, the number of communications to the deviate rises continuously, and differences between the last two time intervals are significant at the 12 per cent level or better for all but the rising *Lo Co Irrel* curves. In three cases (non-rejectors in *Lo Co Rel* and *Lo Co Irrel,* mild rejectors in the *Hi Co Irrel*) there is a slight drop in the final interval. None of these drops is significant.

The theoretical derivations seem as well corroborated as can be anticipated with the

---

ber of communications he had addressed to the deviate was higher in one time interval than in the interval with which it was being compared. Probabilities were then computed by means of binomial expansion.

relatively small number of cases involved. Most of the curves rise, and the only significant declines are the predicted ones.

Communication Patterns to the Mode and Slider

The position of the mode on the scale of perceived difference in Figure 2 should be at zero, the point of no perceived difference between himself and the most of the others in the group. At this point $Pch = 0$, and dependence is at a maximum. There should therefore be no communications to the mode during any meeting in any experimental condition. This conclusion, however, must be qualified by two considerations. (1) As a rule, most, but not all, of the members of any one club were at the modal position. There were slight differences, therefore, between the mode and a few members of the group. (2) A paid participant in the modal role was required to speak once every five minutes. Courtesy would probably demand an occasional response.

We may anticipate, then, that the curve of communication to the mode in all experimental conditions should be a low straight line, parallel to the horizontal time axis. In Table 8, we see that this is the case. The figures in this table are computed on the same basis as those in the previous table. In all conditions only a very small number of communications was addressed to the mode

TABLE 8

MEAN NUMBER OF COMMUNICATIONS ADDRESSED TO THE "MODE" AND "SLIDER" DURING THE COURSE OF THE MEETING

Group	N	Time Interval in Minutes			
		5–15	15–25	25–35	35–45
Hi Co Rel					
Mode	53	0.13	0.06	0.06	0.10
Slider	53	0.53	0.55	0.21	0.17
Lo Co Rel					
Mode	50	0.06	0.10	0.14	0.22
Slider	50	0.30	0.20	0.20	0.20
Hi Co Irrel					
Mode	49	0.18	0.16	0.37	0.12
Slider	49	0.79	0.47	0.20	0.04
Lo Co Irrel					
Mode	46	0.14	0.15	0.13	0.45
Slider	46	0.72	0.63	0.41	0.30

at any time. Fluctuations from a straight line are all within the range of chance expectancy.

Theoretically, communications to the slider present a more complicated picture, for it is impossible to predict exactly the interaction between perceived difference and decreasing absolute difference. But it is reasonable to suggest that communications to the slider should be at about the same level as to the deviate until the slider makes his first shift, and then communications should gradually decrease until by the end of the meeting they are at about the same level for both the slider and the mode. The data presented in Table 8 essentially substantiate these expectations. About 15 minutes after the meeting started the slider shifted from 7 to 5, and finally adopted the modal position between the 35- and 40-minute marks. In all experimental conditions, communications to the slider are at first considerably above the level of communication to the mode and then decline steadily to the level of the mode in the final time interval.[13]

The Frequency of Communication

From the theoretical considerations previously formulated, additional derivations can be made about the magnitude or absolute amounts of communication in each experimental condition. It may be predicted, from the curves of communication in Figure 3, that the amount of communication to the deviate will decrease from *Hi Co Rel* condition to *Lo Co Rel* to *Hi Co Irrel* to *Lo Co Irrel*. And, since the distribution of positions on the love-punishment scale is the same from condition to condition, it may also be anticipated that the mean amounts of communication for meetings, within each condition, will vary in the same order. The data collected with the present observation schedule are, however, inadequate to substantiate or disprove these derivations. It has been postulated that the magnitude of pressures to uniformity are greater on relevant than on irrelevant issues, in high than in low cohesive groups. These derivations will hold *only* for communications that arise from pressures to uniformity, and we can say nothing about communications that arise from other sources. However, people communicate for numberless reasons beyond that of restoring uniformity of opinion. It seems a reasonable assumption that the more irrelevant an issue, the greater will be the number of communications that have sources other than pressures to uniformity. If this analysis of the differences between the discussions of relevant and irrelevant issues is correct, supporting evidence must be found in areas other than the directions and amounts of communication.

Differences between the communication process in relevant and irrelevant conditions are shown in Table 9. Communications in the relevant groups tended to be longer. Slightly more than 30 per cent of all communications in the relevant groups were long communications (more than 30 seconds), and only 21 per cent were long in the irrelevant condition.[14] In addition, discussion in these two conditions went at a different clip. There were far more

---

[13] In the first time interval, though the number of communications to the slider is considerably higher than that to the mode, comparison with Table 7 reveals that the number of slider-directed communications is consistently lower than that to the deviate. Probably this is an artifact of the slider role. In preparing to shift position, the slider probably tended to be somewhat less extreme and emphatic in his defense of position 7.

[14] This difference has a $t = 2.06$, which with 30 *d.f.* is significant at the 5 per cent level.

TABLE 9

INTERRUPTIONS, PAUSES, PERSONAL REFERENCES, AND LONG COMMUNICATIONS
IN ALL CONDITIONS

	Hi Co Rel	Lo Co Rel	Hi Co Irrel	Lo Co Irrel
Per cent long communications	28	33	25	17
Mean interruptions per meeting	67.71	29.86	78.71	82.00
Total pauses	1	1	3	7
Personal history references	18	14	5	8

interruptions in irrelevant than in relevant groups.[15] An interruption is defined as any attempt to break into a speech before it is completed. Oddly enough, in the face of the greater number of communications and the more rapid clip in irrelevant groups, there was a greater number of pauses in the discussions of the irrelevant groups. Though there was no systematic notation of pauses, the observer noted all particularly long, uncomfortable intervals when no one had anything to say. In short, there were marked differences in the character of discussion in the two conditions. Discussion in irrelevant groups might be characterized as cocktail party conversation, fast, brief, clipped, and in bursts; discussion in the relevant groups resembled the board meeting, slow, even-paced, long, and well considered.

Consistent with these characterizations of the process of the meeting are the additional data presented in Table 9 on the relative frequency of personal history references. Reference to personal history may be considered evidence of real involvement in the discussion. In relevant groups, there were more than two and a half times as many personal references as there were in irrelevant groups.[16] Not only were the discussions of the irrelevant groups more glib, but also apparently more superficial.

The marked differences in the manner of relevant and irrelevant groups indicate that communications in irrelevant groups resulted in good part from sources other than pressures to uniformity. The data, therefore, do not serve as an adequate test of the derivations concerning the relative amounts of communication in the various conditions.

SUMMARY

A set of assumptions has been developed which defines the relationships of the constructs dependence and pressures to change, to cohesiveness, relevance, and state of opinion. Both communication and rejection have been coordinated to these constructs. Dependence defines the proportion of the pressures to change that can find public expression, and communication is defined as:

$$Comm = Pch \times Dep$$

Rejection is coordinated to the amount of pressures to change which are not exerted and is defined as:

$$Rej = Pch \times (1 - Dep)$$

These coordinations and the assumptions defining Pch and Dep allow us to make a number of predictions as to the results of the experiment. Predictions about rejection and the evidence supporting them will be reviewed briefly.

1. PERSONS IN THE MODE AND SLIDER ROLES WILL BE REJECTED LESS (IF AT ALL) THAN WILL PERSONS IN THE DEVIATE ROLE. On both the sociometric and committee assignment measures there was no evidence that either the mode or slider was rejected. The deviate, on the other hand, was rejected in all experimental conditions except *Lo Co Irrel*. Where the magnitudes of both *Dep* and *Pch* are low, we anticipate relatively little rejection. Thus, in the *Lo Co Irrel* condition, the sociometric ranking of the deviate was only slightly above the mean, and he was not over-nominated for the correspondence committee.

2. WITH COHESIVENESS HELD CONSTANT, REJECTION WILL BE GREATER IN RELEVANT GROUPS THAN IN IRRELEVANT GROUPS. (*a*) On the committee assignment measure the deviate was assigned to the Correspondence Committee to a far greater extent in the relevant groups than in the irrelevant groups.

(*b*) Though sociometric rankings of the deviate are about the same for the relevant and irrelevant conditions, there is evidence from random sociometric rankings that the intensity of rejection is greater in the relevant than in the irrelevant conditions.

3. WITH RELEVANCE HELD CONSTANT, REJECTION WILL BE GREATER IN HIGH COHESIVE THAN IN LOW COHESIVE GROUPS. (*a*) The mean sociometric ranking of the deviate was considerably higher in both high cohesive

---

[15] The difference between mean number of interruptions in relevant and irrevelant groups is significant at better than the .001 level of significance, with $t = 5.74$ for 30 *d.f.* These measures of interruption and length of communication are relatively independent. Rank order correlations between the two are only $+.39$ in the irrelevant condition and $+.45$ in the relevant condition.

[16] The difference yields a t of 1.89, which with 30 *d.f.* is significant at the 8 per cent level.

conditions than in the corresponding low cohesive conditions.

(*b*) On the committee assignment measure the deviate was nominated to the Correspondence Committee to a greater extent in the *Hi Co Irrel* than in the *Lo Co Irrel* condition. There is no difference, however, between the *Hi Co Rel* and the *Lo Co Rel* conditions. This inconsistency may be explained in terms of the relative nature of the measure. Here, too, the intensity of rejection may be stronger in *Hi Co Rel* than in *Lo Co Rel* groups. There is no immediate evidence, however, to support this argument.

Predictions about patterns of communication follow:

1. *In the* Hi Co Rel *condition, the amount of communication addressed to the deviate by non-rejectors should increase continuously throughout the meeting. Strong rejectors should reach a peak of communication during the meeting and then decline continuously, and mild rejectors should reach a peak somewhat later and then decline.*

2. *In all other experimental conditions, communications to the deviate from strong, mild, or non-rejectors should increase continuously throughout the meeting.*

3. *In all experimental conditions, there should be relatively few communications addressed to persons in the modal role and no increase in communications during the meeting.*

4. *In all conditions, communications to the slider should decrease during the meeting as the slider shifts from a deviate to a modal position.*

The data essentially substantiated all of these predictions. The theory leads to other predictions about the relative magnitudes of communication in each experimental condition. These derivations, however, hold only for communications arising from pressures to uniformity. Since in irrelevant conditions many communications arose from other sources, it is impossible to test these derivations.

REFERENCES

1. Back, K. W. The exertion of influence through social communication. Unpublished Doctor's dissertation, Massachusetts Institute of Technology, 1949.
2. Coch, L., and French, J. R. P., Jr. Overcoming resistance to change. *Hum. Relat.,* 1948, 1, 512–532.
3. Evans, J. Johnny Rocco. *J. abnorm. soc. Psychol.,* 1948, 43, 357–383.
4. Festinger, L., Schachter, S., and Back, K. W. *Social pressures in informal groups: A study of a housing community.* New York: Harper, 1950.
5. Lynd, R. S., and Lynd, H. M. *Middletown, a study in contemporary American culture.* New York: Harcourt, Brace, 1929.
6. Lynd, R. S., and Lynd, H. M. *Middletown in transition.* New York: Harcourt, Brace, 1937.
7. Merei, F. Group leadership in institutionalization. *Hum. Relat.,* 1941, 2, 23–39.
8. Newcomb, T. M. *Personality and social change.* New York: Dryden Press, 1943.
9. Shaw, C. R. (Ed.) *Brothers in crime.* Chicago: Univ. of Chicago Press, 1938.
10. Shaw, C. R. *The jack roller.* Chicago: Univ. of Chicago Press, 1939.
11. Sherif, M. A study of some social factors in perception. *Arch. Psychol.* New York: 1935, No. 187.
12. Sherif, M. *The psychology of social norms.* New York: Harper, 1936.
13. Sherif, M., and Cantril, H. *The psychology of ego-involvements.* New York: Wiley, 1947.
14. Thrasher, F. M. *The gang.* Chicago: Univ. of Chicago Press, 1927.
15. Warner, W. L., and Lunt, P. S. *The social life of a modern community.* New Haven: Yale Univ. Press, 1941.
16. Whyte, W. F. *Street corner society.* Chicago: Univ. of Chicago Press, 1943.
17. Zander, A., and Chabot, J. Unpublished study.
18. Zorbaugh, H. W. *The Gold Coast and the slum.* Chicago: Univ. of Chicago Press, 1929.

Competence and Conformity in the Acceptance of Influence[1] / E. P. Hollander

(*School of International Service, American University*)

When one member influences others in his group it is often because he is competent in a focal group activity. A member may show such competence by individual actions that further the attainment of group goals (cf. Carter, 1954); more specific situational demands may variously favor the ascent of the expediter, advocate, or what Bales and Slater (1955) have termed the task specialist. An additional condition for the acceptance of influence involves the member's perceived adherence to the normative behaviors and attitudes of his group. His record of conformity to these expectancies serves to sustain eligibility of the sort Brown (1936) calls "membership character."

A person who exhibits both competence and conformity should eventually reach a threshold at which it becomes appropriate in the eyes of others for him to assert influence; and insofar as these assertions are accepted he emerges as a leader. But it is still necessary to account for the "nonconformity" that leaders display as they innovate and alter group norms. Certain shifts must therefore occur in the expectancies applicable to an individual as he proceeds from gaining status to maintaining it.

This process has been considered recently in a theoretical model of status emergence (Hollander, 1958). It features the prospect that behavior perceived to be nonconformity for one member may not be so perceived for another. Such differentiations are seen to be made as a function of status, conceived as an accumulation of positively disposed impressions termed "idiosyncrasy credits." A person gains credits, i.e., rises in status, by showing competence and by conforming to the expectancies applicable to him at the time. Eventually his credits allow him to nonconform with greater impunity.[2] Moreover, he is then subject to a new set of expectancies which direct the assertion of influence. Thus, whether for lack of motivation or misperception, his failure to take innovative action may cause him to lose status.[3]

It is readily predictable that in task oriented groups a member giving evidence of competence on the group task should with time gain in influence. If he simply nonconforms to the procedures agreed upon, the opposite effect should be observed. But the sequential relationship of nonconformity to competence is especially critical.

From the model, it should follow that, with a relatively constant level of manifest competence, the influence of a person who nonconforms *early* in the course of group interaction should be more drastically curtailed than in the case of a person who nonconforms *later*. Indeed, a reversal of effect would be predicted in the latter instance. Once a member has accumulated credits, his nonconformity to general procedure should serve as a confirming or signalizing feature of his status, thereby enhancing his influence. Accordingly, it may be hypothesized that given equivalent degrees of task competence, a member should achieve greater acceptance of his influence when he has conformed in the past and is now nonconforming than he should when nonconformity precedes conformity.

Reprinted from *Journal of Abnormal and Social Psychology*, 1960, 61, pages 365–370, by permission of author and publisher, The American Psychological Association.

---

[1] This paper is based upon a study completed under ONR Contract 1849(00), while the author was at the Carnegie Institute of Technology. The views expressed here are those of the author and do not necessarily reflect those of the Department of the Navy.

The considerable assistance of H. Edwin Titus in this study is gratefully acknowledged.

Parts of the paper were reported at the symposium on "Recent Conceptions in Influence and Authority Process," held under the auspices of Division 8 at the 1959 APA Convention.

[2] This is a newer formulation of an observation long since made regarding the latitude provided leaders (e.g., Homans, 1950, p. 416). It is further elaborated in Hollander (1959).

[3] This proposition is consistent with various findings suggestive of the greater social perceptiveness of leaders (e.g., Chowdhry & Newcomb, 1952).

METHOD

Design

Twelve groups, each composed of four male subjects, were engaged in a task involving a sequence of 15 trials. A group choice was required for each trial from among the row alternatives in a 7×7 payoff matrix (see Figure 1). In every group, a fifth member was a confederate whose prearranged response was contrived to be correct on all but four trials, i.e., 2, 3, 6, and 12, thus reflecting considerable competence on the task. All interactions among participants took place through a system of microphones and headsets from partitioned booths. Subjects were assigned numbers from 1 to 5 for communicating with one another. The central manipulation was the confederate's nonconformity to procedures agreed upon by each group in a pretrial discussion. In terms of a division of the 15 trials into three zones—early, middle, and late—of 5 trials each, six treatments were applied: nonconformity throughout, nonconformity for the first two zones, for the first zone alone, for the last two zones, for the last zone alone, and a control with no nonconformity. In one set of treatments the confederate was designated number 5, and in the other number 4, to test possible position effects. Acceptance of the confederate's influence was measured by the number of trials by zone in which his recommended response was accepted as the group's. This was supplemented by postinteraction assessments.

Subjects

The 48 subjects were all juniors in the College of Engineering and Science at the Carnegie Institute of Technology. All had volunteered from introductory psychology sections after being told only that they would be taking part in a study of problem solving in groups. Care was taken in composing the 12 groups so as to avoid either placing acquaintances together or having membership known in advance. Thus, no two subjects from the same class section were used in the same group, and subjects reported at staggered times to different rooms. By the time a subject reached the laboratory room where the experiment was actually conducted, he had been kept apart from the others and was not aware of their identity. The subjects never saw one another during the entire procedure, nor were their names ever used among them.

Instructions and Set

Once seated and assigned a number, every subject was given a sheet of instructions and the matrix used for the task. These instructions fell into two parts, both of which were reviewed aloud with each subject individually, and then with the entire group over the communication network. The first part cautioned the subjects to always identify themselves by number (e.g., "This is Station 3 . . .") before speaking and not to use names or other self-identifying references. The second part acquainted them with the procedures to be used, emphasized the aspect of competition against a "system," and established the basis for evident procedural norms. It read as follows:

1. You will be working with others on a problem involving a matrix of plus and minus values. Everyone has the same matrix before him. The goal is to amass as many plus units as possible, and to avoid minus units. Units are worth 1 cent each to the group; the group begins with a credit of 200 units. You cannot lose your own money, therefore. There will be fifteen trials in all.

2. In any one trial, the task involved is for the group to agree on just *one* row—identified by Able, Baker, Charlie, etc.—which seems to have strategic value. Once the group has determined a row, the experimenter will announce the column color which comes up on that trial. The intersecting cells indicate the payoff. Follow-

	Green	*Red*	*Blue*	*Yellow*	*Brown*	*Orange*	*Black*
Able	−1	−12	+5	−1	−2	+15	−4
Baker	+10	−1	−2	−7	+4	−3	−1
Charlie	−5	+5	−3	+3	−11	−1	+12
Dog	+5	−7	+10	−2	−5	+1	−2
Easy	−4	−1	−1	+1	+13	−10	+2
Fox	−6	+15	−5	−1	−3	−1	+1
George	−1	−1	−2	+10	+4	−2	−8

Fig. 1. Matrix used in group task.

ing this announcement, there will be thirty seconds of silence during which group members can think individually about the best strategy for the next trial, in terms of their notion about the system; note please that there are several approximations to the system, although the equation underlying it is quite complex. But work at it.

3. At the beginning of each trial the group members must report, one at a time, in some order, as to what they think would be the best row choice on the upcoming trial. Members may "pass" until the third time around, but must announce a choice then. Following this, groups will have three minutes on each trial to discuss choices and reach some agreement; this can be a simple majority, or unanimous decision; it is up to the group to decide. If a decision is not reached in three minutes, the group loses 5 units.

4. Before beginning the trials, the group will have five minutes to discuss these points: (a) The order of reporting; (b) How to determine the group choice for a given trial; (c) How to divide up the money at the end. These decisions are always subject to change, if the group has time and can agree. After the 15th trial, group members may have as much as five minutes to settle any outstanding decisions. Then headsets are to be removed, but group members remain seated for further instructions, and the individual payment of funds.

Instruments and Procedure

The matrix was specially constructed for this study to present an ambiguous but plausible task in which alternatives were only marginally discrete from one another.[4] The number of columns and rows was selected to enlarge the range of possibilities beyond the number of group members, while still retaining comprehensibility. The fact that the rows are unequal in algebraic sum appears to be less important as a feature in choice than the number and magnitude of positive and negative values in each; there is moreover the complicating feature of processing the outcome of the last trials in evaluating the choice for the next. All considered, the matrix was admirably suited to the requirements for ambiguity, challenge,

conflict, immediate reinforcement, and ready manipulation by the experimenter.

The confederate, operating as either 4 or 5 in the groups, suggested a choice that differed trial by trial from those offered by other members; this was pre-arranged but subject to modification as required. Since subjects rather typically perceived alternatives differently, his behavior was not unusual, especially during the early trials. For the 11 trials in which the confederate's row choice was "correct," the color that "came up" was contrived to yield a high plus value without at the same time providing a similar value for intersection with another person's row choice. Had his recommendation been followed by the group on these trials, high payoffs would have accrued.

The device of a 5-minute pretrial discussion had special utility for establishing common group expectancies, in the form of procedures, from which the confederate could deviate when called for in the design. Predictable decisions on these matters were reached unfailingly. But their importance lay in having a *public affirmation* of member intent. Thus, on order of reporting, it was quickly agreed to follow the order of the numbers assigned members. Each group, despite minor variants suggested, decided on simple majority rule. Regarding division of funds, equal sharing prevailed, sometimes with the proviso that the issue be taken up again at the end.

In the zones calling for nonconformity, the confederate violated these procedures by speaking out of prescribed turn, by questioning the utility of majority rule, and by unsupported—but not harsh—challenges to the recommendations made by others. He manifested such behaviors on an approximate frequency of at least one of these per trial with a mean of two per trial considered optimum. Thus, he would break in with his choice immediately after an earlier respondent had spoken and before the next in sequence could do so; when there were periods of silence during a trial he would observe aloud that maybe majority rule did not work so well; and he would show a lack of enthusiasm for the choice offered by various others on the matter of basis. Lest he lose credibility and become a caricature, in all instances he chose his moments with care and retained an evident spontaneity of expression.[5]

---

[4] The matrix is an adaptation, at least in spirit, of a smaller one used with success by Moore and Berkowitz (1956).

[5] The same person, H. E. Titus, was the confederate throughout.

RESULTS AND DISCUSSION

The task gave quite satisfactory signs of engrossing the subjects. There was much talk about the "system" and a good deal of delving into its basis, possibly made the more so by the subjects' academic background; the returned matrices were littered with diagrams, notations, and calculations. Though quite meaningless in fact, the confederate's tentative accounts of his "reasoning" were evidently treated with seriousness, perhaps as much because of the contrived time constraint, which prevented probing, as of his jargon regarding "rotations" and "block shifts." In any case, the confederate at no time claimed to have the system completely in hand. He delayed his response from the sixth trial onward to suggest calculation of an optimum choice in the face of conflicting alternatives; and the four trials on which he

was "wrong" were spaced to signify progressive improvement, but not total perfection.

Most pertinent, however, is the fact that there were no manifestations of suspicion concerning the confederate's authenticity. The others seemed to believe that he was one of them and that he was "cracking" the system; the post-interaction data were in full agreement.

Since all of the interactions were available on tape, it was possible to derive a number of indices of acceptance of influence. The most broadly revealing of these appeared to be the frequency of trials on which the confederate's recommended solution was followed.

In Table 1 this index is employed to discern the effects of three major variables. The analysis is arranged by zones (Z) of trials, and in terms of the confederate's nonconformity (NC) in the *current* zone and im-

TABLE 1

MEAN NUMBER OF TRIALS ON WHICH A GROUP ACCEPTS CONFEDERATE'S RECOMMENDED SOLUTION

Confederate's Previous Conformity	Zone I (Trials 1–5)		Zone II (Trials 6–10)		Zone III (Trials 11–15)	
	Non-conforming[a]	Con-forming	Non-conforming	Con-forming	Non-conforming	Con-forming
With Procedural nonconformity in immediate *past* zone	1.67 6[b]	—	3.25 4	3.00 2	4.00 4	5.00 2
Without Procedural nonconformity in immediate *past* zone	—	2.00 6	5.00 2	3.75 4	5.00 2	4.75 4

ANALYSIS OF VARIANCE

Source	SS	df	MS	F
Current Nonconformity	.20	1	.200	—
Zones	47.05	2	23.525	35.01**
Past Nonconformity	3.36	1	3.360	5.00*
Int: Current NC × Z	1.22	2	.610	—
Int: Current NC × Past NC	13.52	1	13.520	20.12**
Int: Z × Past NC	.72	2	.360	—
Int: Current NC × Z × Past NC	4.11	2	2.055	3.06
Residual	16.12	24	.672	
Total	86.30	35		

[a] Confederate showed procedural nonconformity on the trials in this zone.
[b] Indicates number of groups upon which cell is based.
* $p < .05$.
** $p < .001$.

mediate *past* zone.[6] The means given in each cell indicate the number of trials, out of five per zone, on which the confederate's choice was also the group's. In a chi-square test, the effect of position upon this measure was found to be nonsignificant, and is therefore omitted as a distinction in the analysis of variance.

The significant F secured from Zones is in accord with prediction. It reveals the ongoing effect of task competence in increasing the acceptance of the confederate's choice, to be seen in the rising means across zones. While current nonconformity does not yield a significant effect, past nonconformity does. Viewing the table horizontally, one finds that the means for "without" *past* NC exceed the means for "with" *past* NC in all instances but one. Regarding the significant interaction of *current* and *past* NC, the combination "without-without" has a sequence (2.00, 3.75, 4.75) of persistently higher value than has "with-with" (1.67, 3.25, 4.00); this, too, is in line with prediction. Finally, the maximum value of 5.00 in Zone II for the combination "without" *past* NC but "with" *current* NC confirms the key prediction from the model, at least within the context of the relative magnitudes there; the same value is also seen in Zone III for the identical combination; still another reading of 5.00 holds there, however, for the inverse combination, but in a tight range of values quite beyond separation of effects for interpretation.

Considerable consistency was found too in the post-interaction data. On the item "overall contribution to the group activity," 44 of the 48 subjects ranked the confederate first; on the item "influence over the group's decisions," 45 of the 48 ranked him first. Two things bear emphasis in this regard: subjects had to individually write in the numbers of group members next to rank, hence demanding recall; and their polarity of response cut across all six treatments, despite significant differences among these in the actual *acceptance of influence*. That the confederate therefore made an impact is clear; but that it had selective consequences depending upon the

[6] For Zone I, the "past zone" refers to the discussion period. If he was to nonconform there, the confederate would question majority rule and suggest that the division of funds be left until the end rather than agree then on equal shares.

timing of his nonconformity is equally clear.

In detail, then, the findings are in keeping with the predictions made from the model. The operational variable for measuring acceptance of influence was confined to the task itself, but nontask elements are touched as well. In that respect, the findings corroborate the subtle development of differential impressions as a function of even limited interpersonal behavior.

Some unquantified but clearly suggestive data are worth mentioning in this regard. Where, for example, the confederate began nonconforming *after* the first zone, his behavior was accepted with minimal challenge; by the third zone, his suggestion that majority rule was faulty yielded a rubber stamping of his choice. Again, if he had already accrued credit, his pattern of interrupting people out of turn not only went unhindered but was taken up by some others. Quite different effects were elicited if the confederate exhibited nonconformity from *the outset,* notably such comments of censure as "That's not the way we agreed to do it, five."

The findings are especially indicative of the stochastic element of social interaction and its consequence for changing perception. Especially interesting is the fact that these effects are produced even in a relatively brief span of time.

SUMMARY

A study was conducted to test the relationship between competence on a group task and conformity or nonconformity to procedural norms in determining a person's ability to influence other group members. Data were gathered from 12 groups engaged in a problem solving task under controlled conditions. Each was made up of five members one of whom was a confederate who evidenced a high degree of competence during the 15 trials. His nonconformity to the procedural norms agreed upon by the group was introduced at various times, early, middle, or late, in the sequence of trials. Influence was measured by the number of trials (per segment of the entire sequence) in which the confederate's recommended solution was accepted as the group's choice. As a broad effect, it was found that a significant increase in his influence occurred as the trials progressed, presumably as a function of the successive evidences of competence. Past conformity by the confederate was also found to be positively and significantly related to the acceptance of his influence; finally, there was a statistically significant interaction between past and current nonconformity reflected in high influence in the groups in which the confederate had conformed earlier in the sequence of trials but was presently nonconforming. These results were all thoroughly consistent with predictions made from the "idiosyncrasy credit" model of conformity and status.

REFERENCES

Bales, R. F., & Slater, P. E. Role differentiation in small decision-making groups. In T. Parsons, R. F. Bales, *et al.* (Eds.), *Family, socialization, and interaction process.* Free Press of Glencoe, Inc., 1955.

Brown, J. F. *Psychology and the social order.* New York: McGraw-Hill, 1936.

Carter, L. F. Recording and evaluating the performance of individuals as members of small groups. *Personnel Psychol.,* 1954, 7, 477–484.

Chowdhry, Kamla, & Newcomb, T. M. The relative abilities of leaders and non-leaders to estimate opinions of their own groups. *J. abnorm. soc. Psychol.,* 1952, 47, 51–57.

Hollander, E. P. Conformity, status, and idiosyncrasy credit. *Psychol. Rev.,* 1958, 65, 117–127.

Hollander, E. P. Some points of reinterpretation regarding social conformity. *Soc. Rev.,* 1959, 7, 159–168.

Homans, G. C. *The human group.* New York: Harcourt, Brace, 1950.

Moore, O. K., & Berkowitz, M. I. Problem solving and social interaction. *ONR tech. Rep.,* 1956, No. 1. (Contract Nonr-609(16), Yale University Department of Sociology.)

Upward Communication in Experimentally Created Hierarchies[1] / Arthur R. Cohen

In a stimulating experiment on communication in experimentally created hierarchies, Kelley (7) explored some of the relationships between social status, mobility, interpersonal liking, and communication. In his experiment, Kelley set up a two-level hierarchy with varied possibilities of upward or downward mobility at each level, and had his subjects perform a task which presumably necessitated communication among them. Different experimental instructions created four experimental conditions: high status/non-mobility, high status/mobility, low status/non-mobility, and low status/mobility.

Kelley's experiment and others, (1, 11), which define hierarchies in terms of social status, invoke the concept of substitute upward locomotion to explain the communications of persons who are low in the status hierarchy. On the assumption that there is a general drive to move upward in our society (4, 8), one may expect group members to endeavor to move upward in the status hierarchy. Thus, low-status persons may have fantasies about occupying high-status positions and may strive to communicate with high-status persons as a substitute for actual locomotion when actual locomotion is not possible. This is, in effect, a 'status-approximation', theory of upward communication.

Other investigators (3, 6, 9, 10, 12, 13), who place more emphasis on the amount of

Reprinted from *Human Relations,* 1958, 11, pages 41–53, by permission of author and publisher, Tavistock Publications, Ltd.

[1] This experiment was performed as part of the Yale Communications Research Program and was financed by a grant from the Bell Telephone Laboratories. The research program is under the general direction of Carl I. Hovland. The author wishes to express his great indebtedness to Gerard E. McDonnell for his invaluable collaboration in running and analysing the experiment. Thanks are also due to S. Moroff for his statistical aid and to J. W. Brehm and C. I. Hovland for their critical appraisal.

power possessed by persons at different levels in a hierarchy, stress an ego-defensive or self-protective theory of communication. Investigators supporting this approach emphasize the uneasiness often felt by persons with low rank when interacting with those of high rank, because of the power high-ranking individuals possess, and the resultant attempt on the part of the 'lows' to have maximally beneficial relations with 'highs.' This is, in effect, an 'instrumental' theory of upward communication.

By adding the concept of power to that of status, the present report attempts to help clarify the differences between the two low groups of low rank and to highlight a more instrumental view of upward hierarchical communication.

Status may be defined as the amount of desirability and satisfaction inherent in a given position; a high status position is one that is deemed to be more desirable and satisfying to its occupant (7). The concept need not necessarily be defined in terms of any specific relationship between persons of different rank; operationally, high-status persons may be told that their position is the more interesting and important one. Power may be defined as the relative ability to control one's own and others' need satisfaction. High-power persons are able to facilitate or prevent the need satisfaction of those of low power; low-power persons are dependent upon highs for their need satisfaction. It should be emphasized that the crucial characteristic in the relations between persons stemming from differences in their relative degree of power, as distinct from differences in status, is this element of control over need satisfaction. Differences in status, do not, in principle at least, provide the possibility for higher-rank persons to control effectively how well lower-level persons satisfy their needs. We would thus expect persons with low power in a hierarchy to manifest a desire to ensure that the power of the highs will be used in a beneficial fashion, and their communication should reflect this interest in smooth relations and high regard.

When a hierarchy is defined in terms of status, people may attempt to maximize their status in a variety of ways. They may misperceive their position, try to get psycho-

logically closer to those of higher status, not admit to anything that will call a desirable status into question, and so forth. However, if their relations to those of higher rank are not defined in terms of their dependence upon the highs for the rewards inherent in the system, their communication to those highs may not clearly manifest the active attempts at good relations and self-protection *vis-à-vis* the highs which stamps behavior in a hierarchy. It would thus appear that the use of the concept of status without specification of dependence upon highs emphasizes the manifold ways of increasing status without necessary reference to behavior toward those of high rank; implicit in the notion of general status is a lack of functional dependence upon highs. Defining rank in a hierarchy in terms of power differences creates a functional dependence of lows upon highs. An emphasis on power differences points to the lows' behavior toward highs in the interests of need satisfaction, and not merely to their attempts to approximate status in either fantasy or wish-fulfilment.

In addition to desires of low-rank persons for substitute upward locomotion, then, there appears to be pressure that they place upon themselves to have those of high rank behave toward them in a need-gratifying fashion. If an institutional structure provides the possibility for low-rank persons to gain rewards and move into a position where they can exercise control over their own need satisfaction, and if persons of high rank mediate this movement by passing judgements on their performance, we may expect those of low rank to be exceedingly careful in their relations with those of high rank. If, on the other hand, the institutional structure provides no possibility for eventual control over their own need satisfaction on the part of low-rank persons, they should be less concerned about the niceties of their behavior toward persons of high rank who pass judgement on their performance. Thus, we might expect two low-rank groups to differ along these lines: a low group for whom upward mobility is possible should make active efforts to produce good relations with highs; whereas a low group for whom upward mobility is not possible should be more withdrawn and more careless in its attitude toward highs. Though the two low groups are often treated alike, there is good evidence that they differ in the above manner in the results from Kelley's experiment, and Kelley interprets it as such. However, it would seem that the status inductions prevented these differences from emerging sharply and therefore obscured the notion that persons in hierarchical situations behave in a fashion facilitative of need satisfaction. The present report is intended to help clarify the differences between the two groups of low rank.

It was felt by the present investigator that an induction that stressed the lows' lack of power (i.e. their relative inability to control their own and others' need satisfaction) as well as their lack of status, and made their mobility dependent upon highs, would bring about a sharp separation in the behavior of the two low groups and thereby serve to highlight a more instrumental view of upward communication.

Differences in communication between the two low-rank groups should be reflected in perceptions about the general social structure in which they exist. They should also reflect personality differences between individuals within the groups. The concept of power serves as a link between personality and social structure. Though it is essentially a structural concept rooted in the social system, its exercise toward some end always has implications for need satisfaction, thereby raising the question of motivation.

Exploration of the effects upon communication of personality variations within a hierarchy would thus appear to be of crucial theoretical interest. The personality dimension of broadest significance is the concept of general adjustment; variations in degree of adjustment would appear to make for variations in a wide range of behaviors, including hierarchical communication. In addition, the dependent nature of the low-rank position focuses on the individual's predisposition toward regressive behavior as a further determinant of upward communication. Depending upon the person's internal push toward regression, he may highlight or deemphasize a given communication to those of high rank. In effect, general adjustment and specific tendencies toward regression are behavioral predispositions relevant to the low-rank roles; they are highly likely to be cued off by the situational demands of a low position in a hierarchy. The exploration of these personality variables permits some insight into the personality dynamics connected with behavior in certain social roles and helps to provide support for the assumptions made about motivation in the hierarchical social structure.

In order to clarify the differences between the two low-rank groups, the Kelley experiment was replicated in its entirety by the present author. However, since the results concerning the two high-rank groups are very similar to Kelley's results, and since the major theoretical issue concerns the two low-rank groups, only the data for the two low-rank groups will be presented in the present report.

METHOD

Description of the Experiment

Groups of six and eight Ss were divided into equal subgroups and assigned a task which presumably involved communication among them in order to perform in one room a task 'directed' by Ss in another room. Actually, all members performed the same task and reacted to a pre-planned set of standard communications, provided by E, but supposedly initiated by persons in their own and other subgroups. They were all told that members of the other subgroup were of high rank. The members worked at the task for 35 minutes and responded to the prepared messages.

The Ss were told that the experimenters were interested in studying how well groups of people could perform a complicated task when communication among them was limited to written messages. This was made plausible by mentioning that there were many situations in industry and government where people who work in different parts of a building accomplish their joint work by sending memos to one another and that we were interested in such situations.

A fuller description of the general experimental manipulations can be found in Kelley's paper. They were identical in the present experiment except for the following:

1. *Specification of motivation*. A strong need to achieve success and avoid failure was given

so that the power and mobility variations could be effectively introduced and so that the Ss would be involved in the task. The Ss were told in very strong terms that the task was a good index of sensitivity, intelligence, and ability to work together with others, and they were urged to try as hard as they could to do well.

2. *Power induction.* In addition to the specification of status differences among persons (as in Kelley's experiment, Ss were told that their jobs would be unimportant and would lack prestige), low power was also introduced.

After the status inductions, the Ss were told the following: 'Now, how well you do on this job as individuals and as a group will be decided *directly by them* (i.e. the "highs") *and only by them*. It's their messages you are following, and as they are in the best possible spot to evaluate how well you do, your work will be evaluated by them during and after the session. So remember, the decision as to your success or failure will rest *entirely with them*. They will be exercising their power of evaluating your efforts carefully, but firmly. Now, you should all try as hard as possible to do well.'

3. *Mobility inductions.* Half of the low-rank Ss were given the Mobility treatment, half the Non-mobility treatment. In the *Non-mobile condition,* the Ss were told: 'They have much more say over things and probably you'd find their job more interesting and important than your own. It would be nice if some of you could be promoted to their job, but in order for the session to work best, we want to let them stay on it in order for them to get used to it. So, no matter how you do, you'll have to stay on the poorer job throughout the experiment and they will stay on the better one where they rate your performance.'

In the *Mobile condition,* the Ss were told: 'They have much more say over things and probably you'd find their job more interesting and important than your own. But depending upon how well or poorly you are rated by them, you may move up to the other job during the course of the experiment. It hasn't yet been decided how many people should be in each room for the experiment. So some of you may move up to the better

job. Depending upon how well you appear to be doing, you may move up at any time during the experiment.'

4. *Task.* The experimental task required that the Ss plan and build a model city. Ss were given an unstructured terrain on which they could place a number of buildings in order to build an 'ideal' city. The messages they received, presumably from high-rank Ss but in reality from E, directed them in building the city. The task has previously been found to be highly involving and amenable to diverse experimental variations (10).

5. *Post-experimental questionnaires.* After the period allotted to the task, on the pretext that they were going to do another task of the same kind, the Ss were given a short questionnaire asking about their desires to continue the same job or to move to one of 'giving instructions' and whether or not they wished to be eliminated. It being decided that the second task should not be attempted at all, they were asked to fill out the main post-experimental questionnaire.

Subjects

The Ss were Yale College freshmen who were recruited from their dormitories. They participated in the experiment within three months of their arrival on campus. In order to minimize the effects of prior attitudes and past contacts no Ss were placed in the same group if they lived in common dormitory entry ways. This arrangement, together with their recent arrival on campus, made the members of each experimental group comparative strangers to one another. The distribution of the Ss into the experimental groups was as follows: Low Non-Mobile = 30, Low Mobile = 30.

Kinds of Data

1. *Check on motivation.* The degree to which the Ss wanted to do well both before and after the experimental task. Also their desires to remain in the experiment.

2. *Check on experimental manipulations.* (a) *Rank (power and status)*: an index of the degree to which the Ss perceived their jobs to have been of high rank, i.e., powerful, important, and influential, created from their responses to three separate items on the post-experimental questionnaire.

(b) *Mobility:* the Ss' perception of the possibility for them to change from their job to another one during the experiment.

3. *Communication data.* The messages written by the Ss, constituting the main data of the experiment. These were coded into categories paralleling most of Kelley's. Some additional ones relevant to the personality phenomena were also analyzed. The major dimensions coded were:

(a) Number of messages sent, and length of messages sent, to own group and to the higher group.

(b) Number of irrelevant messages: messages coded as having some content irrelevant to the group task such as conjectures about the task, experimenter, or psychology in general; discussion of girls, dating, college affairs; desires for cokes, coffee, beer, and so forth.

(c) Conjectures about the other job: one type of task-irrelevant content concerned purely with conjectures about the nature of the job in the other subgroup such as what they were doing, what their job was like, and how they were going about it.

(d) Critical content: messages critical of the persons to whom they were addressed. These were generally explicit and varied from mild criticism to direct and highly charged hostility about their "writing," the way they were performing, and the directions they gave.

(e) Expressions of confusion about the job: the Ss' general expression of uncertainties about their job and the experimental procedures.

(f) Job suggestions: all messages containing suggestions, recommendations, directives, about how the other person should do the job.

(g) Job questions: specific questions about how to proceed on the job—how details and larger plans were to be carried out.

(h) Desires for support: all requests for support, encouragement, help, friendliness, and the like.

(i) Cohesiveness-building content: overtures to friendship, encouragement, praise, and friendly personal content.

Coding reliabilities on these items appeared to be adequate, ranging from .62 to .91.

4. *Choice of job for second task:* a measure of dissatisfaction with position obtained while the Ss still thought there was to be a second task.

5. *Perceptions of the social structure.* These data were gathered in the post-experimental questionnaire.

(a) Social validity: the degree to which the Ss felt that they had support from others in their own and the upper group for their opinions and ideas.

(b) Attraction to their own group: The Ss' desires to meet with and work with their subgroup again on similar things.

(c) Perception of rejection of own ideas by other group: the degree to which the other group neglected the Ss' ideas and suggestions for the task.

(d) Perceptions of alternative social structure: the degree to which the Ss perceived that there were alternatives to the way the group organization was presently arranged.

6. *Personality measures.* Personality data were gathered several weeks before the experiment. The Blacky Pictures (2) provided data on general psychosexual adjustment. The Blacky test is a modified projective device consisting of a series of pictures that can be shown to individuals or groups. Each picture measures the reactions of the respondent to a major object relationship in psychoanalytic theory. From the Ss' responses one may derive a series of scores indicating degree of disturbance in such areas as oral, oedipal, and so on. In the present research six Blacky pictures were used: oral-erotic, oral-sadistic, anal, oedipal intensity, castration anxiety, and sibling rivalry. An index of general psychosexual disturbance was derived from scores on all six Blacky pictures, indicating the degree to which the S had conflicts which cut across diverse psychosexual areas. The degree to which the S preferred the ego defense of regression against conflicts across all psychosexual areas was assessed by the Defense Preference Inquiry. This measure is given in association with the Blacky pictures and requires that the S rank-order a set of alternatives specifying defense mechanisms for each psychosexual dimension (5).

RESULTS AND DISCUSSION

I. Evidence on the Effectiveness of the Experimental Manipulations

Data from the post-experimental questionnaire indicate that the experimental manipulations were highly effective in creating the assumed differences among the Ss. Persons in both Low Mobile and Low Non-Mobile groups were highly motivated to the same degree, both at the outset and at the conclusion: on an eight-point *a priori* scale, with eight indicating maximum motivation, they both hover at seven. Furthermore, practically no Ss wished to be eliminated from the experiment when given the opportunity to leave.

Both low groups felt that there was a great deal less control and importance inherent in their job than did comparable high-rank Ss ($t = 3.82$, $p<.001$).[2] On the assumption that persons of low rank should be less ready to give orders than those of high rank, data on the communication of job suggestions were examined. The results show that the perceived difference in power and status is reflected in the lows' lesser communication of job suggestions, recommendations, and orders ($t = 3.30$, $p<.01$).

The two low groups differed in their perception of their potential mobility: the Low Mobiles perceived their chances for a change in job during the experiment to have been higher (5.10) than did those in the Low Non-Mobile group (4.20). These means are

[2] All statistical tests in this report are two-tailed tests.

significantly different at beyond the .05 level ($t = 2.05$).

Thus the experimental inductions appear to have produced a common perception of low rank in the low groups, and differing perceptions of opportunities for mobility.

II. Comparison of Low Non-Mobile and Low Mobile Groups

1. *Differences in communication and perception.* When the two low conditions are compared with regard to the total data, striking differences between them are evident. The greater concern of the Low Mobiles with the experimental situation, their suppression of irrelevancies, and their general orientation toward the highs rather than toward the members of their own subgroup stand out clearly.

In *Table 1* it can be seen that while both groups send an almost identical number of words to members of the upper group, the Low Mobiles' messages are significantly longer. When communicating to their own group, the Low Non-Mobiles communicate more words and their messages are significantly longer than those of the Low Mobiles.

Table 2 shows that differences between the groups in their total volume of communica-

TABLE 1

Average Number of Words and Number of Words per Message to Own and Upper Group

	Low Non-Mobile	Low Mobile	t	p
Total number of words to upper group	149.37	148.00	.10	ns
Total number of words to own group	41.17	20.80	3.96	<.001
Number of words per message to upper group	14.44	17.84	2.09	<.05
Number of words per message to own group	9.16	5.74	2.78	<.01

TABLE 2

Average Number of Messages Having General Irrelevant Content and Conjectures About the Job in the Upper Group

	Low Non-Mobile	Low Mobile	t	p
Total irrelevant content	8.07	4.53	3.55	<.01
Irrelevant content to own group	3.70	2.53	2.24	<.05
Irrelevant content to upper group	4.37	2.00	3.98	<.001
Conjectures about job in upper group				
those wanting own job	.37	.78		
those wanting upper job	.69	.38	2.03	<.05

tion appear to be due to the great differences in the amount of irrelevant content they communicate rather than to wholly relevant content. Furthermore, the wide differences with regard to total amount of irrelevant content are due to the amount of irrelevant content communicated to the upper group rather than to their own group. In sum, it appears that the Low Mobiles are more concerned with task-centered communication to the upper level than are Low Non-Mobiles.

If conjectures about the nature of the job in the higher group can be taken as an indication of substitute upward locomotion, it would appear that this process certainly occurs within the general context of instrumental communication. Conjectures increase where locomotion is desired but is not possible (Low Non-Mobiles who want the other job) and where it is possible but not desirable (Low Mobiles who want their job). Thus, substitute upward locomotion may not occur uniformly within a population of low-rank Ss but only among those with low rank whose possibilities for upward movement and desires for such move-

ment are contradictory. Such communication may be viewed as an attempt to project themselves into the high-rank role on the part of those persons who cannot gain high rank and want to, and of those who can potentially gain high rank, but have forsaken it.

When desiring movement into the upper group the Low Mobiles appear not to make many conjectures about the other job; they may be trading off conjectures for actual mobility. For the Low Non-Mobile group, however, where upward promotion is impossible, stronger desires to locomote produce conjectures about the nature of the job in the other room. This may be indirect evidence for a greater concern with the highs on the part of the Low Mobiles.

More direct evidence for the Low Mobiles' greater concern with their relations with the highs is obtained from the data on critical comments. *Table 3* shows that compared to the Low Non-Mobiles the Low Mobiles make fewer total critical comments about the upper group and fewer critical comments about those at the upper level

TABLE 3

AVERAGE NUMBER OF MESSAGES HAVING CRITICAL CONTENT AND PERCENT OF MESSAGES HAVING COHESIVENESS-BUILDING CONTENT DIRECTED TO OWN GROUP

	Low Non-Mobile	Low Mobile	t	p
Critical content about upper group sent directly to them	.97	.33	4.58	<.001
Total critical content about upper group	1.40	.47	3.87	<.01
Cohesiveness-building content to own group				
% sending one or more	47%	27%		
% sending none	53%	73%	Exact test p <.05	

TABLE 4

PERCEPTIONS OF THE SOCIAL STRUCTURE

	Low Non-Mobile	Low Mobile	t	p
Attraction to own group	9.87	9.17	1.50	<.20
Perceived rejection of own ideas by upper group	4.23	3.48	1.80	<.08
Social validity received				
% saying they receive it from own group	46%	25%		
% saying they receive it from upper group	54%	75%	Exact test p <.10	

sent directly to them. Furthermore, the data on cohesiveness-building comments indicate that the Low Mobiles send fewer such comments to members of their own group than do the Low Non-Mobiles.

Additional data on the Ss' perceptions of the social structure show that the Low Mobiles say they receive more social validity from the highs than the Low Non-Mobiles do, they tend to be less attracted to their own group, and they do not feel that the highs reject their ideas so much.

There are no differences with regard to expressions of confusion, desires for support, or job questions, but the data support the assumption that the two low groups behave differently toward the highs. These differences between the two low groups are similar to Kelley's findings that the Low Non-Mobiles are more concerned with their own group and more disruptive of the total group's cohesiveness than the Low Mobiles. In the present experiment the Low Mobiles appear to be behaving in a way guaranteed to promote their chances of being rated favorably by the powerful highs and therefore being moved to the higher group. They are careful about criticism, stay more with the task, and center their attention less on their own group; their greater mobility and their perceptions of the highs as mediating it cause them to behave in this manner. The Low Non-Mobiles, on the other hand, appear to be reacting to a situation where they have low rank but, no matter what they do, they cannot locomote upward. They do work hard, but a good deal of their energy is devoted to irrelevant comments. They are more critical of the highs to their faces and tend to perceive the highs as more threatening and rejecting than the Low Mobiles do. They tend to center their affect and attention on the members of their own group to the neglect of the highs. For them, communication and interaction cannot be instrumental to mobility and, therefore, positive treatment does not have quite the same meaning as it does for the Low Mobiles. Thus, they may be expected to be less concerned about the highs than the Low Mobiles. This evidence can be taken as support for the general hypothesis concerning the differences between the two low groups.

2. *Perceptions of the social structure and communication.* These speculations about the motives of the two low-rank groups can be more firmly anchored if we consider the relationship between various perceptions of the social structure and certain communication variables. Even though the Low Non-Mobiles as a whole receive more social validity from their own group and perceive their job as less powerful than the upper group's, those within the group who really feel that their job is powerless, who see the upper group even less as a source of social validity, but yet who are even more highly motivated to do well, pay *even less* attention to the task and are much more critical of the highs. The data are to be found in *Table 5.*

We have seen that the Low Mobiles tend much more to behave in a friendly fashion. Nevertheless, the data in *Table 6* indicate that when their perceptions of their place in the social structure are such as to make them feel relatively non-mobile and to make them feel that the social structure presents no possibility for them to behave differently with regard to rank and their own need satisfaction, then they tend to behave more like Low Non-Mobiles: they tend to be more critical and to send more irrelevant messages. It would seem that the more the Low Mobiles perceive that their communication cannot be made instrumental to their need satisfaction, the less careful they are about their communication upward.

3. *Personality and communication.* Additional support for the interpretation of the differences between the two low groups can be gained when personality variations within the two groups are related to the communication variables. The data point up a complex interaction between social position and personality factors owing to the different requirements of the different mobility positions.[3] General conflict, as well as specific tendencies toward regression, lead to even stronger dependency behaviors to-

[3] Interpretations concerning the effects of personality factors are based only upon those instances in which differences in communication are related to personality variations. Thus, in *Table 7*, blank cells appear in a number of places where personality differences make no difference in behavior. It was felt that leaving out the findings which produced no differences would make for increased ease in scanning the data.

TABLE 5

AVERAGE NUMBER OF MESSAGES HAVING IRRELEVANT AND CRITICAL
CONTENT ACCORDING TO DIFFERING PERCEPTIONS OF THE
SOCIAL STRUCTURE FOR THE LOW NON-MOBILES

a. *Social validity*

	Irrelevant content	
From own group	10.07	$t = 2.73, p < .01$
From upper group	6.33	

b. *Perceived rank of job*

	Critical content	
High	.93	$t = 2.25, p < .03$
Low	1.81	

c. *Motivation to do well at outset*

	Critical content	
High	1.80	$t = 2.44, p < .02$
Low	.81	

TABLE 6

AVERAGE NUMBER OF MESSAGES HAVING IRRELEVANT AND CRITICAL
CONTENT ACCORDING TO DIFFERING PERCEPTIONS OF THE
SOCIAL STRUCTURE FOR THE LOW MOBILES

a. *Perception of alternatives in social structure*

	Irrelevant content	
Perceive alternatives	3.31	$t = 2.18, p < .04$
Perceive no alternatives	5.98	

b. *Perception of alternatives in social structure*

	Critical content	
Perceive alternatives	.18	$t = 3.41, p < .01$
Perceive no alternatives	.86	

c. *Experimental check on mobility chances*

	Critical content	
Perceive high mobility	.21	$t = 1.96, p = .06$
Perceive low mobility	.67	

ward the other level on the part of the Low Mobiles: they communicate more desires for support and express more confusion. However, when the Low Non-Mobiles are specifically predisposed toward regression, they tend to refrain from asking for support. Whatever desires for support there are appear to be confined to the low regression group. Furthermore, when they are relatively maladjusted, they are even more critical of the other level than usually, they admit less to task confusion and they communicate far more irrelevancies.

The general picture indicates that the Low Non-Mobiles tend to become even more distant from and hostile toward the other level when they are generally disturbed and when they have specific regressive defenses. This is in contrast to the Low Mobiles, who when disturbed and regressive lean even more than they ordinarily do upon those at the upper level. The different mobility possibilities held out by the social system lead to very different effects of personality variations on dependency upon and orientation toward members of the upper group. The interaction between personality and rank in determining com-

TABLE 7

INTERRELATIONSHIP BETWEEN PERSONALITY AND COMMUNICATION FOR
LOW MOBILES AND LOW NON-MOBILES

	Low Non-Mobile		Low Mobile	
1. *Use of regression*				
a. *Desires for support*				
High regression	0	$t = 1.70, p = .10$	1.10	$t = 2.63, p < .02$
Low regression	.62		.10	
b. *Expression of confusion*				
High regression	—		1.20	$t = 1.83, p < .08$
Low regression	—		.25	
2. *General adjustment*				
a. *Irrelevant content*				
High conflict	9.18	$t = 1.74, p < .10$	—	
Low conflict	6.62		—	
b. *Critical content*				
High conflict	1.89	$t = 1.71, p = .10$	—	
Low conflict	1.00		—	
c. *Expressions of confusion*				
High conflict	.17	$t = 2.13, p < .05$	—	
Low conflict	.67		—	
d. *Desires for support*				
High conflict	—		.67	$t = 1.70, p = .10$
Low conflict	—		.20	
e. *Job questions*				
High conflict	—		2.40	$t = 2.91, p < .01$
Low conflict	—		.93	

munication is consistent with the differences between the two groups and may be said to provide support for these differences.

CONCLUSION

When rank in a hierarchy is defined in terms of power or control over need satisfaction as well as general status, those with low rank who can move upward communicate in a way guaranteed to protect and enhance their relations with the highs who exercise that control; those with low rank for whom mobility upward is impossible have less need to communicate to the upper level in such a friendly, promotive, and task-oriented fashion. This difference may not be clearly seen when the hierarchical structure is defined *only* in terms of status differences. When defined in terms of power as well, these differences emerge, and help to give a picture of upward communication in a hierarchy as more than merely serving as substitute upward loco-

motion but more generally as facilitative of need satisfaction.

These assumptions about the different motivations of the two low-rank groups received support from relationships between perceptions of the social structure and communication items. Relationships between personality factors and communication items provide still further evidence for the motivational differences between the two low-rank groups. These personality mechanisms were felt to increase the concern with their dominant motivations on the part of the low-rank groups and to separate them even further in their communication to persons at the other level.

REFERENCES

1. Back, K., Festinger, L., Hymovitch, B., Kelley, H. H., Schachter, S., and Thibaut, J. The methodology of studying rumor transmission. *Hum. Relat.,* Vol. 3, pp. 307–12, 1950.

2. Blum, G. S. A study of the psychoanalytic theory of psychosexual development. *Genet. Psychol. Monogr.*, Vol. 39, pp. 3–99, 1949.

3. Cohen, A. R. Situational structure, self-esteem, and threat-oriented reactions to power. In D. Cartwright (Ed.), *Studies in Social Power*, 1959.

4. Festinger, L. A theory of social comparison processes. *Hum. Relat.*, Vol. VII, pp. 117–40, 1954.

5. Goldstein, S. A projective study of psychoanalytic mechanisms. Unpublished doctoral dissertation, University of Michigan, 1952.

6. Hurwitz, J., Zander, A., and Hymovitch, B. Some effects of power on the relations among group members. In D. Cartwright and A. Zander (Eds.), *Group Dynamics*. Evanston, Ill.: Row Peterson, 1953, London: Tavistock Publications, 1954, pp. 483–92.

7. Kelley, H. H. Communication in experi-

mentally created hierarchies. *Hum. Relat.*, Vol. IV, pp. 39–56, 1951.

8. Maslow, A. H. A theory of human motivation. *Psychol. Rev.*, Vol. 50, pp. 370–96, 1943.

9. Pepitone, A. Motivational effects in social perception. *Hum. Relat.*, Vol. III, pp. 57–76, 1950.

10. Stotland, E. Peer groups and reactions to power figures. In D. Cartwright (Ed.), *Studies in Social Power*, 1959.

11. Thibaut, J. An experimental study of the cohesiveness of underprivileged groups. *Hum. Relat.*, Vol. III, pp. 251–78, 1950.

12. Zander, A., Cohen, A. R., and Stotland, E. *Role Relations in the Mental Health Professions.* Ann Arbor: Institute for Social Research, 1957.

13. Zander, A., and Cohen, A. R. Attributed social power and group acceptance. *J. abnorm. soc. Psychol.*, Vol. 51, pp. 490–2, 1955.

Studies of Interpersonal Bargaining[1] / Morton Deutsch and Robert M. Krauss

(*Bell Telephone Laboratories, Incorporated, Murray Hill, New Jersey*)

INTRODUCTION

A *bargain* is defined in Webster's Unabridged Dictionary as "an agreement between parties settling what each shall give and receive in a transaction between them"; it is further specified that a bargain is "an agreement or compact viewed as advantageous or the reverse." When the term "agreement" is broadened to include tacit, informal agreements as well as explicit agreements, it is evident that bargains and the processes involved in arriving at bargains ("bargaining") are pervasive characteristics of social life.

The definition of "bargain" fits under sociological definitions of the term "social norm." In this light, it may be seen that the experimental study of the bargaining process and of bargaining outcomes provides a means for the laboratory study of the development of certain types of social norms. It is well to recognize, however, that bargaining situations have certain distinctive features which, unlike many other types of social situations, make it relevant to consider the conditions which determine whether or not a social norm will develop as well as to consider the conditions which determine the nature of the social norm if it develops. Bargaining situations highlight for the investigator the need to be sensitive to the possibility that, even where cooperation would be mutually advantageous, shared purposes may not develop, agreement may not be reached, interaction may be regulated antagonistically rather than normatively.

Reprinted from *Journal of Conflict Resolution*, 1962, 6, pages 52–76, by permission of authors and publisher, Department of Journalism, University of Michigan.

[1] This paper was awarded the 1961 Meritorious Essay Prize in Socio-Psychological Inquiry by the American Association for the Advancement of Science. Parts of it have appeared previously in Deutsch and Krauss (1960).

The essential features of a bargaining situation exist when:

1. both parties perceive that there is the possibility of reaching an agreement in which each party would be better off, or no worse off, than if no agreement is reached;
2. both parties perceive that there is more than one such agreement which could be reached; and
3. both parties perceive each other to have conflicting preferences or opposed interests with regard to the different agreements which might be reached.

Everyday examples of a bargaining situation include such situations as: the buyer-seller relationship when the price is not fixed; the husband and wife who want to spend an evening out together but have conflicting preferences about where to go; union-management negotiations; drivers who meet at an intersection when there is no clear right of way; disarmament negotiations.

From our description of the essential features of a bargaining situation it can be seen that, in terms of our prior conceptualization of cooperation and competition (Deutsch, 1949), it is a situation in which the participants have mixed motives toward one another: on the one hand, each has interest in cooperating so that they reach an agreement; on the other hand, they have competitive interests with regard to the nature of the agreement they reach. In effect, to reach agreement the cooperative interest of the bargainers must be strong enough to overcome their competitive interests. However, agreement is not only contingent upon the *motivational* balances of cooperative to competitive interests but also upon the situational and *cognitive* factors which would facilitate or hinder the recognition or invention of a bargaining agreement that reduces the opposition of interest and enhances the mutuality of interest.[2]

The discussion of the preceding paragraph leads to the formulation of two general, closely related propositions about the likelihood that a bargaining agreement will be reached.

1. Bargainers are more likely to reach an agreement, the stronger are their cooperative interests in comparison with their competitive interests in relationship to each other.
2. Bargainers are more likely to reach an agreement, the more resources they have available for the recognition or invention of potential bargaining agreements and the more resources they have for communication to one another once a potential agreement has been recognized or invented.

From these two basic propositions and additional hypotheses concerning the conditions which determine the strengths of the cooperative and competitive interests and the amount of available resources, we believe it is possible to explain the ease or difficulty of arriving at a bargaining agreement. We shall not present a full statement of these hypotheses here but shall instead turn to a description of a series of experiments that relate to Proposition 1.

EXPERIMENT I

The first experiment to be reported here was concerned with the effect of the availability of threat upon bargaining in a two-person experimental bargaining game we have devised.[3] Threat is defined as the expression of an intention to do something which is detrimental to the interests of another. Our experiment was guided by two assumptions about threat:

1. If there is a conflict of interest and a means of threatening the other person exists, there will be a tendency to use the threat in an attempt to force the other person to yield. This tendency will be stronger, the more irreconcilable the conflict is perceived to be.
2. If threat is used in an attempt to intimidate another, the threatened person (if he considers himself to be of equal or superior status) will feel hostility toward the threatener and will tend to respond with counterthreat and/or increased resistance to yield-

---

[2] Schelling, in a series of stimulating papers on bargaining (1957, 1958), has also stressed the "mixed motive" character of bargaining situations and has analyzed some of the cognitive factors which determine agreements.

[3] The game was conceived and originated by the senior author; the junior author designed and constructed the apparatus employed in these experiments. We gratefully acknowledge the expert advice of R. E. Kudlick in the design of the electrical circuitry employed.

ing. We qualify this assumption by stating that the tendency to resist will be greater, the greater the perceived probability and magnitude of detriment to the other and the lesser the perceived probability and magnitude of detriment to the potential resistor from the anticipated resistance to yielding.

The second assumption is based upon the view that to allow oneself to be intimidated, particularly by someone who does not have the right to expect deferential behavior, is (when resistance is not seen to be suicidal or useless) to suffer a loss of social face and, hence, of self-esteem; and that the culturally defined way of maintaining self-esteem in the face of attempted intimidation is to engage in a contest for supremacy *vis-à-vis* the power to intimidate or, minimally, to resist intimidation. Thus, in effect, it can be seen that the use of threat (and if it is available to be used, there will be a tendency to use it) should strengthen the competitive interests of the bargainers in relationship to one another by introducing or enhancing the competitive struggle for self-esteem. Hence, from Proposition 1, it follows that the availability of a means of threat should make it more difficult for the bargainers to reach agreement (providing that the threatened person has some means of resisting the threat). The preceding statement is relevant to the comparison of both of our experimental conditions (described below) of threat, *bilateral* and *unilateral,* with our experimental condition of *nonthreat.* We are hypothesizing that a bargaining agreement is more likely to be achieved when neither party can threaten the other, than when one or both parties can threaten the other.

It is relevant now to compare the situations of bilateral threat and unilateral threat. For several reasons, it seems likely that a situation of bilateral threat is less conducive to agreement than is a condition of unilateral threat. First, the sheer likelihood that a threat will be made is greater when two people rather than one have the means of making the threat. Secondly, once a threat is made in the bilateral case, it is likely to evoke counterthreat. Withdrawal of threat in the face of counterthreat probably involves more loss of face (for reasons

analogous to those discussed above in relation to yielding to intimidation) than does withdrawal of threat in the face of resistance to threat. Finally, in the unilateral case, although the person without the threat potential can resist and not yield to the threat, his position *vis-à-vis* the other is not so strong as the position of the threatened person in the bilateral case. In the unilateral case, the threatened person may have a worse outcome than the other whether he resists or yields; while in the bilateral case, the threatened person is sure to have a worse outcome if he yields but he may insure that he does not have a worse outcome if he does not yield.

Method

Subjects (Ss) were asked to imagine that they were in charge of a trucking company, carrying merchandise over a road to a destination. For each trip they completed they made $.60, minus their operating expenses. Operating expenses were calculated at the rate of one cent per second. So, for example, if it took thirty-seven seconds to complete a particular trip, the player's profit would be $.60 − $.37 or a net profit of $.23 for that particular trip.

Each subject was assigned a name, Acme or Bolt. As the "road map" (see Figure 1) indicates, both players start from separate points and go to separate destinations. At one point their paths coincide. This is the section of road labeled "one-lane road." This section of road is only one lane wide; this means that two trucks, heading in opposite directions, could not pass each other. If one backs up the other can go forward,

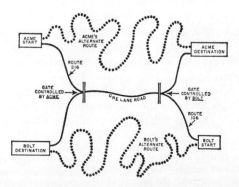

Fig. 1. Subject's road map.

or both can back up, or both can sit there head-on without moving.

There is another way for each subject to reach the destination on the map and this is labeled the "alternate route." The two players' paths do not cross on this route, but the alternate is 56 per cent longer than the main route. Subjects were told that they could expect to lose at least $.10 each time they used the alternate route.

At either end of the one-lane section there is a gate which is under the control of the player to whose starting point it is closest. By closing the gate, one player can prevent the other from traveling over that section of the main route. It is the use of the gate which we will call the threat potential in this game. In the bilateral threat potential condition (*Two Gates*) both players had gates under their control. In a sec-

impulse counter which was pulsed by a recycling timer. When the S wanted to move her truck forward she threw a key which closed a circuit pulsing the "add" coil of the impulse counter which was mounted on her control panel. As the counter cumulated, the S was able to determine her "position" by relating the number on her counter to reference numbers which had been written in on her "road map." Similarly, when she wished to reverse, she would throw a switch which activated the "subtract" coil of her counter, thus subtracting from the total on the counter each time the timer cycled.

S's counter was connected in parallel to counters on the other S's panel and on E's panel. Thus each player had two counters on her panel, one representing her own position and the other representing the other

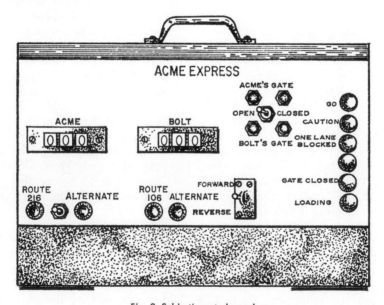

Fig. 2. Subject's control panel.

ond condition of unilateral threat (*One Gate*) Acme had control of a gate but Bolt did not. In a third condition (*No Gates*) neither player controlled a gate.

Subjects played the game seated in separate booths positioned so that they could not see each other but both could see the experimenter. Each S had a "control panel" mounted on a 12" × 18" × 12" sloping-front cabinet (see Figure 2). The apparatus consisted essentially of a reversible

player's. Provision was made in construction of the apparatus to cut the "other player's" counter out of the circuit, so that each S knew only the position of her own truck. This was done in the present experiments.

The only time one player definitely knew the other player's position was when they had met head-on on the one-way section of road. This was indicated by a traffic light mounted on the panel. When this light was on, neither player could move forward un-less the other moved back. The gates were controlled by toggle switches; panel-mounted indicator lights showed, for both subjects, whether each gate was open or closed.

The following "rules of the game" were stated to the Ss:

1. A player who started out on one route and wished to switch to the other route could do so only after first reversing and going back to the start position. Direct transfer from one route to the other was not permitted ex-cept at the start position.
2. In the conditions where Ss had gates, they were permitted to close the gates only when they were traveling on the main route. (That is, they were not permitted to close the gate while on the alternate route or after having reached their destinations.) However, Ss were permitted to open their gates at any point in the game.

Ss were taken through a number of prac-tice exercises to familiarize them with the game. In the first trial they were made to meet head-on on the one-lane path; Acme was then told to back up until she was just off the one-lane path and Bolt was told to go forward. After Bolt had gone through the one-lane path, Acme was told to go forward. Each continued going forward un-til each arrived at her destination. The second practice trial was the same as the first except that Bolt rather than Acme backed up after meeting head-on. In the next practice trial, one of the players was made to wait just before the one-way path while the other traversed it and then was allowed to continue. In the next practice trial, one player was made to take the al-ternate route and the other was made to take the main route. Finally, in the Bilat-eral and Unilateral Threat conditions the use of the gate was illustrated (by having the player get on the main route, close the gate, and then go back and take the alter-nate route). The Ss were told explicitly with emphasis that they did *not* have to use the gate. Before each trial in the game the gate or gates were in the open position.

The instructions stressed an individual-istic motivational orientation. Ss were told to try to earn as much money for them-selves as possible and to have no interest in whether the other player made money or lost money. They were given $4.00 in poker chips to represent their working capital and told that after each trial they would be given "money" if they made a profit or that "money" would be taken from them if they lost (i.e., took more than 60 seconds to complete their trip). The profit or loss of each S was announced so that both Ss could hear the announcement after each trial. Each pair of subjects played a total of twenty trials; on all trials, they started off together. In other words, each trial pre-sented a repetition of the same bargaining problem. In cases where subjects lost their working capital before the twenty trials were completed, additional chips were given them. Subjects were aware that their mone-tary winnings and losses were to be imagi-nary and that no money would change hands as a result of the experiment.

Sixteen pairs of subjects were used in each of the three experimental conditions. The Ss were female clerical and supervisory personnel of the New Jersey Bell Tele-phone Company who volunteered to partici-pate during their working day.[4] Their ages ranged from 20 to 39, with a mean of 26.2. All were naive to the purpose of the ex-periment. By staggering the arrival times and choosing girls from different locations, we were able to insure that our subjects did not know with whom they were playing.

Results[5]

The best single measure of the difficulty experienced by the bargainers in reaching an agreement is the sum of each pair's profits (or losses) on a given trial. The higher the sum of the payoffs to the two players on a given trial, the less time it took them to arrive at a procedure for shar-ing the one-lane path of the main route. (It was, of course, possible for one or both of the players to decide to take the alternate route so as to avoid a protracted stalemate during the process of bargaining. This,

[4] We are indebted to the New Jersey Bell Telephone Company for their cooperation in pro-viding subjects and facilities for this experiment.
[5] We are indebted to M. J. R. Healy for sug-gestions concerning the statistical analysis of these data.

however, always resulted in at least a $.20 smaller joint payoff if only one player took the alternate route, than an optimally arrived at agreement concerning the use of the one-way path.) Figure 3 presents the medians of the summed payoffs (i.e.,

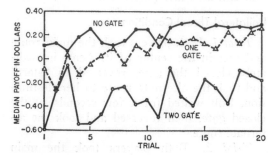

Fig. 3. Median joint payoff (Acme + Bolt) over trials.

Acme's plus Bolt's) for all pairs in each of the three experimental conditions over the twenty trials.[6] These results indicate that agreement was least difficult to arrive at in the No Threat condition, was more difficult to arrive at in the Unilateral Threat condition, and exceedingly difficult or impossible to arrive at in the Bilateral Threat condition. (See also Table 1.)

Figure 4 compares Acme's median profit in the three experimental conditions over the 20 trials; while Figure 5 compares Bolt's profit in the three conditions. (In the Unilateral Threat condition, it was Acme who controlled a gate and Bolt who did not.) It is evident that Bolt's as well as

[6] Medians are used in graphic presentation of our results because the wide variability of means makes inspection cumbersome.

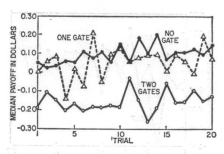

Fig. 4. Acme's median payoff.

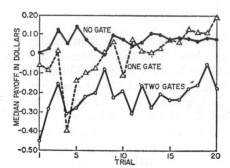

Fig. 5. Bolt's median payoff.

Acme's outcome is somewhat better in the No Threat condition than in the Unilateral Threat condition; Acme's as well as Bolt's outcome is clearly worst in the Bilateral Threat condition. (See Table 1 also.) However, Figure 6 reveals that Acme does somewhat better than Bolt in the Unilateral condition. Thus, if the threat-potential exists within a bargaining relationship it is better to possess it oneself than to have the other party possess it. However, it is even better for neither party to possess it. Moreover, from Figure 5, it is evident that Bolt

TABLE 1

MEAN PAYOFFS SUMMATED OVER THE TWENTY TRIALS

Variable	Means			Statistical Comparisons: p Values[1]			
	(1) No Threat	(2) Unilateral Threat	(3) Bilateral Threat	Over-all	(1) vs. (2)	(1) vs. (2)	(2) vs. (3)
Summed Payoffs							
(Acme + Bolt)	203.31	−405.88	−875.12	0.01	0.01	0.01	0.05
Acme's Payoff	122.44	−118.56	−406.56	0.01	0.10	0.01	0.05
Bolt's Payoff	80.88	−287.31	−468.56	0.01	0.01	0.01	0.20

[1] Evaluation of the significance of over-all variation between conditions is based on an F test with 2 and 45 df. Comparisons between treatments are based on a two-tailed t test.

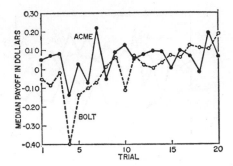

Fig. 6. Acme's and Bolt's median payoff in Unilateral Threat condition.

is better off not having than having a gate even when Acme has a gate: Bolt tends to do better in the Unilateral Threat condition than in the Bilateral Threat condition.

To provide the reader with a more detailed description of what went on during the bargaining game, we present a synopsis of the game for one pair in each of the three experimental treatments.

No Threat Condition

Trial 1. The players met in the center of the one-way section. After some back-and-forth movement Bolt reversed to the end of the one-way section, allowing Acme to pass through, and then proceeded forward herself.

Trial 2. They again met at the center of the one-way path. This time, after moving back and forth deadlocked for some time, Bolt reversed to start and took the alternate route to her destination, thus leaving Acme free to go through on the main route.

Trial 3. The players again met at the center of the one-way path. This time, however, Acme reversed to the beginning of the path, allowing Bolt to go through to her destination. Then Acme was able to proceed forward on the main route.

Trial 5. Both players elected to take the alternate route to their destinations.

Trial 7. Both players took the main route and met in the center. They waited, deadlocked, for a considerable time. Then Acme reversed to the end of the one-way path allowing Bolt to go through, then proceeded through to her destination.

Trials 10 through 20. Acme and Bolt fall into a pattern of alternating who is to go first on the one-way section. There is no deviation from this pattern.

The only other pattern which emerges in this condition is one in which one player dominates the other. That is, one player consistently goes first on the one-way section and the other player consistently yields.

Unilateral Threat Condition

Trial 1. Both players took the main route and met in the center of it. Acme immediately closed the gate, reversed to "start" and took the alternate route to her destination. Bolt waited for a few seconds, at the closed gate, then reversed and took the alternate route.

Trial 2. Both players took the main route and met in the center. After moving back and forth deadlocked for about fifteen seconds, Bolt reversed to the beginning of the one-way path, allowed Acme to pass, and then proceeded forward to her destination.

Trial 3. Both players started out on the main route, meeting in the center. After moving back and forth deadlocked for a while, Acme closed her gate, reversed to "start" and took the alternate route. Bolt, meanwhile, waited at the closed gate. When Acme arrived at her destination she opened the gate, and Bolt went through to complete her trip.

Trial 5. Both players took the main route, meeting at the center of the one-way section. Acme immediately closed her gate, reversed and took the alternate route. Bolt waited at the gate for about ten seconds, then reversed and took the alternate route to her destination.

Trial 10. Both players took the main route and met in the center. Acme closed her gate, reversed and took the alternate route. Bolt remained waiting at the closed gate. After Acme arrived at her destination, she opened the gate and Bolt completed her trip.

Trial 15. Acme took the main route to her destination and Bolt took the alternate route.

Trials 17, 18, 19 and 20. Both players took the main route and met in the center. Bolt waited a few seconds, then reversed to the end of the one-way section allowing Acme to go through. Then Bolt proceeded forward to her destination.

Other typical patterns which developed in this experimental condition included an alternating pattern similar to that described in the No Threat condition, a dominating pattern in which Bolt would select the alternate route leaving Acme free to use the main route unobstructed, and a pattern in which Acme would close her gate and then take the alternate route, also forcing Bolt to take the alternate route.

Bilateral Threat Condition

Trial 1. Acme took the main route and Bolt took the alternate route.

Trial 2. Both players took the main route and met head-on. Bolt closed her gate. Acme waited a few seconds, then closed her gate, reversed to "start," then went forward again to the closed gate. Acme reversed and took the alternate route. Bolt again reversed, then started on the alternate route. Acme opened her gate and Bolt reversed to start and went to her destination on the main route.

Trial 3. Acme took the alternate route to her destination. Bolt took the main route and closed her gate before entering the one-way section.

Trial 5. Both players took the main route and met head-on. After about ten seconds spent backing up and going forward; Acme closed her gate, reversed and took the alternate route. After waiting a few seconds, Bolt did the same.

Trials 8, 9, 10. Both players started out on the main route, immediately closed their gates, reversed to start and took the alternate route to their destinations.

Trial 15. Both players started out on the main route and met head-on. After some jockeying for position, Acme closed her gate, reversed and took the alternate route to her destination. After waiting at the gate for a few seconds, Bolt reversed to start and took the alternate route to her destination.

Trials 19, 20. Both players started out on the main route, immediately closed their gates, reversed to start and took the alternate routes to their destinations.

Other patterns which emerged in the Bilateral Threat condition included alternating first use of the one-way section, one player's dominating the other on first use of the one-way section, and another dominating pattern in which one player consistently took the main route while the other consistently took the alternate route.

Discussion

The results of Experiment I clearly indicate that the availability of a threat potential in our experimental bargaining situation adversely affects the player's ability to reach effective agreements. In terms of our introductory analysis of bargaining as a mixed motive situation (i.e., one in which both competitive and cooperative motivations are acting upon the participants), we can interpret these results as indicating that the existence of threat enhances the competitive aspects of interaction.

These results, we believe, reflect psychological tendencies which are not confined to our bargaining situation: the tendency to use threat (if a means for threatening is available) in an attempt to force the other person to yield when he is seen as an obstruction; the tendency to respond with counter-threat or increased resistance to attempts at intimidation. How general are these tendencies? What are the conditions likely to elicit them? Answers to these questions are necessary before our results can be generalized to other situations. However, we will postpone consideration of the psychological processes which operate in bargaining until we have had an opportunity to examine the results of some further experiments.

EXPERIMENT II

Our discussion thus far has suggested that the psychological factors which operate in our experimental bargaining game are to be found in many real-life bargaining situations. However, it is well to point out an important unique feature of our experimental game: namely, that the bargainers had no opportunity to communicate verbally with one another. Prior research on the role of communication in trust

(Deutsch, 1958, 1960; Loomis, 1959) suggests that the opportunity for communication would ameliorate the difficulty bargainers experience in reaching agreement. This possibility was expressed spontaneously by a number of our subjects in a post-experimental interview. It should be noted, however, that the same research cited above (Deutsch, 1960) indicates that communication may not be effective between competitively oriented bargainers.

To test the effect of communication upon bargaining, we undertook an experiment in which subjects were permitted to talk over an intercom hookup. It was further decided to differentiate Bilateral Communication (both parties permitted to talk) from Unilateral Communication (only one party is permitted to talk).

Method

The experimental apparatus, instructions to the Ss and training procedures here were the same as described in Experiment I. In addition, each S was equipped with a headset (earphones and microphone) hooked into an intercom system. The intercom was so constructed that E could control the direction of Ss' communication. This was necessary so that in the Unilateral Communication condition one S was prevented from talking to the other, but both were able to talk to E when necessary. A filter, built into the intercom's amplification system, distorted voice quality sufficiently to make it unlikely that Ss would recognize one another's voices even if they were previously acquainted, without significantly impairing intelligibility.[7] Ss received the following instructions on communication:

> During the game, when your trucks are en route, you may communicate with each other . . . (Here Ss received instructions on operating the intercom system) . . . In talking to the other player you may say anything you want; or if you don't want to talk you don't have to. You may talk about the game, about what you'd like to happen in the game, what you're going to do, what you'd like the other player to do, or anything else that comes to mind. What you talk about—

[7] In only one group did an S recognize her partner's voice; this group was discarded.

or whether you decide to talk or not—is up to you.

These instructions were modified in the Unilateral Communication condition to indicate that only one player (Acme) would be permitted to talk. Communication was not allowed between trials; only during the actual "trip" were Ss permitted to talk.

The two levels of our communication variable (bilateral and unilateral) were combined with the three levels of threat employed in the previous study to produce a 2×3 factorial experiment. It was necessary to employ such a design to test the possibility that communication might be differentially effective under different conditions of threat.

Five pairs of Ss were entered randomly into each of six treatment conditions. All were female clerical and secretarial employees of the Bell Telephone Laboratories and were, in most respects, comparable to the New Jersey Bell Telephone employees used in Experiment I. Again, Ss were selected from different work areas and arrival times were staggered to prevent Ss from knowing their partner's identity.

Results

An analysis of variance of Experiment II indicates that our communication variable had no effect on the players' ability to reach effective agreements; however the "threat" variable, as in the first experiment, had a significant effect. It should also be noted that the results of this experiment are not significantly different from the findings of Experiment I, where no communication was permitted. For economy of presentation these cross-experiment comparisons will be included with the results of Experiment III below.

Product-moment correlations were computed between frequency of communication for each pair (the number of trials out of twenty in which one or both Ss spoke) and joint payoff. Both over-all and within the threat conditions no significant relation was observed between frequency of communication and payoff. As will be discussed below, only a minimum of communication did occur and quite likely frequency of communication in this situation was determined by characteristics of the Ss which were irrelevant to the achievement of agreement in the bargaining situation.

An additional finding of interest: it will be recalled that in the Unilateral Threat condition Acme was the player possessing the threat potential. Similarly, in the Unilateral Communication condition, it was Acme who was allowed to talk. To ascertain the effect of this double asymmetry we ran an additional five pairs of Ss in a Unilateral Threat–Unilateral Communication condition in which Bolt was given the opportunity to talk, while Acme still possessed the threat potential. A comparison of this group with the standard Unilateral Threat–Unilateral Communication condition revealed no significant differences between them.

We can also examine the gross frequency of talking in the three threat conditions. Each pair of Ss received a score based upon the number of trials on which one or both players spoke to the other. The mean frequency of communication in the three threat conditions is presented in Table 2a. Most talking occurs in the No Threat condition; the rate of talking in the Unilateral and Bi-

lateral Threat conditions is approximately equal. However, these differences, when tested by a one-way analysis of variance, are not large enough to permit a rejection of the null hypothesis.

If we examine frequency of talking in the Unilateral vs. Bilateral Communication conditions we find that, in accordance with expectation, significantly more talk occurs in the bilateral condition ($F = 31.04$, with 1 and 38 d.f.; $p < 0.001$). These means are presented in Table 2b.

We had intended to tape-record our Ss' communications to preserve them for a subsequent content analysis. Unfortunately, breakdowns of the recording equipment and electrical distortions introduced by the bargaining game apparatus rendered this impossible. Thus, except for the impressions gained by E who monitored all communication, these data are lost and any discussion of communication content must necessarily be impressionistic. Modifications of the equipment are presently under way which will correct these difficulties.

In a post-experimental questionnaire and interview we questioned Ss closely in an attempt to ascertain the reason for the paucity of communication. Most of our Ss were at a loss to explain why they did not talk, although almost all acknowledged that they were less than normally talkative. With some probing on E's part, a frequent comment concerned "the difficulty of talking to someone you don't know." Possibly, the communication process normally involves a system of reciprocal expectations by which a speaker has some idea of the effect his words will have on a listener. Even in an encounter between strangers these expectations may be partly derived from such visual cues as appearance, dress, facial expression, etc. All of these cues were absent in the communication between our Ss. Interestingly enough, when Ss were introduced after the experimental session, a great deal of spontaneous chatter ensued. And this was true even of Ss who had not talked at all during the experimental session.

TABLE 2

Frequency of Talking

Table 2a

Frequency of Talking in the Three Threat Conditions

	No Threat	Unilateral Threat	Bilateral Threat
Mean number of trials on which talking occurred	5.7	3.9	3.3

Table 2b

Frequency of Talking in the Bilateral vs. Unilateral Communication Conditions

	Bilateral Communication	Unilateral Communication
Mean number of trials on which talking occurred	5.8	2.7

Discussion

It is obvious from the results of Experiment II that the opportunity to communi-

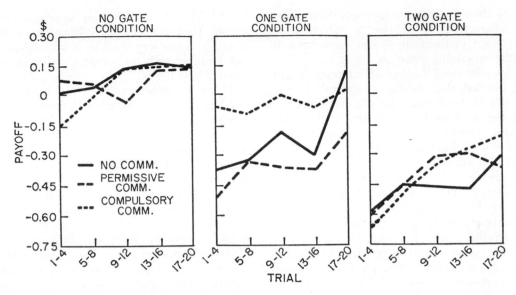

Fig. 7. Mean joint payoffs (Acme + Bolt) in the communication conditions across the three threat conditions.

cate does not necessarily result in an amelioration of conflict in our experimental bargaining situation. Indeed, it should be stated that the *opportunity* to communicate does not necessarily result in communication at all. Actually, little communication occurred; most of our Ss did not utilize their opportunity to communicate.

The results of Experiment II are in line with the finding of Deutsch (1960). Apparently the competitive orientation induced by the threat potential in our situation was sufficiently strong to overcome any possible ameliorating effects of communication. In the No Threat condition, where competitiveness is at a minimum, the advantage gained by the use of communication to coordinate effort was offset by the time consumed by talking. It would seem that the coordination problem posed for the Ss by our experimental game was sufficiently simple to be solvable without communication, given the existence of an appropriate motivational orientation. This will be considered further in our discussion of Experiment III.

EXPERIMENT III

Any straightforward interpretation of the effects of communication upon interpersonal bargaining is difficult to make based on the

results of Experiment II. This is particularly true in view of the fact that the majority of our Ss did not use the opportunity to communicate that was presented to them. Thus, one may speculate that had our Ss in fact communicated, the outcome of Experiment II might have been quite different.

Studies of collective bargaining procedures suggest one of their important values lies in their ability to prevent disputants from breaking off communication (Douglas, 1958). Newcomb (1948) has used the term "autistic hostility" to denote a situation in which a breakdown, or absence, of communication leads to the exacerbation of interpersonal conflict. Rapoport (1960) has stressed the importance of continued communication in resolving international conflict.

Experiment III was undertaken to test the effect of forced, or compulsory, communication.

Method

The experimental apparatus, instructions to the Ss, and training procedures employed here were the same as in Experiment II. Ss received the following instructions on communication (the italicized portions are those which differ from the instructions used in Experiment II):

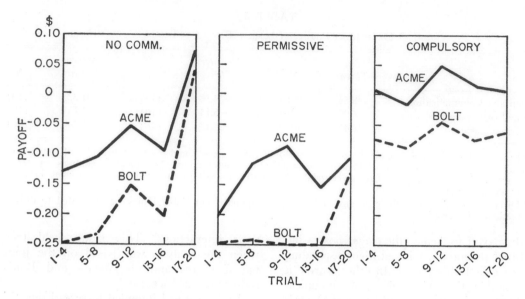

Fig. 8. Acme's and Bolt's mean payoffs in the unilateral threat condition across the three communication conditions.

During the game, when your trucks are en route, you *both will be required* to communicate with each other . . . (Here *S*s received instructions on operating the intercom system) . . . In talking to the other player you may say anything you want. You may talk about the game, about what you'd like to happen in the game, what you're going to do, what you'd like the other player to do, or anything else that comes to mind. What you talk about is up to you. *But remember, you must say something to the other player on every trip.*

In Experiment III only a Bilateral Communication condition was run, again under three levels of threat potential. On trials where either *S* failed to talk, they were reminded by *E* at the conclusion of the trial of the requirement that they talk to the other player on every trial. In no group was it necessary to make this reminder on more than four trials.

Ten pairs of *S*s were entered randomly into each of the three treatment conditions. *S*s were drawn from the same pool used in Experiment II; however, none of the *S*s in this experiment had served in the previous one.

Results

We will refer to the form of communication utilized in Experiment II as Permis-

sive Communication; communication in Experiment III will be called Compulsory Communication; in Experiment I, No Communication was involved. Since in Experiment II no differences were found between our Bilateral and Unilateral Communication treatments, we have combined these two categories to increase the *N* of the Permissive Communication group.

Figure 7 presents the mean joint payoffs (summarized as the averages of four-trial blocks for convenience) for all three experiments. (See also Table 3.) The effectiveness of the Compulsory Communication variable is seen in comparison of groups in the Unilateral Threat condition. Here alone, of all the conditions in which gates are present, does performance approach that of *S*s in the No Threat condition. In the Bilateral Threat condition the competitive motivation present seems too great to be overcome, even by the Compulsory Communication treatment. As was noted above, in the No Threat condition coordination was sufficiently simple that communication failed to produce any visible effect.

We can examine more closely performance in the Unilateral Threat condition. For example, it is possible that the effectiveness of Compulsory Communication as reflected in the joint payoff data is due to an increase

TABLE 3

MEAN JOINT PAYOFFS (ACME + BOLT) PER TRIAL[1]

	No Threat	N	Unilateral Threat	N	Bilateral Threat	N
Permissive Communication	8.54	(10)	−34.58	(15)	−41.32	(10)
Compulsory Communication	6.09	(10)	−5.14	(10)	−41.73	(10)
No Communication*	10.41	(16)	−22.13	(16)	−47.44	(16)

[1] In an analysis of variance, significant ($p < 0.01$) F ratios were found for the "threat" and "communication" main effects and for the "threat × communication" interaction. Additionally, analysis of trend discloses a significant linear effect over trials ($p < 0.01$) for all groups, with no differences between group trends present.

* Discrepancies between these means and means computed from Table 1 may be attributed to different methods of averaging.

in the payoff to Acme (the player possessing a threat potential), without a corresponding increase in Bolt's payoff. In other words, it is possible that Compulsory Communication acts to increase the advantaged player's bargaining power in an asymmetrical situation. Figure 8 breaks down the payoffs of Acme and Bolt in the three communication conditions. Although in all conditions Acme does better than Bolt, the margin of discrepancy does not vary substantially in the three conditions.[8]

An analysis of trend over trials (Grant, 1956) was performed on the data of the three experiments. Over-all, a significant linear component was present, as Figure 7 indicates; however, there were no differences in trend resulting from a partitioning of Ss by the two independent variables or

[8] A one-way analysis of variance of the algebraic difference in payoff (Acme-Bolt) yields a nonsignificant F ratio.

their interactions. This result held true when the analysis was based on the joint payoff scores and on Acme's and Bolt's scores analyzed separately.

Again, we had intended to record our Ss' conversations for later content analysis. The same technical difficulties discussed above continued to cause difficulty. However, in Experiment III we were somewhat more successful in obtaining complete recordings of a small number of our Ss' conversations. In order to give the reader some notion of the sort of conversations which did take place we present below a transcript for selected trials of three pairs of Ss, one in each of the threat conditions, which were judged to be relatively typical. The numbers in parentheses below each conversation represent the payoff to each player on that trial (in imaginary dollars). Positive numbers represent winnings and negative numbers are losses.

NO THREAT CONDITION

Trial	Acme	Bolt
1	I'll stop at 5 so you can go through first . . . I'm backing up for you. (0.01)	(0.19)
2	Okay, wait 6 seconds because I had to back up last time. (0.26)	I'll wait for you at 5. (0.10)
6	(0.27)	I'll wait at 5 this time. (0.09)
7	I'll wait for you at 4 or 5. We might as well alternate 'cause I don't see how we'll make any money any other way. (0.03)	Okay, that's true. (0.25)

Trial	Acme	Bolt
12	Is it my turn to wait for you?	I'll wait for you this time at 5.
	Okay, I couldn't remember whose turn it was. (counting) 13, 14, 15.	Let me know when you reach 15.
	(0.27)	(0.09)
13	I'll wait for you.	All right. I'll let you know at 15.
	Okay. I didn't go on break this morning and boy, am I hungry!	You can start now.
	I'll make 9 cents and you'll make 27. I started a few seconds too late.	
	(0.07)	(0.26)
16		I'll wait at 5 this time and let me know at 13 also.
	Okay. I'll count up so you know. 13, 14, 15.	Okay. Thank you.
	There's no way to make money except by compromising this way.	No, that's the only way and it comes out even that way, usually.
	Except for the first few times.	Yuh.
	(0.27)	(0.09)
17	I'll wait at 5.	Okay. You'll make 9 cents, I'll make 27.
	Yeah. Are you from around here?	Yuh, Summit [a local town]. . . . (counting) 13, 14, 15.
	Thank you. I won't ask you any more because I don't know you.	Okay. No.
	(0.08)	(0.26)
20		I'll wait for you this time.
	Okay. Do you have a watch on?	Yeah.
	What time is it?	Twenty-five after eleven. What number are you on now?
	Twelve.	Okay (counting), 13, 14.
	(counting) 14, 15. You're such a cooperative partner.	What?
	Nice working for such a cooperative partner.	Oh, nice to work with you, too.
	(0.26)	(0.09)

UNILATERAL THREAT CONDITION

Trial	Acme	Bolt
1	Do you intend to take the main route?	Um . . . I'm taking it, but I've stopped. Are you going to close the gate?
	I've closed it already. I'm going to open it.	You finish yet?
	Yes, I have.	
	(0.26)	(0.05)
2		Are you on the main road?
	Yes, I am. I think we're going to meet again. I guess we've met, uh, I'm going to back up.	Where are you?
	I'm backing up	What number are you on?

Trial	Acme	Bolt
	Now I'm on 4.	Oh, all right. I'll go forward.
	I think we met again.	
	(−0.17)	(0.00)
5	My gate's closed.	Uh huh. I noticed.
	It's open now. Oh, we met?	Yes.
	I'm going to reverse.	We met?
	Yes.	Go now.
	I can go?	We'll try.
	No.	No? (laughs)
	Wait a sec. I'll back up some more. Okay. You must almost be there.	
	(−0.12)	(0.06)
6	My gate's closed.	Uh huh. Are you gonna leave it closed?
	No, it's open now. You go . . . . Oh. Oh, we met.	I'll go back.
	Okay.	Try it now.
	Okay, I'm there already.	
	(0.21)	(−0.03)
9	I'll back up.	Okay. I'm there.
	Oh, you're there? You beat me by a hair. I'm only halfway there.	I keep forgetting to push this thing down [probably a reference to switch on intercom].
	Oh.	
	(−0.06)	(0.11)
10	My gate's closed.	Are you there?
	Yes.	All right. You beat me by seven, eight.
	(0.26)	(0.10)
13		Are you there?
	Yeah.	Are you gonna . . . oh, it's open.
	It's open.	
	(0.26)	(0.05)
14	I'll back up.	Try going forward.
	Okay. No.	Not yet?
	You keep coming now.	What, go forward?
	Yeah.	On 15, 16, okay.
	I wonder how many times we're going to play this.	
	(−0.07)	(0.09)
19		Are you going back?
	Yes, are you going forward?	Yes.

Trial	Acme	Bolt
	I'm back. There.	Um, no.
	Oh.	
	(0.01)	(0.18)

Trial	Acme	Bolt
20		You going forward?
	Uh huh.	What number are you on?
	(counting) 10, 11.	10?
	Okay.	You there?
	Yeah, no, we're blocked.	Oh, I'll go back.
	Are you stopped or going back?	I'm going forward.
	Oh, now you're going forward. Oh, I guess we're okay now.	I'm on 9; are you there?
	Yeah.	I think I'm glad I'm not a truck driver.
	(0.20)	(−0.01)

BILATERAL THREAT CONDITION

Trial	Acme	Bolt
1	You decide on your route?	I'm taking the main route.
	I am, too.	Oh, we're stopped. What happens now?
	What did you say?	Did you stop?
	Yeah, the lane is blocked completely.	Well, who's going to back up?
	Well, I don't know. You gonna back up this time?	All right. I'll back up.
	All right.	Your gate is locked.
	I know it's locked.	That wasn't very fair.
	Anything's fair.	Well, what are you going to do?
	I don't have to do anything. I'm going to my destination.	This is not funny.
	(laughs)	At your destination?
	No!	I'll never reach mine at this point.
	I've reached mine.	Well?
	Sit tight.	Planned your next route?
	No, have you?	I've got some ideas.
	Thanks a lot.	I'm getting there slowly but surely.
	(laughs)	
	(−0.95)	(−1.87)

Trial	Acme	Bolt
2		I've got my plan.
	I've got mine, too.	How're you doing?
	Fine. How are you doing?	Oh, I'm fine. I'm not getting any place fast, though.

Trial	Acme	Bolt
	This doesn't move very quick.	Slow trucking.
	That makes two of us.	Where are you now?
	Twenty-seven [on alternate route]. Where are you?	Twenty-four (both laugh). Looks like we both don't trust each other. I'll lose money this game.
	(−0.44)	(−0.54)
5	We're stopped. What are we going to do now?	Oh, I backed up the first time. Now it's your turn.
	All right. What are you going to do?	I'm going to take the alternate route.
	Go right ahead.	Are you going to open your gate?
	No.	What are you going to do now?
	I've got to at least make the loss even.	I hear only one ticking [a reference to noise made by the apparatus].
	(−1.02)	(−0.75)
7		You've got yours closed, too.
	We're both stopped.	Are you going to open your gate?
	Why should I?	I'll do the same next time.
	Is that a threat?	You playing tricks?
	No.	I'll lose five dollars this trip because of you.
	(−1.33)	(−0.75)
9	I see you've got your gate closed. What route are you on?	Why should I tell you?
	Okay, if that's the way you want to play.	No, I'll tell you where I am if you tell me where you are.
	I asked you first.	So am I [sic]. . . . At 17. . . . How far are you?
	I don't believe you.	Have it your way.
	(−1.33)	(−0.75)
13	(Unintelligible)	You had yours closed.
	I think that's my business.	Why don't you open your gate?
	Don't have time.	I'm not getting any place.
	(−0.60)	(−0.23)
14	You have yours shut, too.	What?
	You never let me through.	Let's both open our gates as long as we're going the other way.
	I know you are (sarcastically).	
	(−0.20)	(−0.22)
18	What route are you taking?	(no answer)
	I think we both are going bankrupt.	They [sic] just don't trust each other, right?
	(−0.39)	(−0.50)
20		Your gate's closed again.
	So is yours, so that means you must have taken the alternate route.	Why? What gives you that idea?

Trial	Acme	Bolt
	Well, you wouldn't be crazy enough to go to the main route with my gate closed.	Well, maybe I think I can persuade you to open it.
	You know better than that.	Do I? . . . I get the use of these gates all mixed up. I shut mine when I don't want to and, oh, . . .
	If I go into the trucking business I'm not going to have gates.	
	(−0.21)	(−0.22)

Discussion

In the introduction, we presented our view of bargaining as a situation in which both cooperative and competitive tendencies are present and acting upon the individual. From this point of view, it is relevant to inquire as to the conditions under which a stable agreement of any form will develop. However, implicit in most models of bargaining (e.g., Zeuthen, 1930; Stone, 1958; Cervin, 1961; Suppes and Carlsmith, 1961) is the assumption that the cooperative interests of the bargainers will be sufficiently strong to insure that some form of mutually satisfactory agreement will be reached. For this reason, such models have focused upon the form of the agreement reached by the bargainers. Siegel and Fouraker (1960) report a series of bargaining experiments quite different in structure from ours in which only one of many pairs of subjects was unable to reach agreement. Siegel and Fouraker explain this rather startling statistic as follows:

> Apparently the disruptive forces which lead to the rupture of some negotiations were at least partially controlled in our sessions. . . .
> Some negotiations collapse when one party becomes incensed at the other, and henceforth strives to maximize his opponent's displeasure rather than his own satisfaction. . . . Since it is difficult to transmit insults by means of quantitative bids, such disequilibrating behavior was not induced in the present studies. If subjects were allowed more latitude in their communications and interactions, the possibility of an affront—offense—punitive behavior sequence might be increased [p. 100].

In our experimental bargaining situation, the availability of threat clearly made it more difficult for bargainers to reach a mutually profitable agreement. Indeed, Bilateral Threat presents a situation so conflict-fraught that no amount of communication seems to have an ameliorating effect. These tendencies we believe are not confined to our experimental situation. The "affront—offense—punitive behavior sequence" to which Siegel and Fouraker refer, and which we have observed in our experiment, are common attributes of everyday interpersonal conflict. The processess which underlie them have long been of interest to social scientists and an imposing set of theoretical constructs have been employed to explain them.

Dollard et al. (1939) have cited a variety of evidence to support the view that aggression (i.e., the use of threat) is a common reaction to a person who is seen as the agent of frustration. There seems to be little reason to doubt that the use of threat is a frequent reaction to interpersonal impasses. However, everyday observation indicates that threat does not inevitably occur when there is an interpersonal impasse. We would speculate that it is most likely to occur when the threatener has no positive interest in the other person's welfare (he is either egocentrically or competitively related to the other); when the threatener believes that the other has no positive interest in his welfare; and when the threatener anticipates either that his threat will be effective or, if ineffective, will not worsen his situation because he expects the worst to happen if he does not use this threat. We suggest that these conditions were operative in our experiment; the subjects were either egocentrically or competitively oriented to one another[9] and they felt that they would not be worse off by the use of threat.

Everyday observation suggests that the tendency to respond with counterthreat or increased resistance to attempts at intimidation is also a common occurrence. It is our belief that the introduction of threat into a bargaining situation affects the meaning of yielding. Although we have no data to support this directly, we will attempt to justify it on the basis of some additional assumptions.

Goffman (1955) has pointed out the pervasive significance of "face" in the maintenance of the social order. In this view, self-esteem is a socially validated system which grows out of the acceptance by others of the claim for deference, prestige and recognition which one presents in one's behavior toward others. Thus, the rejection of such a claim would be perceived (by the recipient) as directed against his self-esteem and one which, in order to maintain the integrity of his self-esteem system, he must react against rather than accept.

One may view the behavior of our subjects as an attempt to make claims upon the other; an attempt to develop a set of shared expectations as to what each was entitled to. Why then did the subjects' reactions differ so markedly as a function of the availability of threat? The explanation for this lies, we believe, in the cultural interpretation of yielding (to a peer or subordinate) under duress, as compared to giving in without duress. The former, we believe, is perceived as a negatively valued form of behavior, with negative implications for the self-image of the individual who so behaves. At least partly, this is so because the locus of causality is perceived to be outside the voluntary control of the individual. No such evaluation, however, need be placed on the behavior of one who "gives in" in a situation where no threat or duress is a factor. Rather, we should expect the culturally defined evaluation of such an individual's be-

havior to be one of "reasonableness" or "maturity." Again, this may be because the cause of the individual's behavior is perceived to lie within the individual.

One special feature of our experimental game is worthy of note: the passage of time, without coming to an agreement, is costly to the players. There are, of course, bargaining situations in which the lack of agreement may simply preserve the *status quo* without any worsening of the bargainers' respective positions. This is the case in the typical bilateral monopoly case, where the buyer and seller are unable to agree upon a price (e.g., see Siegel and Fouraker, 1960; Cervin, 1961). In other sorts of bargaining situations, however (e.g., labor-management negotiations during a strike; inter-nation negotiations during an expensive cold war), the passage of time may play an important role. In our experiment, we received the impression that the meaning of time changed as time passed without the bargainers reaching an agreement. Initially, the passage of time seemed to pressure the players to come to an agreement before their costs mounted sufficiently to destroy their profit. With the continued passage of time, however, their mounting losses strengthened their resolution not to yield to the other player. They comment: "I've lost so much, I'll be damned if I give in now. At least I'll have the satisfaction of doing better than she does." The mounting losses and continued deadlock seemed to change the game from a mixed motive into a predominantly competitive situation.

The results of Experiments II and III justify, we believe, a reconsideration of the role of communication in the bargaining process. Typically, communication is perceived as a means whereby the bargainers coordinate effort (e.g., exchange bids, indicate positions, etc.). Usually, little emphasis is given to interaction of communication with motivational orientation. Certainly the coordination function of communication is important. However, as Siegel and Fouraker (1960) point out, free communication may also be used to convey information (e.g., threats, insults, etc.) which may intensify the competitive aspects of the situation.

---

[9] A post-experimental questionnaire indicated that, in all three experimental conditions, the Ss were most strongly motivated to win money, next most strongly motivated to do better than the other player, next most motivated to "have fun," and were very little or not at all motivated to help the other player.

It should be emphasized here that the "solution" of our bargaining problem (i.e., alternating first use of the one-lane section of the main route) is a simple and rather obvious one. Indeed, the sort of coordination of effort required by the game is sufficiently simple to be readily achievable without the aid of communication. (Note that Ss in the No Threat–No Communication conditions did as well as Ss in the two No Threat conditions with communication.) More important than this coordinating function, however, is the capacity of communication to expedite the development of agreements. In this context, agreements serve a function similar to that ascribed by Thibaut and Kelley to the social norm; that is, ". . . they serve as substitutes for the exercise of personal influence and produce more economically and efficiently certain consequences otherwise dependent upon personal influence processes" (Thibaut and Kelley, 1959, p. 130). Effective communication, by this line of reasoning, would be aimed at the development of agreements or, to state it another way, at a resolution of the competitive orientation which produces conflict in the bargaining situation.

One must grant that our Ss were relatively unsophisticated in the techniques of developing agreements under the stress of competition. Possibly persons who deal regularly with problems of conflict resolution (e.g., marriage counselors, labor-management arbitrators, diplomats, etc.) would have little difficulty in reaching agreement, even under our Bilateral Threat condition.

Another barrier to effective communication lies in the reticence of our Ss. As we noted above, our Ss found talking to an unknown partner a strange and rather uncomfortable experience. This factor alone would limit the possibility of any communication, let alone communication which was effective.

The studies reported here are part of an ongoing program of research on the factors affecting interpersonal bargaining. In an experiment presently under way, we are attempting to develop communication procedures which will be effective in ameliorating conflict in the Bilateral Threat condition. Additionally, in projected studies we intend to investigate the effect of other structural factors on bargaining behavior.

It is, of course, hazardous to generalize from a set of laboratory experiments to the problems of the real world. But our experiments and the theoretical ideas which underlie them can perhaps serve to emphasize some notions which, otherwise, have some intrinsic plausibility. In brief, these are the following: (1) There is more safety in cooperative than in competitive coexistence. (2) The mere existence of channels of communication is no guarantee that communication will indeed take place; and the greater the competitive orientation of the parties vis-à-vis each other, the less likely will they be to use such channels as do exist. (3) Where barriers to communication exist, a situation in which the parties are compelled to communicate will be more effective than one in which the choice to talk or not is put on a voluntary basis. (4) If the bargainers' primary orientation is competitive, communication which is not directed at changing this orientation is unlikely to be effective. (5) It is dangerous for bargainers to have weapons at their disposal. (6) Possibly, it is more dangerous for a bargainer to have the capacity to retaliate in kind than for him not to have this capacity, when the other bargainer has a weapon. This last statement assumes that the one who yields has more of his values preserved by accepting the agreement preferred by the other than by extended conflict. Of course, in some bargaining situations in the real world the loss incurred by yielding may exceed the loss due to extended conflict.

REFERENCES

Cervin, V. B. and Henderson, G. P. Statistical theory of persuasion. *Psychological Review,* 68 (1961), 157–66.

Deutsch, M. A theory of cooperation and competition. *Human Relations,* 2 (1949), 129–52.

———. Trust and suspicion. *The Journal of Conflict Resolution,* 2 (1958), 265–79.

———. The effect of motivational orientation upon trust and suspicion. *Human Relations,* 13 (1960), 123–40.

Deutsch, M. and Krauss, R. M. The effect of threat upon interpersonal bargaining. *Journal of Abnormal and Social Psychology,* 61 (1960), 181–9.

Dollard, J. *et al. Frustration and Aggression.* New Haven, Conn.: Yale University Press, 1939.

Douglas, A. Peaceful settlement of industrial and intergroup disputes. *The Journal of Conflict Resolution,* 1 (1957), 69–81.

Goffman, E. On face-work. *Psychiatry,* 18 (1955), 213–31.

Grant, D. A. Analysis of variance tests in the analysis and comparison of curves. *Psychological Bulletin,* 53 (1956), 141–54.

Loomis, J. L. Communication, the development of trust and cooperative behavior. *Human Relations,* 12 (1959), 305–15.

Newcomb, T. R. Autistic hostility and social reality, *ibid.,* 1 (1947), 69–86.

Rapoport, A. *Fights, Games, and Debates.* Ann Arbor, Mich.: University of Michigan Press, 1960.

Schelling, T. C. Bargaining, communication and limited war. *The Journal of Conflict Resolution,* 1 (1957), 19–38.

———. The strategy of conflict: prospectus for the reorientation of game theory, *ibid.,* 2 (1958), 203–64.

Siegel, S. and Fouraker, L. E. *Bargaining and Group Decision Making.* New York: McGraw-Hill, 1960.

Stone, J. J. An experiment in bargaining games. *Econometrica,* 26 (1958), 286–96.

Suppes, P. and Carlsmith, J. M. Experimental analysis of a duopoly situation from the standpoint of mathematical learning theory. Applied Mathematics and Statistics Laboratories, Stanford University, 1960. (Mimeo.)

Thibaut, J. W. and Kelley, H. H. *The Social Psychology of Groups.* New York: John Wiley & Sons, 1959.

Zeuthen, F. *Problems of Monopoly and Economic Warfare.* London: Routledge, 1930.

Experiences in Groups: I[1] / W. R. Bion

Some months ago the Professional Committee of the Tavistock Clinic asked me to take therapeutic groups, employing my own technique. Now, I had no means of knowing what the Committee meant by this, but it was evident that in their view I had "taken" therapeutic groups before. I had, it was true, had experience of trying to persuade groups composed of patients to make the study of their tensions a group task (1), and I assumed the Committee meant that they were willing that I should do this again. It was disconcerting to find that the Committee seemed to believe that patients could be cured in such groups as these. It made me think at the outset that their expectations of what happened in groups of which I was a member were very different from mine. Indeed, the only cure of which I could speak with certainty was related to a comparatively minor symptom of my own— a belief that groups might take kindly to my efforts. However, I agreed; so, in due course, I would find myself sitting in a room with eight or nine other people— sometimes more, sometimes less—sometimes patients, sometimes not. When the members of the group were not patients, I often found myself in a peculiar quandary. I will describe what happens.

At the appointed time members of the group begin to arrive; individuals engage each other in conversation for a short time, and then, when a certain number has collected, a silence falls on the group. After a while desultory conversation breaks out again, and then another silence falls. It becomes clear to me that I am, in some sense, the focus of attention in the group. Furthermore, I am aware of feeling uneasily that I am expected to do something. At this point

Reprinted from W. R. Bion, *Experiences in Groups and Other Papers,* 1961, by permission of author and publishers, Tavistock Publications, London & Basic Books, New York.

[1] Dr. Bion has agreed to a suggestion from the Editorial Committee that he might contribute some descriptive and discursive articles to the scanty literature on the phenomena and dynamics of small groups, without prejudice to a later organization of the material in some other form.

I confide my anxieties to the group, remarking that, however mistaken my attitude might be, I feel just this.

I soon find that my confidence is not very well received. Indeed, there is some indignation that I should express such feelings without seeming to appreciate that the group is entitled to expect something from me. I do not dispute this, but content myself with pointing out that clearly the group cannot be getting from me what they feel they are entitled to expect. I wonder what these expectations are, and what has aroused them.

The friendliness of the group, though sorely tested, enables them to give me some information. Most members have been told that I would "take" the group; some say that I have a reputation for knowing a lot about groups; some feel that I ought to explain what we are going to do; some thought it was to be a kind of seminar, or perhaps a lecture. When I draw attention to the fact that these ideas seem to me to be based on hearsay, there seems to be a feeling that I am attempting to deny my eminence as a "taker" of groups. I feel, and say, that it is evident that the group had certain good expectations and beliefs about myself, and are sadly disappointed to find they are not true. The group is persuaded that the expectations are true, and that my behaviour is provocatively and deliberately disappointing —as much as to say, I could behave differently if I wanted to, and am only behaving like this out of spite. I point out that it is hard for the group to admit that this could be my way of taking groups, or even that I should be allowed to take them in such a way.

At this point the conversation seems to me to indicate that the group has changed its purpose.

While waiting for the group to settle on its new course, it may be useful if I try to offer the reader some explanation of behaviour which may, by this time, puzzle him as much as it does the group. I would not, of course, dream of doing this in a group, but the reader is in a different position from that of the man or woman who has much more evidence to go upon than the written word. Several questions may have occurred to the reader. He may think that my attitude

to the group is artificially naive, and certainly egotistical. Why should a group be bothered by having to discuss irrelevant matters such as the personality, history, career, and so forth, of one individual? I cannot hope to give any kind of full answer to such questions, but will say provisionally that I do not consider that I forced the group to discuss myself, though I do agree that the group was forced to do so. However irrelevant it may appear to be to the purpose of the meeting, the pre-occupation with my personality certainly seemed to me to obtrude itself, unwelcome though that might be to the group or to myself. I was simply stating what I thought was happening. Of course, it may be argued that I provoked this situation, and it has to be admitted that this is quite possible, although I do not think so. But even supposing my observations are correct, it may be wondered what useful purpose is served in making them. Here I can only say I do not know if any useful purpose is served in making them. Nor am I very sure about the nature of this kind of observation. It would be tempting, by analogy with psychoanalysis, to call them interpretations of group transference, but I think any psycho-analyst would agree with me that before such a description could be justified, a great deal of evidence from groups would have to be evaluated. But at least I can plead that observations of this kind are made spontaneously and naturally in everyday life, that we cannot avoid making them, unconsciously if not consciously, and that it would be very useful if we could feel that when we make observations of this kind they correspond to facts. We are constantly affected by what we feel to be the attitude of a group to ourselves, and are consciously or unconsciously swayed by our idea of it. It will be seen at once that it does not follow that one should blurt it out in the way I have so far described myself as doing in the group. This, I confess, must be regarded as peculiar, although if precedent were required, we are all familiar with certain types of people, particularly those who tend to feel persecuted, who behave in this manner. Not a happy precedent, the reader will think, and it will not be long before it is evident that the group thinks so too. But it is necessary now to return to the group, whom we left in the process of changing course.

The first thing that strikes us is the improvement that has taken place in the atmosphere. Mr. X, who has a likeable personality, has taken charge of the group, and is already taking steps to repair the deplorable situation created by myself. But I have given a mistaken impression if I seemed to suggest that we can watch this group in detachment, for Mr. X, who is anxious for the welfare of the group, quite rightly turns his attention to the source of the trouble, which, from his point of view, is myself. You can see that he has a very good idea of tackling at once those elements in his group which are destructive of morale and good fellowship. He therefore asks me directly what my object is, and why I cannot give a straightforward explanation of my behaviour. I can only apologise, and say that, beyond feeling that the statement that I want to study group tensions is probably a very inadequate description of my motives, I can throw no light on his problem; he has a good deal of sympathy from the group when he turns from this very unsatisfactory reply to question one or two others, who seem to be more co-operative and frank than myself. I think, however, I detect some unwillingness on the part of the group to follow his lead wholeheartedly. The dissidents seem to have reassured themselves that the Committee of the Tavistock Clinic must have had some good purpose in saying that I was to take the group; they give the impression that they are determined to believe that experience of a group taken by myself is valuable, in spite of their observations so far.

Nevertheless, Mr. X is having some success. Mr. Y tells him he is a Probation Officer, and has come to get a scientific knowledge of groups, which he feels would be of value to him. Mr. R, though not professionally concerned, has always had an interest in the scientific study of groups. Mr. X, Mr. Y and Mr. R also give some details of their background, and explain why they feel a scientific study would help them.

But now difficulties appear to be arising. Other members of the group are not so forthcoming as Mr. Y and Mr. R. Further-

more, there seems to be some irritation with Mr. X for taking the lead at all. Replies become evasive, and it looks as if even the information that has been obtained was not really quite the information that was wanted. I begin to feel, as the conversation becomes more desultory, that I am again the focus of discontent. Without quite knowing why, I suggest that what the group really wants to know is my motives for being present, and since these have not been discovered, they are not satisfied with any substitute.

It is clear that my interpretation is not welcome. One or two members want to know why I should take curiosity, which would seem to be valid without any further explanation, upon myself. The impression I receive is that very little importance is attached to the view I express as a possible explanation of what is going on. It seems to me either to be ignored, or to be taken as evidence of a warped outlook in myself. To make matters worse, it is not at all clear to me that my observation, however correct, is really the most useful one to make at the moment. But I have made it, and prepare to watch what follows.

I should explain that this bald description does not do justice to the emotional state of the group at this point. Mr. X seems harassed to find his initiative ill-received, and the rest of the group seem to be in varying stages of discomfort. For my part, I have to confess that it is a reaction with which I am familiar in every group of which I have been a member. I cannot, therefore, dismiss it simply as a peculiarity of this group. To me it is clear that whatever the group may think about Mr. X, it has much more serious misgivings about myself. In particular, I suspect that my personality, and especially my capacity for social relationships, and, therefore, my fitness for the role I am expected to fill, is in question. In the group we are contemplating at the moment, discontent with what is taking place, and particularly with my part in producing it, has risen to such a pitch that even the continued existence of the group becomes a matter of doubt to me. For some uncomfortable moments I fear it will all end by my having to explain to the Professional

Committee that their project has broken down through the inability of the group to tolerate my behaviour. I suspect from their demeanour that similar gloomy thoughts, differently orientated, are passing through the minds of the rest of the group.

In the tense atmosphere prevailing my own thoughts are not wholly reassuring. For one thing, I have recent memories of a group in which my exclusion had been openly advocated; for another, it is quite common for me to experience a situation in which the group, while saying nothing, simply ignores my presence, and excludes me from the discussion quite as effectively as if I were not there. On some occasions of this kind of crisis, the reaction has taken the milder form of suggestions that I have already excluded myself from the group, and that I make things difficult by not participating. A reaction as mild as this is quite reassuring, but I cannot forget that when I first attempted to put such methods into operation the experiment was terminated by my removal in fact from my post. I should prefer to believe that on that occasion the dismissal was due to coincidental circumstances, but I remember that, even so, the patients with whom I was dealing had constantly warned me, on what grounds I did not know, that serious attempts were being made to sabotage the scheme. I have, therefore, every reason, in such a situation as I am describing, to believe that the discontent is real, and may easily lead to the disruption of the group.

But on this occasion my anxieties are relieved by a new turn of events. Mr. Q suggests that logical argument at this point would hardly be likely to elicit the information wanted, and, indeed, it is possible that I would rather not explain why I make such an interpretation, because it would run counter to any idea of leaving the group to experience the nature of group phenomena for itself. He argues that, after all, I must have good reason for taking the line I do. The tension in the group is immediately relaxed, and a far more friendly attitude towards myself becomes apparent. It is clear that the group has a high opinion of myself after all, and I begin to feel that I have been perhaps treating the group unfairly by not being more communicative. For a moment I am impelled to make amends by responding to this friendly change with some explanation of my behaviour. Then I check myself, as I realise that the group has simply gone back to its former mood of insisting that hearsay is fact; so, instead of this, I point out that the group now appears to me to be coaxing me to mend my ways and fall in with their wish that my behaviour should conform more to what is expected or familiar to them in other fields. I also remark that the group has, in essence, ignored what was said by Mr. Q. The emphasis has been shifted from what Mr. Q intended to only one part of what he said—namely, that, after all, I was likely to know what I was about. In other words, it has been difficult for an individual member to convey meanings to the group which are other than those which the group wishes to entertain.

This time the group really is annoyed, and it is necessary to explain that they have every right to be. It is perfectly clear that nobody ever explained to them what it meant to be in a group in which I was present. For that matter, nobody ever explained to me what it was like to be in a group in which all the individual members of this group were present. But I have to realise that the only person whose presence has so far been found to be disagreeable is myself, so that any complaints I may have have not the same validity as those of other members. To me it is more than ever clear that there is some quite surprising contradiction in the situation in which I find myself. I, too, have heard rumours about the value of my contribution to groups; I have done my best to find out just in what respect my contribution was so remarkable, but have failed to elicit any information. I can, therefore, easily sympathise with the group, who feel that they are entitled to expect something different from what, in fact, they are getting. I can quite see that my statements must appear to the group to be as inaccurate as views of one's own position in a given society usually are, and, furthermore, to have very little relevance or importance for anybody but myself. I feel, therefore, that I must try to present a broader view of the situation than I have done so far.

With this in view, I say that I think my interpretations are disturbing the group. Furthermore, that the group interprets my interpretations as a revelation of the nature of my personality. No doubt attempts are being made to consider that they are in some way descriptive of the mental life of the group, but such attempts are overshadowed by a suspicion that my interpretations, when interpreted, throw more light on myself than on anything else, and that what is then revealed is in marked contrast with any expectations that members of the group had before they came. This, I think, must be very disturbing, but quite apart from any point of this sort, we have to recognise that perhaps members of the group assume too easily that the label on the box is a good description of the contents.

We must recognise now that a crisis has been reached, in that members may well have discovered that membership of a group in which I am a member happens to be an experience that they do not wish to have. In that way we have to face frankly that members of our group may need to leave, in exactly the same ways as a person might wish to leave a room which he had entered under a mistaken impression. I do not myself believe that this is quite a correct description, because, I remind the group, it was quite clear that in the beginning the group was most unwilling to entertain any idea that they had not properly satisfied themselves of the accuracy of hearsay reports about myself. In my view, therefore, those who felt that they had been misled by others, and now wished to withdraw, ought seriously to consider why they resisted so strongly any statements that seemed to question the validity of their belief in the value of my contributions to a group.

At this point it is necessary that I should say that I consider the emotional forces underlying this situation to be very powerful. I do not believe for a moment that the objective fact—namely, that I am merely one member of a group possessing some degree of specialised knowledge, and in that respect no different from any other member of the group—would be likely to be accepted. The forces opposed to this are far too strong. One external group—that is, the Clinic re-

sponsible for saying that I am to take a group—has given the seal of its authority to a myth of unknown dimensions; but apart from this, I am certain that the group is quite unable to face the emotional tensions within it without believing that it has some sort of God who is fully responsible for all that takes place. It has to be faced, therefore, that no matter what interpretations may be given, by myself or anybody else, the probability is that the group will reinterpret them to suit its own desires, exactly as we have just seen it do with the contribution of Mr. Q. It therefore becomes important to point out that the means of communication within the group are tenuous in the extreme, and quite uncertain in their action. Indeed, one might almost think that it would be less misleading if each individual member of the group spoke a language unknown to the remainder. There would then be less risk of assuming that we understood what any given individual said.

The group has now turned somewhat resentfully, but with more anxiety than resentment, to another member of the group. I get the impression that they are looking to him to be leader, but without any real conviction that he can be leader. This impression is strengthened because the man in question shows every desire to efface himself. The conversation becomes more and more desultory, and I feel that for most of the group the experience is becoming painful and uninteresting. A fresh thought occurs to me, so I pass it on.

I tell the group that it seems to me we are determined to have a leader, and that the leader we want seems to possess certain characteristics against which we match the characteristics of the different individuals we try out. Judging by our rejections, we seem to know perfectly well what we want. At the same time, it would be very difficult to say from our experience so far what these desirable characteristics are. Nor is it obvious why we should require a leader. The time of meeting of the group has been laid down, and really there seem to be no other decisions which the group has to make. One would imagine that a leader was required in order to give effective orders to the group, to implement moment to moment decisions; but if this is so, what is there in our present situation which would make us think that a leader of this kind is required? It cannot be the external situation, for our material needs and our relationships with external groups are stable, and would not seem to indicate that any decisions will be required in the near future. Either the desire for a leader is some emotional survival operating uselessly in the group as archaism, or else there is some awareness of a situation, which we have not defined, which demands the presence of such a person.

If my description of what it is like to be in a group of which I am a member has been at all adequate, the reader will have experienced some misgivings, harboured some objections and reserved many questions for further discussion. At the present stage I wish only to isolate two features of the group experience for inspection; one of these is the futility of the conversation in the group. Judged by ordinary standards of social intercourse, the performance of the group is almost devoid of intellectual content. Furthermore, if we note how assumptions pass unchallenged as statements of fact, and are accepted as such, it seems clear that critical judgment is almost entirely absent. To appreciate this point the reader must remember that he is able to read this account in tranquility, with unfettered use of his judgment. This is not the situation in the group. Whatever it may appear to be on the surface, that situation is charged with emotions which exert a powerful, and frequently unobserved, influence on the individual. As a result, his emotions are stirred to the detriment of his judgment. The group accordingly will often wrestle with intellectual problems which, one believes, the individual could solve without difficulty in another situation—a belief which will later be seen to be illusory. One of the main objects of our study may well turn out to be precisely the phenomena that produce these perturbations of rational behaviour in the group—phenomena whose existence I have only been able to indicate by descriptions of facts that bear less relationship to the object of our study than the lines of a monochrome print do to the colours of a painting in which colour is the all important quality.

The second feature to which I must allude is the nature of my own contribution. It would be satisfying if I could now give a logical account of my technique—the technique the Professional Committee, it will be remembered, wished me to employ—but I am pursuaded that it would also be very inaccurate and misleading. I shall, in the course of these articles, give as accurate a description as I can of what I say and do, but I propose also to indicate what groups think I say and do, and this not merely to illustrate the mental working of a group, but to provide as much material as possible for the reader to use in reaching his own conclusions. I will, however, emphasise one aspect of my interpretations of group behaviour which appears to the group, and probably to the reader, to be merely incidental to my personality, but which is, in fact, quite deliberate—the fact that the interpretations would seem to be concerned with matters of no importance to anyone but myself.

BIBLIOGRAPHY

1. Bion, W. R., and Rickman, J. (1943). Intragroup tensions: their study a task of the group. *Lancet,* ii, 678.

B. The Large Scale Organization

Unlike the context provided by the small group, the large scale organization or bureaucracy represents a social structure characterized by larger numbers of elements (e.g. positions or roles), more formalized patterns of relationship, and a more rigidly defined division of labor. Each of us as individuals in a complex society finds ourselves increasingly brought into direct and indirect contact with various large scale organizations: e.g. as university students, as employees in a large industry, as patients in a hospital, and other similar contacts. Thus this is an increasingly important context for social psychological inquiry.

The growth of large scale organizations, analogous in many respects to the growth of complex societies, may be understood in terms of human efforts to coordinate activities necessary to the functioning of the complex society and thus to their own survival. Within the small group setting, containing few individuals, coordination of action and group integration itself is more easily provided by primary group, informal norms. As the society moves from this relatively simplified structural pattern to one more complex, demanding that increasing numbers of persons be brought into the same sphere of activity, coordination and integration or cohesion must be maintained by some other class of normative arrangements. The shift away from primary group patterns of integration and control to secondary, rational-legal patterns marks the normative shift characterizing the large scale organization. Questions of historical and continuing interest, given this shift towards bureaucratic dominance, have centered around the nature of the normative control exercised, the effects of such structures and control upon organizational cohesiveness and productivity, and upon individual well-being.

The collection of readings included in this section involve both theoretical and empirical articles dealing with the previously mentioned questions. Selznick presents a theory of organizations framed within the structural-functional orientation characteristic of many contemporary sociological theories. Evan and Zelditch present an experimental study of an artificially created organization, while Morse and Reimer present a field experiment conducted on an ongoing organization. The concluding article by Zald deals with an empirical study of a particular type of organization, also characteristic of our complex society.

Foundations of the Theory of Organization /
Philip Selznick (*University of California, Los Angeles*)

Trades unions, governments, business corporations, political parties, and the like are formal structures in the sense that they represent rationally ordered instruments for the achievement of stated goals. "Organization," we are told, "is the arrangement of personnel for facilitating the accomplishment of some agreed purpose through the allocation of functions and responsibilities."[1] Or, defined more generally, formal organization is "a system of consciously coordinated activities or forces of two or more persons."[2] Viewed in this light, formal organization is the structural expression of rational action. The mobilization of technical and managerial skills requires a pattern of coordination, a systematic ordering of positions and duties which defines a chain of command and makes possible the administrative integration of specialized functions. In this context *delegation* is the primordial organizational act, a precarious venture which requires the continuous elaboration of formal mechanisms of coordination and control. The security of all participants, and of the system as a whole, generates a persistent pressure for the institutionalization of relationships, which are thus removed from the uncertainties of individual fealty or sentiment. Moreover, it is necessary for the relations within the structure to be determined in such a way that individuals will be interchangeable and the organization will thus be free of dependence upon personal qualities.[3] In this way, the formal structure becomes subject to calculable manipulation, an instrument of rational action.

But as we inspect these formal structures we begin to see that they never succeed in conquering the non-rational dimensions of organizational behavior. The latter remain at once indispensable to the continued existence of the system of coordination and at the same time the source of friction, dilemma, doubt, and ruin. This fundamental paradox arises from the fact that rational action systems are inescapably imbedded in an institutional matrix, in two significant senses: (1) the action system—or the formal structure of delegation and control which is its organizational expression—is itself only an aspect of a concrete social structure made up of individuals who may interact as *wholes,* not simply in terms of their formal roles within the system; (2) the formal system, and the social structure within which it finds concrete existence, are alike subject to the pressure of an institutional environment to which some over-all adjustment must be made. The formal administrative design can never adequately or fully reflect the concrete organization to which it refers, for the obvious reason that no abstract plan or pattern can—or may, if it is to be useful—exhaustively describe an empirical totality. At the same time, that which is not included in the abstract design (as reflected, for example, in a staff-and-line organization chart) is vitally relevant to the maintenance and development of the formal system itself.

Organization may be viewed from two standpoints which are analytically distinct but which are empirically united in a context of reciprocal consequences. On the one hand, any concrete organizational system is an *economy;* at the same time, it is an *adaptive social structure.* Considered as an economy, organization is a system of relationships which define the availability of scarce resources and which may be manipulated in terms of efficiency and effectiveness. It is the economic aspect of organization which commands the attention of management

Reprinted from *The American Sociological Review,* 1948, 13, pages 25–35, by permission of author and publisher, The American Sociological Association.

[1] John M. Gaus, "A Theory of Organization in Public Administration," in *The Frontiers of Public Administration* (Chicago: University of Chicago Press, 1936), p. 66.

[2] Chester I. Barnard, *The Functions of the Executive* (Cambridge: Harvard University Press, 1938), p. 73.

[3] Cf. Talcott Parsons' generalization (after Max Weber) of the "law of the increasing rationality of action systems," in *The Structure of Social Action* (New York: McGraw-Hill, 1937), p. 752.

technicians and, for the most part, students of public as well as private administration.[4] Such problems as the span of executive control, the role of staff or auxiliary agencies, the relation of headquarters to field offices, and the relative merits of single or multiple executive boards are typical concerns of the science of administration. The coordinative scalar, and functional principles, as elements of the theory of organization, are products of the attempt to explicate the most general features of organization as a "technical problem" or, in our terms, as an economy.

Organization as an economy is, however, necessarily conditioned by the organic states of the concrete structure, outside of the systematics of delegation and control. This becomes especially evident as the attention of leadership is directed toward such problems as the legitimacy of authority and the dynamics of persuasion. It is recognized implicitly in action and explicitly in the work of a number of students that the possibility of manipulating the system of coordination depends on the extent to which that system is operating within an environment of effective inducement to individual participants and of conditions in which the stability of authority is assured. This is in a sense the fundamental thesis of Barnard's remarkable study, *The Functions of the Executive*. It is also the underlying hypothesis which makes it possible for Urwick to suggest that "proper" or formal channels in fact function to "confirm and record" decisions arrived at by more personal means.[5] We meet it again in the concept of administration as a process of education, in which the winning of consent and support is conceived to be a basic function of leadership.[6] In short, it is recognized that control and consent cannot be divorced even within formally authoritarian structures.

The indivisibility of control and consent makes it necessary to view formal organizations as *cooperative* systems, widening the frame of reference of those concerned with the manipulation of organizational resources. At the point of action, of executive decision, the economic aspect of organization provides inadequate tools for control over the concrete structure. This idea may be readily grasped if attention is directed to the role of the individual within the organizational economy. From the standpoint of organization as a formal system, persons are viewed functionally, in respect to their *roles,* as participants in assigned segments of the cooperative system. But in fact individuals have a propensity to resist depersonalization, to spill over the boundaries of their segmentary roles, to participate as *wholes*. The formal systems (at an extreme, the disposition of "rifles" at a military perimeter) cannot take account of the deviations thus introduced, and consequently break down as instruments of control when relied upon alone. The whole individual raises new problems for the organization, partly because of the needs of his own personality, partly because he brings with him a set of established habits as well, perhaps, as commitments to special groups outside of the organization.

Unfortunately for the adequacy of formal systems of coordination, the needs of individuals do not permit a single-minded attention to the stated goals of the system within which they have been assigned. The hazard inherent in the act of delegation derives essentially from this fact. Delegation is an organizational act, having to do with formal assignments of functions and powers. Theoretically, these assignments are made to roles or official positions, not to individuals as such. In fact, however, delegation necessarily involves concrete individuals who have interests and goals which do not always coincide with the goals of the formal system. As a consequence, individual personalities may offer resistance to the demands made upon them by the official conditions of delegation. These resistances are not accounted

[4] See Luther Gulick and Lydall Urwick (editors), *Papers on the Science of Administration* (New York: Institute of Public Administration, Columbia University, 1937); Lydall Urwick, *The Elements of Administration* (New York, Harper, 1943); James D. Mooney and Alan C. Reiley, *The Principles of Organization* (New York: Harper, 1939); H. S. Dennison, *Organization Engineering* (New York: McGraw-Hill, 1931).

[5] Urwick, *The Elements of Administration, op. cit.*, p. 47.

[6] See Gaus, *op. cit.* Studies of the problem of morale are instances of the same orientation, having received considerable impetus in recent years from the work of the Harvard Business School group.

for within the categories of coordination and delegation, so that when they occur they must be considered as unpredictable and accidental. Observations of this type of situation within formal structures are sufficiently commonplace. A familiar example is that of delegation to a subordinate who is also required to train his own replacement. The subordinate may resist this demand in order to maintain unique access to the "mysteries" of the job, and thus insure his indispensability to the organization.

In large organizations, deviations from the formal system tend to become institutionalized, so that "unwritten laws" and informal associations are established. Institutionalization removes such deviations from the realm of personality differences, transforming them into a persistent structural aspect of formal organizations.[7] These institutionalized rules and modes of informal cooperation are normally attempts by participants in the formal organization to control the group relations which form the environment of organizational decisions. The informal patterns (such as cliques) arise spontaneously, are based on personal relationships, and are usually directed to the control of some specific situation. They may be generated anywhere within a hierarchy, often with deleterious consequences for the formal goals of the organization, but they may also function to widen the available resources of executive control and thus contribute to rather than hinder the achievement of the stated objectives of the organization. The deviations tend to force a shift away from the purely formal system as the effective determinant of behavior to (1) a condition in which informal patterns buttress the formal, as through the manipulation of sentiment within the organization in favor of established authority; or (2) a condition wherein the informal controls effect a consistent modification of formal goals, as in the case of some bureaucratic patterns.[8] This trend will eventually result in the formalization of erstwhile informal activities, with the cycle of deviation and transformation beginning again on a new level.

The relevance of informal structures to organizational analysis underlines the significance of conceiving of formal organizations as cooperative systems. When the totality of interacting groups and individuals becomes the object of inquiry, the latter is not restricted by formal, legal, or procedural dimensions. The *state of the system* emerges as a significant point of analysis, as when an internal situation charged with conflict qualifies and informs actions ostensibly determined by formal relations and objectives. A proper understanding of the organizational process must make it possible to interpret changes in the formal system—new appointments or rules or reorganizations—in their relation to the informal and unavowed ties of friendship, class loyalty, power cliques, or external commitment. This is what it means "to know the score."

The fact that the involvement of individuals as whole personalities tends to limit the adequacy of formal systems of coordination does not mean that organizational characteristics are those of individuals. The organic, emergent character of the formal organization considered as a cooperative system must be recognized. This means that the *organization* reaches decisions, takes action, and makes adjustments. Such a view raises the question of the relation between organizations and persons. The significance of theoretical emphasis upon the cooperative *system* as such is derived from the insight that certain actions and consequences are enjoined independently of the personality of the individuals involved. Thus, if reference is made to the "organization-paradox"—the tension created by the inhibitory consequences of certain types of informal structures within organizations—this does not mean that individuals themselves are in quandaries. It is the nature of the interacting consequences of divergent interests

7 The creation of informal structures within various types of organizations has received explicit recognition in recent years. See F. J. Roethlisberger and W. J. Dickson, *Management and the Worker* (Cambridge: Harvard University Press, 1941), p. 524; also Barnard, *op. cit.*, c. ix; and Wilbert E. Moore, *Industrial Relations and the Social Order* (New York: Macmillan, 1946), chap. xv.

8 For an analysis of the latter in these terms, see Philip Selznick, "An Approach to a Theory of Bureaucracy," *American Sociological Review*, Vol. VIII, No. 1 (February, 1943).

within the organization which creates the condition, a result which may obtain independently of the consciousness or the qualities of the individual participants. Similarly, it seems useful to insist that there are qualities and needs of leader*ship,* having to do with position and role, which are persistent despite variations in the character or personality of individual leaders themselves.

Rational action systems are characteristic of both individuals and organizations. The conscious attempt to mobilize available internal resources (e.g., self-discipline) for the achievement of a stated goal—referred to here as an economy or a formal system—is one aspect of individual psychology. But the personality considered as a dynamic system of interacting wishes, compulsions, and restraints defines a system which is at once essential and yet potentially deleterious to what may be thought of as the "economy of learning" or to individual rational action. At the same time, the individual personality is an adaptive structure, and this, too, requires a broader frame of reference for analysis than the categories of rationality. On a different level, although analogously, we have pointed to the need to consider organizations as cooperative systems and adaptive structures in order to explain the context of and deviations from the formal systems of delegation and coordination.

To recognize the sociological relevance of formal structures is not, however, to have constructed a theory of organization. It is important to set the framework of analysis, and much is accomplished along this line when, for example, the nature of authority in formal organizations is reinterpreted to emphasize the factors of cohesion and persuasion as against legal or coercive sources.[9] This redefinition is logically the same as that which introduced the conception of the self as social. The latter helps make possible, but does not of itself fulfill, the requirements for a dynamic theory of personality. In the same way, the definition of authority as conditioned by sociological factors of sentiment and cohesion—or more generally the definition of formal organizations as cooperative

systems—only sets the stage, as an initial requirement, for the formulation of a theory of organization.

STRUCTURAL-FUNCTIONAL ANALYSIS

Cooperative systems are constituted of individuals interacting as wholes in relation to a formal system of coordination. The concrete structure is therefore a resultant of the reciprocal influences of the formal and informal aspects of organization. Furthermore, this structure is itself a totality, an adaptive "organism" reacting to influences upon it from an external environment. These considerations help to define the objects of inquiry; but to progress to a system of predicates *about* these objects it is necessary to set forth an analytical method which seems to be fruitful and significant. The method must have a relevance to empirical materials, which is to say, it must be more specific in its reference than discussions of the logic or methodology of social science.

The organon which may be suggested as peculiarly helpful in the analysis of adaptive structures has been referred to as "structural-functional analysis."[10] This method may be characterized in a sentence: *Structural-functional analysis relates contemporary and variable behavior to a presumptively stable system of needs and mechanisms.* This means that a given empirical system is deemed to have basic needs, essentially related to self-maintenance; the system develops repetitive means of self-defense; and day-to-day activity is interpreted in terms of the function served by that activity for the maintenance and defense of the system. Put thus generally, the approach is applicable on any level in which the determinate "states" of empirically isolable systems undergo self-impelled and repetitive transformations when impinged upon by external conditions. This self-impulsion suggests the relevance of the term "dynamic," which is often used in referring to physio-

[9] Robert Michels, "Authority," *Encyclopedia of the Social Sciences* (New York: Macmillan, 1931), pp. 319 ff.; also Barnard, *op. cit.,* c. xii.

[10] For a presentation of this approach having a more general reference than the study of formal organizations, see Talcott Parsons, "The Present Position and Prospects of Systematic Theory in Sociology," in Georges Gurvitch and Wilbert E. Moore (ed.), *Twentieth Century Sociology* (New York: The Philosophical Library, 1945).

logical, psychological, or social systems to which this type of analysis has been applied.[11]

It is a postulate of the structural-functional approach that the basic need of all empirical systems is the maintenance of the integrity and continuity of the system itself. Of course, such a postulate is primarily useful in directing attention to a set of "derived imperatives" or needs which are sufficiently concrete to characterize the system at hand.[12] It is perhaps rash to attempt a catalogue of these imperatives for formal organizations, but some suggestive formulation is needed in the interests of setting forth the type of analysis under discussion. In formal organizations, the "maintenance of the system" as a generic need may be specified in terms of the following imperatives:

(1) *The security of the organization as a whole in relation to social forces in its environment.* This imperative requires continuous attention to the possibilities of encroachment and to the forestalling of threatened aggressions or deleterious (though perhaps unintended) consequences from the actions of others.

(2) *The stability of the lines of authority and communication.* One of the persistent reference-points of administrative decision is the weighing of consequences for the continued capacity of leadership to control and to have access to the personnel or ranks.

(3) *The stability of informal relations within the organization.* Ties of sentiment and self-interest are evolved as unacknowledged but effective mechanisms of adjustment of individuals and sub-groups to the conditions of life within the organization. These ties represent a cementing of relationships which sustains the formal authority in day-to-day operations and widens opportunities for effective communication.[13] Consequently, attempts to "upset" the informal structure, either frontally or as an indirect consequence of formal reorganization, will normally be met with considerable resistance.

(4) *The continuity of policy and of the sources of its determination.* For each level within the organization, and for the organization as a whole, it is necessary that there be a sense that action taken in the light of a given policy will not be placed in continuous jeopardy. Arbitrary or unpredictable changes in policy undermine the significance of (and therefore the attention to) day-to-day action by injecting a note of capriciousness. At the same time, the organization will seek stable roots (or firm statutory authority or popular mandate) so that a sense of the permanency and legitimacy of its acts will be achieved.

(5) *A homogeneity of outlook with respect to the meaning and role of the organization.* The minimization of disaffection requires a unity derived from a common understanding of what the character of the organization is meant to be. When this homogeneity breaks down, as in situations of internal conflict over basic issues, the continued existence of the organization is endangered. On the other hand, one of the signs of "healthy" organization is the ability to effectively orient new members and readily slough off those who cannot be adapted to the established outlook.

This catalogue of needs cannot be thought of as final, but it approximates the stable system generally characteristic of formal organizations. These imperatives are derived, in the sense that they represent the conditions for survival or self-maintenance of cooperative systems of organized action. An inspection of these needs suggests that organizational survival is intimately connected

---

[11] "Structure" refers to both the relationships within the system (formal plus informal patterns in organization) and the set of needs and modes of satisfaction which characterize the given type of empirical system. As the utilization of this type of analysis proceeds, the concept of "need" will require further clarification. In particular, the imputation of a "stable set of needs" to organizational systems must not function as a new instinct theory. At the same time, we cannot avoid using these inductions as to generic needs, for they help us to stake out our area of inquiry. The author is indebted to Robert K. Merton who has, in correspondence, raised some important objections to the use of the term "need" in this context.

[12] For "derived imperative" see Bronislaw Malinowski, *The Dynamics of Culture Change* (New Haven: Yale University Press, 1945), pp. 44 ff. For the use of "need" in place of "motive" see the same author's *A Scientific Theory of Culture* (Chapel Hill: University of North Carolina Press, 1944), pp. 89–90.

[13] They may also *destroy* those relationships, as noted above, but the need remains, generating one of the persistent dilemmas of leadership.

with the struggle for relative prestige, both for the organization and for elements and individuals within it. It may therefore be useful to refer to a *prestige-survival motif* in organizational behavior as a short-hand way of relating behavior to needs, especially when the exact nature of the needs remains in doubt. However, it must be emphasized that prestige-survival in organizations does not derive simply from like motives in individuals. Loyalty and self-sacrifice may be individual expressions of organizational or group egotism and self-consciousness.

The concept of organizational need directs analysis to the *internal relevance* of organizational behavior. This is especially pertinent with respect to discretionary action undertaken by agents manifestly in pursuit of formal goals. The question then becomes one of relating the specific act of discretion to some presumptively stable organizational need. In other words, it is not simply action plainly oriented internally (such as in-service training) but also action presumably oriented externally which must be inspected for its relevance to internal conditions. This is of prime importance for the understanding of bureaucratic behavior, for it is of the essence of the latter that action formally undertaken for substantive goals be weighed and transformed in terms of its consequences for the position of the officialdom.

Formal organizations as cooperative systems on the one hand, and individual personalities on the other, involve structural-functional homologies, a point which may help to clarify the nature of this type of analysis. If we say that the individual has a stable set of needs, most generally the need for maintaining and defending the integrity of his personality or ego; that there are recognizable certain repetitive mechanisms which are utilized by the ego in its defense (rationalization, projection, regression, etc.); and that overt and variable behavior may be interpreted in terms of its relation to these needs and mechanisms—on the basis of this logic we may discern the typical pattern of structural-functional analysis as set forth above. In this sense, it is possible to speak of a "Freudian model" for organizational analysis. This does not mean that the substantive insights of individual psychology may be applied to organizations, as in vulgar extrapolations from the individual ego to whole nations or (by a no less vulgar inversion) from strikes to frustrated workers. It is the *logic,* the *type* of analysis which is pertinent.

This homology is also instructive in relation to the applicability of generalizations to concrete cases. The dynamic theory of personality states a set of possible predicates about the ego and its mechanisms of defense, which inform us concerning the propensities of individual personalities under certain general circumstances. But these predicates provide only tools for the analysis of particular individuals, and each concrete case must be examined to tell which operate and in what degree. They are not primarily organs of prediction. In the same way, the predicates within the theory of organization will provide tools for the analysis of particular cases. Each organization, like each personality, represents a resultant of complex forces, an empirical entity which no single relation or no simple formula can explain. The problem of analysis becomes that of selecting among the possible predicates set forth in the theory of organization those which illuminate our understanding of the materials at hand.

The setting of structural-functional analysis as applied to organizations requires some qualification, however. Let us entertain the suggestion that the interesting problem in social science is not so much why men act the way they do as why men in certain circumstances *must* act the way they do. This emphasis upon constraint, if accepted, releases us from an ubiquitous attention to behavior in general, and especially from any undue fixation upon statistics. On the other hand, it has what would seem to be the salutary consequence of focusing inquiry upon certain necessary relationships of the type "if . . . then," for example: If the cultural level of the rank and file members of a formally democratic organization is below that necessary for participation in the formulation of policy, then there will be pressure upon the leaders to use the tools of demagogy.

Is such a statement universal in its applicability? Surely not in the sense that one can predict without remainder the nature of all or even most political groups in a democracy. Concrete behavior is a resultant, a complex vector, shaped by the operation of a number of such general constraints. But there is a test of general applicability: it is that of noting whether the relation made explicit must be *taken into account* in action. This criterion represents an empirical test of the significance of social science generalizations. If a theory is significant it will state a relation which will either (1) be taken into account as an element of achieving control; or (2) be ignored only at the risk of losing control and will evidence itself in a ramification of objective or unintended consequences.[14] It is a corollary of this principle of significance that investigation must search out the underlying factors in organizational action, which requires a kind of intensive analysis of the same order as psychoanalytic probing.

A frame of reference which invites attention to the constraints upon behavior will tend to highlight tensions and dilemmas, the characteristic paradoxes generated in the course of action. The dilemma may be said to be the handmaiden of structural-functional analysis, for it introduces the concept of *commitment* or *involvement* as fundamental to organizational analysis. A dilemma in human behavior is represented by an inescapable commitment which cannot be reconciled with the needs of the organism or the social system. There are many spurious dilemmas which have to do with verbal contradictions, but inherent dilemmas to which we refer are of a more profound sort, for they reflect the basic nature of the empirical system in question. An economic order committed to profit as its sustaining incentive may, in Marxist terms, sow the seed of its own destruction. Again, the anguish of man, torn between finitude and pride, is not a matter of arbitrary and replaceable assumptions but is a reflection of the psychological needs of the human organism, and is concretized in his commitment to the institutions which command his life; he is in the world and of it, inescapably involved in its goals and demands; at the same time, the needs of the spirit are compelling, proposing modes of salvation which have continuously disquieting consequences for worldly involvements. In still another context, the need of the human organism for affection and response necessitates a commitment to elements of the culture which can provide them; but the rule of the super-ego is uncertain since it cannot be completely reconciled with the need for libidinal satisfactions.

Applying this principle to organizations we may note that there is a general source of tension observable in the split between "the motion and the act." Plans and programs reflect the freedom of technical or ideal choice, but organized action cannot escape involvement, a commitment to personnel or institutions or procedures which effectively qualifies the initial plan. *Der Mensch denkt, Gott lenkt*. In organized action, this ultimate wisdom finds a temporal meaning in the recalcitrance of the tools of action. We are inescapably committed to the mediation of human structures which are at once indispensable to our goals and at the same time stand between them and ourselves. The selection of agents generates immediately a bifurcation of interest, expressed in new centers of need and power, placing effective constraints upon the arena of action, and resulting in tensions which are never completely resolved. This is part of what it means to say that there is a "logic" of action which impels us forward from one undesired position to another. Commitment to dynamic, self-activating tools is of the nature of organized action; at the same time, the need for continuity of authority, policy, and character are pressing, and require an unceasing effort to master the instruments generated in the course of action. This generic tension is specified within the terms of each cooperative system. But for all we find a persistent relationship between *need* and *commitment* in which the latter not only qualifies the former but unites with it to produce a continuous state of tension. In this

[14] See R. M. MacIver's discussion of the "dynamic assessment" which "brings the external world selectively into the subjective realm, conferring on it subjective significance for the ends of action." *Social Causation* (Boston: Ginn, 1942), chaps. 11, 12. The analysis of this assessment within the context of organized action yields the implicit knowledge which guides the choice among alternatives. See also Robert K. Merton, "The Unanticipated Consequences of Purposive Social Action," *American Sociological Review*, I, 6 (December, 1936).

way, the notion of constraint (as reflected in tension or paradox) at once widens and more closely specifies the frame of reference for organizational analysis.

For Malinowski, the core of functionalism was contained in the view that a cultural fact must be analyzed in its setting. Moreover, he apparently conceived of his method as pertinent to the analysis of all aspects of cultural systems. But there is a more specific problem, one involving a principle of selection which serves to guide inquiry along significant lines. Freud conceived of the human organism as an adaptive structure, but he was not concerned with all human needs, nor with all phases of adaptation. For his system, he selected those needs whose expression is blocked in some way, so that such terms as repression, inhibition, and frustration became crucial. All conduct may be thought of as derived from need, and all adjustment represents the reduction of need. But not all needs are relevant to the systematics of dynamic psychology; and it is not adjustment as such but reaction to frustration which generates the characteristic modes of defensive behavior.

Organizational analysis, too, must find its selective principle; otherwise the indiscriminate attempts to relate activity functionally to needs will produce little in the way of significant theory. Such a principle might read as follows: *Our frame of reference is to select out those needs which cannot be fulfilled within approved avenues of expression and thus must have recourse to such adaptive mechanisms as ideology and to the manipulation of formal processes and structures in terms of informal goals.* This formulation has many difficulties, and is not presented as conclusive, but it suggests the kind of principle which is likely to separate the quick and the dead, the meaningful and the trite, in the study of cooperative systems in organized action.[15]

The frame of reference outlined here for the theory of organization may now be identified as involving the following major ideas: (1) the concept of organizations as coopera-

tive systems, adaptive social structures, made up of interacting individuals, sub-groups, and informal plus formal relationships; (2) structural-functional analysis, which relates variable aspects of organization (such as goals) to stable needs and self-defensive mechanisms; (3) the concept of recalcitrance as a quality of the tools of social action, involving a break in the continuum of adjustment and defining an environment of constraint, commitment, and tension. This frame of reference is suggested as providing a specifiable *area of relations* within which predicates in the theory of organization will be sought, and at the same time setting forth principles of selection and relevance in our approach to the data of organization.

It will be noted that we have set forth this frame of reference within the over-all context of social action. The significance of events may be defined by their place and operational role in a means-end scheme. If functional analysis searches out the elements important for the maintenance of a given structure, and that structure is one of the materials to be manipulated in action, then that which is functional in respect to the structure is also functional in respect to the action system. This provides a ground for the significance of functionally derived theories. At the same time, relevance to control in action is the empirical test of their applicability or truth.

COOPTATION AS A MECHANISM OF ADJUSTMENT

The frame of reference stated above is in fact an amalgam of definition, resolution, and substantive theory. There is an element of *definition* in conceiving of formal organizations as cooperative systems, though of course the interaction of informal and formal patterns is a question of fact; in a sense, we are *resolving* to employ structural-functional analysis on the assumption that it will be fruitful to do so, though here, too, the specification of needs or derived imperatives is a matter of empirical inquiry; and our predication of recalcitrance as a quality of the tools of action is itself a *substantive theory,* perhaps fundamental to a general understanding of the nature of social action.

15 This is not meant to deprecate the study of organizations as *economies* or formal systems. The latter represent an independent level, abstracted from organizational structures as cooperative or adaptive systems ("organisms").

A theory of organization requires more than a general frame of reference, though the latter is indispensable to inform the approach of inquiry to any given set of materials. What is necessary is the construction of generalizations concerning transformations within and among cooperative systems. These generalizations represent, from the standpoint of particular cases, possible predicates which are relevant to the materials as we know them in general, but which are not necessarily controlling in all circumstances. A theory of transformations in organization would specify those states of the system which resulted typically in predictable, or at least understandable, changes in such aspects of organization as goals, leadership, doctrine, efficiency, effectiveness, and size. These empirical generalizations would be systematized as they were related to the stable needs of the cooperative system.

Changes in the characteristics of organizations may occur as a result of many different conditions, not always or necessarily related to the processes of organization as such. But the theory of organization must be selective, so that explanations of transformations will be sought within its own assumptions or frame of reference. Consider the question of size. Organizations may expand for many reasons—the availability of markets, legislative delegations, the swing of opinion—which may be accidental from the point of view of the organizational process. To explore changes in size (as of, say, a trades union) as related to changes in nonorganizational conditions may be necessitated by the historical events to be described, but it will not of itself advance the frontiers of the theory of organization. However, if "the innate propensity of all organizations to expand" is asserted as a function of "the inherent instability of incentives"[16] then transformations have been stated within the terms of the theory of organization itself. It is likely that in many cases the generalization in question may represent only a minor aspect of the empirical changes, but these organizational relations must be made explicit if the theory is to receive development.

In a frame of reference which specifies

needs and anticipates the formulation of a set of self-defensive responses or mechanisms, the latter appear to constitute one kind of empirical generalization or "possible predicate" within the general theory. The needs of organizations (whatever investigation may determine them to be) are posited as attributes of all organizations, but the responses to disequilibrium will be varied. The mechanisms used by the system in fulfillment of its needs will be repetitive and thus may be described as a specifiable set of assertions within the theory of organization, but any given organization may or may not have recourse to the characteristic modes of response. Certainly no given organization will employ all of the possible mechanisms which are theoretically available. When Barnard speaks of an "innate propensity of organization to expand" he is in fact formulating one of the general mechanisms, namely, expansion, which is a characteristic mode of response available to an organization under pressure from within. These responses necessarily involve a transformation (in this case, size) of some structural aspect of the organization.

Other examples of the self-defensive mechanisms available to organizations may derive primarily from the response of these organizations to the institutional environments in which they live. The tendency to construct ideologies, reflecting the need to come to terms with major social forces, is one such mechanism. Less well understood as a mechanism of organizational adjustment is what we may term *cooptation*. Some statement of the meaning of this concept may aid in clarifying the foregoing analysis.

Cooptation is the process of absorbing new elements into the leadership or policy-determining structure of an organization as a means of averting threats to its stability or existence. This is a defensive mechanism, formulated as one of a number of possible predicates available for the interpretation of organizational behavior. Cooptation tells us something about the process by which an institutional environment impinges itself upon an organization and effects changes in its leadership and policy. Formal authority may resort to cooptation under the following general conditions:

16 Barnard, *op. cit.,* pp. 158-9.

(1) When there exists a hiatus between consent and control, so that the legitimacy of the formal authority is called into question. The "indivisibility" of consent and control refers, of course, to an optimum situation. Where control lacks an adequate measure of consent, it may revert to coercive measures or attempt somehow to win the consent of the governed. One means of winning consent is to coopt elements into the leadership or organization, usually elements which in some way reflect the sentiment, or possess the confidence of the relevant public or mass. As a result, it is expected that the new elements will lend respectability or legitimacy to the organs of control and thus reestablish the stability of formal authority. This process is widely used, and in many different contexts. It is met in colonial countries, where the organs of alien control reaffirm their legitimacy by coopting native leaders into the colonial administration. We find it in the phenomenon of "crisis-patriotism" wherein normally disfranchised groups are temporarily given representation in the councils of government in order to win their solidarity in a time of national stress. Cooptation is presently being considered by the United States Army in its study of proposals to give enlisted personnel representation in the court-martial machinery —a clearly adaptive response to stresses made explicit during the war, the lack of confidence in the administration of army justice. The "unity" parties of totalitarian states are another form of cooptation; company unions or some employee representation plans in industry are still another. In each of these cases, the response of formal authority (private or public, in a large organization or a small one) is an attempt to correct a state of imbalance by *formal* measures. It will be noted moreover, that what is shared is the *responsibility* for power rather than power itself. These conditions define what we shall refer to as *formal cooptation*.

(2) Cooptation may be a response to the pressure of specific centers of power. This is not necessarily a matter of legitimacy or of a general and diffuse lack of confidence. These may be well established; and yet organized forces which are able to threaten the formal authority may effectively shape its structure and policy. The organization in respect to its institutional environment—or the leadership in respect to its ranks—must take these forces into account. As a consequence, the outside elements may be brought into the leadership or policy-determining structure, may be given a place as a recognition of and concession to the resources they can independently command. The representation of interests through administrative constituencies is a typical example of this process. Or, within an organization, individuals upon whom the group is dependent for funds or other resources may insist upon and receive a share in the determination of policy. This form of cooptation is typically expressed in informal terms, for the problem is not one of responding to a state of imbalance with respect to the "people as a whole" but rather one of meeting the pressure of specific individuals or interest-groups which are in a position to enforce demands. The latter are interested in the substance of power and not its forms. Moreover, an open acknowledgement of capitulation to specific interests may itself undermine the sense of legitimacy of the formal authority within the community. Consequently, there is a positive pressure to refrain from explicit recognition of the relationship established. This form of the cooptative mechanism, having to do with the sharing of power as a response to specific pressures, may be termed *informal cooptation*.

Cooptation reflects a state of tension between formal authority and social power. The former is embodied in a particular structure and leadership, but the latter has to do with subjective and objective factors which control the loyalties and potential manipulability of the community. Where the formal authority is an expression of social power, its stability is assured. On the other hand, when it becomes divorced from the sources of social power its continued existence is threatened. This threat may arise from the sheer alienation of sentiment or from the fact that other leaderships have control over the sources of social power. Where a formal authority has been accustomed to the assumption that its constituents respond to it as individuals, there may be a rude awakening when organization of those constituents on a non-governmental basis creats nuclei of power which are able effectively to demand a sharing of power.[17]

The significance of cooptation for organ-

[17] It is perhaps useful to restrict the concept of cooptation to formal organizations, but in fact it probably reflects a process characteristic of all group leaderships. This has received some recognition in the analysis of class structure, wherein the ruling class is interpreted as protecting its own stability by absorbing new elements. Thus Michels made the point that "an aristocracy cannot maintain an enduring stability by sealing itself off hermetically." See Robert Michels, *Umschichtungen in den herrschenden Klassen nach dem Kriege* (Stuttgart: Kohlhammer, 1934), p. 39; also Gaetano Mosca, *The Ruling Class* (New York: McGraw-Hill, 1939), p. 413 ff. The alliance or amalgamation of classes in the face of a common threat may be reflected in formal and informal cooptative responses among formal organizations sensitive to class pressures. In a forthcoming volume, *TVA and the Grass Roots,* the author has made extensive use of the concept of cooptation in analyzing some aspects of the organizational behavior of a government agency.

izational analysis is not simply that there is a change in or a broadening of leadership, and that this is an adaptive response, but also that *this change is consequential for the character and role of the organization.* Cooptation involves commitment, so that the groups to which adaptation has been made constrain the field of choice available to the organization or leadership in question. The character of the coopted elements will necessarily shape (inhibit or broaden) the modes of action available to the leadership which has won adaptation and security at the price of commitment. The concept of cooptation thus implicitly sets forth the major points of the frame of reference outlined above: it is an adaptive response of a cooperative system to a stable need, generating transformations which reflect constraints enforced by the recalcitrant tools of action.

A Laboratory Experiment on Bureaucratic Authority* /

William M. Evan (*Bell Telephone Laboratories, Murray Hill, New Jersey*)
Morris Zelditch, Jr. (*Stanford University*)

In this experiment an effort is made to separate the rational and legal components of Weber's theory of bureaucratic authority, and to vary the dimension of authority of knowledge while holding authority of office constant. A small part of a fictitious research organization is simulated. Three statuses are activated: project director, coding supervisor, and coder. The hypotheses tested are that (a) if an official holds office without commensurate knowledge, subordinates would not accord legitimacy to the official's authority; (b) the erosion of the supervisor's authority would have negative effects both on the subordinates' performance and on their conformity to technical rules and commands; (c) conformity to administrative rules and commands would not be affected by treatment differences. The results confirmed the relationship between the independent variable and conformity. The relationship with legitimacy was found to be unexpectedly complex. The anticipated relationship with performance was not confirmed.

A significant recent trend in organization theory is the separation of the dimensions in Weber's construct of bureaucracy. Udy, for

example, has recently obtained illuminating results from a cross-cultural analysis of production organizations in which "bureau-

Reprinted from *The American Sociological Review*, 1961, 26, pages 883–893, by permission of authors and publisher, The American Sociological Association.

* Revised version of a paper read at the annual meeting of the American Sociological Association, Chicago, Illinois, September, 1959. We wish to

acknowledge our indebtedness to the Council for Research in the Social Sciences of Columbia University for a grant which defrayed part of the cost of the experiment. We are also immensely grateful to the following graduate students at Columbia University whose enthusiasm and competence made this experiment possible: Sanci Cohen Michael, project assistant; Koya Azumi, Joan Dulchin, cratic" properties, such as hierarchy and the existence of an administrative staff, are shown to be independent of "rational" properties of formal organization, such as limited objectives and segmental participation.[1] Similarly, Gouldner has made an effort to separate "rational" from "legal" components of bureaucratic authority in defining the "representative" and the "punishment-centered" types of bureaucracy.[2] In this paper we report a laboratory experiment intended to contribute to this trend in organization theory.

THE PROBLEM

The *rational* component of bureaucratic authority refers to the use of technical knowledge in the allocation of means to the efficient attainment of ends. "Bureaucratic administration," says Weber, means "the exercise of control on the basis of knowledge. This is the feature of it which makes it specifically rational."[3] The *legal* component of authority relates to the normative order which regulates relations among incumbents of a graded system of offices. To ensure impersonal and impartial administration, authority is vested in the office and not in the office-holder. The claims to legitimacy of such an authority system are based on a belief in the validity of the normative order and in the right of the office-holder to issue commands. Thus, Weber's "rational-legal"

system of bureaucratic authority may be interpreted as having two dimensions, "the authority of knowledge" and "the authority of office."[4]

As a consequence of his ideal-type method, Weber treated these dimensions as perfectly correlated; bureaucratic authority rests on office, but offices[5] are filled solely on grounds of merit. Parsons was perhaps the first to point out that the two dimensions of authority are conceptually, and even empirically, independent.[6] If they are dichotomized and conceived to be independent, four types can be identified. Each type can be illustrated by an empirical case:

Type 1. The ideal type: the qualified official.
Type 2. Knowledge without office: the staff specialist in industrial organizations.
Type 3. Office without knowledge: the "lay" administrator in professional organizations.
Type 4. Neither office nor knowledge: the "job holder."

Type 2 has received a considerable amount of attention, and its strains are well known.[7] Conflict would probably be very much greater if organizations did not develop structural arrangements to accommodate to this strain. Barnard, for example, thought that knowledge without office could not command obedience; but it could exercise influence through institutionalized advisory relations.[8] Thus the staff-line arrangement may be an accommodation which actually reduces the degree of disruption inherent in

---

Theodore Ernst, Jerald Hage, Paul Lehrman, John Lofland, John Michael, Jane Mullins, Elaine Rosenbaum Meyer, and Robert Smith. We also wish to thank Morton Deutsch and Stanley H. Udy, Jr. for especially helpful comments on the manuscript. For a discussion of the methodological aspects of this experiment, see Morris Zelditch, Jr. and William M. Evan, "Simulated Bureaucracies: A Methodological Analysis," in Harold Guetzkow, editor, *Simulation of Social Systems,* Englewood Cliffs, N.J.: Prentice-Hall, 1962.

[1] Stanley H. Udy, Jr., " 'Bureaucracy' and 'Rationality' in Weber's Organization Theory: An Empirical Study," *American Sociological Review,* 24 (December, 1959), pp. 791–795.

[2] Alvin W. Gouldner, *Patterns of Industrial Bureaucracy,* Glencoe, Ill.: The Free Press, 1954, pp. 19–24; see also "Organizational Analysis," in Robert K. Merton, Leonard Broom and Leonard S. Cottrell, Jr., editors, *Sociology Today,* New York: Basic Books, 1959, pp. 402–403 and 413–417.

[3] A. M. Henderson and Talcott Parsons, editors, *Max Weber: The Theory of Social and Economic Organization,* New York: Oxford University Press, 1947, p. 339.

[4] Authority of office also entails a body of experience and knowledge of a non-technical character which is distinguishable from authority of knowledge. Administrative knowledge, as it may be called, includes not only "official secrets" but access to information about rules and policy decisions which is generally confined to certain categories of statuses in an organization.

[5] "Office" is used as an abbreviation of "authority of office" and "an office" is used for a status in an organization which has authority of office. Note that some statuses in an organization do not have office, hence the term is not synonymous with "status."

[6] Henderson and Parsons, *op. cit.,* "Introduction" by Talcott Parsons, pp. 58–60, note 4.

[7] Cf. Melville Dalton, "Conflicts between Staff and Line Managerial Officers," *American Sociological Review,* 15 (June, 1950), pp. 342–351.

[8] Chester I. Barnard, *The Functions of the Executive,* Cambridge, Massachusetts: Harvard University Press, 1938, pp. 174–175.

having members in an organization who have knowledge without office.

Type 3, although perhaps not as well understood, is also very common. In hospitals, for example, authority is frequently in the hands of persons with either equal or less knowledge than those over whom it is exercised. The accommodation may be very similar to that known for Type 2. Goss reports that the staff in a large teaching and research hospital distinguishes between problems of administration and problems of a technical nature. With respect to the former, superiors may give commands and they will be obeyed; with respect to the latter they may give only advice.[9]

In the experiment reported here the problem of office without knowledge is investigated in an artificial professional bureaucracy which is not permitted the accommodations observed in natural situations. The knowledge differential between supervisors and subordinates is varied, office remaining constant. The effects predicted are probably consistent with Weber's analysis and also with Barnard's.[10] The effects examined are: (a) the performance of subordinates; (b) the beliefs of subordinates regarding the legitimacy of their superior's authority; (c) the conformity of subordinates to the rules of the organization and to the commands of their superiors. The first two dependent variables are explicitly considered by Weber; the third is implicitly recognized as an organizational problem. We expect all three variables to be negatively affected by office without knowledge, and we expect legitimacy—the willingness of subordinates to accept the authority of their superiors as valid —to play the role of an intervening variable. We also hypothesize that subordinates will discriminate among the commands of their superiors, considering some of these actions to be primarily *administrative* and others to

be primarily *technical*. The negative effects of office without knowledge should be confined to the latter.

DESIGN OF THE EXPERIMENT

In designing this experiment we attempted to simulate some features of an actual organization. Although we used college students as subjects, we did not recruit them in their role as students or as experimental subjects. Instead, we "hired" 45 students as part-time employees, at the rate of $1.25 an hour, to code the face sheet of a questionnaire supposedly distributed nationally by a fictitious survey organization called *National Social Surveys, Inc.* The knowledge differential between superordinate and subordinate was manipulated by varying the responses of coding supervisors to questions asked by the subjects. To make sure that some questions were asked, a set of "traps" was created; that is, subjects were given a code book that did not provide the solution to certain coding problems. Coders were told that in such cases the decision was the responsibility of the coding supervisor whom they never saw but with whom they could communicate by telephone. Communication with supervisors was mediated by telephone for two reasons: (a) to simulate one of the features of an organization which distinguish it from a small group;[11] and (b) to avoid contaminating the experimental variable of knowledge differential with other variables such as the supervisor's personality or his other statuses, for example, ethnic, religious, racial, etc.

An effort was made to reduce the number of calls that concerned matters other than the trap questions in order to have a uniform administration of the experimental stimulus. A pretest indicated how to avoid many such calls, but they were not entirely eliminated. Coding supervisors were given a standard set of responses to each trap, varying for each treatment, and a general set of instructions for dealing with other calls, which also varied with each treatment.

The sequence of the experiment may be

[9] Mary E. W. Goss, *Physicians in Bureaucracy: A Case Study of Professional Pressures on Organizational Roles,* Columbia University: Unpublished Doctoral Dissertation, 1959. See also William M. Evan, "Some Consequences of a Discrepant Authority Relationship," *Proceedings and Summaries of the 23rd Annual Meeting, New York State Psychological Association* (May, 1960), pp. 32–34.

[10] See Barnard, *op. cit.,* and "Functions and Pathology of Status Systems in Formal Organizations," in W. F. Whyte, editor, *Industry and Society,* New York: McGraw-Hill, 1946.

[11] Cf. Harold Guetzkow and Anne E. Bowes, "The Development of Organizations in a Laboratory," *Management Science,* 3 (July, 1957), pp. 380–381.

divided into three time periods which we may label t_0, t_1 and t_2. In t_0 three coders at a time were instructed by one of the experimenters, identified as the project director, in both the practice of coding and in the rules of the organization. The introductory statement describing the organization emphasized the professional and non-profit nature of the organization, and the importance of avoiding DK's and NA's. It read, in part, as follows:

> National Social Surveys, Inc. is a non-profit research organization sponsored by several universities. It is dedicated to the discovery of scientific knowledge about human behavior, principally through the use of sample surveys. To realize this objective, it takes great pains to recruit personnel who will conduct research of the highest caliber. All personnel of the organization, whether directors of projects, coding supervisors, or coders, are expected to perform their work in accordance with traditional scientific standards of objectivity, accuracy, and integrity. Imagination as well as meticulousness are requirements of scientific research.
>
> As a coder for National Social Surveys, you perform operations which are of critical importance for the conduct of a research project. Errors in coding diminish the validity of the data which have been collected with great care and at a great cost. To avoid errors, *please read the following coding and operating instructions carefully.*

The experimenter also stressed calling the supervisor if difficulty was encountered. This instruction period, in which each subject also practiced coding, took about one-half hour. At the end, the subject was given a code book, a statement of the organization's rules, a batch of questionnaires to code, code sheets, and time sheets on which to keep a record of his work.

The three subjects were then taken to separate rooms. It was explained that efficiency was greater if each coder worked independently. We did this to eliminate the effects of group interaction among subjects. However, in each room there was an observer to record spontaneous comments and nonverbal behavior of the subjects. The observer, if he was asked, said he was working on a different project and knew nothing about the project on which the subjects were working. His behavior was unobtrusive and he was not recognized as an observer.

In t_1 all subjects were exposed to technically competent supervisors for about 45 minutes. The supervisors were confederates of the experimenters. This period had several functions: it permitted the coder to establish a standard of comparison where otherwise he might not be able to discriminate incompetent responses; it increased the homogeneity of the subjects by giving them at least some common prior experience with the organization; and finally, in order to reduce heterogeneity due to differences in intelligence and personality differences such as degree of authoritarianism, which we were unable to measure before allocation of treatments to subjects, we wanted repeated measurements on the same individuals.

The beginning of t_2 was signalled when the supervisor called the coder, announced that he had to leave, and assigned him to another supervisor on another extension. The supervisors were then rotated among subjects to control for variations in the personalities of the confederates. At the same time, a messenger brought a new batch of questionnaires to ensure that all subjects started t_2 with the same task. The allocation of both confederates and treatments was random, yielding a randomized complete blocks design in which the confederates in the role of second supervisor are the blocks.

The independent variable was translated into three experimental treatments: exposure to a superior-knowledge supervisor, to an equal-knowledge supervisor, and to an inferior-knowledge supervisor. In the superior-knowledge treatment the coding supervisor exhibited special resources and special knowledge of his job; he invariably replied to the coder's questions with a rational and occasionally a technical justification for his decision. In the equal-knowledge treatment the coding supervisor exhibited about as much knowledge as the coder himself had by that time: the supervisor sometimes indicated this by asking the coder what he thought and by arriving at a decision with the aid of the code book, thus evidencing no resources superior to those of the coder. In the inferior-knowledge treatment the supervisor always said he was uncertain and advised the coder to code the problematic item "no answer."[12]

In addition to their responses to trap-items, which constitute technical orders, the supervisors in each period gave certain administrative orders, common to all treatments, concerning the signing of code sheets and the keeping of time sheets.

After the 45 minutes of t_2 elapsed, coders were visited by interviewers who identified themselves as representatives of a management research organization studying *National Social Surveys, Inc.* The interviewer asked questions designed to obtain evaluations of the supervisors, perceptions of incorrect decisions, the grounds for obeying such decisions, the beliefs regarding the right of the supervisors to hold their jobs and their right to expect obedience. The interviewer then explained the experiment to the subject. All but three of the subjects responded to the explanation in good humor. These three, and others who were really in need of a part-time job and were disappointed to learn that it was an experiment, were placed on actual coding jobs on other projects. In designing the experiment, we were mindful of the ethical problems involved and took precautions to minimize the chances of any harmful effects on the subjects.

[12] We intended to have 15 subjects in each treatment; the actual distribution of subjects is 15 in the superior-knowledge treatment, 14 in the equal-knowledge treatment, and 16 in the inferior-knowledge treatment.

The experiment was completed in three days during the Easter vacation in order to reduce contamination from interaction of students. Subjects were instructed not to talk about the experiment until they returned to school.

RESULTS

Validation of the Independent Variable. Despite some success during the pretest, we were concerned that the independent variable might not be induced. The equal-knowledge treatment appeared particularly difficult to discriminate from the inferior-knowledge treatment, and it was not clear how much effect the personality of the supervisor would have on heterogeneity within treatment. To validate the independent variable we used several items of information: how the coders evaluated the t_2 supervisors compared to the t_1 supervisors on a 10-point scale of technical competence; how they evaluated themselves compared to both their supervisors on the same scale; how many of their supervisors' decisions they perceived as wrong; and how they spontaneously reacted during the trial as recorded by the observers.

On all four indicators the inferior and superior levels of knowledge were clearly differentiated (see Table 1). The equal level of knowledge, however, does not fall half-way between the inferior and superior levels. On three of the four indicators it is differen-

TABLE 1

VALIDATION OF THE INDEPENDENT VARIABLE

Indicator	Treatment: Second Supervisor's Level of Knowledge*			Mood-Brown Analysis of Variance[13]		
	Inferior	Equal	Superior	Treatment χ^2	df	P
Wrong decisions perceived:						
Increase in number	2.0	1.6	−0.3	16.88	2	<.01
Evaluation of 1st and 2nd supervisors:						
Mean difference	5.0	3.3	0.2	22.13	2	<.01
Evaluation of self and 2nd supervisor:						
Mean difference	2.7	1.5	−3.2	20.06	2	<.01
Spontaneous negative comments:						
Increase in number	10	8	3	3.72**	2	.10<P<.20

* Block means, block χ^2, and the χ^2 for interaction are not shown. No block or interaction effects were significant.

** Significance computed by a straightforward χ^2 rather than by Mood-Brown analysis of variance.

tiated from the inferior and superior levels sufficiently to consider it a separate treatment, but it is consistently closer to the inferior level of knowledge than to the superior level. Nor can the equal-knowledge treatment be accurately thought of as "equal"; subjects in this treatment see themselves as 1.5 points *more* competent than their second supervisors.

Despite these difficulties with the equal level of knowledge, all treatment differences, with the exception of spontaneous gestures and comments, are statistically significant. This indicates that the treatments differentiated among subjects. No block differences are significant, indicating that supervisors played their roles well enough to eliminate effects of their own personalities. And no interaction effects are significant, indicating that supervisors played all roles equally well so that no particular supervisor combined with any particular knowledge-level had some effect not predictable from the main effects of the experiment.

Performance. We expected that performance would be differentiated by treatment; we found that it was not. We used two measures of performance. First, we measured the coder's rate of speed. The amount of time actually spent coding, after subtracting the time spent on telephone calls to the supervisors, was divided by the number of questionnaires completed for each time period. We then subtracted the rate in t_2 from the rate in t_1, yielding a measure of the increasing rate of speed of the coder between the two periods. There was no difference by either treatment or block. Second, we measured the per cent of "non-trap" items that were coded incorrectly in the two coding periods, subtracting the rate in the first period from the rate in the second period. This yields a measure of increasing error from t_1 to t_2. Here also there were no treatment or block differences.

We were, of course, surprised by the lack of performance results, despite the fact that a number of experiments with organizational variables find equally little result in the area of performance.[14] We first checked our randomization, thinking that more intelligent subjects might have been assigned to the inferior-knowledge treatment, counteracting the treatment effects. But the tendency, although not statistically significant, is actually for them to be in the superior-knowledge treatment. We then thought that the nature of the task was such that more intelligent subjects would be more adversely affected by its routine character than the less intelligent subjects. But the correlation of ability —indicated by verbal and mathematical scores on the College Entrance Board Examination—with the distribution of performance differences is almost exactly zero.

Other possibilities suggest themselves. First, there simply may not have been enough time for performance effects to show themselves. Second, performance of such a routine task, with such limited variation in its time-and-motion aspects, may have been an insensitive indicator of treatment effects. Third, it is quite possible that the negative findings are real. The market situation of the "employees" of this particular "organization" may have led them to perform as well as possible, independently of their reactions to their supervisors. They were interested in short-run job opportunities, did not have quickly-marketable skills in other labor markets, and possibly regarded their initial performance as a "test" on which subsequent employment was contingent. The result

---

[13] Almost all of the distributions in this experiment are markedly platykurtic, which led us to use nonparametric methods throughout. Kurtosis affects particularly the power of the parametric test. See, for example, A. B. L. Srivastava, "The Effect of Nonnormality on the Power of the Analysis of Variance Test," *Biometrika,* 46 (June, 1959), pp. 114–122. The Mood-Brown two-way analysis of variance, based on median tests, was used for the following reasons: (1) for cell sizes greater

than two it is distribution-free; (2) it is not disturbed by unequal cell sizes; (3) the more familiar Friedman two-way analysis of variance by ranks demands too great a cost in degrees of freedom; and (4) the interpretation of interaction effects in the Friedman test is disturbed by more than one observation per cell. See G. W. Brown, and A. M. Mood, "On Median Tests for Linear Hypotheses," in J. Neyman, editor, *Second Berkeley Symposium on Mathematical Statistics and Probability,* Berkeley, California: University of California Press, 1951; A. M. Mood, *Introduction to the Theory of Statistics,* New York: McGraw-Hill, 1950, pp. 402–406; and M. W. Tate and R. C. Clellands, *Non-parametric and Short-cut Statistics,* Danville, Ill.: Interstate Printers and Publishers, 1957, pp. 115–129.

[14] Guetzkow and Bowes, *op. cit.,* p. 393; see also Harold Guetzkow and William R. Dill, "Factors in the Organizational Development of Task-Oriented Groups," *Sociometry,* 20 (September, 1957), p. 179.

might have been like that described by Goode and Fowler, who found that productivity in a feeder plant which employed primarily handicapped, non-unionized workers was independent of morale. Workers could be easily fired, found it difficult to get other jobs, and consequently produced at a high level of efficiency despite low morale.[15]

Conformity to Technical Rules and Commands. The most important technical rule of the organization concerned telephoning the supervisor when a coding problem was encountered. We had expected that subjects in the inferior- and equal-knowledge treatments would be more likely to violate this rule than those in the superior treatment. There was, in fact, a tendency in all three groups to telephone the supervisor less in t_2 than in t_1. But, while the drop-off rate in the inferior treatment is more rapid than the drop-off rate in the superior treatment, the treatments are not significantly different in this respect (see Table 2). Otherwise, our expectations concerning technical rules and orders were generally confirmed.

Our most marked result in the area of nonconformity was in the "trap-error" rates.

[15] William J. Goode and Irving Fowler, "Incentive Factors in a Low Morale Plant," *American Sociological Review,* 14 (October, 1949), pp. 619–624.

By a "trap-error" we mean coding errors on trap-items only. The three treatments differ significantly in the number of trap-errors made, i.e., in the number of acts of non-conformity (see Table 2). This effect appears to be due to three distinct factors. First, there is some tendency for subjects in the inferior treatment to telephone less often, and thus to discover the correct response less often, even though this tendency is not statistically significant. Those who guess at the code and do not telephone very often guess incorrectly. Second, there is some tendency for subjects actually to disobey the instructions of their supervisor in the inferior treatment and to guess at an answer rather than code it NA. We will call this overt or active disobedience. Third, and most important, there is a distinct tendency to passive or covert disobedience; many subjects, told to code a response NA, manage to code NA incorrectly or fail to code the item at all.[16] Covert disobedience

[16] This is rather difficult to detect after the fact, but not impossible. For example, in one trap-item occupational skill-level and prestige are to be coded for an occupation that does not appear listed in the code book. The inferior-knowledge supervisor instructs the coder to code it DK, which is a 9 in column 4 and an X in column 5. Many subjects in this treatment make the error of coding either 9 only or X only, or code $9XX$, there being a vacant space in column 6. These are called errors but they are hardly direct acts of disobedience.

TABLE 2

CONFORMITY: MEAN DECREASE IN "TRAP" CALLS,* MEAN INCREASE IN ERROR,**
AND MEAN INCREASE IN DISOBEDIENCE***

Conformity	Treatment: Second Supervisor's Level of Knowledge****			Mood-Brown Analysis of Variance		
	Inferior	Equal	Superior	Treatment χ^2	df	P
Mean decrease in "trap" calls	−.26	−.21	−.15	5.69	6	.30<P<.50
Mean increase in "trap" error	2.50	1.36	1.53	10.81	2	P<.01
Mean increase in disobedience	1.25	0.57	0.00	8.31	2	.01<P<.02

    * Decrease in trap calls is measured by subtracting the per cent of items on which the coder telephones the supervisor in the second coding period from the per cent on which he telephones in the first coding period. The base of the percentage is the number of trap-items on which it was *possible* for the coder to telephone; the base was adjusted for individuals who did not complete a sufficient number of questionnaires to code all trap items.
    ** Non-conformity is measured here by subtracting the number of trap-errors in the first coding period from the number in the second.
    *** If, on a given trap-item, a subject telephoned his supervisor, was instructed how to code an item, but then made an error of any kind in coding that item, the error was defined as disobedience to the supervisor's instructions. The number of acts of disobedience in the first period was subtracted from the number in the second.
    **** To save space, block means, block χ^2 and interaction χ^2 are omitted. No block or interaction effects were significant.

accounts for most of the disobedience that occurs. There are, in all treatments combined, 59 acts of disobedience—that is, instances in which the subject telephones his supervisor, is instructed by the supervisor, and then makes a trap-error. Only twenty-seven per cent of these instances are overt acts of disobedience; i.e., instances in which the error is due to the subjects apparently attempting to violate directly the supervisor's instruction. Covert and overt non-conformity combined differ significantly by treatment (see Table 2).

Conformity to Administrative Rules and Commands. Concerning administrative rules and commands, we had expected that there would be no differences in conformity by treatment. By and large this expectation was borne out. In the coding-instruction period subjects were told to sign their full names on each code sheet after completion of each questionnaire. In the middle of t_2 the second supervisor changed this rule, prescribing initials in the place of full signatures. Subjects were also directed by the coding-instructor (who was identified as the project director, it will be recalled) to record the time, on time sheets, after every 10 completed questionnaires. The second-period supervisor changed this rule to every five minutes. A third administrative rule remained constant throughout; this was an instruction to draw a line through errors and re-code correctly on the same code sheet, never erasing or destroying code sheets.

With respect to two of these indicators, the results are clear-cut; with respect to the third, the results are in the same direction but the data are unreliable. There are no treatment differences in conformity to the signature order; nor is erasing of errors on code sheets differentiated by treatment. The time sheet data are inconclusive because the recording by both subjects and observers was sufficiently unclear that reliable coding of the results was not possible.

These negative results, as in the case of the performance results, may be due to the brief time of the trials rather than to the true absence of treatment effects.

Legitimacy of Technical Commands. The process of legitimation is complex and as yet little understood. We had intended to avoid the difficult question of how it operates by measuring only its end-product, legitimacy of the supervisor's authority—that is, belief in the obligation to obey his commands. But regardless of what subjects thought of their supervisors, in post-session interviews virtually no one questioned the supervisor's right to expect obedience to his commands even where subjects said they thought the decisions embodied in these commands were wrong.

This result made conclusive analysis of the process intervening between treatments and effects almost impossible. First, since no attempt had been made before the experiment to conceptualize the legitimation process, very few indicators of it were available for analysis. Those that were available were in some respects contaminated. Second, because components of the legitimation process had not been intentionally manipulated, a complete set of replicates for all appropriate contrasts could not be obtained with the available results. Third, the hypotheses which would guide such an analysis were in danger of being both result-guided and *ad hoc*.

Yet some of the post-session interview responses did yield clues to the operation of this process, and we made an effort to trace the intervening process as far as the data permitted. To guard against result-guided, *ad hoc* interpretation, new hypotheses were grounded as far as possible in the original conceptualization of the experiment.

At least three components of the process of legitimation are probably at work in the experiment. One is the subject's judgment that the supervisor has authority of office. While we have no indicator of this judgment, there were no differences in this variable incorporated into treatments and there should be no effects due to it. A second component is the subject's judgment that the supervisor has authority of knowledge. This is indicated by a post-session question in which subjects were asked, for each supervisor, if the supervisor had a right to his job. A third component is the subject's conception of the basis on which legitimacy should be accorded in this particular type of organization. This would include, for example, their views regarding the relative importance of knowledge vs. office as a basis of legitimacy. This is indicated by the reasons subjects gave for their feeling an obligation to obey.

As one would expect, feelings about the supervisor's right to his job were sharply differentiated by treatment (see Table 3). Quite unexpectedly, the basis on which legitimacy was granted also differed by treatment. Responses to interviewer probes into the obligation to obey were classified as: (1) *bureaucratic,* if subjects stressed legal obligations of their status ("I was hired to obey," or "It's his job to give orders") or bureaucratic principles of organization ("Organizations must have hierarchies"); (2) *professional,* if subjects stressed expertise of the supervisor ("The supervisor knows more about it") or the scientific goals of the survey ("uniform categories and consistent decisions ensure valid results"); and (3) *mixed* responses, if subjects mentioned both. The instructions during coder-training had clearly stressed the professional goal of the organization. But the treatments shifted the basis on which subjects accorded legitimacy from "professional" to "bureaucratic" grounds (see Table 4). Only 2 per cent of those who obeyed the first supervisor on "bureaucratic" grounds changed in response to the second supervisor, but there was a marked shift of those who obeyed the first supervisor on "professional" grounds if they were subjected to the inferior- or equal-knowledge treatment.

The way in which these two components of the legitimation process interacted is difficult to discern in the experiment because shifts in "right to office" responses were associated with shifts in "basis of legitimacy" responses. The two were completely independent in the initial period of the experiment ($\phi = .06$, $\chi^2 = 0.17$, $.50 < P < .70$), but in t_2 there was a marked increase in their association ($\phi = .44$, $\chi^2 = 4.63$, $.02 < P < .05$). This association was brought about by two kinds of shifts: (1) subjects who gave "bureaucratic" responses in t_1 and felt the first supervisor had a right to his job were likely to remain "bureaucratic" and feel the second supervisor did *not* have a right to his job if they received the inferior- or equal-knowledge treatment; (2) subjects who gave "professional" or "mixed" responses in t_1 and felt the supervisor had a right to his job were likely to change both responses if they received the inferior- or equal-knowledge treatment.

That "right to job" responses did act as an intervening variable in the experiment is evident from their relation to conformity. Shifts on this item from "yes" in t_1 to "qualified yes" or "no" in t_2 were significantly related to increases in disobedience. This effect was independent of any effects due to shifts in the "basis of legitimacy." Among those who did not shift the basis on which they granted legitimacy, subjects who shifted "right to job" response, compared with

TABLE 3

CHANGES IN CONCEPTIONS OF LEGITIMACY: SUBJECTS' JUDGMENT OF RIGHT TO JOB OF FIRST AND SECOND SUPERVISORS

Subjects' Judgment of Right to Job		Treatment: Second Supervisor's Level of Knowledge			
of 1st Sup.	of 2nd Sup.	Inferior	Equal	Superior	Total
		(N = 16)	(N = 14)	(N = 15)	(N = 45)
Yes	Yes	13%	36%	67%	38%
Yes	Qual. Yes, No	81%	43%	7%	44%
Qual. Yes, No	Qual. Yes, No	..	..	13%	4%
Any NA		6%	21%	13%	13%
	Total	100%	100%	100%	99%

$\chi^2 = 15.53$; df = 2; P < .001.
χ^2 was computed after removing rows 3 and 4.
Qual. Yes = Qualified Yes.

TABLE 4

CHANGES IN CONCEPTIONS OF LEGITIMACY: SUBJECTS' GROUNDS FOR BELIEF IN
LEGITIMACY OF FIRST AND SECOND SUPERVISORS

Subjects' Grounds for Legitimation		Treatment: Second Supervisor's Level of Knowledge			Total
of 1st Sup.	of 2nd Sup.	Inferior	Equal	Superior	
		(N = 16)	(N = 14)	(N = 15)	(N = 45)
P, M	P, M	12%	..	47%	20%
P, M	Bur.	38%	36%	7%	27%
Bur.	P, M	..	..	7%	2%
Bur.	Bur.	38%	36%	12%	29%
Any NA		12%	28%	27%	22%
	Total	100%	100%	100%	100%

$\chi^2 = 14.80$: df $= 4$; $.01 < P < .001$.
χ^2 was computed after removing rows 3 and 5.
P = Professional. Bur. = Bureaucratic, M = Mixed.

subjects who did not, had a significantly higher increase in disobedience ($H = 3.88$; $.02 < P < .05$).[17] There were very few subjects who shifted the basis on which they granted legitimacy and at the same time remained constant in "right to job" response.

It is therefore impossible to say how this variable would operate independently. But it is possible to examine its interaction effects. Our conjecture was that shifts in basis of according legitimacy would dampen the effects of shifts in "right to job," since authority of office would replace authority of knowledge as the more important criterion for granting legitimacy. There was no difference, however, between those who shifted on both variables and those who shifted only "right to job" responses ($H = 0$).

Legitimacy of Administrative Rules and Commands. The post-session interview probed into beliefs regarding legitimacy of administrative rules and commands as well as into beliefs regarding legitimacy of technical commands. As we had anticipated, there was no difference in beliefs regarding legitimacy of administrative rules and com-

mands by treatment. Almost all subjects felt obliged to obey a supervisor's decisions about administrative matters, just as they had about technical matters. Unlike the case of technical commands, however, the grounds for legitimacy also were not differentiated by treatment. Subjects generally advanced "bureaucratic" rather than "professional" justifications for obeying administrative rules and commands.

SUMMARY AND CONCLUSION

The purpose of the present experiment is to separate the *rational* and *legal* components of Weber's theory of bureaucratic authority, and to vary the dimension of authority of knowledge while holding authority of office constant. Hypotheses concerning the effects of variations in authority of knowledge on performance, conformity, and legitimacy are suggested by Weber's theory.

In order to separate systematically the two dimensions under controlled conditions, and also to observe systematically instances in which officials without knowledge gave technical as well as administrative commands, a small part of a fictitious research organization was simulated. Three statuses in this organization were activated: a project director, a status occupied by one of the experimenters who appeared only during a training session; a coding supervisor, a status

[17] Where only one-way analysis of variance was required, the Kruskal-Wallis H-test was used. See W. H. Kruskal and W. A. Wallis, "The Use of Ranks in One-criterion Variance Analysis," *Journal of American Statistical Association,* 47 (December, 1952), pp. 583–621; and the very convenient description in S. Siegel, *Nonparametric Statistics for the Behavioral Sciences,* New York: McGraw-Hill Book Co., 1956, pp. 184–193.

occupied by confederates of the experimenters; and a coder, a status occupied by naive subjects, hired at $1.25 an hour for what they thought were real jobs. The main operative unit of the organization was the supervisor-coder relationship. Other parts of the organization were simulated by occasional inputs to this unit, and beliefs about the organization were manipulated by information given in the instruction period. The organization was "professional" in its goals, but clearly the subjects were not themselves professionals nor oriented to careers in this organization, despite efforts to induce a professional attitude in the instruction period. Various extraneous sources of variation were eliminated by (1) a before-after design, to remove effects of individual differences in subjects; and (2) extreme simplification of the organizational context— e.g, communication by telephone only, elimination of interaction between subordinates —to eliminate contaminating organizational processes.

The independent variable was manipulated by varying supervisors' responses to requests for decisions made by subjects who were faced with "traps" in the coding process. "Traps" were built into the task by presenting coding situations for which no solutions were provided in instructions in the code book.

We hypothesized that (a) if an official held office without commensurate knowledge, subjects would not accord legitimacy to the official's authority; (b) that this erosion of the supervisor's authority would have negative effects both on the subordinates' performance and on their conformity to technical rules and commands; (c) but that conformity to administrative rules and commands would not be affected by treatment differences.

The following results were actually obtained:

(1) The treatments did not differentiate performance measures.

(2) Marked treatment differences appeared in rates of conformity to technical commands, particularly in "covert" non-conformity.

(3) Treatment differences in rates of conformity were accounted for in part by shifts in the belief that the supervisor had a right to occupy his office.

(4) The treatments induced subjects to change the grounds appropriate to defining legitimate authority in such an organization. Subjects in inferior- and equal-knowledge treatments were likely to shift from *"professional"* to *"bureaucratic"* bases of legitimacy.

(5) Almost all subjects, regardless of treatment, felt obligated to obey commands of their supervisor, even though for different reasons.

(6) No treatment effects were observed in either conformity to, or in beliefs regarding legitimacy of, administrative rules and commands.

As for the significance of the experiment: many important questions are suggested simply by observing that both office without knowledge and knowledge without office empirically occur. For example, what are the consequences of these combinations of office and knowledge for different kinds of organizations? Under what conditions does one occur rather than the other? What are the possible variations in the structural arrangements through which organizations accommodate to discrepant combinations of office and knowledge? These questions presuppose that discrepant combinations of office and knowledge will pose a "problem" in the absence of certain kinds of socially-structured accommodations. In general, our experiment seems to confirm this proposition, which suggests that the questions based on it are meaningful and are likely to provide fruitful lines of inquiry.

Organizational experiments,[18] such as the one presented here, obviously need not be confined to authority problems, critical as these are for any organization. They can also revolve around problems of division of labor, types of rewards, reward differentials, or any of a large number of other organizational variables. It seems to us likely that if experimental sociologists succeed in designing theoretically-significant simulations of organizational structures and organizational processes, they will considerably accelerate progress in a field already developing rapidly.

[18] For examples of noteworthy organizational experiments, see Donald F. Clark and Russell L. Ackoff, "A Report on Some Organizational Experiments," *Operations Research,* 7 (May–June, 1959), pp. 279–293; C. West Churchman and Philburn Ratoosh, "Innovation in Group Behavior," *Management Science Nucleus,* Working Paper No. 10 (January, 1960) dittoed.

The Experimental Change of a Major Organizational Variable[1] /

Nancy C. Morse (*The Merrill Palmer School*)
and Everett Reimer (*Office of Personnel, Commonwealth of Puerto Rico*)

This experiment is one in a series of studies of social behavior in large-scale organizations undertaken by the Human Relations Program of the Survey Research Center. Its primary aim is to investigate the relationship between the allocation of decision-making processes in a large hierarchical organization and (*a*) the individual satisfactions of the members of the organization, (*b*) the productivity of the organization.

The results of several previous studies suggested that the individual's role in decision-making might affect his satisfaction and productivity. The effectiveness of decision-making in small groups shown by Lewin, Lippitt, and others (4, 5) and the successful application of small-group decision-making to method changes in an industrial setting by Coch and French (1) both indicated the pos-

Reprinted from *Journal of Abnormal and Social Psychology,* 1956, 52, pages 120–129, by special permission of the publisher, The American Psychological Association.

[1] This is a short description of an experiment done while the authors were on the staff of the Human Relations Program of the Survey Research Center, University of Michigan. Financial support for field work and analysis of the data came from the Rockefeller Foundation, the Office of Naval Research Contract No. N6 onr-232 Task Order II, and the company in which the research was done. In addition to the authors the field staff of the experiment included: Arnold Tannenbaum, Frances Fielder, Gilbert David, Arlene Kohn Gilbert, Barbara Snell Dohrenwend, Ann Seidman, Jean Kraus Davison, and Winifred Libbon. The analysis staff included: Nancy Morse, Arnold Tannenbaum, Arlene Kohn Gilbert, and Ruth Griggs. The experiment will be described fully in a book now in preparation. Floyd H. Allport provided extensive assistance on the theoretical problems of the study. The experiment was under the general direction of Daniel Katz, director of the Human Relations Program during the field phase of the experiment, and Robert Kahn, director of the Human Relations Program during the analysis phase. The authors wish to express their appreciation to the staff members on the experiment and to the people in the company who cooperated in the experiment. They also want to thank particularly Daniel Katz, Robert Kahn, Arnold Tannenbaum, Carol Kaye, and Jane Williams for their helpful comments and criticisms of this article.

sibilities for enlarging the role of the rank and file in the ongoing decision-making of an organization. The practical experience of Sears, Roebuck and Co. with a "flat," administratively decentralized structure, described by Worthy (8), pointed in the same direction, as did the survey findings by Katz, Maccoby, and Morse (2) that supervisors delegating greater authority had more productive work groups. The logical next step seemed to be the controlled testing of hypotheses concerning the relationship between role in organizational decision-making and two aspects of organizational effectiveness: satisfaction and productivity. Two broad hypotheses were formulated:

Hypothesis I. An increased role in the decision-making processes for rank-and-file groups increases their satisfaction (while a decreased role in decision-making reduces satisfaction).

Hypothesis II. An increased role in decision-making for rank-and-file groups increases their productivity (while a decreased role in decision-making decreases productivity).

Both these hypotheses deal with the effects on the rank and file of different hierarchical allocations of the decision-making processes of the organization. The rationale for the satisfaction hypothesis (I) predicts different and more need-satisfying decisions when the rank and file has decision-making power than when the upper echelons of the hierarchy have that power. Furthermore, the process of decision-making itself is expected to be satisfying to the majority of people brought up in American traditions. Underlying the productivity hypothesis (II) was the consideration that local unit policy-making would increase motivation to produce and thus productivity. Motivation should rise when productivity becomes a path for greater need satisfaction. The productivity hypothesis predicts a higher degree of need satisfaction (as does Hypothesis I) *and* an increase in the degree of dependence of satisfactions upon productivity under conditions of greater rank-and-file decision-making. It is expected that when rank-and-file members work out and put into effect their own rules and regulations, their maintenance in the organization (and thus their satisfactions) will depend much more directly upon their performance.

PROCEDURE

The experiment was conducted in one department of a nonunionized industrial organization which had four parallel divisions engaged in relatively routine clerical work. The design involved increasing rank-and-file decision-making in two of the divisions and increasing upper-level decision-making in the other two divisions. The time span was one and one-half years: a before measurement, one-half year of training of supervisors to create the experimental conditions, one year under the experimental conditions, and then remeasurement. The two pairs of two divisions each were comparable on relevant variables such as initial allocation of the decision-making processes, satisfaction and productivity, as well as on such background factors as type of work, type of personnel, and type of supervisory structure.

The rank-and-file employees were women, mostly young and unmarried, with high school education. The usual clerk's plans were for marriage and a family rather than a career. The population used in the analysis except where noted is a subgroup of the clerks, the "matched" population. These clerks were present throughout the one and one-half year period, and their before and after questionnaires were individually matched. While they comprise somewhat less than half of the clerks present in these divisions at any one time, they are comparable to the total group, except on such expected variables as length of time in the division, in the work section, and on the job.

One aspect of the work situation should be mentioned, as it bears on the adequacy of the setting for a test of the productivity hypothesis. The amount of work done by the divisions was completely dependent upon the flow of work to them, i.e., the total number of units to be done was not within the control of the divisions. With volume fixed, productivity depends upon the number of clerks needed to do the work, and increased productivity can be achieved only

by out-placement of clerks or by foregoing replacement of clerks who leave for other reasons.

The Development of the Experimental Conditions

Creating the experimental programs included three steps: (a) planning by research staff and company officials; (b) introducing the programs to the division supervisory personnel and training of the supervisors for their new roles; and (c) introduction to the clerks and operation under the experimental conditions.

The experiment was carried out within the larger framework of company operations. The introduction, training, and operations were in the hands of company personnel. The experimental changes were not made through personnel shifts; the changes were in what people did in their jobs with respect to the decision-making processes of the organization.

Two main change processes were used in both the Autonomy program, designed to increase rank-and-file decision-making, and in the Hierarchically-controlled program, designed to increase the upper management role in the decision-making processes. First, there were formal structural changes to create a new organizational environment for the divisions in each program. In both programs the hierarchical legitimization of new roles preceded the taking of the new roles.[2] In the Autonomy program authority was delegated by upper management to lower levels in the hierarchy with the understanding that they would redelegate it to the clerical work groups. In the Hierarchically-controlled program, authority was given to the higher line officials to increase their role in the running of the divisions and to the staff officials to increase their power to institute changes within the two divisions in that program. Second, there were training programs for the supervisors of the divisions to ensure that the formal changes would result in actual changes in relations between people. (For a longer description of the change programs see Reimer [6].)

---

[2] Weber and others have used the word "legitimization" to refer to the acceptance by subordinates of the authority of superiors. We are using the word in quite a different sense. By hierarchical legitimization we mean the formal delegation of authority by superiors to subordinates. This delegation *legitimizes* the subordinates' utilization of this authority.

Measurement

The results of the changes were gauged through before and after measurements and through continuing measurements during the experimental period. The major emphasis was on the attitudes and perceptions of the clerks as reflected in extensive questionnaires. In addition, the training programs and the operations phase of the experiment were observed. Before and after interviews were conducted with the supervisory personnel of the division. Data from company records such as productivity rates, turnover figures, etc., were also included.

The data reported here will be confined to material most pertinent to the testing of the two hypotheses. For other related aspects of the experiment, see Tannenbaum's study of the relationship of personality characteristics and adjustment to the two programs (7), Kaye's study of organizational goal achievement under the Autonomy program (3), as well as forthcoming publications.

RESULTS[3]

Success of Experimental Manipulation

The first question was to discover whether or not the change programs were successful in creating the conditions under which the hypotheses could be tested. Two types of data are pertinent. The first is descriptive data concerning the actual operations of the two programs. The second is perceptual data from the clerical employees themselves indicating the degree to which they saw changes in their role in organizational decisions.

The operations of the divisions in fact changed in the direction expected. In the Autonomy program the clerical work groups came to make group decisions about many of the things which affected them and which were important to them. The range of the decisions was very great, including work methods and processes, and personnel matters, such as recess periods, the handling of tardiness, etc. Probably the most important area

in which the clerks were not able to make decisions was the area of salary. Some of the work groups were more active in the decision-making process than others, but all made a very great variety of decisions in areas important to them. In the Hierarchically-controlled program the changes decreased the degree to which the employees could control and regulate their own activities. One of the main ways in which this greater limitation was manifested was through the individual work standards that staff officials developed for the various jobs. Also the greater role of upper line and staff officials in the operation of the divisions meant that the indirect influence which the clerks could have on decisions when they were made by division managers and section supervisors was reduced.

The clerks were operating under different conditions in the two programs as the result of the experimental changes, but did they perceive these changes? The method of measuring the perception of changes in decision-making was by asking clerks about their part and about the part of people above their rank in decisions with respect to a wide variety of areas of company operations, or company systems. The following questions were asked about each major area of company operations or system: "To what degree do company officers or any employees of a higher rank than yours decide how the _____ System is set up and decide the policies, rules, procedures or methods of the _____ System?" (followed by a line with the landmark statements: not at all, to a slight degree, to some degree, to a fairly high degree and to a very high degree) and, "To what degree do you and the girls in your section decide how the _____ System is set up and decide the policies, rules, procedures or methods of the _____ System?" (followed by a line with the same landmark statements as the first question).

The extreme degree of perceived hierarchical control of the decision-making processes would be shown by the clerks answering that employees of a higher rank than theirs made the decisions, "to a very high degree" and the clerks made them "not at all." Table 1 shows the number of systems where there are half or more of the clerks endorsing

---

[3] For the statistical tests used in this section, we have assumed that the individuals were randomly chosen, while the selection of individuals by divisions undoubtedly results in some clustering effect. The levels of significance should, therefore, be considered as general guides rather than in any absolute sense.

TABLE 1

NUMBER OF COMPANY SYSTEMS IN WHICH CLERKS
PERCEIVE VERY HIGH UPPER LEVEL CONTROL
OF DECISION-MAKING ALLOCATION

	Number of Systems in which Half or More Clerks Gave Specified Response		
	Before	*After*	
	All Divs	*Program I Divs*	*Program II Divs*
Response			
Upper levels decided policies to a very high degree	20	7	24
Clerks did not decide policies at all	25	9	23
Total number of systems measured	27	24	24

these two statements for the before situation and for the two experimental situations. (The Autonomy program is designated in Table 1 and thereafter as Program I and the Hierarchically-controlled program as Program II.) Questions were asked for 27 company systems in the before measurement and 24 systems in the after measurement.

Table 1 shows that the clerks perceived the decision-making processes for most of the company operations measured as located at hierarchical levels above their own, prior to the introduction of the experimental changes. The experimental changes in the Autonomy program divisions resulted in their seeing decision-making activities as much less exclusively confined to levels above theirs. The changes in the Hierarchically-controlled program were less striking but they resulted in the clerks judging that all of the systems about which they were asked in the after situation had their policies molded to a very high degree by people above their level.

The relative role of the hierarchy compared to the rank and file as perceived by the clerks was measured by assigning scores from 1 to 9 for the landmark positions on the scales for the two questions and then dividing the score for upper-level decision-making by the score for rank-and-file decision-making. The theo-

retical range for the resulting index is from 9.0 to 0, with numbers less than 1 indicating greater local control than upper-level control. Table 2 includes the average index scores for the systems from the before and after measurements calculated by division.

Table 2 indicates the change in the divisions in the Autonomy program toward

TABLE 2

EFFECT OF CHANGE PROGRAMS ON PERCEPTION OF
DECISION-MAKING ALLOCATION

Experimental Groups	*Index of Perceived Decision-Making Allocation*				
	Before Mean	*After Mean*	*Diff.*	*SE Diff.*	*N*
Program I					
Div. A	5.69	4.39	−1.30**	.24	61
Div. B	6.49	4.08	−2.41**	.26	57
Average	6.08	4.24	−1.84**	.18	118
Program II					
Div. C	6.15	6.87	+ .72**	.22	44
Div. D	6.78	7.13	+ .35	.26	44
Average	6.41	7.00	+ .59**	.17	88

NOTE:—Higher values correspond to perception of predominance of upper levels of organization in decision-making.
** Significant at the 1% level.

greater perceived rank-and-file role in decision making, but also shows that the upper levels are seen as still having the major role in the after situation. (The downward shift in perceived decision-making control in the Autonomy program is significant above the 1 per cent level by the Student's t test for paired data. A statistically significant, but slight, change toward greater upper-level control took place in the Hierarchically-controlled program.)

Both Tables 1 and 2 show that the clerks in the Autonomy program perceive as predicted a significant shift away from upper-level control when their before-after answers are compared, and that the clerks in the Hierarchically-controlled program see some increase in upper-level control over policy-making, even though it was already perceived as highly controlled from above before the experiment.

These measures of successful experimental manipulation suggest that the conditions in the two programs are sufficiently different to permit tests of the experimental hypotheses.

Hypothesis I

This hypothesis states that an increase in the decision-making role of individuals results in increased satisfactions, while a decrease in opportunity for decision-making is followed by decreased satisfaction. The general hypothesis was tested for a variety of specific areas of satisfaction. The attitudinal areas to be reported include: (a) self-actualization and growth, (b) satisfaction with supervisors, (c) liking for working for the company, (d) job satisfaction, (e) liking for program. Student's one-tailed t test for paired data was used for tests of significance. Results reaching the 5 per cent level or above are considered significant.

Self-actualization. One of the hypotheses of the study was that greater opportunity for regulating and controlling their own activities within the company structure would increase the degree to which individuals could express their various and diverse needs and could move in the direction of fully exploiting their potentialities. An increase in upper-management control on the other hand was predicted to decrease the opportunities for employee self-actualization and growth.

Five questions were used to measure this area: 1, Is your job a real challenge to what you think you can do? 2, How much chance does your job give you to learn things you're interested in? 3, Are the things you're learning in your job helping to train you for a better job in the company? 4, How much chance do you have to try out your ideas on the job? 5, How much does your job give you a chance to do the things you're best at? These five items, which were answered by checking one position on a five-point scale, were intercorrelated and then combined to form an index.[4] Table 3 shows the means for the four divisions and two groups on the self-actualization and growth index.

While both groups of clerks indicated that their jobs throughout the course of the ex-

[4] The items were intercorrelated by the tetrachoric method. When these correlations were converted to z scores the average intercorrelation was .62, corrected for length of test, a reliability index of .89 was obtained.

TABLE 3

Effect of Change Programs on Feelings of Self-Actualization on Job

Experimental Groups	Index of Perceived Self-Actualization				
	Mean Before	Mean After	Diff.	SE Diff.	N
Program I					
Div. A	2.67	2.74	+.07	.09	52
Div. B	2.18	2.39	+.21*	.11	47
Average	2.43	2.57	+.14*	.07	99
Program II					
Div. C	2.43	2.24	−.19	.14	43
Div. D	2.30	2.23	−.07	.10	38
Average	2.37	2.24	−.13*	.07	81

Note:—Scale runs from 1, low degree of self-actualization to 5, a high degree.
* Significant at the 5% level, one-tailed t test for paired data.

periment did not give them a very high degree of self-actualization, the experimental programs produced significant changes. In the Autonomy program, self-actualization increased significantly from before to after, and a corresponding decrease was shown in the Hierarchically-controlled program. At the end of the experimental period, the Autonomy program is significantly higher on this variable than the Hierarchically-controlled program.

Satisfaction with supervision. A variety of indices were developed in order to test the hypothesis that the Autonomy program would improve satisfactions with supervisors and that the Hierarchically-controlled program would reduce such satisfactions. Two general types of attitudes were separately measured: (a) satisfaction with relations with supervisors and (b) satisfaction with supervisors as a representative. These two types of attitudes were studied before and after the experimental period with respect to three levels of supervision: the first-line supervisor, the assistant manager of the division, and the manager of the division. The following three questions were asked for each of these levels in order to tap the clerks' degree of satisfaction with relations with supervisors:

1. How good is your supervisor (assistant manager, manager) at handling people?

2. Can you count on having good relations with your supervisor (assistant manager, manager) under all circumstances?

3. In general, how well do you like your supervisor (assistant manager, manager) as a person to work with?

These three questions were combined to form indices of satisfaction with relations with supervisors, assistant manager, and manager. (The items were intercorrelated for the satisfaction with relations with supervisor index. Through converting to z scores, the average intercorrelation of items is found to be .78. Correcting for length of test, i.e., using three items to form the index rather than one, the reliability index is .91 with an N of 360.)

Table 4 shows that in general there was a shift toward greater satisfaction with supervisors in the Autonomy program and toward less satisfaction with supervisors in the Hierarchically-controlled program. The divisions, however, show certain characteristic differences in satisfaction at the outset and shift in the expected direction to different degrees.

Both divisions in the Hierarchically-controlled program show a decrease in satisfaction with the first-line supervisor, although the changes are not statistically significant. The after differences between the Autonomy and the Hierarchically-controlled programs are, however, significant.

Satisfaction with relations with both the assistant manager and the manager increased significantly in the Autonomy program and decreased significantly in the Hierarchically-controlled program. Each of the divisions within the groups likewise shifted in the hypothesized directions for the two managerial indices. In the Autonomy program the assistant manager index shifted in the right direction for both divisions, but the changes were not statistically significant when each division was tested separately.

Thus while the employees were generally quite satisfied with their relations with their different supervisors, the experimental programs did have the expected effects of increasing the satisfactions of those in the Autonomy program and decreasing the satisfaction of those in the Hierarchically-controlled program. The effects of the programs appear to be most evident in attitudes toward the

TABLE 4

Effect of Change Programs on Satisfaction with Relations with Three Levels of Supervision

Experimental Groups	Index of Satisfaction				
	Mean Before	Mean After	Diff.	SE Diff.	N
Relations with Supervisor					
Program I					
Div. A	4.18	4.15	−.03	.09	62
Div. B	3.19	3.50	+.31*	.14	54
Average	3.71	3.80	+.09	.08	116
Program II					
Div. C	3.80	3.67	−.13	.11	46
Div. D	3.43	3.29	−.14	.16	45
Average	3.64	3.48	−.16	.10	91
Relations with Assistant Manager					
Program I					
Div. A	3.49	3.61	+.12	.12	59
Div. B	3.97	4.11	+.14	.11	53
Average	3.71	3.86	+.15*	.08	112
Program II					
Div. C	3.80	3.34	−.46**	.12	43
Div. D	3.57	3.22	−.35**	.11	43
Average	3.64	3.28	−.36**	.08	86
Relations with Manager					
Program I					
Div. A	3.84	4.11	+.27**	.08	62
Div. B	4.04	4.20	+.16*	.09	52
Average	3.93	4.15	+.22**	.06	114
Program II					
Div. C	3.23	2.59	−.64**	.15	43
Div. D	3.87	3.37	−.50**	.13	40
Average	3.50	3.01	−.49**	.10	83

Note:—Degree of Satisfaction with Relations with Supervision: five point scale ranging from 1, low degree of satisfaction to 5, high degree of satisfaction.

* Significant at the 5% level one-tailed t test for paired data.
** Significant at the 1% level.

managerial level and least marked in attitudes toward the first-line supervisors, probably because the managers occupy the key or pivotal positions in the structure (see Kaye, [3]).

The second type of attitude toward supervisors measured was satisfaction with the supervisors as representatives of the employees. Three questions were asked employees as a measure of this type of satisfaction:

1. How much does your supervisor (assistant manager, manager) go out of her (his) way to help get things for the girls in the section?

2. How effective is she (he) in helping you and the other girls get what you want in your jobs?

3. How much does your supervisor (assistant manager, manager) try to help people in your section get ahead in the company?

These three items were intercorrelated for the attitudes toward the supervisor as a representative index and the average intercorrelation was .83 with a corrected reliability of .94 (N of 340).

The findings for the three levels of supervision on the satisfaction with supervisors as representatives index are shown in Table 5.

The employees' attitudes toward their supervisors as effective representatives of their interests show significant changes in the predicted directions in the two programs. Those in the Autonomy program became more satisfied than they had been previously, while those in the Hierarchically-controlled program became less satisfied. On satisfaction with the first-line supervisor as a representative both Division B in the Autonomy program and Division D in the Hierarchically-controlled program shifted significantly in the hypothesized directions, although the other two divisions did not shift significantly. The two program groups were not matched on degree of satisfaction with manager and assistant manager as a representative at the beginning of the experiment, as there was significantly more satisfaction in the Autonomy program divisions than there was in Program II. However, the changes for both groups of divisions were statistically significant and in the predicted direction. For attitude toward manager all of the division differences are in the predicted direction and all except Division D are statistically significant.

Satisfaction with the company. One general question was used to measure company satisfaction: "Taking things as a whole, how do you like working for _____ (the name of the company)?"

TABLE 5

The Effect of Change Programs on Satisfaction with Three Levels of Supervision as Representatives of Employees

Experimental Groups	Index of Satisfaction				
	Mean Before	Mean After	Diff.	SE Diff.	N
Supervisor as Representative of Employees					
Program I					
Div. A	3.98	4.06	+.08	.12	59
Div. B	2.91	3.43	+.52**	.14	49
Average	3.48	3.74	+.26**	.09	108
Program II					
Div. C	3.73	3.67	−.06	.13	45
Div. D	3.52	3.16	−.36*	.18	41
Average	3.59	3.43	−.16	.11	86
Assistant Manager as Representative of Employees					
Program I					
Div. A	3.32	3.75	+.43**	.14	51
Div. B	3.54	3.76	+.22*	.13	53
Average	3.43	3.75	+.32**	.09	104
Program II					
Div. C	3.07	2.81	−.26*	.12	41
Div. D	3.23	2.92	−.31*	.13	42
Average	3.15	2.86	−.29**	.10	83
Manager as Representative of Employees					
Program I					
Div. A	3.82	4.37	+.55**	.11	57
Div. B	3.76	3.96	+.20*	.10	53
Average	3.79	4.17	+.38**	.07	110
Program II					
Div. C	2.70	2.19	−.51**	.13	41
Div. D	3.14	2.92	−.22	.16	30
Average	2.92	2.52	−.40**	.10	71

NOTE:—Five-point scale ranging from 1, low degree of satisfaction to 5, high degree of satisfaction.
* Significant at the 5% level one-tailed t test for paired data.
** Significant at the 1% level.

The answers for this question presented in Table 6 indicate an increase in favorableness toward the company under the Autonomy program and a decrease under the Hierarchically-controlled program.

All of the changes are significant in the predicted direction, except for the before-after difference in Division B which is only at the 10 per cent level of significance.

TABLE 6

The Effect of Change Programs on Satisfaction with the Company

Experimental Groups	Index of Satisfaction with Company				
	Before Mean	After Mean	Diff.	SE Diff.	N
Program I					
Div. A	4.16	4.32	+.16*	.09	62
Div. B	3.83	4.02	+.19	.13	53
Average	4.01	4.18	+.17*	.08	115
Program II					
Div. C	4.04	3.80	−.24*	.14	46
Div. D	4.26	3.95	−.31**	.12	43
Average	4.15	3.88	−.27**	.09	89

Note:—Five point scale, ranging from 1, low degree of satisfaction to 5, high degree of satisfaction.
* Significant at the 5% level one-tailed t test for paired data.
** Significant at the 1% level.

Job satisfaction. Three questions were used as an index of job satisfaction:

1. Does your job ever get monotonous?
2. How important do you feel your job is compared with other jobs at (the company)?
3. In general, how well do you like the sort of work you're doing in your job?

These three questions showed an average intercorrelation of .47 with a corrected reliability of .73 (N of 369). The results on this index are reported in Table 7.

While the trend for the changes in job satisfaction are in the direction predicted, the differences are not sufficiently great to be statistically significant except for Division C. The lack of change in job satisfaction in the Autonomy program may be due to the fact that the job content remained about the same. It is also possible that the increases in complexity and variety of their total work were offset by a rise in their level of aspiration, so that they expected more interesting and varied work.

Satisfaction with the program. In the after measurement additional questions were asked concerning attitudes toward the programs. Most of these questions were open-ended and required the employee to write her response in her own words. Although less than half of the clerks taking the after measurement filled

TABLE 7

The Effect of Change Programs on Job Satisfaction

Experimental Groups	Index of Job Satisfaction				
	Before Mean	After Mean	Diff.	SE Diff.	N
Program I					
Div. A	3.29	3.29	0	.08	58
Div. B	3.03	3.09	+.06	.09	55
Average	3.16	3.19	+.03	.06	113
Program II					
Div. C	3.14	2.94	−.20*	.10	42
Div. D	3.12	3.07	−.05	.12	46
Average	3.13	3.00	−.13*	.07	88

Note:—Five-point scale, ranging from 1, low degree of satisfaction to 5, high degree of satisfaction.
* Significant at the 5% level one-tailed t test for paired data.

them out, the results on questions relevant to the satisfaction hypothesis deserve brief mention. The clerks in the Autonomy program typically: wanted their program to last indefinitely, did not like the other program, felt that the clerks were one of the groups gaining the most from the program and described both positive and negative changes in interpersonal relations among the girls. The clerks in the Hierarchically-controlled program, on the other hand, most frequently: wanted their program to end immediately, liked the other program and felt that the company gained the most from their program. Not one single person in the Hierarchically-controlled program mentioned an improvement in interpersonal relations as a result of this program. All of the noted changes were for the worse, with increases in friction and tension being most frequently mentioned.

Taking all of these results on the attitudinal questions together, the first hypothesis would appear to be verified. Increasing local decision-making increased satisfaction, while decreasing the role of rank-and-file members of the organization in the decision-making decreased it.

Hypothesis II

This hypothesis predicts a direct relationship between degree of rank-and-file decision-making and productivity. Thus, in order for the hypothesis to be verified, productivity should increase significantly in the Autonomy program, and should decrease significantly in the Hierarchically-controlled program.

We have previously described the problems of assuming a direct relationship between motivation to produce and productivity in a situation in which volume is not controllable by employees and level of productivity depends upon the number of people doing a fixed amount of work. The Autonomy program was handicapped by both the fact that increasing productivity required reducing the size of their own work group and the fact that the upper management staff and line costs were not included in the measure of costs per volume of work.

The measure of productivity, then, is a measure of clerical costs. These clerical costs are expressed in percentage figures, calculated by dividing the actual clerical costs by a constant standard of cost expected for that volume. Since this way of estimating productivity makes the higher figures indicate lower productivity, we have reversed the signs for purposes of presentation. The results for this measure are shown in Table 8.

The clerical costs have gone down in each division and thus productivity has increased.

TABLE 8

Comparison of the Four Divisions on Clerical Productivity for Year Control Period and Year Experimental Period

		Index of Productivity			
Experimental Groups	*Mean Control Period*	*Mean Experimental Period*	*Diff. %*	*SE Diff.*	*N*
Program I					
Div. A	46.3%	55.2%	+ 8.9**	1.3%	12
Div. B	51.0	62.0	+11.0**	1.3	12
Average	48.6	58.6	+10.0**	1.2	24
Program II					
Div. C	50.2	63.2	+13.0**	1.2	12
Div. D	46.8	62.0	+15.2**	1.1	12
Average	48.5	62.6	+14.1**	.9	24

Note:—Higher values correspond to greater productivity.
** Significant at the 1% level.

All these increases in productivity are statistically significant (by t tests). In addition, the productivity increase in the Hierarchically-controlled program is significantly greater than that in the Autonomy program. These increases in productivity do not seem to be acounted for by a general rise in productivity throughout the company, since the divisions outside the experimental groups which were most comparable to them showed no significant gain in productivity during this period. The rise in productivity appears to be the result of the experimental treatments. The two divisions initially low in productivity showed the greatest differential change. Division D increased its productivity the most of the four while Division A increased the least.

A second measure of the organizational costs of the two programs is the degree of turnover which could be attributed to on-the-job factors. A method of control and regulation which reduces clerical costs, but which produces the hidden costs of training new employees is of greater cost to the organization than would at first appear evident. In this company turnover, however, is not high and much of the turnover that does occur is due to personal reasons (marriage, pregnancy, etc.) rather than on-the-job reasons. Out of the 54 employees who left the company from the four divisions during the time of the experiment, only nine resigned for other jobs or because of dissatisfaction. Out of these nine, however, all but one were in the Hierarchically-controlled program. In the exit interviews conducted by the company personnel department 23 of the girls leaving made unfavorable comments about pressure, work standards, etc. Nineteen of these girls were from the Hierarchically-controlled program.

These results indicate that the productivity hypothesis is clearly not verified in terms of direct clerical costs, since the Hierarchically-controlled program decreased these costs more than the Autonomy program, contrary to the prediction. The indirect costs for the Hierarchically-controlled program are probably somewhat greater. But even when this is considered the evidence does not support the hypothesis.

DISCUSSION

The results on productivity might suggest a "Hawthorne effect" if it were not for the satisfaction findings. The increase in satisfaction under the Autonomy program and the decrease under the Hierarchically-controlled program make an explanation of productivity changes in terms of a common attention effect unlikely.[5]

The Hierarchically-controlled program reduced staff costs by ordering reductions in the number of employees assigned to the tasks. Increases in productivity for Divisions C and D were brought about as simply as that. This temporary increase in one measure of productivity is not surprising and is traditional history in industry. In the Autonomy program, decrease in costs was more complex but can be simply stated as follows. The Autonomy program increased the motivation of the employees to produce and thus they did not feel the need for replacing the staff members who left the section. In addition, they were willing to make an effort to try to outplace some of their members in other jobs which they might like. The reductions in staff in the two programs came about in different ways. Those occurring by order in the Hierarchically-controlled program surpassed in number those occurring by group decision in the Autonomy program, but it is not clear how long the superiority of the Hierarchically-controlled program would have lasted.

The results of the experiment need to be placed in a larger theoretical framework in order to contribute to the understanding of the functioning of large-scale organizations. We shall first consider briefly the role and function of the social control processes, as it is these processes which were changed by the experimental manipulations.

The high degree of rationality which is characteristic of the institutional behavior of man is achieved through a complex system for controlling and regulating human behavior. Hierarchy is a requirement because

human beings must be fitted to a rational model. There are essentially two functions which the usual hierarchy serves: a *binding-in* function and a *binding-between* function. By *binding-in* we mean insuring that there will be individuals present to fill the necessary roles. The role behavior required by the organization must be a path to individual goals. Money is the most important means used for binding-in, but all ways to motivate a person to enter and remain in the system are means of binding-in. By *binding-between* we mean the insurance of the rationality of action, that is, the setting up and continuation of institutional processes which will accomplish the ends for which the organization is designed. The role behavior of individuals must be integrated into a pattern to produce interrelated action directed toward the goals of the organization. The development of assignments, work charts, job specifications, etc., are but a few examples of the many means used by organizations for binding-between.

Any means for controlling and regulating human behavior in a large organizational setting, then, needs to serve these two functions. The experiment shows that the allocation of decision-making processes to the upper hierarchy results in a greater emphasis on the binding-between function, while the function of binding-in is handled by an external reward system. Such a direct stress on the binding-between function was shown in the Hierarchically-controlled program and resulted in the increase in productivity (an indication of binding-between) and a decrease in employee satisfaction (an indication of degree of binding-in) and some increase in turnover (another indication of binding-in).

The greater allocation of the decision-making processes to the rank-and-file employees in the Autonomy program resulted in an emphasis on both the binding-between and the binding-in functions. Thus there was both an increase in productivity and an increase in satisfaction. While the program is addressed primarily to the binding-in function, in such a context the binding-between function is also served.

The problems of the Hierarchically-controlled system are maintaining the employee

[5] It is unlikely that even in the Hawthorne experiment the results were due to attention. There were a number of changes in addition to an increase in attention, including relaxation of rules, better supervisors, no change in piece rates despite raises in productivity—to name a few.

effectively "bound-in" to the organization and continuing favorable relations between the supervisory personnel who have involvement in the organization and the rank and file who must do the work. Indications of these problems are dissatisfaction, distortions in communications up the hierarchy, the tendency to "goof off" and cut corners in the work, and the greater turnover.

The Autonomy program is an integrated means of handling both the binding-between and the binding-in functions, but it requires in the long run that the organization be willing to grant employee decision-making in the key areas of binding-in such as pay and promotions. The granting of "safe" areas of decision-making and the withholding of "hot" ones is not likely to work for long. It is necessary for the rank and file to be sufficiently bound-in to the organization for them to want to make decisions which are rational for the system. But the rationality of their decisions will also depend upon the orientation of the key supervisors whose values they will interiorize. (Thus the clerks in Division B were more organizationally oriented than those in Division A—see Kaye [3].)

SUMMARY

A field experiment in an industrial setting was conducted in order to test hypotheses concerning the relationship between the means by which organizational decisions are made and (a) individual satisfaction, and (b) productivity.

Using four parallel divisions of the clerical operations of an organization, two programs of changes were introduced. One program, the Autonomy program involving two of the divisions, was designed to increase the role of the rank-and-file employees in the decision-making processes of the organization. The other two divisions received a program designed to increase the role of upper management in the decision-making processes (the Hierarchically-controlled program). The phases of the experiment included: (a) before measurement, (b) training programs for supervisory personnel lasting approximately 6 months, (c) an operations period of a year for the two experimental programs, and (d) after measurement. In addition, certain measurements were taken during the training and operational phases of the experiment. Findings are reported on the question of the experimental "take" and on the general hypotheses on individual satisfactions and productivity. Briefly, it was found that:

1. The experimental programs produced changes in decision-making allocations in the direction required for the testing of the hypotheses.
2. The individual satisfactions of the members of the work groups increased significantly in the Autonomous program and decreased significantly in the Hierarchically-controlled program.
3. Using one measure of productivity, both decision-making systems increased productivity, with the Hierarchically-controlled program resulting in a greater increase.

The relationship of the findings to the so-called "Hawthorne effect" is examined and the experimental programs and their results are considered in the light of a theoretical description of the role of the control and regulation processes of large organizations.

REFERENCES

1. Coch, L., & French, J. R. P., Jr. Overcoming resistance to change. Hum. Relat., 1948, 1, 512–532.
2. Katz, D., Maccoby, N., & Morse, Nancy. Productivity, supervision and morale in an office situation. Ann Arbor: Survey Res. Center, Univer. of Michigan, 1950.
3. Kaye, Carol. The effect on organizational goal achievement of a change in the structure of roles. Ann Arbor: Survey Res. Center, 1954 (mimeographed).
4. Lewin, K. Group decisions and social change. In G. E. Swanson, T. M. Newcomb, & E. L. Hartley (Eds.). Readings in social psychology (2nd Ed.). New York: Holt, 1952, 459–473.
5. Lippitt, R., & White, R. K. An experimental study of leadership and group life. In G. E. Swanson, T. M. Newcomb, & E. L. Hartley (Eds.). Readings in social psychology (2nd Ed.). New York: Holt, 1952, 340–354.

6. Reimer, E. *Creating experimental social change in an organization.* Ann Arbor: Survey Res. Center, 1954 (mimeographed).

7. Tannenbaum, A. *The relationship between personality variables and adjustment to contrasting types of social structure.* Ann Arbor: Survey Res. Center 1954 (mimeographed).

8. Worthy, J. C. Factors influencing employee morale. *Harvard Bus. Rev.,* 1950, 28, 61–73.

The Correctional Institution for Juvenile Offenders: An Analysis of Organizational "Character"[1] /

Mayer N. Zald (*University of Chicago*)

INTRODUCTION

During the last decade the sociological study of large organizations has emphasized the limitations of Weber's ideal-type of bureaucracy as a model of organizational behavior. Moving away from a focus on bureaucracy and its pathologies, organizational research has begun to examine the variety of factors that affect and limit different types of organizations. The purpose of this paper is to describe the juvenile correctional institution as one type of large-scale social organization.*

First of all, institutions for delinquents share with other organizations, such as hospitals, certain attributes usually associated with communities. Secondly, they belong to a class of large-scale social organizations that have multiple goals, and thus have functional problems like these organizations. Thirdly, correctional institutions are of interest because of their critical role in our society's attempt to minimize anti-social behavior.

In this paper the major patterns of similarity and dissimilarity between correctional institutions and other types of organizations will be delineated and explained. Further, some of the dimensions along which correctional institutions vary among themselves will be indicated. A "character analysis" of these organizations, as systems of action, may make it possible (a) to summarize and integrate a scattered body of knowledge; (b) to specify areas where research is needed; and (c) to set forth some concepts and dimensions that may be useful in such research.

The concept of organizational "character," most fully developed by Philip Selznick (30), stresses interdependencies, commitments, fixed limitations and capacities of different types of organizations. Using the concept of organizational "character" the present analysis aims at a middle range level of theoretical abstraction.**

To describe the "character" of correctional institutions we will discuss their goals, their relationships to the larger community, and, finally, their internal structures.***

THE GOALS OF CORRECTIONAL INSTITUTIONS

Like universities, mental hospitals and some other large-scale social organizations, correctional institutions can be said to have

Reprinted from *Social Problems,* 1960, 8, pages 56–67, by permission of author and publisher, The Society for the Study of Social Problems.

[1] This paper was written as part of an ongoing project supported by research grant M-2104, from the National Institute of Mental Health, Public Health Service. Morris Janowitz and Robert Vinter, directors of the project at the University of Michigan, have greatly aided the author by their critical comments on earlier drafts of the paper. The conceptual framework of the project is included here. The general hypotheses which the project attempts to test are stated in a previous publication by Vinter and Janowitz (35).

* The terms large-scale organization and organization are used interchangeably in this paper.

** Francis Scott has recently discussed mental hospitals and prisons within a Parsonian framework (27). The analysis presented here will be less inclusive.

*** On occasion this analysis uses studies of mental hospitals as well as prisons. Paucity of organizational research on juvenile correctional institutions, as well as similarities among these organizations justifies this extension. Pertinent recent studies include those of McCleery 16; 17) and Sykes (33) for prisons, Belknap (1), Caudill (3), Stanton and Schwartz (31), and the book edited by Greenblatt, Levinson, and Williams (11) on mental hospitals.

multiple goals. Their prime functions are to incarcerate—that is, establish custody over —the offender *and* to rehabilitate the delinquent. These goals may be incompatible because maximization of one may lead to inadequate fulfillment of the other. Business firms, in contrast, typically have one primary goal and several secondary goals or "functions" that are usually evaluated in relation to the primary goal.

It is often said that mental hospitals and, to a lesser extent, prisons are moving from an emphasis on incarceration and punishment to an emphasis on treatment and rehabilitation. Institutions for delinquents have had a goal of rehabilitation from the beginning. Bowler and Bloodgood (2, p. 9) point out that the first Houses of Refuge in Boston, New York, and Philadelphia were quite clear in their emphasis upon rehabilitation as the primary goal of the organization. The earliest state institutions combined emphasis on rehabilitation with a covert goal of custody. Advocates of military training, of farming, of vocational programs all visualized their programs as rehabilitative. Society has become more humanitarian and less repressive in its concepts of social control. As social welfare, mental hygiene, and social science concepts have spread, the general public and the expanding mental health professions have pressed for the implementation of treatment goals, even though the details of treatment techniques have in themselves been subject to considerable debate among contending professional groups.

In many states physical punishment and repressive controls have been legally denied the juvenile institution, and rehabilitative goals have been formally established. Yet it is rarely the case that correctional institutions can also abandon custodial goals. A variety of legal statutes govern the admission and retention of the offender by the institution, and assignment of the delinquent is often intended to protect the community. Rehabilitative goals have not been substituted for custodial goals in most cases; rather they have been added to organizational goals. It is possible, therefore, to place a given institution on a continuum whose poles are defined by goal ratios in which custody or rehabilitation predominate. Most institutions may be

characterized by the degree of dominance of one goal over the other. However, knowledge of the goal ratio alone is insufficient for understanding the structures of the institutions. Institutions with similar goal ratios may stress differing means. Thus one treatment-oriented institution may stress the casework relationship as the primary means while another might stress the utilization of the milieu. One custodial institution might stress negative sanctions for running away while another might not allow opportunities for escape.

All of the diverse functions associated with these two goals are not inherently in conflict. A custodially-oriented institution, for example, could use techniques usually associated with treatment to achieve discipline and control (36; 23). Conversely, custodial control may be a prerequisite in some cases for effective rehabilitation. In certain situations custodial needs and therapeutic needs might dictate similar policies or decisions. But it is also true that they might dictate divergent solutions. If the multiple goals of the organization have not been clearly delineated and their relationship defined, the potentiality of organizational conflict is raised. That is, consensual validation of the norms and rules and of their relative importance will be absent.

In a formal sense an organization may be said to have split or multiple goals when the goal-setting agents—those who charter the organization and to whom the highest organizational authorities are responsible—conceive of the organization as having multiple purposes or functions. However, the actual degree of dominance of one goal over another is not wholly determined by the chartering agents. Even if they were to specify quite precisely the relative emphasis upon goals that were to be expected, the organization might not be able to realize this goal ratio. Depending upon its resources, structure, personnel, and clientele, the institution might be more or less successful in attaining its goals. Moreover, in many cases there may be a large degree of indeterminancy in the charter. Internal and external pressure groups may argue for one or another interpretation of the goals at various times and for policies which support their interpretations

(7). The existence of the two major goals of custody and rehabilitation heighten the possibility of conflicting occupational role groups and the development of conflicting policies. The manner in which multiple goals affect the relation of the institution to the larger society and how they affect the structure and effectiveness of the organization will be discussed in later sections.

THE ORGANIZATION AND THE EXTERNAL ENVIRONMENT

The relation of an organization to its environment may profitably be discussed in terms of (1) external factors that affect the input of facilities and legitimation, (2) the process of evaluation of the output of the organization, and (3) factors that affect the demographic characteristics of staff and clientele.

Sources of Legitimation and Facilities. Resource inputs to an organization are of several different kinds and effect the autonomy or independence of an organization. The designation of organizations as autonomous is largely a matter of degree. Any organization exists in a matrix of intricate relations with the larger society and must meet certain standards in order to exist. One organization may be said to be more autonomous than another to the extent that it has greater control over its environment, has more freedom in determining its own goals, judging its own effectiveness, and perpetuating its own personnel. An organization may have a narrowly limited area of operation and yet be largely autonomous in its operation. The converse may also be true. A correctional institution organized under a department of corrections is ordinarily less autonomous than is an institution less directly related to a department of government. The more a private institution depends on a limited number of sources for facilities, the more its autonomy is limited.

Public institutions receive facilities— money and capital investment—from legislative and judicial units of government or their administrative agents, while private institutions are primarily dependent upon charitable organizations or fund raising drives. Both public and private institutions receive legitimation from the state and from professional and lay associations. As sources of facilities, legislatures operate primarily with reference to two criteria: the tenor of the times and the pressure of the budget. The variability of both of these factors is conducive to organizational instability.

Facilities for public institutions are often channeled through a state agency responsible for all organizations of a similar type. Operating through a state department has both advantages and disadvantages for an organization. On the one hand it allows all of the correctional institutions to be treated as a single power unit rather than as fragmented institutions. It is a further advantage to give the job of organizational defense into a separate department of government with prestige and a staff of civil servants. However, this arrangement necessitates meeting standards set by an external agency directly responsible for the institution's continual effectiveness. Since the agency is more likely to accept rehabilitative goals, is not in direct contact with the clients, is more often in contact with standard-setting national welfare agencies, such as the Children's Bureau, we would expect the operating organizations to develop defensive patterns of relating to the parent agency. This should be especially true of the more custodially oriented organizations.

There is little research in this area. The literature on public administration treats of somewhat similar situations in its discussion of central office-field office relations, but there are no systematic studies of the relationship of correctional institutions to their administrative departments.

Private institutions, although relatively more autonomous in establishing organizational policy and acquiring personnel, have the complex problem of insuring the receipt of facilities through fund raising associations and foundations.

Etzioni (9) has recently traced the implications, for both society and organizations, of receiving financial support from a source different from the payment of clients for services received. Almost all public and many private organizations fall into this category. As compared with business organizations, such organizations should have

problems in harmonizing the possibly conflicting interests of clients and sponsors.
First, there is not a necessary relationship
between the quality of service rendered to
clients and the input of resources. Secondly,
clients sent to these organizations are usually
involuntary participants.

Evaluation of Output. It is obvious that
any large-scale organization must satisfy the
needs of others in the society by its output if
it is to continue in existence. Organizational
stability is dependent upon how successful it
is in fulfilling its custodial and rehabilitative
tasks with the allotted resources. Unlike a
private business which may go into bank-
ruptcy if it fails to offer a satisfactory product, correctional institutions monopolistically
meet a continuing need of our society. Thus,
lack of organizational success in satisfying
this need is more likely to lead to a turnover
of executive personnel.

The output of the correctional organization is evaluated by the agencies directly in
contact with it, and, more diffusely, by the
general public. The broader public usually
becomes involved in the organization only
when: (1) the organization does not maintain control over those committed to it, as
reflected in riots or escapes; (2) some level
of care dictated by the standards of the times
is not maintained; (3) public norms of humanitarian treatment are violated. Public
officials, professional associations, and cru-
sading journalists may bring pressure to
bear when the second and third conditions
occur as judged by professional criteria.
Ohlin and Pappenfort have pointed out that
there are many possible incidents which
could be used to threaten organizational
stability. Only a few of these are actually
turned into crises, sometimes by external
organizations or associations (22).

The rehabilitative output of the organization can be judged in terms of several criteria. It can be judged by evaluating the
recidivism rate of released clients, by evaluating the "personality" changes occurring
while in the institution, or by evaluating the
degree to which the organization meets
standards (empirical or theoretical) which
are supposed to insure success. At best, however, rehabilitation seems to "pay off" to the
society at large only in the long run. How-

ever, when there are either runaways or
other "incidents" the larger public is quick
to apply pressure. Since control and rehabilitation are not always compatible and since
rehabilitation is a vague and difficult to
establish criterion, a continuous pressure for
emphasizing control instead of rehabilitation
is implied, if an institution is to be free of
demands for reorganization.

In addition to official agencies directly related to the institution, various professional
associations influence operations by establishing standards for their members and for
organizations utilizing the members' services. Social work, psychiatric, correctional,
medical, and educational associations all formulate standards which can be utilized in
defense of their functions, and which are
related to their "professional images." Sociologists have, unfortunately, rarely studied
the relationships *between* organizations. As
Levine, White, and Pierson note, sociologists
make many assumptions about the interaction of organizations, but few study it
directly (14). Ohlin's paper "Interest Group
Conflict and Correctional Objectives," is one
of the few exceptions to this generalization
(20).

An institution may attempt to create
sources of support by coopting elements of
the local community (29). Cooptation may
involve the formation of citizens' advisory
committees or the encouragement of volunteer activities for the institution. Such
devices, while helping to create a stable relationship with the community, may also lead
to lessened organizational autonomy, problems of internal coordination, and others.

*Demographic Characteristics of Staff and
Clients.* The external environment effects
not only the type and amount of resources
allocated to the institution but also affects its
personnel and clientele. The state of the local
labor market may markedly affect the character of institutional personnel. For instance,
a college community can provide staff at the
lower levels quite different from an industrial community in terms of their orientation
toward juvenile offenders. This does not imply that college students *per se* are more desirable as rehabilitative employees. Rather, a
college community provides a large number
of potential employees whose ideologies may

be more compatible with the rehabilitative philosophy, but whose student status precludes high salary demands. However, use of college students leads to high turnover and other instabilities (15, p. 23). Further, the opportunity for various types of activities, for both clients and staff, will vary from community to community. The size of the local community may also determine the off-the-job social relations of the staff. The isolation of some institutions increases the dependence of the staff upon each other for social activity, heightening the communal aspects of the institution.

The characteristics of the clients are to an even greater extent affected by the environment of the institution. Clients are provided the organization by the courts. Operating under mandates from the legal system, the courts must determine who among their clientele are to be sent to correctional institutions and how the clients are to be treated. This complex decision involves a variety of factors, such as the available capacity of institutions in the area, the nature of the offense and the available ways of dealing with the offender. The nature of this decision may be systematic apart from the requirements for admission formally set by an institution. For example, offenders may be sent to the institution in the absence of a reasonable alternative and not with the intention of thereby protecting society or rehabilitating delinquents. If this were a constant practice, it would affect organizational operation at several points including, among others, its discharge policy and process, its training program, its distribution of facilities, and the nature of its clientele. Some of these problems have been dealt with in social work research concerning the intake and referral systems of agencies. However, this research tends to be administrative rather than sociological.

The type of community from which the delinquent comes may also influence his values and orientations. The physical isolation of the correctional institution also contributes to the degree of deprivation that the delinquent feels; e.g., he may be deprived of contacts with family and peers.

Client characteristics together with the input of facilities largely determine the degree

to which various organizational goals can be pursued. If, as workers in the field claim (13, p. 34) delinquents have become more aggressive, brutal, and acting-out in their antisocial acts, more organizational activity may have to be devoted to meeting custodial requirements in order to placate the surrounding community.

THE INTERNAL SYSTEM

Within an institution power and resources are distributed to maintain stability and attain goals. However, depending upon the distribution of power and the ideology of key personnel goals may be redefined and reshaped to differing specifications than those held by the governing board of the institution. The translation of goals into organizational practice can be shown by discussing three sets of interpersonal relationships; (1) staff relationships with other staff, (2) staff relationships with clients, and (3) client relationships with clients.

Staff-Staff Relations. The formal table of organization of the correctional institution defines the positions and the authority relations among positions that are supposed to characterize the institution. At a minimum, the table indicates a superintendent and an assistant superintendent; teachers, a nurse; a business and maintenance staff; and a staff variously called cottage parents, attendants, or supervisors. Even the most custodial institution for delinquents must have teachers, for in most states the law requires that children under sixteen years of age go to school. As institutions adopt contemporary modes of differentiating and treating delinquents, psychologists, psychiatrists, and social workers are added to the staff. The formal organization is not synonymous with the actual organization, nor is it complete. Any discussion of the internal structure of a correctional institution must include an analysis of the informal structure of the staff—as well as the social organization of the clientele. McCleery (16, 17), John and Elaine Cummings (11, pp. 50–72) and Novick (19) have shown that even on the formal level, however, the correctional institutions with different goal orientations will differ sharply in their authority structures; decentralization of power tending to be greater in rehabilitative institutions.

The existence in the organization of more than one goal raises the probability of role behavior having to meet diverse criteria. It allows conflict to develop between position occupants whose individual tasks are associated with the divergent goals. Thus, cottage parents and counselors whose performances largely are judged, respectively, in terms of their contributions to custodial and rehabilitative goals and whose pespectives are largely shaped by these goals, will often find themselves in conflict (37). "Interest groups" may form in any organization. But the value of their effects on the organization can usually be determined by reference to the dominant goal. In correctional institutions a group may develop an ideology, defenses, and norms which further its goal and its power and prestige at the expense of another group's goals and power (1, pp. 123–144; 23; 36).

Correctional institutions with marked custodial orientations are characterized by the relatively high actual power of the cottage parent and custodial staff, while institutions with predominantly rehabilitative orientations raise the power level of rehabilitative positions, defining custodial roles in relation to the rehabilitative function and lowering the power of the cottage staff. In many cases, where the definition of goals is in flux and unstable, inter-group conflict may be chronic or the external and internal necessities of control will emphasize custodial goals by default. For example, eligibility for discharge, in theory a rehabilitative decision, may be manipulated by the custodial staff as a control sanction.

Even if inter-group conflict is minimal, conflicting role expectations of the administration may lead to intra-role conflict. Thus the cottage counselors at one of the schools described in the MacIver report on institutions for delinquents seem to be subject to extreme role strain (16, p. 23). Cressey (8) and Grusky (13) have described such conflicts in a prison setting and in the setting of a minimum security camp. In less custodial institutions the cottage parent is generally asked to maintain control but is not, from his point of view, given the sanctions to do his job right.

Since correctional institutions are often in an unstable relation to their environment, superintendents typically find a good deal of their time taken up with organizational defense; that is, with protecting the organization and maximizing the receipt of facilities and legitimation (36). The superintendent may be led to abrogate his authority to personnel that insure organizational stability. The combination of chronic pressure to economize, the inherent difficulty of evaluating the efficacy of rehabilitative policy, and the need to maintain organizational stability and control create recurring pressures that minimize the rehabilitative orientation. However, there is evidence that various organizations of personnel and policy are compatible with a given budget, and, furthermore, that adequate funds do not insure rehabilitative organization (21).

A typical bifurcation occurs along professional-nonprofessional lines. Part of the staff is highly educated, trained, middle class, and professionally oriented, while another part tends to be poorly trained, have little education and is of lower class origin. Status distinctions may lead to restricted communication between groups, turning each into a closed social unit similar to the status-linked groupings in hospitals.

Adult members of lower status groups have difficulty gaining access to higher status groups. In contrast, many organizations provide defined channels of mobility by which members can rise in the organization. Blocked upward mobility increases the individual's dependence on his own status group for support and solidifies the group as a unit for social control. This tends to raise the power of key custodial personnel through their ability to reward or punish individuals dependent on them. Thus effective institutionalization of rehabilitative policy is further blocked. Barriers to communication and interaction are probably lowest between the maintenance staff and the custodial staff, allowing informal patterns of cooperation to develop. Some institutions have developed committee mechanisms to help bridge this gap (5, 19).

Staff-Client Relations. As compared with

most organizations in our society, staff-client relationships differ significantly in the juvenile correctional institution. Basic to this difference are four characteristics: (1) clientele and staff form a community; (2) the clients typically are drawn from a low social class and are social deviants; (3) staff are in a clearly superordinate position in relation to clients; and (4) adult and adolescent cultures are markedly divergent in our society. The fact that the staff associate almost continuously with the clients means that relationships tend to diffuseness, particularism, and affectivity; staff may easily develop warm relationships with some boys and none at all with others. This is in contrast with most bureaucratic organizations in which the relationships with clients tend towards specificity, universalism, and affective-neutrality. In most correctional institutions the cottage personnel tend to interact on a more intimate, diffuse, and personalized basis with the delinquents than do the rehabilitative, professional staff. The professional staff tend to interact on a segmented and specific basis with the clients (12). Thus, in many ways, lower level staff have more chance to establish warm, supportive relationships than anyone else, which according to current theory, are necessary for changing identifications and values. Yet, the demands of the role of the cottage parent and his own attitudes may only reinforce the boys' estrangement from society. Cottage staff find themselves confronted with the problem of managing from 15 to 70 boys. They must accomplish routine housekeeping, keep order, and prevent escapes. Unlike prisons, juvenile institutions usually do not even provide a wall to contain the delinquents. Few sanctions are available to the cottage staff; they have little training, often get little positive support from the professionals or the administration, and are most readily evaluated in terms of the visible criteria of control and cleanliness.

The correctional institution must maintain discipline and minimize violence in a population that has demonstrated its own lack of personal controls. The difficulty of maintaining control will vary with the age, sex, and traits of the delinquents that the institution serves. Since rewards may be largely controlled by staff, they have the opportunity to develop a variety of reward structures to achieve ends. However, the reward structure is a reflection not only of the ends sought but also of staff perspectives on what means will achieve these ends. This entails a view of the nature of the clientele and how they will respond (an implicit learning and behavior theory).

As stated by Gilbert and Levinson (11, pp. 20–36), the custodial orientation gives rise to an ideology that focuses upon the inherent nature of the client's difficulty and his lack of malleability. The ideology stresses rigid distinctions between types of people and the use of authoritarian techniques of interpersonal control. In contrast, the ideology of rehabilitation and therapy focuses on the socio-psychological causes of deviancy, on malleability and on permissiveness in interpersonal relations.

The utilization of sanction structures and interpersonal relationships congruent with these ideologies may have great effect upon client attitudes and upon client informal organization (12; 27). Client attitudes may be hostile to the organization, or docile but distant, or cooperative and cynical, or cooperative and personally involved in the institution's program. An instructive comparison of attitudes can be made from the description of attitudes reported by Clemmer (4, p. 152) and McCorkle, Elias and Bisby (18, pp. 109–157). Our knowledge in this area has been gained predominantly with prison populations. We would expect anti-social and anti-organizational attitudes to be less crystallized for juvenile offenders than for adult criminals. Therefore, the institution should be able to have a greater effect upon the former.

Staff-client relations in an institution with custodial goals tend to be more restrictive than in a rehabilitative institution. They are more "rule-oriented" and work to maintain social distance between staff and client. In ideal form they serve to maintain an objective fairness. At worst, favoritism and individual bargaining take place (32).

Client-Client Relations. Rehabilitation implies a substitution of positive social values for anti-social values. Yet it has long been said that the major product of penal institutions is the teaching of criminal values. If it is assumed that the juvenile delinquent is more amenable to change than the adult offender and is less committed to anti-social patterns, then the values esteemed by the client informal organization may be crucial in negating or supporting delinquent behavior patterns.

The incoming delinquent is completely dependent upon other offenders and upon staff for all social gratifications and deprivations, and for many definitions of cognitive reality. Thus, other clients serve as a major socialization agent to organizational practices and perspectives. As in any social system, clients rank actors and behave towards them in terms of a set of relevant criteria. The new client must, if he or she is to gain status and its rewards, adequately meet these criteria.

To a certain extent status criteria are imported into the organization. Instrumental and socio-emotional leadership have a degree of similarity in both delinquent and nondelinquent peer groups. Sophistication, athletic ability, personal appearance, strength, personality characteristics are all brought with the boy into the organization. However, the criteria that may be most affected by institutional practices are also those that are most relevant to rehabilitative goals. For instance, client organization may stress "con" values —the unfairness of society and staff, and the necessity of proving one's worth by anti-social behavior; or it may stress the necessity of facing reality, being fair, and proving one's worth by socially approved means.

Like the mental hospital which must accommodate the hospital to the patient, correctional institutions with rehabilitative aims cannot merely force the offender to accommodate to it. They require voluntaristic participation and identification. We would expect client organization to favor attitudes that support goals of rehabilitation the more the clients perceive the staff as working for the interests of the clients.* When there is not this perception overt compliance may take place, but covertly rehabilitative goals are sabotaged. Professional staff working in

predominantly custodial institutions have often found themselves being "used" by the other staff and by the clients.

Some kind of *modus vivendi* must be reached between client leadership and staff in any institution if perpetual crisis is to be avoided. Staff in an institution have something to bargain with. They can "sell" prerogatives, positions, and psychological rewards. And what they "sell" influences not only the ranking criteria but also the structure of client organization. Structures can be found ranging from those that are hierarchically organized around the control of violence and communication to those that are less rigid and decentralized (16; 38). The multiple goals of most institutions affect client structure by: (1) introducing inconsistencies into the relationships between staff and clients; (2) allowing clients to play off one staff group against the other; and (3) by presenting client organization with an unstable situation. The existence of conflicting staff groups contributes to the breakdown of a rigid client structure by giving access to facilities to clients who are not among the more influential of the clients, thus breaching the monolithic client system of more custodial institutions of prisons.

The ability of the institution to affect client organization is also dependent upon the personality structure of the offender. Reiss's investigations would imply that the "Relatively Integrated" delinquent should be more adaptive than either the "Defective Super-Ego" or the "Weak Ego" offender (25; 26). Since the delinquent sub-culture supports the values of the peer group, the problem of the correctional institution is to structure the situation so that the anti-social values of the primary group are replaced by more positive ones (6). Rehabilitation of the "Defective Super-Ego" and the "Weak Ego" offender may well require both extinction of delinquent values and development of socially approved values by therapeutic techniques.

CONCLUSIONS

We have attempted to delineate the character of correctional institutions for delinquents. Reflecting a growing body of literature, the analysis has stressed the fact, that,

---

* In many ways delinquents stand in a relation to the organization similar to the primary members of military or industrial organizations. Their identification with the organization seems to be a crucial determinant of their organizational behavior.

like other large-scale organizations, these dependent institutions are involved in a web of relationships with the external environment.

Strategically, the analysis has proceeded from the characteristics of the goals and the external environment to the structured relationships of the staff and their effects upon client behavior. Some of the characteristics which are most striking about correctional institutions are (a) the critical climate of opinion in which they operate; (b) the fact that they are resource-deprived institutions; (c) the abstract quality of rehabilitative goals and the difficulty of proving one technique to be more successful than another; (d) the multiplicity of functions assigned the institutions; and finally (e) the fact that these are "total institutions."

Correctional institutions will vary along many of the dimensions discussed. For example, we should not expect all local communities to have equal tolerance of escapees. The size of the community, its history, and other factors will condition its reaction to the institution. Similarly we should not expect all guards or cottage parents to develop ideologies congruent with the goals of the organization. Future research must be directed at ascertaining the conditions under which the phenomena herein described occur.

REFERENCES

1. Belknap, Ivan. *Human Problems of a State Mental Hospital* (New York: McGraw-Hill, 1956).
2. Bowler, Alida C., and Bloodgood, Ruth S. *Institutional Treatment of Delinquent Boys, Part I. Treatment Programs of Five State Institutions* (Washington, Children's Bureau Publication No. 228, 1935).
3. Caudill, William. *The Psychiatric Hospital as a Small Society* (Cambridge: Harvard, 1958).
4. Clemmer, Donald. *The Prison Community* (Boston: Christopher, 1940).
5. Craig, Leita P. Reaching delinquents through cottage committees. *Children,* 6 (July-August, 1959), 129–134.
6. Cressey, Donald R. Contradictory theories in correctional group therapy programs. *Federal Probation,* 18 (June, 1954), 20–25.
7. ———. The nature and effectiveness of correctional techniques. *Law and Contemporary Problems,* 23 (Autumn, 1958), 754–771.
8. ———. Contradictory directives in complex organization: the case of the prisons. *Administrative Science Quarterly,* 4 (June, 1959), 1–19.
9. Etzioni, Amitai. Administration and the consumer. *Administrative Science Quarterly,* 3 (September, 1958), 251–264.
10. Goffman, Erving. The characteristics of total institutions, in *Symposium on Preventive and Social Psychiatry* (Washington: Government Printing Office, 1957), 43–84.
11. Greenblatt, Milton, Daniel G. Levinson, and Richard Williams (eds.). *The Patient and the Mental Hospital* (Glencoe, Ill.: Free Press, 1957).
12. Grusky, Oscar. *Treatment Goals and Organizational Behavior: A Study of an Experimental Prison Camp,* unpublished Ph.D. dissertation (Ann Arbor, The University of Michigan, 1957).
13. Juvenile delinquency, *Interim Report of the Committee on the Judiciary, U.S. Senate* (Washington: Government Printing Office, 1954).
14. Levine, Sol, Paul E. White, and Carol L. Pierson. Interaction among organizations (paper delivered at the 1959 meetings of the American Sociological Society).
15. MacIver, Robert M., director. Three residential treatment centers. *Interim Report No. IX of the Juvenile Delinquency Evaluation Project of the City of New York* (March, 1958).
16. McCleery, Richard H. *Policy Change in Prison Management* (Lansing: Governmental Research Bureau, Michigan State University, 1957).
17. ———. Communication patterns as a basis for a system of authority and power (paper prepared for the SSRC seminar on corrections, undated).
18. McCorkle, Lloyd W., Albert Elias, and F. Lovell Bisby. *The Highfields Story* (New York: Henry Holt, 1958).
19. Novick, A. G. Training school organization for treatment. *The Proceedings of the National Association of Training Schools*

and Juvenile Agencies, 54 (Chicago, 1958), 72–80.

20. Ohlin, Lloyd E. Interest group conflict and correctional objectives (paper prepared for the Ad Hoc Committee on Correctional Organization of the SSRC, April, 1957).

21. ———. The reduction of role conflict in institutional staff. *Children,* 5 (March–April, 1958), 65–69.

22. Ohlin, Lloyd E., and Donnell Pappenfort. Crisis, succession and organizational change (mimeographed paper, 1956).

23. Powelson, Harvey, and Reinhard Bendix. Psychiatry in Prisons. *Psychiatry,* 14 (February, 1951), 73–86.

24. Redl, Fritz. The meaning of therapeutic milieu, symposium in Greenblatt, Milton, Daniel G. Levinson, and Richard Williams (eds.). *The Patient and the Mental Hospital* (Glencoe, Ill.: Free Press, 1957), 503–516.

25. Reiss, Albert. Social correlates of psychological types of delinquency. *American Sociological Review,* 17 (December, 1952), 710–718.

26. ———. Delinquency as the failure of personal and social control. *American Sociological Review,* 16 (April, 1951), 196–207.

27. Schrag, Clarence. Leadership among prison inmates. *American Sociological Review,* 19 (February, 1954), 37–42.

28. Scott, Frances G. Action theory and research in social organization. *American Journal of Sociology,* 64 (January, 1959), 386–96.

29. Selznick, Philip. *TVA and the Grass Roots* (Berkeley: University of California Press, 1949).

30. ———. *Leadership and Administration: a Sociological Interpretation* (Evanston: Row Peterson, 1957).

31. Stanton, Alfred H., and Morris Schwartz. *The Mental Hospital* (New York: Basic Books, 1954).

32. Sykes, Gresham. The corruption of authority and rehabilitation. *Social Forces,* 34 (March, 1956), 257–62.

33. ———. *The Society of Captives: A Study of a Maximum Security Prison* (Princeton: Princeton University Press, 1958).

34. Vinter, Robert D. Juvenile correctional institution executives: a role analysis (mimeographed paper, 1958).

35. Vinter, Robert D., and Morris Janowitz. Effective institutions for juvenile delinquents: a research statement. *Social Service Review,* 33 (June, 1959), 118–131.

36. Vinter, Robert D., and Roger Lind. *Staff Relationships and Attitudes in a Juvenile Correctional Institution* (Ann Arbor: School of Social Work, 1958).

37. Webber, George H. Conflicts between professional and non-professional persons in institutional delinquency treatment. *Journal of Criminal Law, Criminology, and Police Science,* 48 (June, 1957), 26–43.

38. Weeks, H. Ashley, and Oscar W. Ritchie. *An Evaluation of the Services of the State of Ohio to its Delinquent Children and Youth* (Columbus: Bureau of Educational Research, Ohio State University, 1956).

39. Wells, Fred L., Milton Greenblatt, and Robert W. Hyde. As the psychiatric aide sees his work and problems. *Genetic Psychology Monographs,* 53 (February, 1956), 3–75.

C. The Community

Moving upwards along a dimension of inclusiveness, we come next to consider the community as a legitimate, though often ignored, context for behavior of relevance to the social psychological investigator. As with the other levels of social context discussed, it is oftentimes easier to point to one than to offer a more general, abstract definition. Speaking very generally, however, the community is a geographically based system of relationships and interdependencies which serves as a source of supply for member sustenance needs, including typically the location of living and working.

The "character" of the community, its power, leadership or control structure, and its manner of organization (e.g. residential patterning, central and suburban areas, etc.) all provide important areas of investigation. Historically, the emergence of "the city" and the consequent problems which developed from this emergence have occupied the attention of both historians and sociologists. For some time, sociologists were concerned

with characterizing areas of the city and relating these to crime, delinquency, and mental illness rates. More recently, concern with the power structure of the community, and particularly with the relationship between this structural property and the political characteristics of the community has been in increasing evidence in the literature.

In general, the social psychologist has ignored the context of the community in his studies, focusing most of his attention on the small group and the larger culture itself. The inclusion of readings dealing with this context, then, must draw heavily from the more sociologically oriented investigations.

The two readings included present both theoretical (Greer) and empirical approaches (Form & Sauer) to studying the community context. Although the readings most heavily concentrate upon the power structure of the community, the theoretical presentation by Greer deals with some broader community characteristics and processes.

The Social Structure and Political Process of Suburbia* / Scott Greer (*Northwestern University*)

The basic characteristics differentiating suburban areas from the central city, as developed in current literature, are related through a theory of social organization. This approach derives spatially-based social organization from population type and the social consequences of spatial aggregation. The social-political structure of suburbia is conceptualized at three organizational levels, concentric in scope: the neighborhood, the local residential community, the municipality. From their differential relations with structures at the first two levels, empirically and conceptually defined types of "local actors" are developed. Their relative involvement in the local political process is specified. A series of hypotheses deduced from the general argument specifies the relations between (1) population type, (2) household type, (3) participational type, and (4) political behavior in the local system.

Three aspects of suburban society are emphasized in the recent literature: the demographic characteristics of the population, the associational structure, and the political structure. Suburban population tends to be more middle-class, ethnic, and family-centered than that of the central city; in the suburb the neighborhood and perhaps the local community are more important *loci* of association than in the city; and suburbia characteristically has smaller governmental units than the cities, and has more of them.

General theory is hazy, unarticulated, and incomplete with respect to the manner in which these three aspects of suburban society are related. Those committed to each approach neglect the others, or assume a non-existent integration. Duncan and Reiss, who emphasize differences in population composition, accept political boundaries as meaningful for their analyses.[1] Those who are more concerned with ecological processes derive demographic differences from ecological position and the economic dependence of suburbs upon the central city, paying little attention to the political structures which contain and define their data.[2] On the other hand, Robert Wood's recent treatment of suburban political structure emphasizes the political form of the municipality in the suburbs as a determinant for both recruitment to suburbia and the staying power of the suburban governmental enclaves.[3] Wood does not, however, explore the interrelations between political structure and the variables emphasized by the demographers and ecologists; again, a "loose fit" is assumed. Finally, recent work by Bell postulates a "quest for community" which implies that associational structure is a major selective factor in migration to suburbia and a stabilizing factor in the suburban trend, but one which cannot be subsumed under the "housing market" or the "political climate" of suburbia.[4]

In this paper an effort is made to integrate and order these three aspects of suburbia and to develop a systematic theory of the relationships among population type, associa-

Reprinted from *The American Sociological Review,* 1960, 25, pages 514–526, by permission of author and publisher, The American Sociological Association.

* An expanded and revised version of a paper read at the annual meeting of the American Sociological Association, September, 1959. I wish to thank, for their critical reading and creative suggestions, Aaron Cicourel and Harold Guetzkow of Northwestern University, and Wendell Bell of The University of California, Los Angeles.

[1] Otis Dudley Duncan and Albert J. Reiss, Jr., *Social Characteristics of Rural and Urban Communities: 1950,* New York: Wiley, 1956.

[2] E.g., Walter T. Martin, "The Structuring of Social Relationships Engendered by Suburban Residence," *American Sociological Review,* 21 (August, 1956), pp. 446–453.

[3] Robert C. Wood, *Suburbia, Its People and Their Politics,* Boston: Houghton Mifflin, 1959. See especially Chapter 4, "The Nature of Suburbia."

[4] Wendell Bell, "Social Choice, Life Styles, and Suburban Residence," in W. A. Dobriner, editor, *The Suburban Community,* New York: Putnam's, 1958, pp. 225–247.

tional patterns, communication system, and political structure congruent with the present state of research findings and capable of further test and evaluation. The paper emphasizes the organizational level of analysis, and concentrates upon the explanation of the immediate organizational structure—that is, the spatially defined group as it exists in the suburbs.

This strategy differs from several current and traditional approaches. It does not move directly from the most general levels of societal structure to the observables (ordinarily the person-to-person relationship) or *vice versa,* as is common in the work of Durkheim, Parsons, Riesman, Weber, and other analysts of large-scale society.[5] Nor does this approach assume away the nature of interaction, as in much work by contemporary ecologists.[6] Both general theory and ecology are "macroscopic" approaches which emphasize the congruity and interdependence of social trends at a high level of abstraction. If, however, one takes seriously the intermediate-level constructs implied by these approaches—social class, bureaucracy, and occupational strata—one finds striking anomalies when studying the local community. Thus suburbanites, disproportionately made up of white-collar bureaucrats (the "organization men" and the "other directed"), are precisely the people who cling

most fiercely to the autonomy of the small municipalities when merger with the central city is in question. Their involvement in large-scale organizational systems does not determine their behavior in the community. In view of the viability or staying power of the suburban communities, one must ask: To what extent is this behavior appropriate to occupational scenes transferred, if at all, to the residential area? To raise this question is to require that the relevant area of social action, the residential community itself, be approached with a conceptual scheme appropriate to its own characteristics as a field for social action.

Thus, the strategy adopted here is to move from the macro-level, using census data for an aggregate description, but spelling out the steps by which one reaches the micro-level of household organization. This procedure provides a method of analyzing the social structure of the suburb—neighborhood, local residential community, and municipality. Such an approach then leads back to the macro-level. Indexes based upon census data, however, now become measures of conditions under which spatially defined social groups become probable.[7]

POPULATION TYPE AND LIFE STYLE

The transformation of a predominantly agricultural and rural nation into an increasingly metropolitan nation may be summarized as an increase in societal scale. Many sequences of change are fundamental causes of this process and many secondary changes ensue.[8] For present purposes, changes in the kind of *differentia* which cut across the societal unit are emphasized. Occupation, for example, is a rather unimportant differentiator within small-scale society, and ethnic variations are usually absent. In modern cities, however, nothing

[5] Emile Durkheim, *Suicide,* translated by John A. Spaulding and George Simpson, edited with an Introduction by George Simpson, Glencoe, Ill.: Free Press, 1951; Talcott Parsons, *The Social System,* Glencoe, Ill.: Free Press, 1952; David Riesman, Reuel Denney, and Nathan Glazer, *The Lonely Crowd,* New Haven: Yale University Press, 1950; Max Weber, *The Theory of Social and Economic Organization,* translated by A. M. Henderson and Talcott Parsons, edited with an Introduction by Talcott Parsons, New York: Oxford University Press, 1947. To bring matters up to date, see the work of the Detroit Area Study, which moves immediately from individual characteristics to such societal dimensions as the stratification system: *A Social Profile of Detroit, 1956, A Report of the Detroit Area Study of the University of Michigan,* Ann Arbor: Detroit Area Study, Department of Sociology and the Survey Research Center of the Institute for Social Research, 1957.

[6] Amos H. Hawley, *Human Ecology: A Theory of Community Structure,* New York: Ronald, 1950; Otis Dudley Duncan and Beverly Duncan, "Residential Distribution and Occupational Stratification," *American Journal of Sociology,* 60 (March, 1955), pp. 493–503; Leo F. Schnore, "The Growth of Metropolitan Suburbs," *American Sociological Review,* 22 (April, 1957), pp. 165–173.

[7] In the exposition of the theory that follows, the author has assumed the dogmatic but simplifying device of expressing many discrete hypotheses as valid propositions. These hypotheses, couched in testable form, conclude this paper.

[8] See, e.g., Fred Cottrell, *Energy and Society,* New York: McGraw-Hill, 1955; Godfrey and Monica Wilson, *The Analysis of Social Change,* Cambridge: At the University Press, 1954; Eshref Shevky and Wendell Bell, *Social Area Analysis,* Stanford: Stanford University Press, 1955.

is more impressive than the differences in culture, life chances, deference, and power associated with variations in occupation and ethnic identity.

A third dimension emphasized here is urbanism, or life style. By urbanism we refer to the life-ways of sub-segments which have become differentiated on a continuum ranging from a familistic to an extremely urban mode of life.[9] Such a continuum first emerged from the analysis of census tract populations, and the indexes developed to measure it apply to such aggregates.[10] Toward the urban end of the continuum are neighborhoods of apartment houses with single persons, childless couples, and one-child families predominating; toward the other end are single-family dwelling units inhabited by families with several children, in which the woman, not a member of the labor force, plays the role of wife and mother. This definition of urbanism, emphasizing household organization and its consequences, excludes much that is usually encompassed in the term, but this limited meaning appears to be especially relevant to the present analysis of spatially defined groups in the metropolis.

The familistic type of neighborhood approximates, of course, the typical image of suburbia. Although suburbs have no monopoly of such populations, they tend to be more consistently inhabited by familistic households than any other part of the urban agglomeration. One important reason for such concentration lies in the demand and supply of sites for family living. Studies of suburban residents indicate the high evaluation they place on the physical and social facilities for child-rearing and home-making, including the prerequisite for this life, private space, indoors and out. The site demanded is one which allows for the play of children in safe and "pleasant" places, space for growing flowers, vegetables, and grass, for keeping pets, for patio exercise, and the like.[11] With the existing patterns of land allocation in urban regions, however, a large area per person is available at moderate price only on the outskirts of the built-up districts. To be sure, the relationship between demand and supply is far from perfect; as Schnore implies, many persons might settle for equivalent lodgings in the middle of the city.[12] But the point is moot—until new, single-family dwellings, rather than high-rise public housing developments, replace the tenements and row-houses near the centers, we will not know how many "suburbanites" are fleeing the city and how many are forced to move outward because no other acceptable housing is available. Meanwhile, the family-oriented population continues to seek and find its sites on the growing edge of the city.

The local associational structure of a population can be derived from such sociological characteristics as family-orientation, for contiguity indicates the likelihood of contact, homogeneity indicates the likelihood of similar interests, and population type indicates the specific content which may plausibly be inferred for those interests.[13] Thus the use

---

[9] The term *urbanism* is used to refer to a concept Shevky has denoted as "urbanization" and Bell as "family status" or "familism." In general, urbanism implies that the higher the index reading, the nearer the approach to an ideal typical "urbanism as a way of life." Both the earlier terms are awkward, have disturbing connotations in the literature, and are sometimes downright misleading.

[10] The index of urbanism is discussed in Shevky and Bell, *op. cit.*, pp. 17 and 55–56. For evidence of the independence and importance of this dimension, see the factor analysis studies: Wendell Bell, *A Comparative Study of the Methodology of Urban Analysis,* unpublished Ph.D. thesis, University of California, Los Angeles, 1952; Maurice D. Van Arsdol, Jr., Santo F. Camilleri, and Calvin Schmid, "The Generality of Urban Social Area Indexes," *American Sociological Review,* 23 (June, 1958), pp. 277–284. For a test of the index, using sample survey data, see Scott Greer and Ella Kube, "Urbanism and Social Structure," in Marvin Sussman, editor, *Community Structure and Analysis,* New York: Crowell, 1959, pp. 93–112.

[11] See the findings reported by Bell (in Dobriner, *op. cit.*) and by Richard Dewey in "Peripheral Expansion in Milwaukee County," *American Journal of Sociology,* 53 (May, 1948), pp. 417–422. Seventy-two per cent of Bell's respondents who had moved from Chicago into two middle-rank suburbs listed physical characteristics as a reason for moving to the suburbs; 50 per cent of their responses reflected improvement in privacy and geographical space. Dewey's respondents gave as reasons for their move, in order, "better for children," "less congested," "cleaner," and "larger lot," as the four most popular ones.

[12] Schnore, *op. cit.* A polemical statement of the possibility is found in William H. Whyte, Jr., "Are Cities Un-American?" in Editors of *Fortune, The Exploding Metropolis,* Garden City, N.Y.: Doubleday, 1958.

[13] This argument is presented in another context by Wendell Bell in "A Probability Model for the Measurement of Ecological Segregation," *Social Forces,* 32 (May, 1954), pp. 357–364.

of indexes which aggregate persons by geographical sub-areas implies contiguity and the relative homogeneity of the residential neighborhood. Specifically, the urbanism index developed by Shevky and Bell as a measure of average life-style yields social attributes of the geographically defined sub-population, hypothesized here as crucial for spatially-based social interaction.[14] The less urban and more familistic the neighborhood, the more important is the dwelling unit as a site for everyday life, and for a particular kind of life.

The type and rate of interaction, however, is not specified in detail by this set of statements. All that is proposed, at this point in the argument, is that spatially defined interaction is related to the familistic character of the suburban population. In order to translate such interaction into social structure and political process, it is necessary to relate the gross variations in population type to a theory of spatially defined organization.

THE ORGANIZATIONAL STRUCTURE OF THE SUBURBS

The bifurcation of work and residence is sometimes taken as one of the defining characteristics of the suburban population.[15] But this bifurcation holds for most of the population in a metropolis; any local residential area is segmental in nature. Because a living area is the site for some, but not all, of the basic social activities of its residents, Janowitz calls it the "community of limited liability."[16] Such a community, however, encompasses some very crucial structures and therefore has constraining force—which allows the social scientist some predictive and explanatory power.

The definition of social organization used in the present discussion emphasizes functional interdependence. As the unit of analysis, we shall emphasize the spatially defined group. The locality group, or community, is

thus viewed as a special case of the social form elsewhere defined as "an aggregate in a state of functional interdependence, from which emerges a flow of communication and a consequent ordering of behavior."[17]

Geographical contiguity, however, has no self-evident sociological meaning. It may become the basis for interdependence only when it constitutes a field for social action. We consider below three such fields, concentric in scope: the neighborhood, the local residential community, and the municipality. Using the definition of the group stated above, we ask three questions about each of these levels of organization: What constitutes the functional interdependence of the members? What are the channels of communication and the contents of the communication flow? What kind of ordered behavior results?

The neighborhood.—If the residents of a neighborhood consist of households with familistic ways of life (and consequently similar interests) existing in close proximity, there is a high probability of intersecting trajectories of action. Since surrounding households constitute important and inescapable parts of any given household's organizational environment, there emerge problems of social order, maintenance, and aid. Specifically, it is necessary to regulate the play of children, child-adult relations, and adult-adult relations to the degree that these represent possible blocks to the orderly performance of the household's way of life. To the extent that contiguous sites overlap visually, aurally, and (sometimes) physically, it is also necessary to regulate the use of the sites. The unsightly yard, the noises of the night, the dangerously barricaded sidewalk may constitute such blocks. Finally, similarity of life routines indicates a probable similarity of equipment and tasks: thus the interchangeability of parts is possible. This may range from the traditional borrowing of a cup of bourbon to the baby-sitting pool.

To be sure, similar problems arise in the apartment house districts characterized by a highly urban way of life, but the structure of the neighborhood and the nature of the

---

[14] By relative homogeneity we mean no more than the probability that differences by a chosen criterion are greater between areas than is true within each area.

[15] See, e.g., Martin, *op. cit.*

[16] Morris Janowitz, *The Community Press in an Urban Setting,* Glencoe, Ill.: Free Press, 1952. See esp. Chapter 7, "The Social Dimensions of the Local Community."

[17] Scott Greer, *Social Organization,* New York: Random House, 1955. The spatially defined group and the changing nature of the urban sub-community are discussed in Chapters 4 and 5.

population result in different kinds of order. The lower rate of communication, due to lack of common or overlapping space, and the separation of routines in time, result in a greater dependence upon formal norms (rules of the building, laws of residency) and upon formal authorities. Thus the apartment house manager, or even the police, may be useful for the maintenance of order and the site. (Their utility, from household to *concierge* to police, is evident in the reliance placed upon such organizations by the state in various European countries.) In the suburbs, however, life-style and the relationships among the sites force inter-household communication.

Communication in the neighborhood may take place at many levels, but in viewing the suburban neighborhood as an organizational unit we shall emphasize casual interaction among those whose paths necessarily intersect. In the adjoining backyards, at bus stops, and local commercial facilities, considerable social interaction is well nigh unavoidable. This interaction may become elaborated into relatively permanent cliques —kaffeeklatsch groups, pools, and the like— and frequently results in a network of close friendships. These differ from "neighboring," or participation in the neighborhood organization, just as friendship within any organization differs from the ongoing structure of activity common to the aggregate.

The resulting patterns of behavior, the structured action, probably vary a good deal according to the type of neighborhood; however, the ubiquity of the phrase "the good neighbor" seems to indicate some generalized role system and normative structure.[18] Orderliness, accessibility in time of need, and cleanliness are salient characteristics rooted in the functional interdependence discussed above. Individual members conform to such norms (whether or not they love their neighbors) because the norms facilitate their ongoing household enterprises.

But the neighborhood is a microcosm. Nor is it the only spatially based social structure mediating between the household and the

metropolis. The neighborhood then is a precipitate of interacting households; participation in it does not necessarily indicate a role in the larger local area as community or as political unit. The neighborhood produces, at the least, some order among the small enclave of residents, and communication relevant to the nearby scene.

The local residential area.—Neighbors in the suburbs tend to have similar interests, for their ways of life have similar prerequisites, while in the local residential area interdependence results when similar interests are transformed into common interests, based upon the common field in which they operate. Spatial aggregates are the distributing units for many goods and services— public schools, commercial services, and various governmental aids and are frequently available to the individual only through his residence in a geographically delimited aggregate. To the degree that this is true of vital resources, the population of a local residential area is functionally interdependent.[19] At the same time space, as the site of common activities (street, sidewalk, park, playground), is a base of interdependence, as in the neighborhood.

The local residential community as here defined includes a number of neighborhoods. It may or may not be coterminous with a political unit. What is its minimal organizational structure? Communication relevant to the area ordinarily takes place through two channels, the community press and voluntary

---

[18] The norms may vary of course by social rank and ethnicity; to simplify the argument the effects of these dimensions are considered irrelevant to the major hypotheses. Social rank is discussed in a later section.

[19] The reader may question the existence of such "local areas" as social fact. However, scattered evidence indicates that the map of the city breaks down into sub-units for the residential population, whether or not these are congruent with ecologically defined "natural areas." The nature and consequences of economic decentralization are explored by Foley, of social and economic decentralization by Janowitz. See Donald L. Foley, "The Use of Local Facilities in a Metropolis," *American Journal of Sociology,* 56 (November, 1950), pp. 238–246, and *Neighbors or Urbanites? The Study of a Rochester Residential District,* Rochester, N.Y.: University of Rochester, 1952; and Janowitz, *op. cit.* A more recent study reports a strong definition of sub-areas among residents of Boston. See Laurence Ross, *The Local Community in the Metropolis,* unpublished Ph.D. thesis, Harvard University, 1959. Furthermore, 98 per cent of the residents of suburban St. Louis County accept the notion and give a distinctive name to their residential area (unpublished research report, Metropolitan St. Louis Survey).

organizations. While each is a communication channel, we shall stress the communications function of the press and the action
function of the voluntary organization.

The local community press in the suburbs,
widely distributed and widely read, is a medium available to almost all residents of most
local areas.[20] Its utility stems directly from
the interdependence of activities within the
local area; supported by local merchants, it
provides support in turn for the various
formal organizations which constitute the
"community." To be sure, all areas are not
now serviced by a community press, but so
useful is the medium (and consequently, so
lucrative) that it is rapidly "covering" the
suburban areas of contemporary cities. As
the press develops where there is a market
for its services, this should occur most consistently and widely among the familistic
populations.

The suburban paper is quite similar to that
described by Janowitz—parochial in its interests, reporting almost exclusively upon
local happenings, translating metropolitan
events into their effects on the local area,
seldom reporting national events.[21] Such
local personages as merchants, bureaucrats,
and organizational leaders constitute the
actors on this stage. Insofar as the local area
is a social fact, the latter is reflected in the
press and at the same time reinforced in the
process of reflection, for the press in perpetuating lines of communication stabilizes
norms and roles. If it is chiefly a merchan-
dising mechanism in its economic function,
it is also a public platform for the area in
its social and political functions.

But what of the local area without a separate government? In this case, what kind of
structured action is indicated as the third
term in the definition of the area as a social
structure? Noting again that spatially defined organization in the residential area is
loose, unstructured, and does not engage all

of the residents, here we emphasize participation in the local formal organizations.
Such organizations are segmental in their
membership and purposes; they include
those residents who are dependent upon
them for basic necessities to their way of life.
Community-oriented organizations, improvement associations, child-centered organizations, some fraternal and service clubs are
examples. They are particular to the area,
their membership is largely limited to those
living there, and they are instruments of persuasion and control with respect to various
community problems, projects, and festivals.
Furthermore, if there is no political structure
they are the *only* existing structures through
which an interdependence specific to the area
(issuing in local problems), communicated
through the press (as "community issues"),
become manifested in social action.

The suburban municipality.—The typical
political structure of metropolitan suburbia
viewed as a whole is a crazy-quilt of many
small municipalities having various eccentric
shapes and displaying little obvious order in
their boundaries. It is likely, however, that
many of these municipalities are roughly
coterminous with one or more social communities of the kind discussed above. To the
degree that this is the case, the seemingly
arbitrary lines on the map may come to represent social communities. The congruence
of municipal boundaries with a local residential community permits the translation of
common interests into a polity. The common
field of activity (and the various segmental
interests sited in this field) is contained
within a formal organizational structure having the power to control, within wide limits,
some of the basic goods and services of the
residents. Thus streets, parks, schools (and,
to a degree, commercial and residential development) are not only sources of interdependence—their control is so structured
as to allow effective action by the interdependent population. Furthermore, taxation,
police power, and other governmental attributes are assigned to the local municipality.

Where such is the case, an additional level
is added to the structured action which results from interdependence and the flow of
communication within the residential community: political action, within a political

[20] Thus 84 per cent of Janowitz's respondents
were readers of their local press (*op. cit.*). Similar
findings are reported for a Los Angeles suburban
sample: of those who received the paper (85 per
cent) over 92 per cent were regular readers; see
Scott Greer and Ella Kube, *Urban Worlds: A
Comparative Study of Four Los Angeles Areas,*
Los Angeles: Laboratory in Urban Culture, 1955
(processed).

[21] Janowitz, *op. cit.*

community.[22] Communication now incorporates well defined political norms and roles, the latter including the governmental official, political leader, voter, local taxpayer, and so on. But this type of organizational structure does not displace the kinds of voluntary community organizations indicated earlier. Certain modes of action tend to become allocated to the governmental organization; others remain the functions of private and semi-private groups (including the neighborhoods).

The organizational structure of suburbia may be summarized as follows: (1) The overlapping activities of households result in the neighborhoods, which exist as a kind of network spreading throughout the familistic population (for neighborhoods overlap as do households, and the neighborhood structure of a metropolis frequently resembles St. Augustine's definition of God, an infinite circle whose center is everywhere and whose periphery is nowhere). (2) Larger residential areas with a degree of functional interdependence constitute "communities of limited liability." They exhibit communication

[22] This does not imply an automatic evolution which presumes that through time interdependence must result in communication and order. The precise processes by which organizational structures evolve are not spelled out here; they would be desirable but are not essential to the purposes of the present paper.

through informal relations and the community press, and action through voluntary private and semi-private organizations. (3) In many cases, political units are roughly coterminous with, or include, one or more social communities. Neighborhoods are probably nearly omnipresent, though a network need not include all households; so are communities, but they vary widely in degree of organization; political communities may or may not exist. In the summary presented in Table 1, each analytical category is sketched in for each organizational level.

RELATIONS BETWEEN ORGANIZATIONAL LEVELS IN SUBURBIA

The four types of organization discussed above—household, neighborhood, local residential area, municipality—are, generally, of ascending order as to size and descending order as to the probability of face-to-face or "primary" relations. They are also arranged in an order which indicates an increasing possibility of common "public" interest and action and, therefore, of policy relevance. Thus as formal policy becomes possible, representation rather than universal participation is a necessity.

The neighborhood, as the first level beyond the individual household, is very likely

TABLE 1
SOCIAL-POLITICAL SRUCTURES OF SUBURBIA

	Source of Interdependence	Channels of Communication	Structured Action
Neighborhood:	Overlapping field Similar interests	Informal interaction Casual visiting	Regulated interaction Maintenance of the site Mutual aid
Local Area:	Common field Common interests	Community press Local organizations Informal interaction	Segmental interests protection Diffuse community action (outside political structure)
Municipality:	Common field Common interests Common organizational structure coterminous with both	Local governmental functions Local political organizations Local non-political organizations Community press Informal interaction	Law-abiding (local), tax-paying Voting, holding office Attending meetings Use of bureaucratic structure for complaints and appeals Organization of electoral campaigns

to generate interhousehold friendships and visiting patterns; neighboring then may be part of the informal communication flow of the area. The neighborhood, however, is not apt to form polity beyond the conventional "rules of the road," nor is it apt to be a representational unit for any larger collectivity. The social products of the neighborhood *per se* are small-scale order, mutual aid, and friendship. The lack of a formal structure oriented to the collective needs and problems of the inhabitants probably facilitates the performance of those minimal tasks discussed earlier: the informal and, indeed, often unspoken norms relevant to the group allow for considerable flexibility and effective control of deviation. But unformalized norms and unspecialized roles are suitable only for a given routine, and preferably one requiring little precision. The self-ordering of the neighborhood is an ordering of routine interaction, with wide limits of tolerance.

For these reasons, the neighborhood is not formally related to any other level of spatially based organization: it is too small to constitute an administrative sub-unit of a larger system and too informal to constitute a base for independent representation in a larger system. The interaction of households produces a luxuriant network of neighborhoods in the suburbs, but these have little direct significance for the polity.[23] Their chief contribution to other organizational systems is one of communication: they are a site for conversational ferment.

The household is related to the larger local area through formal organizations sited in the area. These include public and business structures and such "auxiliary" voluntary formal organizations as PTA and service club, as well as voluntary organizations built upon independent functional bases. In general, local organizations are concerned with common activities of specific segments of the residential population in the area.[24] The same household activities and interests which produce involvement in these area-wide segmental organizations also produce interest in the flow of local communication through informal relationships and the community press. Thus household members are differentially related to local formal organizations, while their reading of the press (and conversation with others) permits a familiarity with the organizations and actors of the local area as a whole.

In the present approach, the agencies of local government, although they possess distinctive political functions, are also viewed as segmental structures. For, despite its conventional identity with a geographical space and its population, local government has only limited powers and duties and affects only a small part of the residents' activities.

The non-governmental organizational structure of the local area is related to the suburban municipality through the congruence of fields of action (and convergence or conflict of interests) between voluntary organizations and governmental agencies. Possible interrelations of the two kinds of structures include, for example, the use of private organizations as representatives of community interests before the government, the overlapping leadership role within both government and private organizations, and the private organization as a political faction or party. Each of these would strengthen the argument that the local government is "truly representative of the community"; at the same time, each would have important consequences for the effectiveness of, and the constraints upon, local governmental agencies in dealing with problems and issues.

Thus, we should expect an overlapping membership between voluntary organizations and the municipal electorate. If the members of local organizations are exceptionally sensitive to community news as reported in the press, and if at the same time the community press reports governmental affairs extensively and frequently, the per-

[23] The reader will recall the widely reported relationship between the voting of respondents and their neighbors; however, the significant variables in the present discussion are quite different. Reference here is to *participation* (not direction of vote) in *local* elections, while neighbors are distinguished from friends (the latter is a sub-category). Near-dwelling friends may indeed influence voting in Presidential elections; this is not the proposition presented above.

[24] They may be coded as: child-centered, community-political, and fraternal-service, for those most intimately related to the affairs of the local residential area. The remaining voluntary organizations may be usefully coded as either work-related or church-related.

sons most active in local voluntary organizations should be highly informed about the *dramatis personae* of community polity. Insofar as they are committed members of common interest organizations, they would be particularly aware of governmental decisions, for these frequently affect voluntary organizations. And, even though they do not read the local paper, they should be unusually aware of information concerning the local residential community through their organizational activities, neighboring, and local friendships.

In short, neighborhood structures involve a large proportion of the suburban population, are loosely related to the local area communication system, but are not formally related to larger organizational networks. The local residential community and the municipality both involve a smaller proportion of the population (and one that is largely composed of the same individuals), but their scale and functions are such that they "stand for" the total population with respect to many basic activities.

TYPES OF RELATIONSHIP TO COMMUNITY ORGANIZATION

If there are predictable and orderly relationships between households, neighborhoods, residential communities, and municipalities, we can spell out the possible logical combinations, and can examine the distribution of community roles and the consequences for forms of behavior other than those built into the typology. In constructing types we emphasize neighborhood, local area, and governmental structure.

From the previous discussion may be deduced three levels of relationship to local social structure: (1) involvement in the small-scale system of the neighborhood, (2) a role in segmental structures based upon certain interests common to some people in the local area, and (3) a place in the flow of communication representing the local area "as a whole."

Dichotomizing each attribute for simplicity yields eight logically possible combinations. Some of these, however, are inconsistent with the framework sketched out earlier. If we consider separately the possible relations between neighborhood interaction, community roles, and access to the communication flow, the theory, with its emphases upon the communication functions of neighboring and of the local press and the social consequences of roles in local organizations, leads to the conclusions that there are no necessary relationships between (1) neighboring and community roles and (2) neighboring and reading the local press, but that there *is* a necessary relationship between a community role and participation in the communication network, either through neighboring or the press or both. A person with a role in the local organizational network but who neither reads the paper nor visits with his neighbors behaves inconsistently with the general hypothesis.

Following the procedures and qualifications discussed above results in the "organizational types" presented in Table 2. The rubrics in the right-hand column of the table are something more than summaries and something less than fully explicated types.

TABLE 2

"Organizational Types" in Suburbia

	Neighborhood Interaction	Local Community Role	Access to Communication Flow	Type
I.	Yes	Yes	Yes	Multi-level participator
II.	Yes	Yes	No	Community actor (A)
III.	No	Yes	Yes	Community actor (B)
IV.	Yes	No	Yes	Neighborhood actor (A)
V.	Yes	No	No	Neighborhood actor (B)
VI.	No	No	Yes	Voyeur
VII.	No	No	No	Isolate
VIII.	No	Yes	No	Error

The local "isolate," on the one hand, and the "multi-level participator," on the other, are clearly extremes. "Neighborhood actors" have defined positions only within the neighborhood system (although they may read the paper for gossip and entertainment). "Voyeurs" read the papers only as spectators of the community; they do not hold positions in role-systems and are otherwise comparable to isolates. "Community actors" may avoid their neighbors but, through common commitments, may still participate in area-wide formal organizations.

Population type and organizational type. —Certain associations are implied by the theory. Life style as the basis for similar interests at the neighborhood level and for common interests at the local area level should be a key variable in producing associational patterns. Thus, considering the urbanism dimension of the geographical sub-area as a rough measure of life style among contiguous populations, we expect neighboring to increase consistently as urbanism declines. Within a sample from neighborhoods at a given level of urbanism, however, variation in neighboring should be a result of variation in the life style of individual households: neighboring should increase with homeownership, number of children in the family, presence of wife in the household during the day. (The opposite extreme is the single person or childless couple with a working wife, who live in a rented apartment.)

One may object that the latter attributes of individual households would be a simpler and more reliable index than the urbanism of the geographical sub-area, clearly a possibility. However, neighborhoods are aggregates of persons in given sub-areas, and such aggregates cannot be inferred from a sample that is random with respect to neighborhood. If individual household attributes are the only data, we cannot allow for "the neighboring type of people" who live in areas where most women work, there are few children, and neighboring is difficult.[25] Contrariwise, considering only the average nature of the

[25] Greer and Kube, *op. cit.,* report a diminution in neighboring among non-working women, as the proportion of working women in a neighborhood increases. They explain this as a consequence of declining opportunities for neighboring.

neighborhood, we lose the deviants within it. For these reasons, both aggregate and household attributes are significant.

The same logic should lead to similar relationships between the urbanism of the residential population and membership in local organizations. Commitment to the area, as measured by commitment to home, public schools, and other household investments, should increase as urbanism declines. Within the households residing in given types of area, however, those who are most concerned with the local residential area should be most apt to belong to formal organizations of a "community" nature.

The prediction of discrepancy between neighboring and activity in community organizations is based upon the hypothesis that in some familistic areas the neighborhood interaction system includes persons whose interests are deviant (for example, the post-parental couple, the non-family female), but that such interaction does not necessarily lead to a concern with broader community interests. And, *vice versa,* persons may be "good citizens" in the community at large although they are not involved with immediate neighbors. Thus urbanism should be related to both neighboring and community participation, but not necessarily through the identical group of actors.

Finally, the urbanism of the neighborhood should be associated with access to the local communication flow. The same variations in household commitment producing increased participation in neighborhood and local area organizational networks should increase the value of communication relevant to the residential community. As a consequence of these relationships, the constructed types of local "actors" (see Table 2) should vary with the urbanism of the neighborhood. Moving from urban districts towards familistic suburbs, we should find an increasing proportion of the adult population involved in the small-scale neighborhood and in the larger residential area as organizational systems—with isolates becoming a decreasing proportion.

A note on social rank.—A relationship is often postulated between participation in formal community organizations and social rank (occupation, education, and income levels of the respondents or their neighborhoods or both). With social rank, however, as with age and sex, we are dealing with role variations which cut across the larger society, and these should have about the same effect *within* each type of neighborhood and, within the neighborhood, within each category of local actors. When social rank is controlled, therefore, community participational type should remain a major differentiator with respect to involvement and competence in the affairs of the local residential area.

Nevertheless, we would expect more community actors in upper-status neighborhoods, and among persons with more education, income, and with higher prestige occupations, for these persons may be expected to have more organizational memberships. At each level of social rank, however, the urbanism of the neighborhood should be salient, for it reflects the variations in life style relevant to spatially defined organization. Thus isolates should vary little by social rank, once the urbanism of the neighborhood is controlled. The chief effect of decreasing social rank would then be a decrease in community-level actors and an increase in neighborhood-level actors. Lower-status neighborhoods of low urbanism would be, not so much "massified and fragmented," as organized on the small-scale basis of the neighborhood. At each level of social rank, urbanism should make a major difference in the distribution of participational types.

This theory leads then to the proposition that urbanism *as such* has an independent predictive power for the identification of types of community actors because it indicates aspects of the population conducive to a greater or lesser generation of spatially defined groups. A corollary proposition is that type of community actor is a more powerful predictive instrument for many kinds of *local* organizational behavior than the social rank of the resident or his neighborhood and municipality.

Governmental structure.—It was indicated above that governmental structure adds another organizational level, provides a "mold" for community activity, a focus for the policy-oriented, and a set of roles· for the actors on the stage of the local community press. As an additional segmental organiza-tion, local government is a voluntary formal organization in that it provides further opportunities for involvement in the residential area's affairs. Therefore, if residential sub-areas are classified by organizational and governmental structure, we should expect the following rank order of competence and involvement in local affairs : areas with (1) autonomous organizational and governmental structures, (2) autonomous organizational but not governmental structures, (3) autonomous governmental but not organizational structures, and (4) areas with neither structure. Type (1) would include the sub-urban municipality which is a "social fact" as well as a governmental artifact; (2) would include the "local communities" in the unincorporated suburbs; (3) would probably be found in the areas now surrounded by the central city but still retaining political autonomy or in the areas immediately contiguous to the more urban neighborhoods of the city; (4) would be found, for the most part, in the central city.

Such a scheme points up the probability that incorporation will tend to increase public communication and action within a familistic area, for government summarizes many segmental common interests. If we consider the further possibility of applying the organizational types presented earlier to the probabilities of interaction within the political system, the analysis becomes more pertinent to the general problem of relating political and non-political social systems.

POLITICAL SYSTEM AND RESIDENTIAL COMMUNITY

Three general types of actors summarize the seven types presented in Table 2: isolates, neighborhood actors, and community actors. These terms are used below as short-hand for the description of organizational conditions and memberships producing each type.

With respect to the political and proto-political processes in suburbia, we may ask: To what degree does the suburban population participate in a local political system? Participation here refers to *competence* (the possession of adequate and accurate information on the political process) and *involvement* (including voting in local elections).

Interaction within the community-wide system is a clue to probable involvement in the polity (and, consequently, voting, electioneering, standing for office, and other manifestations). We assume that the action role is pursued only within a group context, and that the membership groups available in the suburbs are the various community-wide organizations. Such membership is thus considered a prerequisite to involvement in community politics; similarly involvement emerges from a functional commitment to the local area at other levels. Involvement, however, does not necessarily imply competence. We consider competence as the probable result of participation in the flow of communication *relevant to the community-wide system*. This may result from informal interaction (friendship or neighboring) or the community press or both. The general types of community actors should behave quite differently within the role system of the local municipality.—These hypotheses are suggested by the following tabular presentation:

	Involvement	Competence
Isolates	Low	Low
Neighborhood actors	Higher	Higher
Community actors	Highest	Highest

The difference between political settings is crucial for testing the general hypothesis of organizational scale. If the three types of actors are further categorized by the political structure of their residential areas, isolates should differ little in their competence, whether they live in unincorporated or incorporated areas: they should be largely incompetent. Neighbors should be relatively incompetent in each area. But community actors in the incorporated areas should have more knowledge about community organization, for there is more to know. For example, they should know a larger number of leaders, for their governmental structure provides such parochial leaders. When political leaders are subtracted from their knowledge, however, they should have a general back-

log of information on local leadership quite similar to those who live in unincorporated areas: organization type should be a predictor when political structure is controlled.

Two implications may be drawn from this discussion which are relevant to the current controversy about metropolitan governmental reform. First, the areas in which a viable, small-scale, local governmental process is likely are those of familistic populations, within which there are many community actors and few isolates—whether or not such areas are now incorporated. Second, the strength of the resistance to the "merger" of the central city and the suburbs should be found concentrated in those areas with a strong organizational network involving a large proportion of the adults in the residential community. In fact, the rank order of opposition should be correlated with the rank order, stated above, of competence and involvement in local affairs by areal attributes. At the low end of the resulting continuum would be those who live in the highly urban neighborhoods of the central city, for whom the local residential community has little meaning—and these persons are usually strong supporters of metropolitan "integration."

SOME DERIVED HYPOTHESES

Further applications of the theoretical scheme are possible and tempting. It is desirable at this point, however, to apply the theory to some derived observational requirements. The following hypotheses, implicit or explicit in the above discussion, merely illustrate a much larger number of possibilities. They are now being tested against data from a large-scale survey of the suburban population of one of the major metropolitan areas.[26] The hypotheses are stated briefly, but are consistent with the foregoing theoretical presentation.

Urbanism, life-style, and organizational participation.—Thirty-four specific hypotheses under this category may be presented as the following six propositions:

(a) Despite the varying effects of social

[26] The results of this analysis are to be reported in a forthcoming paper.

rank, ethnicity, and the characteristics of individual municipalities, urbanism is negatively related to neighboring, participation in formal organizations situated in the area, readership of the local press for local community news, and the incidence of community actors; urbanism is positively related to the incidence of isolates and voyeurs (hypotheses 1 through 6).

(b) When urbanism is controlled, social rank is positively related to the incidence of community actors, and negatively related to the incidence of neighborhood actors (hypotheses 7 and 8).

(c) Despite the varying effects of unit characteristics, the presence of children in the household is positively related to neighboring, participation in formal organizations situated in the area, and the incidence of community actors; it is negatively related to the incidence of isolates and voyeurs (hypotheses 8 through 11).

(d) When the presence of children in the household is controlled (and despite the varying effects of other unit characteristics), urbanism continues to have discriminating power with respect to the six participational variables indicated in (a) above (hypotheses 12 through 17).

(e) When the urbanism of the census tract of residence is controlled (and despite the varying effects of other unit characteristics, the presence of children in the household has discriminating power with respect to the participational variables indicated in (a) above (hypotheses 17 through 22).

(f) Despite the varying effects of other unit variables, urbanism and the presence of children in the household are conducive to the same types of organizational participation. Specifically, extremely high participation rates characterize those who live in low urban areas and have children, with respect to neighboring, belonging to local organizations, and reading the local press; the opposite holds for those without children in highly urban areas. With respect to the constructed types, the most community actors and the fewest isolates and voyeurs inhabit low urban neighborhoods with children in the households; the opposite holds for high

urban neighborhoods among childless households (hypotheses 23 through 34).

Organizational participation and political behavior.—Forty additional specific hypotheses are stated as the following seven more general formulations:

(a) Because it indicates involvement in the local area as an organizational system, participation in local organizations is positively related to voting, naming local leaders, and knowing the electoral rules. Because it indicates participation in the flow of communication in the area, readership of the press is related to naming leaders and knowing the rules. This also holds for neighboring with respect to naming leaders and knowing the rules. Neither neighboring nor readership of the press has a strong relationship with voting when organizational membership and the other unit of the pair is controlled (hypotheses 35 through 43).

(b) When the logically possible combinations are reduced to five, isolates (who neither read, neighbor, nor belong), voyeurs (who neither neighbor nor belong but who read the press), neighborhood actors (who neighbor but do not belong), deviants (who belong but neither neighbor nor read the press), and community actors (who belong and either neighbor, read, or do both), the following relative distributions result:

| | Competence | | Involve-ment |
| | | Knows | |
Type	Names	Rules	Votes
Isolates	−	−	−
Voyeurs	+	+	−
Neighbors only	+	+	+
Community actors	++	++	++
Deviants	−	−	+

(Hypotheses 44 through 58.)

(c) When age, sex, and education (as an index of social rank) are controlled, each age, sex, and educational category will manifest the same variation by organization type (hypotheses 59 through 64).

(d) If competence and involvement are considered simultaneously, those competent and not active should be concentrated among the voyeurs, those active and not competent among the deviants, those active and competent among the community actors, those neither active nor competent, among the isolates (hypotheses 65 through 68).

(e) The rank order of the distribution of community actor types should be (1) local area coinciding with municipality, (2) local area without municipality, (3) municipality without local area, and (4) district with neither residential area organization nor political structure (hypothesis 69). This, in turn, should result in a similar rank order of ability to name leaders (hypothesis 70). The same rank order should hold for resistance to metropolitan integration movements (hypothesis 71).

(f) With incorporation controlled, the organizational types should have similar ability to name local leaders (hypothesis 72).

(g) If political office-holders and past office-holders are eliminated, organizational types in incorporated and unincorporated areas should have similar abilities to name local leaders, although a somewhat larger number should be able to do so in the incorporated areas. Therefore, naming of non-political leaders should be related to the urbanism of the area (hypotheses 73 and 74).

Organized Labor's Image of Community Power Structure* /
William H. Form and Warren L. Sauer (*Michigan State University*)

INTRODUCTION

Community power structure may be defined as that network of relations obtaining between individuals and organizations which affect decisions regarding issues or actions of community wide importance. Much of the recent research in the area of community power has focused on the reputed power of local elites to influence the decision-making process.[1] These studies see power in personal terms, and decision making within a context of interpersonal relations. Several criticisms have been levelled at this position.[2] First, it ignores the broader organizational context of power in the community. Thus ethnic groups and labor unions may have power even though unrepresented among the local elites. Second, the elites may not form a solidary clique which controls decisions.[3] Third, the elite themselves may or may not have an accurate perception of the local power arrangements which may affect their exercise of influence. It is this last area, the images of community power held by local elites, in which this research is interested.

Systematic data on this point are scarce. Social scientists generally agree that businessmen not only control the American community but know that they do.[4] Yet business leaders and some social scientists decry the unrestricted power of organized labor.[5]

Reprinted from *Social Forces*, 1960, 38, pages 332–341, by permission of authors and publisher, The University of North Carolina Press.

* This study was done under the auspices of the Labor and Industrial Relations Center of Michigan State University.

[1] See Floyd Hunter, *Community Power Structure* (Chapel Hill: The University of North Carolina Press, 1953); Roland J. Pelligrin and Charles H. Coates, "Absentee-owned Corporations and Community Power Structure," *The American Journal of Sociology*, LXI (March 1956), 413–419; Floyd Hunter, Ruth C. Schaffer, and Cecil G. Sheps, *Community Organization* (Chapel Hill: The University of North Carolina Press, 1956).

[2] Robert A. Dahl, "A Critique of the Ruling Elite Model," *The American Political Science Review*, LII (June 1958), 463–469; James S. Coleman, *Community Conflict* (Glencoe, Illinois: The Free Press, 1957); William H. Form and Delbert C. Miller, *Industry, Labor, and Community* (New York: Harper and Brothers, forthcoming 1960).

[3] See Delbert C. Miller, "Decision-Making Cliques in Community Power Structures: A Comparative Study of an American and English City," *The American Journal of Sociology*, LXIV (November 1958), 299–310; William H. Form and William V. D'Antonio, "Integration and Cleavage Among Community Influentials in Two Border Cities," *The American Sociological Review*, 24 (December 1959), pp. 804–814.

[4] See among others Robert S. Lynd and Helen M. Lynd, *Middletown in Transition* (New York: Harcourt, Brace and Company, 1937); C. Wright Mills, *The Power Elite* (New York: Oxford University Press, 1956); Thorstein Veblen, *Absentee Ownership* (New York: Viking Press, Inc., 1938); Hunter, *op. cit.*

[5] See Edward H. Chamberlain *et al.*, *Labor Unions and Public Policy* (Washington: American Enterprise Association, 1958).

Labor leaders also generally picture the local community as the handmaiden of business. Yet during expansive moods, they claim to represent an important power bloc. If, as Riesman and Bell suggest, there is no fixed hierarchical structure of power nationally and locally,[6] the images of community power held by local influentials may decisively determine local decision making. The broad images of community power held by top influentials in business, organized labor, and the professions in a middle-sized community are currently being analyzed. A comparison of these images seems to be requisite for understanding the local dynamics of issue resolution.[7] This paper focuses on the image of community power held by top labor influentials in a midwestern city.

Despite labor's increasing economic, political, and social power, there is disagreement about (a) its place in community power structure, and (b) its image of that structure.

(a) Several studies have sought to assess the place of organized labor in the local community directly. McKee's pioneer study of Steelport (a city of 40,000)[8] showed that the CIO had won formal political control after 1945, but had not altered the basic strength and prestige of business. However, the consolidation of the Catholic Church, ethnic groups, and labor unions into a bloc foreshadowed changes in power alignments. Hart indicated that the UAW in Windsor (population 100,000) was disengaging itself from management-dominated organizations and substituting union-sponsored activities to meet the social needs of the workers.[9] In Illini City, (population 70,000) Wray found

that the unions (despite increased bargaining strength) had not genuinely influenced the programs of local associations. Union representatives there were absorbed into business organizations such as the Chamber of Commerce.[10] In Steeltown (population 14,000) the unions traditionally used their strength to settle economic and grievance problems, and not political, welfare, educational, or other problems. Yet in a crisis situation, they had power resources which had not been manifested earlier.[11] In Jonesville (population 10,000) the unions had not expanded their activities beyond the narrowest limits of collective bargaining and had failed to become a significant force in community life.[12] Somewhat the same situation existed in Regional City (population 331,000)[13] and in the satellite city of Cibola (population 20,000).[14] Whether the differences among these localities represent differences along a single scale of development can only be determined by making longitudinal studies of communities containing important structural differences in size, degree of unionization, and related variables.[15]

(b) The authors are unaware of systematic empirical studies of labor's image of the structure of community power and its place in it. There are, of course, many partial descriptions of the national scene. In Mills' study of labor leadership he reported that three-quarters of them believed that business, because of its monetary strength, had more weight than labor organizations. Labor saw its power as derived from its potential voting strength, if properly organized.[16] Union of-

[6] David Riesman, *The Lonely Crowd* (New Haven: Yale University Press, 1951); Daniel Bell, "America's Un-Marxist Revolution," *Commentary,* 7 (March 1949), pp. 207–215.

[7] See Benjamin M. Selekman, *Labor Relations and Human Relations* (New York: McGraw-Hill Book Co., Inc., 1947), pp. 195–199.

[8] James McKee, Organized Labor and Community Decision Making; A Study in the Sociology of Power (unpublished Ph.D. dissertation, University of Wisconsin, 1953); also "Status and Power in the Industrial Community," *The American Journal of Sociology,* LVIII (January 1953), 364–370. The population of the communities reported on apply for the time of the studies.

[9] C. W. M. Hart, "Industrial Relations Research and Social Theory," *Canadian Journal of Economics and Political Science,* XV (February 1949), 53–73.

[10] See Donald E. Wray, "The Community and Labor-Management Relations," *Labor-Management Relations in Illini City* (Champaign: Institute of Labor and Industrial Relations, 1953).

[11] Charles R. Walker, *Steeltown* (New York: Harper and Brothers, 1950), pp. 42–45.

[12] W. L. Warner and others, *Democracy in Jonesville* (New York: Harper and Brothers, 1949).

[13] Hunter, *Community Power Structure.*

[14] Robert O. Schultze and Leonard Blumberg, "The Determination of Local Power Elites," *The American Journal of Sociology,* LXIII (November 1957), 290–296.

[15] See Albert J. Reiss, Jr., "Some Logical and Methodological Problems in Community Research," *Social Forces,* XXXIII (October 1954), 51–57.

[16] C. Wright Mills, *The New Men of Power* (New York: Harcourt, Brace and Company, 1948), pp. 133–137.

ficials at the local level were reported to be more suspicious of business than state and national officials.[17] In *The Power Elite* he suggests that labor nationally wants a "share of the directorate" and the status that goes along with it. Labor's image of the power structure or its role in it, however, is not clearly specified.[18] In "Labor Leaders and the Power Elite," Mills suggests that labor sees itself as a pressure group and, by inference, that it envisions the structure of power as a force field of pressure groups, in which labor wants a bigger share. "They seek greater integration at the upper levels of the corporate economy [and want] to join owners and managers in running the corporate enterprise system."[19]

Daniel Bell asserts that "labor looks upon itself as a cowering minority often at the mercy of a marauding business class, which is intent on wiping out all of its gains. In its rhetoric and in its propaganda, these images still stand paramount. On the other side of the coin, businessmen have a distorted image of a coherent trade union movement powerfully allied with the 'intellectuals' in an effort to change the social character of the society."[20] Whether these are, in fact, the images held is problematical. It is therefore urgent to find what the images are as well as whether business and labor act on the basis of them.[21]

RESEARCH PROBLEMS

The hypotheses we attempted to test are:

1. Labor perceives the community power structure as composed primarily of an inte-

grated management clique which controls the outcome of most significant community issues.

As corollaries: (a) labor sees management's community goals as motivated by specific economic interests; (b) labor views itself as an association which is tangential to the community power structure.

2. Variations in labor's image of its community power are accounted for by the age, community involvement, union position, and degree of influence among union personnel. Older ex-AFL union leaders, those who participate heavily in local organizations, and those who hold high offices and have great influence in the union perceive the local power structure as less business dominated than the younger unionists, ex-CIO officials, those who hold lower union posts, and those who have less influence in union circles.

The first hypothesis was postulated on the premise that unions currently occupy a position in the community similar to minority or ethnic groups.[22] The second hypothesis was based on the assumption that the perception of cleavage in a power structure is reduced by the greater community involvement which accompanies increased age, participation, power, and prestige.[23]

METHODS AND SAMPLE

The main source of data was an interview with the union representatives considered to be most influential in community affairs. The preliminary slate of respondents consisted of consensual nominations provided by a panel comprised of two knowledgeables from mass communication, industry, government, and professors at Michigan State University interested in local industrial relations. The list of names was further corroborated and expanded during interviews with the labor influentials themselves. The interviews, conducted in 1957, were designed to obtain data in four general areas.

1. Participation in community organizations and its self-evaluations:
   a. Evaluation of the local community

[17] *Ibid.*, p. 141.
[18] C. W. Mills, *The Power Elite* (New York: Oxford University Press, 1956), pp. 264–265. Here Mills comes closest to specifying labor's image of its own power.
[19] C. Wright Mills, "Labor Leaders and the Power Elite," in *Industrial Conflict*, edited by Arthur Kornhauser, Robert Dubin, and Arthur M. Ross (New York: McGraw-Hill Book Co., Inc., 1954), p. 152.
[20] "The Language of Labor," *Fortune*, 44 (September 1951), p. 256.
[21] The broader study is also concerned with business' view of the community power structure, as well as an organizational analysis of the place of both labor and business in the structure. See William H. Form, "The Place of Organized Labor in Community Power Structure," *Industrial and Labor Relations Review*, 12 (July 1959), pp. 526–539.

[22] The usefulness of such a proposition is suggested by Melvin Seeman, "The Intellectual and the Language of Minorities," *The American Journal of Sociology*, LXIV (July 1958), 25–35.
[23] See Mills, *The New Men of Power*.

b. Amount and nature of community participation
c. Attitudes toward community participation
d. Priority of community participation goals
e. Estimate of opposition to labor's community activities
f. Responses to the opposition

2. Self-evaluation of its power in the context of local issues:
   a. Evaluation of effectiveness in policy making
   b. Past community achievements
   c. Ranking of issues facing the community
   d. Position on issues and probable influence on their resolution

3. Nature of the "opposition" in the context of local issues and objectives:
   a. Specification of issues important to business
   b. Differences in labor and management's community objectives
   c. Degree of consensus with management on local issues
   d. Degree to which labor is consulted on emerging issues and projects

4. Substantive image of the community power structure:
   a. Composition and social solidarity of the top decision-makers
   b. Composition of the strongest interests groups
   c. The place of organized labor among decision makers and interests groups
   d. Strategies used by decision makers and interests groups and their sense of community responsibility
   e. Estimate of labor's over all community strength vis-a-vis business

RESEARCH SITE

Lansing, Michigan is a city of 120,000 and the capitol of the state.[24] Its main "industries" are automobile manufacturing, metal manufacturing, and government. Previous to World War I the auto plants were locally owned. The largest plants (Oldsmobile, Fisher Body, Motor Wheel, Reo, John Bean) are now absentee-owned. However, most of the forges and auto-parts plants are still locally owned and hire about 40 percent of the industrial labor force.[25] About 80,000 people are currently employed in the city, 20,000 in automobile and metal manufacturing concerns. About half of all workers reside outside the city. About 20,000 workers belong to former CIO unions, and 4,000 to former AFL unions. The United Automobile Workers (UAW) is the main union in the city. Officers of that and other international unions frequently visit the capitol to contact legislators and government officials. This, together with the proximity of Detroit, facilitates contacts between local and international union officers. Since World War II, the UAW has encouraged the locals to become involved in the entire institutional life of the city and challenge the dominance of business and industry.

Unlike many other middle-size cities in the industrial east and midwest, Lansing contains a relatively small proportion of foreign-born and Negro workers. Native-born workers constitute about ninety percent of the labor force. Over two-thirds of them are descendants from early New England migrants, later German migrants, and more recently migrants from the rural South. Southern-born workers probably comprise ten percent of the labor force and Negroes only four or five percent. Lansing has been a remarkably stable community despite a rapid growth after World Wars I and II. It is estimated that seven-tenths of the manual workers own their own homes. Local, state, and national elections have consistently gone Republican since the city's founding in 1859. A recent survey indicated that the residents like the city because it is small, conservative, and friendly.[26] In summary, the city contains a conservative native-born working class, many of whose members belong to the UAW, a dynamic and ideologically oriented union dedicated to contest management's influence in local, state, and national affairs.

---

[24] For a further description of the city see Sigmund Nosow, "Labor Distribution and the Normative System," *Social Forces*, XXXV (October 1956), 20–31; Eli Chinoy, *Automobile Workers and the American Dream* (New York: Doubleday and Co., 1955).

[25] In a study by the author and Sigmund Nosow of a sample of 580 workers in the community, two-fifths were employed in locally owned plants. See Nosow, *loc. cit.*

[26] See Joel Smith and William H. Form, Urban Identification and Disidentification (unpublished manuscript).

FINDINGS

Profile of Labor Influentials

Despite every effort to get respondents to identify persons of great power and influence in local union circles irrespective of union office, all nominations consisted of people who currently occupied important union offices: *viz.*, heads of the local central bodies, locally stationed regional representatives of the internationals, and presidents, business agents, and treasurers of the locals. The rather sharp break in the number of votes received by the top and bottom twenty suggests that there are only twenty top labor influentials in the community.

Table 1 summarizes the chief characteristics of the 39 labor influentials who were interviewed. Their median age was slightly under fifty years. The overwhelming majority were native born and reared in small villages and cities in Michigan and nearby states. After obtaining some high school education they came to Lansing in search of employment. As a whole they displayed remarkably little geographic and occupational mobility, largely remaining in the same community, the same industry, and the same job. Compared to most manual workers they participated quite heavily in local community organizations both in the past and in the present.[27]

Most respondents immediately joined the unions when given the opportunity. They became appointive or elective officers from the very beginning. Although they typically held more than one union office from the beginning, the number of offices they currently held increased with the level of their present position in the union hierarchy. Their community affiliations did not decrease with time, but tended to shift away from "private" organizations (*e.g.*, Elks, Odd Fellows) to organizations in which they participated as union representatives (*e.g.*, Community Chest). In the past they constituted a socially intimate and cohesive group. Presently, their relations seem more restricted to their official duties. This career pattern typified the top

[27] Cf. Toimi E. Kyllonen, "Social Characteristics of Active Unionists," *The American Journal of Sociology*, LVI (May 1951), 528–533.

TABLE 1

GENERAL AND UNION BACKGROUND OF LABOR INFLUENTIALS

	Number	Percent
A. General Background:		
1. Median number of votes received as union influentials:		
Top third	22	
Middle third	5	
Low third	2	
2. Median age, years	48	
3. Education:		
Eight years or less	4	10
Some high school	24	62
Some college	11	28
4. Community of socialization (size):		
Under 5,000	14	36
5,000–50,000	17	43
50,000 or more	8	21
5. Median years lived in community	27	
6. Median number of present community organizational affiliations	3.3	
7. Median number of past community organizational affiliations	3.0	
B. Union Background:		
1. Ex AFL unions	15	38
Ex CIO unions	24	62
2. Union positions:		
District, regional, or international	12	31
High local officers	20	51
Lesser local officers	7	18
3. Tenure as union officials:		
20 years or more	11	28
10–19 years	14	36
Less than 10 years	14	36
4. Union offices:		
Median number of union offices, present	4.5	
Median number of union offices, past	4.3	

twenty more than the bottom twenty influentials.

Disposition Toward Community Participation

While participation in community organizations does not automatically lead to social power, it is often a condition for widespread influence.[28] All influentials revealed, in response to direct and indirect questioning, that it was important for organized labor to participate in as many community organizations as possible.[29] They further indicated a favorable disposition toward the community as a place to live and as a place for unions to prosper. Three-fifths asserted without solicitation that labor is well organized, or that it is accepted and well represented in community organizations. About two-fifths (see Table 2) indicated that they currently officially represented labor in local associations. However, the group was equally split on the desirability of expanding labor participation. Those who wanted it were asked why it had not been realized. Over half of these (11 individuals) perceived the situation in power terms, as resulting from outside opposition or insufficient power on the part of labor to force acceptance. Yet half of all the respondents admitted, on direct questioning, that there was no opposition to labor's community participation.

The relation between social participation and social power was partially perceived by the respondents. All of them felt that it was more important for the unions to participate in some organizations rather than in others. Health and welfare agencies were given the highest priority followed closely by political and governmental agencies. When asked directly how they ranked political participation, three-quarters, ranked it highest—equally as important as the improvement of wages and economic security.

Evaluation of Community Participation

Respondents were asked whether they, personally, and whether organized labor in general, significantly influenced policies of local community organizations. All answered affirmatively on both scores. Local health and welfare organizations were singled out as areas of most influence, followed by political and governmental agencies. Almost no other associations were mentioned. In speci-

fying the nature of their influence, equal proportions (30 percent) indicated that they made organizations undertake new goals or made them more effective in attaining their traditional objectives. Only a small minority felt they were successful in getting organizations to support union activities and getting them to consult with unions prior to undertaking projects.

What labor felt it achieved by community participation provides clues to its self-image of power. The data in Table 2-D clearly reveal that labor saw its most important achievements in the area of private health and welfare services. Almost all of the respondents singled out labor's efforts in raising money for the Community Chest and increasing the effectiveness of the associated agencies. About half suggested that this resulted directly from the pressure they exerted. Only a quarter felt that labor had secured increased strength in the political and governmental area.[30] Since participation in institutional routines sometimes clouds ideological objectives, the panel was asked to name the most important problems and issues facing the community. Three-quarters of the influentials maintained that there was consensus within labor on the primary community issues and that labor would influence their resolution. Yet Table 2-E indicates that only one-third of the issues they named could be classified as traditional labor issues, *viz.,* improved educational and welfare services, equitable taxation, better housing, and more employment in that order. Two-thirds of the issues identified are not usually associated with labor's traditional goals, *viz.,* more parking space, better transportation planning, annexation, and civic improvements. These, in fact, were the primary objectives of local businessmen as determined by subsequent interviewing.

The Character of the Opposition

Clearly, community problems and issues were not conceived in oppositional terms because over seven-tenths of the labor influen-

---

[28] McKee, *op. cit.*

[29] In response to the question, "Are there organizations in the community in which labor should not participate?" only one-quarter answered affirmatively. The justification for labor participation was that it represented the largest segment of the community.

[30] This self-evaluation is rather accurate. An over all appraisal of labor's strength in various institutional sectors showed it to be strongest in the welfare arena and weakest in the political. See Form, *op. cit.,* "The Place of Organized Labor in Community Power Structure."

TABLE 2

LABOR'S SELF IMAGES OF COMMUNITY PARTICIPATION

	Number	Percent
A. Official union representatives in community organizations	17	43
B. Indication of opposition to labor's community participation	21	55
C. Indication of union influence on policies of community organizations	34	87
D. Most important achievements of organized labor in community affairs:		
Raised effectiveness of health and welfare fund drives	17	44
Improved health and welfare services	17	44
Acquired representation in community agencies	11	28
Improved prestige and community image of organized labor	10	26
Improved political position of labor	10	26
Improved economic conditions	9	23
Affected school board policies	4	10
Other	3	8
E. Most important issues facing the community:		
Traditional labor issues:	(32)	(82)
Housing, slum clearance, unemployment	6	16
Improved health and welfare services	9	23
Local gov't—inequitable taxes and administration	6	16
Educational improvement	11	28
Non-traditional labor issues:	(59)	(151)
Improved parking facilities	24	62
Improved transportation planning	14	36
Civic improvements (civic center, new hotels, etc.)	8	21
Annexation	13	33
F. Comparisons with management:		
1. Relative economic stake in community participation		
Management has a greater stake	12	31
Stakes are equal	9	23
Labor has a greater stake	10	26
Other	5	13
Not ascertained	3	8
Total	39	101
2. Relative interest in becoming involved in community affairs		
Management has greater interest	12	31
Interest is equal	15	38
Labor has greater interest	8	21
Other	4	10
Total	39	100
3. Relative unity in community participation goals		
Management more united	17	44
Equally united	11	28
Labor more united	11	28
Total	39	100

tials agreed that the issues they named were also considered the most pressing by the community representatives of business. When pressed to specify *any* general differences in the community objectives of labor and management, one-quarter indicated that no differences existed. An equal proportion felt that differences developed only over the methods of achieving identical goals. Almost two-fifths asserted that the goals of labor and management differed, mainly in the area of governmental objectives and tax policies.

A clue to the nature of the cleavage, if any, in community power arrangements revolved around the consultation process. Only one-quarter of the labor influentials indicated that they were consulted from the beginning on any of the community problems, issues, or projects which they listed. One-half asserted that labor was not usually brought in from the beginning to make policy on broad community issues. Despite this exclusion, they did not feel that labor lacked power. The question was posed, "What organizations do you feel have the most weight in getting things done or preventing some things from getting done in Lansing?" Both organized labor and the Chamber of Commerce were named by seven-tenths of the respondents. Many other business and management groups were also named, such as the board of realtors, local industries, the local newspaper, religious groups, service clubs, and the downtown businessmen's association in that order. When asked directly to compare the relative influence of management and labor in community affairs, three-quarters unequivocally asserted that management had greater influence.[31]

Why does management have more community power in labor's eyes? The latter were asked to compare the relative economic stake, interest, and internal unity of the two interest groups in community participation. As Table 2-F shows, no substantial agreement was found among the influentials on these items. About equal proportions asserted that labor had more, less, and the same economic stake as management in community participation. Although a plurality (two-fifths) felt that labor and management had equal interest in community involvement, most of the remaining felt that management was more interested. When asked to compare the internal unity of the groups, over two-fifths asserted that management had more solidarity, and the remaining were equally split in feeling that labor was more united and that no difference existed. In

view of these disagreements they were asked whether labor carefully selected community issues on which to use its influence. Two-thirds asserted that labor committed its resources on all important community issues.

Images of the Decision Makers and Decision-Making Process

The image of the organizational texture of community power was supplemented by probing for the image of decision makers. The first problem was to find the degree of labor representation among these decision makers. The sample was asked to "name ten or more persons who, singly or collectively, have enough influence and power to put across a major project or settle a major issue in the community." The consensual list of fifty names provided by the respondents was designated as "top influentials." The top ten who received most votes were designated as "key influentials."[32]

One-fifth of both the top and key influentials were labor union officials, a much higher estimate than others were willing to accord labor.[33]

A series of questions found in Table 3 were then posed to ascertain how this group of top influentials was perceived.[34] The questions were designed to ascertain whether the group was perceived as a small solidary clique which acted autonomously and secretively to secure its own narrow interests, or whether it was a non-solidary entity comprised of persons acting openly in response to broad community needs.[35] The evidence, although not decisive, tends to point to the "responsible model" of decision makers. Two-thirds of the labor influentials felt that the top decision makers were "the same small crowd of people working together" on most of the issues confronting the community. This "crowd" was not perceived as having autonomous power, because three-

---

[31] When asked to compare this pattern to Detroit, respondents were split in believing that labor was stronger in Detroit and seeing no differences between the cities.

[32] These concepts were jointly worked out with Delbert C. Miller of Indiana University.

[33] In a slate of forty top influentials drawn from a community-wide panel, labor had only two representatives.

[34] Compare these questions with those used by Hunter, *op. cit.*, Pelligrin and Coates, *op. cit.*, and Miller, *op. cit.*

[35] A typology of the internal organization of the top influentials as related to the organizational structure of power is elaborated in Form and Miller, *op. cit.*

TABLE 3

LABOR'S IMAGE OF THE COMMUNITY DECISION-MAKING SYSTEM

	Number	Percent
A. In your judgment, do you feel that the big community decisions tend to be made by the same small "crowd" of people working together, or do these people change according to the issue confronting the community?		
Same group	26	67
Group changes	9	23
Other	4	10
Total	39	100
B. Do the people who make important community decision do this pretty much on their own or do they have to get approval for their actions from the organizations to which they belong?		
Can act on their own	8	21
Must get organizational approval	29	74
Other	2	5
Total	39	100
C. Are important issues usually quietly solved without the public knowing what they are or are they usually brought out in the open?		
Issues are made public	17	43
Depends on issues	12	31
Issues resolved privately	7	18
Other	3	8
Total	39	100
D. Do you feel the people involved in making big decisions have a broad sense of community responsibility or are they more concerned with protecting or furthering their own interests?		
Broad community responsibility	18	46
Further own interests	9	23
Depends on issue, situation, or persons	12	31
Total	39	100
E. Do labor or management community representatives generally have a broader sense of community responsibility?		
Labor more responsible	12	31
Equally responsible	19	48
Management more responsible	3	8
Other	5	13
Total	39	100

quarters of the respondents felt its members had to obtain organizational approval prior to committing themselves.[36] The respondents did not agree on the question of whether the top influentials resolved issues privately or publicly. About half felt that issues were generally or sometimes resolved behind closed doors, and an almost equal proportion felt that they were generally brought out in the open. Similar disagreement arose in response to inquiries concerning the sense of community responsibility found among the top influentials. About half felt that the influentials acted responsibly, and the other half were split on whether they always or sometimes acted to further their own interests.

Further probing revealed that half of the interviewees felt that management and labor

[36] This may be a generalization of the practice of local General Motors officials to consult with central Detroit offices prior to committing themselves and of union officials consulting with the local AFL-CIO council prior to taking action.

exhibited the same sense of community responsibility, but more of the remaining insisted that labor leaders had a greater sense of community responsibility (Table 2-E). Despite these disagreements on the nature of local power arrangements, labor influentials are not ready to abandon the present system. They were almost unanimous in asserting that labor is better off to go along with the present system and not establish an independent community program.

Internal Differences

The second guiding hypothesis was concerned with internal differences in the perceptions of the labor influentials. The latter were divided into "high" and "low" categories for age, union position, number of votes received as influentials, and amount of community participation. It was hypothesized that those in the "high" categories would perceive the local power structure as less management-dominated. As a corollary, they would perceive labor as a more integral part of the local power system. In general, older unionists received more votes as labor influentials and held higher union positions. Higher influentials also represented labor in more community organizations.[37]

Most of the responses of the "high" and "low" groups did not differ statistically. Where differences were found, more labor power was perceived by the "high" group of labor influentials. For example, more of them listed more union officers among top community influentials, and more of them asserted that labor's power in community affairs was equal to management's.

The reverse of our hypothesis was found in the area concerned with internal cleavages in the local power structure. More cleavage was perceived by the "high" than the "low" categories of labor influentials. A significantly larger proportion of the former observed that there were organizations and activities in the community from which labor was excluded. Larger proportions of them also indicated

[37] In two by two tables for the variables age and influence, the chi square was 4.3, p = <.05, C = .49. For union position and number of votes as influentials; $\chi^2 = 11.7$, p = <.01, C = .70. For level of influence and community participation; $\chi^2 = 13.3$, p = <.01, C = .79. See Thomas McCormick, *Elementary Social Statistics* (New York: McGraw-Hill Book Co., Inc., 1941), pp. 206–209.

that management's community representatives would disagree with their list of the most urgent issues confronting the city. The over-all pattern then seemed to be that labor influentials who were most involved in community decision making were conscious of their own influence and ascribed greater power to labor. Their proximity to the sources of community power seemed to make them more aware of the cleavages still existing between labor and management.

CONCLUSIONS

Only about twenty labor officials out of a union membership of 25,000 were actively involved in community affairs and seriously concerned about labor's place in the local power structure. The first hypothesis, that labor perceives the community power structure as an integrated management clique which controls the outcome of the significant local issues was substantiated to a limited degree. While acknowledging management's general dominance of the local community, labor sees itself within the power structure and not tangential to it. Although it feels excluded from initiating local projects and issues, it insists it has a powerful voice when it enters a contest. The cleavage between itself and management is not seen in a firm oppositional context. Neither is local participation generally viewed as a contest with management and other groups. Labor defines its goals as the attainment of a better social welfare system in a context of growing political power. Management's community goals are not seen as differing much from labor's. In fact, they evince a reluctance to impute crude economic motives to management's community participation.

Variations in the backgrounds of union influentials were slightly related to their perceptions of the local power scene. There was a slight tendency for those who were most involved in community activities to recognize the shape and reality of business power more sharply. Increased recognition of labor's power tended to reinforce feelings of cleavage between it and business in community affairs. There was little evidence that animosities in collective bargaining were carried over into community participation.

Among the labor influentials interviewed there was remarkably little stereotypical imagery either of itself or management. Indeed, there were large variations and even contradictions in their images of the local power arrangements. Labor sees itself committed to community participation and to solving the problems attending it. Its present limited participation is perceived as resulting from internal problems rather than from the opposition of management or other groups. Most union officials appraise their community operations as effective but some realize they are ineffective in getting others to support independent labor goals. In short, labor has made friends, but has not influenced them.

Labor evidences almost no desire to have a distinctive community program. Traditional labor goals in the community are given at best a secondary priority and management's objectives are generally endorsed. Labor's ideology is essentially one of co-operating with other groups in conserving and improving the present community organizations. Although it sees few allies, labor assesses itself as a potentially powerful organization. What it wants most is to be consulted on community problems from the beginning. Many labor influentials suspect that their limited prestige and power results from business' greater interest, activity, and economic concern with community problems.

Labor influentials believe they discern a small active "clique" of decision makers who mediate most community projects and issues. Labor has a small and inadequate representation in this "clique." The clique is not ascribed independent power to make decisions, and it is perceived as operating publicly and in a socially responsible manner. Although its members are not as selfless as labor, they are not people with narrow economic self-interests. This indeed is how labor prefers to perceive itself.

D. Culture and Society

The largest, most inclusive social context with which we deal in this collection of readings involves the culture and society. At this level of inclusiveness we have already contained the preceding three social contexts of the small group, the large scale organization, and the community. In addition, however, it is possible to focus upon other aspects of society, such as its role and class structure, its symbolic value structure or ideology, its modal personality structure, and other components of subculture within the larger society.

From the anthropologist and ethnologist we have descriptions of hundreds of human cultures and societies detailing enumerable characteristics, ranging from mythology through highly specific child-training procedures. From the sociologist we have further descriptions of cultures and societies, typically larger, more complex and modern than those characterizing much of the anthropological work. Each, however, is describing a patterned or structured series of relationships which have been abstracted from observed behaviors of individuals and groups, and which form the basis of what is referred to as the culture of a particular society.

Although we are using the two terms culture and society somewhat interchangeably to refer to this most inclusive context, it is possible to differentiate between "society," referring to a specifically located geographic and political entity, and "culture," referring to these abstracted, patterned modes of cognition and relationship which characterize that society.

The readings included in this section focus upon some of the features of culture and society which are most salient to the social psychologist. The selections by Goode and by Getzels and Guba focus upon an aspect of the role structure of the social system. By differentiating two types of subcultures within the non-unitary, complex, larger culture, Yinger's article calls attention to the important differences in the normative relationship to the larger culture which characterize these two broad classes of subcultural units.

The Vogt and O'Dea selection brings us somewhat around the full swing towards our beginnings in cognitive theory as they see the value orientations of a group as providing a framework or context (a world view) into which the solutions to daily problems are placed. Although their study occurs within a community context, their concern with general value orientations or ideology provides a valuable insight into the functioning of such orientations on the broader societal level.

The Inkeles, Hanfmann, and Beier selection presents a specific example of modal personality research. As was previously discussed in the section on socialization, modal personality, basic personality structure, and national character studies assume the existence of some common or basic personality-value core within a given cultural system. The Inkeles *et al* article examines this issue further, paying particular attention to its relationship to individual adjustment within a given social system.

The final article in this section, by Young, provides an example of the comparative approach to the study of culture. Young examines a specific cultural practice, the male initiation ceremony, offering a functional interpretation of this practice.

A Theory of Role Strain* / William J. Goode (*Columbia University*)

When social structures are viewed as made up of roles, social stability is not explicable as a function of (a) the normative consensual commitment of individuals or (b) normative integration. Instead, dissensus and role strain—the difficulty of fulfilling role demands—are normal. In a sequence of role bargains, the individual's choices are shaped by mechanisms, outlined here, through which he organizes his total role system and performs well or ill in any role relationship. Reduction of role strain is allocative or economic in form, but the economic model is different. "Third parties" interact with an individual and his alter, to keep their bargain within institutionalized limits. The larger social structure is held in place by role strains. The cumulative pattern of all such role bargains determines the flow of performances to all institutions. The research utility of this conception is explained.

The present paper is based on the general view that institutions are made up of role relationships, and approaches both social action and social structure through the notion of "role strain," the felt difficulty in fulfilling role obligations. Role relations are seen as a sequence of "role bargains," and as a continuing process of selection among alternative role behaviors, in which each individual seeks to reduce his role strain. These choices determine the allocations of role performances to all institutions of the society. Within the limited compass of this paper, only a few of the possible implications of role strain as a theoretical approach can be explored.

The widespread notion that institutions are made up of roles is fruitful because it links a somewhat more easily observable phenomenon, social behavior, to an important but less easily observable abstraction, social structure. In functionalist terms, this notion also links the observed acts and inferred values of the individual with the institutional imperatives or requisites of the society. At the same time, by focusing on the elements in the individual's action decision, it avoids the pitfall of supposing that people carry out their obligations because these are "functional" for the society.

Approaching role interaction in terms of role strain offers the possibility of buttressing more adequately the empirical weaknesses of the most widely accepted theoretical view of society,[1] according to which the

Reprinted from *The American Sociological Review*, 1960, 25, pages 483–496, by permission of author and publisher, The American Sociological Association.

* Completed under National Institute of Mental Health Grant No. 2526-S.
I am indebted to several of my colleagues for criticism of this and related papers, and especially to Amitai Etzioni, Johan Galtung, Robert K. Merton, Charles H. Page, Morris Zelditch, and Hans L. Zetterberg.

[1] I prefer to call this the "Lintonian model" (Ralph Linton, *The Study of Man*, New York: Appleton-Century, 1936), although Linton is not,

continuity of social roles, and thus the maintenance of the society, is mainly a function of two major variables: the normative, consensual commitment of the individuals of the society; and the integration among the norms held by those individuals. Although this view is superior to earlier ones,[2] it fails to explain how a complex urban society keeps going[3] because it does not account for the following awkward empirical facts:[4]

1. Some individuals do not accept even supposedly central values of the society.
2. Individuals vary in their emotional commitment to both important and less important values.
3. This value commitment varies by class strata, and by other characteristics of social position, for example, age, sex, occupation, geographic region, and religion.
4. Even when individuals accept a given value, some of them also have a strong or weak "latent commitment" to very different or contradictory values.[5]
5. Conformity with normative prescriptions is not a simple function of value commitment; there may be value commitment without conformity or conformity without commitment.
6. When individuals' social positions change,

they may change both their behavior and their value orientations.
7. The values, ideals, and role obligations of every individual are at times in conflict.

Under the current conception of roles as units of social structures, presumably we should observe the role decisions of individuals in order to see how the society continues. On first view, as can be seen from the above list of points, the basis of social stability or integration seems precarious, and the decisions of the individual puzzling. For even when "the norms of the society" are fully accepted by the individual, they are not adequate guides for individual action. Order cannot be imposed by any *general* solution for all role decisions, since the total set of role obligations is probably unique for every individual. On the other hand, the individual may face different types of role demands and conflicts, which he feels as "role strains" when he wishes to carry out specific obligations.

In the immediately following sections, the major sources and types of role strain are specified, and thereafter the two main sets of mechanisms which the individual may use to reduce role strain are analyzed.

TYPES OF ROLE STRAIN

It is an axiom, rarely expressed, of social theory that the individuals who face common role obligations *can* generally fulfill them. Indeed, most theories of stratification and criminality require such an assumption, and common opinion uses it is a basis for its moral demands on the individual. We may suppose, as a corollary, that there are theoretical limits to the specific demands which societies may make of men. In addition, the "theorem of institutional integration"[6] is roughly correct as an orienting idea: people generally *want* to do what they are supposed to do, and this is what the society needs to have done in order to continue.

Yet, with respect to any given norm or

of course, the creator of this model. Rather, he summed up a generation of thought about social structure in a clear and illuminating fashion, so that for many years the definitions and statements in this book were widely cited by both anthropologists and sociologists. Of course, "everyone knows" these weaknesses, but our basic model is not thereby changed to account for them.

[2] For a systematic statement of several earlier models, see Talcott Parsons, *The Structure of Social Action,* New York: McGraw-Hill, 1937, Chapter 2.

[3] For an earlier discussion relevant to this paper, see William J. Goode, "Contemporary Thinking about Primitive Religion," *Soziologus,* 5 (1955), pp. 122–131; also in Morton Fried, editor, *Readings in Anthropology,* New York: Crowell, 1959, Vol. II, pp. 450–460.

[4] For a good exposition of certain aspects of dissensus as they apply to American society, see Robin W. Williams, *American Society,* New York: Knopf, 1956, esp. pp. 352 ff.

[5] Charles H. Page has reminded me that role diversity is not confined to modern societies, as the work of functionalist anthropologists (e.g., Malinowski's *Crime and Custom* and Benedict's *Patterns of Culture*) has shown. This empirical fact is of considerable theoretical consequence, especially for the relations between adjacent social strata or castes, or between conquerors and the conquered.

[6] This is the label which Talcott Parsons has suggested for the view, generally accepted since Durkheim's *Division of Labor,* that the maintenance of the society rests on desires of individuals to do things which must be done if the society is to survive. *The Social System,* New York: Free Press of Glencoe, Inc., 1949, pp. 36–43.

role obligation; there are always some persons who cannot conform, by reason of individuality or situation: they do not have sufficient resources, energy, and so on. A wider view of all such obligations discloses the following types or sources of role strain:

First, even when role demands are not onerous, difficult, or displeasing, they are required at particular times and places. Consequently, virtually no role demand is such a spontaneous pleasure that conformity with it is always automatic.

Second, all individuals take part in many *different* role relationships, for each of which there will be somewhat different obligations.[7] Among these, there may be either contradictory performances required (the bigamous husband; the infantry lieutenant who must order his close friend to risk his life in battle) or conflicts of time, place, or resources. These are conflicts of allocation (civic as against home obligations).

Third, each role relationship typically demands *several* activities or responses. Again, there may be inconsistencies (what the husband does to balance his family budget may impair his emotional relations with the members of his household). There may be different but not quite contradictory norms which may be applied to the various behavioral demands of the same role (the clergyman as the emotionally neutral counselor, but as a praising or condemnatory spiritual guide). Perhaps most jobs fall into this category, in that their various demands create some strain as between the norms of quantity and quality, technical excellence and human relations skills, and universalism and particularism.

Finally, many role relationships are "role sets," that is, the individual engages, by virtue of *one* of his positions, in several role relationships with different individuals.[8]

The individual is thus likely to face a wide, distracting, and sometimes conflicting array of role obligations. If he conforms fully or adequately in one direction, fulfillment will be difficult in another. Even if he feels lonely, and would like to engage in additional role relationships, it is likely that he cannot fully discharge all the obligations he already faces. He cannot meet all these demands to the satisfaction of all the persons who are part of his total role network. Role strain—difficulty in meeting given role demands—is therefore normal. In general, *the individual's total role obligations are overdemanding.*

Consequently, although the theorem of institutional integration, or the assumption of norm commitment, offers an explanation for the fulfillment of the duties imposed by a single norm, it does not account for the integration of an individual's total role system, or the integration among the role systems of various individuals, which presumably make up the social structure. The individual's problem is how to make his whole role system manageable, that is, how to allocate his energies and skills so as to reduce role strain to some bearable proportions. For the larger social structure, the problem is one of integrating such role systems—by allocating the flow of role performances so that various institutional activities are accomplished.

THE REDUCTION OF ROLE STRAIN: EGO'S CHOICE

A sensitizing or orienting notion in functionalist as well as system theory—perhaps more properly called one element in the definition of a "system"—is that a strain is likely to be associated with some mechanisms for reducing it.[9] The individual can

---

[7] In this paper, I distinguish role and status on the basis of only "degree of institutionalization": all role relations are somewhat institutionalized, but statuses are more fully institutionalized.

[8] Cf. Robert K. Merton, *Social Theory and Social Structure,* New York: Free Press of Glencoe, Inc., 1957, pp. 369 ff. For its use in an empirical study, see Mary Jean Huntington, "The Development of a Professional Self Image," in R. K. Merton *et al.,* editors, *The Student-Physician,* Cambridge: Harvard University Press, 1957, pp. 180 ff.

[9] Merton's "mechanisms" operate to *articulate* role sets; see Robert K. Merton, "The Role Set: Problems in Sociological Theory," *British Journal of Sociology,* 8 (June, 1957), pp. 113 ff. Here, we are concerned with a more general problem, which includes role sets as a special source of role strain. Moreover, Merton is concerned with only one of our problems, integrating the total role systems of all individuals in a demarcated social system; while we are, in addition, concerned with the problem of the individual in integrating his own role system. Several of our mechanisms, then, are parallelled by Merton's. Compartmentalization partly corresponds,

utilize two main sets of techniques for reducing his role strain: those which determine whether or when he will enter or leave a role relationship; and those which have to do with the actual role bargain which the individual makes or carries out with another.

Ego's Manipulation of His Role Structure.—Ego has at his disposal several ways of determining whether or when he will accept a role relationship:

1. *Compartmentalization:* This may be defined on the psychological level as the ability to ignore the problem of consistency. Socially, role relations tend toward compartmentalization because the individual makes his demands on another and feels them to be legitimate, in specific situations where he can avoid taking much account of the claims on that person. There seems to be no overall set of societal values which explicitly requires consistency or integration from the individual. The process of compartmentalization works mainly by (a) location and context and (b) situational urgency or crisis. The latter process permits the individual to meet the crisis on its own terms, setting aside for the moment the role demands which he was meeting prior to the crisis.

2. *Delegation:* This may be seen, at least in part, as one way of achieving compartmentalization. If, for example, secular counseling is inconsistent with the clergyman's moral leadership role, he may be able to delegate it. If secular manipulation by a church is inconsistent with its sacredness, it may delegate some secular acts to lay leaders or to specialized religious orders. A wife may delegate housekeeping, and some of the socialization and nursing of the child. Note, however, that the societal hierarchy of values is indicated by what may *not* be delegated: for example, the professor may not hire a ghost writer to produce his monographs, and the student may not delegate examinations.

3. *Elimination of role relationships:*[10] Curtailment may be difficult, since many of our role obligations flow from our status positions, such as those in the job or family, which are not easily eliminated. Of course, we can stop associating with a kinsman because of the demands he makes on us, and if our work-group sets norms which are too high for us to meet we can seek another job. Aside from social and even legal limits on role curtailment, however, some continuing role interaction is necessary to maintain the individual's self-image and possibly his personality structure: for example, many people feel "lost" upon retirement—their social existence is no longer validated.

4. *Extension:* The individual may expand his role relations in order to plead these commitments as an excuse for not fulfilling certain obligations. A departmental chairman, for example, may become active in university affairs so that he can meet his colleague's demands for time with the plea that other duties (known to his colleagues) are pressing. In addition, the individual may expand his role system so as to *facilitate* other role demands, for instance, joining an exclusive club so as to meet people to whom he can sell stocks and bonds.

5. *Obstacles against the indefinite expansion of ego's role system:* Although the individual may reduce his felt strain by expanding his role system and thereby diminishing the level of required performance for any one of his obligations, this process is also limited: After a possible initial reduction, *Role strain begins to increase more rapidly with a larger number of roles than do the corresponding role rewards or counterpayments from alter.* This differential is based on the limited role resources at individual's commands. The rewards cannot increase at the same rate as the expansion even if at first he increases his skill in role manipulation, because eventually he must begin to fail in some of his obligations, as he adds more relationships; consequently, his alters will not carry out the counter-per-

---

for example, to two of his—observability of the individual's role activities and observability of conflicting demands by members of the role set. Our mechanism of hierarchy or stratification, assigning higher or lower values to particular role demands, corresponds to two of Merton's—the relative importance of statuses and differences of power among members of the role set.

[10] This, again, is a general case of which Merton's "abridging the role-set" is a special example (*ibid.,* p. 117).

formances which are expected for that role relationship. Consequently, he cannot indefinitely expand his role system.

6. *Barriers against intrusion:* The individual may use several techniques for preventing others from initiating, or even continuing, role relationships—the executive hires a secretary through whom appointments must be made, the professor goes on a sabbatical leave. The administrator uses such devices consciously, and one of the most common complaints of high level professionals and executives is that they have no time. This feeling is closely connected with the fact that they *do* have time, that is, they may dispose of their time as they see fit. Precisely because such men face and accept a wider array of role opportunities, demands, and even temptations than do others, they must make more choices and feel greater role strain. At the same time, being in demand offers some satisfaction, as does the freedom to choose. At lower occupational ranks, as well as in less open social systems where duties are more narrowly prescribed, fewer choices can or need be made.

Settling or Carrying Out the Terms of the Role Relationship.—The total role structure functions so as to reduce role strain. The techniques outlined above determine whether an individual will have a role relationship with another, but they do not specify what performances the individual will carry out for another. A common decision process underlies the individual's sequence of role performance as well as their total pattern.

1. *The role relationship viewed as a transaction or "bargain":* In his personal role system, the individual faces the same problem he faces in his economic life: he has limited resources to be allocated among alternative ends. The larger social system, too, is like the economic system, for the problem in both is one of integration, of motivating people to stop doing X and start doing Y, whether this is economic production or religious behavior.

Because economic structures are also social structures, and economic decisions are also role decisions, it might be argued that economic propositions are simply "special cases" of sociological propositions.[11] In a more rigorous methodological sense, however, this claim may be viewed skeptically, since at present the former body of propositions cannot be deduced from the latter.[12] Rather, economic theory may be a fruitful source of sociological ideas, because its theoretical structure is more advanced than that of sociology. Since the precise relation between economic and sociological propositions is not yet fully ascertained, economic vocabulary and ideas are mainly used in the succeeding analysis for clarity of presentation, and the correctness of propositions which are developed here is independent of their possible homologs in economics.[13] In this view, economic performance is one type of role performance, a restricted case in which economists attempt to express role performance, reward, and punishment in monetary terms.[14] In both, the individual

[11] Some structural differences between the two cases, however, should be noted: (1) There are specialized economic *producers,* for example, wheat farmers who offer only one product on the market, but no corresponding sociological positions in which the individual offers only one type of role performance. Some political, religious, military, or occupational leaders do "produce" their services for a large number of people, but they must all carry out many other roles as well in the "role market." Every adult must take part as producer in a minimum number of such role markets. (2) Correspondingly, in the economic sphere all participate in several markets as *buyers;* in the role sphere they act in several markets as *both* sellers and buyers. (3) Correlatively, our entrance into the economic *producer* or *seller* activities may be long delayed, and we may retire from them early if we have enough money, but as long as we live we must remain in the role market: we need other people, and they demand us. (4) We may accumulate enough money so as to be able to purchase more than we can use, or produce more than we can sell, in the economic sphere; but in the role system we probably always ask more on the whole than our alters can give, and are unable to give as much as they demand.

[12] The most elaborate recent attempt to state the relations between the two is Talcott Parsons and Neil J. Smelser, *Economy and Society,* New York: Free Press of Glencoe, Inc., 1956.

[13] Again, however, correctness is independent of their origin. It is equally clear that they parallel certain conceptions of psychodynamics, but again their sociological value is independent of their usefulness in that field.

[14] Anthropologists have noted for over a generation that economic theory needs a more general framework to take account of the non-monetary aspects of economic action in non-Western societies. Cf. Bronislaw Malinowski, "Primitive Economics of the Trobriand Islanders," *Economic Journal* 31

must respond to legitimate demands made on him (role expectations, services, goods, or demands for money) by carrying out his role obligations (performances, goods, or money payments). Through the perception of alternative role strains or goods-services-money costs, the individual adjusts the various demands made upon him, by moving from one role action to another. Both types of transactions, of course, express *evaluations* of goods, performances, and money.

In his role decisions, as in his economic decisions, the individual seeks to keep his felt strain, role cost, or monetary and performance cost at a minimum, and may even apply some rationality to the problem. At the same time, a variety of pressures will force him to accept some solutions which are not pleasant. His decisions are also frequently habitual rather than calculated, and even when calculated may not achieve his goal. Rather, they are the most promising, or the best choice he sees. Since the analysis of such behavior would focus on the act and its accompanying or preceding decision the research approach of "decision analysis" seems appropriate to ascertain the course of events which led to the act.[15]

In role behavior, we begin to experience strain, worry, anxiety, or the pressures of others if we devote more time and attention to one role obligation than we feel we should, or than others feel we should. This strain may be felt because, given a finite sum of role resources, too much has already been expended; or because the individual feels that relative to a given value the cost is too high. The relative strength of such pressures from different obligations determines, then, the individual's role allocation

pattern within his total role system. This system is the resultant of all such strains. Analysis of role allocation requires, of course, that we know the individual's *internal* demands, that is, the demands which he makes on himself, and which thus contribute to his willingness to perform well or not.[16]

The process of strain allocation is facilitated somewhat, as noted above, by ego's ability to manipulate his role structure. On the other hand, the structure is kept in existence by, and is based on, the process of allocation. For example, with reference to the norms of adequate role performance, to be considered later, the White child in the South may gradually learn that his parents will disapprove a close friendship with a Negro boy, but (especially in rural regions) may not disapprove a casual friendship. The "caste" role definitions state that in the former relationship he is over-performing, that is, "paying too much." Such social pressures, expressed in both individual and social mechanisms, are homologous to those in the economic market, where commodities also have a "going price," based on accepted relative evaluations. Correspondingly, the individual expresses moral disapproval when his role partner performs much less well than usual, or demands far more than usual.

In all societies, the child is taught the "value of things," whether they are material objects or role performances, by impressing upon him *that* he must allocate his role performances, and *how* he should allocate them.[17] These structural elements are considered in a later section.

2. *Setting the role price in the role bargain:* The level of role performance which the individual finally decides upon, the "role price," is the resultant of the interaction be-

---

(March, 1921), pp. 1–16. See also Malinowski's earlier article, "The Economic Aspects of the Intichiuma Ceremonies," *Festskrift Tillagnad Edward Westermarck*, Helsingfors: 1912; and *Argonauts of the Western Pacific,* London: Routledge, 1922. Also Raymond Firth, *Primitive Economics of the New Zealand Maori,* New York: Dutton, 1929. For a discussion of the interaction of economic roles and religious roles, see William J. Goode, *Religion Among the Primitives,* New York: Free Press of Glencoe, Inc., 1951, Chapters 5, 6.

15 See the several discussions in Paul F. Lazarsfeld and Morris Rosenberg, editors, *The Language of Social Research,* New York: Free Press of Glencoe, Inc., 1955, pp. 387–448.

16 Price in an elementary economics textbook, determined by the intersection of supply and demand, requires no such datum (i.e., why or whence the demand is not relevant), and thus the model is simpler than the role model. However, more sophisticated economics, as well as the economic practitioner, must distinguish various components or sources of demand.

17 Doubtless, however, the lessons can be made more explicit and conclusive when the "value" can be expressed in dollars rather than in the equally intangible (but more difficult to measure) moral or esthetic considerations.

tween three supply-demand factors: (a) his pre-existing or autonomous norm commitment—his desire to carry out the performance; (b) his judgment as to how much his role partner will punish or reward him for his performance; and (c) the esteem or disesteem with which the peripheral social networks or important reference groups ("third parties") will respond to *both* ego's performance and to alter's attempts to make ego perform adequately.

The individual will perform well ("pay high") if he *wants* very much to carry out this role obligation as against others. He will devote much more time and energy to his job if he really enjoys his work, or is deeply committed normatively to its aims. The individual's willingness to carry out the role performance varies, being a function of the intrinsic gratifications in the activity, the prospective gain from having carried out the activity, and the internal self-reward or self-punishment from conscience pangs or shame or a sense of virtue, or the like.

With reference to what ego expects alter to do in turn, he is more likely to over-perform, or perform well if alter can and will (relative to others) reward ego well or pay him well for a good or poor execution of his role obligations. Thus, my predictions as to what will make my beloved smile or frown will affect my performance greatly; but if she loves me while I love her only little, then the same smiles or frowns will have less effect on my role performances for her.[18] Similarly, as will be noted below in more detail, alter's power, esteem, and resources affect ego's performance because they allow alter to punish or reward ego more fully. The individual perceives these consequences cognitively and responds to them emotionally. If, then, the individual aspires to be accepted by a higher ranking individual or group, he may have to perform more adequately than for one of his own rank. This last proposition requires a further distinction. Alter may be able, because of his position, to reward ego more than alter rewards others in a similar status,

but this additional reward may be no more than a socially accepted premium for extra performance. On the other hand, the additional reward may sometimes be viewed by those others as beyond the appropriate amount. Or the individual may over-perform in one activity of his role relationship to compensate for a poor performance in another—say, the poor breadwinner who tries to be a good companion to his children. Such further consequences of higher performance and higher reward may at times be taken into account by both role partners in making their role bargain.

If alter asks that ego perform consistently better than he is able or willing to do, then he may ease his allocation strain by severing his relationship with that individual or group and by seeking new role relationships in which the allocation strain is less.[19]

3. *Limitations on a "free role bargain":* The third component in ego's decision to perform his role bargain is the network of role relationships—"the third party" or parties—with which ego and alter are in interaction. If either individual is able to exploit the other by driving an especially hard role bargain, such third parties may try to influence either or both to change the relationship back toward the "going role price." Not only do they feel this to be their duty, but they have an interest in the matter as well, since (a) the exploiting individual may begin to demand that much, or pay that little, in his role relations with them; and (b) because the exploited individual may thereby perform less well in his role relations with them. These pressures from third parties include the demand that either ego or alter punish or reward the other for his performances or failures.[20]

It is not theoretically or empirically clear

[18] Cf. Willard Waller's "Principle of Least Interest" in Willard Waller and Reuben Hill, *The Family*, New York: Dryden, 1952, pp. 191–192.

[19] Cf. Leon Festinger's Derivation C, in "A Theory of Social Comparison Processes," *Reprint Services No. 22*, Laboratory for Research in Social Relations, University of Minnesota, 1955, p. 123. Also see No. 24, "Self-Evaluation as a Function of Attraction to the Group," by Leon Festinger, Jane Torrey, and Ben Willerman.

[20] Note, for example, the potential "seduction" of the mother by the child; the mother wishes to please the child to make him happy, and may have to be reminded by others that she is "spoiling" him.

whether such third parties must always be a limited reference group, or can at times be the entire society. Many of the norms of reference groups appear to be special definitions or applications of similar norms of the larger society. Certain groups, such as criminal gangs or power cliques in a revolutionary political party, may give radical twists of meaning to the norms of the larger society. Under such circumstances, the interaction of pressures on ego and alter from various third parties can be complex. We suppose that *which* third party is most important in a given role transaction between ego and alter is a function of the degree of concern felt by various third parties and of the amount of pressure that any of them can bring to bear on either ego or alter.

STRUCTURAL LIMITS AND DETERMINANTS

Strain-Reducing Mechanisms.—The individual can thus reduce his role strain somewhat: first, by selecting a set of roles which are singly less onerous, as mutually supportive as he can manage, and minimally conflicting; and, second, by obtaining as gratifying or value-productive a bargain as he can with each alter in his total role pattern.

As the existence of third parties attests, however, both sets of ego's techniques are limited and determined by a larger structural context within which such decisions are made. Not all such structural elements reduce ego's role strain; indeed, they may increase it, since they may enforce actions which are required for the society rather than the individual. Essentially, whether they increase or reduce the individual's role strain, they determine which of the first set of mechanisms ego may use, and on what terms. Similarly, they determine whether ego and alter may or must bargain freely, to either's disadvantage, or to what extent either can or must remain in an advantageous or costly bargaining position. The most important of such elements are perhaps the following:

1. *Hierarchy of evlauations:* Social evaluations are the source of the individual's evaluations, but even if only the frequently occurring types of choices are considered,

such evaluations reveal complex patterns.[21] Some sort of overall value hierarchy seems to be accepted in every society, but aside from individual idiosyncrasies, both situational and role characteristics may change the evaluation of given acts. Indeed, all individuals may accept contradictory values in some areas of action, which are expressed under different circumstances. Here, the most important of these qualifying factors are: (a) the social position of ego (one should pay some respect to elders, but if one is, say, 30 years of age, one may pay less); (b) the social position of alter (the power, prestige, or resources of alter may affect ego's decision); (c) the content of the performance by ego or alter (mother-nurse obligations are more important than housekeeper-laundress duties); and (d) situational urgency or crisis. When ego gives the excuse of an urgent situation, alter usually retaliates less severely. However, when several crises occur simultaneously, the allocation of role performances is likely to be decided instead by reference to more general rankings of value.[22]

These illustrations suggest how structural factors help to determine ego's willingness to perform or his performance, in an existing role relationship (Type 1b), and though they reduce his uncertainty as to what he should or must do, they also may increase his obligations. At the same time, these same factors also determine in part whether or when ego will include the relationship at all (Type 1a) in his total role system (for example, a noted physicist should engage in a technical correspondence with a fellow physicist, but may refuse to appear on a popular television show; even a passing stranger is expected to give needed aid in a rescue operation).

This set of interacting factors is complex, but gives some guidance in role interaction.

[21] Norman Miller has used data from the Cornell Values Study to show how various combinations of social positions affect expressions of value in *Social Class Differences among American College Students,* Ph.D. thesis, Columbia University, 1958.

[22] In an unpublished paper on "doubling" (the living together of relatives who are not members of the same nuclear family), Morris Zelditch has used approximately these categories to analyze the conditions under which the claim to such a right is likely to be respected.

Since there is a loose, society-wide hierarchy of evaluations, and both individuals and their reference groups or "third parties" may be committed to a somewhat different hierarchy of values, at least the following combinations of evaluations may occur:

EVALUATIONS OF:

EVALUATIONS BY:	Task Content	Rank of Alter	Situational Urgency
Society			
Reference Groups or Third Parties			
Alter			
Ego			

2. *Third parties:* Though third parties figure most prominently in the bargaining within an existing role relationship, especially those which are more fully institutionalized (statuses), they also take part in ego's manipulation of his role structure, since they may be concerned with his total social position. For example, families are criticized by kinsmen, neighbors, and friends if they do not press their children in the direction of assuming a wider range of roles and more demanding roles as they grow older.

3. *Norms of adequacy:* These define what is an acceptable role performance.[23] Norms of adequacy are observable even in jobs which set nearly limitless ideals of performance, such as the higher levels of art and science, for they are gauged to the experience, age, rank, and esteem of the individual. For example, a young instructor need not perform as well as a full professor; but to achieve that rank he must perform as well as his seniors believe they performed at his rank. Such norms also apply to the total system of roles assumed by the individual. The individual may criticize another not only when the latter's specific performance fails to meet such criteria, but also when the latter's range of roles is too narrow (the

wife complains, "We never go out and meet people") or too wide (the husband complains, "You take care of everything in the community except me").

The individual must assume more roles in an urban society than in primitive or peasant society, and the norm of functional specificity applies to a higher proportion of them. This norm permits individuals to bargain within a narrower range, but also, by limiting the mutual obligations of individuals (and thus tending to reduce role strain), it permits them to assume a larger number of roles than would otherwise be possible. This, then, is a role system basis for the generally observed phenomenon of *Gesellschaft* or secondary relations in urban society.

4. *Linkage or dissociation of role obligations in different institutional orders:* The fulfillment of role obligations in one institutional order either rests on or requires a performance in another.[24] Thus, to carry out the obligations of father requires the fulfillment of job obligations. Such doubled obligations are among the strongest in the society, in the sense that ego may insist on rather advantageous terms if he is asked to neglect them in favor of some other obligation. Linking two institutional orders in this fashion limits ego's freedom to manipulate his role system.

At the same time, there are barriers against combining various roles, even when the individual might find such a linkage congenial. (For example: a military rule against officers fraternizing intimately with enlisted men; a regulation forbidding one to be both a lawyer and a partner of a certified public accountant). In an open society, some role combinations are permitted which would be viewed as incongruous or prohibited in a feudal or caste society.

Such pressures are expressed in part by the punishments which the individual may have to face if he insists on entering disapproved combinations of roles. The barriers against some combinations also apply to a special case of role expansion: entrance into certain very demanding statuses, those

[23] This mechanism is akin to, though not identical with, Merton's "mutual social support among status occupants." Merton, "The Role Set . . . ," *op. cit.,* p. 116.

[24] I have described this mechanism of institutional integration in some detail in *Religion Among the Primitives, op. cit.,* Chapters 5–10.

which require nearly continuous performance, are subject to frequent crises or urgencies, and are highly evaluated.[25] Even in our own society there are not many such statuses. The combination of two or more sets of potential crises and responsibilities would make for considerable role strain, so that few individuals would care to enter them; but in addition organizational rules sometimes, and common social attitudes usually, oppose such combinations.—The priest may not be a mother; the head of a hospital may not be a high political leader.

5. *Ascriptive statuses:* All statuses, but especially ascriptive statuses, limit somewhat ego's ability to bargain, since social pressures to conform to their norms are stronger than for less institutionalized roles. Some of these require exchanges of performances between specific individuals (I cannot search for the mother who will serve my needs best, as she cannot look for a more filial child) while others (female, Negro, "native American") embody expectations between status segments of the population. The former are more restrictive than the latter, but both types narrow considerably the area in which individuals can work out a set of performances based on their own desires and bargaining power. Because individuals do not usually leave most ascriptive statuses, some may have to pay a higher role price than they would in an entirely free role market, or may be able (if their ascription status is high in prestige and power) to exact from others a higher role performance.[26] The psychological dimensions of these limitations are not relevant for our discussion. It should be noted, however, that at least one important element in the persistence of personality patterns is to be found in these limitations: the role structure remains fairly stable because

the individual cannot make many free role bargains and thus change his role system or the demands made on him, and consequently the individual personality structure is also maintained by the same structural elements.[27]

6. *Lack of profit in mutual role deviation:* Since two role partners depend in part on each other's mutual performance for their own continuing interaction with other persons, mutual role deviation will only rarely reduce their role strain. It might be advantageous to me if my superior permits me to loaf on the job, but only infrequently can he also profit from my loafing. Consequently, both ego and alter have a smaller range of choices, and the demands of the institutional order or organization are more likely to be met. When, moreover, in spite of these interlocking controls, ego and alter do find a mode of deviation which is mutually profitable—the bribed policeman and the professional criminal, the smothering mother and the son who wants to be dependent—concerned outsiders, third parties, or even a larger segment of the society are likely to disapprove and retaliate more strongly than when either ego or alter deviates one-sidedly.

On the other hand, there is the special case in which ego and alter share the same status—as colleagues or adolescent peers, for example. They are then under similar pressures from others, and may seek similar deviant solutions; they may gang together and profit collectively in certain ways from their deviation.[28]

Less Desirable Statuses: Efforts to Change the Role Bargain.—The preceding analysis of how ego and alter decide whether, when, or how well they will carry out their role obligations permits the deduction of the proposition that when an individual's norm commitment or desire to perform is *low* with respect to a given status

---

[25] Perhaps the third characteristic is merely a corollary of the first two.

[26] Although the matter cannot be pursued here, it seems likely that in economic terms we are dealing here with the phenomena of the "differentiated product"—ego cannot accept a given role performance from just anyone, but from the specific people with whom he is in interaction—and of oligopoly—ego can patronize only a limited number of suppliers or sellers. Moreover, with respect to certain roles, both supply and demand are relatively inelastic.

[27] Cf. C. Addison Hickman and Manford H. Kuhn, *Individuals, Groups, and Economic Behavior,* New York: Dryden, 1956, p. 38.

[28] Albert K. Cohen has discussed one example of this special case at length in *Delinquent Boys,* New York: Free Press of Glencoe, Inc., 1955. It requires, among other factors, special ecological conditions and the possibility of communication among those in the same situation.

—in our society, many women, Negroes, and adolescents reject one or more of the obligations imposed on them; perhaps slaves in all societies do—then alter must bring greater pressure to bear on him in order to ensure what alter judges to be an adequate performance. If the individual does underperform, he is less likely to have strong feelings of self-failure or disesteem; he may feel no more than some recognition of, and perhaps anxiety about, possible sanctions from alter.

Individuals are especially conscious that they are "training" others in both child and adult socialization, if those others are suspected of being weakly committed to their role obligations. Thus, most Whites in the South have for generations held that all Whites have an obligation to remind the Negro by punishment and reward that he "should keep in his place," and that punishment of the Negro is especially called for when he shows evidence that he does not accept that place. It is the heretic, not the sinner, who is the more dangerous. It is particularly when the members of a subordinate status begin to deny normatively their usual obligations that third parties become aroused and more sensitive to evidence of deviation in either performance or norm commitment. On the other hand, individuals in a formerly subordinate status may, over time, acquire further bargaining power, while those in a superior status may gradually come to feel less committed to the maintenance of the former role pattern.

THE FAMILY AS A ROLE BUDGET CENTER

For adult or child, the family is the main center of role allocation, and thus assumes a key position in solutions of role strain. Most individuals must account to their families for what they spend in time, energy, and money outside the family. And ascriptive status obligations of high evaluation or primacy are found in the family. More important, however, is the fact that family members are often the only persons who are likely to know how an individual is allocating his *total* role energies, managing his whole role system; or that he is spending "too much" time in one role obligation and

retiring from others. Consequently, family relations form the most immediate and persistent set of interactions which are of importance in social control. Formal withdrawal from these relationships is difficult, and informal withdrawal arouses both individual guilt feelings and pressures from others.

Moreover, since the family is a role allocation center, where one's alters know about one's total role obligations and fulfillments, it also becomes a vantage point from which to view one's total role system in perspective. Because it is a set of status obligations which change little from day to day and from which escape is difficult, role alternatives can be evaluated against a fairly stable background. Consequently, other family members can and do give advice as to how to allocate energies from a "secure center." Thus it is from this center that one learns the basic procedures of balancing role strains.

Finally, family roles are "old shoe" roles in which expectations and performances have become well meshed so that individuals can relax in them. In Western society, it is mainly the occupational statuses which are graded by fine levels of prestige, just as achievement within occupations is rewarded by fine degrees of esteem. It is not that within jobs one is held to standards, while within families one is not.[29] It is rather that, first, socialization on the basis of status ascription within the family fits individual expectations to habitual performances and, second, rankings of family performances are made in only very rough categories of esteem. The intense sentiments within the family cushion individual strain by inducing each person to make concessions, to give sympathy, to the others. Of course, greater strain is experienced when they do not. These status rights and obligations become, then, "role retreats" or "role escapes," with demands which are felt to be less stringent, or in which somewhat more acceptable private bargains have been made among the various members of the group. One's per-

[29] See Melvin Tumin's discussion of incentives in various non-occupational statuses in "Rewards and Task Orientations," *American Sociological Review,* 20 (August, 1955), pp. 419–422.

formance is not graded by the whole society, and one's family compares one's family performance to only a limited extent with that of other people in other families.

The existence of unranked or grossly ranked performance statuses or roles may permit the individual to give a higher proportion of his energy to the ranked performance statuses. The institutions which contain such statuses vary. For example, in contemporary Western society, the layman's religious performances, like his familial performances, are ranked only roughly, but at one time evaluation of the former was more differentiated. However, familial performance apparently is never ranked in fine gradation in any society.[30] Here, an implicit structural proposition may be made explicit: the greater the degree of achievement orientation in a system of roles, the finer the gradation of prestige rankings within that system or organization.[31]

ROLE STRAIN AND THE LARGER SOCIAL STRUCTURE

Social structures are made up of role relationships, which in turn are made up of role transactions. Ego's efforts to reduce his role strain determine the allocation of his energies to various role obligations, and thus determine the flow of performances to the institutions of the society. Consequently, the sum of role decisions determines what *degree* of integration exists among various elements of the social structure. While these role performances accomplish whatever is done to meet the needs of the society, never-

[30] Partly because of the difficulty of outsiders observing crucial performances within it; partly, also, because of the difficulty of measuring relative achievement except in universalistic terms, as against the particularistic-ascriptive character of familial roles. Note, however, the creation by both Nazi Germany and Soviet Russia of a family title for very fertile mothers (an observable behavior).

[31] Note in this connection the case of China, the most family-oriented civilization. In comparison with other major civilizations, the Chinese developed a more complex ranking of kinship positions—and a more explicit ranking of familial performances. (See Marion J. Levy, Jr., *The Family Revolution in Modern China*, Cambridge: Harvard University Press, 1949, esp. Chapter 3). Various individuals have figured in Chinese history as "family heroes," that is, those who performed their family duties exceedingly well.

theless the latter may not be adequately served. It is quite possible that what gets done is not enough, or that it will be ineffectively done. As already noted, the role demands made by one institutional order often conflict with those made by another—at a minimum, because the "ideal" fulfillment in each is not qualified by other institutional demands and would require much of any person's available resources. Many such conflicting strains frequently result in changes in the social structure. Within smaller sub-systems, such as churches, corporations, schools, and political parties, the total flow of available personal resources may be so disintegrative or ineffective that the system fails to survive. In addition, the total role performances in some societies have failed to maintain the social structure as a whole.

Thus, though the sum of role performances ordinarily maintains a society, it may also change the society or fail to keep it going. There is no necessary harmony among all role performances, even though these are based ultimately on the values of the society which are at least to some extent harmonious with one another. Role theory does not, even in the general form propounded here, explain why some activities are ranked higher than others, why some activities which help to maintain the society are ranked higher, or why there is some "fit" between the role decisions of individuals and what a society needs for survival.

The total efforts of individuals to reduce their role strain within structural limitations directly determines the profile, structure, or pattern of the social system. But whether the resulting societal pattern is "harmonious" or integrated, or whether it is even effective in maintaining that society, are separate empirical questions.

SUMMARY AND CONCLUSIONS

The present paper attempts to develop role theory by exploiting the well-known notion that societal structures are made up of roles. The analysis takes as its point of departure the manifest empirical inadequacies, noted in the first section, of a widely current view of social stability, namely, that the continuity of a social system is mainly a function of two major variables: (a) the normative, consensual commitment of the individuals of the society; and (b) the integration among the norms held by those individuals. Accepting dissensus, nonconformity, and conflicts among norms and roles as the usual state of affairs, the paper develops the idea that the total role system of the individual is unique and over-demanding. The individual cannot satisfy fully all demands, and must move through a continuous sequence of role decisions and bargains, by which he attempts to adjust these demands. These choices and the execution of the decisions are made somewhat easier by the existence of mechanisms which the individual may use to organize his role system, or to obtain a better bargain in a given role. In addition, the social structure determines how much freedom in manipulation he possesses.

The individual utilizes such mechanisms and carries out his sequences of role behaviors through an underlying decision process, in which he seeks to reduce his role strain, his felt difficulty in carrying out his obligations. The form or pattern of his process may be compared to that of the economic decision: the allocation of scarce resources—role energies, time, emotions, goods—among alternative ends, which are the role obligations owed by the individual. The role performances which the individual can exact from others are what he gets in exchange.

It is to the individual's interest in attempting to reduce his role strain to demand as much as he can and perform as little, but since this is also true for others, there are limits on how advantageous a role bargain he can make. He requires some role performance from particular people. His own social rank or the importance of the task he is to perform may put him in a disadvantageous position from which to make a bargain. Beyond the immediate role relationship of two role partners stands a network of roles with which one or both are in interaction, and these third parties have both a direct and an indirect interest in their role transactions. The more institutionalized roles are statuses, which are backed more

strongly by third parties. The latter sanction ego and alter when these two have made a free role bargain which is far from the going role price. The demands of the third parties may include the requirement that ego or alter punish the other for his failure to perform adequately.

Under this conception of role interaction, the bargains which some individuals make will be consistently disadvantageous to them: the best role price which they can make will be a poor one, even by their own standards. However, no one can ever escape the role market. The continuity of the individual's total role pattern, then, may be great even when he does not have a strong normative commitment to some of his less desirable roles. Like any structure or organized pattern, the role pattern is held in place by both internal and external forces—in this case, the role pressures from other individuals. Therefore, not only is role strain a normal experience for the individual, but since the individual processes of reducing role strain determine the total allocation of role performances to the social institutions, the total balances and imbalances of role strains create whatever stability the social structure possesses. On the other hand, precisely because each individual is under some strain and would prefer to be under less, and in particular would prefer to get more for his role performances than he now receives, various changes external to his own role system may alter the kind of role bargains he can and will make. Each individual system is partly held in place by the systems of other people, their demands, and their counter-performances—which ego needs as a basis for his own activities. Consequently, in a society such as ours, where each individual has a very complex role system and in which numerous individuals have a relatively low intensity of norm commitment to many of their role obligations, changes in these external demands and performances may permit considerable change in the individual's system.

The cumulative pattern of all such role bargains determines the flow of performances to all social institutions and thus to the needs of the society for survival. Nevertheless, the factors here considered may not in fact insure the survival of a society, or of an organization within it. The quantity or quality of individual performances may undermine or fail to maintain the system. These larger consequences of individual role bargains can be traced out, but they figure only rarely in the individual role decision.

With respect to its utility in empirical research, this conception permits a more adequate delineation of social structures by focussing on their more observable elements, the role transactions. This permits such questions as: Would you increase the time and energy you now give to role rela-

tionship X? Or, granted that these are the ideal obligations of this relationship, how little can you get away with performing? Or, by probing the decision, it is possible to ascertain why the individual has moved from one role transaction to another, or from one role organization to another. Finally, this conception is especially useful in tracing out the articulation between one institution or organization and another, by following the sequence of an individual's role performance and their effects on the role performances of other individuals with relation to different institutional orders.

Role, Role Conflict, and Effectiveness: An Empirical
Study* / J. W. Getzels and E. G. Guba (*The University of Chicago*)

Although the concepts of *role* and *role conflict* have received increasing attention in recent years, achieving the status of central constructs in the work of Parsons, Shils, and others,[1] they have remained theoretical terms largely untried by realistic experimental application. The few empirical studies that have been made, notably those by Stouffer and Toby,[2] are neatly contrived, but fail to do more than barely approximate real life situations. Korber among others is critical of this approach, maintaining that the experimental stories invented for the research "depict unrealistically simplified

and inadequate situations."[3] And Stouffer himself confesses the need "for studies which can be made in settings closer to actual life than paper and pencil tests."[4]

The present investigation sought to avoid the shortcomings of contrived situations by working within a real life setting. Specifically, it was concerned with examining the relationships existing in the military situation between two highly organized roles, those of officer and of teacher; the conflict between these roles when held by a single individual; and the consequences of such conflict for the effective management of one of the roles. The primary goal of the phase of the study being reported here was not to provide substantive data regarding the specific situation under analysis, but to work out a method for investigating role conflict in a real life setting and to test a number of hypotheses implicit in the indicated role theory.

SOME RELEVANT ASPECTS OF ROLE THEORY

The role theory considered here is part of the larger framework recently proposed for

Reprinted from *The American Sociological Review,* 1954, 19, pages 164–175, by permission of the senior author and publisher, The American Sociological Association.

* This research was supported in whole or in part by the United States Air Force under Contract No. AF 18(600)–5 monitored by the Air Research and Development Command.

[1] See, for example, Talcott Parsons, *The Social System,* New York: The Free Press of Glencoe, Inc., 1951, p. 280 f.; Talcott Parsons and Edward A. Shils (eds.), *Toward a General Theory of Action,* Cambridge: Harvard University Press, 1951, *passim;* Jackson Toby, "Some Variables in Role Conflict Analysis," *Social Forces,* XXX (March, 1952), pp. 323–327.

[2] Samuel A. Stouffer, "An Analysis of Conflicting Social Norms," *American Sociological Review,* XIV (December, 1949), pp. 707–717; Samuel A. Stouffer and Jackson Toby, "Role Conflict and Personality," *American Journal of Sociology,* LVI (March, 1951), pp. 395–406.

[3] George W. Korber, "Role Conflict and Personality," Letter to the Editor, *American Journal of Sociology,* LVII (July, 1951), pp. 48–49.

[4] Samuel A. Stouffer, "Reply to Korber," Letter to the Editor, *American Journal of Sociology,* LVII (July, 1951), p. 49.

the development of a "unified conceptual scheme for theory and research in the social sciences."[5] Three basic terms are of immediate applicability: (1) *actor,* the individual considered in abstraction from his personality and roles, (2) *role,* the set of complementary expectations regarding the actor in his interaction with other individuals, (3) *personality,* the system of need-dispositions reacting to the alternatives presented by the existence of the different roles.

Broadly conceived, the theory holds that an actor's behavior may best be understood as a function of role and personality. Consider, for example, an actor who finds himself alone in a completely isolated locale. Within the practical limits of the situation it is possible for the individual to satisfy his every want provided only that it is environmentally feasible. But introduce upon the scene a second individual who has it within his power to hinder or help the original actor (ego) in the attainment of desired goals. Now whenever ego acts, he must take into account the possible reactions of the other actor (alter). He builds up a set of expectations regarding alter's reactions, and he will modify his own proposed activity in terms of these expectations in order to assure himself of alter's approval or at least to avoid his active disapproval.

In the meantime, of course, alter has in a similar manner been building his own set of expectations with regard to ego. As a result of their interaction, both ego and alter will revise their expectations of one another to conform more nearly to the reality of which each has some evidence. In the end each actor inhabits a number of well-defined roles, the definition of the roles stemming not alone from the actor who fills the roles but from his alter who holds the expectations. Deviance from a role brings disapproval and negative sanction; conformity, approval and position sanction.

This elementary exposition of role and role expectation may be extended to the interaction of individuals in a larger collectivity. Each individual occupies a number of roles defined by his group. To the extent

that an actor properly meets the expectations of his roles, he meets with approval; to the extent that he fails to meet these expectations, he is held eccentric and at extremes liable to negative sanctions. Since the actor filling the role is himself a member of the group that defines the role, he will in general share the expectations of the role, and the expectations will have for him a legitimacy that stems from mutual acceptance. The actor thus feels an internal obligation to conform to the role, even when in some respects the role expectations run counter to his own needs.

In certain situations *role conflicts* occur. That is, the situations are so ordered that an actor is required to fill simultaneously two or more roles that present inconsistent, contradictory, or even mutually exclusive expectations. The actor cannot realistically conform to these expectations. He is then forced to choose one of several alternatives: he may abandon one role and cling to the other, he may attempt some compromise between the roles, or he may withdraw either physically or psychologically from the roles altogether. In any event, over any long-term period he cannot fully meet the expectations of all roles, and to the extent that he fails to meet the expectations, he is judged *ineffective* in the management of one or another of the roles by the defining groups.

The severity of role conflict is dependent on two factors. One is the *relative incompatibility* of expectations between roles. Consider here two roles x' and x'' containing in common expectations $x,$ but differing in that role x' also contains expectations y and role x'' expectations $z.$ By common expectations is meant that a single act will suffice to meet the requirements of two or more roles. The elements y and z differ, however, and some of these elements may be contradictory or even mutually exclusive so that conformity to y_1 makes conformity to z_1 impossible. Severity of role conflict will ordinarily increase as y and z are enlarged relative to $x.$ The other factor determining severity of role conflict is the *rigor* with which expectations are defined within a given situation. How flexible or rigid are

[5] Talcott Parsons and Edward A. Shils (eds.), *op. cit.,* p. 4.

the limits set by the defining group within which their expectations may satisfactorily be met? For example, both the military and civilian have certain expectations regarding appropriate dress for certain occasions, but the limits within which the military may meet these expectations are usually much more restricted than is the civilian. Expectations may also vary in rigor from situation to situation. Teachers, for example, are expected to dress neatly. But this expectation may vary from "always wear a white shirt and tie" in one community, to "dress appropriately to the occasion" in another. If in this latter instance the teacher happens also to be a member of an informal club where sport dress is ordinarily worn, he will be in much more conflict in the first situation than in the second.

There is another element in the analysis of role conflict that cannot be lost sight of, and that is *personality*. No role is defined merely for a single actor. It is possible to fill the same role with a variety of actors, provided only that they possess the required technical competence. The crucial differences in behavior are a function of the interaction between the different personalities and the role expectations. The extent to which conflict is felt is also a function of differences in personality structure. In the case of the dress of teachers previously cited, it is clear that the intensity of reactions to the conflict and the mode of adjustment might be considerably different for an actor with a flexible personality and for one with a rigid personality.

The portions of the theory that are especially pertinent to this study may be summarized as follows: Role conflicts ensue whenever an actor is required to fill two or more roles whose expectations are in some particulars inconsistent. The severity of the conflict is a function *situationally* of the relative incompatibility and rigor of definition of the expectations, and *personalistically* of certain adjustive mechanisms of the individual filling the roles. An actor who is in conflict must necessarily ignore some of the expectations of one or more of the roles, and to the extent that he does so, he is held to be ineffective.

THE PROBLEM AND HYPOTHESES

There is a reciprocal relationship between theory and research. On the one hand, theory facilitates the selection of meaningful problems and provides hypotheses to be applied to and tested by empirical study. On the other hand, if the research problems are so formulated in terms of systematic concepts the resulting empirical data will not only be of value in practical application but will contribute to the validity and revision of the theory. In these terms, the present study has two major objectives: (1) to investigate a given social situation—in this instance a teaching situation—with reference to such concepts provided by the theory outlined in the preceding section as *role, role conflict, personality,* and *effectiveness;* (2) to examine a number of hypotheses founded in the theory in the light of the empirical data supplied by (1), thus providing a test of the applicability and validity of the theory itself. In effect, of course, the two objectives are different sides of the same coin.

The setting chosen for the study was the Air Command and Staff School of Air University, Maxwell Air Force Base, consisting of nine courses or "schools." Aside from considerations of interest on the part of the school, there was an over-riding experimental reason for the choice of this locale: The military setting offers an excellent *real situation* laboratory for testing role theory since role and role expectations are defined and acted out with a clarity not readily available elsewhere to the observer. Indeed, each actor in a military institution carries his role visibly on his shoulder.

With reference then to the specific situation under analysis, the theory pointed to three major issues for investigation: (1) the identification of the role conflicts inherent in the Air University situation, (2) the ordering of schools and instructors as a function of the number and kind of these role conflicts attributable to them, (3) the discovery of relationships between the kinds and number of role conflict and the characteristics of the schools and instructors, and more especially in the case of the latter, between the intensity of role conflict and effectiveness in the instructor role.

In this connection, a crucial distinction must be made between the *extent* of role conflict in the situation and the *intensity* of role conflict in the actor. It is perfectly clear that a situation may involve much potential conflict yet theoretically not involve any given actor within the situation in the conflict. For example, a community may pay its teachers only lower-class salaries but expect them to live according to middle-class standards. The situation contains incompatible expectations and is therefore one of potential conflict. A teacher, however, who has a private income, though recognizing the conflict as existing in the situation, may himself not be involved in it to any degree whatsoever.

Three general hypotheses of relevance to the issues under investigation are:

1. With respect to situational differences, the *extent* of role conflict as seen by the actors is a function of the number and magnitude of incompatible expectations placed upon or held by the actors.

2. With respect to individual differences, the greater the *intensity* of an actor's involvement in role conflict the greater his relative *ineffectiveness* in at least one of the roles.

3. The *intensity* of an actor's involvement in role conflict is systematically related to certain personal and attitudinal characteristics.

THE METHOD

The Air Command and Staff School of Air University is composed of nine teaching divisions or schools and staffed by some 300 officer-instructors and supervisory personnel. It provides advanced training at the general and specific functional levels to several thousand officers a year. The procedures used in the study may be outlined as follows:

1. *Identification of the complaints, frustrations, and dissatisfactions of instructors.* Two-hour intensive interviews were conducted with a sample of fourteen officer-instructors representing all teaching units, and all military ranks from Lieutenant to Colonel. In addition, less lengthy interviews were conducted with a number of the administrative personnel of the school. The assumption was that some of the dissatisfactions might have their source in role conflict.

2. *Identification of the major role conflicts for study.* The texts of the interviews obtained in (1) were abstracted into separate statements, each describing a particular dissatisfaction. These statements were then sorted in two ways: according to the *content* of the dissatisfaction, e.g. difficulty of obtaining a field command upon re-assignment from Air University, and according to the *roles* engaged in the conflict producing the dissatisfaction, e.g. the requirements of a *field officer* versus present experience as an *academic instructor*. (In the sorting process, a number of statements having only a tenuous relationship to role conflict or involving not a conflict between two existing roles but between an existing role and an idealized role were discarded.) When the sorting was finished it was clear that the single major conflict was between the *officer* role and the *teacher* role, and this became the conflict for experimental study.

3. *Construction of the role conflict instruments.* Two role-conflict instruments were required: first, a situational instrument measuring the *extent* of conflict from *school to school;* and second, a personalistic instrument measuring the intensity of conflict from *officer-instructor to officer-instructor* within each school.

The crucial factors in the conflict under study were categorized into four major problem areas. Each item for the experimental instruments had the following form: (a) A statement of a complaint relevant to one of the areas. The statement was derived from the interview material. (b) A contrasting statement to clarify the nature of the complaint. This contrasting statement often referred to a civilian school situation. (c) Specific reference to the situation at Air University. The following are the four major problem areas and sample items for each area:

(i) Procedures. The items in this area reflect the conflict when officers who wear the mark of their differential status in clear sight are required to be "democratic" in the classroom without regard to the visible differences in military status. Traditionally a military organization is ordered in terms of rank and managed by command rather than consensus. However, there is a strong educational tradition that "democratic" teaching is the best teaching.[6] Attempts are made to operate classes at the Air Command and Staff School in a more or less informal, group process, "democratic" manner, where differences in military rank are minimized. This situation may be conducive to conflict in some officer-instructors.

Typical items are:

12. While the purpose of committee work among instructors is to arrive at decisions through the free interchange of ideas, this purpose is frequently not fulfilled by committees at Air University since junior officers cannot persist in disagreeing with their military superiors.

27. The mixture of democratic and military procedures at Air University leaves the instructor in the ambiguous position of never knowing when to act on his own initiative and when to be guided by S.O.P. (Standard Operating Procedures.)

(ii) Rank. The items in this area reflect the officer-instructor's problems in responsibility, authority, professional status and salary. The officer typically receives these as a function of his military rank earned in the field, while the teacher receives these largely as a function of his experience, training, and ability in the classroom. Confusion of these at Air University, as for example when a Colonel with little educational training and a Lieutenant with considerable educational experience perform the same instructional duties, may give rise to conflicts both for higher and lower ranking officer-instructor.

Typical items are:

31. It is a shortsighted policy to rate instructors at Air University solely in terms of factors relating to effectiveness as officers, largely ignoring factors relating to effectiveness as instructors.

[6] The use of the term "democratic" in this sense is viewed with some misgivings, since it has come to have a strong connotation of a value judgment. Here it simply refers to an interdependence in subordinate-superordinate organization, with communication proceeding in both directions with relatively equal force and freedom.

41. Since all instructors at Air University perform the same job, it is unfortunate that they are paid as if they were filling field assignments involving differentiated duties and risks.

(iii) Career. The items in this area represent problems arising when professional Air Force officers are required to perform an academic assignment they do not visualize as contributing to the advancement of their military careers. Promotion at Air University is held to be slow because of the generally high calibre of all the personnel stationed there, and in any case promotion is not ordinarily a function of teaching proficiency. There is in addition the feeling among officer-instructors that the way up the career ladder is by assignment to field command rather than to an academic service position.

Typical items are:

37. Compared with a tour of duty in a field command, a tour at Air University is a gap in the career of a professional Air Force officer.

44. In spite of a good record as a teacher, an instructor at Air University with no overseas or combat experience has little chance for promotion.

(iv) Assignment. The items in this area reflect the problems arising when personnel subject to the assignment regulations of the Service find themselves assigned to Air University against their wishes, or are required to teach subject-matter in which they have no interest or feel no competence.

13. While an instructor at a civilian institution who occupies a teaching assignment outside his major specialty may reasonably expect this to be temporary, an instructor at Air University in similar circumstances must consider his position relatively permanent, since no effective channels for reassignment exist.

19. Unlike instructors at civilian institutions, whose teaching duties are likely to be determined on the basis of their professional competence, instructors at Air University are often assigned to courses on the basis of the vacancies which happen to exist at a particular time.

Forty-six items were included in each of the two experimental inventories, twelve from each of the first three categories and ten from the fourth.[7] The choice of items was guided by the frequency with which the problem stated in the item was mentioned in the interviews. The two inventories contained exactly the same items, in the same order. They differed only in that on the first instrument the respondent was required to indicate the proportion of instructors in his school who would agree with the item, and on the second instrument the respondent was required to indicate how much he personally was troubled by the situation described in the item. The respondents were asked to react to each item on a six-point scale as shown at bottom of page.

Inventory I

The statement as made would be agreed to at my school by:

0—practically none of the instructors
1—a small proportion of the instructors
2—some of the instructors
3—a considerable number of the instructors
4—many of the instructors
5—very many of the instructors

Inventory II

The situation described in the statement troubles me:

0—not at all
1—to a small degree
2—to some degree
3—to a considerable degree
4—to a great degree
5—to a very great degree

Inventory I was thus designed to yield a measure of situational differences, and Inventory II, a measure of personal differences. Two assumptions are involved in these procedures: (1) The greater the number of instructors reported being aware of a conflict, the more prevalent or *extensive* it is, and (2) The more troubled a given instructor reports feeling about a situation, the more *intensely* involved he is in the conflict portrayed by the situation.

4. *The Personal Questionnaire and the*

Effectiveness Criterion. In addition to the role-conflict inventories, a third instrument —the Personal Questionnaire—was developed. This was designed to obtain the following types of material from the respondents:

(a) *Descriptive* information such as age, rank, educational training, and current duties.

(b) *Attitudinal* information such as interest in the goals of Air University, feelings of adequacy or inadequacy in their work and sentiments toward the educational procedures.

(c) *Ratings* of fellow-instructors as either below average or above average in teaching effectiveness.

This material was used to describe the sample, to select characteristics typical of personnel in conflict as measured by Inventory II, and to provide criterion data for the analysis of the relationship between role-conflict and effectiveness in the instructor role.

The technique of colleague inter-rating as the criterion of teacher effectiveness was adopted for several reasons: (1) None of the standard officer rating forms seemed especially relevant to teaching ability, and even if they were, the ratings were so uniformly high and displayed such little variability that they were statistically unfeasible. (2) Limitations of time and opportunity ruled out the possibility of making a full-scale study of the problem and providing a reliable and valid rating instrument. (3) Most important, because of the policy at Air University that all instructors systematically visit each other's classes and try out all their lectures before their colleagues, the instructors were in particularly favored positions to make valid judgments of their fellows.

5. *Administration of Instruments and Subjects.* The instruments were self-administering. They were distributed to the officer-instructors through the regular message-center facilities of the Schools and the completed forms were returned to the research staff at the University of Chicago by mail. There was a week's interval between the distribution of Inventory I and the dis-

---

[7] The categories were derived from the interview data, and were used for convenience of item writing. No claim of unidimensionality of items is made, and, in fact, there is evidence to show that conflict in one area of a situation tends to spread to the entire situation. The areas therefore cannot be thought of as independent.

TABLE 1

MEAN SCORES ACHIEVED ON A SAMPLING OF INVENTORY I ITEMS BY TWO GROUPS OF SCHOOLS

Item No.	Group C (2 Schools)	Group A (2 Schools)	Item
8	3.723	1.072	While at civilian institutions the professional status of an instructor is determined on the basis of training, experience, and ability, at Air University it is determined on the basis of the comparatively irrelevant factor of rank earned in the field.
7	2.889	0.536	While academic freedom is a privilege which a teacher normally enjoys, instructors at Air University have no such freedom in so far as they are obliged to follow the "authoritative folder."
29	4.226	2.014	Military rank rather than teaching experience or competence too often determines the position that an officer will receive at Air University.
26	4.278	2.072	It frequently happens at Air University that competent teachers have low military rank while poorly qualified teachers have high military rank.
11	2.556	0.449	Since instructors at Air University have different military ranks, it is difficult for them to achieve the social give and take that exists among instructors at civilian institutions.
42	2.778	0.956	The recognition given to an instructor at Air University may depend more on the insignia on his collar than on his knowledge of the subject matter and his teaching efficiency.
25	3.111	1.319	Although an officer is trained in military planning, it does not follow that he is equipped to do the kinds of educational planning, such as curriculum making, which Air University requires of him.
10	2.722	0.942	Although the existing policy at Air University expects instructors to function democratically, individual civilian and military school administrators seem to be free to exempt themselves from this policy without regard for dissenting opinions.

tribution of Inventory II and the Personal Questionnaire.

Of the 266 officer-instructors canvassed, 200 or approximately 75 per cent completed and returned Inventory I, and 169 or approximately 64 per cent completed and returned Inventory II and the Personal Questionnaire. Although no claim is made regarding the representativeness of the sample, in terms of the known factors of rank and school assignment, the sample parallels the total population of officer-instructors very closely.

RESULTS

The data obtained will be presented under the following four headings:

1. *Specific Conflicts.* Was the method successful in bringing to light conflicts that were meaningful to the officer-instructor respondents?

2. *Schools.* Were there systematic differences among the nine schools in the extent of role-conflict as measured by Inventory I (Hypothesis 1)?

3. *Effectiveness.* What was the relation-

ship between the intensity of role-conflict of the officer-instructors and role ineffectiveness (Hypothesis 2)?

4. *Individual Differences.* What was the nature of the relationship between the intensity of role-conflict and certain of the descriptive and attitudinal variables (Hypothesis 3)?

1. *Specific Conflict.* Each of the items included in the experimental instruments describes a conflict expressed or implied during personal interviews. However, the mere fact that an item was included could not by itself be taken as evidence that the given conflict was necessarily meaningful or widespread among the schools. The first question asked of the data was therefore: Is there evidence for the existence and meaningfulness of the situations described in the Inventories?

Table 1 lists a sampling of the more discriminating items and gives the mean Inventory I scores for each item as achieved by two groups of schools. It will be noted that for one group an item may have a mean in excess of 4.000 on a scale ranging from 0.000 to 5.000, while for the other group the item may have a very much smaller mean. In addition, it may be noted that some items (for example, items 26 and 29) are scored quite high in all schools, while other items (for example, items 7 and 11) are scored quite high in one group of schools but not in the other. Moreover, it will be noted that in spite of these inter-item variations, one group of schools scores systematically higher on *all* items without exception. It is clear that the items were responded to systematically rather than randomly; they have meaning for the respondents and relevance for the Air University situation. The relative extent of the various conflicts may be judged from the magnitude of the means presented in Table 1. Further evidence of the systematic nature of the responses by schools and by individual will be found in the following sections.

2. *Schools.* A mean conflict score was obtained for each of nine schools by averaging the Inventory I scores for the instructors within each school. These mean scores are shown in Table 2.

Table 2 demonstrates the extent of the

TABLE 2

MEAN SCORES FOR INVENTORY I FOR EACH OF THE NINE SCHOOLS

School	Mean Score
A–1	0.918
A–2	1.162
B–1	1.414
B–2	1.455
B–3	1.500
B–4	1.600
B–5	1.650
C–1	2.067
C–2	2.400

differences in role conflict among the various schools. The schools may be placed into three groups: the "A" group with mean scores near 1.0, designated as the *low* conflict group; the "B" group with mean scores near 1.5, designated as the *medium* conflict group; and the "C" group with mean scores in excess of 2.0, designated as the *high* conflict group. The differences in scores between schools in the A group and schools in the C group are statistically significant beyond the .01 level (as determined by analysis of variance and separate "t" tests). The differences *within* any of the groups do not even approach significance. The difference between the extreme schools of group B, i.e. between B–1 and B–5, is not as great as the difference between school A–2 and B–1 or between B–5 and C–1. It seems safe to conclude that the three groups show high internal homogeneity and relatively marked differences from one another.

Is there any way to account for the striking differences between the schools in group A and group C? It will be recalled that Hypothesis 1 suggested that "with respect to situational differences, the *extent* of role conflict as seen by the actors is a function of the number and magnitude of incompatible expectations placed upon or held by the actors." The question then resolves itself into: do the schools at the extremes in role conflict as determined by the present method represent different *kinds* of schools within the Air University setting? The answer is that they do. The schools with least conflict are military in nature, being concerned with weapons, tactics, and such, without counterpart in civilian educational institutions. The schools with most conflict are perhaps the two least military of the schools, being concerned with bookkeeping, legalistics and other subjects having real counterparts in civilian educational institutions.

Two different types of personnel are involved in the two kinds of schools. All the schools at Air University are of course designed for the advanced training of officers. But the former two schools are directly concerned with the teaching of field operations, while the latter two schools are concerned with the teaching of more or less civilian subject matter. The officer-instructors teaching in the latter schools are competent in content areas having their counterparts in civilian schools. Although presently officers, the instructors have themselves received a major part of their training as civilian professional people, in business or law schools and the like. In short, in addition to the roles of officer and instructor they have also internalized and are accustomed to the expectations of the civilian professional statuses they occupy.

An examination of the items discriminating most sharply between the high and the low conflict schools as presented in Table 1 will make the distinction clear. Consider, for example, item 29, "Military rank rather than teaching experience or competence too often determines the position that an officer will receive at Air University." The military content instructor who holds himself an officer first, and an instructor only secondarily, is not likely to believe that rank too often determines the position of a member of the staff at Air University. Air University is a military institution, and how else but by rank is position to be determined? Besides, highest military rank probably is truly a concomitant of greatest experience and competence in the military content type of school.

Observe in contrast the civilian content instructor who may hold himself a lawyer or accountant first, and an officer only secondarily, at least while at Air University. Position within a teaching situation becomes for him a function of professional experi-

ence, educational background, knowledge of subject matter, and the like. Rank earned in the field is a relatively lesser if not irrelevant consideration. He feels cheated if educational status, authority, and recognition are based on rank or other military criteria rather than on the criteria ordinarily applied to him as a professional person. For him military rank rather than professional experience or competence does indeed "too often" determine position at Air University. These difficulties are reflected in the higher conflict scores of the schools in group C.

3. *Role Effectiveness.* The distributions of scores for Inventory I and Inventory II were compared with the ineffectiveness ratings obtained from the instructor interratings. The hypothesis under test was that "the greater an actor's involvement in role conflict, the greater the relative ineffectiveness." Although the hypothesis predicts a relationship between conflict and ineffectiveness, it does not follow that lack of conflict is related to effectiveness. Accordingly, the hypothesis was tested by comparing ineffective instructors with *all* other instructors.

To permit the required analysis, a *low* conflict group and a *high* conflict group were defined for both Inventories, the high group including all individuals with a mean item score of 1.7 or greater, the low group including all individuals with a score of 0.5 or less. The number of "ineffective" and of "other" instructors falling into each of these categories was determined, and the frequencies were compared by chi-square test. The results are shown in Table 3.

It will be seen from this table that the empirical findings bear out the theoretical expectations: The individuals experiencing conflict are also the relatively ineffective ones. It will be noted also that Inventory I, designed as a situational instrument, has no predictive value for the personalistic criterion of effectiveness, while Inventory II, the personalistic instrument, shows a significant relationship. Thus, although Inventory I and Inventory II undoubtedly overlap in some respects, they function quite differently with respect to this criterion.

These data provide excellent supporting evidence for the validity of the theory,

TABLE 3

COMPARISON OF HIGH AND LOW CONFLICT SCORES WITH ROLE INEFFECTIVENESS
RATINGS

| Inventory | Comparison Group | Frequencies and Per Cent Falling In | | Chi-Sq. | Probability |
		Low Conflict Group	High Conflict Group		
I	Ineffective	4(21)	15(79)	0.027	.80–.90
	All others	26(30)	60(70)		
II	Ineffective	8(40)	12(60)	6.120	.01–.02
	All others	60(72)	23(28)		

methods, and instruments. The criterion was of course imperfect, and it is not unreasonable to assume that higher relationships might have resulted if a more objective and reliable criterion had been available. It seems clear, however, that ineffectiveness in the performance of a role is related to the degree of personal involvement in role conflict.

It may also be noted that although the chi-square calculations were made for extreme groups, a relatively large number of cases were included. For Inventory I, 105 cases or 53 per cent of the total number were used, and for Inventory II, 103 or 62 per cent of the cases were used. Thus the findings are based on a fairly large proportion of the cases and are not contingent upon a small group of extreme isolates.

4. *Individual Differences.* In addition to the effectiveness material, certain descriptive and attitudinal data gathered by the Personal Questionnaire were analyzed for relationships with conflict scores on Inventory II. Comparison groups were formed for each datum, either by dividing the distribution at the mean for continuous variables (such as age), or by using the natural groups for dichotomous or categorical variables (such as rank). The groups were compared in terms of their mean Inventory II conflict scores by means of t tests. On the basis of these analyses, it is possible to describe instructors who tend to have significantly *higher* conflict scores (as measured by Inventory II) as follows:

1. Instructors who have been officers for nine years or less, as compared with officers of more than nine years service ($P = .05–.10$).

2. Instructors who are not rated (i.e. not on flying status and not receiving flying pay) as compared with rated instructors ($P = .05–.10$).

3. Instructors who have been overseas 27 months or less, as compared with instructors of longer overseas service ($P = .05–.10$).

4. Instructors who did not volunteer for duty at Air University, as compared with instructors who did volunteer ($P = .05$).

5. Instructors who were not given an opportunity to refuse assignment to Air University, as compared with instructors who had such opportunity ($P = .05$).

6. Instructors assigned to teach in a course not in line with their felt interests, as compared with instructors not so assigned ($P = .01–.02$).

7. Instructors assigned to teach in a course not in line with their felt competence, as compared with instructors not so assigned ($P = .01$).

The results with respect to the descriptive and attitudinal variables are entirely in the expected direction. Consider, for example, the fact that greater conflict scores are obtained by officer-instructors who did not volunteer for teaching duty, who did not have an opportunity to refuse the assignment, who are required to teach subject matter not in line with their interests, and who feel that they are teaching material not within their sphere of competence. The relationship between the indicated factors and intensity of conflict in the situation is logically consistent. Instructors teaching against their wishes, interests, felt competencies may reasonably be expected to be less tolerant of the situational pressures described in the role conflict inventories. That the findings are in fact precisely of this order tends not only to confirm the specific hypothesis under examination but lends support to the general framework and techniques on which the study as a whole is based.

DISCUSSION

Theoretical considerations suggest two variables as crucial to the analysis of role conflict: a situational variable and a personalistic variable. Situationally, it was postulated that the *extent* of role conflict varied as a function of the incompatibility of the role expectations. Differential role expectations were known to exist among the several schools under study according to their task and personnel. The measured differences in the extent of role conflict among these schools conformed to the theoretical expectations. It was postulated that the *intensity* of involvement in role conflict varied as a function of certain individual and attitudinal characteristics, and that there was a systematic relationship between the intensity of involvement in role conflict and role effectiveness. The empirical data were again in line with the theoretical expectations.

The foregoing findings do not, however, explicate the points of articulation between role conflict, personality, and effectiveness. The fact that the indicated relationships have been shown to exist does not by itself provide an understanding of the mechanisms involved in the relationship. The question here is: Since many situations do objectively contain role conflicts, what is the nature of successful and unsuccessful resolution of the conflicts for the individual? More specifically with reference to the present study, how did individuals who resolved the situational conflicts differ in the handling of the conflicts from those who did not resolve the conflicts successfully?

Detailed study is now in progress along the lines laid down by the foregoing problem, but certain preliminary observations

may be presented here.[8] Theoretically, an individual in a role conflict situation may resolve the conflict—always omitting the possibility of changing the situation or withdrawing from it entirely—either by compromise or exclusion. He may attempt to stand midway between the conflicting roles, giving equal due to both roles, shifting from one to another as he believes the occasion demands, or he may choose one role as his significant frame of reference and assimilate all other roles in the situation to it. In actual practice it would seem that the situation at Air University—and one may well wonder whether this is not general to most situations—establishes the latter alternative as the one more likely to find acceptance. There seems to be a *major role* to which one must commit himself in order to determine his action at choice points, despite contrary expectations attaching to other roles he may simultaneously occupy.

If, for example, an officer has elected to remain in service and to make a career of being a professional military man, he has by this act chosen a major role for himself in the same sense as has the academician, lawyer, or teacher. With the choice comes a set of expectations that his group holds binding upon him and that cannot be ignored without liability to severe sanctions from the group. When an officer is confronted with role conflict in which the officer role is one of the conflicting roles, successful handling of the conflict requires him to make his decisions in accordance with the expectations of the officer role, even at considerable cost to successful fulfillment of the other roles.

What then about the choice of the alternative role, that of teacher as the major role in the situation under study? Or more generally, of two possible roles within a situation what are the criteria for the choice of the appropriate major role for the individual? The concept of *major role* achieves significance here when taken in conjunction

---

[8] Data are now being gathered in a further study at Air University. These studies are part of a series outlined earlier by one of the authors. See J. W. Getzels, "A Psycho-Sociological Framework for the Study of Educational Administration," *Harvard Educational Review*, XXII (Fall, 1952), pp. 235-46.

with two additional concepts, that of *legitimacy of expectations* and of *congruence of needs and expectations*.

Ackerman[9] has already pointed out that the extent to which a role is successfully handled is a function of the degree of overlap between the role expectations and the actor's own needs. The individual is most likely to handle best from among several roles the one whose expectations are most nearly congruent with his needs. In fact, the individual will ordinarily seek out a role or create one that permits the expression of specific personality needs. An actor, therefore, placed in a role conflict situation, will probably choose as his major role the one that is most compatible with his needs and will assimilate other competing roles to it as the frame of reference.

In many instances, especially in situations that are relatively laissez-faire or permissive in structure, the choice of major role in terms only of personal need proves a sufficient criterion. In general, however, the choice cannot be left so cavalierly to personal need alone. Personal need is a necessary but not sufficient criterion. It is in this connection that the concept of *legitimacy of expectations* must be applied.

No matter what major role an actor may select, he must face the realities of the situation in which he finds himself. He cannot long ignore the legitimate expectations of others upon him without retaliation from them. None of the Air University officer-instructors, whatever his personal predilection, may with impunity overlook the fact that he is part of a military organization. Moreover, it is clear that he will eventually (perhaps soon) be reassigned to a military command rather than to another teaching position—at most the tour of duty at the University is three years. That the situation is so ordered places added legitimacy upon the officer role over and above the instructor role.

In addition then to the often-recognized personalistic criterion of congruence of needs and expectations for the choice of an appropriate major role, there is the equally significant situational criterion of legitimacy of expectations. If the individual chooses as his major role the one that is also the legitimate role in the situation he is less likely to be affected by conflicts or the threat of sanctions than when he chooses some alternate role. The instructor in a military establishment who thinks of himself as an officer first and as a teacher second is not too disturbed by conflicting expectations from the teacher role. He assimilates all expectations to his major role. He is, to use again the instance of the most discriminating item in the present study, not troubled that "military rank rather than teaching experience or competence too often determine the position that an officer will receive at Air University." Indeed, as has been remarked, he will ask how else is position to be determined in the military setting. Certainly not by such ephemeral requirements as teaching accomplishment, for after all, an officer may be a teacher for a few years, but he is an officer for a lifetime. An officer may be required to perform a variety of tasks, and if one of them involves teaching, it may be subsumed under the officer role. The officer role is the more legitimate role, and if the officer-instructor makes all his decisions at choice points in terms of this role, he will not be called to task for having erred.

Consider, on the other hand, the officer-instructor who thinks of himself as a teacher first and an officer second. He is stripped of a general frame of reference for decision making. Unlike his colleagues, he is very troubled that "military rank rather than teaching experience too often determines position" in his school. He is troubled too that the "recognition given an instructor may depend more on the insignia on his collar than on his knowledge of the subject matter." And so on. He is troubled because he is making decisions in terms of the teacher role when the dominant expectations and the appropriate decisions in the situation, whether he likes it or not, are made in terms of the officer role. The officer-instructor at Air University who chooses as his major role the instructor rather than the officer role is more likely to be involved in

---

[9] Ackerman, Nathan W., "Social Role and Total Personality," *American Journal of Orthopsychiatry,* XXI (January, 1951), pp. 1–17.

conflict because his major role is not also the legitimate role. It is noteworthy that it is the officer-instructor trained in a civilian specialty, say lawyer, and required to teach this civilian subject matter who is in more conflict than the officer-instructor trained in a military specialty teaching military subject matter. And it is the officer-instructor with many years service as officer, that is at least well committed to the military role, who is in less conflict at Air University than the officer-instructor with less service as officer.

There has been a tendency to place emphasis in the study of role effectiveness on the relative congruence of personality needs and role expectations. This, it seems to us,

is a necessary condition but by no means a sufficient one. It is also necessary that the expectations that are engaged by the needs be the more legitimate ones within the total setting. We would hold that in a role conflict situation the sufficient conditions for role effectiveness, technical skill aside, are twofold: the congruence of personality needs and role expectations *and* the choice of a major role that is the more legitimate one. Further clarification of the effective handling of role conflict might well be pushed forward within the three concepts involved in these conditions: the choice of major role, the congruence of needs and expectations, and the legitimacy of expectations within the situation.

Contraculture and Subculture / J. Milton Yinger (*Oberlin College*)

Current sociological work makes extensive use of the concept of subculture—in the analysis of delinquency, adolescence, regional and class differences, religious sects, occupational styles, and other topics. In the study of these areas, our understanding has been increased by seeing norms that vary from more general standards as manifestations, in part, of distinctive sub-societies. Unfortunately, however, the term subculture is used in several different ways. In over 100 sources reviewed here, three clearly different meanings are found, with resultant imprecision in its application. A new term contraculture, *is suggested in order to distinguish between normative systems of sub-societies and emergent norms that appear in conflict situations. The usefulness of this distinction is explored with reference to several substantive areas of research.*

In recent years there has been widespread and fruitful employment of the concept of subculture in sociological and anthropological research. The term has been used to focus attention not only on the wide diversity of norms to be found in many societies but on the normative aspects of deviant behavior. The ease with which the term has been adopted, with little study of its exact meaning or its values and its difficulties, is indicative of its utility in emphasizing a sociological point of view in research that has been strongly influenced both by individual-

istic and moralistic interpretations. To describe the normative qualities of an occupation, to contrast the value systems of social classes, or to emphasize the controlling power of the code of a delinquent gang is to underline a sociological aspect of these phenomena that is often disregarded.

In the early days of sociology and anthropology, a key task was to document the enormous variability of culture from society to society and to explore the significance of the overly simplified but useful idea that "the mores can make anything right." In recent years that task has been extended to the study of the enormous variability of culture *within* some societies. It is unfortunate that "subculture," a central concept in this

Reprinted from *The American Sociological Review*, 1960, 25, pages 625–635, by permission of author and publisher, The American Sociological Association.

process, has seldom been adequately de-fined.[1] It has been used as an *ad hoc* concept whenever a writer wished to emphasize the normative aspects of behavior that differed from some general standard. The result has been a blurring of the meaning of the term, confusion with other terms, and a failure frequently to distinguish between two levels of social causation.

THREE USAGES OF SUBCULTURE

Few concepts appear so often in current sociological writing. In the course of twelve months, I have noted over 100 books and articles that make some use, from incidental to elaborate, of the idea of "subculture." The usages vary so widely, however, that the value of the term is severely limited. If chemists had only one word to refer to all colorless liquids and this led them to pay attention to only the two characteristics shared in common, their analysis would be exceedingly primitive. Such an analogy overstates the diversity of ideas covered by "subculture," but the range is very wide. Nevertheless three distinct meanings can be described.

In some anthropological work, subculture refers to certain universal tendencies that seem to occur in all societies. They underlie

culture, precede it, and set limits to the range of its variation. Thus Kroeber writes: "Indeed, such more or less recurrent near-regularities of form or process as have to date been formulated for culture are actually subcultural in nature. They are limits set to culture by physical or organic factors."[2] In *The Study of Man,* Linton uses subculture to refer to various pan-human phenomena that seem to occur everywhere. Thus good-natured and tyrannical parents may be found in societies that differ widely in their family patterns.[3] This use shades off into other concepts that are similar but not iden-tical: Edward Sapir's "precultural" and Cooley's "human nature" refer to biological and social influences that underlie all cul-tures.[4] Since subculture is only rarely used today to refer to this series of ideas, I shall exclude them from further consideration, with the suggestion that the use of Sapir's term "precultural" might well clarify our thinking.

Two other usages of subculture represent a much more serious confusion. The term is often used to point to the normative systems of groups smaller than a society, to give emphasis to the ways these groups differ in such things as language, values, religion, diet, and style of life from the larger society of which they are a part. Perhaps the most common referent in this usage is an ethnic enclave (French Canadians in Maine) or a region (the subculture of the South),[5] but

---

[1] There are a few formal definitions. For ex-ample: "The term 'subculture' refers in this paper to 'cultural variants displayed by certain segments of the population.' Subcultures are distinguished not by one or two isolated traits—they constitute relatively cohesive cultural systems. They are worlds within the larger world of our national culture." (Mirra Komarovsky and S. S. Sargent, "Research into Subcultural Influences upon Per-sonality," in S. S. Sargent and M. W. Smith, edi-tors, *Culture and Personality,* New York: The Viking Fund, 1949, p. 143.) These authors then refer to class, race, occupation, residence, and re-gion. After referring to sub-group values and language, Kimball Young and Raymond W. Mack state: "Such shared learned behaviors which are common to a specific group or category are called *subcultures.*" (*Sociology and Social Life,* New York: American Book, 1959, p. 49.) They refer then to ethnic, occupational, and regional variations. Blaine Mercer writes: "A society contains numer-ous subgroups, each with its own characteristic ways of thinking and acting. These cultures within a culture are called *subcultures.*" (*The Study of Society,* New York: Harcourt-Brace, 1958, p. 34.) Thereafter he discusses Whyte's *Street-corner So-ciety.* Although these definitions are helpful, they fail to make several distinctions which are devel-oped below.

[2] A. L. Kroeber, "The Concept of Culture in Science," *Journal of General Education,* 3 (April, 1949), p. 187. See also Clyde Kluckhohn's refer-ence to this idea in "Culture and Behavior," in Gardner Lindzey, editor, *Handbook of Social Psy-chology,* Cambridge: Addison-Wesley, 1954, Vol. 2, p. 954; and A. L. Kroeber in "Problems of Proc-ess: Results," in Sol Tax *et al.,* editors, *An Ap-praisal of Anthropology Today,* Chicago: Univer-sity of Chicago Press, 1953, p. 119.

[3] Ralph Linton, *The Study of Man,* New York: Appleton-Century, 1936, p. 486. See also his *The Cultural Background of Personality,* New York: Appleton-Century-Crofts, 1945, pp. 148–151. Else-where in *The Study of Man,* Linton uses subculture in a different sense, similar to the second usage de-scribed below.

[4] Edward Sapir, "Personality," in *Encyclopedia of the Social Sciences,* New York: Macmillan, 1931, Vol. 12, p. 86; Charles H. Cooley, *Human Nature and the Social Order,* revised edition, New York: Scribner, 1922.

[5] See, e.g., John K. Morland, *Millways of Kent,* Chapel Hill: University of North Carolina Press, 1958; Julian Steward, *The People of Puerto Rico,*

the distinctive norms of much smaller and more temporary groups (even a particular friendship group) may be described as a subculture. Kluckhohn, for example, refers to "the subculture of anthropologists" and Riesman to "subcultures among the faculty."

This second meaning, which itself contains some ambiguities, as we shall see, must be distinguished from a third meaning associated with it when the reference is to norms that arise specifically from a frustrating situation or from conflict between a group and the larger society. Thus the emergent norms of a delinquent gang or the standards of an adolescent peer group have often been designated "subcultural." In addition to a cultural dimension, this third usage introduces a social-psychological dimension, for there is direct reference to the personality factors involved in the development and maintenance of the norms. Specifically, such personality tendencies as frustration, anxiety, feelings of role ambiguity, and resentment are shown to be involved in the creation of the subculture. The mutual influence of personality and culture is not a distinctive characteristic of this type of subculture, of course, for they are everywhere interactive. Thus:

> Tendencies for parents to respond harshly to their children's aggressive behavior, for instance, if common to the members of a society, are to be referred equally to the culture and to the modal personality of the parents. But the result in the developing child is not a foregone conclusion: present knowledge suggests that under specifiable conditions outcomes as different as rigid politeness or touchy latent hostility may follow. These consequences in turn may lead to cultural elaborations that seem superficially remote from the cultural starting point, yet are dynamically linked with it. . . .[6]

As this quotation suggests, culture and personality are always empirically tied together. Yet the nature of the relation is not the same in all cases. The term subculture, when used in the third way described here, raises to a position of prominence one particular kind of dynamic linkage between norms and personality: the creation of a series of inverse or counter values (opposed to those of the surrounding society) in face of serious frustration or conflict. To call attention to the special aspects of this kind of normative system, I suggest the term *contraculture*. Before exploring the relationship between subculture and contraculture, however, the range of meanings given subculture even when it is limited to the second usage requires comment.

SUBCULTURE AND ROLE

The variety of referents for the term subculture is very wide because the normative systems of sub-societies can be differentiated on many grounds. The groups involved may range from a large regional subdivision to a religious sect with only one small congregation. The distinctive norms may involve many aspects of life—religion, language, diet, moral values—or, for example, only a few separate practices among the members of an occupational group. Further distinctions among subcultures might be made on the basis of time (has the subculture persisted through a number of generations?), origin (by migration, absorption

Champaign: University of Illinois Press, 1956; Charles Wagley and Marvin Harris, "A Typology of Latin American Subcultures," *American Anthropologist,* 57 (June, 1955), pp. 428–451; Evon Z. Vogt, "American Subcultural *Continua* as Exemplified by the Mormons and Texans," *American Anthropologist,* 57 (December, 1955), pp. 1163–1172; Murray Straus, "Subcultural Variations in Ceylonese Mental Ability: A Study in National Character," *Journal of Social Psychology,* 39 (February, 1954), pp. 129–141; Joel B. Montague and Edgar G. Epps, "Attitudes Toward Social Mobility as Revealed by Samples of Negro and White Boys," *Pacific Sociological Review,* 1 (Fall, 1958), pp. 81–84; Hylan Lewis, *Blackways of Kent,* Chapel Hill: University of North Carolina Press, 1955; Robin M. Williams, Jr., *American Society,* New York: Knopf, 1951, Chapter 10; T. S. Langner, "A Test of Intergroup Prejudice Which Takes Account of Individual and Group Differences in Values," *Journal of Abnormal and Social Psychology,* 48 (October, 1953), pp. 548–554.

[6] Brewster Smith, "Anthropology and Psychology," in John Gillin, editor, *For a Science of Social Man,* New York: Macmillan, 1954, p. 61. See also Talcott Parsons and Edward A. Shils, editors, *Toward A General Theory of Action,* Cambridge: Harvard University Press, 1951, esp. the monograph by the editors; and Ralph Linton's preface to Abram Kardiner, *The Psychological Frontiers of Society,* New York: Columbia University Press, 1945.

by a dominant society, social or physical segregation, occupational specialization, and other sources), and by the mode of relationship to the surrounding culture (from indifference to conflict). Such wide variation in the phenomena covered by a term can be handled by careful specification of the several grounds for sub-classification. Confusion has arisen not so much from the scope of the term subculture as from its use as a substitute for "role." Only with great effort is some degree of clarity being achieved in the use of the role concept and the related terms "position" and "role behavior."[7] Were this development retarded by confusion of role with subculture it would be unfortunate. All societies have differentiating roles, but only heterogeneous societies have subcultures. Role is *that part of* a full culture that is assigned, as the appropriate rights and duties, to those occupying a given position.[8] These rights and duties usually interlock into a system with those of persons who occupy other positions. They are known to and accepted by all those who share the culture. Thus the role of a physician is known, at least in vague outline, by most persons in a society and it is seen as part of the total culture. (This is not to prejudge the question of role consensus, for there may be many non-role aspects of being a physician.) But subculture is not tied in this way into the larger cultural complex: it refers to norms that set a group apart from, not those that integrate a group with, the total society. Subcultural norms, as contrasted with role norms, are unknown to, looked down upon, or thought of as separating forces by the other members of a society. There are doubtless subcultural aspects of being a physician—normative influences affecting his behavior that are not

part of his role, not culturally designated rights and duties. But the empirical mixture should not obscure the need for this analytic distinction.

Along with confusion with the role concept, subculture carries many of the ambiguities associated with the parent concept of culture. In much social scientific writing it is not at all clear whether culture refers to norms, that is, to expected or valued behavior, or to behavior that is widely followed and therefore normal in a statistical sense only. This dual referent is particularly likely to be found in the work of anthropologists. Perhaps because their concepts are derived largely from the study of relatively more stable and homogeneous societies, they draw less sharply the distinction between the statistically normal and the normative. Sociologists are more apt to find it necessary to explore the tensions between the social order and culture, to be alert to deviations, and they are therefore more likely to define culture abstractly as a shared normative system. Yet much of the commentary on subculture refers to behavior. In my judgment this identification is unwise. Behavior is the result of the convergence of many forces. One should not assume, when the members of a group behave in similar ways, that cultural norms produce this result. Collective behavior theory and personality theory may also help to account for the similarities.

CONTRACULTURE

Failure to distinguish between role and subculture and vagueness in the concept of culture itself are not the only difficulties in the use of the idea of subculture. Perhaps more serious is the tendency to obscure, under this one term, two levels of explanation, one sociological and the other social-psychological, with a resulting failure to understand the causal forces at work. On few topics can one get wider agreement among sociologists than on the dangers of reductionism. If a psychologist attempts to explain social facts by psychological theories, we throw the book (probably Durkheim) at him; we emphasize the "fallacy of misplaced concreteness." In view of the

[7] See, e.g., Neal Gross, Ward S. Mason, and A. W. McEachern, *Explorations in Role Analysis,* New York: Wiley, 1958; F. L. Bates, "Position, Role, and Status: A Reformulation of Concepts," *Social Forces,* 34 (May, 1956), pp. 313–321; Robert K. Merton, "The Role-Set: Problems in Sociological Theory," *British Journal of Sociology,* 8 (June, 1957), pp. 106–120; S. F. Nadel, *The Theory of Social Structure,* New York: Free Press of Glencoe, Inc., 1957; Theodore R. Sarbin, "Role Theory," in *Handbook of Social Psychology, op. cit.,* Vol. 1, Chapter 6.

[8] It is possible, of course, for a subculture to specify roles within its own system.

widespread neglect of socio-cultural factors in the explanation of behavior, this is a necessary task. It makes vitally important, however, keen awareness by sociologists that they also deal with an abstract model. Perhaps we can reverse Durkheim's dictum to say: Do not try to explain social psychological facts by sociological theories; or, more adequately, do not try to explain *behavior* (a product of the interaction of sociocultural and personality influences) by a sociological theory alone. Yablonsky has recently reminded us that an excessively sociological theory of gangs can result in our seeing a definite group structure and a clear pattern of norms where in fact there is a "near-group," with an imprecise definition of boundaries and limited agreement on norms.[9] Carelessly used, our concepts can obscure the facts we seek to understand.

To see the cultural element in delinquency or in the domination of an individual by his adolescent group, phenomena that on the surface are non-cultural or even "anti-cultural," was a long step forward in their explanation. But it is also necessary to see the non-cultural aspects of some "norms"— phenomena that on the surface seem thoroughly cultural. Our vocabulary needs to be rich enough to help us to deal with these differences. The tendency to use the same term to refer to phenomena that share *some* elements in common, disregarding important differences, is to be content with phyla names when we need also to designate genus and species.

To sharpen our analysis, I suggest the use of the term contraculture wherever the normative system of a group contains, as a primary element, a theme of conflict with the values of the total society, where personality variables are directly involved in the development and maintenance of the group's values, and wherever its norms can be understood only by reference to the relationships of the group to a surrounding dominant culture.[10] None of these criteria

definitely separates contraculture from subculture because each is a continuum. Subsocieties fall along a range with respect to each criterion. The values of most subcultures probably conflict in some measure with the larger culture. In a contraculture, however, the conflict element is central; many of the values, indeed, are specifically contradictions of the values of the dominant culture. Similarly, personality variables are involved in the development and maintenance of all cultures and subcultures, but usually the influence of personality is by way of variations around a theme that is part of the culture. In a contraculture, on the other hand, the theme itself expresses the tendencies of the persons who compose it. Finally, the norms of all subcultures are doubtless

---

[9] Lewis Yablonsky, "The Delinquent Gang as a Near-Group," *Social Problems*, 7 (Fall, 1959), pp. 108–117.

[10] By the noun in "contraculture" I seek to call attention to the normative aspects of the phenomena under study and by the qualifying prefix to call attention to the conflict aspects. Similar terms are occasionally found in the literature, but they are either defined only by their use in context or are used differently from the meaning assigned to contraculture in this paper. Harold D. Lasswell uses the term "countermores" to refer to "culture patterns which appeal mainly to the *id* . . ." (*World Politics and Personal Insecurity*, New York: McGraw-Hill, 1935, p. 64). He then designates "revolutionists, prostitutes, prisoners, obscene and subversive talk"—which scarcely suggest a clear analytic category. In *World Revolutionary Propaganda*, New York: Knopf, 1939, Lasswell and Dorothy Blumenstock discuss the use of inverse values as a revolutionary propaganda weapon and comment on the presumed vulnerability of deprived persons to the countermores stressed in this propaganda. In *Power and Society*, New Haven: Yale University Press, 1950, p. 49, Lasswell uses the term somewhat differently: "*Countermores* are culture traits symbolized by the group as deviations from the mores, and yet are expected to occur." A certain amount of bribery, for example, is "normal" "and must be included by the candid observer as part of culture."

At various points, Talcott Parsons more nearly approaches the meaning of the concept contraculture as used here, although more by implication than by direct definition, and without distinguishing it from the concept of subculture. Referring to the ideological aspects of a subculture, he writes: "In such cases of an open break with the value-system and ideology of the wider society we may speak of a 'counter-ideology.'" (*The Social System*, New York: Free Press of Glencoe, Inc., 1951, p. 355.) And later: "If, however, the culture of the deviant group, like that of the delinquent gang, remains a 'counter-culture' it is difficult to find the bridges by which it can acquire influence over wider circles" (p. 522). It is not clear from these uses how counter-ideology and counter-culture are to be defined; but the important place Parsons gives to the element of ambivalence in his use of the concept subculture suggests that he has in mind something similar to our concept of contraculture in his use of these various terms. (See *ibid.*, p. 286.)

affected in some degree by the nature of the relationship with the larger culture. A subculture, as a pure type, however, does not require, for its understanding, intensive analysis of interaction with the larger culture; that is, its norms are not, to any significant degree, a product of that interaction. But a contraculture can be understood only by giving full attention to the interaction of the group which is its bearer with the larger society. It is one thing to say that the subculture of the rural, lower-class Negro encourages slow, inefficient work. It is another thing to say, with Charles S. Johnson, that such a norm represents "pseudo-ignorant malingering," a contracultural way of describing the same phenomenon. Johnson stressed the conflict element, the extent to which the norm was a product of interaction of white and Negro. There is certainly value in emphasizing the subcultural source of some of the values of southern Negroes. Against racist views or individual explanations, the sociologist opposes the subcultural: If they strive less, have different sexual mores, or otherwise vary from standards of the dominant society, it is in part because they have been socialized in accordance with different norms. But this is not enough, for their similar behavior may be interpreted in part as a shared response to a frustrating environment.

Empirically, subcultural and contracultural influences may be mixed, of course. Delinquency and adolescent behavior almost certainly manifest both influences. The need, however, is to develop a clean analytic distinction between the two in order to interpret the wide variations in their mixture.

ADOLESCENT SUBCULTURE AND CONTRACULTURE

The utility of the distinction between contraculture and subculture can be tested by applying it to several research problems where the concept of subculture has been widely used. There is an extensive literature that interprets the behavior of adolescents substantially in these terms.[11] In the words

of Havighurst and Taba: "Recent studies of adolescents have emphasized the fact that boys and girls in their teens have a culture of their own with moral standards and with moral pressures behind those standards. This culture has been called the 'adolescent peer culture.'"[12] Or Riesman: "All the morality is the group's. Indeed, even the fact that it is a morality is concealed by the confusing notion that the function of the group is to have fun, to play. . . ."[13] A close reading of the literature on adolescent culture reveals at least four different levels of interpretation, often only partially distinguished:

1. There is a cultural level, in which the roles of adolescent boys and girls are described, or the specialties (in Linton's sense) are designated. There is no reason to introduce concepts other than role or specialty to refer to norms that are generally accepted by elders and youths alike as appropriate to youth.

2. On the subcultural level, there are norms that manifest some separate system of values accepted within the adolescent group. These norms are not part of the role of youth. In part they are unknown to the elders; in part they conflict with standards accepted by the elders. They are learned, not by socialization in the total society, but by interaction within the sub-society of youth. Thus interests, games, speech patterns, and aesthetic tastes may be com-

---

[11] See Talcott Parsons, *Essays in Sociological Theory Pure and Applied,* New York: Free Press of Glencoe, Inc., 1949, Chapter 5; Howard Becker, *German Youth: Bond or Free,* New York: Oxford, 1946; S. N. Eisenstadt, *From Generation to Generation. Age Groups and the Social Structure,* New York: Free Press of Glencoe, Inc., 1956; David Riesman *et al., The Lonely Crowd,* New Haven: Yale University Press, 1950; R. J. Havighurst and Hilda Taba, *Adolescent Character and Personality,* New York: Wiley, 1949; Kingsley Davis, "The Sociology of Parent-Youth Conflict," *American Sociological Review,* 5 (August, 1940), pp. 523–534; Ralph Linton, "Age and Sex Categories," *American Sociological Review,* 7 (October, 1942), pp. 589–603; Joseph R. Gusfield, "The Problem of Generations in an Organizational Structure," *Social Forces,* 35 (May, 1957), pp. 323–330. For some contradictory evidence, see W. A. Westley and Frederick Elkin, "The Protective Environment and Adolescent Socialization," *Social Forces,* 35 (March, 1957), pp. 243–249; and Elkin and Westley, "The Myth of Adolescent Culture," *American Sociological Review,* 20 (December, 1955), pp. 680–684.

[12] *Op. cit.,* p. 35.

[13] *Op. cit.,* p. 72.

municated among an age-group with little reference to the larger culture.

3. There are currents of fashion or of other collective behavior that sweep through an adolescent group, strongly influencing the behavior of its members.[14] Although it is difficult to distinguish fashion from culture —many empirical phenomena have aspects of both—it is wise to keep them apart conceptually. This is not always done. The terminology of Riesman is closer to that of fashion than of culture, but the net impression of his analysis is that he is thinking of control by the peer group primarily as a cultural phenomenon.[15] And the sentence following the one quoted above from Havighurst and Taba reads: "Boys and girls, desiring the approval of their age mates, follow the fashions of the peer culture in morals, dress, and speech. . . ." If the peer group influence stems from fashion, then strictly speaking it is not culture. The two differ to some degree in their origins, their functions, and their consequences.[16]

4. Many analyses of the control exercised by a youth group over its members employ the *concept* of contraculture, although the terminology and the assumptions are often those of subculture or culture. There is emphasis on the cross-pressures which young people feel: they want to be adults, yet fear to leave the securities of childhood; they experience contradictory adult treatment—a demand for grownup behavior here, the prevention of it there; ambiguity of self-image leads to efforts to prove oneself a fullfledged adult; there is sexual frustration. The peer group may help one to struggle with these cross-pressures, as described by Parsons: "Perhaps the best single point of reference for characterizing the youth culture lies in its contrast with the dominant pattern of the adult male role. By contrast with emphasis on responsibility in this role, the orientation of the youth culture is more or less specifically irresponsible."[17] This irresponsibility cannot be understood simply as another cultural norm, as part of the "role" of youth, although these are Parsons' terms. It must be studied in the context of strain, of role ambiguity. Some sociologists explain this irresponsibility as merely a manifestation of the youth culture, thus obscuring the personality factors also involved. The description and analysis of an adolescent subculture, to be sure, are an important contribution to the sociology of youth. Many adolescents spend a great deal of time in groups that sustain norms different from those of the adult world; and adults often respond to the behavior that follows these norms in an "ethnocentric" way. To rely on a subcultural explanation alone, however, is to disregard the emergent quality of many of the standards and to minimize the fact that they are often in direct conflict with adult standards (which most adolescents themselves will soon accept).

This sharp conflict of values requires explanation. Parsons states the facts clearly: "Negatively, there is a strong tendency to repudiate interests in adult things, and to feel at least a certain recalcitrance to the pressure of adult expectations and disciplines. . . . Thus the youth culture is not only, as is true of the curricular aspects of formal education, a matter of age status as such but also shows signs of being a product of tensions in the relationship of younger people and adults."[18] At several other points Parsons develops the "reaction" theme and later uses the concept of "reaction-formation."[19] Should these various phenomena be subsumed under the concept of culture? It is one thing for a society to train its youth to certain ways of behaving. It is quite another for a youth group to develop inverse values in an effort to struggle with role

---

[14] See Harold Finestone, "Cats, Kicks, and Color," *Social Problems,* 5 (July, 1957), pp. 3–13. Here the "cat" among some Negroes is seen as "the personal counterpart of an expressive social movement."

[15] See Riesman, *op. cit.,* esp. Chapter 3, "A Jury of Their Peers."

[16] The desirability of keeping distinct the analytic concepts of culture and collective behavior, including fashion, cannot be elaborated here. See Herbert Blumer, "Collective Behavior," in A. M. Lee, editor, *Principles of Sociology,* New York: Barnes and Nobel, 1951; Ralph H. Turner and Lewis M. Killian, *Collective Behavior,* Englewood Cliffs, N.J.: Prentice-Hall, 1957; Edward Sapir, "Fashion," *Encyclopedia of the Social Sciences,* New York: Macmillan, 1931, Vol. 6, pp. 139–144; Georg Simmel, "Fashion," *American Journal of Sociology,* 62 (May, 1957), pp. 541–558.

[17] Parsons, *op. cit. Essays . . . ,* p. 92.

[18] *Ibid.,* pp. 92–93.

[19] See *ibid.,* pp. 101–102, 189–190, 342–345, 355.

ambiguities and strains. The adolescent may experience both as normative sanctions; but that should scarcely lead the social analyst to disregard their differences. I suggest the term contraculture in order to indicate the normative *and* the conflict aspects of this type of situation.

DELINQUENT CONTRACULTURE

The usefulness of separating subcultural and contracultural influences is seen particularly clearly in the analysis of delinquency and of criminality generally. Perhaps in no other field were there more substantial gains in understanding made possible by the introduction of a sociological point of view to supplement and to correct individualistic and moralistic interpretations. There is little need to review the extensive literature, from *Delinquent Gangs to Delinquent Boys,* to establish the importance of the normative element in criminal and delinquent behavior. It is a mistake, however, to try to stretch a useful concept into a total theory. A "complex-adequate" analysis[20] may seem less sharp and definitive than one based on one factor, but it is likely to be far more useful. Cohen's excellent work,[21] although labelled as a study of the culture of the gang, does not overlook the psychogenic sources of delinquency. In fact, his explanation of the origins of the subculture (contraculture) and its functions for the lower class male makes clear that the norms of the gang are not learned, accepted, and taught in the same way that we learn what foods to eat, what clothes to wear, what language to speak. The very existence of the gang is a sign, in part, of blocked ambition. Because tensions set in motion by this blockage cannot be resolved by achievement of dominant values, such values are repressed, their importance denied, counter-values affirmed. The gang member is often ambivalent. Thwarted in his desire to achieve higher status by the criteria of the dominant society, he accepts criteria he can meet; but the

reaction-formation in this response is indicated by the content of the delinquent norms—non-utilitarian, malicious, and negativistic, in Cohen's terms. This negative polarity represents the need to repress his own tendencies to accept the dominant cultural standards. This is not to say that the values of the gang cannot be explained partially by cultural analysis, by some extension of the idea that "the mores can make anything right." But I suggest that Cohen's multiple-factor analysis might have been clearer, and less subject to misinterpretation, had he introduced the concept of contraculture alongside the concept of subculture. One reviewer, for example, completely disregards the "negative polarity" theme:

> In an overall summary, cultural delinquency is a phenomenon of culture, society, and sociocultural experience. It is a positive thing: members of the several social classes are socialized, but there is a differential content in the socialization. Delinquency is not a negative thing; it is not a result of the breakdown of society, nor of the failure to curb criminal instincts, nor of the failure of the family, the church, or the school. The same set of concepts, the same social processes, and the same set of logical assumptions account for both delinquency and lawfulness. Since delinquency is of this character, it is unnecessary to invent any pathology to account for it.[22]

This statement neither adequately represents Cohen's thesis nor encourages us to explore a number of important questions: Why do only some of those who are exposed to the delinquent "subculture" learn it?[23] Why do those who follow the subculture often manifest ambivalence and guilt feelings?[24] Why do many of the same patterns of behavior occur in areas and among groups where the presence of the subculture is much less clear

[20] See Robin M. Williams, Jr., "Continuity and Change in Sociological Study," *American Sociological Review,* 23 (December, 1958), pp. 619–633.

[21] Albert K. Cohen, *Delinquent Boys,* New York: Free Press of Glencoe, Inc., 1955.

[22] Frank Hartung, in a review of *Delinquent Boys, American Sociological Review,* 20 (December, 1955), p. 752.

[23] See Solomon Kobrin, "The Conflict of Values in Delinquency Areas," *American Sociological Review,* 16 (October, 1951), pp. 653–661; Alex Inkeles, "Personality and Social Structure," in Robert K. Merton *et al.,* editors, *Sociology Today,* New York: Basic Books, 1959, p. 254.

[24] See Gresham M. Sykes and David Matza, "Techniques of Neutralization: A Theory of Delinquency," *American Sociological Review,* 22 (December, 1957), pp. 664–670.

(middle-class delinquency)?[25] What is the significance of the fact that the delinquent subculture is not only different from but in part at least a reversal of the values of the dominant culture? The use of a purely sub-cultural model of analysis discourages or even prevents the raising of these questions and thus precludes adequate answers to them.

Cohen and Short have dealt with several of these issues by suggesting the need for a typology. Specifically for the study of delinquency, they propose five types of sub-cultures: the parent male (the central pattern described in *Delinquent Boys*), the conflict-oriented, the drug addict, the semi-professional theft, and the middle-class sub-cultures.[26] Although the criteria of classification are not entirely clear, these categories are primarily descriptive. The concept of contraculture might be added to this list as a type of subculture, if the one distinctive criterion used to designate a subculture is the presence in a sub-society of a normative system that separates it from the total society. Such a procedure does not seem, however, to produce an adequate taxonomy. If the shift is made from description to analysis, or from an interest in the content of norms to their etiology, an important difference emerges between subculture and contraculture: the one set of norms derives from standard socialization in a sub-society; the other stems from conflict and frustration in the experience of those who share many of the values of the whole society but are thwarted in their efforts to achieve those values.

It should be stressed once more that these are analytic concepts, no one of which is adequate to handle the empirical variations of delinquent behavior. Failure to recognize the abstract quality of our conceptual tools leads to unnecessary disagreements. When Miller describes the "Lower Class Culture as a Generating Milieu of Gang Delinquency," for example, he points to an important series of influences that derive from

the value system of the lower-class community.[27] In his effort to emphasize this aspect of the etiology of delinquency, however, he tends to overlook the kind of evidence reported by Sykes and Matza, Cohen, Finestone, Yablonsky, the McCords, and others concerning collective behavior and personality variables.[28] Surely the evidence is now rich enough for us to state definitively that delinquency is a multi-variable product. The task ahead is not to prove that it stems largely from cultural or sub-cultural or contracultural influences, but to spell out the conditions under which these and other factors will be found in various empirical mixtures.[29]

CONTRACULTURAL ASPECTS OF CLASS AND OCCUPATION

The same admixture of the concepts of culture, subculture, and contraculture is found in the extensive literature on occupations and classes. Doubtless all three forces

[25] John I. Kitsuse and David C. Dietrick, "Delinquent Boys: A Critique," *American Sociological Review,* 24 (April, 1959), pp. 208–215.

[26] See Albert Cohen and James Short, "Research in Delinquent Subcultures," *The Journal of Social Issues,* 14, 3 (1958), pp. 20–37.

[27] Walter B. Miller, "Lower Class Culture as a Generating Milieu of Gang Delinquency," *The Journal of Social Issues,* 14, 3 (1958), pp. 5–19.

[28] In addition to the studies of Sykes and Matza, Cohen, Finestone, and Yablonsky cited above, see William McCord and Joan McCord, *Origins of Crime. A New Evaluation of the Cambridge-Somerville Youth Study,* New York: Columbia University Press, 1959.

[29] In a recent manuscript, Sykes and Matza suggest that delinquent behavior can profitably be studied as an exaggerated expression of certain "subterranean values" of the dominant society (the search for excitement, the use of "pull" to get by without too much work, and aggression). This idea deserves careful study. The main research task is to discover the conditions which promote selective and exaggerated attention to these values at the cost of neglect of the more prominent "public" values. It seems likely that this task will lead to the incorporation of the "subterranean values" thesis into the larger complex of theories of delinquency. The thesis raises a question of terminology in connection with the present paper: At what point does exaggerated emphasis on a value become a counter-value by virtue of the exaggeration? *Some* cultural support can be found in a complex society for many patterns of behavior that are not fully valued. A society may accept or even applaud a pattern that is used to a limited degree while condemning its extravagant use. And the meaning of the pattern in the life of the individual when found in culturally approved degree differs from what it is when the pattern becomes a dominant theme. To discover why some subterranean values are raised into a style of life, therefore, requires more than cultural analysis. (See Gresham M. Sykes and David Matza, "Juvenile Delinquency and Subterranean Values," unpublished manuscript, 1960.)

are found in many instances, and the research task is to untangle their various influences. It may stretch the meaning of the term too far to speak of the *position* of the "middle-class member," with its culturally designated role specifications; although in relatively stable societies the usage seems appropriate. In such societies, many of the rights and obligations of various status levels are culturally defined. In more mobile class systems, however, subcultural and contracultural norms become important. Our understanding of the American class system has certainly been deepened in the last twenty years by the descriptions of differences, among classes, in value perspectives, time orientations, levels of aspiration, leisure-time styles, and child rearing practices.[30]

The introduction of the concept of subculture has helped to avoid class derived biases in the interpretation of the wide variations in these phenomena. In class analysis as in the study of deviations, however, there may be some over-compensation in the effort to eliminate the distortions of a middle-class and often rural perspective.[31] There is evidence to suggest that differences between classes are based less upon different values and norms than the subcultural approach suggests. The "innovations" of lower-class members, to use Merton's term,

are not simply subcultural acts defined as innovative by middle-class persons. They are in part responses to a frustrating situation. They are efforts to deal with the disjunction of means and ends. When the disjunction is reduced, the variations in value and behavior are reduced. Thus Rosen found, "surprisingly," that Negroes in the Northeast made higher scores on an "achievement value" test than his description of Negro "culture" led him to expect. This may indicate that the low achievement response is less the result of a subcultural norm than a protest against a difficult situation. If the situation improves, the achievement value changes.[32] Stephenson's discovery that occupational plans of lower-class youth are considerably below those of higher-class youth, but that their aspirations are only slightly lower, bears on this same point. His data suggest that the classes differ not only in norms, but also in opportunity.[33] Differences in behavior, therefore, are only partly a result of subcultural contrasts. The lower educational aspirations of lower-class members are also found to be in part situationally induced, not simply normatively induced. When the situation changes, values and behavior change, as Mulligan found in his study of the response of the sons of blue-collar workers to the educational opportunities of the GI Bill, and as Wilson reports in his investigation of the aspirations of lower-class boys attending higher-class schools and upper-class boys attending lower-class schools.[34]

[30] Of the many studies in this area, see Charles McArthur, "Personality Differences Between Middle and Upper Classes," *Journal of Abnormal and Social Psychology,* 50 (March, 1955), pp. 247–254; Melvin L. Kohn, "Social Class and Parental Values," *American Journal of Sociology,* 64 (January, 1959), pp. 337–351; A. B. Hollingshead and Frederick C. Redlich, *Social Class and Mental Illness,* New York: Wiley, 1958; Clyde R. White, "Social Class Differences in the Uses of Leisure," *American Journal of Sociology,* 61 (September, 1955), pp. 145–151; John A. Clausen and Melvin L. Kohn, "The Ecological Approach in Social Psychiatry," *American Journal of Sociology,* 60 (September, 1954), pp. 140–151; A. B. Hollingshead, *Elmtown's Youth,* New York: Wiley, 1949; Louis Schneider and Sverre Lysgaard, "The Deferred Gratification Pattern: A Preliminary Study," *American Sociological Review,* 18 (April, 1953), pp. 142–149; Urie Bronfenbrenner, "Socialization and Social Class Through Time and Space," in Eleanor E. Maccoby *et al.,* editors, *Readings in Social Psychology,* New York: Holt, 1958, pp. 400–425.

[31] C. Wright Mills, "The Professional Ideology of Social Pathologists," *American Journal of Sociology,* 49 (September, 1943), pp. 165–180.

[32] Bernard C. Rosen, "Race, Ethnicity, and the Achievement Syndrome," *American Sociological Review,* 24 (February, 1959), pp. 47–60. It is highly important, in aspiration studies, to compare, not absolute levels, but the extent of aspiration above the existing level of individuals or their families. A low absolute target for lower-class members may require a larger *reach* than a higher target for middle-class persons. See Leonard Reissman, "Levels of Aspiration and Social Class," *American Sociological Review,* 18 (June, 1953), pp. 233–242.

[33] Richard M. Stephenson, "Mobility Orientation and Stratification of 1,000 Ninth Graders," *American Sociological Review,* 22 (April, 1957), pp. 204–212.

[34] Raymond A. Mulligan, "Socio-Economic Background and College Enrollment," *American Sociological Review,* 16 (April, 1951), pp. 188–196; Alan B. Wilson, "Residential Segregation of Social Classes and Aspirations of High School Boys," *American Sociological Review,* 24 (December, 1959), pp. 836–845.

In short, our thinking about differences in behavior among social classes will be sharpened if we distinguish among those differences that derive from role influences, those based on subcultural variations, and those that express contracultural responses to deprivation. The proportions will vary from society to society; the research task is to specify the conditions under which various distributions occur. One would expect, to propose one hypothesis, to find more contracultural norms among lower-class members of an open society than in a similar group in a closed society.

The interpretation of differential behavior among the members of various occupational categories can also be strengthened by the distinctions made above. Here the contrast between role and subculture is especially useful. The role of a teacher consists of the rights and duties that *integrate* him into a system of expected and established relationships with others. The teaching subculture, on the other hand, insofar as it exists, *separates* teachers from the cultural world of others. It is either unknown to others or, if known, a source of disagreement and perhaps of conflict with others. There are also contracultural aspects of some occupational styles of life. In interpreting the differences between the values of jazz musicians and "squares," for example, Becker writes: "their rejection of commercialism in music and squares in social life was part of the casting aside of the total American culture by men who could enjoy privileged status but who were unable to achieve a satisfactory personal adjustment within it."[35] Their style of life, in other words, can be understood only by supplementing the cultural and subcultural dimensions with the conflict theme. Cameron develops the same point. Although he makes no use of the term subculture, he describes the differentiating norms of the dance-band group, presumably a result of the "esoteric" aspects of their art, the differences in their time schedule, and the like. But he also describes the *contra* aspects of some of the norms, and suggests that they derive from the fact that

early recruitment ties the jazz musician to the adolescence problem.[36]

CONCLUSION

Poorly defined terms plague research in many areas, particularly in the specification of relationships between sociological and social psychological levels of analysis. Thus "anomie" is still used to refer both to a social structural fact and to a personality fact, although this confusion is gradually being reduced. "Role" may refer, alternately, to rights and duties prescribed for the occupants of a position or to individual performance of that position. And subculture, I have suggested, is used to designate both the traditional norms of a sub-society and the emergent norms of a group caught in a frustrating and conflict-laden situation. This paper indicates that there are differences in the origin, function, and perpetuation of traditional and emergent norms, and suggests that the use of the concept contraculture for the latter might improve sociological analysis.

Hypotheses to guide the study of subculture can most profitably be derived from a general theory of culture. As an illustration, it may be hypothesized that a subculture will appear, in the first instance, as a result of mobility or an extension of communication that brings groups of different cultural background into membership in the same society, followed by physical or social isolation or both that prevents full assimilation.

Hypotheses concerning contracultures, on the other hand, can best be derived from social psychological theory—from the study of collective behavior, the frustration-aggression thesis, or the theory of group formation. One might hypothesize, for example, that under conditions of deprivation and frustration of major values (in a context where the deprivation is obvious because of extensive communication with the dominant group), and where value confusion and weak social controls obtain, contracultural norms will appear. One would expect

[35] Howard S. Becker, "The Professional Dance Musician and His Audience," *American Journal of Sociology,* 57 (September, 1951), pp. 136–144.

[36] W. B. Cameron, "Sociological Notes on the Jam Session," *Social Forces,* 33 (December, 1954), pp. 177–182.

to find, according to these propositions, many subcultural values among southern rural Negroes. Among first and second generation urban Negroes, however, one would expect an increase in contracultural norms. Both groups are deprived, but in the urban situation there is more "value leakage" from the dominant group, more value confusion, and weakened social controls.[37]

The subculture of the sociologist requires

sophistication about the full range of human behavior. This desideratum has led to the proposition that the vast diversity of norms believed in and acted upon by the members of a modern society is not a sign of value confusion and breakdown but rather an indication that urban life brings into one system of interaction persons drawn from many cultural worlds. One unanticipated consequence of the sociological subculture may be that we exaggerate the normative insulation and solidarity of these various worlds. An important empirical question concerns the extent and results of their interaction.

[37] There are numerous alternative ways in which the protest against deprivation can be expressed. Delinquency and drug addiction often have a contracultural aspect; but somewhat less clearly, political and religious movements among disprivileged groups may also invert the values of the influential but inaccessible dominant group. Thus the concept of contraculture may help us to understand, for example, the Garveyite movement, the Ras Tafari cult, and some aspects of the value schemes of lower-class sects. (See, e.g., Liston Pope, *Millhands*

and Preachers, New Haven: Yale University Press, 1942; and George E. Simpson, "The Ras Tafari Movement in Jamaica: A Study of Race and Class Conflict," *Social Forces,* 34 (December, 1955), pp. 167-170.)

A Comparative Study of the Role of Values in Social Action in Two Southwestern Communities* /

Evon Z. Vogt (*Harvard University*)

and Thomas F. O'Dea (*Massachusetts Institute of Technology*)

It is one of the central hypotheses of the Values Study Project that value-orientations play an important part in the shaping of social institutions and in influencing the forms of observed social action. By value-orientations are understood those views of the world, often implicitly held, which define the meaning of human life or the "life situation of man" and thereby provide the context in which day-to-day problems are

solved.[1] The present article is an outgrowth of one phase of the field research carried out in western New Mexico. It presents the record of two communities composed of people with a similar cultural background and living in the same general ecological setting.

The responses of these two communities to similar problems were found to be quite different. Since the physical setting of the two villages is remarkably similar, the explanation for the differences was sought in the manner in which each group viewed the situation and the kind of social relationships and legitimate expectations which each felt appropriate in meeting situational challenges. In this sphere of value-orientations a marked difference was found. Moreover, the

Reprinted from *The American Sociological Review*, 1953, 18, pages 645–654, by permission of the senior author and publisher, The American Sociological Association.

* The authors are indebted to the Rockefeller Foundation (Social Science Division) for the financial support of the research reported in this paper as part of the Comparative Study of Values in Five Cultures Project of the Laboratory of Social Relations at Harvard University. We also wish to express our appreciation to Ethel M. Albert, Wilfrid C. Bailey, Clyde Kluckhohn, Anne Parsons, and John M. Roberts for criticisms and suggestions in the preparation of the paper.

[1] Clyde Kluckhohn, "Values and Value-Orientations in the Theory of Action: An Exploration in Definition and Classification," *Toward a General Theory of Action,* edited by Talcott Parsons and E. A. Shils, Cambridge: Harvard University Press, 1951, p. 410.

differences in response to situation in the two cases were found to be related to the differences between the value-orientations central to these communities.

We do not deny the importance of situational factors. Nor do we intend to disparage the importance of historical convergence of value-orientations with concrete situations in explaining the centrality of some values as against others and in leading to the deep internalization of the values we discuss. But the importance of value-orientations as an element in understanding the situation of action is inescapably clear. All the elements of what Parsons has called the action frame of reference—the actors, the means and conditions which comprise the situation, and the value-orientations of the actors enter into the act.[2] The primacy of any one in any individual case does not permit generalization. Yet the present study testifies to the great importance of the third element—the value-orientations—in shaping the final action which ensues.

FOCUS OF THE INQUIRY

The inquiry is focused upon a comparison of the Mormon community of *Rimrock*[3] with the Texan community of *Homestead*, both having populations of approximately 250 and both located (forty miles apart) on the southern portion of the Colorado Plateau in western New Mexico. The natural environmental setting is virtually the same for the two villages: the prevailing elevations stand at 7,000 feet; the landscapes are characterized by mesa and canyon country; the flora and fauna are typical of the Upper Sonoran Life Zone with stands of pinyon, juniper, sagebrush, and blue gramma grass and some intrusions of Ponderosa pine, Douglas fir, Englemann spruce and Gambel oak from a higher life zone; the region has a steppe climate with an average annual precipitation of 14 inches (which varies

greatly from year to year) and with killing frosts occurring late in the spring and early in the autumn.[4] The single important environmental difference between the two communities is that Rimrock is located near the base of a mountain range which has elevations rising to 9,000 feet, and a storage reservoir (fed by melting snow packs from these higher elevations) has made irrigation agriculture possible in Rimrock, while in Homestead there is only dry-land farming. Today both villages have subsistence patterns based upon combinations of farming (mainly irrigated crops of alfalfa and wheat in Rimrock, and dry-land crops of pinto beans in Homestead) and livestock raising (mainly Hereford beef cattle in both villages).

Rimrock was settled by Mormon missionaries in the 1870's as part of a larger project to plant settlements in the area of northern Arizona. Rimrock itself, unlike the Arizona sites, was established as a missionary outpost and the intention of the settlers was the conversion of the Indians, a task conceived in terms of the *Book of Mormon,* which defines the American Indian as "a remnant of Israel."

The early settlers were "called" by the Church, that is, they were selected and sent out by the Church authorities. The early years were exceedingly difficult and only the discipline of the Church and the loyalty of the settlers to its gospel kept them at the task. Drought, crop diseases, and the breaking of the earth and rock dam which they had constructed for the storage of irrigation water added to their difficulties, as did the fact that they had merely squatted on the land and were forced to purchase it at an exorbitant price to avoid eviction. The purchase money was given by the Church authorities in Salt Lake City, who also supplied 5,000 pounds of seed wheat in another period of dearth. The original settlers were

---

[2] Talcott Parsons, *The Structure of Social Action,* New York: Free Press of Glencoe, Inc., 1949, pp. 43–86; *Essays in Sociological Theory,* New York: Free Press of Glencoe, Inc., 1949, pp. 32–40; *The Social System,* New York: Free Press of Glencoe, Inc., 1951, pp. 3–24.

[3] "Rimrock" and "Homestead" are pseudonyms used to protect the anonymity of our informants.

[4] For additional ecological details on the region see Evon Z. Vogt, *Navaho Veterans: A Study of Changing Values,* Peabody Museum of Harvard University, Papers, Vol. XLI, No. 1, 1951, pp. 11–12; and John Landgraf, *Land-Use in the Rimrock Area of New Mexico: An Anthropological Approach to Areal Study,* Peabody Museum of Harvard University, Papers, forthcoming, 1953.

largely from northern Utah although there were also some converts from the southern states who had been involved in unsuccessful Arizona settlements a few years earlier.

As the emphasis shifted from missionary activities to farming, Rimrock developed into a not unusual Mormon village, despite its peripheral position to the rest of Mormondom. Irrigation farming was supplemented by cattle raising on the open range. In the early 1930's the Mormons began to buy range land, and Rimrock's economy shifted to a focus upon cattle raising. Today villagers own a total of 149 sections of range land and about four sections of irrigated or irrigable land devoted to gardens and some irrigated pastures in the immediate vicinity of the village. The family farm is still the basic economic unit, although partnerships formed upon a kinship basis and devoted to cattle raising have been important in raising the economic level of the village as a whole. In recent years some of the villagers—also on the basis of a kinship partnership—purchased the local trading post which is engaged in trading with the Indians as well as local villages business. In addition to 12 family partnerships which own 111 sections of land, there is a village cooperative which owns 38 sections. Privately-owned commercial facilities in the village include two stores, a boarding house, two garages, a saddle and leather shop, and a small restaurant. With this economic variety there is considerable difference in the distribution of wealth.

The Church is the central core of the village and its complex hierarchical structure, including the auxiliary organizations which activate women, youth, and young children, involves a large portion of the villagers in active participation. The church structure is backed up and impenetrated by the kinship structure. Moreover, church organization and kinship not only unify Rimrock into a social unit, they also integrate it into the larger structure of the Mormon Church and relate it by affinity and consanguinity to the rest of Mormondom.

Rimrock has been less affected by secularization than most Mormon villages in Utah and is less assimilated into generalized American patterns.[5] Its relative isolation has both kept such pressures from impinging upon it with full force and enhanced its formal and informal ties with the Church, preserving many of the characteristics of a Mormon village of a generation ago.

Homestead was settled by migrants from the South Plains area of western Texas and Oklahoma in the early 1930's. The migration represented a small aspect of that vast movement of people westward to California which was popularized in Steinbeck's *Grapes of Wrath* and which was the subject of investigation by many governmental agencies in the 1930's and 1940's.[6] Instead of going on to California, these homesteaders settled in a number of semi-arid farming areas in northern and western New Mexico and proceeded to develop an economy centered around the production of pinto beans. The migration coincided with the period of national depression and was due in part to severe economic conditions on the South Plains which forced families to leave their Texas and Oklahoma communities, in part to the attraction of land available for homesteading which held out the promise of family-owned farms for families who had previously owned little or no land or who had lost their land during the depression. The land base controlled by the homesteaders comprises approximately 100 sections. Each farm unit is operated by a nuclear family; there are no partnerships. Farms now average two sections in size and are scattered as far as twenty miles from the crossroads center of the community which contains the two stores, the school, the post office, two garages, a filling station, a small restaurant, a bean warehouse, a small bar, and two church buildings. Through the years, farming technology has shifted almost completely from horse-drawn implements to mechanized equipment.

With the hazardous farming conditions (periodic droughts and early killing frosts) out-migration from Homestead has been

[5] Lowry Nelson, *The Mormon Village*, Salt Lake City: University of Utah Press, 1952, pp. 275–85.
[6] See especially the reports of the Tolan Committee, U.S. Congress, "House Committee to Investigate the Interstate Migration of Destitute Citizens," 76th Congress, 3rd Session, Volume 6, Part 6, 1940.

relatively high. A few of these families have gone on to California, but more of them have moved to irrigated farms in the middle Rio Grande Valley and entered an agricultural situation which in its physical environmental aspects is similar to the situation in the Mormon community of Rimrock.

THE MORMON CASE

In broad perspective these two villages present local variations of generalized American culture. They share the common American value-orientations which emphasize the importance of achievement and success, progress and optimism, and rational mastery over nature. In the Mormon case, these were taken over from the 19th century American milieu in western New York where the Church was founded, and reinterpreted in terms of an elaborate theological conception of the universe as a dynamic process in which God and men are active collaborators in an eternal progression to greater power through increasing mastery.[7] The present life was and is conceived as a single episode in an infinity of work and mastery. The result was the heightening for the Mormons of convictions shared with most other Americans. Moreover, this conception was closely related to the belief in the reopening of divine revelation through the agency first of Joseph Smith, the original Mormon prophet, and later through the institutionalized channels of the Mormon Church. The Mormons conceived of themselves as a covenant people especially chosen for a divine task. This task was the building of the kingdom of God on earth and in this project—attempted four times unsuccessfully before the eventual migration to the west—much of the religious and secular socialism of the early 19th century found a profound reflection. The Mormon prophet proposed the "Law of Consecration" in an attempt to reconcile private initiative with cooperative endeavor. Contention led to its abandonment in 1838 after some five years

of unsuccessful experiment. Yet this withdrawal did not limit, but indeed rather enhanced, its future influence in Mormon settlement. The "Law of Consecration" was no longer interpreted as a blueprint prescribing social institutions of a definite sort, but its values lent a strong cooperative bias to much of later Mormon activity.[8] In the context of the notion of peculiarity and reinforced by out-group antagonism and persecution, these values became deeply embedded in Mormon orientations. The preference for agriculture combined with an emphasis upon community and lay participation in church activities resulted in the formation of compact villages rather than isolated family farmsteads as the typical Mormon settlement pattern.[9]

While Rimrock and Homestead share most of the central value-orientations of general American culture, they differ significantly in the values governing social relationships. Rimrock, with a stress upon community cooperation, an ethnocentrism resulting from the notion of their own peculiarity, and a village pattern of settlement, is more like the other Mormon villages of the West than it is like Homestead.

The stress upon *community cooperation* in Rimrock contrasts markedly with the stress upon *individual independence* found in Homestead. This contrast is one of emphasis, for individual initiative is important in Rimrock, especially in family farming and cattle raising, whereas cooperative activity does occur in Homestead. In Rimrock, however, the expectations are such that one must show his fellows or at least convince himself that he has good cause for *not* committing his time and resources to community efforts while in Homestead cooperative action takes place *only* after certainty has been reached that the claims of other individuals upon one's time and resources are legitimate.

Rimrock was a cooperative venture from the start, and very early the irrigation com-

---

[7] The data from Rimrock are based upon seven months field experience in the community during 1950–51. Additional data on this community will be provided in O'Dea's forthcoming monograph on *Mormon Values: The Significance of a Religious Outlook for Social Action.*

[8] The "Law of Consecration" became the basis of the Mormon pattern of cooperative activity also known as "The United Order of Enoch." Cf. Joseph A. Geddes, *The United Order Among the Mormons,* Salt Lake City: Deseret News Press, 1924; Edward J. Allen, *The Second United Order Among the Mormons,* New York: Columbia University Press, 1936.

[9] Nelson, *op. cit.,* pp. 25–54.

pany, a mutual non-profit corporation chartered under state law, emerged from the early water association informally developed around—and in a sense within—the Church. In all situations which transcend the capacities of individual families or family combinations, Rimrock Mormons have recourse to cooperative techniques. Let us examine four examples.

The "tight" land situation. Rimrock Mormons, feeling themselves "gathered," dislike having to migrate to non-Mormon areas. However, after World War II the 32 returned veterans faced a choice between poverty and under-employment or leaving the community. This situation became the concern of the Church and was discussed in its upper lay priesthood bodies in the village. It was decided to buy land to enable the veterans to remain. The possibilities of land purchase in the area were almost nonexistent and it appeared that nothing could be done, when unexpectedly the opportunity to buy some 38 sections presented itself. At the time, the village did not have the needed 10,000 dollars for the down payment, so the sum was borrowed from the Cooperative Security Corporation, a Church Welfare Plan agency, and the land was purchased. The patterns revealed here—community concern over a community problem, and appeal to and reception of aid from the general authorities of the Church—are typically Mormon. However, Mormon cooperation did not end here. Instead of breaking up the purchased land into plots to be individually owned and farmed, the parcel was kept as a unit, and a cooperative Rimrock Land and Cattle Company was formed. The company copied and adapted the form of the mutual irrigation company. Shares were sold in the village, each member being limited to two. A quota of cattle per share per year to be run on the land and a quota of bulls relative to cows were established. The cattle are privately owned, but the land is owned and managed cooperatively. The calves are the property of the owners of the cows. The project, which has not been limited to veterans, supplements other earnings sufficiently to keep most of the veterans in the village.

The graveling of the village streets. The streets of Rimrock were in bad repair in the fall of 1950. That summer a construction company had brought much large equipment into the area to build and gravel a section of a state highway which runs through the village. Before this company left, taking its equipment with it, villagers, again acting through the Church organization, decided that the village should avail itself of the opportunity and have the town's streets graveled. This was discussed in the Sunday priesthood meeting and announced at the Sunday sacrament meeting. A meeting was called for Monday evening, and each household was asked to send a representative. The meeting was well attended, and although not every family had a member present, practically all were represented at least by proxy. There was considerable discussion, and it was finally decided to pay 800 dollars for the job which meant a 20 dollar donation from each family. The local trader paid a larger amount, and, within a few days after the meeting, the total amount was collected. Only one villager raised objections to the proceedings. Although he was a man of importance locally, he was soon silenced by a much poorer man who invoked Mormon values of progress and cooperation and pledged to give 25 dollars which was 5 dollars above the norm.

The construction of a high school gymnasium. In 1951 a plan for the construction of a high school gymnasium was presented to the Rimrock villagers. Funds for materials and for certain skilled labor would be provided from state school appropriations, providing that the local residents would contribute the labor for construction. The plan was discussed in a Sunday priesthood meeting in the church, and later meetings were held both in the church and in the schoolhouse. Under the leadership of the principal of the school (who is also a member of the higher priesthood), arrangements were made whereby each able-bodied man in the community would either contribute at least 50 hours of labor or 50 dollars (the latter to be used to hire outside laborers) toward the construction. The original blueprint was extended to include a row of classrooms for the high school around the large central gymnasium.

Work on the new building began in late

1951, continued through 1952, and is now (in 1953) nearing completion. The enterprise was not carried through without difficulties. A few families were sympathetic at first but failed to contribute full amounts of either labor or cash, and some were unsympathetic toward the operation from the start. The high school principal had to keep reminding the villagers about their pledges to support the enterprise. But in the end the project was successful, and it represented an important cooperative effort on the part of the majority.

The community dances. The Mormons have always considered dancing to be an important form of recreation—in fact a particularly Mormon form of recreation. Almost every Friday evening a dance is held in the village church house. These dances are family affairs and are opened and closed with prayer. They are part of the general Church recreation program and are paid for by what is called locally "the budget." The budget refers to the plan under which villagers pay 15 dollars per family per year to cover a large number of entertainments, all sponsored by the Church auxiliary organization for youth, the Young Men's Mutual Improvement Association, and the Young Women's Mutual Improvement Association. The budget payment admits all members of the family to such entertainments.

Observation of these dances over a six months period did not reveal any tension or fighting. Smoking and drinking are forbidden to loyal Mormons, and those who smoked did so outside and away from the building. At dances held in the local school there has been evidence of drinking, and at times fighting has resulted from the presence of non-villagers. But on the whole the Rimrock dances are peaceful family affairs.

Rimrock reveals itself responding to group problems *as a group.* The economic ethic set forth by Joseph Smith in the Law of Consecration is seen in the dual commitment to private individual initiative (family farms and family partnerships in business and agriculture) and to cooperative endeavor in larger communal problems (irrigation company, land and cattle company, graveling the streets, and construction of school gymnasium). For the Mormons, co-

operation has become second nature. It has become part of the institutionalized structure of expectations, reinforced by religious conviction and social control.

THE HOMESTEADER CASE

The value-stress upon individual independence of action has deep roots in the history of the homesteader group.[10] The homesteaders were part of the westward migration from the hill country of the Southern Appalachians to the Panhandle country of Texas and Oklahoma and from there to the Southwest and California. Throughout their historical experience there has been an emphasis upon a rough and ready self-reliance and individualism, the Jacksonianism of the frontier West. The move to western New Mexico from the South Plains was made predominantly by isolated nuclear families, and Homestead became a community of scattered, individually-owned farmsteads—a geographical situation and a settlement pattern which reinforced the stress upon individualism.

Let us now examine the influence of this individualistic value-orientation upon a series of situations comparable to those that were described for Rimrock.

The "tight" land situation. In 1934 the Federal Security Administration, working in conjunction with the Land Use Division of the Department of Agriculture, proposed a "unit re-organization plan." This plan would have enabled the homesteaders to acquire additional tracts of land and permit them to run more livestock and hence depend less upon the more hazardous economic pursuit of dry-land pinto bean farming. It called for the use of government funds to purchase large ranches near the Homestead area which would be managed cooperatively by a board of directors selected by the community. The scheme collapsed while it was still

[10] The data from Homestead are based upon a year's field work in the community during 1949–50. Additional data on this community will be provided in Vogt's forthcoming monograph on *The Homesteaders: A Study of Values in a Frontier Community.* See also Vogt, "Water Witching: An Interpretation of a Ritual Pattern in a Rural American Community," *Scientific Monthly,* LXXV (September, 1952).

in the planning stages, because it was clear that each family expected to acquire its own private holdings on the range and that a cooperative would not work in Homestead.

The graveling of the village streets. During the winter of 1949–50 the construction company which was building the highway through Rimrock was also building a small section of highway north of Homestead. The construction company offered to gravel the streets of Homestead center if the residents who lived in the village would cooperatively contribute enough funds for the purpose. This community plan was rejected by the homesteaders, and an alternative plan was followed. Each of the operators of several of the service institutions—including the two stores, the bar, and the post office—independently hired the construction company truck drivers to haul a few loads of gravel to be placed in front of his own place of business, which still left the rest of the village streets a sea of mud in rainy weather.

The construction of a high school gymnasium. In 1950 the same plan for the construction of a new gymnasium was presented to the homesteaders as was presented to the Mormon village of Rimrock. As noted above, this plan was accepted by the community of Rimrock, and the new building is now nearing completion. But the plan was rejected by the residents of Homestead at a meeting in the summer of 1950, and there were long speechs to the effect that "I've got to look after my own farm and my own family first; I can't be up here in town building a gymnasium." Later in the summer additional funds were provided for labor; and with these funds adobe bricks were made, the foundation was dug, and construction was started—the homesteaders being willing to work on the gymnasium on a purely business basis at a dollar an hour. But as soon as the funds were exhausted, construction stopped. Today a partially completed gymnasium, and stacks of some 10,000 adobe bricks disintegrating slowly with the rains, stand as monuments to the individualism of the homesteaders.

The community dances. As in Rimrock, the village dances in Homestead are important focal points for community activity. These affairs take place several times a year in the schoolhouse and are always well-attended. But while the dances in Rimrock are well-coordinated activities which carry through the evening, the dances in Homestead often end when tensions between rival families result in fist-fights. And there is always the expectation in Homestead that a dance (or other cooperative activity such as a picnic or rodeo) may end at any moment and the level of activity reduced to the component nuclear families which form the only solid core of social organization within the community.

The individualistic value-orientation of the homesteaders also has important functional relationships to the religious organization of the community. With the exception of two men who are professed atheists, all of the homesteaders define themselves as Christians. But denominationalism is rife, there being ten different denominations represented in the village: Baptist, Presbyterian, Methodist, Nazarene, Campbellite, Holiness, 7th Day Adventist, Mormon, Catholic, and Present Day Disciples.

In the most general terms, this religious differentiation in Homestead can be interpreted as a function of the individualistic and factionalizing tendencies in the social system. In a culture with a value-stress upon independent individual action combined with a "freedom of religion" ideology, adhering to one's own denomination becomes an important means of expressing individualism and of focusing factional disputes around a doctrine and a concrete institutional framework. In turn, the doctrinal differences promote additional factionalizing tendencies, with the result that competing churches become the battleground for a cumulative and circularly reinforcing struggle between rival small factions within the community.[11]

To sum up, we may say that the strong commitment to an individualistic value-orientation has resulted in a social system in which inter-personal relations are strongly

[11] This relationship between churches and factionalizing tendencies has also been observed by Bailey in his unpublished study of a community in west Texas, in the heart of the ancestral home region of the present residents of Homestead. Cf. Wilfrid C. Bailey, "A Study of a Texas Panhandle Community; A Preliminary Report on Cotton Center, Texas," Values Study Files, Harvard University.

colored by a kind of factionalism and in which persons and groups become related to one another in a competitive, feuding relationship. The homesteaders do not live on their widely separated farms and ignore one another, as it might be possible to do. On the other hand, they do not cooperate in community affairs as closely as does a hive of bees. They interact, but a constant feuding tone permeates the economic, social and religious structure of the community.

RELATIONSHIP BETWEEN THE TWO COMMUNITIES

Although there is some trading in livestock, feed, and other crops, the most important contacts between the two communities are not economic but are social and recreational. The village baseball teams have scheduled games with one another for the past two decades, and there is almost always joint participation in the community dances and in the summer rodeos in the two communities. Despite Mormon objections to close associations with "gentiles," there is also considerable inter-dating between the two communities among the teen-age groups, and three intermarriages have taken place.

In general, the homesteaders envy and admire the Mormons' economic organization, their irrigated land, and more promising prospects for good crops each year. On the other hand, they regard the Mormons as cliquish and unfriendly and fail completely to understand why anyone "wants to live all bunched up the way the Mormons do." They feel that the Mormons are inbred and think they should be glad to get "new blood" from intermarriages with homesteaders. They add, "That Mormon religion is something we can't understand at all." Finally, the homesteaders say that Mormons "used to have more than one wife, and some probably still do; they dance in the church, they're against liquor, coffee, and tobacco, and they always talk about Joseph Smith and the *Book of Mormon.*"

The Mormons consider their own way of life distinctly superior to that of the homesteaders in every way. Some will admit that the homesteaders have the virtue of being more friendly and of "mixing more with others," and their efforts in the face of farming hazards are admired, but Homestead is generally regarded as a rough and in some ways immoral community, especially because of the drinking, smoking, and fighting (particularly at dances) that takes place. They also feel that Homestead is disorganized and that the churches are not doing what they should for the community. For the past few years they have been making regular missionary trips to Homestead, but to date they have made no conversions.

COMPARISONS AND CONCLUSIONS

In the case of Rimrock and Homestead, we are dealing with two communities which are comparable in population, in ecological setting, and which are variants of the same general culture. The two outstanding differences are: (a) irrigation versus dry-land farming and associated differences in settlement pattern, compact village versus isolated farmstead type;[12] (b) a value stress upon cooperative community action versus a stress upon individual action. The important question here involves the relationship (if any) between these two sets of variables. Is the cooperation in Rimrock directly a function of an irrigation agriculture situation with a compact village settlement pattern, the rugged individualism in Homestead, a function of a dry-land farming situation with a scattered settlement pattern? Or did these value-orientations arise out of earlier historical experience in each case, influence the types of communities which were established in western New Mexico, and later persist in the face of changed economic situations? We shall attempt to demonstrate that the second proposition is more in accord with the historical facts as we now know them.

Nelson has recently shown that the general pattern of the Mormon village is neither a direct function (in its beginnings) of the requirements of irrigation agriculture, nor of the need for protection against Indians on the frontier. Rather, the basic pattern was a social invention of the Mormons, motivated by a sense of urgent need to prepare a dwelling place for the "Savior" at "His

12 Cf. Nelson, *op. cit.,* p. 4.

Second Coming." The "Plat of the City of Zion" was invented by Joseph Smith, Sidney Rigdon, and Frederick G. Williams in 1833 and has formed the basis for the laying out of most Mormon villages, even those established in the Middle West before the Mormons migrated to Utah.[13]

It is very clear that both the compact village pattern and the cooperative social arrangements centered around the church existed before the Mormons engaged in irrigation agriculture and had a strong influence upon the development of community structure not only in Utah but in the Mormon settlements like Rimrock on the periphery of the Mormon culture area. There is no objective reason in the Rimrock ecological and cultural setting (the local Navahos and Zunis did not pose a threat to pioneer settlements in the 1880's) why the Mormons could not have set up a community which conformed more to the isolated farmstead type with a greater stress upon individualistic social relations. Once the Mormon community was established, it is clear that the cooperation required by irrigation agriculture of the Mormon type and the general organization of the church strongly reinforced the value stress upon communal social action.

It is of further significance that as the population expanded and the Rimrock Mormons shifted from irrigation agricultural pursuits to dry-land ranching in the region outside of the Rimrock valley, the earlier cooperative patterns modeled on the mutual irrigation company were applied to the solution of economic problems that are identical to those faced by the homesteaders. Moreover, in midwestern and eastern cities to which Mormons have recently moved, church wards have purchased and cooperatively worked church welfare plan farms.

In Homestead, on the other hand, our evidence indicates that the first settlers were drawn from a westward-moving population which stressed a frontier-type of self-reliance and individualism. They were searching for a place where each man could "own his own farm and be his own boss." Each family settled on its isolated homestead claim, and there emerged from the beginning an iso-

lated farmstead type of settlement pattern in which the nuclear family was the solidary unit. The service center which was built up later simply occupied lots that were sold to storekeepers, filling station operators, the bartender, and others, by the four families who owned the four sections which joined at a crossroads. Only two of these four family homes were located near the service center at the crossroads. The other two families continued to maintain their homes in other quarters of their sections and lived almost a mile from "town." In 1952 one of the former families built a new home located over a mile from the center of town, and commented that they had always looked forward to "getting out of town."

There is no objective reason in the Homestead ecological setting why there could not be more clustering of houses into a compact village and more commuity cooperation than actually exists. One would not expect those farmers whose farms are located 15 or 20 miles from the service center to live in "town" and travel out to work each day. But there is no reason why those families living within 2 or 3 miles of the village center could not live in town and work their fields from there. In typical Mormon villages a large percentage of the farms are located more than three miles from the farm homes. For example, in Rimrock over 31 per cent, in Escalante over 38 per cent, and in Ephriam over 30 per cent of the farms are located from three to eight or more miles from the center of the villages.[14]

It is clear that the homesteaders were operating with a set of individualistic property arrangements (drawn, of course, from our generalized American culture) and that their strong stress upon individualism led to a quite different utilization of these property patterns (than was the case with the Mormons) and to the establishment of a highly scattered type of community. Once Homestead was established, the individualism permitted by the scattered dry-land farming pattern, and encouraged by the emphasis upon the small nuclear family unit and upon multi-denominationalism in church affiliation reacted on and strongly reinforced the

[13] Nelson, *op. cit.*, pp. 28–38.

[14] See Nelson, *op. cit.*, pp. 99 and 144 for data on Escalante and Ephriam.

value stress upon individual independence. It is evident that the homesteaders continue to prefer this way of life, as shown by their remarks concerning the "bunched up" character of a Mormon village and the fact that a number of families have recently moved "out of town" when they built new houses.

Of further interest is the fact that when homesteader families move to irrigated farms in the middle Rio Grande Valley, the stress upon individual action tends to persist strongly. They do not readily develop cooperative patterns to deal with this new setting which is similar to the situation in the irrigated valley of the Mormons at Rimrock. Indeed, one of the principal innovations they have been promoting in one region along the Rio Grande where they are replacing Spanish-Americans on the irrigated farming land is a system of meters on irrigation ditches. These meters will measure the water flowing into each individual farmer's ditches, and effectively eliminate the need for more highly organized cooperative arrangements for distributing the available supply of water.

In conclusion, we should like to reiterate that we are strongly cognizant of situational factors. If the Rimrock Mormons had not been able to settle in a valley which was watered by melting snow packs from a nearby mountain and which provided the possibilities for the construction of storage reservoir, they certainly could not have developed an irrigation agricultural system at all. In the case of Rimrock, however, the actual site of settlement was selected from among several possible sites in a larger situation. The selection was largely influenced by Mormon preconceptions of the type of village they wished to establish. In fact, Mormons chose the irrigable valleys throughout the inter-montane west. On the other hand, the physical environmental features for the development of irrigation were simply not present in the Homestead setting, and the people had no alternative to dryland farming. There is no evidence to suggest that had they found an irrigable valley, they would have developed it along Mormon lines. In fact, the homesteaders' activities in the Rio Grande Valley suggest just the opposite. It is clear that the situational facts did not *determine* in any simple sense the contrasting community structures which emerged. Rather, the situations set certain limits, but within these limits contrasting value-orientations influenced the development of two quite different community types. It would appear that solutions to problems of community settlement pattern and the type of concrete social action which ensues are set within a value framework which importantly influences the selections made with the range of possibilities existing within an objective situation.

Modal Personality and Adjustment to the Soviet Socio-Political System[1] / Alex Inkeles, Eugenia Hanfmann, and Helen Beier

Two main elements are encompassed in the study of national character.[2] The first step is to determine what modal personality patterns, if any, are to be found in a particular national population or in its major subgroups. In so far as such modes exist one can go on to the second stage, studying the interrelations between the personality modes and various aspects of the social system.

Reprinted from *Human Relations*, 1958, 11, pages 3–22, by permission of the senior author and publisher, Tavistock Publications, Ltd.

[1] Revised and expanded version of a paper read at the American Psychological Association Meetings in San Francisco, Sept. 1955. Daniel Miller read this early version and made many useful com- ments. The authors wish to express their warm appreciation for the prolonged support of the Russian Research Center at Harvard. Revisions were made by the senior author while he was a Fellow of the Center for Advanced Study in the Behavioral Sciences, for whose support he wishes to make grateful acknowledgment.

[2] For a discussion of the basic issues and a review of research in this field see Alex Inkeles and Daniel J. Levinson (17).

Even if the state of our theory warranted the drafting of an 'ideal' research design for studies in this field, they would require staggering sums and would probably be beyond our current methodological resources. We can, however, hope to make progress through more restricted efforts. In the investigation we report on here we studied a highly selected group from the population of the Soviet Union, namely, former citizens of Great Russian nationality who 'defected' during or after World War II. We deal, furthermore, mainly with only one aspect of the complex interrelations between system and personality, our subjects' participation in an adjustment to their Communist socio-political order.[3] We find that certain personality modes are outstanding in the group, and believe that we can trace their significance for our subjects' adjustment to Soviet society.

SAMPLE AND METHOD

An intensive program of clinical psychological research was conducted as part of the work of the Harvard Project on the Soviet Social System.[4] The Project explored the attitudes and life experiences of former Soviet citizens who were displaced during World War II and its aftermath and then decided not to return to the U.S.S.R. Almost 3,000 completed a long written questionnaire, and 329 undertook a detailed general life history interview. The individuals studied clinically were selected from the latter group. Criteria of selection were that the interviewee seemed a normal, reasonably adjusted individual who was relatively young, had lived most of his life under Soviet conditions, and was willing to undertake further intensive interviewing and psychological testing.

The group studied clinically included 51 cases, forty-one of whom were men. With the exception of a few Ukrainians, all were Great Russians. Almost half were under 30, and only 8 were 40 or older at the time of interview in 1950, which meant that the overwhelming majority grew up mainly under Soviet conditions and were educated in Soviet schools. Eleven had had a minimum education of four years or less, 22 between four and eight years, and 18 advanced secondary or college training. In residence the group was predominantly urban but if those who had moved from the countryside to the city were included with the rural, then approximately half fell in each category. As might be expected from the education data, the group included a rather large proportion of those in high-status occupations, with 11 professionals and members of the intelligentsia, 7 regular army officers, and 9 white-collar workers. Sixteen were rank-and-file industrial and agricultural workers, and five rank-and-file army men. In keeping with the occupational pattern but running counter to popular expectations about Soviet refugees, a rather high proportion were in the Party (6) or the Young Communist League (13). Again running counter to popular expectations about refugees, the group was not characterized by a markedly high incidence of disadvantaged family background as reflected either in material deprivation, the experience of political arrest, or other forms of repression at the hands of the regime. Ten were classified as having been extremely disadvantaged, and 15 as having suffered minor disadvantage.

All of the Soviet refugees have in common their 'disaffection' with Soviet society. The clinical group included mainly the more 'active' defectors who left Soviet control on their own initiative, rather than the 'passive' who were removed by force of circumstance. Thirty-four had deserted from the military[5] or voluntarily departed with the retreating German occupation armies. In general, however, the clinical group was not more vigorously anti-Communist than

[3] For analysis of another aspect of the psychological properties of this group, see Eugenia Hanfmann (12).
[4] The research was carried out by the Russian Research Center under contract AF No. 33(038)-12909 with the former Human Resources Research Institute, Maxwell Air Force Base, Alabama. For a general account of the purposes and design of the study see: R. Bauer, A. Inkeles, and C. Kluckhohn (2). The clinical study was conducted by E. Hanfmann and H. Beier. A detailed presentation is given in the unpublished report of the Project by E. Hanfmann and H. Beier (13).

[5] This was in part a result of our selection procedure. The larger project was particularly interested in post-war defectors, almost all of whom came from the Soviet military occupation forces in Germany. Half of the men fell in that category.

the other refugees. They overwhelmingly supported the principles of the welfare state, including government ownership and state planning, and credited the regime with great achievements in foreign affairs and economic and cultural development. They refused to return for much the same reasons given by other refugees: fear of reprisal at the hands of the secret police, because of former oppression, opposition to institutions like the collective farm, or resentment of the low standard of living and the absence of political freedom. In psychological adjustment, finally, they seemed to reflect fairly well the tendency toward adequate adjustment which characterized the refugees as a whole.

With regard to the parent refugee population, then, the clinical group was disproportionately male, young, well educated, well placed occupationally and politically, and 'active' in defecting.[6] In its internal composition, the sample was also unbalanced in being predominantly male, but otherwise gave about equal weight to those over and under 35, in manual vs. white-collar occupations, from urban or rural backgrounds, with education above or below the advanced secondary level.

Each respondent was interviewed with regard to his childhood experience, some aspects of his adult life, and his adjustment to conditions in a displaced persons' camp. Each took a battery of tests which included the Rorschach, TAT, a sentence-completion test of 60 items, a 'projective questions' test including eight of the questions utilized in the authoritarian personality study, and a specially constructed 'episodes' or problem-situations test. We regard the use of this battery of tests as a matter of special note, since most attempts to assess modal tendencies in small-scale societies have relied upon a single instrument, particularly the Rorschach. The various tests differ in their sensitivity to particular dimensions or levels of personality, and differentially reflect the

impact of the immediate emotional state and environmental situation of the subject. By utilizing a series of tests, therefore, we hope that we have in significant degree reduced the chances that any particular finding mainly peculiar to the special combination of instrument, subject, and situation will have been mistakenly interpreted as distinctively Russian. In addition the use of this battery enables us to test our assumptions in some depth, by checking for consistency on several tests.

Each test was independently analysed according to fairly standard scoring methods, and the results were reported separately.[7] In reporting their results, however, each set of analysts made some observations on the character traits which seemed generally important to the group as a whole. Further, in drawing these conclusions the analysts made use of a criterion group of Americans matched with the Russian sample on age, sex, occupation, and education. The availability of such test results posed a challenge as to whether or not these general observations, when collated and analysed, would yield any consistent patterns for the group as a whole.

To make this assessment we selected the eight major headings used below as an organizing framework. We believe that they permit a fairly full description of the various dimensions and processes of the human personality, and at the same time facilitate making connections with aspects of the social system. These categories were, however, not part of the design of the original clinical research program,[8] and were not used by the analysts of the individual instruments. While this circumstance made for lesser comparability between the tests, it acted to forestall

---

[6] The young post-war defectors on the whole did prove to be less stable and more poorly adjusted. Apart from this issue of adjustment or 'integration', however, they shared with the rest of the sample much the same range of outstanding personality traits. Therefore, no further distinctions between that group and the rest are discussed in this paper. See E. Hanfmann and H. Beier (13).

[7] On the 'Episodes Test' a detailed report has been published, see Eugenia Hanfmann and J. G. Getzels (14). A brief account of results on the Projective Questions has also been published in Helen Beier and Eugenia Hanfmann (4). The other results were described in the following as yet unpublished reports of the Project, which may be examined at the Russian Research Center: Beier (3), Rosenblatt et al. (21), Fried (10), Fried and Held (11), Roseborough and Phillips (20).

[8] The basic categories were suggested to A. Inkeles by D. J. Levinson in the course of a seminar on national character, and are in part discussed in Inkeles and Levinson (17). They were somewhat modified for the purposes of this presentation.

the slanting of conclusions to fit the analytic scheme. The statements in the conclusions drawn by the analysts of each instrument were written on duplicate cards, sorted, and grouped under all the categories to which they seemed relevant. The evidence with regard to each category was then sifted and weighed, and where there were ambiguous findings the original tables were re-examined for clarification. Relevant impressions based on the interviews were also drawn on. Similarities and differences between those in our sample and the matching Americans aided in grasping the distinctive features of the Russian pattern. On this basis a characterization of the group was developed under each heading of the analytic scheme.

It should be clear that the sketch of modal personality characteristics presented below is not a simple and direct translation of particular test scores into personality traits. Rather, it is an evaluative, summary statement, following from the collation and interpretation of conclusions drawn from each test, conclusions which were in turn based both on test scores and on supplementary qualitative material. The word modal should not be taken too literally in this context. We have relied on some tests scores when only a small proportion of the sample manifested the given response or pattern of responses, if this fits with other evidence in developing a larger picture. In stating our findings we have been freer with the evidence than some would permit, more strict than others would require. We attempted to keep to the canons of the exact method, without neglecting the clinical interpretations and insights. In this way we hoped to arrive at a rich and meaningful picture of the people studied, a picture that would provide an adequate basis for an analysis of their adjustment to the socio-political system.

BRIEF SKETCH OF RUSSIAN MODAL PERSONALITY CHARACTERISTICS

1. Central Needs[9]

Since all human beings manifest the same basic needs, we cannot assert that some need is unique to a given national popula-

[9] See H. Murray (18). We do not strictly follow Murray in our use of the 'need' terminology.

tion. Among these universal needs, however, some may achieve greater strength or central importance in the organization of the personality, and in this sense be typical of the majority of a given group.

Probably the strongest and most pervasive quality of the Russian personality that emerged from our data was a need for *affiliation*. By this we mean a need for intensive interaction with other people in immediate, direct, face-to-face relationships, coupled with a great capacity for having this need fulfilled through the establishment of warm and personal contact with others. Our subjects seemed to welcome others into their lives as an indispensable condition of their own existence, and generally felt neither isolated nor estranged from them. In contrast to the American subjects, the Russians were not too anxiously concerned about others' opinion of them and did not feel compelled to cling to a relationship or to defend themselves against it. Rather, they manifest a profound acceptance of group membership and relatedness. These orientations were especially prevalent in test situations dealing with relations between the individual and small face-to-face groups such as the family, the work team, and the friendship circle.

Closely linked with the need for affiliation is a need for *dependence* very much like what Dicks (5) spoke of as the Russians' 'strong positive drive for enjoying loving protection and security', care and affection. This need shows not only in orientation towards parents and peers, but also in the relations with formal authority figures. We did not, however, find a strong need for submission linked with the need for dependence, although Dicks asserts it to be present. In addition there is substantial evidence for the relatively greater strength of *oral* needs, reflected in preoccupation with getting and consuming food and drink, in great volubility, and in emphasis on singing. These features are especially conspicuous by contrast with the relative weakness of the more typically compulsive puritanical concern for order, regularity, and self-control. However, our data do not permit us to stress this oral component as heavily as does Dicks, who regards it as 'typical' for the culture as a whole.

Several needs rather prominent in the records of the American control group did not appear to be of outstanding importance in the personality structure of the Russians. Most notable, the great emphasis on *achievement* found in the American records was absent from the Russian ones. Within the area of interpersonal relations our data lead us to posit a fairly sharp Russian-American contrast. Whereas the American records indicate great strength of need for *approval* and need for *autonomy,* those needs were rather weakly manifested by the Russians. In approaching interpersonal relations our American subjects seemed to fear too close or intimate association with other individuals and groups. They often perceived such relations as potentially limiting freedom of individual action, and therefore inclined above all to insure their independence from or autonomy within the group. At the same time the Americans revealed a strong desire for recognition and at least formal acceptance or approval from the group. They are very eager to be 'liked,' to be regarded as an 'all right' guy, and greatly fear isolation from the group. Finally we note that certain needs important in other national character studies were apparently not central in either the American or the Russian groups. Neither showed much need for dominance, for securing positions of superordination, or for controlling or manipulating others and enforcing authority over them. Nor did they seem markedly distinguished in the strength of hostile impulses, of desires to hurt, punish, or destroy.

2. Modes of Impulse Control

On the whole the Russians have relatively *high awareness* of their impulses or basic dispositions—such as for oral gratification, sex, aggression, or dependence—and, rather, *freely accept* them as something normal or 'natural' rather than as bad or offensive.[10] The Russians show evidence, furthermore, of *giving in* to these impulses quite readily and frequently, and of *living them out.* Although they tended afterwards to be penitent and

admit that they should not have 'lived out' so freely, they were not really punitive towards themselves or others for failure to control impulses. Of course, this does not mean complete absence of impulse control, a condition that would render social life patently impossible. Indeed, the Russians viewed their own impulses and desires as forces that needed watching, and often professed the belief that the control of impulses was necessary and beneficial. The critical point is that the Russians seemed to rely much less than the Americans on impulse control to be generated and handled from within. Rather, they appear to feel a need for aid from without in the form of guidance and pressure exerted by higher authority and by the group to assist them in controlling their impulses. This is what Dicks referred to as the Russian's desire to have a 'moral corset' put on his impulses. The Americans, on the other hand, vigorously affirm their ability for *self-control,* and seem to assume that the possession of such ability and its exercise legitimates their desire to be free from the overt control of authority and the group.

In this connection we may note that the review of individual cases revealed a relative lack of well-developed *defensive structures* in many of the Russian subjects. Mechanisms that serve to counteract and to modify threatening feelings and impulses—including isolation, intellectualization, and reaction formation—seem to figure much less prominently among them than among the Americans. The Russians had fewer defenses of this type and those they had were less well established.

3. Typical Polarities and Dilemmas

Within certain areas of feelings and motives individuals may typically display attitudes and behavior that belong to one or the opposite poles of the given variable, or else display a preoccupation with the choice of alternatives posed by these poles. Such preoccupation may be taken to define the areas of typical dilemmas or conflicts, similar to the polarized issues, such as 'identity vs. role diffusion' and 'intimacy vs. isolation', which Erikson (6) found so important in different stages of psychological maturation.

In our Russian subjects we found a con-

---

10 Such a statement must of course always be one of degree. We do not mean to say that such threatening impulses as those toward incest are present in the awareness of Russians or are accepted by them more than by Americans.

scious preoccupation with the problem of *trust vs. mistrust* in relation to others. They worried about the intentions of the other, expressing apprehension that people may not really be as they seem on the surface. There was always the danger that someone might entice you into revealing yourself, only then to turn around and punish you for what you have revealed. Another typical polarity of the Russians' behavior is that of *optimism vs. pessimism,* or of faith vs. despair. One of our projective test items posited the situation that tools and materials necessary for doing a job fail to arrive. In responding to this item our Russian subjects tended to focus on whether the outcome of the situation will be good or bad for the actor, while the Americans at once sprang into a plan of action for resolving the situation. Finally, we may include under the typical polarities of the Russians' attitude that of *activity vs. passivity,* although in the case of this variable we found little indication of a sense of a conscious conflict. However, the subjects' choice of alternatives in the projective tests tended to be distributed between the active and the passive ones, while the Americans' preference for the active instrumental response was as clear-cut and strong as was their generally optimistic orientation.

The pronounced polarities of the Russians' orientation lend support to Dicks's assertion that 'the outstanding trait of the Russian personality is its contradictoriness— its ambivalence' (5). Two qualifications, however, must be kept in mind. First, the strength of our Russian subjects' dilemmas may have been greatly enhanced by the conditions of their lives, both in the Soviet Union and abroad. Second, the American subjects also show some involvement in problematic issues, though they were different from the Russian ones. Thus the problem of 'intimacy vs. isolation' or 'autonomy vs. belongingness', to which we have already alluded, seemed a major dilemma for Americans whereas it was not such an issue for the Russians.

4. Achieving and Maintaining Self-Esteem

In their orientations toward the self, the Russians displayed rather low and *unintense self-awareness* and little painful self-con-

sciousness. They showed rather high and *secure self-esteem,* and were little given to self-examination and doubt of their inner selves. At the same time they were not made anxious by examination of their own motivation or that of others, but rather showed readiness to gain insight into psychological mechanisms. The American pattern reveals some contrasts here, with evidence of acute self-awareness, substantial self-examination, and doubting of one's inner qualities.

We were not able to discern any differences between Americans and Russians in the relative importance of *guilt* versus *shame* as sanctions. There were, however, some suggestive differences in what seemed to induce both guilt and shame. The Americans were more likely to feel guilty or ashamed if they failed to live up to clear-cut 'public' norms, as in matters of etiquette. They were also upset by any hint that they were inept, incompetent, or unable to meet production, sports, or similar performance standards. The Russians did not seem to be equally disturbed by such failures, and felt relatively more guilty or ashamed when they assumed that they had fallen behind with regard to moral or interpersonal behavior norms, as in matters involving personal honesty, sincerity, trust, or loyalty to a friend. These latter qualities they value most highly and they demand them from their friends.

5. Relation to Authority[11]

Our clinical instruments presented the subjects with only a limited range of situations involving relations with authority. These did not show pronounced differences in basic attitudes between Russians and Americans, except that Russians appeared to have more fear of and much less optimistic expectations about authority figures. Both of these manifestations might, of course, have been mainly a reflection of their recent experiences rather than of deeper-lying dispositions. Fortunately, we can supplement the clinical materials by the life history interviews which deal extensively with the in-

[11] Relations to authority may be thought of as simply one aspect of a broader category—'conceptions of major figures'—which includes parents, friends, etc. We have included some comments on the Russians' perceptions of others under 'cognitive modes' below.

dividual's relations with authority. A definite picture emerges from these data. Above all else the Russians want their leaders—whether boss, district political hack, or national ruler—to be warm, nurturant, considerate, and interested in the individuals' problems and welfare. The authority is also expected to be the main source of initiative in the inauguration of general plans and programs and in the provision of guidance and organization for their attainment. The Russians do not seem to expect initiative, directedness, and organizedness from an average individual. They therefore expect that the authority will of necessity give detailed orders, demand obedience, keep checking up on performance, and use persuasion and coercion intensively to insure steady performance. A further major expectation with regard to the 'legitimate' authority is that it will institute and enforce sanctions designed to curb or control bad impulses in individuals, improper moral practices, heathen religious ideas, perverted political procedures, and extreme personal injustice. It is, then, the government that should provide that 'external moral corset' which Dicks says the Russian seeks.

An authority that meets these qualifications is 'good' and it does what it does with 'right'. Such an authority should be loved, honored, respected, and obeyed. Our Russian subjects seemed, however, to expect that authority figures would in fact frequently be stern, demanding, even scolding and nagging. This was not in and of itself viewed as bad or improper. Authority may be, perhaps ought to be, autocratic, so long as it is not harshly authoritarian and not totally demanding. Indeed, it is not a bad thing if such an authority makes one rather strongly afraid, make one 'quake' in expectation of punishment for trespassing or wrongdoing. Such an authority should not, however, be arbitrary, aloof, and unjust. It should not be unfeeling in the face of an open acknowledgement of one's guilt and of consequent self-castigation. Indeed, many of our subjects assumed that authority can in fact be manipulated through humbling the self and depicting oneself as a weak, helpless person who needs supportive guidance rather than harsh punishment. They also assumed that authority may be manipulated by praise or fawning, and seduced through the sharing of gratificatory experiences provided by the supplicant—as through the offer of a bottle of liquor and the subsequent sharing of some drinks. Russians also favor meeting the pressure of authority by evasive tactics, including such devices as apparently well-intentioned failure to comprehend and departures from the scene of action.

Throughout their discussions of authority our respondents showed little concern for the preservation of precise forms, rules, regulations, exactly defined rights, regularity of procedure, formal and explicit limitation of powers, or the other aspects of the traditional constitutional Anglo-Saxon approach to law and government. For the Russians a government that has the characteristics of good government listed above justifies its right to rule by virtue of that performance. In that case, one need not fuss too much about the fine points of law. By contrast, if government is harsh, arbitrary, disinterested in public welfare—which it is apparently expected to be more often than not—then it loses its right to govern no matter how legal its position and no matter how close its observance of the letter of the law.

6. Modes of Affective Functioning

One of the most salient characteristics of the Russian personality was the high degree of their *expressiveness* and emotional aliveness. On most test items the Russian responses had a stronger emotional coloring, and they covered a wider range of emotions, than did the American responses. Their feelings were easily brought into play, and they showed them openly and freely both in speech and in facial expression, without much suppression or disguise. In particular they showed a noticeably greater *freedom and spontaneity in criticism* and in the expression of hostile feelings than was true for the Americans. There were, further, two emotions which the Russians showed with a frequency far exceeding that found in the Americans—*fear,* and *depression* or despair. Many of the ambiguous situations posited in the tests were viewed by them in terms of danger and threat, on the one hand, and of privation and loss, on the other. Undoubtedly this was in good part a reflection of the tense social situation which they had experienced in the Soviet Union, and of their depressed status as refugees, but we believe that in addition deeper-lying trends were here being tapped. These data provide some evidence in support of the oft-noted prevalence of depressive trends among the Russians.

7. Modes of Cognitive Functioning

In this area we include characteristic patterns of perception, memory, thought, and imagination, and the processes involved in forming and manipulating ideas about the world around one. Of all the modes of personality organization it is perhaps the most subtle, and certainly in the present state of theory and testing one of the most difficult to formulate. Our clinical materials do, however, permit a few comments.

In discussing people, the Russians show a keen *awareness of the 'other'* as a distinct entity as well as a rich and diversified recognition of his special characteristics. Other people are usually perceived by them not as social types but as concrete individuals with a variety of attributes distinctly their own. The Russians think of people and evaluate them for what they are rather than in terms of how they evaluate ego, the latter being a more typically American approach. The Russians also paid more attention to the 'others' ' basic underlying attributes and attitudes than to their behavior as such or their performance on standards of achievement and accomplishment in the instrumental realm.

Similar patterns were evident in their perception of interpersonal situations. In reacting to the interpersonal relations 'problems' presented by one of the psychological tests they more fully elaborated the situation, cited more relevant incidents from folklore or their own experience, and offered many more illustrations of a point. In contrast, the Americans tended more to describe the formal, external, characteristics of people, apparently being less perceptive of the individual's motivational characteristics. The Americans also tended to discuss interpersonal problems on a rather generalized and abstract level. With regard to most other types of situation, however, especially problems involving social organization, the pattern was somewhat reversed Russians

tended to take a rather broad, sweeping view of the situation, *generalizing* at the expense of detail, about which they were often extremely vague and poorly informed. They seemed to feel their way through such situations rather than rigorously to think them through, tending to get into a spirit of grandiose planning but without attention to necessary details.

8. Modes of Conative Functioning

By conative functioning we mean the patterns, the particular behavioral forms, of the striving for any valued goals, including the rhythm or pace at which these goals are pursued and the way in which that rhythm is regulated. In this area our clinical data are not very rich. Nevertheless, we have the strong impression that the Russians do not match the Americans in the vigor of their striving to master all situations or problems put before them, and to do so primarily through adaptive instrumental orientations. Although by no means listless, they seem much more *passively accommodative* to the apparent hard facts of situations. In addition, they appeared less apt to persevere systematically in the adaptive courses of action they did undertake, tending to backslide into passive accommodation when the going proved rough. At the same time, the Russians do seem capable of great bursts of activity, which suggests the bi-modality of an *assertive-passive pattern* of strivings in contrast to the steadier, more even, and consistent pattern of strivings among the Americans.

To sum up, one of the most salient characteristics of the personality of our Russian subjects was their emotional aliveness and expressiveness. They felt their emotions keenly, and did not tend to disguise or to deny them to themselves, nor to suppress their outward expression to the same extent as the Americans. The Russians criticized themselves and others with greater freedom and spontaneity. Relatively more aware and tolerantly accepting of impulses for gratification in themselves and others, they relied less than the Americans on self-control from within and more on external socially imposed controls applied by the peer group or authority. A second outstanding characteristic of the Russians was their strong need for intensive interaction with others, coupled with a strong and secure feeling of relatedness to them, high positive evaluation of such belongingness, and great capacity to enjoy such relationships. The image of the 'good' authority was of a warm, nurturant, supportive figure. Yet our subjects seemed to assume that this paternalism might and indeed should include superordinate planning and firm guidance, as well as control or supervision of public and personal morality, and if necessary, of thought and belief. It is notable, in this connection, that in the realm of conative and cognitive functioning orderliness, precision of planning, and persistence in striving were not outstandingly present. Such qualities were rather overshadowed by tendencies toward over-generalizing, vagueness, imprecision, and passive accommodation. Countering the image of the good authority, there was an expectation that those with power would in fact often be harsh, aloof, and authoritarian. The effect of such behavior by authority is alienation of loyalty. This fits rather well with the finding that the main polarized issues or dilemmas were those of 'trust vs. mistrust' in relations with others, 'optimism vs. pessimism', and 'activity vs. passivity', whereas the more typically American dilemma of 'intimacy vs. isolation' was not a problem for many Russians. Though strongly motivated by needs for affiliation and dependence and wishes for oral gratification—in contrast to greater strength of needs for achievement, autonomy, and approval among the Americans—our Russian subjects seemed to have a characteristically sturdy ego. They were rather secure in their self-estimation, and unafraid to face up to their own motivation and that of others. In contrast to the Americans, the Russians seemed to feel shame and guilt for defects of 'character' in interpersonal relations rather than for failure to meet formal rules of etiquette or instrumental production norms. Compared with the Americans, however, they seemed relatively lacking in well-developed and stabilized defenses with which to counteract and modify threatening impulses and feelings. The organization of their personality depended for its coherence much more heavily on their intimate relatedness to those around them, their capacity to use others' support and to share with them their emotions.

RELATIONS OF MODAL PERSONALITY AND THE SOCIO-POLITICAL SYSTEM

In the following comments we are interpreting 'political participation' rather broadly, to cover the whole range of the individual's role as the citizen of a large-scale national state. We therefore include his major economic and social as well as his specifically political roles. This may extend the concept of political participation too far for most national states, but for the Soviet Union, where all aspects of social life have been politicized, it is the only meaningful approach. Specifically, the questions to which we address ourselves are as follows.

Assuming that the traits cited above were widespread among the group of Great Russians studied by our project, what implications would this have for their adjustment to the role demands made on them by the social system in which they participated? To what extent can the typical complaints of refugees against the system, and the typical complaints of the regime against its own people, be traced to the elements of non-congruence between these personality modes and Soviet social structure?

A full answer to these questions would involve us in a much more extensive presentation and a more complex analysis than is possible here. We wish to stress that our analysis is limited to the Soviet socio-political system as it typically functioned under Stalin's leadership (see Bauer *et al.*, 2, and Fainsod, 7), since this was the form of the system in which our respondents lived and to which they had to adjust. To avoid any ambiguity on this score we have fairly consistently used the past tense. We sincerely hope that this will not lead to the mistaken assumption that we regard the post-Stalin era as massively discontinuous with the earlier system. However, to specify in any detail the elements of stability and change in post-Stalin Russia, and to indicate the probable effects of such changes on the adjustment of Soviet citizens to the system, is beyond the scope of this paper. As for the personality dimensions, we will discuss each in its relations to system participation separately, rather than in the complex combinations in which they operate in reality. Only those of the personality traits cited above are discussed that clearly have relevance for the individual's participation in the socio-political system.

Need Affiliation. Virtually all aspects of the Soviet regime's pattern of operation seem calculated to interfere with the satisfaction of the Russians' need for affiliation. The regime has placed great strains on friendship relations by its persistent programs of political surveillance, its encouragement and elaboration of the process of denunciation, and its assignment of mutual or 'collective' responsibility for the failings of particular individuals. The problem was further aggravated by the regime's insistence that its élite should maintain a substantial social distance between itself and the rank-and-file. In addition, the regime developed an institutional system that affected the individual's relations with others in a way that ran strongly counter to the basic propensities of the Russians as represented in our sample. The desire for involvement in the group, and the insistence on loyalty, sincerity, and general responsiveness from others, received but little opportunity for expression and gratification in the tightly controlled Soviet atmosphere. Many of the primary face-to-face organizations most important to the individual were infiltrated, attacked, or even destroyed by the regime. The break-up of the old village community and its replacement by the more formal, bureaucratic, and impersonal collective farm is perhaps the most outstanding example, but it is only one of many. The disruption and subordination to the state of the traditional family group, the Church, the independent professional associations, and the trade unions are other cases in point. The regime greatly feared the development of local autonomous centers of power. Every small group was seen as a potential conspiracy against the regime or its policies. The system of control required that each and all should constantly watch and report on each other. The top hierarchy conducted a constant war on what it scornfully called 'local patriotism', 'back-scratching',

and 'mutual security associations', even though in reality it was attacking little more than the usual personalizing tendencies incidental to effective business and political management. The people strove hard to maintain their small group structures, and the regime persistently fought this trend through its war against 'familieness' and associated evils. At the same time it must be recognized that by its emphasis on broad group loyalties, the regime probably captured and harnessed somewhat the propensities of many Russians to give themselves up wholly to a group membership and to group activity and goals. This is most marked in the Young Communist League and in parts of the Party.

Need Orality. The scarcity element that predominated in Soviet society, the strict rationed economy of materials, men, and the physical requirements of daily life seem to have aroused intense anxieties about further oral deprivation that served greatly to increase the impact of the real shortages that have been chronic to the system. Indeed, the image of the system held by most in our sample is very much that of an orally depriving, niggardly, non-nurturant leadership. On the other hand, the regime can hope to find a quick road to better relations with the population by strategic dumping or glutting with goods, which was to some extent attempted during the period of Malenkov's ascendancy, although perhaps more in promise than reality.

Need Dependence. The regime took pride in following Lenin in 'pushing' the masses. It demanded that individuals be responsible and carry on 'on their own' with whatever resources were at hand, and clamored for will and self-determination (see Bauer, 1). Clearly, this was not very congruent with the felt need for dependent relations. At the same time the regime had certain strengths relative to the need for dependence. The popular image of the regime as one possessed of a strong sense of direction fits in with this need. Similarly it gained support for its emphasis on a massive formal program of social-welfare measures, even if they were not too fully implemented. This directedness has a bearing also on the problem of submission. Although the regime had the quality of a firm authority able to give needed direction, it did not gain as much as it might because it was viewed as interested in the maximation of power *per se*. This appears to alienate the Russian as he is represented in our sample.

The Trust-Mistrust Dilemma. Everything we know about Soviet society makes it clear that it was extremely difficult for a Soviet citizen to be at all sure about the good intentions of his government leaders and his immediate supervisors. They seemed always to talk support and yet to mete out harsh treatment. This divided behavior pattern of the leadership seemed to aggravate the apparent Russian tendency to see the intentions of others as problematical and to intensify the dilemma of trust-mistrust. On the basis of our interviews one might describe this dilemma of whether or not to grant trust as very nearly *the* central problem in the relations of former Soviet citizens to their regime. The dilemma of optimism vs. pessimism, of whether outcomes will be favorable or unfavorable, presents a very similar situation.

The Handling of Shame. The regime tried exceedingly hard to utilize public shame to force or cajole Soviet citizens into greater production and strict observance of the established rules and regulations. Most of our available public documentary evidence indicates that the regime was not outstandingly successful in this respect. Our clinical findings throw some light on the reason. The regime tried to focus shame on non-performance, on failures to meet production obligations or to observe formal bureaucratic rules. To judge by the clinical sample, however, the Russian is little shamed by these kinds of performance failures, and is more likely to feel shame in the case of moral failures. Thus, the Soviet Russian might be expected to be fairly immune to the shaming pressures of the regime. Indeed, the reactions of those in our sample suggest the tables often get turned around, with the citizen concluding that it is the regime which should be ashamed because it has fallen down in these important moral qualities.

Affective Functioning. The general expansiveness of the Russians in our sample, their easily expressed feelings, the giving in to impulse, and the free expression of criticism, were likely to meet only the coldest reception from the regime. It emphasized and rewarded control, formality, and lack of feeling in relations. Discipline, orderliness, and strict observance of rules are what it expects. Thus, our Russian subjects could hope for little official reward in response to their normal modes of expression. In fact, they could be expected to run into trouble with the regime as a result of their proclivities in this regard. Their expansiveness and tendency freely to express their feelings, including hostile feelings, exposed them to retaliation from the punitive police organs of the state. And in so far as they did exercise the necessary control and avoided open expression of hostile feelings, they experienced a sense of uneasiness and resentment because of this unwarranted imposition, which did much to color their attitude to the regime.

Conative Functioning. The non-striving quality of our Russian subjects ties in with the previously mentioned characteristics of dependence and non-instrumentality. The regime, of course, constantly demanded greater effort and insisted on a more instrumental approach to problems. It emphasized long-range planning and deferred gratification. There was a continual call for efforts to 'storm bastions', to 'breach walls', 'to strive mightily'. With the Russian as he is represented in our sample, it does not appear likely that the regime could hope to meet too positive a response here; in fact it encountered a substantial amount of rejection for its insistence on modes of striving not particularly congenial to a substantial segment of the population. Indeed, the main influence may have been exerted by the people on the system, rather than by the system on them. Soviet official sources have for many years constantly complained of the uneven pace at which work proceeds, with the usual slack pace making it necessary to have great, often frenzied, bursts of activity to complete some part of the Plan on schedule, followed again by a slack period. It may well be that this pattern results not only from economic factors such as the uneven flow of raw material supplies, but that it also reflects the Russian tendency to work in spurts.

Relations to Authority. In many ways the difficulties of adjustment to the Soviet system experienced by our subjects revolved around the gap between what they *hoped* a 'good' government would be and what they *perceived* to be the behavior of the regime. Our respondents freely acknowledged that the Soviet leaders gave the country guidance and firm direction, which in some ways advanced the long-range power and prestige of the nation. They granted that the regime well understood the principles of the welfare state, and cited as evidence its provision of free education and health services. The general necessity of planning was also allowed, indeed often affirmed, and the regime was praised for taking into its own hands the regulation of public morality and the conscious task of 'raising the cultural level' through support of the arts and the encouragement of folk culture.

Despite these virtues, however, the whole psychological style of ruling and of administration adopted by the Bolsheviks seems to have had the effect of profoundly estranging our respondents. A great gulf seemed to separate the rulers and the ruled, reflected in our respondents' persistent use of a fundamental 'we'-'they' dichotomy. 'They' were the ones in power who do bad things to us, and 'we' were the poor, ordinary, suffering people who, despite internal differences in status or income, share the misfortune of being oppressed by 'them'. Most did not know that Stalin had once asserted that the Bolsheviks could not be a 'true' ruling party if they limited themselves 'to a mere registration of the sufferings and thoughts of the proletarian masses' (23). Yet our respondents sensed this dictum behind the style of Soviet rule. They reacted to it in charging the leaders with being uninterested in individual welfare and with extraordinary callousness about the amount of human suffering they engender in carrying out their plans. Our subjects saw the regime as harsh and arbitrary. The leaders were characterized as cold, aloof, 'deaf' and unyielding to popular pleas, impersonal and distant from the people's problems and desires. The regime was seen not as firmly guiding but as coer-

cive, not as paternally stern but as harshly demanding, not as nurturant and supportive but as autocratic and rapaciously demanding, not as chastening and then forgiving but as nagging and unyieldingly punitive.

The rejection of the regime was however by no means total, and the Bolshevik pattern of leadership was in many respects seen not as totally alien but rather as native yet unfortunately exaggerated. This 'acceptance' did not extend to the coldness, aloofness, formality, and maintenance of social distance, which were usually rejected. It did, however, apply to the pressures exerted by the regime, which were felt to be proper but excessive. Coercion by government was understandable, but that applied by the regime was not legitimate because it was so harsh. The scolding about backsliding was recognized as necessary, but resented for being naggingly persistent and caustic. And the surveillance was expected, but condemned for being so pervasive, extending as it did even into the privacy of one's friendship and home relations, so that a man could not even hope to live 'peacefully' and 'quietly'. The elements of acceptance within this broader pattern of rejection have important implications for the future of the post-Stalin leadership. They suggest that the regime may win more positive support by changing the mode of application of many of its authoritarian and totalitarian policies without necessarily abandoning these policies and institutions as such. Indeed in watching the public behavior of men like Khrushchev and Bulganin one cannot help but feel that their style of leadership behavior is much more congenial to Russians than was that of Stalin.

The preceding discussion strongly suggests that there was a high degree of incongruence between the central personality modes and dispositions of many Russians and some essential aspects of the structure of Soviet society, in particular the behavior of the regime. Most of the popular grievances were clearly based on real deprivations and frustrations, but the dissatisfactions appear to be even more intensified and given a more emotional tone because they were based also on the poor 'fit' between the personality patterns of many Soviet citizens and the 'personality' of the leaders as it expressed itself in the institutions they created, in their conduct of those institutions and the system at large, and in the resultant social climate in the U.S.S.R.

SOCIAL CLASS DIFFERENTIATION

Since personality traits found in the Russian sample are merely modal rather than common to the group at large, it follows that sub-groups can meaningfully be differentiated by the choice of appropriate cutting points on the relevant continua. As a way of placing the individuals in our sample on a common scale, three elements from the total range of characteristics previously described were selected. They were chosen on the grounds that they were most important in distinguishing the Russians as a group from the Americans, and also because they seemed meaningfully related to each other as elements in a personality syndrome. The three characteristics were: great strength of the drive for social relatedness, marked emotional aliveness, and general lack of well-developed, complex, and pervasive defenses. The two clinicians rated all cases for a combination of these traits on a three-point scale. Cases judged on the basis of a review of both interview and test material to have these characteristics *in a marked degree* were placed in a group designated as the 'primary set'. Individuals in whom these characteristics were clearly evident, but less strongly pronounced, were designated as belonging to a 'variant' set. The 'primary' and 'variant' sets together constitute a relatively homogeneous group of cases who clearly revealed the characteristics that we have described as 'modal'. All the remaining cases were placed in a 'residual' category, characterized by markedly stronger development of defenses, and in most instances also by lesser emotional expressiveness and lesser social relatedness. This group was relatively the least homogeneous of the three because its members tended to make use of rather different combinations of defenses without any typical pattern for the set as a whole. Subjects placed in the 'residual' group appeared to differ more from those in the 'variant' set than the 'primary' and the 'variant' sets differed from each other. However, even the 'residual' pattern was not separated from the others by a very sharp break: emotional aliveness and relatedness to people were present also in some members of this group. Each of our 51 cases was assigned to one of four social-status categories on the basis of occupation and education. All those in group A were professionals and higher administrative personnel most of whom had university training, and all those in the D group were either peasants, or unskilled or semi-skilled workers with no more than five years of education. Placement in the two intermediary categories was also determined by the balance of occupation and education, group B consisting largely of white-collar workers and semi-professional and middle supervisory personnel, and group C of more skilled workers with better education.

Table I gives the distribution of cases among the three personality types within

TABLE 1

STATUS DISTRIBUTION OF PERSONALITY TYPES AMONG FORMER SOVIET CITIZENS

| | *Personality Type* | | | |
Status	Primary	Variant	Residual	Total
A	—	1	12	13
B	2	8	6	16
C	3	4	2	9
D	8	3	2	13
Total	13	16	22	51

each of the four status groups. It is evident that the primary pattern has its greatest strength in the lower classes, becomes relatively less dominant in the middle layers, and plays virtually no role at all in the top group. The 'residual' pattern predominates at the top level and is very rare among peasants and ordinary workers.[12]

Since the distinctive patterns of adjust-

[12] The method of assigning the cases to the three psychological groups was holistic and impressionistic. It is of interest to note, therefore, that when more exact and objective techniques were used on the Sentence Completion Test to rate a similar but larger sample of refugees on some differently defined personality variables, the relationship between occupation and education and the personality measures was quite marked in three out of five variables. See M. Fried (10).

ment to the Soviet system by the various socio-economic groups will be the basis of extensive publications now in progress, we restrict ourselves here to a few general observations. First, we wish to stress that, as our interviews indicate, both the more favored and the rank-and-file share substantially the same range of complaints against the regime, find the same broad institutional features such as the political terror and the collective farm objectionable, and view the same welfare features such as the system of education and free medical care as desirable. In spite of these common attitudes our data suggest that personality may play a massive role with regard to some aspects of participation in and adjustment to the socio-political system. The educational-occupational level attained and/or maintained by an individual in an open-class society is one of the major dimensions of such participation. This is particularly the case in the Soviet Union, where professional and higher administrative personnel are inevitably more deeply implicated in the purposes and plans of the regime, are politically more active and involved, and are subjected to greater control and surveillance. It seems plausible that persons in whom the affiliative need was particularly strong, expressiveness marked and impulse control weak, and the defensive structures not well developed or well organized would be handicapped in competition for professional and administrative posts in any society; they certainly could not be expected to strive for or to hold on to positions of responsibility in the Soviet system.

The pattern of marked association between certain traits of personality and educational-occupational level clearly invites a question as to whether the personality really affected the level attained and held, or whether the appropriate personality traits were merely acquired along with the status. This question raises complex issues which we cannot enter into here. We do wish to point out, however, that the characteristics on which our psychological grouping was based belong to those that are usually formed at an early age and are relatively long enduring and resistant to change. At first glance this affirmation of the early origins of the patterns described seems to be inconsis-

tent with their observed association with educational-occupational level. However, the contradiction exists only if one assumes that obtaining a higher education and a superior occupation in Soviet society is a matter either of pure chance or exclusively of ability, unrelated to family background and the person's own attitudes and strivings. The data on stratification and mobility in Soviet society show, however, that persons born into families of higher social and educational level have a much better chance than do others to obtain a higher education and professional training (Feldmesser, 8; see also Inkeles, 15). Consequently, many people of the professional and administrative class grew up in families of similar status, and in those families were apparently reared in a way different from that typical of the peasant and worker families.[13] Presumably this produced enduring effects on their personality formation, which were important prior to exposure to common educational experience.

In addition, mobility out of the lower classes may have been mainly by individuals whose personality was different, for whatever reason, from that of the majority of their class of origin. Such differences can easily express themselves in a stronger drive for education and for a position of status. We must also allow for the role played by the regime's deliberate selection of certain types as candidates for positions of responsibility. Finally, there is the less conscious 'natural selection' process based on the affinity between certain personality types and the opportunities offered by membership in the élite and near-élite categories. In this connection we are struck by the relative distinctness of the highest status level in our sample, since only one person with either of the two variants of the modal personality of the rank-and-file shows up among them. These results bear out the impression, reported by Dicks, of radical personality differences and resultant basic incompatibilities between the ruled population and the rulers. The latter, we assume, are still further re-

---

[13] For a detailed discussion of *class differences* in the child-rearing values of pre-Soviet and Soviet parents see Alice Rossi (22).

moved from the 'modal pattern' than are our subjects in the élite group.

We have yet to deal with the question of how far our observations concerning a group of refugees can be generalized to the Soviet population and *its* adjustment to the Soviet system? The answer to this question depends in good part on whether personality was an important selective factor in determining propensity to defect among those in the larger group who had the opportunity to do so.[14] It is our impression that personality was not a prime determinant of the decision not to return to Soviet control after World War II. Rather, accidents of the individual's life history such as past experience with the regime's instruments of political repression, or fear of future repression because of acts which might be interpreted as collaboration with the Germans, seem to have been the prime selective factors. Furthermore, such experiences and fears, though they affected the loyalty of the Soviet citizen, were not prime determinants of his pattern of achievement or adjustment in the Soviet socio-political system.[15] The refugee population is not a collection of misfits or historical 'leftovers'. It includes representatives from all walks of life and actually seemed to have a disproportionately large number of the mobile and successful.

Though we are acutely aware of the smallness of our sample, we incline to assume that the personality modes found in it would be found within the Soviet Union in groups comparable in nationality and occupation. We are strengthened in this assumption by several considerations. First, the picture of Russian modal personality patterns which emerges from our study is highly congruent with the traditional or classic picture of the Russian character reported in history, literature, and current travellers' accounts.[16] Second, much of the criticism directed by the regime against the failings of the population strongly suggests that some of the traits we found modal to our sample and a source of strain in its adjustment to the system are widespread in the population and pose an obstacle to the attainment of the regime's purposes *within* the U.S.S.R. Third, the differences in personality between occupational levels are consistent with what we know both of the general selective processes in industrial occupational systems and of the deliberate selective procedures adopted by the Soviet regime. Because of the methodological limitations of our study, the generalization of our findings to the Soviet population must be considered as purely conjectural. Unfortunately we will be obliged to remain on this level of conjecture as long as Soviet citizens within the U.S.S.R. are not accessible to study under conditions of relative freedom. We feel, however, that, with all their limitations, the findings we have reported can be of essential aid in furthering our understanding of the adjustment of a large segment of the Soviet citizens to their socio-political system and of the policies adopted by the regime in response to the disposition of the population.

REFERENCES

1. Bauer, R. *The New Man in Soviet Psychology.* Cambridge, Mass.: Harvard University Press, 1952.
2. ———, Inkeles, A., and Kluckhohn, C. *How the Soviet System Works.* Cambridge, Mass.: Harvard University Press, 1956.
3. Beier, Helen. The responses to the Rorschach test of the former Soviet citizens. Unpublished Report of the Project. Russian Research Center, March 1954.
4. Beier, Helen, and Hanfmann, Eugenia. Emotional attitudes of former Soviet citizens as studied by the technique of projec-

[14] It is impossible to estimate accurately how many former Soviet citizens had a real chance to choose not to remain under Soviet authority. The best available estimates suggest that at the close of hostilities in Europe in 1945 there were between two and a half and five million former Soviet citizens in territories outside Soviet control or occupation, and of these between 250,000 and 500,000 decided and managed to remain in the West. See G. Fischer (9).

[15] Evidence in support of these contentions is currently being prepared for publication. A preliminary unpublished statement may be consulted at the Russian Research Center: A. Inkeles and R. Bauer (16).

[16] After this article was completed we discovered a report based almost entirely on participant observation which yielded conclusions about modal personality patterns among Soviet Russians extraordinarily similar to those developed on the basis of our tests and interviews. See: Maria Pfister-Ammende (19).

tive questions. *J. abnorm, soc. Psychol.*, Vol. 53, pp. 143–53, 1956.

5. Dicks, Henry V. Observations on contemporary Russian behavior. *Hum. Relat.*, Vol. V, pp. 111–74, 1952.

6. Erikson, Erik. *Childhood and Society.* New York: Norton, 1950.

7. Fainsod, Merle. *How Russia is Ruled.* Cambridge, Mass.: Harvard University Press, 1953.

8. Feldmesser, R. The persistence of status advantages in Soviet Russia. *Amer. J. Sociol.*, Vol. 59, pp. 19–27, July 1953.

9. Fischer, G. *Soviet Opposition to Stalin.* Cambridge, Mass.: Harvard University Press, 1952.

10. Fried, Marc. Some systematic patterns of relationship between personality and attitudes among Soviet displaced persons. Unpublished Report of the Project. Russian Research Center, October 1954.

11. ———, and Held, Doris. Relationships between personality and attitudes among Soviet displaced persons: a technical memorandum on the derivation of personality variables from a sentence completion test. Unpublished report of the project. Russian Research Center, August 1953.

12. Hanfmann, Eugenia. Social perception in Russian displaced persons and an American comparison group. *Psychiatry,* Vol. XX, May 1957.

13. ———, and Beier, Helen. Psychological patterns of Soviet citizens. Unpublished Report of the Project. Russian Research Center, August 1954.

14. ———, and Getzels, J. G. *Interpersonal Attitudes of Former Soviet Citizens as Studied by a Semi-Projective Method. Psychol. Monogr.,* Vol 69, No. 4, whole number 389, 1955.

15. Inkeles, A. Stratification and social mobility in the Soviet Union: 1940–1950. *Amer. sociol. Rev.,* Vol. 15, pp. 465–79, August 1950.

16. ———, and Bauer, R. Patterns of life experiences and attitudes under the Soviet system. Russian Research Center, October 1954.

17. ———, and Levinson, Daniel J. National character: the study of modal personality and sociocultural systems. In G. Lindzey (Ed.), *Handbook of Social Psychology,* Vol. II, pp. 977–1020. Cambridge, Mass.: Addison-Wesley, 1954.

18. Murray, H. *Explorations in Personality.* New York: Oxford University Press, 1938.

19. Pfister-Ammende, Maria. Psychologische Erfahrungen mit sowetrussischen Fluchtlingen in der Schweiz. In M. Pfister-Ammende (Ed.), *Die Psychohygiene: Grundlagen und Ziele.* Bern: Hans Huber, 1949.

20. Roseborough, H. E., and Phillips, H. P. A comparative analysis of the responses to a sentence completion test of a matched sample of Americans and former Russian subjects. Unpublished Report of the Project. Russian Research Center, April 1953.

21. Rosenblatt, Daniel, Slaiman, Mortimer, and Hanfmann, Eugenia. Responses of former Soviet citizens to the thematic apperception test (TAT): an analysis based upon comparison with an American control group. Unpublished report of the project. Russian Research Center, August 1953.

22. Rossi, Alice. Generational differences among former soviet citizens. Unpublished Ph.D. thesis in sociology, Columbia University, 1954.

23. Stalin, J. *Leninism.* New York: Modern Books, Vol. I, pp. 95–6, 1933.

The Function of Male Initiation Ceremonies: A Cross-Cultural Test of an Alternative Hypothesis[1] / Frank W. Young

A recent explanation of male initiation ceremonies interprets them as a means of controlling potentially disruptive emotions generated in childhood. The main evidence supporting this hypothesis consists of a cross-culturally based association between male initiation ceremonies and a combination of two customs: a close mother-son sleeping arrangement and a postnatal taboo on the mother's sex relations. This essentially Freudian interpretation is, however, not the only possible one. A counter hypothesis explains initiation as the dramatization of the sex-role characteristic of societies with a high degree of male solidarity. The two "child-rearing practices" are better interpreted as aspects of the organization of polygynous families. The exclusive mother-child sleeping arrangement is simply another way of looking at the father's absence, and the postnatal taboo is a norm that protects wives from too frequent pregnancies. The spuriousness of the association is demonstrated empirically, and a similar interpretation, proposed as a substitute for the first hypothesis, is also rejected.

Many "culture and personality" studies depend on theories which characterize personality as a system of intervening variables or mechanisms by which one aspect of culture—usually child-training practices—influences another aspect such as religious beliefs or particular institutions. Although this view has been criticized[2] and contradictory evidence on some points has been published,[3] it has been difficult to put the theory to a decisive test because so much of its support is in the form of clinical or anthropological

evidence that cannot be replicated. There is need for a test which differentiates between a Freudian hypothesis and an alternative, and which, in turn, rejects one but not the other under conditions that are rigidly controlled.

The opportunity for such a test is provided by the appearance of a study by John W. M. Whiting, Richard Kluckhohn, and Albert Anthony in which they test on a sample of fifty-six societies a hypothesis that links certain childhood situations to the presence of male initiation rites.[4] They assert that when the infant sleeps on its mother's bed for a year or more, strong feelings of dependency develop. Similarly, if there is a postnatal taboo of a year or more on the mother's sex relations, when the husband finally returns to his wife the displacement of the dependent boy from his mother's close care generates deep hostility. Both these emotions may become disruptive to society when the boy matures. Adolescence is a particularly dangerous period because at that age the boy is called upon to participate in men's work, independent of his mother's support. At this age he also handles weapons. Since all societies must maintain social control of disruptive behavior, an institutional

Reprinted from *The American Journal of Sociology*, 67, 1962, pages 379–396, by Frank W. Young by permission of The University of Chicago Press. Copyright 1962 by University of Chicago. Printed in U.S.A.

[1] This paper is an expanded version of one read at the 1960 meeting of the American Anthropological Association and was supported by PHS Small Grant #M 3740A. I am indebted to my wife, Dr. Ruth C. Young, for her analytic assistance and to Mrs. John A. Beagles and Miss Joan Brownell for ably coding the bulk of the data. Millicent R. Ayoub, Albert S. Anthony, Jules Henry, John Hitchcock, Kimball Romney, Leigh Triandis, and John M. Whiting kindly supplied unpublished data or other information on which this research depended. I am indebted to Orrin Klapp and Morris Daniels for helpful criticism.

[2] Cf. H. Orlansky, "Infant Care and Personality," *Psychological Bulletin*, XLVI (1949), 1–48, and A. R. Lindesmith and A. L. Strauss, "A Critique of Culture-Personality Writings," *American Sociological Review*, XV (1950), 587–600.
[3] W. H. Sewell, "Infant Training and the Personality of the Child," *American Journal of Sociology*, LVIII (1952), 15–59.

[4] "The Function of Male Initiation Ceremonies at Puberty," in E. Maccoby, T. M. Newcomb, and E. L. Hartley (eds.), *Readings in Social Psychology* (New York: Henry Holt & Co., 1958), pp. 359–70.

mechanism of control is functionally necessary. The initiation ceremonies of primitive peoples may be interpreted as such a mechanism. Hazing and genital operations assert the authority of men over the adolescent boy; the separation of boys from women and submission to tests of fortitude breaks the boys' psychological dependency. A demonstrable association exists between the four initiation customs and the two child-training practices.

It is clear that the foregoing "disruptive emotion" hypothesis follows the classic Freudian framework of impulsive man assailed by a frustrating culture. Although Whiting *et al.* reject a specific Oedipal explanation, their modification is still in the Freudian tradition, and the many general criticisms that have been made of that framework still apply. For instance, it is assumed that the emotions generated in childhood somehow maintain themselves until adolescence, despite the great variety of experience between the two periods. It is further assumed that the two- or three-year-old boy is capable of the complex emotions and perceptions that are postulated by the theory; that is, when the father returns the displaced boy is able to infer that the father is to blame, even though it was the mother who allowed the father to return. Third, it is assumed that initiation ceremonies are primarily inhibitory and that this function is almost completely determined by the peculiar patterning of two small aspects of family organization.

Before introducing an alternative explanation based on symbolic interaction theory, it should be acknowledged that Whiting has already abandoned the disruptive emotion hypothesis (a shift that became known to the author after the termination of the study reported here) and has substituted what may be called a "sex-role conflict" hypothesis. The latter explanation of the empirical association between initiation ceremonies and child care depends on a particular concept of identification, namely: "the process of identification consists of the covert practice of the role of an envied status. In learning-theory terms, identification consists (*a*) of learning a role by rehearsal in fantasy or in play rather than by actual performances, and (*b*) such rehearsal is motivated by envy of

the incumbent of a privileged status."[5] The initiation ceremony is now interpreted as an institution that resolves a cross-sex identification. The child having a close sleeping relation with his mother (the post-natal taboo is disregarded in the second interpretation) comes to envy her status, which in turn leads to a feminine identification. If he lives in a society where the rule of residence is patrilocal, however, at five or six years of age he perceives that men have the enviable status, which leads him to a male identification. The resulting conflict must be resolved with the help of a social institution.

In view of the second hypothesis, criticism and empirical rejection of the disruptive emotion explanation is more pertinent rather than less so, because the second hypothesis is basically like the first. For example, despite the term identification, the sex-role conflict hypothesis involves the same assumptions regarding childhood emotions and the competence of the child to make complex interpretations. Thus, Whiting argues that when the boy sleeps with the mother he comes to identify with her as a result of his recognition that her status is different from his and that hers is enviable, while if the parents sleep together, the boy identifies with them both to about the same degree. But is not the opposite interpretation equally plausible? If a child thinks at all, is it not more likely that he would be satisfied when he has his mother all to himself and would feel relatively deprived when he must share her with the father? Would he not therefore identify with her when the father is present? Similarly, the interpretation of patrilocal residence is dubious. Even granted that in patrilocal societies men have higher status, it does not follow that such status is any more readily perceived than in matrilocal societies. At any rate, the best study available indicates that males play the instrumental role in all societies, regardless of rule of residence.[6] At least, then, the child must

[5] Roger V. Burton and John W. M. Whiting, "The Absent Father: Effects on the Developing Child," paper read at the 1960 meeting of the American Psychological Association.

[6] See Morris Zelditch, Jr., "Role Differentiation in the Nuclear Family: A Comparative Study," in T. Parsons and R. F. Bales, *Family: Socialization and Interaction Process* (New York: Free Press of Glencoe, Inc., 1955), 307–351.

discriminate between the instrumental role of the men and their prestige. Finally, the sex-role conflict hypothesis still assumes that initiation ceremonies are inhibiting—at least Whiting implies this when he uses the term "brainwash" to characterize their function—although now the ceremony also functions to reinforce the boy's male identification, presumably as a result of the hazing and genital operations, which prompt the youth to envy the status of his tormentors.

The present study uses the cross-cultural methodology employed in the Whiting research, and whenever possible uses his coding of items, although this coding, since it is derived from another theoretical framework, tends to work against the test. The same sample is used with the exception of the Khalapur Rajputs and the Druze, inasmuch as these are a caste and a religious group respectively and do not qualify as communities, the basic unit of the present analysis.[7]

AN ALTERNATIVE FORMULATION

According to the symbolic interaction explanation,[8] the function of initiation is to stabilize the boy's sex role at a time when it is particularly problematical, although not in the manner suggested by Whiting. Thus, one's sex role becomes problematical insofar as its definition does not provide sufficient guidance in the diverse social interactions allowed or prescribed by society. Inasmuch as societies have a sexual division of labor and some form of marriage, a well-defined sex role becomes functionally necessary when the boy nears the threshold of participation in such social patterning. However, some societies pose still another socialization problem which is that sex role must conform to more specific requirements imposed by a high degree of male solidarity. Such solidarity may be defined as the co-operation of the men in maintaining a definition of their situation as one that is not only different from that of women, but which involves organized activities requiring the loyalty of all males. Although solidarity is a matter of degree, a crucial threshold develops when the men of a village come to see themselves as a consciously organized group with the power to exclude or discipline its membership. Inasmuch as explanation of the development of male solidarity is outside the scope of this paper, it is sufficient to say that it appears to be an ecological problem in the sense that the physical and social environment determines the degree of cohesion: The environment must permit a simple and stable definition of the situation. Solidarity would not be expected among Eskimo men where the food supply is so meager and diverse that males rarely act in concert. At the other extreme, modern societies have such complex environments that an undifferentiated interpretation is rarely possible. Rather, male solidarity should occur in the "middle-level" societies where the variety of food exploitation patterns is limited and where the resources may be exploited by co-operative groups. Moreover, it is among such societies that intergroup hostilities conducive to male solidarity are possible. In nomadic communities hostility tends to be individualized while in com-

[7] The general methodology of these studies is reviewed in John W. M. Whiting, "The Cross-cultural Method," in Gardner Lindzey (ed.), *Handbook of Social Psychology* (Cambridge: Addison-Wesley Publishing Co., 1954), 523–31. The specific sample used here is described in Whiting, Kluckhohn, and Anthony, *op. cit.* The following considerations bear on the level of reliability and freedom from bias of this study: (*a*) After a period of training, the two coders extracted the data from the ethnographies for fifteen societies. Data that did not attain a level of agreement of 85 per cent were omitted from the schedule, which was revised at that point. Lack of funds precluded a complete reliability study. (*b*) Four coders worked on the different parts of the data, which means that an adequate level of reliability must have been obtained, since the hypotheses hold despite the negative influence of any random error introduced. (*c*) Data coded by Murdock and Whiting *et al.* were used, introducing different frames of reference which, if anything, worked against the hypotheses. (*d*) In general, the variables used in this study are gross categories, and are therefore probably more reliable.

[8] The theory proposed here is simply a specification of that already developed by Durkheim, Radcliffe-Brown, G. H. Mead, W. I. Thomas, H. S. Sullivan, A. R. Lindesmith, A. L. Strauss, N. Foote, and E. Goffman, all of whose work is too well known to require citation. This line of thought has recently been reviewed and creatively extended by Hugh Dalziel Duncan (see his "The Development of Durkheim's Concept of Ritual and the Problem of Social Disrelationships" in Kurt H. Wolff (ed.), *Émile Durkheim, 1858–1917* (Columbus: Ohio State University Press, 1960), pp. 97–117.

plex societies armies are made up of men from diverse communities. Only in relatively stable, autonomous communities would combat groups include all the males of the village and only those. Of course, as male cohesion develops it is likely that the "approved" interpretation of the environment becomes oversimplified, and if a notion like "all whites are our enemies" develops, then the phenomenal environment may operate to further consolidate the group.

In societies with a high degree of male solidarity, stabilization of sex role is not complete until the boy identifies with the male group, since such identification is a major component of the sex role. Identification is here defined as the process of taking as one's own the cluster of social meanings held by a person or group. Identification requires first that the identifier have sufficient skill in symbolic interaction (usually not acquired until early adolescence) to comprehend the symbolic environment and, second, that he recognize that his society requires him to learn certain specific clusters of social meanings, such as those involved in one's sex role. Strength of identification is determined by the degree to which the identifier cooperates in creating and maintaining the definition of the situation and by the degree of clarity given the social meanings by the group or person generating them.

Given the foregoing assumptions, it might appear that identification with a solidary male group is easy compared to learning the relatively vague attitudes required for participation in work and the family and hence that initiation ceremonies should be unnecessary for the more organized male structure. But the relative clarity of meanings held by the cohesive males is not apparent to the candidate. Typically, the male activities are hidden from the uninitiated. Moreover, once the meanings of the male group are accessible, internalization must be achieved rapidly and precisely. There is no long period of inculcation by way of games, sharing in sex-segregated work, or the differentiated expectations of others. Neither is there the allowable deviation that occurs in most family and work organization. Therefore, the social meaning of male solidarity must be dramatized in a memorable way and the candidate must participate intensely in the presentation. Furthermore, the rest of the community must be alerted to his new status so they can respond appropriately. What could be more impressive to both the youth and the community than to be publicly subincised or to be the center of attention of a group of village men intent upon beating him severely? It is a mistake to interpret initiation ceremonies in terms of culture-bound notions of pain or mutilation. The ethnographic accounts strongly suggest that, given the proper attitude, these are probably accepted with the same equanimity that a woman submits to beauty care or a man to being tattooed. Similarly, tests of fortitude and social separation (the ethnographic accounts give no basis for Whiting's phrase "separation from women") are another way of dramatizing the boy's new status. Not only does he give a performance to the community, but his separation before or after the performance reminds the community by his absence of his new presence.

The solidarity hypothesis may be empirically tested by cross-tabulation of the child-training items and initiation ceremonies when male solidarity is controlled. Although this hypothesis ultimately requires a recoding of both the child-training items and Whiting's empirical definition of initiation rites, they are adequate for the present test. The only new factor, then, is male solidarity. Empirically it is defined by the presence of an organization in which all adult males are expected to participate and from which women are excluded. The organization must be institutionalized to the point of having its own building or a taboo that protects open meetings from the perception of women or uninitiated boys. The definition includes the cases of the Hopi and Dahomeans where there are a number of male organizations of essentially the same type. It is assumed that such reduplication occurs in larger communities simply as an adaptation to the larger population. When the organizations develop differentiated purposes, they do not qualify.

The cross-tabulation of these three factors is shown in Table 1 and follows the format of the Whiting et al. article. It is clear that when male solidarity is controlled, no relation

TABLE 1

RELATIONS OF MALE INITIATION CEREMONIES TO EX-
CLUSIVE MOTHER-SON SLEEPING ARRANGEMENT AND
POSTNATAL TABOO WHEN PRESENCE OF EXCLUSIVE
MALE ORGANIZATION IS CONTROLLED

Exclusive Male Organization	Mother-Son Sleeping	Post-natal Taboo	No. of Societies Having at Least One or Four Initiation Customs*	
			Present	Absent
Present	+	+	11	1
	+	−	1	1
	−	+	2	0
	−	−	2	0
			16	2
Absent	+	+	3	4
	+	−	0	2
	−	+	1	4
	−	−	0	22
			4	32

* Genital operations, hazing, seclusion from women, and tests of manliness.

remains between the typology of child-care items and the presence of initiation ceremonies. The relative efficiency of prediction of the disruptive emotion and solidarity hypotheses is .45 and .70 respectively, as measured by Goodman and Kruskal's[9] lambda and giving Whiting *et al.* the benefit of the doubt on the predictions of the positive-negative combinations of child-care items, even though they made no prediction about these. Essentially the same cross-tabulation applies to the sex-role conflict hypothesis, except that the postnatal taboo is dropped out and the presence of patrilocal residence (as against matrilocal and a general category labeled ambilocal) is substituted. The efficiency of the prediction based on these factors is only .40 compared, as before, to .70 for the more parsimonious solidarity variable. Unfortunately a cross-tabulation of

[9] Leo A. Goodman and William H. Kruskal, "Measures of Association for Cross-Classifications," *Journal of American Statistical Association*, XLIX (1954), 732–64. Lambda varies from zero to one. Although tables of significance are as yet unavailable, this makes no difference in the present case where all the tests used the same sample.

these variables with male solidarity controlled is not feasible due to the paucity of cases.

Among a number of possible objections to these results, one demands immediate analysis: Is the relation between male solidarity and initiation ceremonies tautological? As usual, answers may be given at different levels of abstraction. If the question refers to the concrete level of indicators, then the answer is certainly negative. If the only index of male solidarity was the presence of a specific male organization, one might object that the initiation ceremony is merely an aspect of the organization's activities. But as defined here, male solidarity is more than a specific organization and is indicated in other ways, such as group hunting, organization for local warfare, etc. Moreover, many initiation ceremonies have no apparent relation to the activities of the male organization, and even if they did, it still does not follow that the *degree* of dramatization (the dependent variable) is an integral part of the organization's activities. If, however, the question refers to the conceptual level, there is room for doubt. Of course, there is nothing in either of the two concepts—male definition of the group situation and dramatization of status—that necessarily implies the other, but it might be argued that at a high level of abstraction initiation ceremonies are simply another way of talking about the boundary-maintaining activities of a given, although abstractly conceived, group. Whether this is so or not requires a much deeper theoretical and empirical probing, but the important implication remains unchallenged. If initiation ceremonies and group solidarity are simply different aspects of the same social structure, then it is even more doubtful that an explanation of these in terms of the events of childhood is sufficient. Certainly the basic features of social structure are not determined by events that are consequences of that very structure. Rather, an ecological explanation, such as has been suggested, would appear more plausible.

A RECONCEPTUALIZATION OF INITIATION CEREMONIES

The cross-tabulation in Table 1 shows that when male solidarity is controlled, the association between the child-care items and initiation ceremonies is dissolved. But the indicators of the initial association were based on the rejected hypothesis. It remains now to reconceptualize both of these in terms of the new framework and to show that male solidarity is an even stronger determinant when these variables are recoded.

The solidarity hypothesis would define initiation ceremonies as the more dramatic forms of sex-role recognition. So conceived, initiation ceremonies involve a patterned performance designed to convey a particular impression to an audience. Such dramatization of sex role takes a variety of forms, combining particular customs like tattooing, tooth filing, beatings, fasting, special taboos, social isolation, gifts, dances, participation in raids, circumcision, subincision, etc., in ways that have always attracted the attention of anthropologists. Examples of undramatic sex-role recognition are the informal delineation that results from differentiated subsistence activities among Koryak men and women, the adolescent boy's shift of resi-

dence to a youth camp among the Nyakyusa, and the formalized—but undramatic coeducation in our own society. However, not all customs of the adolescent period are relevant to the social recognition of sex role, and the following rules delineate the limits: (a) the custom must occur periodically in the same general form and be supervised at least in part by the adults of the society, (b) it must apply to all adolescent males and only to these—ceremonies including females do not qualify—and (c) of a series of initiation ceremonies, only the most elaborate, as measured by the scale, is to be coded. Such rules would exclude the tooth filing among children in Alor, the festivities surrounding the young men in wartime Japan who went into the military, the unpatterned hazing of Maori warrior novices, and the marriage-initiation pattern of the Khalapur Rajputs (although they were excluded on other grounds). One major implication of these operational rules is the rejection of the view that initiation marks the attainment of full adult status. There is of course an intimate connection between sex role and responsible adulthood, and in a few societies the recognition of the two statuses merges. But in the large majority, consensual validation of responsible adult status is withheld by prohibitions on marriage, speaking in councils, full participation in warfare, etc., until late adolescence.

These criteria defined a large pool of items, some of which formed a Guttman scale (Table 2). Step 1 of the scale includes all the minimal recognition customs, such as gift-giving, a change of name, festive attention, etc, that are periodically maintained with the help of adults. Such public recognition usually lasts less than a day and involves a group no larger than the immediate family. The second and third steps may be taken together to reflect individualized dramatization of the initiate. Social seclusion and decoration and/or performance call attention to the personality of the youth. The last two items also combine to form a general category of "group participation," with the fifth step reflecting an emotionally charged group response. It is significant that items like circumcision, subincision, etc., did not scale, probably because the coding was not sensi-

TABLE 2

SCALE OF DEGREES OF DRAMATIZATION OF MALE INITIATION CEREMONIES

Step	Item	Per Cent of Societies	Scale Error
1	Customary minimal social recognition (gift, party, change of name, etc.)	100	0
2	Social seclusion (physical and/or social separation such as initiation camp, isolation or taboo on social contact)	75	0
3	Personal dramatization (initiate is ceremonially dressed and/or gives public performance)	55	2
4	Organized social response (group dresses ceremonially and/or performs)	35	1
5	Emotionalized social response (beating or severe hazing)	30	0
	Total cases	(20)	

tive to their precise dramatic context, which is the basis of the scale. Circumcision in itself, as our own society demonstrates, is not necessarily dramatic. Needless to say, none of the scale items occurs in societies with undramatic sex role recognition.

Although the scale has a high coefficient of reproducibility (.97), the small number of cases and the fact that some of the steps contain only one or two societies detracts from its internally demonstrated validity. However, at least two relationships between the scale and other data reinforce its interpretation as an undimensional measure. First, essentially the same scale applies to females, and holds for the thirty-four societies of this sample that have dramatic initiation ceremonies for that sex. Second, an elaborate dramatization is most likely to occur when there are a number of initiates, rather than just one, a fact which would also support the present interpretation.

However, a more important consideration is the theoretical plausibility of the scale. The three basic steps appear to reflect an increasing amount of social preparation. The easiest thing the adults can do is make a simple gesture, such as a gift. If they wish to call more attention to the boy, but still keep the effort small, they can separate him socially. Further elaboration can be achieved by dramatizing the initiate's person, or by organizing the whole group. Only in the more elaborate forms is there a strong emotional display.

The scale takes on special significance in view of Whiting's interpretation of initiation as "brainwashing." It is difficult to see how these items would support such an interpretation, as indeed, it is difficult to see how the four items chosen by Whiting et al. (especially when only one of the four need be present) qualify as a social mechanism for resolving a sex-role conflict. It must be admitted, however, that there is an almost total overlap between the presence of initiation ceremonies as coded by Whiting et al. and as indicated by the scale. In fact, nineteen of the twenty cases are identical. The scale rejects one society (Chiracahua) which Whiting et al. coded as having initiations and adds another (Yap) which they excluded. Such correspondence is reasonable, nonetheless, since all the four items used by Whiting et al. are ways of dramatizing sex role. The crucial point is that the four-item index excludes a host of customs that anthropologists and the scale would include.

If the scale of dramatic sex-role recognition is substituted for the four-item index in Table 1, and is used simply to indicate the presence or absence of dramatic customs, there is an increase in the measure of prediction efficiency of the solidarity hypothesis, bringing it to .80 in comparison with .45 for the disruptive-emotion hypothesis, where there is no change. The next step is to relate degrees of solidarity to degrees of dramatization, but because of the small number of cases in the present sample, only a trend shows up

MALE SOLIDARITY AND FAMILY ORGANIZATION

In addition to replacing the interpretation of initiation ceremonies required by the two Freudian hypotheses, the solidarity hypothesis calls for a reinterpretation of the childhood experience items. It has already been shown that the two aspects of what may now be labeled "absent-father family organization" have no empirical relation to initiation ceremonies when male solidarity is controlled. Why, then, was there even a correlation to begin with? It is important, first, to examine the actual data. An "exclusive mother-infant sleeping arrangement" means that the mother keeps the child on her own mat for at least a year and usually until the child is weaned. Often the mother lives in a special hut, a pattern that is frequent when there is polygyny. But these same facts have another side. From the adult point of view an exclusive sleeping arrangement is simply another way of saying that the father is absent. While it is true that the mother need not keep the child on her own mat when the father is away, the two situations are usually the same in practice and it is doubtful whether it would be possible to code the distinction, given present data, even if it existed. Perhaps then, the real question is why the father is absent. The mere fact of polygyny is almost a sufficient explanation. Although it is conceivable that a husband might continue to sleep with a wife who is nursing an infant, considerations of sleeping convenience are enough to explain why he stays with other wives. But even in those cases where the husband has no other wives he may not stay with his new family, but go instead to the men's house where life is probably more exciting and at least quieter. And what of the postnatal taboo? It also makes sense in this context as a norm for controlling the frequency of pregnancy, since polygynous wives typically maintain separate households and gardens, and must be free to work. This interpretation is tested in Table 3 by a cross-tabulation of the relation of the father to a nursing wife with the presence of an exclusive male organization and the extent of polygyny.[10] The absent-father family pattern was empirically defined by the combination of both the exclusive mother-son sleeping arrangement and the postnatal taboo, since to rely on only one of these items would admit too many cases where the family type was undeveloped. The distribution of the cases (lambda is .42) indicates that when general polygyny and a male organization are both present, the absent-father family pattern is likely to occur. It is still relatively frequent if only general polygyny exists. In the two cases where a male organization is present but there is no polygyny, we should expect the presence of a men's house where the husband can stay. In fact they (the Yapese and Fijians) do have such houses. Similarly, the society (Ooldea) that does not have the absent-father family pattern despite the presence of a male organization ought not to have a men's house, as indeed is the case. However, this sort of refinement in terms of sleeping quarters may not be carried too far. In some societies, the men sleep apart from their wives despite the lack of men's house while in other societies they do not make use of the clubhouse in this manner. Also, such refinement unduly reduces the already small number of cases.

The foregoing discussion has been extended more than might ordinarily be necessary because it is important to show how faulty operationalization leads to false conclusions. These customs of household organization apply only to adults. Any inference from them to the personality of the child is just that. Admittedly it is difficult to index infant behavior directly, but there are descriptions of boy's play, attitudes, etc., which might serve better. The burden of proof is at least on those who see such a connection. Indeed, it should have been there at the outset. To assume that childhood experiences index personality tendencies is

---

[10] The data on polygyny are taken from G. P. Murdock's invaluable "World Ethnographic Sample" (*American Anthropologist*, LIX [1957], 664–87). His categories of "general," "sororal," and "non-sororal" polygyny were combined for the first category in the table, and his "limited" and "limited . . . but sororal" constitute the second category.

tantamount to defining as true the crucial link in the theory.

The only problem remaining is why polygyny should be associated with male solidarity. Although various hypotheses might be offered, the simplest one is that it takes the work of many women to support the activities of solidary males.

SOME BASIC ISSUES

There are many loose ends to this study, such as the relation of female initiation to female solidarity, the relation of solidarity to the division of social labor and to more particular ecological factors, the prediction of degrees of dramatization, and the relation of other customs, such as the couvade, to types of household organization. Preliminary findings on all of these factors appear to support the solidarity hypothesis and

TABLE 3

RELATION OF FATHER'S SEPARATION FROM NURSING WIFE TO EXTENT OF POLYGYNY AND PRESENCE OF EXCLUSIVE MALE ORGANIZATION

	Father Typically Separated from Nursing Wife	
Extent of Polygyny	Yes	No
Exclusive male organization present:		
Polygyny, 20 per cent or more	7	1
Limited polygyny, under 20 per cent	3	1
Monogamy	2	4
Total	12	6
Exclusive male organization absent:		
Polygyny, 20 per cent or more	5	8
Limited polygyny, under 20 per cent	1	8
Monogamy	1	13
Total	7	29

will be published elsewhere. Enough has been said, however, to permit an analysis of some basic issues.

In the image of man and society that stands behind the two Freudian hypotheses, personality is conceptualized as "mediat-ing" between "maintenance systems" and "projective systems." An example given by Whiting illustrates the paradigm: In societies with extended family households, in contrast to mother-child households, mothers tend to indulge infants.[11] Such high indulgence is in turn associated with the belief that human beings can influence the gods. In this example, the organization of the household is part of the maintenance system. The kind of personality found in different household organizations is said to be reflected in the amount of maternal indulgence, and since this indicator is associated with attributes of the gods, it is asserted that personality interacts with the projective system. Initiation ceremonies can be similarly fitted into this paradigm: polygyny is part of the maintenance system and, as Table 3 shows, is associated with an exclusive mother-child sleeping arrangement. The feminine identification alleged to result from this infant experience is a variable of personality which interacts with other variables, particularly male identification. Initiation ceremonies, interpreted as part of the projective system, help to resolve the resultant personality conflict. If childhood training is interpreted as predisposing the child to accept a certain social order, the cases are analogous, although the meaning of "projective" thereby becomes ambiguous. However, the basic point is clear: Whiting's particular hypothesis concerning initiation ceremonies, whether in its first or second form, is to be taken as only one instance of a general paradigm, as a specific derivation from a general theory. Now, if we could be sure that his explanation of initiation ceremonies was a rigorous deduction from this theory, then a negative test of the hypothesis would invalidate the parent structure. But such precision may not be assumed at the present stage of the social sciences, so it is necessary to examine directly, if only theoretically, the basic conceptualization. It may be criticized on several fundamental counts.

In the Whiting model, the direction of causation moves from the subsistence in-

[11] In John W. M. Whiting, "Socialization Process and Personality" in Francis L. K. Hsu (ed.), *Psychological Anthropology* (Homewood, Ill.: Dorsey Press, 1961), 358 ff.

stitutions to the personality of the child and thence to the wider social order. Although the possibility is admitted that some sequences by-pass the childhood events, they are exceptions to the rule. Such a framework poses at the outset complex methodological problems. An adequate test of any derived hypothesis should follow the causal sequence from the events in the economy of one generation to the interaction of the next generation with the prevailing ideology. An experiment lasting some twenty years or more is indicated, and it is difficult to believe that adequate controls could be instituted during this period.

But a more substantive question bears on the assumption that social determinants can be generated or transmitted through the mechanisms of childhood personality. For a hundred years or more social scientists have agreed that society exists in and through communication, and it was tacitly assumed that this was adult communication. There were good reasons for this assumption that children do not fully participate in society, that is, in the symbolic environment of a group of people making a living in a particular locality. Since children are not physically able to participate in adult work, they are excluded from full involvement in the symbolic environment. Such participation, there is good reason to believe, is a precondition to adequate comprehension of social meanings. Phrasing this criticism another way, can any modern conception of society disregard the vast accumulation of evidence and theory regarding social control, institutionalization, leadership, and all the other processes that adults appear to maintain? The situation is analogous to that pointed out by Hume in discussing whether we should accept the truth of miracles. If such a belief requires the rejection of a larger body of scientific generalization, we are well advised to disbelieve.

But even if the Whiting model granted that "babies don't make culture," as Ellsworth Faris once said, it would still be inadequate. For it appears that the scheme postulates an essentially wordless communication. In both hypotheses, the child assimilates a crucial meaning of his experience quite early in life, certainly before his language skill is fully developed. In the discussion of how the four customs of the initiation ceremony operate, it is implied that the experience of isolation, tests of fortitude, etc., convey particular meanings. Again, in the sex-role conflict hypothesis the boy learns by exposure to genital operations and hazing that identification with males is preferable to identification with females. Phrased generally, the individual is placed in a behavioral situation, and "he gets the message."

Maintaining the position that meaning is conveyed without words is at least awkward. How then does the boy maintain his male identification after his initiation when there is no high-status group to envy? To say that the youth is always inferior to someone invalidates the particular choice of patrilocal residence and the mother-son sleeping arrangement as determinants. Whiting might invoke secondary reinforcement—a wordless variety—but such reinforcement can only account for the narrowest conception of identification. For if male role means anything it means participating in the legal, religious, military, and kinship structures—all of which involve words and consensus—in ways that are different from the activity of females. Sex, dominance, or aggression may or may not be part of the male role, but participation in certain social sectors in prescribed ways always is. At the very least, the empirical association between male solidarity and initiation would appear to imply words and demand an explanation in terms of them.

It appears, then, that Whiting's conception of cultural and personality integration can do without words only if a narrow concept of identification is employed. But it is questionable whether the social sciences can do without a broad, social definition of male identification. How are we to explain the modal shifts in behavior as a person changes roles even when the situation remains the same? How are we to deal with the identical responses made to different stimulus situations? Words seem quite necessary as carriers of the complex and flexible cluster of meanings that appear to be involved in the male role.

However, it is very likely that Whiting

would agree that the conventional symbolism of language is necessary for the flexible behavior characteristic of the socialized adult. Secondary reinforcement might be invoked to connect the behavioral situations with the associated words. Perhaps the contrary implication in his empirical research is simply an operational problem, to be remedied by better data. But if this is so, major theoretical problems remain. Concepts like status envy and identification must be broadened to include social meanings and the theory must explain how these meanings are learned. In the present case, initiation ceremonies may not be labeled "brainwashing" and described with no reference to the manipulation and dramatization of ideas that is part of the meaning of that term.

There is another characteristic of Whiting's conception of meaning that may be noted. The model places great emphasis on the isomorphism of the behavioral situation and the meaning that it conveys. Thus, infants that are indulged by their mothers come to believe that the gods will indulge them too. When a boy is displaced from his mother's bed by his father, he believes he is being deprived (rather than favored by both). When, during initiation, a boy is socially isolated, he comprehends that he must give up his dependence on women, and when he is circumcised he is confirmed in his male status through an experience impossible for women. Of course, not all the ascribed meanings reflect this congruency, but there is a strong trend in this direction, reminiscent of early Freudian dream interpretation. However, this implicit assumption is untenable if for no other reason than the lack of enough isomorphisms in the world to account for social behavior. Even if there were, it would require great methodological sophistication to find the connections. For instance, does a digging stick convey the idea of a man or a woman? Admittedly the assumption of isomorphism between situation and meaning is not crucial to the theory, but it does tell us something about Whiting's disinterest in purely conventional symbolism.

A third line of criticism questions whether any theory that explains social facts in terms of parallel individual experiences can adequately account for the uniformities of group behavior. This question, posed long ago by Durkheim, has never been satisfactorily answered by advocates of person-specific theories. In the present case, for instance, it is agreed that all societies that initiate boys do so uniformly. The exceptions are few and clearly deviant. Now, in terms of the sex-role conflict hypothesis each boy sleeps near his mother, comes to identify with her, and later, if he lives in a patrilocal society, comes to envy the status of the men and to identify with them. But do all boys follow this sequence? It has already been shown that the exclusive mother-child sleeping arrangement is a concomitant of polygyny. But even in polygynous societies not all men have multiple wives and some of the monogamous men very likely sleep at home with their nursing wives. Of what use is initiation to these boys? It does no good to claim that the norm of polygyny exerts a general influence, because the hypothesis requires that each boy experience a close relationship with his mother. Neither is it sufficient to say that some boys have no conflict but go along with initiation anyway, because such a loophole vitiates the hypothesis and undermines the whole task of explanation.

Actually, this criticism of person-specific theories has been implicit in a methodological complaint often lodged against cross-cultural research. It has been argued that a social norm is not an adequate index of individual behavior. There is no assurance that individual behavior is uniform, and the very notion of a norm implies that it will not be. But this stricture had little force as long as investigators obtained correlations between two or more social norms and made a plausible explanation of how individual behavior might operate. On the other hand, the criticism has great force when it is stated, not as an operational problem, but as a fundamental deficiency of a whole class of theory. Regardless of correlations, person-specific theories cannot explain uniformities of behavior like participation in initiation ceremonies.

What then is the alternative conceptual framework? Admittedly symbolic interactionism is still in its early stages of development and requires much more elaboration.

But such a conceptual framework would assert that society is a complex of groups within groups—even the smallest primitive community is differentiated—and that each of these subgroups tends to maintain its organization intact in the context of the whole and vis-à-vis the other sub-groups. The individual members co-operate to maintain a given definition of the group situation and to communicate it successfully, often by dramatization, to the other groups, which constitute audiences. This interplay always appeals to overriding principles of the social order since few subgroups can afford the destruction of the larger structure. Over and above this organized conversation is the grammar of language itself. This combined structural backbone helps to maintain the contingencies in vocabulary that carry clusters of social meaning.

The relations of the individual to these symbolic structures is one of varying modes and degrees of participation, and the organization of roles acquired in the course of such participation is the basis of personality. Although personality may be said to affect social structure indirectly through individually promulgated social innovation, to say that modal personality has an independent effect on the shared system of beliefs makes no sense in these terms. Personality is linked to culture not as a mediator and converter of signals in the manner of a television relay station, but as a special and intense organization of a field of symbols. The degree and mode of each individual's participation in society determine "how much" personality he will have and whether he will reorganize his portion of the symbolic environment in a way that might later affect the whole.

In the picture of society suggested above there is little that is new. The novelty lies in the application of this conceptual framework to the phenomena of initiation. Male solidarity has already been defined as the consensus of the men regarding the purpose and activities of the group. Although the present study does not directly index these shared meanings, the ethnographic accounts strongly suggest that definite religious, military, and fraternal attitudes exist and are expressed in the ritual activity, regalia, and mythology. These meanings must be maintained by adults inasmuch as, quite aside from the taboos barring the uninitiated, children cannot comprehend these meanings fully until after early adolescence. Granted that games, observation, and conversation serve as an introduction to adult symbolic structures, the inculcation of these is weak and partial. Certainly this line of thought would reject the unconscious learning asserted by the Freudians to occur during the first several years of life.

Initiation ceremonies are viewed as a mechanism for maintaining the consensus of the males. If the boys did not undergo initiation or if some were allowed to avoid it, the male definition of the situation might be distorted or weakened. It is for this reason that initiation is required of all boys in a community. The ceremony insures conformity by involving the candidate in an intense co-operation with men in the symbolic process. Initiation is the first and perhaps most memorable step in a continued participation in an organized symbolic structure. So long as a man participates in it, the social meanings he has internalized remain strong and he plays his sex role with confidence in diverse situations. The rituals themselves only remind him of what it means to be a man in his society; in themselves they contain no meaning. On this view circumcision is not different in kind from a gift, a new name, a dance, etc. It differs in degree only insofar as its acquisition has a more dramatic and emotional context. Thus, almost anything can figure in the initiation ceremony. The sound of a bull roarer or some test of endurance have an intrinsic dramatic quality. Lacking such, the effect may be heightened by hiring a specialist to direct the ceremony or by encouraging the women to wail.

An initial implication of this conception of initiation ceremonies is that empirical work on ritual must allow for the wide variety of symbolic contents; it may not be limited to particular customs. More generally, it suggests that other rituals might profitably be viewed in terms of a dramaturgical framework. The essence of this approach, it should be noted, is the analysis of the function of rituals for groups, not individuals.

article, offering a framework which provides guidance, suggests an important avenue through which

SECTION THREE

Social Issues and

Social Problems

Investigating the important relationship between
the individual and the social contexts for his behavior, the field of social psychology is necessarily
brought into areas which are directly concerned with
pressing social issues and problems. In this final
section, we have included four articles building upon
the previous "approaches" and "contexts" and dealing with four different areas of public concern.

The article by Sampson *et al.* examines the issue of
mental hospitalization by providing a framework
based upon the study of families undergoing this
particular life crisis.

The concept of *anomie,* referring to a state of
normlessness, in which the individual is lacking or is
disconnected from his usual, normative ties with
others, is related to social structural variables in the
article by Mizruchi. The anomic individual, lacking
rootedness and social ties to control and integrate his
behavior and to provide him with necessary social
supports, falls easy prey to many forms of moral
and mental illness. How this psychological state is
related to one's position in the social structure offers
another example of a social psychological approach
to an important social problem.

Bordua's article presents a sociological interpretation of delinquency, an obvious social issue of
increasing importance. He views delinquency as a
subcultural, or in Yinger's terms, a contracultural,
phenomena. This more sociological approach provides
insights into this problem which are often lost by an
overly psychological approach, in which delinquent

behavior is seen as the outcome of a distorted, or abnormal personality.

The final article, by Pettigrew, examines the issue of desegregation and the present and hoped for future role of the social psychologist in studying this area. By offering the concept, *latent liberal,* Pettigrew suggests an important avenue for social psychological research and intervention.

Family Processes and Becoming a Mental Patient[1] / Harold Sampson, Sheldon L. Messinger, and Robert D. Towne[2]

Both before and after hospitalization a type of accommodative pattern usually evolves between a disturbed person and his family and ultimately permits or forces him to remain in the community in spite of severe difficulties. It is the disruption of this pattern which eventually brings a disturbed person to psychiatric attention. Two patterns of accommodation between schizophrenic patients and their families are identified, the disruption of these patterns are documented, and the consequences of these patterns for the nature of the pathway to the mental hospital are examined.

Becoming a mental patient is not a simple and direct outcome of "mental illness"; nor is hospitalization in a mental institution, when and if it comes, the automatic result of a professional opinion. Persons who are, by clinical standards, grossly disturbed, severely impaired in their functioning, and even overtly psychotic may remain in the community for long periods without being "recognized" as "mentally ill" and without benefit of psychiatric or other professional attention. It is clear that becoming a mental patient is a socially structured event.[3] The research reported here is directed to increasing our understanding of the nature and significance of this structuring as it mediates the relations between individuals and the

more formal means of social control. The research explores (*a*) the relationship between patterns of family means for coping with the deviant behavior of a member who later becomes a mental patient and (*b*) efforts of the future patient or members of his family to secure professional help.

The broad nature of this latter relationship may be inferred from a number of published findings. Yarrow and her colleagues have documented the monumental capacity of family members, before hospitalization, to overlook, minimize, and explain away evidence of profound disturbance in an intimate.[4] The post-hospital studies of the Simmons group have suggested that high "tolerance for deviance" in certain types of families is a critical determinant of the likelihood of poorly functioning and sometimes frankly psychotic former patients avoiding rehospitalization.[5] Myers and Roberts found that few mental patients or their families sought or used professional assistance before hospitalization until the problems they encountered became unmanageable.[6] Whit-

Reprinted from *The American Journal of Sociology,* 68, 1962, pages 88–96, by Harold Sampson, Sheldon L. Messinger, and Robert D. Towne by permission of The University of Chicago Press and the senior author. Copyright 1962 by University of Chicago. Printed in U.S.A.

[1] This report is based on a study carried out by the California Department of Mental Hygiene and partially supported by Grant No. 3M–9124 from the National Institute of Mental Health.

[2] Thanks are due to David Ross, Florine Livson, Mary-Dee Bowers, Lester Cohen, and Kate S. Dorst for their substantial contributions to the research for this study.

[3] Erving Goffman, in "The Moral Career of the Mental Patient," *Psychiatry,* XXII (May, 1959), 123–42, discusses a variety of "career contingencies" that may intervene between deviant behavior and hospitalization for mental illness. Also see the articles in *Journal of Social Issues,* XI (1955), ed. John A. Clausen and Marian Radke Yarrow, under the general title of "The Impact of Mental Illness on the Family." August B. Hollingshead and Fredrick C. Redlich (*Social Class and Mental Illness: A Community Study* [New York: John Wiley & Sons, Inc., 1958], chap. vi, "Paths to the Psychiatrist") also emphasize this point.

[4] Marian Radke Yarrow, Charlotte Green Schwartz, Harriet S. Murphy, and Leila Calhoun Deasy, "The Psychological Meaning of Mental Illness in the Family," *Journal of Social Issues,* XI (1955), 12–24. Also see Charlotte Green Schwartz, "Perspectives on Deviance—Wives' Definitions of Their Husbands' Mental Illness," *Psychiatry,* XX (August, 1957), 275–91; Hollingshead and Redlich, *op. cit.,* esp. pp. 172–79; and Elaine Cumming and John Cumming, *Closed Ranks* (Cambridge, Mass.: Harvard University Press, 1957), esp. pp. 91–108.

[5] See Ozzie G. Simmons, *After Hospitalization: The Mental Patient and His Family* (Hogg Foundation for Mental Health, n.d.) and the several studies by the Simmons group cited there.

[6] Jerome K. Myers and Bertram H. Roberts, *Family and Class Dynamics* (New York: John Wiley & Sons, Inc., 1959), pp. 213–20. These find-

mer and Conover reported that the occasion for hospitalization was ordinarily not recognition of "mental illness" by the patient or his family but inability to cope with disturbed behavior within the family.[7]

These observations and our own permit two inferences. First, both before and after hospitalization some type of accommodative pattern ordinarily evolves between a disturbed person and his family which permits or forces him to remain in the community in spite of severe difficulties. Second, it is the disruption of this pattern which eventually brings a disturbed person to psychiatric attention.[8] An investigation of typical family accommodations to the deviant behavior of future patients, and how these accommodations collapse, should therefore contribute to our understanding of the ways in which individuals and the intimate social networks of which they are members are rendered less and more accessible to institutionalized devices of social control. Specifically, it should provide us with a glimpse of those dynamic family processes which determine a future mental patient's accessibility to community, particularly psychiatric intervention; these same processes determine the accessibility of the family. It should also contribute to our understanding of the meaning of such intervention to the

future patient and his family. Such family accommodations pose strategic problems for the persons who constitute and man community remedial facilities. These are problems seldom taken into explicit or systematic account by such persons—problems beyond but related to the pathology of the patient.

We shall be concerned here with two phases in the relationship between the future patient and his family and with the connections between these phases and the course of events leading to hospitalization. The first phase consists of the evolution of a pattern of accommodation within the family to behavioral deviance on the part of the future patient.[9] The second phase consists in the disruption of this pattern of accommodation. Our observations are derived from a study of seventeen families in which the wife-mother was hospitalized for the first time in a large state mental institution and therein diagnosed as schizophrenic.[10] We established a research relationship with both patient and spouse at the time of admission and continued to see them regularly and frequently throughout hospitalization, and for varying periods extending to more than two years following first release. We conducted about fifty interviews with the members of each marital pair, including typically

---

ings also suggest that lower-class families are better able to contain an extremely disturbed person for long periods of time than are middle-class families; the latter call on outside help more rapidly when "major psychotic decompensation" occurs. This would follow from the argument presented by Talcott Parsons and Renée Fox in "Illness, Therapy, and the Modern Urban American Family," *Journal of Social Issues,* VIII (1953), 31–44.

[7] Carroll A. Whitmer and Glenn C. Conover, "A Study of Critical Incidents in the Hospitalization of the Mentally Ill," *Journal of the National Association of Social Work,* IV (January, 1959), 89–94 (see also Edwin C. Wood, John M. Rakusin, and Emanuel Morse, "Interpersonal Aspects of Psychiatric Hospitalization," *Archives of General Psychiatry,* III [December, 1960], 632–41).

[8] Another inference we have made, and which we discuss elsewhere, is that an important set of effects of community devices of social control pertain to family patterns of accommodation. In important ways, it is through these that individuals are controlled, rather than by direct action (Harold Sampson, Sheldon L. Messinger, and Robert D. Towne, "The Mental Hospital and Family Adaptations," *Psychiatric Quarterly,* 36 [1962], 704–19).

[9] This phase emphasizes one side of a complicated reciprocity between family relations and the deviance of family members. We have focused on the other side of this reciprocity—family relations as they sustain and promote deviant behavior—elsewhere (see Robert D. Towne, Sheldon L. Messinger, and Harold Sampson, "Schizophrenia and the Marital Family: Accommodations to Symbiosis," *Family Process,* 1 [1962], 304–18, and Robert D. Towne, Harold Sampson, and Sheldon L. Messinger, "Schizophrenia and the Marital Family: Identification Crises," *Journal of Nervous and Mental Diseases,* CXXXIII [November, 1961], 423–29). There is a large and growing literature on this topic, particularly as it concerns schizophrenia, much of which is referred to in the various citations to be found in *The Etiology of Schizophrenia,* ed. by Don D. Jackson (New York: Basic Books, Inc., 1960).

[10] Detailed characteristics of the families studied may be found in Harold Sampson, Sheldon L. Messinger, and Robert D. Towne, "The Mental Hospital and Marital Family Ties," *Social Problems,* IX (Fall, 1961), 141–55. In two of seventeen cases, a brief psychiatric hospitalization in a county hospital had occurred earlier; in a third case, the woman had been hospitalized in a private sanitarium for one month earlier in the same year she entered the state institution.

one or more joint interviews. Other relatives, psychiatrists, physicians, hospital personnel, and other remedial agents who had become involved with the patient or family over the years were also interviewed. Interview materials were supplemented by direct observation at home and in the hospital, and by such medical and social records as we could locate and gain permission to abstract.

These methods, which are described more fully elsewhere,[11] enabled us to reconstruct the vicissitudes of these marital families from courtship through marriage, child-bearing and child-rearing, eventual hospitalization of the wife, and well into the period following the patient's first release. We shall focus here on a longitudinal analysis of two patterns of accommodation which evolved between these women and their families prior to hospitalization and the disruption of these patterns. The patterns are exemplified by eleven and four cases, respectively; two of the seventeen families do not appear to be adequately characterized by either pattern. In order to present the patterns in some detail, our analysis will be developed in terms of selected families exhibiting each type of accommodation. This does not exhaust the empirical variety to be found even in the limited number of cases studied here. In the concluding section, however, emphasis will be placed on common patterns of relationship between future mental patients and their immediate interpersonal communities, as well as on the conditions under which these patterns deteriorate and collapse.

THE UNINVOLVED HUSBAND AND SEPARATE WORLDS

In the first situation, exemplified by eleven families, the marital partners and their children lived together as a relatively independent, self-contained nuclear family, but the marital relationship was characterized by mutual withdrawal and the construction of separate worlds of compensatory involvement. At some point during the marriage, usually quite early, one or both of the partners had experienced extreme dissatisfaction with the marriage. This was ordinarily

accompanied by a period of violent, open discord, although in other cases, the dissatisfaction was expressed only indirectly, through reduced communication with the marital partner. Whatever the means of managing the dissatisfaction when it occurred, in each of these families the partners withdrew and each gradually instituted a separate world. The husband became increasingly involved in his work or in other interests outside the marital relationship. The wife became absorbed in private concerns about herself and her children. The partners would rarely go out together, rarely participate together in dealing with personal or family problems, and seldom communicate to each other about their more pressing interests, wishes, and concerns. The marriage would continue in this way for some time without divorce, without separation, and without movement toward greater closeness. The partners had achieved a type of marital accommodation based on interpersonal isolation, emotional distance, and lack of explicit demands upon each other. This accommodation represented an alternative to both divorce and a greater degree of marital integration.

It is a particularly important characteristic of this type of family organization that pathological developments in the wives were for a time self-sustaining. The wife's distress, withdrawal, or deviant behavior did not lead to immediate changes of family life but rather to an intensification of mutual withdrawal. In this setting, the wives became acutely disturbed or even psychotic, without, for a time, very much affecting the pre-existing pattern of family life. This is exemplified in the following cases:

In the evenings, Mr. Urey worked on his car in the basement while his wife remained upstairs, alone with her sleeping children, engaged in conversations and arguments with imaginary others. This situation continued for at least two years before Mrs. Urey saw a psychiatrist on the recommendation of her family physician. Another two years elapsed before Mrs. Urey was hospitalized. During this period, Mr. Urey became ever less concerned with his wife's behavior, accepting it as a matter of course,

[11] *Ibid.*

and concerned himself with "getting ahead" in his job.

For two years prior to hospitalization, Mrs. Rand was troubled by various somatic complaints, persistent tension, difficulty in sleeping, a vague but disturbing conviction that she was a sinner, and intermittent states of acute panic. Mr. Rand was minimally aware of her distress. He worked up to fourteen hours a day, including weekends, in his store, and eventually a second job took him out of the home three evenings a week. On those infrequent occasions when his wife's worries forced themselves on his attention, he dismissed them curtly as absurd, and turned once again to his own affairs.

In these families the patterned response to distress, withdrawal, or illness in the wife was further withdrawal by the husband, resulting in increasing distance between, and disengagement of, the marital partners. These developments were neither abrupt nor entirely consistent, but the trend of interaction in these families was toward mutual alienation and inaccessibility of each partner to the other. In this situation, early involvement of the wife in a professional treatment situation was limited by her own withdrawal and difficulty in taking the initiative for any sustained course of action in the real world, as well as by the husband's detachment.

This pattern of mutual withdrawal eventually became intolerable to one or the other partner, pressure for a change was brought to bear, and the family suffered an acute crisis. In some cases, pressure for change was initiated by the husband. In other cases, such pressure was initiated by the wife in the form of increasing agitation, somatic and psychic complaints, and repeated verbal and behavioral communications that she was unable to go on. However the pre-hospital crisis was initiated, and whether it signaled a desire for increased or reduced involvement by the initiating partner, the change indicated an incipient collapse of the former pattern of accommodation.

In four of the eleven cases considered here, the pre-hospital crisis was primarily precipitated by a shift in the husband's "tolerance for deviance." In two of these cases, the wives had been chronically and

pervasively withdrawn from role performances and at least periodically psychotic. One husband, in the midst of job insecurities and a desire to move to another state to make a new start, pressed his wife to assume more responsibility. Another husband, approaching forty years of age, reassessed his life and decided that the time had come to rid himself of a wife whom he had long considered "a millstone around my neck." These husbands sought medical or psychiatric assistance specifically to exclude their wives from the family; the two wives were passively resistant to hospitalization. The explicit attitude of the husbands was that they wished the hospital to take their wives off their hands.

In the other two cases, the disruption of the earlier accommodation was associated with the establishment, by the husband, of a serious extra-marital liaison. Here, as in the two cases referred to above, there appeared to be no marked change in the wife's conduct prior to this indication of a desire by the husband for total withdrawal.

Virtually identical family processes were apparent in those cases where the manifest illness of the wife was itself the source of pressure for change, the harbinger of the collapse of the prior marital accommodation. The wife's illness intruded itself into family life, at first with limited impact, but then more insistently, like a claim which has not been paid or a message that must be repeated until it is acknowledged. The wife's "complaints" came to be experienced by the husband as, literally, complaints to him, as demands upon him for interest, concern, and involvement. These husbands, however, uniformly initially struggled to preserve the earlier pattern, that is, to maintain uninvolvement in the face of demands which implicitly pressed for their active concern. Thus, as the pre-hospital crisis unfolded, the wife's manifest illness assumed the interpersonal significance of a demand for involvement, and the husband's difficulty in recognizing her as seriously disturbed had the interpersonal significance of a resistance to that demand. The excerpt cited earlier from the Rand case illustrates this process if we add to it the observation that during these two years Mrs. Rand's difficulties recurrently came to the husband's attention in the form of momentary crises which compelled at least the response of curt dismissal.

In this situation, the husband initially assumed a passive or indifferent attitude toward his wife's obtaining professional help. But if she became involved with a psychiatrist, physician, minister, or social worker who took some interest in her life situation, the husband became concerned with the treatment in a negative way. The treatment "wasn't necessary," it "wasn't helping," it "cost too much money." In addition to these deprecations was a hint of alarm that the treatment would challenge the husband's pattern of uninvolvement.[12] For example, Mr. Rand, whose working schedule was mentioned earlier, worried that his wife's psychiatrist might support her complaint that he did not spend enough time at home. Thus the involvement of the wife with a psychiatrically oriented helper was experienced by the husband, at least initially, as a claim upon himself—for money, for concern, and most centrally, for reinvolvement. We have reported elsewhere[13] that there is some basis for this feeling. The treatment process, especially during hospitalization, does tend to induct the husband into the role of the responsible relative, and thereby presses for the re-establishment of reciprocal expectations which had been eroded in the earlier family accommodation.

In most of these cases, these processes led to more extreme deviance on the part of the wife which eventually came to the attention of the larger community, thereby resulting in hospitalization. For example, Mrs. Urey, who had been actively psychotic for some time, was hospitalized only after she set fire to her home. In brief, the wife's distress is at first experienced by the husband as an unwarranted demand for his reinvolvement in the marital relationship, he withdraws further, and her behavior becomes more deviant.

We may conclude this section with a few more general remarks. The pre-hospital crisis, in each of these cases, marked, and

was part of, the disruption of a pattern of accommodation which had been established between the marital partners. The disruption was in effect initiated by one of the partners and resisted by the other.[14] The former accommodation and the way in which it came to be disrupted were important determinants of the processes of "recognizing" the wife as mentally ill, of seeking and using professional help, and of moving the wife from the status of a distressed and behaviorally deviant person within the community to that of a mental patient. These processes, in fact, can only be understood within the context of these family patterns. The problems of early intervention in cases of serious mental illness and of effective intervention in the later crises which ordinarily do come to psychiatric attention cannot even be formulated meaningfully without consideration of these interpersonal processes which determine when, why, and how sick persons become psychiatric patients.

THE OVERINVOLVED MOTHER AND THE MARITAL FAMILY TRIAD

In a contrasting situation found in four cases, the marital partners and their children did not establish a relatively self-contained nuclear family. Rather, family life was organized chronically or periodically around the presence of a maternal figure who took over the wife's domestic and child-rearing functions.[15]

This organization of family life was a conjoint solution to interlocking conflicts of the wife, husband, and mother. In brief, these mothers were possessive and intrusive, motivated to perpetuate their daughters' dependency, and characteristically disposed to assume the "helpful" role in a symbiotic in-

[12] In one case, the psychiatrist urged the husband to seek treatment for himself.

[13] Sampson *et al.*, "The Mental Hospital and Marital Family Ties," *op. cit.*

[14] Wood, Rakusin, and Morse, *op. cit.*, have arrived at a related conclusion on the basis of an analysis of the circumstances of admission of forty-eight patients to a Veterans Administration hospital. "There is also evidence to suggest that hospitalization can for some patients be a way of demanding that those close to them change their behavior, just as it can be an expression by relatives that they are dissatisfied with the patient's behavior."

[15] This person was the wife's mother in three cases, her mother-in-law in the fourth. This distinction is not critical in the present context, and we shall refer to "the wife's mother," etc.

tegration with her. The daughters ambivalently pressed for the establishment or maintenance of a dependent relationship with their mothers and struggled to break the inner and outer claims of the maternal attachment. The husbands responded to anxieties of their own about the demands of heterosexual intimacy and marital responsibility, as well as their own ambivalent strivings toward maternal figures, by alternately supporting and protesting the wives' dependence on the maternal figure. The resulting family organization, in which the mother was intermittently or continuously called upon for major assistance, represented an alternative to both a relatively self-contained, independent nuclear family and to marital disruption with the wife returning to live within the parental family.

In direct contrast to the family accommodation described in the preceding section, the wives in "triadic" families did not quietly drift into increasing isolation and autism. Here, sickness or withdrawal by the wife were occasions for intense maternal concern and involvement. This development was ordinarily abetted by the husband. The resulting situation, however, would come to be experienced as threatening by the wife. She would come to view her mother as interfering with her marriage and her fulfilment of her own maternal responsibilities, as restricting her freedom, and as preventing her from growing up. At this point a small but often violent rebellion would ensue, and the husband would now participate with his wife to exclude the mother from family life. Such cycles of reliance on the mother followed by repudiation of her recurred over the years with only minor variations.

This accommodation complicated seeking and using professional help, but in a distinctively different way than in the family setting depicted earlier. Here, the family accommodation included this patterned response to withdrawal, illness, or distress in the wife: the mother replaced the wife in her domestic and child-care functions, and established with the wife a characteristic integration involving a helpless one who needs care and a helpful one who administers it; the husband withdrew to the periphery of the family system, leaving the wife and mother bound in a symbiotic interdependency.

In this patterned response, outside help was not simply superfluous but constituted an actual threat to the existing interdependency of mother and daughter (by implying that it was inadequate, unnecessary, or even harmful), whereas in the type of family accommodation previously described, treatment was experienced as a threat to the husband's uninvolvement; here, treatment was a threat to the mother's involvement.

It was the failure of this family accommodation which led to the wife's contact with the physician or psychiatrist. This failure occurred when, simultaneously, the wife rebelled against the maternal attachment but could not establish with her husband the previously effective alternative of temporary repudiation of that attachment. The following example demonstrates these processes:

> Mrs. Yale became anxious, confused, and unable to cope with the demands of daily life in the context of increasing withdrawal by her husband combined with increasing inner and outer pressure for reinvolvement with her mother. Her mother, Mrs. Brown, was living with the marital family, tending the house, caring for the child, and remaining by the side of her troubled daughter night and day. Mr. Yale had become increasingly involved in shared interests with a circle of male friends, and felt disaffected from family life.
>
> Mrs. Brown later characterized this period to the research interviewer: "I think Mary resented me because I tried to help and do things for her. She didn't want me to help with her work. She didn't seem to want me around–sort of resented me. She kept saying she wanted to be on her own and that she didn't have confidence because I was always doing things for her. She even resented me doing the dishes. I just wanted to help out." At this point, Mrs. Brown considered her daughter to be seriously emotionally disturbed, and thought psychiatric help would be advisable.

In such cases, the behavior which led family members to doubt the young woman's sanity consisted of hostility, resentment, and accusatory outbursts directed toward the mother. In these violent outbursts toward the maternal figure, the daughter was indeed "not herself." It was at just this point that the daughter's behavior constituted a disruption of the former family pattern of accommodation and led toward involvement with outside helpers. The mother might now view outside helpers as potential allies in re-establishing the earlier interdependency. The psychiatrist, however, was unlikely to fulfill the mother's expectations in this regard, and then he became an heir to the husband in the triadic situation, a potential rival to the mother-daughter symbiosis.

Shortly after outpatient treatment began, Mrs. Brown took her daughter on an extended vacation which effectively interrupted the treatment, detached the daughter from her incipient attachment to the psychiatrist, and re-established the pattern of mother-daughter interdependency with the husband at the periphery of involvement.

We may summarize, then, certain connections between this type of family accommodation and the use of professional help prior to hospitalization. The initial response to the family to the wife's distress was to attempt to reinstate a familiar pattern: a drawing together of mother and daughter in symbiotic interdependency and a withdrawal of the husband to the periphery of the family. This accommodation was disrupted by the eruption of the daughter's formerly ego-alien resentment toward her mother, and at this point the latter was likely to view physicians or psychiatrists as potential allies in restoring the former equilibrium. The psychiatrist, however, was unlikely to play this part and became, for the mother, a rival to the interdependency. For the daughter, also, this meaning of treatment invested it with the dangerous promise of a possible separation from the maternal figure. In this drama, the husband was likely to play a relatively passive if not a discouraging role, affording the wife little if any support in what she experienced as a threatening and disloyal involvement outside the family.

The way in which the hospitalization of the wife came about, in the collapse of this family accommodation, also provided contrasts to the processes depicted in the preceding section. As the pre-hospital crisis developed, the wife sought to withdraw from continuing intolerable conflict in the triadic situation. At first, the wife felt impelled to choose between regressive dependency on a maternal figure and the claims of her marital family, but was unable to either relinquish the former or achieve inner and outer support for the latter. Both alternatives were transiently affirmed and repudiated in the period preceding hospitalization, but in time she came to feel alienated from *both* mother and husband, and driven toward increasing *psychic* withdrawal. This process did not resolve her conflicts or remove her from the triadic field, and in time she herself pushed for physical removal.

Thus, in two of the four triadic cases, the wife herself, with a feeling of desperation, explicitly requested hospitalization. In a third case, the disturbed wife was brought to a psychiatrist in the company of both mother and husband, refused to return home with them after the appointment, and was thereupon hospitalized. In the fourth case, the wife was initially co-operative to a hospitalization plan, but equivocation by the husband and psychiatrist delayed action, and the wife gave herself and her daughter an overdose of drugs, thereby precipitating the hospitalization. This last case resembles the most common pattern described in the preceding section, in which the wife is driven to extreme deviance which comes to the attention of the larger community and compels hospitalization. But the secondary pattern, in which a husband takes primary initiative for hospitalizing a reluctant wife because she has become a "millstone around my neck," was entirely absent.

DISCUSSION

The career of the mental patient and his family ordinarily comes to the attention of treatment personnel during the course of an "unmanageable" emergency and fades from view when that emergency is in some way resolved. Prior to this public phase of the crisis, and often again after it, the disturbance of the patient is contained within a community setting. It is the collapse of accommodative patterns *between* the future patient and his interpersonal community which renders the situation unmanageable and ushers in the public phase of the pre-hospital (or rehospitalization) crisis.

Our analysis has been addressed to ways in which two particular organizations of family life have contained pathological processes, to the ways in which these organizations were disrupted, and to the links between family dynamics and recognition of illness, seeking and using professional help, and the circumstances of mental hospitalization. The analysis carries us beyond the observations that families often "tolerate" deviant behavior, may resist "recognition" that the future patient is seriously disturbed, and may be reluctant to use help, toward a systematic view of "typical" accommodations around deviance and typical patterns of crisis.

It is, of course, by no means evident how typical the patterns we have described may be. Although the analysis is confined to certain marital family organizations and does not entirely exhaust our own empirical materials, we suggest that the presentation does touch upon two common situations encountered in work with the mentally ill and their families. In the first situation, the future patient and his immediate interpersonal community move from each other, effect patterns of uninvolvement, and reciprocate withdrawal by withdrawal. The future patient moves, and is moved, toward exclusion from interpersonal ties and from any meaningful links to a position in communal reality. This situation, as we have seen, is compatible with very high "tolerance for deviant behavior," which may permit an actively psychotic patient to remain *in* the community while not psychosocially *of* it.

The accommodation may be disrupted by a shift in the "tolerance" of the interpersonal community, however determined,[16] or from the side of the future patient by increasing agitation which signals an attempt to break out of inner and outer isolation. Here, hospitalization is a possible route toward further disengagement of the patient from his interpersonal community, or conversely, toward

re-establishment of reciprocal expectations compatible with re-engagement. Whatever the outcome, a strategic therapeutic problem is posed by the chronic pattern of mutual disinvolvement and withdrawal.

In the second situation, the future patient and a member of his immediate interpersonal community become locked in mutual involvement, effect patterns of intense interdependency, and reciprocate withdrawal by concern. The future patient moves and is moved toward a bond in which interlocking needs tie the participants together rather than isolate them. This situation is also compatible with high tolerance for deviant behavior, but here because the deviance has become a necessary component of the family integration. It is this type of family process, rather than the first type, which has attracted most psychiatric interest,[17] although there is no reason from our data to suppose that it is the more common.

In the cases observed the disruption of this accommodation took the form of an ego-alien movement by the future patient against the claims of the overwhelming attachment. Here, hospitalization is at once a route of escape from intolerable conflict in the interpersonal community, and a potential pathway toward re-establishing the earlier pattern of accommodation. The strategic therapeutic problem posed is the contrasting one of modification of a chronic pattern of intense involvement.

The observations reported do not yield precise knowledge as to how psychiatric intervention might routinely be brought about early in the development of a serious mental illness, whether or when this is advisable, and how intervention might be more effective later on. The observations indicate, rather, that we must confront these questions in their real complexity, and investigate more closely and persistently than heretofore the characteristic ways in which families cope with severe psychiatric disturbances, the ways in which these intra-family mechanisms are disrupted, and the significance of the family dynamics which form the crucial background of the eventual encounter between patient and clinician.

---

[16] The determinants may be extraneous to inherent family processes. Thus, in a case not included in the present sample, the movement of a family from farm to city altered the family's capacity to retain a psychotic young man and precipitated his hospitalization.

[17] See Jackson (ed.), *op. cit.*

Social Structure and Anomia in a Small City /

Ephraim Harold Mizruchi (*State University of New York, Cortland*)

Interest recently has been focused on Durkheim's concept of anomie and Merton's theory of social structure and anomie. Srole's scale of anomia has been utilized in several studies; some doubt remains regarding support for Merton's notions. The present study based on a survey of a small city replicates in part some of the earlier work and tests Merton's hypothesis. Significant associations are reported between Srole's anomia and social class, class identification, and formal and informal social participation. It is held that anomia is not peculiar to large urban environments. Finally, it is hypothesized that the relatively lower classes have a greater tendency to anomia due to socially structured differential access to supportive subsystems as well as the inaccessibility of means for the achievement of socially desired ends.

Considerable interest has been shown in recent years in Durkheim's concept of *anomie* and sociological journals have carried more and more papers devoted to theoretical formulations and empirical application of this concept.[1] Merton's essays[2] have stimulated a good deal of thought regarding the sources of anomie in the social structure, and Srole's scale of anomia has precipitated a number of studies of this phenomenon.[3]

The present paper is directed in part toward a replication of some of the earlier studies in this sphere, and attempts to assess relationships between anomia and a series of sociologically significant independent variables. Somewhat more standardized measures than usual are used in analyzing data drawn from the very small city. Srole's Scale of Anomia is used as an index of social psychological anomie, Hollingshead's two factor Index of Social Position as an

index of class,[4] and Chapin's Social Participation Scale as an index of participation in formally organized voluntary associations.[5]

As Bell has noted, there is some question concerning the empirical support of Merton's hypothesis that the discrepancy between desired ends and inaccessibility of the means for achieving these ends leads to greater anomie in the relatively lower-class segments of the population.[6] Thus Srole[7] and Roberts and Rokeach[8] have reported con-

---

Reprinted from *The American Sociological Review*, 1960, 25, pages 645–654, by permission of author and publisher, American Sociological Association.

[1] See, e.g., *American Sociological Review*, 24 (April, 1959), which contains four papers dealing with some aspect of this concept.

[2] Robert K. Merton, "Social Structure and Anomie," in *Social Theory and Social Structure*, New York: Free Press of Glencoe, Inc., 1949, 1957, Chapter 4. The revised edition of this volume (1957) also extends the discussion into other areas in "Continuities in the Theory of Social Structure and Anomie," Chapter 5.

[3] Leo Srole, "Social Integration and Certain Corollaries: An Exploratory Study," *American Sociological Review*, 21 (December, 1956), pp. 709–716.

[4] A. B. Hollingshead, "Two-Factor Index of Social Position," New Haven, Conn., 1956, mimeographed. For a assessment of the usefulness of the ISP and other measures of social stratification in upstate New York, see Walter Boek *et al Social Class, Maternal Health and Child Care*, Albany: New York State Department of Health, 1957.

[5] F. Stuart Chapin, *Social Participation Scale*, Minneapolis: University of Minnesota Press, 1952. This is a revision of Chapin's original scale published as part of *The Measument of Social Status*, Minneapolis: University of Minnesota Press, 1933.

[6] Wendell Bell, "Anomie, Social Isolation, and the Class Structure," *Sociometry*, 20 (June, 1957), pp. 105–116.

[7] Leo Srole, *op. cit.*, p. 715. In Srole's first report on the A scale, "Social Dysfunction, Personality and Social Distance Attitudes," presented at the annual meeting of the American Sociological Society, 1951, the index of class is based on the respondent's educational level. In the paper referred to here Srole uses a combination of education and occupation. The reported relationship between class and anomia is not as high (−.30) as might be expected from Merton's hypothesis. In the absence of an explanation for the item weighting in the combined class scale we *suspect* that the discrepancy between Srole's results and those reported below is due to the nature of his scale.

[8] A. H. Roberts and M. Rokeach, "Anomie, Authoritarianism, and Prejudice," *American Journal of Sociology*, 62 (January, 1956), pp. 355–358.

flicting results, the former's findings supporting the Merton thesis and the latter's questioning it. Bell and, more recently, Meier and Bell, have shown that class and anomia are inversely associated, thus supporting Srole's findings.[9] The present study provides still another test of Merton's hypothesis.

A second interest of this investigation is the relationship between anomia and relative social isolation. The findings, as in the case of Bell's study, suggest that social isolation, if indicated by lack of participation in formal and informal associations, is associated with anomia.

Finally, this paper reflects a concern with the extent to which anomia exists in a given population and, more specifically, in small communities as contrasted with the large urban areas previously studied.

METHOD AND SCALE

Data for the study were gathered in 1958 as part of an adult education survey in a small upstate New York city (population about 20,000).[10] Items were included in the interview schedule designed to elicit information for the testing of sociological hypotheses. The interviews were conducted by college students enrolled in the writer's classes. The interviewers received elaborate instruction in interview techniques, but the precise nature of the study was not explained to them until all of the data were gathered.

The sampling unit was the dwelling and the respondent was designated as the male or female head of household selected alternately in every other unit. Where this was not possible the interviewer selected a male or female residing in the unit over 18 years of age.

The units were selected according to a standardized systematic sampling procedure, which provided data on at least two re-spondents living in each block. Accordingly, every eighth dwelling unit listed in the city directory (revised two years preceding the study) was designated as part of the sample. Commercial addresses were excluded from the count. In all, 618 completed interviews were obtained representing a response rate of almost 73 per cent. Approximately ten per cent of the households in the city are represented in the sample.

As Meier and Bell, for example, have pointed out, there is a lack of consensus regarding the usage of the term "anomia."[11] It is beyond the scope of the present paper to attempt a conceptual analysis of the various usages of "anomia" and "anomie."[12] It is possible, however, to differentiate two broad analytical levels: the sociological, which represents Durkheim's "classic" focus of attention; and the social psychological, which is the level being investigated by Srole, Bell, and others.[13] Our usage follows Srole's which refers to a continuum of eunomia-anomia, representing "the individual's generalized, pervasive sense of 'self-to-others belongingness' at one extreme compared with 'self-to-others distance' and 'self-to-others alienation' at the other pole of the continuum."[14]

Srole's scale includes five statements with which the respondent may either agree or disagree. Following his suggestion, however, five other items were interspersed among the A scale statements to reduce the possibility of the respondent operating under or developing an "acquiescence set."[15] Thus, in

[9] Bell, op. cit.; Dorothy L. Meier and Wendell Bell, "Anomie and Differential Access to the Achievement of Life Goals," American Sociological Review, 24 (April, 1959), pp. 189–202.

[10] For a report on the adult education phase of the study, see Ephraim H. Mizruchi and Louis Vanaria, "Who Participates in Adult Education?" Adult Education, 10 (Spring, 1960), pp. 141–143.

[11] Meier and Bell, op. cit., p. 191 n.

[12] A limited conceptual analysis is represented by the writer's Ph.D. thesis, in process, Purdue University, tentatively entitled, "Social Class, Social Participation and Anomia in a Small City." The present paper represents a preliminary analysis and interpretation of some of the data used in the thesis. I am indebted to the Danforth Foundation for a Teacher Study Grant and The Research Foundation of the State University of New York for a grant-in-aid.

[13] As Srole notes, op. cit., p. 712. Both Robert M. MacIver in The Ramparts We Guard, New York: Macmillan, 1950, and Harold D. Lasswell in "The Threat to Privacy," in R. M. MacIver, editor, Conflict of Loyalties, New York: Harper, 1952, use social psychological definitions of the term.

[14] Srole, op. cit., p. 711.

[15] Personal communication from Leo Srole, whom I thank for his helpful suggestions in relation to the A scale and his comments on a first draft of the present paper.

the following list, presented in the same wording and order as they were to the respondents, statements 2, 4, 6, 8, and 10 are taken from A scale items while the others were devised by the writer:

1. Teachers should be allowed to hold public office.
2. Most public officials (people in public office) are not really interested in the problems of the average man.
3. Unemployment usually results from the attempts of politicians to control private enterprise.
4. These days a person doesn't really know whom he can count on.
5. Delinquency is not as serious a problem as the papers play it up to be.
6. Nowadays a person has to live pretty much for today and let tomorrow take care of itself.
7. College professors tend to be radical when it comes to politics.
8. In spite of what some people say, the lot (situation) (condition) of the average man is getting worse, not better.
9. If the steel industry is responsible for the present recession, then the government ought to nationalize it.
10. Most people don't really care what happens to the next fellow.

Only the "Agree" responses to the A scale items were scored. A score of 5 represents the extreme anomic response, a score of 0 the extreme non-anomic response.

FINDINGS

Social Class and Anomia: Objective.—As noted above, some doubt remains regarding the relationship between anomia and social class. Is the association an inverse one, as Srole and Bell report, or is it "negligible," as Roberts and Rokeach suggest? Different indices of class were used in these three studies, which probably accounts for some of the discrepancy between the findings. No standard index of social class has as yet been applied systematically in the various attempts to evaluate its role in relation to anomia.

In the present study Hollingshead's two-factor Index of Social Position is utilized as a measure of social class.[16] In this measure, a modification of his three-factor scale,[17] occupation is given a weight of 7, education a relative weight of 4. The occupational scale itself is a modification of the Edwards scale which takes into account the differences among kinds of professionals and "the sizes and economic strengths of businesses."[18] The scale yields a distribution into five classes. The findings concerning the relationship between these classes and anomia are presented in Table 1 and 2. A clear and marked association between class and anomia thus results when a social class scale is used as an index of class. Both the Chi-square analysis (Table 1) and the test for the significance of the differences between means (Table 2) are consistent with Merton's hypothesis.

Although these findings lend support to Merton's theory of social structure and

[16] Hollingshead, "Two-Factor Index of Social Position," *op. cit.*
[17] August B. Hollingshead and Frederick C. Redlich, *Social Class and Mental Illness,* New York: Wiley, 1958, pp. 390–391.
[18] *Ibid.,* p. 390.

TABLE 1

RELATION BETWEEN ANOMIA SCORE AND OBJECTIVE CLASS POSITION*

| Anomia Score | Social Class | | | | | | | | Total N |
| | I and II | | III | | IV | | V | | |
	N	e	N	e	N	e	N	e	
0	54	(26.1)	38	(34.2)	51	(62.9)	20	(39.8)	163
1–2	31	(40.3)	62	(52.7)	107	(96.8)	51	(61.2)	251
3–5	9	(27.6)	23	(36.1)	68	(66.3)	72	(42.0)	172
Total	94		123		226		143		586

Chi-square = 87.31, 6 d.f., P < .001.
* The cells in this table as well as those which follow are grouped in conformity with the requirement that no more than 20 per cent of the cells in a chi-square table may have an expected frequency of less than 5.

TABLE 2

Mean Anomia Score for Each Social
Class Group

Class (ISP)	Mean Anomia Score	Significant Differences
I	.49	
II	1.04	I– II P<.01
III	1.34	II–III P<.01
IV	1.81	III–IV P<.01
V	2.40	IV– V P<.01

anomie they do not, in themselves, provide a replication of the studies cited above. This requires the introduction of some controls into the analysis.[19]

The major discrepancy between the findings of Srole, on the one hand, and Roberts and Rokeach, on the other, on class and anomia appears to be the result in part at least of the measures used as indices to class. Although it seems that the measures used in both cases are somewhat less than adequate, replication of those findings which are central to the controversy—the relationship between income and anomia—is nevertheless in order.

Roberts and Rokeach found that, when

[19] I thank Wendell Bell for his careful reading of two drafts of this paper and for his constructive criticisms, almost all of which have been incorporated. I also gratefully acknowledge the assistance of my students, especially Marilyn Hymson, Naomi Leff, Leo Nolan, Laurence Apeland, Robert Fragnoli, Charles Perfetti, Carol Ziegler, and Marianne Lont.

holding education constant, the relationship between income and anomia is negligible (.22). An attempt to replicate this part of their study was made; the results are presented in Table 3. As the controlled analysis shows, no association holds between income and anomia for those segments of the population whose educational attainment is below the college level. Yet it is quite clear that there is such an association for those who have attended college.

While Roberts and Rokeach's finding is supported in some measure, an important qualification should be noted. Neither their data nor those presented here lend support nor provide an adequate basis for rejection of Merton's or Srole's formulations of the relationship between class and anomia. They do, however, provide a lead to an important and related question. If income is the major means of attaining the worldly goods associated with success in contemporary American society, then income should be systematically related to anomia. Our findings suggest that income alone does not determine whether or not persons become anomic, but that expectations regarding income—the principal *means* of achieving success—play a significant role in the process. Persons who have attended college have greater income expectations, and when the latter are not realized a greater tendency to anomia results. The present findings, interpreted in this way, not only are generally consistent with Meier and Bell's notions but raise an interesting ques-

TABLE 3

Relation between Anomia Score and Income with Education Held Constant

Anomia Score	Grade School				High School				College			
	Income More than $5000		Income $5000 and less		Income More than $5000		Income $5000 and less		Income More than $5000		Income $5000 and less	
	N	e	N	e	N	e	N	e	N	e	N	e
0	7	(5.6)	7	(8.4)	38	(36.0)	30	(32.3)	56	(49.6)	20	(26.4)
1–2	26	(22.0)	29	(33.0)	76	(69.0)	56	(62.8)	46	(43.1)	20	(22.9)
3–5	29	(34.4)	57	(51.6)	26	(35.0)	41	(31.9)	9	(18.3)	19	(9.7)
Total	62		93		140		127		111		59	

N = 155
Chi-square = 2.54, 2 d.f.,
   P < .20

N = 267
Chi-square = 7.62, 2 d.f.,
   P < .03

N = 170
Chi-square = 37.82, 2 d.f.,
   P < .001

tion directly related to Durkheim's theory. This too is beyond the scope of the present paper.

Social Class and Anomia: Subjective.— In Meier and Bell's study it was found that anomia is inversely associated with class *identification.* In an effort to test this relationship in the context of this study, comparable data were gathered. Thus respondents were asked to rank themselves along a class continuum from "Very Low" to "Very High." Table 4 presents the results of the analysis of these self-rankings.

A marked and significant inverse relationship between class identification and anomia supports the findings of Meier and Bell. There is a tendency, however, for those respondents who fall into both the very high (I and II) and the very low (IV and V) categories on the objective scale to place themselves in the "average" position on the identification scale. Thus, although roughly 16 per cent of the respondents are in classes I and II objectively only eight per cent perceive of themselves as "High," and whereas 63 per cent are in classes IV and V objectively only 11 per cent rank themselves as "Low." In spite of these variations, the direction of class self-identification and its association with anomia are apparent.

Social Participation and Anomia.—Bell reports that relative social isolation, as reflected in low frequencies of participation in both formal and informal associations, is associated with high anomia. However, these relationships do not hold for the higher economic status groups as measured by an ecological index. Thus Bell found no significant differences between frequent and infrequent participants in informal groups in the highly ranked neighborhoods, and a difference in these same neighborhoods for members as compared with non-members at less than the .05 level of probability. Bell writes: "These findings, relating informal and formal participation to anomie, are not so convincing as one would desire, but they offer some evidence in favor of the hypothesis that social isolation may result in personal disorganization."[20]

In an effort to test this hypothesis, the Chapin Social Participation Scale as an index of formal social participation and the replies to two questions on the interview schedule were utilized. The questions read: "Do you generally go out one or more evenings a week for activities like a card club, bowling, or something of that sort?" and "Do you usually spend one or more evenings a week out with friends or having friends in?"[21] The frequency of these activities was recorded. As Table 5 indicates, there is a marked and significant inverse association between formal social participation and anomia.

Bell has shown, however, that this relationship is not uniform throughout the class structure. It should also be noted that all of his respondents were men. In an attempt to reassess this finding, the relationship between anomia and social participation was

[20] Bell, *op. cit.,* p. 110. It should be noted that anomia may not be synonymous with "personal disorganization," as Bell views it.

[21] This question is a modification of one devised by Renee Marks and Francis Ianni for use in the Upstate New York Social Science Research Project on Poliomyelitis, with which the writer was associated.

TABLE 4

RELATION BETWEEN ANOMIA SCORE AND SELF-RANKED CLASS POSITION

| Anomia Score | Self-Ranked Class Position | | | | | | | |
| | "High" | | "Average" | | "Low" | | | |
	N	e	N	e	N	e	Total
0	23	(12.9)	122	(125.1)	11	(18.0)	156
1–2	17	(20.7)	210	(201.3)	24	(28.9)	251
3–5	8	(14.4)	134	(139.6)	32	(20.1)	174
Total	48		466		67		581

Chi-square = 52.53, 6 d.f., P < .001

TABLE 5

RELATION BETWEEN ANOMIA SCORE AND CHAPIN SOCIAL PARTICIPATION SCORE

	Chapin Social Participation Score (in Points)						
	8+		1–7		0 (None)		
Anomia Score	N	e	N	e	N	e	Total
0	83	(59.8)	36	(40.2)	49	(68.0)	168
1–2	101	(92.9)	72	(62.5)	88	(110.6)	261
3–5	36	(67.3)	40	(45.3)	113	(76.4)	189
Total	220		148		250		618

Chi-square = 36.8   P < .001

TABLE 6

RELATION BETWEEN ANOMIA SCORE AND THE CHAPIN SOCIAL PARTICIPATION SCORE
CONTROLLING OBJECTIVE CLASS POSITION

	Chapin Scores for Social Class Positions I, II, III						
	8+		1–7		0 (None)		
Anomia Score	N	e	N	e	N	e	Total
0	59	(50.0)	15	(21.2)	18	(20.8)	92
1–2	52	(50.6)	26	(21.4)	15	(21.0)	93
3–5	7	(17.4)	9	(7.4)	16	(7.2)	32
Total	118		50		49		217

Chi-square = 23.8, 4 d.f., P < .001

	Chapin Scores for Social Class Positions IV, V						
	8+		1–7		0 (None)		
Anomia Score	N	e	N	e	N	e	Total
0	21	(16.6)	19	(18.1)	31	(36.4)	71
1–2	43	(36.8)	46	(40.2)	69	(80.9)	158
3–5	22	(32.6)	29	(35.7)	89	(71.7)	140
Total	86		94		189		369

Chi-square = 13.7, 4 d.f., P < .01

tested holding both class and sex constant. Table 6 indicates that the controlled analysis fails to support Bell's finding that this relationship does not hold for the higher classes. Furthermore, as Table 7 shows, formal social participation and anomia are uniformly associated when sex is controlled.

The relationship between *informal* social participation and anomia, on the other hand, is less uniform. Using the two types of informal associations referred to in the questions quoted above, separate analyses were made. Both participation in informal activities and in informal friendship associations appear to be significantly associated in the initial analysis (Table 8).

Holding class constant, however, no uniform pattern emerges. While the relationships between informal activities and anomia reach acceptable levels of significance for both class groupings, they are .01 for classes IV and V but only .05 for classes I, II, and III (See Tables 9 and 10). Similarly, the associations between friendship associations and anomia vary somewhat by class groupings. The relationship for classes IV and V

TABLE 7

RELATION BETWEEN ANOMIA SCORE AND THE CHAPIN SOCIAL PARTICIPATION SCORE
WITH SEX HELD CONSTANT

Anomia Score	*Males* Chapin Scores 8+		1–7		0 (None)		
	N	e	N	e	N	e	Total
0	37	(23.5)	11	(16.6)	17	(24.9)	65
1–2	15	(25.3)	15	(17.9)	40	(26.8)	70
3–5	33	(36.2)	34	(25.5)	33	(38.3)	100
Total	85		60		90		235

Chi-square = 27.1, 4 d.f., P < .001

Anomia Score	*Females* Chapin Scores 8+		1–7		0 (None)		
	N	e	N	e	N	e	Total
0	46	(35.8)	25	(23.8)	30	(41.4)	101
1–2	20	(41.1)	25	(27.3)	71	(47.6)	116
3–5	68	(57.1)	39	(37.9)	54	(66.0)	161
Total	134		89		155		378

Chi-square = 33.0, 4 d.f., P < .001

TABLE 8

RELATION BETWEEN ANOMIA SCORE AND FREQUENCY OF PARTICIPATION IN INFORMAL ASSOCIATIONS

Weekly Informal Associations

Activity-Oriented

Anomia Score	3+		1–2		0		
	N	e	N	e	N	e	Total
0	5	(7.1)	66	(50.0)	97	(110.9)	168
1–2	12	(11.0)	81	(77.7)	168	(172.3)	261
3–5	9	(7.9)	37	(56.3)	143	(124.8)	189
Total	26		184		408		618

Chi-square = 17.30, 4 d.f., P < .01

Friendship-Oriented

Anomia Score	3+		1–2		0		
	N	e	N	e	N	e	Total
0	22	(23.8)	95	(86.8)	46	(52.4)	163
1–2	35	(37.2)	147	(135.7)	73	(82.0)	255
3–5	31	(27.0)	79	(98.5)	75	(59.6)	185
Total	88		321		194		603

Chi-square = 12.18, 4 d.f., P < .02

TABLE 9

RELATIONS BETWEEN ANOMIA SCORE AND PARTICIPATION IN WEEKLY ACTIVITY-ORIENTED
ASSSOCIATIONS CONTROLLING OBJECTIVE CLASS POSITION

Weekly Activity-Oriented Associations

Chapin Scores for Social Class Positions I, II, III

Anomia Score	2+		1		0		Total
	N	e	N	e	N	e	
0	12	(13.9)	21	(16.4)	54	(56.7)	87
1–2	19	(14.2)	15	(16.8)	55	(58.0)	89
3–5	2	(4.9)	3	(5.8)	26	(20.3)	31
Total	33		39		135		207

Chi-square = 8.87, 4 d.f., P < .05

Chapin Scores for Social Class Positions IV, V

Anomia Score	2+		1		0		Total
	N	e	N	e	N	e	
0	15	(9.5)	20	(14.4)	32	(43.0)	67
1–2	18	(22.1)	39	(33.3)	98	(99.6)	155
3–5	18	(19.4)	18	(29.3)	100	(87.4)	136
Total	51		77		230		358

Chi-square = 15.30, 4 d.f., P < .01

TABLE 10

RELATION BETWEEN ANOMIA SCORE AND PARTICIPATION IN WEEKLY FRIENDSHIP-ORIENTED
ASSOCIATIONS CONTROLLING OBJECTIVE CLASS POSITION

Weekly Activity-Oriented Associations

Chapin Scores for Social Class Positions I, II, III

Anomia Score	2+		1		0		Total
	N	e	N	e	N	e	
0	21	(18.7)	30	(28.0)	12	(16.3)	63
1–2	23	(26.4)	43	(39.6)	23	(23.0)	89
3–5	10	(8.9)	8	(13.4)	12	(7.7)	30
Total	54		81		47		182

Chi-square = 6.88, 4 d.f., P < .15

Chapin Scores for Social Class Positions IV, V

Anomia Score	2+		1		0		Total
	N	e	N	e	N	e	
0	23	(24.0)	25	(20.2)	19	(22.9)	67
1–2	58	(55.7)	50	(47.1)	48	(53.1)	156
3–5	48	(49.3)	34	(41.7)	56	(47.0)	138
Total	129		109		123		361

Chi-square = 12.63, 4 d.f., P < .02

reaches the .02 level of significance but only .15 for the I, II, III grouping. These data, then, lend support to Bell's finding that anomia and informal social participation are not as closely related in the high as in the low economic status groups.[22] The question of whether or not this lack of uniformity is of any sociological significance is discussed below. At this point it should be stressed that, with the noted exception, all of the present findings either approach acceptable levels of significance or exceed these limits and that the data present overall uniformities with respect to group affiliation and anomia.[23]

Sex and Anomia.—Meier and Bell suggest that women *may* be more anomic than men.[24] But this depends presumably on whether or not women accept goals (especially those other than being a housewife) which they are prevented from reaching due to their sex.

In this study, although knowledge of the respondents' goals are not known, the statistical relationship between sex and anomia was measured. The chi-square test of association yields the lowest measure of any of the calculations (Chi-square $= .12$, d.f., $P > .90$, $N = 615$, 237 males and 378 females), which does not support the hypothesis that sex and anomia are associated.

Urbanism and Anomia.—In their concluding remarks Meier and Bell, in reference to comments made by Greer and Kube, suggest that anomia is not necessarily a characteristic peculiar to urban life, as some sociologists have argued.[25] Typical of the latter view is the following statement taken from Louis Wirth's widely read essay:

> The superficiality, the anonymity, and the transitory character of urban social relations make intelligible, also, the sophistication and the rationality generally ascribed to city-dwellers. Our acquaintances tend to stand in a relationship of utility to us in the sense that the role which each one plays in our life is overwhelmingly regarded as a means for the achievement of our own ends. Whereas the individual gains, on the one hand, a certain degree of emancipation or freedom from the personal and emotional controls of intimate groups, he loses, on the other hand, the spontaneous self-expression, the morale, and the sense of participation that comes with living in an integrated society. This constitutes essentially the state of *anomie,* or the social void, to which Durkheim alludes in attempting to account for the various forms of social disorganization in technological society.[26]

This statement, which appears to have been directly derived from Georg Simmel,[27] re-

---

[22] Bell, *op. cit.* An hypothesis currently being studied by the writer is that two aspects of affiliation are at work in both formal and informal associations. Quantity and quality of interaction provides one dimension of support in the prevention of anomia. More significantly, I believe, is the role of associations in the reinforcement of community norms and sentiments. Since formal associations have a greater tendency to be organized about community projects they are more likely to reflect in their activities the normative system of the community than that of a sub-group. Additional data are being analyzed in which two classifications of formal associations are utilized: one focusing on functions for the participants classifies voluntary associations as *instrumental, instrumental-expressive, and expressive* (following C. Wayne Gordon and Nicholas Babchuk, "A Typology of Voluntary Associations," *American Sociological Review,* 24 [February, 1959], pp. 22–29) ; the other focuses on functions for the community as a system (derived from Sherwood D. Fox, *Social Structure and Voluntary Associations in the United States,* Ph.D. thesis, Harvard University, 1952). Fox classifies associations as *majoral, minoral,* and *medial,* depending upon their primary functions for a given social system. Gordon and Babchuk's typology, it should be noted, does not include a purely *integrative* function for the participant in relation to the community and its institutions.

[23] Additional support for this generalization is the finding that, although no association was found between type of religious affiliation and anomia, a significant relationship holds between church and synagogue membership and anomia (Chi-square $=$ 22.86, 2 d.f., $P < .001$, $N = 608$). It would appear that it does not matter to which church one belongs as long as one belongs. This echoes the American value system as described by Will Herberg in *Protestant—Catholic—Jew,* New York: Doubleday, 1956. On this point, see also William H. Whyte, Jr., *The Organization Man,* New York: Doubleday (Anchor Books), 1956; and Louis Schneider and Sanford M. Dornbusch, *Popular Religion,* Chicago: University of Chicago Press, 1958.

[24] Meier and Bell, *op. cit.,* p. 201, and personal communication from Wendell Bell.

[25] *Ibid.,* p. 201; and the reference is to Scott Greer and Ella Kube, "Urbanism and Social Structure," in M. Sussman, editor, *Community Structure and Analysis,* New York: Crowell, 1959.

[26] "Urbanism as a Way of Life," *American Journal of Sociology,* 44 (July, 1938), p. 12.

[27] "The Metropolis and the Mental Life" in Kurt Wolff, editor and translator, *The Sociology of Georg Simmel,* New York: Free Press of Glencoe, Inc., 1950.

flects the influence of the German romanticists on Toennies, Simmel, and others, and its persistence, as Shils points out, in contemporary sociological thought.[28]

The present study of a small city, located in a county in which the rural population accounts for 43 per cent of the total,[29] represents a community tending more to the rural-village pole of the conventional continuum than has been the case in the studies of anomia cited above. Our data, consequently, provide at least a preliminary test of the proposition that anomia is primarily a characteristic of large urban areas.

The following percentages represent the total distribution of anomia scores for the sample of 618 cases: 0(27.2), 1(21.5), 2(20.7), 3(16.0), 4(10.7), and 5(3.9). Thus only about 27 per cent of the population can be described (according to the criteria used here) as being completely non-anomic while over 30 per cent may be classed as anomic (that is, those having scores of 3 or more on the Srole scale). It appears that the differences between dwellers of large urban areas and those of less urbanized communities have often been exaggerated.

DISCUSSION

The present study is directed toward a test of the hypothesis that differential access to the means for the achievement of socially prescribed goals results in a differential distribution of anomie in the social structure; and, in some measure, replicates and extends studies of the relationship between Srole's anomia and social participation. The data again reveal a relationship between class and anomia. But they do not provide a full test

of Merton's theory since we have *assumed*, as have the authors of the studies cited above, that the respondents have similar life goals. Merton himself makes this assumption. Further research, taking this problematic situation into account, would be useful in making a more complete assessment of Merton's theory. Although the associations between class and anomia and between social participation and anomia are both statistically significant, we have no clear explanation, at this point, of why or in what way they are related. An adequate explantion awaits a sound causal analysis of the frequently noted relationship between social class and social participation. Such an analysis is now being attempted by the writer.

Whatever the causes, however, important processes can be noted. Several studies, including the present investigation, show that formal social participation is directly associated with social class.[30] Thus the relatively lower-class sections of the population are cut off from a variety of social situations which would bring them into contact with other members of the community. Precisely why this occurs still remains to be explained. It appears that access to those groups which provide a bridge between the individual and the community is limited for members of the lower classes as a result of both voluntary and involuntary processes. Knupfer has suggested that the "underdogs" lack the confidence necessary for interaction in these situations and thus limit their activities.[31] Hollingshead's study of "Elmtown" describes how lower-class adolescents are denied access to a variety of social situations.[32] A voluntary pattern of avoidance probably emerges from this lack of confidence, on the one hand, and "involuntary avoidance" results from rejection patterns practiced by members of the middle classes.

What are the functions of participation in formal associations for the participants? Our data suggest that a latent function of such

[28] Edward A. Shils, "Daydreams and Nightmares: Reflections on the Criticism of Mass Culture," *Sewanee Review,* 65 (Fall, 1957), pp. 587–608. The concern with the presumed effects of urbanism in the realm of social pathology continues as a source of controversy in spite of studies which fail to support these notions. See, e.g., Ellen Winston, "The Assumed Increase of Mental Disease," *American Journal of Sociology,* 40 (January, 1935), pp. 427–439; and Herbert Goldhamer and Andrew Marshall, *Psychosis and Civilization,* New York: Free Press of Glencoe, Inc., 1953.

[29] U.S. Bureau of the Census, *County and City Data Book, 1956,* Washington, D.C.: U.S. Government Printing Office, 1957, p. 202.

[30] In the present study, Chi-square = 72.58, 6 d.f., $P < .001$, N = 585.

[31] Genevieve Knupfer, "Portrait of the Underdog," *Public Opinion Quarterly,* 11 (Spring, 1947), pp. 103–114.

[32] August B. Hollingshead, *Elmtown's Youth,* New York: Wiley, 1949.

participation is the provision of a means of preventing personal demoralization through interaction: these groups serve as buffers against social psychological anomia.[33] This function is also a characteristic of other types of collectivities: the store-front church for the lower-class rural migrant in the city. *Landsmanschaften* for the ethnic immigrant, beatnik and other bohemian groups for many youthful and not so youthful persons and so on. But the number of affiliations and

[33] This function is hypothesized for other types of groups in Ephraim H. Mizruchi, "Bohemianism and the Urban Community," *Journal of Human Relations* (Autumn, 1959), pp. 114–120.

the degree of interaction are less for the lower than for the higher classes. It may be argued, then, that interaction between members of the lower classes and those groups which provide them with a feeling of belonging to a community is limited.

If these speculations are correct then the members of the lower classes lack access to the sources which provide support against personal malintegration. Not only do they have a greater tendency to anomia as a result of the relative inaccessibility of the means for attaining socially desired ends but from socially structured differential access to supportive sub-systems as well.

Delinquent Subcultures: Sociological Interpretations of Gang Delinquency / David J. Bordua

Group delinquency has been of theoretical interest to American sociology for more than half a century. During that time, four major interpretations of the origins of gang delinquency and delinquent subcultures have emerged. The classical view developed by Thrasher focuses on the development of spontaneous groups under conditions of weak social control and social disorganization. Two other views, somewhat akin, emphasize the adjustment problems of lower class boys and stress respectively the status deprivation of such boys when they fail to place well according to the middle class measuring rod and the alienation produced when opportunities to achieve universally demanded success goals are denied lower class boys. Another view is that of the lower class street gang and its way of life as the adolescent version of a more general adult life style, namely, lower class culture. There is a noticeable tendency in the recent theories to emphasize irrational explanations of gang delinquency, to view the boys who participate as driven rather than attracted, and polemical pressures have tended to produce extreme theoretical interpretations.

The problem of group delinquency has been a subject of theoretical interest for American sociologists and other social observers for well over a half century. In the course of that period, the group nature of delinquency has come to be a central starting point for many theories of delinquency, and delinquency causation has been seen by some sociologists as pre-eminently a process whereby the individual becomes associated

with a group which devotes some or all of its time to planning, committing, or celebrating delinquencies and which has elaborated a set of lifeways—a subculture—which encourages and justifies behavior defined as delinquent by the larger society.

In addition to the processes whereby an individual takes on the beliefs and norms of a pre-existing group and thereby becomes delinquent—a process mysterious enough in itself in many cases—there is the more basic, and in many respects more complex, problem of how such groups begin in the first place. What are the social conditions that

Reprinted from *Annals of American Academy of Political and Social Science*, 1961, 388, pages 119–136, by permission of author and publisher, The American Academy of Political and Social Science.

facilitate or cause the rise of delinquency-carrying groups? What are the varying needs and motives satisfied in individuals by such groups? What processes of planned social control might be useable in preventing the rise of such groups or in redirecting the behavior and moral systems of groups already in existence? All these questions and many others have been asked for at least two generations. Within the limits of this brief paper, it is impossible to present and analyze in detail the many answers to these questions which have been put forward by social scientists. What I can do is single out a few of the major viewpoints and concentrate on them.

In its more well-developed and extreme forms, gang or subcultural delinquency has been heavily concentrated in the low status areas of our large cities. The theoretical interpretations I will discuss all confine themselves to gang delinquency of this sort.

THE CLASSICAL VIEW

Still the best book on gangs, gang delinquency, and—though he did not use the term—delinquent subcultures is *The Gang* by Frederick M. Thrasher, and his formulations are the ones that I have labeled "the classical view." Not that he originated the basic interpretative framework, far from it, but his application of the theoretical materials available at the time plus his sensitivity to the effects of social environment and his willingness to consider processes at all behavioral levels from the basic needs of the child to the significance of the saloon, from the nature of city government to the crucial importance of the junk dealer, from the consequences of poverty to the nature of leadership in the gang still distinguish his book.[1]

Briefly, Thrasher's analysis may be characterized as operating on the following levels. The ecological processes which determine the structure of the city create the interstitial area characterized by a variety of indices of conflict, disorganization, weak family and neighborhood controls, and so on. In these interstitial areas, in response to universal childhood needs, spontaneous play groups

[1] Frederick M. Thrasher, *The Gang* (Chicago: University of Chicago Press, 1927).

develop. Because of the relatively uncontrolled nature of these groups—or of many of them at least—and because of the presence of many attractive and exciting opportunities for fun and adventure, these groups engage in a variety of activities, legal and illegal, which are determined, defined, and directed by the play group itself rather than by conventional adult supervision.

The crowded, exciting slum streets teem with such groups. Inevitably, in a situation of high population density, limited resources, and weak social control, they come into conflict with each other for space, playground facilities, reputation. Since many of their activities, even at an early age, are illegal, although often not feloniously so—they swipe fruit from peddlers, turn over garbage cans, stay away from home all night and steal milk and cakes for breakfast, play truant from school—they also come into conflict with adult authority. Parents, teachers, merchants, police, and others become the natural enemies of this kind of group and attempt to control it or to convert it to more conventional activities. With some groups they succeed, with some they do not.

If the group continues, it becomes part of a network of similar groups, increasingly freed from adult restraint, increasingly involved in intergroup conflict and fighting, increasingly engaged in illegal activities to support itself and to continue to receive the satisfactions of the "free" life of the streets. Conflict, especially with other groups, transforms the play group into the gang. Its illegal activities become more serious, its values hardened, its structure more determined by the necessity to maintain eternal vigilance in a hostile environment.

By middle adolescence, the group is a gang, often with a name, usually identified with a particular ethnic or racial group, and usually with an elaborate technology of theft and other means of self-support. Gradually, the gang may move in the direction of adult crime, armed robbery, perhaps, or other serious crimes.

Prior to that time, however, it is likely to have engaged in much stealing from stores, railroad cars, empty houses, parents, drunks, almost anywhere money or goods are available. The ready access to outlets for stolen goods is of major importance here. The junk dealer, especially the junk wagon peddler, the convenient no-questions-asked attitudes of large numbers of local adults who buy "hot" merchandise, and the early knowledge that customers are available all help to make theft easy and profitable as well as morally acceptable.[2]

Nonutilitarian?

It is appropriate at this point to deal with a matter that has become important in the discussion of more recent theories of group delinquency. This is Albert K. Cohen's famous characterization of the delinquent subculture as nonutilitarian, by which he seems to mean that activities, especially theft, are not oriented to calculated economic ends.[3]

Thrasher makes a great point of the play and adventure quality of many illegal acts, especially in the pregang stages of a group's development, but he also describes many cases where theft has a quite rational and instrumental nature, even at a fairly early age.

The theft activities and the disposition of the loot make instrumental sense in the context of Thrasher's description of the nature of the group or gang. Much theft is essentially for the purpose of maintaining the group in a state of freedom from adult authority. If a group of boys lives days or even weeks away from home, then the theft of food or of things which are sold to buy food is hardly nonutilitarian. If such a group steals from freight cars, peddles the merchandise to the neighbors for movie money, and so on, this can hardly be considered nonutilitarian. The behavior makes sense as instrumental behavior, however, only after one has a picture of the general life led by the group. Boys who feed themselves by dupli-

cating keys to bakery delivery boxes, creep out of their club rooms right after delivery, steal the pastry, pick up a quart of milk from a doorstep, and then have breakfast may not have a highly developed sense of nutritional values, but this is not nonutilitarian.

Such youngsters may, of course, spend the two dollars gained from selling stolen goods entirely on doughnuts and gorge themselves and throw much of the food away. I think this largely indicates that they are children, not that they are nonutilitarian.[4]

Let us look a little more systematically at the Thrasher formulations, however, since such an examination can be instructive in dealing with the more recent theories. The analysis proceeds at several levels, as I have mentioned.

Levels of Analysis

At the level of the local adult community, we may say that the social structure is permissive, attractive, facilitative, morally supportive of the gang development process.

It is permissive because control over children is weak; attractive because many enjoyable activities are available, some of which are illegal, like stealing fruit, but all of which can be enjoyed only if the child manages to evade whatever conventional controls do exist.

[2] One of the charms of Thrasher's old-time sociology is the fashion in which fact intrudes itself upon the theorizing. For example, he tells us that there were an estimated 1,700 to 1,800 junk wagon men in Chicago, most of whom were suspected of being less than rigid in inquiring about the source of "junk." *Ibid.*, p. 148. He also does some other things that seem to have gone out of style, such as presenting information on the age and ethnic composition of as many of the 1,313 gangs as possible. *Ibid.*, pp. 73, 74, 191–193.

[3] Albert K. Cohen, *Delinquent Boys: The Culture of the Gang* (New York: Free Press of Glencoe, Inc., 1955), pp. 25, 26.

[4] The examples cited above are all in Thrasher along with many others of a similar nature. In general, views of the nature of gang activity have shifted quite fundamentally toward a more irrationalist position. Thus, the gang's behavior seems to make no sense. Underlying this shift is a tendency to deal almost entirely with the gang's subculture, its values, beliefs, and the like, to deal with the relationships between this subculture and presumed motivational states which exist in the potential gang members before the gang or protogang is formed, and to deal very little with the developmental processes involved in the formation of gangs. Things which make no sense without consideration of the motivational consequences of gang membership are not necessarily so mysterious given Thrasher's highly sensitive analysis of the ways in which the nature of the gang as a group led to the development—in relation to the local environment—of the gang culture. Current theory focuses so heavily on motive and culture to the exclusion of group process that some essential points are underemphasized. It would not be too much of a distortion to say that Thrasher saw the delinquent subculture as the way of life that would be developed by a group becoming a gang and that some recent theorists look at the gang as the kind of group that would develop if boys set about creating a delinquent subculture.

In another sense, the local environment is attractive because of the presence of adult crime of a variety of kinds ranging from organized vice to older adolescents and adults making a living by theft. The attraction lies, of course, in the fact that these adults may have a lot of money and live the carefree life and have high status in the neighborhood.

The local environment is facilitative in a number of ways. There are things readily available to steal, people to buy them, and places to hide without adult supervision.

The environment is morally supportive because of the presence of adult crime, as previously mentioned, but also for several additional reasons. One is the readiness of conventional adults to buy stolen goods. Even parents were discovered at this occasionally. The prevalence of political pull, which not only objectively protected adult crime but tended to undercut the norms against crime, must be mentioned then as now. The often bitter poverty which turned many situations into matters of desperate competition also contributed.

Additionally, many gang activities, especially in the protogang stage, are not seriously delinquent and receive adult approval. These activities include such things as playing baseball for "side money" and much minor gambling such as penny pitching. Within limits, fighting lies well within the local community's zone of tolerance, especially when it is directed against members of another ethnic group.

At the level of the adolescent and pre-adolescent groups themselves, the environment is essentially coercive of gang formation. The presence of large numbers of groups competing for limited resources leads to conflict, and the full-fledged adolescent gang is pre-eminently a conflict group with a high valuation of fighting skill, courage, and similar qualities. Thus, the transition from spontaneous group to gang is largely a matter of participating in the struggle for life of the adolescent world under the peculiar conditions of the slum.

At the level of the individual, Thrasher assumes a set of basic needs common to all children. He leans heavily on the famous four wishes of W. I. Thomas, security, response, recognition, and new experience, es-

pecially the last two. Gang boys and boys in gang areas are, in this sense, no different from other boys. They come to choose different ways of satisfying these needs. What determines which boys form gangs is the differential success of the agencies of socialization and social control in channeling these needs into conventional paths. Thus, due to family inadequacy or breakdown or school difficulties, coupled with the ever present temptations of the exciting, adventurous street as compared to the drab, dull, and unsatisfying family and school, some boys are more available for street life than others.

Finally, it should be pointed out that the gang engages in many activities of a quite ordinary sort. Athletics are very common and highly regarded at all age levels. Much time is spent simply talking and being with the gang. The gang's repertory is diverse—baseball, football, dice, poker, holding dances, shooting the breeze, shoplifting, rolling drunks, stealing cars.

This is more than enough to give the tenor of Thrasher's formulations. I have purposely attempted to convey the distinctive flavor of essentially healthy boys satisfying universal needs in a weakly controlled and highly seductive environment. Compared to the deprived and driven boys of more recent formulations with their status problems, blocked opportunities (or psychopathologies if one take a more psychiatric view), Thrasher describes an age of innocence indeed.

This is, perhaps, the most important single difference between Thrasher and some—not all—of the recent views. Delinquency and crime were attractive, being a "good boy" was dull. They were attractive because they were fun and were profitable and because one could be a hero in a fight. Fun, profit, glory, and freedom is a combination hard to beat, particularly for the inadequate conventional institutions that formed the competition.

WORKING CLASS BOY AND MIDDLE CLASS MEASURING ROD

If Thrasher saw the gang as being formed over time through the attractiveness of the free street life and the unattractiveness and moral weakness of the agencies of social control, Albert K. Cohen sees many working class boys as being driven to develop the delinquent subculture as a way of recouping the self-esteem destroyed by middle-class-dominated institutions.

Rather than focusing on the gang and its development over time, Cohen's theory focuses on the way of life of the gang—the delinquent subculture. A collective way of life, a subculture, develops when a number of people with a common problem of adjustment are in effective interaction, according to Cohen. The bulk of his basic viewpoint is the attempted demonstration that the common problem of adjustment of the lower class gang boys who are the carriers of the delinquent subculture derives from their socialization in lower class families and their consequent lack of preparation to function successfully in middle class institutions such as the school.

The institutions within which the working class boy must function reward and punish him for acceptable or unacceptable performance according to the child-assessing version of middle class values. The middle class value pattern places great emphasis on ambition as a cardinal virtue, individual responsibility (as opposed to extreme emphasis on shared kin obligations, for example), the cultivation and possession of skills, the ability to postpone gratification, rationality, the rational cultivation of manners, the control of physical aggression and violence, the wholesome and constructive use of leisure, and respect for property (especially respect for the abstract rules defining rights of access to material things).[5]

The application of these values adapted to the judgment of children constitutes the "middle class measuring rod" by which all children are judged in institutions run by middle class personnel—the school, the settlement house, and the like. The fact that working class children must compete according to these standards is a consequence of what Cohen, in a most felicitous phrase, refers to as the "democratic status universe" characteristic of American society. Everyone is expected to strive, and everyone is measured against the same standard. Not

everyone is equally prepared, however, and the working class boy is, with greater statistical frequency than the middle class boy, ill prepared through previous socialization.

Cultural Setting

Social class for Cohen is not simply economic position but, much more importantly, a set of more or less vertically layered cultural settings which differ in the likelihood that boys will be taught the aspirations, ambitions, and psychological skills necessary to adjust to the demands of the larger institutions.

Cohen goes on to describe this predominantly lower working class cultural setting as more likely to show restricted aspirations, a live-for-today orientation toward consumption, a moral view which emphasizes reciprocity within the kin and other primary groups and correlatively less concern with abstract rules which apply across or outside of such particularistic circumstances. In addition, the working class child is less likely to be surrounded with educational toys, less likely to be trained in a family regimen of order, neatness, and punctuality. Of particular importance is the fact that physical aggression is more prevalent and more valued in the working class milieu.

When a working class boy thus equipped for life's struggle begins to function in the school, the settlement, and other middle-class-controlled institutions and encounters the middle class measuring rod, he inevitably receives a great deal of disapproval, rejection, and punishment. In short, in the eyes of the middle class evaluator, he does not measure up. This is what Cohen refers to as the problem of status deprivation which constitutes the fundamental problem of adjustment to which the delinquent subculture is a solution.

Self-derogation

But this deprivation derives not only from the negative evaluations of others but also from self-derogation. The working class boy shares in this evaluation of himself to some degree for a variety of reasons.[6] The first of

---

[5] Albert K. Cohen, *op. cit.*, pp. 88–93.

[6] In presenting the theoretical work of someone else, it is often the case that the views of the original author are simplified to his disadvantage. I have tried to guard against this. At this point

these is the previously mentioned democratic status universe wherein the dominant culture requires everyone to compete against all comers. Second, the parents of working class boys, no matter how adjusted they seem to be to their low status position, are likely to project their frustrated aspirations onto their children. They may do little effective socialization to aid the child, but they are, nevertheless, likely at least to want their children to be better off than they are. Third, there is the effect of the mass media which spread the middle class life style. And, of course, there is the effect of the fact of upward mobility as visible evidence that at least some people can make the grade.

In short, the working class boy is subjected to many social influences which emphasize the fact that the way to respect, status, and success lies in conforming to the demands of middle class society. Even more importantly, he very likely has partly accepted the middle class measuring rod as a legitimate, even superior, set of values. The profound ambivalence that this may lead to in the individual is simply a reflection of the fact that the larger culture penetrates the lower working class world in many ways.

Thus, to the external status problem posed by devaluations by middle class functionaries is added the internal status problem of low self-esteem.

This, then, is the common problem of adjustment. Given the availability of many boys similarly situated, a collective solution evolves, the delinquent subculture. This subculture is characterized by Cohen as non-utilitarian, malicious, and negativistic, characterized by versatility, short-run hedonism, and an emphasis on group autonomy, that is, freedom from adult restraint.

These are, of course, the direct antitheses of the components of the middle class measuring rod. The delinquent subculture functions simultaneously to combat the enemy

without and the enemy within, both the hated agents of the middle class and the gnawing internal sense of inadequacy and low self-esteem. It does so by erecting a counter-culture, an alternative set of status criteria.

Guilt

This subculture must do more than deal with the middle-class-dominated institutions on the one hand and the feelings of low self-esteem on the other. It must also deal with the feelings of guilt over aggression, theft, and the like that will inevitably arise. It must deal with the fact that the collective solution to the common problem of adjustment is an illicit one in the eyes of the larger society and, certainly, also in the eyes of the law-abiding elements of the local area.

It must deal, also, with the increasing opposition which the solution arouses in the police and other agencies of the conventional order. Over time, the subculture comes to contain a variety of definitions of these agents of conventionality which see them as the aggressors, thus legitimating the group's deviant activities.

Because of this requirement that the delinquent subculture constitute a solution to internal, psychological problems of self-esteem and guilt, Cohen sees the group behavior pattern as being overdetermined in the psychological sense and as linking up with the mechanism of reaction formation.

Thus, the reason for the seeming irrationality of the delinquent subculture lies in the deeply rooted fears and anxieties of the status deprived boy. I have already discussed the shift from Thrasher's view of delinquency as attractive in a situation of weak social control to the views of it as more reactive held by some modern theorists. Cohen, of course, is prominent among these latter, the irrationalists. It is extremely difficult to bring these viewpoints together at all well except to point out that Cohen's position accords well with much research on school failure and its consequences in damaged self-esteem. It does seem unlikely, as I will point out later in another connection, that the failure of family, school, and neighborhood to control the behavior of Thrasher's boys would result in their simple withdrawal from

---

in Cohen's formulation, however, I may be over-simplifying to his benefit. In view of the considerable struggle over the matter of just what the working class boy is sensitive to, I should point out that Cohen is less than absolutely clear. He is not as unclear, however, as some of his critics have maintained. For the best statement in Cohen's work, see *Delinquent Boys*, pp. 121–128.

such conventional contexts without hostility and loss of self-regard.

Cohen emphasizes that not all members of an ongoing delinquent group are motivated by this same problem of adjustment. Like any other protest movement, the motives which draw new members at different phases of its development will vary. It is sufficient that a core of members share the problem.

The analysis of the delinquent subculture of urban working class boys set forth in *Delinquent Boys* has been elaborated and supplemented in a later article by Cohen and James F. Short.[7]

Other Delinquent Subcultures

Responding to the criticism that there seemed a variety of kinds of delinquent subcultures, even among lower class urban youth, Cohen and Short distinguish the parent-male subculture, the conflict-oriented subculture, the drug addict subculture, and a subculture focused around semiprofessional theft.[8]

The parent subculture is the now familiar subculture described in *Delinquent Boys*. Cohen and Short describe it as the most common form.[9]

> We refer to it as the parent sub-culture because it is probably the most common variety in this country—indeed, it might be called the "garden variety" of delinquent subculture—and because the characteristics listed above seem to constitute a common core shared by other important variants.

In discussing the conditions under which these different subcultures arise, Cohen and Short rely on a pivotal paper published in 1951 by Solomon Kobrin.[10] Dealing with the differential location of the conflict-oriented versus the semiprofessional theft subculture,

Kobrin pointed out that delinquency areas vary in the degree to which conventional and criminal value systems are mutually integrated. In the integrated area, adult criminal activity is stable and organized, and adult criminals are integral parts of the local social structure—active in politics, fraternal orders, providers of employment. Here delinquency can form a kind of apprenticeship for adult criminal careers with such careers being relatively indistinct from conventional careers. More importantly, the interests of organized criminal groups in order and a lack of police attention would lead to attempts to prevent the wilder and more untrammeled forms of juvenile violence. This would mean, of course, that crime in these areas was largely of the stable, profitable sort ordinarily associated with the rackets.

LOWER CLASS BOY AND LOWER CLASS CULTURE

The interpretation of the delinquent subculture associated with Albert Cohen that I have just described contrasts sharply in its main features with what has come to be called the lower class culture view associated with Walter B. Miller.[11] Miller disagrees with the Cohen position concerning the reactive nature of lower class gang culture.[12]

> In the case of "gang" delinquency, the cultural system which exerts the most direct influences on behavior is that of the lower class community itself—a long-established, distinctively patterned tradition with an integrity of its own—rather than a so-called "delinquent sub-culture" which has arisen through conflict with middle class culture and is oriented to the deliberate violation of middle class norms.

[7] Albert K. Cohen and James F. Short, Jr., "Research in Delinquent Sub-Cultures," *Journal of Social Issues*, Vol. 14 (1958), No. 3, pp. 20–36.

[8] For criticism in this vein as well as for the most searching general analysis of material from *Delinquent Boys*, see Harold L. Wilensky and Charles N. Lebeaux, *Industrial Society and Social Welfare* (New York: Russell Sage Foundation, 1958), Chap. 9.

[9] Cohen and Short, *op. cit.*, p. 24. The characteristics are those of maliciousness and so on that I have listed previously.

[10] Solomon Kobrin, "The Conflict of Values in Delinquency Areas," *American Sociological Review*, Vol. 16 (October 1951), No. 5, pp. 653–661.

[11] See the following papers, all by Walter B. Miller: "Lower Class Culture as a Generating Milieu of Gang Delinquency," *Journal of Social Issues*, Vol. 14 (1958), No. 3, pp. 5–19; "Preventive Work with Street Corner Groups: Boston Delinquency Project," *The Annals of the American Academy of Political and Social Science*, Vol. 322 (March 1959), pp. 97–106; "Implications of Urban Lower Class Culture for Social Work," *The Social Service Review*, Vol. 33 (September 1959), No. 3, pp. 219–236.

[12] Walter B. Miller, "Lower Class Culture as a Generating Milieu of Gang Delinquency," *op. cit.*, pp. 5, 6.

What, then, is the lower class culture Miller speaks of and where is it located? Essentially, Miller describes a culture which he sees as emerging from the shaking-down processes of immigration, internal migration, and vertical mobility. Several population and cultural streams feed this process, but, primarily, lower class culture represents the emerging common adaptation of unsuccessful immigrants and Negroes.

> It is the thesis of this paper that from these extremely diverse and heterogeneous origins (with, however, certain common features), there is emerging a relatively homogeneous and stabilized native-American lower class culture; however, in many communities the process of fusion is as yet in its earlier phases, and evidences of the original ethnic or locality culture are still strong.[13]

In his analysis, Miller is primarily concerned with what he calls the hard core group in the lower class—the same very bottom group referred to by Cohen as the lower-lower class. The properties of this emerging lower class culture as described by Miller may be divided into a series of social structural elements and a complex pattern of what Miller calls focal concerns.

Focal Concerns

The first of the structural elements is what Miller calls the female-based household, that is, a family form wherein the key relationships are those among mature females (especially those of different generations but, perhaps, also sisters or cousins) and between these females and their children. The children may be by different men, and the bi-

ological fathers may play a very inconsistent and unpredictable role in the family. Most essentially, the family is not organized around the expectation of stable economic support provided by an adult male.

The relationship between adult females and males is characterized as one of serial mating, with the female finding it necessary repeatedly to go through a cycle of roles of mate-seeker, mother, and employee.

Closely related to and supportive of this form of household is the elaboration of a system of one-sex peer groups which, according to Miller, become emotional havens and major sources of psychic investment and support for both sexes and for both adolescents and adults. The family, then, is not the central focus of primary, intimate ties that it is in middle class circles.

In what is surely a masterpiece of cogent description, Miller presents the focal concerns of lower class culture as trouble, toughness, smartness, excitement, fate, and autonomy. His description of the complexly interwoven patterns assumed by these focal concerns cannot be repeated here, but a brief discussion seems appropriate.[14]

Trouble is what life gets you into—especially trouble with the agents of the larger society. The central aspect of this focal concern is the distinction between law-abiding and law-violating behavior, and where an individual stands along the implied dimension either by behavior, reputation, or commitment is crucial in the evaluation of him by others. Toughness refers to physical prowess, skill, masculinity, fearlessness, bravery, daring. It includes an almost compulsive opposition to things seen as soft and feminine, including much middle class behavior, and is related, on the one hand, to sex-role identification problems which flow from the young boy's growing up in the female-based household and, on the other hand, to the occupational demands of the lower class world. Toughness, along with the emphasis on excitement and autonomy, is one of the ways one gets into trouble.

---

[13] Walter B. Miller, "Implications of Urban Lower Class Culture for Social Work," *op. cit.,* p. 225. Miller seems to be saying that the processes of sorting and segregating which characterized American industrial cities in the period referred to by Thrasher are beginning to show a product at the lower end of the status order. In this, as in several other ways, Miller is much more the inheritor of the classical view, as I have called it, than are Cohen or Cloward and Ohlin. Miller shows much the same concern for relatively wholistic description of the local community setting and much the same sensitivity to group process over time. Whether his tendency to see lower class culture in terms of a relatively closed system derives from differences in fact due to historical change or primarily to differences in theoretical perspective is hard to say.

[14] This description of the focal concern is taken from Walter B. Miller, "Lower Class Culture as a Generating Milieu of Gang Delinquency," *op. cit.,* especially Chart 1, p. 7. In this case especially, the original should be read.

Smartness refers to the ability to "con," outwit, dupe, that is, to manipulate things and people to one's own advantage with a minimum of conventional work. Excitement, both as an activity and as an ambivalently held goal, is best manifested in the patterned cycle of the weekend night-on-the-town complete with much drink and sexual escapades, thereby creating the risk of fighting and trouble. Between weekends, life is dull and passive. Fate refers to the perception by many lower class individuals that their lives are determined by events and forces over which they have little or no control. It manifests itself in widespread gambling and fantasies of "when things break for me." Gambling serves multiple functions in the areas of fate, toughness, smartness, and excitement.

The last focal concern described by Miller is that of autonomy—concern over the amount, source, and severity of control by others. Miller describes the carrier of lower class culture as being highly ambivalent about such control by others. Overtly, he may protest bitterly about restraint and arbitrary interference while, covertly, he tends to equate coercion with care and unconsciously to seek situations where strong controls will satisfy nurturance needs.

Growing Up

What is it like to grow up in lower class culture? A boy spends the major part of the first twelve years in the company of and under the domination of women. He learns during that time that women are the people who count, that men are despicable, dangerous, and desirable. He also learns that a "real man" is hated for his irresponsibility and considered very attractive on Saturday night. He learns, too, that, if he really loves his mother, he will not grow up to be "just like all men" but that, despite her best efforts, his mother's pride and joy will very likely turn out to be as much a "rogue male" as the rest. In short, he has sex-role problems.

The adolescent street group is the social mechanism which enables the maturing boy to cope with a basic problem of feminine identification coupled with the necessity of somehow growing up to be an appropriately hated and admired male in a culture which maximizes the necessity to fit into all male society as an adult. The seeking of adult status during adolescence, then, has a particular intensity, so that manifestations of the adult culture's focal concerns tend to be overdone. In addition, the street group displays an exaggerated concern with status and belongingness which is common in all adolescent groups but becomes unusually severe for the lower class boy.

The street group, then, is an essential transition mechanism and training ground for the lower class boy. Some of the behavior involved is delinquent, but the degree to which the group engages in specifically delinquent acts, that is, constructs its internal status criteria around the law-violating end of the trouble continuum, may vary greatly depending on local circumstances. These include such things as the presence and salience of police, professional criminals, clergy, functioning recreational and settlement programs, and the like.

Like Thrasher, Miller emphasizes the wide range of activities of a nondelinquent nature that the gang members engage in, although, unlike Thrasher's boys, they do not do so because of poor social control, but because of the desire to be "real men."

Participation in the lower class street group may produce delinquency in several ways:[15]

1. Following cultural practices which comprise essential elements of the total pattern of lower class culture automatically violates certain legal norms.
2. In instances where alternative avenues to similar objectives are available, the non-law-abiding avenue frequently provides a greater and more immediate return for a relatively smaller investment of energy.
3. The "demanded" response to certain situations recurrently engendered within lower class culture involves the commission of illegal acts.

Impact of Middle Class Values

Miller's approach, like the approaches of Thrasher and Cohen, has its strengths and weaknesses. Miller has not been very successful in refuting Cohen's insistence on the

[15] Walter B. Miller, "Lower Class Culture as a Generating Milieu of Gang Delinquency," *op. cit.*, p. 18.

clash between middle class and lower class standards as it affects the sources of self-esteem. To be sure, Cohen's own presentation of just what the lower class boy has or has not internalized is considerably confused. As I have remarked elsewhere, Cohen seems to be saying that a little internalization is a dangerous thing.[16] Miller seems to be saying that the involvements in lower class culture are so deep and exclusive that contacts with agents of middle class dominated institutions, especially the schools, have no impact.

Actually, resolution of this problem does not seem so terribly difficult. In handling Cohen's formulations, I would suggest that previous internalization of middle class values is not particularly necessary, because the lower class boys will be told about them at the very time they are being status-deprived by their teachers and others. They will likely hate it and them (teachers and values), and the process is started. On the other hand, it seems unlikely that Miller's lower class boys can spend ten years in school without some serious outcomes. They should either come to accept middle class values or become even more antagonistic or both, and this should drive them further into the arms of lower class culture.

This would be especially the case because of the prevailing definition of school work as girlish, an attitude not at all limited to Miller's lower class culture. With the sex-role identification problems Miller quite reasonably poses for his boys, the demands of the middle class school teacher that he be neat and clean and well-behaved must be especially galling.[17] In short, it seems to me inconceivable that the objective conflict between the boys and the school, as the most crucial example, could end in a simple turning away.

Miller also seems to be weak when he insists upon seeing what he calls the hard core of lower class culture as a distinctive form and, at the same time, must posit varieties of lower class culture to account for variations in behavior and values. This is not necessarily a factually untrue position, but it would seem to underemphasize the fluidity and variability of American urban life. It is necessary for him to point out that objectively low status urban groups vary in the degree to which they display the core features of lower class culture, with Negroes and Irish groups among those he has studied displaying it more and Italians less.

Validity of Female Base

Miller seems so concerned that the features of lower class culture, especially the female-based household, not be seen as the disorganization of the more conventional system or as signs of social pathology that he seems to overdo it rather drastically. He is very concerned to show that lower class culture is of ancient lineage and is or was functional in American society. Yet, at the same time, he says that lower class culture is only now emerging at the bottom of the urban heap. He also forgets that none of the low status groups in the society, with the possible exception of low status Negroes, has any history of his female-based household, at least not in the extreme form that he describes.[18]

A closely related problem is posed by Miller's citation of cross-cultural evidence, for example, "The female-based household is a stabilized form in many societies—frequently associated with polygamy—and is found in 21 per cent of world societies."[19] I do not doubt the figure, but I question the implication that the female-based household as the household form, legitimated and normatively supported in societies practicing polygamy, can be very directly equated with a superficially similar system existing on the margins of a larger society and clearly seen as deviant by that larger society.

[16] David J. Bordua, *Sociological Theories and Their Implications for Juvenile Delinquency* (Children's Bureau, Juvenile Delinquency: Facts and Facets, No. 2; Washington, D.C.: U.S. Government Printing Office, 1960), pp. 9–11.

[17] For evidence that lower class Negro girls seem to do much better than boys in adjusting to at least one middle class institution, see Martin Deutsch, *Minority Group and Class Status as Related to Social and Personality Factors in School Achievement* (Monograph No. 2, The Society for Applied Anthropology; Ithaca, New York: The Society, 1960).

[18] E. Franklin Frazer, *The Negro Family in the United States* (Chicago: University of Chicago Press, 1939).

[19] Walter B. Miller, "Implications of Urban Lower Class Culture for Social Work," *op. cit.,* p. 225 fn.

Surely, in primitive societies, the household can count on the stable economic and judicial base provided by an adult male. The very fact that such a household in the United States is under continuous and heavy pressure from the law, the Aid to Dependent Children worker, and nearly all other agents of the conventional order must make for a very different situation than in societies where it is the accepted form. In such societies, would mothers generally regard men as "unreliable and untrustworthy" and would the statement "all men are no good" be common?[20] Surely, such an attitude implies some awareness that things should be otherwise.

All this is not to argue that tendencies of the sort Miller describes are not present nor to underestimate the value of his insistence that we look at this way of life in its own terms—a valuable contribution indeed—but only to ask for somewhat greater awareness of the larger social dynamics that produce his lower class culture.

Danger of Tautology

Finally, a last criticism of Miller's formulations aims at the use of the focal concerns material. There seems more than a little danger of tautology here if the focal concerns are derived from observing behavior and then used to explain the same behavior. One would be on much safer ground to deal in much greater detail with the structural roots and reality situations to which lower class culture may be a response. Thus, for example, Miller makes no real use of the vast literature on the consequences of prolonged instability of employment, which seems to me the root of the matter.

These criticisms should not blind us to very real contributions in Miller's position. Most importantly, he tells us what the lower class street boys are for, rather than just what they are against. In addition, he deals provocatively and originally with the nature of the adult culture which serves as the context for adolescent behavior. Finally, he alerts us to a possible historical development that has received relatively little attention— the emergence of something like a stable American lower class. This possibility seems

[20] *Ibid.*, p. 226.

to have been largely neglected in studies of our increasingly middle class society.

SUCCESS GOALS AND OPPORTUNITY STRUCTURES

The last of the major approaches to the problem of lower class group delinquency to be considered here is associated with Richard A. Cloward and Lloyd E. Ohlin.[21] Stated in its briefest form, the theory is as follows: American culture makes morally mandatory the seeking of success goals but differentially distributes the morally acceptable means to these success goals, the legitimate opportunities that loom so large in the approach.[22]

This gap between culturally universalized goals and structurally limited means creates strain among lower class youths who aspire to economic advancement. Such strain and alienation leads to the formation of delinquent subcultures, that is, normative and belief systems that specifically support and legitimate delinquency, among those boys who blame the system rather than themselves for their impending or actual failure. The particular form of delinquent subculture —conflict, criminal, or retreatist (drug-using)—which results depends on the nature of the local neighborhood and, especially, on the availability of illegitimate opportunities, such as stable crime careers as models and training grounds.

The criminal subculture develops in stable neighborhoods with much regularized crime present; the conflict form develops in really disorganized neighborhoods where not even illegitimate opportunities are available; the retreatist, or drug-use, subculture develops among persons who are double failures due either to internalized prohibitions against violence or theft or to the objective unavailability of these solutions.

Intervening between the stress due to

[21] The full statement of the approach is in Richard A. Cloward and Lloyd E. Ohlin, *Delinquency and Opportunity* (New York: Free Press of Glencoe, Inc., 1960) ; see also Richard A. Cloward "Illegitimate Means, Anomie and Deviant Behavior," *American Sociological Review,* Vol. 24 (April 1959), No. 2, pp. 164–176.
[22] For the original version of this formulation, see Robert K. Merton, *Social Theory and Social Structure* (rev. and enl.; New York: Free Press of Glencoe, Inc., 1951), Chaps. 4, 5.

blocked aspirations and the creation of the full-fledged subculture of whatever type is a process of collectively supported "withdrawal of attributions of legitimacy from established social norms."

This process, coupled with the collective development of the relevant delinquent norms, serves to allay whatever guilt might have been felt over the illegal acts involved in following the delinquent norms.

Since the argument in *Delinquency and Opportunity* is, in many ways, even more complicated than those associated with Cohen, Short, and Miller, I will discuss only a few highlights.[23]

Potential Delinquents

On the question of who aspires to what, which is so involved in the disagreements between Cohen and Miller, Cloward and Ohlin take the position that it is not the boys who aspire to middle class status—and, therefore, have presumably partially internalized the middle class measuring rod—who form the raw material for delinquent subculture, but those who wish only to improve their economic status without any change in class membership. Thus, it is appropriate in their argument to say that the genitors of the delinquent subcultures are not dealing so much with an internal problem of self-esteem as with an external problem of injustice. Cohen says, in effect, that the delinquent subculture prevents self-blame for failure from breaking through, the reaction formation function of the delinquent subculture. Cloward and Ohlin say that the delinquent norm systems are generated by boys who have already determined that their failures, actual or impending, are the fault of the larger social order.[24]

[23] Large segments of *Delinquency and Opportunity* are devoted to refutations of other positions, especially those of Cohen and Miller. I felt that, at least for the present paper, criticizing in detail other people's refutations of third parties might be carrying the matter too far. It should be pointed out, however, that the tendency to take extreme positions as a consequence of involvement in a polemic which is apparent in Miller's work seems even more apparent in the Cloward and Ohlin book.

[24] Richard A. Cloward and Lloyd S. Ohlin, *Delinquency and Opportunity, op. cit.* For the problem of types of aspiration and their consequences, see, especially, pp. 86–97. For the matter of self-blame and their system blame for failure, see pp. 110–126.

This insistence that it is the "system blamers" who form the grist for the subcultural mill leads Cloward and Ohlin into something of an impasse, it seems to me. They must, of course, then deal with the determinants of the two types of blame and choose to say that two factors are primarily relevant. First, the larger culture engenders expectations, not just aspirations, of success which are not met, and, second, there exist highly visible barriers to the fulfillment of these expectations, such as racial prejudice, which are defined as unjust.

These do not seem unreasonable, and, in fact, in the case of Negro youth, perhaps, largely fit the case. Cloward and Ohlin, however, are forced for what seems overwhelmingly polemical reasons into a position that the feeling of injustice must be objectively correct. Therefore, they say (1) that it is among those actually fitted for success where the sense of injustice will flourish and (2) that delinquent subcultures are formed by boys who do not essentially differ in their capacity to cope with the larger institutions from other boys. This point deserves some attention since it is so diametrically opposed to the Cohen position which states that some working class boys, especially lower working class boys, are unable to meet the demands of middle-class-dominated institutions.

It is our impression that a sense of being unjustly deprived of access to opportunities to which one is entitled is common among those who become participants in delinquent subcultures. Delinquents tend to be persons who have been led to expect opportunities because of their potential ability to meet the formal, institutionally-established criteria of evaluation. Their sense of injustice arises from the failure of the system to fulfill these expectations. Their criticism is not directed inward since they regard themselves in comparison with their fellows as capable of meeting the formal requirements of the system. It has frequently been noted that delinquents take special delight in discovering hypocrisy in the operation of the established social order. They like to point out that it's "who you know, not what you know" that enables one to advance or gain coveted social rewards. They become convinced that bribery, blackmail, fear-inspiring pressure, special influence, and similar factors are more important than the publicly avowed criteria of merit.[25]

Delinquents and Nondelinquent Peers

On the same page in a footnote, the authors go on to say that the research evidence indicates "the basic endowments of delinquents, such as intelligence, physical strength, and agility, are the equal of or greater than those of their non-delinquent peers."

The material in these quotations is so riddled with ambiguities it is difficult to know where to begin criticism, but we can at least point out the following. First, Cloward and Ohlin seem to be confusing the justificatory function of delinquent subcultures with their causation. All of these beliefs on the part of gang delinquents have been repeatedly reported in the literature, but, by the very argument of *Delinquency and Opportunity,* it is impossible to tell whether they constitute compensatory ideology or descriptions of objective reality.

Second, Cloward and Ohlin seem to be victims of their very general tendency to ignore the life histories of their delinquents.[26] Thus, there is no way of knowing really what these subcultural beliefs may reflect in the experience of the boys. Third, and closely related to the ignoring of life history material, is the problem of assessing the degree to which these gang boys are in fact prepared to meet the formal criteria for success. To say that they are intelligent, strong, and agile is to parody the criteria for advancement. Perhaps Cohen would point out that intelligent, agile, strong boys who begin the first grade using foul language, fighting among themselves, and using the

school property as arts and crafts materials do not meet the criteria for advancement.

It is quite true that members of highly sophisticated delinquent gangs often find themselves blocked from whatever occupational opportunities there are, but this seems, often, the end product of a long history of their progressively cutting off opportunity and destroying their own capacities which may begin in the lower class family, as described by either Cohen or Miller, and continue through school failure and similar events. By the age of eighteen, many gang boys are, for all practical purposes, unemployable or need the support, instruction, and sponsorship of trained street-gang workers. Participation in gang delinquency in itself diminishes the fitness of many boys for effective functioning in the conventional world.[27]

If, indeed, Cloward and Ohlin mean to include the more attitudinal and characterological criteria for advancement, then it seems highly unlikely that any large number of boys trained and prepared to meet these demands of the occupational world could interpret failure exclusively in terms which blame the system. They would have been too well socialized, and, if they did form a delinquent subculture, it would have to perform the psychological function of mitigating the sense of internal blame. This, of course, would make them look much like Cohen's boys.

In short, Cloward and Ohlin run the risk of confusing justification and causation and of equating the end with the beginning.

All of this is not to deny that there are real obstacles to opportunity for lower class boys. There are. These blocks on both the performance and learning sides, are a major structural feature in accounting for much of the adaptation of lower class populations. But they do not operate solely or even pri-

---

[25] *Ibid.,* p. 117.

[26] This is the most fundamental weakness in the book. The delinquents in Thrasher, Cohen, and Miller were, in varying degrees, once recognizably children. Cloward and Ohlin's delinquents seem suddenly to appear on the scene sometime in adolescence, to look at the world, and to discover, "Man, there's no opportunity in my structure." It is instructive in this connection to note that the index to *Delinquency and Opportunity* contains only two references to the family. One says that the family no longer conducts occupational training; the other criticizes Miller's ideas on the female-based household.

[27] Here, again, Thrasher seems superior to some of the modern theorists. He stressed the fact that long-term involvement in the "free, undisciplined" street life with money at hand from petty theft and with the days devoted to play was not exactly ideal preparation for the humdrum life of the job. Again, Thrasher's sensitivity to the attitudinal and subcultural consequences of the gang formation and maintenance process truly needs reintroduction.

marily on the level of the adolescent. They create a social world in which he comes of age, and, by the time he reaches adolescence, he may find himself cut off from the larger society. Much of the Cloward and Ohlin approach seems better as a theory of the origins of Miller's lower class culture. Each generation does not meet and solve anew the problems of class structure barriers to opportunity but begins with the solution of its forebears.[28] This is why reform efforts can be so slow to succeed.

Some Insights

The positive contributions of the Cloward-Ohlin approach seem to me to lie less on the side of the motivational sources of subcultural delinquency, where I feel their attempts to clarify the ambiguities in Cohen have merely led to new ambiguities, but more on the side of the factors in local social structure that determine the type of subcultural delinquency.

The major innovation here is the concept of illegitimate opportunities which serves to augment Kobrin's almost exclusive emphasis on the differentially controlling impact of different slum environments. I do think that Cloward and Ohlin may make too much of the necessity for systematic, organized criminal careers in order for the illegitimate opportunity structure to have an effect, but the general argument has great merit.

In addition to the concept of illegitimate opportunities and closely related to it is the description, or speculation, concerning historical changes in the social organization of slums. Changes in urban life in the United States may have truly produced the disorganized slum devoid of the social links between young and old, between children and

older adolescents which characterized the slums described by Thrasher. Certainly, the new conditions of life seem to have created new problems of growing up, though our knowledge of their precise impact leaves much to be desired.

CONCLUSION

This paper should not, I hope, give the impression that current theoretical interpretations of lower class, urban, male subcultural delinquency are without value. Such is far from the case. Many of my comments have been negative since each of the theorists quite ably presents his own defense, which should be read in any case. In fact, I think that this problem has led to some of the most exciting and provocative intellectual interchange in all of sociology in recent years. I do believe, however, that this interchange has often been marred by unnecessary polemic and, even more, by a lack of relevant data.

As I have indicated, there have been some profound changes in the way social theorists view the processes of gang formation and persistence. These, I believe, derive only partially, perhaps even unimportantly, from changes in the facts to be explained. Indeed, we must wait for a study of gangs which will approach Thrasher's in thoroughness before we can know if there are new facts to be explained. Nor do I believe that the changes in viewpoint have come about entirely because old theories were shown to be inadequate to old facts. Both Cohen and Cloward and Ohlin feel that older theorists did not deal with the problem of the origins of delinquent subcultures, but only with the transmission of the subculture once developed.[29] A careful reading of Thrasher indicates that such is not the case.

All in all, though, it does not seem like much fun any more to be a gang delinquent. Thrasher's boys enjoyed themselves being chased by the police, shooting dice, skipping school, rolling drunks. It was fun. Miller's

---

[28] Parenthetically, the Cloward and Ohlin position has great difficulty in accounting for the fact that lower class delinquent subculture carriers do not avail themselves of opportunities that do exist. The mixed success of vocational school training, for example, indicates that some fairly clear avenues of opportunity are foregone by many delinquent boys. For Negro boys, where avenues to the skilled trades may indeed be blocked, their argument seems reasonable. For white boys, I have serious question. In fact, the only really convincing case they make on the aspiration-blockage, system-blame side is for Negroes.

[29] Albert K. Cohen, *Delinquent Boys, op. cit.,* p. 18; Richard A. Cloward and Lloyd E. Ohlin, *Delinquency and Opportunity, op. cit.,* p. 42.

boys do have a little fun, with their excitement focal concern, but it seems so desperate somehow. Cohen's boys and Cloward and Ohlin's boys are driven by grim economic and psychic necessity into rebellion. It seems peculiar that modern analysts have stopped assuming that "evil" can be fun and see gang

delinquency as arising only when boys are driven away from "good."[30]

[30] For a more thorough commentary on changes in the view of human nature which, I think, partly underlie the decline of fun in theories of the gang, see Dennis Wrong, "The Oversocialized View of Man" *American Sociological Review,* Vol. 26 (April 1961), No. 3, pp. 183–193.

Social Psychology and Desegregation Research[1] /
Thomas F. Pettigrew (*Harvard University*)

What one hears and what one sees of southern race relations today are sharply divergent. Consider some of the things that occur in interviews with white Southerners.

"As much as my family likes TV," confided a friendly North Carolina farmer, "we always turn the set off when they put them colored people on." But as the two of us were completing the interview, a series of famous Negro entertainers performed on the bright, 21-inch screen in the adjoining room. No one interrupted them.

A rotund banker in Charleston, South Carolina, was equally candid in his remarks: "Son, under no conditions will the white man and the black man ever get together in this state." He apparently preferred to ignore the government sponsored integration at his city's naval installation, just a short distance from his office.

Another respondent, this time a highly educated Chattanooga businessman, patiently explained to me for over an hour how race relations had not changed at all in his city during the past generation. As I left his office building, I saw a Negro policeman directing downtown traffic. It was the first

Negro traffic cop I had ever seen in the South.

The South today is rife with such contradictions; social change has simply been too rapid for many Southerners to recognize it. Such a situation commands the attention of psychologists—particularly those in the South.

There are many other aspects of this sweeping process that should command our professional attention. To name just two, both the pending violence and the stultifying conformity attendant with desegregation are uniquely psychological problems. We might ask, for instance, what leads to violence in some desegregating communities, like Little Rock and Clinton, and not in others, like Norfolk and Winston-Salem? A multiplicity of factors must be relevant and further research is desperately needed to delineate them; but tentative early work seems to indicate that desegregation violence so far has been surprisingly "rational." That is, violence has generally resulted in localities where at least some of the authorities give prior hints that they would gladly return to segregation if disturbances occurred; peaceful integration has generally followed firm and forceful leadership.[2]

Research concerning conformity in the present situation is even more important. Many psychologists know from personal experience how intense the pressures to conform in racial attitudes have become in the

Reprinted from *American Psychologist,* 1961, 16, pages 105–112, by permission of author and publisher, The American Psychological Association.

[1] This paper was given as an invited address at the Annual Meeting of the Southeastern Psychological Association, Atlanta, Georgia, March 31, 1960. The author wishes to express his appreciation to Gordon W. Allport of Harvard University, E. Earl Baughman of the University of North Carolina, and Cooper C. Clements of Emory University for their suggestions.

[2] Clark (1953) predicted this from early border-state integration, and a variety of field reports have since documented the point in specific instances.

present-day South; indeed, it appears that the first amendment guaranteeing free speech is in as much peril as the fourteenth amendment. Those who dare to break consistently this conformity taboo must do so in many parts of the South under the intimidation of slanderous letters and phone calls, burned crosses, and even bomb threats. Moreover, this paper will contend that conformity is the social psychological key to analyzing desegregation.

It is imperative that psychologists study these phenomena for two reasons: first, our psychological insights and methods are needed in understanding and solving this, our nation's primary internal problem; second, this process happening before our eyes offers us a rare opportunity to test in the field the psychological concomitants of cultural stress and social change. Thus I would like in this paper to assess some of the prospects and directions of these potential psychological contributions.

ROLE OF SOCIAL SCIENCE IN THE DESEGREGATION PROCESS TO DATE

The role of social science, particularly sociology and psychology, in the desegregation process has been much publicized and criticized by southern segregationists.[3] Many of these critics apparently think that sociology is synonymous with socialism and psychology with brainwashing. In any event, their argument that we have been crucially important in the Supreme Court desegregation cases of the fifties is based largely on the reference to seven social science documents in Footnote 11 of the famous 1954 *Brown vs. Board of Education* decision. It would be flattering for us to think that our research has had such a dramatic effect on the course of history as segregationists claim, but in all truth we do not deserve such high praise.

In making their claim that the 1954 decision was psychological and not legal, the

segregationists choose to overlook several things. The 1954 ruling did not come suddenly "out of the blue"; it was a logical continuation of a 44-year Supreme Court trend that began in 1910 when a former private in the Confederate Army, the liberal Edward White, became Chief Justice (Logan, 1956). When compared to this backdrop, our influence on the 1954 ruling was actually of only footnote importance. Furthermore, the language and spirit of the 1896 *Plessy vs. Ferguson,* separate-but-equal decision, so dear to the hearts of segregationists, were as immersed in the jargon and thinking of the social science of that era as the 1954 decision was of our era. Its 1896, Sumnerian argument that laws cannot change "social prejudices" (Allport, 1954, pp. 469–473) and its use of such social Darwinism terms as "racial instincts" and "natural affinities" lacked only a footnote to make it as obviously influenced by the then current social science as the 1954 ruling.

A final reason why we do not deserve the flattering praise of the segregationists is our failure to make substantial contributions to the process since 1954. The lack of penetrating psychological research in this area can be traced directly to three things: the lack of extensive foundation support, conformity pressures applied in many places in the South that deter desegregation research, and the inadequacy of traditional psychological thinking to cope with the present process. Let us discuss each of these matters in turn.

A few years ago Stuart Cook (1957) drew attention to the failure of foundations to support desegregation research; the situation today is only slightly improved. It appears that a combination of foundation fears has produced this situation. One set of fears, as Cook noted, may stem from concern over attacks by southern Congressmen on their tax free status; the other set may stem from boycotts carried out by some segregationists against products identified with the foundations. In any case, this curtailment of funds is undoubtedly one reason why social scientists have so far left this crucial process relatively unstudied. Recently, however, a few moderate sized grants have been made for work in this area; hopefully, this is the

---

[3] For instance, once-liberal Virginius Dabney (1957, p. 14), editor of the *Richmond Times-Dispatch,* charged that "the violence at Little Rock . . . never would have happened if nine justices had not consulted sociologists and psychologists, instead of lawyers, in 1954, and attempted to legislate through judicial decrees."

beginning of a reappraisal by foundations of their previous policies. And it is up to us to submit competent research proposals to them to test continually for any change of these policies.

It is difficult to assess just how much damage has been done to desegregation research in the South by segregationist pressures. Probably the number of direct refusals to allow such research by southern institutions outside of the Black Belt has actually been small. More likely, the greatest harm has been rendered indirectly by the stifling atmosphere which prevents us from actually testing the limits of research opportunities. Interested as we may be in the racial realm, we decide to work in a less controversial area. Perhaps it is less a matter of courage than it is of resignation in the face of what are thought to be impossible barriers. If these suspicions are correct, there is real hope for overcoming in part this second obstacle to desegregation research.

In some situations, there should be little resistance. In racially integrated veterans' hospitals, for instance, much needed personality studies comparing Negro and white patients should be possible. In other situations, the amount of resistance to race research may be less than we anticipate. Since Little Rock, many so-called "moderates" in the South, particularly businessmen, have become more interested in the dynamics of desegregation. This is not to say that they are more in favor of racial equality than they were; it is only to suggest that the bad publicity, the closing of schools, and the economic losses suffered by Little Rock have made these influential Southerners more receptive to objective and constructive research on the process. It is for this reason that it is imperative the limits for the southern study of desegregation be tested at this time.

Finally, psychological contributions to desegregation research have been restricted by the inadequacy of traditional thinking in our discipline. More specifically, the relative neglect of situational variables in interracial behavior and a restricted interpretation and use of the attitude concept hinder psychological work in this area.

The importance of the situation for racial interaction has been demonstrated in a wide variety of settings. All-pervasive racial attitudes are often not involved: many individuals seem fully capable of immediate behavioral change as situations change. Thus in Panama there is a divided street, the Canal Zone side of which is racially segregated and the Panamanian side of which is racially integrated. Biesanz and Smith (1951) report that most Panamanians and Americans appear to accommodate without difficulty as they go first on one side of the street and then on the other. Likewise in the coal mining county of McDowell, West Virginia, Minard (1952) relates that the majority of Negro and white miners follow easily a traditional pattern of integration below the ground and almost complete segregation above the ground. The literature abounds with further examples: southern white migrants readily adjusting to integrated situations in the North (Killian, 1949), northern whites approving of employment and public facility integration but resisting residential integration (Reitzes, 1953), etc. Indeed, at the present time in the South there are many white Southerners who are simultaneously adjusting to bus and public golf course integration and opposing public school integration. Or, as in Nashville, they may have accepted school integration but are opposing lunch counter integration.

This is not to imply that generalized attitudes on race are never invoked. There are some Panamanians and some Americans who act about the same on both sides of the Panamanian street. Minard (1952) estimated about two-fifths of the West Virginian miners he observed behave consistently in either a tolerant or an intolerant fashion both below and above ground. And some whites either approve or disapprove of all desegregation. But these people are easily explained by traditional theory. They probably consist of the extremes in authoritarianism; their attitudes on race are so generalized and so salient that their consistent behavior in racial situations is sometimes in defiance of the prevailing social norms.

On the other hand, the "other directed" individuals who shift their behavior to keep in line with shifting expectations present the real problem for psychologists. Their racial attitudes appear less salient, more specific, and more tied to particular situations. Conformity needs are predominantly important for these people, and we shall return shortly to a further discussion of these conformists.

One complication introduced by a situational analysis is that interracial contact itself frequently leads to the modification of attitudes. A number of studies of racially integrated situations have noted dramatic attitude changes, but in most cases the changes involved specific, situation-linked attitudes. For example, white department store employees become more accepting of Negroes in the work situation after equal status, integrated contact but not necessarily more accepting in other situations (Harding & Hogrefe, 1952). And *The American Soldier* studies (Stouffer, Suchman, DeVinney, Star, & Williams, 1949) found that the attitudes of white army personnel toward the Negro as a fighting man improve after equal status, integrated contact in combat, but their attitudes toward the Negro as a social companion do not necessarily change. In other words, experience in a novel situation of equal status leads to acceptance of that specific situation for many persons. Situations, then, not only structure specific racial behavior, but they may change specific attitudes in the process.

One final feature of a situational analysis deserves mention. Typically in psychology we have tested racial attitudes in isolation, apart from conflicting attitudes and values. Yet this is not realistic. As the desegregation process slowly unfolds in such resistant states as Virginia and Georgia, we see clearly that many segregationist Southerners value law and order, public education, and a prosperous economy above their racial views. Once such a situation pits race against other entrenched values, we need to know the public's hierarchy of these values. Thus a rounded situational analysis requires the measures of racial attitudes in the full context of countervalues.[4]

A second and related weakness in our psychological approach is the failure to exploit fully the broad and dynamic implications of the attitude concept. Most social psychological research has dealt with attitudes as if they were serving only an expressive function; but racial attitudes in the South require a more complex treatment.

In their volume, *Opinion and Personality,* Smith, Bruner, and White (1956) urge a more expansive interpretation of attitudes. They note three attitude functions. First, there is the *object appraisal* function; attitudes aid in understanding "reality" as it is defined by the culture. Second, attitudes can play a *social adjustment* role by contributing to the individual's identification with, or differentiation from, various reference groups. Finally, attitudes may reduce anxiety by serving an expressive or *externalization* function.

> Externalization occurs when an individual . . . senses an analogy between a perceived environmental event and some unresolved inner problem . . . [and] adopts an attitude . . . which is a transformed version of his way of dealing with his inner difficulty (pp. 41–44). (Reprinted with permission of John Wiley & Sons, Inc.)

At present the most fashionable psychological theories of prejudice—frustration-aggression, psychoanalytic, and authoritarianism—all deal chiefly with the externalization process. Valuable as these theories have been, this exclusive attention to the expressive component of attitudes has been at the expense of the object appraisal and social adjustment components. Moreover, it is the contention of this paper that these neglected and more socially relevant functions, particularly social adjustment, offer the key to further psychological advances in desegregation research.[5]

The extent to which this psychological concentration on externalization has influenced the general public was illustrated recently in the popular reaction to the swastika desecrations of Jewish temples. The perpetrators, all agreed, must be juvenile hoodlums, or "sick," or both. In other words,

---

[4] A popular treatment of this point has been made by Zinn (1959).

[5] Though this paper emphasizes the social adjustment aspect of southern attitudes toward Negroes, the equally neglected object appraisal function is also of major importance. Most southern whites know only lower class Negroes; consequently their unfavorable stereotype of Negroes serves a definite reality function.

externalization explanations were predominantly offered.[6] Valid though these explanations may be in many cases, is it not also evident that the perpetrators were accurately reflecting the anti-Semitic norms of their subcultures? Thus their acts and the attitudes behind their acts are socially adjusting for these persons, given the circles in which they move.

Much less the public, some sociologists, too, have been understandably misled by our overemphasis on externalization into underestimating the psychological analysis of prejudice. One sociologist (Rose, 1956) categorically concludes:

> There is no evidence that . . . any known source of "prejudice" in the psychological sense is any more prevalent in the South than in the North (p. 174).

Two others (Rabb & Lipset, 1959) maintain firmly:

> the psychological approach, as valuable as it is, does not explain the preponderance of people who engage in prejudiced behavior, but do *not* have special emotional problems (p. 26).

Both of these statements assume, as some psychologists have assumed, that externalization is the only possible psychological explanation of prejudice. These writers employ cultural and situational norms as explanatory concepts for racial prejudice and discrimination, but fail to see that conformity needs are the personality reflections of these norms and offer an equally valid concept on the psychological level. To answer the first assertion, recent evidence indicates that conformity to racial norms, one "known source of prejudice," is "more prevalent in the South than in the North." To answer the second assertion, strong needs to conform to racial norms in a sternly sanctioning South, for instance, are *not* "special emotional problems." Psychology is not just a science of mental illness nor must psychological theories of prejudice be limited to the mentally ill.

[6] Such explanations also serve for many anti-Semitic observers as an ego-alien defense against guilt.

CONFORMITY AND SOCIAL ADJUSTMENT IN SOUTHERN RACIAL ATTITUDES

Evidence of the importance of conformity in southern attitudes on race has been steadily accumulating in recent years. The relevant data come from several different research approaches; one of these is the study of anti-Semitism. Roper's (1946, 1947) opinion polls have twice shown the South, together with the Far West, to be one of the least anti-Semitic regions in the United States. Knapp's (1944) study of over 1,000 war rumors from all parts of the country in 1942 lends additional weight to this finding. He noted that anti-Semitic stories constituted 9% of the nation's rumors but only 3% of the South's rumors. By contrast, 8.5% of the southern rumors concerned the Negro as opposed to only 3% for the nation as a whole. Consistent with these data, too, is Prothro's (1952) discovery that two-fifths of his white adult sample in Louisiana was quite favorable in its attitudes toward Jews but at the same time quite unfavorable in its attitudes toward Negroes. But if the externalization function were predominant in southern anti-Negro attitudes, the South should also be highly anti-Semitic. Externalizing bigots do not select out just the Negro; they typically reject all out-groups, even, as Hartley (1946) has demonstrated, out-groups that do not exist.

Further evidence comes from research employing the famous F Scale measure of authoritarianism (Adorno, Frenkel-Brunswik, Levinson, & Sanford, 1950). Several studies, employing both student and adult samples, have reported southern F Scale means that fall well within the range of means of comparable nonsouthern groups (Milton, 1952; Pettigrew, 1959; Smith & Prothro, 1957). Moreover, there is no evidence that the family pattern associated with authoritarianism is any more prevalent in the South than in other parts of the country (Davis, Gardner, & Gardner, 1941; Dollard, 1937). It seems clear, then, that the South's heightened prejudice against the Negro cannot be explained in terms of any regional difference in authoritarianism. This is not to deny, however, the importance of the F Scale in predicting individual differences; it appears to correlate with prejudice in southern samples at approximately the same levels as in northern samples (Pettigrew, 1959).

The third line of evidence relates conformity measures directly to racial attitudes. For lack of a standardized, nonlaboratory measure, one study defined conformity and deviance in terms of the respondents' social characteristics (Pettigrew, 1959). For a southern white sample with age and education held constant, potentially conforming respondents (i.e., females or church attenders) were *more* anti-Negro than their counterparts (i.e., males or nonattenders of church), and potentially deviant respondents (i.e., armed service veterans or political independents) were *less* anti-Negro than their counterparts (i.e., nonveterans or political party identifiers). None of these differences were noted in a comparable northern sample. Furthermore, Southerners living in communities with relatively small percentages of Negroes were less anti-Negro than Southerners living in communities with relatively large percentages of Negroes, though they were *not* less authoritarian. In short, respondents most likely to be conforming to cultural pressures are more prejudiced against Negroes in the South but not in the North. And the percentage of Negroes in the community appears to be a fairly accurate index of the strength of these southern cultural pressures concerning race.

Thus all three types of research agree that conformity to the stern racial norms of southern culture is unusually crucial in the South's heightened hostility toward the Negro.[7] Or, in plain language, it is the path of least resistance in most southern circles to favor white supremacy. When an individual's parents and peers are racially prejudiced, when his limited world accepts racial discrimination as a given of life, when his deviance means certain ostracism, then his anti-Negro attitudes are not so much expressive as they are socially adjusting.

This being the case, it is fortunate that a number of significant laboratory and theoret-

ical advances in the conformity realm have been made recently in our discipline. Solomon Asch's (1951) pioneer research on conformity, followed up by Crutchfield (1955) and others, has provided us with a wealth of laboratory findings, many of them suggestive for desegregation research. And theoretical analyses of conformity have been introduced by Kelman (1958, 1961), Festinger (1953, 1957), and Thibaut and Kelley (1959); these, too, are directly applicable for desegregation research. Indeed, research in southern race relations offers a rare opportunity to test these empirical and theoretical formulations in the field on an issue of maximum salience.

Consider the relevance of one of Asch's (1951) intriguing findings. Asch's standard situation, you will recall, employed seven pre-instructed assistants and a genuine subject in a line judgment task. On two-thirds of the judgments, the seven assistants purposely reported aloud an obviously incorrect estimate; thus the subject, seated eighth, faced unanimous pressure to conform by making a similarly incorrect response. On approximately one-third of such judgments, he yielded to the group; like the others, he would estimate a 5-inch line as 4 inches. But when Asch disturbed the unanimity by having one of his seven assistants give the correct response, the subjects yielded only a tenth, rather than a third, of the time. Once unanimity no longer existed, even when there was only one supporting colleague, the subject could better withstand the pressure of the majority to conform. To carry through the analogy to today's crisis in the South, obvious 5-inch lines are being widely described as 4 inches. Many Southerners, faced with what appears to be solid unanimity, submit to the distortion. But when even one respected source—a minister, a newspaper editor, even a college professor—conspicuously breaks the unanimity, *perhaps* a dramatic modification is achieved in the private opinions of many conforming Southerners. Only an empirical test can learn if such a direct analogy is warranted.

Consider, too, the relevance of recent theoretical distinctions. Kelman (1958, 1961), for example, has clarified the concept of conformity by pointing out that three separate

[7] Similar analyses of South African student data indicate that the social adjustment function may also be of unusual importance in the anti-African attitudes of the English in the Union (Pettigrew, 1958, 1960).

processes are involved: *compliance, identifi-cation,* and *internalization.* Compliance exists when an individual accepts influence not be-cause he believes in it, but because he hopes to achieve a favorable reaction from an agent who maintains surveillance over him. Identification exists when an individual ac-cepts influence because he wants to establish or maintain a satisfying relationship with another person or group. The third process, internalization, exists when an individual ac-cepts influence because the content of the behavior itself is satisfying; unlike the other types of conformity, internalized behavior will be performed without the surveillance of the agent or a salient relationship with the agent. It is with this third process that Kel-man's ideas overlap with authoritarian the-ory.

We have all witnessed illustrations of each of these processes in the acceptance by Southerners of the region's racial norms. The "Uncle Tom" Negro is an example of a compliant Southerner; another example is furnished by the white man who treats Negroes as equals only when not under the surveillance of other whites. Identification is best seen in white Southerners whose re-sistance to racial integration enables them to be a part of what they erroneously imagine to be Confederate tradition. Such identifiers are frequently upwardly mobile people who are still assimilating to urban society; they strive for social status by identifying with the hallowed symbols and shibboleths of the South's past. Southerners who have internal-ized the white supremacy dictates of the cul-ture are the real racists who use the issue to gain political office, to attract resistance group membership fees, or to meet person-ality needs. Southerners with such contrast-ing bases for their racial attitudes should re-act very differently toward desegregation. For instance, compliant whites can be expected to accept desegregation more readily than those who have internalized segregationist norms.

On the basis of this discussion of con-formity, I would like to propose a new con-cept: *the latent liberal.* This is not to be confused with the cherished southern notion of the "moderate"; the ambiguous term "moderate" is presently used to describe everything from an integrationist who wants

to be socially accepted to a racist who wants to be polite. Rather, the latent liberal refers to the Southerner who is neither anti-Semitic nor authoritarian but whose conformity hab-its and needs cause him to be strongly anti-Negro. Through the processes of compli-ance and identification, the latent liberal continues to behave in a discriminatory fash-ion toward Negroes even though such be-havior conflicts with his basically tolerant personality. He is at the present time *il*liberal on race, but he has the personality potenti-ality of becoming liberal once the norms of the culture change. Indeed, as the already unleashed economic, legal, political, and so-cial forces restructure the South's racial norms, the latent liberal's attitudes about Negroes will continue to change. Previously cited research suggests that there are today an abundance of white Southerners who meet this latent liberal description; collec-tively, they will reflect on the individual level the vast societal changes now taking place in the South.

SOME SUGGESTED DIRECTIONS FOR FUTURE PSYCHOLOGICAL RESEARCH ON DESEGREGATION[8]

We are in serious need of research on the Negro, both in the North and in the South. Most psychological research in this area was conducted during the 1930s and directed at testing racists' claims of Negro inferiority. But the most sweeping advances in American Negro history have been made in the past generation, requiring a fresh new look—par-ticularly at the Negro personality.

Two aspects of this research make it com-plex and difficult. In the first place, the race of the interviewer is a complicating and not as yet fully understood factor. Further methodological study is needed on this point. Moreover, special problems of control are inherent in this research. Not only are there some relatively unique variables that must be considered (e.g., migration history, differen-tial experience with the white community, etc.), but such simple factors as education are not easy to control. For instance, has the average graduate of the southern rural high

---

[8] For other suggestions, see the important analy-sis of desegregation by Cook (1957).

school for Negroes received an education equal to the average graduate of such a school for whites? No, in spite of the South's belated efforts to live up to separate-but-equal education, available school data indicate that the graduates have probably not received equivalent educations. Yet some recent research on Negro personality has been based on the assumption that Negro and white education in the South are equivalent (e.g., Smith & Prothro, 1957).

Fortunately, the Institute for Research in the Social Sciences at the University of North Carolina has embarked on a large study of many of these content and methodological problems. It is to be hoped that their work will stimulate other efforts.

Some of the most valuable psychological data now available on desegregation have been collected by public opinion polls. But typically these data have been gathered without any conceptual framework to guide their coverage and direction.

For example, one of the more interesting poll findings is that a majority of white Southerners realize that racial desegregation of public facilities is inevitable even though about six out of seven strongly oppose the process (Hyman & Sheatsley, 1956). The psychological implications of this result are so extensive that we would like to know more. Do the respondents who oppose desegregation but accept its inevitability have other characteristics of latent liberals? Are these respondents more often found outside of the Black Belt? Typically, we cannot answer such questions from present poll data; we need to build into the desegregation polls broader coverage and more theoretical direction.

The third direction that psychological research in desegregation could usefully take concerns measurement. Save for the partly standardized F Scale, we still lack widely used, standardized field measures of the chief variables in this realm. Such instruments are necessary both for comparability of results and for stimulation of research; witness the invigorating effects on research of the F Scale, the Minnesota Multiphasic Inventory, and the need achievement scoring scheme. Mention of McClelland's need achievement scoring scheme should remind

us, too, that projective and other indirect techniques might answer many of these measurement requirements—especially for such sensitive and subtle variables as conformity needs.

Finally, the definitive interdisciplinary case study of desegregation has yet to be started. Properly buttressed by the necessary foundation aid, such a study should involve comparisons before, during, and after desegregation of a wide variety of communities. The interdisciplinary nature of such an undertaking is stressed because desegregation is a peculiarly complex process demanding a broad range of complementary approaches.

Any extensive case project must sample three separate time periods: before a legal ruling or similar happening has alerted the community to imminent desegregation, during the height of the desegregating process, and after several years of accommodation. Without this longitudinal view, desegregation as a dynamic, ongoing process cannot be understood. This time perspective, for instance, would enable us to interpret the fact that an overwhelming majority of Oklahoma whites in a 1954 poll sternly objected to mixed schools, but within a few years has accepted without serious incident integrated education throughout most of the state (Jones, 1957).

A carefully selected range of communities is required to test for differences in the process according to the characteristics of the area. Recent demographic analyses and predictions of the South's school desegregation pattern (Ogburn & Grigg, 1956; Pettigrew, 1957; Pettigrew & Campbell, 1960) could help in making this selection of communities. Comparable data gathered in such a selected variety of locations would allow us to pinpoint precisely the aspects of desegregation unique to, say, a Piedmont city, as opposed to a Black Belt town.

Compare the potential value of such a broad research effort with the limited case studies that have been possible so far. Low budget reports of only one community are the rule; many of them are theses or seminar projects, some remain on the descriptive level, all but a few sample only one time period, and there is almost no comparability of instruments and approach. A comprehensive case project is obviously long overdue.

This has been an appeal for a vigorous empirical look at southern race relations. Despite segregationists' claims to the contrary, social psychological contributions to desegregation research have been relatively meager. There are, however, grounds for hoping that this situation will be partly corrected in the near future—particularly if psychologists get busy.

Foundations appear to be re-evaluating their previous reluctance to support such research. And we can re-evaluate our own resignation in the face of barriers to conduct investigations in this area; the tragedy of Little Rock has had a salutary effect on many influential Southerners in this respect.

Recognition of the importance of the situation in interracial behavior and the full exploitation of the attitude concept can remove inadequacies in the traditional psychological approach to the study of race. In this connection, an extended case for considering conformity as crucial in the Negro attitudes of white Southerners was presented and a new concept—the latent liberal—introduced. One final implication of this latent liberal concept should be mentioned. Some cynics have argued that successful racial desegregation in the South will require an importation of tens of thousands of psychotherapists and therapy for millions of bigoted Southerners. Fortunately for desegregation, psychotherapists, and Southerners, this will not be necessary; a thorough repatterning of southern interracial behavior will be sufficient therapy in itself.

REFERENCES

Adorno, T. W., Frenkel-Brunswik, Else, Levinson, D. J., & Sanford, N. *The authoritarian personality.* New York: Harper, 1950.

Allport, G. W. *The nature of prejudice.* Cambridge, Mass.: Addison-Wesley, 1954.

Asch, S. E. Effects of group pressure upon the modification and distortion of judgments. In H. Guetzkow (Ed.), *Groups, leadership and men.* Pittsburgh: Carnegie, 1951.

Biesanz, J., & Smith, L. M. Race relations of Panama and the Canal Zone. *Amer. J. Sociol.,* 1951, 57, 7–14.

Clark, K. B. Desegregation: An appraisal of the evidence. *J. soc. Issues,* 1953, 9, 1–76.

Cook, S. W. Desegregation: A psychological analysis. *Amer. Psychologist,* 1957, 12, 1–13.

Crutchfield, R. S. Conformity and character. *Amer. Psychologist,* 1955, 10, 191–198.

Dabney, V. The violence at Little Rock. *Richmond Times-Dispatch,* 1957, 105, September 24, 14.

Davis, A., Gardner, B., & Gardner, Mary. *Deep South.* Chicago: Univer. Chicago Press, 1941.

Dollard, J. *Caste and class in a southern town.* New Haven: Yale Univer. Press, 1937.

Festinger, L. An analysis of compliant behavior. In M. Sherif & M. O. Wilson (Eds.), *Group relations at the crossroads.* New York: Harper, 1953.

Festinger, L. *A theory of cognitive dissonance.* Evanston, Ill.: Row, Peterson, 1957.

Harding, J., & Hogrefe, R. Attitudes of white department store employees toward Negro co-workers. *J. soc. Issues,* 1952, 8, 18–28.

Hartley, E. L. *Problems in prejudice.* New York: King's Crown, 1946.

Hyman, H. H., & Sheatsley, P. B. Attitudes toward desegregation. *Scient. Amer.,* 1956, 195, 35–39.

Jones, E. City limits. In D. Shoemaker (Ed.), *With all deliberate speed.* New York: Harper, 1957.

Kelman, H. C. Compliance, identification, and internalization: Three processes of attitude change. *J. conflict Resolut.,* 1958, 2, 51–60.

Kelman, H. C. *Social influence and personal belief.* New York: Wiley, 1961.

Killian, L. W. Southern white laborers in Chicago's West Side. Unpublished doctoral dissertation, University of Chicago, 1949.

Knapp, R. H. A psychology of rumor. *Publ. opin. Quart.,* 1944, 8, 22–37.

Logan, R. W. The United States Supreme Court and the segregation issue. *Ann. Amer. Acad. Pol. Soc. Sci.,* 1956, 304, 10–16.

Milton, O. Presidential choice and performance on a scale of authoritarianism. *Amer. Psychologist,* 1952, 7, 597–598.

Minard, R. D. Race relations in the Pocahontas coal field. *J. soc. Issues,* 1952, 8, 29–44.

Ogburn, W. F., & Grigg, C. M. Factors related

to the Virginia vote on segregation. *Soc. Forces,* 1956, 34, 301–308.

Pettigrew, T. F. Demographic correlates of border-state desegregation. *Amer. sociol. Rev.,* 1957, 22, 683–689.

Pettigrew, T. F. Personality and sociocultural factors in intergroup attitudes: A cross-national comparison. *J. conflict Resolut.,* 1958, 2, 29–42.

Pettigrew, T. F. Regional differences in anti-Negro prejudice. *J. abnorm. soc. Psychol.,* 1959, 59, 28–36.

Pettigrew, T. F. Social distance attitudes of South African students. *Soc. Forces,* 1960, 38, 246–253.

Pettigrew, T. F., & Campbell, E. Q. Faubus and segregation: An analysis of Arkansas voting. *Publ. opin. Quart.,* 1960, 24, 436–447.

Prothro, E. T. Ethnocentrism and anti-Negro attitudes in the deep South. *J. abnorm. soc. Psychol.,* 1952, 47, 105–108.

Rabb, E., & Lipset, S. M. *Prejudice and society.* New York: Anti-Defamation League of B'nai B'rith, 1959.

Reitzes, D. C. The role of organizational struc-

tures: Union versus neighborhood in a tension situation. *J. soc. Issues,* 1953, 9, 37–44.

Roper, E. United States anti-Semites. *Fortune,* 1946, 33, 257–260.

Roper, E. United States anti-Semites. *Fortune,* 1947, 36, 5–10.

Rose, A. M. Intergroup relations vs. prejudice: Pertinent theory for the study of social change. *Soc. Probl.,* 1956, 4, 173–176.

Smith, C. U., & Prothro, J. W. Ethnic differences in authoritarian personality. *Soc. Forces,* 1957, 35, 334–338.

Smith, M. B., Bruner, J. S., & White, R. W. *Opinion and personality.* New York: Wiley, 1956.

Stouffer, S. A., Suchman, E. A., DeVinney, L. C., Star, Shirley A., Williams, R. M., Jr. *Studies in social psychology in World War II.* Vol. 1. *The American soldier: Adjustment during army life.* Princeton: Princeton Univer. Press, 1949.

Thibaut, J. W., & Kelley, H. H. *The social psychology of groups.* New York: Wiley, 1959.

Zinn, H. A fate worse than integration. *Harper's,* 1959, 219, August, 53–56.

Index

Index

A

Aaronson, Helene, 197n.
ABC's of Scapegoating, 278
Abeles, Milton, and Schilder, Paul, 235n.
"Absent Father: Effects on the Developing Child," 501n.
"Absentee-owned Corporations and Community Power Structure," 427n.
Absentee Ownership, 427n.
Achievement motivation, 141–52
Ackerman, Nathan W., 463
Ackoff, Russell L., and Clark, Donald F., 391n.
Adolescence and the verbal self, 48–49
Adolescent Character and Personality, 469n.
Adorno, T. W., Frenkel-Brunswik, Else, Levinson, D. J., and Sanford, R. N., 199, 257n., 277, 287, 551
Adult Education, 524n.
Adulthood and the verbal self, 48–49
"Affect and Cognition in Attitude Structure and Attitude Change," 253n.
After Hospitalization: The Mental Patient and His Family, 515n.
Age groups and stages of conceptual development, 17 (*table*), 19–20, 21, 23, 25
"Age and Sex Categories," 469n.
Albert, Ethel M., 475n.
"Alienation from Interaction," 265n.
Allen, Edward J., 478n.
Allinsmith, W., 198, 199, 201, 208, 212
Allinsmith, W., and Greening, T. C., 161
Allport, Floyd H., 392n.
Allport, G. W., 126, 278, 547n., 548
American Anthropologist, 466n., 507n.
American Economic Review, 95n.
American Journal of Orthopsychiatry, 463n.
American Journal of Sociology, 71n., 79n., 219n., 229n., 415n., 416n., 418n., 427n., 428n., 429n., 431n., 452n., 470n., 473n., 474n., 500n., 515n., 523n., 531n., 532n.
American Political Science Review, 427n.
American Psychological Association, 113n.
American Psychologist, 288n., 547n.
American Society, 440n., 466n.
American Sociological Association, 78n.
American Sociological Review, 72n., 78n., 83n., 219n., 220n., 223n., 225n., 231n., 371n., 373n., 377n., 381n., 382n., 414n., 415n., 416n., 427n., 439n., 449n., 452n., 464n., 469n., 471n., 473n., 475n., 500n., 523n., 524n., 531n., 539n., 543n., 547n.
American Soldier, The, 550
"American Subcultural *Continua* as Exemplified by the Mormons and Texans," 466n.
"America's Un-Marxist Revolution," 428n.
Ames, Louise B., and Ilg, Frances L., 17, 18, 19, 20, 23

"Analysis of Affective-Cognitive Consistency," 256n.
"Analysis of Complaint Behavior," 266n.
"Analysis of Conflicting Social Norms," 452n.
Analysis of Social Change, 415n.
Anderson, N. H., *et al.,* 294
Angyal, A., 134
Animal psychology, trend in, 121–24, 137
    activity and manipulation, 122
    changing conceptions of drive, 122–24
    exploratory behavior, 121–22
Annals of the American Academy of Political and Social Science, 533n., 539n.
Anomia, *see* "Social Structure and Anomia in a Small City"
"Anomie, Authoritarianism, and Prejudice," 523n.
"Anomie and Differential Access to the Achievement of Life Goals," 524n.
"Anomie, Social Isolation, and Class Structure," 523n.
Anthony, A. A., *et al.,* 155, 500, 501
Anthropology, 2, 3, 8, 29, 185, 438
"Anthropology and Psychology," 466n.
Appraisal of Anthropology Today, 465n.
"Approach to a Theory of Bureaucracy," 373n.
Archives of General Psychiatry, 516n.
Archives of Psychology, 229n.
"Are Cities Un-American?" 416n.
Argonauts of the Western Pacific, 444n.
Arkoff, A., and Vinacke, W. E., 302–11
Aronfreed, Justin, 186, 197–218, 199, 201, 206, 208
Aronson, Elliot, 15
Arrowood, A. John, and Kelley, Harold H., 302–11
Asch, S. E., 58, 101, 104, 105, 106, 107, 265n., 552
"Assumed Increase of Mental Disease," 532n.
Atkinson, J. W., 141n., 142, 151
Atkinson, J. W., and Litwin, G. H., 142, 150, 151
Atkinson, J. W., and Raphelson, A. C., 143
"Attitude Change and Attitude Structure," 252n.
"Attitude Change as a Function of Response Restriction," 266n.
Attitude change, *see* "Principle of Congruity in the Prediction of Attitude Change"
Attitude, concept of, 236–98
    readings, 237–98
Attitude dynamics, *see* "Structural Theory of Attitude Dynamics"
"Attitude and Motivation," 249n.
Attitude Organization and Change, 256n.
"Attitudes Toward Social Mobility as Revealed by Samples of Negro and White Boys," 466n.
Authoritarian Personality, The, 103, 257n.
"Authority," 374n.
"Authority Structure in a Mental Hospital Ward," 76n.
Automobile Workers and the American Dream, 430n.

ΑΣΣΤ
37

Ρ - ΣΤ